Pacific Northwest

including Western Canada and Alaska

THE ROUGH GUIDE

£1.00

Pages loose SMT

D1344667

There are more than eighty Rough Guide titles covering
destinations from Amsterdam to Zimbabwe

Forthcoming titles include
China • Corfu • Jamaica • New Zealand • South Africa
Southwest USA • Vienna • Washington DC

Rough Guide Reference Series
Classical Music • The Internet • Jazz • Rock • World Music

Rough Guide Phrasebooks
Czech • French • German • Greek • Italian • Mexican Spanish
Polish • Portuguese • Spanish • Thai • Turkish • Vietnamese

Rough Guides on the Internet
http://www.roughguides.com/
http://www.hotwired.com/rough

Rough Guide Credits

Text editors:	Greg Ward and Alison Cowan
Series editor:	Mark Ellingham
Editorial:	Martin Dunford, Jonathan Buckley, Jo Mead, Samantha Cook, Amanda Tomlin, Annie Shaw, Lemisse al-Hafidh, Catherine McHale, Paul Grey, Vivienne Heller, Alan Spicer (Online UK), Andrew Rosenberg (Online US)
Production:	Susanne Hillen, Andy Hilliard, Melissa Flack, Judy Pang, Link Hall, Nicola Williamson, David Callier, Helen Ostick
Publicity:	Richard Trillo, Simon Carloss (UK), Jean-Marie Kelly, Jeff Kaye (US)
Finance:	John Fisher, Celia Crowley, Catherine Gillespie
Administration:	Tania Hummel, Margo Daly

Acknowledgments

Tim: The staff at Alberta House and British Columbia House in London; *Greyhound*; Mandy Wheelwright; Madeleine Tucker; and very special thanks to James and Vicky Ballantyne.

Phil: For their generous support and wise advice, Jim Bocci at the Portland Visitors' Association; Susan Bladholm at the Oregon Economic Development Dept; and Carrie Wilkinson at Washington State Tourism. Also thanks as usual to Cathy Rees for her endurance and Emma Rees for her company.

Thanks also to Wendy Ferguson for permission to draw on her original accounts of Washington and Oregon, and to Tim Perry for his Alaska research; Jean Muchnick and David Leffman; Sharon Gaiptman and Linda Mickel in Alaska; Daniel Czaran in Seattle; Paul Gray for diligent proofreading and Ally Scott for help with production; Micromap; and all those involved in editing successive drafts – Jonathan Buckley, David Reed, Martin Dunford, Greg Ward and Alison Cowan.

The publishers and authors have done their best to ensure the accuracy and currency of all information in *The Rough Guide to the Pacific NW*; however, they can accept no responsibility for any loss, injury, or inconvenience sustained by any traveller as a result of information or advice contained in the guide.

This first edition published 1994 and reprinted in June 1995 and August 1996 by Rough Guides Ltd, 1 Mercer Street, London WC2H 9QJ.
Distributed by The Penguin Group:

Penguin Books Ltd, 27 Wrights Lane, London W8 5TZ
Penguin Books USA Inc., 375 Hudson Street, New York 10014, USA
Penguin Books Australia Ltd, 487 Maroondah Highway, PO Box 257, Ringwood, Victoria 3134, Australia
Penguin Books Canada Ltd, 10 Alcorn Avenue, Toronto, Ontario, Canada M4V 1E4
Penguin Books (NZ) Ltd, 182–190 Wairau Road, Auckland 10, New Zealand

Rough Guides were formerly published as Real Guides in the United States and Canada.

Illustrations in Part One and Part Three by Edward Briant.
Basics and Contexts illustrations by Henry Iles.
Typeset in Linotron Univers and Century Old Style to an original design by Andrew Oliver.
Printed in the United Kingdom by Cox & Wyman Ltd (Reading).

© Tim Jepson and Phil Lee 1994
592pp.
Includes index.
A catalogue record for this book is available from the British Library.

ISBN 1-85828-092-3

Pacific Northwest
including Western Canada and Alaska

THE ROUGH GUIDE

written and researched by
Tim Jepson and Phil Lee

with additional accounts by
Wendy Ferguson and Tim Perry

THE ROUGH GUIDES

CONTENTS

Introduction vii

PART ONE — BASICS — 1

Getting There from Britain and Ireland 3
Getting There from Australasia 7
Getting There from North America 9
Entry Requirements for Foreign Visitors 14
Insurance, Health and Personal Safety 18
Costs, Money and Banks 21
Telephones, Time Zones and Mail 24
Information and Maps 27
Getting Around 30
Disabled Travellers 40
Senior Travellers 42

Travelling with Children 43
Women Travellers 44
Gay and Lesbian Travellers 45
Accommodation 46
Outdoors 52
Food and Drink 59
Sports 63
Entertainment and Media 64
Festivals and Public Holidays 66
Climate and When To Go 67
Directory 69

PART TWO — GUIDE — 71

■ 1	**PORTLAND AND WESTERN OREGON**	**73**
■ 2	**EASTERN OREGON**	**122**
■ 3	**SEATTLE AND WESTERN WASHINGTON**	**141**
■ 4	**THE CASCADES AND EASTERN WASHINGTON**	**202**
■ 5	**VANCOUVER AND VANCOUVER ISLAND**	**229**
■ 6	**SOUTHERN BRITISH COLUMBIA**	**313**
■ 7	**CALGARY AND THE CANADIAN ROCKIES**	**348**
■ 8	**NORTH TO THE YUKON**	**441**
■ 9	**ALASKA**	**483**

PART THREE — CONTEXTS — 545

Historical Framework 547
Northwest Wildlife 555
Books 563

Index 567

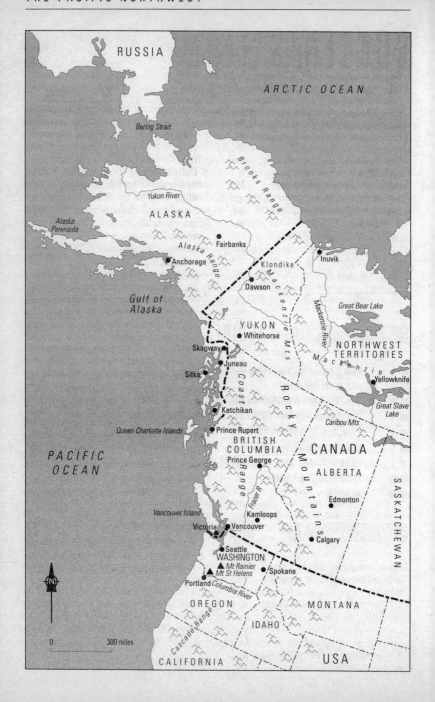

INTRODUCTION

ew areas of North America owe so little to national and provincial boundaries as the **Pacific Northwest**. A loosely defined region cutting across the western redoubts of both the United States and Canada, it is isolated by geography from the rest of the continent and tends to look westward to the Pacific Ocean for its identity. Extending from Oregon and Washington in the south, then hopscotching through British Columbia and the Canadian Rockies, via the Yukon, to the icy tip of Alaska, it encompasses varied and awe-inspiring landscapes. Mountains, lakes and pristine wilderness are the finest features, with abundant wildlife offering the chance to see creatures – from whales to wolves – in their natural habitats, but it is also a region of high historical adventure, intriguing native American and Inuit cultures, superb cuisine (seafood in particular), state-of-the-art museums and some of the most urbane and civilized cities in North America.

Leading the way in this last respect are **Vancouver** and **Seattle**, both dynamic, cosmopolitan and instantly likeable – destined to be pivotal points of any trip. Vancouver is preceded by a well-deserved reputation as one of the world's most beautiful cities, cradled in a mountain and seafront setting that provides its laidback citizens with hedonistic possibilities ranging from hiking, skiing and sailing to world-class theater, outdoor summer festivals and the more simple West Coast pleasures of bar-hopping and beach-bumming. Seattle, though somewhat grittier, also benefits from a dramatic setting: its hilly suburbs bump around the deep blue of the Pacific Ocean, while its busy, bristling center is alive with great restaurants and some of the finest live-music nightspots around.

Of the smaller cities, environmentally aware **Portland** is easily the nicest: the height of gentility, its downtown peopled by latte-drinking urbanites and graced with whimsical street sculptures. Although less compelling as cities in their own right, Calgary, Victoria and Anchorage each merit a couple of days before heading into the surrounding backcountry. Cow-town **Calgary** comes alive during its famous Stampede, but also boasts a glittering oil-funded downtown, an appealing base for trips to the Rockies and the fine sights in southern Alberta. On Vancouver Island, **Victoria** offers an ersatz taste of old England, an affectation that fails to overshadow one of North America's finest museums. **Anchorage**, the capital of Alaska, though hardly picturesque, has a sense of extremes and of life on the edge, with the longest of summer days, the sharpest of winters.

Despite the attractions of the cities, the chances are you will spend much of your time exploring the **landscapes** for which the Pacific Northwest is famed. Embracing North America's highest mountains and largest glaciers, these include not only the majestic peaks, thundering rivers and endless forests you might expect, but also sun-scorched patches of near-desert, spatulate river deltas and wetlands, smoking volcanoes, huge swathes of Arctic tundra, and benignly rippling grasslands. Many form wilderness areas unrivalled elsewhere on the continent, vast reaches of country untouched by the twentieth century, yet at the same time rendered accessible to casual visitors by a network of superbly run national, state and provincial **parks**.

Almost any of these will provide enough jaw-dropping scenery, hiking trails and outdoor pursuits to last several lifetimes. The highlight of Oregon is its magnificent sand- and rock-strewn coastline, while inland the Cascade Mountains shelter elegiac **Crater Lake**. In Washington you can choose from the wild fast-ness that is the **Olympic Peninsula**, with its glacial peaks, rainforests, and storm-tossed shore, and the northern continuation of the Cascades, including **Mount St Helens**, whose dramatic eruption captured world headlines in 1980. Across the Canadian border, the Rockies carry the mountains in a huge north-ward sweep towards the Yukon, displaying some of their grandest scenery within Alberta's **Banff** and **Jasper** national parks. Offshore, enclaves like **Vancouver Island**, the **Queen Charlottes** and the **San Juan** archipelago offer a unique blend of mountain and maritime landscapes. Further north, the **Yukon** provides a foretaste both of **Alaska**'s dramatic landscapes – vast glaciers nestling between ferociously cold mountains, and caribou roaming across the tundra – and of the often individual-cum-eccentric outlook of the people who choose to live on one of the world's last frontiers.

Where to go

Any one of these areas could easily occupy a two- or three-week trip, particularly if you're seduced by the appeal of Alaska, the stunning diversity of the Olympic Peninsula, or the legendary beauty of the Canadian Rockies. If you're planning to tour, however, certain key **itineraries** stand out, facilitated by roads that probe even the most remote areas, a reasonable public transport system (better in the Canadian parts of the region), and a network of ferries that cobwebs most of the coast. Many people travel the so-called **Inside Passage**, one of the world's great sea journeys, taking boats from Bellingham, Vancouver Island and other points up the coast to ride all or part of the way north to Alaska – the entire journey takes two and a half days. The same destinations can be reached (less expensively) by road, driving the 1500-mile **Alaska Highway** up through Alberta and British Columbia to Fairbanks, the still wilder **Cassiar Highway** through northern BC, the **Klondike Highway** to Dawson City, site of the Klondike gold rush, or the **Dempster Highway** across the Arctic Circle and Yukon tundra to Canada's Northwest Territories. For any of these long overland journeys, you'll need plenty of time, a spirit of adventure – and patience to cope with the featureless stretches. By comparison, exploring Washington and Oregon requires less endurance – the distances between the main centers are much shorter, the terrain more accessi-ble. A favorite is the spindly highway that pips and squeaks its way along the magnificent coast or, if you're in a hurry, you can thump along the main interstate which runs north–south just inland. Coming from the east, your best bet is to follow the route of the old Oregon Trail, across the plains and down the Columbia River Gorge, itself a fine aperitif to the region's scenic splendors.

Perhaps the best way to see the Pacific Northwest, however, is to combine a city or two with a mixture of land and sea routes, getting acquainted with some of the better-known scenery en route. Permutations, of course, are endless: thus you might visit Seattle before heading to the mountains of the Cascades (and then hit the Inside Passage ferries from Bellingham), spend time in Calgary before visiting the Canadian Rockies, or hole up in Vancouver before tackling southern British Columbia or Vancouver Island.

The vastness of the region, and its resultant climatic variations, make it difficult to generalize about the best time to go, although you should bear in mind that during winter some areas – such as the higher peaks and passes of the mountain ranges – are altogether inaccessible, while many more are simply unbearably cold. For more guidance on when to plan a visit, together with details of average temperatures and rainfall, see p.67.

PART ONE

THE
BASICS

GETTING THERE FROM BRITAIN AND IRELAND

Four major cities in the Pacific Northwest are accessible by non-stop flights from the United Kingdom – Calgary, Edmonton, Vancouver and Seattle. Your choice of carrier is more limited than to other North American destinations, but you're sure to find an appropriate option if you're prepared to take into account direct flights (which may land once or twice en route, but keep the same flight number throughout their journey), and flights via such "gateway cities" as San Francisco and Toronto.

Non-stop flights to **Seattle** or **Vancouver** from London take ten or eleven hours; London–**Calgary** and London–**Edmonton** flights take around eight hours. Following winds ensure that return flights are always around an hour shorter than outward journeys. Because of the time difference between Europe and the Northwest, flights usually leave Britain around noon, which means you land in mid-afternoon, local time; flights back from Calgary tend to arrive in Britain early in the morning, and from Seattle in time for lunch.

FARES AND AIRLINES

Britain remains one of the best places in Europe to obtain flight bargains, though **fares** vary widely according to season, availability and the current level of inter-airline competition. As a general indication, prices to **Seattle** range from about £170 single (£300 return) in low season to about £300 (£500 return) in high season: fares to **Calgary** vary between £180 (£325) and £265 (£445). There are no direct flights to **Alaska** from Europe. Most services are routed through Seattle, which is likely to prove expensive at around £335 one-way in low season (£550 return) or £410 (£665) in summer.

The comments that follow can only act as a general guide, so be sure to shop around carefully for the best offers by checking the travel ads in the Sunday papers and, in London, scouring *Time Out* and the *Evening Standard*. Giveaway magazines aimed at young travellers, such as *TNT*, are also useful.

Stand-by deals are few and far between, and don't give great savings: in general you're better off with an **Apex** ticket. The conditions on these are pretty standard whoever you fly with – seats must be booked 21 days or more in advance, and you must stay for a minimum of seven nights; tickets are normally valid for up to six months. Some airlines also do a less expensive **Super-Apex** ticket, which can cost up to £100 less than an ordinary Apex but often must be booked thirty days in advance and is only valid for up to 21 days; usually, it's also non-refundable or changeable. With an **open-jaw** ticket you can fly into one city and out of another; fares are calculated by halving the return fares to each destination and adding the two figures together. This makes a convenient option for those who want a fly-drive holiday – though you are likely to incur high drop-off charges if you leave a rental car in a city other than the one where you picked it up (see p.37).

Generally, the most expensive time to fly is **high season**, roughly between June and August and during the period around Christmas. May and September are slightly less pricey, and the rest of the year is considered low season and cheaper still. Keep an eye out for slack season bargains, and, additionally, make sure to check the exact dates of the seasons with your operator or airline; you might be able to make major savings by shifting your departure date by a week – or even a day. **Weekend rates** for all flights tend to be £30–50 more expensive than those in the week.

Whenever you travel, the competition between carriers always makes it worth phoning

NON-STOP FLIGHTS FROM THE UK TO THE NORTHWEST

Air Canada ☎0800/181313

From **Heathrow** to Calgary (4 weekly), Edmonton (3 weekly), and Vancouver (daily); and from **Manchester** to Calgary, Edmonton and Vancouver (all 1 weekly).

British Airways
London ☎081/897 4000
Glasgow ☎041/332 9666
Manchester ☎061/228 6311
Belfast ☎0345/222 111

From **Heathrow** to Vancouver (4 weekly) and Seattle (5 weekly).

Canadian Airlines International ☎0345/616 767

From **Gatwick** to Calgary (3 weekly), Edmonton (2 weekly), Vancouver (2 weekly).

United ☎081/990 9900

From **Heathrow** to Seattle (daily in high season).

---

the **airlines** direct to check on **current deals** they may be offering, which will often undercut even the Apex fares. Plenty of **agents**, such as those listed below, also specialize in low-cost and unofficially discounted flights. Especially if you're under 26 or a student, they may be able to knock up to fifty percent off the regular Apex fares, thus bringing prices down as low as £300 return.

Once in North America, a **Visiting US and Canada Airpass** (VUSA) can be a good idea if you want to do a lot of travelling. These are only available to non-US and Canadian residents, and must be bought before reaching North America (see p.34).

COURIER FLIGHTS

It is possible for those on a very tight budget to travel as **couriers**. Most of the major courier firms offer opportunities to travel for up to fifty percent off the cheapest fare (as low as £200 return to the Northwest) in return for delivering a package. There'll be someone to check you in and to meet you at your destination, which minimizes any red-tape hassle. However, you'll have to travel light, with only a cabin-bag, and accept tight restrictions on travel dates – stays of more than a fortnight are rare. For phone numbers, see below or check the Yellow Pages.

PACKAGES

Packages – fly-drive, flight/accommodation deals and guided tours (or a combination of all three) – can work out cheaper than arranging the same trip yourself, especially for a short-term stay. To take a typical example, ten days in Vancouver and the Rockies, including your return

flight, costs around £850 per person. Drawbacks include the loss of flexibility and the fact that you'll probably be made to stay in hotels in the mid-range to expensive bracket, even though less expensive accommodation is almost always readily available.

High street travel agents have plenty of brochures and information about the various combinations available. Most charter deals from agents include accommodation along with the flight. Prices are based on two or more people travelling together; and this can be such a bargain that even if you do end up paying for a hotel room, which, of course, you don't have to use, it may still be cheaper than the standard fare. Flight-only deals do turn up at the last minute to fill unused seats; scan high street travel agents for the latest offers.

FLY-DRIVE

Fly-drive deals, which give cut-rate (sometimes free) car rental when buying a transatlantic ticket from an airline or tour operator, are always cheaper than renting on the spot and give great value if you intend to do a lot of driving. On the other hand, you'll probably have to pay more for the flight than if you booked it through a discount agent. Competition between airlines and tour operators means that it's well worth phoning to check on current special promotions.

Northwest Flydrive, PO Box 45, Bexhill-on-Sea, East Sussex TN40 1PY (☎0424/224400), offers excellent deals for not much more than an ordinary Apex fare. Several of the companies listed in the box on p.6 offer similar packages. However, there will often be little to choose between them; the most important determining factors are the current strength of the US or Canadian dollar against the pound, and your destination in the Northwest. The lowest rates start at around £65 per week for a small family saloon, working up to £150 per week for an estate. Be sure that you're getting unlimited mileage, and watch out for hidden extras, such as local taxes, "drop-off" charges, which can be as much as a week's rental, and Collision Damage Waiver insurance. Remember, too, that while you can drive in Canada and the States with a British licence, there can be problems renting vehicles if you're under 25. For complete car-rental and driveaway details, see "Getting Around" (p.37).

FLIGHT AND ACCOMMODATION DEALS

There are no end of **flight and accommodation** packages to all the major Northwestern cities; although you can do things cheaper independently, you won't be able to do the same things cheaper. Pre-booked accommodation schemes, under which you buy vouchers for use in a specific group of hotels, are not normally good value – see p.47.

TOURING AND ADVENTURE PACKAGES

A simple and exciting way to see a chunk of the Northwest's Great Outdoors, without being hassled by too many practical considerations, is to take a specialist **touring and adventure package**, which includes transport, accommodation, food and a guide. Some of the more adventurous carry small groups around on minibuses and use a combination of budget hotels and camping (equipment, except sleeping bag, is provided). Most also have a food kitty of perhaps £25 per week, with many meals cooked and eaten communally, although there's plenty of time to leave the group and do your own thing.

TrekAmerica (☎0869/38777) is one UK-based company to offer excellent deals; trips currently on offer include the 14-day "Mountie" expedition, which takes in Seattle, Vancouver and the national parks of the Canadian Rockies (£475–523, not including transatlantic flight), and the 26-day "Klondike", driving from Washington to Alaska and taking the ferry back (£977–1075).

CRUISES

For many visitors, the main reason to come to the Northwest is to enjoy a **cruise** along the spectacular Pacific coast. Possibilities range from short trips from Seattle to the islands of the Puget Sound (see p.164), or to and around Vancouver Island from Vancouver (see p.35), up to the magnificent three-day voyage on the **Alaska Marine Highway** from Bellingham, Washington, to Skagway in Alaska (see p.35 and p.487).

Such trips can in theory be arranged on the spot, but you won't save significant amounts of money by doing so, and in any case almost any excursion longer than a half-day ferry ride is likely to be booked up months ahead – most of them as block bookings by major tour operators. If you plan to take a long (half-day plus) cruise, it

---

FLIGHT AGENTS IN BRITAIN

Low-Cost Flight Agents

Campus Travel, 52 Grosvenor Gdns, London SW1 ☎071/730 210. *Also many other branches around the country.*

Council Travel, 28A Poland St, London W1 ☎071/437 7767

STA Travel, 86 Old Brompton Rd, London SW7 ☎071/937 9971. *Offices nationwide.*

Trailfinders, 194 Kensington High St, London W8 ☎071/938 3232

Travel Cuts, 295 Regent St, London W1 ☎071/637 3161

Specialist Flight Operators

Globespan ☎0737/773171

Jetsave ☎0342/322771

Travel Express ☎0273/835095

Unijet ☎0444/458181

Major Courier Firms

CTS Ltd ☎071/351 0300

DHL ☎081/890 9393

Polo Express ☎081/759 5383

SPECIALIST HOLIDAY OPERATORS

Airtours
Helmshore, Rossendale
Lancs BB4 4NB   ☎0706/260000

AmeriCan Adventures
45 High St, Tunbridge Wells
Kent TN1 1XL   ☎0892/511894

Bon Voyage
18 Bellevue Rd, Southampton
Hants SO1 2AY   ☎0703/330332

British Airways Holidays, Atlantic House
Hazelwick Ave, Three Bridges, Crawley
West Sussex RH10 1NP   ☎0293/572704

Contiki Travel
Wells House, 15 Elmfield Rd
Bromley, Kent BR1 1LS   ☎081/290 6422

Destination USA
41–45 Goswell Rd
London EC1V 7EH   ☎071/253 2000

Enterprise
Groundstar House, London Rd, Crawley
West Sussex RH10 2HB   ☎0293/560777

Explore Worldwide
I Frederick St, Aldershot
Hants GU11 1LQ   ☎0252/319448

Green Tortoise
PO Box 24459
San Francisco, CA 94124   ☎415/821-0803

Greyhound
Sussex House, London Rd, East Grinstead
West Sussex RH19   ☎0342/317317

Premier
Westbrook, Milton Rd
Cambridge CB4 1YQ   ☎0223/355977

Sierra Club
c/o Outings Dept, 730 Polk St
San Francisco, CA 94110   ☎415/776-2211

Thomson
Greater London House, Hampstead Rd
London NW1 7SD   ☎071/387 6534

Top Deck
131 Earls Court Rd
London SW5   ☎071/244 8641

TransAmerica
3A Gatwick Metro Centre, Balcombe Rd
Horley, Surrey RH6 9GA   ☎0293/774441

Trek America
Trek House, The Bullring, Deddington
Oxford OX15 OTT   ☎0869/38777

Unijet
"Sandrocks", Rocky Lane, Haywards Heath
West Sussex RH16 4RH   ☎0444/459191

Virgin Holidays
The Galleria, Station Rd, Crawley
West Sussex RH10 1WW   ☎0293/617181

definitely makes sense to arrange it as far in advance as possible, through one of the many companies whose brochures litter the offices of high-street travel agents; some of which are listed above.

FLIGHTS FROM IRELAND

Other than charter deals, seasonal bargains and all-in packages which may be on offer from high street travel agents, the cheapest flights from Ireland to Seattle and, less frequently, Portland (alone among the major cities of the Pacific Northwest) are available – especially if you're

under 26 or a student – from *USIT*. Student/youth fares are around IR£100 less than standard Apex fares.

Aer Lingus (in partnership with a US airline, principally *TWA*) fly daily from Dublin to Seattle (Apex fare IR£550) and daily to Portland (IR£760), via a gateway city (usually New York).

To fly from Ireland to Anchorage, Vancouver, Edmonton and Calgary you'll almost certainly be routed through London.

USIT can be contacted at Aston Quay, O'Connell Bridge, Dublin 2 (☎01/679-8833), while *Aer Lingus* is at 41 Upper O'Connell Street, Dublin 1 (☎ 01/837-7777 or 837-0191).

GETTING THERE FROM AUSTRALASIA

Other than charter deals, seasonal bargains and all-in packages which may be on offer from high street travel agents, the cheapest flights from Australasia to the US are available from the specialists listed below.

From **Australia**, *Canadian Airlines* fly daily from Sydney, in conjunction with *Qantas*, to **Vancouver**; the free return side trip included can take you on to **Seattle**, LA or San Francisco for A$1690 in low season (A$2040 high season). There are also through services from Sydney to **Calgary** (A$1863/2212) or **Edmonton** (A$1886/2335). *United Airlines* offer the most comprehensive service to West Coast

AIRLINES AND AGENTS IN AUSTRALASIA

Adventure World
73 Walker St, Sydney ☎008/221 931
101 Great South Rd, Auckland ☎09/524-5118

Air New Zealand
Air New Zealand House, Queen St
Auckland ☎09/357-3000

Anywhere Travel
345 Anzac Parade, Kingsford
Sydney ☎02/663-0411

Brisbane Discount Travel
360 Queen St, Brisbane ☎07/229-9211

British Airways
64 Castlereagh St, Sydney ☎02/258-3300
Dilworth Building, Queen St/Customs St
Auckland ☎09/367-7500

Budget Travel
PO Box 505, Auckland ☎09/309-4313

Exodus Expeditions
81A Glebe Point Rd, Sydney ☎008/800 724

Flight Centres
Circular Quay, Sydney ☎02/241-2422
Bourke St, Melbourne ☎03/650-2899
205–225 Queen St, Auckland ☎09/309-6171
152 Hereford St, Christchurch ☎03/379-7145
50–52 Willis St, Wellington ☎04/472-8101

Northwest
309 Kent St, Level 13, Sydney ☎02/290-4455

Passport Travel
320b Glenferrie Rd, Malvern
Melbourne ☎03/824-7183

Qantas
Qantas International Centre, International Square
Sydney ☎02/236-3636

Snowscene
3360 Pacific Highway, Springwood
NSW ☎008/777 053

STA Travel
209 King St, New Town, Sydney ☎02/519-9866
256 Flinders St, Melbourne ☎03/347-4711
10 High St, Auckland ☎09/309-9723
233 Cuba St, Wellington ☎04/385-0561

Thai International Airways
Kensington Swan Building, 22 Fanshawe St
Auckland ☎09/377-0268

Topdeck Travel
45 Grenfell St, Adelaide ☎08/410-1110

Tymtro Travel
Wallaceway Shopping Centre
Chatswood, Sydney ☎02/411-1222

United
5th Floor, 10 Barrack St, Sydney ☎02/237-8888
7 City Rd, Auckland ☎09/379-3800

destinations, flying daily to LA and three times a week to San Francisco for A$1842/2156, with connections to **Seattle** or **Vancouver** for the same price; to **Portland** (A$2160/2474); to **Calgary** (A$2015/2329); to **Edmonton** (with *Canadian Pacific* via Vancouver; A$2038/2352); and to **Anchorage** (A$2597/2911). You're allowed two stopovers, can change the dates of travel after booking, and, at a discount, can break the journey to accommodate alternative travel methods between points on your way up the coast.

From **New Zealand**, *Air France* fly weekly to Los Angeles (with a two-night stopover in Tahiti) for a low NZ$1600; an extra NZ$570 buys three flight coupons valid in the continental US, or NZ$620 if you need to reach Alaska. *United* also fly from Auckland to San Francisco/Los Angeles for NZ$1699; three internal flight coupons, to include Anchorage, bring the cost to NZ$2870.

Of the travel agents listed in the box above, *Adventure World*, *Exodus* and *Snowscene* are particularly recommended for their organized package vacations to the Northwest.

GETTING THERE FROM NORTH AMERICA

See "Getting Around", p.30, for details of transportation **within the Pacific Northwest**. For more information on **getting to Alaska**, see p.486.

Travelling to the Northwest from anywhere else in North America is straightforward, but any means of transportation other than flying is likely to be inordinately time-consuming without necessarily saving significant amounts of money. Vancouver and Seattle are very much the major points of access; Anchorage in Alaska no longer plays the pivotal role in connecting international air routes that it once did.

BY AIR

The principal airports in the Northwest are those at **Seattle**, **Portland**, **Vancouver**, **Calgary**, and **Edmonton**. Major US air carriers such as *American*, *Delta*, *United*, *Continental*, and *Northwest* regularly fly to them all from other cities **in the US**, though services to Seattle and Portland tend to be both more direct and more frequent. *Air Canada* and *Canadian Airlines International* should be your first choice for frequent service from major cities **in Canada**.

With the major carriers involved in inc(r)easing price wars, it's always worth checking the Sunday newspapers for current fare bargains, as well as getting in touch with such discount travel agents as *STA Travel* or *Council Travel* (addresses listed on p.10). The best value **ticket** to buy is the **APEX** (Advanced Purchase Excursion Fare), which has to be purchased two to three weeks ahead of your departure date and requires a Saturday night stayover. Fares are cheaper still if you travel on "off" days such as Monday and Tuesday.

FROM EASTERN AND CENTRAL US

Although it's always hard to quote exact fares, travellers from **New York** can expect to pay anywhere from $468 to $648 round-trip for flights to Seattle or Portland (though APEX fares on *Mark Air* drop as low as $388); between $447 and $527 for flights to Calgary; $527–700 to Edmonton; and $400–700 to Vancouver. From **Chicago**, fares to Seattle and Portland average $440; Calgary ranges from $299 to $377; Edmonton should cost around $370, and Vancouver $424.

TOLL-FREE NUMBERS IN THE US AND CANADA

Air BC	☎1-800/663-8868	Kenmore Air	☎1-800/543-9595
Air Canada	☎1-800/776-3000	Mark Air	☎1-800/627-5247
Alaska Airlines	☎1-800/426-0333	Morris Air	☎1-800/444-5660
American Airlines	☎1-800/433-7300	Northwest	☎1-800/225-2525
America West	☎1-800/235-9292	Reno Airlines	☎1-800/736-6247
Canadian Airlines International	☎1-800/426-7000	Tower Air	☎1-800/221-2500
Canadian Partner	☎1-800/426-7000	United Airlines	☎1-800/241-6522
Continental	☎1-800/231-0856	United Express	☎1-800/241-6522
Delta	☎1-800/221-1212	US Air	☎1-800/428-4322
Horizon Air	☎1-800/547-9308		

The lowest fare to **Anchorage** from New York is $692 on *Mark Air*, while *United* charges from $725 to $1500. From Chicago to Anchorage costs between $500 and $700.

FROM THE WEST COAST

Competition between regional airlines on the West Coast serves to bring fares down to attractive levels. For example, a San Francisco–Seattle round trip on *Mark Air* is $140; Los Angeles–Portland is $198 on *Reno*. With the bigger carriers, these fares usually run more like $200 to $350. Flights from Los Angeles to Calgary and Vancouver average $300–600; Edmonton is similar at $350–580. Alaska fares from California are higher, at from $500 to $850 to Anchorage. Flights from Seattle to Anchorage usually cost around $450 round-trip.

FROM CANADA

Flights on *Air Canada* leave **Toronto** daily for Vancouver – costing around Can$500 round-trip. Through fares to Seattle and Portland average Can$669, and rates from Montréal are similar.

At present, no airline flies direct from Canada to Anchorage. The only routing is through the US,

---

DISCOUNT AGENTS IN THE US AND CANADA

Council Travel
Nationwide US student travel organization.
Head office:
205 E 42nd St, New York, NY 10017 (☎212/661-1450).

Other main offices at:
530 Bush St, Suite 700, San Francisco, CA 94108 (☎415/421-3473);

14515 Ventura Blvd, Suite 250, Sherman Oaks, CA 91403 (☎818/905-5777);

1138 13th St, Boulder, CO 80302 (☎303/447-8108);

3300 M St NW, 2nd Floor, Washington, DC 20007 (☎202/337-6464);

1153 N Dearborn St, Chicago, IL 60610 (☎312/951-0585);

729 Boylston St, Suite 201, Boston, MA 02116 (☎617/266-1926);

1501 University Ave SE, Room 300, Minneapolis, MN 55414 (☎612/379-2323);

2000 Guadalupe St, Suite 6, Austin, TX 78705 (☎512/472-4931);

1314 Northeast 43rd St, Suite 210, Seattle, WA 98105 (☎206/632-2448).

Travel Cuts
Canadian student travel organisation.
Head Office: 187 College St, Toronto, ON M5T 1P7 (☎416/979-2406).

Other main offices at:
MacEwan Hall Student Centre, University of Calgary, Calgary, AB T2N 1N4 (☎403/282-7687);

12304 Jasper Av, Edmonton, AB T5N 3K5 (☎403/488-8487);

Student Union Building, Dalhousie University, Halifax, NS B3H 4J2 (☎902/494-2054);

1613 rue St Denis, Montréal, PQ H2X 3K3 (☎514/843-8511);

1 Stewart St, Ottawa, ON K1N 6H7 (☎613/238-8222);

2383 Ch Ste Foy, Suite 103, Ste Foy, Quebec, PQ G1V 1T1 (☎418/654-0224);

Place Riel Campus Centre, University of Saskatchewan, Saskatoon SA S7N 0W0 (☎306/975-3722);

501–602 W Hastings, Vancouver BC V6B 1P2 (☎604/681-9136);

University Centre, University of Manitoba, Winnipeg MA R3T 2N2 (☎204/269-9530).

STA Travel
Worldwide specialist in independent travel.
☎1-800/777-0112 (nationwide information number).

Main offices at:
48 E 11th St, New York, NY 10003 (tele-sales ☎212/477-7166);

7202 Melrose Ave, Los Angeles, CA 90046 (tele-sales ☎213/934-8722);

ASUC Travel Center, MLK Jr Bldg, 2nd Floor, UC, Telegraph at Bancroft Way, Berkeley, CA 94720 (☎510/642-3000);

166 Geary St, Suite 702, San Francisco, CA 94108 (☎415/391-8407);

273 Newbury St, Boston, MA 02116 (☎617/266-6014);

3730 Walnut St, Philadelphia, PA 19104 (☎215/382-2928).

using *Alaska Airlines* to get from Seattle to Anchorage. Thus a flight from Toronto would take you through both Vancouver and Seattle, at a round-trip APEX fare of Can$786.

BY TRAIN

The only reason to consider travelling to the Pacific Northwest **by train** from the other side of the North American continent – and it's by no means a bad reason, at that – is if you think of the rail journey as an enjoyable part of your vacation in itself. Services are nothing like as frequent as they used to be, and not necessarily any less expensive than a flight.

ACROSS THE USA

For travellers who wish to cross the **USA** by rail, **Amtrak** has daily service to the Pacific Northwest aboard the *Empire Builder*, which takes a northern route from Chicago to Seattle; the *Pioneer*, which travels from Chicago to Seattle via Denver and Portland; and the *Coast Starlight*, which begins in Los Angeles and makes stops throughout western Oregon and Washington en route to Seattle.

Fares are generally more expensive than *Greyhound* buses over the same routes – and sometimes also pricier than air travel. One-way fares don't vary according to season – a one-way cross-country trip costs around $250 – but round-trip journeys can be much cheaper between September and May (excluding the Christmas period). **Discounts** are available to senior citizens (15 percent, Mon–Thurs only); travellers with disabilities (25 percent); and children from two to fifteen accompanied by an adult (half-fare): children under two travel free. You can also cut costs dramatically with Amtrak's **All-Aboard America** fares, which allow three stopovers and a maximum trip duration of 45 days. These divide the US into three regions, Eastern, Central, and Western, with the latter covering Washington and Oregon. The fare within any one region is $199, rising to $299 if you travel within and between two regions, and $399 among three.You must plan your itinerary beforehand, as well as your exact dates. The route may not be changed once travel has begun, though specific times and dates can be altered, at no cost, later on in the trip. Details of the **USA Rail Pass**, sold only to foreign travellers (including Canadian citizens – and US citizens who can prove they live abroad)

and operating according to slightly different zones, can be found on p.35.

Always **reserve** as far in advance as possible; *Amtrak* recommends two to three months in advance for summer travel. All passengers must have seats, and some trains, especially between major cities, are booked solid. Supplements are also payable, for **sleeping compartments** (which cost around $100 per night for one or two people, including three full meals), and for the plush *Metroliner* carriages, for example. Even standard *Amtrak* carriages are surprisingly spacious, and there are additional dining cars and lounge cars (with full bars and sometimes glass-domed 360° viewing compartments).

> For all **Amtrak** information, call ☎1-800/USA-RAIL.
> For all **Via rail** information, call ☎1-800/561-7860 in Canada, or ☎1-800/665-0200 in the US.

ACROSS CANADA

The railroad may have created modern **Canada**, but passenger services are now few and far between – at the beginning of 1990 over half the services of the Montréal-based **VIA rail Canada** were eliminated at a stroke, and remaining fares increased dramatically. Like *Amtrak*, trains are notoriously slow and delays common as passenger services give way to freight, however, rail travel can still be highly rewarding, especially on trains with special "dome cars" that allow an uninterrupted roof-top view of the countryside.

One of the saddest losses of the *VIA* cutbacks was the legendary **Canadian** train that followed the Canadian Pacific lines across the country daily from Montréal to Vancouver via Calgary and Banff in Alberta. Today's *Canadian* now departs three times weekly from Toronto, and though it still crosses the Northwest, its route follows the more northerly *Canadian National* lines. These take it to Edmonton and Jasper in Alberta, and then on to Vancouver via Prince George and Kamloops in BC, passing en route – like its predecessor – through some of the grandest scenery in the Canadian Rockies. A one-way ticket from Toronto to Vancouver costs Can$474 between mid-June and mid-September.

For further details of *VIA* rail services within western Canada, including the thrice-weekly *Skeena* from Jasper, Alberta to the British

Columbia port city of Prince Rupert, see p.30; for information concerning Canrail passes – available to visitors from outside Canada, and to Canadian and US citizens who can show they are domiciled abroad – see p.35.

BY BUS

Options for long-distance **bus travel** to the Pacific Northwest are basically limited to *Greyhound* (☎1-800/231-2222) and the funkier *Green Tortoise* (see box below). Ordinarily, the one-way three-day coast to coast *Greyhound* trip costs around $200, though a one-way APEX ticket from New York to Seattle, bought 14 days in advance and with a host of restrictions on travel times, can be as low as $110. The only real reason to go *Greyhound* is if you want to visit other places en route; Greyhound's *AmeriPass*, valid for unlimited travel within a certain time, costs $250 for 7 days, $350 for 15 days and $450 for 30 days (see p.34 for reduced rates for overseas travellers).

In Canada, *Greyhound* offers regular intercity bus routes along the Trans-Canada Highway from Toronto and Montréal to Vancouver and Calgary (Can$272 from Toronto to Vancouver, which takes 2 days and 17 hours; $232 Toronto–Calgary, in 2 days). Seats can be reserved in advance and tickets purchased by mail. The Montréal-based *Voyageur* company runs regularly between Montréal and Vancouver (☎514/842-2281).

The *Alaska Direct Bus Line* (☎1-800/770-6652) runs a marathon trip from Minneapolis/St Paul to Anchorage via North Dakota, Alberta and the Yukon. One-way fares start from $250.

BY CAR

Driving your own car (or renting one) may maximize your freedom and flexibility, but, once again, if you're travelling cross-country you'll need to allow plenty of time. If you do use your own car, make sure your insurance is up to date and that you are completely covered. In Canada, automobile insurance with covering of Can$2,000,000 is mandatory. General advice and help with route planning can be had from either the **American Automobile Association** *(AAA)*, 100 AAA Drive, Heathrow, FL 327746-5080 (☎AAA-HELP or 1-800/222-4357) or the **Canadian Automobile Association** *(CAA)* at 60 Commerce Valley Drive East, Thornhill, Ontario L3T 7PQ (☎416/7713111).

If you don't have a car, or you're not sure whether the car you do have will make the distance, consider working with an **automobile transit company**, who match drivers with car owners who need their cars moved from one city to another. The only expenses are gas, food, tools and lodging, and the company's insurance covers any breakdowns or damages. You must be at least 21, have a valid driver's licence and agree to drive about 400 miles per day on a fairly direct route. For more information, contact *Auto Driveaway,*

GREEN TORTOISE

One alternative to Long-Distance Bus Hell is the slightly counter-cultural **Green Tortoise**, whose buses, furnished with foam cushions, bunks, fridges and rock music, run between Los Angeles, San Francisco and Seattle (including a new "commuter" line from Seattle to Los Angeles, where you can board at any point). In summer, they also cross the United States from New York and Boston, transcontinental trips which amount to mini-tours of the country, taking around a dozen days (at a current cost of around $299–349, not including food), and allowing plenty of stops for hiking, river-rafting, and hot springs. Other organized *Green Tortoise* excursions include a 35-day trip from San Francisco north to **Alaska**, the latter with a ferry ride along the Inside Passage and side-trips into the Canadian Rockies (35 days, $1700, plus $250 for food). To be sure of a place on any ride, book one or two months in advance, though most services have space at departure. Deposits of around $100 are required for most trips.

Main Office:		New York	☎212/431-3348
PO Box 24459, San Francisco, CA 94124		Portland	☎503/225-0310
☎415/821-0803 or 1-800/227-4766.		San Francisco	☎415/821-0803
Seat Reservation Numbers		Santa Barbara	☎805/569-1884
Boston	☎617/265-8533	Santa Cruz	☎408/462-6437
Eugene	☎503/937-3603	Seattle	☎206/324-7433
Los Angeles	☎310/392-1990	Vancouver	☎604/732-5153

310 S Michigan Ave, Chicago, IL 60604 (☎1-800/
346-2277), or *Anthony's Driveaway*, PO Box 502,
62 Railroad Ave, East Rutherford, NJ 07073
(☎201/935-8030). Provided you're prepared either
to give plenty of advance notice, or to wait, you
should get the route you want.

American citizens planning to drive their own
cars into Canada should be certain to carry
proper owner registration and proof of insurance
coverage. The *Canadian Non-Resident Inter-
Provincial Motor Vehicle Liability Insurance Card*,
available from any US insurance company, is
accepted as evidence of financial responsibility
in Canada.

Toll-free numbers for **car rental** companies
are listed on p.38.

PACKAGE TOURS

If you're happy to have everything planned for
you, including transportation, a **package tour**
can make your vacation much easier; if you don't
yet know what you want to do, they're worth
checking out for ideas. Free-spirited, adventure-
some types may appreciate the convenience of
the "independent packages" put together by
airlines such as *American Airlines* (*Fly AAway
Vacations*; ☎1-800/321-2121), *United Airlines*
(*Vacation Planning Center*, ☎1-800/328-6877), or
Air Canada (*Tour Department*; ☎1-800/776-3000).

For details of the wide range of **cruises** that
explore the magnificent Pacific coast, all the way
north to Alaska, see p.33, or contact the tour
operators listed in the box below.

TOUR OPERATORS IN NORTH AMERICA

American Express Vacations
Box 5014, Atlanta   in GA ☎1-800/556-5454
GA 30302   elsewhere ☎1-800/241-1700

Contiki Holidays
300 Plaza Alicante, Suite 900
Garden Grove, CA 92640   ☎714/740-0808

Cosmos/Globus Gateway
150 S Los Robles Ave   ☎818/449-0919
Suite 860, Pasadena, CA   ☎1-800/556-5454

Gray Line of Seattle
720 S Forest St
Seattle, WA 98134   ☎206/624-5813

Holland America Westours
300 Elliott Ave W   ☎206/281-3535
Seattle, WA 98119   ☎1-800/426-0327

Maupintour
1515 St Andrews Drive   ☎913/843-1211
Lawrence, KS 66046   ☎1-800/255-4266

Suntrek Tours America
PO Box 1190
Rohnert Park, CA 94928   ☎1-800/292-9696

Trek America
PO Box 1338
Gardena   ☎1-800/221-0596

ENTRY REQUIREMENTS FOR FOREIGN VISITORS

The same form can be used by citizens of most European countries, provided their passports are up to date, and covers entry into the US across the land borders with Canada.

However, prospective visitors from Ireland, Australia, New Zealand, and all other parts of the world require a valid passport and a **non-immigrant visitor's visa**. To obtain a visa, fill in the application form available at most travel agents and send it with a full passport to the nearest US Embassy or Consulate. Visas are not issued to convicted criminals and anybody who owns up to being a communist, fascist or drug dealer.

VISAS

The visa situation for British travellers who plan to visit the Pacific Northwest is straightforward; no one who holds a full UK passport (not a British Visitor's Passport) requires a visa to enter Canada or the United States for a period of ninety days or less.

UNITED STATES

The **United States** has speeded up its immigration procedures in the last few years by using the **Visa Waiver Scheme** instead of requiring visas. Eligible visitors have to fill in a **visa waiver form**, which is provided either by travel agencies, or by the airline during check-in, or on the plane, and must be presented to immigration on arrival.

CANADA

British citizens, as well as citizens of the European Union (EU), Scandinavia and most British Commonwealth countries do *not* need an entry visa to visit **Canada**: all that is required is a full valid passport. However, admission is normally granted for a period of up to ninety days. If you plan a longer trip, Canadian immigration officials *may* permit stays of up to a maximum of six months: check with the Canadian High Commission for details before you leave.

IMMIGRATION CONTROLS

Standard immigration regulations apply to all visitors. During the flight, you'll be handed an **immigration form** (and a customs declaration: see below), which must be given up at immigration control once you land. The form requires details

US AND CANADIAN TRAVELLERS

United States and Canadian citizens are in a particularly privileged position when it comes to crossing the border into one another's countries. For a brief excursion, you do not necessarily need even a passport, just some form of ID; if you're obviously setting off on a longer trip, you should carry a passport, and if you plan to stay for more than ninety days you need a visa too.

Bear in mind that if you cross the border in your car, trunks and passenger compartments are subject to spot searches by the customs personnel of both countries, though this sort of surveillance is likely to decrease as remaining tariff barriers fall over the next few years. At present, though, officers at the more obscure entry points on the border – and there are several in the Northwest – can be real sticklers, so expect to be delayed. Remember, too, that both nationalities are legally barred from seeking gainful employment in each other's country.

Americans who visit Canada for at least 48 hours and haven't made an international trip in 30 days can bring back goods to the value of $400. Gifts valued at less than $40 that do not contain tobacco or alcohol can be brought into Canada; those valued at more than $40 are subject to regular import duty on the excess amount. The US Customs Service (☎202/927-6724) can help with any queries. Canadian citizens should contact External Affairs at ☎613/957-0275.

US EMBASSY AND CONSULATES IN CANADA

Embassy
100 Wellington St, Ottawa, ON K1P 5T1 ☎613/238-5335

Consulates
Suite 1050, 615 Macleod Trail
Calgary, AB ☎403/266-8962

Suite 910, Cogswell Tower, Scotia Square
Halifax, NS ☎902/429-2480

Complex Desjardins, South Tower
Montréal, PQ ☎514/281-1468

2 Place Terrace Dufferin
Québec City, PQ ☎418/692-2095

360 University Ave
Toronto, ON ☎416/595-1700

1095 West Pender St
Vancouver, BC ☎604/685-4311

US EMBASSIES AND CONSULATES ELSEWHERE

UK

5 Upper Grosvenor St
London W1 ☎071/499 9000

3 Regent Terrace
Edinburgh EH7 5BW ☎031/556 8315

Queens House, 14 Queen St
Belfast BT1 6EQ ☎0232/328239

Australia
Moonhah Place
Canberra ☎62/270 5000

Denmark
Dag Hammerskjöld Allé 24
2100 Copenhagen ☎31/ 42 31 44

Ireland
42 Elgin Rd, Ballsbridge
Dublin ☎01/687122

Netherlands
Museumplein 19
Amsterdam ☎020/310 9209

New Zealand
29 Fitzherbert Terrace, Thorndon
Wellington ☎04/722 068

Norway
Drammensveien 18
Oslo ☎22 44 85 50

Sweden
Strandvägan 101
Stockholm ☎08/783 5300

of where you are staying on your first night (if you don't know, write "touring") and the date you intend to **leave** the US or Canada. If you give the name and address of a friend, don't be surprised if immigration check. You should be able to prove that you have enough money to support yourself while in the US or Canada; something in the region of $250 cash per week is considered sufficient. Anyone revealing the slightest intention of working while in either country – or admitting to being HIV positive or having AIDS – is likely to be refused admission.

Part of the immigration form will be attached to your passport, where it must stay until you leave, when an immigration or airline official will detach it.

CUSTOMS

Customs officers will relieve you of your customs declaration and check whether you're carrying any fresh foods. You'll also be asked if you've visited a farm in the last month: if you have, you

could well lose your shoes. The **duty-free allowance** if you're over 17 in the US and over 19 in Canada is 200 cigarettes and 100 cigars (50 cigars in Canada), and a liter of spirits (you must be over 21 in the US to bring in spirits).

As well as foods and anything agricultural, the USA prohibits travellers from bringing in any articles from North Korea or Cuba. Canada and the US forbid the importation of such things as obscene publications, protected wildlife species, and pre-Columbian artefacts. Anyone found to be carrying drugs into either country will not only face prosecution but be entered in the records as an undesirable and probably denied entry for all time.

EXTENSIONS

The date stamped on your immigration form is the latest you're legally allowed to stay. Leaving a few days later may not matter, especially if you're heading home, but more than a week or so can result in a protracted, rather unpleasant,

FOREIGN EMBASSIES AND CONSULATES IN THE US

Great Britain

Embassy:
3100 Massachusetts Ave NW
Washington DC 20008
☎202/462-1340

Consulates:
33 N Dearborn St
Chicago, IL 60602
☎312/346-1810

3701 Wilshire Blvd, #312
Los Angeles, CA 90010
☎213/385-7381

1001 S Bayshore Drive, #2110
Miami, FL 33131
☎305/374-1522

845 Third Ave
New York, NY 10022
☎212/745-0200

1 Sansome St, #850
San Francisco, CA 94104
☎415/981-3030

Australia

1601 Massachusetts Ave NW
Washington DC 20036-2273
☎202/797-3000

Canada

501 Pennsylvania Ave NW
Washington DC 20001
☎202/682-1740

Denmark

3200 Whitehaven St NW
Washington DC 20008
☎202/234-4300

Ireland

2234 Massachusetts Ave NW
Washington DC 20008
☎202/462-3939

Netherlands

4200 Linnean Ave NW
Washington DC 20008
☎202/244-5300

New Zealand

37 Observatory Circle NW
Washington DC 20008
☎202/328-4800

Norway

2720 34th St NW
Washington DC 20008
☎202/333-6000

Sweden

600 New Hampshire Ave NW, #1200
Washington DC 20037
☎202/944-5600

For details of foreign consulates **in the Pacific Northwest**, see the relevant city accounts for **Seattle**, **Portland**, **Vancouver**, **Calgary** and **Edmonton**.

interrogation from officials which may cause you to miss your flight. Overstaying may also cause you to be turned away next time you try to enter the US or Canada.

To get an extension before your time is up, apply in the United States to the nearest **US Immigration and Naturalization Service** (INS) office, or in Canada to a **Canada Immigration Centre**, preferably in writing well before the end of the authorized visit (their address will be under the Federal Government Offices listings in the phone book). They will assume that you're working illegally and it's up to you to convince them otherwise. Do this by providing evidence of ample finances, and, if you can, bring along an upstanding American or Canadian citizen to vouch for you. You'll also have to explain why you didn't plan for the extra time initially.

WORK AND STUDY

Anyone planning an extended legal stay in the United States or Canada should apply for a special working visa at any Canadian or American Embassy/High Commission before setting off. Different types of visas are issued, depending on your skills and length of stay, but unless you've got relatives (parents or children over 21) or a prospective employer to sponsor you, your chances are at best slim.

Illegal work is nothing like as easy to find as it used to be, especially in the States now that the government has introduced fines of up to $10,000 for companies caught employing anyone without the legal right to work in the US. Even in traditionally more casual establishments such as restaurants, bars and fish canneries, things have really tightened up, and if you do find work it's likely to be of the less visible, poorly paid kind – washer-up instead of waiter.

Students have the best chance of prolonging their stay in either country. One way is to get on to an Exchange Visitor Programme in the US, for which participants are given a J-1 visa that entitles them to take paid summer employment and apply for a social security number. However, you should note that most of these visas are issued for jobs in American **summer camps**, which aren't everybody's idea of a good time; they fly you over, and after a summer's work you end up with around $500 and a month to blow it in. If you live in Britain and are interested, contact *BUNAC* (16 Bowling Green Lane, London EC1; ☎071/251 3472), or *Camp America* (37 Queens' Gate, London SW7; ☎071/589 3223). If you want to **study** at an American or Canadian university, apply to that institution directly; if they accept you, you're more or less entitled to unlimited visas so long as you remain enrolled in full-time education.

INSURANCE, HEALTH AND PERSONAL SAFETY

INSURANCE

Though not compulsory, **travel insurance** is *essential* for **foreign travellers**. The US has as yet no national health system, and you can lose an arm and a leg (so to speak) having even minor medical treatment; Canada has an excellent health service, but non-residents have to pay anything from $50 to $1000 a day to use it. There is no free treatment, and in some Canadian provinces doctors and hospitals actually add a surcharge to treatment meted out to foreigners.

Insurance policies can be bought through any high street travel agent or insurance broker, though the cheapest in Britain are generally *Endsleigh*, 97–107 Southampton Row, London WC1 (☎071/436 4451), *Touropa*, 52 Grosvenor Gardens, London SW1W 0NP (☎071/730 2101), or *Columbus Travel Insurance* (071/375 0011). Elsewhere in the world, try your nearest *STA* or *Travel Cuts* office (addresses on p.5 and p.10).

On all policies, read the small print to ensure the cover includes a sensible amount for medical expenses – this should be at least £1,000,000, which will cover the cost of an air ambulance to fly you home in the event of serious injury or hospitalization.

American and Canadian travellers should find that their **health insurance** should cover any health charges or costs; you may well consider it essential however to be covered against the loss of your possessions or money as well. Many bank and charge accounts include some form of coverage, and insurance may also be included if you pay for your trip with a credit card. Check any insurance policies you already have before taking out a new one. If you do want a specific travel insurance policy, there are numerous kinds to choose from. **Trip cancellation-and-interruption** insurance protects you in the event you are unable to undertake or complete your trip; **default** or **bankruptcy** insurance protects you against a supplier's failure to deliver. Consider the first one if your airline ticket or package tour doesn't allow changes or cancellations. The amount of coverage should equal or exceed the cost of your trip. Read the fine print carefully. You are advised to pay for your trip with a credit card; that way you can refuse to pay the bill on your return if services haven't been rendered.

In the event that you do incur medical expenses, save all the **forms** to support a claim for subsequent reimbursal. Remember also that time limits may apply when making claims after the fact, so promptness in contacting your insurer is highly advisable.

TRAVEL INSURANCE AGENTS IN NORTH AMERICA

Carefree Travel Insurance
100 Garden City Plaza, PO Box 9366
Fifth Floor, Garden City   ☎516/294-0220
NY 11530   or ☎1-800/323-3149

Travel Guard
1145 Clark St   ☎715/345-0505
Stevens Point, WI 54481   or ☎1-800/826-1300

The Travellers Companies
1 Tower Square   ☎203/277-0111
Hartford, CT 06183   or ☎1-800/243-3174

Wallach and Company, Inc
107 W Federal St, Box 480   ☎703/687-3166
Middleburg, VA 22117   or ☎1-800/237-6615

World Access
6600 W Broad St   ☎804/285-3300
Richmond, VA 23230   or ☎1-800/955-4002

HEALTH ADVICE FOR FOREIGN TRAVELLERS

If you have a serious **accident** while in the US or Canada, emergency medical services will get to you quickly and charge you later. For emergencies or ambulances in both countries, dial ☎911 (or whatever variant may be on the information plate of the pay phone). Note, though, that in parts of rural Canada you may still have to call ☎0 for the operator instead.

Should you need to see a **doctor**, lists can be found in the Yellow Pages under "Clinics" or "Physicians and Surgeons". A basic consultation fee is $50–75, payable in advance. Medications aren't cheap either – keep all your receipts for later claims on your insurance policy.

Many **minor ailments** can be remedied using the fabulous array of potions and lotions available in **drugstores**. Foreign visitors should bear in mind that many pills available over the counter at home need a prescription in the US and Canada – most codeine-based painkillers, for example – and that local brand names can be confusing; ask for advice at the **pharmacy** in any drugstore.

Travellers from Europe do not require **inoculations** to enter the US or Canada.

See p.55 for advice on the specific health issues entailed by travelling in the Great Outdoors in the Pacific Northwest.

CRIME AND PERSONAL SAFETY

No one could pretend that North America is trouble-free, though in the Northwest – and in its Canadian component in particular – crime is far less of a problem than it is elsewhere. Away from the urban centers, crime is low-key – perhaps the odd bar brawl in a rough and ready small town. Even the lawless reputation of larger American cities tends to be exaggerated, and most parts of these cities, by day at least, are fairly safe; at night, though, a few areas should be off-limits. By being careful, planning ahead and taking good care of your possessions, you should, generally speaking, have few real problems.

Foreign visitors tend to report that the police are helpful and obliging when things go wrong, although they'll be less sympathetic if they think you brought the trouble on yourself through carelessness.

MUGGING AND THEFT

Remember that although theft is rare, especially in Canada and Alaska, it's still a good idea to be aware of the potential threat of **mugging**. It's impossible to give hard and fast rules about what to do if you're confronted by a mugger. Whether to run, scream or fight depends on the situation – but most local people would just hand over their money. Of course, the best thing would be simply to avoid being mugged, and there are a few basic rules worth remembering: *don't* flash your money around; *don't* peer at your map (or this book) at every street corner, thereby announcing that you're a lost stranger; even if you're terrified or drunk (or both), *don't* appear so; avoid dark streets, especially ones you can't see the end of; and in the early hours stick to the roadside edge of the pavement so it's easier to run into the road to attract attention. If you have to ask for directions, choose your target carefully. Another idea is to carry a wad of cash, perhaps $50 or so, separate from the bulk of your holdings so that if you do get confronted you can hand over something of value without it costing you everything.

If the worst happens and your assailant is toting a gun or (more likely) a knife, try to stay calm: remember that he (for this is generally a male pursuit) is probably scared, too. Keep still, don't make any sudden movements – and hand over your money. When he's gone, you should, despite your shock, try to find a phone and dial ☎**911** (the emergency number in both Canada and the US), or hail a cab and ask the driver to take you to the nearest police station. Here, report the theft and get a reference number on the report to claim insurance and travellers' check refunds. If you're in a big city, ring the local help line or *Travelers Aid* (their numbers are listed in the phone book) for sympathy and practical advice. For specific advice for women in case of mugging or attack, see p.44.

Another potential source of trouble is having your **hotel room burgled**. Always store valuables in the hotel safe when you go out; when inside keep your door locked and don't open it to anyone you are suspicious of; if they claim to be hotel staff and you don't believe them, call reception on the room phone to check.

Needless to say, having bags snatched that contain travel documents can be a big headache, none more so for foreign travellers than **losing your passport**. If the worst happens, go to the

STOLEN TRAVELLERS' CHECKS AND CREDIT CARDS

Keep a record of the numbers of your **travellers' checks** separately from the actual checks; if you lose them, ring the issuing company on the toll-free number below.

They'll ask you for the check numbers, the place you bought them, when and how you lost them and whether it's been reported to the police. All being well, you should get the missing checks reissued within a couple of days – and perhaps an emergency advance to tide you over.

Emergency Numbers

Mastercard (*Access*)	☎1-800/999-0454
American Express (TCs)	☎1-800/221-7282
(credit cards)	☎1-800/528-4800
Diners Club	☎1-800/234-6377
Thomas Cook	☎1-800/223-7373
Visa	☎1-800/227-6811

nearest embassy or consulate and get them to issue you a **temporary passport**, basically a sheet of paper saying you've reported the loss, which will get you out of Canada or America and back home.

CAR CRIME

Crimes committed against tourists driving **rented cars** in a few parts of North America – especially Florida and California – may have garnered headlines around the world in recent years, but they remain rare in the Pacific Northwest. In major urbanized areas, any car you rent should have nothing on it – such as a particular licence plate – that makes it easy to spot as a rental car. When driving, under no circumstances stop in any unlit or seemingly deserted urban area – and especially not if someone is waving you down and suggesting that there is something wrong with your car. Similarly, if you are "accidentally" rammed by the driver behind, do not stop immediately but drive on to the nearest well-lit, busy area and phone the emergency number (☎911) for assistance. Keep your doors locked and windows never more than slightly open. Do not open your door or window if someone approaches your car on the pretext of asking directions. Hide any valuables out of sight, preferably locked in the boot or in the glove compartment (any valuables you don't need for your journey should be left in your hotel safe).

In the rougher areas of Seattle, several motorists have been gunned down in recent years for sounding their car horns at (young male) drivers who have blocked traffic by halting their vehicles in the middle of the road in order to talk to friends.

COSTS, MONEY AND BANKS

To help with planning your vacation, this book contains detailed price information for lodging and eating throughout the Northwest. Prices are given in either US or Canadian dollars as appropriate, with a label – US$ or Can$ – where confusion may arise. The two currencies do not have a one-for-one exchange rate; as this book went to press one Canadian dollar was worth about seventy-five US cents. Not surprisingly, Canadian shops and hotels are often prepared to accept US dollars, but not vice versa. Unless otherwise stated, the hotel price codes (explained on p.46) are for the cheapest double room in high season, exclusive of any local taxes, while meal prices include food only and not drinks or tip. For museums and similar attractions, the prices we quote are for adults; children usually get in half-price or free.

Even when the exchange rate is at its least advantageous (see below), most western European visitors find virtually everything – accommodation, food, fuel, cameras, clothes and more – to be better value in the US, and to a lesser extent Canada, than it is at home. However, if you're used to travelling in the less expensive countries of Europe, let alone in the rest of the world, you shouldn't expect to scrape by on the same minuscule budget once you're in the Northwest. You should also be prepared for regional variances; most prices in tourist areas, or in the far north, for example, tend to be above those in the rest of the region; Alaska in particular is consistently around twenty percent more expensive than Washington and Oregon.

Accommodation is likely to be your biggest single expense. Few hotel or motel rooms in the cities of either country cost under US$35 – it would be more usual to pay something like US$55 – and rates in rural areas are little cheaper. Although hostels offering dorm beds – usually for US$10 to $15 – are reasonably common, they're by no means everywhere, and in any case they save little money for two or more people travelling together. Camping, of course, is cheap, ranging from free to perhaps US$18 per night, but while an excellent prospect in the Northwest's great outdoors, is rarely practical in or around the big cities.

As for **food**, US$15 a day is enough to get an adequate life-support diet, while for a daily total of around US$30 you can dine pretty well. Beyond this, everything hinges on how much sightseeing, taxi-taking, drinking and socializing you do. Much of any of these – especially in a major city – and you're likely to be getting through upwards of US$50 a day.

The rates for **travelling** around using buses, trains and even planes, may look cheap on paper, but the distances involved are so great that costs soon mount up. For a group of two or more, renting a **car** can be a very good investment, not least because it will enable you to stay in the ubiquitous budget motels along the interstates instead of expensive city-center hotels.

In almost every state and province, **sales tax**, at rates varying up to fifteen percent, is added to virtually everything you buy in shops, but it isn't part of the marked price (for more details, see p.69). Alberta, with its big oil revenues, has no sales tax, but like most areas levies a **hotel rooms tax** (usually between five and ten percent), and like all of Canada levies the national seven percent **Goods and Services Tax** (GST). However, note that a GST **rebate** is available to visitors for **accommodation expenditure** over $100 during a maximum period of one month. This can add up to a significant amount, so take the trouble to pick up claim forms, available from many shops, hotels or from any Canadian embassy. Return them, with **all receipts**, to Revenue Canada, Customs and Excise, Visitors' Rebate Program, Ottawa, Canada K1a 1J5.

MONEY: A NOTE FOR FOREIGN TRAVELLERS

Regular upheaval in the world money markets causes the relative value of the **US and Canadian dollar** against the currencies of the rest of the world to vary considerably. Generally speaking, one **pound sterling** will buy between US$1.40 and $1.80 and between Can$1.80 and $2.10; the value of one **Canadian dollar** fluctuates between 75¢ and US$1.

BILLS AND COINS

US and Canadian currency comes in **bills** worth $1, $5, $10, $20, $50 and $100, plus various larger (and rarer) denominations. In the United States, confusingly, all are the same size and same green color, making it necessary to check each bill carefully. In Canada the notes all have different colors and designs. There is also a new Canadian $2 bill, whilst the country's $1 bill is being phased out and replaced by a gold-colored coin known as a "**loonie**" (after the bird on one face).

The dollar is made up of 100 cents in **coins** with the same names in both countries: 1 cent (known as a **penny**), 5 cents (a **nickel**), 10 cents (a **dime**) and 25 cents (a **quarter**). Very occasionally in the US you might come across **JFK half-dollars** (50¢), **Susan B Anthony dollar coins**, or a **two-dollar bill**. Change (quarters are the most useful) is needed for buses, vending machines and telephones, so always carry plenty.

TRAVELLERS' CHECKS

US dollar travellers' checks are the best way to carry money, for both North American and foreign visitors; they offer the great security of knowing that lost or stolen checks will be replaced. Only if you're restricting your travels to Canada alone is it worth taking Canadian dollar checks.

Although it's not always easy to change checks for cash in the US, there's no real need to do so. In neither country are you likely to have any problems using the better-known checks, such as *American Express* and *Visa*, in shops, restaurants and gas stations (don't be put off by "no checks" signs, which only refer to personal checks). Be sure to have plenty of the $10 and $20 denominations for everyday transactions.

Banks in both countries are generally open from 10am until 4pm Monday to Thursday, and 10am to 6pm on Friday, although the trend is towards longer opening hours and Saturday morning opening. Until recently, banks in the US were organized along state lines, so even the largest US banks only had branches in a single state. This is rapidly changing, but it can still be an awkward task to keep track of who's who. In Canada, travellers' checks can be cashed at most major banks, though the commission charged (which usually incorporates both a flat fee and a percentage levy) varies substantially. In general, you do better to change large amounts occasionally than small amounts frequently. For converting **foreign currency** in either country,

exchange bureaux such as *Thomas Cook* or *American Express*, always found at airports, tend to charge less commission. Rarely, if ever, do hotels change foreign currency.

Emergency phone numbers to call if your checks and/or credit cards are stolen are listed on p.20.

PLASTIC MONEY AND CASH MACHINES

If you don't already have a **credit card**, you should think seriously about getting one before you set off. For many services, it's simply taken for granted that you'll be paying with plastic. When renting a car (or even a bike) or checking into a hotel you may well be asked to show a credit card to establish your creditworthiness – even if you intend to settle the bill in cash. **Visa**, **Mastercard** (known elsewhere as **Access**), **Diners Club**, **Discover** and **American Express** are the most widely used.

With *Mastercard* or *Visa* it is also possible to **withdraw cash** at any bank displaying relevant stickers, or from appropriate automatic teller machines (**ATMs**) – though you're charged immediate interest for what is effectively a cash loan. *Diners Club* cards can be used to cash personal checks at *Citibank* branches. *American Express* cards can only get cash, or buy travellers' checks, at *American Express* offices (check the Yellow Pages) or from the travellers' check dispensers at most major airports. Most **Canadian** credit cards issued by hometown banks will be honored in the US and vice versa.

North American holders of ATM cards are likely to discover that their cards work in the machines of certain banks in other states and provinces (check with your bank before you leave home). Not only is this method of financing safer, but at around only a dollar per transaction it's economical as well.

Most major credit cards issued by **foreign banks** are accepted in the US and Canada, as well as cash-dispensing cards linked to international networks such as *Cirrus* and *Plus* – once again, check before you set off, as otherwise the machine may simply gobble up your plastic friend. Overseas visitors should also bear in mind that fluctuating exchange rates may result in spending more (or less) than expected when the item eventually shows up on a statement.

Each of the two main networks operates a toll-free line to let customers know the location of their nearest ATM; *Plus System* is ☎1-800/THE-PLUS, *Cirrus* is ☎1-800/4CI-RRUS.

EMERGENCIES

Assuming you know someone who is prepared to send you money in a crisis, the quickest way is to have them take the cash to the nearest **Western Union** office (information on ☎1-800/325-6000 in the US, or ☎0800/833833 in the UK) and have it instantaneously **wired** to the office nearest you, subject to the deduction of ten percent commission. **Thomas Cook** provides a similar service.

It's a bit less expensive to get a bank to transfer cash by cable, while if you have a few days' leeway, sending a postal money order, which is exchangeable at any post office, through the mail is cheaper still. The equivalent for foreign travellers is the **international money order**, for which you need to allow up to seven days in the international air mail before arrival. An ordinary check sent from overseas takes 2–3 weeks to clear.

Foreigners in difficulties have the final option of throwing themselves on the mercy of their nearest national **Consulate** (see p.16), who will – in worst cases only – repatriate you, but will never, under any circumstances, lend you money.

TELEPHONES, TIME ZONES AND MAIL

Although visitors from overseas have always tended to be impressed by the speed and efficiency of communications in North America – with the exception of the US mail – matters are not exactly improving. The break-up of "Ma Bell"'s monopoly has left a plethora of competing telephone companies which often appear to prioritize local and domestic calls over international links.

TELEPHONES

Public telephones in the US and Canada invariably work, and in cities at any rate can be found everywhere – on street corners, in railway and bus stations, hotel lobbies, bars and restaurants. They take 25¢, 10¢ and 5¢ coins. The cost of a **local call** from a public phone (within a limited radius, rather than the entire area covered by any one code) varies, from a minimum of 25¢ – when necessary, a voice comes on the line telling you to pay more.

Some numbers covered by the same area code are considered so far apart that calls between them count as **non-local** (*zone calls*). These cost much more and usually require you to dial 1 before the seven-digit number. Pricier still are **long-distance calls** (ie to a different area code), for which you'll need a stack of change. Non-local calls and long-distance calls are much less expensive if made between 6pm and 8am, and calls from **private phones** are always much cheaper than those from public phones. Detailed rates are listed at the front of the **telephone directory** (the White Pages, a copious source of information on many matters).

USEFUL NUMBERS

Emergencies ☎911 (US and Canada); ask for the appropriate emergency service: fire, police or ambulance

Long-distance directory information
(US and Canada) ☎1 (Area Code)/555-1212

Directory enquiries for toll-free numbers
(US and Canada) ☎1-800/555-1212

INTERNATIONAL TELEPHONE CALLS

International calls can be dialled direct from private or (more expensively) public phones. You can get assistance from the **international operator (☎1-800/874-4000)**, who may also interrupt every three minutes asking for more money, and call you back for any money still owed immediately after you hang up. The **lowest rates** for international calls to Europe are between 6pm and 8am, when a direct-dialled three-minute call will cost roughly $5.

In **Britain**, it's possible to obtain a free **BT Chargecard** (☎0800/800 838), using which all calls from overseas can be charged to your quarterly domestic account. To use these cards in the US, or to make a **collect call** (to "reverse the charges"), contact the local operator: *AT&T* ☎1-800/445-5667; *MCI* ☎1-800/444-2162; or *Sprint* ☎1-800/800-0008.

The telephone code to dial **TO the US and Canada** from the outside world is 1.
To make international calls **FROM the US and Canada**, dial 011 followed by the country code:

Australia 61	**Ireland** 353	**Sweden** 46
Denmark 45	**Netherlands** 31	**United Kingdom** 44
Germany 49	**New Zealand** 64	

TELEPHONE AREA CODES WITHIN THE NORTHWEST

Alaska (AK)	907
Alberta (AB)	403
British Columbia (BC)	604
Northwest Territories (NWT)	403 and 819
Oregon (OR)	503
Washington (WA) Seattle	206
Eastern Washington	509
Yukon (YT)	403

Making telephone calls from **hotel rooms** is always a lot more expensive than from a payphone, though some hotels offer free local calls from rooms – ask when you check in. An increasing number of phones accept **credit cards**, while anyone who holds a credit card issued by a major North American bank can obtain an **AT&T** (or similar) **charge card**, sometimes known as an **affinity card** (information on ☎1-800/874-4000 ext 359).

Many government agencies, car rental firms, hotels and so on have **toll-free numbers**, which always have the prefix ☎1-800. Generally these can be dialled from anywhere in mainland North America, but in the Northwest you may find the line is toll-free only within either the US or Canada, but not both. Phone numbers with the prefix ☎1-900 are pay-per-call lines, generally quite expensive and almost always involving either sports or phone sex.

States and provinces within the Northwest have different **area codes** – three-digit numbers which must precede the seven-figure number if you're calling from abroad or from a region with a different code. In this book, we've highlighted the local area codes at appropriate moments in the text, and they're also listed in the box above. On any specific number we give, we've only included the area code if it's not clear from the text which one you should use, or if a given phone number lies outside the region currently being described.

MAIL SERVICES

Post offices in the United States are usually open Monday to Friday from 9am until 5pm, and Saturday from 9am to noon; in Canada they open Monday to Friday from 8.30am to 5.30pm, and on Saturdays from 9am to noon. **Stamps** can also be bought from automatic vending machines, the lobbies of larger hotels, airports, train stations, bus terminals and many retail outlets and newsstands. Mailboxes are blue in the US, red in Canada. Ordinary **mail** costs 29¢ for a letter weighing up to an ounce in the US (95¢ to post mail abroad), 43¢ in Canada (and 86¢ abroad). Addresses must include the **zip**, or **postal code**, as well as the sender's address on the envelope. **Air mail** between the US and Europe generally takes about a week. Postcards cost 40¢, aerograms are 45¢, while letters weighing up to half an ounce (a single thin sheet) are 50¢. There is no separate air mail rate in Canada for mail sent abroad: **aerogrammes** (86¢) can only be mailed to destinations in Canada. Mail sent **Priority Courier** from Canada should reach US cities (Can$23.50 per document) the following day, and international destinations in two days (Can$63).

The last line of the address is made up of an abbreviation denoting the state or province (Washington is "WA", the Yukon is "YT", for example, though you can spell it in full if you're unsure; see the list in the phone codes box) and a multi-digit number – the zip code (US) or postal code (Canada) – denoting the local post office (codes in Canada have a mix of numbers and letters). Letters which don't carry a code are liable to get lost or at least delayed; if you don't know it, phone books carry a list for their service area, and post offices – even in Europe – have directories.

Letters can be sent c/o **General Delivery** in both the US and Canada (what's known elsewhere as **poste restante**) to the one relevant post office in each town or city (for larger cities, we list these in the *Guide*), but *must* include the zip code and will usually only be held for thirty days (fifteen days in Canada) before being returned to sender – so make sure there's a return address on the envelope. If you're receiving mail at someone else's address, it should include "c/o" and the regular occupant's name; otherwise it, too, is likely to be returned. Letters will also be held at **hotels** – mark such mail "Guest Mail, Hold For Arrival". If you hold an *American Express* card or travellers' checks you can have mail sent to *Amex* offices throughout the Northwest (label such mail "client letter service", and confirm arrangements in advance). Others can pick up mail from *Amex* for a small fee (we give addresses of *Amex* offices in the larger cities). For details on the service call ☎1-800/528-4800.

The rules covering the sending of **parcels** are very rigid: all packages have to be in special containers bought from post offices and must be sealed according to their instructions, which are given at the start of the Yellow Pages. To send anything out of the country, you'll need a green **customs declaration form**, available from a post office.

TELEGRAMS AND FAXES

To send a **telegram** (sometimes called a *wire*), don't go to a post office but to a *Western Union* office in the US, or a *CN/CP Public Message Centre* in Canada (listed in the Yellow Pages). Credit card holders can dictate messages over the phone. In Canada you can also phone in **telepost** messages, a guaranteed next-day or sooner service to anywhere in Canada or the US. **International telegrams** cost slightly less than the cheapest international phone call: one sent in the morning from North America should arrive at its overseas destination the following day. For domestic telegrams ask for a **mailgram**, which will be delivered to any address in the country the next morning.

Public **fax** machines, which may require your credit card to be "swiped" through an attached device, are found in the US at photocopy centers and, occasionally, bookstores. An international fax service, **Intelpost**, is available at larger Canadian post offices.

TIME ZONES

The Northwest spreads over three different time zones; the **Mountain** zone covers Alberta and is two hours behind the East Coast, seven behind Britain; the **Pacific Standard** zone includes Oregon, Washington, BC, Yukon and is three hours behind New York, eight behind London. **Alaska** is a further hour behind the Pacific zone.

INFORMATION AND MAPS

The most useful source of information on the Northwest is the enormous range of free maps, leaflets and brochures distributed by each of the various state and provincial tourist offices (see box below). Write well in advance of your departure, and be as specific as possible about your interests. Most maps issued by park and tourist offices will be sufficient for the trails recommended in this book, but for the backcountry or long distance paths you must track down more detailed maps.

The USTTA – United States Travel and Tourism Administration – has offices all over the world, usually in US embassies and consulates. These serve mainly as clearing houses, stocking vast quantities of printed material, but are unable to help with specific queries. In Britain, you can only contact them by telephone, on ☎071/495 4466 (Mon–Fri 10am–4pm). Canadian embassies, consulates and high commissions offer similar services, and can generally respond to specific questions. Many provinces also keep extremely helpful offices abroad: in Britain you should definitely contact **Alberta House**, 1 Mount St, London W1Y 5AA (☎071/491 3430) and **British Columbia House**, I Regent St, London SW1 4NS (☎071/930 6857) before you leave.

Visitor centers go under a variety of names through out the Northwest (in BC, for example, they're called **infocentres**) but they all provide details on the area (typically open Mon–Fri 9am–5pm, Sat 9am–1pm). In the US they're often known as the "Convention and Visitors Bureau" (CVB); in smaller towns, many operate under the auspices of the **Chamber of Commerce**, who promote local business interests. **Park** visitor centers (again the name varies) should invariably be your first port-of-call in any national, state or provincial park. Staff are usually outdoors experts, and can offer invaluable advice on trails, current conditions and outfitting or adventure possibilities. Most large communities also have **free newspapers** carrying entertainment listings.

STATE TOURIST OFFICES

Alaska
Alaska Division of Tourism, PO Box 11081, Juneau, AK 99811; ☎907/465-2010

Alberta
Alberta Tourism, PO Box 2500, Edmonton, Alberta, T5J 2Z4; ☎403/427-4321 or 1-800/661-8888

British Columbia
Tourism British Columbia, Parliament Buildings, Victoria, BC V8V 1X4; ☎604/387-1642, 1-800/888-8835 or 1-800/663-6000 (US)

Northwest Territories
NWT Dept of Tourism, Yellowknife, Northwest Territories X1A 2L9; ☎403/873-7200 or 1-800/661-0788

Oregon
Oregon Tourism Division, 775 Summer St NE, Salem OR 97310; ☎503/378-3451 or 1-800/547-7842

Washington
Washington State Tourism Development Division 101 General Administration Building, PO Box 42513, Olympia WA 98504-2513; ☎206/586-2102 or 1-800/544-1800

Yukon Territory
Tourism Yukon, PO Box 2703, Whitehorse, Yukon Y1A 2C6; ☎403/667-5340 or 1-800/661-0788 (US and Canada)

MAPS

The **free maps** issued by each state, provincial or local tourist offices are usually fine for general driving and route planning. To get hold of one, either write to the office directly or stop by any visitor center. *Rand McNally* produces good commercial maps of the US and Canada, bound together in their *Rand McNally Road Atlas*, or printed separately for individual states and provinces. Excellent atlases of individual American

MAP OUTLETS IN THE UK

London

National Map Centre, 22–24 Caxton St, SW1 (☎071/222 4945);

Stanfords, 12–14 Long Acre, WC2 (☎071/836 1321);

The Travellers Bookshop, 25 Cecil Court, WC2 (☎071/836 9132).

Edinburgh

Thomas Nelson and Sons Ltd, 51 York Place, EH1 3JD (☎031/557 3011).

Glasgow

John Smith and Sons, 57–61 St Vincent St (☎041/221 7472).

Maps by **mail or phone order** are available from *Stanfords* (☎071/836 1321).

MAP OUTLETS IN NORTH AMERICA

Chicago

Rand McNally, 444 N Michigan Ave, IL 60611 (☎312/321-1751).

Montréal

Ulysses Travel Bookshop, 4176 St-Denis (☎514/289-0993).

New York

British Travel Bookshop, 551 5th Ave, NY 10176 (☎1-800/448-3039 or 212/490-6688);

The Complete Traveler Bookstore, 199 Madison Ave, NY 10016 (☎212/685-9007);

Rand McNally, 150 East 52nd St, NY 10022 (☎212/758-7488);

Traveler's Bookstore, 22 West 52nd St, NY 10019 (☎212/664-0995).

San Francisco

The Complete Traveler Bookstore, 3207 Fillmore St, CA 92123 (☎415/923-1511);

Rand McNally, 595 Market St, CA 94105 (☎415/777-3131).

Seattle

Elliot Bay Book Company, 101 South Main St, WA 98104 (☎206/624-6600).

Toronto

Open Air Books and Maps, 25 Toronto St, M5R 2C1 (☎416/363-0719).

Vancouver

World Wide Books and Maps, 1247 Granville St. (☎604/687-3320).

Washington DC

Rand McNally, 1201 Connecticut Ave NW, Washington DC 20036 (☎202/223-6751).

Note that *Rand McNally* now have 24 stores across the US; phone ☎1-800/333-0136 (ext 2111) for the address of your nearest store, or for **direct mail** maps.

MAP OUTLETS IN AUSTRALIA

Adelaide

The Map Shop, 16a Peel St, Adelaide, SA 5000 (☎08/231 2033).

Brisbane

Hema, 239 George St, Brisbane, QLD 4000 (☎07/221 4330).

Melbourne

Bowyangs, 372 Little Bourke St, Melbourne, VIC 3000 (☎03/670 4383).

Perth

Perth Map Centre, 891 Hay St, Perth, WA 6000 (☎09/322 5733).

Sydney

Travel Bookshop, 20 Bridge St, Sydney, NSW 2000 (☎02/241 3554).

states – simply the best for drivers – are produced by *DeLorme Mapping*, PO Box 298, Freeport, Maine (☎207/865-4171). They currently cover 26 states, including Washington, Oregon and Alaska, at an average cost of $15 per book; with one of these, you won't need to buy any local maps unless you're hiking. In Canada, the **Canada Map Office**, 615 Booth St, Ottawa, Ontario K1A 0E9 (☎613/952-7000) publish two main series of maps, 1:250,000 and 1:50,000 (ideal for hiking and canoeing), and supply map indexes to identify the map you'll need.

The well-equipped bookstores that you'll find in Seattle, Vancouver, Portland and all large towns, as well as camping shops, and park ranger stations in national parks, state parks and wilderness areas, will all sell good-quality local **hiking** maps for $3 to $5. Among the best of the many small companies producing such maps, at the necessary 1:50,000 level of detail, is *Earthwalk Press*, 2239 Union St, Eureka, CA 95501 (☎1-800/828-MAPS).

In the US, the *American Automobile Association* (*AAA*; ☎1-800/336-4357), based at 1000 AAA Drive, Heathrow, Florida 32746, provides free maps and assistance to its members, and to British members of the *AA* and *RAC*.

GETTING AROUND

The vast distances between the towns and villages of the Northwest make it essential to think carefully in advance about how you intend to travel from place to place. *Amtrak* in the US and *VIA rail* in Canada, provide skeletal but often scenic national rail services, together with a handful of private lines. *Greyhound* in both the US and Canada provide good bus links between the major cities, while the boats of *BC Ferries*, *Washington State Ferries* and the *Alaska Marine Highway* offer stunning trips up and down the Northwest coast.

It has to be said, however, that things are always easier if you have a **car**. Many of the most spectacular and memorable destinations in the Pacific Northwest are rural destinations far removed from the cities, and remain aloof of public transportation. Even if a bus or train can take you to the general vicinity of one of the great National Parks, for example, it can be nearly impossible to explore the area without your own vehicle. For that matter, the cities themselves can be so large, and so heavily car-oriented, that the lack of a vehicle can seriously impair your enjoyment.

BY TRAIN

Travelling by **rail** is not a terribly viable way of getting around the Northwest, though if you have the time it can be a pleasant and relaxing experience. Neither the American **Amtrak**, nor the shrinking Canadian **Via rail** networks serve many centers these days, and services are generally restricted to one or two trains a day on a few days each week. That said, the train is by far the most comfortable – and often the most scenic – way to go, and long-distance rides especially can be a great opportunity to meet people.

AMTRAK AND ALASKA

Details of the various *Amtrak* routes that connect the states of **Washington** and **Oregon** with the rest of the United States, together with information on *Amtrak*'s pricing and reservation policies, can be found on p.11.

The days when the railroad linked hundreds of communities throughout **Oregon** and **Washington** are long gone, but among a handful of surviving lines, the most scenic is the *Coast Starlight*, which picks its daily way up the coast from Los Angeles and California's Oakland (for bus connections from San Francisco) to cross the Oregon border near Klamath Falls. From here, the train pulls across the Cascade Mountains for Eugene, Salem and Portland, travelling on to reach Washington state at Vancouver, from where it continues to Seattle. The *Coast Starlight* terminates here – although there are speculative plans to re-open the line up to Vancouver, in Canada. There are two other regional rail lines and each runs daily across the Cascade Mountains: the *Empire Builder* (from Chicago) links Spokane, in eastern Washington, with either (depending on your chosen route) Portland or Seattle. Alternatively, the *Pioneer* (also out of Chicago) loops around through Idaho and shadows the route of the old Oregon Trail on its way between Oregon's Ontario, Baker City, La Grande and Pendleton. West of here, the railroad tracks along the Columbia River Gorge to reach Portland – where it pauses before the onward trip up the coast to Seattle.

In **Alaska**, the *Alaska Railroad Company* (*ARRC*, ☎1-800/544-0552 or 907/265-2623), North America's most northerly railway, connects Seward and Whittier in the south with Anchorage, Fairbanks, and the Denali National Park. The ride between Anchorage and Fairbanks, with a stop in Denali, costs $130 in either direction. Further south, the private *White Pass and Yukon* railway is a short and expensive line connecting Skagway (and its ferry system) and Bennett in British Columbia, with bus services providing onward travel from Bennett to Whitehorse in the Yukon and points in Alaska.

VIA RAIL

Transcontinental rail travel across Canada – insofar as it still exists – is covered in detail on p.11. The most spectacular part of the old *Canadian* route is now the preserve of a private operator, **Rocky Mountaineer Railtours** (☎1-800/665-7245), who run packages between Banff and Vancouver (and Jasper), taking in the Canadian Rockies between Lake Louise and Yoho National Park before continuing through the mountains of Glacier and Revelstoke national parks. These tours, which are swiftly booked out, run from June to September and cost around Can$420 one way for two (about Can$750 return), plus a supplement of around Can$40 for travel between Calgary and Banff (prices include light meals and a night's hotel accommodation in Kamloops).

The other surviving *VIA* line in the Northwest runs from **Jasper to Prince Rupert** (via Prince George), another scenic line, and also a useful means of connecting with *BC Ferries* and the *Alaska Marine Highway* at Prince Rupert for boats to Vancouver Island, Alaska, and Bellingham (WA). Additionally there is **BC Rail**, a provincially administered line in British Columbia that runs daily summer trains from **Vancouver to Prince George** via Lillooet (3 daily off season). Stations are not shared with *VIA rail* in Prince George, but a shuttle bus allows you to make connections with *VIA rail* services to Jasper, Kamloops, Prince Rupert and Edmonton. At the time of writing, the joint *VIA-Amtrak* line between **Seattle and Vancouver** was closed (and replaced by a bus service), though there are plans to re-open the rail link.

Fares on *VIA* and *BC Rail* are slightly more reasonable than *Amtrak*, though generally still more expensive than the equivalent *Greyhound* journey. Prices vary according to whether you

travel **coach** (second) — with reclining seat for sleeping; **section** (first), with large seats that become curtained bunks at night; **roomettes**, a private single with toilet and bed that folds from the wall; or **bedrooms**, spacious two-person cabins with armchairs, large windows, table, toilet, wardrobe and a bunk bed. Return (round-trip) fares are simply double the price of single tickets.

Discounts of 33 percent on coach fares are available in Alberta and BC, between November and mid-December, and from early January to late April, though you must buy your ticket a week in advance. Ten percent reductions are also available for students and the over-60s; two- to eleven-year olds are half fare (accompanied by an adult); and people with disabilities and their companions are charged a single fare (though a letter is required from a doctor stating the companion is necessary).

BY BUS

If you're travelling on your own, and making a lot of stops, **buses** are by far the cheapest way to get around. The main long-distance service is **Greyhound** in both the US and Canada (though *Greyhounds* in each country are run by separate companies). *Greyhound* buses link all major cities and many smaller towns in the Northwest, with *Greyhound*'s BC and Alberta coverage being particularly extensive (there's even a bus up the Alaska Highway). The exceptions are in the Yukon (where the *Greyhound* network stops at Whitehorse) and Alaska. However, various smaller companies provide a surprisingly good service in these northern regions, together with similar companies on Vancouver Island, in Banff National Park, along the BC coast, and elsewhere (see box, "Northwest Bus Companies"). Shoestring and vaguely alternative buses like **Green Tortoise** (see box on p.12) are also increasingly a feature of the Yukon, Alaska and Canadian Rockies national parks, where several enterprising companies are providing inexpensive connections to trailheads, to hostels, and between main towns. Check hostel infoboards or visitor centers for details, as such companies inevitably go in and out of business fairly quickly.

Out in the country, buses are fairly scarce, sometimes appearing only once a day, and here you'll need to plot your route with care. But along the main highways, buses run around the clock to

NORTHWEST BUS COMPANIES

Alaska Direct Bus Line (☎1-800/770-6652). Services to and from Haines and Skagway, via Whitehorse and Tok, to Anchorage and Fairbanks.

Alaskon Express (☎907/277-5581). Services between Anchorage, Fairbanks, Tok, Haines, Skagway and Whitehorse.

Brewster Transportation (☎403/260-0719). Banff to Jasper via Lake Louise, plus connections from Banff to Calgary and Calgary airport.

Caribou Express (☎907/278-5776). Services from Anchorage to Fairbanks.

Clallam Transit (☎206/452-4511). Services around Washington's Olympic Peninsula.

Denali Express (☎907/274-8539). Services from Anchorage and Fairbanks to Denali.

Empire Trailways (☎509/624-4116 or 1-800/351-1060). For eastern Washington.

Gold City Tours (☎403/993-5175). Buses on the Dempster Hwy from Dawson City (Yukon) to Inuvik (NWT).

Gray Lines of Alaska (☎1-800/544-2206). Services throughout Alaska and the southern Yukon.

Gray Lines of Seattle (☎206/624-5077). Daily bus service between Seattle and Victoria, via the *Washington State* ferry at Anacortes.

Greyhound America (☎1-800/231-2222). Services throughout Washington and Oregon.

Greyhound Lines of Canada (☎403/265-9111). Services in Alberta, mainland BC and the Yukon as far as Whitehorse.

Homer and Seward Bus Lines (☎907/278-0800). Services to Seward and Homer on Alaska's Kenai Peninsula.

Island Coach Lines (☎604/385-4411). Services on Vancouver Island.

Island Transit (☎678-7771). Free services round Whidbey Island.

Jefferson Transit (☎385-4777). Services around Washington's Olympic Peninsula.

Lane Transit (☎687-5555). Services in and around Eugene.

Norline Coaches (☎403/993-5331). Whitehorse to Dawson City service in the Yukon.

Northwestern Trailways (☎1-800/366-3830). California connections to Reno, Boise and Spokane. Spokane to Calgary and Seattle. Seattle to Vancouver, BC and Portland. Also other eastern Washington services.

Pacific Coach Lines (☎604/662-5074). Services from Vancouver to Vancouver Island, on Vancouver Island and the southern BC coast.

Pacific Transit System (☎875-9418 or 642-9418). Services up and down the Washington coast – from Aberdeen to Astoria (Oregon).

Pika Shuttle Co Ltd (☎1-800/363-0096). Shuttle connections between youth hostels in Banff and Jasper national parks.

Quick Coach Lines (☎604/244-3744 or 1-800/665-2122). Express services from SeaTac airport to Seattle, Bellingham and Vancouver.

a fairly full timetable, stopping only for meal breaks (almost always fast-food dives) and driver change-overs. *Greyhound* and other buses are slightly less uncomfortable than you might expect, except perhaps in northern BC and the Yukon, where *Greyhounds* have only about a dozen seats, the rest of the bus being given over to freight. It's feasible to save on a night's accommodation by travelling overnight and sleeping on the bus – though you may not feel up to much the next day.

To avoid possible hassle, lone female travellers in particular should take care to sit as near to the driver as possible, and to arrive during daylight hours, since bus stations are often in fairly dodgy areas. It used to be that any sizeable community would have a *Greyhound* station, but these days – although some places have the post office or a gas station doubling as the bus stop and ticket office – many have had their bus service cancelled altogether. In remoter settlements, buses do not make scheduled stops, but will halt at specified **flag stops** if there is anyone waiting; you must be sure of the correct location, as drivers are not obliged to stop anywhere else.

Greyhound have finally introduced a seat-booking system in the US; you can reserve with a credit card up to seven days in advance, and have the ticket mailed to you, or make a reservation on the spot up to 24 hours in advance. In Canada a **Seat-Selection** scheme operates between the larger cities, principally Calgary, Edmonton and Vancouver in the Northwest. This allows you to book a specified seat on the bus for just Can$1, though you must do so in person at the bus depot. Extra buses are also automatically laid on in Canada if the first bus is full, so you can always be sure of reaching your destination.

Fares average 10¢ a mile, which can add up quickly – for example, around US$19 from Portland to Seattle, and Can$70 from Vancouver to Calgary. For long-trip travel riding the bus costs a little less than the train in both countries, though considering the time involved in some journeys – and the preponderance of discount air fares – it's not always that much cheaper than flying. However, the bus is the best deal if you plan to visit a lot of places: **Ameripasses** for domestic travellers are good for unlimited travel nationwide for 7 days ($250), 14 days ($350) and 30 days ($450); the reduced rates for foreign travellers are on p.34, together with details of *Greyhound*'s **Canada Pass**, which allows unlimited *Greyhound* travel in Canada.

Greyhound produces a condensed **timetable** of major country-wide routes, but do not distribute it to travellers; to plan your route, pick up the free route-by-route timetables from larger stations in both the United States and Canada.

BY PLANE

Taking a plane is much the quickest way to get about the Northwest, with a plethora of smaller, regional airlines competing on obviously lucrative routes – *Air BC*, *Canadian Partner*, *Horizon Air* and *United Express*, for example, connect Seattle, Portland, Vancouver and Victoria in various permutations.

If you plan ahead, flying can work out reasonably cheap, often costing less than the train – especially if you take into account how much you save not having to pay for food and drink while on the move – and only a little more than the bus. As well as turning what might be a full day's $35 bus journey in either country into a quick and scenic $75 flight of under an hour, air travel can also – as in the case of many places in Alaska and the Yukon – be the *only* way of moving around the region. Generally you have to start with a larger operator such as *Canadian*, who have a remarkable network of far north destinations, and then follow up with one of the many connecting mid-sized companies.

Often the pages of local Sunday newspapers list ticket bargains for longer flights, and if you've planned carefully **VUSA** tickets and individual airline **passes** can save money (see box). Any good **travel agent**, especially student and youth-oriented travel ones like *Council Travel* and *STA*, can usually get you a much better deal than the airlines themselves. Phone the airlines to find out routes and schedules, then buy your ticket using the **Fare Assurance Program**, which processes all the ticket options to find the cheapest fare, taking into account the requirements of individual travellers. One agent using the service is *Travel Avenue* (☎1-800/333-3335). Few stand-by fares are available, and the best discounts are usually offered on tickets booked and paid for at least two weeks in advance, which are almost always non-refundable and hard to change.

> See p.9 for a list of **toll-free airline numbers** in the US and Canada.

BY FERRY

Ferries play an important role in transportation in the Pacific Northwest – in fact in some areas, they're effectively the *only* affordable way to travel. Alaska's state capital of Juneau, for example, can only be reached via water or air. Around Seattle and Vancouver, boats transport thousands of commuters a day to and from work, but for visitors, they're a novelty: an exhilarating way to experience the sheer scenic splendor of the area. Ferry travel can be expensive, however, when you bring a car along.

The voyage up the coast to Alaska, along the so-called **Inside Passage**, forms the cornerstone of many visitors' trips. Two separate ferry systems run boats along all or part of this journey – the Canadian-based **BC Ferries**, who also link with the Queen Charlotte Islands off the BC coast, and the more extensive American-run **Alaska Marine Highway**. Further south, **Washington State Ferries** operate a virtual monopoly on shorter crossings in and around the Puget Sound, and also connect with Canada's Vancouver Island.

Foot passengers using any of these companies should have few problems boarding boats, but if you're taking a car or hope to grab a cabin on longer journeys, you'll usually have to have booked places on summer sailings many months in advance. Contact the ferry companies directly for booking information (see box). When space allows, both Inside Passage companies allow backpackers to pitch their tents or unroll sleeping

GREYHOUND CANADA PASS AND AMERIPASSES

Foreign visitors intending to travel extensively by *Greyhound* in the Northwest, or to venture further afield in the US or Canada, can buy a *Greyhound* **Ameripass** or **Canada Pass**, offering unlimited travel within a set time limit, before leaving home: most travel agents can oblige. In the UK, the *Ameripass* costs £50 (4-day), £90 (7-day), £135 (15-day) or £180 (30-day). The *Canada Pass* costs £92 (7-day), £120 (15-day) and £165 (30-day).

Greyhound's office for both American and Canadian passes and information is at Sussex House, London Road, East Grinstead, West Sussex RH19 1LD (☎0342/317317). Extensions can be bought for the *Ameripass* for the 7- and 15-day passes for £12, but **must** be bought in the UK. No extensions are available for the Canada Pass.

The first time you use your pass, it will be dated by the ticket clerk (which becomes the commencement date of the ticket), and your destination is written on a page which the driver will tear out and keep as you board the bus. Repeat this procedure for every subsequent journey.

AIR PASSES

The main American airlines, *Air Canada* and *Canadian Airlines* (and *British Airways* in conjunction with *USAir*) all offer VUSA (Visiting US and Canada) **air passes** for visitors who plan to fly a lot within the US and Canada: these have to be bought in advance, and in the UK are usually sold with the proviso that you cross the Atlantic with the relevant airline. All the deals are broadly similar, involving the purchase of at least two or three **coupons** (for around £170; around £65 for each additional coupon), each valid for a flight of any duration in the US and Canada.

In Canada *Canadian* have the strongest domestic connections, plus a good variety of passes. The best **unlimited** pass within the Canadian northwest is the *Air BC* **Western Canada AirPass**, available from UK and other foreign travel agents before departure. *Northwest* is the strongest operator in Washington and Oregon, whilst *AlaskaAir* is the mainstay of that state's domestic network.

The **Visit USA** scheme entitles foreign travellers to a 30 percent discount on any full-priced US domestic fare, provided you buy the ticket before you leave home.

bags in the boat's gym or **solarium**, not only a comfy alternative to the deck, but also a great way of meeting people.

BC FERRIES

BC Ferries, also known as the "Friendship Fleet", operate 38 ships to serve 42 ports of call along the coast of British Columbia, from tiny two-minute lake crossings in the interior to the endless shuttles that ply back and forth across the Georgia Strait between Vancouver and Vancouver Island. Its most popular sailing, however, is the *Queen of the North* boat, which operates year-round along a portion of the **Inside Passage**, taking around 10 hours to connect Port Hardy on the northern tip of Vancouver Island (see box p.303) with Prince Rupert, where passengers can join Alaskan ferries heading north or *VIA rail* trains setting off east through the Rockies. The journey leaves four times weekly in summer, when reservations are

strongly recommended, and once weekly in winter. Passenger rates are about Can$90 one-way.

The company's other long-haul route is the 7-hour MV *Queen of Prince Rupert* ferry from Prince Rupert to the **Queen Charlotte Islands** (see box p.448), with daily sailings in summer (around Can$20 for foot passengers). It also runs several boats from Vancouver to **Vancouver Island**, the most heavily-used the Tsawwassen to Swartz Bay (for Victoria) and Horseshoe Bay to Nanaimo crossings (see "Getting to Vancouver Island", p.262). Numerous smaller boats criss-cross between the **Gulf Islands** that lie scattered between Vancouver Island and the BC mainland.

ALASKA MARINE HIGHWAY

Although run by a single company, the **Alaska Marine Highway** consists of two unconnected ferry systems. The **Southeast** network runs from Bellingham, WA up the Inside Passage to

AMTRAK RAIL PASSES

Overseas travellers (including Canadian citizens – and US citizens if they can prove they live abroad) to the United States have a choice of the following **rail passes**, which can be bought at *Amtrak* stations in the US on production of a passport issued outside the US or Canada. The **Coastal Pass** permits unlimited train travel on the east and west coasts, but not between the two.

	15-day (June–Aug)	**15-day** (Sept–May)	**30-day** (June–Aug)	**30-day** (Sept–May)
East or **Far West**	$188	$168	$239	$219
West	$238	$198	$299	$269
Coastal	–	–	$209	$189
National	$318	$218	$399	$319

CANRAIL PASSES

Visitors from outside Canada (including US and Canadian citizens only if they can demonstrate that they live abroad) can cut rail costs in Canada with a **Canrail Pass**, which allows twelve days unlimited *VIA* coach class travel within a 30-day period. However, *VIA* have a quota system on some lines restricting seats allocated to pass holders, so booking is still essential on busier lines – especially the Edmonton to Vancouver route. Passes are available for two periods: between October and May they cost Can$349 full-fare and Can$319 for over-60s and under-24s, between June and September the rates rise to Can$510 and Can$460 respectively. All prices are subject to a seven percent federal tax. You can buy these passes abroad (see below for details) or from any *VIA* station (with proof of foreign national status), though passes bought at stations are some Can$50 more expensive if you don't buy seven days in advance.

SPECIALIST RAIL AGENTS

UK		**Ireland**	
Compass Travel	☎0733/53809	*Eurotrain*	☎01/741 777
Destination Marketing	☎071/978 5212	**Australia**	
Explorers Travel	☎0753/681999	*Walshes World*	☎02/232-7499
Long-Haul Leisurail	☎0733/51780	**New Zealand**	
Thistle Air Ltd	☎0563/71159	*Atlantic & Pacific*	☎071/978-5212

Skagway in Alaska. The whole trip takes around three days (usually with a Friday start), and like the shorter *BC Ferries* run (see above) provides a medley of stupendous coastal landscapes and the chance of spotting a host of marine and other wildlife (including whales). En route the boat calls at smaller centers, notably Ketchikan, Wrangell, Petersburg, Juneau and Haines (smaller boats from these places serve smaller villages in turn). Thus they follow the same route as the luxury cruise ships, but at half the cost. Staterooms are available, but usually sell out quickly. Otherwise, there is plenty of room to sleep in the public lounges or on deck. All boats have free showers, cafés and a heated solarium for passengers without cabins. (Note that a separate *AMH* ferry runs from Prince Rupert (BC) to Skagway: the Bellingham boat does *not* call at Prince Rupert en route for Skagway.)

Tickets can be bought to all destinations en route, and while stopovers are encouraged, it is cheaper to fix your itinerary when buying a ticket. Tickets between ports are reasonable – typically US$20–30 for a three-hour trip, though you also need to factor in extras for food and transporting bikes and kayaks (prices for the last two can be almost half the price of a normal ticket). A through ticket from Bellingham to Skagway currently costs $246 for foot passengers, $656 for a small car (the Prince Rupert–Skagway ferry costs $120 for foot passengers). Car reservations should be made *six* months in advance; a waiting list for **standby** car places opens in Bellingham at 8.30am on the Monday before a sailing, though **walk-on** foot passengers should find a place if they have tickets by Thursday. For standby information call ☎206/676-8445. Check-in is three hours before departure. Standby passengers risk being off-loaded at each port to make way for booked passengers.

AMH ferries on the separate **Southwest**, or south central network, work out a bit pricier than those from Bellingham. Although they take in what is arguably even more stunning scenery, trips do involve sailing the open sea, which can get very choppy. They link the communities of Cordova, Valdez, Whittier (for Anchorage), Seward, Homer, Kodiak, and the Aleutian Islands.

OTHER FERRIES

The largest of the many other Northwest ferry companies is **Washington State Ferries**, whose commuter-oriented fleet of 25 ferries handles more than 23 million passengers per year. They run between Anacortes, WA and Sidney, BC (for Victoria and Vancouver Island); from Anacortes to the San Juan Islands; and between Seattle and points on the Kitsap Peninsula. Reservations are not accepted and you should try to avoid peak commuter travel times.

Black Ball Transport runs from Port Angeles, WA to Victoria, with a crossing time of 90 minutes and no reservations, while **Clipper Navigation** operates three passenger-only jet catamarans between Seattle and Victoria. Two increasingly popular boats provide unforgettable trips off Vancouver Island: the **MV Lady Rose** from Port Alberni, which runs through the gorgeous seascapes of the Pacific Rim National

---

NORTHWEST FERRY COMPANIES

Alaska Marine Highway, PO Box 25535, Juneau 99802-5535 (☎907/465-3941from outside North America; ☎1-800/642-0066 from the US, except Washington state ☎1-800/585-8445; ☎1-800/665-6444 from Canada).

Alaska Northwest Travel Service, Inc, 130 Second Ave S, Edmonds, WA 98020 (☎206/775-4504). An agent for Alaska and British Columbia ferries as well as a full service travel agency specializing in Alaska; they can book ferries and offer advice on itineraries.

BC Ferries, 1112 Fort St, Victoria, BC V8V 4V2 (☎604/386-3431 in Victoria; ☎604/669-1211 in Vancouver).

Black Ball Transport, 430 Bellevue St, Victoria, BC V8V 1W9 (☎604/386-2202; ☎206/457-4491 in Port Angeles).

Clipper Navigation, 2701 Alaskan Way, Pier 69, Seattle, WA 98121 (☎1-800/888-2535).

Washington State Ferries, 801 Alaskan Way, Seattle, WA 98104 (☎206/464-6400 or 1-800/843-3779).

For details of the **Alaska Pass**, which allows unlimited transportation on participating ferries, trains, and buses in Alaska and the Yukon, call ☎1-800/248-7598 in North America or ☎0800/898285 in the UK. See also p.488.

Park (see p.291), and the **Uchuck III**, a World War II minesweeper-turned-ferry, which patrols the villages of the island's northwest coast (see p.301).

BY CAR

Although the weather may not always be ideal, and towns in the far north lie beyond the reach of the road, the appeal of cruising the open highway, preferably in an open-top convertible with the radio blaring, is as strong in the Northwest as it is across most of North America. Apart from anything else, a car makes it possible to choose your own itinerary and to explore the wide-open landscapes that may well provide your most enduring memories of the region.

The Northwest holds some of the continent's greatest highways – especially the infamous 1500-mile **Alaska Highway** and the Rockies' awe-inspiring **Icefields Parkway**. In addition you can experience the thrill of the frontier on a string of increasingly travelled wilderness roads, including the **Cassiar Highway** through northern BC, the **Dempster** across the Arctic Circle, and the **Top of the World Highway** from the old goldfields of the Klondike which crosses the high mountain tundra into Alaska. In Washington, the **Cascade Loop** enables travellers to penetrate the heart of the spectacular Cascade Mountains, while the **Columbia River Gorge** drive in Oregon explores the dramatic bluffs, ravines and waterfalls of the Columbia River.

The main border crossing between the US and Canada by car is on I-5 at Blaine, Washington, 30 miles south of Vancouver; immigration procedures are usually quick and simple, with the crossing open 24 hours a day.

CAR SAFETY

Special factors associated with driving in the Northwest, however, are essential to take on board. Many northern roads, especially in the northern reaches of the Alaskan Interior, are **gravel**-topped, and often in poor condition. Dust and flying stones are major **hazards**, as are subsidence caused by ice (**frost heaves**) and the thundering heavy lorries that use such routes with little regard for automobiles. **Weather** is another potential danger, with severe snow falls possible in some areas even in August, and dense fog plaguing the coast of Washington and Oregon. If you're heading north radiators and headlights should be protected from stones and insects with a wire screen and headlight covers. *Always* carry a spare tire and fan belt, gas can (preferably full), fill up at every opportunity, and check where the next fuel is available (on the Cassiar or Dempster it could be literally hundreds of miles away). It goes without saying your car should be in excellent shape: it's also a good idea to carry flares, jack and a good set of tools and wrenches. These precautions may sound over the top, but after you've travelled a few northern roads, and seen the desolation to either side, they'll make more sense – and they might also save your life.

In the **cities**, a car is by far the most convenient way to negotiate your way around, especially as public transit can be scarce. Many Northwestern cities sprawl for so many miles in all directions that your hotel may be miles from the sights you came to see, or perhaps simply on the other side of a freeway which there's no way of crossing on foot. Even in smaller towns the motels may be six miles or more out along the highway, and the restaurants in a brand-new shopping mall on the far side of town.

See p.20 for advice on **car crime**.

CAR RENTAL

Conditions for **renting a car**, together with the rental companies, are virtually identical in both Canada and the US. It is *vital* to note, however, that the majority of these companies are going to be extremely reluctant to rent cars if they know you're intending to travel on gravel roads (don't think they won't notice if you do – the dents in the paintwork will be a dead giveaway). Ask what arrangements they might be able to make, and if they refuse, rent a car from the northern-based outlets who tend to be understanding (and whose cars are probably both more robust and more battered into the bargain). Pick-ups are a great standby in such circumstances.

Drivers wishing to rent cars are supposed to have held their licences for at least one year; people under 25 years old may encounter problems, and will probably get lumbered with a higher than normal insurance premium (around $15 per day extra). Car rental companies (listed below) will also expect you to have a credit card; if you don't have one they may let you leave a hefty **deposit** (at least $200) but don't count on it. The likeliest tactic for getting a good deal is to phone the major firms' toll-free 800 numbers and ask for their best rate – most will try to beat the offers of their competitors, so it's worth haggling. Rental rates tend to be higher on the islands (especially the Queen Charlottes) and to rise the further north you travel.

In general the lowest rates are available at the airport branches – $149 a week for a subcompact is a fairly standard budget rate. Always be sure to get free unlimited mileage, and be aware that leaving the car in a different city to the one in which you rent it can incur a **drop-off charge** that can be as much as $200 or more. Also, don't automatically go for the cheapest rate, as there's a big difference in quality of cars from company to company; industry leaders like *Alamo* and *Hertz* tend to have newer, lower-mileage cars, often with air-conditioning and stereo cassette decks as standard equipment – no small consideration on the 1500 miles of the Alaska Highway.

Alternatively, various **local** companies rent out new – and not so new (try *Rent-a-Wreck*) – vehicles. They are certainly cheaper than the big chains if you just want to spin around a city for a day, but free mileage is not often included, so they work out far more costly for long-distance travel. Addresses and phone numbers are documented in the Yellow Pages.

When you rent a car, read the small print carefully for details on **Collision Damage Waiver (CDW)**, sometimes called Liability Damage Waiver (LDW), a form of insurance which often isn't included in the initial rental charge but is well worth considering. This specifically covers the car that you are driving yourself – you are in any case insured for damage to other vehicles. At $9 to $13 a day, it can add substantially to the total cost, but without it you're liable for every scratch to the car – even those that aren't your fault. Some credit card companies (*AMEX* for example) offer automatic CDW coverage to anyone using their card; read the fine print beforehand in any case. Increasing numbers of

CAR RENTAL COMPANIES

IN THE US AND CANADA

Alamo	☎1-800/327-9633	**National**	☎1-800/227-7368
Avis (Canada)	☎1-800/268-2310	**Payless**	☎1-800/729-5377
Avis (US)	☎1-800/722-1333	**Rent-a-Wreck**	☎1-800/535-1391
Budget (Canada)	☎1-800/268-8900	**Snappy**	☎1-800/669-4800
Budget (US)	☎1-800/527-0700	**Thrifty**	☎1-800/367-2277
Dollar	☎1-800/421-6868	**Tilden** (Canada)	☎1-800/361-5334
Enterprise	☎1-800/325-8007	**Tilden** (US)	☎1-800/227-7368
Hertz (Canada)	☎1-800/263-0600	**Value**	☎1-800/468-2583
Hertz (US)	☎1-800/654-3131		

IN THE UK

Alamo	☎0800/272 200	**Europcar**	☎081/950 5050
Avis	☎081/848 8733	**Hertz**	☎081/679 1799
Budget	☎0800/181 181	**Holiday Autos**	☎071/491 1111

DRIVING FOR FOREIGNERS

UK nationals can **drive** in the US and Canada on a full UK driving licence (International Driving Permits are not always regarded as sufficient). Fly-drive deals are good value if you want to **rent** a car (see p.4), though you can save up to 60 percent simply by booking in advance with a major firm. If you choose not to pay until you arrive, be sure you take a written confirmation of the price with you. Remember that it's safer not to rent a car straight off a long transatlantic flight; and that standard rental cars have **automatic transmissions**.

It's also easier and cheaper to book **RVs** in advance from Britain. Most travel agents who specialize in the US and Canada can arrange RV rental, and usually do it cheaper if you book a flight through them as well. A price of £400 for a five-berth van for two weeks is fairly typical.

NORTH AMERICAN DRIVING TERMS

Antenna	Aerial	*Parking brake*	Hand brake
Divided highway	Dual carriageway	*Parking lot*	Car park
Fender	Bumper/Car wing	*Speed zone*	Area where speed limit decreases
Freeway	Limited access motorway	*Stickshift*	Gear stick/manual transmission
Gas(oline)	Petrol	*Trunk*	Boot
Hood	Bonnet	*Turn-out*	Lay-by
No standing	No parking or stopping	*Windshield*	Windscreen

states are requiring that this insurance be included in the weekly rental rate, and are regulating the amounts charged to cut down on rental car company profiteering; companies are also becoming more particular about checking up on the driving records of would-be renters and refusing to rent to high-risk drivers.

If you **break down** in a rented car, there should be an emergency number pinned to the dashboard. If you're on a main road, sit tight and wait for the RCMP, highway patrol or state/provincial police, who cruise by regularly. Raising your car hood is recognized as a call for assistance, although women travelling alone should be wary of doing this. Another tip is to rent a **mobile telephone** from the car rental agency – you often only have to pay a nominal amount until you actually use it, and in larger cities they increasingly come built in to the car, but having a phone can be reassuring at least, and a potential lifesaver should something go terribly wrong.

If you take a rental car across the US–Canada border, keep a copy of the contract with you. It should bear an endorsement stating that the vehicle is permited entry into the other country.

RENTING AN RV

Recreational Vehicles or **RVs** – which range from a basic camper on the back of a pickup truck to a huge juggernaut equipped with multiple bedrooms, bathrooms and kitchens – can be rented from around US$400 per week (plus mileage charges). Though good for groups or families travelling together, these can be unwieldy on the road. Also, rental outlets are not as common as you might expect, as people tend to own their RVs. On top of the rental fees, take into account the cost of gas (some RVs do twelve miles to the gallon or less) and any drop-off charges, in case you plan to do a one-way trip across the country. Also, it is rarely legal simply to pull up in an RV and spend the night at the roadside; you are expected to stay in designated parks that cost up to $20 per night. Regulations for dumping and overnighting are especially strict in all national, state and provincial parks.

The *Recreational Vehicle Rental Association*, 3251 Old Lee Highway, Fairfax VA 22030 (☎703/591-7130 or 1-800/336-0355), publishes a newsletter and a directory of rental firms. A couple of the larger companies offering RV rentals are *Cruise America* (☎1-800/327-7799) and *Go! Vacations* (☎1-800/845-9888).

HITCHHIKING

Although in Alaska and backwoods Canada, locals and travellers alike often hitchhike to get around, we do not feel it would be responsible to recommend hitchhiking under any circumstances.

BY BIKE

As a rule, **cycling** is a cheap and healthy method to get around the Northwest, whether it's in the parks – you'll find that most have rental outlets and designated mountain bike trails – or in the big **cities**, some of which have cycle lanes and local buses equipped to carry bikes (strapped to the outside). *Greyhound* will take bikes (so long as they're in a box), and *VIA rail* and *Amtrak* make small charges for their transportation. Carriage charges on ferries, however, are more expensive: check with individual companies for rates and conditions (see "By Ferry", p.36). In **country areas**, roads are usually well maintained and with wide shoulders. A number of companies across the region organize multiday cycle tours, either camping out or staying in country inns; we've mentioned local firms where appropriate. Many individual states and provinces (notably Oregon) issue their own cycling guides; contact the tourist offices listed on p.27.

For more casual riding, bikes can be **rented** for $15 to $30 per day, or at discounted weekly rates, from outlets which are usually found close to beaches, university campuses, or simply in areas that are good for cycling, although rates in heavily touristed areas can be much higher. Local visitor centers should have details. Before setting out on a **long-distance cycling** trip, you'll need a good-quality, multispeed bike, panniers, tools and spares, maps, padded shorts, a **helmet** (not a legal obligation but a very good idea), and a route avoiding major highways and interstates (on which cycling is unpleasant and usually illegal). Of **problems** you'll encounter, the main one is traffic – RVs driven by buffoons who can't judge their width, and huge eighteen-wheelers (logging trucks are a menace in much of the Northwest) which scream past and create intense back-draughts capable of pulling you out into the middle of the road.

DISABLED TRAVELLERS

By international standards, the US and Canada are accommodating for travellers with mobility problems or other physical disabilities. All public buildings have to be wheelchair accessible and provide suitable toilet facilities, almost all street corners have dropped kerbs, public telephones are specially equipped for hearing-aid users, and most public transit systems have such facilities as subways with elevators, and buses that "kneel" to let people board.

Most states and provinces provide information for disabled travellers – contact the tourism departments on p.27. The *Handicapped Travel Division* of the *National Tour Association*, 546 East Main St, PO Box 3071, Lexington KY 40596 (☎606/253-1036), can put you in touch with organizations facilitating travel for the disabled, or see the list below. The annual *British Columbia Accommodation Guide* includes a list of hotel facilities for guests with disabilities. Larger **hotels,** including most *Holiday Inns,* have at least one or two suites designed specifically for their disabled guests, and the entire *Red Roof, Best Western, Embassy Suites, Radisson* and *Journey's End* chains are fully accessible to travellers with disabilities. *Motel 6* is a budget chain with access at most of its locations.

The **Golden Access Passport**, issued without charge to permanently disabled US citizens, gives free lifetime admission to all national parks. *Easy Access to National Parks*, by Wendy Roth and Michael Tompane ($15 from the Sierra Club, 730 Polk St, San Francisco CA 94110; ☎415/776-2211), details every national park for people with disabilities, senior citizens and families with children; in most parks at least a couple of trails are wheelchair accessible. *Disabled Outdoors* (2052 W 23rd St, Chicago IL 60608; ☎708/358-4160) is a quarterly magazine specializing in facilities for disabled travellers who wish to explore the great outdoors; their friendly office serves as a clearing-house for all related information.

GETTING AROUND

Most **airlines**, transatlantic and within the US and Canada, do whatever they can to ease your journey, and will usually let attendants of more seriously disabled people accompany them at no extra charge (*Air Canada* is the best-equipped Canadian carrier). The *Americans with Disabilities Act 1990* obliged all air carriers to make the majority of their services accessible to travellers with disabilities within five to nine years.

Almost every **Amtrak train** includes one or more coaches with accommodation for handicapped passengers. **VIA rail** offer a particularly outstanding service: apart from considerable support and help, *all* trains can accommodate wheelchairs that are no larger than 81cm by 182cm and weigh no more than 114kg without notice. Guide dogs travel free and may accompany blind, deaf or disabled passengers in the carriage. Try to give 24 hours' notice. Hearing or speech-impaired passengers can get information from *Amtrak* on ☎1-800/523-6590, and from *VIA rail* on ☎ 1-800/268-9503.

Greyhound, however, is not to be recommended. Buses are not equipped with lifts for wheelchairs, though staff will assist with boarding (intercity carriers are required by law to do this), and the "Helping Hand" scheme offers two-for-the-price-of-one tickets to passengers unable to travel alone (carry a doctor's certificate). *Greyhound* in Canada allow free travel for companions of blind passengers.

Both *BC Ferries* and the *Alaska Marine Highway* offer discount cards to disabled travellers on their **ferries**; for $10 the latter also offers a two-year pass good for free standby travel on all boats from October to April, and on some boats from May to September. *BC Ferries* allow a companion to travel free unless the disabled passenger is taking a car onto the ferry. For full details contact the companies directly (see p.36).

The *American Public Transit Association*, 1201 New York Avenue, Suite 400, Washington DC 20005 (☎202/898-4000), provides information about the accessibility of **public transit** in cities.

The *American Automobile Association* (see p.12) produces the *Handicapped Driver's Mobility Guide* for **disabled drivers** (available from *Quantum-Precision Inc*, 225 Broadway, Suite 3404, New York NY 10007). The larger car rental companies provide cars with hand-controls at no extra charge, though only on their full-size (ie most expensive) models; reserve well in advance.

USEFUL ORGANIZATIONS FOR DISABLED TRAVELLERS

Access Alaska, 3710 Woodland Drive, Suite 900, Anchorage, AK 99517 (☎907/248-4777). Information and referral to disabled visitors to Alaska.

Barrier Free Alaska, 7233 Madelynne Drive, Anchorage, AK 99504-4656 (☎907/337-6315). Information about facilities accessible to disabled travellers throughout the state.

BC Coalition of People with Disabilities, 204-456 W Broadway, Vancouver (☎604/875-0188). Advice and assistance for travellers in BC.

Canadian Paraplegic Association, 780 SW Marine Drive, Vancouver, BC V6P 5YT (☎604/324-3611). Information on touring British Columbia for travellers with disabilities. Also at 520 Sutherland Drive, Toronto M4G 3V9 (☎416/422-5640).

Challenge Alaska, Box 110065, Anchorage, AK 995110065 (☎907/563-2658). Recreational opportunities (such as cross-country skiing, kayaking, camping, swimming, etc) for people with disabilities.

Directions Unlimited, 720 N Bedford Rd, Bedford Hills, NY 10507 (☎914/241-1700). Travel agency with expertise in tours and cruises for the disabled.

Easter Seal Society, 521 Second Ave W, Seattle, WA 98119 (☎206/281-5700). Publishers of *Access Seattle*, a free guide to the city's services for the disabled.

Evergreen Travel Service, 4114 198th Ave, Suite 13, Lynnwood, WA 98036 (☎1-800/435-2288 or 206/776-1184 in WA). *Wings on Wheels* tours for those in wheelchairs, *White Cane* tours for the blind, and tours for the deaf. It also makes group and independent arrangements for travellers with any disability – anything from bus tours to fishing trips – to all parts of the Northwest.

Junior League, 4838 SW Scholls Ferry Rd, Portland, OR 97225 (☎503/297-6364). Publishers of *Circling the City – a Guide to the Accessibility of Public Places in and near Portland*.

Mobility International, PO Box 3551, Eugene, OR 97403 (☎503/343-1248). Answers transport queries and operates an exchange program for disabled people.

Oregon Disabilities Commission (☎1-800/358-3117 or 503/230-1225 in OR). Advice and information for disabled visitors to Oregon.

Outdoors Forever, Box 4811, East Lansing, MI 48823 (☎517/337-0018). A new organization aimed at making the outdoors more accessible to the disabled.

Redmond Travel, 16979 Redmond Way, Redmond, WA 98052 (☎206/885-2210). Travel agency with a special *Wheelchair Journeys* division.

Shared Outdoor Adventure Recreation (*SOAR*, ☎503/238-1613). Listings of recreational activities available to the disabled traveller.

Society for the Advancement of Travel for the Handicapped (*SATH*, 345 Fifth Ave #610, New York, NY 10016 (☎212/447-7284). A non-profit travel-industry grouping which includes travel agents, tour operators, hotel and airline management, and people with disabilities. They will pass on any enquiry to the appropriate member; allow plenty of time for a response.

Twin Peaks Press, Box 129, Vancouver, WA 98666 (☎206/694-2462 or 1-800/637-2256). Publishers of the *Directory of Travel Agencies for the Disabled* ($19.95) listing more than 370 agencies worldwide; *Travel for the Disabled* ($14.95); the *Directory of Accessible Van Rentals* and *Wheelchair Vagabond* ($9.95), loaded with personal tips.

Western Institute for the Deaf, 2125 W Seventh Ave, Vancouver, BC V6K IX9 (☎604/736-7391 or 736-2527). Advice for the hearing-impaired.

Whole Persons Tours, PO Box 1084, Bayonne NJ 07002 (☎201/858-3400). Travel agency specializing in disabled group tours.

SENIOR TRAVELLERS

For many senior citizens, retirement brings the opportunity to explore the world in a style and at a pace that is the envy of younger travellers. As well as the obvious advantages of being free to travel during the quieter, more congenial and less expensive seasons, and for longer periods, anyone over the age of 62 can enjoy the tremendous variety of discounts on offer to those who can produce suitable ID. *VIA rail*, *Amtrak* and *Greyhound*, for example, offer (smallish) percentage reductions on fares to older passengers.

Any US citizen or permanent resident aged 62 or over is entitled to free admission for life to all national parks, monuments and historic sites, using a **Golden Age Passport**, which can be issued free at any such site. This free admission applies to all accompanying travellers in the same car – a welcome encouragement to families to travel together. It also gives you a fifty percent reduction on park user fees such as camping charges.

The *American Association of Retired Persons*, 601 E St NW, Washington DC 20049 (☎1-800/227-7737 or 202/434-2277), membership of which is open to US residents aged 50 or over for an annual fee of $8, organizes group travel for senior citizens and can provide discounts on accommodation and vehicle rental. The *National Council of Senior Citizens*, 1331 F St NW, Washington DC 20004 (☎202/347-8800), is a similar organization with a yearly membership fee of $15.

TRAVELLING WITH CHILDREN

Travelling with kids in the more populated parts of the Pacific Northwest is relatively problem-free; children are readily accepted – indeed welcomed – in public places across the region, hotels and motels are well used to them, most state and national parks organize children's activities, and every town or city has clean and safe playgrounds.

Restaurants make considerable efforts to encourage parents in with their offspring. All the national chains offer bolster chairs and a special kids' menu, packed with huge, excellent-value (if not necessarily healthy) meals – cheeseburger and fries for 99¢, and so on.

Virtually all museums and tourist attractions offer reduced rates for kids. Most large cities have natural history museums or aquariums, and quite a few have hands-on children's museums.

State tourist bureaux can provide specific information, and various guidebooks have been written for parents travelling with children – such as the very helpful *Trouble Free Travel with Children* (US$6.95), available through Publishers Group West.

GETTING AROUND

Children under two years old **fly** free on domestic routes, and for 10 percent of the adult fare on international flights – though that doesn't mean they get a seat, let alone frequent-flier miles. When aged from 2 to 12 they are usually entitled to half-price tickets.

Travelling **by bus** may be the cheapest way to go, but it's also the most uncomfortable for kids. Under-2s travel (on your lap) for free; ages 2 to 4 are charged 10 percent of the adult fare, as are any toddlers who take up a seat. Children under 12 years old are charged half the standard fare.

Even if you discount the romance of the railroad, **taking the train** is by far the best option for long journeys – not only does everyone get to enjoy the scenery, but you can get up and walk around, relieving pent-up energy. Most cross-country trains have sleeping compartments, which may be quite expensive but are a great adventure. Children's discounts are much the same as for bus or plane travel.

Most families choose to travel **by car**; if you're hoping to enjoy a driving vacation with your kids, it's essential to plan ahead. Don't set yourself unrealistic targets; pack plenty of sensible snacks and drinks; plan to stop (ie don't make your kids make you stop) every couple of hours; arrive at your destination well before sunset; and avoid travelling through big cities during rush hour. Also, it can be a good idea to give an older child some responsibility for route-finding – having someone "play navigator" is good fun, educational and often a real help to the driver. If you're doing a fly-drive vacation, note that when **renting a car** the company is legally obliged to provide free car seats for kids.

Recreational Vehicles (RVs) are also a good option for family travel, successfully combining the convenience of built-in kitchens and bedrooms with freedom of the road (see "Getting Around" on p.39).

LOST AND FOUND

Wherever you are, be sure to keep track of one another – it's no less terrifying for a child to be lost at some big sight than it is for him or her to go missing at the mall. Whenever possible agree a meeting place *before* you get lost, and it's not a bad idea, especially for younger children, to attach some sort of wearable ID card.

Another good idea is to tell your kids to stay where they are, and not to wander; if *you* get lost, you'll have a much easier time finding each other if you're not all running around anxiously.

WOMEN TRAVELLERS

Women's support centers, bookstores, bars and organizations across the Northwest provide testimony to the continuing, and widespread commitment to female emancipation in the US and Canada.

Practically speaking, a woman **travelling alone** in the Northwest, especially in cities such as Seattle and Vancouver, is not usually made to feel conspicuous, or liable to attract unwelcome attention. But as with anywhere, particular care has to be taken at night: walking through unlit, empty streets is never a good idea, and if there's no bus service, take cabs.

In the major urban centers, provided you listen to advice and stick to the better parts of town, going into **bars** and **clubs** alone should pose few problems: there's generally a pretty healthy attitude towards women who do so and your privacy will be respected. Gay and lesbian bars are usually a trouble-free and welcoming alternative.

However, **small towns** and redneck mining and lumber centers in the north and interior are not blessed with the same liberal or indifferent attitudes toward lone women travellers. People seem to jump immediately to the conclusion that your car has broken down, or that you've suffered some terrible tragedy; in fact, you may get fed up with well-meant offers of help. If your **vehicle breaks down** in a country area, walk to the nearest house or town for help; on interstate highways or heavily travelled roads, wait in the car for a police or highway patrol car to arrive. One increasingly available option is to rent a portable telephone with your car, for a small additional charge – a potential lifesaver.

Rape statistics are outrageously high, and it goes without saying that you should *never* **hitch** alone – this is widely interpreted as an invitation for trouble, and there's no shortage of weirdos prepared to give it. Similarly, if you have a car, be careful who you pick up: just because you're in the driving seat doesn't mean you're safe. Avoid travelling alone at night by public transport – deserted bus stations, if not actually threatening, will do little to make you feel secure – and wherever possible you should team up with a fellow traveller. There really is security in numbers. On *Greyhound* buses, follow the example of other lone women and sit as near to the front – and the driver – as possible (new bookings schemes should make it possible to select seats in such positions in advance; see "By Bus" p.31). Should disaster strike, all major towns have some kind of rape counselling service; if not, the local RCMP or sheriff's office should arrange for you to get help and counselling, and, if necessary, get you home.

In the States a central group protests women's issues; lobbying by the National Organization for Women (featuring Gloria Steinem and Betty Friedan) has done much to effect positive legislation. NOW branches, listed in local phone directories, can provide referrals for specific concerns such as rape crisis centers and counselling services, feminist bookstores, and lesbian bars. Principal offices include 15 W 18th St, 9th Floor, New York NY 10011; 425 13th St NW, Washington DC 20004; and 3543 18th St, San Francisco CA 94110.

The annual ***Index/Directory of Women's Media*** (published by the Women's Institute for the Freedom of the Press, 3306 Ross Place NW, Washington DC 20008; ☎202/966-7793), lists women's publishers, bookstores, theater groups, news services and media organizations, and more, throughout the United States.

Further back-up material can be found in ***Places of Interest to Women*** ($8; Ferrari Publications, PO Box 35575, Phoenix AZ; ☎602/863-2408), an annual guide for women travelling in the US, Canada and elsewhere.

GAY AND LESBIAN TRAVELLERS

Although the big cities of the Pacific Northwest have healthy and conspicuous gay scenes – gay life in Seattle centers on Capitol Hill, in Vancouver it's based around Denham and Davie, and Portland too has a number of gay and lesbian bars and clubs – the gay community tends to be more of a forceful pressure group rather than the major power-player it is, say, in San Francisco. Gay politicians, and even police officers, are however more than a novelty, and representation at most levels is a reality.

Things change as quickly in the gay and lesbian scene as they do everywhere else, but we've tried to give an overview of local **resources**, **bars** and **clubs** in each of the major cities. Head into the backwoods in both countries and life more than looks like the Fifties – away from large cities homosexuals are still oppressed and commonly reviled, and gay travellers would regrettably be well advised to watch their step to avoid hassles and possible aggression.

Of national **publications** to look out for, most of which are available from any good bookstore, by far the best are the range produced by *Bob Damron in San Francisco* (PO Box 422258, San Francisco CA 94142; ☎1-800/462-6654 or 415/255-0404). These include the *Address Book*, a pocket-sized yearbook full of listings of hotels, bars, clubs and resources for gay men, costing $15; the *Women's Traveller*, which provides simi-lar listings for lesbians ($11); and the *Road Atlas*, which shows lodging and entertainment in major cities ($14).

Another useful lesbian publication is *Gaia's Guide* (132 W 24th St, New York NY 10014; $6.95), a yearly international directory with a lot of US information. In Oregon, the monthly magazine, *Lavender Network*, covers local gay and lesbian activities, and is sold in most liberal bookstores. In Vancouver, the free monthly *Angles* magazine, available from many bookstores, offers detailed listings of gay and lesbian events.

NORTHWEST GAY AND LESBIAN ORGANIZATIONS

Many larger towns and cities have help, advice and information lines for gays and lesbians. These organizations should provide useful starting points for travellers wanting more information locally.

Calgary: *Gay Lines Calgary*, 223-12th Ave Sw (☎403/234-8973).

Portland: *Phoenix Rising*, 620 SW 5th-710 (☎503/223-8299).

Seattle: *Gay Counseling Service*, 200 W Mercer, Suite 300 (☎206/282-9307).

Vancouver: *Gay and Lesbian Switchboard*, 2-1170 Bute St (☎604/684-6869).

Victoria: *Victoria Gay and Lesbian Line* (☎604/361-4900).

ACCOMMODATION

Accommodation costs will form a significant proportion of the expenses for any traveller exploring the Northwest. Depending on your priorities, you may choose to economize by concentrating on the wide range of budget accommodation detailed in this book, but we've also tried to highlight as many as we can of the truly memorable hotels and B&Bs that are scattered throughout the region.

A dormitory bed in a **hostel** usually costs between US$6 and $20. However, with basic room prices away from the major cities tending to start at around US$30 per night, groups of two or more will find it little more expensive to stay in the far more abundant motels and hotels. Many places will set up a third single bed for around US$10 on top of the regular price, reducing costs

for three people sharing. On the other hand, the lone traveller will have a hard time of it: "singles" are usually double rooms at an only slightly reduced rate.

Since inexpensive beds in tourist areas tend to be taken up quickly, always **reserve in advance**, especially in and around the region's national parks. If you get stuck try **visitor centers**: most offer free advice and will either book accommodation for you or perhaps provide a "courtesy phone" to call round after vacancies. Big resorts, like Banff and Lake Louise in the Rockies, often have privately run central reservations agencies which will (for a fee) find you a room in your chosen price range.

Reservations are only held until 5pm or 6pm unless you've told the hotel you'll be arriving late. However, it's worth confirming **check-in times**, particularly in busy areas, where your room may not be available until late afternoon. Most of the larger chains have an advance booking form in their brochures and will make reservations – and often offer discounts – if you move on to another of their premises; alternatively you can take advantage of the toll-free phone numbers of the national organizations (see list on p.48) that handle bookings for properties across the country.

Wherever you stay, you'll be expected to **pay in advance**, at least for the first night and

---

ACCOMMODATION PRICE CODES

Throughout this book, accommodation prices have been graded with the symbols below, according to the cost of the least expensive double room.

However, with the exception of the budget motels and lowliest hotels, there's rarely such a thing as a set rate for a room. A basic motel in a seaside or mountain resort may double its prices according to the season, while a big-city hotel in Seattle or Vancouver which charges $200 per room during the week will often slash its tariff at the weekend when all the business types have gone home. As the high and low seasons for tourists vary widely across the region – as a rule prices are higher the further north you go – astute planning can save a lot of money. Remember, too, that a third person in a double room usually costs only a few dollars.

Only where we explicitly say so do these room rates include local taxes.

①	up to US$30	up to Can$40	⑤	US$80–100	Can$100–125
②	US$30–45	Can$40–60	⑥	US$100–130	Can$125–175
③	US$45–60	Can$60–80	⑦	US$130–180	Can$175–240
④	US$60–80	Can$80–100	⑧	US$180+	Can$240+

perhaps for further nights too, particularly if it's high season and the hotel's expecting to be busy. Payment can be in cash or in dollar travellers' checks, though it's more common to give a credit card imprint and sign for everything when you leave. Virtually every state and province has a sales or **room tax**: all go under different names, but all have the effect of adding a few dollars to the advertised price of a room.

In major cities **campgrounds** tend to be on the outskirts if they exist at all, but there are excellent opportunities for camping in the many parks and country areas all over the region. A more detailed overview of the practical and safety considerations associated with "rough" or wilderness camping is given in the "Outdoors" section beginning on p.52.

HOTELS

Hotels in both Canada and the United States tend to fall into three categories: high-class five-star establishments in big cities and major resort areas; mid-range, often chain-owned establishments; and grim downtown places, often above a bar.

Top-of-the range hotels can be very grand indeed, catering to rich tourists in the resorts and business travellers in the cities. Rooms in high season cost anywhere between US$150 and US$500, though US$250 would get you a first-class double anywhere in the Northwest, and rates in all these hotels can fall as low as US$100 off-season.

Mid-range Canadian and American hotels usually belong to one of the big chains, and offer standard-issue modern facilities, often in a downtown location, plus a touch more comfort than the middling motels. You should be able to find a high-season double for around US$80.

Bottom-bracket hotels – those costing around US$25 to US$40 – are mostly hangovers from the days when liquor laws made it difficult to run a bar without an adjoining restaurant or hotel. Found in many medium- and small-sized towns, they have the advantage of being extremely central, but the disadvantage that the money-generating bars come first, with the rooms usually an afterthought. Many have strip joints or live music likely to pound until the small hours, and few pay much attention to their guests, many of whom are long-stay clients as seedy as the hotel itself.

HOTEL DISCOUNT VOUCHERS

For the benefit of overseas travellers, many of the higher-rung hotel chains offer **pre-paid discount vouchers**, which in theory save you money if you're prepared to pay in advance. To take advantage of such schemes, British travellers must purchase the vouchers in the UK, at a usual cost of between £30 and £60 per night for a minimum of two people sharing. However, it's hard to think of a good reason to buy them; you may save a nominal amount on the fixed rates, but better-value accommodation is not exactly difficult to find in the Northwest, and you may well regret the inflexibility imposed upon your travels.

MOTELS

It is consistently easy to find a basic **motel** room in most of the Northwest. Drivers approaching any significant town are confronted by lines of motels along the highway, with prominent neon signs flashing their rates. Along the major routes the choice is phenomenal. Only in the far north are places thinner on the ground, and US visitors should be warned that the remote areas of western Canada have fewer accommodation possibilities than their equivalent areas in the US. Don't assume that because a town is prominent on the map it's going to have rooms: check first. In most towns mentioned in this book we've recommended particular establishments, but you can also assume that there are a whole lot more we haven't got the space to list. Only where there is a genuine shortage of accommodation have we explicitly said so.

Motels may be called inns, lodges, or motor hotels, but most amount to much the same thing; reliable and reasonably priced places on the main highways just outside towns or cities. There are few differences between Canadian and American versions, many chains being common to both countries, though prices across the board are generally a few dollars higher in Canada, and the choice at the bottom end of the market is a little more limited. The budget ones are pretty basic affairs, but in general there's a uniform standard of comfort everywhere – double rooms with bathroom, TV and phone – and you don't get a much better deal by paying, say, US$50 instead of $35. Over US$50 or Can$60, the room and its fittings simply get bigger and better, and there'll probably be a swimming pool which guests can use for free. Paying over US $100 or Can$125 brings you into the decadent realms of the en-suite jacuzzi. Not many budget hotels or motels bother to compete with the ubiquitous diners and offer **breakfast**, although there's a trend towards providing free self-service coffee and sticky buns. Ritzier spots may have a restaurant, but generally you can expect nothing in the way of food and drink beyond a drinks machine.

During **off-peak periods** (usually October to April) many motels and hotels struggle to fill their rooms, and it's worth **haggling** to get a few dollars off the asking price. Staying in the same place for more than one night usually brings further reductions. Some places have cheap triple or quadruple berth rooms, and most are fairly relaxed about introducing an extra bed into a "double" room. Many places also offer a Family Plan, whereby youngsters sharing their parents' room stay free. Additionally, pick up the many **discount coupons** which fill tourist information offices. Read the small print, though: what appears to be an amazingly cheap room rate sometimes turns out to be a per-person charge for two people sharing and limited to midweek. As a rule of thumb, prices drop in the larger towns and cities the further you move from down-town. In the Northwest's more remote areas, or in hiking or resort towns, remember that many places are likely to close off-season.

BED AND BREAKFAST

Over the last decade or so, **bed and breakfast** has become a popular option in both Canada and the United States, as a luxurious (but usually less expensive) alternative to conventional hotels. Sometimes B&Bs – also known as **guesthouses** and **inns** – are just a couple of furnished rooms in someone's home, and even the larger estab-lishments tend to have no more than ten rooms, without TV and phone but often laden with flow-ers, stuffed cushions and an almost over-contrived homey atmosphere. In many parts of the Northwest, you may find yourself in a "heri-tage home" of great charm, or in some stunning mountain location.

The price you pay for a B&B – which varies from $40 to $200 in both Canada and the US – always includes a huge and wholesome breakfast (sometimes a buffet on a sideboard, but more often a full-blown cooked meal). The crucial determining factor is whether or not each room has an en-suite bathroom; most B&Bs feel obliged to provide private bath facilities: those that do tend to cost between $60 and $80 per night for a double. At the top end of the price spectrum, the distinction between a "hotel" and a "bed and breakfast inn" may amount to no more than that the B&B is owned by a private individual rather than a chain.

HOTEL, HOSTEL AND MOTEL CHAINS

Many of the hotel and lodging chains listed below are found all over the Northwest (in Canada and the US), and publish handy free directories (with maps and illustrations) of their properties. If you stay one night in one of their properties, many offer discounts on subsequent overnight stops in their establish-ments elsewhere. Although we've indicated typical room rates (using the codes explained on p.46), bear in mind that the location of a particular hotel or motel has a huge impact on the price.

American Youth Hostel Association (①)	☎202/783-6161	**Hilton Hotels** (⑤ and up)	☎1-800/445-8667
Best Western (③–⑥)	☎1-800/528-1234	**Holiday Inns** (⑤ and up)	☎1-800/465-4329
Budgetel (③)	☎1-800/428-3438	**Howard Johnson** (③–④)	☎1-800/654-2000
Canadian Youth Hostel Association (①)	☎613/748-5638	**Marriott Hotels** (⑥ and up)	☎1-800/228-9290
Comfort Inns (④–⑤)	☎1-800/221-2222	**Motel 6** (②)	☎505/891-6161
Econolodge (②)	☎1-800/446-6900	**Ramada Inns** (④ and up)	☎1-800/272-6232
Embassy Suites Hotels (⑥)	☎1-800/362-2779	**Select Inns** (②)	☎1-800/641-1000
Fairfield Inns (③)	☎1-800/228-2800	**Stouffer Hotels** (⑤ and up)	☎1-800/468-3571
Hallmark Inns (③)	☎1-800/251-3294	**Super 8 Motels** (②–③)	☎1-800/800-8000
Hampton Inns (④)	☎1-800/426-7866	**Travelodge** (②)	☎1-800/255-3050
		YMCA (Canada) (①)	☎613/237-1320
		YMCA (US) (①)	☎1-800/922-9622

B&B establishments tend to open and close with greater rapidity than hotels, but those that last are often booked up well in advance. Local visitor centers can usually provide current listings; many, such as Vancouver's, keep catalogues bulging with photographs to help you choose a property. In some areas, B&Bs have grouped together to form central **booking agencies**, making it much easier to find a room in advance; we've given addresses for these where appropriate.

YS AND YOUTH HOSTELS

Although hostel-type accommodation is not as plentiful in the US and Canada as it is in Europe and elsewhere, provision for backpackers and low-budget travellers is particularly strong in the hiking and outdoors areas of Canada's Northwest and Alaska. Aside from the odd private hostel in the larger cities, there are four basic kinds of hostel: YMCA/YWCA hostels (known as "Ys"), which offer mixed-sex or, in a few cases, women-only accommodation, the official **Canadian Hostelling Association** (*CHA*) and **mini-hostel** network, the **American Youth Hostel** (*AYH*) network, and the growing **AAIH** (*American Association of Independent Hostels*) organization.

Note that the *International Youth Hostel Federation* (*IYHF*) – to which the *CHA* and *AYH* are affiliated – has recently changed is name to **Hostelling International**. As a result the *CHA* and *AYH* are now properly called *Hostelling International-America* (*HI/AYH*) and *Hostelling International-Canada* (*HI-C*). The old names and acronyms linger in the Northwest, however, and we have retained them throughout the *Guide*.

YMCAS AND YWCAS

Prices in **YMCAs** in both countries range from around $15 for a dormitory bed to $50 for a single or double room. Ys offering accommodation (and not all do, many being basically health clubs) are sometimes in older buildings in less than ideal neighborhoods, but they're usually conveniently downtown, and in Canadian cities in particular many have recently had sparkling face-lifts. Facilities can include a gymnasium, a swimming pool, and an inexpensive cafeteria, while the quality of accommodation matches that of many motels, and invariably exceeds that of other hostel-type lodgings. Dorm beds are sometimes available, but the trend now is increasingly to single, double and even family units, though many *YWCAs* will still only accept women. There's no consistent policy as to whether Ys accept children.

YOUTH HOSTELS

To stay in a hostel in either country, you're supposed in theory to be an *IYHF* member: in practice you can join the *IYHF* on the spot, or rely on most hostels making a slightly higher charge for non-members (though members are usually given priority). Most places offer communal recreational and cooking facilities, plus pillows and blankets, though in simpler places you're expected to provide your own sleeping bag and towels. Especially in high season, it's advisable to **reserve ahead** by writing to the relevant hostel and enclosing a deposit. Some hostels will allow you to use a **sleeping bag**, though officially *AYH* affiliates should insist on a **sheet sleeping bag**.

The hostel scene in **Canada** is currently in a state of flux, and the old ways are passing: hostels are **open** later and longer – lock-outs during the day are now rare, and curfews, or "quiet times" (typically 11pm–7am) are less stringent (though a three-day limit can still be imposed on stays). Increasingly efficient **booking schemes** are also being set up, meaning you can often book into smaller hostels from the big hostels in Calgary, Banff, Edmonton, Seattle and Anchorage. Some major hostels now accept credit card and fax bookings, though the more common way to secure a booking (vital at places like Lake Louise) is still to send a deposit for the first night's stay or an *IYHF* Advance Booking Voucher, available from any *IYHF* office or specialist travel agents – though check that the hostel you're after accepts them.

Almost half of the **CHA**'s 60 or so hostels are in Alberta and British Columbia, and together with their ten AYH-Alaskan counterparts, they often offer the *only* accommodation in more remote areas. Additionally there are a growing number of **unaffiliated hostels** which nonetheless feature in *CHA* and Alaskan *AYH* literature and are often aspiring to full hostel status. Hostels are graded in four categories (basic, simple, standard and superior) and rates range between US$8 and US$14 (Can$14–25) a night. Although dorm beds are still mostly available, there has recently been a move to single, double and four-bed rooms, effectively turning many hostels into extremely reasonably priced hotels. Bigger and newer hostels, notably Banff and Lake Louise, have excellent and well-priced cafeterias. **Mini-hostels** tend to be private homes, or tiny commercial hotels with small breakfast included. Prices are about US$7 (Can$10–20), sometimes with a surcharge for non-members, and you must have your own sleeping bag. A full current list is available from most larger hostels. The official *CHA Hostelling Handbook* is available from affiliated hostels or direct from the *CHA*, National Office, 333 River Rd, Tower A-3, Vanier City, Ottawa, Ontario L1L 8H9 (☎613/748-5638).

In **Washington** (nine hostels) and **Oregon** (seven), hostels are fewer and further between, with most located either in cities or in coastal towns, though a smattering can be found in good hiking country. In both states, hostels still tend to observe the old hostelling niceties – a limited check-in time (usually 5–8pm) and strict daytime lockouts (9.30am–5pm). **Rates** range between $8 and $15 per night depending on grade and location; non-members, and those without an *AYH Hostelling International* card, pay a few dollars extra.

The official *AYH/Hostelling International Handbook* can be picked up from affiliated hostels or direct from the *AYH National Office*, PO Box 37613, Washington DC 20013-7613 (☎202/783-6161).

YOUTH HOSTEL INFORMATION

Local youth hostel information can be found at the following *CHA* and *AYH* offices:

Alaska, Alaska Council, 700 H St, Anchorage, AK 99501 (☎907/562-772).

Alberta, Southern District: 203, 1414 Kensington Rd NW, Calgary, AB T2N 3P9 (☎403/283-5551; Fax 403/283-6503).

Northern District: 10926-88th Ave, Edmonton AB, T6G 0Z1 (☎403/432-7798; Fax 403/733-7781).

British Columbia, 1515 Discovery St, Vancouver, BC V6R 4K5 (☎604/224-7177; Fax 604/224-4852).

Oregon, Oregon Council, 1520 SE 37th Ave, Portland, OR 97214 (☎503/235-9493).

Washington, Washington State Council, 419 Queen Anne Ave N, Suite 101, Seattle, WA 98109 (☎206/281-7306).

The *Hostelling Handbook for the USA and Canada*, produced each May, lists over four hundred hostels and is available for $2 plus $1 postage from Jim Williams, *Sugar Hill House International House Hostel*, 722 Saint Nicholas Ave, New York, NY 10031 (☎212/926-7030).

Overseas travellers will find a comprehensive list of hostels in the *International Youth Hostel Handbook*. In the UK, it's available from the **Youth Hostel Association** headquarters/shop, at 14 Southampton St, London WC2 (☎071/836 1036), where you can also buy a year's *IYHF* membership for £9 (under-18s £3).

CAMPING

Few areas of North America offer as much scope for **camping** as the Pacific Northwest. Most urban areas have a campground, and all national parks and the large proportion of state and provincial parks have outstanding government-run sites. Most state and provincial tourist material covers campgrounds in some detail. In many wilderness areas and in the vast domain of Canada's Crown Lands and the United States' public land you can camp pretty much anywhere you want (ask permission or get a permit wherever possible). We've covered this **wilderness camping** in more detail under "Outdoors" on p.53.

As well as plenty of campgrounds, there are plenty of people intending to use them: take special care plotting your route if you're camping during public holidays or the high season, or hoping to stay at some of the big campgrounds near lake or river resorts, or in any of the national parks (this applies both to main and backcountry campgrounds). Either aim to arrive early in the morning or book ahead – we've given phone numbers wherever this is possible (see below). And check that the site is **open** – many campgrounds only operate seasonally, usually from May to October.

There are several **types of campground**. At the bottom of the pile are **municipal campgrounds**, usually basic affairs with few facilities, which are either free or cost only a few dollars – typically $5 per tent, $10 per RV, though these are usually tent places only. **Private campgrounds** run the gamut: some are as basic as their municipal cousins, others are like huge outdoor pleasure domes with shops, restaurants, laundries, swimming pools, tennis courts, even saunas and jacuzzis. Best-known among the latter is the family-oriented *KOA* network, with campgrounds across the Northwest; the company publishes an annual directory of its campgrounds in both countries (*Kampgrounds of America*, Billings, MT 59114-0558; ☎406/248-7444). Lone or budget travellers may appreciate their facilities but not their commercial atmosphere.

As for **price**, private campgrounds have several ways of charging. Some charge by the vehicle; others per couple; comparatively few on a per tent or per person basis. Two people sharing a tent in either country might typically pay anything between $5 and $15 each, though an average price would be nearer $5–7. Where we've given a price it is for two people sharing a tent. Booking is almost always an option in a private campground.

Campgrounds in national or other **parks** are run by national, state or provincial governments (see also "Wilderness Camping" on p.53). Most are well turned out and the bulk are open officially from May to September. In practice many are open longer (though may be unserviced out of season), and in the bigger national parks, you'll find the occasional site serviced for **winter camping**. **Prices** vary from $5 to $15 per tent in both countries depending on location, services

and the time of the year – prices may be higher during July and August.

Campgrounds in the major parks, especially close to towns, usually offer a full range of amenities for both tents and RVs, and often have separate sites for each. As a rule, though, provincial or state sites and more remote national park campgrounds tend to favor tents and offer only water, stores of firewood and pit toilets. Hot showers, in particular, are rare. But all park campgrounds, of course, invariably score highly on their scenic locations. Most state, federal or provincial campgrounds in both Canada and the US fill the bulk of their pitches on a **first-come, first-served** basis, though reservations are possible in Alaska (and often essential in high season), and there is a growing trend elsewhere for park campgrounds to introduce a high-season reservation system.

Whatever type of campground you use, check the small print for the number of **unserviced** (tent) sites, as many places cater chiefly for recreational vehicles (RVs), providing them with **full or partial hookups** for water and electricity (or "serviced sites"). Anywhere describing itself as an "RV Park" ought to be avoided completely.

OUTDOORS

The Pacific Northwest is scattered with fabulous backcountry and wilderness areas, coated by dense forests, crossed by mighty whitewater rivers, and capped by majestic mountains and vast glaciers. Opportunities for outdoor pursuits are almost limitless, and the facilites to indulge them some of the best on the continent. We've concentrated on the most popular activities – hiking, skiing and rafting – and on the region's superlative national parks. Whatever activity interests you, be sure to send off to the various state and provincial tourist offices for information before you go. Once you're in the Northwest you can rely on finding outfitters, equipment rental, charters, tours and guides to help you in most areas.

THE PARKS SYSTEM

Protected backcountry areas in both Canada and the United States fall into a number of potentially confusing categories. **National parks** in both countries are large federally controlled areas of great natural beauty and/or historical significance. **National monuments** in the States and **national historic sites** in Canada and the US tend to be outstanding geological or historical features covering much smaller areas than national parks and not having quite the same facilities or broad tourist appeal; National seashores, lakeshores and so on are self-explanatory. The tracts of **national forest** that often surround national parks are also federally administered, but are much less protected, and usually allow some limited logging and other land-based industries – ski resorts and mining the most common.

National parks are usually supervised locally by a ranger (US) or warden (Canada) based at a park office or a **park information center** (the terminology may vary from park to park). These should be your first port-of-call, certainly if you intend to fish, camp or climb in the backcountry, pursuits which in both countries usually require a **permit**. Most offer information and audio-visual displays on flora, fauna and outdoor activities, and virtually all employ highly experienced staff who can provide firsthand advice on your chosen trail or pursuit. **Regulations** common to all parks

include a total ban on firearms, hunting, snowmobiles or off-road vehicles, the feeding of wildlife, and the removal or damaging of any natural objects or features.

Most national park regulations relating to the care of the environment and campground behavior are usually applicable to **state** (US) or **provincial** (Canada) parks. These are usually, but not always, smaller areas of outstanding natural beauty than national parks, or sites of specific geological or geographical importance. They are run by the states or provinces of each country, while various government departments administer a whole range of wildlife refuges, national scenic rivers, recreation areas and the like. In the United States the **Bureau of Land Management (BLM)** has the largest holdings of all, most of it open rangeland, but also including some enticingly out-of-the-way reaches.

While any of the above areas will have at least basic facilities for **camping** (see below), many national and smaller parks have few towns and extremely limited **supplies and services**. In general, the better known a place is, the more likely it will be to have some semblance of the comforts of home, with shops and petrol stations and lodges – all of which are handy but can detract from the natural splendor. Elsewhere, particularly in Alaska's protected areas, southeast Oregon, and Canada's Yoho and Jasper parks, it's as well to be aware that food, petrol and shelter can be literally tens, if not hundreds of miles away. The parks' superb back-up – in the shape of maps, brochures and visitor centers – can often obscure the fact that these are wild places. Some planning is essential, even if it's just making sure you have enough petrol in the tank to get you to the next known gas station. Weather can also turn, even in summer: it's not been unknown, for example, for people to have become trapped by snow and died in their cars on the famous Banff to Jasper Icefields Parkway, a heavily travelled route that nonetheless reaches heights of almost 8000 feet and has just one service stop in over 150 miles.

ENTRANCE FEES

In **Canada** all motor vehicles, including motorbikes, must buy a **Park Permit** before entering a national park, usually from a roadside booth at

STATE AND PROVINCIAL PARK OFFICES

While park visitor centers and ranger/warden stations provide excellent information on individual parks, it can be useful – either on the spot or before you go – to contact the regional offices below for both general and specific queries (especially on camping arrangements) in the national and smaller parks within individual states and provinces.

Alaska

Alaska State Division of Parks,
Old Federal Building,
Anchorage, AK 99510 ☎907/762-2617

Public Lands & National Parks Information Center,
605 W Fourth Ave, Suite 105,
Anchorage, AK 99501 ☎907/271-2737

Public Lands Information Center,
250 Cushman Suite 1A,
Fairbanks, AK 99701 ☎907/451-7352

Public Lands Information Center,
Box 359,
Tok, AK 99780 ☎907/883-5667

US Fish and Wildlife Service (for campgrounds in
National Wildlife Refuges), 1011 E Tudor Rd,
Anchorage, AK 99503 ☎907/271-4126

United States Forest Service (for campgrounds in
national forests), 1675 C St,
Anchorage, AK 99501 ☎907/271-4126

Alberta

Canadian Parks Service (for all national parks in
Alberta and BC), 520, 220 Fourth Ave SW,
Calgary AB T2P 3H8 ☎403/292-4401

Provincial Parks Information, Standard Life Centre,
1660, 10405 Jasper Ave,
Edmonton T5J 3N4 ☎403/427-9429

British Columbia

BC Provincial Parks Service,
800 Johnson St, Second Floor,
Victoria, BC V8V 1X4 ☎604/387-5002

Canadian Parks Service (Yoho, Glacier and
Revelstoke): see Alberta above.

Oregon

Oregon State Parks and Recreation Dept,
525 Trade St SE,
Salem, OR 97310 ☎503/378-6305

Campsite information:
For the state parks inside OR (March–Labor Day,
daily 8am–4.30pm) ☎1-800/452-5687
For Portland and outside OR ☎503/238-7488

*Forest Service Regional HQ, Pacific Northwest
Region,* 319 SW Pine St, PO Box 3623,
Portland, OR 97208 ☎503/222-2877

Washington

*National Park Service/USDA Forest Pacific
Northwest Region,* Outdoor Recreation Information
Office, 1018 First Ave, Seattle,
WA 98104 ☎206/442-0170

*Washington State Parks and Recreation
Commission,* 7150 Cleanwater Lane, KY-11
Olympia, WA 98504-5711 ☎206/753-2027
or May–Aug, in WA ☎1-800/562-0990
May–Aug, outside WA ☎206/753-2116

the point where the road crosses the park boundary. People entering on foot, bicycle, boat or horseback are exempt, and there are exemptions for vehicles passing straight through certain parks without stopping overnight. An annual permit, valid whenever you buy it until March of the following year, costs Can$30; a four-day permit costs Can$10; and a day permit Can$5. Permits bought for one national park are valid for all other Canadian national parks. Provincial parks are usually free.

Comparable arrangements obtain in the **United States**, though here pedestrians and cyclists also have to pay a small entrance fee, and many areas of specific US national parks do not charge for admission. If you plan to visit more than a couple of national parks (where the standard fee per carload is between US$3 and US$10), buy a **Golden Eagle passport**, which gives unlimited access to (almost) any national park or monument, and costs $25 for a calendar year. Special free passes are available for disabled travellers and senior citizens – see p.40 and p.42 respectively. Most US state parks are free.

WILDERNESS CAMPING

If your time and money are limited, but you want to get a feel for the wilderness, one of the best options is to backpack or tour around by car, **camping** out at night and cooking your own meals (on a camp stove, if local regulations allow). If you don't fancy roughing it all the way, there is also a wide selection of public and commercially run **campgrounds** in or very near areas of great beauty, together with special federally run campgrounds in national parks. Every state or province produces comprehensive lists of the campgrounds in its parks: we've mentioned the most useful or most scenic in the *Guide*.

Park and wilderness campgrounds usually range from **primitive** (a flat piece of ground that may or may not have a water tap, and may charge nothing at all) to **semi-primitive**, which usually provide wood, water and pit toilets, and where "self-registration" is the norm and a small fee (around $5) is left in the box provided. In bigger park campgrounds like Banff and Lake Louise, the facilities match and often exceed those of big commercial campgrounds, with shops, restaurants and washing facilities, and nightly rates in both countries of around $15.

Campgrounds in national parks are bound by special rules, and in both Canada and the US are always federally run concerns administered by the National Parks Services: there are no private sites. Some are for tents, some for RVs only, and most parks have at least one site which remains open for basic **winter camping** (check all opening times carefully: most park sites open only from around mid-May to mid-September). Fees depend on facilities, and currently run from around US$5 (Can$7) per tent (semi-primitive) to around US$10 (Can$18) for those with electricity, sewage, water and showers. Advance booking is being introduced into some provincially run parks, but generally sites in national parks are filled on a first-come, first-served basis. Booking is possible however – and highly recommended – in the **Alaskan parks**: the *Alaska Public Lands Information Centers* at Anchorage (☎907/271-2737), Fairbanks (☎907/451-7352) and Tok (☎907/883-5667) offer information on the parks in question and details of how to book (but do not actually make reservations).

Official permission is required in both countries for **backcountry camping**, whether you're rough camping or using designated primitive or semi-primitive sites, in order to enable the authorities to keep a check on people's whereabouts and to regulate the numbers. In Canada you must obtain an **overnight permit** from a park center (or the park warden office if the center is shut out of season). These are either free or cost Can$1–2, in addition to any campground fees you may also have to pay. In certain wilderness areas

of the States, including the backcountry reaches of most national parks, you need a **Wilderness Permit** (either free or US$1), available from the nearest park rangers' office.

Note, however, that while registration and permits are obligatory, other regulations for rough camping vary enormously and arrangements are still being finalized in many parks. Some parks, like Jasper in the Canadian Rockies, for example, allow backcountry camping only in tightly defined sites: others, like nearby Banff, have a special **primitive wildland** zone where you can pitch tent within a designated distance of the nearest road or trailhead. Throughout the Canadian parks, though, a quota system operates in the more popular backpacking areas: no more permits will be issued once a set number have been allocated for a particular trail or backcountry campground.

When **camping rough**, check that fires are permitted before you start one (they are not on the Arctic tundra of Alaska and the Yukon); even if they are, try to use a campstove in preference to local materials – in some places firewood is scarce, although you may be allowed to use deadwood. In wilderness areas, try to camp on previously used sites. Where there are no toilets, **bury human waste** at least eight inches into the ground and two hundred feet from the nearest water supply and campground. It'll be hard to do, but also try to avoid using toilet paper if possible (leaves, stones and acceptable bio-safe soaps are alternatives). Never wash directly into rivers and lakes – use a container at least 50 feet from either, and try to use a biodegrable soap. It is *not* acceptable to burn any rubbish: the preferred practice is to **pack out**, or carry away all rubbish, the ideal being to leave no trace whatsoever of your presence.

HIKING

The Pacific Northwest boasts some of North America's finest hiking, and whatever your abilities or ambitions you'll find a walk to suit you almost anywhere in the region. All the national and provincial or state parks have well-marked and remarkably well-maintained trails, and a visit to any park center or local tourist office will furnish you with adequate **maps** of local paths. Park trails are usually sufficiently well marked not to need more detailed maps for short walks and day hikes. If you're entering into the backcountry, though, try to obtain the appropriate maps (see p.28). For key hiking areas we've given a brief summary of the best hikes in the appropriate parts of the *Guide*, though with over 1500km of paths in Canada's Banff National Park alone, recommendations can only scratch the surface. Be sure to consult park staff on other good walks, or to pick up the **trail guides** that are widely available for most of the region's prime walking areas.

Wherever you're hiking, and at whatever altitude, it goes without saying that you should be **properly prepared and equipped** and treat all terrain — not just the mountains — with the respect it deserves. Good boots, waterproof jacket and spare food and warm clothing are all essential. Be prepared for sudden changes of weather, for encounters with wildlife, especially **bears**, which flourish throughout the entire state of Alaska and in much of the Canadian Rockies (see p.409), and for the sort of health considerations now sadly a fact of life in North American backcountry (see below). Outdoor clothing can be bought easily in most towns, and in most mountain areas there's a good chance of being able to **rent** tents and specialized cold-weather gear.

MAIN HIKING AREAS

In picking out the Northwest's prime walking areas we've chosen the parks which are accessible by road (or by boat, as is sometimes the case in Alaska), where maps and guides are available, where the trail system is developed, and where you can turn up up without too much planning or special wilderness training.

Some of the best-known and most developed of these are the national parks of the **Canadian Rockies** in Alberta and British Columbia. Thousands of well-kept and well-tramped trails criss-cross the "big four parks" — Banff, Jasper, Yoho and Kootenay — as well as the smaller but no less spectacular or approachable Glacier, Revelstoke and Waterton Lakes national parks. Scope for hiking of all descriptions is almost limitless, as it is in the national parks of Washington, most dramatically among the glacial peaks of the **North Cascades** and around the highest Cascade mountain of them all, **Mount Rainier**. Most of the five national parks in **Alaska** are trail-less, but the scenery is equally awe-inspiring, especially among the giant glaciers and volcanoes of **Wrangell-St Elias** and in the wide-open spaces of **Denali**.

Smaller areas dotted all over the region boast walking possibilities out of all proportion to their size. In Oregon, pint-sized **Crater Lake National Park** presents some of the Pacific Northwest's most stunning scenery, while Washington's **Mount St Helens Volcanic Monument** bears remarkable charred and dusty testimony to the force of the eruption that blew the mountain to pieces in 1980. In British Columbia, which has some of the best smaller protected areas, all the following provincial parks offer day hikes, short strolls and longer trails that could keep you happy for a week or more: **Wells Gray**, north of Kamloops; **Kokanee Glacier**, near Nelson; **Manning**, east of Vancouver; **Garibaldi**, north of Vancouver; and **Strathcona**, on Vancouver Island. Virtually every coastal Alaskan town, especially those in the southeast such as **Sitka**, **Haines**, **Cordova**, and **Homer**, boasts its own network of trails.

LONG-DISTANCE FOOTPATHS

In areas with highly developed trail networks, seasoned backpackers can blaze their own **long-distance footpaths** by stringing together several longer trails. Recognized long-haul trails, however, are relative rare, though more are being designated yearly. One of the best is the **Chilkoot Trail** from Dyea in Alaska to Bennett in British Columbia, a 53-kilometer hike that closely follows the path of prospectors en route to the Yukon during the 1898 gold rush. Another increasingly popular path is the **West Coast Trail**, which runs for 80km along the edge of Vancouver Island's Pacific Rim National Park; a southern equivalent is the **Oregon Coast Trail**, hugging the 360 miles of coastline from the Columbia River to the Californian border. The **Pacific Crest Trail**, a 2620-mile path from Mexico to the Canadian border, offers manageable one- or two-week stretches in Oregon and Washington (with a network of cabins if you're not camping). The 150-mile **Oregon Desert Trail**, across the southeast portion of the state, is still under construction, and will eventually form part of a putative long-distance desert trail from Canada to Mexico. Most trails have a growing body of guides to help you with practicalities and route-finding.

HIKING AND HEALTH

Hiking at **lower elevations** should present few problems, though the thick swarms of **insects** you're likely to encounter near any body of water, particularly in Alaska and the Yukon, can drive you crazy. April to June is the **blackfly** season, and the **mosquitoes** are out in force from July until about October: *DEET* (not on sale in Alaska) and *Avon Skin-so-soft* handcream are two fairly reliable repellents. Before you go, you could try taking three times the recommended dosage of Vitamin B, and continuing with the recommended dosage while you're in the region – it's been shown to cut bites by 75 percent. Burning coils or candles containing allethrin or citronella can help if you're camping or picnicking. Once bitten, an antihistamine cream like phenergan is the best antidote. On no account go anywhere near an area posted as a blackfly mating ground – people have died from bites sustained when the monsters are on heat.

If you develop a large rash and flu-like symptoms in the backcountry, you may have been bitten by a **tick** carrying **lyme borreliosis** (or "lyme tick disease"). This is a problem spreading with alarming speed through North America, and it's particularly prevalent in wooded country. Check with the local tourist authority. The condition is easily curable, however, so see a doctor, but if left can lead to nasty complications. Ticks – tiny beetles that plunge their heads into your skin and swell up – can sometimes leave their heads inside, causing blood clots or infections, so get advice from a park ranger if you've been bitten. If the prospect of tick encounter fills you with horror, invest in a strong tick repellent and wear long socks, trousers and sleeved shirts when walking.

One very serious backcountry problem you must confront camping is **Giardia** (or "Beaver Fever"), a water-borne bacteria causing an intestinal disease, of which the symptoms are chronic diarrhoea, abdominal cramps, fatigue and loss of weight. Treatment at that stage is essential; much better to avoid catching it in the first place. **Never drink** from rivers, streams or glaciers, however clear and inviting they may look (you never know what unspeakable acts people – or animals – further upstream have performed in them); **water** that doesn't come from a tap should be boiled for at least five minutes, or cleansed with an iodine-based purifier (such as *Potable Aqua*) or a Giardia-rated filter, available from any camping or sports store. Neither ordinary filters nor standard water purification tablets will remove the bacteria.

Beware, too, of **poison oak**, an allergenic shrub that grows all over the Pacific Northwest, usually among oak trees. Its leaves come in groups of three and are distinguished by prominent veins and shiny surfaces (waxy green in spring, rich red and orange in fall). It causes open blisters and lumpy sores up to ten days after contact. If you come into contact with it, wash your skin (with soap and cold water) and clothes as soon as possible – and don't scratch: the only way to ease the itching is to smother yourself in calamine lotion or to take regular dips in the sea. In serious cases, hospital emergency rooms can give antihistamine or adrenaline jabs.

There's also a danger of being bitten or stung by various **poisonous creatures**. You'll soon know if this happens. Current medical thinking rejects the concept of cutting yourself open and attempting to suck out venom; whether snake, scorpion or spider is responsible, you should apply a cold compress to the wound, constrict the area with a tourniquet to prevent the spread of venom, drink lots of water and bring your temperature down by resting in a shady area. Stay as calm as possible and seek medical help **immediately**.

Hiking at **higher elevations**, as in the 14,000-feet peaks of Alaska and the Rockies, you need to take especial care: late snows are common, even into July, and in spring there's a real danger of avalanches, not to mention meltwaters making otherwise simple stream crossings hazardous. Altitude sickness, brought on by the depletion of oxygen in the atmosphere, can affect even the fittest of athletes. Take it easy for the first few days you go above seven thousand feet; drink lots of water, avoid alcohol, eat plenty of carbohydrates, and protect yourself from the increased power of the sun. Watch out for signs of **exposure** – mild delirium, exhaustion, inability to get warm – and on snow or in high country during the summer take a good **sun-block**.

SKIING

Wherever there's hiking in the Northwest, there's also usually **skiing**. Washington has sixteen ski areas, mostly in the **Cascades**, and many within easy striking distance of Seattle. Oregon boasts **Mount Batchelor**, offering some of North America's finest skiing, and **Mount Hood**, where you can ski well into the summer. For details of

SKIING – HOW TO SAVE MONEY

The Northwest features some of the best ski terrain in the world, but without careful planning a ski vacation can be horribly expensive. In addition to the tips listed below, phone (toll-free) or write in advance to resorts for brochures, and when you get there, scan local newspapers for money-saving offers.

- Visit during early or late season to take advantage of lower accommodation rates.
- The more people in your party, the more money you save on lodgings. For groups of four to six, a condo unit costs much less than a standard motel.
- Before setting a date, ask the resort about package deals including flights, rooms and ski passes. This is the no-fuss and often highly economical way to book a ski vacation.
- Shop around for the best boot and ski rentals – prices often vary significantly.
- If you have to buy tickets at the resort, save money by purchasing multiday tickets.
- If you're an absolute beginner, look out for resorts that offer free "never-ever" lessons with the purchase of a lift ticket.
- Finish your day's skiing in time to take advantage of happy hours and dining specials, which usually last from 4pm until 7pm.

all these areas contact the *Pacific Northwest Ski Areas Association*, PO Box 2325, Seattle, WA 98111-2325 (☎206/623-3777). Increasingly, however, it is the big resorts in the Canadian Rockies and British Columbia's Coast Ranges that are grabbing the headlines. Resorts such as **Whistler**, north of Vancouver – with North America's longest vertical run – and **Lake Louise** in Banff National Park, are widely acknowledged to offer some of the finest skiing anywhere in the world. Furthermore, both these areas, together with countless others in the Rockies, are less than 90 minutes from major cities, making them readily and cheaply accessible.

Despite the expense involved, **heli-skiing** is also taking off, a sport that involves a helicopter drop deep into the backcountry (or to the actual summits of mountains) followed by some of the wildest and most exhilarating off-piste skiing you're ever likely to experience. The main centres, again, are mostly in the Rockies and Coast Mountains, though it's one of the fastest growing adventure sports in the region; contact visitor centers for details of packages and outfitters.

US and Canadian **ski packages** are available from most foreign travel agents, while companis and hotels in many Northwest cities organize their own mini-packages to nearby resorts. It is, however, perfectly feasible to organize your own trips, but be sure to book well ahead if you're hoping to stay in some of the better known resorts. In the first instance, contact state or provincial tourist offices in the Northwest, or their offices abroad (see p.27); most publish regional ski and winter sports directories. On the spot, visitor centers in ski areas open up in the winter to help with practicalities, and most towns have ski shops to buy or rent equipment. **Costs** for food, accommodation and ski passes, in Canada at least, are still fairly modest by US and European standards (see the box for some cost-cutting tips). Generally you can rent equipment for about Can$15 per day, and expect to pay perhaps another Can$40 per day for lift tickets. A cheaper option is **cross-country skiing**, or ski-touring. Backcountry ski lodges dot mountainous areas, offering rustic accommodation, equipment rental and lessons, from as little as Can $10 a day for skis, boots and poles, up to about $100 for an all-inclusive weekend tour.

FISHING

The Pacific Northwest is **fishing** nirvana. While each area has its dream catches, from the arctic char of Alaska to the Pacific salmon of Washington and British Columbia, excellent fishing can be found in most of the region's super-abundant lakes, rivers and coastal waters. Most towns have a fishing shop for equipment, and any spot with fishing possibilities is likely to have companies running boats and charters. As with every other type of outdoor activity, states and provinces publish detailed booklets on outfitters and everything that swims within the area of their jurisdiction.

Contact the following offices to confirm current conditions, regulations and prices for fishing throughout the Northwest.

Alaska

Fish and Game Licensing, PO Box 25526, AK 99802-5525 (☎907/465-2376). Non-resident licences $10 (daily), $15 (3-day), $30 (14-day), $50 (annual).

Alberta

Fish and Wildlife Service, 9945 108th St, Edmonton T5K 2G6 (☎403/427-3590). Non-resident licences Can$15 for Canadians (annual), $30 for non-Canadians (annual).

British Columbia

Fish and Wildlife Information, Ministry of Environment, 780 Blanshard St, Victoria, BC V8V 1X4 (☎604/387-9737). Non-resident licences Can$22.50 (6 days), $35 (annual).

Oregon

Department of Fish and Wildlife, 2501 SW First Ave, PO Box 59, Portland 97207 (☎503/229-5400). Non-resident licences $35.75 (annual) plus $5.50 for each salmon, steelhead, sturgeon and halibut tagged.

Washington

Department of Fisheries, PO Box 43135, Olympia 98504-3135 (☎206/902-2200). Non-resident food use licence $10 (annual), plus $4 for salmon and $3 for sturgeon tags; game fishing licence ($48).

Yukon

Department of Renewable Resources, Fish and Wildlife Branch, 10 Burns Rd, PO Box 2703, Whitehorse Y1A 2C6 (☎403/667-5221). Non-resident licence Can$5 (daily), $20 (6-day), $35 (annual).

Fishing in Canada and the US is governed by a medley of **regulations** that vary from state to state, and province to province. These are baffling at first glance, but usually boil down to the need for a non-resident permit for freshwater fishing, and another for salt-water (see box above). These are obtainable from most local fishing or sports shops for about US$45 (Can$30) and are valid for a year. Short-term (one- or six-day) licences are also available in some areas. In a few places you may have to pay for extra licences to go after particular fish, and in Canadian national parks you need a special additional permit. There may also be quotas or a closed season on certain fish. Shops and visitor centers always have the most current regulations, which you should check before you set out.

ADVENTURE TRAVEL

The opportunities for active travelling in the Northwest are all but endless, from whitewater rafting down the Rogue, Kenai and Fraser rivers, to mountain biking in the volcanic Cascades, polar-bear watching in Inuvik, horse riding in the Cariboo, and ice-climbing on the glacial monoliths of Alaska, Mount Rainier and the Columbia Icefields. While an exhaustive listing of the possibilities could fill another volume of this book, certain places have an especially high concentration of adventure opportunities, notably the Rockies' parks, the Yukon, the Cascades and Alaska. We occasionally recommend guides, outfitters, and local adventure tour operators, but a quick visit to any local visitor or park center should provide you with reams of material on just about any outdoor activity you care to name.

FOOD AND DRINK

The sheer number of restaurants, bars, cafés and fast-food joints in the Northwest is staggering, but for the most part there's little to distinguish the mainstream urban cuisines of the region's towns and cities: in both Canada and America, shopping malls, main streets and highways are lined with pan-American food chains, each trying to outdo each with their bargains and special offers. However, this overall uniformity is leavened in the bigger cities by a plethora of ethnic restaurants, and places that specialize in Pacific Northwestern seafood dishes. Even out in the country – the domain of often grim family-run diners – you'll find the odd ethnic or seafood restaurant to save the day.

BREAKFAST

Breakfast is taken very seriously all over the Pacific Northwest, and with prices averaging between US$4 and US$7 (Can$5–10) it can be very good value. Whether you go to a café, coffee shop or hotel snack bar, the breakfast menu, on offer until around 11am, is a fairly standard fry. **Eggs** are the staple ingredient: "sunny side up" is fried on one side leaving a runny yolk; "over" is slipped over in the pan to stiffen the yolk; and "over easy" is flipped for a few seconds to give a hint of solidity. Scrambled, poached eggs and omelettes are popular too. The usual meat is **ham or bacon**, streaky and fried to a

crisp, or skinless and bland **sausages**. Whatever you order, you nearly always seem to receive a dollop of fried potatoes, called **hash browns** or sometimes **home fries**. Other favorite breakfast options include **English muffins** or, in posher places, **bran muffins**, a glutinous fruitcake made with bran and sugar, and **waffles or pancakes**, swamped in butter with lashings of maple syrup.

Whatever you eat, you can wash it down with as much **coffee** as you can stomach: for the price of the first cup, the waiters will keep providing free refills until you beg them to stop. The coffee is either **regular** or **decaf** and is nearly always freshly ground, though lots of the cheaper places dilute it until it tastes like dish water. As a matter of course, coffee comes with cream or **half-and-half** (half cream, half milk) – if you ask for skimmed milk, you're often met with looks of disbelief. **Tea**, with either lemon or milk, is also drunk at breakfast, and the swisher places emphasize the English connection by using imported brands – or at least brands which sound English.

LUNCH AND SNACKS

Between 11.30am and 2.30pm many big-city restaurants offer **specials** that are generally excellent value. In Chinese and Vietnamese establishments, for example, you'll frequently find rice and noodles, or dim sum feasts for $4 to $6, and many **Japanese** restaurants give you a chance to eat sushi for under $10, far cheaper than usual. **Pizza** is also widely available, from larger chains like *Pizza Hut* to family-owned restaurants and pavement stalls. Favorites with white-collar workers are **café-restaurants** featuring whole- and vegetarian foods, though few are nutritionally dogmatic, serving traditional seafood and meat dishes and sandwiches too; most have an excellent selection of daily lunch specials for around $7.

For quick **snacks** many **delis** do ready-cooked meals from $3, as well as a range of sandwiches and filled bagels. Alternatively, shopping malls sometimes have **ethnic fast-food stalls**, a healthier option than the inevitable **burger chains**, whose homogenized products have colonized every main street in the land. Regional snacks are all things nautical – from salmon and halibut to clams and shrimps.

COPING AS A VEGETARIAN

In the big cities at least, being a **vegetarian** in Canada and the United States presents few problems. Cholesterol-fearing North Americans are turning to healthfoods in a big way, and most towns of any size boast a wholefood or vegetarian café, while America's Mexican restaurants tend to include at least one vegetarian item on their menus. However, don't be too surprised in rural areas if you find yourself restricted to a diet of eggs, cheese sandwiches (you might have to ask them to leave the ham out), salads and pizza. If you eat fish the Northwest's ubiquitous salmon will become a staple, though some apparently "safe" foods such as baked beans, and the nutritious-sounding red beans and rice, often contain bits of diced pork. None of the major fast-food chains includes a vegetarian burger on its menu, but the Mexicanesque *Taco Bell*, which boasts outlets as far north as Fairbanks, sells meatless tostadas and burritos.

Some city **bars** are used as much by diners as drinkers, who turn up in droves to gorge themselves on the free **hors d'oeuvres** laid out between 5pm and 7pm from Monday to Friday in an attempt to grab commuters. For the price of a drink you can stuff yourself with pasta and chilli. **Brunch** is another deal worth looking out for, a cross between breakfast and lunch served up in bars at the weekend from around 11am to 2pm. For a set price ($8 and up) you get a light meal and a variety of complimentary cocktails or wine.

MAIN MEALS AND SPECIALTIES

While the predictable burgers, piles of ribs or half a chicken, served up with salads, cooked vegetables and bread, are found everywhere, you should aim to explore the diverse regional cuisines of the Pacific Northwest when it comes to the main meal of the day. **Beef** is especially prominent in Alberta, while **fish and seafood** – anything from salmon and lobster to king crab, oysters and shrimp – dominate the menus of just about all the coastal areas. **Salmon**, especially, is predominant, either served straight or stuffed, or sometimes in unlikely mixes with pasta. **Shellfish** are also popular, notably **clams**, Washington's highly rated **Dungeness crab** – smoother and

COFFEE HOUSES

Coffee houses play an increasingly important role in social interaction in the Northwest – especially in Seattle, which has literally hundreds. Most specialize in **espressos**, though **latté**, made with milk and served in a tall glass, is also a favorite. Such is the emphasis on coffee throughout the region that even in far-flung Alaskan villages the local café may well serve top-notch cappuccinos and espressos.

creamier than the average crab – and, most strikingly, Puget Sound **geoduck** (pronounced "gooeyduck"), huge molluscs of intensely phallic appearance that are often served coyly chopped up. In the far north regions you may well come across some of the most exotic offerings – things like **arctic char** and **caribou** steak.

Ethnic variations are endless, especially in the big cities of Seattle and Vancouver. **Chinese** food is everywhere, and can be among the cheapest available. **Japanese** is not far behind, at least in Vancouver and Seattle, and is not quite as expensive – or fashionable – as it once was. As Pacific Rim immigration gathers pace, other Far Eastern imports are currently making headway, especially Thai, Indonesian and **Vietnamese** cuisines. **Italian** food is popular, and can still be cheap in the "Little Italy" of Vancouver. Away from simple pastas, however, it can become expensive, particularly if you venture into the world of exotic pizza toppings and specialist Italian cooking catching on fast in major cities. **French** food, too, is available, though always pricey, the favored cuisine of the urban rich. **Indian** restaurants are making an increasing showing, but again are still only restricted to the bigger centers. Be on the lookout also for **Native American** restaurants, a slowly growing breed, where you enjoy the likes of venison, buffalo and black-husked wild rice.

More generally, **Californian cuisine** has made its presence felt throughout the region. Geared towards health and aesthetics, it's basically a development of French *nouvelle cuisine*, utilizing the wide mix of fresh, locally available ingredients. The theory is to eat only what you need, and what your body can process. Vegetables are harvested before maturity and steamed to preserve both vitamins and flavor. Seafood comes from oyster farms and the

NORTH AMERICAN FOOD TERMS FOR OVERSEAS VISITORS

A la mode	With ice cream	*Hot cakes*	Pancakes
Au jus	Meat served with a gravy made from its own juices	*Jello*	Jelly
		Jelly	Jam
Biscuit	Similar to a scone, eaten as an accompaniment to a meal	*Muffin*	Small cake made with bran and/or fruit and other sweeteners
BLT	Bacon, lettuce and tomato toasted sandwich	*Nachos*	Tortilla chips with melted cheese
Broiled	Grilled	*Pecan pie*	Pastry shell filled with pecan nuts and syrupy goo
Brownie	A fudgy, filling chocolate cake	*Popsicle*	Ice lolly
Burrito	Folded *tortilla* stuffed with refried beans or beef and grated cheese	*Pretzels*	Savory circles of glazed pastry
		Salsa	Chillis, tomato, onion and cilantro, in varying degrees of spiciness
Check, Tab	Bill		
Chips	Potato crisps	*Sashimi*	Thinly sliced raw fish eaten with soy sauce or *wasabi*
Cilantro	Coriander		
Clam chowder	A thick soup made with clams and other seafood	*Seltzer*	Fizzy/soda water
		Sherbet	Sorbet
Club sandwich	Large, overstuffed sandwich	*Shrimp*	Prawns
Cookie	Sweet biscuit	*Soda*	Generic term for any soft drink
Crawfish (also *crayfish*)	Crustacean, resembling a baby lobster	*Squash*	Marrow
		Steamers	Steamed clams, served with butter
Eggs:			
sunny side up	fried on one side only	*Sub*	French-bread sandwich
over	flipped over to stiffen the yolk	*Sushi*	Japanese specialty; raw fish wrapped with rice in seaweed
over easy	flipped for a few seconds only		
Eggplant	Aubergine	*Tacos*	Folded, fried *tortillas*, stuffed with chicken, beef, etc
Enchiladas	Soft *tortillas* filled with meat and cheese or chilli and baked		
English muffin	Toasted bread roll, like a crumpet	*Tamales*	Corn meal dough with meat and chilli, baked in a corn husk
Fajitas	Soft *taco*-like flour *tortilla* stuffed with shrimp, chicken or beef	*Tempura*	Seafood and vegetables deep fried in batter
Frank	Frankfurter (hot dog)	*Teriyaki*	Chicken or beef, marinated in soy sauce and grilled
(French) fries	Chips		
Frijoles	Refried beans, ie mashed fried pinto beans	*Tortillas*	Maize dough pancakes used in most Mexican dishes
Half-and-half	Half cream, half milk	*Waldorf salad*	Celery, chopped apple and walnuts served on lettuce leaves with mayonnaise
Hash browns	Fried chopped or grated potato		
Hero, Hoagie	French-bread sandwich		
Home Fries	Thick-ciut fried potatoes	*Zucchini*	Courgettes

catches of small-time fishers, and what little meat there is tends to be from animals reared on organic farms. One result has been the creation of a clutch of expensive – very expensive – restaurants in the big cities, another has been to stimulate the development in Washington and Oregon of **Northwest Cuisine**, with its emphasis on fish. Similar attitudes – and influences – to food and nutrition also underpin the scores of vaguely counter-cultural restaurants that dot the Pacific Northwest, often owned by former Sixties' "Love Children".

Mexican food is common in the US Northwest (and increasingly in Vancouver and Calgary). Day or night, this is one of the cheapest types of food to eat: even a full dinner with a few drinks will rarely be over $10 except in the most upmarket place. Mexican food in the States is different from that in Mexico, making more use of fresh meats and vegetables, although the essentials are the same: rice and pinto beans, often served refried (ie boiled, mashed and fried), with variations on the **tortilla**, a very thin corndough or flour pancake that is wrapped around the food and eaten by hand (a **burrito**); folded, fried and filled (a **taco**); rolled, filled and baked in sauce (an **enchilada**); or fried flat and topped with a stack of food (a **tostada**). Meals are usually served with complimentary **nachos** (chips) and a hot **salsa** dip. The **chile relleno** is a good vegetarian option – a green pepper stuffed with cheese, dipped in egg batter and fried.

DRINKING

Across the Northwest, **bars** and cocktail lounges occasionally live up to the *Cheers*-celebrated popular image: long dimly lit counters with a few punters perched on stools before a bartender-cum-guru, and tables and booths for those who don't want to join in the drunken bar-side debates. Mostly, though, they vary enormously, from the male-dominated, rough-edged drinking holes concentrated in the blue-collar parts of cities, lumber and mining towns (often annexed to a seedy hotel), to the far more fashionable city establishments which provide food, live entertainment and an inspiring range of cocktails.

BUYING AND CONSUMING

To buy and consume alcohol in the US, you must be 21, and you may be asked for ID even if you look older. In Alberta the legal drinking age is eighteen, and nineteen in BC and the Yukon. In Canada, though, it's rare to be asked for ID, except at government-run liquor shops, which hold a virtual monopoly on the sale of alcoholic beverages direct to the public. Buying is easier in Washington and Oregon, where laws are more relaxed: wine and beer are sold by most supermarkets and groceries. Hard liquor attracts tighter regulation, and in Washington must be purchased

from a state liquor store. Across the Pacific Northwest, bars usually stay open until 1.30am.

BEER AND WINE

American **beer** tends to be limited to fizzy and tasteless national brands like *Budweiser*, *Miller* and *Coors;* Canada has two national brands, *Molson* and *Labatts*, each marketing remarkably similar products under a variety of names – Labatts Blue, Molson Canadian, Molson Export, drinks that inspire, for reasons that elude most foreigners, intense loyalty. Fortunately there are alternatives. Of especial interest to travellers, **micro-breweries** and **brewpubs** are springing up all over the western US, in which you can drink excellent beers, brewed on the premises and often not available anywhere else. These are usually friendly and welcoming places, and almost all serve a wide range of good-value, hearty **food** to help soak up the drink. Brands to look out for in particular include Henry Weinhard's, one of the best and most widely available; ESB and Red Hook Ale in Seattle; Grants in Yakima; Deschutes Black Butte Porter in Bend, Oregon; Alaskan Amber Ale; and the product of any of Portland's dozen fine breweries.

Costs are fairly uniform until you hit the far north, where prices generally are above the odds. Expect to pay around US$1.25 or Can$1 for a glass, and anything from US$1.75 or Can$2 to US$4 and Can$6 for bottled imports. Don't forget that six-packs from supermarkets and liquor stores are much more reasonable, and that in all but the most pretentious bars, several people can save money by buying a **pitcher** of beer: prices start around US$4 or Can$6; measures are usually a quart or half gallon (about one and two litres respectively).

As for **wine and wineries**, production is considerable in the US portions of the Northwest, mainly east of the mountains in Washington's Yakima Valley (see p.219), where the excellent local wines are sold by grape-type rather than by vineyard, and in Oregon's Willamette Valley. We've given details of various tours and tastings in the appropriate pages. Various wineries also experiment with fruits and berries, producing tasty concoctions made from raspberry, loganberry, blackberry and rhubarb. Parts of the Okanagan in BC produce acceptable wines, though most of the time you'll find yourself drinking the stuff more for the novelty of knocking back Canadian wine than for its intrinsic merits.

SPORTS

Besides being good fun, catching a base-ball game on a summer afternoon or joining in with the screaming throngs at a football or ice-hockey game, can give a real sense of the peculiar characters who inhabit the various cities of the Pacific Northwest. Professional sports almost always put on the most spectacular shows, but big games between college rivals, minor league base-ball games – even Friday-night high-school football – provide an easy and enjoyable way to get on intimate terms with a place.

BASEBALL

Baseball, because the teams play so many games – 162 in total, usually five or so a week throughout the summer – is probably the easiest sport to catch when travelling in the United States, and it's also among the cheapest sports to watch (at around $7 a seat), with tickets usually easy to come by. The **Seattle Mariners** (☎206/628-3555), who play in the American League, are the Northwest's big deal, but watch out for minor league or so-called "Farm teams" such as the Portland Beavers, Calgary Cannons, Vancouver Canadians and Edmonton Trappers. Even Alaska has its own semi-professional clubs, and Fairbanks hosts the celebrated "Midnight Sun" game which pitches off at midnight each June 21.

FOOTBALL

Pro football is quite the opposite of baseball – tickets are expensive and difficult to get (if the team is successful). Of the teams in the Northwest, only the Seattle Seahawks have made the big time, their nearest Canadian rivals being second division outfits in the Canadian Football League (the British Columbia Lions, Calgary Stampeders and Edmonton Eskimos). **College football** is a passionate affair too, with Seattle's University of Washington Huskies, one of the best in their class, being enthusiastically supported.

ICE HOCKEY

Ice hockey ignites the passions of virtually all Canadians – and many Americans as well. Three of the best of the National Hockey League's teams are from the Northwest – the Calgary Flames (☎403/261-0455), Edmonton Oilers (☎403/474-8561) and Vancouver Canucks (☎604/254-5141). Portland's Winter Hawks and Seattle's Thunderbirds play in the lesser Western Hockey League.

With players hurtling around at 50kph, and the puck clocking speeds of 160kph, it's a tremendous sport to watch live, the adrenalin rush increased by the relaxed attitude to physical contact on the rink – "I went to see a fight and an ice-hockey game broke out" is how the old adage runs. Teams play around ninety games over a season that runs from October to May. Tickets for all but the biggest games are usually available, though it's always an idea to try and obtain seats in advance: prices start at around $10.

BASKETBALL

Basketball, on both the college and pro level, also focuses local attention and emotions. The major Northwest teams with a following and showing in the National Basketball Association include the Portland Trailblazers (☎503/234-9291), who play at the Memorial Coliseum, and the Seattle Supersonics (☎206/281-5800), based at the Coliseum in the Seattle Center.

SPORTING SEASONS	
Baseball	April–Sept
Basketball	Nov–May
Football	Sept–Jan
Ice Hockey	Oct–May

ENTERTAINMENT AND MEDIA

Visitors touring the Pacific Northwest are, in terms of entertainment and media, liable to find themselves travelling through a fairly homogenized cultural landscape: American-style images and icons predominate, a hegemony that's only shattered at the edges by the region's many minorities – who are, at least, given some degree of influence in Canada's state-subsidized TV stations and film productions.

MUSIC

All the major cities and some of the larger towns of the Northwest have good **live music** scenes – with differences of emphasis arising from the comparative local popularity of C&W, R&B, Rock and Roll, Rock, Jazz and, in Seattle at least, Cajun music. It's also Seattle that possesses the Pacific Northwest's real claim to musical fame for – setting aside local lad Jimi Hendrix – this is where **grunge** music really hit the big time through local bands like Nirvana, Soundgarden and Pearl Jam. Despite the suicide of Kurt Cobain, the grunge scene is still thriving and has gone some way to making the city one of the more fashionable metropolises in the US.

FILM AND THEATER

Europeans who want to be ahead of the crowds back home should take in a film or two while in the Northwest; Hollywood **movies** are generally on show three to six months before they would reach them back home. Most cities have good movie theaters downtown – the biggest, especially Seattle, have some excellent alternative cinemas, too – though in smaller places you often have to make your way out to the multiscreen venues in the malls on the edge of town. Sadly, you don't come across many drive-ins these days.

Theater is very hit and miss in the big cities, though Seattle has a well-deserved reputation for the quality of its repertory and independent theater groups. The larger college towns tend to feature well-funded performances of Shakespeare and the usual canon, while throughout the region – even in the most backwoods areas – local companies provide their own stimulating alternatives.

Most major cities have at least one **comedy club**. Standards vary enormously; in some, sexist xenophobes pander to the basest of prejudices; in others the material is fresh, incisive and above all funny. We've listed some of the best venues, though as ever you should consult the local entertainment weeklies.

NEWSPAPERS

In the US, no national **newspapers** (with the exception of the business-oriented *Wall Street Journal* and the lesser *USA Today*) possess much clout. As a consequence, local city papers such as Seattle's *Post-Intelligencer* and the quirky *Anchorage Times* can be very good indeed. Canada, by contrast, has the *Globe and Mail*, an Ontario broadsheet also published in a western edition and available more or less everywhere in BC, Alberta and the Yukon. National news magazines are also available, principally *Maclean's* in Canada, and *Time* and *Newsweek* in the United States.

Most Canadians and Americans still prefer their newspapers grainy, inky and local. Every large town has at least one morning and/or evening paper, generally excellent at covering its own area but relying on agencies for foreign – and even national – reports.

One good thing most newspapers share is their low cost – normally US35¢ (Can50¢) to US50¢ (Can75¢), with the enormous Sunday editions selling for around US$2 (Can$2.50). Newspapers are sold from vending machines on street corners; outside big cities, newsagents are very rare.

Every community of any size has at least one **free newspaper**, found in street distribution bins or in shops and cafes. These can be handy sources for bar, restaurant and nightlife information, and we've mentioned the most useful titles in the relevant cities.

TV

For low-budget travellers, watching cable **television** in an anonymous motel room may well be the predominant form of entertainment. Bar local stations, the Canadian Broadcasting Corporation (CBC) and one or two public broadcasting channels in Canada, the TV of the Pacific Northwest is effectively the TV of mainstream America.

American, and by implication Canadian TV, can be quite insanely addictive; it certainly comes in quantity, and the quality of the best of it can keep you watching indefinitely. With perhaps thirty-odd channels to choose from, there's always something to grab your attention. The schedules are packed with sycophantic chat shows, outrageous quizzes and banal sitcoms, persistently interrupted by commercials. As for **news** coverage, local reports are comprehensive: a couple of hours each night, usually from 5pm until 6pm and 10pm until 11pm. The hour of national and international news which normally follows tends to be much less thorough, and world events which don't directly affect the US barely get a look-in.

Cable TV is widely found in motels and hotels, although sometimes you have to pay a couple of dollars to watch it. Most cable stations are worse than the major networks (*ABC*, *CBS* and *NBC*), though some of the more specialized channels are consistently interesting. The *ARTS* channel broadcasts enjoyable, if po-faced, arts features, imported TV plays and the like. *CNN* (*Cable Network News*) offers round-the-clock news, *HBO* (*Home Box Office*) shows recent big-bucks movies, *AMC* (*American Movie Company*) shows old black-and-white films, and *ESPN*

exclusively covers sport. Finally, there's *MTV* (*Music Television*), which, with the exception of its slots on rap, heavy metal and the like, is wearingly mainstream and mostly inane.

RADIO

Radio stations are even more abundant than TV channels, and the majority, again, stick to a bland commercial format. Except for news and chat, stations on the **AM** band are best avoided in favor of **FM**, in particular the nationally funded public and college stations, found between 88 and 92 FM. These provide diverse and listenable programming, be it bizarre underground rock or obscure theater, and they're also good sources for local nightlife news.

Though the large cities boast good specialist **music** stations, for most of the time you'll probably have to resort to skipping up and down the frequencies, between re-run Eagles tracks, country and western tunes, fire-and-brimstone Bible thumpers and crazed phone-ins. Driving through rural areas can be frustrating; for hundreds of miles you might only be able to receive one or two (very dull) stations. It's not usual for car rental firms to equip their vehicles with cassette players.

FESTIVALS AND PUBLIC HOLIDAYS

Someone, somewhere is always celebrating something in the USA or Canada, although apart from national holidays, few festivities are shared throughout the respective countries. Instead, there is a disparate multitude of local events: art and craft shows, county fairs, ethnic celebrations, music festivals, rodeos, sandcastle building competitions, and many others of every hue and shade.

PUBLIC HOLIDAYS

The biggest and most all-American of the US **national festivals and holidays** is **Independence Day**, on the Fourth of July, when the entire country grinds to a standstill as people get drunk, salute the flag and partake of firework displays, marches, beauty pageants and more, all in commemoration of the signing of the Declaration of Independence in 1776. **Canada Day** three days earlier is similar, but is accompanied by slightly less nationalistic fervor. **Halloween** (October 31) lacks patriotic overtones, and is not a public holiday despite being one of the most popular yearly flings. More sedate is **Thanksgiving Day**, on the last Thursday in November in the US, the second Monday in October in Canada. This big event of the year is essentially a domestic affair, when relatives return to the familial nest to stuff themselves with roast turkey, and (supposedly) fondly recall the first harvest of the Pilgrims in Massachusetts – though in fact Thanksgiving was already a national holiday before anyone thought to make the connection.

On the national **public holidays** listed below, shops, offices, banks and government buildings are liable to be closed all day. Many states and provinces also have their own additional holidays, and in some places Good Friday is a half-day holiday. Such holidays are movable feasts, their dates changing slightly from year to year. The traditional season for tourism runs from Memorial Day in the US, Victoria Day in Canada to Labor Day (around Sept 5 in both countries) or even Thanksgiving; some tourist attractions, information centers, motels and campgrounds are only open during that period.

NATIONAL HOLIDAYS IN THE NORTHWEST

IN THE US
New Year's Day
Martin Luther King's Birthday (Jan 15)
President's Day (third Mon in Feb)
Easter Monday
Memorial Day (last Mon in May)
Independence Day (July 4)
Labor Day (first Mon in Sept)
Columbus Day (second Mon in Oct)
Veterans' Day (Nov 11)
Thanksgiving Day (last Thurs in Nov)
Christmas Day

IN CANADA
New Year's Day
Good Friday
Easter Monday
Victoria Day (Mon before May 25)
Canada Day (July 1)
Labour Day (first Mon in Oct)
Thanksgiving (second Mon in Oct)
Remembrance Day (Nov 11)
Christmas Day
Boxing Day (Dec 26)

CLIMATE AND WHEN TO GO

Despite a reputation for rain and dreariness, the climate of the Pacific Northwest is characterized by wide variations, not just from region to region and season to season, but also day to day and even hour to hour. Most weather patterns are produced by westerly winds sweeping in from the Pacific, but the region's mountain ranges and the extreme northerly latitudes of Alaska and the Yukon produce climates and microclimates that can range from the near desert conditions of parts of southern BC and eastern Oregon to the arctic onslaught frequently experienced by far northern communities.

It is, of course, possible to make certain generalizations. Temperatures tend to rise the further south you go, and to fall the higher you climb, while the climate along either coast is, on the whole, milder and more equable than inland. Mountains, throughout the region, are powerful influences on climate.

Oregon and **Washington** display mixtures of weather, with gentle blue-skied summers, but often dismally grey and wet periods, particularly on the west side of the Cascade Mountains between October and June. Winters, while soggy, are rarely cold, temperatures hovering above freezing point. The drizzle stops east of the mountains, and the temperatures become more extreme – pleasant in spring, less so in summer, and with colder winters. The coastal peaks of Washington's Olympic Peninsula ensure that this is the wettest area of either state – wet enough to foster temperate rainforests.

The prairies of **Alberta**, some of the region's most benign-looking landscapes, ironically experience some of the continent's wildest climatic extremes, suffering the longest, harshest winters, but also some of the finest, clearest summers. Extremes are also more marked between the south and north of the region, with far lower temperatures in winter in the north. Winter skiing brings lots of people to the **Rockies**, where weather is related closely to altitude and position: colder higher up, drier on the more easterly slopes (see p.364 for details of Chinooks, the

AVERAGE TEMPERATURES (°F) AND RAINFALL

		Jan	Feb	March	April	May	June	July	Aug	Sept	Oct	Nov	Dec
Anchorage	av. max temp	19	27	33	44	54	62	65	64	57	43	30	20
	av. min temp	5	9	13	27	36	44	49	47	39	29	15	6
	days of rain	7	6	5	4	5	6	10	15	14	12	7	6
Edmonton	av. max temp	15	22	34	52	64	70	74	72	62	52	34	21
	av. min temp	-4	1	12	28	38	45	49	47	38	30	16	5
	days of rain	12	9	10	8	12	15	14	12	9	9	11	12
Fairbanks	av. max temp	-2	11	23	42	59	71	72	66	54	35	12	1
	av. min temp	-20	-10	-4	17	35	46	48	44	33	18	-5	-16
	days of rain	10	6	6	4	9	10	13	15	10	11	10	7
Portland	av. max temp	44	48	54	61	66	72	77	77	71	62	53	46
	av. min temp	34	36	39	43	47	53	56	56	52	47	41	37
	days of rain	19	17	17	14	13	10	3	4	8	12	17	19
Seattle	av. max temp	45	48	52	58	64	69	72	73	67	59	51	47
	av. min temp	36	37	39	43	47	52	54	55	52	47	41	38
	days of rain	18	16	16	13	12	9	4	5	8	13	17	19
Vancouver	av. max temp	41	44	50	58	64	69	74	73	65	57	48	43
	av. min temp	32	34	37	40	46	52	54	54	49	44	39	35
	days of rain	20	17	17	14	12	11	7	8	9	16	19	22

To convert °F to °C, subtract 32 and multiply by 5/9

curious warm winds associated with the eastern Rockies). Summer is still the busiest time in these mountains, however, especially July and August, the months that offer the best hiking conditions (though snow can linger even on popular low-lying trails as late as June). Lower-slope hiking can be better in spring and early summer, when there are less insects too.

Much of **British Columbia** (and Washington's Olympic Peninsula) bears the brunt of Pacific depressions, making it one of the region's damper areas, though southwestern parts of the province enjoy remarkably benign weather: the fruit- and wine-producing Okanagan valley has a Californian climate of long hot summers and mild winters, while the area to the north around Kamloops experiences near desert conditions.

The popular coastal regions of **Alaska**, such as the Kenai Peninsula and the southeast, enjoy a maritime climate not dissimilar to that of Washington's Puget Sound. June and July usually yield the best weather, though there's always a good chance of rain – Ketchikan in the extreme southeast receives an average annual rainfall of 165 inches. May and September, when room rates are much lower and the temperatures

only slightly chillier, can be just as good times to go. Winters across the **Yukon** and **Alaskan Interior** are bitterly cold, with temperatures rarely rising above freezing for months on end (-10°F is an average, -70°F a possibility), but precipitation year-round is among the region's lowest (making the "dry" cold slightly more bearable). Summers, by contrast, are short but surprisingly warm, and spring – though late – can produce outstanding displays of wild flowers across the tundra. In the extreme north of Alaska, for example, the sun doesn't set for 82 days from late May to early August, producing inland temperatures in the 90s°F. At the same time, summers can also throw up dreadfully cold and wet days. Another problem are the voracious swarms of mosquito and blackfly that can blight trips into the backcountry.

For detailed daily **weather forecasts in the US**, tune in to TV's 24-hour *Weather Channel*. Many smaller stations offer similar services, especially in popular hiking and skiing areas such as the Canadian Rockies. Such areas usually also offer special phone lines for up-to-the-minute forecasts. Be sure to check weather before setting off on longer hikes: conditions can change quickly and dramatically in mountain regions.

DIRECTORY

ADDRESSES Generally speaking, roads in built-up areas in both Canada and the United States are laid out on a grid system, creating "blocks" of buildings. The first one or two digits of a specific address refer to the block, which will be numbered in sequence from a central point, usually downtown; for example, 620 S Cedar Avenue will be six blocks south of downtown. It is crucial, therefore, to take note of components such as "NW" or "SE" in addresses; 3620 SW Washington Boulevard will be a very long way indeed from 3620 NE Washington Boulevard.

AIRPORT TAX This is invariably included in the price of your ticket.

CIGARETTES AND SMOKING Both the US and Canada are strongly concerned about smoking's detrimental effects on health, with smoking now severely frowned upon. Most cinemas are non-smoking, restaurants are usually divided into non-smoking and smoking sections, and smoking is universally forbidden on public transport – including almost all domestic airline flights. Work places, too, tend to be smoke-free zones, so employees are reduced to smoking on the street outside. Cigarettes are more than twice as expensive in Canada as they are in the US.

DATES In the American style, the date 1.8.95 means not August 1 but January 8.

ELECTRICITY 110V AC in both the US and Canada. All plugs are two-pronged and rather insubstantial. Some European-made travel plug adaptors don't fit American sockets.

FLOORS The *first* floor in the US and Canada is what would be the ground floor in Britain; the *second* floor would be the first floor, and so on.

ID Should be carried at all times. Two pieces should suffice, one of which should have a photo: a passport and credit card(s) are your best bets.

MEASUREMENTS AND SIZES The US has not gone metric, so measurements are in inches, feet, yards and miles; weight in ounces, pounds and tons. American pints and gallons are about four-fifths of Imperial ones. Clothing sizes are always two figures less what they would be in Britain – a British women's size 12 is a US size 10 – while British shoe sizes are 1½ below American ones. Canada, by contrast, officially uses the metric system (though many people still use the old Imperial system): distances are in kilometers, temperatures in degrees Celsius, and food, petrol and drink are sold in grams, kilograms and liters.

TAX Be warned that federal and/or state and provincial **sales** or **services taxes** are added to virtually every good or service purchased in both the US and Canada, but isn't generally part of the marked price. The actual rate varies from place to place, though Alaska, Alberta and Oregon have no *local* sales tax. **Hotel tax** will add 5 to 15 percent to most bills. See also p.21.

TEMPERATURES Given in Fahrenheit in the US, in Celsius in Canada.

TIME ZONES See p.26.

TIPPING Many first-time visitors to North America think of tipping as a potential source of huge embarrassment. It's nothing of the sort; tipping is universally expected, and you quickly learn to tip without a second thought. You really shouldn't depart a bar or restaurant without leaving a tip of *at least* 15 percent (unless the service is utterly disgusting). The whole system of service is predicated on tipping; not to do so causes a great deal of resentment, and a short paypacket for the waiter or waitress at the end of the week. About the same amount should be added to taxi fares – and round them up to the nearest 50¢ or dollar. A hotel porter who has lugged your suitcases up several flights of stairs should get $3 to $5. When paying by credit or charge card, you're expected to add the tip to the total bill before filling in the amount and signing.

VIDEOS The standard format of video cassettes in North America is different from that in Britain. You cannot buy videos in the US or Canada compatible with a video camera bought in Britain.

METRIC CONVERSION TABLE

	1 centimetre (*cm*) = 0.394in	1 inch (*in*) = 2.54cm
		1 foot (*ft*) = 30.48cm
1 metre (*m*) = 100cm	1 metre = 39.37in	1 yard (*yd*) = 0.91m
1 kilometre (*km*) = 1000m	1 kilometre = 0.621 miles	1 mile = 1.610km
1 hectare = 10,000 square metres	1 hectare = 2.471 acres	1 acre = 0.4 hectares
	1 litre = 0.22 UK gal	1 UK gallon (*gal*) = 4.55 litres
	1 litre = 0.26 US gal	1 US gallon (*gal*) = 5.46 litres
	1 gramme (*g*) = 0.035oz	1 ounce (*oz*) = 28.57g
1 kilogramme(*kg*) = 1000g	1 kilogramme = 2.2lb	1 pound (*lb*) = 454g

PART TWO

THE

GUIDE

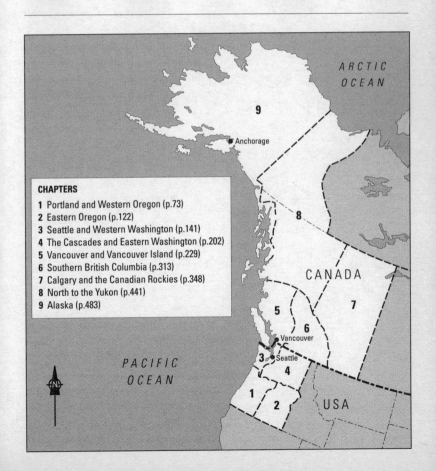

CHAPTERS

1 Portland and Western Oregon (p.73)
2 Eastern Oregon (p.122)
3 Seattle and Western Washington (p.141)
4 The Cascades and Eastern Washington (p.202)
5 Vancouver and Vancouver Island (p.229)
6 Southern British Columbia (p.313)
7 Calgary and the Canadian Rockies (p.348)
8 North to the Yukon (p.441)
9 Alaska (p.483)

ARCTIC
OCEAN

9

● Anchorage

8

CANADA

7

5

6
● Vancouver

3 ● Seattle

4

1

2

USA

PACIFIC
OCEAN

N

CHAPTER ONE

PORTLAND AND WESTERN OREGON

For nineteenth-century pioneers, driving in their covered wagons across the mountains and deserts of the Oregon Trail, the green **Willamette Valley**, running for just over a hundred miles parallel to and just inland from the Pacific coast, was the promised land. Rich and fertile, it became the home of Oregon's first settlements and towns, and the valley is still at the heart of the state's social, political and cultural existence. Most of Oregon's population is concentrated here, either in the cities strung along the river or in the hinterland of rural villages, and many remain dependent on agriculture and forestry – the twin pillars of what has always been a resource-based economy.

In early days, the produce of Oregon's farms and forests spawned a handful of trading centers, bustling townships such as Oregon City, Eugene, Albany and, most successful of all, Portland, from where ships left for Europe and the east coast laden with raw materials. It was the lack of safe anchorages along the storm-battered coast that dictated the creation of these Willamette River ports, all of which had access to the Pacific via the Columbia River. Even now, Coos Bay is Oregon's only major coastal town.

It was, however, a different sort of natural resource that boosted the local economy sky-high. In 1852, **gold** was unearthed on the Rogue River, in the south of the state, and during the subsequent Gold Rush the prospectors' colony of Jacksonville was even touted as the state capital. However, the gold gave out in the 1880s, and Oregon, boosted by the injection of cash, resumed its more pedestrian agricultural progress. Only latterly have tourism, electronics and hydroelectricity provided some diversification, and those pockets of industrialization that do exist remain pint-sized.

A sense of pastoral continuity, rare in the Pacific Northwest, underpins the slight (semi-humorous) disdain expressed by many well-established Oregonians for their neighbors to the south. This hauteur is demonstrated by frequent reference to an apocryphal signpost on the Oregon Trail: the route to California was marked by a cairn of shimmering quartz, the other by a marker with the legend "To Oregon". The pioneers who could read (and were therefore, so the assumption goes, respectable and hardworking) came to Oregon; the rabble went south.

TOLL-FREE INFORMATION NUMBER

Oregon Tourism Division ☎ 1-800/547-7842.
The telephone **area code** for all Oregon is ☎503.

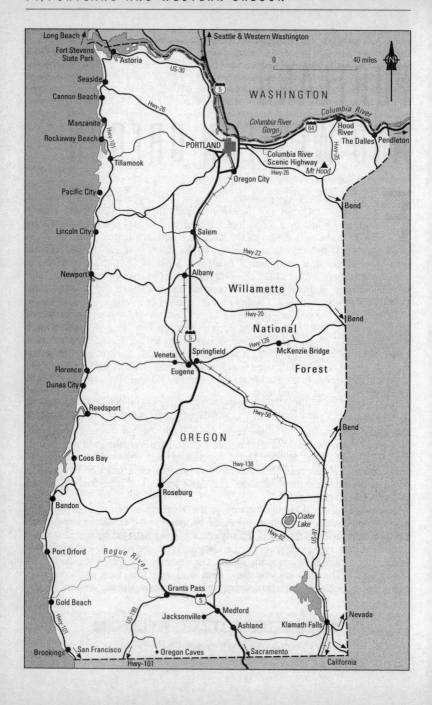

This self-image, along with the magnificent scenery of the Pacific coast, explains why hundreds of Americans disenchanted with mainstream culture, have in the last thirty years, congregated in Oregon. Most visibly, they have combined with a string of reformist governors to stave off the worst excesses of urban development, keeping the downtowns of the two largest cities, **Portland** and **Eugene**, to manageable proportions, friendly to pedestrians, joggers and cyclists alike. Each of these cities, at either end of the Willamette Valley, merits a two- or three-day stay, though Portland is particularly agreeable. A relaxed and easy-going place, it offers a fine assortment of museums, art galleries, coffee houses, and amiable nightlife.

Both Portland and Eugene are also within easy striking distance of the **Cascade Mountains**, once the final barrier to incoming pioneers, but now a major recreation area, where the forested slopes and severe peaks feature a superbly rugged terrain, criss-crossed by walking trails and liberally strewn with campgrounds and mountain lodges. The most popular tourist route here is along the **Columbia River Gorge** flanking **Mount Hood**.

In the opposite direction, west from the valley across a slender line of scenic hills and forests, lies the 340-mile **Oregon Coast**, a magnificent preamble (if you're heading north) to the stunning land- and seascapes of the rest of the Pacific Northwest. Don't expect too much from Oregon's resorts – most are pretty dull, and scores of campgrounds within the string of state parks make better alternatives – but concentrate instead on a shoreline boasting great stretches of sandy beach interrupted by weather-beaten headlands, Sahara-like sand dunes and mysterious-looking sea stacks. On a sunny day (and there are many) the trip along the coast is exhilarating – though some claim foggy and stormy days are even better.

Getting around

With *Greyhound* and, to a lesser extent, *Amtrak* linking major towns, and local bus services extending the network, **getting around** on public transportation is less of a problem here than in other parts of the Northwest, but there are large areas that you just can't cover without your own vehicle. The coast especially is ideal for cycling but obviously, a car will make things much easier – particularly as hitching is illegal in Oregon. The mountains and rivers of western Oregon provide opportunities for all sorts of watersports, from fishing to windsurfing (best on the Columbia River at the town of **Hood River**) and whitewater rafting –

ACCOMMODATION PRICE CODES

All accommodation prices in this book have been coded using the symbols below, corresponding to US dollar prices in the US chapters and equivalent Canadian dollar rates in the Canadian chapters. Prices are for the least expensive double rooms in each establishment, and only include local taxes where we explicitly say so.

For a full explanation see p.46 in *Basics*.

① up to US$30	④ US$60–80	⑦ US$130–180
② US$30–45	⑤ US$80–100	⑧ US$180+
③ US$45–60	⑥ US$100–130	

THE OREGON TRAIL

President Thomas Jefferson, who had a clearer conception than any of his contemporaries of the opportunities presented by the vast lands west of the Missouri, surreptitiously funded the **Lewis and Clark expedition** of 1804, which crossed the continent to the Pacific Ocean. Surreptitiously, because the **Oregon Country**, as the coastal strip between Russian Alaska and Spanish California was then known, was already claimed by the British, based in Canada. This territorial dispute dragged on until 1846, by which time the British claim to the region south of the 49th Parallel (present-day Washington and Oregon) had become academic, swept away by the rising tide of overland immigration launched by pioneer-farmers, the majority of whom came from the Midwest, just east of the Missouri.

The migrants – or **movers**, as they're often called – were inspired not so much by Lewis and Clark, as by the missionaries who went west to Christianize the "Indians" in the 1830s, travelling with their wives and children in simple covered wagons. They sent back glowing and widely circulated reports of the Oregon Country's mild climate, fertile soil and absence of malaria, and confirmed that the lands of the West Coast were well forested. This was at the time considered a necessary prerequisite for successful farming; the treeless (and therefore unfamiliar) prairie – the "great American Desert" – was not thought to be worth plowing.

When the Senate in 1842 came close to ratifying legislation giving generous land grants to Oregon Country settlers, the rush was on. In the spring of 1843, one thousand would-be migrants gathered at Independence and Westport on the banks of the Missouri, to prepare for what is now known as the **Great Migration**. The pioneers were a remarkably homogeneous bunch, nearly all experienced farmers, travelling in family groups in ordinary ox-pulled farm wagons with flimsy canvas roofs. Only too aware of the difficulties of the journey, the movers voted in wagon train leaders (after the first hundred miles – nobody wanted to be saddled with a charlatan), and established camp rules to govern everything from the grazing of livestock to the collection of fuel (usually buffalo dung).

Traversing almost two thousand miles of modern Nebraska, Wyoming and Idaho, they cajoled their wagons across rivers, struggled over mountain passes, chopped their way through forests, and paused at the occasional frontier fort or missionary station to recuperate. Finally, after three months on the trail, they built rafts which, with the assistance of local Native Americans, they steered from The Dalles down the treacherous lower reaches of the Columbia River. Despite orders to the contrary from the British-owned Hudson's Bay Company, **John McLoughlin**, head of Fort Vancouver, helped the newcomers to recover from their ordeals. Their arrival doubled Oregon's American population, and pushed the US government into the creation of the **Oregon Territory** just five years later.

Over the next thirty years, further waves of settlers swelled the population of the Willamette Valley by some fifty thousand. Precious little survives today to remember them by, but out in eastern Oregon, one or two hillsides still show the ruts made by the wheels of their wagons (see Baker City, p.129).

on the Rogue River from **Gold Beach**. For hikers, there are literally hundreds of walking trails, ranging from the shortest of afternoon strolls to full-scale expeditions on either of two long-distance trails – the **Oregon Coast Trail**, right along the coast, and a portion of the 2600-mile **Pacific Crest Trail** running from Mexico to Canada across Oregon's Cascades.

PORTLAND

Oregon's Portland was named after Portland, Maine, as the result of a coin toss between its two ardent East Coast founders in 1843 ("Boston" was the other option). It was then no more than a clearing in the woods, but its location on a deep part of the Willamette River, near a hinterland of fertile valleys, made it a perfect trading port, and the town grew fast, expanding quickly and replacing its humble clapboard houses with ornate Florentine facades and Gothic bursts of twirling towers and gables. Through the nineteenth century it was a raunchy, bawdy shipping and railway town, notorious for its gambling, prostitution and opium dens. However, when the new ports in Puget Sound to the north – principally Seattle – gained ascendancy, Portland declined, leaving behind huge swathes of derelict riverside warehouses and rail yards, linked by dozens of heavy-duty bridges spanning the Willamette River.

As a consequence, city planners in the Seventies faced a downtown in tatters, part-gentrified, part low-life waterfront, its historic buildings decayed or sacrificed to parking lots and expressways. Portland scrupulously salvaged what was left of its nineteenth-century past, while risking the odd splash of post-modernist architectural color, and undertook much assiduous gap-filling, even to the extent of grassing over a riverside highway to convert it into a park. Meanwhile a levy on new construction funded all manner of public art – most obviously in the folksy and whimsical life-size statues that now decorate downtown streets. Pockets of seediness remain, but nowadays much of the downtown area bears the stamp of these renewal projects, with redbrick replacing concrete, cycle routes and an extensive public transit system replacing cars. There's a way to go yet perhaps but, overlooked by extensive parkland on the green West Hills, ecology-conscious, arts-conscious Portland is an attractive and very liveable city.

Arrival and information

Portland International Airport (PDX) is 15 miles northeast of the city: get into town either on the express *Raz* bus, which drops off regularly at major downtown hotels (every 30min from 5am to midnight; $7), or more cheaply on a local *Tri-Met* bus #12 ($1.25), coded "purple rain" – both leave from right outside the airport's doors.

Arriving by car, I-5 will bring you into the city from the north or south, I-84 from the east: aim for Burnside Street, which channels traffic through downtown; heading south on I-5, take the City Center/Morrison Bridge exit; northbound, the Front Avenue exit. The terminals for *Greyhound*, 550 NW Sixth Ave at Glisan (☎243-2323), and *Amtrak*, 800 NW Sixth Ave (☎273-4865), are conveniently situated within walking distance of the center. *Green Tortoise* (☎225-0310) drop off and pick up downtown at 616 SW College and Sixth, near *University Deli Café*.

Information
The **visitor center**, along the river in the glassy World Trade Center, 26 SW Salmon St at Front (Mon–Fri 8.30am–5pm, Sat 9am–3pm; ☎222-2223 or 1-800/962-3700), can provide good free maps and lots of other useful information on anything from state parks, cycle routes and bus timetables to lists of forthcoming events.

City transportation

Portland's a compact city and you can see much of it on foot, but, if only to get to where you're staying, you may have to avail yourself of the excellent public transit system. The *Tri-Met* **bus system** is based at the downtown "transit malls": two bus-shelter-lined stretches along Fifth Avenue (southbound) and Sixth Avenue (northbound). Each shelter is labelled with a symbol – brown beaver, blue snowflake, purple rain – which serves as a code for the route; video displays and telephones inside the shelters give more information. Though designed for simplicity, the system can still be pretty confusing: contact the **Tri-Met Customer Assistance Office**, close by on Pioneer Courthouse Square (Mon–Fri 9am–5pm; ☎238-4888; for disabled citizens ☎238-4952), to get sorted out. Buses (and Max, see below) are free in the downtown zone – "Fareless Square"– edged by the Willamette to the north and east, and I-405 to the south and west. Outside here, fares are between 95¢ and $1.25 – pay the driver exact change; transfers for onward travel within the same zone (there are 3 fare zones altogether) are free. The *Tri-Met* office sells day tickets (all zones) for $3.25 and books of ten tickets at a discount – $11.50, all zones. There's a *Tri-Met* trip planning line too (☎238-7433; Mon–Fri 7.30am–5.30pm).

Max, Portland's light railway, shunts tourists around downtown and the old town area, then carries commuters over the river through the northeast neighborhoods as far as suburban Gresham – you'll see its tracks along the streets. Vintage **streetcars** have returned to trundle along the downtown streets, just as they did until 1905; the present fleet are working replicas of the originals. They operate every 30 minutes, between 10am and 5.30pm, rattling up Yamhill, across Eleventh Avenue, down Morrison and along First Avenue before heading over the river to the Lloyd Center. *Rose City Riverboat Cruises* (☎234-6665) operate tours of Portland Harbor once or twice daily (except Mon; $10.50 per adult), as well as once-weekly trips up the Willamette River to Oregon City (see p.93) – $22 per adult.

The City

The Willamette River divides Portland in half: the downtown area, where you'll probably spend most time, is on the west bank, while the east is mostly residential. **Downtown Portland** – mostly the southwest quadrant – focusing on Pioneer Courthouse Square, is a compact mix of gleaming new offices and old plasterwork, punctuated by grassy strips of small parks and liberally sprinkled with statues. It's here you'll find the malls, the department stores, theaters, the main museums. Just north along the riverfront are the restored nineteenth-century buildings of **Old Town**, where smart new restaurants and shops face groups of streetpeople crowded around the Salvation Army mission.

Restaurants and coffee houses cluster in downtown and in the quaint **Nob Hill** district, a mile northwest of the town center, and further out west **Washington Park** offers leafy trails, formal gardens, a couple of museums and the best city views.

Downtown Portland

When the sun shines, **Pioneer Courthouse Square** is Portland's focal point, cluttered with music and people; in colder weather, only teenagers hang around

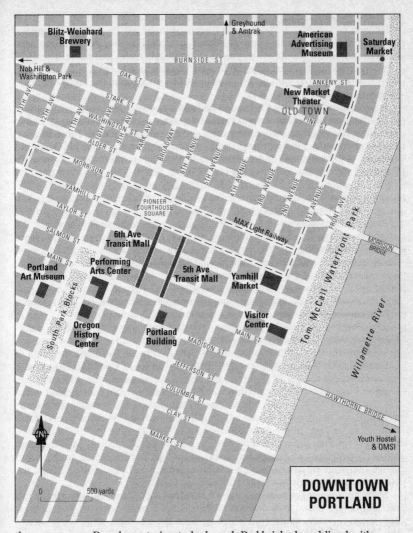

DOWNTOWN
PORTLAND

the corner near Broadway, trying to look cool. Red-bricked, and lined with curving shelves of steps, the square is the modern centerpiece of downtown's new look (it used to be a nasty asphalt parking lot), and brightly upstages the solid nineteenth-century **Pioneer Courthouse** behind. North from here, along Fifth and Sixth avenues, the redbrick and smoked-glass **transit malls** are another keystone of the city's renovations: stretches of street are lined with hi-tech bus shelters, a study in user-friendliness.

Leading off Pioneer Square, **Broadway**, more than any other street, pulls together Portland's mix of old grandeur and new wealth. Great, white movie palaces (relics from the Roaring Twenties) share the street with pricey hotels such as the modern *Hilton*, towering on an ugly, bunker-like pedestal. One of the old cinemas, the grand *Portland*, has been restored as the **Arlene Schnitzer Concert Hall**, part of the new **Portland Center for the Performing Arts** complex and home to Oregon's symphony orchestra, opera and ballet. The main arts center building is next door, an opulent construction of brick and dark glass, topped with a spectral light dome. Look up as you walk round the foyer – the blue dashes in the dome change color.

A paved arcade between the concert hall and arts center leads to a sedate group of buildings around a long strip of elm-lined grass – dotted with bronze statues of Theodore Roosevelt and other luminaries – that's called the **South Park Blocks**. Across the block, next to the grandiose columned front of the old **Masonic Temple**, is the long, low, understated facade of 1930s architect Pietro Belluschi's **Portland Art Museum** (Tues–Sat 11am–5pm & Sun 1–5pm; $4.50, but free first Thurs of month 4–9pm). Founded in 1892, the museum's collection is wide-ranging and well laid-out, spacious galleries displaying haunting Northwest Indian masks, squat Mexican statues, ancient Chinese figures, ornately framed portraits of European aristocrats – and, proudly displayed, one of Monet's *Waterlilies*. It's an above-average art museum, and very popular, especially during the "Museum After Hours" sessions on Wednesday night, when there's (usually good) jazz in the entrance hall and food and wine on sale. Opposite the museum, beside an old, ivy-covered church, the **Oregon History Center** (Mon–Sat 10am–6pm & Sun noon–5pm; $3.00) is worth a peep for its displays on Oregon's covered-wagon past and its excellent little bookshop, round the back on Broadway. The research library here is the definitive source of information on Oregon's history.

The South Park Blocks are often crowded with students from the small **Portland State University**, whose modern campus lies three blocks west. Back down Madison Street, at the junction with Fifth Avenue, is Portland's one sight of national, if not world, renown – architect Michael Graves's **Portland Building**, a squarely-sat concoction of concrete, tile and glass, adorned with pink and blue tiling and pale blue rosettes. It's quite possible to walk straight past without realizing this is anything special, but on closer examination it's certainly an eclectic structure, an uninhibited (some say flippant) re-working of classical and other motifs that was one of the most talked-about US buildings of the 1980s. Portland positively relished the controversy, and, in a burst of civic zeal, hoisted the enormous copper figure of *Portlandia* (a sort of Portlandian *Liberty*) on to the porch above the main entrance – where she kneels, one hand clutching a trident, the other reaching down towards the Fifth Avenue transit mall.

Stretching along the eastern edge of Downtown Portland, the **riverfront** has recently been rescued from over a century of burial beneath wharves, warehouses, and, more recently, an express highway. Now the mile-long strip, re-christened the **Tom McCall Waterfront Park** – after Governor McCall, a key figure in the 1970s movement to improve the city – is lined by trees which will eventually screen promenaders from the less-than-inspiring view of the ugly east bank. Midway along the popular walking and cycling path that winds through the park, the modern, grey and glassy **World Trade Center** (home of the **visitor center**) looms over the gushing fountains of the Salmon Street Springs. A couple of blocks over, around First and Yamhill, the small **Yamhill Historic District** is lined with 1890s buildings. **Yamhill Marketplace** (actually built in 1982, on the site of a nineteenth-century farmer's market) has a couple of fruit and vegetable stalls, though most of its stands now serve hot food, making it a popular lunch spot.

Old Town

Old Town, along the river between the Morrison and W Burnside bridges, was where Portland was founded in 1843, and by the 1860s wealthy Portlanders were edging the streets with grand, Italianate cast-iron facades. But the area tended to flood, and when the railroad came in 1883 the town center soon shifted away from the river; the big, ornate buildings became warehouses and the area plummeted down the social scale. "Improvement" schemes in the 1950s almost finished the district off, and gaps lined with peeling plaster still show where buildings were pulled down to make way for parking lots. Recent attempts at rejuvenation have been more tactful, and the area is now an odd mixture of restoration work, housing a glut of bistros and boutiques, and old-style dereliction. Along W Burnside Street, and especially around the large Salvation Army mission at Ankeny and Second, the well-heeled and the down-and-out eye each other dubiously – in a division that is – for Oregon – uncomfortably sharp.

Among Old Town's surviving turn-of-the-century buildings, the heavy sandstone stonework and terracotta friezes of the **Dekum Building**, at Third and Washington, are of special note. Dating from 1892, the building was finished in the Richardson Romanesque style, representing an influential departure from the cast-iron preoccupation of the 1880s. Across the street, the **Postal Building** of 1900 continues the sandstone theme while nearby, at Stark and Third, the Gothic Revival **Bishop's House** is also worth a moment, built in 1879 for the city's Catholic archbishop.

The best time to come to Old Town is at weekends, when the **Saturday Market** (March–Dec Sat 10am–5pm, Sun 11am–4.30pm) packs the area under the west end of the Burnside Bridge with arts and crafts stalls, street musicians, spicey foods and lively crowds. In the middle of this, the **Skidmore Fountain** at First and Ankeny is Old Town's focal point, a bronze basin raised by caryatids above a granite pool, designed to provide European elegance for the citizens – and water for hardworked nineteenth-century horses. Across an angular plaza, an ornamental colonnade salvaged from the pediments, arches, columns and other remnants of demolished local buildings stretches from the side of the **New Market Theater**, a combination of theater and vegetable market that has been restored and is now full of cafés. Not far from here, the **American Advertising Museum**, 9 NW Second Ave (Wed–Fri 11am–5pm, Sat & Sun noon–5pm; $3), gives a fascinating account of the rise of advertising, beginning with the printed posters that engendered all kinds of social phenomena, from the rise of the cornflake to the rush of volunteers to World War II, moving on to tapes of old radio adverts and videos of classic TV ads. The museum also hosts some lively and intelligent temporary exhibits.

Chinatown and Nob Hill

Away from the river, up W Burnside Street, an ornate, even tacky, oriental gate at Fourth Avenue marks the entrance to what's left of Portland's **Chinatown**. By the late nineteenth century, expanding Portland had the second-largest Chinese community in the US, but white unemployment in the 1880s led, as elsewhere, to racist attacks. Chinese workers were threatened, their homes dynamited or burned, and most were forced to leave; there's little to see here today. Heading northwest, towards the *Greyhound* and *Amtrak* stations, you soon reach a sleazy district that's long been the haunt of drug dealers, addicts, and prostitutes. Yet things are changing. Affronted by this eyesore, the city council are revamping the area, closing down the flophouses, moving the poor out and extending the iron grip of respectability.

Back on Burnside, crossing the North Park Blocks, it's a few minutes' walk to **Powell's Books** at Burnside and Tenth (Mon–Sat 9am–11pm, Sun 9am–9pm), one of the largest bookstores on the West Coast – five full floors of new and secondhand books so overwhelming that floorplans are given out at the entrance. Up the street from *Powell's* another local institution, the **Blitz-Weinhard Brewery** at 1133 W Burnside St, fills up most of the surrounding blocks in order to brew the Northwest's most popular lagers and ales, including *Henry Weinhard's Private Reserve*; free 30-minute tours and tastings are given on weekdays (June–Sept, 1pm, 2pm, 3pm & 4pm; Oct–May 1pm, 2.30pm & 4pm; ☎222-4351). Many of the other old warehouses and industrial premises – especially in the nearby **Pearl District** around Twelfth and Hoyt – have been converted by artists and craftspeople into studios and loft spaces, a change evident in the many good galleries emerging here, such as *Image Gallery Inc*, 1307 NW Glisan.

A bus ride away, the **Nob Hill** district (often simply called the "Northwest Section") stretches from Burnside Street along a dozen blocks of NW 23rd Avenue and NW 21st Avenue. The name was borrowed from San Francisco, imported by a grocer who hoped the area would become as fashionable as the Nob Hill back home. It did, almost, and a few multicolored wooden mansions add a San Franciscan tinge – though the main interest up here are the dozens of cafés and restaurants, which are among the city's best.

The West Hills and Washington Park

Directly behind Nob Hill, the wooded bluffs of the **West Hills** hold the elegant houses of Portland's wealthy, some of which are visible from the window of the brightly painted "zoo bus" (#63 from the downtown transit mall) as it winds along its special route towards **Washington Park**. Set aside for public use in 1871, much of the park is green, leafy and twined with trails; it's also home to a **zoo** (summer daily 9.30am–7pm, gates close earlier in other seasons; $3), whose star turn is its Asian elephants. The zoo has a sizeable breeding herd and, in 1962, witnessed the first birth of an Asian elephant in the western hemisphere. An **Elephant Museum** details the sad effects of the ivory trade, while the ambitious Africa exhibition attempts to give a comprehensive view of the continent, including giraffes, rhinos and birds as part of an African environment. Come here on a Wednesday night in summer, and you'll catch the weekly **Zoo Jazz** concert (free with admission to the zoo), followed on Thursdays by a **Zoo Grass** (bluegrass) session (☎226-1561 for details). Next door, the **World Forestry Center** (daily 10am–5pm; $1.50) goes in for lively exhibits, not least in the seventy-foot "talking" tree which introduces the museum. Beyond it, among other things, is a collection of chunks from most of North America's native trees, and a dramatic push-button reconstruction of the "Tillamook Burn", a fire that ravaged one of Oregon's coastal forests in the 1930s.

A miniature train ($2) connects the zoo with two formal gardens further north in the park. The **International Rose Test Gardens** are at their best between May and September, when eight thousand rose bushes cover layered terraces with a gaudy range of blooms. Home of America's oldest and largest rose-growing society, the city at one point in its early days had more rose bushes than people, and Portland now calls itself the "City of Roses". During the crowded and colorful **Rose Festival** each June, everyone flocks to Burnside Bridge to watch a big parade that makes the claim seem fair enough. On the hill above, the **Japanese Gardens** (summer daily 10am–6pm, winter daily 10am–4pm; $3.50) are more subtle, with cool, green shrubs reflected in pools, and an abstract sand and stone garden making minimal use of color.

If you've got a car, you might consider driving the few miles northwest from the park to the opulent **Pittock Mansion** (daily noon–4pm, closed early Jan; $3.50), set in its own park the other side of W Burnside Street at 3229 NW Pittock Drive – there's a bus from downtown, but it drops you half a mile from the entrance. Henry Pittock came to Portland in 1853 as a sixteen-year-old printer's devil; eight years later he became editor of *The Oregonian*, still Oregon's most influential newspaper, and in 1909 started to build this enormously flashy chateauesque home, furnishing rooms in styles alternately Jacobean, Victorian and French Renaissance.

East of the river

While the west side of the Willamette River provided a deep port, the **east side** was too shallow for shipping and the area remained undeveloped for the first fifty years of Portland's life. The Morrison Street Bridge crept across the river at the end of the last century, since when most of Portland's population has lived here, in various neighborhoods that are almost entirely residential. Restaurants, bars, nightclubs and the youth hostel are its most obvious features, but of a few things to see, the **Oregon Museum of Science and Industry (OMSI)**, at 1945 SE Water and Clay, is worthwhile. It's a lavish and ambitious complex that invites participation – kids thump, jump and shout at the more robust exhibits, and play astronauts to discover the mysteries of gravity (Sat–Wed 9.30am–5.30pm, Thurs & Fri 9.30am–9pm; $6.50). Other exhibition areas house the *Murdock Sky Theater* planetarium and the *Omnimax Theater* with its five-storey dome-shaped film screen (show times ☎797-4000). Bus #63 serves the site. Also on this side of the river, way out at SE 28th Ave and Woodstock, the **Crystal Springs Rhododendron Garden** (daily, dawn–dusk; free, but $2 Thurs–Mon 10am–6pm; bus #19), opposite ivy-covered **Reed College** provides colorful strolling in March, April and May. And in the far northeast, **The Grotto**, the sanctuary of Our Sorrowful Mother, at NE 85th and Sandy Blvd (daily 8am–dusk; free), contains a marble replica of Michelangelo's *Pieta*; surrounded by candles and set in a cave in a cliff face, it now forms the centerpiece of an eccentric outdoor church and monastic complex.

Accommodation

Dozens of **motels** can be found off the Interstates and along Sandy Boulevard, northeast of the center, but – for a few dollars more – you're far better staying in a downtown hotel or in one of the city's scattering of cozy **B&Bs**. Several low-price old hotels are scattered around the downtown area, but most are fairly shabby, inside and out; a better bargain is a room at the **hostels** or, for women, the downtown YWCA.

Hostels

Ben Stark International Hostel, 1022 SW Stark St at Tenth (☎274-1033). Pretty grim, but fairly central hostel. Dormitory accommodation. Emergencies only. ①.

Portland International AYH Hostel, 3031 SE Hawthorne Blvd (☎236-3380). Across the river in a lively neighborhood of cafés and pubs. Dorm beds, in a surprisingly cheery old Victorian house, with separate dorms for men and women, plus family room (reservations recommended); open 7–9.30am and 5–11pm; dining room; bike storage; fully equipped kitchen. Take bus #5 from SW Fifth Ave. ①.

YWCA, 1111 SW Tenth Ave (☎223-6281). Clean and central – right next to the downtown arts center – but its very few rooms are often booked solid months in advance. For women only. ①.

Hotels, motels and B&Bs

Clinkerbrick House, 2311 NE Schuyler (☎281-2533). Peaceful and quiet, but a way out from the center, this nicely decorated, 1908 red-brick Dutch Colonial bed-and-breakfast inn has a lovely garden and comfortable rooms. ④.

General Hooker's House, 125 SW Hooker St (☎222-4435). Small and relaxed bed-and-breakfast inn. Evening cocktails on the roofdeck. ③–④.

Governor Hotel, SW Tenth at Alder St (☎224-3400 or 1-800/554-3456). Fine luxury hotel conveniently situated a few blocks north of the riverfront. Housed in splendidly refurbished hotel and 1920s-Italian Renaissance office building. Watch out for the mural of Lewis and Clark in the lobby. ⑦.

Heathman Hotel, 1009 SW Broadway at Salmon (☎241-4100 or 1-800/551-0011). Portland's top hotel, this restored downtown landmark would be a standout anywhere, with its elegant, teak-panelled interior and generous amounts of marble and brass, especially in the high-style wainscoted lobby bar. Substantial discounts for weekend stays. You'd pay twice the price for a lot less were it in a ritzier locale. A real treat. ⑦–⑧.

Imperial Hotel, 400 SW Broadway (☎228-7221). Respectable downtown hotel with comfortable doubles. ④.

Mallory Hotel, 729 SW 15th Ave at Yamhill (☎223-6311 or ☎1-800/228-8657). Old and well-worn, with comfortable if slightly spartan doubles, just a few blocks from Pioneer Square. ④.

Mark Spencer Hotel, 409 SW 11th Ave at Stark (☎224-3293). Standard issue hotel with steady doubles. ③.

Portland Inn, 1414 SW Sixth Ave at Clay (☎221-1611). Modern, reasonably priced rooms beside the transit mall. ④.

Riverside Inn, 50 SW Morrison (☎221-0711). For a river view at a reasonable price, this is the best bet. Overlooking the riverfront promenade, and near the Old Town district, with fairly plain modern rooms. ⑤.

Travelodge, 949 E Burnside St (☎234-8411). Standard, no-frills motel, just half a mile east of Pioneer Square. ③.

Unicorn Inn Motel, 3040 SE 82nd St (☎774-1176). Far from the thick of things (off I-205 at exit 19) but cheap, clean and comfortable. Cable TV and pool. ②.

Vintage Plaza Hotel, 422 SW Broadway (☎228-1212 or ☎1-800/243-0555). Central extravagance with luxurious bi-level suites. ⑦.

Eating

Friendly and unpretentious are the two words that come to mind most often to describe Portland's **restaurants**, the bulk of which are concentrated in the downtown area, with quite a few in the Nob Hill area to the northwest and a handful on the less-touristed east side of the river, on and around Hawthorne Boulevard. There's a surprisingly good range of top-notch places, with fresh fish dishes, especially salmon, the local specialty, and many more down-to-earth, bistro-style neighborhood joints, as good for quaffing local brews and vintages as they are for tasty meals. For flavorful fast food at low prices, pop into either of two popular local chains, *Hot Lips Pizza* (based at 1909 SW Sixth Ave) or the Mexican-food *Macheezmo Mouse* (723 SW Salmon St), both of which have branches all over town.

Inexpensive

B Moloch Heathman Bakery and Pub, 901 SW Salmon St (☎227-5700). Great pizzas – topped with all manner of designer ingredients – plus salads and daily specials, and some of the Northwest's best micro-brewed beers, around twenty on tap.

Basta's, 410 NW 21st Ave (☎274-1572). Tasty pastas and lip-smacking desserts.

Besaw's Café, 2301 NW Savier St at 23rd Ave (☎228-2619). Old-fashioned, NY-style bar and grill. Lots of dark wood panelling, good-sized burgers, steaks and sandwiches, plus onion rings to kill for.

Caffe Café, 808 SW Tenth Ave (☎243-1461). Everything here is homemade, from the soup to the puddings. Great value.

Cisco and Pancho's, 107 NW Fifth Ave (☎223-5048). Lively, inexpensive Tex-Mex restaurant with free live jazz or blues most evenings.

Hamburger Mary's, 840 SW Park St (☎223-0900). Relaxed and occasionally bizarre burger and salad bar with a decidedly non-conformist clientele.

Metro on Broadway, 911 SW Broadway St (☎295-1200). A dozen distinct low-priced stands offer food from around the world, under one roof.

Old Wives' Tales, 1300 E Burnside St (☎238-0470). Feminist café with great breakfasts, sandwiches and innovative vegetarian food; it's also the place to find out about local women's issues.

Rose's, 315 NW 23rd Ave (☎227-5181). Long-established family-run place, as near to a Jewish New York City deli as you get in the Northwest. Bagels, blintzes, and a killer *kreplach* soup.

Vat and Tonsure, 822 SW Park Ave (☎227-1845). Beat Generation hangout, where the animated conversations are energized by good-sized portions of bistro-style food, copious amounts of wine, and reasonable prices.

Moderate to expensive

Brasserie Montmartre, 626 SW Park Ave (☎224-5552). Pseudo-Left Bank, Paris-in-the-1930s bistro, with free live jazz and very good food – it's the only place in Portland where you can get fresh pasta with pesto and scallops at 2am.

Bread and Ink Café, 3610 SE Hawthorne Blvd (☎239-4756). Bustling morning to night, this spacious café puts together an anarchically varied menu of bagels, burritos, and Mediterranean food; come on Sunday for the special Jewish brunch or one of Portland's best breakfasts.

Heathman Hotel Restaurant, 1009 SW Broadway (☎241-4100). Power breakfasts and pricey dinners featuring the finest of Northwest cuisine.

Jake's Famous Crawfish, 401 SW 12th Ave (☎226-1419). For nearly 100 years this polished wood oyster bar has been Portland's prime spot for fresh seafood, though at weekends it's packed and veers toward singles bar territory. The food, especially the daily fish specials, is excellent and not exorbitantly priced, but be sure to save room for dessert.

L'Auberge, 2601 NW Vaughn St (☎223-3302). One of the classiest restaurants on the West Coast, serving up exquisitely prepared traditional French dishes with a *nouvelle* emphasis on fresh local ingredients; *prix fixé* meals start at a reasonable $35, plus wine. The upstairs bar is surprisingly cozy and unpretentious – on Sunday night they show old movies on the walls – and has a good value menu of burgers, grilled fish and salads.

McCormick and Schmick's, 235 SW First Ave at Oak (☎224-7522). Another of Portland's many excellent fish restaurants, with a variety of ultra-fresh nightly specials; there's also a lively oyster bar, where besides bivalves you can get a range of burgers and pasta dishes.

Drinking and nightlife

Though sometimes clogged with cars and clubbers on summer weekends, Portland's streets can seem pretty quiet at night. However, there's generally a lot more going on here than you might at first think. **Coffee houses** – including some of the best in the US – and dozens of **bars** form the fulcrum of a lively scene, and the city is a beer-drinker's heaven, with dozens of local microbreweries proof of the resurgence of the Northwest's proud brewing traditions.

Music is another thing Portland does well, with a handful of decent folk and rock clubs and some good jazz and blues – downtown, on and off-Broadway, is the place to head. *The Downtowner*, available free on most street corners, has up-to-the-minute listings of what's on and where, as does the "A & E" section of Friday's *Oregonian* newspaper, the main local rag.

Coffee houses

Anne Hughes Coffee Room, inside *Powell's Books*, 1005 W Burnside St (☎228-4651). Not too big on atmosphere, but brought to life by the many earnest characters leafing through their books and partaking of caffeine.

Café, 737 SW Salmon St (☎227-1794). Very central downtown café, with a fine selection of powerful coffees.

Coffee People Immediate Care Center, 817 NW 23rd Ave (☎226-3064). "Good coffee – no backtalk" is the motto, and they deliver, at least on the first count. Excellent espresso, straight up or smothered in whipped cream. For a real eye-opener, try the "Depth Charge" filter coffee supercharged with a shot of espresso.

Panini, 620 SW Ninth Ave (☎224-6001). Espresso bar serving good Italian sandwiches.

Papa Hayden's, 701 NW 23rd Ave (☎228-7317). Chic, upscale ice-cream café that brews up some good coffees to wash down their sugar-shock-inducing desserts, including a world-class chocolate mousse.

Rimsky Korsakoffee House, 707 SE 12th Ave (☎232-2640). Looks like someone's house from the outside, but inside live chamber music enlivens a very pleasant if slightly cliqueish café.

Bars and pubs

B Moloch Heathman, 901 SW Salmon St (☎227-5700). Always crowded downtown brew-pub pouring some of Oregon's finest pints – from Widmer's weisen lagers to Deschutes's Black Butte Porters, and every shade in between. They also serve excellent pizzas – see p.85.

Bridgeport Brewpub, 1313 NW Marshall St (☎241-7179). Huge old warehouse that's now one of the city's largest and liveliest beer bars, pouring pints of homebrewed Bridgeport Ale. There's food too, including a top-rated, malt-flavored pizza.

Dublin Pub, 6821 SW Beaverton Hwy (☎279-2889). Traditional Irish pub, with regular live folk music, including bagpipes, and well-kept pints of Guinness.

East Bank Saloon, 727 SE Grand Ave (☎231-1659). Rowdy sports bar with an occasionally obnoxious, very male clientele; the best place, other than courtside, to watch a Rip City Portland Trailblazers basketball game.

Portland Brewing Company and Brewpub, 1339 NW Flanders (☎222-7150). Features the beers and ales of one of the city's more renowned micro-breweries.

Produce Row Café, 204 SE Oak St (☎232-8355). Just across the river among the still-working fruit-and-vegetable warehouses, with about a million different beers and gigantic sandwiches to help soak it up. Pool tables and a varied crowd keep things interesting.

Virginia Café, 725 SW Park Ave (☎227-0033). Step back into the 1940s for $1 drinks and plush wooden booths in this popular downtown bar; open all day (with budget food), but the later it gets, the more interesting the crowd.

Rock venues

Eli's Hard Rock Café, 424 SW Fourth Ave (☎223-4241). What you'd expect.

LaLuna, 215 SE Ninth Ave (☎242-5862). Showcase for some of the best bands in town.

Melody Ballroom, 615 SW Alder (☎232-2759). Cavernous old dancehall that's become one of Portland's prime venues for up-and-coming pop bands and touring indie stars.

The Roseland Theater, 8 NW Sixth Ave (☎224-7469). Portland's prime mid-sized venue; tickets usually around $15.

Satyricon, 125 NW Sixth Ave (☎243-2380). Somewhat intimidating post-punk club that mixes live bands, performance art and various oddball acts. In a seedy neighborhood, but inexpensive (cover free–$10) and with filling bar food.

X-Ray Café, 214 W Burnside St (☎721-0115). Anarchic punk club in Old Town storefront; all ages, no alcohol, low (or no) cover.

Blues and folk venues

Bojangles, 2229 SE Hawthorne (☎233-1201). Hosts some of the best touring artists.

Café Vivo, 555 SW Oak Ave (☎228-8486). Lively jazz and blues venue.

Dandelion Pub, 1033 NW 16th at Marshall (☎223-5366). Bluesy, pub-rock venue way out in the warehouse wilderness of the Northwest waterfront.

East Avenue Tavern, 727 E Burnside St (☎236-6900). Located about half a mile east of the river, with nightly Irish, folk or bluegrass music.

Key Largo, 31 NW First Ave (☎223-9919). Tropical decor, steamy dance floor, and the hottest blues bands. Cover at weekends only.

Jazz venues

Benson Hotel, 309 SW Broadway (☎228-2000). Regular live jazz in chic and high-priced downtown hotel dating from 1912.

Brasserie Montmartre, 626 SW Park Ave (☎224-5552). Nightly live jazz for the price of a dinner or a drink (see "Eating" above for more).

Dakota Café, 239 SW Broadway (☎241-4151). Relaxed downtown club that has live bands most nights.

Parchman Farm, 1204 SE Clay St (☎235-7831). Intimate club with good pizzas and great jazz most nights. No cover.

Nightclubs and discos

The City, 13 NW 13th Ave (☎224-2489). Portland's largest and liveliest gay nightclub, with huge dance floors and occasional live acts. Thurs–Sun only, until 4am Fri and Sat; cover $5–10.

Quest, 126 SW Second Ave (☎479-9113). Portland's biggest disco, mostly under-18 and all under-21: no alcohol allowed. Cover under $5.

Red Sea Reggae African Club, 318 SW Third Ave (☎241-5450). Small dance floor hidden away in the back of an Ethiopian restaurant, grooving most nights to DJed reggae and rockers tunes. No cover, strong drinks.

Classical music, theater and cinema

The *Portland Center for the Performing Arts* on Broadway, coupled with the opulently restored *Arlene Schnitzer Concert Hall* next door, forms the nucleus of Portland's **arts scene**. For up-to-date what's on and ticket information, call ☎248-4496; the *Oregonian* and the *Downtowner* carry listings and reviews. The **Oregon Symphony Orchestra** (☎228-4294) perform at the Concert Hall from September to April; tickets range from $15–40 for evening performances, but you can catch a Sunday afternoon concert for as little as $7. At other times, the Concert Hall is used for visiting acts – classical, jazz, country and rock. Keep an eye open for **free concerts**, especially in Pioneer Courthouse Square or at the zoo in the summer, and year round at the *Old Church*, Eleventh and Clay downtown, every Wednesday at noon.

The *Portland Center for the Performing Arts* is also the best place to catch **theater** in Portland. One of its two small auditoria, the cherry-wood-panelled *Intermediate Theater*, is also the main venue for the local chamber orchestra and ballet companies; the other, the hi-tech *Winningstad Theater*, is used by, among others, the *New Rose Theater*, based at 904 SW Main St (☎222-2487), who tend to keep to the classics. A few blocks away at SW Third and Clay, the *Civic Auditorium* (☎248-4496) is a venue for big musical extravaganzas, operas and anything else that needs a large stage. You'll find **cinema** listings in the *Downtowner* and the *Oregonian*, but for stuff out of the mainstream try the *Northwest Film Center*, 1219 SW Park Ave in the Art Museum (☎221-1156), or *Movie House*, 1220 SW Taylor St (☎224-4595); both show foreign and art films.

Listings

Airlines *Air Canada* (☎1-800/776-3000); *Alaska Airlines*, 530 SW Madison (☎224-2547 or 1-800/426 0333); *American Airlines*, 1216 SW Sixth Ave (☎1-800/433-3700); *British Airways* (☎1-800/247-9297); *Delta*, 1210 SW Sixth Ave (☎225-0830); *Lufthansa* (☎1-800/645-3880); *Northwest Airlines*, 910 SW Second Ave (domestic ☎1-800/225-2525; international ☎1-800/447-4747); *Qantas* (☎1-800/227-4500); *United Airlines*, 502 SW Madison (1-800/241-6522).

American Express Travel Service with **poste restante**, 1100 SW Sixth St (☎226-2961). There are automatic cash dispensers at the airport.

Banks Central branches include *First Interstate Bank*, 1300 SW Fifth Ave (☎225-2613), and *US Bank of Oregon*, 321 SW Sixth Ave (☎275-7393).

Basketball The Portland Trailblazers play at the Memorial Coliseum, 1401 N Wheeler (☎234-9291).

Bike Rental *Cascadden's Mountain Sports*, 1533 NW 24th (☎224-4746).

Books *Powell's City of Books*, 1005 W Burnside St (Mon–Sat 9am–11pm, Sun 9am–9pm; ☎228-4651), is a huge book-lined labyrinth of new and secondhand books. There's a branch, *Powell's Travel Store* (Mon–Sat 9am–7pm, Sun 10am–5pm; ☎228-1108), directly on Pioneer Square, where you can buy travel guides and maps.

Car Rental *Avis*, 330 SW Washington (☎227-0220); *Budget*, 2033 SW Fourth Ave (☎649-6500); *Dollar Rent a Car*, 132 NW Broadway (☎228-3540); *Hertz*, 1009 SW Sixth Ave (☎249-5727); *Thrifty*, 632 SW Pine St (☎227-6587).

Consulates Belgium, 520 SW Yamhill (☎228-0465); the British Consulate (☎227-5669) seems to exist only as an answerphone, redirecting you to Seattle or Los Angeles; Germany, 200 SW Market (☎227-0220); Netherlands, 4555 N Channel (☎228-0131); Norway, 5441 SW Macadam (228-8828); Sweden, 1600 SW Fourth (☎224-4155);

Gay & Lesbian Helpline (☎683-2428) The *Phoenix Rising Foundation*, at 630 SW Fifth Ave, Suite 710 (☎223-8299), is a gay and lesbian counselling and health center.

Hospital *The Good Samaritan Hospital and Medical Center*, 1015 NW 22nd Ave (information ☎229-7711, emergency dept ☎229-7260).

Laundromat *Springtime Laundry*, 2942 SE Hawthorne Blvd (☎235-5080), not far from the youth hostel; *Starting Point Laundromat*, 302 NW Sixth (☎222-3316), two blocks south of the *Greyhound* station.

Police 1111 SW Second Ave (796-3097); 222 Second Ave at Main St (☎294-2300).

Post Office 715 NW Hoyt St (☎223-6906), zip code 97209 (Mon–Fri 8.30am–8pm, Sat 8.30am–5pm).

State Parks *Oregon State Parks Office*, 3554 SE 82nd (Mon–Fri 9am–4.30pm; ☎731-3293 or ☎1-800/452-5687).

Taxi *Broadway Cabs* (☎227-1234) or *Portland Taxi Co* (☎256-5400).

Tours *Gray Line*, PO Box 17306 (☎285-9845) operate a range of summer bus tours visiting Oregon's beauty spots. Examples are tours of Mount Hood/Columbia Gorge (8hr; $30; 3 weekly) and the North Oregon coast (9hr; $30; 2 weekly). The Columbia Gorge bus/boat trip (8hr; $35; 4 weekly) includes a 2-hr cruise on the "sternwheeler" out of Cascade Locks. Further details from the visitor center.

Women's Crisis and Rape Lines Rape line ☎235-5333. There's also an office at 3020 E Burnside St (Mon–Fri 9am–4pm; ☎232-9751) offering counselling to women who've been raped; Metro crisis line (☎223-6161).

Women's politics *National Organization for Women*, 8700 SW 26th (☎462-0272).

WESTERN OREGON

East of Portland, just beyond the city's outlying suburbs, waterfalls cascade down mossy cliffs along the delightful **Columbia River Gorge**, and south of here the twisting path of an old pioneer road leads through more gorgeous scenery around **Mount Hood**.

Travellers heading south through Oregon toward California have the choice of two main parallel routes, which we trace in separate sections in the pages that follow. I-5 races south from Portland, through the Willamette Valley, passing by a number of medium-sized towns such as **Salem**, the state capital, and attractive **Eugene**, both of which lie along the river with the forested Cascade Mountains right on their doorstep. Further south still, **Crater Lake National Park**, a pristine alpine lake held within the shell of a burnt-out volcano, sits on the crest of the Cascades, only an hour's drive east of I-5, while near the California border, tiny **Ashland**'s summer-long Shakespeare Festival acts as a magnet for arts-oriented travellers.

The other alternative is to head down the Oregon **coast**, which – though rarely warm enough for sun and sea bathing – offers some of Oregon's finest scenery. Several highways link it with the Willamette Valley. As for towns, there are a couple of working ports – grim and grimy **Coos Bay** and **Astoria**, which benefits from a couple of good museums and a clutch of fine Victorian mansions – but most, like **Seaside**, **Newport** and, best of all, **Bandon** and **Cannon Beach** are small resorts, busy in summer, half-deserted out of season, when only storm-watchers come to see the wind lash stupendous waves against the rocks.

The Columbia River Gorge and Mount Hood

Carved by the Columbia River as it powered through volcanic layers to the sea, the **Columbia River Gorge**, stretching 44 miles from the Sandy River – 15 miles east of Portland – to Hood River was scoured deep and narrow by huge glaciers and rocks during the Ice Age. Now it's covered with green fir and maple trees, which turn fabulous shades of gold and red in the fall. Narrow white waterfalls cascade down its sides over mossy fern-covered rocks. To its south, the forested slopes of **Mount Hood** become increasingly lonely as you follow the path of the old pioneer Barlow Road back towards Portland. The best way to see the gorge is by **car**; *Greyhound* buses run along the gorge, stopping at **Cascade Locks**, but they take the freeway and you really want to be on the smaller, more scenic route. *Gray Line* run day **tours** from Portland during the summer for around $30 (☎285-9845), although they don't really allow you time to do the waterfalls justice, and it's frustrating not to have time to follow the trails.

For this reason, too, it's much better not to attempt the gorge and Mount Hood in one day, whatever the tourist leaflets say. A nice **Mount Hood Loop** takes you round the most dramatic sections of both areas (turn south from the gorge onto Hwy-35 at Hood River, then west on Hwy-26), but if you want to do any walking, you'll need two days for this trip. No matter when you come, be sure to get out of the car (or off your bike) and walk the many trails, otherwise the gorge can be somewhat disappointing: it's not breathtakingly sheer-walled or deep, but it does have dozens of waterfalls and countless other cascades and streams, all flowing through the lushly forested ravine.

The Columbia River Gorge

A tired Lewis and Clark were the first whites to pass through the **Columbia River Gorge**, floating down it on the last stage of their 1804 trek across the continent. Just forty years later it had become the perilous final leg of the Oregon Trail, negotiated by pioneer families on precarious rafts. Thereafter, when gold was discovered in eastern Oregon, the Columbia turned into a lifeline for pioneering miners and farmers and a prime target for a lucrative transportation monopoly, when a Portland-based company put steamboats on the river, and was soon raking in profits from the dependent (and bitter) residents of the arid east. By the 1880s, the steamboats were already carrying tourists, too.

The advent of car-borne tourism prompted the construction of the **Columbia River Scenic Highway** in 1915 – and this is still the road you should take through the gorge. The old road, now bypassed by I-84 (and *Amtrak* trains), is by far the most popular day out from Portland and so can be quite busy, especially at the weekend. Even then it doesn't take much effort to escape the crowds that congregate round the parking lots beneath the waterfalls and at the *Crown Point Vista House*, where there's a panoramic view out over the gorge, and much background information. Most people come from Portland via I-84, getting off at the Troutdale exit and following the signs along the Sandy River; there are however several other access points, including one towards the east end of the Scenic Highway at Multnomah Falls.

The tallest and most famous of the many falls along the highway, two-tier **Multnomah Falls** plummets 542 feet down a mossy rockface, collects in a pool, then falls another 70 feet to the ground. Apparently, when a sickness once threatened the Multnomah tribe, the chief's daughter threw herself over the falls to appease the Great Spirit, and you're supposed to be able to see her face in the mist. The rustic stone and timber *Multnomah Falls Lodge* (actually a gift shop and restaurant) has been catering for legend-enamored tourists since 1925.

Multnomah Falls can get quite packed, but several much less visited and equally impressive cascades lie within easy striking distance. Immediately to the west, **Wahkeena Falls** is the starting point for a number of hiking trails into the backcountry of the Mount Hood National Forest, as well as the two-mile "Perdition Trail", which takes you high above Wahkeena and offers views of Multnomah. East of Multnomah the powerful torrent of **Horsetail Falls** is balanced by the quieter and prettier **Pony Tail Falls**, upstream at the end of an easy mile-long trail. Perhaps the best of the many short hikes within the gorge heads up **Oneonta Gorge**, half a mile west of Horsetail Falls, following a shallow stream along the bottom of the sheerest of the Columbia Gorge's many side-canyons.

Back on I-84, five miles east of the Scenic Highway, **BONNEVILLE** is the site of a massive dam, a WPA project that's the first of the chain of dams which made the Columbia River the biggest producer of hydroelectric power in the world (for more on the Columbia dams, and Woody Guthrie, who wrote a series of songs about them, see p.226). There's a **visitor center** and **fish ladder** here (daily 10am–5pm; free). Four miles on, at **CASCADE LOCKS**, a toll bridge marks the legendary site of the native Americans' **Bridge of the Gods**. The story goes that a natural stone bridge once crossed the water here, but it was misused by sparring gods and the Great Spirit broke it down again; a small **museum** (May–Sept daily noon–5pm), in Marine Park, fills in the details, and has a modest assortment of pioneer memorabilia.

Hood River

The next bridge across the Columbia River abuts the town of **HOOD RIVER**, which is, depending upon the time of year, one of the most popular windsurfing, mountain biking and cross-country skiing centers in the Pacific Northwest. Though the town itself isn't exactly pretty – just a few modern blocks sandwiched between the gorge and I-84 to the north and the Hood River to the east – the outdoor recreation opportunities partly compensate. By the Columbia Gorge bridge, just beyond the east end of the town, the **visitor center** (Mon–Sat 9am–4pm; ☎1-800/336-3530 or 386-2000) has all the details, including lists of recommended outfitters and excursion organizers. Close by, you can rent a windsurfer for around $40 per day from the *Rhonda Smith Windsurfing Center* (☎386-9463), which also gives lessons and has a café right on the river near the main launching spot, under the bridge. In town, *Discover Bicycles*, in the back of the Dill Building at 1020 Wasco St (☎386-4820), one block up from I-84, rents out mountain bikes and can suggest which of the many nearby trails might be most to your taste. If you just want to see the scenery, ride the Mount Hood Railroad (☎386-3556; $15) halfway up the mountain; trains leave for the twenty-mile trip from the *Amtrak* station near the mouth of the river at the east end of town (April–Dec, Tues–Sun at 10am & 2.30pm).

Practicalities

After dark, join the sailors and bikers for a pint of Full Sail Ale in the *Hood River Brewing Company*, 506 Columbia St (☎386-2247), or sample the barbecue ribs at the *Mesquitery*, 1219 12th St (☎386-2002). For a **place to stay**, there's the clean and good-value *Vagabond Lodge,* 4070 Westcliff Drive (☎386-2992; ③), where you should ask for a room overlooking the river, as well as the plush *Columbia Gorge Hotel* (☎336-5566; ⑦) next door, built for the lumber king Simon Benson in 1921. There are also a handful of pricey B&Bs, such as the *Lakecliff Estate* (☎386-7000; ⑤) at 3820 Westcliff Drive, off I-84 half a mile west of Hood River, where the food is as excellent as the view over the gorge. There's a good-sized Forest Service **campground** at Lost Lake 23 miles southwest of town: follow Hwy-281 and Road #13.

The Dalles

From Hood River, Hwy-35 heads south to Mount Hood (see below), Hwy-141 heads north towards Washington's Mount St Helens (see p.207), and I-84 continues upriver to the ugly industrial township of **THE DALLES**, an old military outpost, halting point on the Oregon Trail and later, gold mining town that's now the closest settlement to the **Dalles Dam**, just beyond. Until the dam was built, the water tumbled over a series of rocky shelves called **Celilo Falls**, used by Native Americans as fishing grounds since prehistoric times, and the source of much aboriginal lore ("the great fishing place of the Columbia", Washington Irving, drawing on the experience of early fur-traders, called it). Celilo Falls were flooded when the Dalles Dam opened in 1957, to the anguish of local Native Americans; the compensation money went to build the *Kah Nee Tah* resort east of the Cascades (see p.132). Close to where the falls used to be, on the Washington side of the river, about six miles upstream from the dam, the village of **WISHRAM** was a great Indian trading center: ancient petroglyphs are relics of its one-time cultural role, though there's little else here today. A few miles further east, across the river on Hwy-97, is Washington State's Maryhill Museum (see p.220).

Mount Hood

The barren gulches and escarpments framing the Columbia River on either side of The Dalles herald the sagebrush plateaux of Eastern Oregon. But, the most spectacular part of the gorge is long gone – way back west – and there's a good case for turning south from Hood River towards **Mount Hood**, the tallest of the Oregon Cascades, thereby avoiding The Dalles altogether. Hwy-35 runs through the Hood River Valley (fruit-growing country, whose specialty is red Anjou pears), climbing out of the valley and up the mountain, with lovely views, until it comes to the highest point on the loop road, **Barlow Pass**, named after Samuel Barlow, a wagon train leader who pioneered a new finish to the Oregon Trail. The Columbia River Gorge was impassable by wagon, and pioneers had previously been forced to carry all their goods around Celilo Falls, then float down the river on rafts – or to pay extortionate rates to the two boats operating on the river. In 1845, Barlow led his party off to blaze a new trail around the south side of Mount Hood. They were trapped by snow while chopping their way through thick forests, and had to leave their wagons behind in the struggle to reach the Willamette Valley before they starved or froze. But Barlow returned a year later to build the **Barlow Road** (much of which is still followed by Hwy-26), and many migrants chose to brave its steep ridges, where wagons frequently skidded out of control and plummeted downhill, rather than face the Columbia. Barlow grew rich on his endeavors. To the irritation of many pioneers, he charged them $5 a wagon to use his road, while his partner completed the rip-off at the end of the trail, in the one and only general store.

Beyond Barlow Pass, Hwy-35 leads into Hwy-26, and shortly afterwards there's a turning up the mountain towards **Timberline Lodge** (☎272-3311; conventional and bunk rooms; ③–⑤), solidly built in stone and furnished with craftwork in wood, textiles, wrought iron and mosaic – like Bonneville Dam, a New-Deal job-creation scheme. During winter Timberline is the headquarters of a busy ski-resort, and you can rent ski equipment; in summer there's plenty of hiking. The lodge was used as the location of Kubrick's horror film *The Shining*.

The Willamette Valley

South of Portland, I-5 cuts through a series of inland valleys towards the Californian border, stringing through the region's main towns – though it bypasses historic **Oregon City** on the outskirts of Portland, once the end of the Oregon Trail and the first state capital. **Salem**, a quiet nineteenth-century milltown, is the modern capital, while at the southern end of the Willamette Valley, **Eugene** is Oregon's second largest city, a lively university town within easy striking distance of some of the Cascades' finest forest and wilderness scenery. East of the valleys, **Crater Lake National Park** is the region's one real tourist attraction, a deep blue lake cradled in an old volcano.

There are fast and frequent bus services up and down I-5, with *Greyhound* stopping at most places, and *Green Tortoise*'s twice-weekly bus providing an alternative. *Amtrak* links up Salem, Albany, Eugene and Klamath Falls before swinging south into California.

Oregon City

Set beside the confluence of the Willamette and Clackamas rivers, about thirteen miles south of Portland, **OREGON CITY** is, in a sense, where the state began. This was the end of the Oregon Trail and the first capital of the Oregon Territory – though ironically enough it was actually founded by the British-owned Hudson's Bay Company during the early nineteenth-century Anglo-American scramble to settle the Northwest. Today, the split-level town consists of an unappealing modern section, down by the river, and – up above – an uptown area of old wooden houses set on a bluff, that's ascended by both steep streets and steps.

It's on this compact, gridiron upper level that you'll find the town's two main sights. The small **Oregon Trail Interpretive Center** at Fifth and Washington (Mon–Sat 10am–4pm, Sun noon–4pm; $2), commemorates the often dangerous route followed by the pioneer wagon-trains of the 1840s with exhibits and a short film, eagerly presented by the volunteer staff. Nearby, among a number of nineteenth-century wooden mansions, the restored **McLoughlin House** at 713 Center St (Tues–Sat 10am–4pm, Sun 1–4pm; $3) was the home of Dr John McLoughlin, head of the Hudson's Bay Company, the town's founder, and something of a local hero. Ignoring political antagonisms, he provided the Americans who survived the Oregon Trail with food, seed, and periodic rescue from hostile Indians. He's now regarded as one of Oregon's founding fathers, and although his main base was north of here in the town of Vancouver, Washington, he retired to Oregon City in 1846. The house has been refurnished in period style, with a good scattering of McLoughlin's own possessions; he and his wife are buried in the grounds. Of lesser interest, the **Ermatinger House,** 619 Sixth St (Tues–Sat 10am–4pm; $1.50), dating from 1845, was where the name of "Portland" was chosen on the flip of a coin; and, just down the street at no 603, is the **Stevens–Crawford Museum** (Tues–Sun 10am–4pm; $3), an historic 1907 home, restored to something of its original appearance.

Salem

The build-up of motels and fast-food chains that ushers you into **SALEM**, some 50 miles south of Portland and the state capital of Oregon, doesn't really prepare you for the city's humble size. In fact Salem is a small and rather low-key little town, content dutifully to point visitors around its quota of attractions – the Capitol building, Mission Mill Village and Willamette University – but not particularly expecting them to linger. It was founded by the Methodist missionary Jason Lee, who set up Oregon's first US mission a few miles north of Salem in 1834. Lee originally intended to convert the Native Americans, but his sermons went down better with the white fur-traders who had retired to farm in the area, and Lee, deciding white settlement was the best way to further the cause, requested more recruits. The Methodist Missionary Board sent a shipful of pioneers, and, usefully, the machinery for a grist mill and a sawmill, which Lee set up by a dam in Salem, building himself a house nearby and thus laying the cornerstone for the present town. His ideal of a self-sufficient Willamette farming community was advanced further when an enterprising pioneer managed to herd a flock of high-grade sheep over the Oregon trail in 1848 – no mean feat in itself. The woollen mills that resulted, worked mostly by local women, sprang the rural valley into the industrial age – and Salem, like Oregon City, became established as a workaday mill town, leavened only by the presence of the state legislature.

The Town

Downtown Salem has a compact collection of nineteenth-century low-slung redbrick, the showpiece of which is the 1869 **Reed Opera House**, at Court and Liberty, once the center of local cultural and political activity and now a classy mall, full of antique shops. But a short walk from the downtown shopping area is the town's real centerpiece, the tall, white, Vermont marble **Capitol Building**, finished in 1938 and topped with a gold-leaf pioneer, axe in hand, eyes towards the west. At the entrance, there's a marble carving of explorers Lewis and Clark processing regally towards (presumably) the Willamette Valley, its caption – "Westward the Star of Empire Takes its Way" – an odd sort of motto, considering the amount of blood and effort spent throwing out the British only a few years before Lewis and Clark set off. Inside are murals celebrating the state's beginnings, and on the floor there's a large bronze version of the state seal, in which wheat, a covered wagon and trading ships symbolize the new Oregon state of 1859, under the wings of a bald eagle. There are regular tours round the Capitol – the **information desk** inside the rotunda has the times – but the tower remains out of bounds for the moment as a result of earthquake damage sustained in March 1993. Back outside, manicured gardens surround the building, with statues of Jason Lee and Dr McLoughlin on the east side.

Next to the Capitol, verdant **Willamette University** is the oldest university in the West, originally a mission school set up by Jason Lee. But to get a more vivid (albeit prettified) glimpse of Salem's early history, head a few minutes' walk further out of downtown to **Mission Mill Village**, off 12th St at 1313 Mill St, which groups a nineteenth-century woollen mill, a small museum and the old frame houses of two early pioneers with a café and several small shops. There's a **visitor center** here too (Mon–Fri 9am–5pm, Sat 10am–4pm; ☎1-800/874-7012 or 581-4325). Around the back, the modest **Marion Museum of History** (Tues–Sat 9.30am–4.30pm; $1) has an exhibit on the Kalapuyan, who lived in the Willamette

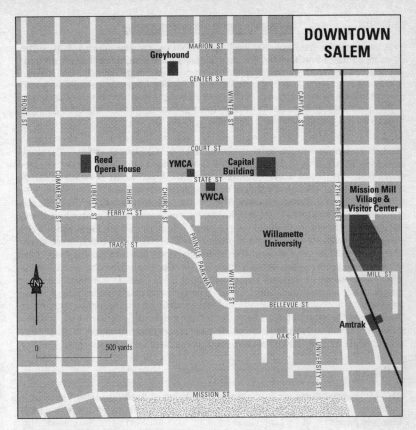

Valley until a combination of white settlers, the Klickitat and disease drove them out. As much as ninety percent of the native population were killed by a nineteenth-century malaria epidemic. The museum's pride and joy is a rickety 125-year-old canoe, a rare Native American relic hollowed out, in the traditional manner, by hot coals.

Practicalities

Only an hour from Portland, and easy to reach along the main I-5 corridor, Salem can be visited on a day trip from Portland or, better, on the way south towards Eugene and Ashland. The *Greyhound* station is convenient at 450 Church St NE (☎362-2428), and the *Amtrak* station is at 13th and Oak (☎588-1551); *Cherriots* buses, 183 High St NE (☎588-2877), provide a local bus service. There are plenty of **motels** around: although most of them are far from the city center, downtown options include the no-frills *City Center Motel*, 510 Liberty St, south of Trade St (☎364-0121; ②), and the pricier *Execulodge*, nearby at 200 Commercial St SE and Trade (☎363-4123 or 1-800/452-7879; ④). The *Hampshire House Bed and Breakfast*, a short walk north of downtown at 975 D St NE and Capitol (☎370-7181; ③), offers two simple bedrooms in a leafy, suburban part of town. The best

> ### COVERED BRIDGES
>
> Pioneers in the area around Albany put roofs over their bridges to protect the wooden trusses from the Oregon rain, lengthening the bridge's life-span from ten to thirty years or more – a tradition which continued until fairly recently. The privacy they afforded earned them the nickname of "kissing bridges". It's unlikely you'll want to hunt down all thirteen of the covered bridges in the vicinity of Albany, but five, mostly dating from the 1930s, are clustered together around tiny **Scio**, roughly twelve miles east of town along Hwy-226.

budget option for women is probably the *YWCA*, 768 State St (☎581-9922; single rooms only; ①), next to the university – though much of its space goes to longer-term residents. Space is even tighter at the *YMCA*, 685 Court St (☎581-9622; ①), two blocks away, though it's always worth a try.

Among several **campgrounds**, there's the commercial *KOA*, 3700 Hagers Grove Rd SE (☎581-6736 or 1-800/826-9605), southeast of the center beside exit #253 on I-5. However, about 20 miles east of Salem, the **Silver Falls State Park** campground, 20024 Silver Falls Highway (☎873-8681), has a much more attractive location. The area around the university does not turn up the busy **food** scene you might expect, though the *Ram Border Café*, 515 12th St SE (☎363-1904), is a pleasant bar and restaurant, open until 2am. Downtown, the *Court Street Daily Lunch*, 347 Court St at Liberty, is a good old-fashioned diner, complete with original furnishings and fittings dating from the Fifties and Sixties. And, down the street at 471 Court, is the more upbeat *Governor's Cup*, where a filling meal will set you back about $10; *La Margarita*, 545 Ferry St SE at High (☎362-8861), is lively and enjoyable, mesquite grilling being its specialty.

Albany

The I-5 interstate cuts straight through the heart of the Willamette Valley from Salem to Eugene, while the old Hwy-99 potters through smaller towns at a more leisurely pace.

Sticking to I-5, the first major town south of Salem is **ALBANY**, which, despite its industrial profile, has a good-looking concentration of late nineteenth-century wooden mansions and churches, over three hundred in all. These are reminders of the town's heyday as a transportation center, when Albany's merchants prospered exporting the products of the Willamette Valley. Most of the town's grand old houses remain in private hands, and are rarely – if ever – open to the public, but a walking tour of the more distinguished parts of town still makes for an enjoyable diversion. The **visitor center**, 300 SW Second Ave (☎928-0911 or 1-800/526-2256) has maps and pamphlets detailing tours of the three main historic districts, and of the area's **covered bridges**.

Eugene

An excellent base for exploring the neighboring Willamette National Forest, or for visiting the coast, **EUGENE** – and its industrial annexe Springfield, just across the Willamette River – dominate the lower end of the Willamette Valley, serving as a study in opposites: one the haunt of students, joggers and white-collar workers; the other a gritty blue-collar lumber town. The former was named after Eugene Skinner, the first person to build a homestead in the area around 1846, his success based on the abundant supply of timber rather than the ferry service he ran for local farmers – sunken logs and gravel bars were a constant hazard. Eugene has become Oregon's second largest center, and has been a prime cultural focus since travelling theater groups began to stop here on their way between Portland and San Francisco in the late nineteenth century.

Arrival and information

Getting to Eugene is easy: the *Greyhound* terminal is at Tenth and Pearl (☎344-6265); *Amtrak* pull in at Fourth and Willamette (☎485-1092); while *Green Tortoise* stop two to four times weekly at 14th and Kincaid (by the University) on their way to and from Seattle (☎937-3603 or 1-800/227-4766). The local bus service, *Lane Transit District* (*LTD;* ☎687-5555), have a central boarding-point and information center (Mon–Fri 6.30am–11pm; Sat & Sun 9am–5.30pm) at Tenth and Willamette – pick up a route map from *7-11* stores. Fares are 75¢ per journey during weekdays – 50¢ after 7pm and at weekends. Day passes cost $1.90 and advance purchase tokens (sold in fives) give a small discount.

There's a **visitor center** at 305 W Seventh Ave (Mon–Fri 8.30am–5pm; ☎484-5307 or ☎1-800/547-5445), between Lincoln and Lawrence streets – it's signposted from the highway. They have all sorts of leaflets on Eugene and the surrounding Lane County, which extends from the Cascades to the Oregon coast. Of special interest are the cycle route details, information on local wineries and covered bridge sightseeing routes.

The Town

Though short on sights, Eugene's homely downtown of partly pedestrianized modern shopping malls and offices is spick and span and almost devoid of highrise developments. It's here, bordered by the river to the north and east, and clustered on either side of its north–south axis, Willamette Street, that you'll find many of the town's best restaurants and bars. The **University of Oregon** campus in the city's southeast corner (you can walk or catch a local bus from downtown) provides more and lends a youthful – and cost-conscious – feel to the place. The university also has a very decent **Museum of Art** (Wed–Sun noon–5pm; free), whose highlight is a strong Asian collection, plus contemporary Northwest and American paintings.

Eugene puts on a highly watchable display of its social diversities at its two big markets, especially the weekly **Saturday Market** between Eighth and Oak (April–Dec), which began in 1970 as a local crafts market but has since expanded into something of a carnival, with live music and street performers. Tie-dye and wholefoods set the tone, but rastas, skateboarders, punks and students join the hippies, and make a cheerful throng. **Fifth Street Public Market** (to the north at Fifth and High), though more touristy, is another lively affair, its three levels of shops around a brick inner courtyard (actually a clever conversion of an old chicken-processing plant) selling arts, crafts, and clothes, as well as a huge assortment of ethnic food, from Chinese to Mexican to fish and chips. **Skinner Butte Park**, north of downtown along High Street, is leafy and green and worth a look for the Shelton Murphy House, an 1888 Queen Anne Victorian with a sharply pointed spire and all manner of ornate flourishes.

Eugene is also something of a **sports** capital: the city and university have hosted the US Olympic Track and Field Trials; the *Nike* sports shoes company was started here; locals even claim to have started the jogging revolution in the 1970s. Trails and paths abound for runners and cyclists, both in the city center and along leafy river banks. In fact, if you intend to spend some time here, a bike's a good way to get around: you can rent one for $3 an hour, $15 a day, from *Pedal Power,* 545 High St (☎687-1775), between Fifth and Sixth Ave – a credit card or $250 cash deposit is required. Some **university sports facilities** are open to the public (☎346-3014 for details) and the *EMU Waterworks Co,* 1395 Franklin Blvd (☎686-4386), rents out **canoes and kayaks** in the summer.

Accommodation

Palatable budget accommodation is concentrated on and around Franklin Boulevard, off I-5 near the university, although Eugene's bed and breakfasts are generally more distinctive than its hotels and motels. The basic hotels clustered around Sixth and Seventh avenues, just west of Lincoln, are in the town's seediest area and are probably best avoided. The nearest **campground** is the *KOA,* off I-5 at Coburg, just north of Eugene, but there are far better campgrounds east of Eugene in the Willamette National Forest.

Angus Inn Motel, 2121 Franklin (☎342-1243). Standard motel near the university. ③.

Barron's Motor Inn, 1859 Franklin (☎342-6383). Handy for the Interstate. ③.

Campus Cottage, 1136 E 19th Ave (☎342-5346). A plush antique-furnished bed and breakfast one block south of the university. ⑤.

Eugene Hilton, 66 E Sixth Ave (☎342-2000). By far the best downtown option, if you can afford it: a sparkling new tower block where many of the rooms have superb views out across the valley. ⑥.

Eugene Motor Lodge, 476 E Broadway (☎344-5233). Budget motel. ②.

Franklin Inn, 1857 Franklin (☎342-4804). A reasonably priced motel by the university. ②.

Maryellen's Guest House, 1583 Fircrest (☎342-735). A peaceful bed and breakfast, near campus on the east side of Hendricks Park. ④.

Eating

With over fifteen thousand students to feed, Eugene is well supplied with **cafés and restaurants**, both around the campus and **downtown**, where there's more choice.

Café Zenon, 898 Pearl St (☎343-3005). An upbeat bistro with marble-topped tables, tile floors and an eclectic though pricey menu ranging from (tasty) pasta to (bland) curry.

Excelsior Café, 754 East 13th Ave (☎342-6963). Classy and expensive, but popular for its quality French cuisine.

Govinda's, at Eighth and Lincoln (☎686-3531). A popular and inexpensive vegetarian/vegan restaurant.

Guido's, 801 E 13th St (☎343-0681), out near the university. Offers decently priced Italian food, plus chart music on Wednesday, Friday and Saturday nights.

Jo Federigo's Café & Jazz Bar, 295 East Fifth Ave (☎343-8488). Stick to the Italian dishes and enjoy the nightly live jazz.

Keystone Café, 395 W Fifth St at Lawrence (☎342-2075). Inexpensive high-quality American and Mexican food.

Oregon Electric Station, 27 E Fifth Ave (☎485-4444). Housed in a tastefully refurbished station building and featuring live music at the weekend. Delicious lunches served in the bar, but the restaurant is over-priced.

Steelhead Brewery and Café, 199 E Fifth Ave (☎686-BREW). This reasonably priced establishment has its beer brewed on the premises as a tasty accompaniment to sandwiches, burgers and pizzas.

Sy's New York Pizza, 1211 Alder (☎686-9598). Some of the best pizza in town.

Willie's on Seventh Street, 388 West Seventh Ave (closed Sun; ☎485-0601). Worth trying for good and filling lunches and dinners.

Nightlife and festivals

For **evening entertainment** lots of bars have live music but the city's showpiece is the *Hult Performing Arts Center*, Seventh and Willamette (☎687-5000), which features everything from Bach to blues, its annual Bach Festival in late June drawing musicians from all over the world; call the 24-hour Concert Line, ☎342-5746, for an update. The older *WOW Hall,* 291 W Eighth St (☎687-2746), once a meeting hall for the Industrial Workers of the World (or "Wobblies"), is more informal, featuring up-and-coming bands across the musical spectrum, with some vigorous Saturday night dancing. Other venues include the *Erb Memorial Union Ballroom*, 13th and University (☎346-4000), which features a wide range of acts, and the lively *Rock'n'Rodeo*, a country bar/club at Seventh and Willamette (☎683-5160).

Eugene's biggest event of the year is the **Oregon Country Faire** ($10 a day), held ten miles west on US-126 in Veneta over three days on the second weekend in July – a big, crowded hippy-flavored festival of music, arts, food and dancing that's well worth making the effort to get to. Traffic for the fair is heavy, and even with a car you might be better taking Eugene's local *LTD* buses, which run to Veneta every 30 minutes during the fair for 25¢. There's another big summer festival at Cottage Grove, twenty miles south of Eugene on I-5. This, the **Bohemia Mining Days**, in the third week of July, recalls the nineteenth-century gold strike of one James Bohemia Johnson.

For further details of local events and gigs, consult the free broadsheet the *Eugene Weekly*.

Willamette National Forest

Within easy striking distance of Eugene is the **Willamette National Forest**, a great slab of wilderness and forested mountain slope that occupies a one-hundred-mile strip on the western side of the Cascade Mountains, tipped by the high lava fields around McKenzie Pass. Four major highways, running west–east, leave the Willamette Valley to access the forest as well as its many hiking trails and campgrounds, and two link Eugene (and Salem) with Bend in eastern Oregon (see p.135). In Eugene, the *Willamette National Forest Office*, at 211 E Seventh Ave (Mon–Fri 9am–4.30pm; ☎465-6521), carries a full range of maps, trail details and information, as do the other US Forest Service offices at, among several, Blue River (☎822-3317) and McKenzie Bridge (☎822-3381), both tiny settlements on Hwy-126. It's this same highway, traversing the **McKenzie River Valley**, that's the most popular route into the National Forest from Eugene, tracking along the river bank, through miles of fruit and nut orchards, before reaching **McKENZIE BRIDGE**, fifty miles east of town.

Here you'll find the start of the **McKenzie River National Recreation Trail**, a clearly marked, 27-mile route that follows the course of the McKenzie River, passing patches of old-growth forest, lava flows and waterfalls on its way to the main northern trailhead on the Old Santiam Wagon Road, a couple of miles from the junction of Hwy-126 and US-20. The trail is a fine introduction to the local scenery and, as the footpath also runs near the road, you can reach and walk more manageable portions quite conveniently. Other, less-frequented trails begin near McKenzie Bridge too, plus more old favorites such as the short footpath to the spectacular **Proxy Fall**, and further afield, the easy half-mile **Lava River Trail**, which has intriguing views of several sorts of lava flow near McKenzie Pass.

Parts of the McKenzie River also offer excellent **whitewater rafting** and boating. Several Eugene/Springfield-based companies organize excursions – contact the *McKenzie River Raft Company*, 7715 Thurston Road, Springfield (☎747-9231), or *Dean Helfrich & Sons*, 2415 N 17th Place, Springfield (☎747-8401).

Most of the National Forest's **campgrounds** operate on a first-come, first-served basis; there's a leaflet, available from the forest offices, listing them all, including the dozen or so near McKenzie Bridge. Among local **inns** and **lodges**, which are thin on the ground, the most distinguished is *Holiday Farm*, 54455 McKenzie River Drive (☎822-3715; ⑥), off Hwy-126 at Rainbow, 45 miles from Eugene. The food here is excellent, and many of the cottages are right by the banks of the river – the resort was a favorite retreat for President Herbert Hoover in the late 1920s. The *Cedarwood Lodge*, just outside McKenzie Bridge (☎822-3351; ④), is more mundane. *Lane Transit* run regular **bus** services out of Eugene up along Hwy-126 as far as McKenzie Bridge.

Crater Lake National Park

The Northwest's best-looking volcanic crater, located south of the Willamette National Forest and just ninety scenic miles east of I-5 along the Umpqua Valley, sits high up in the Cascade Range, where the shell of Mount Mazama holds **Crater Lake**; blue, deep and resoundingly beautiful. For half a million years Mount Mazama sent out periodic sprays of ash, cinder and pumice, later watched apprehensively by Klamath Indians, who saw in them signs of a war between two gods, Llao and Skell, and kept well clear. The mountain finally burst, blowing its one-time peak over eight states and three Canadian provinces in an explosion many times greater than the more recent Mount St Helens blast. A cone-like mini-volcano began to grow again within the hollowed mountain-top, but when the mountain cooled the basin was filled by springs and melted snow, and the growth, now dormant, became an island in what's now Crater Lake. In its snow-covered isolation, the lake is awe-inspiring, especially in summer, when wildflowers bloom, wildlife (deer, squirrels, chipmunks, elks, even bears) emerges from hibernation, and boats run out across the lake to the lightly forested shores of **Wizard Island**.

Though it's a stop well worth making, Crater Lake National Park, set high in the mountains, is not easy to reach: you'll need a car, and of the two approach roads, the northern entrance (off Hwy-138 from Roseburg on I-5) is closed by snow from mid-October to late June, as is the 33-mile **"Rim Drive"** road around the crater's edge. The southern access road (off Hwy-62, which leads off US-97), is kept open all year, though of course the higher hiking trails – of which there are many – are snow-covered for much of the year, and except in summer are used mainly by cross-country skiers.

At the north end of the lake, the steep, mile-long **Cleetwood Trail** leads to the shore, the only way down from the Rim Drive, and to the pleasure boats which make regular, two-hour cruises round the lake (late June–early Sept 10am–4pm; $10). The southern approach road brings you to the lake and tiny **Rim Village**,

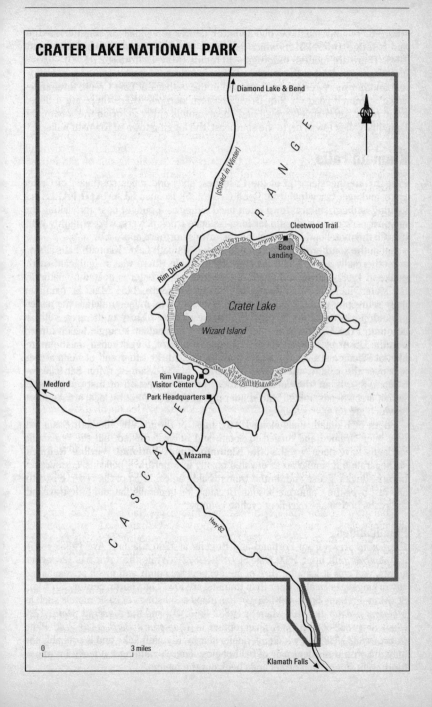

CRATER LAKE NATIONAL PARK

Diamond Lake & Bend

(closed in Winter)

RANGE

Cleetwood Trail

Boat Landing

Rim Drive

Crater Lake

Wizard Island

Medford

Rim Village Visitor Center

Park Headquarters

CASCADE

Mazama

Hwy-62

0   3 miles

Klamath Falls

where there's not much beyond a **visitor center** (open daily in summer), a café, and a **lodge** (☎594-2511), which is closed for repairs and refurbishment until 1995. There are modern **lodgings** – 40 rooms (May–Oct; ☎594-2511; ④) – plus a large **campground** at the hamlet of Mazama, near the park's southern entrance, and another more remote campground in the outback at Lost Creek, three miles down a branch road off Rim Drive's eastern portion, where there are a dozen basic plots. Alternatively, you'll find cheap motels either in, or on the way to, the Umpqua Valley towns or, to the southeast, the logging town of Klamath Falls.

Klamath Falls

Past the southeastern tip of the Cascades, sixty-odd miles southeast of Crater Lake, and over twice that from Bend (see p.135), isolated **KLAMATH FALLS** is a logging and agricultural town often used either as a budget base for visiting the national park or as a pit-stop for long-distance truck drivers, whose mighty vehicles fill the motel parking lots along the town's northern approach.

Set at the southern tip of enormous Upper Klamath Lake, Klamath Falls sits on a geothermally active – and geologically unstable (there was a significant earthquake in 1993) – area, and much of the small town center is heated by naturally hot water, including the **Klamath County Museum**, 1451 Main St (summer daily 9am–6pm; winter Mon–Sat 8am–5pm; free). The museum details the underground quirks and runs through the sparse pioneer history of the area, with an account of the **Modoc War** – a bitter nineteenth-century struggle which turned into the US Army's most expensive Indian campaign, fought mostly in the maze-like lava beds just over the Californian border. At the other end of Main Street, just over the bridge, the **Favell Museum**, 125 W Main St (Mon–Sat 9.30am–5.30pm; $3), is an idiosyncratic, cluttery private collection of vast quantities of Indian arrowheads, mixed with renderings of the Old West by local artists, more of which are on sale upstairs.

South of Klamath Falls along US-97, most of the marshy Klamath Basin has now been drained and turned to potato and onion farmland, but the remaining wetlands have been saved as the **Klamath Basin National Wildlife Refuges**, six separate but similar areas devoted mostly to waterfowl – pelicans, cormorants, herons, ducks, geese and, in the winter, bald eagles. Most of the reserve is actually just over the California border. Because it's generally flat and little travelled, the roads here make excellent cycling country.

Practicalities

Greyhound arrive from Portland and Eugene at 1200 Klamath Ave (☎882-4616), and *Amtrak* pull in at 1600 Oak St (☎884-2822). While the town has few actual sights, you can at least be sure of an inexpensive **room** and meal: prices, aimed at working-class locals rather than tourists, are low. The **visitor center**, 507 Main St (Mon–Fri 9am–5pm; ☎884-5193), has maps and listings of basic motels such as *Molatore's Motor Inn*, 100 Main St (☎882-4666; ②), and the *Maverick Motel*, 1220 Main St (☎882-6688; ②). A nicer option is *Thompson's B&B*, 1420 Wild Plum Court (☎882-7938; ③), which overlooks nearby Klamath Lake and is probably the only inn with a resident pair of bald eagles. There's nothing too fancy by way of **food**: walk along Main Street and check out the menus.

South from Eugene to the California border

Back on the western side of the Cascades, the Umpqua and Rogue river valleys are forested basins in a mountainous region, scattered with logging and agricultural towns such as outdoors-oriented **Grants Pass**, a popular base for whitewater river rafting along the turbulent Rogue River. This same river was also a major **gold mining** area: **Jacksonville**, now a partly restored relic of Gold Rush times, had its improbable beginnings after a prospector's mule kicked up a gold nugget in 1852. Nearby **Ashland** hosts the Oregon Shakespeare Festival, a spring and summer dose of Shakespeare and more contemporary drama.

Oakland

Tiny **OAKLAND**, fifty tedious miles south from Eugene and a mile east of I-5, was once a major stopping point on the stagecoach line from Sacramento to Portland. Today it's a quiet rural hamlet, whose halcyon days are recalled by the neon-free, old wooden storefronts of Locust Street, the main drag. Here, at no 130, you'll find the local **history museum** (daily 1–4.30pm), housed in the former grocery store and post office, while City Hall around the corner has town plans and walking tips, pointing out what happened where and when among the various redbrick buildings.

For **food**, *Tolly's*, 115 Locust St (☎459-3796), features an antique ice cream parlor, gift shop and candy counter downstairs, and a restaurant up above; close by is the *Medley Market* deli and soda fountain.

Roseburg

Fifteen miles south of Oakland, the hilly lumber town of **ROSEBURG** is the urban center of the fertile Umpqua Valley. There's not much to see downtown – though the older storefronts and timber houses are worth a few minutes – but the **Douglas County Museum** (Tues–Sat 10am–4pm, Sun noon–4pm; free), along I-5 (exit 123) on the south side of town, portrays the lives of the loggers with great effect, and has a library on the ground floor where you can pore over old photos and books.

If you break your journey here, **eat and drink** at the friendly *Little Brother's Pub*, 428 SE Main St (☎672-0912); the *Café Espresso*, 368 SE Jackson St at Douglas (Mon–Fri; ☎672-1859), serves the best coffee in town. There are several bargain-basement **motels** on Stephens St, not far from the **Greyhound** depot at 835 SE Stephens (☎673-5326), while the more comfortable *Garden Villa Motel*, 760 NW Garden Valley Blvd (☎672-1601; ③), is off I-5 on the north side of town.

The **visitor center**, 410 SE Spruce St (Mon–Fri 9am–5pm; ☎672-9731), has the low-down on everything in and around Roseburg, including route maps of the area's covered bridges as well as the five local **wineries** open for tours and tastings.

Around Roseburg: the North Umpqua River Valley

East of Roseburg, Hwy-138 leads the ninety miles to the Crater Lake National Park (see above) via the **North Umpqua River Valley** and **National Forest**. The river is famous for its fishing – trout, salmon and steelhead – and whitewater rafting, and any of several Roseburg outfitters will supply your every need. For national forest maps and hiking trail details stop at the **ranger station** (☎496-3532) in **GLIDE**, eighteen miles east of town, where the turbulent watery basin called Colliding Rivers marks the confluence of the North Umpqua and Little rivers. Further east, **STEAMBOAT** is noteworthy for the riverside cottages and cabins of the *Steamboat Inn* (☎498-2411; ⑤–⑦) – which also has an excellent restaurant (dinners by reservations only) – although most visitors to the national forest opt for one of the dozen or so **campgrounds** that lie dotted along the road. A couple of the best are deep in the heart of the forest around **Diamond Lake**, a high-altitude, deep-blue rectangle of water 76 miles out of Roseburg (and not far from Crater Lake – see p.100). From here, a difficult four-mile trail leads to the summit of Mount Thielsen, or you can settle for the easier stroll round the lakeshore.

Grants Pass

Leaving Roseburg, I-5 snakes its way the seventy miles south to **GRANTS PASS**, set beside the Rogue River as it tumbles vigorously from the Cascade Mountains to the sea. Like Gold Beach at the river's mouth (see p.119), Grants Pass seems to earn its living by strapping its visitors into bright orange life-jackets, and packing them in to rafts to bounce over the river's whitewater rapids. A half-day's rafting or kayak tour will cost around $35, a full day $45 – the **visitor center**, 1501 NE Sixth St (☎476-7717 or 1-800/547-5927) can provide brochures from the more than two dozen licensed (and therefore safer) river guides operating from the town; you can rent paddle-boats and canoes, too.

With such exciting surroundings, the town is rather on the dull side, mostly modern, neon-lit shops with a few old brick buildings and churches dating from the turn of the century. Hwy-99, the old main route through the valley, cuts along Seventh Street (northbound) and Sixth Street (southbound), holding the bulk of the town's budget accommodation, such as the *Flamingo Inn* at 728 NW Sixth St (☎476-6601; ②) and the *Travelodge*, 748 SE Seventh St (☎476-7793; ③).

Thrilling though rafting undoubtedly is, it's easier to concentrate on the scenery around the Rogue River Canyon on foot: the forty-mile Rogue River Trail begins (or ends, if you're coming from the coast – see p.120) at Grave Creek, 27 miles to the northwest of Grants Pass. It's a sweaty walk in summer, and muddy to the point of impassability in winter, but in spring or autumn it's an excellent trek for serious walkers, and there are regular campgrounds on the way. There's more easily accessible **camping** sixteen miles east of town in the **Valley of the Rogue State Park** (I-5 exit 45A).

The Oregon Caves

Hwy-199 leaves I-5 at Grants Pass, and wanders down the Illinois River Valley towards the Northern Californian coast. At the small town of **CAVE JUNCTION**, 30 miles from Grants Pass, there's a turning for the **Oregon Caves**, tucked in a wooded canyon at the end of a narrow, twisting road. The caves were discovered in 1874, when a deerhunter's dog chased a bear into a hole in the mountainside, but they only became famous when the poet Joaquin Miller described his 1909 visit in such ringing phrases that "the marble halls of Oregon" were preserved as Oregon's only national monument.

Inside, the caves – actually, one enormous cave with smaller passages leading off it, totalling three miles in length – are the stuff of geology lessons. The marble walls were created by the centuries-long compression of mucky lime, mud and lava, then carved out over the eons by subterranean water. Limestone dissolved into the remaining water, and long years of steady dripping have created elaborate formations from the lime deposits: clinging stalactites hang from the ceiling, some met by stalagmites to form columns, while rippled flows of rock run from the walls. The caves are open year round, and are always cool, so you'll need extra clothes: hours vary according to season – call the nearby *Caves Chateau* hotel on ☎592-3400 for an update. You have to go in with the hour-long tour ($6): while you're waiting (tours leave regularly but can get full in the summer, when it's wise to turn up early in the day), you could go on one of the two nature trails that ramble up the mountain above the caves and look out magnificently over the surrounding Siskiyou Mountains.

Eight miles from Cave Junction, twelve miles from the cave, the **Fordson Home Hostel**, 250 Robinson Rd (☎592-3203), offers a cheap bed ($8, but you need to book in advance), **camping**, free use of bicycles and $2 discount off entry to the caves for non-Americans with the hostel's stamp on their *IYHA* cards. There's plenty of other camping around, best at the two US Forest Service campgrounds near the caves. The *Gold Leaf Resort*, 7901 Caves Highway (☎592-3406; ③), has motel-style rooms and there's always the *Caves Chateau* hotel itself (mid-June to Sept; ☎592-3400; ④), a grand 1930s timber lodge tucked into a wooded canyon.

Medford and Jacksonville

Heading south inland on I-5 rather than toward the coast on Hwy-199, it's a short journey from Grants Pass to **MEDFORD**, the Rogue River Valley's urban center – an industrial goliath squatting among huge paper mills and piles of sawdust. Best passed through as quickly as possible, there's a turning here for smaller and prettier **JACKSONVILLE**, five miles west. The largest of Oregon's 1850s Gold Rush towns, a flourishing and boisterous prospectors' town-cum-supply-center for just thirty years, Jacksonville saw its fortunes take a nose-dive when the gold boom ended: it crumbled, quietly, until it was old enough to attract tourists, and now the whole town has been restored and is listed as a national historic landmark.

The **Jacksonville Museum**, on Fifth Street in the County Courthouse (summer daily 10am–5pm; winter closed Mon; $2), sometimes stages performances of pioneer scenes in nineteenth-century costume, and, like the **Children's Museum** next door, has exhibits on the town's chief celebrity, Pinto Colvig – who provided the voices of Goofy and Pluto in the Disney films. If you're around in July and August, look out for the **Britt Music Festival** (☎773-6077 or 1-800/882-7488 for further info), which fills the town with musicians and dancers (and visitors). Jazz, classical, bluegrass and folk music plays everywhere, and accommodation – always pricey here – becomes impossible (you'll find cheaper beds in Ashland). At Jacksonville's small **visitor center** (☎899-8118) inside the old railway depot, at Oregon and C streets, you can pick up a free walking-tour map of the town. Jacksonville boasts a clutch of quaint **B&Bs** in restored old homes: the swankiest is the *Old Stage Inn*, 883 Old Stage Rd (☎899-1776 or 1-800/US-STAGE; ⑤), housed in a century-old converted farmhouse. The *McCully*

House Inn, 240 E California St (☎899-1942; ④), dating from 1861, is a good second choice. Another option is the plush *Jacksonville Inn*, 175 E California St (☎889-1900; ⑤–⑥), located right in the center of town. For **food**, the *Bella Union*, a refurbished saloon at 170 W California (☎899-1770), has a wide-ranging and imaginative menu, while the lounge menu of the *Jacksonville Inn* is superb and not too expensive – try the veal piccata.

Ashland and the Shakespeare Festival

Throughout Oregon, the small town of **ASHLAND** is identified with the works of Shakespeare, a bizarre cultural anomaly among the timber and dairy-farming towns of the state's rural, folksy south. The idea of an **Oregon Shakespeare Festival** came to a local teacher, Angus Bowmer, fifty years ago, and now throughout the summer Shakespeare T-shirts and mugs fill the shops, and actors in Elizabethan costume pack audiences into a half-timbered replica of sixteenth-century London's open-air *Fortune Theatre* – here the **Elizabethan Theater** – while Shakespearian (and other) plays are staged in indoor venues from February to October.

Despite the obvious phoniness of it all, Ashland is nowhere near as tacky as Shakespeare's birthplace in England, and in some ways has the distinct edge. Performance standards are high, and there's some excellent contemporary fringe theater around – not to mention pleasant cafés and a young, friendly atmosphere when the nearby Southern Oregon State College is in session. Ashland's setting, between the Cascade and the Siskiyou mountains, is magnificent, enabling good skiing in the winter and river rafting in summer.

Lithia Park is appealing too: stretching around the Elizabethan theater close to Ashland's two main streets of shops and cafés, it was designed by John McLaren (of Golden Gate fame) with shrubs, trails and a brook, its spreading trees sheltering both family picnics and meditating hippies. The park was created during Ashland's pre-festival incarnation as a spa-town, a project of New York advertising mogul, Jesse Winburne. He overestimated the appeal of the nasty-tasting local Lithia Spring water, and the spa idea failed, but it did lodge the germ of Ashland's potential as a tourist town.

Seeing the plays

The **festival** runs from February to October. Shakespeare is performed at the *Elizabethan* and the modern *Angus Bowmer* theaters, both in Lithia Park, while the smaller *Black Swan*, opposite the park off Pioneer Street, tends to stage contemporary plays. Ticket information for all three is available from the *Oregon Shakespeare Festival*, 15 Pioneer St (☎482-4331; Tues–Sun) – expect to pay anywhere from $12 to $30. Lots of performances sell out in advance, but you can sometimes pick up half-price tickets on the day, and the *Elizabethan* sells standing-only tickets for $8. Contemporary drama comes cheaper ($8–12): try the *Actors' Theatre of Ashland*, 295 E Main St (☎482-9659; tickets from the *Blue Dragon* bookshop), or the *Oregon Cabaret Theatre*, in a renovated pink church at First and Hagerdine (☎488-2902).

Practicalities

Greyhound (☎482-2516) stops in the center of Ashland at 91 Oak St; *Rogue Valley Transport* (☎799-BUSS) runs local buses between Ashland, Jacksonville and

Medford. The **visitor center**, 110 E Main St (Mon–Fri 9am–5pm; ☎482-3486), has bus schedules and other information about the area. For **accommodation**, the Ashland *AYH Youth Hostel*, 150 N Main St (☎482-9217 – book ahead), or one of the **motels** out along Siskiyou Blvd, should suffice – try the *Palm Motel*, at no 1065 (☎482-2636; ②); or the *Ashland Motel*, no 1145 (☎482-2561; ③). There are also some motels along Main Street, the cheapest being the *Manor Motel*, 476 N Main St (☎482-2246; ②). Otherwise accommodation in the town is relatively expensive, especially the numerous B&Bs which charge up to $150 for a double room.

There are also quite a few good places to **eat and drink**, ranging from soup-and-sandwich spots such as the *Ashland Bakery Café*, 38 E Main St (☎482-2117), to more upscale haunts such as the *Monet* French restaurant, 36 S Second St (☎482-1339); the best place to drink is the *Rogue Brewery*, 31 S Water St just off N Main St (☎488-5061), which has a dozen of Oregon's best micro-brewed beers as well as pizzas and nightly live music.

The Oregon coast

Although I-5 is much the quickest route south from Portland to California, the **Oregon coast** is more scenic – and not as busy as you might expect. The warmer weather draws the tan-seeking masses to California (summer temperatures on the Oregon coast stay in the sixties and seventies), leaving Oregonians and their visitors to wander their elongated shoreline with barely a crowd in sight. While holiday homes and extensive logging operations detract somewhat from the natural beauty, the entire coast is public land: when private ownership threatened to turn Oregon's beaches into havens for the rich during the Sixties, the state passed a bill preserving the lot for "free and uninterrupted" public use. State park after state park lines the shore, scattering campgrounds thickly; there's a strategically useful hostel in lively **Bandon**, and extensive and often isolated beaches offer a multitude of free activities, from beachcombing for Polynesian glass floats and sea-carved driftwood, to shell-fishing, whale-watching, or, in winter, storm-watching. This isn't to say that Oregon has escaped commercialism: small fishing towns, hard-hit by decline, are jumping on to the tourism bandwagon, and it's a lucky traveller who finds a cheap room without booking ahead in July and August, especially in the more beguiling resorts – Cannon Beach, Manzanita, and Bandon.

Give or take the odd logging truck, the coast is almost perfect for cycling (pick up the *Oregon Coast Bike Route* map from any tourist board, which also shows inclines, wind directions and other handy information for cyclists). US-101 follows the coast closely right down to the Californian border, sometimes offering spectacular panoramas, and it's possible to make diversions onto the many, smaller "scenic loop" roads that cling to the clifftops or wind through the inland forests.

Most places can be reached by bus: *Greyhound* run up the coast as far as **Lincoln City**, then cut inland to Portland, from where *Raz Buses* branch out on a coastal loop to **Seaside** and north to **Astoria**. But this leaves a sizeable gap in the northern third of the coast, some of which is covered by a local bus service but the rest of which – between Lincoln City and Cannon Beach – is completely inaccessible by public transportation.

FOOD FORAGING ALONG THE COAST

With patience, the beaches can yield a hearty meal – though there are often limits on the numbers of shellfish and crabs you're allowed to catch, so you'll need to check for local restrictions. You need, also, to know what you're looking for. There are several sorts of **clams**: razor clams are the hardest to catch, moving through the sand remarkably quickly; others are easier game. Gapers, found at a depth of 14 to 16 inches, and softshells, found 8 to 14 inches deep in firmer mud flats, both have meaty and rather phallic-looking "necks"; cockles don't have these (a decided advantage if you're at all squeamish) and are also the easiest to dig, lying just below the surface. Arm yourself with bucket and spade and find a beach where other people are already digging – obviously a likely spot.

Cleaning and cooking gapers and softshells is not for the faint-hearted. You immerse them in fresh warm water until the neck lengthens and the outer skin will slip off easily, then prize the entire clam out of its shell with a sharp knife, peel off the outer skin from the neck, and slit lengthwise. Split open the stomach, remove all the cark material and gelatinous rod and cook as preferred – steamed, fried, battered or in a chunky chowder soup. Cockle clams are much less messy; you just steam them in fresh or salt water until their shells open – some people prefer them almost raw.

For **crabbing**, you'll need to get hold of a crab ring (often rentable) and scrounge a piece of fish for bait. You lower the ring to the bottom of the bay from a boat, pier or dock – and wait. The best time to crab is an hour before or an hour after low and high tides; you're not allowed to keep babies (less than 5.75 inches across) or females (identified by a broad round flap on the underside – the male flap is narrow). To cook a crab, boil it in water for twenty minutes, then crack it, holding its base in one hand, putting your thumb under the shell at midpoint, and pulling off its back. Turn the crab over to remove the leaf-like gills and "butter" from its center – then pick the meat from its limbs.

Astoria

Set at the mouth of the Columbia River, northwest of Portland, **ASTORIA** was the first American attempt at colonizing the West Coast. It was founded as a private commercial venture by the millionaire John Jacob Astor, who wanted to set up a massive Pacific business empire, trading for furs in Alaska. Established in 1811, "Fort Astoria" struggled on for a painful year and a half, beset by natural disasters, internal feuding and supply-line difficulties before selling out to the British: Washington Irving made the best of the saga in his chunky novel *Astoria*. There's a small replica of the old fort at 15th and Exchange, but nowadays Astoria is really a working port, with enough on the historical side to attract a few tourists, but little of the candy-floss razzmatazz of the communities further south.

Arriving from Portland on US-30, the road into Astoria – Marine Drive – runs parallel with the waterfront – a rough place during the nineteenth century, crammed with saloons and brothels, many of which had built-in trap-doors for shanghaiing drunken customers, who might wake up halfway across the Pacific, sold into an unexpected naval career. Shanghaiing got so out of hand at one point that workers on quayside canneries had to carry guns to get themselves safely to the nightshift. It's all much tamer now, though the odd drunk sailor still rolls out of the downtown bars. Exhibits from Astoria's seafaring past are on display at the huge sail-shaped **Columbia River Maritime Museum**, at 17th and Marine Drive (daily 9.30am–5pm; $5), including the red-hulled lightship Columbia that was used to guide ships over the treacherous bar at the mouth of the Columbia River.

From Marine Drive, numbered streets climb towards the uptown area, where wealthy nineteenth-century merchant sea captains and politicians built their elegant mansions, well away from the noise of the port. Several still stand along Franklin and Grand avenues, and **Flavel Mansion**, 441 Eighth St at Duane (summer daily 10am–5pm, winter daily 11am–4pm; $4), has been restored and refurnished in the style of its turn-of-the-century owner, Captain George Flavel, who made his fortune piloting ships across the Columbia River bar. The house's cresting balconies, shingles, wraparound verandas and hipped roofs are a fine example of Queen Anne architecture. The admission charge here also covers the **Heritage Museum**, 1618 Exchange Ave in the old City Hall (same hours), which houses exhibits on the region's history.

High above the town, on top of Coxcomb Hill (follow the signs up 15th and then Coxcomb Drive), the **Astoria Column** is coated with a faded mural depicting the town's early history: inside, a spiral staircase leads up to a magnificent view across the town and the river, as far north as Mount St Helens. Near the column, a concrete replica of an **Indian Burial Canoe** – hundreds of the original wooden versions once littered the banks of the Columbia River – serves as a memorial to Chief Comcomly of the Chinook tribe. He was on fairly amicable terms with the first settlers, one of whom even married his daughter, until he caught his son-in-law hoeing potatoes (woman's work in the chief's opinion). Another of Comcomly's relatives turns up in the saga of **Jane Barnes**, a barmaid from Portsmouth who arrived on an English ship in 1814 to become, Astorians claim, the first white woman in the Northwest. Proposed to by Comcomly's son, among others, Jane turned him down, wreaking havoc with local race relations. None the less, local taverns still nominate honorary barmaid Janes to take part in **Jane Barnes Day**, held in the second week of May.

Practicalities

The *Raz/Greyhound* station is at 364 Ninth St (☎325-5641), connected twice daily with Portland via Seaside to the south. A local bus service, run by *Pacific Transit* (☎206/642-9418), makes connections with the south Washington coast as far as Aberdeen, and *North Coast Transit* (☎738-7083) has a weekday service south to Cannon Beach. The **visitor center** (summer Mon–Sat 8am–6pm, Sun 9am–5pm; Sept–May Mon–Fri 8am–5pm, Sat & Sun 11am–4pm; ☎325-6311), at 111 W Marine Drive, near the base of the US-101 bridge over the Columbia River, is well signposted and well stocked – and its "Walking Tour" leaflet is particularly good ($2.50).

Astoria's pride and joy are its **bed and breakfasts**, mostly housed in the splendid old mansions of the upper town. Among several, there's the enjoyable *Franklin Street Station*, 1140 Franklin at 11th St (☎325-4314; ④/⑤), where three of the six rooms have river views; the *Inn-Chanted*, 707 Eighth St (☎325-5223; ⑤); and the good-looking *Martin and Lilli Foard House*, 690 17th St (☎325-1892; ⑤). But best of all is the *Astoria Inn*, a mile or so east of the town center at 3391 Irving Ave (reservations recommended; ☎325-8153; ⑤); this 1890s farmhouse has sumptuous views out across the Columbia, and footpaths leave the grounds to climb into the surrounding woods. If you're on a tighter budget, several cheap (and pretty grim) **motels** are clustered round the bridge – try the *Lamplighter*, 131 W Marine Drive (☎325-4051; ②), or the *City Center Motel*, 495 Marine Drive (☎325-4211; ②). There's a **youth hostel** on the other side of the Columbia River about four miles away in Washington's Fort Columbia State Park (see p.190), and **camping** in Fort Stevens State Park (see below).

For **food** try the *Pacific Rim Restaurant*, 229 W Marine Drive (☎325-2233), somewhat shabby-looking but near the visitor center and with excellent pasta and pizza. More centrally, the tiny *Columbian Café*, 1114 Marine Drive, has tasty vegetarian and seafood dishes, though the opening hours are as erratic as the menu, while close by is the waterfront *Feed Store* restaurant, at the foot of 11th St (☎325-0279), where the service is good and the meals are filling.

Fort Clatsop and Fort Stevens

Having finally arrived at the mouth of the Columbia River in November 1805, the explorers Lewis and Clark needed a winter base before the long trudge back east. They built **Fort Clatsop** (summer daily 8am–6pm, winter daily 8am–5pm; $4), beside a tributary river six miles southwest of Astoria (off today's US-101) and had a thoroughly miserable time there. It rained on all but 12 of their 106 days, and most of the party caught fleas. Lewis and Clark's log stockade has been reconstructed and the visitor center has a good film show on the expedition. In the summer, staff don furs and britches and act out a "living history" program.

Ten miles west of Astoria off US-101, **Fort Stevens State Park** is a massive recreational area occupying a narrow peninsula that juts out into the Columbia, separating the river from the ocean. There are trails, lakes, camping and miles of beaches, on one of which lies the **wreck of the Peter Iredale**, a British schooner that got caught out by high winds in 1906. Fortifications were first put up at Fort Stevens to guard against Confederate raiders entering the Columbia River during the Civil War, though **Battery Russell** was part of World War II defences. It did, in fact, get shelled one night by a passing Japanese submarine, which makes it, incredibly, the only military installation on the mainland US to have been fired on by a foreign power since 1812. A small **Military Museum**, one mile north of the campground, details this and other events (mid-May to Sept daily 10am–6pm; Oct to mid-May Wed–Sun 10am–4pm).

Seaside

Sixteen miles down the coast from Astoria, **SEASIDE** is a small-town resort, full of amusement arcades, hot dogs, cotton candy and all the other things its name suggests. The local authorities have recently tried to spruce the place up, tidying the main street, Broadway, and promoting Seaside as a conference center. But they haven't entirely suceeded, and it's really the enduring tackiness that lends the town its character.

Not surprisingly, the long sandy **beach** provides the main focus in town and it won't take long to exhaust Seaside's other few features. Behind the beach is the two-mile boardwalk (actually concrete), divided into the North and South Prom by The Turnaround, at the foot of Broadway, where a bronze sculpture pays homage to Lewis and Clark. From their winter camp at Fort Clatsop, three members of the Lewis and Clark expedition ventured south to Seaside to spend a tedious few weeks boiling down gallons of seawater to make salt – vital to preserve meat for the journey back. This hard labor is commemorated by a rock replica of their salt cairn, just east of the South Prom on Lewis and Clark Way. The small **Historical Museum**, at 570 Necanicum Drive (daily 10.30am– 4.30pm), north of the Convention Center, details other aspects of the town's history, from a smattering of Clatsop artifacts to the foundation of Seaside as Oregon's first coastal resort in the early 1870s.

Practicalities

Seaside is served by the twice-daily *Raz* route between Portland and Astoria, which stops at 325 S Holladay Drive and Broadway (☎738-5121); *North Coast Transit* (☎738-7083) services leave from the same intersection, heading north to Astoria and south to Cannon Beach, Mondays to Fridays only. Further details, and general information, are available from the helpful **visitor center**, 7 N Roosevelt, at Broadway (summer Mon–Fri 8am–6pm, Sat 10am–4pm, Sun noon– 4pm; shorter hours in winter; ☎738-6391 or 1-800/444-6740).

There are plenty of **motels**, but also lots of tourists in summer; as elsewhere along the coast, book ahead. The *Riverside Inn*, 430 S Holladay Drive (☎738-8254; ③), officially a bed and breakfast, is a good cut above the average motel; the *Mariner-Holladay Motel*, 429 S Holladay Drive (☎738-3690; ②–③) next door, is cheaper, while the luxurious *Shilo Inn*, 30 North Prom (☎738-9571; ⑥), occupies a prime oceanside location – it's the poshest place in town. There's nothing too remarkable by way of **food**, though plenty of low-priced restaurants and cafés line Broadway, one of the best being *Dooger's*, 505 Broadway at Franklin (☎738-3778), where you should stick to the seafood.

Cannon Beach

Nine miles south of Seaside, **CANNON BEACH** is a more upmarket resort. The town, which takes its name from several cannon that washed on to the beach from the wreck of a USS warship, the *Shark*, in 1846, now sees itself as a refined and cultured place, and has building regulations to match – there are no neon signs, and even the supermarket is tastefully draped with Fifties advertisements for coffee and cigarettes. On the tiny main street, painters sell their work from weathered cedar galleries, while tourists and visiting Portlanders wander from bookshop to bistro. The resort is at its liveliest during the great annual **Sandcastle Competition**, a one-day event held late May or early June: what Cannes is to film, Cannon Beach is to sandcastle-building, and past subjects have included dinosaurs, sphinxes, even the Crucifixion. Photographs of past master-pieces are on display at the **visitor center**, at Spruce and Second (Mon–Fri 11am–5pm, Sun 11am–4pm; ☎436-2623), which also has a very good range of practical information.

The wide and long sandy beach is dominated by the great, black monolith of **Haystack Rock**, crowned with nesting seagulls and puffins while starfish, mussels and other shellfish shelter at its base. But increasing numbers of tourists wandering among the sea-creatures has caused ecological consternation, and now, during the summer, volunteers are strategically placed with information and binoculars. To escape the crush, head the four miles north to **Ecola State Park**, where dense conifer forests decorate the basaltic cliffs of Tillamook Head. The park has several walking trails, a beach and a primitive, hikers-only campground.

Practicalities

Cannon Beach is served by the *North Coast Transit* service from Astoria or Seaside, Monday through Friday. **Accommodation** is always tight over the summer, and booked solid during the sandcastle competition. The *Mcbee Motel*, 888 S Hemlock St (☎436-2569; ②–③) and *Hidden Villa*, 188 E Van Buren St (☎436-2237; ②–③), are both close to the beach. The *Blue Gull Inn,* 632 S Hemlock St (☎436-2714; ③–④), is somewhat more expensive, but does have a sauna, while the *Cannon Beach Hotel*, 1116 S Hemlock at Gower (436-1392; ③–④) has an informal boarding-house air that's a big improvement on most of its motel-style rivals.

For **food**, the outlook is good: *Lazy Susan Café*, 126 N Hemlock St (☎436-2816), opposite the *Coaster Theater*, does excellent health-food brunches and lunches; *Osburn's Deli*, just down the road at 240 N Hemlock St (☎436-2234), has a good deli selection and sidewalk seats; the *Bistro*, 263 N Hemlock St (☎436-2661), has a tasty range of fresh seafood and the town's best bar.

South to Lincoln City

South of Cannon Beach, the highway threads through the wooded hills that overlook the ocean, passing a string of State Parks on the way. At the first two, the **Tolovana** and **Arcadia** waysides, there are excellent sandy beaches, and the third, **Oswald West**, incorporates two sharp, densely forested headlands, Cape Falcon and **Neah-Kah-Nie Mountain**, which has been linked with legends of buried treasure since a Spanish galleon was wrecked here in the 1700s. There's a steep two-mile track to the top of Neah-Kah-Nie, and the park also possesses a beach and primitive **campground** (mid-March to Oct), a fifteen-minute walk from the parking lot.

Manzanita

Continuing south, there are magnificent views out along the coast as US-101 twists round the precipitous mass of Neah-Kah-Nie. Down below, some fifteen miles from Cannon Beach, lies **MANZANITA,** the prettiest resort for miles, a few mainly modern blocks framed by a splendid sandy beach – a good spot for windsurfers – and pine-studded dunes. Close to the beach, the best place to stay is the *Inn at Manzanita*, 67 Laneda St (☎368-6754; ⑤), whose eight units are spacious and comfortable. There are cheaper and more mundane options too – such as the *Coachman Motor Inn*, 114 Laneda St (☎368-5245; ③–④) – as well as **camping** at **Nehalem Bay State Park** just south of town. Inland, accessed by narrow paved roads, the **Tillamook State Forest** stretches vast and green, having recovered from the 1933 forest fire, which devoured five hundred square miles of timberland in a week-long blaze – economically disastrous for the nearby logging communities. The scorched area, known as the Tillamook Burn and made worse by later fires, prompted Oregon to begin state-managed forestry, and a massive scheme was launched to replant the trees, completed in 1973.

Tillamook

Further south still, the ugly sprawl of Rockaway Beach mars the beauty of the adjacent beach, whose white and windswept sands extend for almost six miles. Beyond is Garibaldi, a tacky-looking fishing town, and then **TILLAMOOK**, a plain dairy town whose two cheese-making factories are trying hard to turn themselves into tourist attractions. Two miles north of the town on US-101, a quick glimpse of workers in wellington boots bent over large vats of orange-colored Tillamook cheddar is all you get in the **Tillamook County Creamery Association** before the factory's cavernous gift shop/restaurant takes over. Further along US-101, the **Blue Heron French Cheese Factory** is slightly less gimmicky and has wine tasting – but in either factory you have to be fiendishly skilful with a cocktail stick to spear a sizeable free cheese sample (and the cheese is pretty bland anyway). A **visitor center**, 3705 Hwy-101, across the parking lot from the Tillamook Creamery (summer Mon–Fri 9am–5pm, Sat & Sun 2–5pm; shorter hours in winter; ☎842-7525), provides information and sticks accommodation lists on the door when it's closed. Downtown, the **Tillamook County Pioneer Museum**, at Second and Pacific (summer Mon–Sat 8.30am–5pm, Sun noon–5pm; winter closed Mon; $1), in the old county courthouse, has displays on wildlife and pioneer life, including a portrayal of logging developments from the beginning of the century, with a full-size fire-watch station.

Most of the **motels** are on Hwy-101 in the north of town, such as the inexpensive *Coastway Motel*, 1910 Hwy-101 (☎842-6651; ③), and the pricier *Shilo Inn*, 2515 Main St (☎842-7971; ④). There are no regular bus services covering the eighty-mile stretch of coast between Cannon Beach and Lincoln City.

Scenic loop roads to Lincoln City

Leading west out of Tillamook, the 35-mile clifftop detour around the **Three Capes Scenic Loop** is much more exciting than the main route down US-101. The loop begins by climbing **Cape Meares**, on the southern arm of broad **Tillamook Bay** (once called "Murderer's Harbor" after Indians killed a sailor from Gray's expedition here in 1788). The restored **lighthouse** (Wed–Sun 11am–6pm), built at the end of the last century, has a small photo exhibition inside, and outside you have a truly magnificent view of the rocky coast. Further on, **Cape Lookout State Park** incorporates **Netarts Bay**, a shallow and narrow stretch of water that's a favorite spot for clamming and crabbing – the bay is protected from the Pacific by a slender sandspit. At the south end of the bay is the park's **campground** and further south again is the cape that gives the park its name, a wooded headland crossed by a 2.5-mile trail that offers superb views.

Back on the highway, it's a few miles south to Cape Kiwanda, a steep sandstone promontory that's partly protected by a monolithic sea stack, **Haystack Rock**. The headland makes up most of the Kiwanda State Park, near the tiny town of Pacific City, a desultory sort of place whose only distinction is its **dory fleet** of special fishing boats which can be launched through the surf straight into the oncoming breakers. Overhead, hang-gliders often launch themselves off the cape, landing (they hope) on the wide sandy beach. Shortly after Pacific City you rejoin US-101 to proceed to Neskowin, where there's a turning for another detour, the **Cascade Head Scenic Loop**, this one taking you inland through forest and farmland coming out at the one-shop town of Otis, home to the *Otis Café* (☎994-2813), an excellent and inexpensive small-town café.

Lincoln City

There's no avoiding **LINCOLN CITY** – probably the ugliest town on the coast – without swinging miles inland. Actually the merged version of five small beach towns, run together in 1965, Lincoln City rattles along the highway for seven and a half congested, motel-lined miles. One faint ray of interest is the **kite-flying**: conditions along the long, windswept beach are often excellent, and there are a couple of major kite-flying festivals – one in spring, on Mothers' Day weekend, the other in September. The *Catch the Wind Kite Shop* (☎994-9500) coastal chain have their headquarters here at 266 SE US-101; they have kites in all shapes and colors and for all different types of wind conditions. **Lacey's Doll and Antique Museum**, 3400 N US-101 (daily; summer 8am–5pm, otherwise 9am–4pm; $2), has Dolly Parton and Shirley Temple dolls among its bizarre exhibits.

Behind Lincoln City is **Devil's Lake**, whose unenticing waters curve round towards the ocean beside US-101 at NE Sixth Drive, off which you'll find the busy **campgrounds** of Devil's Lake State Park. The 100-foot "D" River, sometimes inaccurately claimed as the shortest river in the world, links the lake with the ocean. The boat dock adjoining the campground rents out paddle boats. From behind the bridge over the "D" River, you can walk to the beach with its myriad colorful kites and windsocks fluttering in the sky.

Practicalities

Greyhound buses, 316 SE US-101 (☎994-8418), reappear here, running to Portland and south down the coast, so you might even end up staying – especially since Lincoln City will have rooms long after other beach towns are full up. The **visitor center**, (Mon–Fri 9am–5pm, Sat 10am–5pm, Sun 10am–4pm; ☎994-2164 or 1-800/452-2151) has lists of bargain-basement motels, such as the clean and fairly reasonable *City Center Motel*, 1014 NE US-101 (☎994-2612; ②), but most of these are strung out along the noisy main drag. Better – and pricier – alternatives are nearer the beach – try the *Sea Horse Oceanfront Motel*, 2039 NW Harbor Drive (☎994-2101 or 1-800/662-2101; ③–④), or the *Seagull Motel*, along the street at no 1511 (☎994-2948 or 1-800/422-0219; ②–⑥). The food is as you might expect, with exceptions to the mediocre rule including the seafood at *Barnacle Bill's*, 2174 NW US-101 (☎994-3022), and *Kyllo's*, 2733 NW US-101 (☎994-3179).

The coast to Newport

Beyond Lincoln City, US-101 skirts Siletz Bay before slicing down to Depoe Bay, a small harbor town at the start of one of the most beautiful stretches of the coast. Turning off the highway two miles south of town, the daunting scenery is best appreciated along the **Otter Creek Loop**, a four-mile section of the old coast road which edges its way precariously around the sheer rock walls of **Cape Foulweather**. The cape was discovered and named by a jaded Captain Cook, whose historic expedition up the Pacific Coast had nearly been dispatched to a watery grave by a sudden Northwest storm – the wind up here can reach 100mph. Further on a turning leads to the **Devil's Punchbowl** – and state park – a sandstone cave whose roof has fallen in, the sea foaming up cauldron-like at high tide and receding to reveal pools of sea-creatures. Back on the highway, you soon reach the magnificent sands of **Beverly Beach**, part of which is designated a state park with camping and picnic facilities, and further south still, just before Newport, there's a turning to **Yaquina Head Lighthouse** (summer daily noon–5pm; 50¢). This gives an unsurpassed view of the coast, overlooking **Agate Beach**, where winter storms toss up agates from gravelly beds under the sea. If you walk along the beach towards the sun on an outgoing tide, the agates (after a winter storm, at least) sparkle up at you: moonstone agates are clear, carnelians are bright red and transparent, and ribbon agates have colored layers. Local shops provide both information and more accessible agates.

Newport

Like so many other coastal fishing towns, **NEWPORT** has been turned into a bustling, often crassly commercial resort, though here at least there are remnants of more vigorous times, from the working harbor along Bay Boulevard – home to one of Oregon's more successful fishing fleets – to the turn-of-the-century timber houses of the old bayfront nearby. Some of the tourist industry packaging is also surprisingly chic, especially the smart grey wood, dark glass and sophisticated neon logos of the *Mariner Square* tourist development. And there's an artsy undertone to the place as well, manifest in the oceanfront Visual Arts Center and the new Performing Arts Center, both on Nye Beach.

Geographically, Newport sits on a narrow neck of land separating the Pacific from Yaquina Bay to the south of town. Visitors take a look at Bay Boulevard, overloooking Yaquina Bay, but it's the ocean that really pulls the crowds, thronging the beaches up as far as **Nye Beach**, a mile or two north of the river mouth, where you've more than enough space to breathe. On the south side of arching Yaquina Bay bridge, the **Mark O Hatfield Marine Science Center** (daily; summer 10am–6pm, winter 10am–4pm; free), on Marine Science Drive, is the base of Oregon State University's coastal research, and various curious sea-creatures swim around in display tanks; next door the brand-new, state-of-the-art **Oregon Coast Aquarium** (same times) has more entertaining and educational displays.

Practicalities

Newport's a nice place to stay over: there's a pleasant, relaxed feel to the town, some appealing cafés and restaurants, and a couple of good budget **accommodation** options, the highlight of which is the *Sylvia Beach Hotel*, 267 NW Cliff (☎265-9231; ①–④). Named after the owner of the *Shakespeare and Co.* bookstore in Paris during the Twenties and Thirties, the hotel aims to encourage modern would-be writers – there's a cozy attic library, and dorm beds go for $25 a night, including breakfasts. Other rooms are decorated in the styles of various writers (the Poe room has a guillotine over the bed), but they're small and pricey. As far as **motels** go, it's the usual story – less of the roar of the sea, and more of the roar of US-101. The best of them is probably the *Penny Saver*, 710 N Coast Highway (☎265-6631; ②). The *Puerto Nuevo Inn*, 544 SW US-101 (☎265-5767; ③–④), is new and has good rooms with a view of the sea. There are popular **campgrounds** in Beverly Beach State Park (☎265-9278) north of town (see above), and in the South Beach State Park (☎867-4715), two miles south of the bridge.

Maps with complete motel and campground listings are available from the **Chamber of Commerce**, 555 SW Coast Highway (summer Mon–Fri 8.30am–5pm, Sat & Sun 10am–4pm; winter Mon–Fri 8.30am–5pm; ☎265-8801 or 1-800/262-7844; ③–④). *Greyhound* pulls in at 956 SW Tenth St (☎265-2253). For **food**, the *Whale's Tale*, 452 SW Bay Blvd (☎265-8660), has a varied menu (German, Greek, Cajun, vegetarian), live music at weekends – and a large piece of whale's vertebrae suspended from the ceiling. At lunchtime the *Boardwalk Café* on Bay

Blvd (☎265-5028) serves good soups, sandwiches and desserts. Nearby, the *Canyon Way Restaurant and Bookstore*, 1216 SW Canyon Way (☎265-8319), is another pleasant place; at Nye Beach, the *Chowder Bowl*, 728 NW Beach Drive (☎265-7477), is good value, as is the Italian *Don Petrie's*, 613 NW Third (☎265-3663), across the road.

Cape Perpetua and the Sea Lion Caves

South of Newport, the huge **Siuslaw National Forest** closes in around the highway, its creeks and rivers threaded by shady forest roads, while the coastline is scattered with campgrounds and state park beaches. **Cape Perpetua**, 25 miles out from Newport, is the center of one of the most spectacular stretches of the Oregon coast. The drive along US-101 is incredibly scenic, with dense forests climbing above the anything-but-pacific surf crashing against the rocks below. Numerous hiking trails loop around from the well-marked **Cape Perpetua Visitor Center** (daily 10am–4pm; ☎547-3289), just off US-101, the most impressive being the strenuous four-mile trek to the cape's 800-foot-high summit. There's a forest service **campground** close by, beside Cape Creek, and there's more hiking, and camping, at **Washburne State Park**, eight miles south. Here, and at the adjoining **Devil's Elbow State Park**, the tidepools and beaches of the shoreline flank **Heceta Head** where the lighthouse, an 1893 Queen Anne-style structure, looks far too petite to withstand the endless onslaught of the sea.

A few minutes' drive further south, the **Sea Lion Caves** (summer daily 8am–dusk; winter daily 9am–dusk; ☎547-3111; $5) are the year-round home of hundreds of sea lions, who sprawl over the rocks during the summer breeding season but in the winter hide away in a massive cave, whose rock walls echo the combined roar of sea and beast; access is by stairs and an elevator. Beyond the caves, the views along US-101 get less incredible, the natural splendor having all but vanished (only for a while, though) by the time you reach Florence, roughly midway along the Oregon coast.

Florence and the dunes

FLORENCE, at the mouth of the Siuslaw River, eleven miles south of the Sea Lion Caves, was once a Siuslaw settlement; nowadays, the town doesn't look like much from the highway, but azaleas and rhododendrons grow wild along the roadside (there's an annual **Rhododendron Festival** in the third week of May, when they're all in bloom), and the **Old Town**, along the harbor front, has been pleasantly revamped.

Practicalities

Greyhound **buses** drop off at 2107 US-101 (☎997-8782), just north of the town center, and there's a **Chamber of Commerce** – good for information on the dunes (see below) – at 270 US-101 (☎997-3128), just north of the river bridge. **Accommodation** is on the pricey side, though the *Money Saver Motel*, 170 US-101 (☎997-7131; ②) near Old Town, and the *Silver Sands Motel*, 1449 US-101 (☎997-3459; ②) are good budget options; *Driftwood Shores*, 88416 First Ave (☎997-8263 or 1-800/824-8744; ⑤), north of town at Heceta Beach, is Florence's only beachfront resort, with fairly standard, sea-view doubles. Florence's bed and breakfasts compare favorably with the motels – try *Johnson House*, one block north of the river at 216 Maple St (☎997-8000; ④), where the food is excellent, the vegetables home-grown; or the twee *Edwin K*, on the west edge of the Old Town at 1155 Bay St (997-8360; ④).

For **food**, head down to the Old Town waterfront, just north of the US-101 bridge, where the *Harbour House Café*, 1368 Bay St (☎997-6816), and the more upmarket *Bridgewater Restaurant*, across the street (☎997-9405), do a top-notch range of fresh seafood.

The dunes

It's **the dunes**, beginning just south of Florence, that dominate the coast as far as Coos Bay: 41 miles of shifting sandhills, punctuated with pockets of forests and lakes. It's thought they were formed by the crumbling of the sandstone mountains back in the interior, with the rivers washing the sediment down to the coast where it dried out on the beach before being picked up and drifted into dunes by the prevailing winds. The best way to explore the dunes is on foot, and there are many hiking trails (taking you far away from the manic buggy riders), including the **Tahkenitch/Three Mile Lakes Trail**, a six-mile loop through dunes, lakes and forest. The trail begins at the Tahkenitch Lake **campground**, seven miles to the north of Reedsport, where the **Oregon Dunes National Recreation Area Information Center**, at the intersection of US-101 and Hwy-38 (summer Mon–Fri 8am–4.30pm, Sat & Sun 10am–5.30pm; winter Mon–Fri 8am–4.30pm; ☎271-3611), has masses of information on hiking, camping and wildlife.

Alternatively, you can, if you must, rent ATVs ("all-terrain vehicles") from *Sandland Adventures*, on US-101 at Tenth St, behind the *Shell* station back in Florence ($25 for the first hour, $50 deposit; ☎997-8087); *Sand Dunes Frontier*, 83960 US-101 S, Florence (☎997-3544), offers a comparable service and organizes dune buggy excursions.

Coos Bay and around

The dunes end as the coastline curves into narrow, V-shaped **Coos Bay**, which groups around its deep natural harbor the merged industrial towns of North Bend and Coos Bay, and the smaller fishing town of Charleston. Forestry and shipping are the economic mainstays here. You'll pass the huge plant of **Weyerhauser**, the biggest name in the Northwest timber industry, on US-101 in North Bend: it offers tours of its sawmill if you're interested. Heavy freighters pull in to pick up shiploads of timber further on in **COOS BAY**, the largest and most industrial town along the Oregon coast. If you want to stop off here, there are factory tours of the **House of Myrtlewood**, just off US-101 at First St (☎267-7804), where rare myrtlewood, indigenous to southwest Oregon, is carved by craftspeople. The main **visitor center** (☎756-4613) is on Sherman Ave, near the south foot of the McCullough Bridge. *Greyhound* stops at 275 N Broadway (☎267-6517). Lots of **motels** are scattered along US-101.

Some eight miles southwest of North Bend, along a byroad following the southern shore of the bay, the small and rather tatty sports-fishing town of **CHARLESTON** is surrounded by a trio of parks, connected by a four-mile cliff-top hiking trail. Enclosed by sandstone cliffs, **Sunset Bay** three miles west of Charleston, is shallow, protected and ideal for swimming, while next to it, **Shore Acres State Park** was once the estate of a shipping tycoon – his lavish mansion burnt down, but the formal gardens survived, laid out with exotic plants and open to the public. South of Shore Acres, **Cape Arago** offers whale-watching, and a view of the seals and sea lions who breed on nearby reefs: tidal pools around the cape's coves house anemones, purple sea urchins, starfish and crabs. More wildlife can be seen at the **South Slough National Estuary Sanctuary**, also near Charleston. These 26 miles of forest and tideflats preserve numerous plants, animals and birds, and are thought to be the inspiration for a local Native American legend about "Baldiyasa" – the place where life began.

Back on the main highway, US-101 stays inland after skirting the southern tip of Coos Bay, slipping through the forested interior on its way to Bandon.

Bandon

Twenty-odd miles south of Coos Bay, easy-going, small-town **BANDON**'s combination of old town restoration work and New Age style make it a far more intriguing place to pass a day or two. Since former habitués of Haight Ashbury and Venice Beach in California moved up here in the late Sixties, the town has grown into something of an arts and crafts center, and "far-out" theories abound. Equipped with one of the state's largest metaphysical bookstores, *Winter River*, Bandon stands, according to a local New Age chiropractor, directly on a ley-line going from the Bering Sea to the Bahamas, making it one of the earth's "acupuncture points".

Located rather more obviously at the mouth of the Coquille River, Bandon was originally a Native American settlement, but the town only developed in the mid-nineteenth century with the onset of the Gold Rush. This century began rather ominously when townsfolk dynamited Tupper Rock, a sacred tribal site located behind today's Jetty Rd on the west edge of town, to build the sea wall, and the town was cursed to burn down three times: it's happened twice so far, in 1914 and 1936, and the superstitious are still waiting. In 1990, the site was deeded back to the Indians, in order to ward off any more bad vibes.

Bandon's main attraction today is its rugged **beach**, whose unusual rock formations – magnificent in stormy weather – have given rise to Native American legends, anthropomorphic notions such as Face Rock being a young woman frozen by an evil sea spirit. In the town, Bandon's history is on display at the **Coquille River Museum**, in the Coast Guard building overlooking the river, near the west end of First St (Tues–Sat noon–4pm; $1). Further out, there's **swimming** at Bradley Lake, a fresh water lagoon sheltered by trees and sand dunes two miles south along Beach Loop Road (there's no signpost – look for a layby on the bend just before Blue Jay Campground) or you can go clamming in the mud-flats of the Coquille River, and crabbing from the town pier. Cranberries are big business in Bandon – you'll see them growing in bogs – and the annual extravaganza here is the **Cranberry Festival** held over four days in late September and early October, featuring a parade, square dancing and a food fair with numerous recipes for the rampant red berry.

Practicalities

Overlooking the harbor, the *Sea Star Guest House*, at 375 Second St (☎347-9632; ③–⑤), is a good **place to stay**, and offers reductions out of season. The *Sea Star Hostel*, at the same address and run by the same management, offers the best budget accommodation – it's the only *AYH* hostel in the state that doesn't have a curfew. Alternatively, Beach Loop Road, running along the coast south of town, is lined with resort hotels and motels: try the *Sunset Resort*, no 1755 (☎347-2543; ②–⑤), or the commodious *Inn at Face Rock*, no 3225 (☎347-9441 or 1-800/638-3092; ③–④). There's **camping** just north of town across the river at **Bullards Beach State Park** (☎347-2209), where a refurbished 1896 lighthouse stands guard over miles of marshy wilderness. You can **eat** great seafood at *Andrea's Old Town Café* (☎347-3022), two blocks from the hostel on Baltimore, while the small *Sea Star bistro* in the hostel itself does an excellent range of meals from $9 and up. The **visitor center** (June–Oct daily 10am–5pm; Nov–May daily 10am–4.30pm; ☎347-9616) is right off US-101 in the town center. Their daily *Coffee Break* free newssheet lists local news and activities, and they also have a handy walking-tour map of the town.

Port Orford

Towns become fewer and further between as you travel south from Bandon along US-101. The first major stop, after 26 miles, is **PORT ORFORD**, a desultory little fishing-port-cum-resort. Its only attraction is **Battle Rock**, a much-trampled-over rocky outcrop which was the site of an early struggle between white settlers, the crew of the steamship *Sea Gull*, and local Native Americans, Rogue Indians, in 1851. It's beside US-101 on the south side of town next door to the seasonal **visitor center** (☎332-8055).

   Greyhound stop by the "K" foodstore at Ninth and Oregon and, if you break your journey here, you can choose from three basic **motels**, one of which is the *Castaway*, 545 W Fifth St (☎332-4502; ③). But you're probably better off **camping** at either of two state parks, the first being **Cape Blanco**, nine miles north of town off US-101, where you can walk down to the lighthouse at the tip of the headland and also inspect several pioneer relics – a cemetery, a church and the two-story **Hughes House** (daily except Tues & Wed 10am–5pm) of 1898. The second park, beside US-101 six miles south of town, is **Humbug Mountain**, comprising a mighty coastal headland whose 1756-foot summit is reached along a three-mile switchback trail.

Gold Beach and the Rogue River

South of Port Orford, grass-covered and partly forested mountains sweep smoothly to the shoreline. The wild and scenic **Rogue River** reaches the sea at **GOLD BEACH**, a small and undistinguished town largely devoted to packing visitors off on rafts and jet-boats, up canyons and through roaring rapids into the depths of the **Siskiyou National Forest**. During the summer, *Mail Boat Hydro-Jets* (☎247-7033 or 1-800/458-3511) and *Jerry's Rogue Jets* (☎247-4571 or 1-800/451-3645) charge roughly the same for either a six-hour trip as far as the town of Agness and back ($27), or a longer eight-hour trip, which bounces you over stretches of white water ($65); times include two-hour lunch breaks at a mountain resort, but food isn't included in the price.

   If you don't fancy a boat-trip, but want to see something of the mountains, head to the **Shrader Old Growth Forest**, nine miles east of town via Jerry's Flat Road, which winds along the south bank of the river. It's one of the few coastal groves never to have been logged, so the dense stands of cedar and fir are a haven for a variety of wildlife, notably the threatened Spotted Owl. A mile-long trail winds through the forest, and there's a pamphlet which describes the various features of this rare undisturbed environment – which seems all the more special after you've passed through the clear-cut hillsides on the way here. If you're a good hiker, you might also consider the forty-mile **Rogue River Trail**, which follows the bank of the river twelve miles inland, eventually linking up with other routes to reach all the way to Grave Creek, 27 miles northwest of Grants Pass (see p.104). There are several **campgrounds** and **lodges** on the way, including the good-quality *Lucas Lodge* (☎247-7443; ③) in Agness, 32 miles up-river, which welcomes weary hikers with all-you-can-eat chicken and home-grown corn-on-the-cob dinners for $10. All the lodges require reservations; the best time to walk the trail is in the spring before summer temperatures turn the river valley into a heated cauldron. Details on this and other hikes are available from the Gold Beach **Ranger District Office** (Mon–Fri 9am–5pm; ☎247-6651), 1225 S Ellensburg Ave on the south side of town. Less adventurously, the **Curry County Museum** (June–Sept Tues–Sat noon–4pm; Oct–May Sat noon–4pm; free) at 920 S Ellensburg Ave has old pictures of the town.

Practicalities

Gold Beach **visitor center**, also at 1225 S Ellensburg Ave (Mon–Fri 9am–5pm; ☎247-7526 or 1-800/525-2334), has all manner of practical information on the town including maps, bus timetables and motel lists. The nicest of the **motels** are the clean and quiet *River Bridge Inn* (☎247-4533; ②), just off US-101 at the south end of the Rogue River Bridge, and the more expensive *Gold Beach Resort* (☎247-7066; ⑤), 1330 S Ellensburg Ave, near the south end of town, where many of the spacious rooms overlook the ocean. Another option is the oceanside *Inn at Nesika Beach Bed & Breakfast* (☎247-6434; ④), west of US-101 down Nesika Road, five miles north of Gold Beach. For **food**, try the fish at *The Captain's Table*, 1295 S Ellensburg (☎247-6308), or the pizzas and burgers of the *Crow's Nest*, 565 N Ellensburg. Gold Beach *Greyhound* have a kiosk on the north side of town one block off Ellensburg at 310 Colvin St and Caughell (☎247-7246).

Brookings

Down towards the California border is Oregon's "banana belt" – of which **BROOKINGS**, 29 miles south of Gold Beach, is the capital. Warmed by drifting thermal troughs from the Californian coast, this area is unusually sunny (often over 70°F in January) making it popular with retirees, and the local industry is, appropriately enough, the genteel art of flower growing – most of North America's Easter lilies are grown here, and some of the local azaleas are over twenty feet high and three hundred years old, inspiring the annual **Azalea Festival** on Memorial Day weekend at the end of May. *Greyhound* (☎469-3326) stops at Cottage and Pacific, and there's a **visitor center** (Mon–Fri 9am–5pm; ☎469-3181) on the left hand side of US-101, opposite the shopping mall. But a quick look at the harbor is all Brookings really merits, and there's little here to keep you from the **beaches and state parks** that stretch out on both sides of the town.

The coastline immediately north of Brookings, especially along the ten-mile stretch of **Samuel Boardman State Park**, is magnificently rugged, the roadway dangling above rocky coves and giving sweeping views out over the Pacific. There isn't much between Brookings and California, but just over the border are the Jedediah Smith Redwoods, forming the northern reaches of the **Redwood National Park** where you'll find the world's first-, third- and sixth-highest trees. You have to pass through part of the park to make the loop to the Oregon Caves and Grants Pass on Hwy-199, the only way over the mountains.

travel details

Trains
From Portland to Baker (1 daily; 7hr 15min); Boise, Idaho (1 daily; 10hr); The Dalles (1 daily; 1hr 40min); Eugene (1 daily; 2hr 30min); Klamath Falls (1 daily; 6hr 30min); La Grande (1 daily; 6hr 15min); Los Angeles (1 daily; 29hr); Pendleton (1 daily; 4hr), Salem (1 daily; 1hr 15min); Seattle (3 daily; 4hr), with buses on to Vancouver, Canada; Tacoma (3 daily; 3hr).

Buses
Greyhound services **from Portland** include buses to Albany (5 daily; 1hr 40min); Ashland (3 daily; 7hr 50min); Bend (1 daily; 4hr 25min); Eugene (7 daily; 3hr); Grants Pass (4 daily; 6hr 45min); Klamath Falls (2 daily; 7hr 15min); Medford (6 daily; 7hr 25min); Olympia (6 daily; 2hr 30min); Roseburg (4 daily; 4hr 50min); Salem (7 daily; 1hr); Seattle (9 daily; 4hr 10min); Spokane (2 daily; 10hr 30min); Vancouver, BC (2 daily; 9hr 30min).

A further two *Greyhound* buses per day run from **Portland** to Lincoln City (2hr 45min), Newport (3hr 45min), Florence (5hr 10min), Bandon (7hr 20min), Gold Beach (8hr 50min), Klamath Falls (11hr), and San Francisco (20hr).

Green Tortoise run 2–4 buses weekly **from Portland** to Ashland (10hr), Eugene (3hr 15min), San Francisco (20hr) and Seattle (5hr).

If you're continuing south to California, the **Rough Guide to California** is an invaluable companion.

CHAPTER TWO

EASTERN OREGON

E ast of the Cascades, Oregon grows wilder and less hospitable. The temperature rises, the drizzle stops, and green valleys give way to scrubby sageland, bare hills and stark rock formations, surrounded on occasion by impenetrable forest. Though nowhere near as popular a destination as the lush coastal areas, the region still has its attractions, particularly in the north. At the **John Day Fossil Beds**, prehistoric skeletons of plants and animals lie embedded in crumbly red and green rock. Further northeast, small-town farming and ranching communities such as **Pendleton**, site of the famous **Pendleton Round-Up** rodeo, and **Baker City**, make good places to break the long journey east to the snow-capped **Wallowa Mountains** overlooking the long deep slash of **Hells Canyon**. In the south, around the small but pleasant town of **Bend**, ancient volcanoes have produced the oddly scarred landscape of the **Lava Lands** – though it comes as a surprise to most first-time visitors that the rest of southeastern Oregon is barren desert and virtually uninhabited.

None of this terrain looked very promising to early immigrants, who hurried on along the Oregon Trail to the prime farmland further west. One bemoaned "This barren, God-forsaken country is fit for nothing but to receive the footprints of the savage and his universal associate the coyote". Those settlers who did brave the east found homesteading a precarious, stockaded affair; at one point it was forbidden altogether by officials who feared for the safety of the white pioneers, and saw the Cascades as "a valuable separation of the races". Petty restrictions were swept away in the early 1860s, when the discovery of gold in Baker and Grant counties prompted a short-lived **gold rush**. To feed the miners, herds of cattle were driven over the Cascades from the Willamette Valley, thousands of animals flourishing on the bunchgrass and meadowgrass of the interior. The native population was displaced, in a series of skirmishes that escalated into successive mini-wars and only fizzled out when the indigenous inhabitants were confined to reservations.

Later, there was more violence, this time between the cattle ranchers and their rivals, the sheep farmers. Cattlemen formed themselves into terrorist squads, and "Sheepshooters" associations committed dire atrocities on the woolly usurpers during Eastern Oregon's "range wars". Sheep and cows now safely graze side by side, and some small towns still celebrate their cowboy roots with annual rodeos — though the great sheep and cattle empires of the late nineteenth century have mostly faded away, especially in northeast Oregon which, with its milder climate and moisture-holding soils, has proved ideal for wheat-growing.

TELEPHONE NUMBERS
Oregon Tourism Division ☎ 1-800/547-7842.
The telephone **area code** for all Oregon is ☎503.

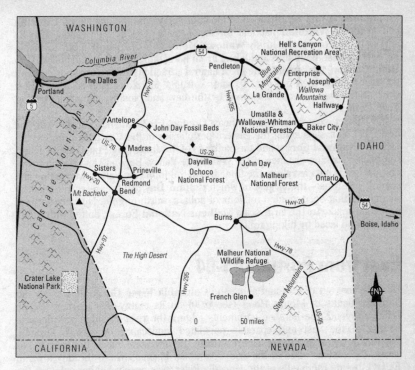

Eastern Oregon's **public transportation** is thin on the ground: *Greyhound* run east from Portland along the Columbia River, serving Pendleton, La Grande and Baker in the northeast corner on the way to Boise, Idaho. A second route from Portland dips through the mountains to Bend. *Amtrak* parallels *Greyhound* to Pendleton, La Grande and Baker, and crosses the Cascades below Eugene to run south to California via Klamath Falls. Local bus services are negligible, and hitching is illegal throughout Oregon. If you want to explore, you'll really need a car – especially if you've come here for the wide-open spaces, in which case you'll also need to escape the mostly mundane **motels** of the highways for the many **campgrounds** of the wilderness.

NORTHEAST OREGON

The remoteness and isolation of **northeast Oregon** can be romantic, though the long-distance driving involved in all but the most cursory of visits is exhausting. The main west–east highway, I-84, leaves The Dalles (see p.92) to track along the bleak gulches of the Columbia River Gorge before cutting southeast to slip past a trio of small towns – **Pendleton**, **La Grande** and **Baker City** – en route to **Ontario**, abutting the Idaho border. Much of I-84 follows the course of the **Oregon Trail** (see p.76), and several of the wayside markers that trace the pioneers' progress detail the problematic crossing of the forested **Blue**

Mountains beyond Pendleton, now incorporated within the giant-sized **Umatilla** and **Wallowa-Whitman** national forests. Leaving I-84 at La Grande, Hwy-82 snakes its way east to the lovely **Wallowa Mountains** at **Joseph**, a tiny township set tight against mountains and lakes. From here, difficult forest roads head on to **Hells Canyon**, the region's one great natural attraction, though the shorter – and far easier – approach is from the south, off I-84 and along Hwy-86 from Baker City; on the way you can also drop by the new and plushly ambitious **Oregon Trail Center**.

For shorter excursions into northeast Oregon, US-26, the other main road, is a better bet as it slips along the eastern peripheries of the Cascades bringing the **Ochoco National Forest** and the badlands of the **John Day Fossil Beds** within reasonable striking distance of the Willamette Valley. Beyond Dayville, however, Hwy-26 heads out east along the thin strip of the John Day Valley, whose tiny and infrequent towns – the largest of which is **John Day** itself – are surrounded by mountains that once yielded millions of dollars' worth of gold. Nowadays, these mountains make up the large-scale **Malheur National Forest**, dotted with campgrounds and laced by hiking trails.

East from Portland: I-84

Heading east out of Portland along the **Columbia River Gorge**, I-84 skirts the northern flanks of Mount Hood (see p.90) on its eighty-mile journey to The Dalles. Beyond, the harsh escarpments edging the river broaden and deepen, hinting at the vast and sparsely populated landscapes of eastern Oregon. Eventually, about 160 miles from Portland, the interstate leaves the river to cut across the eastern edge of the arid Columbian Plateau, where the tiny town of **ECHO**, beside the banks of the Umatilla River, was once a halting point on the **Oregon Trail**. Here, the pioneers faced a difficult choice: they could opt to travel over to the Columbia River and head west by Indian canoe or Hudson's Bay Company bateaux, but the trip was fraught with danger. As Jesse Applegate, one who chose this route, explained, "the river was so wild, so commotional, so fearful and exciting, had not death been there [it was] worth a month of ordinary life". And so most decided to head overland across the plateau, hurrying along from spring to stream in the hope that they would prove strong enough to survive the intense heat and suffocating dust or, if they arrived later, quick enough to beat the snows.

Pendleton

Set within a wide ring of hills just east of Echo, **PENDLETON** cultivates its cowboy reputation, and there's a great build-up to its immensely popular annual **Pendleton Round-Up**. Traditional rodeo stuff – bareback riding, steer roping and of course the bucking bronco – is mixed with extravagant pageantry, parades and a few dubious cultural hybrids ("the American Indian Beauty Contest") for four days in mid-September; tickets from the *Round-Up Association*, PO Box 609, Pendleton, OR 97801 (☎276-2553 or 1-800/45-RODEO; $6–15 per rodeo session). At other times, you can see the evidence – including photos, costumes, saddles and a one-time star horse, now stuffed – at the **Round-Up Hall of Fame**, SW

Court Ave on the Round-Up grounds (summer Tues–Sun 10am–4pm; free). To dress the part, make your way to *Hamley's*, 30 SE Court St, purveyors of Western clothing since 1883.

As well as the Round-Up, Pendleton is known for its woollen goods: sheep-farming gained a hold on the local economy after the ugly days of the nineteenth-century range wars. However, the turn-of-the-century **Pendleton Woolen Mills**, 1307 SE Court Place (Mon–Fri 8am–4.45pm, Sat 9am–1pm; guided tours Mon–Fri only; ☎276-6911), does nothing more exciting than initiate you into the mysteries of mechanized carding, spinning, warp dressing and weaving – disappointing considering it was the mill that put Pendleton on the map. Far more enjoyable is the **Pendleton Underground**, at the corner of SW First and Emigrant Ave (Mon–Sat 8am–5pm; $10), where ninety-minute guided tours explore the town's extensive network of subterranean passageways. To begin with, the tunnels were built to insulate citizens from the inclement climate, but they soon assumed other purposes and were used through Prohibition as saloons, card-rooms and brothels, as well as housing for the area's much-abused Chinese, who were – when they walked the streets – the object of indiscriminate pot shots from drunken cowboys. The tour is brought to life not so much by the tunnels themselves – or by the rather amateurish dioramas – but by a superb commentary full of insights into the life and times of early Pendleton, when the town had 32 saloons and 18 bordellos: for example, the Chinese ran the laundries and used water directly from their mouths to iron and press – a spitting motion that inflamed Caucasian sensibilities to such an extent that the Chinese were obliged to work out of sight. A short walk away, enjoyable old photographs at the **Umatilla County Museum**, 108 SW Frazer (Tues–Sat 10am–4pm), further illustrate the town's early history.

Practicalities

Pendleton's long and narrow downtown runs west to east beside the Umatilla River. Avenues – principally Court, Dorion and Emigrant – run parallel with the river and intersect with the town's numbered streets, which fall either side of Main St. *Greyhound* is at 320 SW Court Ave (☎276-1551), and *Amtrak* at Main St and Frazer Ave.

The **visitor center**, at 25 SE Dorion Ave (Mon–Fri 9am–5pm; ☎276-7411 or 1-800/547-8911), has maps, leaflets and lists of local accommodation. Local **motels** are reasonably priced (except during the Round-Up, when you should book as far in advance as possible), but also pretty grim, with the *Longhorn*

ACCOMMODATION PRICE CODES

All accommodation prices in this book have been coded using the symbols below, corresponding to US dollar prices in the US chapters and equivalent Canadian dollar rates in the Canadian chapters. Prices are for the least expensive double rooms in each establishment, and only include local taxes where we explicitly say so.

For a full explanation see p.46 in *Basics*.

①	up to US$30	④	US$60–80	⑦	US$130–180
②	US$30–45	⑤	US$80–100	⑧	US$180+
③	US$45–60	⑥	US$100–130		

Motel, 411 SW Dorion Ave (☎276-7531; ②), close to the *Greyhound* station, typical among them; you may prefer the *Motel 6*, 325 SE Nye Ave (☎276-3160; ②), perched on a hill beside exit 210 off I-84. Next door, the fanciful *Red Lion Motor Inn*, 304 SE Nye Ave (☎276-6111; ⑤), comes complete with a kitsch Western-style interior and balconied rooms with great views out over the hills. Alternatively, the *Swift Station Inn B&B*, downtown at 602 SE Byers (☎276-3739; ④), has large pleasant rooms.

Pendleton's **restaurants** tend to be plain, all-American affairs featuring burgers, steaks, baked potatoes and huge breakfasts; you'll find several on Main Street including the *Rainbow Bar and Grill*, 209 Main St (☎276-4120), where the walls are covered with intriguing Round-Up memorabilia. The best place to eat is *Raphael's Restaurant*, 233 SE Fourth St (☎276-8500; lunch Tues–Fri, dinner Tues–Sat), noted for its Native American-influenced cuisine and applewood-smoked prime rib.

The Blue Mountains

Leaving Pendleton, it's just forty miles north to Washington's Walla Walla (see p.221) or you can continue southeast on I-84, cutting across the Umatilla River Valley before climbing up into the **Blue Mountains**. It took the wagons of the early emigrants three or four days to cross this band of mountains; they would pause at what is now **Emigrant Springs State Park** to wait for stragglers and to prepare themselves for the descent into the valley below. For many this was a frightening place: the thick forest was confusing and the cries of the cougars during the night demoralizing. Today, there's a **campground** here, and another on the other side of the mountains at **Hilgard Junction State Park**, where thousands of early emigrants bedded down before tackling the steep climb ahead.

The Blue Mountains incorporate large chunks of the **Umatilla** and **Wallowa-Whitman** national forests. A confusing web of rough forest roads cobweb the mountains leading to the remotest of peaks and river valleys. Among the more accessible detours, you can reach the forests, creeks, and peaks – and primitive campground – of **North Fork Umatilla Wilderness** by heading east from Pendleton along the Umatilla River via Gibbon.

La Grande

On the east side of the Blue Mountains is the distinctly shaped **Grande Ronde Valley** – large, round, flat and rimmed by mountains. Now mostly drained to become farmland, the valley was once a marsh, a breeding place for birds, but fatally boggy to the wheels of pioneer wagons, forcing the Oregon Trail to keep to the higher but tougher ground edging the hills. The economic center of the valley is **LA GRANDE**, a simple lumber-and-railway town, whose only claim to fame is the **Hot Lake Mineral Springs**, eight miles from town on Hwy-203 (Wed–Sun 1–4pm; $7; bring a bathing costume). The springs offer relaxing sessions in naturally heated mineral baths or saunas at a resort on the shore of a hot lake – the steam hanging in clouds over the water. The lake was once a summer gathering place for Native American tribes, who used it as a medicinal spa. Later, pioneers took a break from the Oregon Trail here, and in 1864 an hotel was built, which later became a hospital, and was then converted into the present spa – still equipped with the long turn-of-the-century hall of cast-iron bath tubs in which you sit and soak.

Surrounded by trim suburbs, La Grande's slender downtown is little more than one long main drag, Adams Ave (US-30). This runs roughly parallel to and west of I-84, linked to it by Island Ave. The **visitor center**, at 2111 Adams Ave (Mon–Fri 8.30am–5pm; ☎963-8588 or 1-800/848-9969), can supply maps and information about the area. *Greyhound* services from Portland stop at *Carefree Travel*, 2108 Cove Ave (Mon–Fri 8am–noon & 4.30–6pm, Sat 8am–noon; ☎963-5165), a turning off Island Ave a couple of blocks east of Adams; the *Amtrak* station is near the northern end of Adams at Depot and Jefferson streets. La Grande is also the gateway to Enterprise and Joseph in the Wallowa Mountains (see below), to which *Wallowa Valley Stage Line* (☎569-2284), who use the *Greyhound* pick-up point, provide a daily (except Sun) service.

Motels clustered along Adams Ave include *Broken Arrow Lodge*, no 2215 (☎963-7116; ②), and *Stardust Lodge*, no 402 (☎963-4166; ②); **B&B** can be had at the luxurious *Stange Manor Inn*, a refurbished timber magnate's house at 1612 Walnut St (☎963-2400; ④). There's **camping** at Morgan Lake, two miles west of town down B Avenue. **Restaurants** are concentrated on and around Adams Ave too: try the *Golden Harvest*, off Adams at 214 Greenwood St (☎963-3288), which serves excellent Chinese food, or *Mamacita's* at 110 Depot St (☎963-6223), the best place for Mexican dinners.

The Wallowa Mountains

Rather than thumping on down I-84 towards Idaho, consider heading north and then east from La Grande on Hwy-82, the road into the **Wallowa Mountains**, one of Eastern Oregon's loveliest and least discovered areas. The seventy-mile highway takes you through such tiny backwater towns as **ELGIN** – where the only solid-looking building doubles as police station and one-time **Opera House**, its ornately embossed tin ceiling and plush seats a curious dash of old-time opulence – and descends into the Wallowa Valley until the High Wallowa mountains come spectacularly into sight.

ENTERPRISE, in a region of small farming towns, hints at underlying sophistication – perhaps it's the cozy, well-stocked bookstore. The **visitor center** here (Mon–Fri 9am–5pm) is housed in a kiosk at the Court House in the town's small mall; a nice restaurant, *A Country Place on Pete's Pond*, is tucked around the back of town on Montclair St (☎426-3642). The weekend after Labor Day in early September is given over to celebration of **Hells Canyon Mule Days**, with bizarre mule parades, mule rodeos and other competitions.

Joseph

Located at the northern tip of glacially carved Wallowa Lake about six miles to the south of Enterprise, the hamlet of **JOSEPH**, with the mountains rearing behind, is a perfect spot to spend the night and a good base for exploring the surrounding scenery or continuing on to Hells Canyon. The **Wallowa County Museum** on Main St (summer daily 10am–5pm; free) stands in an old, stone corner building dating from 1888, which used to house Wallowa County's first

CHIEF JOSEPH AND THE NEZ PERCÉ

The original inhabitants of the land on which modern Joseph now stands were the **Nez Percé**, so called by French-Canadian trappers for their shell-pierced noses. The Nez Percé came into conflict with the US government soon after settlers started to move into the Wallowa Valley in the early 1870s. The discovery of gold, and white pressure for more space, led to a proposed treaty under which ninety percent of tribal land would be taken away. Chief Joseph refused to sign, pointing out that this was sacred land, where the tribe's ancestors were buried (you can still visit the grave of Old Chief Joseph, the chief's father, by Wallowa Lake). After much bureaucratic chopping and changing, the government decided to go ahead with their plans anyway, and gave the band thirty days to get out of the valley before the army moved in. Chief Joseph asked for more time, to round up stock and avoid crossing the Snake River at a high and dangerous time, but the general in charge, fearing delay (and knowing abandoned stock would fall to white ranchers), refused: the band had to leave cattle and horses behind, and more livestock drowned on the perilous river-crossing.

In the angry aftermath, a handful of white settlers were murdered, and the sad march to the reservation became a dramatic combination of flight and guerilla warfare, the Nez Percé group (the bulk of whom were women, children and old people) out-manoeuvering army columns over twice their strength in a series of hair's-breadth escapes, almost as far as the relative safety of the Canadian border. The flight had its bizarre moments – a group of tourists in search of the Wild West wandered into the Nez Percé warpath in Yellowstone National Park. But only thirty miles from the border, the band were cornered, and Chief Joseph (reportedly) made his much-quoted speech of surrender:

> *Hear me my chiefs! I am tired. My heart is sick and sad. From where the sun now stands I will fight no more forever.*

The Nez Percé had been told they would be put on a reservation in Idaho; instead, they were taken to Kansas, where marshy land caused a fatal malaria epidemic. The survivors were brought back to the Idaho reservation, though Chief Joseph and a few others were taken to the Colville reservation in Washington, where the Chief eventually died in 1904, having campaigned consistently to return with what was left of his people to the Wallowa Valley.

bank, the office of the daily newspaper and a private school. Exhibits on the ground floor, such as a wigwam and native clothing, detail the history of the Nez Percé, and Chief Joseph, for whom the town is named. The upper story is devoted to the pioneers, with the womenfolk and children receiving (for once) their fair share of attention.

Joseph holds a couple of **motels** – *Indian Lodge*, 201 Main St (☎432-2651; ②), and *Mountain View*, 91094 Joseph Hwy (☎432-2982; ②) – but for just a little more money, the friendly *Bed, Bread and Trail Inn* **B&B**, 700 S Main St (☎432-9765; ③), includes a big morning feed. The lakeside *Wallowa Lake Lodge*, 60060 Wallowa Lake Hwy (☎432-9821; ④–⑤), is another comfortable option. In the summer – and especially on weekends – try to book a room in advance. The best local restaurant is *Vali's Alpine Deli and Restaurant*, five miles south at 59811 Wallowa Lake Hwy (summer Tues–Sun, winter Sat & Sun; ☎432-5691), where the specialty is mouth-watering Hungarian food. *Pam's Country Inn Restaurant*, 500

Main St (☎432-1195), is a reasonable second choice. *Wallowa Valley Stage Line* (☎432-3531) run a van service from La Grande (Mon–Sat), stopping in Joseph at the *Chevron* station.

The beauty of the Wallowa area attracts artists, and a few years ago a bronze foundry was set up in Joseph to cast sculptors' work in metal. Its success has drawn craftspeople to the area and encouraged the development of local talent. Finished works are on display at the **Eagle Mountain Gallery**, 107 SW First St, where they have information on tours of the foundry.

Around Joseph: Eagle Cap Wilderness

A mile or so south of Joseph, mountain-rimmed, tourist-populated **Wallowa Lake** is supposedly inhabited by an Oregonian version of the Loch Ness monster. At its far end, **Wallowa Lake State Park** has **camping** (reservations advised; ☎432-2185), and houses the bottom terminal of the **Wallowa Lake Tramway** (summer daily 10am–4pm; $10) – a cable-car system that hoists you up into the mountains where short trails lead to magnificent overlooks. Much of the mountain scenery south of the lake belongs to Wallowa National Forest's **Eagle Cap Wilderness** area, where granite peaks soar high above glaciated valleys, alpine lakes and meadows and – on the lower slopes – thick forests. A number of well-used trails lead up the river valleys to the tiny lakes that punctuate the wilderness; the five-mile hike to **Minam Lake** is a particular favorite, though you'll get more seclusion by carrying on to **Blue Lake**, a lung-wrenching mile further south. But be warned that backcountry hiking and camping here really is remote – so contact the Eagle Cap Ranger District office, 612 SW Second St (☎426-3104) by Hwy-82 in Enterprise, for details and advice, or the Wallowa Valley Ranger District office, one mile north of Joseph on Hwy-82 (☎432-2171).

During the summer months, various **Pack Stations** at Wallowa Lake, Joseph, Enterprise, Elgin and elsewhere in the northeast offer single- and multi-day mule tours into the Eagle Cap Wilderness. You can also arrange to be transported to a remote mountain lake or some such spot, and picked up again a few days later. The cheapest half-day trips are $30; an organized tour – including food and most of the necessary gear – costs perhaps $100 per person per day.

Several forest roads lead east from Joseph to **Hells Canyon** (see also p.131), the deepest gorge on the continent. Though the southern approach via Baker City (see below) is far more practicable, if you have four-wheel drive you can reach the ultimate viewpoint from this side. **McGraw Lookout**, southeast of Joseph, is east off forest road 39 along bumpy forest road 3965; but the most dramatic prospect of all can be had from **Hat Point**, 54 miles northeast of town: take Little Sheep Creek Highway to the hamlet of Imnaha, then drive a further 24 miles along a rough, slow, unpaved road which ends at **Hat Point Lookout Tower** – and campground – high above the canyon's riverbed. Alternatively, if you continue north from Imnaha, forest road 4260 brings you to the start of the four-mile **Nee-Me-Poo Trail**, which twists its way down to the Snake River, at the bottom of the canyon, following the path of Chief Joseph and the Nez Percé as they left their Wallowa Valley home.

Forest road 39, the **Wallowa Mountain Loop**, offers a hair-raising, nerve-jangling shortcut to Hwy-86 at the southern end of Hells Canyon; get advice about road conditions before you set out at the **Hells Canyon National Recreation Area Headquarters**, above the post office at the junction of Hwy-82 and Hwy-3 in Enterprise (☎426-4978; see p.127).

Baker City

From La Grande, I-84 runs 44 miles south through low-lying rangeland to **BAKER CITY** (usually just "Baker"), a substantial redbrick town which outlived the gold-boom days of the 1860s – commemorated by the nuggets displayed in the **US National Bank** at 2000 Main St (Mon–Fri 10am–5pm) – to prosper from agriculture and livestock rearing. From 1876 into the 1890s, enormous herds of cattle and sheep would assemble here, headed for the dinner plates of the East, and there's a pint-sized statue in honor of the **American Cowboy** in the city park at Campbell and Grove. In a corner of the park, several rusty metal spikes survive as relics from nineteenth-century horseshoe-throwing contests.

Opposite the park, the **Oregon Trail Regional Museum**, 2475 Grove St (summer daily 9.30am–5pm; $1.50), has precious little to do with the early pioneers – though the Oregon Trail did pass near here – and is more a motley assortment worth of Western bric-à-brac, the real highlight being an extraordinary collection of rocks. Precious stones, agates, minerals, petrified woods, fossils and shells crowd the shelves, and, in a dark room, fluorescent crystals glow weirdly under ultra-violet light.

Among the sagebrush foothills five miles east of town off Hwy-86, the **Oregon Trail Interpretive Center** ambitiously attempts to recreate the early emigrants' life on the trail (daily 9am–6pm; free). Contemporary quotations with matching illustrations and dioramas are well used, dealing with a wide variety of subjects – from marital strife to the pioneers' impact on Native Americans – and background sound tapes, as well as a short video, further set the scene. Outside, you can wander down the hill to examine wheel ruts left by the pioneers' wagons and staff sometimes recreate a wagon camp.

Practicalities

To reach downtown Baker, leave I-84 at exit 304 and follow Campbell to Main St, where you should turn left. *Greyhound* is beside I-84 at 515 Campbell (☎523-5011), about twenty minutes' walk from Main St; the **visitor center**, across the street at 490 Campbell (summer Mon–Fri 8am–6pm, Sat 8am–4pm; winter Mon–Fri 8am–5pm; ☎523-3356 or 1-800/523-1235), is good for local information plus hiking and camping ideas for the Wallowa-Whitman National Forest and Hells Canyon. The *Amtrak* station is on the opposite side of town at the far end of Broadway.

Baker has its share of standard **motels**, such as the *Super 8*, near the visitor center at 250 Campbell St (☎523-8282; ③); the *Western*, 3055 Tenth St (☎523-3700; ③); and the *Eldorado Inn*, 695 Campbell St (☎523-6494; ③). But you're better off staying at one of the local **B&Bs**, especially the comfortable old house that's now the *A Demain B&B*, 1790 Fourth St at Valley (☎523-2509; ④); the food's great here too. For dinner, try the popular *Brass Parrot*, 2190 Main St (☎523-5355), where you should stick to the traditional American dishes. The *Blue and White Café*, 1825 Main St (☎523-6792; closed Sun), is full of old regulars, lingering over their 10¢ coffees and cinnamon rolls.

Moving on from Baker

Despite its distant location, Baker is something of a crossroads: from here, Hwy-7 heads west across the Blue Mountains for Hwy-26 and the John Day Valley (see p.133), while Hwy-86 covers the seventy miles east to Hells Canyon (see below), passing by the Oregon Trail Interpretive Center. Heading southeast, I-84 makes its dreary way to **ONTARIO**, seventy miles away on the Idaho border. Ontario is duller than dull, a suitably remote spot, so it was thought, to build relocation centers for several thousand Japanese Americans who were bundled out here during World War II. Of the town's **motels**, the *Howard Johnson Lodge*, 1249 Tapadera Ave (☎889-8621; ③), is the trimmest and most comfortable; full listings are available at the **visitor center**, 88 SW Third Ave (☎889-8012).

Hells Canyon

East of Baker, along the Idaho border, the Snake River has carved the prodigious gorge known as **Hells Canyon**. Though a thousand feet deeper than the Grand Canyon, it lacks something of the latter's overwhelming impact because it's what's called a low-relief canyon, edged by a series of gradually ascending false peaks rather than sheer cliffs. But it's impressive enough, with Idaho's Seven Devils mountain range rising behind and the river glimmering in its depths. Since prehistoric times, the canyon's hot and sheltered depths have provided a winter sanctuary for wildlife and local Indians, and stone tools and rock-carvings have been found at old Nez Percé village sites.

Though the Nez Percé are long gone, the canyon area is now preserved for wildlife and backpackers as the **Hells Canyon National Recreation Area**: deer, otters, mink, black bears, mountain lions and whole herds of elk live here, along with less attractive, even poisonous, beasties – rattlesnakes and black widow spiders. Most of the canyon area is designated wilderness land, where mechanical vehicles are banned above water-level (boats along the Snake are allowed); so the only way to explore is on foot or on horseback. Roads do lead through the rest of the recreation area, but they tend to be rough and slippery, and many are closed by snow for much of the year: it's best to check with the **Wallowa-Whitman National Forest Headquarters** at 1550 Dewey Ave in Baker (☎523-6391), before you set out. They (and some information offices in surrounding towns) will be able to supply you with maps and a complete list of hiking trails and **camping** facilities.

Halfway, and the canyon by boat

Readily reached along Hwy-86, tiny and tin-roofed **HALFWAY**, near the Canyon's southern end (you can also get here – just about – by taking the Wallowa Mountain Loop Road from the north), is forty miles south of the Oxbow Dam, making it a good base for exploring the southern end of the canyon: reserve a room at the *Halfway Motel* (☎742-5722; ②) or the lovely rural *Clear Creek Farm* B&B (call for directions; ☎742-2233 or 742-2238; ③) if you plan to stay.

Hwy-86 winds towards the canyon from Halfway, meeting the Snake River at Oxbow Dam, where a Forest Service road leads on to Hells Canyon Dam, the launching-point for **jet boat** and **raft** trips through the canyon. In summer, *Hells Canyon Adventures Inc* (☎785-3352) and *Hells Canyon Challenge* (☎569-2445) run motorboat tours (daily tours $40–70; two-day tours $150). The boats take you skimming over white-water rapids between the deceptively low, bare hills, past rocks faintly colored with ancient Indian rock carvings, to an old homestead where pioneers once tried to eke a living out of the dry, lonely canyonland. The companies also operate a "drop-off" service, taking you to hiking trails along the canyon and picking you up later in the day or the week (costing from $20 per person).

East from Portland: US-26

US-26 from Portland leaves the path of the old Barlow road halfway around the base of Mount Hood (see p.90), to dip southeast through miles of forest into the **Warm Springs Indian Reservation**, within which the scenery changes from mountain forest to the hot, dry landscape of the east. Near the reservation's southeast edge, you pass a turning for the very popular **Kah-Nee-Ta** resort, the "Gift of the Gods" – a catchy, but ironic, piece of hyperbole for what is in fact a canny project set up by the Confederated Tribes of Warm Springs and financed by federal compensation for the flooding of their ancestral fishing grounds at Celilo Falls along the Columbia River. Native culture here is packaged into a jolly tourist product (accommodation in tepees, Indians dancing in feathered head-dresses while the audience munches vast quantities of traditionally baked salmon), and the venture is widely hailed as a commercial success.

Madras, Redmond and Sisters

The wealth of buried fossils and agates around **MADRAS,** on US-26 ten miles beyond the Warm Springs Reservation, makes it popular with so-called "rock-hounds" or amateur excavators: the **visitor center** at 197 SE Fifth St (☎475-2350) has details if you want to go digging; and you'll see signs advertising agates for sale all along the road. US-97 runs south from Madras along the eastern foot of the Cascades for 27 miles before reaching the small, plain town of **REDMOND**, where Hwy-126 cuts off west towards Sisters.

A tourist town with a pseudo-Western high street, but beautifully set, **SISTERS** is genuinely exciting during the annual **rodeo**, held on the second weekend in June, which draws big crowds to watch the cowboys hang grimly on to tough, mean-looking bulls; contact the **visitor center**, 150 W Cascade (☎549-0251). You'd be lucky to find a room during the rodeo, but Sisters has several mundane motels, with *Sisters Motor Lodge*, 600 W Cascade (☎549-2551; ②), the least expensive. For food, *Ali's*, 100 W Cascade (☎549-2545), offers inexpensive snacks and lunches, while *Pandrea's*, 100 E Cascade (☎549-6081), has excellent pizzas.

The white-capped triple peaks of "Faith", "Hope" and "Charity", the **Three Sisters Mountains**, behind the town, provide a stunning backdrop. Two roads lead into the mountains from Sisters, both eventually climbing over high Cascade passes to the west side of the mountains. The dramatic southern route along Hwy-242 (open in summer only) heads straight across the mountains to **McKenzie Bridge** and the **Mckenzie River Valley** on Hwy-126 (see p.99). The other road, US-20/Hwy-126, skirts the highest peaks to fork after **Santiam Pass**, with US-20 proceeding down into the Willamette Valley and Hwy-126 going south to meet Hwy-242 at the McKenzie Valley. Both are beautiful drives through dense mountain forests, with hiking trails and campsites en route.

Ochoco National Forest and the John Day Fossil Beds

Back on US-26, in dreary **PRINEVILLE**, twenty miles east of Redmond, the **Prineville Ranger District Station**, 2321 E Third St (☎447-9641), provides maps, hiking and camping information on the neighboring **Ochoco National Forest**, one of Oregon's less-visited beauty spots. Here, ponderosa and lodgepole

ANTELOPE AND THE BHAGWAN

These days, there's nothing much to see at **ANTELOPE**, fifty or so miles east of the Warm Springs Reservation on Hwy-218. However, the town's story is probably the most bizarre and well known in Oregon's recent history. In 1981, followers of the Indian guru, Bhagwan Shree Rajneesh, bought the old **Big Muddy Ranch**, twenty miles east of Antelope, converting it to an agricultural commune. Dressed exclusively in shades of red – and thus sometimes known as "the orange people" – Bhagwan's followers were a middle-class lot, mostly graduates in their thirties who came from all over the world. The commune's mish-mash of eastern philosophy and western Growth Movement therapies raised great (and initially sympathetic) interest across Oregon – and eyebrows in conservative Antelope. Despite the commune's agricultural success in what still is a relatively depressed region, relations disintegrated fast, especially when Rajneeshis took over the town council; and the appearance of Rajneeshi "peace patrols" clutching semi-automatic weapons did little to restore confidence in the guru's good intentions.

The Rajneeshis' hold on the community was, however, fairly short-lived. Just before the local county elections, the Rajneeshis began a "Share a Home" project that involved bussing in street-people from across the US and registering them to vote here. Many vagrants later turned up in neighboring towns (without the promised bus ticket home), saying they'd been conned, drugged or both, and creating big problems for the local authorities. Worse, an outbreak of salmonella-poisoning in the nearby town of The Dalles turned out to have been part of a Rajneeshi strategy to lay their voting opponents low. When the law eventually moved in on the commune – by now, in early shades of Waco, an armed fortress – they discovered medical terrorism (more poisoning, the misdiagnosis of AIDS) had been used on Rajneeshi members themselves in an internal power-struggle. The culprits were jailed and commune members dispersed. The Bhagwan, after a bungled attempt to flee the country, was deported to India and his notorious fleet of Rolls Royces sold off, along with the ranch, to pay debts. By 1986, embattled Antelope was quiet again. A plaque on a new memorial flagpole in the town center, dedicated to the triumph of the Antelope community over the "Rajneesh invasion", is the only sign that anything ever happened.

pine are scattered over a mountainous terrain studded with canyons and volcanic plugs, one of which, **Twin Pillars**, is at the end of a strenuous five-mile hike through the Mill Creek Wilderness area. To reach the trailhead at the *Wildcat Campground*, go nine miles east of Prineville on US-26 and then turn north for the eleven-mile trip up Mill Creek Road. Lots of other rough forestry roads lace the forest, leading to a handful of other notable trails, but most people stick to US-26 and dash through the Ochoco to emerge into the John Day River Valley, a bare, sun-scorched landscape of ochers and beige typical of much of eastern Oregon.

Valley apart, several other features of the immediate area are named after **John Day** – a fur-trapper from the Astoria colony in the west of Oregon, who fell victim to the elements and local native Americans and was later discovered wandering lost and naked by another party of trappers – including a river, a town and most importantly the **John Day Fossil Beds**, a little way north of US-26. Made up of three separate sites, these carefully excavated areas of strange-colored rock-forms hold some of the most revealing fossil formations in the US. Trails wind through barren hills over crumbly textured earth, and information plaques point out the various geological and paleontological oddities. The fossils date from the period just after the extinction of the dinosaurs: before the Cascade Mountains raised their rain-blocking peaks to the west, a sub-tropical rainforest covered this land in a dense jungle of palms, ferns and tropical fruits, inhabited by unlikely creatures that predate the evolution of current species – *Hpertragulus*, a tiny, mouse-sized deer, *Diceratherium*, a cow-sized rhinoceros, and *Miohippus*, a small, three-toed horse. As the Cascades sputtered into being, volcanic ash poured down on the forest, mixing with the rain to make a thick, muddy poultice, which fossilized bits of the leaves and fruit. Other layers trapped the bones and teeth of the animals. Paleontologists, who first visited the area in the 1860s, have been able to put together a massive epic of evolution and extinction.

The three sites of the fossil beds are spread far apart, and vary greatly in accessibility. You'd have to be a real fossil fanatic to push up to the rocky **Clarno** unit, fifty miles northeast of Madras near Antelope. However, the **Painted Hills** unit, down a (marked) side road off US-26 six miles west of the one-horse town of Mitchell, is more accessible, though the interest here lies as much in the hills themselves as the relics embedded in them: striped in shades of rust and brown, they look like sandcastle mounds, the smooth surface quilted with rivulets worn by draining water. Close up, the hills are frail, their clay surface cracked by dryness; the colors become brighter when it rains and the pores in the earth close up.

Another 28 miles further east, the final section of the fossil beds, **Sheep Rock**, takes its name from the volcanic capstone which looms like the Matterhorn over the John Day River Valley. The staff at **Cant Ranch visitor center** (daily 8.30am–5pm), housed in the ranch-house of an old sheep farm at the foot of the rock, can tell you more than you ever wanted to know about prehistory, and there are plenty of fossils on display. Two miles north of the visitor center a turning leads to the **Blue Basin** canyon, where the rock is more of a pale, greeny color, mixed with the soft, crumbly dark red of the painted hills. The half-mile **Island in Time** trail takes you into the "blue basin" itself – a rock-surrounded natural amphitheater – past perspex-covered fossil exhibits, including a tortoise that hurtled to its death millions of years ago and a saber-toothed cat.

John Day town and Malheur National Forest

Centered around a bright, white-painted wooden nineteenth-century church, small, dry **JOHN DAY**, 38 miles east of Sheep Rock, is, despite having only 2100 inhabitants, the largest town along US-26. Like many of the towns around here, this was originally a Gold Rush settlement, founded when gold was discovered at nearby Canyon Creek in 1862. Along with the rush of hopeful white miners came Chinese immigrants, often to work sites abandoned as unprofitable by the wealthier whites. Despite high-pitched racial tensions across the Northwest, a Chinese herbalist, "Doc" Ing Hay made quite a name for himself treating patients of both races, and his two-story house (which was also the local shop, temple and opium and gambling den) is now open as the **Kam Wah Chung & Co Museum** (summer only; Mon–Thurs 9am–noon & 1–5pm, Sat & Sun 1–5pm; $1.50), next to the City Park on the northwest side of town.

A few miles southeast of town, the **Strawberry Mountain Wilderness** is one of the most scenic portions of the **Malheur National Forest**, which surrounds the John Day Valley. Here, among the pine trees, alpine lakes sit beneath snow-capped mountains that rise to over 9000 feet, providing a remote home for the Rocky Mountain elk. Several forest roads lead to the hiking trails and (mostly primitive) campgrounds of the wilderness, with one of the more popular approaches being the eleven-mile drive south from Prairie City (east of John Day on US-26) along forest road 6001. This takes you to the **Strawberry Campground**, close to several trailheads: the two-mile hike to Little Strawberry Lake is a particular delight.

If you're not into camping, then John Day is where you're likely to stay: try the inexpensive *Gold Country Motel*, 250 E Main St (☎575-2100; ②), the *Budget 8*, 711 W Main St (☎575-2155; ②), or the more comfortable *Best Western Inn*, 315 W Main St (☎575-1700; ④). Information on and maps of the Malheur National Forest are obtainable at the **visitor center**, 281 W Main St (Mon–Fri 9am–5pm; ☎575-0547).

East of John Day

US-26 leaves the John Day Valley just east of Prairie City, climbing over the Blue Mountains to reach the arid buttes and plains that extend southeast to the Idaho border. In the middle of the mountains, Hwy-7 branches off to travel east to Baker City, wriggling past old gold-mining settlements and quasi-**ghost towns** such as **SUMPTER**, where the dredging equipment still looks poised for action. Throughout the summer, a reinstated **steam train** leaves Sumpter for a five-mile excursion up the valley, passing by disfiguring gold-dredge tailings. There are three runs a day and the round trip costs $8; further details on ☎894-2268.

BEND AND THE SOUTHEAST

You can't go far along the Cascades' eastern slopes without encountering some manifestation of the mountains' massive volcanic power. Nowhere is quite as impressive as Washington's Mount St Helens, but here among Oregon's Cascades the green, alpine scenery is everywhere counterpointed by stark cones and lava flows, especially in the **Lava Lands** area that surrounds **Bend**, the southeast's one sizeable town. Bend itself is a young and lively place, full of ski bums in winter and mountain bikers all summer long, with a number of good cafés, bars and restaurants as well as Eastern Oregon's best brewery.

Fortunately, you don't have to venture far into the vast Great Basin desert of **southeastern Oregon** if you just want to get a taste of it: the **High Desert Museum**, one of the best natural history museums in the US, is right outside Bend. If you've got a car, or a bike and strong legs, however, you may well want to explore the empty spaces, which spread east from Bend all the way into Nevada and Idaho; Bend itself is about the only place you can get to using public transportation.

Bend

A convenient mid-point between the Cascade Mountains and the wilder landscapes to the east, **BEND** is really your best base in Eastern Oregon, giving access both to Cascade grandeur and the eerie landscape of Oregon's untouched desert reaches. These surroundings, rather than the town itself, are the main attraction, though Bend (easily reached by *Greyhound* from Portland) is a pleasant enough little place, its gridiron downtown set on a bend in the

Deschutes River. Early hunting trails struck away from the river-path here, and hunters came to know the place as "farewell bend" – a name which stuck until an impatient post office abbreviated it.

It was a turn-of-the-century East Coast entrepreneur who transformed Bend from a ramshackle scattering of half-deserted ranches and small houses into a real town, and its development thereafter followed the rickety, uneven pattern of the Western frontier (cars came here before gaslights or electricity). The recent explosion of interest in leisure pursuits, especially following the development of the ski resort on nearby **Mount Bachelor**, shot Bend to its current popularity with the more sophisticated western part of the state, and now outdoorsy Oregonians pour in from the Willamette Valley, roof-racks laden with skis, mountain bikes or fishing tackle.

To orient yourself, drive up Pilot Butte, just east of downtown off US-20, and you'll get a panorama over Bend to the white-topped Cascades and across the dry bumps of the Lava Lands.

Practicalities

The **Central Oregon Welcome Center** (Mon–Sat 9am–5pm, Sun 11am–3pm; ☎382-3221 or 1-800/547-6858) along US-97 on the north side of town has maps, accommodation listings, and piles of pamphlets on outdoor recreation opportunities in the surrounding area. Rent a mountain bike and get information on the many local trails from *Mt Bachelor Bike and Sport*, 1244 NW Galveston Ave (☎382-4000) west of the river. As is the case almost everywhere in Eastern Oregon, getting around without a car is far from ideal. *Greyhound* will get you here (at midnight) from Portland, and their station is a long way east of town at 2045 E Hwy-20 (☎382-2151); there's no *Amtrak* service.

The many **motels** along Third St (US-97), such as the *Royal Gateway*, 475 SE Third St (☎382-5631; ②), and the *Sonoma Lodge*, 450 SE Third St (☎382-4891; ②), are pretty inexpensive, but they tend to fill up by the end of the day, especially at weekends. *Motel West*, 228 NE Irving St (☎389-5577; ②), behind the *Sizzler* restaurant, is quieter and more central. The *Mill Inn*, 642 NW Colorado St (☎389-9198; ③), is a very pleasant and reasonably priced B&B. There's **camping** during the summer in *Tumalo State Park* (☎388-6055), five miles along US-20 northwest of town, and at numerous sites in the Deschutes National Forest.

As far as **eating** goes, Bend has several pricey little bistros such as the *Old Bend Blacksmith Shop and Broiler*, 211 NW Greenwood Ave (☎388-1994; Tues–Sat only) – which serves classy American homecooking – and the *Pine Tavern Restaurant*, 962 NW Brooks St (☎382-5581). *D&D Bar and Grill* at 927 NW Bond St (☎382-4592), and *Arvard's Lounge and Café*, opposite at no 928 (☎389-0990), serve up big portions of diner food at low prices. Lots of places along Bond Street are good for a **drink**, but no beer drinker will want to miss the chance to sample some of the Northwest's best micro-brewed ales and stouts at the *Deschutes Brewery*, 1044 NW Bond St (☎382-9242), which also does a good range of pastas, pizzas and salads.

Mount Batchelor and the Cascades Lake Highway

Bend owes a good slice of its new-found success to the development of the Northwest's largest ski-resort at **Mount Batchelor**, 22 miles southwest of town on Hwy-372. The season runs from around mid-November to as late as July, snowfall permitting (snow reports on ☎382-7888), and you can rent cross-country and downhill skis (details on ☎382-2442 or 1-800/829-2442). The main ski lift runs in summer, so from Memorial Day onwards sightseers can reach the top without exerting themselves excessively. On a clear day, the view of the Cascades is stupendous.

Mount Batchelor is also the first stop on the **Cascade Lakes Highway**, or "Century Drive" – a hundred-mile mountain loop road which winds around Cascade lakes, giving access to trailheads into the **Three Sisters** (see p.132), or further south, the **Waldo Lake** wilderness areas and a sprinkling of campgrounds. Check with the **Deschutes National Forest Office**, 1230 NE Third St (☎388-5664), or the Lava Lands visitor center (see below) in Bend for details.

The High Desert Museum

Whether or not you intend to travel through Oregon's sandy southeast, it's well worth spending half a day in the fascinating **High Desert Museum**, three miles south of town off Hwy-97 (daily 9am–5pm; $5; ☎382-4754). Unfortunately, however, no bus runs here. As much a zoo as a museum, this account of natural life in Oregon's arid interior sets out its best exhibits around an outdoor path, where pens and pools of creatures – otters, birds of prey, comically ambling porcupines – are interspersed with displays of trees and shrubs, and historical exhibits. A pioneer log cabin and a sheep-herder's wagon stand as relics of a lonely nineteenth-century life spent guarding the animals against natural perils and sheep-shooting cowboys during the "range wars". Try to time your visit for one of the daily talks or (more fun) the otter feedings: call for details.

The exhibits on the region's geography and history are displayed very effectively in several rooms, with the **Spirit of the West Gallery** being particularly noteworthy. Historical scenes of life as it used to be are reproduced in faithful detail, even down to the taped birdsong and chirping crickets. The first scene is of a Paiute Indian settlement beside a swamp; you then see the fur traders on the Snake River Plateau and at the fortified trading station, followed by the arrival of the first settlers in northeastern Nevada. Then come the land surveyors of central Oregon and the gold miners: you wander through the narrow mining shafts into one of the former towns. Through doorways and dusty windows you see a Chinese grocery store, the bank, a photographic studio and other shops in Silver City, Idaho. The last room is devoted to the **buckaroos**, the cowboys who roamed the open range well into this century.

The Lava Lands

Characterized by weird formations of solidified lava, the **Lava Lands** cover a huge area of central Oregon, stretching roughly from Madras way down to Fort Rock in the south. But the concentration of geological oddities in the Bend area makes this the Lava Lands' focal point. The volcanic forms – neat conical buttes, caves and solidified trees – date back seven thousand years to the eruptions of Mounts Newberry and Mazama (today's Crater Lake; see p.100), which dumped enormous quantities of ash and pumice across the region. The process is depicted in a series of dioramas, complete with dramatic narrative and collapsing plastic peaks, at the **Lava Lands visitor center** (summer daily 9am–5pm; ☎593-2421), eleven miles south of Bend on Hwy-97. Histrionic history aside, the visitor center is an excellent source of maps and practical information on the many hiking trails that wind through the lava country. Also, right on its doorstep is the large, dark cinder cone of **Lava Butte**, breached by a gush of molten lava which spilled over the surrounding land. A trail from the visitor center leads through the cracked moonscape of the lava flow, and a road spirals to the top of the butte, giving an overview of dark green pine forest interrupted by chocolate-colored lava. The butte is cratered at the top, the basin-like hole tinged red where steam once oxidized the iron in the rock; an **interpretive center** nearby explains the mini-volcano's geological impact.

A mile south of the Lava Lands visitor center, just east of US-97, the **Lava River Cave** (summer daily 8.30am–6pm; $1, plus 50¢ for a lamp) takes you down a long, subterranean passage into the volcanic underworld. The cave was created by a rush of molten lava during the turbulent Ice Age. Most of the lava eventually cooled and hardened around the hottest, still-molten center of the flow; when this drained away, it left an empty lava-tube, over a mile long, discovered only when a part of the roof fell in. There are supposedly all kinds of formations along the cave, but even with a lantern it's hard to see much beyond the next few steps. However, the long cave has an eerie atmosphere – though it's cold even in summer and you'll need extra clothes and stout shoes.

South of the cave (and a bumpy twelve miles off US-97 down an unpaved forest road, no 9720), the **Lava Cast Forest** contains the casts – easily seen on a one-mile loop trail – formed when, centuries ago, lava poured into a forest of Ponderosa pines, leaving empty moulds when the trees disintegrated. This batch of lava came from what was once the towering Mount Newberry, but is now the sagging **Newberry Crater** (the narrow county road no 21 leads to the crater east off US-97, 24 miles south of Bend). When the mountain finally collapsed, worn out by long years of deluging its surroundings in lava, two lakes were formed, **Paulina** and **East Lake**. Trails lead through the crater area, including the **Trail of Glass**, which travels around a mass of glassy, volcanic obsidian, used by ancient peoples to form tools. Other trails lead around the lakes and into the surrounding hills; there are several **campgrounds** here too.

Southeast Oregon

Seldom visited, Oregon's big, arid southeast is mostly barren land, part-coated with dry sagebrush and punctuated with great flat-topped, cowboy-movie rocks and canyons. Early exploration of the area was mostly accidental: the best-known tale of desert wanderings is that of the **Blue Bucket Mine Party** of 1845, who left the Oregon Trail in search of a short cut and got lost in the parched land with neither food nor water. Most of them were eventually rescued, and caused great excitement with an account of a big nugget of gold, discovered in the bottom of a blue bucket of water brought by children from a creek: members of the party went back to look for the lost gold mine, but it was never found. Despite this and other widely known tales of hardship, unscrupulous promoters conned homesteaders into settling the land around Bend by painting rich pictures of the land's farming potential. In fact, the desert homesteaders faced a bleak, lonely country where water was scarce, dust blew in clouds and gardens turned green in the spring only to wilt under the summer sun – a grim life, which few could stick for long. When World War I broke out, most homesteaders left to take jobs in the new war industries. Today the area is barely populated – although it was, incidentally, around here that the earliest signs of human life in Oregon have been found.

Excavations at **FORT ROCK** (seventy-odd miles south of Bend off Hwy-31) have uncovered ancient sandals, woven from sagebrush nine thousand years ago.

Southeast Oregon's only major west–east highway is US-20, which runs the 260 miles from Bend to Ontario. Especially on a hot summer's day, this is a long and arduous drive across a deserted landscape, whose brain-numbing emptiness is only interrupted by the occasional battered hamlet, boasting a couple of rusting fuel pumps and (maybe) a café: fill up with gas, pack extra water and check your car before you set off. The halfway point is marked by **BURNS**, a welcome watering hole that's the biggest settlement for miles. The town was once surrounded by colossal cattle ranches owned by autocratic figures like Pete French, who – in the 1880s, at the height of his success – had 45,000 head of cattle roaming over 200,000 acres of grazing land. Items from his ranch house are displayed, among pioneer bygones, at the **Harney County Museum**, 18 W D St (May to mid-Oct Tues–Fri 9am–5pm, Sat 9am–noon; $1.50).

From Bend, one *Greyhound* bus a day heads along US-20 stopping at Burns and eventually Ontario; details on ☎573-2736. For tourist information ask at the **visitor center**, also at 18 W D St (☎573-2636). Burns has a handful of modest **motels**, including the *Royal Inn*, 999 Oregon Ave (☎573-5295; ②), and the *Silver Spur*, 789 N Broadway (☎573-2077; ②), as well as the rather more comfortable *Best Western Ponderosa*, 577 W Monroe (☎573-2047; ③). Almost everyone thinks the *Pine Room Café*, 543 W Monroe (☎573-6631), is the best place to eat.

There's not much else to do in town – and the journey on to Ontario is really very tedious, but you can leave the barren spaces behind by heading north on US-395 for the seventy-mile trip to John Day (see p.134).

Around Burns: Malheur National Wildlife Refuge

In the middle of the high desert, thirty minutes' drive south of Burns, the **Malheur National Wildlife Refuge**, centered on lakes Malheur and Harney, is an important bird refuge: cranes, herons, hawks, swans, ducks and geese, among over 300 species, stop off here in this giant-sized, soggy marshland during their spring and fall migrations. The refuge does not have any marked trails, and hiking is both difficult – through the swampy, mosquito-infested terrain – and severely restricted during the nesting season from March to July; so bring binoculars and use your car. The refuge **information center** on the southern edge of Lake Malheur (Mon–Fri 7am–3.30pm; ☎493-2612) provides maps, wildlife information and advice on good vantage points. To get there from Burns, drive 25 miles south on Hwy-205 and turn left along the byroad towards Princeton.

Beyond the turning, Hwy-205 continues past southerly portions of the refuge to reach the end-of-the-world hamlet of Frenchglen, sixty miles from Burns, the starting point for a hair-raising loop-road up **Steens Mountain**. The dirt road, open summer only, follows a gradual slope up this massive basaltic fault-block, giving way at the top to abrupt views into craggy gorges, and over the hard sands of the **Alvord Desert**, stretching away to the east. Just north of where the loop-road rejoins Hwy-205, another route cuts off west through the even more desolate expanse of the **Hart Mountain Antelope Refuge**, where you should keep an eye peeled for spritely Pronghorns.

The *Frenchglen* **hotel** (March–Oct; ☎493-2825; ②) is a small white frame house built in 1914 as a stagecoach stopping point; reservations are recommended. The *Page Springs* **campground** is about four miles to the southeast.

travel details

Trains
From Portland one train daily calls at The Dalles (1hr 40min), Pendleton (4hr), La Grande (6hr 15min), Baker City (7hr 15min), and Ontario (9hr 15min).

Buses
From Portland to Baker (2 daily; 6hr); Bend (2 daily; 4hr 30min); La Grande (2 daily; 5hr); Ontario (2 daily; 9hr); Pendleton (2 daily; 4hr).

CHAPTER THREE

SEATTLE AND WESTERN WASHINGTON

Likeable, liveable **Seattle**, the commercial and cultural capital of the state of Washington, has become one of the most fashionable destinations in the United States. The appeal of its fine Pacific Coast setting is compounded by the excellence of its restaurants, the vitality of its nightlife, and its flourishing performing arts scene (as exemplified by the international fame of its locally grown grunge bands). All this from humble and comparatively recent origins: Seattle's first hesitant economic steps, in the 1850s, were based on the export of timber, shuttled down the coast to the burgeoning cities of California. Other primary products, especially fish, played a supporting role, and together they formed the foundations of Western Washington's first industrial boom. Nowadays the region is sustained by the latter-day high-tech companies and an ongoing economic and cultural reorientation towards the Pacific Rim.

West of Seattle, across **Puget Sound**, is the region's other star turn, the **Olympic Peninsula**, where inaccessible, glacier-draped mountains poke up high above dense temperate rainforests, all fringed by the wild, rocky and remote Pacific Coast. Seattle is also the hub of a ferry system that offers glorious rides to the wood-clad hills and rolling farmland of the islands and peninsulas that pepper the sea as it stretches north towards Canada. This beautiful area is at its most beguiling among the **San Juan Islands**, a cluttered archipelago incorporating the lovely state parks of **Orcas** and the tranquil charm of **Lopez Island**.

Throughout Western Washington, vast forests shelter all kinds of wildlife, remote islands scatter the sea, driftwood-strewn beaches are unchanged since the Native Americans used them to launch whaling canoes; and, edging the region to the east, the Cascade Mountains provide a snow-capped backdrop. Despite the sunny-side-up claims of the tourist authorities, the climate is very wet for most of the year, with just a brief respite in July and August. Don't let this put you off, though: even seen through a haze of fine grey drizzle, the scenery is incredibly beautiful, and you should try to tackle at least a few hiking trails (well laid-out, easy to follow and available in manageably short versions). Otherwise Washington's great, green outdoors with its vast expanses of trees can just make you feel very small indeed.

TELEPHONE NUMBERS

Washington State Tourism Development Division: ☎1-800/544-1800.
The **telephone code** for Seattle and Western Washington is ☎206.

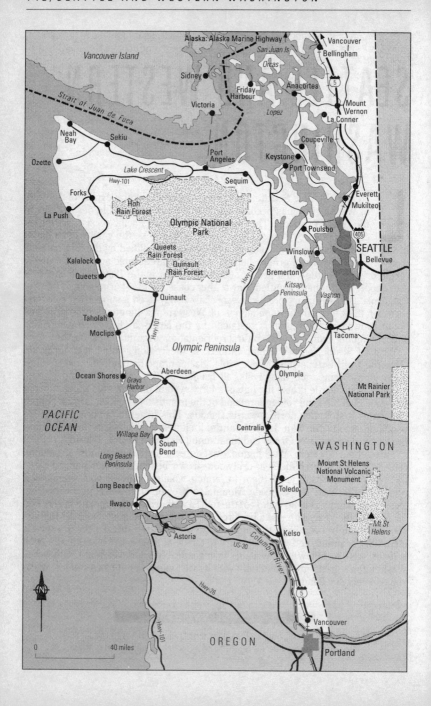

The remoteness of much of the region means that you'll need a car (or bike, if you've got strong legs) to get to some of the most enticing parts, though the ferries will carry you around the waterways, and *Greyhound* provides useful links between the main towns (*Amtrak* only serves the larger cities). Limited local bus services extend the network.

SEATTLE

Curved around the shore of Elliott Bay, with Lake Washington behind and the snowy peak of Mount Rainier hovering faintly in the distance, **Seattle** is beautifully set, its insistently modern skyline of shiny glass skyscrapers gleaming out across the bay, emblem of two decades of vigorous urban renewal. In many ways, it feels like a new city, still groping for a balance between its smart high-rises and a downbeat streetlife that reflects its tough port past. Its old central working-class areas, narrowly saved from the jaws of the bulldozer by popular outcry, have been restored as colorful historic districts, and have become a focus of urban sophistication with a strong artsy and intellectual undertow.

Considering its pre-eminent standing in the economic and cultural life of the Pacific Northwest, Seattle's **beginnings** were inauspiciously muddy. Flooded out of its first location on Alki Beach, the small logging community that was established here in the 1850s built its houses on stilts over the soggy ground of what's now the Pioneer Square historic district. The early settlement was first called "Duwamps", but changed its name to "Seattle" in honor of a friendly native, Chief Sealth. Both moniker and settlement survived the skirmishes and ambushes of the **Puget Sound War** of 1855–56, a conflict that resulted in local natives being consigned to reservations.

Afterwards, as the surrounding forest was gradually felled and the wood sawn and shipped abroad, Seattle grew slowly as a timber town and port, but it was a place with a problem: there weren't enough women. The enterprising Asa Mercer, the president (and only instructor) of the fledgling state university, took himself off east to bring back potential brides. Mercer made two trips, returning with 57 women, some of whom seem to have had a real shock: "[We were met by men] who looked like grizzlies in store clothes, their hair slicked down like sea otters", complained one.

It was, however, the Klondike Gold Rush of 1897 that put Seattle firmly on the national map and boosted its shipbuilding trade. The city was soon a large industrial center, one that to this day holds a significant place in US labor history. Trade unions grew strong and the Industrial Workers of the World or "Wobblies" made Seattle a main base, coordinating the country's first general strike in 1919, during the period of high unemployment which followed the end of World War I.

World War II brought a new impetus to growth, and the decades since have seen Seattle thrive as the economic center of the booming Pacific Northwest. Today Seattle is among the most prosperous cities in the US, comparatively immune to the downturn in the economy everywhere else. Still, there's a sharp contrast between the obvious wealth and power of Seattle's many high-tech companies – such as Boeing, the world's biggest manufacturer of airplanes, and Microsoft, the world leader in computer software – and the very high levels of homelessness. This, combined with Seattle's surprisingly large and visible community of teenage runaways, serves as an all-too-tangible reminder that not everyone shares in the city's good fortune. However, these signs of poverty are confined to small pockets of the city: you may be advised to avoid some of the areas along the southwest shore of Lake Washington below US-90, but elsewhere you can enjoy the "**Emerald City**" surrounded by the trinkets of its prosperity and its coastal beauty.

Arrival and information

Seattle/Tacoma's **Sea-Tac Airport** is fourteen miles south of downtown; after customs, your luggage is taken away again to be put on a conveyor belt and you take the underground train to the main terminal, where there's a small **visitor's information kiosk** (daily summer 9.30am–7pm, winter 8.30am–1pm) in front of the baggage carousel. Outside, the *Gray Line Airport Express* **bus** ($7; pay the driver) leaves every twenty minutes (5am–midnight) – sometimes more frequently – for the half-hour journey downtown, dropping off at major hotels, though further along, the local *Metro* bus makes regular runs along much the same route for $1.10 and takes only ten minutes more. Bus #194 connects with the bus tunnel terminal at Third Ave and University, while the slower #174 runs down to Second Ave. Major **car rental** firms have airport branches, and operate shuttles to their pick-up points: once you're behind the wheel, Hwy-99, the Pacific Highway, leads into town. You can also pick up a car downtown – see "Listings" for details.

Arriving **by car**, you'll probably come in on **I-5**, the main north–south highway between the Canadian border and California; for downtown, take the Stewart St or Union St exit. The **Amtrak** station at Third Ave and Jackson St (☎464-1930), south of downtown near the International District, and the **Greyhound** station, at Eighth Ave and Stewart St (☎624-3456), east of downtown, are both a bus-ride from downtown accommodation. *Green Tortoise*, with between two and four runs per week to and from Portland and San Francisco, drops off and picks up at Ninth Ave and Stewart St (☎324-7433).

Local Puget Sound **ferries** arrive at the pier at the foot of Marion St, downtown; long-distance sevices from British Columbia dock north of downtown at Alaskan Way and Clay St.

Information

The **Seattle-King County Visitor's Bureau**, inside the Washington State Convention Center at Seventh Ave and Pike (Mon–Fri 8.30am–5pm; ☎461-5840), has racks of brochures on Seattle and Washington state, as well as handy free maps and local bus timetables. The free official travellers' guide, *Destination Washington*, provides a comprehensive list of the state's accommodations.

City Transit

Getting around Seattle's downtown area is best done on foot or by taking advantage of the free **bus** services (some of which run underground along Third Ave). Cross out of the free zone – to the University District for example – and you pay the driver as you get off; come back in and you pay as you enter. Single fares are

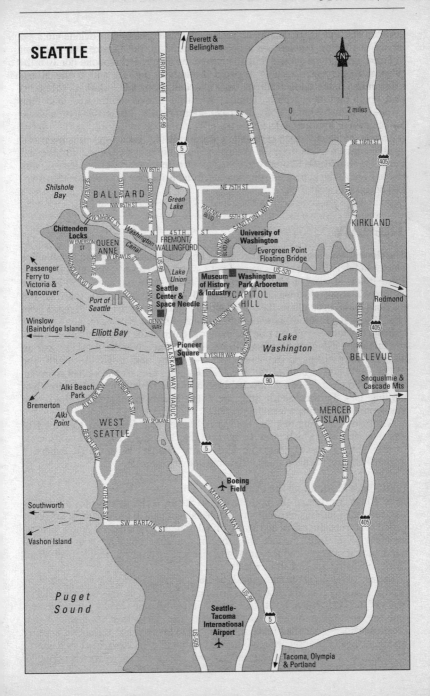

SEATTLE

Everett &
Bellingham

AURORA AVE N

US-99

NE 125TH ST

NE 116TH ST

I-5

405

NW 85TH ST

*Shilshole
Bay*

BALLARD

NE 75TH ST

Green
Lake

NE 75TH ST

KIRKLAND

MARKET ST

GREENWOOD AVE N

15TH AVE

SEAVIEW

NW MARKET ST

NW 65TH ST

NE 45TH ST

RAVENNA BLVD

55TH ST

SAND POINT WAY NE

Chittenden
Locks

W EMERSON ST

Washington Canal

QUEEN
ANNE

45TH ST

FREMONT/
WALLINGFORD

University of
Washington

MONTLAKE BLVD NE

MAGNOLIA BLVD

15TH AVE

W DRAVUS

Evergreen Point
Floating Bridge

Passenger
Ferry to
Victoria &
Vancouver

US-99

QUEEN ANNE AVE N

Lake
Union

Museum
of History
& Industry

Washington
Park Arboretum

US-520

Redmond

Port of
Seattle

ELLIOTT AVE

Seattle
Center &
Space Needle

CAPITOL
HILL

12TH AVE

BELLEVUE WAY SE

405

Winslow
(Bainbridge Island)

Elliott Bay

DENNY
WAY

Pioneer
Square

E MADISON ST

LAKE WASHINGTON BLVD E

Lake
Washington

BELLEVUE

ALASKAN WAY VIADUCT

E YESLER WAY

4TH AVE S

90

Snoqualmie &
Cascade Mts

Alki Beach
Park

ALKI AVE SW

HARBOR AVE SW

MERCER
ISLAND

Bremerton

*Alki
Point*

WEST
SEATTLE

BEACH DR SW

SW SPOKANE ST

MERCER WAY

MERCER WAY

I-5

405

Southworth

47TH AVE SW

SW BARTON ST

Boeing
Field

E MARGINAL WAY S

Vashon Island

*Puget
Sound*

US-99

Seattle-
Tacoma
International
Airport

US-509

5

Tacoma, Olympia
& Portland

0   2 miles

between 85¢ and $1.60, depending on the zone and time of day; tickets are valid for an hour. **Day passes** are a good deal at $1.70, but they're only valid on holidays and at the weekend; buy them from the driver. Ticketbooks (for 10 or 20 rides at 15 percent discount) are sold throughout the city and at the **Metro Customer Assistance Offices**, 821 Second Ave and Marion (Mon–Fri 8am–5pm) and the Transit Tunnel, Westlake Station, Fifth Ave and Pine (Mon–Fri 9am–5.30pm). Both also have information and timetables (☎553-3000 for 24-hr Rider information).

Largely of novelty value, a mile-long **monorail** (80¢ each way) runs overhead on thin concrete stilts from the Westlake Shopping Center Mall at Fifth Ave and Pine St to the Seattle Center, while vintage **streetcars** (part of the Metro – fares 85¢ to $1.60) travel up and down the waterfront, from Pier 70 to Pioneer Square – and beyond.

The City

The **downtown** core of **SEATTLE** would be a predictable collection of tall office blocks and department stores were it not for two enclaves of color and character: **Pike Place Market**, a busy, crowded morass of stalls and cafés, and **Pioneer Square**, a small old-town area of restored redbrick, lined with taverns. The fabulous views over Elliott Bay, too, help to lighten the feel – best perused from along **the waterfront**, despite its clutter of tourist shops.

From downtown, you can ride the monorail north to the **Seattle Center**, where the futuristic, flying-saucer-topped tower of the **Space Needle** presides over an assortment of theaters, museums and the opera house. To the south, the distinctive concrete bulk of the **Kingdome** sports arena/concert hall maroons the small Southeast Asian-dominated **International District** behind its stretch of parking lots. Further south still, the huge **Museum of Flight** charts the development of air travel from Icarus on.

A couple of outlying districts tend to be livelier than downtown: **Capitol Hill** has cafés and bars which form the heart of the city's gay scene (and holds some of the best city parks); and the **University District** is, as you'd expect, a students' district of cheap cafés with some uptempo nightlife.

Pike Place Market and the Waterfront

Pike Place Market, at the bottom of Pike Street, is rightly downtown Seattle's biggest attraction. Buskers and street entertainers play to busy crowds, smells of coffee drift from the cafés, and stalls are piled high with lobsters, crabs, salmon, vegetables and fruit. Further into the long market building, craft stalls sell handmade jewellery, woodcarvings and silk-screen printing, while small shops stock a massive range of ethnic foods.

Farmers first brought their produce here in 1907, lowering food prices by selling straight from the barrow. The market boomed in the poverty-stricken years of the Depression, but by the Sixties it had become shabby and neglected, and the authorities decided to flatten the area altogether. Architect Victor Steinbrueck led a horrified protest: he wanted to preserve the turn-of-the-century buildings, and, more importantly, the whole character of the market as a source of affordable provisions for the elderly and the poor. There was a period of confrontation between the two lobbies, but in 1971 Seattlites voted overwhelmingly to keep the market. Now restored, it still provides low-priced food, thereby preserving its roots – though, perhaps inevitably, upscale restaurants catering to tourists and local yuppies are fast creeping in, undeterred by the surrounding area's porno theaters and teenage prostitutes.

Stairs in the market lead down to the **Hillclimb**, which descends past more shops and cafés to the **Waterfront**. The harbor's no longer deep enough for modern ocean-going ships, and much of the old waterfront has been turned over to the tourist trade while the port's real business goes on to the north and south. Almost opposite the Hillclimb, **Pier 59** is one of a line of old wooden jetties which once served the tall ships; it now houses Seattle's **Aquarium** (daily summer 10am–7pm, winter 10am–5pm; $6.50), which provides some lively information on marine life in the Sound, an underwater viewing dome and a pool of playful sea otters and seals. A combined ticket (for $10.80) also admits you to **Omnidome** next door (daily 10am–8.30pm; $5.95 for two films), showing films featuring clever graphics, or natural dramas such as the eruption of Mount St Helens.

South of Pier 59, the waterfront is lined with souvenir shops, restaurants and fish and chips stands, the most famous of which – though it has declined since the death of owner-founder Ivar Haglund – *Ivar's Acres of Clams*, comes complete with its own special stop ("Clam Central Station") on the **waterfront streetcar** (85¢), which carries tourists along the bay in restored vintage carriages. The waterfront gets back to business at Pier 52, where **Colman Dock** is the terminal for the *Washington State Ferries* (see "Listings" for ferry information), and a good place to watch them pull in and out – though it can get somewhat frantic in the rush hour with commuters crossing from suburban homes over the bay.

Seattle Art Museum

100 University St. Tues, Wed, Fri & Sat 10am–5pm, Thurs 10am–9pm, Sun noon–5pm. $5.

Close to Pike Place Market down along First Avenue, the gleamingly new **Seattle Art Museum** was completed in 1991 to a design by Robert Venturi. The Philadelphian architect took his commission seriously: he wanted to create a museum which was "popular yet esoteric, closed but open, [and] monumental yet inviting". To effect his purpose, Venturi's limestone- and terracotta-faced building has a 48-foot *Hammering Man* sculpture plonked outside the front door as a "tribute to the working man".

Inside the four-story building, a grand staircase leads from the lobby to the upper galleries, under the watchful eye of Chinese sculptures of camels, rams and guards. The second level is given over to temporary exhibitions and the third – and most diverting – boasts an eclectic collection of African, Asian, Oceanian, Levantine and Native American pieces: among many, there are extraordinary masks and fetishes from Guinea and Congo, and, from the Pacific Northwest, rattles and clappers, gargoyle-like wooden pipes, canoes, prow ornaments, more dancing masks and several enormous totem poles from British Columbia. The fourth floor traces the development of "Art in Europe and the United States", beginning with a handful of ancient Mediterranean artefacts, but the modern stuff is more eye-catching, mostly in its awfulness and/or inaccessibility. Look out for the elemental *Coloured Shouting* of Gilbert and George with a script that reads "The decadent artists stand for themselves and their chosen few... a crude denial of the life of the people".

Pioneer Square and around

Walk a few blocks inland from the ferry terminal and you come to **Pioneer Square** (actually an area of a few blocks focusing on First Avenue and Yesler Way) – Seattle's oldest section and another spot that had a close brush with the demolition balls of the Sixties. The restoration work is more glossy here than at Pike Place Market, and the square's old red brick, black wrought iron and heavy stonework bear the unmistakable hallmark of a well-tended historic district, with bookstores and galleries adding a veneer of sophistication. Rock music resounds from a group of lively taverns at night (see "Nightlife"), but by day there's little evidence of the more rumbustious aspects of the city's past. It was here in the mid-1800s that Henry Yesler erected the Puget Sound's first steam-powered sawmill, felling trees at the top of a nearby hill and rolling the logs down what's now Yesler Way, and was then known as the "skid road". Drunks and down-and-outs gathered here in the later years of the Depression and the term "skid row" passed into its present usage – or at least that's Seattle's version.

The whole district was razed in 1889 when a pot of boiling glue turned over in a cabinetmaker's shop and set the wooden buildings and streets ablaze. Rebuilding, the city resolved an unsavory problem with the sewage system (which had a nasty habit of flowing in reverse when the tide was high in the bay) by regrading the level of the land, with the result that entrances to the surviving brick buildings now came in at the old first-floor level. The ground floors, now below the earth, connected by underground passages, became a literal underworld that was soon a prime location for illicit activities (such as drinking during Prohibition). These passages were reopened in the Sixties, and can be explored on the 90-minute **Underground Tours** which leave more or less once an hour (late morning to mid-afternoon) from *Doc Maynard's* tavern, 610 First Ave (☎682-4646 for times and reservations; $5.50) – by far the most amusing way to find out about Seattle's seamy past, with witty guides taking an offbeat look at the city's history before leading you underground.

A couple of blocks from *Doc Maynard's*, at 117 South Main St, the **Klondike Gold Rush National Park** (daily 9am–5pm; free) is not a park at all, but a small museum where a free film and a few artefacts portray the 1897 rush which followed the discovery of gold in the Klondike region of Canada (see p.470). As soon as the first ship carrying Klondike gold docked in the city, Seattle's sharp-eyed capitalists espied massive trading potential in selling groceries, clothing, sledges and even ships to the gold-seekers, and launched a formidable publicity campaign, bombarding inland cities with propaganda billing Seattle above all other ports as the gateway to Yukon gold. It worked: prospectors streamed in, merchants (and con-men) scented easy profit, the population escalated and traders made a fortune. The dog population fared less well, as many a hapless mutt was harnessed to a sledge while gold-seekers practised "mushing" up and down Seattle's streets before facing Yukon snow. Jack London's novel *The Call of the Wild* puts the canine point of view, and gold fever is gloriously sent up in the Charlie Chaplin film *The Gold Rush* – shown free at the museum on weekend afternoons.

Almost opposite the museum, the large cobblestoned square of **Occidental Park** – with its off-putting groups of the drunk and destitute – displays four recently erected totem poles carved with the grotesque, almost cruel, features of creatures from Northwest Native American legends.

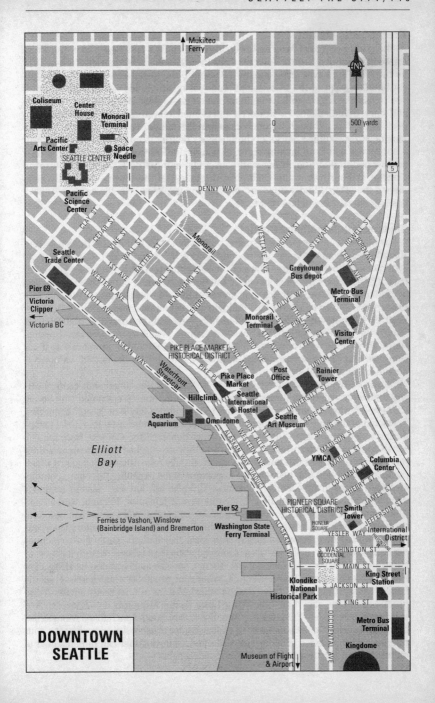

Mukilteo Ferry

N

500 yards

5

Coliseum

Center House

Monorail Terminal

Pacific Arts Center

Space Needle

SEATTLE CENTER

Pacific Science Center

DENNY WAY

CLAY ST

CEDAR ST

VINE ST

WALL ST

BATTERY ST

BELL ST

1ST AVE

WESTERN AVE

ELLIOTT AVE

Monorail

WESTLAKE AVE

VIRGINIA ST

STEWART ST

HOWELL ST

BOREN AVE

TERRY AVE

Seattle Trade Center

Pier 69
Victoria Clipper

Victoria BC

BLANCHARD ST

LENORA ST

OLIVE WAY

6TH AVE

PINE ST

Greyhound Bus depot

Metro Bus Terminal

ALASKAN WAY

Monorail Terminal

3RD AVE

Visitor Center

PIKE PLACE MARKET HISTORICAL DISTRICT

Waterfront Streetcar

PIKE PL

PIKE ST

Pike Place Market

Post Office

UNION ST

Rainier Tower

Hillclimb

Seattle International Hostel

UNIVERSITY ST

Seattle Aquarium

Omnidome

POST ALLEY

WESTERN AVE

Seattle Art Museum

SENECA ST

SPRING ST

Elliott Bay

ALASKAN WAY VIADUCT

MADISON ST

MARION ST

YMCA

COLUMBIA ST

Columbia Center

CHERRY ST

JAMES ST

JEFFERSON ST

Ferries to Vashon, Winslow (Bainbridge Island) and Bremerton

Pier 52

Washington State Ferry Terminal

ALASKAN WAY

PIONEER SQUARE HISTORICAL DISTRICT

PIONEER SQUARE

YESLER WAY

Smith Tower

International District

S WASHINGTON ST

OCCIDENTAL SQUARE

S MAIN ST

Klondike National Historical Park

S JACKSON ST

King Street Station

S KING ST

OCCIDENTAL AVE

Metro Bus Terminal

Kingdome

Museum of Flight & Airport

DOWNTOWN SEATTLE

The business district

At the corner of Yesler Way and Second Ave, Seattle's first skyscraper, the white terracotta-trimmed **Smith Tower**, edges the city's financial district. Built in 1914 by the New York typewriter mogul, L C Smith, the tower was, for years, the tallest building west of the Mississippi. Today it mostly holds private offices, but if you're passing it's worth looking in on the elegant lobby, decked out with marble and carved Indian heads. Restored brass-lined elevators serve an observation deck at the top, although it's often closed to the public. To the north, the prestigious new glassy office blocks of the business district loom over the Smith Tower – not on the whole an inviting sight, although the **Rainier Tower**, balanced on a narrow pedestal at Fourth Ave and University, and the dark, 76-story **Columbia Center**, at Fourth Ave and Columbia, the tallest of the towers (and aptly nicknamed the "Darth Vader building" or "the box the Space Needle came in"), have passing interest as engineering feats.

Chinatown/International District

A few blocks south of Pioneer Square, your way is blocked by the huge concrete **Kingdome**, Seattle's main sports and concerts arena, and the home of its Seahawks football team and Mariners baseball team. The Kingdome's spread of parking lots seems to signal an end to the downtown area, but pushing on east up S Jackson St, past the redbrick clocktower of the old railway station, the concrete expanses soon give way to the build-up of restaurants and ethnic grocers of Seattle's **Chinatown** – officially (and blandly) labelled the **International District** due to the presence of other far-eastern groups. Aside from some good restaurants, for a city with a strong history of Southeast Asian immigration it's a rundown and rather scrappy neighborhood, its tawdry blocks dotted with streetpeople and few actual sights.

Seattle's Chinatown hasn't always been desolate. In the nineteenth century this was an overcrowded and unruly district, its boarding houses crammed with young Chinese men who'd come over to earn money in the city's mills and canneries. Suspicion of the area's gambling halls and opium dens overflowed into racial hatred during a depression in the 1880s: federal laws debarred the Chinese from full citizenship and in the Northwest, Chinese workers were attacked and threatened, their homes burned. The Seattle authorities did eventually rake up an armed guard which made a belated and botched attempt to prevent mobs expelling the entire community (as happened in Tacoma), but most Chinese left anyway, leaving behind a depleted and scarred population. Later influxes of Japanese, Filipino, Korean and Thai immigrants, and more recently Vietnamese, Laotian and Cambodian newcomers, went some way to restoring a trace of the district's nineteenth-century vigor, but Chinatown has been regarded locally with some trepidation – partly due to increasing gang activity. In reality the area is more shabby than unsafe, though it is best to take care after dark. The focus of the district, insofar as it has one, is **Hing Hay Park** at Maynard and South King St, where an ornate oriental gateway stands beneath a large and rather faded dragon mural. But there's not really anything else to see beyond the absorbing little **Wing Luke Asian Museum** at 407 Seventh Ave and Jackson St (Tues–Fri 11am–4.30pm, Sat & Sun noon–4pm, closed Mon; $2.50, free Thurs), which goes some way to explaining local Asian-American history, with reference to the career of Wing Luke, the first Chinese-American to be elected to public office in Seattle, in 1962.

The Museum of Flight
9404 E Marginal Way. Daily 10am–5pm, until 9pm Thurs; $5.

The best and biggest of Seattle's museums, the **Museum of Flight** more than makes up for the twenty-minute bus ride (#174) south from downtown through the port's dreary industrial hinterland. As the birthplace of the Boeing company, Seattle has its own stake in aviation history, and has invested heavily in this huge museum, partly housed in the 1909 "Red Barn" that was Boeing's original manufacturing plant. The displays, accompanied by detailed information plaques and three separate filmshows, take in everything from the dreams of the ancients, through the work of the Wright brothers, with a working model of the windtunnel they used, to the growth of Boeing itself, with part of the Red Barn laid out as an early designer's workshop. The best bit of the museum is the huge glass-and-steel Great Gallery, big as a football field and hung with twenty full-sized aircraft – tiny, fragile-looking mail planes and a red sportscar that can apparently be given wings in minutes. There's also a replica of the Mercury space capsule that took John Glenn into space in 1962. Behind the gallery, museum staff hand out eggboxes and plasticine for the construction of model planes – one way to learn aerodynamics.

Southwest to Alki Beach
Southwest of downtown, on the other side of Elliott Bay (take bus #37 from downtown), the flat little peninsula of **Alki Point** is where Seattle's founders first tried to settle when they weighed anchor in the Puget Sound, optimistically christening their community "New York Alki" – New York "by and by" in the Chinook language. Defeated by floods and the lack of space, the town soon shifted over to what's now Pioneer Square, changing its name to Seattle after a friendly neighborhood chief. The peninsula's now a residential district, interesting only if you want to join the promenaders and cyclists along the narrow strip of **Alki Beach**, which offers pleasing views of Elliott Bay with the city skyline behind and the Olympic Mountains to the west. You can swim here too, but the water's pretty cold.

The Seattle Center
As you head north from Pike Place Market, downtown peters out around Virginia Street, beyond which lies a district once occupied by Denny Hill and now flattened into the **Denny Regrade**. Considering the momentous effort that went into knocking the hill down, it's a shame that nothing interesting has been built here – though the area around Bell Street, known as **Belltown**, has some character, its tough taverns now rubbing shoulders with upmarket cafés with French names. This apart, the regrade is probably best viewed from the window of the **monorail**, which runs from the Westlake Shopping Mall at Fifth Ave and Pine St downtown (80¢ one way), crosses the area on concrete supports, and ends up inside the **Seattle Center**.

The Seattle Center is an inheritance from the 1962 World's Fair, whose theme was "Century 21" (hence the idea of the spindly Space Needle tower, the fair's – and now Seattle's – adopted symbol). Since then the site of the fair has become a sort of culture-park, collecting the city's symphony, ballet and opera, a couple of theaters and a museum alongside the Space Needle, and a small amusement park.

The monorail drops you close to the **Space Needle** (observation deck daily summer 8am–midnight, winter 9am–midnight; $6). Though reminiscent of the

Star Trek era of space-fascination, this still exudes a fair amount of glamor, especially at night, when it's lit up and Seattle's well-to-do come to eat at its revolving restaurant. The view from the observation deck, where there's a (pricey) bar, is unmatched, and this is much the best place to get an overall orientation of the city and its surroundings.

Center House is next to the terminal also, an unappetizingly dark mall-like building, and the unlikely home of the first-rate **Seattle Children's Museum** as well as *The Group*, the city's leading multicultural theater group. Close by, the excellent **Pacific Science Center** (summer daily 10am–6pm; rest of year Mon–Fri 10am–5pm, Sat & Sun 10am–6pm; $5.50), is easily recognizable by its distinctive white arches. This is much livelier than it sounds, full of bright, innovative and often noisy exhibits on a huge range of science-based topics, from robotic and submarine technology to a model of the Puget Sound area, exploring its ebbs and tides; there's a planetarium and an IMAX theater inside here too.

Capitol Hill

Of all Seattle's neighborhoods, **Capitol Hill**, a fifteen-minute bus-ride east of downtown, has probably raised the most eyebrows over the years. Since young gays, hippies and assorted radicals moved in over the Sixties and Seventies, this has been the city's closest thing to an alternative center, fulcrum of the arts scene and chancier night-time activities. In fact, the shops and cafés around **Broadway**, the main street, are now pretty mainstream and, despite black leather jackets slung over teenage shoulders, the neighborhood's days at the cutting edge of Seattle Bohemia are probably over. Still, the concentration of easy-going restaurants, coffee houses and bars provides good day-time café-sitting and night-time drinking (see "Eating" and "Nightlife"), and if you're gay this is still very much the place to be – though homophobic violence can happen here as disturbingly often as it does anywhere in the US.

The northern end of the Capitol Hill district is, by contrast, quietly wealthy, mansions built on Gold Rush fortunes and trimmed with immaculate lawns sitting sedately around the shrubs and trees of **Volunteer Park**, named in honor of those who volunteered for the Spanish–American War of 1898. The lovely 1912 glass **Conservatory** here (daily summer 10am–7pm, winter 10am–4pm; free) packs an immediate aesthetic punch: divided into galleries simulating different climates (jungle, desert, rainforest, etc), it has a sweltering mix of perfect flowers and shrubs, and a huge collection of orchids. Also in the park, the old **Water Tower** can be climbed for a grand (and free) panorama across Seattle, albeit through wire mesh.

Ten blocks east of Volunteer Park, **Washington Park** stretches away to the north, encompassing the **University of Washington Arboretum**, whose assortment of trees shades footpaths and cycle tracks – a huge, leafy invitation for summer walks and picnics, and especially beautiful in fall when the trees turn brilliant shades of red and gold. At the south end of the park, is the immaculately designed **Japanese Tea Gardens** (March–Nov daily 10am to around dusk; $1.50), a landscape of neat ornamental lakes and flower-strewn banks.

The University District

Across Union Bay from the park, the **University District** (aka the "U" district) is livelier than Capitol Hill: a busy hotchpotch of coffee houses, cinemas, clothes, book and record shops, all catering to the tastes and budgets of the University of

Washington's 35,000 students. The area centers on University Way, known as "The Ave" and lined with cheap ethnic restaurants plus the cavernous *University Bookstore* – an excellent place to get the lowdown on the student scene.

The sprawling **campus** itself is more serene, its sedate nineteenth-century buildings and landscaped grounds overlooking Union Bay. There are a couple of museums here: the pale brick **Henry Art Gallery**, at NE 15th Ave and NE 41st St (Tues–Sun 10am–5pm, until 9pm Thurs; $3), houses American and European paintings from the last two centuries, and mounts small innovative shows, often drawing on local work. The **Thomas Burke Memorial Museum**, on the north-western corner of the campus at 17th Ave and NE 45th St (daily 10am–5pm, until 10pm Thurs; $3), has carved totem poles, painted wooden masks from the Northwest coast, plaited-fiber fans from Polynesia and sorcery charms from New Guinea. Across Montlake Bridge, back on the other side of Lake Union, the **Museum of History and Industry**, at 2700 24th Ave East and East Shelby (daily 10am–5pm; $3), has a gallery reconstructing Seattle in the 1880s, with homes, storefronts and a free film, though this is rather out on a limb (bus #25 from downtown drops you fairly near) – enthusiasts only.

Lake Washington Canal, Ballard and other northern parts of town

The U district and Seattle's other northern neighborhoods – working west, Fremont/Wallingford, Green Lake/Greenwood and Ballard – are sliced off from the rest of town by water. Lake Union, in the middle, is connected to the larger Lake Washington to the east, and the sea to the west by the eight-mile-long **Lake Washington Ship Canal**. Built at the turn of the century to carry ships to safe harbors on the inland lakes, the canal was used during World War I to safeguard battleships from exposure to attack in the more open Elliott Bay. If you have an hour to spare, the procession of boats passing from salt water to fresh through a set of canal locks called the **Hiram M Chittenden Locks**, near the mouth of the canal, makes pleasant viewing (bus #17 from downtown), and migrating salmon bypass the locks via the **fish ladder**, a sort of piscine staircase laid out with viewing windows. In peak migrating season (late summer for salmon, fall and early winter for trout) the water behind the locks is full of huge, jumping fish.

East of the locks is Salmon Bay, on the south side of which, beside NW 15th Avenue's Ballard Bridge, is **Fisherman's Terminal**, crowded with the boats of Seattle's fishing fleet; you can buy freshly caught fish here. On the northern side of Salmon Bay, **Ballard** (reachable by several buses from downtown) was settled by Scandinavian fishermen. The **Nordic Heritage Museum**, 3014 NW 67th St (Tues–Sat 10am–4pm, Sun noon–4pm; $3), outlines their history from poverty in rural Scandinavia, through immigration problems at Ellis Island and New York tenements to arrival in the West, in a series of rather musty tableaux in the basement of an old school. Bar a couple of nightspots (see p.161), there's little else to see here, though if you do find yourself passing further east, along the northern shore of Lake Union, look out for **Gasworks Park**, at N Northlake Way and Wallingford, where the rusting black towers of an old gasworks have been left as "urban sculpture" and the slag heaps grassed over to make kite-flying mounds; on summer evenings skateboarders bring ghetto-blasters, and their music echoes round the old industrial site. The park sticks out into the middle of Lake Union at the foot of the **Fremont/Wallingford** district, a largely white and comparatively prosperous neighborhood that extends north (on the west side of I-5) into the quiet residential streets of **Green Lake/Greenwood**. Here, at 5500 N Phinney

Ave and N 55th St, you'll find the **Woodland Park Zoo** (daily summer 9.30am–6pm, winter 9.30am–4pm; $3; bus #5 from First Ave and Union St), an open zoo with naturalish habitats for the animals and, oddly enough, a memorial rock in the African savanna area paying tribute to **Jimi Hendrix**, local lad made world-famous rock guitarist. Hwy-99 separates the zoo from the rest of **Woodland Park**, which extends northeast around Green Lake, a popular haunt for local joggers.

Lake Washington and the eastern outskirts

Until it was bridged, **Lake Washington** isolated the city from the countryside and small farms to the east. Ferries laden with farm produce made slow progress across the water, and the lake became a sort of tradesmen's entrance to the city while the center of Seattle looked towards the big commercial ships docking in Elliott Bay. All this changed when two long, floating bridges, one built in the Forties, the second in the Sixties, opened up commuting possibilities: business people poured across, tripling the population of one-time rural towns **Bellevue**, **Kirkland** and **Redmond** and turning them into affluent city suburbs. Redmond became the world headquarters of software giants Microsoft; Kirkland built plush leisure facilities along its waterfront; and Bellevue quickly outgrew its suburban status to become the state's fourth largest city with its own smart business district and shopping area, the showpiece of which is the expensively stocked **Bellevue Square Mall**. Malls and lake views aside, these three towns have little to recommend them, though neighboring **Mercer Island**, in the middle of Lake Washington, is a pleasant, leafy interlude just a few minutes' drive from downtown along I-90.

Accommodation

There's no shortage of hotel space in Seattle, but it can be difficult to find the middle ground between smart, expense-account-type places – some of which are superb – and the seedy dives of the down-and-out. The standard-issue **motels** lining the highways on the outskirts of town are reliable, if predictable, but you'll sniff far more of Seattle's flavor by staying at a **Bed and Breakfast**. Mostly homey and comfortable, these lie scattered amongst the city's neighborhoods with a concentration in the **Capitol Hill** district on the northeast edge of downtown. Most B&Bs take reservations direct, but others use an agency who will require a deposit (credit cards will do) with your booking, which should be made well in advance: try the *Pacific Bed & Breakfast Agency*, 701 NW 60th St (☎784-0539), or the *Washington Bed and Breakfast Guild*, 2442 NW Market St (☎548-6224), which has members across the state as well as in Seattle.

Budget travellers are in for a treat at the Seattle International **Hostel** on the waterfront, but otherwise low-price, downtown accommodation is usually grim and occasionally risky. If you want to **camp**, try *Fay Bainbridge State Park* (☎842-3931) at the northeast end of Bainbridge Island (see p.000), where there are a handful of basic sites.

Hotels and motels

Alexis Hotel, 1007 First Ave at Madison (☎624-4844). Medium-sized hotel downtown near the waterfront. All the luxuries, from jacuzzis to real wood-burning fireplaces, but no views from this tastefully restored early twentieth-century building. ⑦.

The Edgewater, Pier 67 at Wall St and Alaskan Way (☎728-7000). Seattle's only waterfront hotel is a treat. Rates soar if you want a room overlooking Puget Sound. ⑦–⑧.

Mercer Island Travelodge, 7645 Sunset Hwy, Mercer Island (☎232-8000). Simple, comfortable motel doubles. About five miles east of downtown, just off I-90 on Lake Washington's Mercer Island, a leafy, low-key island-suburb. ③.

Moore Hotel, 1926 Second Ave at Virginia St (☎448-4851). Grim and basic hotel with unsettling nightlife just outside the front door. But it is low-priced and right downtown, a stone's throw from Pike Place Market. ②.

Motel 6, 18900 S 47th Ave (☎241-1648). The lowest prices of the nationally known motels, but it is some distance out of town near the airport; exit 152 from I-5. ①.

Pacific Plaza, 400 Spring St (☎623-3900). Newly renovated 1920s hotel, halfway between Pike Place Market and Pioneer Square. Unambitious doubles. ④.

St Regis Hotel, 116 Stewart St at Second Ave (☎448-6366). Scruffy but centrally located hotel across the street from the Pike Place Market. It's a risky area at night, but fine during the day. Very basic doubles. ②.

Seattle Hotel, 315 Seneca St (☎623-5110). Modern, downtown hotel, with reasonably priced doubles. ④.

Stouffer Madison Hotel, 515 Madison St at Sixth Ave (☎583-0300). Massive, luxurious hotel at the southeast edge of downtown. ⑦.

Super 8 Motel, 3100 S 192nd St (☎433-8188 or 1-800/800-8000). Standard motel doubles out near the airport. ②.

Woodmark Hotel, 1200 Carillon Point, Kirkland (☎822-3700 or 1-800/822-3700). Located in the wealthy suburb of Kirkland, seven miles east of downtown on the shores of Lake Washington, this splendid modern hotel is the height of luxury, but it's only worth the price if you're in one of the lakeside rooms (or suites). ⑧.

Bed and Breakfasts

Chelsea Station Bed & Breakfast Inn, 4915 N Linden Ave (☎547-6077). Opposite the south entrance of Woodland Park Zoo, northwest of downtown across Lake Union. Good-quality doubles, with king beds. ④.

College Inn, 4000 NE University Way in the U district (☎633-4441). Very popular, basic B&B above its own restaurant and bar. Rates include full breakfast. A students' and backpackers' favorite. ④.

Gaslight Inn, 1727 15th Ave at Howell (☎325-3654). Capitol Hill landmark home converted into attractive B&B, with its own swimming pool. ④.

Green Gables Guesthouse, 1503 W Second Ave (☎282-6863). Refurbished turn-of-the-century villa near Seattle Center. Rather twee, but the food is delicious compensation. Four rooms. ④.

Lake Union B&B, 2217 N 36th St (☎547-9965). Three blocks north of Gasworks Park, this 2-roomed B&B offers ample and luxurious accommodation. Parking can be a pain. ⑤.

ACCOMMODATION PRICE CODES

All accommodation prices in this book have been coded using the symbols below, corresponding to US dollar prices in the US chapters and equivalent Canadian dollar rates in the Canadian chapters. Prices are for the least expensive double rooms in each establishment, and only include local taxes where we explicitly say so.

For a full explanation see p.46 in *Basics*.

①	up to US$30	④	US$60–80	⑦	US$130–180
②	US$30–45	⑤	US$80–100	⑧	US$180+
③	US$45–60	⑥	US$100–130		

Roberta's Bed & Breakfast Inn, 1147 E 16th Ave at Prospect (☎329-3326). Plushly furnished Capitol Hill B&B on quiet residential street near Volunteer Park. Five double rooms. ⑤.

Salisbury House, 750 16th E Ave at Aloha (☎328-8682). Capitol Hill location for this grand maple-floored, high-ceilinged B&B. Four doubles. ⑤.

Hostels

Commodore Hotel, 2013 Second Ave (☎448-8868). Bargain-basement, cheerless downtown hotel in chancy location. Dormitory, hostel-like, beds at $12; also singles and doubles. ①.

Green Tortoise Backpackers' Guesthouse, 715 N Second Ave at Roy (☎322-1222). New uptown hostel, partly owned by the alternative bus company, two blocks north of the Seattle Center. Bus #15 or #18 from *Amtrak*, #1, #2 or #13 from *Greyhound*. $10 dorms, also private doubles. ①–②.

Seattle International AYH Hostel, 84 Union St, behind Pike Place Market (☎622-5443). Comfortable and well equipped, with dorm beds for $14 (*AYH* members) or $17 (non-members) a night. Midnight curfew, and you'll need a sheet sleeping bag. Closed 10am–5pm. Full membership required and reservations advisable from June to September. ①.

Vashon Island AYH Hostel, 12119 SW Cove Rd, Vashon Island (May–Oct; ☎463-2592). Rural Vashon Island is a thirty-minute ferry ride (Mon–Sat) from Seattle's Pier 50. A refreshing break from the city; see p.164 for details.

YMCA, 909 Fourth Ave (☎382-5000). By far the best option if you want your own room, clean and safe and open to men and women. Dorm beds (which are reserved for *AYH* members) cost $17, also private singles and doubles. ①–②.

YWCA, 1118 Fifth Ave (☎461-4888). For women only, and slightly older (and cheaper) than the *YMCA*. Large clean rooms with or without private bath. ②.

Eating

You don't have to spend a fortune in Seattle to **eat** extraordinarily well: among the coffee shops of Capitol Hill, the bargain-rate restaurants of the University District, and above all at Pike Place Market there are excellent pickings. **Seafood** is the city's specialty – salmon, trout and crab among a host of less familiar (to East Coast and European eyes) creatures that will set your mouth watering (or guessing). Seattle's wide ethnic mix is reflected in the restaurants and cafés too, while the health food/vegetarian influence is as strong as you might expect in a major Pacific Coast metropolis.

Pike Place Market

During the day, there's no better place to find food than **Pike Place Market**, which extends over several city blocks below First Avenue – between Virginia and Pike streets – with the **Main Arcade** below the corner of Pike Street and Pike Place, directly opposite the **Corner** and **Sanitary** market buildings.

Meals and snacks are obtainable either in picnic form from the stalls and ethnic/wholefood groceries, or served up in cafés and restaurants. Everything's informal – it's part of the market's much-vaunted democratic air – and there are lots of places to choose from, all crowding the market's narrow corridors, although on a busy Saturday, it's not so much where you want to eat, but more a case of finding a vacant stool or table. However, the market starts to close down at around 6pm (and most stalls and cafés don't open on Sunday), after which Pike Place is a less tempting (and slightly threatening) prospect.

Athenian Inn, main floor of Main Arcade (☎624-7166). Something of an institution, this café's window tables, overlooking Puget Sound, are much sought after. Breakfast (especially the hash) is popular, and the lengthy menu is matched by an extensive beer list. Mon–Sat 6.30am–7pm.

El Puerco Lloron, on the Hillclimb (☎624-0541). A low-price, authentic Mexican restaurant. Daily, 11.30am to 8pm or 9pm.

Lowell's Restaurant, main floor of Main Arcade (☎622-2036). Join the stallholders for an early breakfast at this well-established café-restaurant, well known for the quality of its coffee and seafood: try the oysters. Daily 7am–5pm.

Place Pigalle, on the staircase behind *Pike Place Fish*, Main Arcade (☎624-1756). Once a tough working-men's bar, but now a restaurant serving up medium-priced French cuisine and seafood. Mon–Sat 11.30am–10pm.

Three Girls Bakery, lower floor of Sanitary Market (☎622-1045). Superb and filling sandwiches on freshly baked bread served at either the take-out window or the lunch counter. Mon–Sat 7am–6pm.

In and around Pioneer Square

Though a fine place for live music and drinking (see p.160), **Pioneer Square** isn't so hot for inexpensive food: the taverns all serve light meals because they have to by law and, generally speaking, it's pretty mediocre stuff. The square and the adjoining **business district** do, however, boast several of Seattle's finest restaurants, while the neighboring **International District** features a range of Chinese and Vietnamese cuisine to suit any pocket-book.

Al Boccalino, 1 Yesler Way (☎622-7688). One of the best Italian restaurants in town, with high prices to match. Closed Sun; reservations recommended.

Bangkok House, 606 S Weller (☎382-9888). Fine Thai cuisine with delicious satays. Inexpensive.

Chau's Chinese Restaurant, 310 S Fourth Ave (☎621-0006). Cantonese cuisine with the emphasis on seafood. Inexpensive.

Dahlia Lounge, 1904 Fourth Ave (☎682-4142). Between Stewart and Virginia streets east of Pike Place Market. One of the most expensive restaurants in town, but the seafood is definitely something special, forming the centerpiece of an inventive menu. Reservations are advisable.

Elliott Bay Café, 101 S Main St (☎682-6664). Reasonably priced wholefood served up in the cozy book-lined basement of the *Elliott Bay Book Company* bookstore, until 10pm (5pm Sun). You're welcome to browse while you eat.

Hon's Restaurant, 416 S Fifth Ave (☎623-4470). Chinese and Vietnamese dishes.

House of Hong, 409 S Eighth St at Jackson (☎622-7997). Massive restaurant serving some of the best Chinese food around. Inexpensive.

Metropolitan Grill, 818 Second Ave (☎624-3287). Superior steaks in a long and handsome bar that's a favorite destination for after-hours business people.

Mikado, 514 S Jackson St (☎622-5206). Classy Japanese restaurant with a good sushi bar. Closed Sun.

New Orleans Creole Restaurant, 114 First Ave (☎622-2563). You really come here for the live music, but the medium-priced Cajun cuisine isn't bad at all: stick to the gumbo and crayfish.

Tai Tung, 659 S King St (☎622-7372). Popular Cantonese restaurant, one of the International District's oldest.

Trattoria Mitchell, 84 Yesler Way (☎623-3885). Low-price, heaped portions of Italianate food served until 4am Tuesday through Saturday.

Viet My, 129 Prefontaine Place South (☎382-9923). Just off Fourth Ave at Washington. Delicious, inexpensive Vietnamese food in unpretentious surroundings.

Capitol Hill

Options at **Capitol Hill** include laid-back ethnic café-restaurants and chic little coffee houses: locals are inordinately fond of coffee, milky "lattes" being the favorite tipple. The inexpensive norm around here is interrupted by the occasional exclusive bistro.

B&O Espresso, 204 E Belmont (☎322-5028). Lively coffee house with some great desserts.

Byzantion, 601 E Broadway (☎325-7580). Good quality Greek dishes at reasonable prices. The omelettes are a delight.

Cause Célèbre Café, 524 E 15th Ave at Mercer (☎323-1888). First-class wholefood served to a cheerful mix of straight and gay customers. The Sunday brunch is a real treat and there's a fine selection of coffees.

Deluxe Bar and Grill, 625 E Broadway (☎324-9697). Casual restaurant serving nachos, salads and pasta at outdoor tables.

Dilettante, 416 E Broadway (☎329-6463). Pleasurable coffee house specializing in chocolate concoctions.

Gravity Bar, first floor of Broadway Market, 401 E Broadway at Thomas (☎325-7186). Splendid and imaginative vegetarian food served in chic, modernistic surroundings. Also downtown at 113 Virginia St and First Ave (☎448-8826).

Kokeb, 926 12th Ave (☎322-0485). Simple restaurant offering low-priced and spicy Ethiopian dishes. At the south end of the district.

Matzoh Momma, 509 E 15th Ave at Republican (☎324-6262). Quality Jewish deli-restaurant with doorstep-sized sandwiches.

Piecora's Pizzaria & Pastaleria, 1401 E Madison St (☎322-9411). The district's favorite pizza parlor.

Rovers, 2808 E Madison St at 28th Ave (closed Sun & Mon; ☎325-7442). Exquisite (and very expensive) French-style cuisine featuring local delicacies like Ellensburg lamb, rabbit and seafood (try the sturgeon).

Siam on Broadway, 616 E Broadway at Roy St (☎324-0892). Tasty Thai delicacies at reasonable rates. Very popular, so be prepared to wait in line.

The University District

An obvious locale for inexpensive eating, the **University District** has lots of bargain-basement ethnic restaurants, especially Chinese, Greek, Italian, Mexican, Thai and Vietnamese. Finding somewhere good to eat is simply a question of walking up and down University Way – between about NE 40th and NE 50th streets until you find what you want. Expect to be harassed (however peacefully) by panhandlers.

Ave!, 4743 University Way (☎527-9830). Standard Italian food in well-established restaurant.

College Inn Cafe, 4000 University Way (☎633-4441). Beneath the *College Inn*, this diner serves filling, traditional meals till late at night. A favorite budget choice.

Continental, 4549 University Way (☎632-4700). Popular Greek restaurant where the food is a lot better than the decor.

Costas, 4559 University Way (☎633-2751). Filling Greek meals at low prices.

Grand Illusion Espresso and Pastry, 1405 NE 50th St at University Way (☎523-3935). Cozy, vegetarian adjunct to the *Grand Illusion* arts cinema. A good spot to sit with the Sunday papers (which they provide).

Sunlight Café, 6403 NE Roosevelt Way (☎522-9060). Busy and reasonably priced vegetarian café-restaurant on the northwest edge of the district at NE 63rd St.

Nightlife and entertainment

Jimi Hendrix was born in Seattle (his *Spanish Castle Magic* celebrated a now-defunct local nightclub), and Ray Charles came here to make his name. But nothing in the city's musical history could anticipate the impact of **grunge**, which sprang out of Seattle when Washington-born **Nirvana** hit the big time in late 1991. Kurt Cobain's suicide in April 1994 may turn out to have marked the end of an era, but for some years, the success of Nirvana, phenomenal and immediate, made Seattle the hippest city in the States, revitalized the local band scene and attracted many imitators. These pretenders to the underground crown (of thorns) are the ones you can expect to see in the taverns and clubs of Seattle's **live music** scene today, the big names having moved on to international heights.

The estimable *Q Magazine* produced a working definition of grunge: "A rock style which straddles both heavy metal and indie and studiously avoids the crisply articulated melody, the cheerful rhythmic skip and the casual but smart stage attire". It is, as they say, something of an acquired taste – and it's certainly loud – but, much to its credit, grunge almost always eschews the cock-rock lyrics of its heavy-metal cousin in favor of more thought-provoking material, with punk and nihilistic themes and undertones.

If grunge isn't your scene, you'll still find Seattle's nightlife, taken on its own easy-going terms, lively and convivial. The famous (in all types of music) often appear at the *Paramount* downtown (see listings below), but otherwise scores of taverns and clubs showcase local and West Coast bands of (non-grunge) repute, usually for a small cover. The emphasis is on **rock & roll** or **rhythm & blues**, with a good dash of **jazz**, enthusiastically delivered and accompanied by **dancing** where there's room. All-round it makes for a warmly down-to-earth and unpretentious scene, where a good proportion of the audience show up in jeans and there's little scope for posing. There are, of course, the dress-up video-dance places you'd find in any city, but they're less typically local and certainly less fun.

As far as **drinking** goes, there's an enormous variety of potential venues, ranging from **taverns** (which in Washington sell beer and wine but not spirits) to **bars**, which sell everything but must be attached to a restaurant.

On the **arts** front things are relatively sophisticated, particularly in the realm of **theater**. A dozen or so bright and innovative theater groups rework the classics and provide up-to-the-minute and cosmopolitan plays, and the city's a magnet for hopeful young actors, many of whom are marking time behind the craft stalls in Pike Place Market. There's also a fair demand for art and rerun **movies**, shown in the city's wonderful collection of tiny, atmospheric cinemas.

SeattleWeekly, 75¢ from boxes on the streets, is good for movie reviews, theater and arts **listings**, and the what's on sections of the Friday editions of *The Seattle Times* or *Seattle Post Intelligencer* contain live music details. *Ticketmaster* (☎628-0888) can supply **tickets** for most sporting and arts events, with payment taken against your credit card over the phone, while their *Discount Ticket Booth* (☎233-1111) opens at 10am to sell same-day tickets at heavily reduced rates, cash only. *Ticket/Ticket*, Pike Place Market information booth, First Ave and Pike (Tues–Sun noon–6pm; ☎324-2744), offers a similar service, selling theater and concert tickets at half price, but they won't tell you what they have over the telephone, so you have to turn up in person.

Drinking, live music and dancing

Downtown, there's no better introduction to the tavern scene than **Pioneer Square**, where a cluster of lively establishments often host jazz and rhythm & blues bands. Walk around outside until you hear something you like, and look out for "joint cover nights" staged every month or so, where you can get into five or six venues for as many dollars. Several of the key underground/grunge-rock taverns and clubs are also easy to reach, grouped together near Pike Place Market, with others dotted around Seattle's **northern districts**, where there's plenty of reggae and folk music too. **Capitol Hill**'s drinking-places span the range, from chic yuppie bars to the smoky pool-table-and-ripped-jean scene, but the district is most distinctive as a coffee-house habitat and as the focus for the gay scene (see also "Gay Seattle" below).

Downtown

Central Tavern, 207 S First Ave (☎622-0209). Live blues and R&B acts nightly from around 9pm.

Crocodile Café, two blocks north of Pike Place Market, at 2200 Second Ave and Blanchard, (☎448-2114; performance information ☎441-5611). All sorts of stuff here – from jazz, rock and R&B to poetry readings and grunge; one of the hippest places in town. Diner on the premises. Normal cover $8.

Dimitriou's Jazz Alley, 2037 Sixth Ave at Lenora (☎441-9729). Best jazz joint in town, showcasing international stars as well as up-and-coming brilliants. Stylish club; mediocre food (Tues–Sun 7pm–midnight).

Doc Maynard's Public House, 610 First Ave (☎682-4649). A refurbished Pioneer Square tavern with a magnificent, giant-sized wooden bar. Popular with tourists. Bands, mostly R&B, on Friday and Saturday nights.

New Orleans Creole Restaurant, 114 S First Ave (☎622-2563). Anything from Cajun through to ragtime, with some big-name jazz bands at the weekend.

Off-Ramp, 109 E Eastlake Ave (☎628-0232). Venue for Nirvana's legendary four-hour concert of 1990 – aficionados swear it was the best they ever gave – this rough-edged club (mostly) keeps the grunge faith. At Denny Way and Stewart St, by I-5.

OK Hotel Café, 212 S Alaskan Way (☎621-7903). Once a mushers' favorite, the place is more diverse today, with its winning (grunge) ways mixed in with some of the most avant-garde (read ear-splitting/melody-eschewing) bands around.

Old Timer's Café, 620 First Ave (☎623-9800). Narrow and crowded tavern with nightly blues and jazz acts.

Pacific Northwest Brewing Company, 322 S Occidental Ave (☎621-7002). Tasty range of microbrews. Outside tables. Always popular, but packed out after Kingdome events.

Paramount, 901 Pine St (☎682-1414). Venue for the really big names.

RKCNDY, 1812 N Yale Ave (☎623-0470). Big and boisterous – grunge, punk and heavy metal acts a regular feature. Gay nights and some well-known faces too. Pronounced "rock candy".

Virginia Inn, 1937 First Ave (☎728-1937). Young professionals and old timers mix in this easy-going bar near Pike Place Market at First and Virginia.

Vogue, 2018 First Ave (☎443-0673). Rings in your nipples and studs in your nose will help you blend into this alternative/grunge/punk club. Between Virginia and Lenora streets.

Capitol Hill

Comet Tavern, 922 E Pike St just off Broadway (☎323-9853). No-frills bar with smoky pool tables and student-wannabe-nihilist crowd.

Encore Restaurant and Lounge, 1518 11th Ave (☎324-6617). Hard-liquor bar popular with lesbians and gay men.

Hombres Saloon, 1413 14th Ave (☎323-2158). Pleasant neighborhood gay tavern. Pool, pinball and darts; crowded at the weekend.

Neighbors, 1509 Broadway at E Pike (☎324-5358). Gay hangar-like disco. Very popular.

Re-Bar, 1114 E Howell St at Boren Ave (☎233-9873). Probably the best dance spot in Seattle starting nightly at 9pm. Soul and hip-hop are particular favorites, but the music changes emphasis nightly. Mostly gay – especially on "Queer Disco Nights"– but heteros come here in force too. Near Denny Way intersection just west of I-5.

Timberline, 2015 Boren Ave (☎622-6220). Premier Country & Western nightspot for gays, lesbians and "friends of goodwill". On the west edge of Capitol Hill.

Tug's Belmont Tavern, 518 E Pine St (☎323-1145). Hot and sweaty video dance bar with largely gay clientele.

Wild Rose Tavern, 1021 E Pike St (☎324-9210). A popular venue for lesbians, with decent food and often live music or entertainment.

University District, Fremont/Wallingford and Ballard

Backstage, 2208 NW Market St (☎781-2805; box office ☎789-1184). Basement club in Ballard staging quality jazz, rock, reggae and folk acts, some of national renown.

Big Time Brewery and Alehouse, 4133 NE University Way (☎545-4509). Microbrews and antique hardwood floors make this a popular student haunt.

Blue Moon Tavern, 712 NE 45th St (no phone). In U district, on east side of I-5. Wild and woolly bar famed as the one-time hang-out of Ginsberg and Kerouac. It maintains its arty/intellectual reputation. Grateful Dead hogs the tape deck each and every Sunday night. Wide range of local beers.

College Inn, 4000 NE University Way at NE 40th St (☎633-4441). Busy basement bar with finely tuned juke box. Below the diner and guest house of the same name. Mostly students.

Murphy's Pub, 1928 N 45th St, Wallingford (☎634-2110). Has a massive beer list and live folk, often Irish, for no cover.

New Melody Tavern, 5213 NW Ballard Ave (☎782-3480). In Ballard near the Salmon Bay waterfront. Showcases classy folk acts, from bluegrass through to Cajun, though it loses in atmosphere because of its barn-like size. Square dancing on Monday nights.

Old Ballard Firehouse, 5429 NW Russell Ave at NW Market (☎784-3516). Nightly live music in this Ballard venue, mainly local bands of a blues, reggae and rock disposition. Salsa/Latin evenings also. Whopping dance floor.

Owl Café, 5140 Ballard Ave (☎784-3640). Great blues acts, with cover charge averaging $5. Closed Sunday.

Sharky's Beach Bar, 7001 NW Seaview Ave (☎784-5850). Dancing is the big deal here, especially to rock and roll. In Ballard's Shilshole Bay Marina, just north of where the Lake Washington Ship Canal joins the sea.

Dance, classical music and opera

The **Seattle Center** is the base for the city's cultural institutions: the *Pacific Northwest Ballet* (☎441-9411), the *Seattle Symphony Orchestra* (☎443-4747) and the *Seattle Opera* (☎389-7676), take it in turns to use the Opera House there. Tickets go for anything between $15 and $65, and, particularly for the Opera, tend to sell out in advance; you can sometimes get returns – occasionally at reduced prices – just before performances start.

Theater

Theater is Seattle's strongest suit, with numerous small groups performing serious drama alongside the visiting Broadway shows.

Alice B Theater, 1100 E Pike St, Third Floor (☎322-5423). One of the largest gay and lesbian acting troupes on the west coast with performances all year.

A Contemporary Theater (*ACT*), 100 W Roy St, north of the Seattle Center near Queen Anne Hill (☎285-5110). Showcase for mostly modern mainstream drama. May–Dec.

Empty Space, 3509 Fremont Ave North (☎547-7500). Adventurous cosmopolitan dramas and sparse versions of the classics.

Fifth Avenue Theater, 1308 Fifth Ave (☎625-1900). Hosts glamorous musicals – anything less gets lost in the restored movie palace's flamboyant proportions.

The Group, based in Center House, Seattle Center (☎441-1299). Seattle's most right-on stuff, regularly plunging into tough social and political issues.

New City, 1634 11th Ave at Pine (☎323-6800). Capitol Hill's neighborhood playhouse.

Seattle Repertory Company (☎443-2222). Oldest and most established company, performing popular contemporary material, with a good dash of the classics, at the Seattle Center's *Bagley Wright Theater*. No performances June–Sept.

Film

Seattle has the usual first-release venues, prime among which are the *Varsity*, 4329 University Way (☎632-3131), and the big *Metro Cinemas* complex, 45th and Roosevelt (☎633-0055) – both in the U district and offering several screens. But the city also has a number of small, independent movie theaters, many concentrated in the U and Capitol Hill districts in rickety old buildings, showing a selection of left-of-field and foreign films, particularly in May when the annual **Seattle International Film Festival** takes place (check local papers for specific listings).

Egyptian, 801 E Pine St (☎323-4978). Housed in an old Masonic Temple, the art deco HQ of the annual film festival.

Grand Illusion, 1403 NE 50th St at University Way (☎523-3935). Tiny place in the U district.

Harvard Exit, 807 E Roy St (☎323-8986). Cozy little venue, showing festival films.

Neptune, 45th and Brooklyn (☎633-5545). With a lobby decked out to match its name, this film theater works its way through classic double features.

Seven Gables Theater, 911 NE 50th St at Roosevelt Way (☎632-8820). Art-house movie theater.

Gay Seattle

Focusing on the Capitol Hill district, Seattle's **gay scene** is lively and well organized. The best source of information is the weekly *Seattle Gay News*, a high-quality paper with plenty of local resource information and listings of all that's current; pick up a copy at a decent downtown bookshop, or the predominantly gay bookstores mentioned below. Gay and lesbian nightspots and theater are included in our general listings above.

Gay and lesbian resources

Bookstores stocking a wide range of gay and lesbian books, poetry, magazines and videos include *Red and Black Books*, at 430 E 15th Ave (☎322-7323), and *Beyond the Closet Bookstore*, 1501 Belmont Ave at E Pike St (☎322-4609), which also hosts occasional readings.

More general information on lesbian groups and events is available from the *Lesbian Resource Center*, at 1208 E Pine St (☎322-3953), while counselling services are offered by the rather primly named *Seattle Counselling Service for Sexual Minorities* (☎282-9307) and the *Gay Men's Health/Support Group* (☎322-7043).

Festivals

Seattle has several outstanding **festivals**. For four days at the beginning of September, the musicians, actors and dancers of the **Bumbershoot**, the city's premier Arts Festival, take over the Seattle Center; schedule details on ☎682-4FUN. **Seafair** is the biggest party of the lot, a three-week shindig celebrating Seattle's maritime connections, with a selection of activities from children's parades and berserk boat races to the gay community's *Unofficial Seafair Tacky Tourist Queen City Cruise*. From mid- to late September, the **Puyallup Fair** (☎841-5045) is held in Puyallup about 30 miles south of the city. It's a sort of cross between a giant-sized amusement arcade and an agricultural fair, with performances by some of the biggest stars of the C&W world.

Listings

Airlines *British Airways*, 1304 Fourth Ave (☎1-800/247-9297); *Delta*, 410 University St (☎433-4711 or 1-800/221-1212); *Northwest Airlines*, 402 University Ave (☎433-3500 or 1-800/441-1818); *TWA*, 1001 Fourth Ave (☎447-9400); *United*, 1225 Fourth Ave (☎ 441-3700 or 1-800/722-5243).

Airport *Sea-Tac International Airport*, 18612 S Pacific Hwy (general information ☎433-5217).

Air Tours *Chrysler Air*, E 1325 Fairview Ave (☎329-9638), operate 20-minute seaplane tours over Seattle every day (weather permitting) for $30 per person.

American Express 600 Stewart St (Mon–Fri 9am–5pm; ☎441-8622).

Banks Major branches include *Bank of California*, 910 Fourth Ave (☎587-6100); *First Interstate*, 999 Third Ave (☎575-1200); *US Bank*, 723 First Ave (☎461-7444).

Bike Rental None downtown: try *Gregg's*, 7007 Woodlawn Ave in Green Lake (☎523-1822), *Alki Bikes*, 2611 SW California near Alki Beach (☎938-3322), or *Second Gear*, 5601 NE University Way (☎527-1536).

Bookshops The *University Bookstore*, 4326 University Way in the U district (☎634-3400), is the city's biggest general bookshop; the *Elliott Bay Book Company*, 101 S Main St in Pioneer Square (☎624-6600), is convenient and cozy. *Metsker Maps*, 702 First Ave (☎623-8747), has a comprehensive selection of local and regional maps; *Wide World Books and Maps*, out at 1911 N 45th St (☎634-3453), features one of the city's best assortments of travel guides and literature.

Car Rental *Budget*, near the airport at 17808 Pacific Hwy (☎682-2277); and downtown at Westlake & Virginia (☎682-2277). *Dollar*, airport: 17600 Pacific Hwy (☎433-6777); and downtown: Seventh Ave and Stewart (☎682-1316). *Enterprise*, airport: 15607 Pacific Hwy (☎246-1953); and downtown: 2116 Westlake Ave (☎382-1051). *Penny*, 15058 Pacific Hwy, Sea-Tac (☎246-9828). *Thrifty*, airport: 18836 Pacific Hwy (☎246-7565); and downtown: 801 Virginia St (☎625-1133).

City Tours *Gray Line* (☎626-5208) runs guided city tours by coach, covering all major sights with copious commentary. The full 6-hour experience costs $27 (April–Sept only), the 3-hour trip $18 (all year). They also offer ten-hour excursions to Mount Rainier daily from May to early October, $34 each. Rather more fun, but necessarily less comprehensive, are the *Gray Line* cruises of the Chittenden locks departing Pier 57 daily (3hr; $21; ☎623-4252). Pick-up and drop-off is at major downtown hotels. *Seattle Harbor Tours* (☎623-1445) operate frequent one-hour boat trips round Elliott Bay all year. Departures from Pier 55; $11 each – though the ordinary commuter services of *Washington State Ferries* (☎464-6400) offer pretty much the same view, and they're a lot cheaper.

Consulates *British*, eighth floor of the First Interstate Center at Third and Madison (☎622-9255), surprisingly friendly, though they may well refer you to the dragons in LA; *Canadian*, Plaza 600 Suite 412 (☎443-1777); *Danish*, 1809 Seventh Ave (☎682-6101); *German*, 600 University St (☎682-4312); *Norwegian*, Joseph Vance Building, Third Ave and Union (☎623-3957); *Swedish*, Joseph Vance Building, Third Ave and Union (☎622-5640).

Dentist 24-hr emergency answering service ☎624-4912; also, *Yesler Terrace Medical Dental Clinic*, 102 Broadway (☎625-9260).

Doctor *Virginia Mason Fourth Avenue Clinic*, Fourth Ave and University (Mon–Fri 7am–6pm; ☎223-6490).

Emergencies ☎911.

Ferries *Washington State Ferries*, tickets from Pier 52, Colman Dock (☎464-6400), run to Bainbridge Island, Vashon and Bremerton, on the Kitsap Peninsula. *Victoria Clipper*, tickets from Pier 69 (☎448-5000), run to Canada's Victoria.

Fishing *Sport Fishing of Seattle* (☎623-6364) run seven-hour saltwater fishing trips into Puget Sound daily from May to September. Tackle, bait and license are included with the $62 charge.

Hospital *Northwest Hospital*, 1550 N 115th St (☎364-0500). For minor injuries, try the *Country Doctor Community Clinic*, 500 E 19th Ave (☎461-4503); women can use the *Arcadia Women's Health Center*, 112 E Boylston St (☎323-9388).

Laundromats The youth hostel and the *YMCA* both have much nicer facilities than the sleazy ones on the streets, such as the 24-hr laundromat beneath the *St Regis Hotel*, 116 Stewart St. In the U district, there's a *Wash'n'Shop* behind the *Pay'n'Save* shop at 4522 NE Brooklyn Ave at 45th St (☎548-1321).

WESTERN WASHINGTON FERRIES

The network of subsidized routes operated by **Washington State Ferries** provides a wonderful way to explore the islands and peninsulas of the Puget Sound and points north to the Canadian border. Even with a vehicle, costs aren't too steep, while bicycles are taken on board for a minimal fee. In many cases, fares are collected in just one direction (usually westbound) and the return trip is "free". However, drivers can't make advance reservations, so it's a good idea (especially in summer) to reach the ferry port a couple of hours before departure. Timetables and fare details are available at every ferry dock, including Seattle's Pier 52, or you can call ☎1-800/84 FERRY (statewide), or ☎464-6400 (in Seattle).

The two most popular and useful services are the one between **Port Townsend**, on the Olympic Peninsula, and Whidbey Island's **Keystone** (every 45min; 30min), and another that leaves mainland **Anacortes**, about 90 miles north of Seattle, every one or two hours for the **San Juan** archipelago, docking at Lopez (after1hr), Orcas (1hr 30min), and San Juan Island (2hr 10min). The round-trip fare for vehicle and driver in peak season is just $20. Two of the daily San Juan ferries from Anacortes in summer, and one in winter, continue to **Sidney**, Canada. An average-sized vehicle, along with the driver, costs around $30 each way, extra adult passengers $6 each.

No car and passenger ferry services operate to Canada from **Seattle**, but the high-speed, passenger-only **Victoria Clipper** from the city's Pier 69 (summer 3–4 daily, winter 1 daily; ☎448-5000 or 1-800/888-2535) takes just two and a half hours to reach **Victoria**, on Vancouver Island (see p.264). Fares are $49 one-way, $79 round-trip.

For details of the three-day **Alaska Marine Highway** ride from **Bellingham** to **Skagway**, see p.34 and p.192.

Library *Seattle Public Library*, 1000 Fourth Ave (Sept–May Mon–Thurs 9am–9pm, Fri–Sat 9am–6pm, Sun 1–5pm, June–Aug closed Sun; ☎386-4636).

Pharmacy *LD Bracken Prescription Pharmacy*, 1303 Fourth Ave (☎622-2110).

Post Office/poste restante The main post office is at Union St and Third Ave downtown (Mon–Fri 8am–5.30pm; ☎442-6255); zip code 98101.

Rape Crisis Line (☎632-7273) 24 hours; *Battered Women Crisis Hotline* ☎522-9472; *Domestic Violence Hotline* ☎1-800/562-4800.

Resource Center for the Handicapped 20150 NE 45th Ave (☎362-2273).

Sailing From their base on the southwest shore of Lake Union, the *NW Outdoor Center*, 2100 N Westlake Ave (☎281-9694), rents kayaks by the hour, half-day and full day; from the Center it's a short paddle to the Washington Ship Canal. *Sail Seattle* (☎624-3931) run regular sail boat excursions out into Puget Sound from Pier 56; $20 for an hour and a half, $37 for two and a half hours.

Sport Seattle's main sports arena is the **Kingdome**, a few blocks south of Pioneer Square at S King St and S Second Ave. It's home to baseball's Mariners and football's Seahawks. Information and ticket sale details on ☎628-0888. Basketball's Seattle Supersonics are based at the Coliseum in the Seattle Center (☎281-5800).

Taxis *Broadway Cab*, 3736 S Rainier Ave (☎622-4800); *Yellow Cab*, 912 N Dexter Ave (☎622-6500).

Traveler's Aid On the sixth floor of the *YMCA*, 909 Fourth Ave between Madison and Marion St (Mon–Fri 8.30am–9pm, Sat–Sun 1–5pm; ☎461-3888).

Weather 24-hour report on ☎526-6087.

Around Seattle

Puget Sound and its easterly neighbor Lake Washington stretch their clutter of tiny islands and ragged peninsulas **around Seattle**, making boats and bridges an essential part of everyday life. Seattle has only been able to spread by means of boats (there's one boat for every six Seattlites), with the result that most commuters pass over one stretch of water or another on their way to work. You can take advantage of these commuter **ferries** to make the quick crossing from Seattle to **Bainbridge Island** and **Vashon**, both of which make relaxing detours – especially for the cyclist – and are useful as stepping stones, the one to the national parks of the Olympic Peninsula (see p.181) via the **Kitsap Peninsula**; the other, less appealingly, to Tacoma (see p.170). The downside is for the motorist: the ferries tend to clog up with vehicles, while the bridges across Lake Washington just can't cope with the volume of traffic and soul-destroying tailbacks develop at the slightest mishap.

Back on the mainland, the countryside abutting Seattle (once you've cleared its sprawling suburbs) is of little appeal – and certainly can't compete with the dramatic panoramas offered by the Cascade Mountains, beginning with Snoqualmie Falls (see p.216) about twenty-five miles east of downtown. To the north, I-5 scuttles on to its intersection with Hwy-526: turn west for the three-mile detour to the huge **Boeing Plant** (90-min weekday tours, ring for reservations; ☎342-4801), where wide-bodied 767 and 747 jets are visible at various stages of construction in a plant as big as 57 football pitches.

If you're dependent on **public transportation**, be aware that, although the ferry services are fast and frequent, there are hardly any local bus services and, without a car or bicycle, you'll be struggling.

Bainbridge Island

Few commuters are blessed with as pleasant a trip as the **Bainbridge Island** set, who wake up to a serene half-hour on the ferry, the city skyline drawing gradually closer across Elliott Bay. This is such a delightful journey that the island itself (green and rural, but mostly private land) is for most of its visitors simply an excuse for the ferry ride. *Washington State Ferries* leave about every hour from Pier 52 downtown (return tickets around $4 foot passenger, $7 vehicle and driver; avoid rush hours), landing in **WINSLOW** – a town so small that once you've admired the harbor, you'll doubtless be ready to head back to Seattle. An alternative is to cycle the island's narrow country roads – Bainbridge is only ten miles from top to bottom – and **camp** in *Fay Bainbridge State Park* (☎842-3931) on the north shore.

The Kitsap Peninsula

Behind Bainbridge Island, sprawling messily into the middle of Puget Sound, lurks the **Kitsap Peninsula**, a jagged spit of land bristling with defence projects: there's an ammunition dump, a naval submarine base, a torpedo-testing station, and the large naval shipyards of Bremerton – which can also be reached by ferry direct from Seattle.

All of these add up to a fair dollop of military might, but luckily the peninsula has better-looking areas too, spreading out along **Hwy-305**, the handiest route from Seattle to the Olympic Peninsula. This road leaves Bainbridge Island at its northern end by Agate Passage Bridge, on the Kitsap side of which is **Port Madison Indian Reservation**.

Suquamish

Just beyond the Agate Passage Bridge, the first right off the highway down a country road leads the couple of miles to the village of **SUQUAMISH**, the burial place of Chief Sealth, who gave his name to "Seattle" and was the tribal leader when the first whites arrived. Two large dugout canoes mark his grave against the incongruous background of a white wooden church, and a plaque proclaims him "The firm friend of the whites" – something of a dubious accolade, considering how things turned out. Half a mile away, the **Old Man House State Park** marks the site of the Suquamish people's cedar longhouse, which stretched along the shore for 500 feet with a width of about 50 feet: the government had it burnt down in 1870 to eliminate communal living, that great enemy of private-property civilization.

A couple of minutes' drive out of Suquamish brings you to the fascinating **Suquamish Museum** (May–Sept daily 10am–5pm; Oct–April Fri–Sun 11am–4pm; $2.50), off Hwy-305 on Sandy Hook Rd. The museum traces the history of the Suquamish, who occupied much of the Kitsap Peninsula until white settlers arrived. Chief Sealth chose to avoid conflict with his new neighbors, but it didn't do much good, and his people received an appallingly bad deal from the carve-up of their land. But the tone of the museum is moderate, interspersing exhibits of native canoes and old photographs with quotations from tribal elders, whose recorded voices also overlay a slideshow that portrays the schizophrenic lifestyle of present generations, caught between traditional values and the hegemonic culture.

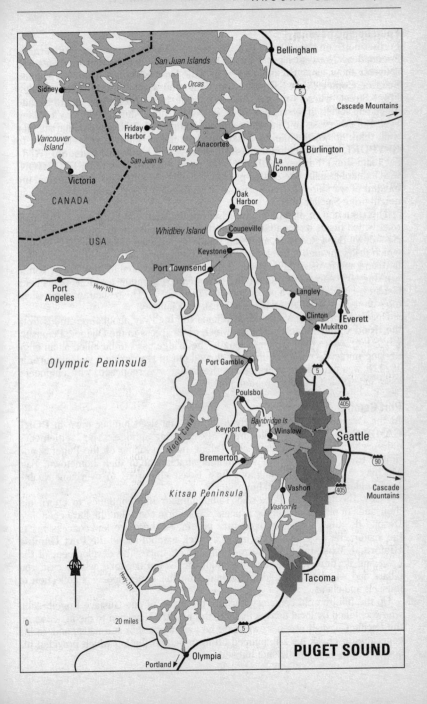

PUGET SOUND

Poulsbo and beyond

Further north on Hwy-305, **POULSBO** makes a bid for the passing tourist trade. Founded by Norwegians, it exploits its heritage by decking out the cafés and souvenir shops along the main street in "little Norway" kitsch. There's a **Marine Science Center** (Mon–Sat 10am–4pm, Sun noon–4pm; $2), on the harborside's Front Street, where you can observe marine fauna from close quarters, and togged-up locals greet visitors in fancy Nordic dress during mid-May's Viking Fest. But otherwise you'll soon be hurrying north – though proto-militarists may well think it worthwhile to make the excursion south across the bay to **KEYPORT**, site of the proud-of-its-torpedoes **Naval Undersea Museum** (Wed–Sat 10am–4pm). Further south still is the naval shipyard town of **BREMERTON**, with its hard-as-nails bars, tattoo parlors, visitable warship, naval museum and the handful of warships that comprise the "Mothballed Fleet", held in readiness in neighboring Sinclair Inlet.

There's a choice of routes onwards from Poulsbo: you can keep to the main road which heads its mundane way north, or four miles from town you can turn right down Bond Road and, after four hundred yards, left along **Big Valley Road**, which drifts through a lovely river valley of antique wooden farmhouses, rolling farmland and forested hills. Here, at the clearly signposted **Manor Farm Inn**, a working farm surrounds a charming picket-fenced farmhouse of 1890 that's been tastefully converted into a plush hotel (☎779-4628; ⑦). The restaurant is excellent too – altogether a delightful place to break your journey.

Heading north, Big Valley Road rejoins the highway about three miles from the **Hood Canal Floating Bridge**, which gives access to the Olympic Peninsula (see p174). More than a mile in length, the bridge used to be billed as an engineering miracle – until a chunk of it floated out to sea during a violent storm in 1979. It was over three years before the bridge was reopened, with engineers' assurances that it had been reinforced.

Port Gamble

At the far north of Kitsap, on Hwy-104, the pint-sized lumber town of **PORT GAMBLE** is about a mile from the floating bridge. The settlement's entrepreneurial founders, Pope and Talbot, made a killing on the Puget Sound timber trade, but satisfied a sentimental attachment to their hometown, East Machias, Maine, by shipping out East Coast elm trees to overhang quaint, New-England-style clapboard houses.

Below the town, the Pope and Talbot lumber mill continues to churn out thousands of planks and, in the process, keeps firm control of the local economy. Despite the town's nineteenth-century prettiness, there are few concessions to the visitor, the only diversions being a quick gambol round the **Port Gamble Historical Museum** (daily 10am–4pm), which traces the development of the town and its timber trade, and the adjoining **General Store**, whose cast iron pillars and wooden floors accommodate – on the upper floor – a collection of mussels and clams.

Up the hill, the old cemetery harbors the grave of one Gustave Engelbrecht, who was killed by local natives in 1856, the first US Navyman to die in action on the Pacific Coast. It was his own fault: he took a pot shot at a native and, in his eagerness to check his kill, jumped up from behind the log which provided his cover, only to be promptly shot himself.

Vashon Island

From Pier 50 in Seattle, it's a 25-minute ferry ride (Mon–Sat; foot passengers only; $3.50 return) to rural **Vashon Island**, a small, cycleable island where there's little to do but unwind and explore the country roads. Once you've worked up an appetite with a cycle or hike, head for the tasty wholefood of the *Dog Day Café* (Tues–Sat; ☎463-6404) in **VASHON**, the tiny crossroads village and the island's only focal point. It's about four miles from the jetty. Three miles or so further south, the upmarket wholefood of the *Sound Food Restaurant* (☎463-3565) brings Seattlites over for weekend brunch – and there's live music on a Saturday night. From here, you can cycle the extra couple of miles southeast, over a narrow causeway, to the hillier terrain of secluded **Maury Island**.

Vashon has several **B&Bs** (details from the visitor center in Seattle) and the **Vashon Island AYH Hostel**, 12119 SW Cove Rd (May–Oct; ☎463-2592; ①; reservations advised – office hours noon–10pm). The hostel is a good twenty-minute walk from the ferry dock – head down the main island road and take the signposted turning on the right – or you can call ahead for a free pick-up. Surrounded by forest, the hostel's covered wagons and tepees provide family accommodation, as well as rooms for couples; a log cabin is used as a dorm, with rates starting at $8 for members ($11 non-members). Free bicycles are provided for cycling the island.

If you'd rather not return directly to Seattle, then carry on to Tahlequah, Vashon's southern tip, where *Washington State Ferries* sail every hour or so to Point Defiance on the northern outskirts of Tacoma (see below). Incidentally, you only have to pay to get to the island – leaving is free.

WESTERN WASHINGTON

Seattle faces Elliott Bay, roughly the mid-point of **Puget Sound**, which hooks deep into Washington like an inland sea, its islands, bays and inlets sheltering every kind of watercraft, from yachts and schooners to fishing trawlers and merchant ships. For the most part, the Sound borders a bucolic landscape of rolling farmland trimmed by forested hills and ridges, but on either side of Seattle the shoreline is blemished by a suburban-industrial sprawl that's the by-product of its economic success. **South of Seattle**, I-5, the main north–south highway, skids past the mess, running parallel to the Sound to round its southern end at blue-collar **Tacoma**, where heavy industry has caused a worrying amount of contamination. Further south, I-5 clears the pollution to reach the dignified government buildings of **Olympia**, the down-beat state capital and, racing on past the volcanic remains of Mount St Helens (see Chapter 4), the rebuilt Hudson's Bay Company fur-trapping colony at **Vancouver**. Beyond is Portland, Oregon, one hundred and seventy miles from Seattle.

Cross an island or two **west from Seattle**, and you come to the **Olympic Peninsula**, fringed with logging communities and circled by the US-101 highway. The rugged mountains at its core rise high above the lush vegetation of the mountain slopes which, in their turn, give way to the magnificent rainforests of the western valleys, and miles of wilderness beaches on the Pacific edge. This is amazing stuff, but you'll need to get off the beaten track to see the best of it.

Washington's **lower coast**, to the south, is more accessible but not as appealing, splodged with industrial towns and holiday resorts.

North of Seattle, mundane towns and villages dot the coast, all within easy striking distance of both the sumptuous peaks of the Cascade Mountains (see Chapter 4) and the smattering of beautiful islands that stretch west towards Canada. At the weekend, Puget Sounders escape from the cities to the rural parts of **Whidbey Island**, or further north to the beautiful **San Juan Islands**, among which **Orcas** boasts the most stunning scenery while **Lopez** is something of a rural idyll, its quiet country roads ideal for cycling.

To see the best of Western Washington you'll need your own **vehicle**, though it is possible to work your way round by ferry, the occasional *Greyhound* and local bus. The region's many **B&Bs** offer the most distinctive accommodation, along with scores of **campgrounds**, many of which occupy fine wilderness locations.

South of Seattle on I-5

Tacoma, Washington's second-largest city, is the state's most heavily industrialized corner, with old steel mills and chemical plants rusting away along the once beautiful Puget Sound shoreline. Apart from the gorgeous **Point Defiance Park** at its northern tip, it's all quite run-down and eminently missable. When Tacoma (and Seattle) boomed in the early 1900s, **Olympia**, the state capital, was left out, its sole money-spinner (apart from politics) the *Olympia Brewing Company*, which set itself up just south of town in 1896 – and is rumored to attract more visitors than the government buildings. Beyond Olympia, **I-5** skirts the western foothills of the Cascades, passing **Mount Rainier** and **Mount St Helens** (see Chapter 4), and in the far south, near the Columbia River and the Oregon border, tiny **Vancouver**, the first European settlement in the Pacific Northwest.

Tacoma

TACOMA has a massive credibility problem. The city council claims it's simply unfortunate that "aroma" rhymes with Tacoma, but the "smelly" label has stuck, making industrial Tacoma the butt of Northwest jokes. There's some truth behind it too: Tacoma's deep Commencement Bay (thought by nineteenth-century explorers to be far superior to anything Seattle had to offer) was recently listed by the Environmental Protection Agency as one of the USA's most dangerously polluted areas, and the *Asarco* copper refinery has just closed after years of spewing large quantites of arsenic. Along with industry, the military are also close at hand, in the shape of the enormous Fort Lewis Army Base and McChord Air Force Base on the south side of town. The redevelopment project that's trying to turn around the tawdry downtown area hasn't been a spectacular success – and many locals are keen to keep to the suburbs after dark.

Indeed, it's the shabby side of the city that strikes you first: whether you come in by car or bus, you'll pass along sleazy Pacific Avenue with its pawn-shops, boarded-up buildings and prostitutes lingering in the doorways. Pacific is a major artery, dividing the sloping town center from the industrial area below around the port. On the way in you'll pass the enormous blue-grey roof of the **Tacoma Dome**, an ugly sports and concerts venue of which the city (adopting it as a symbol) is inordinately proud. Things improve slightly in the main downtown area, to the left of Pacific, with the new **Broadway Plaza** pedestrian area and its centerpiece, the elegant white **Pantages Center**, at Ninth and Broadway, a 1918 Vaudeville theater reopened in 1983 as Tacoma's Performing Arts Center; it now stages ballet, plays and concerts. A short walk from here at 12th and Pacific, the **Tacoma Art Museum** (Mon–Sat 10am–4pm, Sun noon–5pm; free) has a few Renoirs, a Pissarro and a Degas among American paintings and Chinese jade and robes. North of downtown, the **Washington State Historical Society Museum**, though scheduled to be relocated, is presently at 315 N Stadium Way (Tues–Sat 9am–4.30pm, Sun 2–5pm; $2, free Tues); its displays run thoroughly through Washington's history and include temporary exhibitions related to the state, such as photos of Makah people, paintings from the logging era, and quilts made by pioneer women.

Heading away from downtown to the north, Ruston Way follows the curve of Commencement Bay past the now-abandoned tall chimney of the poisonous *Asarco* copper plant. At the tip of this jutting piece of land, **Point Defiance Park** – beaten only by New York's Central Park as the USA's largest city open space – has beaches, gardens, and roads and trails through acres of shady virgin forest as green and lush as the more high-profile rainforests of the Western Washington coast, as well as a number of more specific attractions. These include a **Zoo and Aquarium** (daily summer 10am–7pm; winter 10am–4pm; $3.50); **Camp Six** (Memorial Day to Labor Day only, Mon–Fri 11am–5pm, Sat & Sun 11am–6pm; free), a reconstructed logging camp with bunk houses, old logging equipment and a restored and functioning steam engine; and **Fort Nisqually** (museum building daily summer noon–6pm, winter 1–4pm, grounds open longer; free) – a reconstruction of the trading post set up by the Hudson's Bay Company in 1833, in the pre-settlement days of the fur traders, when American entrepreneurs were beginning to threaten the monopoly of the British company. Fort Nisqually was seen as a key British foothold in what later became Washington state – an area which the British originally intended to keep.

Practicalities

Set squarely on the main north–south route between Seattle and Portland, Tacoma is easy to visit – and, if you're using public transportation, hard to avoid. The *Greyhound* station is in the heart of town at 1319 Pacific Ave and S 13th St (☎383-4621); the *Amtrak* station at 1001 Puyallup Ave is a mile or so south of downtown, near I-5; **local buses** run by *Pierce Transit* (☎581-8000 or 1-800/562-8109) serve the Tacoma area. *Pierce Transit* also connect with Seattle's local *Metro* buses, offering a bargain-rate route between the two cities. I-5 loops towards the central area; take exit 133 for downtown. Transit and city maps are available at the **Chamber of Commerce**, 950 Pacific Ave, Suite 300 (Mon–Fri 8.30am–5pm; ☎383-2459).

With Seattle just 35 miles up the highway and Point Defiance Park connected by regular ferry with Vashon Island (see above), it's unlikely that **accommodation** in Tacoma will be a priority. Hotels downtown are either pricily smart for the business community or grim in the extreme, with your best option being the plush *Sheraton Tacoma Hotel*, next to the enormous convention center at 1320 Broadway Plaza, between 13th and 15th on Broadway (☎572-3200; ⑥); ask for a room with a view over Commencement Bay. Across the bay, five miles northeast of downtown, there's **camping** (as well as coastal hiking and a beach) at **Dash Point State Park**, 5700 SW Dash Point Rd, Federal Way (☎593-2206).

For **entertainment**, it's worth checking what's on at the Pantages Center (☎591-5894). The *Antique Sandwich Company*, 5102 N Pearl at 51st (☎752-4069), near Point Defiance Park, is an offbeat **café** which has huge pots of tea and often features live folk or classical music in the evenings. Closer to downtown, *Engine House No 9*, at 611 N Pine St (☎272-3435), is a lively tavern/café bedecked with firemen's helmets and crowded with locals, consuming excellent pizza, carrot cake and the like with their beer until the early hours.

Olympia and around

Thirty miles southwest of Tacoma, **OLYMPIA** is dominated by the state government's Capitol buildings. No more than a muddy little logging community when it was picked as Washington's capital in 1853 (settlers had only reached the Puget Sound the decade before), Olympia – like Salem, its Oregon counterpart – hasn't grown into the metropolis hoped for by its founders, and after the bustle and industry of Seattle and Tacoma, the town seems sleepy and quiet.

The Washington State Capitol buildings, grouped on a "campus" to the south of downtown (exit 105A on I-5), make Olympia worth a visit, if only to wonder at the sheer energy of the pioneers, who plotted something along the lines of London's St Paul's Cathedral in what was then a backwoods beset by native discontent. Only completed in 1928, after 34 years in the making, the **Legislative Building** (daily 10am–3pm; hourly guided tours; free) is the one to see: an imposing Romanesque structure topped with a high stone dome, and hung with a massive brass Tiffany chandelier among a plethora of gaudy furnishings and fittings – a colossal walnut table, French velvet drapes, bronze-cast doors of gargantuan proprtions and such like. Epic murals were originally planned for the interior, and the *Twelve Labors of Hercules* by Michael Spafford is indeed up on the walls of one of the government chambers – though Washington's pious legislators were apparently so shocked by the "pornographic" images of the painting that their immediate reaction was to spend $15,000 covering it up with hardboard and curtains, which have since been removed.

Behind Capitol Campus is slender **Capitol Lake**, the southernmost segment of a deep inlet that defines the western and northern perimeters of **downtown** Olympia, which starts down the hill from the campus and ends by the harborside. There's nothing very exciting here, just a few blocks of shops and restaurants presided over by the chateau-like **Old Capitol**, its turreted roofs and arched windows facing a grassy square at Seventh Ave and Washington.

Eight blocks south of Capitol Campus, the small **Washington State Capital Museum**, 211 W 21st Ave (Tues–Fri 10am–4pm, Sat & Sun noon–4pm; donation), set in the Mediterranean-style 1920s mansion of the wealthy Lord family, juxtaposes a restored well-to-do dining room with displays of Native American basketwork and natural history exhibits, inadvertently exposing the chasm between the two cultures.

Tumwater

A mile or two south of Capitol Campus, across the narrow neck of Capitol Lake, tiny **TUMWATER** was Washington's first pioneer community, settled in 1845 by an intrepid group who saw the potential in harnessing the power of the tumbling waters – from which the town takes its name – of the Deschutes River, at a point so near the open sea. One of their leaders was George Bush, a black ex-employee of the Hudson's Bay Company who was persuaded to leave his farm and return west by his Missouri neighbors. The party had intended to settle in the Willamette Valley, but on the journey they learnt that the Oregon government, in their desire to avoid the slavery question, had passed a raft of discriminatory legislation – "all Negros and mulattos to be flogged once every six months until [they] quit the territory" – a build-up to the Exclusion Law that prohibited black immigration in 1849. Bush took the hint, and chose Washington instead.

Tumwater Historical Park marks the site of the original settlement, and here you'll also find, at Deschutes Way and Grant St, the small white house of one of the early pioneers, a certain Nathaniel Crosby, grandfather of Harry, otherwise Bing Crosby. Just to the south and smelling strongly of hops, the **Olympia Brewery** (tours and tastings daily 8am–4.30pm; free) overlooks Tumwater Falls, once a rich salmon fishing site for the Nisqually tribe. Finding the park and the brewery is surprisingly difficult, considering they're tucked so close to the east side of I-5 (exit 103). The simplest approach is from Olympia: take Capitol Way/Boulevard out of town, turn right down Custer Way and follow the signs; you'll hit the brewery first.

Wolf Haven International Reserve

Southeast of Tumwater on Capitol Boulevard/Old Hwy-99, it's about eight miles to Offutt Lake Road, where a left turn leads to the **Wolf Haven International Reserve** (May–Sept daily 10am–5pm; Oct–April Wed–Sun 10am–4pm). Established in 1982 to provide a safe breeding ground for the threatened North American timberwolf, and a sanctuary and open-air hospital for wolves shot or poisoned by livestock ranchers, the Wolf Haven has grown into a 65-acre facility that's now home to over forty of these surprisingly affectionate, sociable creatures.

Close-up, educational **tours** ($5) are given hourly throughout the day, but the best time to come is for the Friday and Saturday night "Howl-Ins" (May–Sept 7–9pm; $6; ☎264-4695 or 1-800/448-9653), when storytellers evoke various wolf-related myths and legends, especially those of the Native Americans; when darkness falls, a sort of call-and-response kicks off between the audience and the nearby wolves, baying their heads off at the rising moon.

Olympia practicalities

Olympia is on I-5 and easily accessible by car or bus; *Greyhound* (☎357-5541) are downtown at Capitol Way and Seventh Ave, about five blocks north of the Capitol Campus. The *Amtrak* station, at Rich Rd and 83rd St, is about eight miles southeast of town and not on a bus route. Elsewhere, *Intercity Transit* provides a **local bus** service around Olympia and Tumwater (☎786-1881 for route and timetable information), including a free and frequent shuttle service between Capitol Campus and downtown (Mon–Fri 7am–6pm). On other routes, the adult fare is 50¢, and a one-day pass costs just $1. *IT*'s **customer service** office is downtown at 105 Columbia St and Fourth Ave (Mon–Fri 7am–7pm, Sat 8am–5pm).

The **visitor center** (Mon–Fri 8am–5pm; ☎586-3460) is at the entrance to the Capitol Campus, 14th Ave and Capitol Way. The best **place to stay** is the *Harbinger Inn*, 1136 E Bay Drive (☎754-0389; ③), a turn-of-the-century balconied B&B with views out over the Puget Sound; it's about a mile north of downtown, and reservations are recommended. A good second choice is the *Westwater Inn*, 2300 Evergreen Park Drive (☎943-4000; ④), overlooking the west side of Capitol

Lake. There's **camping** at forested **Millersylvania State Park** (☎753-1519), two miles east of I-5 (exit 99) and twelve miles south of Olympia.

If you've come here to **eat**, try the *Urban Onion*, 116 Legion Way (☎943-9242), diagonally across the square from the Old Capitol, which serves its own herb and onion bread. Failing that, *The Spar*, a few blocks away at 114 E Fourth Ave (☎357-6444), is a genuine Thirties diner with a long, curved counter.

Centralia and Vancouver, WA

On the hundred-mile sprint down I-5 from Olympia to Oregon, there's little to detain you, though the interstate does give access to the easiest (and main) road into **Mount St Helens** National Park (see p.207). Coming from the north, turn down Hwy-505 at Toledo; approaching from the south, take Hwy-504 near Castle Rock. The two turnings merge east of I-5 for the final approach to the mountain, and the drive takes about ninety minutes each way.

Before you reach either turning (travelling south), the work-a-day, lumber town of **CENTRALIA**, 23 miles from Olympia, is of passing interest as the site of one of the nastiest incidents in the history of Washington's Wobblies (see p.553): during the Armistice Day parade of 1919, several members of the American Legion attacked the town's union building (at 807 N Tower St) and, in the fight that followed, four were shot. Local Wobblies were promptly rounded up and thrown into jail, but vigilantes broke in that night to seize, mutilate and then lynch one of their number, a certain Wesley Everest. To make sure the others took the point, the police laid the body out on the jail floor.

Further south, well beyond the Mount St Helens turnings, modest **VANCOUVER** spreads back from the Columbia River, the state border. Bisected by I-5, the town center is to the west, and to the east (Exit 1C, Mill Plain Blvd) is a credible reconstruction of the Pacific Northwest's first substantial European settlement in the **Fort Vancouver National Historic Site** (daily 9am–4/5pm; $1). Dating from the 1820s, this stockaded outpost of the British-owned Hudson's Bay Company was, for over twenty years, a remote but prosperous station dedicated to the fur trade. Its early occupation was part of the case the British made for including present-day Washington in their territory, although, as American colonists poured into the Willamette Valley, British claims diminished. Finally, when the 49th Parallel was determined as the dividing line between the US and Canada, Fort Vancouver was left stranded on US territory. By 1860 the Hudson's Bay Company had moved out, and the fort and outbuildings disappeared, only to be mapped and rebuilt by archeologists in the 1960s. Rangers give interpretive tours throughout the day, and the site – basically five one-story log structures protected within a rectangular palisade – certainly merits at least a quick look, as does nearby Officers' Row, a string of elegant villas built for US Army personnel between 1850 and 1906.

The Olympic Peninsula

The broad mass of the **Olympic Peninsula** projects across the Puget Sound, sheltering Seattle from the open sea. Small towns are sprinkled around the peninsula's edges, but at its core the Olympic Mountains thrust upwards, shredding clouds as they drift in from the Pacific and drenching the coastal area with rain.

Conditions are wet enough for the dense vegetation of the peninsula's forests to thicken into rainforest in the western river valleys, and both the forests and the lonely Pacific beaches provide habitats for a huge variety of wildlife and seabirds.

It was partly to ensure the survival of a rare breed of elk that Franklin D Roosevelt created a national park here in 1939, and the **Olympic National Park** now has the largest remaining herd of Roosevelt elk in the US. The park protects the heart of the peninsula, but the large areas of forest surrounding it are heavily logged. The issue of economy versus ecology is debated with particular intensity, since it was the timber trade that brought settlers here in the first place, and logging remains crucial for local jobs. Ecologists are now reluctantly favoring tourism as the lesser of environmental evils, and the number of visitors is increasing – a marriage with the tough world of the timber trade echoed throughout the Pacific Northwest.

Victorian **Port Townsend** is the most logical and attractive first stop on the peninsula, accessible by ferry from Whidbey Island or by an hour's drive from Seattle, and restored as a "historic" center, with a lively arts scene. The real industrial engine of the peninsula is **Port Angeles**, linked by *Greyhound* to Seattle and by ferry to Victoria in Canada. West of here, settlements are smaller and fewer. **Neah Bay**, at the northwest corner of the peninsula, is the headquarters of the Makah Indian Reservation; below it, the small logging town of **Forks** is the only community of any size on the Pacific side of the mountains.

The peninsula's main route, **US-101**, loops around the coast. No roads run across the peninsula's mountainous core, though a couple do reach up a fair way into the National Park. You can get from town to town quite well using a combination of *Greyhound* and local buses, but if you want to do any walking, you'll have problems reaching trailheads without your own vehicle. A **car** is by far the best way to explore – on a bike beware of narrow roads, sharp corners and hurtling logging trucks.

Port Townsend

With its brightly painted Victorian mansions, convivial cafés and vigorous cultural (and counter-cultural) scene, **PORT TOWNSEND** has always had aspirations beyond its small-time logging roots. A wannabe San Francisco since the mid-nineteenth century, it was poised for Puget Sound supremacy in the 1890s, when confident predictions of a railway terminus lured in the rich, and Gothic mansions sprung up above the flourishing port. Unfortunately for the investors, the railway petered out before Port Townsend, the hoped-for boom never happened, and the town was left with a glut of stylish residences and a very small business district.

This combination has in recent times turned out to be Port Townsend's trump card, and since the old mansions were bought up and restored in the Sixties, the town has mellowed into an artsy community with hippy undertones and a fair amount of charm. Tourists in search of Victoriana fill plush bed and breakfasts, while jazz fans flock to the annual music festivals, and nearby, two nineteenth-century forts provide ample camping and youth hostel facilities.

Arrival and information

Port Townsend – more than likely your first stop on the Olympic Peninsula – is easy to reach, either by **ferry** from Keystone on Whidbey Island, or by **road** over the Hood Canal Bridge from the Kitsap Peninsula. By **bus**, things get more complicated: *Greyhound*'s first major stop on the peninsula is Port Angeles, further west (Mon–Fri 1 daily); this service pauses at Port Ludlow, just before the Hood Canal Bridge, from where *Jefferson Transit* (☎385-477) operate buses (Mon–Fri 4 daily, Sat & Sun 2 daily) to Port Townsend. The same company has services connecting Port Townsend with Winslow (see p.166), where ferries from Seattle dock. Private **ferry** companies run direct from Port Townsend to Seattle, San Juan Island and Victoria, BC – contact the visitor center for details, or telephone *San Juan Express* (☎1-800/888-2535) and *Clipper Navigation* (☎448-5000).

Port Townsend's angular and compact center occupies a triangle of land jutting out into the sea. The ferry dock is right downtown, just off Water Street, the main drag. Pick up a map and information at the helpful **visitor center**, 2437 Sims Way (Mon–Fri 9am–6pm, summer also Sat & Sun 11am–4pm; ☎385-2722), half a mile west of the town center on Hwy-20; to get around, **rent a bike** from *Sport Townsend,* 215 Taylor St (☎385-6470).

The Town

Port Townsend's physical split – half on a bluff, half at sea-level – reflects Victorian social divisions, when wealthy merchants built their houses uptown, well away from the noise and brawl of the port below. The downtown area is still at the base of the hill, its shops and pleasant cafés centering on **Water Street** – lined with hefty 1890s brick and stonework of which the town is very proud (timber is the obvious building material in these parts and a big brick building was quite a coup for a pioneer town). The City Hall, for example, at the east end of town at Water and Madison, is a heavy redbrick Gothic assertion of civic dignity now housing the **Jefferson County Historical Museum** (Mon–Sat 11am–4pm, Sun 1–4pm; free) – crammed with local bygones, early photographs and mementoes of the sailing ships that made the town prosperous. And from here, it's a short stroll north to the pleasant waterfront bluff of **Chetzemoka Park**, at the foot of Blaine Street.

Doubling back to the museum, take Water Street the three blocks to Taylor, where steps lead towards residential uptown's wooden mansions – some private houses, others converted into upmarket bed-and-breakfast inns. The 1868 **Rothschild House** at Franklin and Taylor (summer daily 10am–5pm; winter weekends 11am–4pm; $2) has been restored with period furnishings, although the **Ann Starrett House** at Adams and Clay (see "Practicalities" below) easily out-Gothics the rest, swarming with gables and an octagonal tower, and an impressively ornate elliptical staircase that has to be seen to be believed. It was built at the end of the boom in 1889.

Fort Worden State Park, two miles north of downtown Port Townsend (*Jefferson Transit* bus #5 from Water Street), was part of a trio of coastal forts built at the beginning of the twentieth century to protect the Puget Sound from invasion by a new breed of steam-powered battleships. It's the best preserved of the three, though the old army buildings make rather bleak viewing (they were used as the set for the film *An Officer and a Gentleman*). Still, the officers' quarters now house the *Centrum Arts Foundation* (☎385-3102 or 1-800/733-3608), which stages lively **festivals**, particularly over the summer: it's especially worth watching out for Jazz Port Townsend towards the end of July, the newer Blues festival in early June and American Fiddler Tunes in early July – book accommodation well ahead for any of these. Most of the shows are held in the new McCurdy Pavilion, a modern auditorium inserted into an old dirigible hangar.

OLYMPIC PENINSULA

Practicalities

Port Townsend is Washington's **B&B** capital, with over a dozen establishments sprinkled among the old villas of the uptown area. The cream of this moderately expensive crop are the comfortably equipped *James House*, 1238 Washington at Harrison (☎385-1238; ⑤); the slightly twee *Heritage House*, 305 Pierce at Washington (☎385-6800; ⑤); the somewhat garish *Ann Starrett House*, 744 Clay at Adams (☎385-3205; ⑤); and the *Old Consulate Inn*, 313 Walker at Washington (☎385-6753; ⑥), once the elegant quarters of the German consul. If your budget isn't that elastic, then there are less expensive places down the hill: try the *Tides Inn*, 1807 Water St (☎385-0595; ④), or the turn-of-the-century *Palace Hotel*, 1004 Water St (☎385-0773 or 1-800/962-0741; ④).

Fort Worden's military buildings now house the *Port Townsend AYH* **youth hostel** (March–Oct; ☎385-0655; ①) offering the town's lowest-priced beds at $9 for *IYHF* members, $12 non-members; office hours are 7.30–9.30am and 5–10pm; there's a **campground** (☎385-4730) here too. Another youth hostel (May–Sept;

☎385-1288) and campground (☎385-1259) can be found twenty miles east of Port Townsend at **Fort Flagler**. Set on the tip of rural Marrowstone Island, with a windswept beach, walking trails and great views out across Puget Sound, this is a fine spot and you're more likely to find space here during the summer than at Fort Worden – partly because there's no public transportation.

The town is the peninsula's best place for **eating and drinking** with a sociable atmosphere that makes for good café-sitting: try breakfast or lunch (Wed–Sun) at the *Salal Café*, 634 Water St (☎385-6532), or *Bread and Roses* at 230 Quincy St (☎385-1044). For more substantial meals, the *Fountain Café*, 920 Washington St, serves classy seafood and pasta, while *The Landfall*, 412 Water St (☎385-5814; Wed–Sun), serves up some quality, low-priced Mexican food. Water Street also holds two good fish-and-chip places, the *Lighthouse Cafe* at no 955 (☎385-1165) and the *Day Star*, no 711 (☎385-1336). In the evenings, *The Back Alley Tavern*, behind the Terry Building at 921 Washington St (☎385-2914), has live music Wednesday to Sunday, as does the cooler *Town Tavern*, 639 Water St.

West via Sequim

South of Port Townsend, Hwy-20 skirts round Discovery Bay to meet US-101 at the start of its journey west along the Olympic Peninsula's narrow coastal plain, with the National Park on one side and the **Strait of Juan De Fuca** on the other. The strait, linking the Pacific with Puget Sound, was once thought to be the fabled **Northwest Passage** on the basis of a chance meeting famous among early seventeenth-century mariners – between an English merchant and a certain Apostolos Valerianos in Venice in 1596. The Greek Valerianos claimed – dubiously enough – to be an exiled Spanish sea-captain by the name of Juan De Fuca and, for good measure, he added that he had sailed from the Pacific to the Arctic Ocean via the strait that bears his (assumed) name today. Thoroughly gulled, explorers sought to follow in his nautical footsteps, and the name stuck.

It's eighteen miles from the junction of Hwy-20 and US-101 to **SEQUIM**, (pronounced "Skwim"), the only town on the rain-soaked peninsula to hold an annual irrigation festival. While drenching everywhere else, the Olympic Mountains cast a "dry shadow" over this area, and the sunshine attracts senior citizens to live here in scores, as evinced by advertisements for lessons in the foxtrot and two-step in downtown windows and the tea-shops with olde-worlde spellings strung along the main drag, Washington Street, which doubles as US-101. The ultra-quaint *Oak Table Café*, one block south of the highway at 292 W Bell and Third Ave (☎683-2179), offers excellent breakfasts and lunches; and the *Hi-way 101 Diner*, 392 W Washington (☎683-3388), has the best burgers in town, served in strikingly kitsch Fifties surroundings.

The **visitor center**, 1192 E Washington Rd (☎683-6197), has information on several local attractions, such as the **Sequim-Dungeness Museum** (daily 9am–4pm; free), downtown at 175 W Cedar St, which exhibits locally found historical and archeological objects, including some of the oldest traces of humanity in the Pacific Northwest, uncovered at nearby Happy Valley. The **Olympic Game Farm** (daily 9am–4 or 5pm; $4), six miles north of Sequim – follow the signs from downtown along Sequim–Dungeness Way – produced the animal stars of Disney classics like *The Incredible Journey* and *Grizzly Adams*. Though it's fascinating to see the peninsula's native bears and cougars close up, the sight of a huge buffalo trailing forlornly after your car in hope of a stale hamburger bun (you can buy bagfuls at the entrance) makes for depressing – and far from essential – viewing.

Dungeness National Wildlife Refuge

There are no such indignities for the wildlife on the **Dungeness Spit**, a long sandspit projecting into the sea six miles northwest of Sequim, beyond the Game Farm. Strewn with rocks and weirdly shaped driftwood, this is a bird refuge and the home of Dungeness crabs, widely thought by shellfish gourmets to provide the ultimate in crabmeat. You can hike to the lighthouse, which has been in use for 125 years, in a day – a round trip of 11 miles – but be sure to take provisions and enough drinking water.

As part of the **Dungeness National Wildlife Refuge**, the tidal zone and parts of the coastal forest adjoining the base of the spit have been placed under protection and are the home of numerous waterfowl. Wild geese come here in winter and spring from the far north. There are several ways to reach the refuge and spit, but the most straightforward is to drive four miles west out of Sequim along US-101, and then turn right for the five-mile journey down **Kitchen-Dick Lane** (subsequently Lotzgesell Rd), through the Dungeness Recreation Area to the protected zone. A half-mile footpath leads from the parking lot through a forest, and there's a viewpoint from which you can usually see Canada.

Port Angeles

Founded by the Spanish in 1791, and named "Puerto de Nuestra Senora de los Angeles" until confused postal clerks insisted one Los Angeles on the West Coast was enough, **PORT ANGELES** – seventeen miles west of Sequim – is the peninsula's main town and the most popular point of entry into the Olympic National Park. Though its setting is lovely, it's very much a working town, the main strip of motels and restaurants making few concessions to quaintness; and although the surrounding scenery and ferry connections to and from Victoria BC bring in the tourists, it's timber that's Port Angeles' real business. Heavy logging trucks roll in bearing tree-trunks, while pulp and paper mills – one at each end of the six-mile waterfront – send a pennant of steam over the town 24 hours a day. However, sheltered by the long arm of the Ediz Hook sandspit, the harbor has its own gritty beauty: industrial chimneys are backdropped by mountains, and out in the bay, cormorants fly over the fishing boats.

As far as sightseeing goes, it's not going to take long to look around: the main sight downtown is **Clallam County Museum**, at Fourth and Lincoln (summer daily 9am–4pm; winter Tues–Fri 9am–4pm; free), housed in the old clock-towered Courthouse (Port Angeles' one showpiece of nineteenth-century architecture) and featuring exhibits on maritime and logging matters. But the town's real attraction is its closeness to the Olympic National Park (see below), and that's where you'll want to go – probably as quickly as possible.

Arrival and information

Port Angeles has the peninsula's best **transportation connections** and, for once, the ferry and bus terminals are close together. *Greyhound*, at 215 N Laurel St (☎452-7611), run a daily (Mon–Fri) service to Seattle, while local *Clallam Transit* buses (☎452-4511, or 1-800/858-3747 outside Port Angeles) criss-cross downtown, go part of the way to Port Townsend (change to a *Jefferson Transit* bus at Sequim), and travel west around the Peninsula to Neah Bay, Forks and La Push. *Black Ball Transport* (☎457-4491) operate car **ferries** and *Victoria Express* (☎452-8088 or 1-800/633-1589) run passenger services to Victoria in Canada for a bargain $5 walk-on fare one-way, $25 with car, from the pier at the foot of Lincoln Street. Opposite is the **visitor center**, 121 East Railroad St (daily summer 7am–10pm, winter 10am–4pm; ☎452-2363), which can provide a mass of information about the town. Port Angeles also houses the **Olympic National Park visitor center** (daily summer 9am–8pm, winter 9am–4pm; ☎452-4501), at the top of Race Street as you head out of town along the signposted route towards the park, an excellent source of the maps and information you'll need if you're planning any hiking.

The town is a good place to get kitted out too: *Pedal 'n' Pack*, 120 E Front St (☎457-1240), rent mountain bikes and organize kayak trips, while *Olympic Mountaineering*, 221 S Peabody St (☎452-0240), rent out climbing, camping and hiking tackle. Local **auto rental** companies offer reasonable rates for one- and two-day rentals – you'll see their billboards round the ferry dock; and *Gray Line* (☎452-5112) run daily three-hour excursions up to Hurricane Ridge (see below), from beside the ferry terminal for $12 throughout the season.

Practicalities

You shouldn't have any problems finding a **motel** in Port Angeles – just behind the harbor, the two parallel one-way main streets, First Street and Front Street, are cluttered with them (though book ahead on summer weekends, when they can all fill up). The rooms at *Aggies*, 602 E Front St (☎457-0471; ③), are palatially large (with thin walls), while the *Dan Dee Motel*, ten blocks south of First along Race Street at 132 E Laurisden Blvd (☎457-5404 or 1-800/833-4620; ②), is less expensive. The nicest place in town is the *Red Lion Bayshore Inn,* 221 N Lincoln St (☎452-9215 or 1-800/547-8010), on the waterfront a block from the ferry landing.

The *House of Health*, 511 E First St (☎452-7494; ①), has **hostel beds** for $10 and discounts on their steam baths and saunas – great for relaxing after a day on the trails. There's plenty of excellent **camping** in the Olympic National Park, though you'll need your own vehicle to reach the campgrounds; six miles south of Port Angeles along Hurricane Ridge Road, the *Heart of the Hills* campground is one of the best .

The tiny *First Street Haven* café, 107 E First at Laurel, is good for breakfast or lunch; for dinner, the innovative vegetarian *Coffee House Restaurant and Gallery*, practically opposite at 118 E First St (☎452-1459), has low prices and a pleasant atmosphere.

Neah Bay and the Makah Reservation

Although the major US-101 heads inland from Port Angeles to skirt the Olympic National Park (see below), it's also possible to follow US-112, clinging precariously to the seventy-mile-long coastline as it approaches **NEAH BAY**, the small and rundown last village of the **Makah**. Neah Bay is also served by *Clallam Transit* buses from Port Angeles.

The bitter history of the Makah is typical of the area: a sea-going tribe, they once lived by fishing and hunting whales and seals, moving from village to village across the western part of the peninsula. Like most Native Americans, the Makah were happy to trade with passing European ships, and even when the Spaniards built a stockade here in 1792 (it was abandoned four months later) the relationship remained cordial and mutually beneficial. The change came when white settlers began to arrive in the 1840s, bringing smallpox with them. Makah social structures were simply swept away by an epidemic of savage proportions. Samuel Hancock, who had built a trading post at Neah Bay in 1850, recorded the tragedy: "The beach for a distance of eight miles was literally strewn with the dead bodies . . . still they continue to die in such numbers that I finally hauled them down the beach at low tide, so they would drift away". Other indignities were to follow: treaties restricted their freedom of movement, white settlers were given vast chunks of their traditional lands, and they were forced to speak English at white-run schools, as missionaries set about changing their religion.

The Makah's tenuous grip on their culture received an unexpected boost in 1970, when a mudslide at the Ozette village site on **Cape Alava**, several miles south of their present reservation, revealed part of an ancient Makah settlement – buried, Pompeii-like, by a previous mudslide some five hundred years before and perfectly preserved. The first people to uncover the remains encountered bizarre scenes of instantaneous ageing – green alder leaves, lying on the floor where they fell centuries ago, shrivelled almost as soon as they were exposed. But eleven years of careful excavation revealed thousands of artefacts: harpoons for whale hunts, intricately carved seal clubs, watertight boxes made without the use of metal, strangely designed bowls, and toys all belonging to a period before trade began with Europeans. Rather than being carted off to the depths of the Smithsonian, these artefacts have remained in Makah hands, and many are now displayed at the purpose-built **Makah Cultural and Research Center** (summer daily 10am–5pm; winter Wed–Sun 10am–5pm; $4), along with a full-size replica house and some beautiful turn-of-the-century photographs of Makah people. The settlement itself has been reburied to preserve it.

Practicalities

A couple of **motels** can be found in the village: the *Thunderbird* (☎645-2450; ③) and the slightly cheaper *Tyee Motel* (☎645-2223; ②). But these aren't particularly clean or pleasant; and you're better off travelling the 17 miles back east to Sekiu for low-key and comfortable *Van Riper's Resort* (☎963-2334; ③), where most of the rooms overlook the sea. The *Breakwater Inn* (☎963-2428), also in Sekiu, serves **meals**.

Olympic National Park

The magnificent **OLYMPIC NATIONAL PARK**, which consists of a huge mountainous section in the middle of the Olympic Peninsula plus a separate sixty-mile strip of Pacific coast further west, is Washington's prime wilderness destination, with boundless opportunities for spectacular camping, hiking and wildlife-watching.

Although the park is best known as the location of the only **temperate rainforests** in North America – see p.185 – the special conditions responsible for producing such forests only prevail at lower altitudes, and into its one and a half million acres are crammed an extraordinarily diverse assortment of landscapes and climate zones. About sixty percent of the peninsula – the areas between about 2000 and 4000 feet – is **montane forest**, dominated by the Pacific silver fir and the Douglas fir. Higher up, the **subalpine forest** of mountain hemlock, Alaska cedar and fir, is broken up by a parkland of intermittent forest and lush meadow, while higher still the mountain slopes and summits constitute a forbidding **alpine zone**. Here, windborne ice crystals feel like flying sandpaper, the hiking trails are only free of snow for about two months a year (roughly late June to August), and mosses and lichens are pretty much the only vegetation.

No roads cross the central segment of the park from one side to the other, but many run into it from separate directions. The text which follows reflects the most logical itinerary, working anti-clockwise around the park on US-101 and making forays into different sections from the various access points along the way.

The **park visitor center**, in Port Angeles (see above), has a comprehensive range of maps and information, and there are other, smaller visitor centers at **Hurricane Ridge** and **Hoh Rainforest**. These main services are supplemented by a string of seasonal **ranger stations** – at Lake Crescent, Ozette, Mora, Kalaloch, Queets, Lake Quinault and elsewhere – as well as the occasional US Forest Service station. Most have a wealth of literature to help plan your visit, including complimentary maps and free visitors' guides – though serious hikers will need far more detailed publications.

Over six hundred miles of **hiking trails** pattern the park, ranging from the gentlest of strolls to lung-wrenching treks. The usual backcountry rules apply: for example, don't drink the water, hide food away from bears, avoid defecating near water, and get a (free) backcountry permit if you're venturing beyond the park's established campgrounds to stay out overnight. Also the weather can be particularly changeable, so always carry raingear, watch the tides on the coast – and don't forget the insect repellent.

The one-horse communities dotting the peninsula offer **motel** accommodation, but, generally speaking, you're better off inside the park, either **camping** – there are 16 established campgrounds (operating on a first-come, first-served basis) and around 50 backcountry sites – or staying in one of the **lodges**, among which there are three of note: Lake Crescent, Lake Quinault and Kalaloch. At all of them, book your room well in advance. If you're dependent on **public transportation**, you'll be struggling, though *Clallam Transit* of Port Angeles (see above) provide a reasonable weekday service to Lake Crescent, Forks, Neah Bay and La Push.

Hurricane Ridge and the Olympic Mountains

On the edge of Port Angeles, the park visitor center is the starting point for the seventeen-mile haul up to **Hurricane Ridge** – passing (after about four miles) the *Heart of the Hills* campground. It's a hell of a drive, as the road wraps itself around precipices until the piercing peaks and glistening glaciers of the **Olympic Mountains** spread magnificently in front of you, a formidably thick band of snow-capped peaks stretching south from Port Angeles, with mighty Mount Olympus the tallest of all at nearly 8000 feet. The Hurricane Ridge visitor center features a large relief map of the area, useful for getting your bearings, and **trails** lead off to more isolated spots – through meadows filled with wild flowers in summer.

The most popular hike is the **Hurricane Hill Trail**, a three-mile round trip to the top of a neighboring hill, where there are great views out across the Strait of Juan De Fuca. Longer alternatives include the strenuous eight-mile hike west, over the mountains through classic alpine and subalpine scenery, to **Lake Mills**, where there's a backcountry campground. East from Hurricane Ridge, a difficult and steep nine-mile dirt road heads off to **Obstruction Peak**, which is noted for its views of Mount Olympus; several trails venture from the end of the road into the valley beyond, with one leading to the **campground** at *Deer Park*.

Lake Crescent and Sol Duc Hot Springs

West of Port Angeles, US-101 slips through low-lying forest on its fifteen-mile journey to glacier-cut **Lake Crescent**, a handsome, hill-trapped fishing lake known throughout the region for its fine Beardslee trout. Just off the highway, beside the lake's southern shore, is **Lake Crescent Lodge** (May to early Nov; ☎928-3211; ④–⑤), whose cabins and motel-style rooms occupy a superb wooded headland poking out into the water. Nearby, the one-mile Marymere Falls Trail leads through old-growth forest to a 90-foot waterfall, and continues up the forested mountain slope, as the two-mile Mount Storm King Trail, to Happy Lake Ridge, where there are magnificent views back over the lake, and a couple of backcountry **campgrounds**. Both the lodge and the seasonal **Storm King Ranger Station** (☎928-3380) nearby, have further hiking (and boating) suggestions.

Just beyond the western tip of Lake Crescent, a paved turning leads the twelve miles south to **Sol Duc Hot Springs**, where mineral water bubbles hot out of the earth, and is channelled into three pools (mid-May to Sept daily 9am–5pm; April to mid-May & Oct Sat–Sun 9am–5pm only; $4.50) at the *Sol Duc Hot Springs Resort* (☎327-3583; ④). The resort, which rents out cabins and motel units, also has **camping** facilities. From the end of the road, a mile beyond the resort, you can continue hiking along the river to **Soleduck Falls**, from where a steep path heads off south along Canyon Creek up into the mountains to the **Seven Lakes Basin**. More ambitious souls can hike across the Bogachiel Peak, past the Hoh Lake and down the Hoh River valley – the site of one of the most visited rain-forest areas (see p.185). Alternatively, you can return to the Sol Duc Springs and make the forty-mile journey west to Forks (see below).

The Peninsula's ocean beaches

The wild, lonely Pacific **beaches** that start near Neah Bay and stretch down the Olympic Peninsula's west side still look much as they did before the pioneers got here: black rocks point out of a grey sea along a coastline inhabited mostly by loons, grebes, puffins and cormorants whose protection is ensured by the incorporation of the coast north of Kalaloch into the Olympic National Park.

With strong currents, cold water and hidden rocks, these beaches aren't really suitable for swimming (especially as floating logs present a real hazard), but the hiking can be magnificent. You do hear the odd horror story about hikers cut off by the tide, so carry a tide-table (usually printed in local newspapers), or copy down times at a ranger station or visitor center, and err on the side of caution. Also, unless you're equipped with a four-wheel drive, avoid the dirt-road access points to the coast, particularly in wet or foggy weather.

From Neah Bay, **Cape Flattery**, at the northern corner of the Makah Reservation is comparatively accessible, at least once you've bumped your way down the hard-to-find unpaved road from Neah Bay. From the end of the road, a half-hour hike leads to the cape which once "flattered" Captain Cook with the hope of finding a harbor, and is the USA's northwesternmost point (excluding Alaska). Below the cape, the constant crashing of the waves has worn caves in the sheer rock of the cliff-face, while opposite on **Tatoosh Island**, coastguards staff a remote lighthouse. From Neah Bay, you can also drive round the base of the cape and south along the coast to crescent-shaped **Shi-Shi Beach**, (pronounced *shy-shy*) which ends in **Point of the Arches**, a dramatic array of rocks tunnelled by waves.

Sixteen miles east of Neah Bay, back along Hwy-112, a rough road leads to the northern tip of **Lake Ozette**, where there's a ranger station (☎963-2725), a **campground**, and two three-mile trails which provide the only access to another stretch of wild coastline, including **Cape Alava**, where the Makah village was buried – though the archeological dig closed in 1981. It's possible to hike the eighteen miles from Cape Alava south to **Rialto Beach**, though you'd have to arrange transportation at both ends, and take good care not to get cut off by the tide. At Rialto Beach, which is itself a narrow sandspit, the coast becomes accessible by road again – there's a turning off US-101 about a mile north of Forks. About six miles from the sea, this road splits into two branches – one above, the other below the Quillayute River. The northern route leads to Rialto Beach via **MORA** – where there's an attractive **campground** and a **ranger station** (☎374-5460) – while the southern branch continues to **LA PUSH**, an eight-hundred-year-old fishing village, also at the river mouth and on the Quileute Indian Reservation. This is now sad and shabby but has a beautiful sandy beach.

Retracing your steps from La Push, watch out for the mile-and-a-half trail (on the right-hand side of the road) leading to **Third Beach**. This is the start of a spectacularly beautiful, 16-mile hike down the coast to the end of the Lower Hoh Road, a rough dirt track that heads inland to join US-101 just south of the turning for the Hoh Rainforest (see below). If you decide to make the trek – and can sort out transportation at both ends – the nearest **ranger station**, at Mora, will provide detailed tide and trail information as well as backcountry permits.

Forks

On the densely forested west side of the peninsula, in between the main body and the coastal portion of the Olympic National Park, the small logging community of **FORKS** is set just east of where the Bogachiel River "forks" into two branches. Despite half-hearted attempts to catch the peninsula's growing tourist trade, Forks is still very much a timber town, hit hard by the gradual decline of the industry, though the Mount St Helens explosion in 1980 created a temporary surge of work, as local loggers headed south to clear acres of blasted trees. Today business is slower, though heavy trucks still pull through the town, unloading logs at local sawmills and hauling sawn lumber away to be shipped out of Port Angeles or Grays Harbor.

When you're surrounded by trees, the history of logging becomes more interesting than you might otherwise think, and it's worth calling in on the **Forks Timber Museum** (May–Nov Tues–Sat 10am–6pm; free) on US-101 at the south end of town, whose broad range of exhibits depicts life in the logging camps of the Twenties and Thirties, when men were based out in the forest, sleeping in bunkhouses and hitting the towns for only a couple of days every month. Inexpensive road-building ended the days of the logging camp after World War II, and various mechanical devices (some on display) made logging less dangerous. The timber trade still inspires innovations – a few years back, a Japanese company tried logging around here by balloon. There's a very good **visitor center** (☎374-2531 or 1-800/44FORKS), with lots of information on hiking in the region, right next door.

Clallam Transit run **buses** between Forks and Port Angeles, with connections to Neah Bay. For **accommodation**, try the *Miller Tree Inn* (☎374-6806 after 4.30pm or at weekends; ③), five hundred yards east of the only set of traffic lights in Forks: it's a relaxed bed and breakfast that lowers its rates in winter. *Olympic Suites* (☎374-5400 or 1-800/262-3433; ③) offer comfortable accommodation on the north side of town. Hostel beds are available 23 miles south of Forks at the *Rain Forest Hostel* (see below).

The Hoh Rainforest

The **Hoh Rainforest**, southeast of Forks, is the most popular of the Olympic rainforest areas, in part because it has the only large **visitor center** (daily 9am–4pm; ☎374-6925), nineteen miles along Upper Hoh Road, which leaves US-101 twelve miles south of Forks. After picking up pamphlets and looking in on the various displays, you can explore the rainforest along two short trails, the three-quarter-mile **Hall of Mosses Trail** or the slightly longer **Spruce Trail**, which reaches the Hoh River on a circuit through the forest. More energetic hikers can follow the 36-mile round-trip **Hoh River Trail** right up to the base of 8000-foot Mount Olympus; climbing the ice-covered peak is a major undertaking, but even if you just want to camp out along the route, be sure to check in with the rangers and get a backcountry permit. Cougars and other beasts are still very much present in the park. Beyond the turn-off for the rainforest, US-101 runs parallel to the lower reaches of the Hoh River, passing the small but very friendly *Rain Forest Hostel* (☎374-2270; ①), which will put mattresses in the barn when its

---

THE RAINFORESTS OF OLYMPIC NATIONAL PARK

Incredible as it may seem in cool Washington, an all-but-unique combination of climatic factors in the river valleys of the west side of the Olympic Peninsula has produced an environment akin to a jungle. **Temperate rainforests** are extremely rare – the only others in the world are located in Patagonia and New Zealand – but here the annual rainfall of 140 inches mixes with river-water running down from the mountains to create the overwhelming growing-power normally associated with much warmer climates. Sitka spruce and maple flourish, all but overwhelmed by the thick, trailing tendrils of clubmosses and lichens, epiphytes whose roots gather nourishment from the drizzly air. On the ground, some three hundred species of plants fight for growing space, crowding the ground with ferns, mushrooms and wood sorrel oozing out of the dense, moist soil. The rainforests intermingle with the lowland forests of Western hemlock and Douglas fir, among which are the park's largest trees – in fact the world's biggest Douglas fir is to be found in the Queets Valley.

Several rainforest areas can be visited, notably those in the valleys of the Hoh, Queets and Quinault rivers (see above and below). The only way to get through the rainforests is on the specially cleared, and in places paved, **trails**, although these tend to get slippery as moss grows back again – your footwear should grip well. You'll need a **vehicle** to reach any of the trailheads, but there is good **camping** in all three valleys.

twelve beds are full. Further south, the road returns to the coast just after the tiny (and very difficult to reach – the dirt roads are dire) **Hoh Indian Reservation**, set beside the rugged mouth of the river.

Kalaloch and the Queets River Rainforest

Moving on, US-101 runs right along the coast beyond the Hoh River, passing by a continuous strand of windswept beach belonging to the Olympic National Park. At one of the prettiest spots, **KALALOCH**, there are a couple of campgrounds and the very pleasant *Kalaloch Lodge* (☎962-2271; ④), which has a coffee shop, a good restaurant and a motel unit with large, ocean-view rooms. There's also a **ranger station** (☎963-2283) on the south edge of the short built-up strip, which has lots of information and suggestions for hiking trips.

South of Kalaloch, US-101 cuts inland around the Quinault Indian Reservation (see opposite), while the Queets River, and a 25-mile-long dirt road, heads inland to the **Queets Rainforest**, the least visited of the three main rainforest areas. A marked path around the forest provides information about the luxuriant flora and fauna, including the **world's largest Douglas Fir** tree – 220 feet tall and 45 feet in circumference.

Lake Quinault and the Quinault Rainforest

The most easily accessible and perhaps the most beautiful of all the rainforests is the **Quinault Rainforest,** around the shores of Lake Quinault some 30 miles from Kalaloch. The lake itself was already a popular resort area when Teddy Roosevelt visited in the 1900s and decided to proclaim it part of an expanded Olympic National Park – and you only have to glimpse the lake, with its deep blue, creek-fed waters and impenetrably forested surrounds to see why Roosevelt was impressed.

Two access roads lead off US-101, one travelling the length of the north shore, the other the south, but they don't connect until you're well past the lake and further up the river valley – altogether a thirty-mile loop. Dense overgrowth crowds in on the narrow road as it enters the deeper recesses of the forest, but it perseveres (almost all is paved) and the loop – though it makes a perfect mountain bike tour – is negotiable by vehicle.

On the south shore, there's a **ranger station** (☎288-2444), a café or two and the rustic **Quinault Lodge** (☎288-2571 or 1-800/562-6672; ⑤), where Roosevelt stayed. Starting from the ranger station, the **Maple Glade Trail** is one of the best short hikes, climbing along a small stream through textbook rainforest vegetation. The slightly longer **Quinault Rainforest Trail**, beginning at the parking lot west of Willaby Creek, just two miles off US-101, snakes through a wonderful old-growth forest dominated by colossal Douglas firs which keep out the light, turning the undergrowth into a dark and dank mystery. There are fewer trails on the north shore, but the best **camping** is here at *July Creek*.

The Lower Coast

As you leave the west side of the Olympic Peninsula for the **southern part of Washington's coast**, the roads improve but the scenery gradually grows tamer. Wilderness beaches give way to holiday resorts, dense virgin forest to privately owned timber land, thinned by logging and punctuated by bald patches of "clear-cutting", where everything has been flattened. The coastline cuts deeply into the mainland at two points: the bay of **Grays Harbor**, at the center of which lies industrial **Aberdeen**; and at muddy **Willapa Bay**, ringed by oyster beds and wildlife sanctuaries. Just below here, the churning mouth of the Columbia River has formed the narrow sandspit of the **Long Beach Peninsula**, lined with old resorts, a last thrust of the Washington coast before Oregon.

The area is covered by two **local bus** services: *Grays Harbor Transit*, based in Hoquiam (☎532-2770 or 1-800/562-9730), runs north to Lake Quinault, west along the ocean beaches up to Taholah, and as far inland as Olympia to the east. It connects with *Pacific Transit* (☎642-9418) at Aberdeen, which then runs south as far as Astoria in Oregon, taking in Long Beach Peninsula.

South to Grays Harbor

South of the rainforest areas, US-101 loops awkwardly inland around the **Quinault Indian Reservation**. There have been numerous plans to build a coast road here, but the Quinault have so far vetoed them to preserve their beaches from mass invasion. Routes therefore become somewhat contorted, the main highway travels inland as far as Aberdeen, from where US-109 sneaks back up the coast, to end abruptly at Taholah, the main town. There's inevitably some doubling back in what follows – you could avoid it by cutting across to the coast on tiny back roads.

Grays Harbor and Aberdeen

South of the Quinault Reservation, the bay of **Grays Harbor** takes a big bite out of the coastline. The loggers who settled here in the mid-nineteenth century originally meant to stay only until the dense forest within easy reach of the waterfront had been cut down and the area was "logged out". But railways soon made it possible to transport logs from deeper in the forest, and a combination of this and the plentiful fishing – fish-canneries gradually joined the sawmills along the waterfront – led to the development of the industrial town of **ABERDEEN**, named after the settlement's biggest salmon cannery. Now hit by recession in both fishing and forestry, Aberdeen, and the neighboring city of Hoquiam that merges into it, are not the obvious places for a visit; but Aberdeen is making a brave attempt to use its key location (on the way to the ocean beaches) to catch passing tourists. At its heart is the **Grays Harbor Historical Seaport** project (east on Heron Street on the north side of the Chehalis River Bridge). Set on the battered, industrial waterfront, the Seaport project has painstakingly reconstructed the *Lady Washington*, the eighteenth-century sailing ship of Captain Robert Gray, the American trader who discovered Grays Harbor. Built to conform both with original designs and modern Coast Guard safety regulations, the ship is now a floating museum, the cornerstone of a larger scheme to convert the old mills and packing plants of the waterfront into tourist-attracting shops and cafés. A replica of Gray's other ship, the *Columbia Rediviva* (after which the Columbia River is named), is scheduled to follow.

If you want to **stay** in Aberdeen, there are inexpensive **motels** along Wishkah Street, and Grays Harbor Chamber of Commerce operates a useful **visitor center** off US-101 at 506 Duffy St (Mon–Fri 9am–noon & 1–5pm; ☎532-1924 or 1-800/321-1924), which can also help you with local **bus** times. *Grays Harbor Transit* is based at 3000 Bay St in Hoquiam (☎532-2770).

The coast between Aberdeen and the Quinault Indian Reservation

From Aberdeen, Hwy-109 leads around the northern edge of the harbor towards the wide, sandy beaches of the coast; *Grays Harbor Transit* provides a bus service. Coastal weather around here is not usually of a sort to make you reach for the suntan oil, and **clamming** is the main attraction (see p.108 for how to go about it). The right tide can bring out scores of clam-diggers armed with special shovels to dig up razor clams, and the Department of Fisheries sometimes have to impose no-clamming seasons to give the clams a fighting chance (check locally). Clams aside, there's little to draw you to **OCEAN SHORES**, a purpose-built Sixties bid for the convention dollar, which aimed to line its wide streets with Atlantic City-style glitter. Until, that is, the money ran out, leaving the town with neither sleaze nor soul, a tidy holiday and retirement center.

To the north, the wide beach stretches for miles of fine grey sand to **MOCLIPS**, where more resorts overlook the sea. The road ends north of here at **TAHOLAH**, at the center of the Quinault Indian Reservation, which stretches north and east to Lake Quinault. The Quinault nation, made up of the descendants of several Salish-speaking tribes were plonked down here during the 1850s when most of Washington's reservations were created, in the aggressive treaty-making period after Washington was made a territory and the demand by settlers for land increased. In 1969, the Quinault restricted access to its lovely wilderness beaches to protect them from a growing incursion of litter and graffiti, but you can hike through the beaches and forests in groups led by Native American guides; contact the Tribal Office (☎276-8211) in Taholah for details.

South to Willapa Bay

Hwy-105 leads south out of Aberdeen around the lower side of Grays Harbor to **WESTPORT**, which rescued itself from the decline of the commercial fishing industry by vigorous self-promotion as a "salmon capital" (the Northwest has several) – and enough tourists (especially fishermen) come to help the town get by. Further south, the area around **GRAYLAND** is cranberry country: the local peat bogs were converted to cranberry bogs earlier this century by Finnish settlers who shipped vast quantities of vines over from the east and worked in the mills at Aberdeen until the project took off. It's all a bit on the dreary side, though, and you'll probably want to head on south to where the coastline dips into **Willapa Bay**.

Too shallow to succeed as a commercial port (despite the zealous promotions of unscrupulous nineteenth-century property developers), Willapa Bay is much less developed than Grays Harbor: its muddy depths support a profitable underworld of oysters, and much of the bay is now lined with private oyster beds. Conditions here are also good for wildlife, and sections of the **Willapa Wildlife Refuge** are scattered around the bay, including **Long Island** at the lower end, which is home to otters, raccoons, an ancient cedar grove and some two hundred species of birds. The catch is, you can only get to it by private boat and, although there's a **visitor center** across from the island at the south end of the bay on US-101, twelve miles north of Ilwaco, they are rarely able to help with transportation. More accessible is **Leadbetter Point**, at the tip of the Long Beach Peninsula, at the end of Hwy-103, whose combination of forest, dunes, mudflats and marsh attracts sandpipers, turnstones, migrating black Brandt sea geese and the tiny – and rare – snowy plovers, who nest in a section of the dunes that is specially closed off from

April to August. You'll need your own vehicle to get here, as the bus route ends at Oysterville (see below), a few miles short of the reserve.

The Long Beach Peninsula

At the southern end of Willapa Bay, the **Long Beach Peninsula** projects a spindly arm between the mainland and the ocean (*Pacific Transit* run buses up and down it). Lined by 28 miles of uninterrupted beach, and less prone to fog than other parts of Washington's coast, the peninsula's been a holiday destination since steamboats carried vacationing Portlanders down the Columbia River in the 1890s, and seaside towns like **LONG BEACH** have a nostalgia missing from the modern resorts further north. Large wooden figures of sea creatures and the explorers Lewis and Clark (who passed this way) loom over you as you enter the town, and the mix of seaside gimcrackery and history feels almost surreal in **Marsh's Free Museum** (open as a shop). Here, behind the giftshop paraphernalia of buckets, spades and sea-shells, ancient nickelodeons still turn out whimsical tunes for five cents, and antique peep shows line up behind them. There's no real reason to stay – points north have more appealing accommodation – but for a bite to eat, stop at *My Mom's Pie Kitchen*, Pacific Highway and 12th St (closed Mon; ☎642-2342), which produces some tasty crab quiche alongside its range of gooey pies.

About fifteen miles further up the peninsula, **OYSTERVILLE** made a killing in the 1860s and 1870s by shipping oysters to San Francisco, and flogging them to the decadent spirits of the Gold Rush at up to $40 a plate. But demand outstripped supply and, with the oysters decimated, the town slipped into a long decline, leaving little more than the tiny **historic district** of today, with its Victorian houses of shingles and scrollwork set behind trim picket fences. Once you've strolled round town, there's nothing much to do, though you can sample the local delicacy at **Oysterville Sea Farms**, accommodated at the old cannery. You can also head the three miles north on Stockpole Road to the trails and beaches of **Leadbetter Point** state park and, beyond, the wildlife refuge (see above).

To find somewhere good to stay, retrace your steps south on Hwy-103 to **NAHCOTTA**, where the oyster industry has been revived (albeit with the imported Japanese breed) at **Nahcotta Oyster Farm**, 270th and Sandridge. Not far away, the comfortable **hotel-cum-B&B**, the *Moby Dick*, Sandridge Rd at Bay Ave (☎665-4543; ③), is housed in a stolid villa of 1929; and, on the old Nahcotta dock, *The Ark* **restaurant**, 273rd and Sandridge (☎665-4133), serves some of the finest seafood on the peninsula – its oysters are renowned. Further south still, at **KLIPSAN BEACH**, the cozy *Klipsan Beach Cottages*, two miles south of Ocean Park at 22617 Pacific Hwy (☎665-4888; ③), occupy a fine oceanfront location. And, back in Long Beach, the *Sands Lo Motel*, at 1910 Pacific Highway (☎642-2600; ②), is (among many similar establishments) mediocre but low-priced.

The Columbia River mouth

Though there's not much evidence of it now, the area around the Columbia River mouth was once inhabited by the **Chinook**, who evolved "Chinook jargon", an Esperanto-style mix of their own language, French and English that was widely used for trading, and later, for treaty-making – much to the confusion of other tribes who didn't speak it. Its complexities were put to effective use during World War II, when it was employed as a radio code. The Chinook caught white nineteenth-century imaginations with their strangely flattened skulls, as depicted in careful sketches brought back to a curious East by the explorers Lewis and Clark. The effect was achieved by pressing a piece of bark firmly to a baby's (padded) forehead every time it went to bed for about a year, the end result being seen as a sign of aristocratic distinction. Today, the area's Native American past is evidenced mostly by place names and displays in a couple of museums. The town of **ILWACO**, beside the Columbia River just south of Long Beach, was named after Elowahka Jim, the son-in-law of a Chinook chief. Now a rather rundown fishing town, it had a rough reputation at the turn of the century when competition between fishermen with nets and those with traps broke into a series of street battles, the **gillnet wars**, fought with knives and rifles, and ending only when fishtraps were banned on the Columbia in 1935 – a blow to the local economy. A large proportion of the salmon are now caught by sports-fishing tourists. The **Ilwaco Heritage Museum**, at 115 SE Lake St (summer Mon–Sat 9am–5pm, Sun noon–5pm; winter Wed–Sat, Sun; $1.25), has displays on Chinook culture and the history of the cranberry along with the usual pioneer artefacts.

Southwest of Ilwaco, **Cape Disappointment** hooks into the mouth of the wide Columbia River, the boundary with Oregon. Disappointed fur trader John Meares named the cape when he couldn't get his ship over the dangerous sandbar at the river's entrance. In fact, Meares was lucky – over two hundred ships were later wrecked on the sandbar, despite the two nineteenth-century **lighthouses** that were built to stem the death toll. Dredges and jetties have now made the bar much safer, but coastguards still train off the cape, and you can sometimes see their small boats facing massive waves. Near the tip of the cape, **Fort Canby** is one of a chain of military installations whose bunkers and batteries guarded the Pacific coast (and here, of course, the river mouth) from the late nineteenth century through both world wars. Now a state park with plenty of **camping**, Fort Canby contains the dire **Lewis and Clark Interpretive Center** (summer daily 9am–5pm; winter Sat & Sun 10am–3pm; free), which follows the trail of Lewis and Clark through miles of then-unknown territory to their arrival at the Pacific.

US-101 runs east along the Columbia from Ilwaco, eventually crossing an extraordinary four-mile toll bridge into Oregon at Astoria (see p.108). Before the bridge, and just past the tiny town of Chinook, you come to turn-of-the-century **Fort Columbia** (grounds open: summer daily 8am–dusk, winter closed Mon & Tues), now renovated to include another **Interpretive Center**, this one portraying early military life from kitchens and mess halls to squad rooms where the troops slept; there are also displays on Chinook history. The fort's old hospital now houses **Fort Columbia AYH Youth Hostel** (May–Sept; ☎777-8755; ①) – the least expensive lodgings in the area.

North of Seattle

While the wonderfully wild scenery of the Olympic Peninsula provides lingering detours west of Seattle, I-5 speeds north from the city, heading up the coast to Canada. Just north of Seattle's suburban sprawl, industrial **EVERETT** hogs the shoreline, its gritty sprawl bypassed by the interstate as it slips through the town's eastern peripheries to shoot over the marshy delta of the Snohomish River. Some forty miles further north is the I-5/Hwy-20 intersection: head east and you'll soon reach the mountains of the northern (and most dramatic) portion of the Cascade Loop (see p.210); drive west and you'll cross the dull flood plain of the Skagit River on the 15-mile journey to Anacortes (see p.197), passing the side road to La Conner on your way. Of the shoreline settlements, only **La Conner** and **Bellingham** have a modicum of charm, though several – particularly Mukilteo and Anacortes – are useful for ferry connections to the beautiful necklace of islands that stretches west across Puget Sound and the Strait of Juan De Fuca.

The highlight of the islands, beside the bucolic tranquility of **Whidbey Island** – whose flat glacial moraine and protected rural landscape make it ideal for a cycling tour – is the unforgettable scenery of the **San Juan Islands**. *Washington State Ferries* link mainland **Anacortes** with four of the archipelago, of which **Lopez** offers gentle farmland and rolling, forested hills, while **Orcas** and **San Juan Island** boast more dramatic landscapes of lush valleys overshadowed by steep wooded hills. Bellingham is also the starting point of the Alaska Marine Highway (see box below).

The islands are among the region's most popular tourist destinations, so in summer try to book accommodation in advance. There are good **public transportation** links up and down I-5, but once you're on the islands you'll be struggling without a bike or car – local **bus** services do exist, but they're hardly frequent or comprehensive.

La Conner

If you're keen to break your journey somewhere between Seattle and Bellingham, then **LA CONNER** is your best bet. Dating from the 1860s, the old part of town, complete with many of its early facades, straggles along the bumpy waterfront of the Swinomish Channel, a sheltered nautical shortcut between the San Juan Islands and Puget Sound. Before the area was dyked and drained, the whole Skagit delta was a marshy morass prone to flooding, so the original trading post was plonked on a hill, and named by the town's leading landowner after his wife L(ouisa) A(nn) Conner. But when the railroads reached the northwest in the 1880s, La Conner was left an abandoned backwater, its water-borne trade all but dead and gone. The town became the hang-out of odd-balls and counter-culturals, from painters and Wobblies to poets and World War II conscientious objectors.

Since the Seventies, the town has traded on its off-beat reputation and it's this that pulls the tourist dollar – though it's hard, nowadays, to get a glimpse of anything vaguely "alternative" unless you count the town's several art galleries. That said, the waterfront verges on the picturesque, with a neat little bridge over the channel to the Swinomish Indian Reservation, and there are a couple of attractions of passing interest. The restored Victorian **Gauches Mansion**, up the hill on Second St (Fri–Sun 1–5pm; $1), features some fine nineteenth-century furnishings and fittings, and, on the second floor, the **Valley Museum of Northwest Art** showcases the work of local painters. Further up the hill, at 501 S Fourth St, the **Skagit County Historical Museum** (Wed–Sun noon–5pm; $1), holds exhibits on the early days of Skagit County, from a small Native American section to a 1942 doll of Scarlett O'Hara.

Practicalities

La Conner's *Hotel Planter*, 715 First St (☎466-4710; ⑤), has plush and modern doubles – some of which overlook the waterfront – within a remodelled Victorian inn; *La Conner Channel Lodge*, 205 N First St (☎466-1500; ⑤), offers lavish waterside doubles; and the less expensive *Rainbow Inn B&B*, half a mile east of town at 1075 Chilberg Rd (☎466-4578; ③), has attractive rooms in a converted farmhouse.

The *Calico Cupboard* **restaurant**, 720 First St (☎466-4451), is absurdly quaint, but serves excellent lunches and afternoon teas, while *Palmers Pub*, Second St and Washington (☎466-4261), offers filling, inexpensive meals. *La Conner Tavern*, on the waterfront, has the best burgers in town, a wide range of Washington's best beers and live music on the weekend.

Bellingham

Part-industrial, with a dash of Victoriana and a lively university scene, **BELLINGHAM** drapes around its wedge-shaped bay some ninety miles north of Seattle and just eighteen miles south of the Canadian border. It's actually the sum of four smaller communities, whose separate street patterns make a disjointed, hard-to-navigate whole. The most southerly of the four is the revamped ex-railroad town of **Fairhaven** (I-5 exit 250), with its laid-back restaurants and bars and the main ferry terminal (for Victoria and the Alaska Marine Highway). Moving north, exit 252 accesses **Western Washington University**, where the hillside campus has become the setting for contemporary artwork. Billing itself as an "Outdoor Museum", the campus shows off some inventive modern sculpture, including a kinetic "steam sculpture" which blows a white cloud of mist over the grass. A few blocks further north, off exit 253, **downtown** offers nothing

THE ALASKA MARINE HIGHWAY

The **Alaska Marine Highway** is a three-day ferry ride that snakes its fabulous way between wooded, azure-set islands and hard, craggy coast from Washington's **Bellingham** to Alaska's **Skagway**, with stops along the way at Ketchikan, Wrangell, Petersburg, Juneau and Haines. A similar, parallel service starts further north at Canada's Prince Rupert (see p.448). Ferries leave the Bellingham Cruise Terminal every Friday early in the evening from May to September (less frequently in the winter) and arrive in Skagway the following Monday afternoon. The round trip takes about a week. Summer passages from Bellingham to Skagway cost about $240 one-way per passenger, excluding food and berth; a berth in a shared room will set you back another $120 – but you can bring a sleeping bag and find a space on the covered and heated solarium deck; you're even allowed to set up a tent outside the covered area. Vehicles up to 10 feet in length are charged $270, those between 10 feet and 15 feet about $580, in addition to the driver's fare. Space for these should be reserved well (ie months) in advance: summer reservations are accepted from the first working day of December and all the cabins (staterooms) have gone in about a week. Full payment is expected 45 days before departure. Arrive three hours before sailing time. You can usually get a walk-on passage with just a couple of weeks notice by signing up on the waitlist; or you can try at the Bellingham terminal on the day of departure – but don't bank on success.

Further details from **Alaska Marine Highway System**, Bellingham Cruise Terminal, 355 Harris, Suite 101, Bellingham, WA 98225 (☎206/676-8445); or PO Box 25535, Juneau, Alaska 99802-5535 (☎1-907/465-3941 or 1-800/642-0066; FAX 1-907/277-4829). See also pages 34, 487 and 503.

inspiring, though you could drop by the old City Hall, a grandiose 1892 redbrick building, towered and spired, that is now the main part of the **Whatcom County Museum of History and Art**, at 121 Prospect St (Tues–Sun noon–5pm; free). The setting – it overlooks the bay from a bluff – is, however, a lot more inspiring than the collections inside.

Practicalities

If you're driving into downtown Bellingham via I-5, exit 253 leads to Potter Street, where, at no 904, the helpful **visitor center** (summer daily 9am–6pm; winter daily 8.30am–5.30pm; ☎671-3990 or 1-800/487-2032), provides maps and information on the town as well as the surrounding Whatcom County. Arriving by **bus** – Bellingham is a major stop on the Seattle to Vancouver bus route – the *Greyhound* station (☎733-5251) is downtown at 1329 N State St. Almost next door, at Railroad Ave and Magnolia St, *Whatcom County Transit* (☎676-RIDE) operate local services, including #1A (daily except Sat 6am–6pm; 6 hourly; 25¢), which links the downtown station with Fairhaven and the main **ferry** dock, the **Bellingham Cruise Terminal**. From here, *Gray Line Cruises* (☎738-8099 or 1-800/443-4552) run daily passenger-only round-trips to Victoria (mid-May to mid-Oct 1 daily; 3hr each way). The terminal is also the starting point of the *Alaska Marine Highway System* (see box opposite). Bellingham's secondary ferry port, **Squalicum Harbor**, just north of downtown (bus #12A), acts as the operational base of *Island Shuttle Express* (☎671-1137), who run daily passenger-only ferries to the San Juan Islands, calling at Obstruction Pass, on Orcas, and Friday Harbor, the main town on San Juan Island (June to early Sept 1 daily; 1hr 30min/2hr 10min). In good weather, this is a delightful journey.

For somewhere to **stay**, try to stick to the town's **B&Bs**, many of which occupy the flashy villas built by the Victorians. Options include the homey and unpretentious *Decann House*, near Squalicum Harbor at 2610 Eldridge Ave (☎734-9172; ③); the *North Garden Inn*, just south of downtown at 1014 N Garden (☎671-7828; ③), where some of the rooms have great views over the bay; and the polished antique furniture of *The Castle*, in Fairhaven at 1103 15th St and Knox (☎676-0974; ③–④). The usual mundane, low-price **motels** are strung along I-5: take exit 252 for *Motel 6*, 3701 Byron St (☎671-4494; ②). The *Best Western Lakeway Inn*, just west of exit 253 at 714 Lakeway Drive (☎671-1011; ④), is altogether classier.

Among a score of lively **cafés** and **restaurants** in Fairhaven, you'll find *Tony's*, 1101 Harris Ave at 11th St (☎733-6319), a lovely coffee shop, sometimes hosting live music. Across the road *Bullie's*, 1200 Harris Ave (☎734-BULL), has substantial bar food, and scores of beers by the bottle plus a good selection on tap. The *Colophon Café*, 1208 11th St (closes early on Sun; ☎647-0092), features the best vegetarian cuisine around. If you're stranded downtown, try the inexpensive *Pepper Sisters*, 1055 N State St at Holly (☎671-3414), where the highlight of an imaginative menu is the seafood.

Mount Baker

With snow lasting from early November to mid-May, the **Mount Baker** ski area, in the Cascade Mountains 56 miles east of Bellingham, has become Washington's premier resort (ski reports on ☎671-0211), its lifts and runs dotted over several lower slopes in the shadow of the great mountain itself. At 10775 feet, Mount

Baker is the highest peak for miles around, a volcanic behemoth that hisses great clouds of steam whenever its insides are ruffled – the last time was in 1975. Not surprisingly, it has played a leading role in native folklore: the Lummi saw it as a sort of Ararat, the one peak that survived the Great Flood to provide sanctuary for a Lummi "Noah" in his giant canoe.

The main approach road from Bellingham, Hwy-542, loops round the mountain's northern foothills, passing two or three **campgrounds**, before a final, nail-biting fling up through the ski area to Artists Point beyond. From here, a two-mile loop trail leads up lava cliffs to flat-topped Table Mountain, with Baker soaring high above. There are lots of other trails, but this is the basic starter with several possible extensions, such as the difficult trek south along Ptarmigan Ridge to Coleman Pinnacle.

Mount Baker makes an ideal day trip from Bellingham, but if you decide to hang around – and aren't camping – the nearest **accommodation** is roughly 20 miles back down the road in one-horse Glacier: try the basic *Glacier Creek Motel* (☎599-2991; ③); or, if you're in a group, the (10-berth) riverside cabins of *The Logs* (☎599-2711; ④).

Whidbey Island

The sheer cliffs and craggy outcrops, rocky beaches and prairie countryside of **WHIDBEY ISLAND** make it a favorite retreat for the Puget Sound's city-dwellers, who take a tent and head for one of the state parks, or spend pampered weekends in one of Whidbey's luxurious bed and breakfasts. Once considered a key stronghold in the defence of the Sound, the island carries military relics from various eras: nineteenth-century blockhouses built against Native American attack, concrete bunkers from World War II – and in the north, at Oak Harbor, a large-scale naval base housing the sophisticated warfare squadrons of modern air and naval defence whose low-flying jets are an occasional but considerable annoyance. But on the whole the island is peaceful enough, the narrow country roads winding through farmland and small villages. If you're heading north to the San Juan Islands (see p.196), or crossing to Port Townsend and the Olympic Peninsula (see p.174), it's much more pleasant to meander through Whidbey than dash up I-5 or loop around US-101.

Getting to and around Whidbey Island

Coming **from Seattle**, the quickest route onto Whidbey Island is via the Mukilteo ferry; boats to Clinton run every half-hour, take twenty minutes and single fares are around $2 per person, or $4.50 for a vehicle and driver. A second ferry leaves Port Townsend on the **Olympic Peninsula** hourly for Whidbey's Keystone, halfway up the island just south of Coupeville, the main town. The trip takes thirty minutes with single fares costing about $2 per person, or $7 for a vehicle and driver. It's also possible to reach Whidbey **by road** from the north across Deception Pass – take Hwy-20 (the Anacortes road) off I-5. Local **buses** operated by subsidized *Island Transit* (☎678-7771) run free half-hourly services between Whidbey's larger communities and the ferry ports (Mon–Sat 7am–7pm) – though, as with Puget Sound's other islands, you'd be well advised to bring your own vehicle.

Clinton and Langley

Ferries from mainland Mukilteo reach Whidbey's southeast shore at the small town of **CLINTON**. There's nothing much doing here, and you're better off moving on up the main island road (here Hwy-525, later Hwy-20) to take the turning to **LANGLEY**, a prosperous town whose truncated, old-west wooden high street perches on a bluff overlooking the sea. The touch-of-Frank-Lloyd-Wright *Inn at Langley*, 400 First St (☎221-3033; ⑦), is five-star luxury all the way.

Coupeville

COUPEVILLE is a showcase town of immaculately maintained Victorian mansions built by wealthy sea captains drawn from their native New England by the fine, deep harbor of Penn Cove and the abundance of oak and pine trees, which made good money in the lucrative Californian timber trade. Fearing the local Skagit might object to white annexation of their land, the settlers built **Alexander's blockhouse** (at the end of today's Front Street), a small, wooden, windowless building intended to protect them from attack. However, relations remained remarkably peaceful, and the **dugout war canoe** next to the blockhouse was used only in festivals; both the blockhouse and the canoe are cared for by the **Island County Historical Museum** next door.

The character of Coupeville is protected by its location within **Ebey's Landing National Historic Reserve**, which is dedicated to preserving the area's rural appearance and keeping modern development at bay. The first of its kind in the USA, the reserve occupies the middle part of Whidbey Island on either side of Penn Cove, and is named after Isaac Ebey, the son of a pioneer farmer, who rose to prominence as a civil and military leader before coming to a nasty end at the hands of a vengeful party of Alaskan Tlingit.

Ebey's Reserve also includes two old, windblown forts, now state parks. Five miles southwest of Coupeville, close to the Keystone ferry port, **Fort Casey** was built at the end of the nineteenth century as part of a trio of fortifications across the entrance of the Puget Sound, and a formidable barrage of decaying World War II gun emplacements still face starkly out to sea. It's possible to hike the seven or so miles north from here along the bluff-fringed, shingly seashore (part of which is known as Ebey's Landing) to **Fort Ebey**. You can also reach the fort by road: watch for Libbey Rd, a left turn off Hwy-20 three to four miles northwest of Coupeville. Fort Ebey was constructed in 1942 after America's entry into World War II; there are no guns now, but the fortifications remain, giving good views out across the water to the Olympic Mountains.

Practicalities

Many of Coupeville's old villas have been turned into lavish (and quite expensive) **B&Bs**. The tiny **visitor center**, opposite the church at 5 S Main St (Mon–Fri 9am–5pm; ☎678-5434), has the full list, though you may find the staff at the museum more helpful and informed, a bonus when rooms get tight in the summer. Some fine B&B options include the good-looking *Victorian*, 602 N Main St (☎678-5305; ④); the slightly over-fussy twin pink houses of the *Inn at Penn Cove*, 702 N Main St (☎678-8000 or 1-800/688 COVE; ④–⑤); and the posh *Anchorage Inn*, 807 N Main St (☎678-5581; ④). Better still, the comfortably nautical *Capt Whidbey Inn*, 2072 West Captain Whidbey Inn Rd (☎678-4097 or 1-800/ 366-4097; ⑤–⑦) – take Madrona Way from the foot of Main St and keep going for two miles round Penn Cove – is a real delight: built out of local madrone logs in 1907, the main lodge has a superb restaurant offering some of the state's best seafood. Above there are a handful of antique rooms overlooking Penn Cove, while there are cottages and chalets in the surrounding forest. Another charming alternative is *Fort Casey Inn*, three miles south of Coupeville at 1124 S Engle Rd (☎678-8792; ⑤), where duplex accommodation is available in a row of renovated officers' houses on the edge of the state park. If you're on a tighter budget, the *Tyee Motel*, on the edge of Coupeville at 405 S Main St (☎678-6616; ②), has run-of-the-mill doubles; or you can **camp** either pleasantly at Fort Ebey (☎678-4636) or grimly at Fort Casey (☎678-4519) state parks. **Bikes** can be rented from *All Island Bicycles*, 302 N Main St (☎678-3351).

For **food** in Coupeville, the *Knead and Feed* (☎678-5431) is a bakery offering quality sit-down lunches, and *Toby's Tavern* (☎678-4222) is a friendly local bar-cum-restaurant; both are on Front Street near the jetty.

Oak Harbor and Deception Pass

Beyond the reserve, military matters of a modern and more mundane kind dominate the economy of **OAK HARBOR**, Whidbey's largest – and most unappealing – town. The nearby Naval Air Station, built in 1941, is home to the navy's tactical electronic warfare squadrons, and the town's ugly suburban sprawl is best passed straight through. Unless you're stuck for a motel room (try *Auld Holland Inn*, 5681 Hwy-20, ☎675-0724; ③), you'd do much better to continue north to **Deception Pass State Park** where a steel bridge arches gracefully over the narrow gorge between Whidbey and Fidalgo Island, connecting-point (via Anacortes) for the San Juans.

The pint-sized state park, with its splendid hiking trails and **campground** (☎675-2417), occupies the rocky, forested headlands on either side of the gorge, whose turbulent, churning waters are some of the region's most treacherous. Even the intrepid George Vancouver was wary of them, initially deceived (hence the name) into believing he had charted part of the Whidbey "peninsula", rather than the strait that makes it an island.

The San Juan Islands

Northwest of Whidbey Island, midway between the Washington coast and Canada, the lovely **San Juan Islands** scatter across the eastern reaches of the Strait of Juan de Fuca, and entirely upstage the rest of the inlet. Perfect retreats for walking, cycling and generally unwinding (although the weather can be wet), this maze of green islands is the breeding-ground of rare birds and sea creatures: white-headed bald eagles circle over tree tops, and families of Orca ("killer") whales pass close to shore. Farming and fishing communities now share the islands with escapees from the cities, including artists and craftspeople, all in search of tranquillity and solitude. In summer their numbers are swelled by more visitors than the islands can really accommodate, especially on San Juan and Orcas, the largest of the islands. Of the smaller islands, Lopez is a less crowded alternative, but Shaw has little to entice you off the boat.

You'll absolutely need to **book somewhere to stay in advance**: during summer weekends dozens of disappointed travellers end up spending the night at the ferry terminal, something all the tourist authorities work hard to avoid. However, even in July and August, peaceful corners away from the crowds are easy to find.

Getting to the San Juan Islands

Washington State Ferries run about eight boats a day, more in summer, to the San Juan Islands. The ferries only stop at four of the 172 islands, but the slow cruise through the archipelago is a real highlight. Less serene are the long lines of cars that develop at ferry ports in the summer when latecomers inevitably end up waiting for the next boat: it pays for drivers to be two or three hours early; pedestrians and cyclists have less hassle. Summer fares to San Juan Island are around $20 return for a car and driver, $5 for foot-passengers and cyclists, slightly less out of season. Make a note of when the last ferry leaves the island for the mainland, as it can be surprisingly early, especially out of season. Two ferries a day (less in winter) continue on from the islands to Sidney, on Vancouver Island, British Columbia.

All the ferries depart from the terminal complex eight miles west of **ANACORTES**, an unassuming town that's the best bet for overnight accommodation if you're catching an early ferry (the first one leaves before 6am). There's certainly no other reason to linger here, though the waterfront still has a rough-hewn charm – it's home to the state's largest fishing fleet – and the town makes the occasional gesture to the passing tourist trade. *The Majestic*, downtown at 419 Commercial Ave and Fourth (☎293-3355 or 1-800/950-3323; ⑤), is a recently renovated grand old **hotel** of 1889 with polished doubles. Also on Commercial Avenue, a string of **motels** offer more mundane roadside rooms, including the *Holiday Motel*, at no 2903 (☎293-6511; ③), and the more spacious *Islands Motel*, at no 3401 (☎293-4644; ③). Quality **food** for the ferry trip is available at the Italian take-out *Geppetto's*, 3320 Commercial Ave (☎293-5033). Incidentally, **gas** on the islands is considerably more expensive than on the mainland, and you'll save by filling up in Anacortes before you leave.

Lopez

The ferry's first stop is usually **LOPEZ**, a quiet, pastoral retreat where country lanes cobweb rolling hills and gentle farmland. There's nothing special to see, but many claim this is the attraction – and certainly the island, just ten miles long and not more than five wide, never gets as crowded as its larger neighbors, despite being something of a cyclists' paradise.

From the jetty at the island's northern tip, the main road meanders the five miles south to the one and only settlement, **LOPEZ VILLAGE**, a tiny triangle spreading back from the sheltered waters of Fisherman Bay. If you don't have a vehicle, call *Angie's Cabs* (☎468-2227) from the ferry landing. In the village, you can pick up a map at the "Olde Towne Country Store", drop by the modest museum (summer Fri–Sun noon–4pm) and – half a mile away, on the main road along the shore – rent a **bike** from *Lopez Bicycle Works* (☎468-2847), one of several bike-rental stores on the island. Next door, the *Islander Lopez* hotel and resort (☎468-2233; ④–⑤) is the place to **stay**: the best rooms are spacious, with kitchens and splendid sunset views from their imposing balconies; rates are

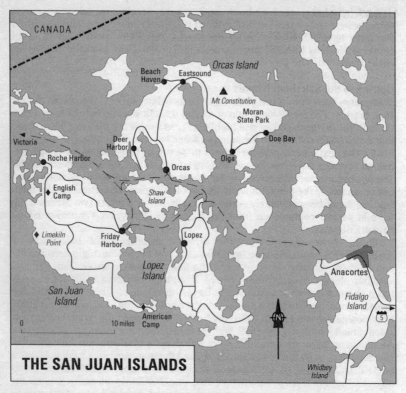

THE SAN JUAN ISLANDS

lower off-season, and there are plans to set up a tepee campground. The *Islander* also rents out a 6-berth fishing boat for around $30 an hour, $150 a day – while neighboring *Dragonfly* (☎468-3699) arrange sea **kayak** trips from $35 a half-day. The hotel will offer advice on visiting the island's homespun industries, from wine-tasting at *Lopez Island Wineries* and jam-licking at *Madrona Farm* to sampling the staggeringly delicious alder-smoked salmon of Greg Larsen's *San Juan Smoked Seafoods*. The *Islander*'s **restaurant** is (only) good for breakfast, but there are a couple of better places back in the village center: *Holly B's Bakery* (June–Sept; ☎468-2133) has fine fresh bread and pastries; and the *Bay Café* (closed Tues; ☎468-3700) offers the most imaginative of mouth-watering dinner dishes including at least one vegetarian choice a day.

Moving on from Lopez Village to the southwest corner of the island, **Shark Reef Park** gives access to an easy walk along the coast's beguiling hills; inland, there's fishing at **Hummel Lake**, and on the east coast at **Spencer Spit State Park** there are beach walks and clamming. The park has a small **campground** (☎468-2251), as does its (slightly) better-equipped twin, **Odlin Country Park** (☎468-2496), near the ferry dock. In between the two, the *Inn at Swifts Bay* (☎468-3636; ⑥), on Port Stanley Road – one mile south of the jetty turn left – is a classy and luxurious **B&B**.

Orcas Island

Horseshoe-shaped **ORCAS ISLAND** is much busier than Lopez, but its holiday resorts are so well tucked into distant coves that the island's peace and quiet is hardly disturbed. The tiny community of **ORCAS**, where the ferry lands, is no exception to this, with little beyond the *Orcas Hotel* (☎376-4300; ⑤) – a grand Victorian building overlooking the ferry landing, its rooms few and pricey, but a good place for a leisurely breakfast. You can rent **bikes** from *Dolphin Bay Bicycles* (☎376-4157 or 376-3093), just up from the dock, and either drive or cycle north through the island's farmlands – the former heart of the state's apple orchards, until Eastern Washington was irrigated.

It's about ten miles from the ferry landing to the island's main town, the run-of-the-mill gathering of mostly modern buildings that's called **EASTSOUND**. Despite its bayside setting, there's little to detain you, and most visitors shoot through on their way to more remote locations. It is, however, a good place to get kitted out: **mopeds** can be rented at *Key Moped Rental*, Prune Alley (☎376-2474), and **bikes** from *Wildlife Cycles*, North Beach Rd at A St (☎376-4708). **Groceries** are available from the *Island Market* foodstore, Prune Alley, and **maps** and **local guides** at *Darvill's Bookstore*, on the main road beside the bay. All these places sit together within the four-block town center.

Eastsound also has several good places to **eat**, including quality Mexican cuisine at *Bilbo's Festivo* restaurant, North Beach and A St (☎376-4728), and sound diner-style food at *Doty's A-1 Café* (☎376-2593), on North Beach just off the main street. If you decide to **stay** the night, your options are limited to two hotels on the west side of town overlooking the bay (and the main road). Of the two, the *Outlook Inn* (☎376-2200; ④–⑤) is the more agreeable. Far better local lodgings are to be found about three miles west of town at the *Beach Haven Resort* (☎376-2288; ④), where fifty-year-old beachfront log cabins line up along a densely wooded, sunset-facing cove; in summer the cabins are only available by the week, but out of season they can be rented on a nightly basis. To get there, head north out of Eastsound along Lover's Lane (the turning near the *Landmark Inn* hotel) and make a left at the sign.

Rising high above the eastern half of Orcas, **Moran State Park** is the island's main attraction, with miles of hiking trails winding through dense forest and open fields around freshwater lakes. **Mount Constitution**, at the heart of the park, is the highest peak on the islands, the summit of which is a steep four-mile hike (or a short drive) up a paved road. The views are as good as you'd expect, looking out as far as Vancouver Island, and back towards snow-capped Mounts Baker and Rainier.

All four **campgrounds** (☎376-2326) in the park fill up early in the summer. You can also camp at **Doe Bay Village Resort (AYH)**, Star Route 86 (☎376-2291 or 376-4755; ①–③), tucked round on the east side of the island about as far from the ferry as you can get: keep to the main road round the park and follow the signs. It's a lovely place, built on a secluded bay, with echoes of its previous incarnation as a "human potential center" still hanging meditatively around its cabins, cottages and hostel dorms. Dorm beds go for $9.50 with *IYHA* membership, $12.50 without – and there are excellent communal facilities, including an open-air **hot tub**, which can also be used by day visitors ($5), plus massage sessions and sea kayak expeditions at about $30 for a half-day's guided trip. There are self-catering facilities at Doe Bay, but, if you're after restaurant food, retrace your steps the four or five miles to **OLGA**, basically a general store, gas station and post office near to *Café Olga* (Mar–Dec daily 10am–6pm; ☎376-5098), where the fruit pies are a specialty. Be warned, though, it's not an undiscovered spot, and bus loads often descend on the place.

San Juan Island

The ferry's last stop is **SAN JUAN ISLAND**, the most visited of the islands, and the only one where the ferry actually drops you in a town. **FRIDAY HARBOR** may be small, but it's the largest town in the archipelago and the best place to rent transport. **Bikes** can be rented from *Island Bicycle* at 380 Argyle (☎378-4941), a few blocks up from the ferry; **mopeds** from *Susie's*, at Nichols and A St (☎378-5244). Ask for advice on cycling routes at the helpful **information center** (winter, daily 8am–4.30pm; longer in summer) at First and Spring, a short walk up from the ferry landing. They also have maps – useful since it's easy to get lost on the island's twisting and badly marked roads.

This taken care of, Friday Harbor's cafés, shops and waterfront make pleasant browsing. Up First Street, the **Whale Museum** (daily summer 10am–5pm, otherwise 11am–4pm; $2.50) has a mass of whale-related artefacts, including paintings, carvings and a whale stained-glass window. The local Orca or "killer" whales are protected by a ban on their capture, which was instituted in 1976, but they're still threatened by pollution. The museum promotes an "Adopt an Orca" programme (there are, apparently, 84 left in the Puget Sound) and monitors whale activities on a "whale hotline" (☎1-800/562-8832): you're asked to call in with any sightings.

Setting off around the island anti-clockwise, the open, windy peninsula that tails off to the south is home to **American Camp**, one of two national parks on the island. Like **English Camp** at the island's northern end, the name derives from the infamous **Pig War**, which briefly put the islands at the center of a very silly international conflict during the last century. When the Canadian border was drawn up in 1846, both the Americans and the British (who still ruled Canada) claimed the San Juans for themselves. This wasn't a great problem, and the American and British residents of the islands lived together fairly amicably until a series of tax squabbles climaxed with an American settler shooting a British pig found munching his garden vegetables. The Americans sent in the infantry; the British responded with warships, and soon 460-odd American soldiers plus cannons were dug in behind a trench opposing five armed British warships carrying over two thousand troops. After a lengthy stalemate, the question was resolved by Kaiser Wilhelm I of Germany in favor of the US, the only casualty being the pig. An information center at American Camp explains the "war" in full. The site itself is a barren affair, pitted with ankle-wrenching rabbit holes, and English Camp, at the greener northern end of the island, makes for a more pleasant walk.

Continuing past the coves and bays on the island's west side, a bumpy gravel road leads to **Lime Kiln Point State Park**, the best place on the island for whale-watching; the odds of a sighting are at their most favorable in summer, when the Orcas come to feed on migrating salmon. The lime kilns that give the park its name are just outside, relics of an era when lime quarrying was big business on the island. Further north, **ROCHE HARBOR** (accessible for $5 each way from Friday Harbor by *Primo Taxi*; ☎378-3550) belongs to the same era –

originally a company town, its gracious white **Hotel de Haro** was built to accommodate visiting lime-buyers in 1887. The hotel, as part of the *Roche Harbor Resort* (☎378-2155; ④), offers slightly down-at-heel doubles – but really you're better off enjoying a quick visit. The attractive wharf is worth a peek, and the hotel can provide directions to the weird **mausoleum** of its founder, a haunting structure set in the woods, incorporating Masonic symbols.

Practicalities

Camping is the obvious way to stay on San Juan Island, but unfortunately neither national park has sites. There's a very pleasant cyclists-only camp, the *Pedal Inn*, five miles form the ferry dock at 1300 False Bay Drive (☎378-3049), while the larger *Lakedale Campground*, is almost five miles from the ferry on Roche Harbor Road and reachable on the *San Juan Tour and Transit Co* bus.

A wide choice of pricey, but comfortable, **B&Bs** includes *Blair House* (☎378-5907; ⑤), an attractively refurbished Victorian villa four blocks from the ferry landing; the plain and simple *Friday's*, on First St (☎378-5848; ③); and the *Wharfeside*, two rooms in a retired sailing boat at K dock (☎378-5661; ⑤).

There are plenty of places to **eat** in Friday Harbor: *Cannery House* (lunch only; ☎378-2500) at the top of First Street has a wonderful view from its outdoor terrace; the *Electric Company*, 175 First St (☎378-4118), is a local tavern which also does food and has live music at weekends; and, if you're setting off early, the *San Juan Donut Shop*, 209 Spring St (☎378-2271), serves hefty breakfasts from 5am.

travel details

Trains

From Seattle to Tacoma (2 daily; 1hr); East Olympia (2; 1hr 45min); Kelso-Longview (2; 3hr); Portland (2; 4hr); Wenatchee (1; 5hr 30min); Spokane (1; 9hr)

Buses

South from Seattle to Tacoma (9; 45min); Olympia (8; 2hr); Longview (5; 3–4hr 30min); Portland (10; 2 express buses 3hr 15min, others up to 5hr). *Green Tortoise* also runs 2–4 times weekly to Portland (4hr 15min).

North from Seattle to Everett (4 daily; 40min); Mt Vernon (4; 1hr 30min); Bellingham (4; 2hr 10min); Vancouver, British Columbia (2; 6hr); Winslow (2 Mon–Fri; 1hr); Poulsbo (2 Mon–Fri; 1hr 15min); Port Ludlow (2 Mon–Fri; 2hr); Sequim (2 Mon–Fri; 2hr 30min); Port Angeles (1 Mon–Fri; 3hr).

Ferries

(All *Washington State Ferries* unless otherwise stated.)

To Alaska from Bellingham (1 weekly; leaves Friday evening, arrives Skagway Monday afternoon).

To Bremerton from Seattle (15 daily; 1hr).

To Port Townsend from Keystone, Whidbey Island (20 daily; 30min).

To the San Juan Islands and Sidney, BC from Anacortes (18 – various routes, including 2 daily to Sidney, BC; to Lopez (1hr); Orcas (1hr 30min); Friday Harbour (2hr); Sidney (3hr).

To Vashon Island: from Point Defiance to Tahlequah (18 daily; 15min); from Fauntleroy, W Seattle, to Vashon (around every half-hour from 5.25am–1.40am; 15min).

To Victoria from Seattle on the *Victoria Clipper* (summer 3–4 daily; winter 1 daily; 2hr 30min); from Port Angeles (*Black Ball Transport* summer 5 daily; spring and autumn 2 daily; 1hr 45min).

To Whidbey Island: from Mukilteo to Clinton (from 5am to 2am every half-hour; 20min); from Port Townsend to Keystone, see above.

To Winslow from Seattle (at least hourly from 6.20am–2.40am; 35min).

CHAPTER FOUR

THE CASCADES AND EASTERN WASHINGTON

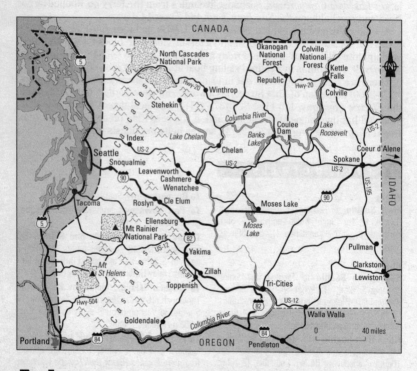

Native American legends say that the thirsty people of **Eastern Washington** once went to the ocean to ask for water. Ocean sent his children Cloud and Rain to water the land, but the people refused to let the spirits return home: Ocean, furious, rescued his offspring and built the **Cascade Mountains** as a great punitive barricade between the people and the sea. Whether or not the gods had a hand in it, the great spine of the Cascades is still a crucial divide, separating the wet, forested, sea-facing regions of the west from the parched prairies and canyonlands of Eastern Washington. Snow-capped and pine-covered, the mountains have a pristine beauty that's best appreciated

> ### TELEPHONE NUMBERS
>
> Washington State Tourism Development Division: ☎1-800/544-1800.
> The area code for the Cascades and Eastern Washington is ☎509.

from one of the many winding hiking trails. **Mount Rainier**, set in its own national park and readily accessible from Olympia or Seattle, has some of the loveliest, while the nearby blasted terrain of **Mount St Helens** – protected as a National Volcanic Monument – offers some of the most dramatic. Hwy-20, the high mountain road that crosses the **North Cascades**, is by far the most spectacular route to the east, dipping into the eastern foothills where small villages like **Winthrop**, **Chelan** and **Leavenworth** make useful bases for exploring the surrounding mountains.

The **East** is a very different proposition: the huge, sagebrush-covered plains, with their exposed buttes and bluffs, and the horizon-filling wheat fields that break them up, conjure cowboy-movie images of the old West. But in fact much of the landscape has changed beyond recognition from early pioneer days, since the exploitation of the Columbia River by the construction of mighty dams – especially the **Grand Coulee Dam**. The East's population is thinly spread, and of the towns only **Spokane**, the largest city east of the Cascades, has much sophistication; others – **Ellensburg**, **Yakima** and **Walla Walla** – are no-nonsense agricultural communities whose residents clearly wonder why on earth you should want to visit. This, in a way, is the attraction: the great, empty region can be fascinating because of its lack of window-dressing, bringing to life the rural America of country music, grain silos, Fifties diners, and battered pick-up trucks, of which there's seemingly one for every resident. It's an interesting enough place to pass through, but you need to be a real die-hard traveller to want to spend much time here.

You'll need a vehicle to explore the North Cascades or see Mounts Rainier and St Helens, but **public transportation** elsewhere in the region is less scanty than you might expect. The larger towns of southeast Washington and Spokane are easy enough to get to on *Greyhound* or *Amtrak*; and *Empire Lines* usefully connect Spokane with smaller towns like Chelan and Grand Coulee, close to the dam, as well as running to more major towns served by *Greyhound*.

THE CASCADE MOUNTAINS

The first bumps of the Cascades surfaced from the sea 35 million years ago, later being torn apart in massive volcanic explosions which gave the present mountain range its fiery birth. Though the snowy peaks that back up almost every Washington view now look the image of serenity, they still conceal a vast and dangerous volcanic power – as **Mount St Helens** proved when it exploded in 1980, killing people, annihilating wildlife over a wide area and deluging the Northwest with ash. Aside from the strangely fascinating scar left by the blast, the Cascades (now largely protected by a series of national parks and national forests that stretch the length of the state) offer mile upon mile of forested wilderness, sheltering all kinds of wildlife and traversed by a skein of beautiful trails –

ACCOMMODATION PRICE CODES

All accommodation prices in this book have been coded using the symbols below, corresponding to US dollar prices in the US chapters and equivalent Canadian dollar rates in the Canadian chapters. Prices are for the least expensive double rooms in each establishment, and only include local taxes where we explicitly say so.

For a full explanation see p.46 in *Basics*.

①	up to US$30	④	US$60–80	⑦	US$130–180
②	US$30–45	⑤	US$80–100	⑧	US$180+
③	US$45–60	⑥	US$100–130		

---

though for all but a few summer months, you'll need snowshoes to follow them. **Mount Rainier National Park** is the most popular access-point, a possible day trip from Seattle and with plenty of facilities. Further north, the remoter **North Cascades** can be reached along Hwy-20, or dipped into from the sunny eastern foothills, where small resort towns – the most agreeable of which is **Chelan** – eagerly await summer tourist-traffic and apple orchards fill sheltered valleys.

Mount Rainier National Park

Set in its own national park, glacier-clad **MOUNT RAINIER** is the tallest and most accessible of the Cascade peaks, and a major Washington landmark. People in Seattle look to see if "the mountain's out", the sign of a clear day, and native Americans living in the shadow of the mountain evolved a complex mythology around it. Rainier appears as a jealous wife magically metamorphosed – a giant mountain mysteriously tamed, its high peak seen as spirit country, inscrutable to human eyes (the summit is wreathed in clouds much of the time). There's a lively movement to re-christen Rainier with a native American name such as *Tahoma*: that would at least avoid the current jokes about the mountain's name actually being a description of its wet weather. The long winter season sees heavy snowfalls; not until late June or July does the snow-line creep up the slopes, unblocking roads and revealing a web of hiking trails. But in summer, when deer and mountain goats appear at the forest edges, small furry marmots emerge among the rocks and newly uncovered meadows sprout alpine flowers, the mountain makes for some perfect – and, if you pick the right trail, not unduly tough – hiking.

Each of the four entrances to the roughly square national park – one in each corner – lead to a distinct section, though in summer it's possible to drive between the main **Nisqually entrance** in the park's southwest corner, and both the smaller entrance to the southeast and the White River entrance in the northeast, reached along Hwy-410. The Nisqually section is the only one kept open year round (for cross-country skiing; the others open when the snow melts around June) and the only part you can see on any kind of public transportation – confined to pricey day trips with *Gray Line* from Seattle (☎626-5208; $34; daily May to early Oct). Admission to the national park is $5 per car, $2 hiker or cyclist; for general information, call ☎569-2211. It's possible to **stay** in the park at either of the two national park lodges in Longmire and Paradise (see below), and there's plenty of **camping**.

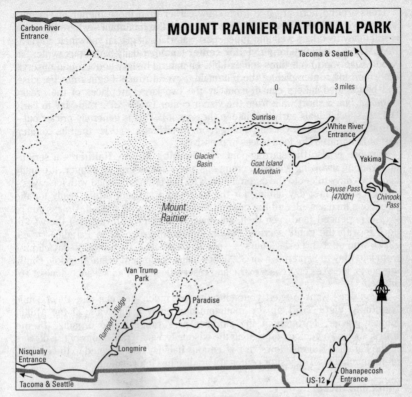

MOUNT RAINIER NATIONAL PARK

Carbon River Entrance

Tacoma & Seattle

0   3 miles

Sunrise

White River Entrance

Glacier Basin

Goat Island Mountain

Yakima

Cayuse Pass (4700ft)

Chinook Pass

Mount Rainier

Van Trump Park

Paradise

Rampart Ridge

Nisqually Entrance

Longmire

Tacoma & Seattle

US-12

Ohanapecosh Entrance

N

The Nisqually entrance: to Longmire and Paradise

The **Nisqually entrance** to the park, around ninety miles southeast of Seattle via I-5, Hwy-7 and then Hwy-706, brings you into the park just short of **LONGMIRE**, a small group of buildings that includes a tiny **wildlife museum** (daily 9am–5pm; free) and a very useful **hiker information center** (summer daily 8am–6pm; closed in winter when services are transferred to the museum) with plenty of information on the thirty-odd trails. In winter you can rent skis in Longmire (skis, boots and poles $11 a day; snowshoes $8), and year round the comfortable and modern *National Park Inn* offers accommodation (③; ☎569-2275 for reservations here and at *Paradise Inn*, below).

Beginning at Longmire, the **Trail of Shadows** is a highly popular, half-hour walk around hillside meadows on a loop trail which takes you past the remains of a long-gone homesteader's cabin. More strenuous hiking trails lead off from the loop – with one following **Rampart Ridge** to reach Van Trump Park beneath the Kautz Glacier; another traversing the side of the mountain – passing a string of campgrounds – to wind its tortuous way to the northwest entrance (and ranger station) at **Carbon River**. From the **Cougar Rock Campground**, a couple of miles up the road from Longmire, you can also hike along the two-mile **Carter Falls Walk** beside the Paradise River.

Trails around here are free from snow earlier than those higher up. In mid-summer you'll probably want to drive further up the mountain – where the snow is still many feet deep well into June – past waterfalls of glacial snowmelt, towards **PARADISE** – where a larger **visitor center** (summer daily 9am–7pm; winter Sat & Sun 10am–5pm) has films and exhibits on natural history and a round observation room for contemplating the mountain. Several routes begin from Paradise, and bedraggled hikers can dry out by the two large fireplaces of the creaky *Paradise Inn*, a short walk from the visitor center (☎569-2275; mid-May to early Oct; ③, special deals early and late in the season). This is generally pricier but – with its folksy 1920s foyer and dining-room furnishings – cozier than its counterpart at Longmire. The food is less impressive.

Paradise is also the starting-point for **climbing Mount Rainier** – a serious undertaking involving ice axes, crampons and some degree of danger. It usually takes two days to get to the summit – with its two craters rimmed with ice-caves – and back: the first day aiming for the base camp at Camp Muir, ready for the strenuous final assault and the descent to Paradise on the second. Unless you're very experienced (and even then, you have to register with rangers) the way to do it is with the guide service, *Rainier Mountaineering Inc* in Paradise (☎569-2227), who offer three-day courses – one day's practice, then the two-day climb – from late May to September for $300. Specialist equipment rental (lug-sole climbing boots, ice axes etc) costs extra, and reservations with an advance deposit are advised.

If you don't want to exert yourself quite that much, you can take the 1.2-mile **Nisqually Vista Trail** up the mountain and enjoy a fine view of the Mount Rainier glacier. Throughout the summer park rangers also organize **theme tours**, such as a geology tour along the Nisqually Vista Trail, a tour of the flowers in the Paradise Hill meadows, or a strenuous half-day tour devoted to the ecology of the mountains. The visitor center at Paradise has information.

Other entrances

In summer it's possible to drive from Paradise along rugged **Stephen's Canyon Road** to the park's southeastern corner, where the **Ohanapecosh visitor center** (summer only, daily 9am–6pm) is set in deep forest, near the trout-packed Ohanapecosh River. A one-and-a-half-mile hiking trail leads along the Grove of the Patriarchs – where some of the trees are over one thousand years old – and another (half-a-mile long) leads off to hot springs that were enjoyed by the first settlers.

South from Ohanapecosh, it's a five-mile trip to US-12, by means of which you can travel east to Yakima (see p.218) or west to both I-5 and the bumpy backroads that lead to the east side of Mount St Helens (see below). In summer, you can also drive north from Ohanapecosh the length of the park to the **White River entrance** in the northeast corner, with its hiker information center (daily summer 8am–4.30pm). From here it's a giddy ride up to the **Sunrise** visitor center (summer only, daily 9am–5pm) and wonderful views of Emmons Glacier and the mountain's crest – and you can continue north to Hwy-410, for Yakima and Seattle; the **Carbon River entrance** in the northwest corner is the least used, with no visitor center and only a few dirt roads. There are **campgrounds** near each entrance; for overnight backpacking away from these you'll need a wilderness permit (free from any ranger or visitor center).

Mount St Helens

The Klickitat who called **MOUNT ST HELENS** *Tahonelatclah* ("Fire Mountain") knew what they were talking about. A perfect snow-capped peak, long popular with scout camps and climbing expeditions, Mount St Helens exploded in May 1980, leaving a blasted landscape and scenes of almost total destruction for miles around. Slowly but surely, the forests are starting to grow again, and the ash is disappearing beneath new vegetation, but the land still bears witness to the incredible force of the eruption.

Mount St Helens has become a major attraction, with most tourists heading for the **Coldwater Ridge visitor center**, immediately northwest of the mountain and reached, travelling north on I-5, by turning off at Hwy-504 (or travelling south, its main feeder road, Hwy-505) roughly halfway between Olympia and Portland. There are three other approach roads also, including Hwy-503 which leads to the park's southwest corner – and in summer it's possible to drive between these secondary entrances across the mountain's south and east flanks, though this is a time-consuming and occasionally nerve-jangling business. Radiating out from the ends of the access roads, a network of **hiking trails** explores every nook and cranny of the mountain, but unless you're indifferent to clouds of dust and ash, a morning or afternoon hike is really enough.

Mount St Helens makes a feasible day trip (of around 200 miles) from either Portland or Olympia, but if you want to avoid a long haul – especially as the access roads are often clogged by vehicles in summer – then **staying overnight** in the area is a good idea. There's the occasional **motel** in the small towns close by the mountain; failing that, you'll have to head back to I-5 where (otherwise unremarkable) Kelso has, among a handful of low-price accommodations, a *Motel 6*, at 106 Minor Rd (☎425-3229; ②). Plenty of **campgrounds** are dotted along the approach roads in the National Forest surrounding the blast area, though the best of the bunch – and the handiest for the mountain – are in the southwest corner of the park, reached via Hwy-503. You can't reach the mountain by public transportation.

Coldwater Ridge

Heading east off I-5, Hwy-504 twists its way through the dark green forests of the Toutle River Valley until bald, spikey trees signal a sudden change: beyond, thousands of grey tree-skeletons lie in combed-looking rows, knocked flat in different directions as the 1980 blast waves bounced off the hillsides. It's a weird and disconcerting landscape, the matchstick-like flattened forest left to rot to regenerate the soil and provide cover for small animals and insects. There are several good vantage points as you progress up the road – notably at **Hoffstadt Bluffs**, where you can make out the path taken by the avalanche of debris that swept down the valley – to the Coldwater Ridge visitor center (daily 9am–6pm; ☎274-2131), which has exhibits, interpretive programs and a free film detailing the eruption. Construction work is gradually pushing Hwy-504 nearer the mountain, and another visitor center at **Johnston Ridge** is scheduled to open in 1996.

From Coldwater Ridge, there's a short, dusty and in places steep trail to **Spirit Lake** which takes a couple of hours to complete; on the way, side trails lead up the mountain for the long and strenuous two-day hike right round the crater peak.

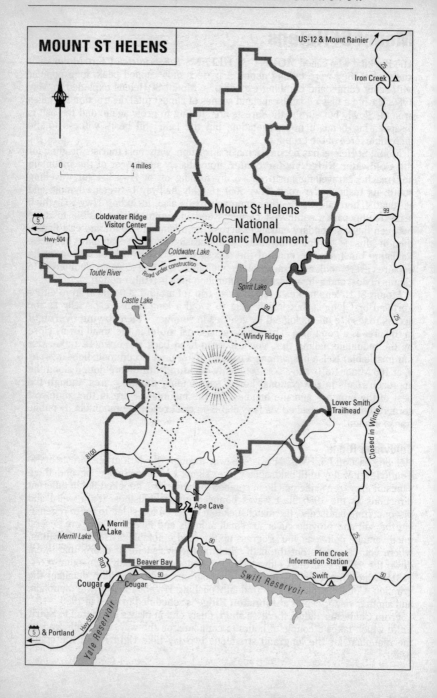

MOUNT ST HELENS

US-12 & Mount Rainier

Iron Creek ▲

25

99

0   4 miles

Coldwater Ridge
Visitor Center

**Mount St Helens
National
Volcanic Monument**

Hwy-504

Coldwater Lake

Road under construction

Toutle River

Spirit Lake

99

Castle Lake

25

Windy Ridge

Lower Smith
Trailhead

Closed in Winter

8100

25

Ape Cave

Merrill
Lake

Merrill Lake

90

8100

Pine Creek
Information Station

Beaver Bay

90

Swift Reservoir

Swift ▲

90

Cougar ●   Cougar

Hwy-503

Yale Reservoir

5 & Portland

THE ERUPTION OF MOUNT ST HELENS

From its first rumblings in March 1980, Mount St Helens became a big tourist attraction. Residents and loggers working on the mountain's forested slopes were evacuated and roads were closed, but by April the entrances to the restricted zone around the steaming peak were jammed with reporters and sightseers – one crew even ducked restrictions to film a beer commercial at the edge of the crater. People in Portland wore T-shirts saying "St Helens is hot" and "Do it, Loowit" (a native American name for the mountain). But the mountain didn't seem to be doing anything much, and impatient residents demanded to be let back to their homes. Even the official line became blurred when Harry Truman, the elderly manager of the Lodge at Spirit Lake, refused to move out, became a national celebrity and was, incredibly, congratulated on his "common sense" by Washington's governor.

It was finally decided on May 17 that home-owners could be allowed in to the restricted zone to collect their possessions, and a convoy was actually waiting at the road-barriers when the mountain finally exploded on May 18 – not upwards, but sideways in a massive lateral blast that ripped a great chunk out of the mountainside. An avalanche of debris slid down the mountain into Spirit Lake, raising it by two hundred feet and turning it into a steaming cauldron of muddy liquid. Heavy clouds of ash and rock suffocated loggers on a nearby slope, and, drifting east, caused a small crop-spraying plane to crash before raining several feet of ash on the town of Yakima.

Fifty-seven people, including the stubborn Harry Truman, died in the eruption. A few were there on official business, taking a calculated risk to survey the mountain, but most had ignored warnings or flouted the restrictions. The wildlife population was harder hit: well over a million wild animals – whole herds of deer and elk, mountain goats, cougar and bear – were killed, and thousands of fish were trapped in sediment-filled rivers whose temperatures rose to boiling point. There were dire economic consequences, too, as falling ash spoiled crops and killed livestock across the state, and millions of cubic feet of timber were lost when forests were destroyed. The long-term effects are less easy to quantify: some have even suggested that the eruption was responsible for climatic changes as far away as Europe.

Other entrances

I-5 intersects Hwy-503 twice just north of Portland, and either exit will do for the journey to both the tiny lakeside settlement of **COUGAR**, where there are a couple of campgrounds, and nearby **Merrill Lake**, on Forest Road 8100, which has another. Closing in on Mount St Helens, it's a further eight miles to the mile-long **Ape Cave**, a tube-like lava cave channelled long ago by the rushing molten lava of an earlier eruption. Ranger-led afternoon tours point out all kinds of geological oddities you'd otherwise miss. It's much colder in the cave than outside, so bring extra clothing. Several forest roads leave the cave to climb the southern slopes of Mount St Helens.

In the summer, you can drive east from Cougar along the mountain's southern slopes to **Pine Creek Information Station** and then head 25 miles north along Forest Road 25 for the final push up Forest Road 99 to **Windy Ridge**, a rocky outcrop with superb views of the crater from its northeast side. You can get even closer on foot: a short hike leads to the long, circular trail round the summit and the easier walk down past Spirit Lake to Coldwater Ridge. Retracing your route to Forest Road 25, it's a few miles north to *Iron Creek campground* and then ten miles more to US-12, by means of which you can reach Mount Rainier (see p.204).

The North Cascades and the Cascade Loop

When Hwy-20 opened up the rugged **North Cascades** to an admiring public in 1972, the towns of the eastern foothills got together and came up with the 300-mile **Cascade Loop**, a route which channels tourist traffic from Hwy-20 through several of their number before sending it west again over US-2. This does make a sensible route for taking in plenty of mountain scenery over a few days, though the return west along I-90 is much faster and just as interesting. The towns themselves, despite gargantuan efforts to rise from the ruins of their industrial past – **Winthrop** has dressed itself up in wild west regalia, while **Leavenworth** has turned Bavarian – have little lasting appeal, and are best treated simply as bases between trips into the gorgeous scenery.

There's immense scope for camping and hiking in the North Cascades, with the remote village of **Stehekin**, reached by boat or plane from the busy lakeside resort of **Chelan**, making a particularly good base. Information on trails and campgrounds in the North Cascades is available from a baffling assortment of government agencies, who have carved up the mountains into three national forests, several recreation and wilderness areas, and the North Cascades National Park – itself divided into a north and south unit on either side of Hwy-20. The free and widely available *Cascade Loop Traveler's Guide* acts as a useful introduction, while detailed hiking information and trail descriptions are best obtained from any ranger station or visitor center. The biggest and most comprehensive of these is the **North Cascades National Park visitor center** (Sun–Thurs 8am–4.30pm, Fri 8am–6pm; closed Sun in winter; ☎206/856-5700), east of I-5 at the junction of Hwy-20 and Hwy-9, on the edge of Sedro Woolley.

The loop is only feasible during the summer, as snow closes the mountain passes and completely covers the hiking trails for much of the year. Unfortunately, there's no bus service over Hwy-20, though *Greyhound* runs along US-2 – through Leavenworth, where you can rent bikes – and I-90. *Empire Lines* buses connect Spokane and Grand Coulee with Wenatchee, the area's largest town, where you can catch up with *Greyhound* or wait for the onward *Empire Lines* service to Chelan. A local line, *LINK*, operate a frequent minibus service between the towns of the eastern foothills, including Chelan, Wenatchee and Leavenworth (☎662-1155 or 1-800/851-LINK).

Over the mountains on Hwy-20

Hwy-20 leaves I-5 about 65 miles north of Seattle at Burlington, running east through the flat, tulip-growing farmlands of the Skagit Valley and past tumble-down barns and farm buildings, before pine forests and mountains finally close in past Sedro Woolley, where you'll find at the Hwy-20 and Hwy-9 junction, the North Cascades National Park visitor center (see above). What few towns there are after this look well past their prime. Cement storage towers, relics from more prosperous days, mark the approach to **CONCRETE** where, at the turn of the century, cement factories were drawn by massive local limestone quarries; production stopped in 1968, and the town's now very quiet. Just east along the highway, in **Rockport State Park**, there's a delightful hiking trail through a forest of fine old Douglas firs and **camping** (☎853-8461). On the park's western edge, a difficult gravel road heads north off Hwy-20 for the eight-mile detour up

Sauk Mountain. It's a two-mile hike from the parking lot to the summit, rewarded by fantastic views out across the mountains and over to Puget Sound.

Back on the highway, it's about four miles to the **Skagit River Bald Eagle Natural Area**, the long-time hunting ground of the bald eagle, the United States' national bird, identifiable by its white head and broad wingspan. They nest year round along the river between Concrete and Marblemount – though winter is really the time to see them, when the birds gather to feed on the river's salmon, easy pickings as they die after spawning. To avoid disturbing the birds, you should stick to the reserve's marked paths.

Minuscule Marblemount is the last chance for ninety miles to fill up on fuel – and the last good place to eat, too, in the roadside *Mountain Song Restaurant* (closed Nov–March; ☎873-2461). Just beyond, set in the forest, you come to a chain of three dams, built across the Skagit River. **NEWHALEM**, near the first, consists of no more than a shop, a restored steam engine, and an **information center** (summer daily 8.30am–5.30pm) for the North Cascades National Park. A few miles up the road, the second dam, **Diablo Dam**, is built at a tricky turn in the river called "Devil's Corner", its name translated into Spanish to cause less offence to early twentieth-century citizens. The road offers a view across the dam and its steep **incline railroad**, built in 1927 to lift men and materials up a near-vertical mountainside and now offering free rides to visitors. A little further east, **Ross Dam**, the largest of the three, created **Ross Lake**, which stretches north for pine-rimmed miles past the Canadian border, surrounded by hiking trails and campgrounds. For longer hikes, look out for **Rainy Pass**, where the Pacific Crest National Scenic Trail crosses Hwy-20: to the north the long-distance trail heads off into the depths of the Okanogan National Forest; to the south it slips along Bridge Creek and curves round the flanks of McGregor Mountain to meet the rough dirt road that, with its five **campgrounds**, leads south to Stehekin at the tip of Lake Chelan (see below). Stopping-points all along the highway boast spectacular views, with one of the most magnificent being **Washington Pass Overlook**, about thirty miles east of Ross Dam, where a short trail from a roadside parking lot leads to a wonderful mountain panorama featuring the jagged, rocky peak of **Liberty Bell Mountain**.

After Washington Pass Overlook, there's a final flurry of mountain scenery before the road reaches the tamer landscapes of the Methow Valley and descends to Winthrop.

Winthrop

Beyond the mountains, Hwy-20 runs straight into **WINTHROP**, landing you among the wooden false fronts, boardwalks, swinging saloon doors and other western paraphernalia that bedecks its main street. Winthrop was actually founded by an East Coast entrepreneur, Guy Waring, who turned up in 1891 with a wagon-load of merchandise and diplomatically named the settlement he founded after John Winthrop, the one-time governor of his native Massachusetts – the state that had provided his backing. Waring was visited by an old Harvard classmate, Owen Wister, and when Wister later wrote *The Virginian*, widely acclaimed as the first Western novel, the book was clearly (in the town's opinion) based on Winthrop. Waring's large log-cabin home, set on a hill behind the main street, is now the **Shafer Museum** (daily mid-May to Sept 10am–5pm; free), its long porch cluttered with old bicycles and rusty farming equipment.

There are some good places to **eat** in Winthrop, the food ranging from Mexican/American meals at the *Duck Brand Cantina* (☎996-2192) to late-night pizza at *Three Fingered Jacks* (☎996-2411), both on the main street. The town has a clutch of modest and slightly over-priced **motels**: the cedar-log *Virginian*, on the main street (☎996-2535; ④), is as good as any. There's more distinguished accommodation nearby at *Sun Mountain Lodge* (☎996-2211; ⑥), where rustic cabins and lodge rooms occupy a grand setting on the edge of the Cascades, nine miles southwest of town along Patterson Lake Road. If you do stay in Winthrop, or want to go horseriding, fishing or whitewater rafting, the **visitor center** (summer only, daily 10am–5pm; ☎996-2125) is well stocked with free literature.

Continuing south along the Methow Valley, passing a couple of campgrounds on your way, it's eleven miles to Winthrop's impoverished neighbor, **TWISP**, whose battered buildings go a good way towards explaining Winthrop's shameless bidding for the tourist trade: whatever you make of the Wild West theme, Winthrop at least looks like a going concern. Shabby Twisp just looks forlorn.

Lake Chelan

South of Twisp, Hwy-20 begins its long and circuitous journey east to Idaho, while Hwy-153 carries on down the Methow Valley for the thirty-mile trip to the Columbia River. From here, both US-97 and US-97Alt shadow the river as it curves south to the short turning that leads over the hills to snake-like **Lake Chelan**. Pint-sized **Chelan**, a popular resort on the southern tip of the lake, is the starting point for trips to **Stehekin**, at the far northern end of the lake and reachable only by boat or seaplane.

The forested hills and mountains that frame Lake Chelan's southern reaches are laced with **hiking trails**, many of which are (fairly) easy to reach from town along bumpy forest roads. Alternatively, you can rent canoes, paddle- and motor-**boats** (as well as bicycles and mopeds) from *Chelan Boat Rentals*, 1210 W Woodin Ave (☎682-4444) – though be warned that the lake experiences sudden squalls. The lake's real pride and joy is, however, the *Lady of the Lake* **passenger ferry** service (☎682-2224), which sails the sixty miles from Chelan up the lake to Stehekin, usually stopping at Lucerne landing to drop supplies for Holden, a Lutheran retreat that occupies the site of an old copper mine in a remote valley to the west. The scenery becomes more impressive the further you go – low, forested hills giving way to the steeply harsh mountains at the heart of the Cascade range. Leaving from the jetty a mile west of town along Woodin Ave, the ferry makes the four-hour trip once daily, May to mid-October (less in winter), sailing at 8.30am and returning to Chelan by 6pm. The round trip costs $21, single $14, and reservations aren't required. The *Lady Express* (1 daily in April & mid-June to Sept, Sat & Sun only mid-May to mid-June, usually 3–4 weekly Oct–March; same number; reservations required) departs at 8.30am and takes just ninety minutes to complete the same trip for $25 per person single, $39 return, with reductions off-season; you can also go up on one boat and return on the other for $38. And, if you're flush, you can seaplane in or out of Stehekin with *Chelan Airways* (☎682-5555), $50 single and $80 return.

Chelan

There's not too much to **CHELAN** itself, but it does boast a couple of quality restaurants, several good-to-excellent hotels and, most important of all, you couldn't wish for a better base for excursions into the mountains.

Your first port of call should be the **visitor center**, near the waterfront at 102 E Johnson Ave (Mon–Fri 9am–5pm, summer only, Sat–Sun 10am–4pm; ☎682-3503 or 1-800/4-CHELAN), where you can pick up all sorts of free information about the town and its mountainous surroundings. They can also provide a list of local accommodations and general hiking advice – though for more detailed trail guidance you should go to the combined USFS and NPS **ranger station**, a five-minute walk over the bridge and along the waterfront from the visitor center, at 428 W Woodin Ave (Mon–Sat 7.45am–4.30pm; USFS ☎682-2576, NPS ☎682-2549).

Campbell's Resort, 104 W Woodin (☎682-2561 or 1-800/553-8225; ⑥), occupies a prime lakeside spot in the center of town, with most of its spacious and comfortable rooms looking out over the water. Other attractive **hotels** include the *Caravel Resort Hotel*, 322 W Woodin (☎682-2582 or 1-800/962-8723; ④); and the self-styled "romantic" (read Victorian furnishings and fittings) *Whaley Mansion B&B*, 415 Third St (☎682-5735 or 1-800/729-2408; ⑤). A less expensive option is the simple *Apple Inn* **motel**, 1002 E Woodin Ave (☎682-4044; ③). The best **restaurant** in town is at *Campbell's Resort*, but for something more informal – and less expensive – head off to *Goochi's*, 104 E Woodin (☎682-2436), which serves mouth-watering pastas and perfect burgers.

Stehekin

The ferry trip from Chelan to **STEHEKIN**, at the lake's mountainous northern tip, is a lovely cruise and an important local transportation link. Otherwise only accessible by hiking trail and seaplane, Stehekin makes an ideal base for **hiking** in the North Cascades. In the village, you can rent bikes and canoes from the *North Cascades Lodge* (☎682-4713), which also runs daily bus tours up to Rainbow Falls, four miles from the landing ($3.50). The NPS operate a seasonal **shuttle-bus** (2–3 daily; $10 each way) deep into the mountains, an exhilarating trip that accesses trailheads and campgrounds as well as following a small portion of the Pacific Crest Trail as it nears Hwy-20. Rooms at the *Lodge* can be hard to get, so it's a good idea to book in advance, as it is at the attractive *Silver Bay Inn* (☎682-2212; ④) close by. For camping and hiking information (and for a wilderness permit – required for some of the trails), visit the **Golden West visitor center** (daily 8am–4.30pm; no phone) in Stehekin, or get advice before you leave Chelan.

Wenatchee

Straddling the Columbia River about forty miles south of Chelan, **WENATCHEE** is Washington's apple capital, the center of an industry that fills the valleys of the eastern foothills with orchards, scattering blossom in the spring. Apple-stalls appear beside the roads in the fall, piled mostly with sweet, outsized *Red Delicious*, the most popular kind in the US – Washington grows nearly half the country's supply. You'll find other varieties too: enormous *Golden Delicious*, tarter red *Winesaps* and giant *Granny Smiths*. Although the warm climate is ideal for apple growing, farmers still protect their fruit from early frosts with metal heaters, their tall fans easily visible from the road.

As apples, rather than tourists, are Wenatchee's main business, the town has for the most part a workaday air, its only gesture towards quaintness a short strip of gaudy Victorian buildings whose cafés and shops cluster at the south end of Mission Street, quite a walk from the town center. More conveniently, the **North**

Central Washington Museum, 127 S Mission St (Mon–Fri 10am–4pm, Sat & Sun 1–4pm; free), has pioneer displays and a (fairly) interesting section devoted to the apple industry, a subject that's developed at the **Washington Apple Commission visitor center** (daily 9am–5pm; free), on the northern outskirts of town at 2900 Euclid Ave, where you can munch away at various varieties for free. Most people only end up at Wenatchee if they're travelling by **bus**, and the *Greyhound* station is downtown on the corner of Second and Chelan (☎662-2183), its premises shared by *Empire Lines*, who run to Chelan and the Methow Valley and some of Eastern Washington. There's also a free local bus service, *LINK* (☎662-1155 or 1-800/851-LINK), shuttling around the towns of the foothills – Wenatchee, Chelan, Leavenworth – from Monday to Saturday; *Amtrak* pull in at the foot of Kittitas St. **Accommodation** is limited to a strip of cheap **motel** rooms along N Wenatchee Avenue.

If you're around in May it's well worth looking in on the **Apple Blossom Festival**, an all-American affair involving carnival floats, interminable marching bands and a semi-official "cruise" where teenagers from miles around cram into cars and pick-up trucks and circle a two-street block from afternoon to night – though this has become something of a law-and-order problem, and the festival's future is under review. At any time, shady **Ohme Gardens** (daily April–Oct 9am to dusk; $4), set on a rocky bluff beside US-97Alt three miles north of town, provide some pleasant relief from the arid scenery with alpine plants, trees and fern-lined pools.

Cashmere

Just before Wenatchee, US-2 branches west into the mountains, towards two more themed villages. The first of these, **CASHMERE**, musters up a reasonably tasteful late-nineteenth-century main street and a small **Pioneer Village** of restored buildings, tucked in a field behind the **Chelan County Museum** – which features displays of stuffed local wildlife and pioneer artefacts.

Cashmere is also famous, at least locally, for its sweet specialty "aplets" and "cotlets" (as in apricot) – not unlike turkish delight and available in free samples from the **Aplets and Cotlets factory**, 117 Mission St (Mon–Fri 8am–5pm, Sat & Sun 10am–4pm).

Leavenworth

Brace yourself as you head west towards **LEAVENWORTH**. Twenty years ago a small timber and railroad town, Leavenworth has warded off economic death by going Bavarian: local motels and stores sport steeply roofed half-timbered "alpine" facades, complete with wooden balconies and window-boxes; wiener schnitzel, sauerkraut and strudels now feature heavily in local menus; and gift shops sell musical boxes, all to the strains of "alpine" folk music – even the super-market bids you *Wilkommen zu Safeway*. This can be fun if you're in the right mood, and even if you're not, you can always escape into the gorgeous mountain scenery.

Orientation couldn't be easier: Leavenworth's main drag, Front Street, runs parallel to US-2, with the rest of the town center sloping south to fill out a small loop in the Wenatchee River. *Greyhound* stop at the west end of town, a ten-minute walk from the **visitor center**, 894 US-2 (Mon–Fri 9am–5pm; ☎548-5807), who have – considering the size of the place – an extraordinarily long list of restaurants and lodgings, though you're still advised to book ahead in summer. You can rent **mountain bikes** from *Leavenworth Ski and Sports Center* (☎548-7864), not far from the *Greyhound* stop at US-2 and Icicle Rd.

The real point of visiting Leavenworth is, however, to **hike** the mountains, and the town's **ranger station** (daily 7.45am–4.30pm; ☎782-1413), on the north side of US-2 at 600 Sherbourne St, has all the details. A series of trailheads – and **campgrounds** – are reached along Icicle Road, which cuts into the mountains from US-2. About eight miles down Icicle Road, the nine-mile-long **Enchantment Lake Trail** heads south to climb Mountaineer Creek for the beautiful lakelets that pepper the mountains up above. Alternatively, a fifty-mile-long round trip via Forest Roads 209 and 207 takes you through the Wenatchee National Forest to **Lake Wenatchee**, a large mountain lake. If you're fit you can cycle the journey, and in summer you can rent boats at the lake or ride horses through the forest. This is also a popular winter-sports area, with some good cross-country skiing.

Practicalities

There are several good places to **stay** downtown, including *Mrs Anderson's Lodging House*, 917 Commercial St (☎548-6173; ③); the *Haus Lorelei Inn B&B*, 347 Division St (☎548-5726; ④), set in a fine countrified location on the edge of downtown; and the *Enzian Motor Inn*, 590 US-2 (☎548-5269 or 1-800/223-8511; ④), which has well-above-average motel accommodation. The grimly spartan *Edelweiss Hotel*, 843 Front St (☎548-7015; ①–②), has hostel-style rooms for as little as $15.

Leavenworth has more than its share of mundane **café-restaurants**, but in with the dross you'll find some tasty surprises: the first-floor *Terrace Bistro*, 200 Eighth St (☎548-4193), leaves the "alpine" cuisine behind for excellent Italian dishes, and *Walter's Other Place*, 820 Commercial St (☎548-6125), offers low-priced quality snacks and meals with the emphasis on Greek foods. To have a Bavarian good-time, eat at *Reiner's Gasthaus*, 829 Front St (☎548-5111), which serves the best German food around.

West from Leavenworth

From Leavenworth, there are two main routes west: US-2 runs through the Cascades over **Stevens Pass** to emerge north of Seattle, just over one hundred miles away, while US-97 heads briefly south via Liberty before joining I-90 for the fast track to Seattle.

Index and Gold Bar

If you want to break your journey along US-2, choose tiny **INDEX**, about halfway and a mile or so beyond the *Mt Index Café*, an old-style diner beside the highway turn-off. Index was once a busy quarry town, noted for its granite, and the rock is still the focal point in the form of the precipitous granite wall that rears up behind the village, sheer enough to be a favorite spot for climbers. No-one could say the *Index Tavern*, the only village bar, is avant-garde. About eight miles further west, **GOLD BAR** was once a hard-edged mining town and railroad settlement where, as anti-Chinese sentiment reached boiling point in the 1890s, a Schindler-like railway engineer shipped terrified Chinese locals out in purpose-built "coffins".

Liberty

Heading south from Leavenworth, US-97 winds through the Swauk Mining District, a remote and mountainous area thoroughly panned and dug for gold in the late nineteenth century – with only limited success. As one of the prospectors wrote home: "There's a lot of gold in that Swauk, but there's a lot of gravel mixed up with it". A couple of miles off the highway, tiny, ramshackle **LIBERTY** is a curious boom-time left-over, an almost-ghost town whose two short rows of mean-looking, false-fronted buildings don't inspire much enthusiasm.

Cle Elum and Roslyn

After joining the westbound I-90, there's little reason to stop off as you race toward Seattle, but there are a trio of attractions, beginning in the dreary, ex-coal mining town of **CLE ELUM**, where *Mama Vallone's Steak House & Inn*, 302 W First St (☎674-5174), is a fine, friendly restaurant with great food.

Rather than returning to I-90 at Cle Elum, consider a short detour to the town's immediate neighbor, **ROSLYN**, an Appalachian look-alike of old timber houses trailing through a forest pocked with old slag heaps, mementoes of the collieries that once produced two million tons of coal a year – the last one closed in 1963. Every inch a company town, no-one seemed bothered about Roslyn until TV "discovered" its unreconstructed appearance and they've been filming *Northern Exposure* here ever since. With its fictional fame have come the sightseers, but it's still an odd, mournful sort of place. The *Roslyn Café* (☎649-2763), bang in the center, serves filling lunches.

North Bend and Snoqualmie Falls

Returning to I-90, the highway crosses the mountains via **Snoqualmie Pass**, the lowest and most traversible of the Cascade passes, long the regular route of traders, trappers and native Americans. About twenty miles further on, with the road scooting down towards the coast, turn off at **NORTH BEND** for the five-mile excursion north along State Route 202 to **Snoqualmie Falls**, as seen during the title sequence of David Lynch's *Twin Peaks*. The falls crash into a rocky gorge, sending up a cloud of white spray. Despite their wild appearance, they're managed by Puget Power electric company, who can adjust the flow to suit their requirements. A trail leads to the thunderous foot of the waterfall past the shiny metal pipes of an underground generating station.

EASTERN WASHINGTON

Big, dry and empty, Eastern Washington has more in common with neighboring Idaho than with the green western side of the state. Faded, olive-colored sagebrush covers mile upon mile of dusty land and huge, reddish flat-topped rocks loom over the farmland-prairies. This is the powerful landscape of a thousand Western movies, and it's impossible not to be stirred by the sheer scale of the scenery. The towns, though, are no-nonsense agricultural and commercial centers, and only **Spokane** has any degree of cultural life. The quickest route across the region is the two-hundred-mile sprint along I-90 from **Ellensburg** to Spokane, but this manages to avoid almost everything of any interest. You're far better off using Spokane as the pivotal point of two routes: one visiting the southern part of the region, the other the north. Ellensburg, directly east of Seattle on I-

90, is a good starting-point for the southern route, beginning with a scoot through the fertile Yakima Valley and dropping by the ex-railway town of **Yakima**. Beyond, you'll want to shoot past the grimly industrial **Tri-cities** (Richland, Pasco and Kennewick) on your way to the **Whitman Mission** National Historic Site. This was once the home of Marcus Whitman, the pioneer missionary who was ultimately killed for his medicinal failings by a vengeful band of Cayuse. The mission is on the edge of the dreary agricultural town of **Walla Walla**, from where you can drive northeast through wheat fields to reach Spokane, possibly taking in **Clarkston**, for boat trips into the depths of **Hells Canyon** – though this is more readily approached from Oregon's Baker City (see p.129). The northern loop leaves the towns of the Cascade foothills – Chelan, Winthrop or Leavenworth – to follow the minor roads that lead to the **Grand Coulee Dam**, one of the biggest concrete structures ever built. From here, it's a manageable drive across the plains to Spokane, or you can detour north to the remote **Colville National Forests**.

There are limited **public transportation** connections: *Amtrak* links Seattle with Wenatchee and Spokane via Everett; *Greyhound* operate two lines from Ellensburg, with one speeding along I-90 to Spokane and the other heading down the Yakima Valley. A useful supplement to *Greyhound* is provided by *Empire Lines*, who connect Spokane with Grand Coulee, close to the dam, and run south to Chelan, Ellensburg and Yakima, and north up US-97 to the Canadian border.

Ellensburg

On the far side of the Cascade Mountains from Seattle, the obvious departure point for a tour of **southeast Washington** is **ELLENSBURG**, a dusty little town with a late-nineteenth-century redbrick core. Like many frontier towns, it was razed by fire in its early wooden-buildings days, then rebuilt itself more solidly in brick – the reason so many of the downtown buildings are branded with the same "1889" date. One such houses the **Kittitas County Museum**, on Third at Pine (Mon–Fri afternoons only; free), featuring rocks, gems and local agates along with native American and pioneer exhibits. Other than that, there's nothing to detain you unless you're around on Labor Day weekend, when the annual **Ellensburg Rodeo** fills the town with stetsoned cowboys and cowgirls, who rope steers, ride bulls and sit on bucking broncos, accompanied by much pageantry and unfurling of star-spangled banners. For tickets, call the Rodeo Ticket Office (☎925-5381 or 1-800/637-2444): prices start at around $9, and include admission to the **Kittitas County Fair**, an odd combination of penned livestock and bright carnival rides that takes place at the same time. Needless to say, you should book accommodation ahead for this.

Greyhound and *Empire Lines* buses stop at Okanogan St and Eighth Ave (☎925-1177). The **visitor center**, a short walk away at 436 N Sprague St (Mon–Fri 8am–5pm; ☎925-3137), can provide a map and advice on **accommodation**, such as the downtown *Regalodge*, in Motel Square, at Sixth and Water (☎925-3116; ②), which has basic doubles. As for **eating**, the art deco *Valley Café*, 105 W Third at Main (☎925-3050), is by far the nicest place in town.

While most visitors speed east out of Ellensburg, disappearing in a cloud of dust along I-90 towards Spokane, others take a slower, more varied route, skirting a large military reservation on their way southeast to the Yakima Valley. There are two roads to choose from – either I-82 or the prettier Hwy-821, which tracks the banks of the Yakima River with wild roses brightening the route in summer.

Yakima

Sprawling **YAKIMA** is the urban hub of the valley, and although its glossy new convention center promotes an upmarket image – "Visit Yakima, the Palm Springs of Washington" – the town isn't about to win any beauty contests. Freight trains still run close to the center, and you get the feeling that the railroad yard might still be the real focus of activity. It certainly was in the nineteenth century, when Yakima shuffled several miles from its original site in pursuit of a vital railroad terminal, meanly located away from the township by a railroad company keen to save every cent: empty prairie was a good deal cheaper than developed land. Outraged citizens protested, but soon bowed to the inevitable, rolling the better houses to the new site on logs to found what the local paper called in 1885 a "Messiah of Commerce" (the old Yakima is now the small neighboring community of Union Gap). The town's attractions are few, but it's a potential base for visiting the Cascades to the west (see "Mount Rainier", p.204), or the wineries of the Yakima Valley to the east (see below).

The town's railroad heritage is invoked at one of a couple of new projects aimed at cheering up the part of downtown that hasn't been scooped into the main mall. Where Yakima Avenue, the main east–west drag, crosses Front Street, **Track 29** is a group of brightly painted 1930s-and-earlier train carriages housing a small collection of shops and food stalls, the vendors leaning sweaty-faced out of cramped kitchens. Next door, **Yesterday's Village** has turned the old Fruit Exchange building into a nostalgic antiques-and-crafts mall – the kind of thing that has worked better in richer, more touristy areas. Across the tracks, located inside the old Union Pacific Railroad station, the *Brewery Pub*, 32 N Front St, serves half a dozen of Grants top-rated ales, lagers and stouts, fresh from the adjacent brewery: be sure to try the hoppy Scottish Ale, or the crisp-tasting local cider, and some of the pub-type **food** in the friendly front room. There's not much else in Yakima to hold your attention, though you might consider the two-mile excursion into the town's southwest suburbs where the **Yakima Valley Museum**, 2105 Tieton Drive (Tues–Fri 10am–5pm, Sat & Sun noon–5pm; $2.50), houses a collection of nineteenth-century buggies, stage coaches and covered Conestoga wagons.

Practicalities

Driving into Yakima along I-82 from Ellensburg, take exit 33 for the town center. *Greyhound* stop downtown at 602 E Yakima Ave (☎457-5131), sharing the depot with *Empire Lines* (same number). A short walk from the bus station is the **visitor center**, at 10 N Eighth St (Mon–Fri 8.30am–5pm, April–Oct also Sat & Sun 9am–5pm; ☎575-1300). They have all the usual information, including details of local wineries open to the public, accommodation lists and route maps of *Yakima Transit* (☎575-6175), who run services (Mon–Sat 7am–7pm) round the city and its suburbs, with a fare-free downtown zone served by brightly painted trolley buses.

Plenty of **motels** line N First St, and the **YWCA**, centrally located at 15 N Naches Ave (☎248-7796; ①), has beds for women only from $15 a night. The *Rio Mirada Motel*, 1603 Terrace Heights Drive (☎457-4444 or 1-800/521-3050; ④), is saved from mediocrity by the views over the Yakima River; take the downtown exit off I-82. For **food**, stick to either the *Brewery Pub* (see above) or *Gasperetti's*, an excellent Italian restaurant at 1013 N First St (closed Mon; ☎248-0628).

The Yakima Valley

To either side of its namesake town, the Yakima Valley turns into fruit- and wine-growing country, where apples, cherries, pears and grapes grow prolifically in what was once sagebrush desert. Though the Yakima Valley's volcanic soil is naturally rich, irrigation is what has made it fertile, and intricate systems of reservoirs, canals and ditches divert water from the Yakima River around the orchards and vineyards. Water rights are a crucial issue for local farmers: priority is given to those who have held land the longest, and in dry years farmers with only junior water rights can find themselves in trouble. Fish can sometimes be left high and dry, too – irrigation channels can drain the river itself to a meagre trickle, too shallow to support migrating salmon.

Heading southeast from Yakima, I-82 tracks along the north bank of the Yakima River before cutting east for the Tri-cities, eighty miles away. En route are the **vineyards** of the Yakima Valley, some twenty of which offer tours and tastings. The visitor center in Yakima can give detailed directions and opening hours.

Zillah

Tiny **ZILLAH**, twelve miles from Yakima, makes a good base for visiting the wine country. Nearby, you'll find the family-run *Bonair* estate (April–Oct daily 10am–5pm; ☎829-6027), noted for its Chardonnay, and, further out, the larger *Covey Run* (Mon–Sat 10am–5pm, Sun noon–5pm; ☎829-6235), which mostly concentrates on Riesling. The oldest vineyard in the valley, established in the 1930s, is *Chateau Ste Michelle* (daily 10am–4pm; ☎882-3928), situated about twenty miles further south on I-82 in Grandview, at W Fifth St and Ave B; they specialize in red wines, particularly Merlot.

In Zillah itself, there's an excellent and inexpensive Mexican **café**, *El Ranchito*, 1319 E First Ave (☎829-5880), catering mostly to the (poorly paid) Hispanic labor employed in the wine-, hop- and fruit-growing field.

Yakima Indian Reservation

The Yakima River marks the northern boundary of the **Yakima Indian Reservation**, a great slab of dry and rugged land that stretches down towards Oregon. US-97 slices through the reservation, at first travelling parallel to I-82 to pass Wapato and, after about twenty miles, the **Yakima Nation Cultural Center** (daily, approximate hours 9am–5pm, closed Jan & Feb; $3; call ☎865-2800 to check opening times), which sits beside the highway just outside Toppenish. Housed in what looks like a stone-built, slate-roofed wigwam, the museum outlines Yakima traditions in a series of dioramas and wall displays. One of the most unusual exhibits is a time-ball, a sort of macramé diary kept by married women as a record of their lives; in old age, major events can be recalled by unravelling the sequence of knots and beads. Deliberately echoing Yakima rituals in its presentation, the museum is sub-titled "The Challenge of Spilyay" – Spilyay being the Yakima version of the god-like coyote figure that crops up in many native American myths. But there's a sadness to the museum's attempts to assert the dignity of the Yakima people, for they were deprived of most of their traditional lands by treaty and war long ago. The ethos behind the brutal skirmishes of the **Yakima War** of the 1850s was summed up by the US Army commander,

Major Gabriel Rains: he would, he declared, make "war forever until not a Yakima breathes in the land he calls his own".

Once out of the museum, you can either move on to Toppenish to return to I-82 near Zillah along State Hwy-22; or head the sixty miles south across the reservation to the Columbia Gorge via US-97.

Maryhill Art Museum

Racing south, US-97 leaves reservation land at Satus Pass to slip down into the Klickitat Valley at Goldendale. Ten miles further on, near the Columbia River, is the region's one real surprise, the extraordinary **Maryhill Museum of Art** (mid-March to mid-Nov daily 10am–5pm; $4), an elaborate house stuffed with the art treasures collected by Sam Hill, an oddball landowner who once planned a Quaker colony here. The Quakers he brought over from Belgium took one look at the parched slopes of the Columbia Gorge and opted out, and he concentrated on the house instead, determined to ensconce his daughter Mary in palatial magnificence. The result is an eclectic collection ranging from Russian icons to native American wickerwork, not to mention one of the best collections of Rodin sculptures in the US. On a nearby hill overlooking the Columbia River, Sam Hill built a miniature copy of **Stonehenge**, a pacifist's tribute to those who died in World War I. Hill believed Stonehenge to be a sacrificial site, its faithful reproduction appropriate as "humanity is still being sacrificed to the god of war".

Richland

I-82 leaves the Yakima Valley at Prosser to slice across the vine-growing country which lies to the west of that cluster of three towns known as the **TRI-CITIES**. Of these, only **RICHLAND** is worth a second glance, and then only for its previous incarnation as the nearest settlement to the now-defunct **Hanford Site**, a massive nuclear energy and research area which fills out a sprawling meander in the Columbia River about thirty miles north of town. During the World War II race for nuclear weapons, the Hanford Site housed a top-secret plant to produce plutonium. The location was carefully selected by the government for its closeness to the Columbia River – providing both cold water for cooling reactors and hydroelectricity from its new dams – and its isolation in the sagebrush-covered wilderness. The sudden arrival of over fifty thousand construction workers from across the US, and the growth of a huge, sprawling makeshift shack-city must surely have made people suspect something was afoot. But apparently very few, perhaps a dozen top scientists and politicians, knew much about what was happening here. During the Sixties and Seventies, work at Hanford shifted from military projects towards the civilian use of nuclear energy, but the Reagan years brought defence back to the fore, a brief boom before the controversies surrounding the nuclear industry precipitated its recent closure. For locals, the economic future looks decidedly grim.

The saga of the town's atomic past is set out at the **Hanford Science Center**, 825 Jadwin Ave in the Federal Building next to the post office in downtown Richland (Mon–Fri 8am–5pm, Sat 9am–5pm; free). The center's computerized exhibits and interactive displays explain the workings of atomic science – rather (perhaps surprisingly) than extolling the benefits of nuclear power. It's unlikely you'll want to hang round Richland for long; the **visitor center** is at 515 Lee Blvd (☎946-1651).

Walla Walla: the Whitman Mission

US-12 follows the Columbia south from the Tri-cities, then cuts east through the wheat and onion fields that surround the college and agricultural town of **WALLA WALLA**. Once the wild scene of Washingon's most disastrous mission outpost, the town is now known for its onions, *Walla Walla Sweets*, which are allegedly mild enough to be eaten raw like apples. Though there's not much to see here now, the town has a crucial historical significance: it was here in 1836 that **Dr Marcus Whitman**, a key figure in the settling of the Northwest, arrived from the East Coast as a missionary, hoping to convert the local Cayuse from their nomadic ways into church-going, crop-growing Christian citizens.

Whitman and his wife Narcissa made little headway with the Cayuse and, like other western missionaries, turned their attention instead to the white settlers who followed in their pioneering footsteps: the Whitmans were the first to drive a wagon this far west. Within a few years the mission became a refuge along the trail, taking in sick and orphaned travellers (including the real-life Sager children of the story book *Children of the Oregon Trail*). The Cayuse eyed the increasing numbers of settlers very warily, and when a measles epidemic decimated the tribe, suspicions grew that they were being poisoned to make way for the whites, particularly as Dr Whitman could help (some) whites but few of the Indians – who had no natural immunity to the disease. Whitman sensed the growing tension, and he must have known of the native belief that medicine-men were directly liable for the deaths of their patients, but he continued to take on even hopeless cases. In November 1847 a band of Cayuse arrived at the mission and murdered Whitman, Narcissa and several others. Fifty more at the mission, mostly children, were taken captive, and although they were later released, angry settlers raised volunteer bands against the Cayuse. When the story hit the newspapers back east, it generated such a tide of fear about native uprisings that the government finally declared the Oregon land (then including Washington) an official US territory, which meant the army could be sent in to protect the settlers – with drastic implications for the original inhabitants.

The site of the **Whitman Mission** (summer daily 8am–8pm, rest of the year 8am–4.30pm; $2), in a lovely little dell seven miles west of Walla Walla off US-12, is bare but effective. The mission itself was burnt down by the Cayuse after the massacre, and simple marks on the ground plus interpretive plaques show its original layout, the place where the Whitman's young daughter drowned in the stream, and the sites of the murders of Marcus and Narcissa. A visitor center by the site shows a film on Whitman's work and the massacre, and is well stocked with books on the subject, including Narcissa Whitman's diary.

When the army arrived, they were stationed at **Fort Walla Walla** (June–Sept Tues–Sun 9am–5pm; May & Oct Sat & Sun 1–5pm; $2), the site of which, at the southwest corner of town, off Myra Road, has been turned into a museum complex. Five enormous shed-like concrete buildings are now home to a collection of relics from the horse-drawn era of agriculture: old ploughs and farm machinery, sturdy wagons and more elegant lightweight buggies, built for nineteenth-century cruising. There are several re-sited and recreated pioneer buildings on the complex too – notably a Babcock Railway Station of 1880.

Practicalities

Once you've seen Walla Walla's two sights (and of the two, the mission's the more interesting), there's not much point in hanging around. *Greyhound* stops at 315 N Second St (☎525-9313), and the **visitor center**, at Sumach and Colville (Mon–Fri 9am–5pm; ☎525-0850), is a couple of blocks away, with maps and listing of lodgings. Of the handful of **motels**, the *Whitman Annex*, 204 N Spokane St (☎529-3400; ②), has reasonably priced rooms a few blocks from the visitor center. The *Green Gable Inn*, 922 Bonsella St (☎525-5501; ④), is a comfortable **B&B** on the east side of the town center one block from Whitman College; take the Clinton exit off US-12.

Walla Walla is something of a crossroads. From here, you can head south over the Oregon border towards Pendleton, La Grande and the lovely Wallowa Mountains (see Chapter Two), retrace your steps west to the Tri-cities to pick up US-395/I-90 for the fast route north to Spokane (see below), or follow US-12 to Clarkston and Lewiston.

Clarkston and Lewiston

US-12 winds its way around the edges of the Blue Mountains to arrive in **CLARKSTON**, an unassuming town at the confluence of the Clearwater and Snake rivers, across which is its bigger neighbor, Idaho's **LEWISTON**. The twin towns date back to the 1860s when gold prospectors bedded down here after the 450-mile ferry trip from the Pacific up the Columbia and Snake rivers – shallow water preventing the boats from continuing along the Clearwater into the gold-bearing hills further east.

Nowadays, it's mainly visited because of its proximity to the northern end of **Hells Canyon**, the deepest gorge on the continent, though the southern approach along Hwy-86 gets you much nearer the most impressive portions (see p.131). It's possible to drive south from Clarkston along the west bank of the river almost as far as the Oregon border, but the road is rough and you're far better off travelling into the canyon by boat. Several Clarkston and Lewiston companies operate **jet boat trips**, with one of the more established being *Snake Dancer Excursions*, 614 Lapwai Road, Lewiston (☎208/743-0890 or 1-800/234-1941), who offer a one-day, 180-mile round trip for $80 per person; departures from Clarkston's Swallows Park boat launch. Alternatively, the equally reputable *Beamer's Hells Canyon Tours*, Lewiston (☎208/743-4800 or 1-800/522-6966), run a similar day-long trip for roughly the same price as well as longer excursions of up to five days. Their boats leave from the Hellsgate State Park Marina about five miles south of town.

For further details and a full list of boat-trip companies, contact the Clarkston **visitor center**, downtown at 502 Bridge St (June–Aug Mon–Fri 9am–7pm, Sat 9am–5pm; Sept–May Mon–Fri 9am–5pm; ☎758-7712 or 1-800/933-2128). For somewhere to **stay**, *Nendels Motel*, 222 Bridge St (☎758-1631; ③), offers clean but spartan doubles; the *Highland House*, 707 Highland Ave (☎758-3126; ④), is an agreeable **B&B** southwest of the center; and the *Quality Inn*, 700 Port Drive (☎758-9500 or 1-800/228-5151; ④), has plush motel-style doubles in a country setting north of the town center, near the Snake River. Clarkston's hardly a gourmet's paradise, but *Fazzari's*, 1281 Bridge St (☎758-3386), has passable spaghetti and better pizzas.

Pullman and the Palouse Region

Moving north from Clarkston, US-195 winds across the agricultural **Palouse** region, where the land undulates into rows of low hills, covered with wave after wave of wheatfields. Thirty miles on, just off the highway, **PULLMAN** is the main town in the area – a college town that dies completely when Washington State University's sixteen thousand students take off for the summer. At other times, the studenty atmosphere is convivial, though you can see what little there is of the place in less than an hour. *Greyhound* stop at NE 115 Olsen St (☎334-1412), and the **visitor center**, N 415 Grand Ave (Mon–Fri 9am–5pm; ☎334-3565 or 1-800/365-6948), can supply information if you're marooned. *Nendels Motor Inn*, 915 SE Main St (☎332-2646; ②), has low-price rooms bang in the center of town.

Beyond Pullman, en route to Spokane, there's more of the seamless wheat and barley fields of the Palouse, interrupted only by a scattering of cone-shaped hills, among which the summit of **Steptoe Butte** – a signposted eight-mile drive east of US-195 – offers a widespread panorama across the rippling land. The butte was named for Colonel Steptoe, whose troops once spent an uneasy night creeping down the hill and through encircling bands of Palouse in an improvised retreat that won him many plaudits (though it's likely the Palouse let him go as annihilation was not their practice). Steptoe's encirclement took the US Army back to the drawing board. The Palouse had better rifles than Steptoe's unit – a state of affairs rectified by the army before they launched a punitive expedition towards Spokane later in 1858.

Spokane

The wide open spaces and plain little towns of Eastern Washington don't really prepare you for **SPOKANE**, fifty miles north of Steptoe Butte. Just a few miles from the Idaho border, it's the region's only real city, and its scattering of grandiose late nineteenth-century buildings – built on the spoils of the Coeur d'Alene silver mines, just across the state divide – sport some unexpectedly elegant, almost colonial touches.

However, Spokane lost its looks badly when its turn-of-the-century heyday gave way to industrial shabbiness and, despite the extensive revamping that went on before the 1974 World's Fair was held here, shades of the down-at-heel freight town still haunt the modern city. It's not the sort of place you're likely to linger very long, but some pleasant parks, the oddness of the architecture and a couple of museums can easily fill a day or so. Spokane is also a good base for visiting the Grand Coulee Dam (see below), eighty miles or so to the west, to which *Empire Line* buses provide a convenient connection.

Arriving and getting around

As you drive into Spokane from the west, I-90 skirts the southern edge of downtown, which is accessed from exit 280A (280B if you're approaching from the east). US-195 (from Clarkston) and US-2 (from Coulee Dam) feed into I-90 west of the city.

Greyhound (☎624-5251) buses use the central and convenient bus depot at 1125 W Sprague and Madison, which they share with *Empire Lines* (☎624-4116 or 1-

800/351-1060). *Amtrak* trains pull in at W First and Bernard (☎624-5144). **Local buses** run by *Spokane Transit Authority (STA)* (☎328-7433) cover the city and its outskirts.

Information, including maps and accommodation lists, is available at the **visitor center**, a short walk from the bus terminal at 926 W Sprague Ave (Mon–Fri 8.30am–5pm; ☎746-3230 or 1-800/248-3220).

The City

Spokane's long and narrow downtown squeezes into the six blocks between I-90 and the Spokane River. The place to make for is **Riverfront Park** – in summer, at least, the town's focal point. Straddling the Spokane River and incorporating the pair of islets in mid-stream, the park was originally planned by Frederick Olmsted, previously responsible for New York's Central Park, who was employed by Spokane's wealthy to landscape the city. Though some of Olmsted's suggestions were followed, big business drew the line at sacrificing their own river access, and for almost a century the banks of the Spokane River were scarred by an ugly tangle of railway lines and buildings – the price for the city's early railroad-based commercial success. But the hundred-acre park was finally laid out in the massive clean-up before the 1974 World's Fair, and is now Spokane's main venue for strolling, picnicking, and general hanging out. An eccentric assortment of attractions includes an old railway clock tower, an antique carousel, a petting zoo, an IMAX theater and a bright and breezy entertainment pavilion.

Slicing through the park, the river tumbles down a series of rocky ledges known as **Spokane Falls**, once a fishing site for the Spokane and later the site of the first pioneer settlement. Early settlers harnessed the churning water to power their mills, and on the far side of the river the **Flour Mill** was an economic cornerstone when it opened in 1896, though it's now been converted to house cutesy shops. Cablecars, known as the **Gondola Skyride** (daily summer 11am–dusk, spring & fall 11am–4 or 5pm; $3), run across the river from the west end of the park, offering panoramic views.

The relics of Spokane's early grandeur are sprinkled all over the town, from the monumental downtown *Davenport Hotel* at Sprague and Post streets, whose heavy flamboyant and internationalist (Tudor chamber, Turkish bath, Bourbon dining room) interior is slowly being restored, to the County Court House, built in the style of a French chateau on the north side of the river. But the main concentration is several blocks southwest of the park on W Riverside Avenue, where heavy neo-Classical facades cluster around Jefferson Street. Further west, the restored **Grace Campbell House**, W 2316 First Ave (Tues–Sat 10am–5pm, Sun 1–5pm), is furnished in a truly tasteless combination of pointedly expensive styles. Next door, and keeping the same hours, the excellent and absorbing **Cheney Cowles Museum** ($3 admission includes Campbell House), intersperses thorough and well-presented displays on Spokane's and Eastern Washington's history with lively contemporary quotes from early residents. There's also a fine collection of prehistoric artwork from Central and South America – weavings, images, odd little dolls – as well as more local stuff, including a number of tableaux showing excruciating-looking native American initiation ceremonies, where the candidates are suspended from hooks embedded in their chests as a test of manhood.

Less than a mile from the museum, **Bing Crosby** pops up again (see p.173) at Gonzaga University, E 502 Boone Ave, which is inordinately proud of its most famous ex-student (recently deposed by Utah Jazz basketball star John Stockton). Bing's family used to live in *Alumni House*, one of the university buildings, and the singer endowed the college with the **Crosby Library**, which sports a shrine to the great man in return. A key from the desk will admit you to a conference room lined with cases of Bing memorabilia – gold discs, sporting awards and suchlike – while a bronze statue of him with golf bag stands outside.

Accommodation

With centrally located hotels and motels, and a youth hostel a short distance away, Spokane caters to all budgets. There's camping at *Riverside State Park campground* (☎456-3964), six miles northwest of the city.

Brown Squirrel AYH hostel, 930 South Lincoln St at Ninth Ave (☎838-5968). A large veran-dahed house in a residential suburb a twenty-minute walk – or a five-minute bus ride (#4 from Howard and Riverside) – south of downtown. Members are charged $10, non-members $13; reservations recommended. ①.

Towne Centre Motor Inn, 901 W First Ave at Lincoln (☎747-1041). No-frills downtown motel. ②.

Travelodge, 827 W First Ave (☎456-8040). Close to the *Towne Centre Motor Inn*, but rather more agreeable. ③.

West Coast Ridpath, 515 W Sprague Ave and Stevens St (☎838-2711 or 1-800/426-0670). Spokane's best hotel. 350 spacious and comfortable rooms – most of those on the upper floors have great views out over town. ⑤.

Food and drink

The restaurants of Spokane are slightly more adventurous than you might expect in Eastern Washington, stimulated by the presence of so many students. As well as the usual breakfast and lunch places, there's plenty of interesting ethnic food on offer, at reasonable prices.

Auntie's Bookstore and Cafe, 313 Riverside Ave (☎838-0206). Home-made soups, salads and desserts in a quiet atmosphere.

Cyrus O'Leary's, 516 W Main St, at the bottom of Bennett Block (☎624-9000). Cheerful place with a long and reasonably priced American menu.

Knights Diner, 2909 N Market St. Beautifully converted old train carriage in whose narrow confines an astoundingly dexterous chef serves generous breakfasts and lunches to eager customers.

Mustard Seed, 245 W Spokane Falls Blvd (☎747-2689). Distinctive oriental cuisine, melding Japanese and Chinese influences.

Niko's, 725 W Riverside Ave (☎624-7444). Best Greek restaurant in town, located several blocks southwest of the park.

Onion Bar and Grill, 302 Riverside Ave (☎747-3852). Beer, wine and fruit daiquiris served across an elegant, polished wooden bar; the food (dressed-up burgers, salads) is quite good, too.

Nightlife and entertainment

Spokane is well-served by a lively mixture of music and sports venues.

Chili D's, 152 S Browne (☎455-9210). Country venue.

The Main Attraction, 116 S Best Rd (☎926-6965). Danceable rock.

Spokane Coliseum, N 1101 Howard St (☎353-6570). Occasional appearances by big-name rock groups; also sporting events, including the odd rodeo.

The Grand Coulee Dam and around

Eastern Washington is seen at its most dramatic in the open, swaggering, big country around the **Grand Coulee Dam**, itself a huge-scale work, around eighty miles west of Spokane or, travelling east, seventy miles from Chelan along Hwy-173 and 174: *Empire Lines* provide daily **bus** connections in both directions.

The dam intercepts the Columbia River at the point where it meets the **Columbia Basin**, an Ice Age disaster area that was scoured and sculpted by ancient floods until it was riven with deep channels called "coulees". These coulees, with their low-lying lakes and skein of rivers, gouge a path south across the state, running east of a giant loop in the course of the Columbia River – basin and river meeting again near Richland. The dam has collected the waters of the basin to create **Banks Lake**, itself occupying a canyon carved long ago when an ice-dam temporarily diverted the Columbia River. Meanwhile, the backed-up river water has swollen to form long, spindly **Lake Roosevelt**, which stretches all the way to the Canadian border, surrounded by campgrounds that serve as useful bases for fishing, sailing and water-skiing.

The dam

Kingpin of the Columbia dams, **Grand Coulee**, begun in 1933, was for a while as much a political icon as an engineering feat. Probably the most ambitious of Roosevelt's New Deal schemes to lift America out of the Depression, it symbolized hope for the Northwest and provided jobs for hundreds of workers from all over the country, notably the dustbowl regions further east, whose unemployed agricultural laborers were migrating west in their hundreds. As folk singer Woody Guthrie had it:

> *Columbia's waters taste like sparklin' wine*
> *Dustbowl waters taste like picklin' brine*

Guthrie worked on the Bonneville Dam lower down the river and was commissioned to write some twenty songs about the Columbia project – one of which, *Roll on, Columbia*, you'll hear ad nauseam in the visitor center (see below). The songs were originally played at local rallies, held to raise investment money, and to combat propaganda from the private power companies whose interests lay in keeping power production in their own hands. Glowing with optimism, the songs underline the promise the dam held for impoverished working people:

> *I'm a farmer's boy, my land's all roots and stumps!*
> *It's gonna take a big 'lectric saw to make 'em jump!*

The dam is now the world's biggest single producer of hydroelectricity, and has certainly controlled flooding lower down the Columbia. But the power-guzzling demands of the new war industries that were attracted to the Northwest during World War II, and the atomic plant at Richland, switched attention and resources from irrigation, and Guthrie's other vision of "green pastures of plenty from dry desert ground" has been much slower to get under way – even now, only half the area originally planned has been irrigated. There's been ecological criticism of the Columbia project too: salmon migration along the river was reduced to a fraction of its pre-dam level, though schemes have since been set up to increase stocks of fish.

The background to the dam's construction is laid out in some detail in the **visitor center**, Hwy-155 on the west side of the dam (daily summer 8.30am–10pm, rest of the year 9am–5pm) with photographs, information and a free film touching on everything from the dangerous working conditions of the Thirties to how the turbines operate. As for the **dam** itself, it's initially something of an anti-climax. Though the world's largest concrete structure, it just doesn't look that big, a trick of the huge-scale scenery that surrounds it; it helps to focus on a car or person on the top for a more impressive perspective. Guided, and self-guided, tours of the dam and its generating plants are available from the visitor center: views of the churning water are quite exciting, but you'll need a fair amount of enthusiasm for things mechanical to appreciate the intricacies of power-generation.

Practicalities

Set against the surrounding scrubland, the leafy streets and shady lawns of **COULEE DAM**, across the dam from the visitor center, are a verdant advertisement for the difference the Grand Coulee's irrigation schemes can make. Otherwise Coulee Dam is a stunningly boring little town, not much more than a dormitory center for the dam's workers, as are its two tiny neighbors – **GRAND COULEE**, which trails up the hill from the visitor center, and **ELECTRIC CITY** next door. Options for food in all three places are pretty dire – Grand Coulee's *Sage Inn*, a slightly tacky diner at 413 Midway Ave (☎633-0550), is better than most. There's a small selection of **motels**: the rooms in Grand Coulee's *Ponderosa Motel*, 10 Lincoln St (☎633-2100; ②), overlook the dam, while the *Sky Deck Motel* (☎633-0290; ②), Hwy-155 in Electric City, sits beside Banks Lake. More appealingly, there's a choice of more than thirty **campgrounds** scattered around Lake Roosevelt, becoming more woody and secluded as you get further north; pick up a map from the dam's visitor center.

Colville National Forest

The most diverting approach to the **Colville National Forest** is along Hwy-25, which can be reached from Coulee Dam via Hwy-174 and then Hwy-2. The national forest covers a huge area, with massive chunks of land spread on both sides of the upper reaches of Lake Roosevelt. Leaving the lake (and Hwy-25) at Kettle Falls, the main access road (Hwy-20) heads east for the remoteness of the national forest's Pend Oreille River, passing a string of campgrounds and hiking trails on the way. Less appealingly, Hwy-20 also travels west for the tiny town of Republic and, ultimately, the dirt roads of the (comparatively small and very isolated) **Okanogan National Forest**.

South along Banks Lake to Dry Falls

South of the Grand Coulee Dam, Hwy-155 follows the shore of Banks Lake through more of the Columbia Basin's big country: endless plains sparsely coated with scrubby vegetation, broken by huge flat-topped rocks, such as **Steamboat Rock**, which now sits in the middle of the lake, only connected to the river bank by a narrow isthmus – watch for the right turn off Hwy-155. The rock has been declared a state park, with a few trails looping half-heartedly over the dry land. It's worth getting out of the car, though: butterflies flit over the sagebrush, brightly colored insects crawl across the path and the odd snake rattles as you walk by.

Banks Lake ends – and Hwy-155 feeds into US-2 – at Dry Falls Dam, named for **Dry Falls**, a few miles further south (take Hwy-17 from the west end of the dam), which had their moment of glory during the Ice Age when the Columbia, temporarily diverted this way, poured a tremendous torrent over a drop twice as high and almost four times as wide as Niagara. It must have been quite a sight, but a waterfall without water is not that impressive, and all you can see today is a wide, bare, canyon-walled hole, the remnants of a lake lurking apologetically in its flat-bottomed depths. A visitor center, beside the highway, gives the background. From Dry Falls Dam, US-2 will take you west towards Chelan (see p.212); while Hwy-17 leads south along the Columbia Basin to I-90.

travel details

Trains
From Spokane one daily to Ephrata (2hr 15min); Wenatchee (3hr 15min); Everett (6hr 25min); Seattle (9hr). Another to Pasco (2hr 40min); Portland (8hr 15min).

Buses
Greyhound

From Seattle to Leavenworth (2 daily; 3hr); Cashmere (2; 3hr 15min); Wenatchee (2; 3hr 30min); Ellensburg (5; 2hr); Yakima (3; 3hr 30min); Toppenish (3; 4hr 25min); Richland (2; 6hr 15min); Walla Walla (2; 7hr); Spokane (4; 6hr).

From Spokane to Portland (1 daily; 9hr, change in Biggs).
From Yakima to Goldendale (1 daily; 1hr 30min); Biggs, Oregon (1; 2hr); Portland (1; 4hr 30min).

Empire Lines

From Spokane to Grand Coulee (1 daily; 2hr), and Wenatchee (1 daily; 4hr 45min) where onward services leave for Chelan, Okanogan and Oroville (1 daily; 1hr/2hr/3hr); and Ellensburg and Yakima (1 daily; 2hr2 0min/3hr).

CHAPTER FIVE

VANCOUVER AND VANCOUVER ISLAND

Vancouver and Vancouver Island are pivotal points in any trip to the Northwest. Rightly preceded by a reputation as one of the world's most beautiful and laid-back cities, Vancouver is the main rival to Seattle as the region's most dynamic metropolis, not only blessed with a superlative natural setting, thriving cultural life and myriad after-dark activities, but also easily accessible and perfectly placed for onward travel to Vancouver Island, mainland British Columbia and the Canadian Rockies. Like Seattle, the city finds itself in the vanguard of trade and cultural ties with the Pacific Rim, links that have reinforced its long-standing economic vigor and deeply rooted multiculturalism. As a result, Vancouver exudes a cosmopolitan and civilized air, its easy-going citizens, outstanding museums and a wealth of opportunities for self-indulgence all likely to keep you in the city for several days.

The obvious excursion is across the Georgia Strait to **Vancouver Island**, home to **Victoria**, British Columbia's modest provincial capital. Swamped by US day-trippers in summer, the city plays up shamelessly to its image as a little piece of "old England", though even if you find this pitch a little hard to swallow, the place is worth at least a day for its superlative museum. The island as a whole, can be a touch disappointing, and you may spend less time than you'd imagined exploring the city's hinterland. For many people the island becomes simply a way-station en route to Prince Hardy, Vancouver Island's terminal for the **ferries of the Inside Passage** (for Prince Rupert and Alaska). If you're not just hurrying through, however, the hiking possibilities and mountain landscapes of the **Strathcona Provincial Park**, and more particularly the tremendous seascapes of the **Pacific Rim National Park**, are both exceptional reasons to linger.

Long before the coming of Europeans, British Columbia's coastal region supported five key **native peoples** – the Kwakiutl, Bella Coola, Nuu-chah-nulth, Haida and Tlingit – all of whom lived largely off the sea and developed a culture in many ways more sophisticated than that of the more nomadic and hunting-oriented tribes of the interior (see box on p.268). European exploration from the late sixteenth to the eighteenth century culminated in the domination of the area by the **Hudson's Bay Company**, a monopoly that antagonized the Americans. The British were prompted to formalize their claim to the region, and the 49th Parallel was agreed as the national boundary, though Vancouver Island, which

TELEPHONE NUMBERS

The **telephone code** for British Columbia is ☎604.
Toll-free Information: Tourism British Columbia ☎1-800/663-6000.

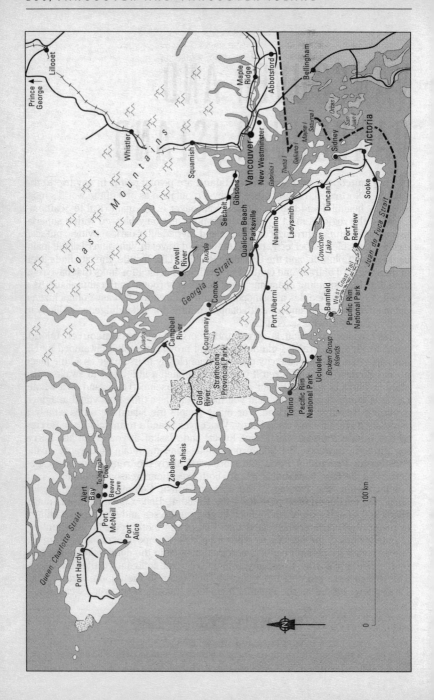

lies partly south of the line, remained wholly British and was officially designated a crown colony in 1849. The discovery of **gold** in the Fraser River and Cariboo regions in the mid-nineteenth century attracted large numbers of hopeful prospectors; their forward base on the mainland eventually became Vancouver.

VANCOUVER

Cradled between the ocean and snow-capped mountains, Vancouver's dazzling downtown district fills a narrow peninsula bounded by Burrard Inlet to the north, English Bay to the west and False Creek to the south, with greater Vancouver sprawling south to the Fraser River. Fringing its idyllic waterfront are fine beaches, a dynamic port and a magnificent swathe of parkland, not to mention the mirror-fronted ranks of skyscrapers that look across Burrard Inlet to the residential districts of North and West Vancouver. Beyond these comfortable suburbs, the Coast Mountains rise in steep, forested slopes, to form a dramatic counterpoint to the downtown skyline – and the most stunning of the city's many outdoor playgrounds.

Vancouver's 1.3 million residents take full advantage of their spectacular surroundings. Whether it's sailing, swimming, fishing, hiking, skiing, golf or tennis, locals don't have to go far to indulge in a plethora of **recreational** activities. Summer and winter alike, the city oozes hedonism and healthy living, typically West Coast obsessions that spill over into sophisticated **arts and culture**. Vancouver claims a world-class museum and symphony orchestra, as well as opera, theater and dance companies at the cutting edge of contemporary arts. Festivals proliferate throughout its mild, if occasionally rain-soaked summer, and numerous music venues provide fertile ground for up-and-coming rock bands and a burgeoning jazz scene.

The city is not all pleasure, however. Business thrives in Canada's third largest and fastest-growing city, much of its prosperity stemming from a **port** so laden with the raw materials of the Canadian interior – lumber, wheat, minerals – that it now outranks New York as North America's largest port, and handles more dry tonnage than the West Coast ports of Seattle, Tacoma, Portland, San Francisco and San Diego put together. The port in turn owes its prominence to Vancouver's much-trumpeted position as a **gateway to the Far East**, and its increasingly pivotal role in the new global market of the Pacific Rim. This lucrative realignment is mirrored by the changing social composition of the city: in the past decade Vancouver has seen an influx of Hong Kong Chinese (the so-called "yacht people"), which has pushed up property prices and strained the city's reputation as an ethnically integrated metropolis.

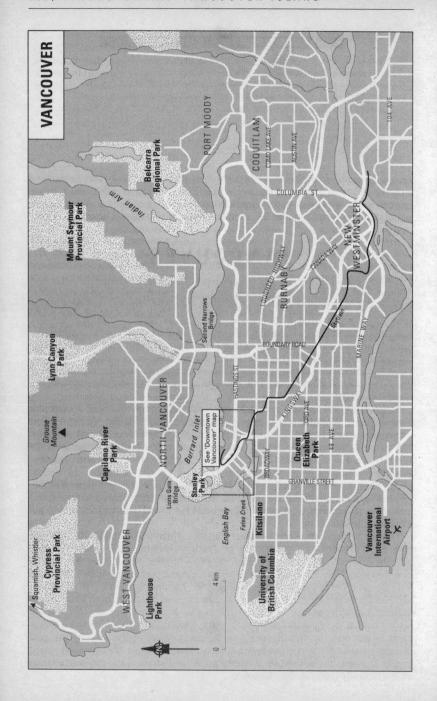

VANCOUVER

Much of the new immigration has focused on Vancouver's **Chinatown**, just one of a number of ethnic enclaves – Italian, Greek, Indian and Japanese in particular – which lend the city a refreshingly gritty quality that belies its sleek, modern reputation. So too do the city's semi-derelict areas, whose worldly low-life characters seem at odds with the glitzy lifestyles pursued in the lush residential neighborhoods. Low rents and Vancouver's cosmopolitan young have also nurtured an unexpected **counterculture**, distinguished by varied restaurants, secondhand stores, avant-garde galleries and one-off clubs and bars – spots where you'll probably have more fun than in many a Northwestern city.

A brief history of Vancouver

Coast Salish natives inhabited about ten villages on the shores of Vancouver's Burrard Inlet before the coming of white people. They were skilled carpenters, canoe makers and artists, but little in the present city – outside its museums – pays anything but lip service to their existence.

Europeans arrived during the eighteenth century, when **Spanish** explorers charted the waters along what is now southwestern British Columbia. In 1778 **Captain James Cook** reached nearby Nootka Sound while searching for the Northwest Passage, creating a British interest in the area and leading to wrangles with the Spanish, though these were quickly settled in Britain's favor when Spain became embroiled in the aftermath of the French Revolution. **Captain George Vancouver** officially claimed the land for Britain in 1792, but stayed only a day – scant homage to a place that was to be named after him a century later.

In 1827 the Hudson's Bay Company set up a fur-trading post at **Fort Langley**, 48km east of the present city; the first white settlement on the mainland, it was none the less kept free of homesteaders, who would have scared off the animals required for the fur trade. Major colonization of the area only came after the Fraser River and Cariboo gold rushes in 1858, when **New Westminster** (now a southern suburb of Vancouver) became the mainland's chief port. In 1862, three British prospectors, unable to find gold, bought a strip of land on the southern shore of Burrard Inlet and – shortsightedly, given the amount of lumber around – started a brickworks; this soon gave way to the Hastings Sawmill and a shanty town of bars which by 1867 had taken the name of **Gastown**. Two years later Gastown became incorporated as the town of **Granville** and prospered on the back of its timber and small coal deposits.

The birth of the present city dates to 1884, when the **Canadian Pacific Railway** decided to make it the terminus of its transcontinental railway. In 1886, on a whim of the CPR president, Granville was renamed Vancouver – only to be destroyed on June 13 that year when fire razed all but half a dozen buildings. This proved a short-lived setback, however, and since the arrival of the first train from Montréal in 1887 the city has never looked back.

Arrival, information and city transit

Vancouver International Airport is situated on Sea Island, 13km south of downtown. International flights arrive at the main terminal, domestic flights at the smaller south terminal. You'll find a **tourist information** booth on Level 2 of the main terminal (daily 6am–midnight) and **foreign exchange** facilities on each level, along with free phone lines to the upmarket hotels. The best way to get into

Vancouver is on the private **Airport Express Bus** (6.15am–12.30am; $8.75; ☎273-9023), known as the "Hustle Bus", which leaves every fifteen minutes from Level 2, stopping at downtown hotels and the bus terminal. (When flying out of Vancouver, note that the *Express Bus* departs from Bay 20 of the bus terminal between 6.25am and 10.40pm; it also calls at the *Hyatt Regency Hotel*, and can be flagged down at the corner of Broadway and Granville.) **Taxis** into town cost about $25–35.

The **public transit** alternative is less expensive ($1.35), slower (1hr) and inconvenient, involving a change of bus – take *Metro Transit* bus #100 to the corner of 71st and Granville (it leaves Level 3 every half-hour), then change to the #20 or 21 which drops off downtown in Granville St.

Vancouver's main **bus terminal** is at 150 Dunsmuir St and Hamilton; to get to downtown, leave by the main entrance and turn left uphill (a 10-min walk), or hop on the SkyTrain (see "Transit", next page) at Stadium station across the road. There are **left luggage** facilities here and a very useful **hotel board**, whose free phone line connects to some of the city's less expensive hotels – some of whom will deduct the taxi fare from the terminal from your first night's bill. Note that *Pacific Coach Lines* (for Victoria, Vancouver Island) and *Maverick Coach Lines* (Whistler, Sunshine Coast and Nanaimo) now operate from the Pacific Central Station (see below).

Arriving by train on **VIA rail** you will enter the city at the Pacific Central Station (☎669-3050) at 1150 Station St; services run to and from Prince Rupert, Prince George and Edmonton and the east via Jasper (3 weekly). There is a chance that the recently closed *VIA/Amtrak* service between Vancouver and recommence – contact the infocentre for the latest.

A second station, belonging to the provincially owned freight-biased **BC Rail** (☎631-3500 or 631-3501) – serving Lillooet (daily) and Prince George (3 weekly) – is located in semi-industrial wasteland at 1311 W First St, in North Vancouver (see "Listings" p.262). Trains arrive late at night, so your best bet for getting into the city is a taxi, unless you can cope with walking the length of Pemberton Ave – about twenty minutes – to catch a #239 bus to connect with the SeaBus; for early-morning departures there's a connecting bus from the bus terminal at 6.20am.

Onward travel options from Vancouver are detailed on p.260.

Information

The **Vancouver Travel Infocentre** is at Pavilion Plaza, 4 Bentall Centre, 1055 Dunsmuir St, near the junction with Burrard (daily June–Aug 8am–6pm; Sept–May 9am–5pm; ☎683-2000 or 1-800/888-8835). As well as information on the city and much of southeastern British Columbia, the office provides **foreign exchange** facilities, *BC Transit* tickets, and tickets to sports and entertainment events. It also has one of the most comprehensive **accommodation services** imaginable, backed up by bulging photo albums of hotel rooms and B&Bs, though staff steadfastly refuse to make recommendations.

Two smaller kiosks open in summer, in the aquarium parking lot in Stanley Park and outside *Eaton's Department Store* on the corner of Georgia and Granville (Sat–Wed 9.30am–5.30pm, Thurs & Fri 9.30am–9pm).

City transit

Vancouver's **public transportation** system is an efficient, integrated network of bus, light-rail and ferry services, all operated by *BC Transit* (☎261-5100 for information, daily 6.30am–11.30pm).

Tickets

Tickets generally cost $1.50 ($2.25 or $3 for longer 2- and 3-zone journeys and the SeaBus during peak hours) and are valid for transfers throughout the system for ninety minutes from the time of issue; day passes, valid only after 9.30am, cost $4.50; monthly passes $50. You can buy tickets individually (or in books of ten and twenty) at stations, *7-Eleven* stores, or any other shop displaying a blue and red *BC Transit* sticker (so-called "Faredealer" outlets). You must carry tickets with you as proof of payment.

Buses and timetables

The invaluable *BC Transit Guide* ($1.25) is available from the infocentre and Faredealer stores, while free **bus** timetables can be found at the infocentre, *7-Eleven* stores and the central library. The free *Discover Vancouver on the Transit* pamphlet is also handy. You can buy tickets on the bus, but make sure you have the right change to shovel into the box beside the driver; you have to ask specially for transfer tickets. Normal buses stop running around midnight, when a patchy "Night Owl" service comes into effect on major routes until about 4am. Blue **West Van** buses also operate in the city (usually to North and West Vancouver destinations), on which *BC Transit* tickets are still valid.

SeaBus

SeaBus ferries ply between downtown and Lonsdale Quay in North Vancouver, a ride that avoids the delays likely to be encountered if you take a bus across the Lions Gate Bridge, but is also a journey definitely worth taking for its own sake: the views of the mountains across Burrard Inlet, the port and the downtown skyline are superb. Two 400-seat catamarans make the crossing every quarter- or half-hour (6.15am–1am), taking about thirteen minutes. Departures are from a terminal housed in the old Canadian Pacific station at the bottom of Seymour Street, downtown, and from Lonsdale Quay in North Van. Bicycles can cross free during off-peak periods; otherwise you need an extra ticket for them.

SkyTrain

Vancouver's single light-rail line – **SkyTrain** – is a model of its type: driverless, completely computerized and magnetically propelled half underground and half on raised track, it covers 22km between the downtown Waterfront station (housed in the CPR building with the SeaBus terminal) and the southeastern suburb of New Westminster. Only the first three or four stations are of any practical use to the casual visitor, but the 27-minute trip is worth taking if only to see how the Canadians do these things – spotless interiors, Teutonic punctuality and fully carpeted carriages.

Ferries

Vancouver also has various small **ferries**, mostly serving False Creek for the Granville Island and Vanier Museum complex. You can pick up the small boats at

---

BUS ROUTES

Some of the more important Vancouver **bus routes** are:

#1 – Gastown–English Bay loop.

#3 & #8 – Gastown–Downtown–Marine Drive.

#4 & #10 – Granville Street–University of British Columbia.

#50 – Gastown–False Creek–Broadway.

#51 – SeaBus Terminal–Downtown–Granville Island.

#19 – Pender Street (Downtown)–Stanley Park.

#20 & #17 – Downtown–Marine Drive; transfer to #100 for the airport.

Some **scenic routes** are worth travelling for their own sakes:

#250 – Georgia Street (Downtown)–North Van–West Van–Horseshoe Bay.

#52 – "Around the Park" service through Stanley Park (April–Oct Sat & Sun only); board at Lost Lagoon or Denman Street.

#351 – Howe Street–White Rock–Crescent Beach (1hr each way).

#210 – Pender Street–Phibbs Exchange; change there for #211 (mountain route) or #212 (ocean views) to Deep Cove.

---

the Arts Club Theatre on Granville Island, the Aquatic Centre at the northern end of the Burrard Bridge, the north foot of the Granville Bridge, the Maritime Museum, the False Creek Yacht Club, and BC Place. For information call *Granville Island Ferries* (☎684-7781) or *Aquabus* (☎874-9930).

The City

Vancouver is a city that neither offers nor requires relentless sightseeing. Its breathtaking physical beauty makes it a place where often it's enough just to wander and watch the world go by – "the sort of town", wrote Jan Morris, "nearly everyone would want to live in." In summer you'll probably end up doing what the locals do – if not actually sailing, hiking, skiing, fishing or whatever, then certainly lying on a beach, lounging in one of the parks or spending time in waterfront cafés.

A handful of sights, however, make worthwhile viewing by any standards. You'll inevitably spend a good deal of time in the **downtown** area and its Victorian-era equivalent, **Gastown**, now a renovated and less than convincing pastiche of its past. **Chinatown**, too, could easily absorb a morning, and contains more than its share of interesting stores, restaurants and rumbustiously busy streets. For a taste of the city's carefree nature, hit **Stanley Park**, a huge area of semi-wild parkland and beaches that crowns the northern tip of the peninsula, or **Granville Island**, by far the most tempting spot for strolling and people-watching. If you prefer a cultural slant on things, a visit to the formidable **Museum of Anthropology** or the other museums of the Vanier Park complex will be rewarding. At a push, you could cram the essentials into a couple of days. If you're here for a longer stay, though, you'll want to venture further out from downtown: trips across Burrard Inlet to **North Vancouver** lend a different panoramic perspective of the city, and lead seamlessly into the mountains and forests that provide Vancouver with its tremendous setting.

Downtown

You soon get the hang of **downtown** Vancouver, an arena of streets and shopping malls centered on **Robson Street**, which on hot summer evenings is like a latterday vision of *la dolce vita* – a dynamic meeting place crammed with cafés, restaurants, late-night stores, and bronzed hunks and lean-limbed blondes cruising in open-topped cars. At other times a more sedate class hangs out on the steps of the Vancouver Art Gallery or glides in and out of the two big department stores, *Eaton's* and *The Bay*, all downtown landmarks.

As a suitable introduction to Vancouver, you could do worse than walk down to the waterfront and **Canada Place**, the Canadian pavilion opened by Charles and Di for Expo '86, and now an architectural anomaly which houses a luxury hotel, cruise ship terminal and two glitzy convention centers.

For all its excess, it makes a superb viewpoint, with stunning vistas of sea and mountains, buzzing boats, helicopters and float planes. In its design, and the way it extends into the harbor, the complex is meant to suggest a ship, and you can walk the building's perimeter as if "on deck", stopping to read the boards that describe the immediate cityscape and the appropriate chapters of its history. Inside are expensive stores, a restaurant, and an IMAX cinema (daily noon–9pm; $6.25; ☎682-6422 for program).

Most of the **Expo site** here and to the east has been levelled or is undergoing rigorous redevelopment. The geodesic dome is a notable exception, but the museum it now houses, **Science World** (daily 10am–5pm; $7 or $11 with Omnimax film) is generally disappointing. Another remnant of Expo is the 60,000-seat **BC Place Stadium** at 1 Robson St, the world's largest air-inflated dome (tours daily at 11am, 1pm & 3pm; $3.50); unless you're there for a sporting event, the "mushroom" or "marshmallow in bondage" of popular parlance isn't worth the bother.

An alternative to Canada Place's vantage point, the **Harbour Centre Building** at 555 W Hastings is one of the city's tallest structures, and is known by locals either as the "urinal" or, more affectionately, the "hamburger" after its bulging upper stories. On a fine day it's definitely worth paying to ride the stomach-churning, all-glass elevators that run up the side of the tower to the fortieth-story observation deck ("The Lookout") for staggering views (March–Sept daily 10am–9pm; $5); admission also entitles you to view a 12-minute gung-ho promotional film, the *Vancouver Discovery Show*.

The Vancouver Art Gallery

Corner of Howe and Robson. Wed, Fri & Sat 10am–5pm; Thurs 10am–9pm; Sun noon–5pm. $4.75; free Thurs 5–9pm.

Centrally located in the imposing old city courthouse, the **Vancouver Art Gallery** at the corner of Howe and Robson looks as if it ought to contain a treasure trove of art, but too much space is given over to dud modern Canadian works. What redeems the place are the powerful and almost surreal works of Emily Carr, who was born on Vancouver Island in 1871 and whose paintings – characterized by deep greens and blues – evoke something of the scale and intensity of the West Coast and its native peoples.

A sparse international collection offers Warhol and Lichtenstein, with token rooms of half a dozen Italian, Flemish and British paintings. The gallery café is excellent.

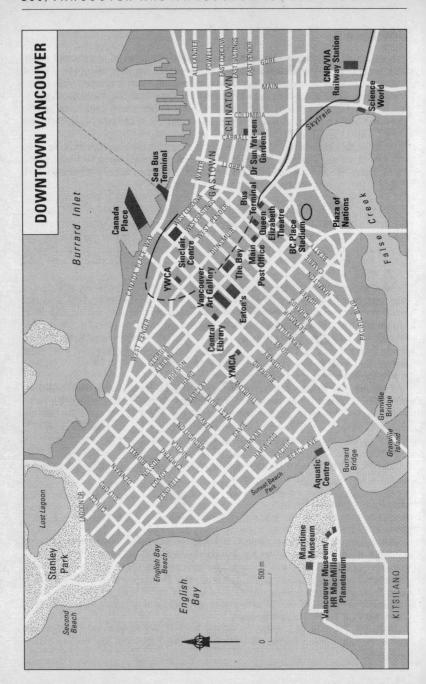

DOWNTOWN VANCOUVER

Burrard Inlet

Sea Bus Terminal

Canada Place

CANADA PLACE WAY

CHINATOWN

ALEXANDER
POWELL
EAST CORDOVA
EAST HASTINGS
EAST PENDER
GORE
MAIN

CNR/VIA
Railway Station

Science World

COLUMBIA

CARRALL

Skytrain

WATER

GASTOWN

ABBOTT

Dr Sun Yat-sen Gardens

WEST CORDOVA
WEST HASTINGS
WEST PENDER

Sinclair Centre

YWCA

Vancouver Art Gallery

DUNSMUR

Bus Terminal

Queen Elizabeth Theatre

The Bay

Eaton's

Main Post Office

BC Place Stadium

Plaza of Nations

False Creek

Central Library

YMCA

WEST PENDER

GEORGIA
ALBERNI
ROBSON
HARO
BARCLAY
NELSON

HAMILTON
CAMBIE
BEATTY

HOMER
RICHARDS
SEYMOUR
GRANVILLE
HOWE
HORNBY
BURRARD
THURLOW

PACIFIC BLVD

WEST BUTE
JERVIS
BROUGHTON
NICOLA
CARDERO
BIDWELL
DENMAN

DAVIE
BURNABY
HARWOOD
PACIFIC
BEACH AVE

Granville Bridge

Granville Island

COMOX
PENDRELL

CHILCO
GILFORD
LAGOON DR

Sunset Beach Park

Aquatic Centre

Burrard Bridge

Lost Lagoon

Stanley Park

English Bay Beach

English Bay

Second Beach

Maritime Museum

Vancouver Museum/ HR MacMillan Planetarium

KITSILANO

500 m

0

N

Gastown

An easy walk east of downtown – five minutes from Canada Place and concentrated largely on Water Street – **Gastown** is a determined piece of city rejuvenation aimed fair and square at the tourist, distinguished by its new cobbles, fake gas lamps, *Ye Olde English Tea Room* and generally overpolished patina. The name derives from "Gassy" Jack Leighton, a retired sailor turned publican who opened a bar in 1867 to service the nearby lumber mills, whose bosses banned drinking on or near the yards. Trade was brisk, and a second bar opened, soon followed by a village of sorts – "Gassy's Town" – which, though swept away by fire in 1886, formed the birthplace of modern Vancouver. Over the years, the downtown focus moved west and something of Gastown's boozy beginnings returned to haunt it, as its cheap hotels and warehouses turned into a skid row for junkies and alcoholics. By the 1970s the area was declared an historic site – the buildings are still the city's oldest – and an enthusiastic beautification program set in motion.

The end product never quite became the dynamic, bustling spot the planners envisaged, but it's worth a stroll for its buskers, Sunday crowds and occasional points of interest. These do not include the hype-laden **steam-powered clock**, the world's first and hopefully last, at the west end of Water Street. It's invariably surrounded by tourists armed with cocked cameras, all awaiting the miniature Big Ben's toots and whistles every fifteen minutes, and bellowing performances on the hour that seem to presage imminent explosion. The steam comes from an underground system that also heats surrounding buildings.

Nearby you'll find the *Town Pump*, one of the city's top music venues (see p.255), and the **Inuit Gallery**, a large commercial showcase of Inuit art at 345 Water St (Mon–Sat 9.30am–5.30pm). The **Western Canadian Wilderness Committee** store and office at 20 Water St provides an interesting stop-off – if you thought BC was people, trees and nature in peace and harmony, this leading conservation group will soon disabuse you.

Probably the most surprising aspect of Gastown, however, is the contrast between its manicured pavements and the down-at-heel streets immediately to the south and east. The bustling hub of **alternative Vancouver**, the area between Gastown and Chinatown is a maze of secondhand clothes stores, bookstores, galleries, new designers and dowdy five-and-dimes. In places, however, this area recalls Gastown's bad old days: unpleasantly seedy, pocked with the dingiest of dingy bars and hotels, and inhabited by characters to match.

Chinatown

Vancouver's vibrant **Chinatown** – clustered mainly on Pender Street from Carrall to Gore, and on Keefer Street from Main to Gore (#22 bus from Burrard) – is a city apart. Vancouver's 100,000 Chinese are expected soon to surpass San Francisco's as the largest Chinese community outside the Far East and are the city's oldest and largest ethnic group after the British-descended majority.

Many crossed the Pacific in 1858 to join the Fraser Valley gold rush; others followed under contract to build the Canadian Pacific Railway. Denied citizenship and legal rights until as recently as 1947, they sought safety and familiarity in a ghetto of their own, where clan associations and societies provided for new arrivals and the local poor – and helped to erect the distinctive houses with recessed balconies and ornamental roofs that have made the area a protected historic site.

Unlike Gastown's gimmickry, Chinatown is all genuine – shops, budget hotels, markets, tiny restaurants and dim alleys vie for attention amid an incessant hustle of jammed pavements and the buzz of Chinese conversation. Striking and unexpected after downtown's high-rise glitz, the district brings you face to face with Vancouver's oft-touted multiculturalism, and helps to explain why Hong Kong immigrants continue to be attracted to the city. There's a seamier side to Chinatown, however, especially at night, and though central districts are fine, lone tourists are better off avoiding Hastings and the back streets.

Apart from the obvious culinary temptations (see "Eating and drinking"), Chinatown's main points of reference are its **markets**. One of the best is *Yuen Fong* at 242 E Pender, where you can find fearsome butchery displays and such edibles as live eels, flattened ducks, hundred-year-old eggs and other delicacies.

Keefer Street is **bakery** row, with lots of tempting stickies on offer such as moon cakes and *bao*, steamed buns with a meat or sweet bean filling. On the corner of Keefer and Main is the *Ten Ren Tea and Ginseng Company*, with a vast range of teas, many promising cures for a variety of ailments (free tastings).

In a similar vein, drop into one of the local **herbalists** to browse among their remedies: snake skins, reindeer antlers, buffalo tongues, dried seahorses and bears' testicles are all available if you're feeling under the weather. *Ming Wo*, at 23 E Pender, is a fantastic cookware shop, with probably every utensil ever devised, while *China West*, 41 E Pender, is packed with slippers, jackets, pens, cheap toys and the like.

Chinatown's chief cultural attraction is the **Dr Sun Yat-sen Garden**, at 578 Carrall St near Pender, billed as the first classical Chinese garden ever built outside China (daily May–Sept 10am–8pm, Oct–April 10am–4.30pm; $3.50). Named after the founder of the first Chinese Republic, who was a frequent visitor to Vancouver, the park was created for the '86 Expo and cost Can$5.3 million, half a million dollars of which came from the People's Republic, along with 52 artisans and 950 crates of materials. The horticultural emissaries, following traditional methods which didn't allow use of a single power tool, spent thirteen months replicating a fourteenth-century Ming garden to achieve a subtle balance of *yin* and *yang;* regular free guided tours explain the Taoist philosophy behind the carefully placed elements.

Alongside the entrance to the garden, the **Chinese Cultural Centre**, Chinatown's community focus and a sponsor of New Year festivities, offers classes and hosts changing exhibitions. Nearby is a small Dr Sun Yat-sen Park (free) which, though less formalized than the Dr Sun Yat-sen Garden, is still a pleasant place to take time-out from Chinatown. Hours are the same as for the garden, and there's an alternative entrance on Columbia St and Keefer.

Stanley Park

One of the world's great urban spaces, **Stanley Park** contributes to Vancouver's particular character. At nearly 1000 acres, it's the largest urban park in North America – less a tame collection of lawns and elms than a semi-wilderness of dense rainforest, marshland and beaches. Ocean surrounds it on three sides, with a road and parallel cycleway/pedestrian promenade following the sea wall right the way around the peninsula for a total of 10.5km. Away from the coastal trail network and two big attractions – the aquarium and the zoo – the interior consists of dense scrub and forest, with few paths and few people.

The peninsula was partially logged in the 1860s, when Vancouver was still a twinkle in "Gassy" Jack Leighton's eye, but in 1886 the newly formed city council – showing typical Canadian foresight and an admirable sense of priorities – moved to make what had become a military reserve into a permanent park. Thus its remaining first-growth forest of cedar, hemlock and Douglas fir, and the swamp now known as Lost Lagoon, were saved for posterity in the name of Lord Stanley, Canada's Governor General from 1888 to 1893.

The park is a simple walk from most of downtown, if a fairly lengthy one from eastern districts. Beach Avenue and Alberni Street are the best entrances if you're on foot, leading to the southern start of the seawall; Georgia Street takes you to the northern entrance. Bus #19 runs to the foot of Alberni Street from points along Pender Street, while the special "Around the Park" service (bus #52) carries on from there hourly at weekends and on holidays (April–Oct), but doesn't run if it's raining. Parking can be problematic, especially on weekends.

Walking around the park provides something of the flavor of life in Vancouver. A good first point of call is the **Lost Lagoon**, a fair-sized lake that started life as a tidal inlet, and got its name because its water all but disappeared at low tide. Odd little sights dot the promenade, all signed and explained, the most famous being the *Girl in a Wetsuit* statue, a lascivious update of Copenhagen's *Little Mermaid*.

If you want a more focused walk, the **Cathedral Trail**, northwest of the Lost Lagoon, takes you past some big first-growth cedars. **Prospect Point**, on the park's northern tip, is a busy spot but worth braving for its beautiful view of the city and the mountains rising behind West Vancouver across the water. Guided **nature walks** depart every Tuesday from the Alberni St bus stop (May, June & Sept at 10am) and from Lumberman's Arch Water Park (July & Aug at 10am & 7pm).

Given the park's size, a **bicycle** affords more flexibility than walking – see "Listings" on p.260 for rental outlets. You can pick up a free cycling map of the park from *Stanley Park Rentals* at 676 Chilco and Alberni (just across from the Alberni St bus stop). Though people do swim in the sea, most bathers prefer to dip in the **swimming pool** next to Second Beach (see box). Facilities of all sorts – cafés, playgrounds, golf, outdoor dancing – proliferate near the downtown margins.

The Children's Zoo and Vancouver Aquarium

The small **Children's Zoo** north of Lost Lagoon is the most visited place in the park, with many farm and other animals allowed to wander in a special open area (daily 10am–5pm; free). The main zoo nearby is far less attractive, and there are repeated calls for its closure on the grounds of cruelty – one look at the obviously distressed and unbelievably mangy polar bears should convert you to the cause.

The neighboring **Vancouver Aquarium** is more ambitious, its six thousand marine species making it Canada's largest (daily summer 9.30am–8pm; winter 10am–5.30pm; $8.50). Certain parts are interesting, even for non-fish enthusiasts – especially the salmon section – but the aquarium, too, has been targetted by animal-rights campaigns for its treatment of performing beluga and killer whales (not to mention cooped-up seals and otters). Given the aquarium's popularity, though, the animal-rights campaigners have a long, uphill battle ahead of them.

VANCOUVER'S BEACHES

Though most of the sand comes from Japan in container ships, Vancouver's **beaches** look and feel like the real thing. All are clean and well kept – the clarity of the water is remarkable, given the size of the port – and the majority have lifeguards during the summer months. The best beaches face each other across False Creek and English Bay, starting with Stanley Park's three adjacent strands: **English Bay Beach**, along Beach Ave; **Second Beach**, to the north, which also features a shallow onshore swimming pool; and **Third Beach**, further north still, the least crowded of the three and the one with the best views of West Vancouver and the mountains.

Across the water to the south and west of the Burrard Bridge, **Kitsilano Beach**, or "Kits", is the busiest and most self-concious of the beaches. It's especially popular with the university, volleyball and body-building crowd, and with the more well-heeled locals. An old hippy and alternative-lifestyle redoubt, it still betrays shades of its past, and with nearby bars and restaurants to fuel the party spirit there's always plenty going on (though there can be a vaguely meat-market sort of atmosphere as well). If it all gets too much, you can retreat to a nearby heated saltwater pool (summer only). **Jericho Beach**, west of Kits and handy for the youth hostel, is a touch quieter and serves as a hang-out for the windsurfing crowd. Still further west, **Locarno Beach** and **Spanish Banks** become progressively less crowded, and mark the start of a fringe of sand and parkland that continues round to the UBC campus. Locals rate Spanish Banks the most relaxed of the city's beaches. Clothing-optional **Wreck Beach** is just off the campus area – ask any student to point you towards the half-hidden access paths. The atmosphere is generally laid-back – though women have been known to complain of voyeurs – and nude pedlars are on hand to sell you anything from pizza to massage and hair-braiding. Finally, **Ambleside**, west of the Park Royal Mall, is the most accessible beach if you're in North or West Vancouver.

Granville Island

Granville Island, huddled under the Granville Street Bridge south of downtown, is the city's most enticing "people's place" – the title it likes for itself – and almost lives up to its claim to be the "heart of Vancouver". Friendly and easy-going, its shops, markets, galleries, marina and open spaces are juxtaposed with a warehouse setting that saves the area from pretentiousness. The island was reclaimed from swampland in 1917 as an ironworks and shipbuilding center, but by the 1960s the yards were derelict and the place had become a rat-infested dumping ground. In 1972 the federal government agreed to bankroll a program of residential, commercial and industrial redevelopment that retained the old false-fronted buildings, tin-shack homes, sea wall and rail sidings. The best part of the job had been finished by 1979 – and was immediately successful – but work continues unobtrusively today, the various building projects only adding to the sense of change and dynamism.

The most direct approach is to take **bus** #50 from Gastown or Granville St. Alternatively, bathtub-sized private **ferries** ply back and forth almost continuously between the island and the Aquatic Centre at the foot of Thurlow St (daily summer 7.30am–10pm; winter 7.30am–8pm; $1), and also connect to Vanier Park (see below). The walk down Granville St and across the bridge is deceptively long, and probably only worthwhile on a fine day. There's an infocentre on the

Island (☎666-5784); you should bear in mind that many of the island's stores and businesses **close** on Mondays.

Virtually the first building you see on the island augurs well: the **Granville Island Brewery**, a small outfit run by a German brewmaster, offers guided tours that include free tastings of its additive-free beers (tours June–Sept regularly 9am–5pm; Oct–May 2pm only; free). Dominant among the maze of shops, galleries and businesses, the **Granville Island Public Market** (Mon–Sat 9am–6pm) is the undisputed highlight of the area. On summer weekends it's where people go to see and be seen, thronged with numerous arts-and-crafts types, and a phalanx of dreadful but harmless buskers. The quality and variety of **food** is staggering, with dozens of kiosks and cafés selling ready-made titbits and potential picnic ingredients. Parks, patios and walkways nearby provide lively areas to sit and eat and soak up the atmosphere. Other spots to look out for include *Blackberry Books* (one of the city's best bookstores), the Water Park (a kids-only playground with hoses to repel intruders) and the *Bridges* pub/restaurant/wine bar, which has a nice outdoor drinking area. **Canoes** can be rented for safe and straightforward paddling in False Creek and English Bay from *Ecomarine Ocean Kayak*, 1688 Duranleau. You might also choose to **walk** from the island along the False Creek sea wall (east) or west to Vanier Park (see below) and Kits Beach.

Vanier Park museum complex

A little west of Granville Island, **Vanier Park** conveniently holds all but one of the city's main museums: the **Vancouver Museum**, the **Macmillan Planetarium** and the **Maritime Museum**. The complex sits on the waterfront at the west end of the Burrard Bridge, near Kitsilano Beach and the residential-entertainment centers of Kitsilano and West Fourth Ave, and Vanier Park itself is a fine spot to while away a summer afternoon. You could easily incorporate a visit to the museums with a trip to Granville Island using the **ferry** (see "City transit", p.235). Coming from downtown, take **bus** #22 from anywhere on Burrard or West Pender – get off at the first stop after the bridge and walk down Chester St to the park.

The Vancouver Museum

1100 Chestnut St. July & Aug daily 10am–5pm; Sept–June Tues–Sun 10am–5pm. $5.

Canada's largest civic museum, the **Vancouver Museum**, traces the history of the city and the lower British Columbian mainland, and invokes the area's past in its very form – the flying-saucer shape of the building being a nod to the conical cedar-bark hats of the Northwest Coast natives. The fountain outside, looking like a crab on a bidet, recalls the animal of native legend which guards the port entrance. Despite being the main focus of interest at Vanier Park, the museum is not as captivating as you'd expect from a city like Vancouver. It claims 300,000 exhibits, but it's hard to know where they all are, and a visit needn't take more than an hour or so. A patchy collection of baskets, tools, clothes and miscellaneous artefacts of native peoples – including a huge whaling canoe, the only museum example in existence – concentrates on the eight thousand years before the coming of white settlers. After that, the main collection, weaving in and out of Vancouver's history up to World War I, is full of offbeat and occasionally memorable insights – notably the accounts of early explorers' often extraordinary exploits, the immigration section (which re-creates what it felt like to travel steerage) and the forestry displays.

The Planetarium and Observatory

The **Macmillan Planetarium**, downstairs from the museum, ranks as one of North America's best (Tues–Sun up to 4 star shows daily; $5–6.50), though its rock and laser extravaganzas (most evenings at 8.30pm) are for fans of the genre only. Also on display – and accorded almost the status of a national shrine – is the favorite piano of cult classical pianist Glenn Gould. The **Gordon Southam Observatory**, next door, is open for public star-gazing on clear nights; astronomers are on hand to show you the ropes and help you position your camera for a "Shoot the Moon" photography session of the heavens (summer daily 7–11pm; winter Fri–Sun 7–11pm; free).

The Maritime Museum

The **Maritime Museum** (daily 10am–5pm; $5), a short walk from the Vancouver Museum, features lovely early photographs evoking turn-of-the-century Vancouver, though the rest of the presentation hardly does justice to the status of the city as one of the world's leading ports. The shabbier displays, however, are redeemed by the renovated *St Roch*, a two-masted schooner that was the first vessel to navigate the famed Northwest Passage in a single season; it now sits impressively in its own wing of the museum, where it can be viewed by guided tour only. Special summer shows spice things up a little, with such dubious activities as hornpipe dancing and shanty-song singalongs (Wed 5–9pm; free) and an annual mid-July open period. Outside the museum on **Heritage Harbour** you can clamber (free of charge) over more restored vessels.

The Museum of Anthropology

Tues 11am–9pm, Wed–Sun 11am–5pm. $5, free on Tues.

Located well out of downtown on the University of British Columbia campus, the **Museum of Anthropology** is far and away Vancouver's most important museum. Devoted largely to the art and culture of the natives of the Pacific Northwest, and those of BC in particular (notably the Haida), its collection of carvings, totem poles and artefacts is unequalled in North America (and ideally should be seen in conjunction with the more general historical native displays of Victoria's Royal British Columbia Museum; see p.267).

Bus #10 from Granville terminates close by: to find the museum, turn right from the bus stand, walk along the tree-lined East Mall to the very bottom (10min), then turn left on NW Marine Drive and walk until you see the museum on the right (another 5min). In the foyer you can pick up a free mini-guide or the larger booklet for $1 – worthwhile to supplement the poor labelling of the exhibits.

Much is made of the museum's award-winning layout, a cool and spacious collection of halls designed by Arthur Erikson; the huge **Great Hall**, inspired by native cedar houses, makes a perfect setting for its thirty-odd **totem poles**. Large windows look out on more poles and reconstructions of Haida houses (which you're free to wander around), against a backdrop of Burrard Inlet and the distant mountains. Most of the poles and monolithic carvings are taken from the coastal tribes of the Haida, Salish, Tsimshian and Kwakiutl, all of which share cultural elements. The suspicion – though it's never confessed – is that scholars really don't know terribly much of the arcane mythology behind the carvings, but the best guess as to their meaning is that the various animals correspond to different clans or the creatures after which the clans were named. To delve deeper into the complexities, it's worth joining an hour-long **guided walk**.

Most of the permanent collection revolves around **Canadian Pacific** cultures, but the **Inuit** and **Far North** exhibits are also outstanding. So, too, are the jewellery, masks and baskets of northern native peoples, all markedly delicate after the blunt-nosed carvings of the Great Hall. Look out especially for the argillite sculptures, made from a jet-black slate found only on BC's Queen Charlotte Islands. The **African** and **Asian** collections are also pretty comprehensive, if smaller, but appear as something of an afterthought alongside the indigenous artefacts.

The museum saves its best for last. Housed in a separate rotunda, **The Raven and the Beast**, a modern sculpture designed by Haida artist Bill Reid, is the museum's pride and joy and has achieved almost iconographic status in the city. Carved from a 4.5-ton block of cedar and requiring the skills of five people over three years, it describes the Haida legend of human evolution with stunning virtuosity, depicting terrified figures squirming from a half-open clam shell, overseen by an enormous and stern-faced raven. However, beautiful as the work is, its rotunda setting makes it seem oddly out of place – almost like a corporate piece of art.

Around the museum

Any number of odds and ends lie dotted around the vicinity of the museum, but they amount to little of real interest. For the exception, turn right out the front entrance and a five-minute walk leads to the **Nitobe Memorial Garden**, a small Japanese garden that might be good for a few minutes of peace and quiet (daily April–Sept 10am–6pm, Oct–March 10am–3pm; $2). Despite its use of many Pacific Northwest species, it's considered the world's most authentic Japanese garden outside Japan. Beyond is the university's **botanical garden**, whose only points of interest for non-gardeners are the macabre poisonous plants of the "Physick" Garden and the swathes of shrubs and huge trees in the Asian Garden. While you're out here, you might also take advantage of the **University Endowment Lands**, on the opposite, west side of the museum. A huge tract of wild parkland – as large as Stanley Park, but used by a fraction of the number of people – the endowment lands boast 48km of trails and abundant wildlife (blacktail deer, otters, foxes and bald eagles). There are few human touches – no benches or snack bars, and only the occasional signpost.

North Vancouver

Perhaps the most compelling reason to visit **North Vancouver** is the trip itself – preferably by *SeaBus* – which provides views not only of the downtown skyline but also the teeming port area, a side of the city that's otherwise easily missed. Most of North Van itself is residential, as is neighboring West Vancouver, whose cosseted citizens boast the highest per capita income in Canada. The other reason to cross to the north shore is to sample the outstanding areas of natural beauty here: **Lynn Canyon**, **Grouse Mountain**, **Capilano Gorge**, **Mount Seymour** and **Lighthouse Park**. All nestle in the mountains that rear up dramatically almost from the waterfront – the proximity of Vancouver's residential areas to genuine wilderness being one of the most remarkable aspects of the city.

Most of North Vancouver is within a single bus ride of **Lonsdale Quay**, the north shore's *SeaBus* terminal. **Buses** to all points leave from two parallel bays immediately in front of you as you leave the boat – blue *West Van* buses are run by an independent company but accept *BC Transit* tickets.

The **Lonsdale Quay Market**, to the right of the buses, is worth a journey whether or not you intend to explore further. While not as vibrant as Granville Island Market, it's still an appealing place, with great food stalls and takeaways, plus walkways looking out over the port, tugs and moored fishing boats.

Lynn Canyon Park

The easiest target for a quick taste of backwoods Vancouver is **Lynn Canyon Park**, a quiet, forested area with a modest ravine which, unlike the more popular Capilano Gorge (see below), you don't have to pay to cross. Several walks of up to ninety minutes take you through fine scenery – cliffs, rapids, waterfalls and an eighty-metre-high bridge over Lynn Creek – all just twenty minutes from Lonsdale Quay. Take **bus** #228 from the quay to its penultimate stop at Peters Street, from where it's a ten-minute walk to the gorge; alternatively, take the #239 to Phibbs Exchange and then the less frequent #229, which drops you about five minutes closer. Before entering the gorge, pop into the **Ecology Centre**, a friendly and informative place where you can pick up maps and pamphlets on park trails and wildlife (daily 10am–5pm).

Grouse Mountain

The trip to **Grouse Mountain** is a popular excursion, partly due to the Swiss-built **cable-car** that runs almost to its 1250-meter summit (daily 10am–9pm; $8.50). A favorite among people learning to **ski** after work, the mountain's brightly illuminated slopes are a North Vancouver landmark on winter evenings. The cable-car terminus has a couple of restaurants and allied tourist paraphernalia, but the views are stunning; another chairlift ($2) takes you the remaining 120m to the summit. Several **trails**, long and short, set off from the top of the cable-car and the summit. Arguably the best hike is to Grouse Lake (1hr); more rugged paths lead into the mountains of the West Coast Range.

Bus #232 (25min) from Lonsdale Quay and *West Van* #247 from Georgia St downtown go direct to the cable-car terminal.

Capilano River Park

Lying just off the approach road to Grouse Mountain, **Capilano River Park**'s most publicized attraction is a seventy-meter-high **suspension bridge** over the vertiginous Capilano Gorge. Though part of the park, the turn-of-the-century footbridge is run as a commercial venture – you can avoid the $5 pedestrian toll by sticking to the paths. More interesting is the **salmon hatchery** just upstream (daily 9am–5pm; free), a provincial outfit designed to help salmon spawn and thus combat declining stocks: it nurtures some two million fish a year. The building is well designed and the information plaques interesting, but it's a prime stop on city bus tours, so the place can often be packed.

Capilano is probably best visited on the way back from Grouse Mountain – from the cable-car station it's an easy downhill walk (1km) to the north end of the park, below the Cleveland Reservoir, source of Vancouver's disconcertingly brown drinking water, and from there marked trails follow the eastern side of the gorge to the hatchery (2km). The area below the hatchery is worth exploring, especially the Dog's Leg Pool (1km) along a swirling reach of the Capilano River, and if you really want to stretch your legs you could follow the river the full 7km to its mouth on the Burrard Inlet. Alternatively, you could ride **bus** #232 to the Cleveland Dam or the main park entrance – the hatchery is reached by a side road (or the Pipeline Trail) from the main entrance.

Mount Seymour Provincial Park

The largest and most easterly of North Vancouver parks, **Mount Seymour Provincial Park** comes closest to the flavor of high mountain scenery. **Bus** #239 from Lonsdale Quay to Phibbs Exchange and then the #215 will take you as far as the Mount Seymour Parkway (1hr) – from there you'll have to make your own way up the thirteen-kilometer road to the heart of the park. The road climbs to over 1000m and ends at a parking lot where boards spell out clearly the trails and mountaineering options available. There's also a café, toilets, a small infocentre (summer only) and a **chairlift** that takes you up to 1200m (July–Aug daily 9am–6pm, Sept–Oct Sat & Sun only 11am–5pm, weather allowing; $3). In winter this is the most popular family and learners' **ski area** near Vancouver.

Many **trails** here are manageable in a day, but be aware that conditions can change rapidly and snow lingers as late as June. One hike goes to the summit of Mount Seymour itself; other good hikes take you to Dog Mountain and Mystery Lake, both about three easy hours' round trip, or Goldie Lake, a half-hour stroll. Views are immense on good days, particularly from the **Vancouver Lookout** on the parkway approach road, where a map identifies the city landmarks below.

Lighthouse Park

Lighthouse Park offers a seascape wilderness at the extreme western tip of the north shore, 8km from the Lion's Gate Bridge. Smooth granite rocks and low cliffs line the shore, backed by huge Douglas firs up to 1500 years old, some of the best virgin forest in southern BC. The rocks make fine sunbeds, though the water out here is colder than around the city beaches. A map at the parking lot shows the two trails to the **lighthouse** itself – you can take one out and the other back, a round trip of about 5km which involves about two hours' walking. Although the park has its secluded corners, it can be disconcertingly busy during summer weekends. The *West Van* #250 **bus** makes the journey from Georgia Street in downtown.

Accommodation

Vancouver has a surprisingly large number of **inexpensive hotels**, but some – mainly in the area east of downtown – are of a dinginess at odds with the city's slick and efficient image. You're a bit better off in the lower price bracket in one of the faintly pleasanter hotels north of the Granville Street Bridge, a tame but central red-light area. **Mid-range hotels** are still reasonable ($65–90), but Vancouver is a tourist city and things can get tight in summer – book ahead for the more popular places. A lot of the nicer options are in the West End, a quiet residential area bordering Stanley Park, five or ten minutes' walk from downtown. Out of season, hotels in all categories drop their prices, and you can reckon on thirty-percent discounts on the prices given below. Remember, too, that the prices below are for doubles: even the smartest hotels will introduce an extra bed into a double room at very little extra cost if there are three of you. **Bed-and-breakfast** accommodation can be booked through agencies, but most of them operate as a phone service only and require two days' notice – in the first resort, use the Infocentre's accommodation service. Though seldom central, B&Bs are likely to be relaxed and friendly, and if you choose well you can have beaches, gardens, barbecues and as little or as much privacy as you want.

In addition to the **hostels**, budget accommodation is available in summer at the **University of British Columbia**, though this is a long way from downtown, and most rooms go to convention visitors – inquire at the Walter Gage Residence in the Student Union Mall (☎822-1010). Vancouver is not a camper's city – the majority of the in-city **campgrounds** are for RVs only and will turn you away if you've only got a tent. We've listed the few places that won't.

Hotels

Austin Motor Inn, 1221 Granville (☎685-7235). Cheap and reasonably cheerful, given the tacky locale. ③.

Barclay Hotel, 1348 Robson and Jervis (☎688-8850). Converted to evoke a chintzy French ambience, and rated one of the city's bargains. ④.

Buchan Hotel, 1906 Haro, near Robson and Denman (☎685-5354). Rooms are small and past their best, but still a genuine bargain given the peaceful downtown location near Stanley Park and English Bay Beach. ④.

Burrard Motor Inn, 1100 Burrard near Helmcken (☎663-0366). A central motel with standard fittings; all rooms look onto a pleasant garden courtyard, and some have kitchens. ④.

Cecil Hotel, 1336 Granville near Burrard Bridge (☎683-8505). The best of the dowdy cluster of hotels at the bottom of Granville St, most of which have tatty bars promising "exotic dancers"; noisy but convenient. ②.

Days Inn Vancouver Downtown, 921 W Pender and Burrard (☎681-4335). Something of a city institution, this old seven-story block in the middle of the financial district has more character than most and lots of original Art Deco touches. ⑤.

Dominion Hotel, 210 Abbott and Water (☎681-6666). A nice, newly decorated old building on the edge of Gastown – ask for one of the new rooms with private bathrooms, preferably well away from the thundering live music. ④.

Holiday Inn Downtown, 1110 Howe St (☎684-2151). Central and large (209 rooms), so a chance of space, and – unlike the dingier hotels – you'll know what to expect. ⑥.

Hotel California, 1176 Granville St (☎688-870). It looks like a no-hoper from the outside, but the rooms have been recently refurbished to block out the rock'n'roll from below. ②.

Kingston Hotel, 757 Richards and Robson (☎684-9024). A well-known bargain two blocks from the bus terminal, its clean and well-decorated interior affecting the spirit of a "European-style" hotel. With the *Sylvia*, the best at its price in the city. Book ahead. Long-stay terms available. ②.

ACCOMMODATION PRICE CODES

All accommodation prices in this book have been coded using the symbols below, corresponding to Canadian dollar rates in the Canadian chapters and equivalent US dollar prices in the US chapters. Prices are for the least expensive double rooms in each establishment, and only include local taxes where we explicitly say so.

For a full explanation see p.46 in *Basics*.

①	up to Can$40	④	Can$80–100	⑦	Can$175–240
②	Can$40–60	⑤	Can$100–125	⑧	Can$240+
③	Can$60–80	⑥	Can$125–175		

BED AND BREAKFAST AGENCIES

A Home Away from Home, ☎873-4888.
Best Canadian, ☎738-7207.
Born Free, ☎298-8815.

Canada West Accommodations, ☎929-1424.
Town and Country, ☎731-5942.

Nelson Place Hotel, 1006 Granville (☎681-6341). Small but reasonably comfortable rooms, though the live music and strippers downstairs aren't especially appealing. ②.

Niagara Hotel, 435 W Pender (☎688-7574). A couple of blocks from the bus station and identifiable by its extraordinary neon waterfall, this is a grim-fronted hotel with small rooms (some with private baths) and very low prices. ②.

Patricia Hotel, 403 E Hastings (☎255-4301). Big, well-known and widely advertised budget choice, but away from downtown in the heart of Chinatown. Clean and newly renovated, it's the best of the many in this area. ②.

Sandman Inn, 180 W Georgia and Homer (☎681-2211). Flagship of a chain with hotels all over western Canada; rooms are only adequate for the price, but it's a big place with good chance of space, and ideally placed next to the bus terminal. ④.

Shatto Inn at Stanley Park, 1825 Comox St (☎681-8920). A small, quiet, family-run place two blocks from the park and beach; some rooms have balconies and/or kitchen units. ③.

Sunset Inn Apartment Hotel, 1111 Burnaby between Davie and Thurlow (☎684-8763). One of the best West End "apartment" hotels and a good spot for a longer stay – spacious rooms (all with kitchens and balconies), laundromat, nearby stores. Ten minutes' walk to downtown. ③.

Sylvia Hotel, 1154 Gilford St (☎681-9321). A local landmark located in a "heritage" building, this is a popular place with a high word-of-mouth reputation – reservations recommended. Two blocks from Stanley Park, it has a snug bar, quiet old-world charm and sea views. ④.

West End Guest House, 1362 Haro near Jervis (☎681-2889). A wonderful small guesthouse (full breakfast included) with an old-time parlor and bright rooms, each with private bathroom; book well in advance. No smoking. ④–⑦.

Hostels

Globetrotter's Inn, 170 W Esplanade, North Vancouver (☎988-5141). Less convenient than the central hostels, though still only two blocks from Lonsdale Quay and the *SeaBus* terminal. Laid-back and a little battered. Dorm $15; single $30; double $40. ①–②.

Vancouver International Hostel (CHA), 1515 Discovery St (☎224-3208). Canada's biggest youth hostel (350 beds) has a superb position by Jericho Beach south of the city – take bus #4 from Granville St to the Jericho Park stop on Fourth Ave. It fills up quickly, occasionally leading to a three-day limit in summer; open all day, with an excellent cafeteria, but the 2am curfew and lights-out are rigidly enforced. Dorm only: $13 members, $18.50 non-members. Free bunks occasionally offered in return for a couple of hours' work. ①.

Vincent's Backpacker's Hostel, 927 Main St (☎682-2441). Friendly and well-known backpacker retreat, with colorful charm and no curfew, but not as clean or well organized as the youth hostel (below). Convenient for bus, train and *SkyTrain* stations. 150 rooms (none with private bath) but you should still book or arrive early (office open 8am–midnight). Dorm $10; single $20; double $25. ①.

YMCA, 955 Burrard St, between Smithe and Nelson (☎681-0221). Less exalted than the *YWCA*, but newly renovated and central. Singles $40; doubles $50. Shared bathrooms, cafeteria, pool and sports facilities; long-term rates available in winter. ②.

YWCA, 580 Burrard and Dunsmuir (☎662-8188 or 1-800/663-1424). A hotel in all but name, with the best value at this price and central location; sports and cooking facilities, cheap cafeteria. Men allowed only with women partners or family. Singles from $45; doubles from $62; triples $63; long-term rates available in winter. ③–④.

Camping

Burnaby Cariboo RV Park, 8765 Cariboo Place, Burnaby (☎420-1722). Has an excellent reputation for its luxurious facilities (indoor pool, jacuzzi, laundromat, free showers). Take Cariboo exit from Hwy 1. Shuttle bus to various sights. $25.

Capilano Mobile Park, 295 Tomahawk, West Vancouver (☎987-4722). The most central site for trailers and tents, beneath the north foot of the Lion's Gate Bridge. Reservations (with deposit) essential June–Aug. $20.

Mount Seymour Provincial Park, North Vancouver (☎986-2261). Lovely spot, but only a few tent sites alongside parking lots #2 and #3. Full facilities July–Sept only. $12.

Richmond RV Park, Hollybridge and River Rd, Richmond (☎270-7878). The best of the year-round outfits, with the usual facilities; take Hwy 99 to the Westminster Highway and follow signs. Open mid-April to mid-Oct. $16–18.

Eating and drinking

Vancouver's ethnic restaurants are some of Canada and the Northwest's finest, and span the price spectrum from budget to blowout. **Chinese** and **Japanese** cuisines have the highest profile (though the latter tend to be expensive), followed by **Italian**, **Greek** and other European imports; **Vietnamese**, **Cambodian**, **Thai** and **Korean** are recent arrivals on the scene (and often provide the best starting points if you're on a tight budget).

Specialist **seafood** restaurants are surprisingly thin on the ground, although those that do exist are of high quality and often remarkably inexpensive. Salmon is ubiquitous in all its forms and at all kinds of restaurants. **Vegetarians** are well served by a number of places, though there is a trend towards the trendy, over-priced and often forgettable restaurants serving so-called Californian ("New American") cuisine. A few West Coast places, however, provide notable exceptions to the rule.

Restaurants are spread around the city, but are thinner on the ground in North and West Vancouver; places in Gastown are generally quite expensive, in marked contrast to Chinatown's bewildering plethora of reasonably priced options. Downtown also offers plenty of chains and choice (the *White Spot* chain is superb if time and money are tight), as do Kitsilano (W Fourth Ave) and neighboring West Broadway.

Cafés, found mainly around the beaches, in parks, along downtown streets, and especially on Granville Island, are at their best in summer. **Little Italy**, the area around Commercial Drive (between Venables and Broadway), is the city's latest hip spot for cheap, cheerful or downright trendy cafés and restaurants (though Little Italy is increasingly becoming "Little Vietnam" and "Little Nicaragua").

The **West End**, around Denman and Davie streets – Vancouver's "gay village" – is also booming, having lost its seedy reputation and gained a wedge of oddball shops and restaurants. The city also has a commendable assortment of **bars**, many a good cut above the functional dives and sham pubs found elsewhere in BC. There is often little distinction between bar, café, restaurant and nightclub: food in some form – usually substantial – is available in most places, while daytime cafés and restaurants also operate happily as night-time bars. In this section we've highlighted places whose main emphasis is food and drink; entertainment venues are listed in the next section.

Cafés and snacks

Alma Street Café, 2505 Alma and Broadway. Cheap and very popular (weekend breakfast queues). Menu changes daily, with emphasis on salads, fish and pasta. Open until 11pm; live jazz on Fri & Sat evenings.

Benny's Bagel and Pretzel Works, 2503 W Broadway & Larch. 24-hour snacks in highly popular laid-back spot.

Bread Garden, 1880 W First at Cypress. Kits' locals love to moan about the slow service, but food in this hyper-trendy deli-café is some of the best – and best-looking – in the city. A great people-watching spot – and it's open 24hr.

Café Calabria, 1745 Commercial Drive. About as close as you can get in Vancouver to a genuine Italian bar.

Café Luxy, 1235 Davie St. Pleasant, easy-going atmosphere. Open until 4am at weekends.

Café S'Il Vous Plait, 500 Robson and Richards. Young, casual and vaguely alternative with good sandwiches, basic home-cooking and local art displays. Open until 10pm.

City Picnics Café, 475 W Hastings. Basic breakfasts at $2.99.

Did's Place, 823 Granville. Popular post-drinking hang-out. Good pizza, loud music. Open until 3am.

Doll and Penny's, 1167 Davie. Fun place with big servings, largely gay clientele (but all welcome); daily drinks specials. Open very late.

Elbow Room, 720 Jervis and Alberni. By general consent, the best basic breakfasts (and pancakes) in the city. Packed at weekends. Daytime only, breakfasts until mid-afternoon.

Gallery Café, Vancouver Art Gallery, 750 Hornby. Relaxed, stylish and pleasantly arty place for coffee, good lunches and healthy, high-quality food (especially desserts). Popular summer patio; no admission to museum required.

Grove Inn, 1047 Denman. Very inexpensive and almost caricatured basic café.

Hamburger Mary's, 1202 Davie. Best burgers in the city. Open all night.

Isadora's, 1540 Old Bridge, Granville Island. Good breakfasts, weekend brunches (frequent queues) and light, creative meals with good veg/wholefood options. Lots of outdoor seating. Open until 10pm.

Joe's Café, 1150 Commercial Drive and William. Lively hang-out, popular with students, artists and local bohos. Open until midnight.

Marine View Coffee Shop, 611 Alexander St at Princess. Moved from its old waterfront site, but still renowned for its seafood: the crab sandwich is the world's best. Arrive early to avoid a wait. Closes at 4pm.

The Only Café, 20 E Hastings and Carrall. People in Vancouver cite this institution, founded in 1912, when they want to prove the city has character. Seafood (the best in town) and potatoes are the only menu items at this budget edge-of-Chinatown café; counter seating, no toilets, no credit cards, no licence, and no messing with the tough service. Closed Sun.

Starbucks, 1100 Robson and Thurlow, 748 Thurlow near Robson, 811 Hornby near Robson, 102-700 W Pender at Granville, and at the *SeaBus* terminal. Hip and sleek espresso bars with downtown's best cups of coffee.

Taf's Café, 829 Granville. Popular alternative spot that attracts punks-and-their-dogs clientele; decent food, juke-box and displays of local art. Open until the small hours.

Chinese restaurants

Grand Garden, 608 Main and Keefer (☎681-4721). Best for lunchtime or late-night noodles – a quick, filling meal for $4. Try the barbecue pork, duck, wonton or fishball noodles in soup.

The Green Door, 111 E Pender and Columbia (☎685-4194). Average Cantonese food, but a legendary city institution whose perfect and seedy atmosphere is redolent of Chinatown in the 1940s. Open Oct–May; unlicensed.

Hon's Wun Tun House, 108-268 Keefer at Gore (☎688-0871). Cheap, basic and popular for the house speciality, "potstickers" – fried meat-filled dumplings.

Kirin Mandarin, 1166 Alberni near Bute (☎682-8833). First of the city's smart Chinese arrivals, co-owned by *Kirin Seafood House*.

Kirin Seafood House, 201-555 W 12th at Cambie (☎879-8083). Almost elegant, but more reasonable than many new-style Chinese places: good, exotic *dim sum* and noodle dishes, and great views of the mountains.

Landmark Hotpot House, 3338 Cambie at 17th (☎873-3338). First Vancouver outlet for a snazzy Hong Kong-based chain; choose from over 70 different noodle dishes.

Ming's, 147 E Pender and Main (☎683-4722). Huge, fancy place which has been the most popular *dim sum* spot for years. Lines start at 11am at weekends; leave your name with host at the top of the stairs and wait for number to be called.

On On Tea Garden, 214 Keefer. A fairly ordinary place with inexpensive, basic food, but for years this was Chinatown's most famous restaurant – it was here that Pierre Trudeau conducted much of his secret courtship of Margaret.

Pink Pearl, 1132 East Hastings near Glen. Big (650 seats), bustling and old-fashioned, highly authentic feel – but in a dingy part of town.

Yang's, 4186 Main and 26th (☎873-2116). A friendly, family-run Mandarin place, this is probably Vancouver's best Chinese (and pricier than most); great Peking duck, some very fiery dishes, plus a noted noodle lunch on Saturdays. Follow the advice of staff when ordering. Dinner daily except Wed; lunch Sat & Sun only.

Italian restaurants

Arriva, 1537 Commercial Drive near Grant (☎251-1177). Classic Italian deli-restaurant with authentic dishes; great *antipasti*.

Barino, 1116 Mainland at Helmcken (☎687-1116). Located in the newly fashionable Yaletown warehouse district, *Barino* is correspondingly trendy, but the northern Italian food is a winner. Prices can be steep.

Fettucini's, 1179 Commercial Drive. Good selection of pasta, fish and chicken dishes.

Gallo D'Oro, 1800 Renfrew and Second Ave. Massive portions of home-cooking. Closed Sun.

Nick's Spaghetti House, 631 Commercial Drive. New management after 30 years in the same family, but still sound food and fun atmosphere. In the heart of Vancouver's small Italian district – take bus #20 from downtown.

The Old Spaghetti Factory, 55 Water St. Part of a popular nationwide chain and better than it appears from outside, with a spacious 1920s Tiffany interior.

Orlando's Fresh Pasta Bar, 220 Abbott. Budget pasta dishes.

Piccolo Mondo, 850 Thurlow and Smithe (☎688-1633). Pricey and excellent food (accompanied by the best selection of Italian wines in the city). The clientele consists of business people at lunch and smoochy couples in the evenings; don't be put off by the grim exterior.

Greek restaurants

Orestes, 3116 W Broadway. Good, basic Greek food.

Simpatico, 2222 W Fourth Ave (☎733-6824). Greek–Italian place decorated with Chianti bottles and portraits of Greek army heroes – but a Fourth Ave fixture since 1969 with some of the city's best pizzas.

Souvlaki Place, 1807 Morton near Denman. A few tables with a lovely view of English Bay. Take-out service available: buy your *falafel* or *souvlaki*, cross to the beach and watch the sun go down. Handy for Stanley Park.

Vassilis, 2884 W Broadway near Macdonald (☎733-3231). Family-run outfit with a high reputation; serves a mean roast chicken. Closed weekend lunchtimes.

West Coast restaurants

Bishop's, 2183 W Fourth near Yew (☎738-2025). All-white decor (plus big splashy paintings) suited to a place that serves refined "contemporary home-cooking" – Italy meets the Pacific Rim and the West Coast. Superb food, with prices to match. Popular; bookings essential.

Chenya, 375 Water near Richards (☎688-4800). Gastown location; formal dining at the rear, more laid-back bistro at the front. Meticulous and innovative fusion of Old and New World food that justifies the claim to be "at the cutting edge of gastronomy": especially lively at lunch.

Raintree, 1630 Alberni near Cardero (☎688-5570). Not necessarily the most exalted food, but probably the first choice if you want an idea of what's going down in the world of "local" West Coast cooking.

Raku, 4422 W Tenth near Trimble (☎222-8188). Tiny, exquisite portions and austere setting, but the crazily eclectic cuisine (Middle East, California, Asia and Caribbean) is immensely popular.

Other ethnic restaurants

Chiyoda, 1050 Alberni at Burrard (☎688-5050). Everything here down to the beer glasses was designed in Japan. The emphasis is on grilled food rather than sushi, and the atmosphere is very chic but convivial.

Dar Lebanon, 678 W Broadway and Heather, 1961 W Fourth and Maple, and 2807 W Broadway and Macdonald. Reasonably priced Lebanese food.

El Mariachi, 735 Denman near Robson (☎683-4982). The city's best Mexican: particularly strong on seafood. Try the chicken with the 28-ingredient *mole* sauce. Dinner only; book at weekends.

Kamei-Sushi, 813 Thurlow and Robson (☎684-4823). Superlative sushi, but at stratospheric prices. Closed weekends.

Momiji, 3550 Fraser near 19th Ave (☎872-2027). Slow service, over-bright lighting, but excellent Japanese food at very low prices. Closed Mon.

Phnom-Penh, 244 East Georgia near Gore (☎682-5777). Excellent seafood and good general introduction to Vietnamese cuisine in a friendly, family-biased restaurant.

Pho Hoang, 3610 Main at 20th (☎874-0810). The first and perhaps friendliest of the many Vietnamese *pho* (beef soup) restaurants that have sprung up all over the city. Choose from 30 varieties of soup; herbs, chillies and lime at plate-side offer added seasoning. No alcohol.

Quilicum, 1724 Davie near Denman (☎681-7044). The city's only restaurant offering genuine Native American cuisine – seaweed, roast caribou, alder-barbecued oysters, barbecued juniper duck with wild rice. Quite expensive. Dinner only.

The Sitar, 564 W Broadway. Inexpensive, reliable Indian.

A Taste of Jamaica, 941 Davie St. Authentic Jamaican food, with reggae accompaniment and red-gold-green decor. Closed Sun lunchtime.

Tojo's, 777 West Broadway at Willow (☎872-8050). Simply the best Japanese food in Vancouver.

Topanga Café, 2904 W Fourth Ave near Macdonald (☎733-3713). A small but extremely popular Mexican restaurant and Vancouver institution.

Vegetarian restaurants

Buddhist Vegetarian, 363 E Hastings. The city's only Chinese vegetarian restaurant.

Circling Dawn Organic Foods, 1045 Commercial Drive (☎255-2326). Full of health and New Age people; sound food and handy noticeboard advertising events, rides, healing and the like.

Concept 2, 724 Nelson St. Organically grown ingredients and West Coast cooking; relaxed atmosphere with live jazz.

The Naam, 2724 W Fourth Ave near Stephens. Hippy hangover, but still the oldest, best and most popular health-food and vegetarian restaurant in the city. Folk music some evenings, outside eating in summer. Open 24hr.

Ruffage, 1280 W Pender. Healthy food; no smoking.

Sweet Cherubim, 3629 W Broadway, 4242 Main St and 1105 Commercial Drive. Good organic and vegetarian restaurants/shops.

Pubs and bars

The Arts Club, 1585 Johnston on Granville Island, and 1181 Seymour and Davie. Both are quietish bars; the former's *Backstage Lounge*, which is part of the theater complex, has a waterfront view and puts on blues and jazz after Wed, Fri & Sat shows.

Bimini's, 2010 W Fourth Ave and Maple. Nice, relaxed pub with occasional live music – Kits Beach's favorite for a drink.

Blarney Stone, 216 Carrall. Gastown location for a lively Irish pub with a genuine feel. Restaurant, live Irish music and dance floor. Closed Sun.

Darby D Dawes, 2001 Macdonald St and Fourth Ave. A pub handy for Kits Beach and the youth hostel, occasionally playing host to the area's more affluent locals. Meals served 11.30am–7pm, snacks until 10pm; live music Fri and Sat evenings, jam sessions on Sat afternoons.

English Bay Café, 1795 Beach and Denman. Good for sunset views of English Bay – the downstairs bistro, not the expensive restaurant upstairs.

La Bodega, 1277 Howe near Davie. One of the city's best and most popular places, with tapas and excellent main courses, but more dedicated to lively drinking. It's packed later on, so try to arrive before 8pm. Closed Sun.

Rose and Thorne, 757 Richards near Georgia. Popular, comfortable and very close to the look and feel of an English pub.

Sylvia Hotel, 1154 Gilford and Beach. Nondescript but easy-going hotel bar, popular for quiet drinks and superlative waterfront views.

Unicorn Pub, 770 Pacific Blvd and Robson. Live music (often of the sing-along variety), British pub food and many different beers, plus a large, popular summer patio.

Nightlife and entertainment

Vancouver gives you plenty to do come sundown, laying on a varied and cosmo-politan blend of **live music** and comedy. Clubs are more adventurous than in many a Northwestern city – with the possible exception of Seattle – particularly the fly-by-night alternative dives in the Italian quarter on Commercial Drive and in the backstreets of Gastown and Chinatown. There's also a choice of smarter and more conventional clubs, a handful of discos and a smattering of **gay** and **lesbian** clubs and bars. Summer nightlife often takes to the streets in West Coast fashion, with outdoor bars and to a certain extent beaches, becoming venues in their own right. Fine weather also allows the city to host a range of **festivals**, from jazz to drama, and the **performing arts** are as widely available as you'd expect in a city as culturally self-conscious as Vancouver.

The most comprehensive **listings** guide to all the goings-on is *Georgia Straight*, a free weekly published on Fridays; the monthly *Night Moves* concen-trates more on live music. For detailed information on **gay and lesbian** events, check out *Angles*, a free monthly magazine available at clubs, bookstores and most of the *Georgia Straight* distribution points. **Tickets** for many major events are sold through *Ticket-Master*, based at 1304 Hornby St and with forty outlets round the city (☎280-4444); they'll sometimes unload discounted tickets for midweek and matinee performances.

Live music, discos and clubs

Vancouver's live-music venues showcase a variety of local bands. Mainstream **rock** groups which have made it from the city – and still play to home fans –

include No Means No, Roots Roundup and Bob's Your Uncle; others hoping to follow them to fame and fortune are Strange But True, Second Nature, Green House, Audio Graffiti, Melancholy Dream and Free-Water Knockout – none of them likely to make it on the strength of their names. (For some reason the city is a fertile breeding ground for **heavy metal** bands, and the fans here are particularly vocal.)

Jazz is currently hot news in Vancouver, with a dozen spots specializing in the genre (ring the Jazz Hot Line at ☎682-0706 for current and upcoming events). And while Vancouver isn't as cowpoke as, say, Calgary, it does have several clubs dedicated to **country**, though most are in the outer suburbs.

Many venues also double as clubs and discos, and as in any city with a healthy alternative scene there are also plenty of fun, one-off clubs that have an irritating habit of cropping up and disappearing at speed. Cover charges are usually nominal, and tickets are often available (sometimes free) at record stores. At the other end of the spectrum, the 60,000-seat *Pacific Coliseum* is on the touring itinerary of most international acts.

Rock venues

Big Bam Boo, 1236 West Broadway near Oak. Piano bar and sushi upstairs; dancing downstairs to Top 40 stuff. Strict dress code and queues Thurs–Sat.

Big Easy, 1055 Homer at Nelson. Large place known for top local bands, smaller touring bands and AOR music at other times.

Commodore Ballroom, 870 Granville and Smithe. Recently given a facelift – but retaining its renowned 1929 sprung dance floor – the city's best midsized venue (room for 1200) has an adventurous music policy, regularly attracting top national and international names. Club nights feature a new DJ every 2–3 weeks.

Cruel Elephant, 23 West Cordova near Carrall. One of the wilder clubs; up-and-coming bands, grunge and indie-type combos.

86 Street Music Hall, 750 Pacific Blvd and Cambie. High-tech place; local Top 40 bands and big-name international gigs. Wed–Sun.

Metro, 1136 W Georgia and Thurlow. Vast, raucous and busy club that hosts local and touring bands. Dubious cabaret features events like "Mr Nude Rock 'n' Roll" – a hen-night favorite. Closed Sun.

Railway Club, 579 Dunsmuir and Seymour. Long-established favorite with a reputation for excellent bookings and casual atmosphere. Has a separate "conversation" lounge, so it's ideal for a drink (and weekday lunches); watch for the Sat jazz sessions (3–7pm). Arrive before 10pm at weekends – the place is tiny – and be prepared for the $10 private club membership fee.

Roxy, 932 Granville and Nelson. Nightly live bands with emphasis on retro 1950s, 1960s and 1970s music. Casual, fun angle with weekly theme parties, old films, comedy turns and a Wednesday "Student Night".

Town Pump, 66 Water and Abbott. Vancouver's best-known music venue, offering a wide range of solid and reliable bands nightly. Convenient mid-Gastown location attracts a varied clientele – it's known as something of a pick-up spot. Bar food and piano lounge until 9pm, when the band strikes up.

Waterfront, 686 Powell. Indie, alternative, rock and jazz bands nightly.

Jazz and blues

Alma Street Café, 2505 Alma St at W Tenth Ave. Wed–Sat sessions feature some of the city's best modern jazz, including top names from the States.

Arts Club Theatre Backstage Lounge, 1585 Johnston, Granville Island. The lounge is a nice spot to hear R&B, jazz and blues, or watch the boats and sunset on False Creek.

Carnegie's, 1619 W Broadway near Fir. Popular bar and grill with top local and imported jazz bands in an upmarket and fake British pub atmosphere. Closed Sun.

Classical Joint Coffee House, 231 Carrall near Water. Intimate and low-key, the city's oldest coffee house is something of a staid home to the local jazz scene, though it also hosts folk and classical events. No alcohol – only chess games as a diversion.

Eldorado, at *Mulhern's Pub*, 2330 Kingsway. Big dance floor, local bands playing R&B, blues and early rock.

Fairview, 898 W Broadway. Local blues and 1950s rock 'n' roll in a pub atmosphere (snacks during the day, good-value evening meals).

Glass Slipper, 185 E 11th Ave at Main. Home of the Coastal Jazz and Blues Society, and so a more lively headquarters for the city's jazz culture than the *Classical*. Lots of contemporary and improvised sessions, often from the house band, the New Orchestra Workshop. Fri, Sat & Sun only.

Hogan's Alley (in *Puccini's Restaurant*), 730 Main St near E Georgia. Local jazz, and blues and R&B in an intimate spot near Chinatown; good Italian food, too. Music Thurs, Fri & Sat.

Hot Jazz Society, 2120 Main St and Fifth. Oldest and most established jazz club in the city. Mainly trad – swing, Dixieland and New Orleans, both local and imported. Good dance floor and big bar. Wednesday is jam night; closed Sun & Mon.

Jake O'Grady's, 3684 E Hastings. Live blues nightly.

Lamplighters Pub, 210 Abbott St. Blues every night.

Landmark Jazz Bar, *Sheraton-Landmark Hotel*, 1400 Robson and Nicola. Large club whose jazz emphasis is shifting slightly to R&B; atmosphere is Bavarian beer-cellar (good, solid food). Live music and dancing Wed–Sat.

Yale Hotel, 1300 Granville and Drake. Seedy neighborhood, but an outstanding venue dedicated exclusively to hard-core blues and R&B. Relaxed air, big dance floor and outstanding local and international names. Noted jam sessions with up to 50 players at a time on Sat (3–8pm) and Sun (3pm–midnight). Closed Mon & Tues.

Country

Boone County Cabaret, 801 Brunette Ave, Coquitlam. Just off the Trans-Canada – take bus #151 – this is suburbia's favorite country music club. No cover Mon–Thurs, and free dance lessons on Mon, Tues & Thurs at 8pm. Closed Sun.

Cheyenne Social Club, Lynnwood Hotel, 1515 Barrow St, North Vancouver. Local country bands Thurs, Fri & Sat.

JR Country Club, Sandman Inn, 180 W Georgia near Cambie. Downtown's main country venue highlights top Canadian bands in fake Old West setting; no cover Mon–Thurs. Closed Sun.

Discos and clubs

Amnesia, 99 Powell St at Columbia. Big, multi-level Gastown disco playing Top 40 music, crammed with bars, video screens and impressive lighting. Closed Tues & Sun.

Graceland, 1250 Richards between Davie and Drake. Bizarre spot for art and fashion crowd. Very loud current dance music, occasional live shows and local avant-garde art on the walls. Closed Sun.

Luv-A-Fair, 1275 Seymour and Davie. Madcap eclectic crowd ranging from punks to drag queens. Boasts excellent dance floor and sound system, plenty of imported videos and Euro-disco, and occasional theme nights and live bands. Closed Sun.

Richard's on Richards, 1036 Richards and Nelson. Probably the city's best-known club/disco, but pretentious and aimed at a chic audience. Long waits and dress code. Thurs–Sat.

Shampers, Coast Plaza at Stanley Park, 1733 Comox St and Denman. The West End's most popular dance floor; also open for lunch, with piano bar music until 9pm.

Sneaky's, 595 Hornby and Dunsmuir. Long-established fifth-story hideaway for late-twenties and thirties age-group.

Soft Rock Café, W Fourth Ave and Cypress. Well-heeled, mainstream dancing, live music and full meals. Popular, with frequent queues. Closed Mon.

Systems, 350 Richards and Hastings. Dedicated dancers, glitzy set-up, big sound and light systems; chart sounds and AOR. Closed Sun.

Waterhouse Cabaret, 871 Beatty St. Mostly black dance music and funkier than many a Vancouver club.

Comedy clubs

Punchlines Comedy Theatre, 15 Water and Carrall. Gastown breeding ground of new talent. "Amateur Night" on Mon, "Comedy Jams" Tues–Thurs. Shows at 9.30pm & 11.30pm; closed Sun.

Yuk Yuk's Komedy Kabaret, Plaza of Nations, 750 Pacific Blvd and Cambie. Hosts top US and Canadian stand-up acts; amateur night on Wed. Shows Wed–Fri at 9pm, plus 11.30pm on Sat & Sun. Closed Mon & Tues.

Gay clubs and venues

Castle Pub, 750 Granville. Quiet gay pub. Closed Sun.

Celebrities Night Club, 1022 Davie and Burrard. Big disco for mixed crowd, but predominantly gay.

Denman Station, 860 Denman off Robson. In an area increasingly becoming a gay "village"; friendly basement bar with game shows, karaoke, darts and the like.

Gandydancer, 1222 Hamilton and Davie. Trendiest and most innovative of the gay clubs. Tues & Wed are contest and cabaret nights; Fri men only.

Heritage House Hotel, 455 Abbott and Pender. Main-floor lounge upstairs and bar downstairs, the latter known as a lesbian bar (Tues–Sat; women only Wed & Fri).

Ms T's Cabaret, 339 West Pender near Richards. Mixed crowd; some live music; Mon–Sat.

Numbers Cabaret, 1042 Davie and Burrard. Good, cruisy disco, movies and pool tables upstairs; mixed downstairs, but very few women. Nightly.

Odyssey, 1251 Howe near Davie. Young and smart. Live music Tues and Wed, disco the rest of the week. Men only on Fri.

Royal, *Royal Hotel*, 1025 Granville at Nelson. The city's oldest gay bar. Extremely crowded, but friendly; live entertainment nightly; few women.

Shaggy Horse, 818 Richards and Robson. Gay club patronized by an older crowd.

Performing arts and cinema

Vancouver serves up enough highbrow culture to please the whole spectrum of its cosmopolitan population, with plenty of unusual and avant-garde performances to spice up the more mainstream presentations you'd expect of a major North American city.

The focus of the city's performing arts is the **Queen Elizabeth Theatre** (☎873-3311 or 665-3050), near the bus station at 649 Cambie and Dunsmuir, which plays host to a steady procession of visiting theater, opera and dance troupes, and even the occasional big rock band. For information on the Vancouver arts scene call the Arts Hotline (☎684-ARTS) or visit their office in the Granville entrance of the **Orpheum Theatre**, Smithe at Seymour (☎665-3050), headquarters of the Vancouver Symphony Orchestra. There's a special line for information relating to dance (☎872-0432).

The western capital of Canada's film industry, Vancouver is increasingly favored by Hollywood studios in their pursuit of less expensive locations and production deals, which may account for the range of **cinemas**. Home-produced and

Hollywood first-run films play in the downtown movie theaters on "Theatre Row" – the two blocks of Granville between Robson and Nelson – and other big complexes, and there's no shortage of arthouse venues for more esoteric productions.

Classical music

Early Music Vancouver (☎732-1610). Early music with original instruments where possible. Concerts all over the city, but especially at the UBC campus during an Early Music Festival held July & Aug.

Festival Concert Society (☎736-3737). Organizes low-priced Sunday morning concerts (jazz, folk or classical) at the *Queen Elizabeth Theatre*.

Vancouver Bach Choir (☎921-8012). The city's top non-professional choir performs three major concerts yearly at the *Orpheum Theatre*.

Vancouver Chamber Choir (☎738-6822). One of only two professional choirs in Canada. Internationally renowned, the choir performs at the *Orpheum* and on some Sun afternoons at the *Hotel Vancouver* ballroom.

Vancouver New Music Society (☎874-6200). Responsible for seven annual concerts of twentieth-century music, usually at the *East Cultural Centre*.

Vancouver Recital Society (☎736-6034). Hosts two of the best and most popular seasons in the city: the summer Chamber Music Festival (at St George's School) and the main *Vancouver Playhouse* recitals (Sept–April).

Vancouver Symphony Orchestra (☎684-9100). Presents most concerts at the *Orpheum*, but also gives free recitals in the summer at beaches and parks, culminating in a concert on the summit of Whistler Mountain.

Drama

Arts Club Theatre (☎687-1644). A leading light in the city's drama scene, performing at three venues: the main stage, at 1585 Johnston St on Granville Island, offers mainstream drama, comedies and musicals; the next-door bar presents small-scale revues and cabarets; and a third stage, at 1181 Seymour and Davie, focuses on avant-garde plays and Canadian dramatists – a launching pad for the likes of Michael J Fox.

Back Alley Theatre, 751 Thurlow near Robson (☎688-7013). In addition to its quality shows (mainly comedies), this intimate venue has achieved a cult status for its "theatresports", a quirky set-up in which teams of actors compete for applause. Improvisation and audience participation are the order of the day.

Firehall Arts Centre, 280 E Cordova and Gore (☎689-0926). Stationed in the alternative and multi-ethnic heart of the city, this is at the forefront of Vancouver's community and avant-garde theater; it also presents mime, music, video and visual arts.

Theatre under the Stars, Malkin Bowl, Stanley Park (☎687-0174). Summer productions here are generally fun and lightweight, but occasionally suffer from being staged in Canada's rainiest city.

Vancouver East Cultural Centre, 1895 Venables and Victoria (☎254-9578). Renowned performance space housed in an old church, utilized by a highly eclectic mix of drama, dance, mime and musical groups.

Waterfront Theatre, 1405 Anderson St (☎685-6217). Home to three resident companies; also holds workshops and readings.

Dance and opera

Anna Wyman Dance Theatre (☎662-8846). Although their repertoire runs the balletic gamut, this group is chiefly dedicated to contemporary dance. In addition to their standard shows, they occasionally put on free outdoor performances at Granville Island and at Robson Square near the Art Gallery.

Ballet British Columbia (☎669-5954). The province's top company, performing – with major visiting companies – at the *Queen Elizabeth Theatre*.

EDAM (☎876-9559). Experimental Dance and Music present modern mixes of dance, film, music and art.

Karen Jamieson Dance Company (☎872-5658). Award-winning company and choreographer; often use Canadian composers and artists, and incorporate Native cultural themes.

Vancouver Opera (☎682-2871). Lays on four lavish productions between October and May at the *Queen Elizabeth Theatre*.

Cinema

Cineplex, in the lower level of the Royal Centre at Georgia and Burrard. Ten-screen complex – the biggest first-run venue in town.

Pacific Cinémathèque, 1131 Howe near Helmcken. Best of the art houses; any film buff will find something to tempt.

Paradise, 919 Granville. The best bargain for first runs.

Ridge Theatre, 3131 Arbutus and 16th Ave. New releases, European films and classic reruns.

Vancouver East Cinema, 2290 Commercial and Seventh. Affiliated to the *Ridge*, with similar program.

Festivals

Warm summers, outdoor venues and a culture-hungry population combine to make Vancouver an important festival city. Recognized as one of the leading events of its kind, Vancouver's annual **International Jazz Festival** (late June to early July) is organized by the enthusiastic Coastal Jazz and Blues Society. Past line-ups have featured such luminaries as Wynton Marsalis, Youssou n'Dour, Ornette Coleman, Carla Bley and John Zorn. In all, some 400 international musicians congregate annually, many offering workshops and free concerts in addition to paid-admission events.

Other music festivals include **Vancouver Folk Festival**, a bevy of international acts centered on Jericho Park's *Centennial Theatre* for three days during the third week of July. For details contact the organizers at 3271 Main St (☎879-2931). Also in July, Vancouver loses its collective head over the **Sea Festival** (☎684-3378), nautical fun, parades and excellent fireworks around English Bay. Further afield in Whistler (see p.308), there's a **Country & Bluegrass Festival** in mid-July.

Drama festivals come thick and fast, particularly in the summer. The chief event – and one that's growing in size and reputation – is the **Fringe Festival**, modelled on the Edinburgh equivalent. It currently runs to 550 shows, staged by ninety companies at ten venues.

There's also an annual **Shakespeare Festival** (June–Aug) in Vanier Park and an **International Comedy Festival** in early August on Granville Island. Many of the city's art-house cinemas join forces to host the **Vancouver International Film Festival**, an annual showcase for over 150 films running from late September to mid-October. Canada's largest independent dance festival, **Dancing on the Edge**, runs for ten days in September at the *Firehall Arts Centre*, featuring the work of fifty of the country's hottest (and weirdest) choreographers.

ONWARDS FROM VANCOUVER

Vancouver is at the hub of transport links to many parts of the Pacific Northwest. Deciding where to move **onward from the city** – and how to go – presents a wealth of possibilities. We've listed the basic alternatives, together with cross references to more detailed accounts of the various options.

Alaska and the Yukon There are no non-stop flights to Alaska from Vancouver (all flights go via Seattle; see p.487). You can **drive** to Alaska through southern British Columbia to Dawson Creek, where you can pick up the Alaska Highway (see p.458) through the Yukon to Fairbanks. Using **public transport** you could take either a *BC Rail* train (see p.31) or *Greyhound* bus to Prince George, connecting with another *Greyhound* to Dawson Creek and Whitehorse (in the Yukon). *Alaskon Express* buses link Whitehorse and Alaskan destinations (see p.32).

To travel to Alaska by **boat** from Vancouver you need first to reach Bellingham (WA), Prince Rupert, or Port Hardy on Vancouver Island (see below).

British Columbia From Vancouver, the southern part of British Columbia is the best part of the mainland to explore (see the chapter "Southern British Columbia"). Two main **road** routes strike east towards Alberta and the Canadian Rockies – the Trans-Canada Highway and Highway 3, both served by regular *Greyhound* **buses**. *VIA* **trains** run through the region via Kamloops to Jasper and Edmonton. Buses and *BC Rail* trains also serve the **Cariboo** region, the duller central part of the province.

Calgary and the Canadian Rockies It takes between ten and twelve hours to drive to Calgary on the Trans-Canada Highway, and about 90 minutes less to reach Banff at the heart of the Canadian Rockies. Special express service *Greyhound* buses operate over the same route (12hr). There is no longer a *VIA rail* passenger service to Calgary. Very frequent one-hour flights connect Vancouver and Calgary.

Seattle Regular 50-minute flights connect Vancouver with Seattle. *Greyhound* or *Quick Shuttle* buses offer a less expensive alternative.

Vancouver Island Numerous **ferries** ply between Vancouver and three points on its eponymous island – Swartz Bay (for Victoria), Nanaimo and Comox. Most leave from Tsawwassen and Horseshoe Bay, terminals about 30 minutes' drive south and west of downtown respectively. As a foot passenger you can buy inclusive bus and ferry tickets from Vancouver to Victoria. Car drivers should make reservations well in advance for all summer crossings (see p.262 for full details of getting to Vancouver Island).

Listings

Airlines *Air Canada*, ☎688-5515; *American Airlines*, ☎222-2532 or 1-800/433-7300; *British Airways*, ☎270-8131; *Canadian Airlines*, ☎682-141; *Continental*, ☎1-800/525-0280; *Delta*, ☎1-800/345-3400; *United*,☎1-800/241-6522.

American Express 1040 W Georgia near Burrard (Mon–Fri 8.30am–5.30pm, Sat 10am–4pm; ☎669-2813). Another office is on the fourth floor of *The Bay* department store, Granville & Georgia (Mon–Fri 9.30am–5pm).

Bike rental *Bayshore Bicycles*, 1876 W Georgia near Denman (☎688-2453); *Robson Cycles*, 1810 Fir at Second (☎731-5552) and 1463 Robson near Broughton (☎687-2777); *Spokes*, 1798 W Georgia at Denman (☎688-5141); *Stanley Park Rentals*, 676 Chilco & Alberni (☎681-5581).

Books *Duthie Books*, 919 Robson St, is the best mainstream bookstore. *World Wide Books and Maps*, 1247 Granville St, specializes in maps, guides and travel.

Buses For long-haul destinations including Seattle, *Greyhound* (☎662-3222); for Victoria and Vancouver Island, *Pacific Coach Lines* (☎662-8074); for the Sunshine Coast, Powell River, Whistler, Pemberton and Nanaimo on Vancouver Island, *Maverick Coach Lines* (☎662-8051 or 1-800/972-6300). For Bellingham Airport, downtown Seattle and SeaTac Airport, *Quick Shuttle* (☎244-3744). Note that only *Greyhound* accepts credit cards and that *Pacific Coach Lines* and *Maverick Coach Lines* operate from the Pacific Central Station, not the central bus depot.

Car rental *Avis*, 757 Hornby near Georgia (☎682-1621); *Budget*, 450 W Georgia St (☎685-0536); *Exotic Car Rentals*, 1820 Burrard at W Second (☎644-9128); *Hertz*, 666 Seymour St (☎688-2411); *Rent-A-Wreck*, 1015 Burrard St (☎688-0001) and 1085 Kingsway near Glen (☎876-5629).

Consulates *Great Britain*, 800-1111 Melville (☎683-4421); *US*, 1075 W Georgia (☎685-4311).

Crisis Centre (☎733-4111); Rape Relief (☎872-8212).

Dentists For the nearest dentists call ☎736-3621. Drop-in dentist *Dentacare* (Mon–Fri only; ☎669-6700) is in the lower level of the Bentall Centre at Dunsmuir & Burrard.

Doctors The College of Physicians will provide the names of three doctors closest to you (☎733-7758). Drop-in service at Medicentre (☎683-8138) in the Bentall Centre (see above).

Emergencies ☎911.

Exchange *Deak International*, 617 Granville near Dunsmuir; *International Securities Exchange*, 1169 Robson near Thurlow.

Ferries *BC Ferries* for services to Vancouver Island, the Gulf Islands, the Sunshine Coast, Prince Rupert, the Inside Passage and the Queen Charlotte Islands; recorded information on ☎669-1211 or 685-1021.

Gay and lesbian switchboard 1-1170 Bute St (☎684-6869).

Hospitals *St Paul's Hospital* is the closest to downtown at 1081 Burrard St (☎682-2344). The city hospital is *Vancouver General* at 855 W 12th near Oak, just south of Broadway (☎875-4111).

Laundromat *Scotty's One Hour Cleaners*, 834 Thurlow near Robson (☎685-7732).

Left luggage At the bus station ($1 per 24hr).

Library 750 Robson and Burrard; Mon–Thurs 9.30am–9.30pm, Fri & Sat 9.30am–6pm. An excellent source of books and free literature on Vancouver, BC and Canada.

Lost property *BC Transit*, ☎682-7887; police (☎665-2232).

Newspapers and magazines US and UK editions at *Manhattan Books and Magazines*, 1089 Robson near Thurlow, and *European News Import*, 1136 Robson.

Optician Same-day service *Granville Mall Optical*, 807 Granville and Robson (☎683-4716).

Parking Main downtown garages are at *The Bay* (entrance on Richards near Dunsmuir), Robson Square (on Smithe and Howe), and the Pacific Centre (on Howe and Dunsmuir) – all are expensive and fill up quickly. A better idea might be to leave your car at the free *Park'n'Ride* in New Westminster (off Hwy 1).

Pharmacies *Shopper's Drug Mart*, 1125 Davie and Thurlow, has the longest hours of any downtown pharmacy – Mon–Sat 9am–midnight, Sun 9am–9pm. *Carson Midnite Drug Store*, 6517 Main at 49th, is open daily until midnight.

Post office Main office at 349 W Georgia and Homer, V6B 3P7 (Mon–Fri 8am–5.30pm; ☎662-5725); branches in *The Bay* and *Eaton's* department stores.

The **Sunshine Coast** northwest of Vancouver, the Sea to Sky Highway to **Whistler** and the **Cariboo** region of the British Columbia interior are covered in a section that begins on p.304.

Taxis *Black Top* (☎731-1111 or 681-2181); *Vancouver Taxi* (☎255-5111 or 874-5111); *Yellow Cab* (☎681-3311 or 681-1111).

Train enquiries *BC Rail* (☎631-3500); *VIA* (☎669-3050 or toll-free Canada only ☎1-800/561-8630).

Weather ☎666-1087.

Women's Resource Centre 1144 Robson near Thurlow (Mon–Fri 10am–2pm; ☎685-3934).

VANCOUVER ISLAND

Vancouver Island's proximity to Vancouver makes it one of western Canada's premier tourist destinations, though its popularity is out of all proportion to what is, in most cases, a pale shadow of the scenery on offer on the Northwest's mainland. The largest of North America's west coast islands, it stretches almost 500km

---

GETTING TO VANCOUVER ISLAND

There are three ways to reach Vancouver Island – by bus and ferry, car and ferry, or air. Most people travelling under their own steam from Vancouver go the first route, which is a simple matter of buying an all-inclusive through ticket to Victoria. More involved crossings to other points on the island, however, whether from the Canadian or US mainlands, are worth considering if you wish to skip Victoria and head as quickly as possible to Port Hardy for the Inside Passage ferry connections, or to Strathcona or Pacific Rim parks.

Foot passengers from Vancouver

Without your own vehicle, the most painless way to Victoria from Vancouver is to buy a **Pacific Coach Lines** *(PCL)* ticket at the Vancouver bus terminal, which takes you, inclusive of the ferry crossing, to Victoria's central bus station. Buses leave hourly in the summer, every two hours in the winter: total journey time is about three and a half hours and a single ticket costs $21.50. The ferry crossing takes 95 minutes, and offers some stunning views as the boat navigates the narrow channels between the Gulf Islands en route. Be sure to keep your ticket stub for reboarding the bus after the crossing. It's also worth stocking up on food on board, as subsidized ferry meals are famously good value (queues form instantly). You can save yourself about $10 by using public transportation at each end and buying a ferry ticket ($6.75) separately, but for the extra hassle and time involved it hardly seems worth it. Bus passengers from the United States can pick up through bus–ferry deals to the island from Seattle.

By car from British Columbia

BC Ferries (☎386-3431; ☎656-0757 for recorded timetable information) operates four routes to the island across the Georgia Strait from mainland British Columbia. Reservations on all are essential in summer if you want to avoid long waits.

The most direct and heavily used by Victoria–Vancouver passengers is the **Tsawwassen to Swartz Bay** connection, the same route used by *Pacific Coach Lines'* buses. Tsawwassen is about a forty-minute drive south of downtown Vancouver; Swartz Bay is the same distance north of Victoria. Ferries ply the route almost continuously from 7am to 9pm. The new *Mid-Island Express* from **Tsawwassen to Nanaimo**, midway up the island, has ten departures daily on the two-hour crossing. More boats cover the **Horseshoe Bay–Nanaimo** route, a 95-

from north to south, but has a population of only 500,000, mostly concentrated around **Victoria**, whose small-town feel belies its role as British Columbia's second metropolis and provincial capital. It is also the most British of Canadian cities in feel and appearance, something it shamelessly plays up to attract its two million – largely American – visitors annually. While Victoria makes a convenient base for touring the island – and, thanks mainly to its superlative museum, it merits a couple of days in its own right – little else here, or for that matter in any of the island's other sizeable towns, is enough to justify an overnight stop.

For most visitors Vancouver Island's main attraction is the great outdoors. The island is a mosaic of landscapes, principally defined by a central spine of snow-capped mountains which divide it decisively between the rugged and sparsely populated wilderness of the west coast and the more sheltered lowlands of the east. Rippling hills characterize the northern and southern tips, and few areas are free of the lush forest mantle that supports one of BC's most lucrative logging

minute journey from a terminal about fifteen minutes' drive from West Vancouver. The fourth route is **Powell River to Comox**, Powell River being some 160km north-west of Vancouver on the Sunshine Coast.

Ferries from the United States
Travellers **from the United States** have several options. *Washington State Ferries* (in BC ☎381-1551 or 656-1531; in Washington ☎206/464-7800) runs ferries **from Anacortes**, ninety minutes north of Seattle, to Sidney, thirty minutes (and 30km) north of Victoria (2 daily in each direction in summer, 1 daily in winter; 3hr–3hr 30min), via Friday Harbor on the San Juan Islands (see p.200). Passenger fares are $6, a car and driver around $35 (car reservations can be made a day in advance by calling ☎206/464-6400).

Black Ball Transport (in BC ☎386-2202; in Washington ☎206/452-8088 or 1-800/633-1589) operates a ferry across the Juan de Fuca Strait between **Port Angeles** on Washington's Olympic Peninsula right to Victoria's Inner Harbour (1–4 daily; 95min). Passenger fares are around US$7 and $30 for cars. Reservations are not accepted. Car drivers should call ahead in summer to get some idea of how long they'll have to wait.

For foot passengers, and day-trippers in particular, a speedier option is *Victoria Rapid Transit*'s hydrofoil service, which also covers the Port Angeles–Victoria Harbour route (1 daily; 55min). Reservations are not accepted, the fare is $20 return and ferries run only from May 23 to Oct 31.

The 300-passenger *Victoria Clipper* catamaran makes four daily trips in each direction between Pier 69 in Seattle and Victoria's Inner Harbour – the only direct ferry between the cities – in about two and a half hours (☎206/448-5000 or 1-800/888-2535 in Seattle). There is one winter sailing in each direction. Tickets prices vary according to season – up to around $55 single, $90 return in summer, about $10 and $20 less respectively in winter.

By air
Several provincial airlines as well as the big two – *Air Canada* and *Canadian* – fly to Victoria, though it's an expensive way to make the journey if you're only coming from Vancouver or Washington State. Open return fares from Vancouver typically run to around Can$115, excursion fares around $75. *Air BC* (1000 Wharf St, Victoria; ☎688-5515) fly the most frequent shuttles between Vancouver and Victoria.

industries. Apart from three minor east–west roads, all the urban centers are linked by a single highway running almost the entire length of the east coast.

Once beyond the main towns of **Duncan** and **Nanaimo**, the northern two-thirds of the island is distinctly underpopulated. Many people are lured by the beaches at **Parksville** and **Qualicum**, while the stunning seascapes of the **Pacific Rim National Park**, protecting the central portion of the island's west coast, and **Strathcona Provincial Park**, which embraces the heart of the island's mountain fastness, are the main destinations. Both offer the usual panoply of outdoor activities, hikers being particularly well served by the national park's **West Coast Trail**, a tough long-distance path.

For a large number of travellers, however, the island is little more than a necessary stop on a longer journey north: thousands annually make the trip to **Port Hardy** at the northern tip to pick up the ferry that follows the so-called **Inside Passage**, a breathtaking trip up the British Columbia coast to Prince Rupert; many venture still further north on the ferries that continue on from Prince Rupert to Skagway and Alaska.

Victoria

VICTORIA has decided it's not named after a queen and an era for nothing, and has gone to town in serving up lashings of fake Victoriana and chintzy commercialism – tea rooms, Union Jacks, bagpipers, pubs and ersatz echoes of empire confront you at every turn. Much of the waterfront area has a quaint, English feel – "Brighton Pavilion with the Himalayas for a backdrop", as Kipling remarked – and Victoria has more British-born residents than anywhere in Canada, but its tourist potential is exploited chiefly for American visitors who make the short sea journey across the border. Despite the seasonal influx and the sometimes atrocious attractions designed to part tourists from their money, it's a small, relaxed place, worth lingering in if only for its inspirational museum – and the city's hosting of the Commonwealth Games in 1994 should raise its international profile. Though often damp, the weather here is extremely mild: Victoria's meteorological station has the distinction of being the only one in Canada to record a winter in which the temperature never fell below freezing.

A brief history of Victoria

Inhabited originally by **Salish natives**, Victoria received its first **white colonists** in 1843 when the Hudson's Bay Company chose the island's southeastern tip as the site of a new fur-trading post, Fort Victoria. British pioneers were brought in to settle the land, several large company farms acting as a focus for immigration. In time, the harbor became a major port for Britain's Pacific fleet, a role it still fulfils for the bulk of Canada's present navy.

Boom came in the 1850s following the mainland gold strikes, when Victoria's port became an essential depot for prospectors heading across the water and into the interior. Military and bureaucratic personnel moved in to ensure order, bring-

---

The **telephone code** for British Columbia is ☎604.
Toll-free Information: Tourism British Columbia ☎1-800/663-6000.

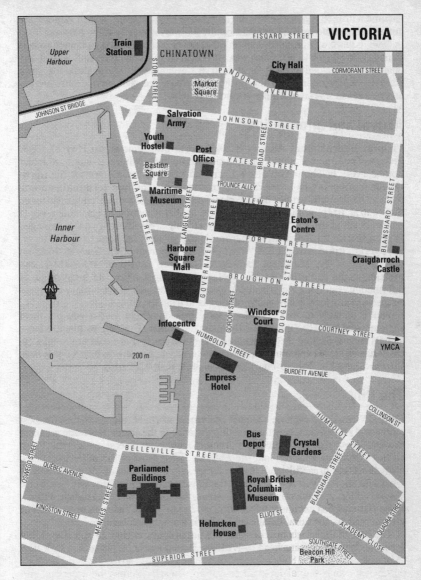

ing Victorian morals and manners with them. Alongside grew a rumbustious shanty town of shops, bars and brothels, one run by "Gassy" Jack Leighton, later to become one of Vancouver's unlikely founders.

Though the gold-rush bubble soon burst, Victoria carried on as a military, economic and political center, becoming capital of the newly created British

Columbia in 1866 – years before the foundation of Vancouver. British values were cemented in stone by the Canadian Pacific Railway, which built the *Empress Hotel* in 1908 in place of a proposed rail link that never came. Victoria's planned role as Canada's western rail terminus was surrendered to Vancouver, and with it any chance of sustained growth or industrial development. These days the town survives almost entirely on the backs of tourists, the civil service bureaucracy and retirees in search of a mild-weathered retreat.

Arrival and information

Victoria International Airport is 20km north of downtown on Hwy 17. *PBM Transport*'s Airporter shuttle bus heads downtown (where it stops at major hotels) every half-hour between 8.15am and 11.45pm; single fare for the thirty-minute journey is $10 (☎383-7311 for information). The **bus terminal** is downtown at 700 Douglas and Belleville, close to the Royal British Columbia Museum; the central **train station** (☎382-2127) is at 450 Pandora Street, about seven blocks north of the *Empress Hotel*, but you'll only arrive there if you've managed to get a seat on the lone daily train from Courtenay and Nanaimo.

Victoria's **infocentre**, at 812 Wharf St, almost in front of the *Empress Hotel* on the harbor (daily, May–Sept 9am–8pm, Oct–April 9am–5pm; ☎382-2127), can probably claim to be the world's best-stocked tourist office. Its huge range of information – on both Victoria and Vancouver Island as a whole – makes as good a reason as any for starting a tour of the island from the city.

You're unlikely to need to take a local **bus** anywhere, but if you do, most services run from the corner of Douglas and Yates. The fare within the large central zone is $1.35 – tickets, including Day Passes ($4) are sold at the infocentre, *7-Eleven* stores and other marked outlets, or you can pay on board if you have the exact fare. For 24-hour information on city transit ☎382-6161.

The City

Central Victoria is very small: almost everything worth seeing, as well as the best stores and restaurants, is within walking distance in the **Inner Harbour** area and the Old Town district behind it. Foremost among its diversions are the Royal British Columbia Museum and the *Empress Hotel*. Most of the other trumpeted attractions are dreadful, and many charge entry fees out of all proportion to what's on show. If you're tempted by the Royal London Wax Museum, Sea World (caged killer whales), Undersea Gardens, Miniature World, English Village, Anne Hathaway's Cottage, the Olde English Inn or any of Victoria's other dubious commercial propositions, details are available from the infocentre.

The best of the area's beaches are well out of town on Hwy 14 and Hwy 1, but for some local swimming head to **Willows Beach** on the Esplanade in Oak Bay, 2km east of Victoria.

The Royal British Columbia Museum

675 Belleville St. May–Sept daily 9.30am–7pm; Oct–April Tues–Sun 10am–5.30pm. $5.

The **Royal British Columbia Museum** is perhaps the best museum in Canada, and is regularly rated among North America's top ten. All conceivable aspects of the province are examined, but the **native peoples** section is probably the definitive collection of a much-covered genre, while the natural history sections – huge re-creations of natural habitats, complete with sights, sounds and smells – are mind-boggling in scope and imagination. Allow at least two trips to take it all in; the entry ticket is valid for 48 hours.

It is clear that thought, wit and a lot of money have gone into the museum. The most popular display is the **Open Ocean**, an in-depth look at the sea and the deep-level ocean. Visitors are admitted at thirty-minute intervals, in groups of ten, into a series of tunnels, dark rooms, lifts and mock-ups of submarines. You take a time-coded ticket and wait your turn, so either arrive early or reckon on seeing the rest of the museum first. Though rather heavy-handed in its "we're-all-part-of-the-cosmic-soup" message, it's still an object lesson in presentation. To capture the essence of life under the sea, the exhibit is also designed to be dark and enclosed, and signs wisely warn you to stay out if you suffer even a twinge of claustrophobia.

The first floor contains **dioramas** of some of the many natural habitats found in British Columbia: the re-created shorelines, coastal rainforests and Fraser Delta landscapes are all incredibly realistic, down to dripping water and cool, dank atmospheres. Audio-visual displays and a tumult of information accompany the exhibits (the beaver film is worth hunting down), most of which focus attention on the province's 25,600km of coastline, a feature of British Columbia usually overlooked in favor of its interior forests and mountains.

Upstairs on the second floor is the mother of all the tiny museums of bric-à-brac and pioneer memorabilia in BC. Arranged eccentrically from the present day backwards, it explores every aspect of the province's **social history** over two centuries. Prominently featured are the best part of an early-twentieth-century town, complete with cinema and silent films, plus comprehensive displays on logging, mining, the gold rush, farming, fishing and lesser domestic details, all the artefacts and accompanying information being presented with impeccable finesse.

The mezzanine third floor has a superb collection of **Native American art, culture and history** (see box below). It's presented in dimmed light, against muted wood walls and brown carpet: precautions intended to protect the fragile exhibits, but which also create a solemn atmosphere in keeping with the tragic nature of many of the displays. The collection divides into two epochs – before and after the coming of Europeans. Successive exhibits illustrate the gradual breakdown of the old ways, culminating in an account of the smallpox epidemic that virtually wiped out in one year a culture that was eight millennia in the making. A revealing section on land and reservations is left for last – the issues are contentious even today. The highlights in this section are many, but try to make a point of seeing the short film footage *In the Land of the War Canoes* (1914), the **Bighouse** and its chants, and the audio-visual display on native myths and superstition.

Helmcken House

Helmcken House (Tues–Sun 10am–5pm; $3.25) stands strangely isolated in Thunderbird Park adjacent to the museum, a predictable heritage offering that showcases the 1852 home, furnishings and embroidery talents of the Helmcken family. Dr John Helmcken was Fort Victoria's doctor and local political bigwig, and his house is a monument to Victorian values. It also contains some of the good doctor's fearsome-looking medical tools, but is probably only of interest if you've so far managed to avoid any of the region's many similar houses. Entrance is by single admission, or with the four-visit pass ($6.50) issued by the Victorian Rediscovery Society (who also run the Carr House, Point Ellice and the Craigflower Farmhouse).

The Parliament Buildings

The huge Victorian pile of the **Parliament Buildings**, at 501 Belleville St, is old and imposing. Beautifully lit at night, the domed building is fronted by the sea and well-kept gardens – a pleasant enough ensemble, though it doesn't warrant the manic enthusiasm visited on it by summer tourists. Designed by the 25-year-old Francis Rattenbury, who was also responsible for the *Empress Hotel* opposite, the building was completed in 1898. Figures from Victoria's grey bureaucratic past are duly celebrated, the main door guarded by statues of Sir James Douglas, who chose the site of the city, and Sir Matthew Baillie Begbie (aka the "Hanging Judge"), responsible for law and order during the heady days of gold fever. Sir George Vancouver keeps an eye on proceedings from the top of the dome. Free tours start from the main steps daily in summer every twenty minutes from 9am

---

NATIVE CULTURES OF THE BRITISH COLUMBIAN COAST

The numerous linguistic groups that inhabit the northwest coast of British Columbia have some of the most sophisticated artistic traditions and the most lavish ceremonials of any North American native group. Traditionally their social organization stemmed from a belief in a mythical time when humans and animals were essentially the same: each tribe was divided into **kin-groups** who were linked by a common supernatural animal ancestor and shared the same names, ritual dances, songs and regalia. Seniority within each kin group was held by chiefs and nobles, who controlled the resources – such as house sites, stands of cedar, and fishing, gathering and hunting territories.

Such privileges, almost unique among Canadian native groups, led to the accumulation of private wealth. Central to the power structure was the ceremonial **potlatch**, which was held in the winter-village, a seasonal resting place for these otherwise nomadic people, located where the supernatural forces were believed to be most accessible. The potlatch marked every significant occasion from the birth of an heir to the raising of a carved pole, and underscored an individual's right to his or her inherited status. Taking its name from the Chinook word for "gift", the potlatch also had the function of **redistributing wealth**. All the guests at the potlatch acted as witnesses to whatever event or object was being validated, and were repaid for their services with gifts from the host chief. Though these gifts often temporarily bankrupted the host, they heightened his prestige and ensured that he would be repaid in kind at a subsequent potlatch.

The most important element of potlatches were the **masked dances** that re-enacted ancestral encounters with supernatural beings, and were the principal means of perpetuating the history and heritage of each kin-group. Created by artists whose innovative ideas were eagerly sought by chiefs in order to impress their guests, the dramatic masks were often elaborate mechanisms that could burst open to reveal the wearer or – like the well-known Cannibal Bird – could produce loud and disconcerting noises.

The **Kwakiutl** produced the most developed potlatches, featuring highly ranked dances like the *hamatsa* or **"cannibal dance"**, whose performers had served a long apprenticeship as participants in less exalted dances. Before the *hamatsa* the initiate was sent to the "Cannibal at the North End of the World", a long period of seclusion and instruction in the snow-bound woods. On returning to the village he would seem to be in a complete cannibalistic frenzy and would rush around biting members of the audience. These apparent victims were all paid for their role, which usually involved cutting themselves with knives to draw blood – and the *hamatsa*

to 5pm (hourly in winter) – precise timings depend on the political business of the moment. Guides are chirpy and full of anecdotes. Look out for the dagger which killed Captain Cook, and the gold-plated dome, painted with scenes from Canadian history.

Beacon Hill Park

The best park within walking distance of the town center is **Beacon Hill Park**, south of the Inner Harbour behind the museum. Victoria's biggest green space, it has lots of paths and quiet corners, and plenty of views over the water to the distant mountains (especially on its southern side). The gardens are a pleasing mixture of well-tended and unkempt, and were a favored retreat of the celebrated Victorian artist, Emily Carr. They also claim the world's tallest totem pole, Mile

would burst blood-filled bladders in his mouth to add to the carnage, while relatives shook rattles and sang to tame him. A fantastic finale came with the arrival of the loudly clacking "Cannibal Birds", dancers dressed in long strips of cedar bark and huge masks, of which the most fearsome was the "Cannibal Raven", whose long straight beak could crush a human skull. The *hamatsa* would then return in ceremonial finery completely restored to his human state.

As elsewhere, **European contact** was disastrous for the coastal peoples. The establishment of fur-trading posts in the early nineteenth century led to the abandonment of traditional economic cycles, the loss of their creative skills through reliance on readily available European goods, the debilitation of alcohol and internecine wars. Though most of BC remains non-treaty, lands on Vancouver Island were surrendered to become the "Entire property of the White people forever" in return for small payments – the Victoria area was obtained for 371 blankets. Infectious disease, the greatest of all threats, reached its peak with the 1862 smallpox epidemic, which spread from Victoria along the coast and far into the interior, killing probably a third of BC's native population.

In this period of decline, potlatches assumed an increased significance as virtually the only medium of cultural continuity, with rival chiefs asserting their status through ever more extravagant displays – even going as far as to burn slaves who had been captured in battle. Excesses such as these and the newly adopted "whiskey feasts" were seen by the **missionaries** as a confirmation that these peoples were enveloped in the "dark mantle of degrading superstition". With BC's entry into confederation the responsibility for the natives fell to the Canadian federal government in faraway Ottawa, much of whose knowledge of the indigenous peoples came from the missionaries. The subsequent **Indian Act**, passed in 1884, prohibited the potlatch ceremony.

For a while the defiant native groups managed to evade detection by holding potlatches at fishing camps rather than the winter-villages, and there were few successful prosecutions until the 1920s. Things came to a head in 1922 with the conviction of 34 Kwakiutl from Alert Bay – all were sentenced to jail terms but a deal was struck whereby all those who surrendered their potlatch regalia were freed. Thirty years later, when potlatching was relegalized, native pressure began to mount for return of these treasures from the collections into which they had been dispersed, but it took a further twenty years for the federal government to agree to return the goods – and then only on condition that they be put on public display. Though the masks totally lose their dramatic emphasis in static exhibitions, many of the local museums have a dual function as community centers, and as such are vital to the preservation of a dynamic native culture.

Zero of the Trans-Canada Highway, and – that ultimate emblem of Englishness – a cricket pitch. Some of the trees are massive old-growth timbers that you'd normally only see on the island's west coast.

Crystal Gardens and Butchart Gardens

The **Crystal Gardens**, behind the bus terminal at 713 Douglas St (daily 10am–5pm; $5.50), was designed on the model of London's destroyed Crystal Palace and was billed on opening in 1925 as housing the "Largest Saltwater Swimming Pool in the British Empire". Now much restored, the greenery-, monkey- and bird-filled greenhouse provides an unaccountably popular tourist spot; only the exterior has any claims to architectural sophistication, and much of its effect is spoilt by the souvenir stores on its ground-floor arcade. Once an upper-crust meeting place, it still plays host to events such as the *Jive and Ballroom Dance Club* and the *People Meeting People Dance*. The daytime attractions are the conservatory-type tea room and tropical gardens. Inhumanely caged birds and monkeys, though, are liable to put you off your scones.

If you're really into things horticultural you'll want to make a trek out to the **Butchart Gardens**, 22km north of Victoria at 800 Benvennto on Hwy 17 towards the Swartz Bay ferry terminal (daily 8am–sunset; $10.50, $1 for readmission within 24hr; take bus #75 for "Central Sahnich" from downtown). Internationally renowned, they were started in 1904 by the wife of a mine-owner to landscape one of her husband's quarries, and now cover fifty breathtaking acres, comprising rose, Japanese and Italian gardens and lots of decorative details. Firework displays every July and August evening provide an added nocturnal temptation.

The Empress Hotel

A town is usually desperate when one of its key attractions is a hotel, but in the case of Victoria the **Empress Hotel**, 721 Government St, is so physically overbearing and plays such a part in the town's appeal that it demands some sort of attention. You're unlikely to be staying here – rooms start at around Can$200 and are largely snapped up by Japanese visitors – but it's well worth wandering through the huge lobbies and palatial dining areas for a glimpse of well-restored colonial splendor. In a couple of lounges there's a dress code – no trainers, dirty jeans or backpacks – but elsewhere you can wander at will without worrying about your appearance. The hotel's **Crystal Lounge** and its lovely Tiffany-glass dome forms the most opulent part of the hotel on view, but the marginally less ornate entrance lounge is *the* place for the charade of afternoon tea. There's also a reasonable bar downstairs, the **Garden Café**, and the so-called **Bengal Lounge** where you can have a curry and all the trimmings for about $10 (the hotel also boasts Victoria's best-appointed toilets). For a splurge try the gentlemen's-club surroundings – Chesterfields and aspidistras – and the champagne-and-chocolate-cake special ($8.50) on offer in the lounge to the left of the entrance lobby.

The rest of the city

Outside the Inner Harbour, Victoria has a scattering of minor attractions that don't fit into any logical tour of the city – and at any rate are only short-stop diversions. Most have a pioneer slant (Regent's Park House, Snooke Regional Museum, Sidney Museum), though if you're looking for old buildings the best is **Craigdarroch Castle**, 1050 Joan Crescent (daily summer 9am–7.30pm; winter

10am–5pm; $5; bus #11 or #14 from downtown). It was built by Robert Dunsmuir, a caricature Victorian politician and coal tycoon who was forced to put up this gaunt Gothic pastiche to lure his wife away from Scotland. There's the usual clutter of Victoriana and period detail, in particular some impressive woodwork and stained glass.

Much the same goes for **Point Ellice House**, 2616 Pleasant St (mid-May to Sept daily except Tues & Wed 10am–5pm; $3.50), magnificently recreated but less enticing because of its shabby surroundings, and for the nearby **Craigflower Heritage Site**, or **Farmhouse**, about 15 minutes' drive from downtown on Admiral's Rd (May–Sept Wed–Sun 10am–4pm; bus #14; $3.25). In its day the latter was the first of Victoria's farming homesteads, marking the town's transition from trading post to permanent community. It was built in 1856 to remind owner Kenneth McKenzie of Scotland, and soon became the foremost social center in the fledgling village – mainly visited by officers because McKenzie's daughters were virtually the only white women on the island.

The **Maritime Museum** at 28 Bastion Square (Mon–Sat 10am–4pm, Sun noon–4pm; $5) is worth a look for the lovely chocolate-and-vanilla building, and for the tiny square itself, the restored heart of Fort Victoria. Displays embrace old charts, uniforms, ships' bells, period photographs, models and the odd native dugout. A minute away is the small **Emily Carr Gallery**, 1107 Wharf St (summer only; Mon–Sat noon–8pm; $2), home to numerous paintings by the province's favorite daughter. The works, housed in Carr's father's old grocery, are an almost surreal amalgam of landscape and native culture, an attempt to preserve "art treasures of a passing race". The **Art Gallery of Greater Victoria**, 1040 Moss St (Mon–Wed & Fri–Sat 10am–5pm, Thurs 10am–9pm, Sun 1–5pm; $4), warrants a visit only if you're a fan of contemporary Canadian paintings or Japanese art.

Accommodation

Victoria fills up quickly in the summer, and most of its budget accommodation is heavily patronized. Top-price hotels cluster around the Inner Harbour area; **hostels** and more downmarket alternatives are scattered all over, though the largest concentration of inexpensive **hotels** and **motels** is around the Gorge Road and Douglas Street areas northwest of downtown. Reservations are virtually obligatory in all categories, but the infocentre's accommodation service will root out a room if you're stuck (☎382-1131 or 1-800/663-3883). They are more than likely to offer you **bed and breakfast**, of which the town has a vast selection; many owners of the more far-flung places will pick you up from downtown. It's also worth consulting specialist B&B agencies: *All-Season* (☎595-2337), *Canada-West* (☎388-4620) or *Garden City* (☎479-9999).

Victoria's commercial **campgrounds** are full to bursting in summer, with most space given over to RVs. Few of these are convenient for downtown anyway – given that you'll have to travel, you might as well head for one of the more scenic provincial park sites. Most are on the Trans-Canada Highway to the north, or on Hwy 14 east of Victoria.

Hotels and motels

Best Western Inner Harbour, 412 Quebec St (☎384-5122). Very convenient and comfortable mid-range hotel. ⑤.

Cherry Bank Hotel, 825 Burdett St (☎385-5380). Deservedly popular budget hotel, marked by dubious red decor and a rotating plastic mermaid on the roof, but excellent rooms and a good breakfast included in the price. Reservations essential. ②.

Crystal Court Motel, 701 Belleville St (☎384-0551). Large, serviceable motel just a block from the Inner Harbour. ④.

Douglas Hotel, 1450 Douglas and Pandora (☎383-4157). Clean, no-frills and slightly rough-edged hotel. Opposite city hall on bus routes #1, 6, 14 and 30. ③.

Helm's Inn, 600 Douglas St (☎385-5767). Popular if gaudily decorated hotel just half a block from the Royal BC Museum. Lower rates off-season. ④.

James Bay Inn, 270 Government and Toronto (☎384-7151). Vying with the *Cherry Bank* as Victoria's best low-cost option, this old Edwardian building was the last home of painter Emily Carr. Simple but adequate rooms, restaurant and *Unwinder* pub in the basement. Located two blocks south of the Government Buildings (buses #5 or 30 to Government and Superior St). Wide variety of rooms at differing prices. ④.

Mayfair Motel, 650 Speed Ave and Douglas (☎388-7337). Small motel 2km north of downtown. ③.

Oak Beach Hotel, 1175 Beach Drive (☎598-4556). Upmarket, mock-Elizabethan hotel on Haro Strait, 6km east of downtown, with good sea and island views. Off-season discounts. Bus #2. ⑤.

Strathcona, 919 Douglas St (☎383-7137). Large, modern downtown hotel, rooms with baths and TVs. ②.

Bed and breakfast

Battery Street Guest House, 670 Battery St (☎385-4632). Central location between Douglas and Government streets, one block from the sea. Popular, so book ahead. ③.

Bryn Gwyn Guest House, 809 Burdett St (☎383-1878). Very central location. ③.

Craigmyle Guest House, 1037 Craigmyle Rd (☎595-5411). Comfortable, friendly antique-furnished home 1.5km walk from downtown; buses #11 or 14 to the corner of Fort St and Joan Crescent. ④.

Glyn House, 154 Robertson St (☎598-0064). Southeast of the city on the marine drive and 3min walk from Gonzales Beach. Period fittings in 1912 home and rooms with private bathrooms, also available for weekly and monthly rentals. ④.

Heritage House, 3308 Heritage Lane (☎479-0892). Popular place in a quiet residential area northwest of downtown. Bus #22 to Grange Rd; reservations essential in summer. ④.

Seaside Cottage, 157 Robertson St (☎595-1047). Overlooking the ocean southeast of the center. ④.

Hostels and student accommodation

Salvation Army Men's Hostel, 525 Johnson St (☎384-3396). Better than it sounds, being clean and modern, but for men only. Rooms are given on a first-come, first-served basis, with doors open at 4pm. Dorm beds are $10, private rooms $20. Weekly and monthly rates available. ①.

University of Victoria (☎721-8395 or 721-8396). Between May and September you can take rooms at the university's nicely situated campus, 20min northeast of downtown near Oak Bay and reached on buses #7 or 14. By phone ask for the University Housing and Conference Services, or register on-site at the Housing Office, near the campus Coffee Gardens. Single and double rooms with shared baths. Rates include breakfast. ②.

Victoria Backpackers' Hostel, 1418 Fernwood Rd (☎386-4471). Battered but laid-back, and less convenient than the youth hostel: take bus #1, 10, 11, 14, 27 or 28 towards Fernwood. $10 dorm beds and private singles and doubles. One bunk room is reserved for women only. No curfew. ①–②.

Victoria YM-WCA Women's Residence, 880 Courtney and Quadra (☎386-7511). Shared cafeteria and sporting facilities, including swimming pool, but single and double rooms for women only. Located a short stroll from downtown and on the #1 bus route. Discounts Oct–May. ③.

Victoria Youth Hostel, 516 Yates and Wharf (☎385-4511). A large, modern, welcoming and well-run place just a few blocks north of the Inner Harbour. Bunk rooms, though, can be noisy. Mon–Thurs 7.30am–midnight, Fri–Sun 7am–2am. Members $13, non-members $18. Bus #23 or #24 from the Johnson Street Bridge. ①.

Campgrounds

Fort Victoria RV and Park Campground, 340 Island Hwy 1A (☎479-8112; $13.50-20). Closest site to downtown, located 6km north of Victoria off the Trans-Canada. Take bus #14 (for Craigflower) from the city center. Free hot showers. 250 sites.

Goldstream Provincial Park, 2930 Trans-Canada Highway (☎387-4363). 20km north of the city, but Victoria's best camping option, with plenty of hiking, swimming and fishing opportunities.

McDonald Provincial Park. A government site with limited facilities 32km from Victoria, but only 3km from the Swartz Bay Ferry Terminal if you've just come off the boat or have a ferry to catch the next morning.

Thetis Lake, 1938 Trans-Canada Highway (☎478-3845). Runs a close second to *Goldstream Park* for the pleasantness of its setting, and is only 10km north of downtown. Family-biased, 100 sites, laundromat and coin-operated showers.

Weir's Beach Resort, 5191 Williams Head Rd (☎478-3323). Enticing beachfront location 24km east of Victoria on Hwy 14.

Eating and drinking

Although firmly in Vancouver's culinary shadow, Victoria still has a plethora of **restaurants** offering greater variety – and higher prices – than you'll find in most other BC towns. **Pubs** tend to be plastic mock-ups of their British equivalents, with one or two worthy exceptions, as do the various **cafés** that pander to Victoria's self-conscious afternoon tea ritual. Good snacks and pastry shops abound, while at the other extreme there are luxury establishments if you want a one-off treat or a change from the standard Canadian menus that await you on the rest of the island. Only Sooke merits its own gastronomic excursion (see p.280).

Cafés, tea and snacks

Barb's Fish and Chips, Fisherman's Wharf off Kingston. Floating shack that offers classic home-cut chips, fish straight off the boat and oyster burgers and chowder to boot.

Blethering Place, 2250 Oak Bay Ave. A local institution and the place to come if you must indulge in the tea-taking ritual. Scones, cakes and dainty sandwiches served up against the background of hundreds of Toby Jugs and Royal Family memorabilia.

C'est Bon Croissant, 10 Bastion Square. Plain and filled croissants to eat in or take out.

Demitasse Coffee Bar, 1320 Blanshard St near Pandora. Popular, elegantly laid-back and vaguely trendy hole-in-the-wall café with excellent coffee, salads, bagels, lunchtime snacks, and an open fire at the back.

Dutch Bakery, 718 Fort St. An institution; pastries and chocolate to take away, or to eat in the popular coffeeshop at the back.

Empress Hotel, 721 Government St. Tea in the lobby here is a singular experience. Tourists and locals alike are on their best behavior amid the chintz and potted plants. No jeans or anoraks.

Goodies, 1005 Broad St (upstairs). Good day or night spot, and handy if you fail to find a table at the nearby *Pagliacci's*. Famed for huge breakfasts, eccentric omelettes and an array of Canadian, Californian and Mexican dishes.

John's Place, 723 Pandora Ave near Douglas. Quick and comprehensive breakfasts until 3pm, inexpensive lunches, free newspapers, comfy booths, great juke-box and occasional live music and dancing at weekends. Interesting clientele from punks to business types.

386-Deli, 1012 Blanshard St. Lunches only (except Fri dinner), with imaginative soup, pasta and dessert menu which changes daily.

Restaurants

Café Latino, 768 Fort St. Plastic tablecloths and apparently shabby ambience don't deter locals, who come here for conventional breakfasts and Latin American-influenced lunches and dinners.

Chez Pierre, 512 Yates St (☎388-7711). Long-established, reliable and expensive French restaurant.

Da Tandoor, 1010 Fort St. Tandoori specialist that shares plaudits with the *Taj Mahal* as the best of Victoria's half-dozen or so Indian restaurants; overlong menu, however, and over-the-top interior.

Flying Rhino, 1219 Wharf St. Organic vegetarian restaurant and shop with friendly and vaguely alternative feel; New Age noticeboard. Mon–Fri 8am–8pm, Sat & Sun 10am–6pm.

Foo Hong's, 564 Fisgard St. Plain but popular joint, and probably the city's best Chinese restaurant, though any in Victoria's tiny Chinatown pales beside its Vancouver equivalent.

Grand Central Café, 555 Johnson St (passageway). Smooth, laid-back ambience and beautiful summer patio provides the setting for modern cuisine with a Cajun and Creole twist.

La Petite Columbe, 604 Broughton St (☎383-3234). Romantic and intimate French restaurant for a splurge at dinner (lunches are more reasonable).

Metropolitan Diner, 1715 Government St. More upmarket than the "diner" tag suggests, with a wildly eclectic menu that blends Californian, French and Far Eastern cuisine in a *nouvelle* mix.

Pagliacci's, 1011 Broad St between Fort and Broughton. The best restaurant in Victoria if you want fast, furious atmosphere, live music, good Italian food and excellent desserts. A rowdy throng begins to gather from the moment the doors are open.

Periklis, 531 Yates St. Greek restaurant with belly dancers, plate-spinning and the like.

Scott's Restaurant, 650 Yates St near Douglas. Genuine diner, cheap breakfast and dinner specials, open 24 hours.

FESTIVALS IN VICTORIA

Summer brings out the buskers and **free entertainment** in Victoria's people-places – James Bay, Market Square and Beacon Hill Park in particular. Annual highlights include:

Dixieland Jazz Festival, held over four days in April. Showcase for about a dozen top international bands.

Jazz Fest, June (☎386-6121). Over a hundred assorted lesser bands perform in Market Square.

Victoria International Festival, July and August (☎736-2119). Victoria's largest general arts jamboree.

Folk Fest, last week of July (☎388-5322). Extravaganza of folk.

First People's Festival, early August (☎387-2134). Celebration of the cultures of Canada's native peoples.

Classic Boat Festival, Aug 30–Sept 1 (☎385-7766). Dozens of wooden antique boats on display.

Fringe Festival, September (☎383-2663). Avant-garde performances of all kinds.

Taj Mahal, 679 Herald St. Good Indian food with chicken, lamb and tandoori specialties.

Wah Lai Yuen, 560 Fisgard St. Cheap and cheerful Chinese with good food, formica tables, open kitchen and plenty of locals.

Bars

Big Bad John's, 919 Douglas St, next to the *Strathcona Hotel*. Victoria's most atmospheric bar: bare boards, a fug of smoke, and authentic old banknotes and IOUs pasted up on the walls.

Pig and Whistle, 634 Humboldt St. One of several hideously mocked-up British pubs, complete with English "bobby" and Pearly King and Queen.

Spinnakers Brew Pub, 308 Catherine St near Esquimalt Rd. Some 40 different beers, including several home-brewed options (occasional tours of the brewery possible). Restaurant, live music nightly and good harbor views draw mixed and relaxed clientele. Take bus #23 to Esquimalt Rd.

Swan's Pub, 506 Pandora Ave at Store St. A highly popular hotel-café-brewery housed in a 1913 warehouse, this is the place to come and watch Victoria's young, successful professionals at play. Several foreign and six home-brewed beers on tap.

Nightlife

Nocturnal diversions in Victoria are tame compared to either Vancouver or Seattle, but there's more to the town than its tea rooms and chintzy shops initially suggest. Other tastes are surprisingly well catered for by a smattering of **live-music** venues and **discos**, which should keep you happy for the limited time you're likely to spend in the city. Jazz is particularly easy to come by – for information on the city's jazz scene, contact the *Victoria Jazz Society* (☎388-4423).

Listings appear in the two main daily newspapers, the *Daily Colonist* and the *Victoria Times*; in the *Monday Magazine*, a free weekly tabloid printed on Wednesday despite its title; and in the fortnightly *Arts Victoria*. The noticeboards at the *Flying Rhino* (see above) have info on more off-beat events. **Tickets** for most offerings are available from the city's main performance space, the *McPherson Playhouse*, 3 Centennial Square, Pandora and Government (☎386-6121).

Clubs and live music

Banana Moon Nite Club, 770 Yates and Blanshard. Rock and "boogie" bands nightly, with a jam session on Sundays.

Esquimalt Inn, 856 Esquimalt Rd. Country seven nights a week, with 3pm jam session each Saturday and Sunday. Take the #23 bus.

The Forge, 919 Douglas St. Biggest, best and noisiest of the hard-rock venues, this club occupies the garish, neon-lit basement of the *Strathcona Hotel*. Music and dancing nightly.

Harpo's, 15 Bastion Square. Easily the best of Victoria's live-music venues, an intimate space which has hosted an eclectic mix of names such as Robert Cray, Billy Bragg and the Wailers. Cover from $5; closed Sun.

Hermann's Dixieland Inn, 753 View St. Dimly lit club thick with Fifties atmosphere which specializes in Dixieland but has occasional excursions into fusion and blues. Mon–Fri 11.30am–2am, Sat 3pm–2am.

La Bohème, 537 Johnson St, opposite Market Square. Occasionally precious coffee bar (downstairs) and restaurant that also hosts wide-ranging live music Tues–Sat.

Pagliacci's, 1011 Broad St. Potpourri of live music starting at 9pm Tues–Sat, in packed and popular restaurant.

The Rail, 2852 Douglas St. Pub-style rock venue located in the *Colony Motor Inn*.

Rumors, 1325 Government St. Gay and lesbian club for drinking and dancing. Closed Sun.

Victoria Folk Music Society, Norway House, 1110 Hillside Ave. Hosts weekly acoustic sets at 8pm.

Discos

Club California, 1318 Broad St. Large upstairs dance floor, lots of big rock video screens, plenty of theme nights.

Julie's Cabaret, 603 Pandora Ave. Standard disco housed in *Monty's Pub* in the Victoria Plaza. Nightly; $3 cover.

Merlin's, 1208 Wharf St. Central waterfront club that attracts early-twenties crowd. Theme nights include a Thurs women's night with male dancers. $3 cover charge after 9.30pm at weekends.

Pier 42, 1605 Store St at Pandora. You may well have to wait in line to join the slightly older crew who frequent the basement disco of *Swan's Pub*. Musical emphasis is on Sixties and Seventies classics and current hits. Tues–Sat.

Spinners, 858 Yates St near Quadra. Expensive club frequented by the 14–19 age-group. Wed–Sat until midnight.

Sweetwaters Niteclub, Market Square off Store St (☎383-7844). Central, upmarket and elegant spot with queues seven days a week and a reputation as a singles club.

Drama

Belfry Theatre, 1291 Gladstone St and Fernwood (☎385-6815). Foremost of Victoria's several highly active companies. Its five-play season in its own playhouse is nationally renowned, and though the program concentrates on contemporary Canadian dramatists, the repertoire runs the gamut of twentieth-century playwrights.

Intrepid Theatre Company, 620 View St (☎383-2663). Responsible for the nine-day September Fringe Festival, featuring some 200 highly varied shows.

Kaleidoscope Theatre, 715 Yates St (☎383-8124). Internationally acclaimed troupe known particularly for its work with young audiences.

Victoria Theatre Guild, 805 Langham Court Rd (☎384-2142). Lightweight musicals, dramas and comedies.

Classical music, opera and dance

Pacific Opera Victoria (☎386-6121). Highly acclaimed company which produces three operas yearly in Feb, April and Sept at the *McPherson Playhouse*.

Victoria Operatic Society, 798 Fairview Rd (☎381-1021). Lightweight operatic performances year round.

Victoria Symphony Orchestra, 846 Broughton Rd (☎385-6515). Numerous concerts annually, usually performed at the nearby *Royal Theatre*.

Listings

Airlines *Air BC* (☎382-9242); *Canadian Airlines* (☎382-6111).

American Express 1701 Douglas St (☎385-8731; Mon, Wed & Sat 9.30am–5.30pm; Tues, Thurs & Fri 9.30am–9pm).

Bike rental *Budget Cycle Time*, 327 Belleville St and 727 Courtney St (☎388-7874); *Explore Victoria*, 1007 Langley St; *Harbour Rentals*, 843 Douglas St and 1223 Wharf St (☎384-2133).

Bookstore *Munro's Books*, 1108 Government St (☎382-2424).

Bus information For services to Vancouver, *Pacific Coast Lines* (☎385-4417); for services on the island, *Island Coach Lines* (☎385-4411) – both at 700 Douglas and Belleville, also an office for *Greyhound* (☎388-5248).

Camping supplies *Jeune Brothers*, 570 Johnson St.

Car rental *Budget*, 843 Douglas St (☎388-5525); *Budget Discount Car Rentals*, 727 Courtney St (☎388-7874); *Hertz*, 901 Douglas St (☎388-4411); *Rent-A-Used-Car*, 752 Caledonian Ave (☎388-6230).

Dentist *Cresta Dental Centre* (☎384-1154) or *Family Dental Centre* (☎384-7711).

Doctors' Directory ☎383-1193.

Equipment rental *Sports Rent*, 3084 Blanshard St (☎385-7368). Rents camping, hiking, climbing and diving gear.

Exchange *The Victoria Conference Centre Currency Exchange*, 724 Douglas St (Mon–Sat 10am–6pm).

Ferries *BC Ferries* (☎386-3431); *Black Ball Transport* (☎386-2202); *Victoria Clipper* (☎382-8100); *Victoria Rapid Transit* (☎361-9144); *Washington State Ferries* (☎381-1551 or 1-800/542-7052).

Gay and lesbian information ☎361-4900.

Hospital *Fairfield Health Centre*, 841 Fairfield Rd (☎389-6300), is three blocks from the *Empress Hotel*; *Victoria General Hospital*, 35 Helmcken Rd (☎727-4212).

Laundromat 812 Wharf St, below the infocentre.

Left luggage At the bus terminal; $1.25 per 24hr.

Lost property Contact Victoria police (☎384-4111) or *BC Transit*'s lost-and-found line (☎382-6161).

Maps and travel guides *Earth Quest Books*, 1286 Broad St (☎361-4533).

Pharmacy *Shopper's Drug Mart*, 1222 Douglas St (daily 8am–9pm); *Save-On Food & Drugs*, 3510 Blanshard St (daily until midnight 362 days a year; ☎384-2333).

Post office 1230 Government and Yates, V8W 1L0 (Mon–Fri 8.30am–5pm; ☎388-3575).

Royal Canadian Mounted Police 625 Fisgard and Government (☎384-4111).

Taxis *Blue Bird Cabs* (☎382-4235); *Crown Taxi* (☎381-2242); *Victoria Taxi* (☎383-7111 or 383-1515). *Preferred Cab* (380-3022) have wheelchair-adapted cabs.

Train information *VIA rail*, 450 Pandora St (☎383-4324 or 1-800/665-8630).

Weather ☎656-3978.

Women's Victoria Contact *Every Woman's Books*, 641 Johnson St (☎388-9411) for books on and by women, and for feedback on what's happening in Victoria's women's and lesbian communities.

The Southern Gulf Islands

Scattered between Vancouver Island and the mainland lie several hundred tiny islands, most no more than lumps of rock, a few large enough to hold permanent populations and warrant a regular ferry service. Two main clusters are accessible from Victoria: the **Southern Gulf Islands** and the San Juan Islands (see p.200). Although both form part of the same archipelago, the latter group is over the border in the US.

You get a good look at the Southern Gulf Islands on the ferry from Tsawwassen to Swartz Bay or Nanaimo – twisting and threading through their coves and channels, the ride sometimes seems a bit too close for comfort. The coastline makes for superb **sailing**, and an armada of small boats criss-cross between the islands for most of the year. Hikers and campers are also well served, and **fishing** is good, with some of the world's biggest salmon having met their doom in the surrounding waters. The climate is mild, though hardly "Mediterranean" as claimed in the tourist blurbs; the vegetation is particularly lush, and there's an abundance of marine wildlife (sea lions, orcas, seals, bald eagles, herons, cormorants). All this has made the Gulf Islands the dream idyll of many people from Washington and BC, whether they're artists, writers, retirees, or drop-outs from the mainstream. For full details of what they're all up to, grab a copy of the local listings, the *Gulf Islander*, distributed on the islands and the ferries.

Getting to the islands

BC Ferries (☎656-0757) sails to five of the Southern Gulf Islands – **Saltspring, Pender, Saturna, Mayne** and **Galiano** – from Swartz Bay, 33km north of Victoria on Hwy 17 (a few others can be reached from Chemainus and Nanaimo, for which see those sections on p.284 and p.285). Reckon on at least two daily crossings to each, but be prepared for all boats to be jammed solid during the summer. If you aim to exploit the many inter-island connections, the company's *Southern Gulf Islands* timetable, widely available on boats and in the mainland infocentres, is invaluable. If you just want a quick, cheap cruise, *BC Ferries* runs a daily four-hour jaunt from Swartz Bay around several of the islands. All the ferries take cars, bikes and motorbikes, though if you have a car you'll need to make a reservation (in Vancouver ☎669-1211; in Victoria ☎386-3431). Bear in mind that there's next to no public transportation on the islands, so what few taxis there are can charge more or less what they wish.

For the San Juans you obviously have to pass through US and Canadian immigration, but you can get good stopover deals on ferries between Sidney on Vancouver Island and Anacortes on the Washington mainland, and foot passengers travel free between the four main islands.

Aim to have your **accommodation** worked out well in advance in summer. Although no reservations are accepted, **campers** should have few problems finding a site, most of which are located in the islands' many provincial parks. At peak times, however, you should arrive before noon to ensure a pitch. For help, use the *BC Accommodations* guide, or contact the Victoria infocentre.

Saltspring Island

SALTSPRING (pop. 5000), the biggest and most-visited of the islands, is served by three ferry terminals: **Fulford Harbour** (from Victoria) and **Vesuvius Bay** (from Crofton, near Duncan) provide links to Vancouver Island; **Long Harbour** has services to points on the BC mainland via other islands. The *Saltspring Island Bus* connects the ferry terminals with **Ganges**, the island's main village. For more complicated journeys call up the 24-hour *Saltspring Taxi* (☎537-9712) or consider **renting a bike** from *Island Spoke Folk* (☎537-4664) in Ganges (for $5 they can arrange for bikes to be waiting for you at the ferry terminal). Locals are a particularly cosmopolitan bunch, the island having been colonized not by whites but by pioneer black settlers seeking refuge from prejudice in the US. If you're here to slum it on a **beach**, the best strips are on the island's more sheltered west side (Beddis Beach, off the Fulford–Ganges road), at Vesuvius Bay and at Drummond Park near Fulford.

Ganges, close to Long Harbour, is a rapidly proliferating assortment of galleries, tourist shops and holiday homes. Community spirit reaches a climax during the annual **Artcraft**, a summer crafts fair that showcases the talents of the island's many dab-handed artisans. The town's **infocentre**, 121 Lower Ganges Rd (May–Sept daily 8am–6pm; ☎537-5252) has details of the island's relatively plentiful **accommodation**, ranging from bed and breakfasts (owners can arrange to pick you up from the ferry) through the so-called "resorts" dotted round the island – usually a handful of houses with camping, a few rooms to rent, and little else. Each of the ferry ports also has a range of mid-price motels. Some of the nicer spots include the *Arbutus Court Motel* at 770 Vesuvius Bay Rd at Vesuvius Bay (☎537-5415; ③); the *Spindrift Resort* at Wellbury Point (☎537-5311; ③), overlooking Long Harbour ferry terminal; and the *Booth Bay Resort*, 375 Baker Rd, Ganges (☎537-5651; ④).

One of the island's better-known places to **eat** is *The Inn at Vesuvius* alongside the ferry at Vesuvius Bay, favored with live music nightly and a great **bar** deck overlooking the harbor. In Ganges the popular *Sweet Arts Patisserie Café* at 112 Lower Ganges Rd (opposite the fire station) has high-quality sandwiches and the like, and healthy picnic supplies can be had from the *Saltspring Nature Works*, 158 Fulford Rd.

The island's best hiking and its top **campground** are to be found in Ruckle Provincial Park, and there's further walking and good views on and around Mount Maxwell.

Galiano Island

Long and finger-shaped, **GALIANO** (pop. 700) is one of the more promising islands to visit if you want variety and a realistic chance of finding somewhere to stay. There are two ferry terminals: **Sturdies Bay**, which takes boats from the mainland, and **Montague Harbour**, which handles the Vancouver Island crossings. The **infocentre** is in the former (May–Sept daily 8am–6pm; ☎539-2233), which also has bike, boat and canoe rentals, motels, bed and breakfasts, and an excellent **campground** at nearby Montague Harbour Provincial Park.

Galiano Gables on Warbler Rd, 3.5km from Sturdies Bay, operates as a **mini hostel** (☎539-2594; non-CHA; ①); turn left up Burrill Rd off the main road after the *Burrill Bros* store. **Rooms** are sometimes available at the *Hummingbird Inn* (☎539-5472; ③), the island's only pub, conveniently close to the ferry on Sturdies Rd (a bus meets boats and also runs out to the provincial park). **Food** is reasonable at the *Hummingbird*; likewise at *La Berengerie*, near Montague Harbour on the corner of Montague and Clanton roads (☎539-5392; ③), a genteel restaurant which also has a few bed-and-breakfast rooms upstairs. For a downy and comfortable stay in peaceful surroundings try the *Woodstone Country Inn* (☎539-2022; ③) on Georgeson Bay Rd close to Montague Harbour Provincial Park. The best choice on the island's quieter northern end is the *Bodega Resort*, at 120 Monasty Rd off Porlier Pass Drive–Cook Drive (☎539-2677; ③), with log cabins set in acres of woods and meadows overlooking the sea.

If you're **canoeing**, stick to the calmer waters, cliffs and coves off the west coast. **Hikers** can walk almost the entire length of the east coast, or climb Mount Sutil (323m) or Mount Galiano (342m) for views of the mainland mountains. The locals' favorite **beach** is at Coon Bay at the island's northern tip.

North and South Pender

The bridge-linked islands of **NORTH** and **SOUTH PENDER** can muster about a thousand people between them, most of whom will try to entice you into their studios to buy arts and crafts. The **infocentre** is at the ferry terminal in **Otter Bay** (May–Sept daily 8am–6pm) on North Pender, home of the *Otter Bay Marina*, where you can rent **bikes** and buy maps for a tour of the islands' rolling, hilly interior. The best **beaches** are at Hamilton (North Pender) and Mortimer Spit (South Pender). **Accommodation**-wise there are plenty of bed and breakfasts, and a wooded **campground** at Prior Centennial Provincial Park. For more upmarket rooms, try the rural *Inn on Pender Island* near Prior Park at 4709 Canal Rd, North Pender (☎629-3353; ③), or *Pender Lodge*, 1325 MacKinnon Rd, North Pender (☎629-3221; ⑤).

Mayne and Saturna islands

MAYNE is the first island to your left if you're crossing from Tsawwassen to Swartz Bay. This may be the only glimpse you'll get, since it's the quietest and most difficult to reach of the islands served by ferries, and has few places to stay. The unspoilt scenery may tempt you out here, however, particularly if you have a bike to explore the web of quiet country roads. The best of several **beaches** is Bennett Bay, a sheltered strip with warm water and good sand; it's reached by heading east from Miner's Bay (5min from the ferry terminal at Village Bay) to the end of Fernhill Rd and then turning left onto Wilks Rd. The island is small enough to explore as a day trip, but the summer-only **infocentre** at Village Bay (daily 8am–6pm) can help you find a bed and breakfast. Other **accommodation** options include the *Root Seller Inn*, a mile south of the ferry terminal at 478 Village Bay Rd (March–Oct; ☎539-2621; ③), and the *Blue Vista Resort*, a few cabins overlooking Bennett Bay on Arbutus Drive (☎539-2463; ③). The summer-only *Tinker's Retreat* on Georgia Point Rd operates as a private **mini-hostel** (☎539-2280; ①).

SATURNA, to the south, is another bed-and-breakfast hideaway: try *Boot Cove Lodge* a couple of miles from the ferry at 130 Payne Rd in Saturna Point, home to a pub, a store and the **infocentre** (May–Sept daily 8am–6pm), which can rent you boats and bicycles. The best local **beach** is at Winter Cove Marine Park (no campground) and there are walking, wildlife and good views to the mainland from Mount Warburton Pike.

Highway 14: Victoria to Port Renfrew

Highway 14 runs west from Victoria to Port Renfrew, lined with numerous beaches and provincial parks, most – especially those close to the city – heavily used during the summer months. The 107-kilometer route is covered in summer by the *Port Renfrew Connector* (☎361-9080), a twice-daily private bus service intended for hikers walking the West Coast Trail (see p.296), but popular for the ride alone. Victoria city buses go as far as **SOOKE** (38km; take #50 to Western Exchange and transfer to #61), best known for its **All Sooke Day** in mid-July, when lumberjacks from all over the island compete in various tests of forestry expertise. The **infocentre** lies across the Sooke River Bridge at 2070 Phillips and Sooke (daily 10am–6pm). This is the last place of any size, so stock up on supplies if you're continuing west. Check out the small **Sooke Region Museum** (daily 10am–5pm) to find out more on the largely logging-dominated local history.

Quite a few people make the trip here just for the **food** at *Sooke Harbour House*, 1528 Whiffen Spit (☎642-3421; ⑦), one of the finest restaurants on the West Coast and frequently lauded as one of the best in the Northwest; it's expensive, but has a surprisingly casual atmosphere. It also has a few top-notch **rooms**.

Beaches beyond Sooke are largely grey pebble and driftwood, the first key stop being **French Beach Provincial Park**, 20km from Sooke. An infoboard here fills in the natural history background, and has maps of trails and the highlights on the road further west. There's good walking on the fairly wild and windswept beach, and camping on the grass immediately away from the shore. Sandy, signed trails lead off the road to beaches over the next 12km to **JORDAN RIVER**, a one-shop, one-hamburger-stall town known for its good surf. Just beyond is the best of the beaches on this coast, part of **China Beach Provincial Park**, reached after a fifteen-minute walk from the road through rainforest.

There's a campground if you're staying over; otherwise you can push on – the road is gravel from here on – past Mystic and Sombrio beaches to **PORT RENFREW**, a logging community that's benefited from being the western starting point of the West Coast Trail. Accommodation, however, is still limited to *Gallaugher's West Coast Fish Camp* on Beach Rd (☎647-5535; ③) and the *Port Renfrew RV Park and Marina* on Parkinson Rd (☎647-5430; $9–11). South of the village on a logging road (6km) is **Botanical Beach**, a sandstone shelf and tidal pool area that reveals a wealth of marine life at low tide.

If you're driving and don't want to retrace your steps, consider taking the gravel logging roads from the village on the north side of the San Juan River to either Shawnigan Lake or the Cowichan Valley. These are marked on most maps, but it's worth picking up the detailed map of local roads put out by the *Sooke Combined Fire Organization* (ask at the Victoria infocentre); heed all warnings about logging trucks.

Highway 1: Victoria to Nanaimo

If you leave Victoria with high expectations of Vancouver Island's lauded scenery, **Highway 1** – the final western leg of the Trans-Canada – will come as a disappointing introduction to the island's southeast coast. After a lengthy sprawl of suburbs, blighted by billboards, the landscape becomes suddenly wooded and immensely lush; unfortunately the beauty is constantly interrupted by stretches of dismal motels, highway junk, and huge swathes of destruction where the road is being widened. **Buses** operated by *Island Coach Lines* make the trip between Victoria and Nanaimo (6 daily). One **train** a day also covers this route and beyond to Courtenay, but it makes a lot of stops and gets booked solid in summer.

Thetis Lake Park, appearing on the right after 10km, is good for swimming; there's a busy beach near the parking lot, but it's quieter round the shore, or beyond at the bottom of the hill on Prior Lake. Prettier still is **Goldstream Provincial Park**, 5km beyond Langford, where you'll find a good **campground** (busy in summer) and a network of marked **trails** designed for anything from five minutes' to an hour's walking. Try the paths to Mount Finlayson for views of the ocean – views you also get if you carry on up the highway, which soon meets Saanich Inlet, a bay with a lovely panorama of wooded ridges across the water. The best-sited **motel** to take in the sea and island vistas is the *Malahat Mountain Oceanview* (☎478-9231; ③), 35km north of Victoria.

A marginally more scenic diversion off the main road takes you to **Shawnigan Lake**, fringed by a couple of provincial parks. If you're biking or are prepared to rough it, note the logging road that links the north end of the lake to Port Renfrew on the west coast.

Duncan

DUNCAN, 60km north of Victoria, begins inauspiciously, with a particularly scrappy section of highway spoiling what would otherwise be an exquisitely pastoral patch of country. Still, the town's Native Heritage Centre merits a stop – unlike the Glass Castle, a messy affair made from glass bottles off the road to the south, and the even sillier "World's Largest Hockey Stick", arranged as a triumphal arch into the town center. It was won at auction by Duncan, in competition with dozens of other cities.

Duncan's **infocentre** is opposite the *Overwaitea* supermarket on the main road (Mon–Fri 8.30am–5pm; ☎746-4636), close to the **bus station**, which has six daily connections to and from Victoria (1hr 10min away). Duncan is not really a place you'd want to consider staying in, but for **meals** you could try *Arbutus*, 195 Kenneth St and Jubilee, much-frequented by locals, or the *White Hart Tea Shop* on Station St. Three kilometers south of town on Hwy 1, the *Pioneer House Restaurant* has a rustic log-cabin feel assisted by a genuine saloon bar transplanted from a period building in Montana. Alternatively, head 10km north of Duncan to the *Red Rooster Diner* (by the *Mount Sicker* petrol station), reputed to be the diner immortalized by Jack Nicholson in *Five Easy Pieces*. It's still a classic – good, inexpensive food, vinyl booths and all the authentic tacky trimmings.

The Native Heritage Centre

The first real reason to pull off the highway is Duncan's brand-new **Native Heritage Centre**, 200 Cowichan Way (May–Sept daily 10am–6pm), on your left in the unmissable wooden buildings next to Malaspina College.

Duncan has long been the self-proclaimed "City of Totems", a reference to a rather paltry collection of poles – arranged mostly alongside the main road – that belong to the Cowichan, historically British Columbia's largest native group. The community still preserves certain traditions, and it's been their energy – along with cash from white civic authorities, attuned to potentially lucrative tourist attractions – that has pulled the project together. Much of the emphasis is on selling native crafts, especially the ubiquitous lumpy woollens for which the area is famous, but you can usually expect to find historical displays and demonstrations of dancing, knitting, carving, weaving and cooking.

British Columbia Forest Museum Park

Vancouver Island is one of the most heavily logged areas in Canada, and the **British Columbia Forest Museum Park**, 1km north of town on Hwy 1 (May–Sept daily 9am–7pm; $4), is run by the province to preserve artefacts from its lumbering heritage. However, with industry bigwigs as museum trustees, you can't help feeling it's designed to be something of a palliative in the increasingly ferocious controversy between loggers and environmentalists. It does a thorough job on trees, though, and if the forestry displays in Victoria's museum have whetted your appetite, you could spend a good couple of hours rounding off your arboreal education. The steam train round the park is a good, if gimmicky, way of getting around. The forest dioramas and the artefacts and archive material in the **Log Museum** are worth a look, and there's also the usual array of working blacksmiths, sawmills, a farmstead, an old logging camp – and a few surviving forested patches where you can take time out.

OLD-GROWTH FORESTS: GOING, GOING, GONE

Although Vancouver Island isn't the only place in North America where environmentalists and the forestry industry are at loggerheads, some of the most bitter and high-profile confrontations have taken place here. The island's wet climate is particularly favorable to the growth of thick **temperate rainforest**, part of a belt that once stretched from Alaska to northern California. The most productive ecosystem on the planet, **old-growth** virgin Pacific rainforest contains up to ten times more biomass per acre than its more famous tropical counterpart – and, though it covers a much smaller area, it is being felled at a greater rate and with considerably less media outrage. Environmentalists estimate that British Columbia's portion of the Pacific rainforest has already been reduced by two thirds; all significant areas will have been felled, they predict, within twelve years. The loggers claim that two thirds survives, but even the Canadian government – largely in thrall to and supportive of the industry – concedes that a mere 3.5 percent of the BC rainforest is currently protected.

The controversy over logging often pits neighbor against neighbor, for 270,000 in the province depend directly or indirectly on the industry, and multinationals like McMillan Bloedel and Fletcher Challenge dominate the scene. **Employment** is a major rallying cry here, and the prospect of job losses through industry regulation is usually enough to override objections. The trend towards **automation** only adds fuel to the argument: by volume of wood cut, the BC forestry industry provides only half as many jobs as in the rest of Canada.

Some **environmental groups** have resorted to such tactics as fixing huge nails in trees at random – these ruin chainsaws and lumber mill machinery, but also endanger lives. The most moderate of the conservation groups, the **Western Canada Wilderness Committee** (WCWC), condemns these acts of environmental vandalism, and instead devotes its energies to alerting the public to the landslide damage and destruction of salmon habitats caused by logging, and the dioxin pollution from pulp mills that has closed 220,000 acres of offshore waters to fishing for shellfish. They point out that the battle is over what they call "the last cookies in the jar", for only eight of the island's 91 watersheds over 12,000 acres have escaped logging; the old-growth bonanza is nearly over, they argue, and the industry might as well wean itself over to sustainable practices now, before it's too late.

The complex forms part of the **Cowichan and Chemainus Ecomuseum**, a vaguely defined park that takes in much of the surrounding region and is intended to preserve its logging heritage – a curiously ill-defined concept that seems to be largely a PR excercise on the part of the logging companies. Ask for details of tours and maps from the Duncan infocentre, or the Ecomuseum office, 160 Jubilee St.

The Cowichan Valley

Striking west into the hills from Hwy 1 north of Duncan, Hwy 18 enters the **Cowichan Valley** and fetches up at Cowichan Lake, the largest freshwater lake on the island. Rather than drive, however, the nicest way up the valley is to walk the eighteen-kilometer **Cowichan Valley Footpath**, following the river from Glenora (a hamlet southwest of Duncan at the end of Robertson Road) to Lake Cowichan Village on the lake's eastern shore. You could do the trip in a day, camp en route, or turn around at Skutz Falls and climb up to the Riverbottom Road to return to Duncan.

A road, rough in parts, circles **Cowichan Lake** (allow 2hr driving time) and offers access to a gamut of outdoor pursuits, most notably fishing – the area is touted as the "Fly-fishing Capital of the World". The water gets warm enough for summer swimming, and there's also ample hiking in the wilder country above. At Youbou on the north shore you can visit the **Pletcher Challenge Heritage Mill**, a working sawmill (tours May–Sept): this area boasts some of the most productive forest in Canada, thanks to the lake's mild microclimate, and lumber is the obvious mainstay of the local economy. On the road up to the lake from Duncan you pass the **Valley Demonstration Forest**, another weapon in the industry's public-relations arsenal, with signs and scenic lookouts explaining the intricacies of forest management.

For details of the area's many tours, trails and outfitters contact the **infocentre** at Lake Cowichan Village (May–Sept daily 9am–8pm; 749-4141). Good, cheap **campgrounds** line the shore, which despite minimal facilities can be quite busy in summer. The biggest and best is at Gordon Bay Provincial Park on the south shore, a popular family place but with a quiet atmosphere and a good sandy **beach**. There are also plenty of hotels, motels and the like in all the lakeside settlements.

Chemainus

CHEMAINUS is the "Little Town That Did", as the billboards for miles around keep telling you. Its mysterious achievement was the creation of its own tourist attraction, realized when the closure of the local sawmill – once among the world's largest – threatened the place with overnight extinction. In 1983 the town's dignitaries commissioned a huge mural recording the area's history. This proved so successful that more panels quickly followed, drawing visitors to admire the artwork – and tempting them to spend money in local businesses. As murals go these are surprisingly good, and if you're driving it's worth the short, well-signed diversion off Hwy 1.

Buses also detour here on the run up to Nanaimo (☎246-3354 for details), and the train drops you right next to a mural. You can also pick up a ferry from Chemainus to the small islands of **Kuper** and **Thetis**. There's a summer-only **infocentre** in town at 9758 Chemainus Rd (May–Sept daily 9am–6pm; ☎246-3944), and if you fancy **staying** – the homey waterside setting is nicer than either Duncan or Nanaimo – try the *Horseshoe Bay Inn*, 9576 Chemainus Rd (☎246-3425; ①). There's also a tiny **mini youth hostel** open year round at 3040 Henry Rd (☎246-4407; ①), about 2km north of town off the Ladysmith road (the wardens, Robert and Vi Matula, can pick you up from the village). There's a kitchen and showers, but you're supposed to bring your own sleeping bag. The best choice for **food** is the *Upstairs Downstairs Café*, 9745 Willow St, with reasonably priced and varied dishes including good vegetarian options.

Ladysmith

LADYSMITH's claim to fame is based solely on an accident of geography, as it straddles the 49th Parallel, the latitude that divides mainland Canada and the US. Canada held onto Vancouver Island only through some hard bargaining, since the logic of the boundary ought to put much of it in the States.

There's little to the place other than the usual motels and garages, though a recent attempt to spruce up the older buildings won it a Western Canada Award of Excellence. Ladysmith's scenic profile, it has to be said, would be considerably higher were it not for a huge sawmill and a waterfront hopelessly jammed with lumber. The **infocentre** at the Black Nugget Museum, 12 Gatacre St (summer only; ☎245-8544), has walking maps of the "heritage center". The **museum** itself (daily noon–4pm; $2) is a restored 1906 hotel stuffed with predictable memorabilia. If you stop off, check out **Transfer Beach Park**, where the water is said to be the warmest in the Pacific north of San Francisco.

Accommodation options include the *Holiday House Motel*, 540 Esplanade St (☎245-2231; ②) overlooking Ladysmith's waterfront, the *Seaview Marine Hotel* (☎245-3768; ②–③), just off the highway 6km south of town, and the *Inn of the Sea*, 3600 Yellow Point Rd (☎245-2211; ④), 13km northeast on the seafront and a popular bolt-hole for weekending Victorians. For **food** call in at the oldest "English-style pub" in BC, the *Crow and Gate* just off the the main road 19km north of the town. The most central campground is the *Sea RV Park and Campground* in Transfer Beach Park overlooking the port (☎245-5344; $13).

Nanaimo

With a population of about 50,000, **NANAIMO** is Vancouver Island's second largest city, the terminal for ferries from Horseshoe Bay and Tsawwassen on the mainland, and a watershed between the island's populated southeastern tip and its wilder, less populated countryside to the north and west. The town itself is unexceptional, though the setting is eye-catching – particularly around the harbor, which bobs with yachts and rusty fishing boats, and allows the first views on the route from Victoria across to the big mountains on the mainland.

Coal first brought white settlers to the region, many of whom made their fortunes here, including the Victorian magnate Robert Dunsmuir, who was given £750,000 and almost half the island in return for building the Victoria–Nanaimo railway – an indication of the benefits that could accrue from the British government to those with the pioneering spirit. Five Salish bands originally lived on the site, which they called **Sney-ne-mous**, or "meeting place", and it was they who innocently showed the local black rock to Hudson's Bay agents in 1852.

The mines are closed, and the town's pockets are now lined by forestry, deep-sea fishing and tourism. It's largely in the pursuit of the last that Nanaimo lays on the annual **Bathtub Race** and **Silly Boat Race**, in which bathtubs are raced (and sunk, mostly) across the 55km to Vancouver. The winner takes the silver Plunger Trophy from the Loyal Nanaimo Bathtub Society. It's all part of the Marine Festival held in the second week of July. More highbrow is the May to June **Nanaimo Festival**, a cultural jamboree that takes place in and around Malaspina College, 900 Fifth St. The town's other minor claim to fame is the Nanaimo bar, a glutinous chocolate confection made to varying recipes and on sale everywhere.

The town's twenty-five or so gardens and small parks, many of them hugging the shore, are perfectly aligned for a seafront breath of air. **Piper's Lagoon Park** offers a windblown, grassy spit, with lots of trails, flowers, rocky bluffs and good sea views: it's off Hammond Bay Road north of the city center. For beaches you could head for **Departure Bay**, off Stewart Avenue north of downtown, which is the main summer hang-out for the town's young and trendy. Plenty of local stores rent a range of marine gear, as well as bikes and boats.

The wildest of the local parks, **Westwood Lake Park**, is good for a couple of hours' lonely hiking and some fine swimming. Tongue-twisting **Petroglyph Provincial Park**, off Hwy 1 well to the south of downtown, is a showcase for Native American stone carvings, many of them thousands of years old – and some spoilt by more recent graffiti.

In Nanaimo itself, only two other sights warrant the considerable amount of energy used to promote them. The **Centennial Museum**, just off the main harbor area at 100 Cameron St (daily 10am–5pm), houses a collection that runs the usual historical gamut of pioneer, logging, mining, native peoples and natural history displays. The best features are the reconstructed coal mine and the interesting insights into the town's cosmopolitan population – a mix of Polish, Chinese, Welsh, Native and English citizens who see themselves today as some of the island's "friendliest folk". The **Bastion**, close by, is a wood-planked tower built by the Hudson's Bay Company in 1853 as a store and a stronghold against native attack, though in the event it was never used for defensive purposes. It's the oldest (perhaps the only) such building in western Canada. These days it houses a small museum of Hudson's Bay memorabilia (daily 10am–5pm); its silly tourist stunt is "the only ceremonial cannon firing west of Ontario" (daily at noon, summer only). This is marginally more impressive than the town's claim to have the most retail shopping space per capita in Canada.

Practicalities

Nanaimo's dingy **bus terminal** (☎753-4371) is some way from the harbor on the corner of Comox and Terminal (behind the *Tally-Ho Inn*), with six daily runs to Victoria, two to Port Hardy and three to Port Alberni, for connections to Tofino and Ucluelet. **BC Ferries** (☎753-1261) sails from Departure Bay, 2km north of downtown (take the Hammond Bay bus #2 to the north end of Stewart Ave), to Tsawwassen (south of Vancouver) and more frequently to Horseshoe Bay on the mainland (7am–9pm, hourly in summer, every two hours off-season; foot passengers $4.75 one way). The town lies on the Victoria–Courtenay rail line and sees two **trains** daily, northbound around 11am and southbound at 3pm: the station is in the center of downtown.

You'll find an **infocentre** on the main highway north of downtown at 266 Bryden St (May–Sept daily 8am–8pm; Oct–April Mon–Fri 9am–5pm; ☎754-8474). They'll help with accommodation referrals, and shower you with pamphlets on the many boat rides and tours to local sawmills, canneries, nature reserves, fishing research stations and so on. You can **rent bikes** and **kayaks** at *North Island Water Sports*, 2755 Departure Bay Rd (☎758-2488).

Numerous **motels** are clustered on the city limits, the best-known of the inexpensive options being the *Colonial*, 950 Terminal Ave on Hwy 1 (☎754-4415; ②), and the *Big 7*, 736 Nicol St (☎754-2328; ①), five minutes south of the center in the downtown area. For more tasteful lodgings, try the *Tally Ho Island Inn*, 1 Terminal Ave (☎753-2241; ④), extremely convenient for the bus terminal, or the *Schooner Cove Resort* (☎468-7691; ④), 26km north of town near Nanoose Bay.

Nanaimo's cheapest beds are at the **CHA youth hostel**, known as the *Thompson*, 1660 Cedar Hwy, 10km south of town (☎722-2251; ①) – take Cedar Bus #11 which drops in front of the hostel, or the free hourly shuttle from the bus terminal (6–9pm). The hostel only sleeps twelve, so call ahead during peak periods, or take advantage of the adjoining campground. There's also a central private ten-bed **mini-hostel**, the *Nicol Street Hostel*, 65 Nicol St (May to early

Sept; ☎753-1188; reservations ☎754-9697; ①), located seven blocks south of the bus terminal and one block south of the Harbour Park Shopping Centre off Hwy 1. A handful of camping spots on the lawn (with ocean views) are also available, plus bike rental. Both hostels charge $10 for members, $15 for non-members.

Other **camping** areas are at Newcastle Island Provincial Park (see below), within walking distance of town, and spread along the main road to the north and south; the best of these – a rural, watery retreat – is the *Brannan Lake Campground*, 6km north of the ferry terminal off Hwy 19 at 4228 Biggs Rd (☎756-0404; from $12). There's also free camping at lovely Nanaimo Lake on Nanaimo Lake Rd about ten minutes south of the town.

The town's best seafood **restaurant** is the *Bluenose Chowder House*, 1340 Stewart Ave (closed Mon), also party to a nice outside terrace. Other reliable choices are *The Grotto*, 1511 Stewart Ave (closed Sun & Mon), up the road near the *BC Ferry* terminal, and *Gina's*, 47 Skinner St, an unmissable Mexican outfit perched on the edge of a cliff and painted bright pink with an electric blue roof. Grab your obligatory Nanaimo bar or other low-cost edibles at the food stands in the **Public Market**, handy for the ferry terminal on Stewart Ave (daily 9am–9pm), or stock up at the big *Overwaitea* supermarket, 2km north of town on Hwy 19.

Newcastle and Gabriola islands

Barely a stone's throw offshore from Nanaimo lies **Newcastle Island**, and beyond it the larger bulk of **Gabriola Island**, both incongruously graced with palm trees: they're beneficiaries of what is supposedly Canada's mildest climate.

Ferries make the crossing every hour on the hour (10am–9pm; $4 round trip) from Maffeo-Sutton Park (the wharf behind the Civic Arena) to Newcastle Island Provincial Park, which has a fine stretch of sand, tame wildlife, no cars, and lots of walking and picnic possibilities. By contrast, there are about fifteen crossings to Gabriola Island (20min), a much quieter place that's home to about 2000 people, many of them artists and writers. The latter offers several beaches – the best are Gabriola Sands and Drumbeg Provincial Park – and lots of scope for scuba-diving, beachcombing and easy walking, plus the added curiosity of the **Malaspina Galleries**, a series of caves and bluffs sculpted by wind and surf. Both islands have numerous **B&Bs** and several **campgrounds**, though if you're thinking of staying the night it's as well to check first with the Nanaimo infocentre.

From Nanaimo to Pacific Rim National Park

North of Nanaimo, Highway 1 is replaced by **Highway 19**, a messy stretch of road spotted with billboards and a rash of motels, marinas and clapboard houses. Almost every last inch of the coast is privately owned, this being the chosen site of what appears to be every British Columbian's dream holiday home. Don't expect, therefore, to be able to weave through the houses, wooden huts and boat launches to reach the tempting beaches that flash past below the highway. For sea and sand you have to hang on for **Parksville**, 37km north of Nanaimo, and its quieter near-neighbor **Qualicum Beach**.

Parksville marks a major parting of the ways: while Hwy 19 continues up the eastern coast to Port Hardy, **Highway 4**, the main trans-island route, pushes west to **Port Alberni** and on through the tremendously scenic Mackenzie Mountains to **Pacific Rim National Park**. *Island Coach Lines* (☎385-4411) runs three **buses** daily from Nanaimo to Port Alberni, where there are connecting services for **Ucluelet** and **Tofino**.

Parksville

The approach to Parksville from the south is promising, heralded by a lonely **infocentre** 6km south of town alongside the entrance to *Craig's Camping*. Thereafter the road takes you through lovely wooded dunes, with lanes striking off eastwards to hidden beaches and a half-dozen secluded **campgrounds**. Four kilometers on, the best of the beaches stretches along **Rathtrevor Beach Provincial Park**. In summer this area is madness – and if you want to lay claim to some of the park's camping space, expect to start queueing first thing in the morning. The 2km of public sand sports all the usual civilized facilities of Canada's tamed outdoors: cooking shelters, picnic spots and walking trails.

Beyond the orange bridge into **PARKSVILLE**, the scenery degenerates into eight blocks of motels and garages. The worst of the development has been kept off the promenade, however, which fronts **Parksville Beach**, whose annual **Sandfest** draws 30,000 visitors per day in July to watch the five-day World Sandcastle Competition (see p.111 for details of a similar event in Cannon Beach, Oregon). The beach offers lovely views across to the mainland and boasts Canada's warmest seawater – 21°C in summer. Though busy, it's as immaculately kept as the rest of the town – a tidiness that bears witness to the reactionary civic pride of Parksville's largely retired permanent population. You'll see some of these worthy burghers at play during August when the town hosts the World Croquet Championships.

For local **information**, Parksville's Chamber of Commerce is clearly signed off the highway in downtown at 1275 East Island Hwy (May–Sept daily 8am–6pm; ☎248-3613). Ask especially for details of the many **hiking** areas and other nearby refuges from the beaches' summer maelstrom, and **fishing**, which is naturally another of the region's big attractions. If you must **stay**, camping offers the best locations. There are a multitude of cheapish identikit **motels** in town and "resort complexes" out along the beaches, though summer vacancies are few and far between. South of Rathtrevor Beach Provincial Park try a pair of cottage resorts which look onto the sea: *Tigh-Na-Mara*, 1095 East Island Hwy (☎248-2072; ④–⑥), and *Graycrest on the Sea*, 1115 East Island Hwy (☎248-6513; ⑤). A touch more upmarket is *Beach Acres*, 1015 East Island Hwy (☎248-3424; ⑤), with its own pool, sandy beach, and good cabins. At the same sort of price, the *Island Hall Resort Hotel*, 181 West Island Hwy (☎248-3225; ⑤), is one of the smarter and better-known downtown establishments, though you'd be just as well off in the neighboring *Sea Edge Motel* (☎248-8377; ④), which shares the *Island Hall*'s beach.

Qualicum Beach

QUALICUM BEACH, says its Chamber of Commerce, "is to the artist of today what Stratford-on-Avon was to the era of Shakespeare" – a bohemian enclave of West Coast artists and writers that has also been dubbed the "Carmel of the North". Both estimations pitch things somewhat high, but compared to Parksville the area has more greenery and charm, and it's infinitely less commercialized.

More a collection of dispersed houses than a town, Qualicum's seafront is correspondingly wilder and more picturesque, skirted by the road and interrupted only by an **infocentre** (the obvious white building midway on the strand), and a couple of well-sited **hotels**: the *Sand Pebble Inn* (☎752-6974; ③) and the *Captain's Inn* (☎752-6743; ③). A cluster of motels sit at its northern end, where the road swings inland, the best being the *Shorewater* (☎752-6901; ③–④). Keep heading north and the road becomes quieter and is edged with occasional **campgrounds**, among which the *Qualicum Bay* and *Spider Lake Provincial Park* sites stand out (both from $8). Twenty-four kilometers north of Qualicum is the area's only half-decent sight, the **Big Qualicum River Fish Hatchery**, a so-called "enhancement center" which encourages salmon to spawn and thus bolster dwindling stocks. A tour of the government-run concern will fill you in on more than you ever wanted to know about salmon.

Highway 4 to Port Alberni

If you've not yet ventured off the coastal road from Victoria, the short stretch of Hwy 4 to Port Alberni offers the first real taste of the island's beauty. The least expensive place to stay along here is the log-cabin-style **mini hostel** (☎248-5694; ①) at 2400 Hwy 4 in **Coombs**, about 10km west of Parksville – take the third entrance past the school on the south side of the main road. Buses will stop here on request, but there are only half a dozen beds – and no cooking facilities – so call in advance.

The first worthwhile stop is **Englishman River Falls Provincial Park**, 3km west of Parksville and then another 9km off the highway. Named after an early immigrant who drowned here, the park wraps around the Englishman River, which tumbles over two main sets of waterfalls. A thirty-minute trail takes in both falls, with plenty of swimming and fishing pools en route. The year-round **campground** is on the left off the approach road before the river, nestled among cedars, dogwoods and lush ferns.

Back on the main highway, a further 8km brings you to **Little Qualicum Hatchery**, given over to chum, trout and chinook salmon, and just beyond it a right turn for **Little Qualicum Falls Provincial Park**, arguably the island's loveliest small park. A magnificent forest trail follows the river as it drops several hundred meters through a series of gorges and foaming waterfalls. A half-hour stroll gives you views of the main falls, but for a longer **hike** try the five-hour Wesley Ridge Trail. There's a sheltered **campground** by the river and a recognized **swimming area** on the river at its southern end.

Midway to Port Alberni, the road passes **Cameron Lake** and then an imperious belt of old-growth forest. At the lake's western end, it's well worth walking ten minutes into **MacMillan Provincial Park** (no campground) to reach the famous **Cathedral Grove**, a beautiful group of huge Douglas firs, some of them reaching 70m tall, 2m thick and up to a thousand years old. The park is the gift of the vast MacMillan timber concern, whose agents have been responsible for felling similar trees with no compunction over the years. Wandering the grove will take only a few minutes, but just to the east, at the Cameron Lake picnic site, is the start of the area's main **hike**. The well-maintained trail was marked out by railway crews in 1908 and climbs to the summit of **Mount Arrowsmith**, a long, gentle twenty-kilometer pull through alpine meadows that takes between six and nine hours. The mountain is also one of the island's newer and fast-developing ski areas. To **stay** locally, head for the *Cameron Lake Resort* (April–Oct; ☎752-6707; ②), based in a park-like setting on the lake: it has seven cottages and a campground ($15).

Port Alberni

Self-proclaimed "Gateway to the Pacific" (and, along with half of Vancouver Island, "Salmon Capital of the World" – see Campbell River, p.299), **PORT ALBERNI** is an ugly town dominated by the sights and smells of its huge lumber mills. It's also a busy fishing port, but its main interest to travellers is as a forward base for Pacific Rim National Park. If you've ever wanted to hook a salmon, this is probably one of the easier places to do so – there are any number of boats and guides ready to help out.

The only conventional sight is the **Alberni Valley Museum**, 4255 Wallace St and Tenth Ave, home to a predictable but above-average logging and Native American collection (daily 10am–5pm; free). For hot-weather swimming, locals head out to **Sproat Lake Provincial Park**, 8km north of town on Hwy 4. It's a hectic scene in summer, thanks to a fine beach, picnic area, and a couple of good campgrounds – one on the lake, the other north of the highway about 1km away. You can also take a guided tour of the world's largest fire-fighting planes or follow the short trails that lead to a few ancient petroglyphs on the park's eastern tip.

Sproat Lake marks the start of the superb scenery that unfolds over the 100km of Hwy 4 west of the town. Only heavily logged areas detract from the grandeur of the Mackenzie Range and the majestic interplay of trees and water. Go prepared, however, as there's no gas or supplies for about two hours of driving.

Practicalities

Island Coach Lines (☎724-1266) runs three **buses** daily to and from Nanaimo, with the terminal on Victoria Quay at 5065 Southgate (though the bus company itself, note, is at 4541 Margaret St). Jump off at the *7-Eleven*, one stop earlier, to be nearer the heart of town. *Orient Stage Lines* (☎723-6924) runs one connection daily from here on to Ucluelet and Tofino in Pacific Rim National Park. *Western Bus Lines* (☎723-3341) and the *Pacheenaht Band Bus Service* (☎647-5521) make connections to Bamfield for the West Coast Trail (see p.296). Help and information on fishing charters, hiking options, minor summer events, or tours of the two local pulp mills, are available at the **infocentre** (daily 9am–6pm; ☎724-6535) off Hwy 4 east of town – look out for the big yellow mural.

For **accommodation** there are the usual motel choices, though if you prefer a good central hotel plump for *The Barclay*, 4277 Stamp Ave (☎724-7171; ③). The *Coast Hospitality Inn*, 3835 Redford St (☎723-8111; ⑤), and *Somass Motel*, 5279 River Rd (☎724-3236; ③), are also both reliable choices. Less expensive, and in more salubrious surroundings 14km west of town on Hwy 4, is the *Westbay* (☎723-2811; ①). There's no local hostel, though the *Friendship Lodge*, 3978 Eighth Ave (☎723-6511; ①), appears to operate as one in all but name: choose between basic doubles or shared small rooms. The infocentre has a list of the constantly changing **bed-and-breakfast** options. **Camping** options include the small and central *Dry Creek Public Campground*, 4850 near Alberni Harbour Quay at Argyle St and Third Ave (May–Sept; ☎723-6011; $5–11), or, further afield, the nicer *China Creek Marina and Campground* (☎723-2657; $10–19), 15km south of the town on Alberni Inlet, which has a wooded, waterside location and sandy, log-strewn beach. Camping at Sproat Lake (see above) is excellent, but busy in the summer.

Eating possibilities are numerous: for **seafood** try the waterfront *Four Winds*, Harbour Quay (☎723-2333), or the more basic fish and chips of *Friar John's*, 4726 Johnston Rd (a few blocks up from Victoria Quay). The *Canal*, 5093 Johnson St, serves good Greek food, and you should find inexpensive lunches at the *Paradise Café*, 4505 Gertrude St, and several deli-bakeries, of which the best are probably the *Mountain View*, 3727 Tenth Ave, and the *Yvette Deli*, 4926 Argyle St.

The MV Lady Rose

The single best thing you can do in Port Alberni is to leave it, preferably on the **MV Lady Rose**, a small, fifty-year-old Scottish-built freighter that plies between Kildonan, Bamfield, Ucluelet and the Broken Group Islands (see p.296). Primarily a conduit for freight and mail, it also takes up to 100 passengers, many of whom use it as a drop-off for canoe trips or the West Coast Trail at Bamfield. You could easily ride it simply for the exceptional scenery – huge cliffs and tree-covered mountains – and for the abundant wildlife (sea-lions, whales, eagles and the like, depending on the time of year).

The boat leaves early most mornings from the Argyle Street Dock at the Alberni Harbour Quay, following a different itinerary on different days of the week, and is back in port by the middle of the afternoon. The nine-hour round trip to Bamfield runs Tuesday, Thursday and Saturday (plus Friday in the summer); the 11-hour ride through the Broken Group Islands to Ucluelet oper-ates on Monday, Wednesday and Friday. Tickets cost $15 to $20 one way, $35 to $40 return, depending how far west you're travelling, and are quickly snapped up in the summer (contact *Alberni Marine Transportation* for information and reser-vations ☎723-8313 or 1-800/663-7192 April–Sept only). Note that smaller boats running more irregular services to the same destinations can occasionally be picked up from Tofino and Ucluelet.

Pacific Rim National Park

Pacific Rim National Park is one of the main reasons to visit Vancouver Island: a stunning amalgam of mountains, coastal rainforest, wild beaches, and unkempt marine landscapes that stretches intermittently for 130km between the towns of Tofino in the north and Port Renfrew to the south. It divides into three distinct areas: **Long Beach**, which is the most popular; the **Broken Group Islands**, hundreds of islets only really accessible to sailors and canoeists; and the **West Coast Trail**, a tough but increasingly popular long-distance footpath. The whole area has also become a mecca for **whale-watching**, and dozens of small compa-nies run charters out from the main villages.

Lying at the north end of Long Beach, **Tofino** is still essentially a fishing village and the best base for general exploration. **Ucluelet** to the south is less attractive, but more geared to accommodating the park's many thousands of annual visitors. **Bamfield**, a tiny and picturesque community still further south, is known mainly as the northern endpoint of the West Coast Trail and as a marine research and whale-watching spot.

Weather in the park is an important consideration, because it has a well-deserved reputation for being appallingly wet, cold and windy – and that's on the good days. An average of 300cm of rain falls annually, and in some places it buckets down almost 700cm, well over ten times what falls on Victoria. So don't count on doing much swimming or sunbathing: think more in terms of spending your time admiring crashing Pacific breakers, hiking the backcountry and maybe doing a spot of beachcombing.

Tofino

TOFINO, most travellers' base in the park, is beginning to show the adverse effects of its tourist influx, but it clearly appreciates that it has a vested interest in preserving the salty, waterfront charm that brings people here in the first place. Crowning a narrow spit, the village is bounded on three sides by tree-covered islands and water, gracing it with magnificent views and plenty of what the tourist literature refers to as "aquaculture". As a service village it fulfils most functions, offering food, accommodation and a wide variety of boat and seaplane tours (most with a whale-spotting dimension). It's easily reached from Port Alberni by the daily *Orient Coach Lines* connection (☎723-6924 for details). *Lake Union Air* operate flights from Seattle to Tofino at around $210 a time (one-way) on Tuesdays and Fridays (journey time is about two hours). *Tofino Airlines Ltd* on First Street in Tofino (☎725-4454) also run excursions and charters as far afield as Seattle and Vancouver.

Sleepy off-season, the place erupts into a commercial frenzy during the summer (unreconstructed hippies and easy-going family groups being the most visible visitors), though there's little to do in town other than walk its few streets and soak up the atmosphere. Thereafter, most people head south to explore Long Beach, or put themselves at the mercy of the boat and plane operators. If you don't go for a general cruise round the coast (about 3hr), the best trip is out to beautiful **Meares Island** (15min by boat), swathed in lush temperate rainforest. The marked **Tribal Park** trail (2hr 30min) meanders among some of the biggest trees you'll ever see, many of them over a thousand years old and up to six meters across. Incredibly, there are plans to log the island, a prospect that has hit national headlines and, needless to say, given rise to considerable opposition.

The other popular trip is to **Hotsprings Cove** (1hr by boat, 15min by float plane), Vancouver Island's only hot springs. A thirty-minute trek from the landing stage, they consist of a small waterfall and four pools, becoming progressively cooler towards the sea. Rough camping is possible, but not encouraged, and a new motel is set to open near the quay.

The relatively quiet **Chesterman's Beach**, by contrast, is walkable from the village, and beyond it lies **Frank Island**, a tempting proposition, but sadly private property (the owners get heartily sick of having to turn people away). For the best (unmarked) local beach, turn right just past the *Dolphin Motel* as you leave Tofino to the south, then drop down from the small parking lot.

PRACTICALITIES

The **infocentre** at 380 Campbell St (May–Sept daily 9am–8pm; ☎725-3414) can give you the exhaustive lowdown on all the logistics of boat and plane tours. They may also be able to get you into one of the village's ever-expanding roster of **bed and breakfasts**, should you be so unwise as to turn up in Tofino without reservations in high summer.

WHALES

Pacific Rim National Park is among the world's best areas for **whale**-watching, thanks to its location on the main migration routes, food-rich waters and numerous sheltered bays. People come from five continents for the spectacle, and it's easy to find a boat going out from Tofino, Ucluelet or Bamfield, most charging around $30 per head for the trip. Regulations prohibit approaching within 100m of an animal but, though few locals will admit it, there's no doubt that the recent huge upsurge in boat tours has begun to disrupt the **migrations**. The whales' 8000-kilometre journey – the longest known migration of any mammal – takes them from their breeding and calfing lagoons in Baja, Mexico, to summer feeding grounds in the Bering and Chukchi seas off Siberia. The northbound migration takes from February to May, with the peak period of passage between March and April. A few dozen animals occasionally abort their trip and stop off the Canadian coast for summer feeding (notably at Maquinna Marine Park, 20min by boat from Tofino). The return journey starts in August, hitting Tofino and Ucluelet in late September and early October. **Mating** takes place in Mexico during December, after which the males turn immediately northwards, to be followed by females and their young in February.

Although killer whales (orcas) are occasionally seen, the most commonly spotted type are **gray whales**, of which some 19,000 specimens are thought to make the journey annually. Averaging 14m in length and weighing 35 to 50 tonnes, they're distinguished by the absence of a dorsal fin, a ridge of lumps on the back, and a mottled blue-gray color. Females have only one offspring yearly, following a gestation period of thirteen months, and, like the males, cruise at only two to four knots – perfect for viewing and, sadly, for capture.

Even if you don't take a boat trip, you might just see whales from the coast as they dive, when you can locate their tails, or during fluking, when the animals surface and "blow" three or four times before making another five-minute dive. There are telescopes at various points along Long Beach, the best known viewpoints being Schooner Cove, Radar Hill, Quistis Point and Combers Beach near Sea Lion Rocks.

The main concentration of **motels**, "cottage resorts" and campgrounds is south of the village, where you can try the excellent *Tofino Swell Lodge*, 340 Olsen Rd (☎725-3274; ②–④), room prices varying according to season, or the *Dolphin Motel* at 1190 Pacific Rim Hwy (☎725-3377; ②). For a bit more class, head for the *Ocean Village Beach Resort* at 555 Hellesen Drive (☎725-3755; ③) just north of Long Beach on the main road, which offers "cottage" accommodation. More central options, all with sea views, are: the *Schooner Motel*, 311 Campbell St (☎725-3478; ③); *Maquinna Lodge Hotel*, 120 First St (☎725-3261; ③); *Pacific Breeze Motel*, 760 Campbell St (March–Oct; ☎725-3269; ③–④); and the *Duffin Cove Resort Motel*, 215 Campbell St (☎725-3448; ③–⑥).

The private **youth hostel**, *Tin Wis Guest House*, 2km from the port at 1119 Pacific Rim Hwy (☎725-3402; ①–④), has a wide variety of bunks and rooms, but no cooking facilities or meals. You can also camp here (from $12), with washing facilities and the possibility of beach barbecues for outdoor cooking. Besides the youth hostel, **camping** options include *Bella Pacifica Resort and Campground* (☎725-3400; from $17, with free hot showers), and *Crystal Cove Beach Resort* (☎725-4213; from $14) – both are by the water about 3km south of Tofino.

The best all-round **restaurant** is *The Loft*, 346 Campbell St, good for breakfast, lunch or dinner, with a friendly atmosphere and outdoor eating in the summer.

The town's most popular choice for coffee and snacks is the *Common Loaf Bake Shop*, 131 First St. In similar vein is the *Alley Way Café*, behind the bank at Campbell & First St, a friendly locals-type of place with newspapers to read and cheap, wholesome food. The *Crab Bar*, 601 Campbell St, sells crab, beer and bread (plus some imaginative salads).

Long Beach

The most easily reached and developed of the park's components, **Long Beach** is just what it says, a long tract of wild, windswept sand and rocky points stretching for about 16km from Tofino to Ucluelet. The snow-covered peaks of the Mackenzie Range rise up over 1200m as a scenic backdrop, and behind the beach grows a thick, lush canopy of coastal rainforest. The white-packed sand itself is the sort of primal seascape that is all but extinct in Europe, littered with beautiful, sea-sculpted driftwood, smashed by surf, broken by crags, and dotted with islets and rock pools oozing with marine life.

As this is a national park, it's all been slightly tamed for human consumption, but in the most discreet and tasteful manner. The best way to get a taste of the area is to walk the beach itself, or to follow any of nine well-maintained **hiking trails**. Most are quite short, though the Half Moon Bay and Shorepine Bog trails are 8km and 10km respectively. Try the South Beach Trail (#4; 1.5km) for admiring the surf, and Half Moon Bay (#2; 10km) for a quieter, sandy bay. All the paths are clearly marked from Hwy 4, but it's still worth picking up a *Hiker's Guide* from the infocentre.

Scenery aside, Long Beach is noted for its **wildlife**, the BC coastline reputedly having more marine species than any other temperate area in the world. As well as the smaller stuff in tidal pools – starfish, anemones, snails, sponges and suchlike – there are large mammals like whales and sea-lions, as well as thousands of migrating birds (especially Oct–Nov), notably pintails, mallards, black brants and Canada geese. Better weather brings out lots of beachcombers (Japanese glass fishing floats are highly coveted), clam diggers, anglers, canoeists, windsurfers and divers, though the water is usually too cold to venture in without a wet suit, and rip currents make swimming dangerous.

PRACTICALITIES

Long Beach's **Pacific Rim National Park Information Centre**, on Hwy 4 3km north of the T-junction for Tofino and Ucluelet (mid-March to early Oct daily 9am–7pm; ☎726-4212), can provide a wealth of material on all aspects of the park, and in summer staff offer guided walks and interpretative programs. Year-round information is available from the Park Administration Office (☎726-7721). Viewing decks with telescopes and lots of well-presented displays are provided at the **Wickaninnish Interpretive Centre** (mid-March to early Oct daily 10am–5pm; ☎726-4212), on your left towards the beach after the infocentre.

There are two park **campgrounds**, the best being *Greenpoint*, set on a lovely bluff overlooking the beach (drive-in; washrooms but no showers; firewood available; $13). However, it's likely to be full every day in July and August, and it's first-come, first-served, so you may have to turn up for several days before getting a spot. There is, however, a waiting-list system, whereby you're given a number and instructions as to when you should be able to return. The other site – more primitive, but equally lovely – is at the northern end of the beach at *Schooner Cove* (outhouses only). The thirty-minute walk from the nearest parking lot

NUU-CHAH-NULTH WHALE HUNTS

All the peoples of the Northwest coast are famed for their skilfully constructed canoes, but only the **Nuu-chah-nulth** – whose name translates roughly as "all along the mountains" – used these fragile cedar crafts to pursue whales, an activity that was accompanied by elaborate ritual. Before embarking on a whaling expedition the whalers had not only to be trained in the art of capturing these mighty animals but also had to be purified through an intensive program of fasting, sexual abstinence and bathing. Whalers also visited forest shrines made up of a whale image surrounded by human skulls or corpses and carved wooden representations of deceased whalers – the dead were thought to aid the novice in his task and to bring about the beaching of dead whales near the village.

When the whaler was on the chase, his wife would lie motionless in her bed; it was thought that the whale would become equally docile. His crew propelled the canoe in total silence until the moment of the harpooning, whereupon they frantically back-paddled to escape the animal's violent death throes as it attempted to dive, only to be thwarted by a long line of floats made from inflated sea lion skins. After exhausting itself, the floating whale was finally killed and boated back to the village, where its meat would be eaten and its blubber processed for its highly prized oil.

reduces demand a little, and also means it tends to be more of a backpackers' hang-out. It too is first-come, first-served ($6). The nearest commercial sites and conventional accommodation are in Tofino and Ucluelet.

Ucluelet

UCLUELET means "People of the Sheltered Bay" and was named by the Nuu-chah-nulth who lived here for centuries to exploit some of the world's richest fishing grounds immediately offshore. Today the port is still dominated by fisheries, which in turn have spawned lumber and canning concerns; these make it a less appealing, if none the less popular base for anglers, whale-watchers, water sports enthusiasts and tourists headed for Long Beach to the north.

Buses and **boats** call at the town from Port Alberni – *Orient Coach Lines* makes the road trip once or twice a day, and the MV *Lady Rose* docks here three days a week (see p.291). There's plenty of **accommodation**, much of it spread along Peninsula Road, the main approach to town from Hwy 4. For full details visit the **infocentre**, 1620 Peninsula Rd (May–Sept daily 9am–6pm; ☎726-4641). Reasonable lodgings include the *Canadian Princess Resort* (☎726-7771; ②–④) on Peninsula Rd, a hotel with one- to six-berth cabins in an old steamer moored in the harbor; the *Sea Side Motel* overlooking the boat basin and marina at 160 Hemlock St (☎726-4624; ③); *Burley's*, 1078 Helen Rd (☎726-4444; ②), a waterfront house; and the least expensive but shabbiest spot in town, the *Ucluelet Hotel*, 250 Main St (☎726-4324; ①). The **public campground** (March–Oct; ☎726-4355; $12–20) overlooks the harbor at 260 Seaplane Base Rd, and the central *Island West Resort RV Park* is at 140 Bay St (☎726-7515; sites $14–18; rooms ③).

Seafood here is as fresh as it comes, and is best sampled at *Smiley's* just across from the *Canadian Princess* on Peninsula Rd, a no-frills, no-decor diner popular with locals. For fish with a Chinese slant, try the *Peninsula Café*, 1648 Peninsula Rd. If you want to walk or see wildlife, the nearest trails are at **Terrace Beach**, just north of the town.

The Broken Group Islands

The only way for the ordinary traveller to approach the hundred or so **Broken Group Islands**, speckled across Barkley Sound between Ucluelet and Bamfield, is by seaplane, chartered boat or the MV *Lady Rose* (see p.291). Boats dock at Gibraltar Island. Immensely wild and beautiful, the islands have a reputation for tremendous wildlife (seals, sea-lions and whales especially), the best **canoeing** in North America, and some of the continent's finest **scuba-diving**. You can rent canoes and gear (contact the *Lady Rose* office or *Sea Kayaking* at 320 Main St, Tofino ☎725-4222), and then take them on board the *Lady Rose* to be dropped off en route. You need to know what you're doing, however – there's plenty of dangerous water – and should pick up the relevant marine chart (*Canadian Hydrographic Service Chart: Broken Group* 3670; $9), available locally. Divers can choose from among fifty shipwrecks claimed by the reefs, rough waters and heavy fogs that beset the aptly named islands.

Eight rough **campgrounds** serve the group, but water is hard to come by: pick up the park leaflet on camping and freshwater locations. A park warden patrols the region from Nettle Island; otherwise the islands are as pristine as the day they rose from the sea.

The West Coast Trail

One of North America's classic walks, the **West Coast Trail** starts 5km south of Bamfield (see opposite) and traverses exceptional coastal scenery for 77km to Port Renfrew. It's no stroll, and though it's becoming very popular it still demands experience, equipment and a fair degree of fitness. Many people, however, do the first easy stage as a day-trip taster from Bamfield. Reckon on five to eight days for the full trip, and be prepared for dreadful weather and poor trail conditions at all times. You will also need to carry camping equipment and all your own food – and cash to pay for ferries and nominal fees for camping on native land.

When it was originally conceived, the trail had nothing to do with promoting the great outdoors. Mariners long ago dubbed this area of coastline the "graveyard of the Pacific", and when the SS *Valencia* went down with all hands here in 1906 the government was persuaded that constructing a trail would at least give stranded sailors a chance to walk to safety along the coast (trying to penetrate the interior's rainforest was out of the question). The path followed a basic telegraph route that linked Victoria with outlying towns and lighthouses, and was kept open by linesmen and lighthouse keepers until the 1960s, when it fell into disrepair. Twenty years ago backpackers began to re-blaze the old trail; some 4000 people now make the trip annually, and the numbers are rising.

Weather is a key factor in planning any trip; the trail is really only passable between June and September (July is the driest month), which is also the only period when it's patrolled by wardens and the only time locals are on hand to ferry you (for a fee) across some of the wider rivers en route.

An increasing amount of literature and route guides is appearing every year (available in most BC bookstores), but for **maps** and **information** visit the main infocentres at Port Alberni (very knowledgeable staff) or Long Beach. The recommended trail map is the 1:50,000 *West Coast Trail, Port Renfrew–Bamfield*, available locally or direct from the Ministry of the Environment, 553 Superior St, Victoria (☎387-1441). Current trail conditions, information and emergency cover are available at Bamfield/Pachena Bay (May–Sept; ☎728-3234) and Port Renfrew (☎647-5434).

Access is also an important consideration. For the northern trailhead at Bamfield take the MV *Lady Rose* from Port Alberni (call ☎723-8313 for current schedule; around $25 one way). *Western Bus Lines*, 4521 Tenth Ave, Port Alberni (Mon, Wed & Fri; ☎723-3341), runs a service along the 100-kilometer gravel road from Port Alberni to the *Tides and Trails Café* in Bamfield. Reservations are a good idea. In addition, the *Pacheenaht Band Bus Service*, 4521 Tenth Ave, Port Alberni (☎647-5521; around $30), runs a summer-only bus service along the same route. The southern trailhead is near Port Renfrew (see p.281).

Bamfield
BAMFIELD, a quaint spot half-raised above the ocean on a wooden boardwalk, has only limited and mainly expensive **accommodation**, so many walkers plan on hitting the trail straight off the bus or boat. If you think you'll need a bed, try to make reservations, especially at the small *Sea Beam,* General Delivery (May–Oct; ☎728-3286) – call anyway for directions or for a taxi pick-up. It runs as a campground and *CHA*-affiliated **hostel** (sites & dorms $15; rooms ②). The setting is tranquil, and it has a small kitchen, common room with open fire and sixteen beds arranged as one-, two- or three-bed dorms: **camping** space is available for 80 tents. Otherwise try the *Bamfield Inn* (Feb–Oct; ☎728-3354; ③) and the seven-room *McKay Bay Lodge* (May–Oct; ☎728-3323; ④), both of which overlook the port. Final choice is *Woods End Lodging*, Wild Duck Rd, six secluded cottages on a two-acre waterfront site (☎728-3383; ③). More places, particularly bed-and-breakfast options, are opening each year.

If you just want to tackle the first stage of the West Coast Trail and return to Bamfield in a day, you can walk the 11km to the **Pachena Lighthouse**, starting from the Ross Bible Camp on the Ohiaht Indian campground at Pachena Beach.

North Vancouver island

It's a moot point where the north of Vancouver Island starts, but if you're travelling on Hwy 19 the sudden lurch into more unspoilt wilderness after Qualicum Beach makes as good a watershed as any. Few of the towns amount to much, and you could head straight up the length of the island to Port Hardy and take the **Inside Passage** ferry up to Prince Rupert – the obvious and most tantalizing itinerary – without missing a lot. Alternatively, you could follow the main highway as far as **Courtenay**, and from there catch a ferry across to the mainland. If you have the means, however, try to get into the wild, central interior, much of it contained within **Strathcona Provincial Park.**

Denman and Hornby islands

North of Qualicum Beach the scenery is uneventful but restful on the eye, graced with ever-improving views of the mainland. Hwy 19 is interrupted by one hamlet, **Buckley Bay**, which consists of a single bed and breakfast and the ferry terminal to **Denman** and **Hornby islands** (18 sailings daily; $15.50 cars, $4 foot passengers) – two outposts described, with some justification, as the "undiscovered Gulf Islands". Big-name celebrities have recently bought property here, complementing a population made up of artists, craftspeople and a laid-back (if wary) mishmash of alternative types (including draft-dodgers from the Vietnam War).

Ferries drop you on Denman, with an infocentre clearly marked on the road from the terminal (☎335-2293). To get to Hornby you need to head 11km across Denman to another terminal, where another 15-minute crossing drops you at Hornby's Shingle Spit dock (most of what happens on Hornby, however, happens at Tribune Bay on the far side of island, 10km distant – try for a lift from a car coming off the ferry if you have no vehicle). There's no public transportation on either island, so you'll need a car or bike to explore: **bikes** can be rented from the *Bike Shoppe* on Denman, 4696 Lacon Rd (☎335-0638), and from the *Zucchini Ocean Kayak Centre* next to the *Co-Op* on Hornby (daily summer; Sat & Sun spring and fall; ☎335-0045 or 335-2033).

Highlights on Denman, the less retrogressive of the islands, are the beaches of the Sandy Island Marine Park and the trails of Boyle Point Park to the Chrome Island Lighthouse. On Hornby you should head for the **Hellivel Provincial Park** and its trails, the best a six-kilometer (1hr 30min) loop to Hellivel Bluffs (with plenty of opportunities to see eagles, herons, spring wildflowers and lots of aquatic wildlife). Whaling Station Bay and Tribune Bay Provincial Park have good beaches (and there's a nudist beach at Little Tribune Bay).

Accommodation is in short supply on both islands, and it's virtually essential in summer to have pre-booked rooms. On Denman the main option is the five-room turn-of-the-century farmhouse, the *Denman Island Guest House and Restaurant*, near the ferry terminal at 3808 Denman Rd (☎335-2688; ③). **Eating** places on the island are concentrated near the ferry, the most noteworthy being the *Denman Island Store and Café*. Hornby has more rooms and campgrounds: *Sea Breeze Lodge*, Fowler Rd (☎335-2321; ⑤); the *Hornby Island Resort*, Shingle Spit Rd (☎335-0136; tents $15; rooms ③); *Bradsdadsland Country Camp and Resort*, 1980 Shingle Spit Rd (☎335-0757; tents $15–17; rooms ③); *Ford's Cove Marina*, Ford's Cove (☎335-2169; tents $12–14; rooms ③, weekly rates only); and the big 120-pitch *Tribune Bay Campsite*, Saltspray Rd (☎335-2359; $14.50–17). At the ferry dock on Hornby are *The Thatch*, a restaurant and deli with great views, and *The Pub*, the island's only spot for alcoholic refreshment (with live music Mon–Wed nights). Across on Tribune Bay the *Co-Op* is the hub of island life, with virtually everything in the way of food and supplies (☎335-1121).

Courtenay

Beyond Buckley Bay is a short stretch of wild, pebbly beach, and then the **Comox Valley**, open rural country that's not as captivating as the brochures might lead you to expect. Of three settlements here – Comox, Cumberland and **COURTENAY** – only the last is of interest, and then only as a ferry link to Powell River on the mainland. The terminal is a good twenty minutes' drive from the town along backroads: if you don't have your own vehicle, you'll have to take a taxi or hold out for the minibus shuttle that leaves the bus depot twice on Tuesday and Friday to connect with sailings. Courtenay is connected to Nanaimo and Victoria by **bus** (4 daily), and is the terminus for **trains** from Victoria (1 daily). If you get stranded in town, there are plenty of **motels** along the strip on the southern approach, close to the **infocentre** at 2040 Cliffe Ave (daily winter 9am–5pm; longer hours in summer; ☎334-3234). The best **camping** is 20km north of Courtenay at Miracle Beach Provincial Park – a vast, and very popular, tract of sand.

The **Comox Valley** scores higher inland, on the eastern fringes of Strathcona Provincial Park (see p.300) and the new **skiing** areas of Forbidden Plateau and Mount Washington. There's plenty of **hiking** in summer, when the Forbidden

Plateau lifts operate at weekends from 11am to 3pm. A great day hike on Mount Washington is the five-hour walk on well-marked trails from the ski area across Paradise Meadows to Moat Lake or Circlet Lake. For details of tougher walks (Battleship Lake, Lady Lake), ask at the infocentre. Access to the trailheads is by minor road from Courtenay.

Campbell River

Of the hundred or so Northwestern towns that claim to be "Salmon Capital of the World", **CAMPBELL RIVER**, 46km north of Courtenay, probably comes closest to justifying the boast. Fish and fishing dominate the place to a ludicrous degree, and you'll soon be heartily sick of pictures of grinning anglers holding impossibly huge chinook salmon. Massive shoals of these monsters are forced into the three-kilometer channel between the town and the mainland, making the job of catching them little more than a formality. The town grew to accommodate fishermen from the outset, centered on a hotel built in 1904 after word spread of the colossal fish that local Cape Mudge natives were able to pluck from the sea. Today about sixty percent of all visitors come to dangle a line in the water. Others come for the scuba-diving (once described by *National Geographic* as the second best in the world). For the casual visitor, the place serves as the main road access to the wilds of Strathcona Provincial Park. If you want to **fish**, hundreds of stores and guides are on hand to help out and rent equipment. The full kit costs about $15 a day, and about $50 for a morning's guidance. Huge numbers of people, however, fish from the new **Discovery Pier**, Canada's first saltwater fishing pier ($1). **Diving** rentals come more expensive; try *Beaver Aquatics* near the Quadra ferry dock in Discovery Bay Marina (☎287-7652). If you merely want to know something about salmon before they end up on a plate, drop in on the **Quinsam Salmon Hatchery**, 5km west of town on the road to Gold River (daily 8am–4pm).

Campbell River's well-stocked **infocentre** is at 1235 Shoppers' Row (daily 9am–6pm; ☎286-0764). Four *Island Coachlines* **buses** daily run to Victoria, but there's only one a day north to Port Hardy and towns en route. The **bus terminal** is on the corner of Cedar and 13th near the Royal Bank (☎287-7151). **Accommodation** is no problem, Campbell River being a resort first and foremost: try the *Super 8 Motel* on the main road south of town (☎286-6622; ③), or the carving-stuffed *Campbell River Lodge*, 1760 North Island Hwy (☎287-7446; ③). You won't be able to escape the fishing clutter common to all hotels unless you head for a **bed and breakfast**, such as *Pier's House B&B*, 670 Island Hwy (☎287-2943; ③). For nice shady **camping** use the *Parkside Campground*, 5km west of town on Hwy 28 (April–Sept; ☎287-3113; laundromat and hot showers; from $12).

There's good seafood at *Shagpokes* in the *Anchor Inn*, 261 Island Hwy (great views), or the *Gourmet by the Sea* on the main road about 15km south of town at Bennett's Point. Budget places to **eat** abound, mainly of the fast-food variety: best burger joint is *Del's Drive-In & Diner*, 1423 Island Hwy, known as somewhere with plenty of local color. For beer and snacks try the *Royal Coachman*, 84 Dogwood St, popular with tourists and townspeople alike.

Quadra Island

Quadra Island is fifteen minutes away from Campbell River and makes a nice respite from the fish. Ferries run roughly hourly from the well-signed terminal out of town. The main excuse for the crossing is the **Kwagiulth Museum and**

Cultural Centre, home to one of the country's most noted collections of potlatch regalia (summer daily 10am–4.30pm; otherwise Tues–Sat; $2). As elsewhere in Canada, the masks, costumes and ritual objects were confiscated by the government in an attempt to stamp out one of the natives' most potent ceremonies, and only came back on condition they would be locked up in a museum.

While on the island you could also walk its coastal **trails**, or climb Chinese Mountain for some cracking views. There's swimming off a rocky beach at **Rebecca Spit Provincial Park**, but the water's warmer and there's a bit of sand at the more distant **Village Bay Park**. Six places offer **accommodation**, including the *Heriot Bay Inn*, on Heriot Bay Rd (☎285-3322; rooms ③; camping from $14), and *Whiskey Point Lodge*, by the ferry dock at 725 Quathioski Cove Rd (☎285-2201; ③).

Strathcona Provincial Park

Vancouver Island's largest protected area, and the oldest park in British Columbia, **Strathcona Provincial Park** is one of the few places on the island where the scenery approaches the grandeur of the mainland mountains. The island's highest point, Golden Hinde (2200m), is here, and it's also a place where there's a good chance of seeing rare indigenous wildlife (Roosevelt elk, marmot and black-tailed deer the most notable examples). Only two areas have any sort of facilities for the visitor – **Forbidden Plateau**, approached from Courtenay, and the more popular **Buttle Lake** region, accessible from Campbell River via Hwy 28. The *Gold River Minibus* will drop you at the head of Buttle Lake, about 40km west of Campbell River (Sun, Tues & Thurs). The rest of the park is unsullied wilderness, but fully open to backpackers and hardier walkers. Be sure to pick up the blue *BC Parks* pamphlet (available from the infocentre at Campbell River and elsewhere): it has a good general map and gives lots of information, such as the comforting fact that there are no grizzly bears in the park.

HIKING IN STRATHCONA

Hiking, it hardly needs saying, is superb in Strathcona, with a jaw-dropping scenic combination of jagged mountains – including Golden Hinde (2200m), the island's highest point – lakes, rivers, waterfalls and all the trees you could possibly want. Seven marked **trails** fan out from the Buttle Lake area, together with six shorter nature walks, most less than 2km long, among which the Lady Falls and Lupin Falls trails stand out for their waterfall and forest views.

All the longer trails can be tramped in a day, though the most popular, the **Elk River Trail** (10km), which starts from Drum Lake on Hwy 28, lends itself to an overnight stop. Popular with backpackers because of its gentle grade, the path ends up at Landslide Lake, an idyllic camping spot. The other highly regarded trail is the **Flower Ridge** walk, which starts at the southern end of Buttle Lake. In the Forbidden Plateau area, named after a native legend that claimed evil spirits lay in wait to devour women and children who entered its precincts, the most popular trip is the **Forbidden Plateau Skyride** to the summit of Wood Mountain where there's a two-kilometer trail to a viewpoint over Boston Canyon. Backcountry camping is allowed throughout the park, and the backpacking is great once you've hauled up onto the summit ridges above the treeline. For serious exploration buy the relevant topographic maps at *MAPS BC*, Ministry of Environment and Parks, Parliament Buildings, Victoria.

You'll see numerous pictures of **Della Falls** around Campbell River, which at 440m are among the world's highest; unfortunately it's a two-day trek with a canoe passage thrown in if you're going to see them.

The approach to the park along Hwy 28 is worth taking for the scenery alone; numerous short trails and nature walks are signposted from rest stops, most no more than twenty minutes' stroll from the car. **Elk Falls Provincial Park** is the first stop, ten minutes out of Campbell River, noted for its gorge and waterfall.

Park practicalities

The **Park Visitor Centre** is located at the junction of Hwy 28 and the Buttle Lake road (May–Sept only); fifteen information shelters around the lake also provide some trail and wildlife information. Buttle Lake has two provincial **campgrounds** (both $8) with facilities, one alongside the park center, the other at Ralph River on the extreme southern end of Buttle Lake, accessed by the road along the lake's eastern shore. Both have good **swimming** areas nearby.

The park's only commercial **accommodation** is provided by the *Strathcona Park Lodge* (☎286-8206 or 286-3122; ④), just outside the Buttle Lake entrance, a weird mixture of hotel, outdoor pursuits lodge, hostel and small nine-site campground ($14–16). For the **hostel** you'll need your own sleeping bag and you must call in advance (pick-ups from Campbell River are sometimes available); rates are about $15 per person, with use of a kitchen. You can also rent canoes, bikes and other outdoor equipment, and sign up for any number of organized tours and activities.

Gold River and Tahsis

There's not a lot happening at **GOLD RIVER,** a tiny logging community 89km west of Campbell River – founded in 1965, the place only has one hotel and a couple of stores – but the ride over on Hwy 28 is superb, and there's the chance to explore the coastline by boat. Every Thursday, year round, the **Uchuck III**, a converted World War II minesweeper, takes mail, cargo and passengers up the coast to Tahsis from the dock at the end of Hwy 28, about 15km southwest of Gold River, returning early evening. It's a lovely trip, with great sea views, tree-covered mountains, and several drop-offs at obscure villages en route. Additional sailings are laid on in July and August (☎283-2325 for information). The local **infocentre** is on Hwy 28 (June–Sept; ☎283-2418).

One of the area's two minor attractions is **Quatsino Cave**, the deepest vertical cave in North America, parts of which are open to the public – for details ask at the infocentre on Village Square Plaza (May–Sept daily 9am–7pm); the other is the **Big Drop**, a stretch of Gold River whitewater known to kayakers worldwide. **Accommodation** is a tad expensive at both the *Gold River Chalet*, 390 Nimpkish Drive (☎283-2244; ④), and the *Ridgeview Motel,* located in a panoramic spot above the village at 395 Donner Court (☎283-2277; ④) – but the *Peppercorn Trail Motel and Campground* on Mill Road (☎283-2443; ①) has cheaper rooms and will let you **camp** for $16.

There are two beautiful roads north from Gold River, both rough, but worth the jolts for the scenery. One provides an alternative approach to **TAHSIS**, which has a single motel if you need to break your journey, the *Tahsis Motel*, Head Bay Rd (☎934-6318; ②). For more background on a lovely part of the coast contact the **infocentre** on Rugged Mountain Rd (summer only; ☎934-6667).

North to Port McNeill, Telegraph Cove and Alert Bay

The main highway north of Campbell River cuts inland and climbs through increasingly rugged and deserted country, particularly after **Sayward**, the one main community en route. Near Sayward is the marvellously oddball **Valley of a Thousand Faces**: 1400 famous faces painted onto cedar logs, the work of a Dutch artist, and more interesting than it sounds (May–Aug daily 10am–4pm; donation). Almost alongside is an RV and tent **campground**, the *White River Court* (☎282-3265; from $10). With a car, you could strike off south from here for 62km to **Schoen Lake Provincial Park**, featuring a couple of forest trails and a well-kept campground.

PORT McNEILL, 180km north of Campbell River and the first real town along Hwy 19, is merely a motel and logging town and not somewhere to spend longer than necessary. By contrast, **TELEGRAPH COVE**, 8km south of Port McNeill and reached by a rough side road, is an immensely likeable place and the best of BC's so-called "boardwalk villages": the whole community is raised on wooden stilts over the waters. As an added bonus, the village has become one of the island's premier **whale-watching** spots, the main attraction here being the pods of orcas (killer whales) that calve locally. Some nineteen of these "families" live at nearby Robson Bight, established as an ecological reserve in 1982. The best outfit for a trip to see them is *Stubbs Island Charters* (☎928-3185), but their daily sailings (June–Oct) are popular, so call well in advance to be sure of a place.

In summer you can buy food at a small café, but otherwise the only provision for visitors is an incongruous new building with shop, ice-cream counter and coffee bar. The only **accommodation** is the large 121-pitch *Telegraph Cove Resorts Campground* (May–Sept; ☎928-3131; $15–18.50) a short walk from the village and one of the best-located sites on Vancouver Island, making reservations essential in summer. The *Hidden Cove Lodge* (☎956-3916; ⑧) at Lewis Point (1km by boat from Telegraph Cove) has four superb lodges, but at $110 to $540 a room is probably beyond the means of most. The *Alder Bay Campground* 6km off Hwy 19 en route for Telegraph Cove from Port McNeill provides 90 grassy tent sites with ocean views (May–Sept; ☎956-4117; reservations recommended; $12).

The breezy fishing village of **ALERT BAY**, on Cormorant Island, is reached by numerous daily ferries from Port McNeill. The fifty-minute crossing sets you back only $2 and in season provides a good chance of seeing whales en route. Despite the predominance of non-native industries (fish processing), half the population of the island is Namgis. The **infocentre** (year round; ☎974-5213) is at 116 Fir St immediately to your right as you come off the ferry. Bear left out of the main part of the village to reach the excellent **U'Mista Cultural Centre** (Mon–Sat 9am–5pm; $3), which houses a collection of potlatch items and artefacts, and shows a couple of award-winning films; you might also come across local kids being taught native languages, songs and dances. The village also claims the world's tallest fully carved **totem pole** (other contenders, say villagers, are all pole and no carving). Also worth a look is the wildlife and weird swamp habitat at **Gator Gardens** behind the bay. Most people come over for the day, but **accommodation** options include the *Orca Inn*, 291 Fir St (☎974-5322; ②) overlooking the sea; *Ocean View Accommodations*, 390 Poplar St, 1km from the ferry terminal (☎974-5457; ③); *Bayside Inn Hotel*, overlooking the waterfront at 81 First St (☎974-5857; ②–④); and *Oceanview Camping* on Alder Rd (☎974-5213; $10).

Port Hardy

Dominated by big-time copper mining, a large fishing fleet and the usual logging concerns, **PORT HARDY** is best known among travellers as the departure point for ships plying one of the more spectacular stretches of the famous **Inside Passage** to Prince Rupert (and thence to Alaska).

If possible, time your arrival to coincide with one of the sailings, which leave every other day in summer and twice weekly in winter. Some **bus** services are scheduled to do this. A daily *Island Coach Lines* bus (☎949-7532 in Port Hardy, ☎385-4411 in Victoria) leaves Victoria early in the morning with a change in Nanaimo, arriving at the Port Hardy ferry terminal in late afternoon; between June and September an extra service operates over the same route on even-numbered dates, departing at noon. *Maverick Coach Lines* (☎753-4371 in Nanaimo, ☎662-3222 in Vancouver) runs an early-morning bus from Vancouver to Nanaimo (inclusive of ferry), connecting with the daily *ICL* bus to Port Hardy. You can **fly** direct from Vancouver International Airport to Port Hardy with *Time Air* (☎279-6611 in Vancouver) or *Air BC* (☎278-3800 in Vancouver).

The Port Hardy **ferry terminal** is actually well away from the town itself at Bear Cove, where buses stop before carrying on to stop opposite the **infocentre**, 7250 Market St (year round; daily 9am–6pm; ☎949-7622). If you stay overnight, leave plenty of time to reach the terminal – sailings in summer are usually around 7.30am. *North Island Transport* provide a shuttle bus service between the ferry

---

THE INSIDE PASSAGE

One of Canada's and the Northwest's great trips, the **Inside Passage** aboard *BC Ferries' Queen of the North*, between Port Hardy and Prince Rupert on the British Columbia mainland, is an inexpensive way of getting what people on the big cruise ships are getting: mountains, islands, waterfalls, glaciers, sea lions, whales, eagles and some of the grandest coastal scenery on the continent. By linking up with the *Greyhound* bus network or the *VIA* rail terminal at Prince Rupert, it also makes a good leg in any number of convenient itineraries around British Columbia. Some travellers will have come from Washington State, others will want to press on from Prince Rupert to Skagway by boat and then head north into Alaska and the Yukon (see p.448 for details on the *Alaska Marine* ferries). It's a good way to meet fellow travellers, particularly if you pitch a tent in the boat's gymnasium, which is set aside for the purpose.

The sea passage takes twenty hours, with one stop at Bella Bella. Be aware that from October 5 to May 25 the sailings in both directions are predominantly at night, which rather defeats the object of the trip. The cost is about $90 single for a foot passenger, $165 for a car; reservations are **essential** throughout the summer season if you're taking a car or want a cabin. Bookings can be made by phone (☎386-3431 in Victoria; ☎669-1211 in Vancouver), fax (☎381-5452 in Victoria) or post (BC Ferry Corporation, 1112 Fort St, Victoria, BC). Include name and address; number in party; length, height and type of car; choice of day-room or cabin; and preferred date of departure and alternatives. Full payment is required up front. Cabins can be reserved by foot passengers, and range from about $35 (2-berth, lower deck) to $75 on the boat deck. If you're making a round trip and want to leave your car behind, there are several supervised lock-ups in Port Hardy: try *Daze Parking* (☎949-7792).

and the town's main hotels (☎949-6300 for information). Otherwise call a taxi (☎949-8000). Many travellers to Port Hardy are in RVs, but there's still some pressure on hotel **accommodation** in summer, and it's as well to call ahead if you're not coinciding with one of the ferry sailings. The cheapest rooms are out of town at the *Airport Inn* (☎949-9424; ②) and at the *Seagate Hotel*, 8600 Granville St (☎949-6348; ②), but you'd be better off in one of the faintly more upmarket central choices like the *North Shore Inn*, 7370 Market St (☎949-8500; ③), and *Thunderbird Inn*, 7050 Rupert St (☎949-7767; ③), the former with nice views of the port and both with potentially sleep-depriving live music. Five minutes south of town at 4965 Byng Rd, in a park-like setting near the river, is the good-value *Pioneer Inn* (☎949-7271; ②). The *Wildwoods* **campground** (☎949-6753) is the perfect tenting option, being within easy walking distance of the ferry. The *Quatse River Campground* (☎949-2395; $12) is at 5050 Hardy Rd opposite the *Pioneer Inn*.

Granville and Market streets have the main **restaurant** concentrations: try *Snuggles*, next to the *Pioneer Inn*, which aims at a cozy English pub atmosphere with live music, drama (Fri nights) and steaks, salads and salmon grilled over an open fire. The infocentre can give you all the details about Port Hardy's tiny but free **museum**, and the immense wilderness of **Cape Scott Provincial Park**, accessible only by foot and supposed to have some of the most consistently bad weather in the world.

NORTH OF VANCOUVER

Although most people will probably move on from Vancouver either to Vancouver Island or southern British Columbia, there are two more excursions from Vancouver on the mainland. The first is the 150-kilometer **Sunshine Coast**, the only stretch of accessible coastline on mainland British Columbia, and a possible springboard to Vancouver Island and the Inside Passage ferry to Prince Rupert. The second is the inland route to **Garibaldi Provincial Park**, containing by far the best scenery and hiking country within striking distance of Vancouver, and the high-profile ski resort of **Whistler**; the road becomes a summer-only route beyond Whistler, but train passengers can forge on through wilder parts all the way to Prince George, the hub of communications in northern British Columbia (see p.444).

The Sunshine Coast

A mild-weathered stretch of sandy beaches, rugged headlands and quiet lagoons backed by forested hills, the **Sunshine Coast** receives heavy promotion – and heavy tourist traffic as a result – though its reputation is over stated and the scenic rewards are slim compared to the interior. In summer, however, this area offers what are reputedly some of Canada's best diving, boating and fishing opportunities, all of which stoke a string of busy villages eager to provide accommodation, run tours and rent anything from bikes to full-sized cruisers.

Highway 101 runs the length of the coast, but it's interrupted at two points by sizeable inlets that entail lengthy ferry crossings. Motorists face enormous long waits to get on the boats in summer (reservations aren't possible), but the crossings present no problems for bus or foot passengers – indeed, they're the best bits of the trip. Given that the area is hardly worth full-scale exploration by car anyway, you might as well go by **bus**; it's perfectly feasible to get to Powell River and back in a day (though it's a long ten-hour day). *Maverick Coach Lines* (☎662-3222) runs two buses daily to Powell River (5hr; $25) and a third as far as Sechelt (2hr; $12).

Along Highway 101

Soon reached and well signposted from North Vancouver, **HORSESHOE BAY** is the departure point for the first of the Hwy 101 **ferry** crossings, a half-hour passage through the islands of fjord-like Howe Sound (regular sailings year round). Ferries also ply from here to Nanaimo on Vancouver Island, with hourly sailings in summer and every other hour in off-season. For information on either of these services contact *BC Ferries* in Vancouver (☎669-1211 or 685-1021), or pick up a timetable from the Vancouver infocentre.

GIBSONS, the terminal on the other side of Howe Sound, is a scrappy place spread widely over a wooded hillside – the nicest area is around the busy marina, where you'll find the **infocentre** at 668 Sunny Crest Rd (year round; daily 9am–6pm; ☎886-2325). Motels abound, but for decent camping hold out for **Roberts Creek Provincial Park**, 8km northwest of the terminal on Hwy 101.

Beyond, the service and supplies village of **SECHELT** is less tourist-oriented than Gibsons, and ongoing development lends the town a messy air which isn't helped by its drab, flat location. Just 4km north, however, **Porpoise Bay Provincial Park** has a campground, a sandy beach, good swimming and a few short woodland trails. The main road beyond Sechelt is very pretty, and offers occasional views to the sea when it's not trapped in the trees. Pender Harbour comprises a collection of small communities, of which **MADEIRA PARK** is the most substantial. Whales occasionally pass this section of coast (which, sadly, has made it the source of most of the whales in the world's aquariums), but the main attractions are fishing and boating.

Earl's Cove is nothing but the departure ramp of the second **ferry** en route, a longer crossing (45min) which again offers fantastic views of sheer mountains plunging into the sea. A short trail (4km) from the adjacent parking lot leads to a viewpoint for the **Skookumchuck Narrows**, where the Sechelt Inlet constricts to produce boiling rapids at the turn of each tide. On board the ferry, look north beyond the low wooded hills – devoid of all human trace – to the immense waterfall which drops off a Lost World-type plateau into the sea.

From Jervis Bay, the opposite landing stage, the country is comparatively less travelled. A couple of kilometers up the road is the best of all the provincial parks in this region, **Saltery Bay Provincial Park.** Everything here is discreetly hidden in the trees between the road and the coast, and the campground – beautifully sited – is connected by short trails to a couple of swimming beaches. The main road beyond is largely enclosed by trees, so there's little to see of the coast, though various **campgrounds** give onto the sea, notably the big *Oceanside* site, 4km short of Powell River, which sits on a superb piece of shoreline (☎485-2435; $10). Although it's given over mainly to RVs, there are a few sites for tents.

Powell River and beyond

Given its seafront location, **POWELL RIVER** inevitably has its scenic side, but its unfocused sprawl and nearby sawmill dampen the overall appeal. The main road cruises past almost 4km of box-like retirement bungalows before reaching the town center – not a terribly captivating resort. If you're catching the **ferry** to Courtenay on Vancouver Island (4 daily; 75min), there's no need to pass through the townsite, as the terminal is 2km to the east at Westview. Some of the **buses** from Vancouver are timed to coincide with the boats; if yours doesn't, you can either walk or call a taxi (☎483-3666). The local **infocentre** (daily 9am–5pm; ☎485-4701), immediately at the end of the wooden ferry pier, can supply a visitor's map with detailed coverage of the many trails leading inland from the coast hereabouts; they can also advise on boat trips on Powell Lake, immediately inland, and tours to Desolation Sound, further up the coast. In the event of having to stay overnight, you can choose from a dozen or so **motels** in town and two at the terminal itself. Of the latter, the *Marine Motel* (☎485-4242; ②), on the left as you look at the ferry, is immensely preferable to the bar and strip-joint opposite. There's a good little diner downstairs, or you can try the **fish-and-chip** shop on the left just beyond the dingier motel, or the *Seaview* immediately above the terminal. For pricier seafood specials the popular choice is the *Beach Gardens Resort Hotel*, 7074 Westminster St, at the extreme eastern edge of Powell River. The most central of several **campgrounds** is the *Willingdon Beach* on the seafront off Marine Avenue at 6910 Duncan St (☎485-2242; $8.50–13.50).

The northern endpoint of Hwy 101 – which, incidentally, starts in Mexico City, making it one of North America's longest continuous routes – is the hamlet of **LUND**, 28km up the coast from Powell River. **Desolation Sound Marine Provincial Park**, about 10km north of Lund, offers some of Canada's best boating and scuba-diving, plus fishing, canoeing and kayaking. There's no road access to the park, but a number of outfitters in Powell River run tours to it and rent all the equipment you could possibly need – try *Westview Live Bait Ltd*, 4527 Marine Ave, for **canoes**; *Coulter's Diving*, 4557 Willingdon Ave, for **scuba gear**; and *Spokes*, 4710 Marine Drive, for **bicycles**. The more modest **Okeover Provincial Park**, immediately north of Lund, has an unserviced campground.

The Sea to Sky Highway

A fancy name for Highway 99 between North Vancouver and Whistler, the **Sea to Sky Highway** has a slightly better reputation than it deserves. Where it undoubtedly scores is in its early coastal stretch, where the road clings perilously to an almost sheer cliff and mountains come dramatically into view on both sides of Howe Sound. Views here are better than along the Sunshine Coast, though plenty of campgrounds, motels and minor roadside distractions fill the route until the mountains of the Coast Range rear up beyond Squamish for the rest of the way to Whistler.

You're better off driving the highway only as far as Garibaldi Provincial Park – the summer-only section between Pemberton and Lillooet is very slow going. Six daily *Maverick Coach Lines* **buses** (☎662-3222) connect Vancouver and Whistler ($20; 3 daily continue to Pemberton), which you can easily manage as a day trip, though a far more interesting and popular way of covering this ground is by

train. *BC Rail* operates a daily passenger service between North Vancouver and Lillooet, calling at Whistler and other minor stations; the train arrives in Lillooet at 1pm and sets off back for Vancouver at 3.30pm, making for an excellent day-trip ($30 return to Whistler, $55.50 return to Lillooet). Another train continues on to Prince George daily between mid-June and late September, and on Sunday, Wednesday and Friday the rest of the year ($140 one way) – a better way to make this journey than by bus via Hope and Cache Creek. Reservations are required if you're travelling beyond Lillooet (☎631-3500).

North Vancouver to Squamish

Road and rail lines meet with some squalor at **BRITANNIA BEACH**, whose **BC Museum of Mining** is the first reason to take time out from admiring the views (May–Aug Wed–Sun 10am–4pm; Sept Sat & Sun 10am–4pm; $5). Clustered around what was, in the 1930s, the largest producer of copper in the British Empire, the museum is housed in a huge, derelict-looking white building on the hillside and is chock-full of hands-on displays, original working machinery and archive photographs.

Beyond Britannia Beach a huge, chimney-surrounded lumber mill hoves into view across Howe Sound to spoil the scenic wonder along this stretch, though **Petgill Lake** makes a nice picnic spot. This is but one of several small coastal reserves, the most striking of which is **Shannon Falls Provincial Park**, signed right off the road and worth a stop for its spectacular 335-metre **waterfall** (5min walk from the road) – though the proximity of the road, plus some commercial fuss and bother, detract a touch.

The sea views and coastal drama end at **SQUAMISH**, not a pretty place, whose houses spread out over a flat plain amid warehouses, logging waste and old machinery. All the town has by way of fame is the rock that literally overshadows it, which is puzzlingly claimed to be the world's "second biggest rock". It's certainly big. If you must be here, come in August when the town holds what it deems to be the World Lumberjack Competition; at all other times this is a pit-stop only. Most of the relevant parts of the town are concentrated on Cleveland Avenue, including the **infocentre** (daily 9am–6pm; longer hours in summer; ☎892-9244), the big *Overwaitea* supermarket and the most central **accommodation**, the *August Jack Motor Inn* on Cleveland Ave (☎892-3504; ③).

The road north of Squamish continues to be a mess, but after about 5km begins to enter the classic river, mountain and forest country of the BC interior. The journey thereafter is a joy, with only the march of electricity pylons and big road-widening schemes to take the edge off an idyllic drive.

Garibaldi Provincial Park

Unless you're skiing, **Garibaldi Provincial Park** is the main incentive to head this way. As you'd expect, it's a huge and unspoilt area which combines all the usual breathtaking ingredients of lakes, rivers, forests, glaciers and the peaks of the Coast Mountains (Wedge Mountain, at 2891m, is the park's highest point). Four rough roads access the park from points along the highway between Squamish and Whistler, but you'll need transportation to reach the trailheads. Pick up the excellent *BC Parks* pamphlet for Garibaldi from the Vancouver tourist office for a comprehensive run-down on all trails, campgrounds and the like.

Unless you're camping, the only accommodation close to the park is at Whistler, though with an early start from Vancouver you could feasibly enjoy a good walk and return the same day.

There are five main areas with trails, of which the **Black Tusk/Garibaldi Lake** region is the most popular and probably most beautiful. Try the trail from the parking area at Rubble Creek to Garibaldi Lake (9km; 3hr one way) or to Taylor Meadows (7km; 2hr 30min). Further trails then fan out from Garibaldi Lake, including one to the huge basalt outcrop of **Black Tusk**, a rare opportunity to reach an alpine summit without any rock climbing. The other hiking areas from south to north are **Diamond Head**, **Cheakamus Lake**, **Singing Pass** and **Wedgemount Lake**. Access to each is clearly signed from the highway, and all have wilderness campsites and are explored by several trails of varying lengths. Outside these small defined areas, however, the park is untrammelled wilderness. Bear in mind there are also hiking possibilities outside the park from Whistler (see below), where in summer you can get a head start on hikes by riding up the ski lifts.

Whistler

WHISTLER is less a town than a full-blown resort. **Whistler Village** is the "downtown", a brand-new and characterless conglomeration of hotels, mountain-gear shops and more loud people in nasty fluorescent clothes than are healthy in one place at any one time. To confuse things, however, a string of smaller resorts straggle a good 6km along Hwy 99 south of the "village", culminating in **Whistler Creek**, home to the main **infocentre** (daily 9am–5pm; longer hours in summer; ☎932-5528) but not terribly useful as a base unless you're skiing. But **skiing**, of course, is what most people are here for, eager to indulge at one of the world's top-ranked resorts, home to the longest vertical run in North America (2100m) and, since 1988, the best summer skiing in the northern hemisphere. If you're not on skis, however, you can still ride one of the two lifts from the village up **Blackcomb Mountain**, where's there's an expensive café, great views and several trailheads. If you're walking, pick up the duplicated sheet of trails from the infocentre or from the smaller kiosks in the village, or better yet buy the 1:50,000 *Whistler and Garibaldi Region* **map**. The two most popular short walks are the **Rainbow Falls** and **Singing Pass** trails.

Practicalities

Soulless and appallingly planned it may be, but Whistler Village has all the facilities of any regular village, with the difference that they all charge more than you'd pay anywhere else. If money's no object, the **infocentre** (see above) will direct you to masses of comfortable chalet accommodation; otherwise call **Whistler Central Reservations** (☎932-4222), who can help find room in an appropriate price bracket. Remember that chalets can put extra beds in double rooms at nominal rates. The **youth hostel** on Alta Lake at 5678 Alta Lake Rd, one of the nicest hostels in BC (☎932-5492; ①), is a signposted forty-minute walk from the infocentre; note that *BC Rail* trains will stop alongside the hostel if you ask the conductor. As it's popular year-round, it's worth reserving space by sending the first night's money as a deposit, or at least calling ahead. All beds are in shared rooms and cost $12 for members, $19.50 for non-members. A little closer to Hwy 99 (behind the *Husky* garage) is the *Backpacker's Guest House*, 2124 Lake

Placid Rd (☎932-1177; ①), with private or shared rooms from $15. Other reasonably priced options include *Seppo's Log Cabin*, 7114 Nestor's Rd (☎932-6696; ①), and the *Fireside Lodge* (☎932-4545; ①) at Nordic Estates, 3km south of the village. Finally, you could try the *Whistler Lodge* (☎228-5851; ③), also in Nordic Estates, which is owned by the University of British Columbia but lets non-students stay from $15; check-in time is from 4pm to 10pm. Best of the **campgrounds** is the *Whistler KOA*, 1km north of the village off Hwy 99 to the right (☎932-5181; $17).

If you're up for **drinking** and **nightlife**, Whistler certainly has plenty of both in winter – and increasingly in summer. People come up for seasonal work from Vancouver, and get together in places like *Tapley's Neighborhood Pub* next to the conference center and the big bar at the main gondola terminal. **Food** is expensive unless you buy your own at the stores in less flashy Whistler Creek: in the village the best place for **snacks** is *Ingrid's Cork and Cheddar* in the "Village Square" opposite the *Alexis Restaurant*: the latter has many claims to being Canada's most kitsch restaurant. *Bart's* restaurant and pub, at the top end of the village, and *The Keg*, in Sundial Place, are reliable steak, salad and salmon type places.

North of Whistler

Hwy 99 funnels down to two slow lanes at **PEMBERTON**, and beyond, whether you're travelling by road or rail, you're treated to some wonderfully wild country in which Vancouver and even Whistler seem a long way away. Patches of forest poke through rugged mountainsides and scree slopes, and a succession of glorious lakes culminate in Sefton Lake, whose hydroelectric schemes feed power into the grid as far south as Arizona, accounting for the pylons south of Whistler.

At the lumber town of **LILLOOET** the railway meets the Fraser River, which marks a turning point in the scenery as denuded crags and hillsides increasingly hint at the *High Noon*-type ranching country to come. In July and August, the rocky banks and bars of the sluggish, mud-colored river immediately north of town are dotted with vivid orange and blue tepees and tarpaulins. These belong to Native Americans who still come to catch, dry and smoke salmon as the fish make their way upriver to spawn – one of the few places where this tradition is continued. The town boasts four central **motels** if you need to stay: best are the *Mile 0 Motel*, 616 Main St (☎256-7511; ③), and the *4 Pines Motel* on the corner of Eighth Ave and Russell St (☎256-4247; ①).

Over the next 100km the **Fraser Valley** is more than enough to justify the price of a train ticket to Prince George. The alpine profile of the Coast Range flattens out into the high, table-topped ridges of the Cariboo Plateau, and the railway looks down to the dry, dustbowl gullies and cliffs of the vast canyon from a vantage point some 1000m above the river. The views are some of the grandest and strangest in the province, taking in huge horizons of bleached ocher soil and deserts of lonely scrubby pasture that belonged once to the so-called **"remittance men"**: the off-beam, half-mad or just plain dangerous sons of nineteenth-century English aristocrats dispatched here on a monthly remittance, or allowance, and encouraged not to get in touch. Several ranches here – some of the biggest in Canada – were long owned by Britons, among them the ranch bought in 1912 by the Marquis of Exeter and run by his son, Lord Martin Cecil, who used it as a base for the Emissaries of Divine Light, a religious group, until his recent death.

The Cariboo

The Cariboo is the name given to the broad, rolling ranching country and immense forests of British Columbia's interior plateau, which extend north of Lillooet between the Coast Mountains to the west and Cariboo Mountains to the east. The region contains by far the dullest scenery in the province, and what little interest it offers – aside from fishing and boating on remote lakes – comes from its **gold-mining** heritage. Initially exploited by fur traders to some degree, the region was fully opened up following the discovery of gold in 1858 in the lower Fraser Valley by prospectors who had made their way north from the Californian goldfields. The building of the **Cariboo Wagon Road**, a stagecoach route north out of Lillooet, spread gold fever right up the Fraser watershed as men leapfrogged from creek to creek, culminating in the big finds at Williams Creek in 1861 and Barkerville a year later.

Much of the old Wagon Road is today retraced by lonely **Highway 97** – the Cariboo Highway – and **VIA rail**, which run in tandem through hour after hour of straggling pine forests and past the occasional ranch and small, marsh-edged lake – scenery which strikes you as pristine and pastoral for a while but which soon leaves you in a tree-weary stupor. If you're forced to stop over, there are innumerable lodges, ranches and motels by the highway, and you can pick up material on the region at the Vancouver tourist office or infocentres en route.

A compact little village surrounded by green pastures and tree-covered hills, **CLINTON** – named after a British duke – marks the start of the heart of Cariboo country. The town has a couple of motels, the most central being the *Nomad* (☎459-2214; ①), and the in-town *Gold Trail RV Park and Campground* (☎459-2519; sites $9–13).

The three tiny settlements beyond Clinton at 70, 100, and **150 MILE HOUSE** are echoes of the old roadhouses built by men who were paid by the mile to blaze the Cariboo Wagon Road – which is doubtless why 100 Mile House is well short of 100 miles from the start of the road. **WILLIAMS LAKE**, a busy and drab transportation town, huddles in the lee of a vast crag on terraces above the lake of the same name, with plenty of motels, boat launches and swimming spots south of the town – but hardly a place you'd want to spend any time in unless you're around on the first weekend in July for its famous **rodeo**.

Highway 20 branches west here, a part-paved, part-gravel road that runs 455km to **BELLA COOLA**. Most of the way is through the interminable forest of the Cariboo Plateau, but the last 100km or so traverses the spectacular high peaks of the Coast Mountains. *Chilcotin Stage Lines*, based at 27-7th Ave South in Williams Lake (☎392-6170), runs **buses** all the way to Bella Coola, where there are a few hotels but no onward sea route: unless you fly out, you'll have to either head back the way you came or pick up one of the ferries on the Inside Passage that stop off at the port. If you want to take a plane, contact *Wilderness Airlines* (☎982-2225 or 1-800/665-9453). Bella Coola's **infocentre** is on the Mackenzie Hwy near town (☎799-5919). **Accommodation** is provided by the *Cedar Inn* (☎799-5316; ②) and *Bella Coola Motel* (☎799-5323; ②), both downtown, and the *Bay Motor Hotel* on Hwy 20 14km east of the town and 1km from the airport (☎982-2212; ②).

North of Williams Lake on Hwy 97, the **Fraser River** begins one of its more scenic stretches, opening with a dramatic stretch of canyon, followed by compelling hills and snatches of river meadows. This also marks the start, however, of some of the most concerted **logging operations** in all British Columbia, presaged by increasing numbers of crude pepper-pot kilns used to burn off waste wood. By **QUESNEL**, home of the "world's largest plywood plant", you're greeted with scenes out of an environmentalist's nightmare: whole mountainsides cleared of trees, piles of sawdust the size of small hills, and unbelievably large lumber mills surrounded by stacks of logs and finished timber that stretch literally as far as the eye can see. If you're stuck for accommodation (there are a dozen hotels) or tempted by any of the many mill tours, contact the **infocentre** in Le Bourdais Park at 703 Carson Ave (year round; ☎992-8716).

Most people who take the trouble to drive this route detour from Quesnel to **Barkerville Provincial Historic Park**, 90km to the east in the heart of the Cariboo Mountains, the site of the Cariboo's biggest gold strike and an invigorating spot in its own right, providing a much-needed jolt to the senses after the sleepy scenery to the south (June–Sept daily 9am–6pm; Oct–May Mon–Fri 9am–6pm; $6). In 1862 a Cornishman named Billy Barker idly staked a claim here and after digging down a few feet was about to pack up and head north. Urged on by his mates, however, he dug another couple of spadefuls and turned up a cluster of nuggets worth $600,000. Within months Barkersville, as it was later dubbed, had become the largest city in the region, and rode the boom for a decade until the gold finally played out. Today numerous buildings have been restored, and the main administrative building has displays on mining methods and the gold rush, together with propaganda on their importance to the province.

If you want to **stay** up here there are just two options, both at **WELLS**, 8km west of the park: *Hubs Motel* (☎994-3313; ①) and the *White Cap Motor Inn* (☎994-3489; ②), the latter also with a few camping spaces for $13.50. The village has a an **infocentre** on Pooley St, part of its small museum (summer only; ☎994-3237).

travel details

Trains

From Vancouver to Jasper (June–Sept daily except Wed; Oct–May 3 weekly; 19hr); Edmonton (3 weekly; 25hr); Prince George (mid-June–Sept 1 daily; rest of year 3 weekly; 13hr 30min); Lillooet (mid-June–Sept 1 daily; rest of year 4 weekly; 5hr 30min); Winnipeg via Edmonton and Saskatoon (3 weekly; 40hr).

From Victoria to Courtenay via Nanaimo (1 daily; 4hr 35min).

Buses

From Vancouver to Calgary via Kamloops (6 daily; 13hr); Calgary via Princeton and Kelowna (2 daily; 18hr); Calgary via Penticton, Nelson and Cranbrook (2 daily; 24hr); Edmonton via Jasper (3 daily; 16hr 30min); Vernon (6 daily; 6hr); Prince George via Cache Creek and Williams Lake (2 daily; 13hr); Powell River (2 daily; 5hr 10min); Whistler (6 daily; 2hr 30min); Pemberton (3 daily; 3hr 10min); Victoria (8 daily; 3hr 30min–5hr); Nanaimo (8 daily; 5hr); Seattle (4 daily; 3hr 30min).

From Victoria to Vancouver (8 daily; 5hr); Nanaimo (6 daily; 2hr 20min); Campbell River (4 daily; 5hr); Port Hardy (1 daily; 9hr 45min); Port Renfrew (2 daily; 2hr 30min).

From Nanaimo to Victoria (6 daily; 2hr 20min); Port Alberni (3 daily; 1hr 20min).

From Port Alberni to Tofino via Ucluelet (1–2 daily; 5hr 30min); Nanaimo (4 daily; 1hr 20min).

Flights

From Vancouver to Victoria (14 daily; 25min); Calgary (20 daily; 1hr 15min); Edmonton (14 daily; 1hr 30min); Portland (5 daily; 1hr 15min); Seattle (15 daily; 50min).

From Victoria to Vancouver (14 daily; 25min); Calgary (4 daily; 1hr 40min).

Note: There are **no** non-stop scheduled flights from Vancouver or Victoria to Alaska: Alaskan flights depart only from Seattle or other US centers.

Ferries

From Vancouver to Victoria (hourly 7am–9pm; 1hr 35min); Nanaimo (16 daily; 1hr 35min–2hr).

From Powell River to Courtenay (4 daily; 1hr 15min).

From Victoria to Vancouver (hourly 7am–10pm; 1hr 35min); Anacortes, Port Angeles and San Juan Islands, USA (1–2 daily; 55min–2hr 30min); Seattle, USA (1–4 daily; 2hr 30min–3hr 30min).

From Courtenay to Powell River (4 daily; 1hr 15min).

CHAPTER SIX

SOUTHERN BRITISH COLUMBIA

The often pristine scenery of **southern British Columbia** more than lives up to most people's image of the wilds of the Northwest. What may come as a surprise, however, is the sheer natural diversity of the region: over and above the mountainous, forested interior lies a jigsaw of landscapes, including genteel farmland, ranching country, immense lakes and even a patch of real desert. British Columbia contains both the Northwest's wettest and its driest climates, and reputedly more species of flora and fauna than the rest of the region put together. The range of recreational possibilities is equally impressive: some of Canada's better ski areas, its warmest lakes and some of its best beaches are all here, not to mention hot springs, hiking, sailing and canoeing galore, and some of the best salmon fishing in the world.

Culturally and logistically, southern British Columbia stands apart from the northern half of the province (covered in Chapter Eight), containing most of the roads, towns, people and accessible sights. Vancouver is also here, a transportation hub for the region. Its size and cosmopolitan zest, however, set it apart, and we deal with the city – and the island – in Chapter Five. Although the area merits exploration for its own sake, many people take the quickest roads through. Unfortunately, both of the major highways confine you to some of its least interesting areas. The most obvious line east, the Trans-Canada Highway, isn't one you want to consider at all unless you're in a real hurry (allow about eight hours from Vancouver to Golden). Nor does Highway 3, rumbling along just north of the US border, offer a convincing alternative (though with ten trans-border road crossings this is the route you'll hit if you're crossing from the States).

In an ideal world you'd pursue a meandering course across the interior, taking in some of the nicer villages and scenery on Highway 3 east of **Hope** as far as **Osoyoos**, and then perhaps cutting north through the **Okanagan**, an almost Californian enclave of orchards, vineyards, warm lakes and rowdy resort towns – a region whose beaches and scorching summers suck in hordes of vacationers from all over Canada and the western United States. Thereafter you have the option of heading north to **Kamloops**, a dullish town, but the interior's transportation hub, from whence you should head north to **Wells Gray Provincial Park,** the finest of BC's provincial parks, and the equal of the national parks to the east. This route,

TELEPHONE NUMBERS

The **telephone code** for British Columbia is ☎604.
Toll-free Information: Tourism British Columbia ☎1-800/663-6000.

however, rather commits you to following the magnificently scenic Highway 5 north to Mount Robson and Jasper (see Chapter Seven), or to Prince George for the push north on the Alaska Highway towards the Yukon. This would mean missing the loveliest area in British Columbia – the **Kootenays** – best accessed from Vernon in the Okanagan on the spectacular and lonely Highway 6 eastbound. Occupying the province's southeastern corner, the Kootenays are an idyllic assortment of mountain-hemmed lakes, tidy old mining towns, quaint villages and a seductive couple of places – **Nelson** and **Kaslo** – you might stay for a few days.

The British explorer **Francis Drake** probably made the first sighting of the mainland by a European during his round-the-world voyage of 1579. Spanish explorers sailing from California and Russians from Alaska explored the coast almost two centuries later, though it was another Briton, **Captain Cook**, who made the first recorded landing in 1778. Captain George Vancouver first mapped the area in 1792–94, hard on the heels of the **Nuu-chah-nulth Convention** of 1790 – a neat piece of colonial bluster which wrested from the Spanish all rights on the mainland as far as Alaska for the British. Exploration of the interior came about during a search for an easier way to export furs westwards to the Pacific, instead of the arduous haul eastwards across the continent. **Alexander Mackenzie** of the North West Company made the first crossing of North America north of Mexico in 1793, followed by two further adventurers, **Simon Fraser** and **David Thompson**, whose names also resonate as sobriquets for rivers, shops, motels and streets across the region.

The **gold rush** centered on the Fraser River in 1858, and the Cariboo region three years later, changed everything, attracting some 25,000 people to the goldfields. The building of the **Cariboo Road** (the present Highway 97) and the **Dewdney Trail** (Highway 3) opened up the interior and contributed to the influx of the so-called **Overlanders** – a huge straggle of pioneers that tramped from Ontario and Québec in the summer of 1862. Britain declared mainland British Columbia a crown colony in 1858 to impose imperial authority on the region and, more importantly, to lay firm claim to the huge mineral wealth which was rightly believed to lie within it. When Canada's eastern colonies formed the Dominion in 1867, though, British Columbia dithered over joining until it received the promise of a railway to link it to the east in 1871 – though the Canadian Pacific didn't actually arrive for another fifteen years.

While British Columbia no longer dithers, it still tends to look to itself – and increasingly to the new economic markets of the Pacific Rim – rather than to the rest of Canada and the US west coast. The francophone concerns of eastern

---

ACCOMMODATION PRICE CODES

All accommodation prices in this book have been coded using the symbols below, corresponding to Canadian dollar rates in the Canadian chapters and equivalent US dollar prices in the US chapters. Prices are for the least expensive double rooms in each establishment, and only include local taxes where we explicitly say so.

For a full explanation see p.46 in *Basics*.

①	up to Can$40	④	Can$80–100	⑦	Can$175–240
②	Can$40–60	⑤	Can$100–125	⑧	Can$240+
③	Can$60–80	⑥	Can$125–175		

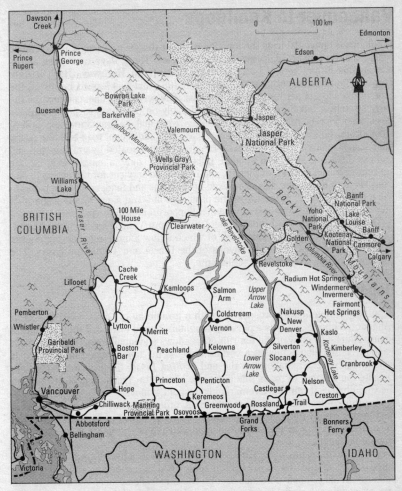

Canada are virtually nonexistent here – there is, for example, just one French school in the entire province. For the most part British Columbians are well-off, both financially and in terms of quality of life, and demographically the province is one of Canada's youngest. If there are flies in the ointment, they're the **environmental pressures** thrown up by an economy which relies on primary resources for its dynamism: British Columbia supplies twenty-five percent of North America's commercial timber, and exports significant amounts of hydro-electric power, fish, zinc, silver, oil, coal and gypsum. Few of these can be exploited without exacting a toll on the province's natural beauty; British Columbians may be well-off, but they're increasingly aware of the environmental price being paid for their prosperity.

Vancouver to Kamloops

Kamloops is unavoidable as the junction of major routes in the region, and can be reached by two main highways from Vancouver. These days most cars, buses and anyone in any sort of hurry take the **Coquihalla Highway** (Hwy 5) from **Hope**, a four-lane superhighway opened in 1987 that has lopped hours off the time it takes to get across British Columbia. The scenery is unexceptional in the early stretches, but things look up considerably on the climb to the Coquihalla Pass, when forests, mountains and crashing rivers make a dramatic reappearance – compromised somewhat by old mines, clearcuts and recent road-building scars. Landscapes change sharply again on the descent, dominated by grazing land and endless lines of arid, half-wooded hills. There's only a single exit, at the supremely missable town of Merritt, and literally no services for the entire 182km from Hope to Kamloops. Come stocked up with gas and food, and be prepared to pay a toll (about $12) at the top of the pass – a wind- and snow-whipped spot that must offer one of the loneliest employment opportunities in the province.

The older, slower (and more scenic) route from Vancouver is on the **Trans-Canada Highway** or **VIA rail**, both of which follow a more meandering course along the lower reaches and canyons of the Fraser and Thompson rivers. The remainder of this section details this route.

Hope

Reputedly christened by prospectors with a grounding in Dante, **HOPE** – as in "Abandon all hope . . ." – is a pleasant mountain-ringed town and the first hint of scenic interest to enliven the flat run of meadows and small towns en route from Vancouver. It's also achieved a certain fame as the town wasted in spectacular fashion by Sylvester Stallone at the end of *First Blood*, the first Rambo movie. Despite the number of roads that converge here – the Trans-Canada, Hwy 3 and the Coquihalla – it remains a remarkably unspoilt stopover.

The **infocentre** (daily summer 8am–8pm, otherwise 9am–5pm; ☎869-2021) is next to the artfully dumped pile of antique farm machinery at 919 Water Ave; the town **museum** shares the same building, and offers the usual memorabilia of Hope's old-timers.

Across the road, the lovely view across the Fraser as it funnels out of the mountains is one of the town's best moments. Fishing, canoeing, and even gold-panning are all popular pastimes around the hundreds of local lakes, rivers and creeks; details are available from the infocentre, which also prints a summary of local hikes. Of these, the **Rotary Trail** (3km) to the confluence of the Fraser and Coquihalla rivers is well-used, as is the more demanding clamber over gravel paths to the top of **Thacker Mountain** (5km).

Another walking expedition worth pursuing is the dark jaunt through the **tunnels** of the abandoned Vancouver–Nelson railway, reached by a short trail from the **Coquihalla Canyon Provincial Park**, 6km northeast of town off Coquihalla Highway. This was one of the backcountry locations used during the filming of *First Blood*, and offers spectacular views over the cliffs and huge sandbars of the Coquihalla Gorge. **Kawkawa Lake Provincial Park**, 3km northeast of Hope off Hwy 3, is also a much-frequented mountain retreat, endowed with plenty of hiking, relaxing and swimming opportunities.

Practicalities

Most of what happens in Hope happens on its single main street, Water Avenue. The *Greyhound* **bus terminal** (☎869-5522) is here, a critical juncture if you're on the bus because you'll have to transfer, depending on whether you're going north to Kamloops or east to Penticton and the Okanagan. Cheap **motels** proliferate along Hwy 3 as you leave town heading east, and though most are much of a muchness, the *Flamingo* (☎869-9610; ①), last on the strip, has a nice piney setting. Closer in on the same road, the *Heritage* (☎869-7166; ②), a lovely grey-wood building smothered in flowers, is also excellent, but slightly more expensive. If you're just off the bus, the nearest place to the terminal – a block to its north – is the *Hope Motor Hotel*, 272 Wallace St (☎869-5641; ③). **Campgrounds**, too, are numerous, but most are some way from downtown. The municipal site is at *Coquihalla Park* (year round; ☎869-5671; $10), off Hwy 3 and reached via Seventh Ave. The top-of-the-pile *KOA Campground* is 5km west of town (March–Oct; ☎869-9857; $16.50–20).

Food facilities and late-night entertainment are extremely limited in what is, despite Vancouver's proximity, still a small-time town. For snacks try the bakery on the main street, or the rock-bottom café in the *Greyhound* station. For more substantial dishes try the *Hope Motor Hotel* and *Lee's Kettle Valley Restaurant*, both on Wallace Street.

The Fraser Canyon

Veering north from Hope, the Trans-Canada runs up the Fraser River valley, squeezed here by the high ridges of the Cascade and Coast ranges into one of British Columbia's grandest waterways. Though it's now a clear-cut transport corridor – the Canadian Pacific Railway also passes this way – the **Fraser Canyon** was long regarded as impassable; to negotiate it, the Trans-Canada is forced to push through tunnels, hug the Fraser's banks, and at times cling perilously to rock ledges hundreds of meters above the swirling waters.

The river is named after **Simon Fraser**, one of Canada's remarkable early explorers, who as an employee of the North West Company travelled its entire 1300-kilometer length in 1808 under the mistaken impression he was following the Columbia. "We had to pass where no man should venture", he wrote, and made most of the journey on foot guided by local natives, pushing forward using ladders, ropes and improvised platforms to bypass rapids too treacherous to breach by boat. Few people felt the need to follow Fraser's example until the discovery of **gold** near Yale in 1858; prospectors promptly waded in and panned every tributary of the lower Fraser until new strikes tempted them north to the Cariboo.

YALE, 15km north of Hope, opens the canyon with a ring of plunging cliffs. Sitting at the river's navigable limit, it was once the largest city in North America west of Chicago and north of San Francisco: during the 1858 gold rush its population mushroomed to over 20,000, a growth only tempered by the end of the boom and the completion of the Canadian Pacific. Today it's a small lumber town of about 250, though a visit to the **Yale Museum** on Hwy 1, known here as Douglas St (summer daily 9am–6pm), offers an exhaustive account of the town's golden age. The **infocentre** is also on Douglas (daily 9am–6pm June–Sept; ☎863-2324). For **rooms** you can't do much better than *Fort Yale Motel* (☎863-2216; ①) at the entrance to the canyon. Some 10km north of the town, the *Colonial Inn* (☎863-2277; ③) offers ten cabins and six sites for tents.

BOSTON BAR, 20km north of Yale, boasts about four motels and is also a center for **whitewater** raft trips down the Fraser as far as Yale. Various companies run several trips a week from May to August; contact *Frontier River Adventure* for details (☎867-9244). Midway between the village and Yale is the famous **Hell's Gate**, where – in a gorge almost 180m deep – the huge swell of the Fraser is squeezed into a 38-meter channel of foaming water that crashes through the rocks with awe-inspiring ferocity. The water here is up to 60m deep and as fast-flowing (8m a second) as any you're likely to see, but to get down to the river there's a certain amount of resort-like commercialism to negotiate and a four-minute ride on the "Air-Tram" to pay for (March–Oct daily; $8). Close by there are also displays on the various provisions made to help migrating salmon complete their journeys, interrrupted over the years by the coming of the road and railway. The Fraser is one of the key runs for Pacific salmon, and every summer and fall they fill the river as they head for tributaries and upstream lakes to spawn.

Cache Creek

CACHE CREEK has a reputation as a hitch-hiker's black hole and is indeed the sort of sleepy place you could get stuck in for days. Locals also say it didn't help that an escaped child murderer, Charles Olsen, was recaptured nearby in 1985 – since when they've been understandably wary of picking up strangers. The town's name is accounted for by a variety of legends, the most romantic version concerning a couple of prospectors who buried a hoard of gold and never returned to pick it up. Sadly, it's likelier to derive from early trappers' more prosaic habit of leaving a cache of supplies at points on a trail to be used later.

Cache Creek is known as the "Arizona of Canada" for its baking summer climate, which settles a heat-wasted somnolence on its dusty streets. The parched, windswept mountains round about are the product of anomalous volcanic intrusions in the regional geology, which left a legacy of resistant rock and semi-precious stones – including jade – that attracts climbers and rock-hounds. Heading east out of town towards Kamloops, the Trans-Canada penetrates more of this strange scenery, shadowing Kamloops Lake and churning sluggishly through a broad, arid valley of scrub and semi-derelict irrigation schemes that do little to soften the rock-strewn bare hills. There's not much to do in Cache Creek, but for local insights visit the **infocentre** on the northwest side of town at 1340 Hwy 97 near the main road junction (summer 9am–6pm; ☎457-5306). If you're stranded, there are about half a dozen **motels**, of which the best is the bizarre *Castle Inn* (☎457-9547; ②). Less eccentric are the *Sandman Desert* (☎457-6284; ②) and *Tumbleweed* (☎457-6522; ②). The nearest **campground** is the *Brookside* (May–Oct; ☎457-6633; $10), 1km east of town on the main highway.

Kamloops

Almost any trip in southern British Columbia brings you sooner or later to **KAMLOOPS**, a town which has been a transport focus from time immemorial – its name derives from the Shuswap word for "meeting of the rivers" – and which today marks the meeting point of the Trans-Canada and Yellowhead (South) highways, Canada's principal transcontinental roads, as well as the junction of the Canadian Pacific and Canadian National railways. The largest interior town (pop. 75,000) in southern British Columbia, it's a fairly unobjectionable place, except when the wind blows from the uptown sawmills – when it smells as if something's been dead for a week – but there's no need to spend any time here if you're travelling by bus or train. If you're camping or driving, however, it makes a convenient provisions stop, especially if you're heading north on Hwy 5 or south on the Coquihalla Highway, neither of which has much in the way of facilities.

Kamloops is determinedly functional and not a place to spend a happy day wandering, but all the same the **Kamloops Museum** (Tues–Sat July–Sept 10am–9pm, Oct–June 10am–4pm; free) is one of the more interesting provincial offerings, with illuminating archive photographs – especially the one of the railway running down the middle of the main street – artefacts, bric-à-brac, period set pieces and an especially well done section on the Shuswap. The stuffed-animal display, without which no BC museum is complete, has a fascinating little piece on the life cycle of the tick presented without any discernible irony. For a more complete picture of local native history and traditions, call at the **Secwepemec Museum**, just over the bridge on Hwy 5 (Mon–Fri 8.30am–4.30pm; donation).

Perhaps the most interesting thing about Kamloops is its surroundings, dominated by strange, bare-earthed brown hills that locals like to say represent the northernmost point of the Mojave Desert. There's no doubting the almost surreal touches of near-desert, which are particularly marked in the bare rock and clay outcrops above the bilious waters of the Thompson River and in the bleached scrub and failing stands of pines that spot the barren hills. Most scenic diversions lie a short drive out of town, and the infocentre has full details of every last local bolthole, with a special bias towards the 200 or so trout-stuffed lakes that dot the hinterland. The nearest and most popular on a hot summer's day is **Paul Lake Provincial Park**, 17km northeast of town on a good paved road, with swimming and a provincial campground.

Practicalities

The **infocentre** is a little out of downtown at Tenth Avenue – to reach it, follow River Street immediately next to the main bridge over the Thompson River (June–Sept daily 8am–8pm; Oct–May Mon–Fri 9am–5pm; ☎828-9500; BC only ☎1-800/667-0143). They have full details of accommodation and recreational opportunities for the town and much of the province, and a particularly useful book of bed and breakfasts. They're also keen to emphasize that Kamloops has *no fort*, this for some reason being something most people come expecting to see.

The **Greyhound terminal** (☎374-1212) is in the Aberdeen Mall, off Hwy 1 a good 6km west of downtown, and is a crucial interchange for buses to all parts of the province; the #3 local bus into town leaves from immediately outside. Kamloops is also served by three weekly **trains** in each direction to Edmonton (via Jasper) and Vancouver. The *VIA rail* office is at 95 Third Ave, behind Landsdowne St, but is open only on days trains are running (☎372-5858).

Kamloops's huge volume of accommodation is aimed fair and square at the motorist and consists of thick clusters of **motels**, most of which blanket the town's eastern margins on Hwy 1 (called "Valleyview" in the *BC Accommodation Guide*) or out on Columbia Street West. The *Thrift Inn* (☎374-2488; ①) is the least expensive, but it's about the last building on eastbound Hwy 1 out of town. You pay a premium for central beds, most of which are on Columbia Street: the

Whistler Inn Apartment Hotel is about as central as you can get, at 375 Fifth Ave (☎828-1322; ②); or try the always reliable *Sandman*, 550 Columbia St (☎374-1218; ②), or the *Fountain Motel*, 506 Columbia St (☎374-4451; ②). There's also a clutch of places around the bus terminal, in case you arrive late and have no inclination to head into town.

The nearest **campground** is the *Silver Sage Tent and Trailer Park* at 771 East Athabasca (☎828-2077; $12–16), but if you've got a car aim for the far more scenic facilities at Paul Lake Provincial Park (see above).

The best **restaurant** is the well-known *Fat Mel's* on Kamloops Square off Seymour and Third Ave – despite some strange signs on the door, it's a good mix of Tex-Mex, Cajun and Italian food, and the atmosphere's lively and friendly. Snack food is cheap and served in generous portions at the popular *Steiger's Swiss Café*, 359 Victoria St, which really is run by Swiss and does good muesli, cappuccino, lots of sticky buns, and excellent bread. If you're on a rock-bottom budget, head for *Barnsey's*, "home of the 50¢ cup of coffee": it's at the back of *Bob's PX Store* at 246 Victoria St. For supermarket stock-ups, the *Safeway* is on the corner of Seymour and Fifth Ave.

Highway 5: Clearwater and Wells Gray

Northbound **Highway 5** (here known as the Yellowhead South Highway) heads upstream along the broad North Thompson River as it courses through high hills and rolling pasture between Kamloops and **Clearwater**, and beyond, in one of the most astounding road routes in this part of the world, follows the river as it carves through the Monashee Mountains from its source near **Valemont**, finally meeting the main Yellowhead Highway (Hwy 16) at Tete Jaune Cache, a total distance of 338km. The entire latter half of the journey is spent side-stepping the immense **Wells Gray Provincial Park**, one of the finest protected areas in British Columbia.

Greyhound **buses** cover the route on their run between Kamloops and Prince George via Clearwater (2 daily in each direction), as do *VIA* **trains**, which connect Kamloops with Jasper via Clearwater (3 weekly). Note that there are other, far less travelled gravel roads into other sectors of the park from **Blue River**, 112 km north of Clearwater on Hwy 5, and from 100 Mile House, on Hwy 97 west of the park.

Valemount and Blue River

Clearwater is by far the best base locally, but the area is so remote there is a good chance the **accommodation** options at **VALEMOUNT** and **BLUE RIVER** may well be useful. At Valemount there's a seasonal **infocentre** at 98 Gorse St on Hwy 5 (June–Sept daily 9am–5pm; ☎566-4846). One block off the highway on Fifth Ave are three motels, the cheapest the *Yellowhead* (☎566-4411; ②); there's little to choose between the others, the *Chalet Continental* (☎566-9787; ③) and *Alpine* (☎566-4471; ③). Two blocks off the main road, the most reasonable choice in the village is the *Ramakada Motel* at 1275 Juniper St (☎566-4555; ①). On Swift Creek adjoining the village is one of two local campgrounds, the *Yellowhead Campsite and Trailer Park* (June–Aug; ☎566-4227; $10). The other, the superior *KOA Campground Valemount*, is on the highway (March–Oct; ☎566-4312; $16.50).

Blue River, a slip of a place, has four options, the least expensive being the *Blue River Motel* on Spruce St (☎673-8387; ①). For a few dollars more try the *Mountain View Motel* on Third Ave and Spruce St (☎673-8366; ②). Top of the pile is a chain hotel, the *Sandman*, on the highway (☎673-8364; ③). The only campground for miles is the *Eleanor Lake Campsite and Trailer Park* on Herb Bilton Way (May–Oct; ☎673-8313; $9–12).

Clearwater

CLEARWATER is a dispersed farming community that's invisible from Hwy 5, and unless you arrive by rail there's no need to drop down to it at all. Everything you need apart from the odd shop is on or just off the junction between the highway and the slip road to the village, including the **bus stop** and the excellent **infocentre** (daily June–Aug 8am–8pm; Sept–May 9am–5pm; ☎674-2646), a model of the genre which has immensely useful information on all aspects of Wells Gray Provincial Park. If you intend to stay locally or do any walking or canoeing, take time to flick through the reference books devoted to accommodation, trails and paddling routes.

Clearwater is the best place to **stay** along Hwy 5 if you're planning on visiting Wells Gray. By far the nicest prospect, thanks to its lovely views over Dutch Lake, is *Jasper Way Inn* (☎674-3345; ①–②), 1km off the highway to the west and well signed from the infocentre; some rooms have cooking facilities. If it's full try the big *Wells Gray Inn* (☎674-2214; ②), close by on the main road; the doubles here are more comfortable, but lack the view. The latter is virtually the only place to **eat** locally. Three **campgrounds** lie within walking distance of the infocentre: the best – again, on the lake – is the *Dutch Lake Resort* (May–Oct; ☎674-3351; $12–15).

Wells Gray Provincial Park

Wells Gray Provincial Park is the equal of any of the Rocky Mountain national parks to the east – it's so untamed that many of its peaks remain unclimbed and unnamed. Wildlife sightings are common throughout the park – especially if you tramp some of the wilder trails, where encounters with black bears, grizzlies and mountain goats are a possibility, not to mention glimpses of smaller mammals such as timber wolves, coyotes, weasels, martens, minks, wolverines and beavers. With some 250km of maintained trails and dozens of other lesser routes, the park is superb for **hiking**. Short walks and day hikes from the park access road are described below, but serious backpackers can easily spend a week or more tramping the Murtle River (14km) and Kostal Lake (26km) trails, among others. Make sure to pick up a free *BC Parks* map-pamphlet at the Clearwater infocentre, and if you're thinking of doing any backcountry exploration you'll want to invest in their more detailed topo maps and guides. **Cross-country skiing** is also possible, but there are only a few groomed routes in the park: details from the infocentre.

Another of the park's big attractions is **canoeing** on Clearwater and Azure lakes, which can be linked with a short portage to make a 100-plus-kilometer dream trip for paddlers; you can rent canoes for long- or short-haul trips from *Clearwater Lake Tours* (☎674-3052). Whitewater rafting down the Clearwater

River is also popular, and half-day to full-week tours can be arranged through the Clearwater infocentre or the two accommodation options below. Several local operators run shorter commercial boat trips around Clearwater Lake, as well as full-scale **tours** featuring horse riding, camping, trekking, fishing, boating, even float-plane excursions around the park – the Clearwater infocentre has the inside story on all of these.

The only indoor **accommodation** in or near the park is at the *Wells Gray Ranch* (May–Oct; ☎674-2792; ④) just before the park entrance, which has ten cabins, and at the slightly larger but equally lonely *Helmcken Falls Lodge* (Jan–March & May–Oct; ☎674-3657; ④–⑤) at the entrance itself, with similar facilities but at slightly higher prices. You'll be lucky to find vacancies in summer, however, unless you've booked. Both of these also have a few pitches for tents, but there's far better roadside **camping** along the park access road at Spahats Creek and in the park at Dawson Falls (just 10 sites) and Clearwater Lake (35 sites) – these last two fill up promptly in season, however. Many backpackers' campgrounds dot the shores of the park's major lakes; *Clearwater Lake Tours* operates a water-taxi service which can drop you off at any site on Clearwater Lake and pick you up at a pre-arranged time.

Sights and hikes along the access road

Even if you're not geared up for the backcountry, the access road to the park from Clearwater opens up a medley of waterfalls, walks and viewpoints that make a day or more's detour extremely worthwhile. It's paved for the first 30km to the park boundary, but the remaining 33km to Clearwater Lake are gravel.

About 8km north of Clearwater, a short walk from the car park at **Spahats Creek Provincial Park** brings you to 61-meter Spahats Falls, the first of several mighty cascades along this route. You can watch the waters crashing down through layers of pinky-red volcanic rock from a pair of observation platforms, which also provide an impressive and unexpected view of the Clearwater Valley way down below. A few hundred meters further up the road, a fifteen-kilometer gravel lane peels off into the **Wells Gray Recreation Area**; a single trail from the end of the road strikes off into alpine meadows, feeding four shorter day-trails into an area particularly known for its bears. This is also the site of a juvenile correction center, which must rank as possibly the most beautiful but godforsaken spot to do time in North America. About 15km further up the main access road, a second four-wheel-drive track branches east to reach the trailhead for **Battle Mountain** (19km), with the option of several shorter hikes like the Mount Philip Trail (5km) en route.

Green Mountain Lookout, reached by a rough, winding road to the left just after the park entrance, offers one of the most expansive roadside panoramas in British Columbia, and it's a sight that will help you grasp the sheer extent of the Canadian wilderness: as far as you can see, there's nothing but an almighty emptiness of primal forest and mountains. Various landscape features are picked out on plaques, and the immediate area is a likely place to spot moose.

The next essential stop is **Dawson Falls**, a broad, powerful cascade (91m wide and 18m high) just five minutes' walk from the road – signed "Viewpoint". Beyond, the road crosses an ugly iron bridge and shortly after meets the start of the **Murtle River Trail** (14km one way), a particularly good walk if you want more spectacular waterfalls.

Immediately afterwards, a dead-end side road is signed to **Helmcken Falls**, the park's undisputed highlight. They're heavily visited, and it's not unknown for wedding parties to come up here to get dramatic matrimonial photos backed by the luminous arc of water plunging into a black, carved bowl fringed with vivid carpets of lichen and splintered trees, the whole ensemble framed by huge plumes of spray wafting up on all sides. At 137m, the falls are two and a half times the height of Niagara – or, in the infoboards' incongruous comparison, approximately the same height as the Vancouver skyline.

Continuing north, the park access road rejoins the jade-green Clearwater River, passing tastefully located picnic spots and short trails that wend down to the bank for close-up views of one of the province's best whitewater rafting stretches. The last sight before the end of the road is **Ray Farm**, home to John Bunyon Ray, who in 1912 was the first man to homestead this area. Though it's not much to look at, the farm offers a sobering insight into the pioneer mentality – Ray's struggle to scrape a living and raise a family in this harsh environment beggars belief – and the wooden shacks are scattered in picturesque ruin in a lovely, lush clearing. The park road ends at **Clearwater Lake**, where there are a couple of boat launches, a provincial campground and a series of short trails clearly marked from the roadhead.

Salmon Arm and the Shuswap

Given the variety of routes across southern BC there's no knowing quite when you'll find yourself in **SALMON ARM**, 108km east of Kamloops, but that's not something that need concern you in planning an itinerary because the town – the largest of the bland resorts spread along Shuswap Lake's 1000km of navigable waterways – has little to recommend it other than sublime views across an arm of the lake. It's a much smaller place than most maps would suggest – and you know you're in trouble when you see signs proclaiming it "Home of the World Famous Non-Irrigated Macintosh Apple". The town is oddly dispersed and has a scrappy and haphazard appearance, but if you're driving towards Revelstoke and the Rockies it makes a natural break along one of the Trans-Canada's more monotonous stretches. To get anything out of it you'll have to pull off the main drag, which is formed by the Trans-Canada itself, and head one block south to the lakeside which, barring a huge sawmill and plywood works, is a pleasant open area with a view of distant hazy hills.

The lake and the surrounding region take their name from the Shuswap, the northernmost of the great Salishan family and the largest single tribe in British Columbia. The name of the town harks back to a time when it was possible to spear salmon straight from the lake, and fish were so plentiful that they were shovelled onto the land as fertiliser. Shuswap still provides an important sanctuary for hatched salmon fry before they make their long journey down the Thompson and Fraser rivers to the sea; the abundance of such lakes, together with ideal water temperatures, free-flowing, well-oxygenated and silt-free tributaries, and plenty of sand and gravel beds for egg-laying, make the Fraser River system the continent's greatest salmon habitat.

One of the few reasons you might make a special journey to the Salmon Arm area is to watch the huge migrations of **spawning salmon** that take place around

---

SALMON

At times it seems impossible to escape the **salmon** in the Northwest, and particularly in British Columbia. Whether it's on restaurant menus, in rivers, or in the photographs of grinning fishermen clutching their catch, the fish is almost as much a symbol of the region as its mountains and forests. Five different species inhabit the rivers and lakes of the Pacific Northwest: **pink, coho, chum, chinook** and, most important of all, the **sockeye**.

Though they start and finish their lives in fresh water, salmon spend about four years in the open sea between times. Mature male and female fish make their epic migrations from the Pacific to **spawn** in the rivers of their birth between June and November, swimming about 30km a day; some chinook travel over 1400km up the Fraser beyond Prince George, which means almost fifty days' continuous swimming upstream. Though the female lays as many as 4000 eggs, only about six percent of the offspring survive: on the Adams River near Salmon Arm, for example, it's estimated that of 4 billion sockeye eggs laid in a typical year, 1 billion survive to become fry (hatched fish about three-quarters of an inch long), of which 75 percent are eaten by predators before becoming smolts (year-old fish), and only five percent of these then make it to the ocean. In effect each pair of spawners produces about ten mature fish; of these, eight are caught by commercial fisheries and only two return to reproduce.

These are returns which clearly put the salmon's survival and British Columbia's lucrative **fishing industry** on a knife-edge. Caught, canned and exported, salmon accounts for two thirds of BC's $1 billion annual revenues from fishing – the largest of any Canadian province, and its third-ranking money-earner after forestry and energy products. Commercial fishing suffered its first setback in British Columbia as long ago as 1913, when large rock slides at Hell's Gate in the Fraser Canyon disrupted many of the spawning runs. Although fish runs were painstakingly constructed to bypass the slides, new pressures have subsequently been heaped on the salmon by mining, logging, urban and agricultural development, and the dumping of industrial and municipal wastes. An increasingly important line of defence, **hatcheries** have been built on rivers on the mainland and Vancouver Island to increase the percentage of eggs and fry that successfully mature. Meanwhile overfishing remains a major concern, particularly as the **drift nets** of Japanese and Korean fleets (intended for neon squid) over the past decade have taken numerous non-designated species, including BC and Yukon salmon. Under intense lobbying from Canada and the US, both nations agreed to a moratorium on large-scale drift nets from June 30, 1992.

October. Anything up to two million fish brave the run from the Pacific up to their birthplace in the Adams River – one of the most famous spawning grounds in the province. During the peak week of the run, around 250,000 visitors come to witness the event. This short stretch of river is protected by **Roderick Haig-Brown Provincial Park**, reached from Salmon Arm by driving 46km west on the Trans-Canada to Squilax and then 5km north on a side road. If you're thinking of dangling a line, pick up the *Fishing in Shuswap* leaflet from the infocentre in Salmon Arm, and don't forget to pick up a licence at the same time.

The best chance of a leg-stretch around here is at **Herald Provincial Park** on the shore opposite Salmon Arm (turn right off Hwy 1 at Tappen, 6km west of town). There's good swimming from a sandy beach, a provincial **campground**, and a lovely fifteen-minute walk culminating at Margaret Falls.

Practicalities

Greyhound **buses** serve Salmon Arm from Vancouver and Calgary (5 daily in each direction) and Kelowna, Vernon and Penticton (2 daily). The bus terminal is at the West Village Mall on Hwy 1, and the **infocentre** (year round Mon–Sat 8.30am–5.30pm; ☎832-6247) is nearby at 70 Hudson Ave NE.

The most convenient of Salmon Arm's many **motels** is the *Village Motel* (☎832-3955; ②), plumb in the heart of downtown. Of several **campgrounds**, the obvious first choice is the *Salmon Arm KOA*, 3km east of town on a big wooded site; its excellent facilities include a heated swimming pool (May–Oct; ☎832-6489; $16–20). The *Salmon River Motel and Campground*, 1km west of downtown at 910-40th St SW (year round; ☎832-3065; rooms ②; sites $12), is also good.

The *Orchard House* **restaurant**, on 22nd St on the east side of town, is popular with locals. For soup, salads and sandwiches, try the central *Eatery* on Alexander St or the *Brass Kettle* out west on the Trans-Canada.

A decidedly alternative form of accommodation is on offer at **Sicamous**, a pleasant but very busy waterfront village east of Salmon Arm along the Trans-Canada. Though crammed with motels and campgrounds, the village is better known for its many **houseboats**; a few rent by the night, but most tend to be let weekly by about half a dozen local agencies.

Highway 97: Westwold to Vernon

Passing through idyllic pastoral landscapes, **Highway 97** is a far better entrance to (or exit from) the Okanagan than the dreary road from Salmon Arm. The grass-green meadows, grazing cattle and low wooded hills here are the sort of scenery pioneers must have dreamed of; most of the little hamlets en route make charming spots to stay, and any number of minor roads lead off to small lakes, each with modest recreational facilities.

The highway peels south off the Trans-Canada 26km east of Kamloops, its first good stops being **Monte Lake**, served by the excellent *Heritage Campground and RV Park* (April–Oct; ☎375-2478; $10) and the equally well-tended and unspoilt public campground at **Monte Lake Provincial Park**. WESTWOLD, 5km beyond, is a dispersed ranching community of clean, old wooden houses and large pastures that present a picture of peaceful rural life.

FALKLAND, 13km beyond, is a tidy, unassuming place whose two **motels** blend easily into its rustic village atmosphere. The nicer of the pair is the *Highland* (☎379-2249; ①) on Adelphi St, but you might also drop into the infocentre (summer only) for lists of local bed and breakfasts. There are also a couple of quiet **campgrounds**. Country lanes lead north and east from here to **Bolean Lake** (10km), served by a small lodge and campground (May–Oct; no phone; rooms ①; tents $10); to **Pillar Lake** (13km) and the *Pillar Lake Resort* (May–Oct; ☎379-2623; rooms ②; campsites from $12); and to **Pinaus Lake** (10km) and its adjacent campground (April–Oct; no phone; $12).

Twelve kilometers short of Vernon, near the junction with the west-side Okanagan Lake road, stands the **O'Keefe Ranch**, a collection of early pioneer buildings and a tidy little museum that's well worth a short stop (May–Oct daily 9am–5pm; extended hours July & Aug; $5). In addition to a proficient summary of nineteenth-century frontier life, the museum contains an interesting section on the role of Native Canadians in the two world wars, when some 25 percent of eligible men immediately volunteered for service – a tour of duty that did little to resolve their national dilemma, which the museum sums up pithily with the observation that they belong to that "unhappy group who lost the old but are unable to obtain the new". Outside, a complete reconstruction of a period street includes a persuasively detailed general store where you can buy oddments from staff in old-time dress. You feel the past most strongly in the church and grave-yard, where a poignant handful of graves – three generations of O'Keefes, who first settled here in 1867 – capture the isolation and closeknit hardship of pioneer life. All the grandchildren died within a few years of each other in the 1980s.

The Okanagan

The vine- and orchard-covered hills and warm-water lakes of the **Okanagan** are in marked contrast to the rugged beauty of British Columbia's more mountainous interior, and have made the region not only one of Canada and the Northwest's most important fruit-growing areas but also a very popular destination with summer vacationers. Despite its high word-of-mouth reputation, it can be disorientating to stumble upon one of the brash towns of the Okanagan after lazing in BC's mountain emptiness. Three main centers – **Vernon**, **Kelowna** and **Penticton**, ranging from north to south along 100-kilometer **Okanagan Lake** – together contain the lion's share of the province's interior population, and all lay on an array of accommodation and mostly tacky tourist attractions.

On the plus side, the almost year-round Californian-style lushness that makes this "the land of beaches, peaches, sunshine and wine" means that, in the relative peace of **off-season**, you can begin to experience the region's potential charms: fruit trees in blossom, quiet lakeside villages and free wine tastings in local vine-yards. Not only that, but you can also expect room rates to be up to fifty percent lower in off-season. Kelowna is the biggest and probably best overall base at any time of the year, but local **buses** link all the towns and *Greyhounds* ply Hwy 97 on their way between Osoyoos and Kamloops or Salmon Arm.

Vernon

The beach scene in **VERNON** is one of the most relaxed in the Okanagan. Located at the junction of highways 6 and 97 near the northern edge of Okanagan Lake, the town attracts fewer of the bucket-and-spade brigade, though the empha-sis on fruit and the great outdoors is still strong, and the main highway through town is crammed with motels, fast-food outlets and ever more garish neon entreaties. On the whole you'll find it easier to find a place to stay here than in Kelowna (see below) – but there are fewer reasons for wanting to do so.

Downtown Vernon concentrates on 32nd Avenue (Hwy 97) and leaves a far more gracious impression than the town's outskirts by virtue of its elegant tree-lined streets and 500 listed buildings. The locals are an amenable and cosmopoli-tan bunch made up of British, Germans, Chinese and Salish, plus an abnormally large number of Jehovah's Witnesses, whose churches seem to have a monopoly on religious observance in the town. The local **museum**, by the clock tower at 3009-32nd Ave, does the usual job on local history (Mon–Sat 10am–5.30pm; free). At the southern entrance to town, **Polson Park** provides a green sanctuary from the crowds, but for beaches you have to head further afield to **Kalamalka Beach** on Kalamalka Lake, south of Vernon, or to **Kin Beach** on Okanagan Lake west on Okanagan Landing Road – both places with adjoining campgrounds.

Other outdoor recreation (but not camping) is on hand at **Silver Star Recreation Area**, a steep 22-kilometer drive to the northeast on 48th Avenue off Hwy 97, where in summer a **ski lift** (July–Sept daily 10am–4pm; $7.50) trundles to the top of Silver Star Mountain for wide views and meadow-walking opportunities; the most used trail wends from the summit back to the base area. Three kilometers from the *Silver Star* complex are the **Cedar Springs Public Hot Springs** (daily noon–11pm; $5).

Practicalities

Vernon's **infocentre** is at 3700-33rd St, one block west of Hwy 97 (daily June–Aug 8am–8pm; Sept–May 9am–5pm; ☎542-1415), along with seasonal offices north and south of town on the main highway. The **Greyhound station** is on the corner of 30th St and 31st Ave (☎545-0527). Local motels may well have **rooms** when nearby towns are full: a sound if bland choice is the *Sandman* at 4201-32nd St (☎542-4325; ②). The *Polson Park Motel* (☎549-2231; ①), opposite the eponymous park on 24th Ave, is one of the cheapest options. The more upmarket *Schell Motel*, 2810-35th (☎545-1351; ②), tempts clients with a pool and sauna. **Campgrounds** near town all get busy, and you may have to trek some way along the lakeshore before you strike lucky; try *Dutch's Tent and Trailer Court* (May–Sept; ☎545-1023; $15) at 15408 Kalamalka Rd, 3km south of Vernon near Kalamalka Beach. Much more rural are the sites at *Cedar Falls Campground* (May–Sept; ☎545-2888; $12) near Cedar Springs Public Hot Springs (see above), and at Ellison Provincial Park, 25km off to the southwest on Okanagan Lake.

The range of **food** is fairly cosmopolitan, especially at the many cafés and sandwich places. Try *Jackie's*, a local favorite on 30th Ave at 34th St, or *Little Hobo* on 30th Ave at 31st St. For something more special, Vernon's top restaurant is *Café Campeache*, 3202-31st Ave (☎542-1518; closed Sun & Mon).

Kelowna

If you're continuing south from Vernon, be sure to take the minor road on the western shore of Okanagan Lake – a quiet detour that offers something of the beauty for which the area is frequently praised but which is pretty hard to find among the commercialism of towns. From the road, weaving in and out of woods and small bays, the lake looks enchanting in the right light. The shore is often steep and there are few places to get down to the water – though you might squeeze a tent between the trees for some unofficial camping.

If you want a summer suntan and cheek-by-jowl nightlife – neither of which you'd readily associate with the British Columbian interior – then **KELOWNA** ("grizzly bear" in the Salish dialect) is probably the place to come. People had such a good time here in the summer of 1988 that the annual Kelowna Regatta turned into a full-blown and very un-Canadian riot, forcing the police to wade in with truncheons and tear gas. The following year people from as far away as Vancouver responded to invitations to a showdown in similar vein, arriving with truckloads of rocks to hurl at the enemy; the main event has since been cancelled, but the beach and downtown bars are as busy as ever. That this modest place should have fostered such an urban-style melée isn't all that surprising. Compared to other interior towns, Kelowna (pop. 70,000) is a sprawling metropolis and, to the unsuspecting tourist, its approaches come as an unpleasant surprise – particularly the grim conglomeration of motels, garages and fast-food joints on Hwy 97 at the north end of town.

That said, the lakefront and beaches, though heavily developed, aren't too bad, and off-season Kelowna can make a good couple of days' respite from mountains and forests. The main attractions are the public beach off **City Park**, a lovely green space that fronts downtown, and the strips along Lakeshore Road south of Kelowna's famed pontoon bridge, which tend to attract a younger, trendier crowd: **Rotary Beach** here is the windsurfers' hang-out, and **Boyce Gyro Park**, just north, is where the town's teenagers practise their preening and petting. Across the bridge and 2km up the lake's west bank, **Bear Creek Provincial Park** is a lovely – and popular – spot with another great beach and campground.

Kelowna owes its prosperity primarily to one man, Father Pandosy, a French priest who founded a mission here in 1859 and planted a couple of apple trees two years later. Much of Canada's **fruit** is now grown in the area – including virtually all the apricots, half the pears and plums, and thirty percent of the apples. The infocentre can point you to dozens of juice, fruit, food and forestry tours, but if you feel like sampling the more hedonistic fruits of Father Pandosy's legacy, consider visiting one of the local **vineyards**, all of them known for their open-handed generosity with free samples after a tour of the premises. **Calona Wines** is Canada's second biggest winery, and it's just six blocks off Hwy 97 at 1125 Richter (summer daily 9am–4pm; tours every 30min), but the infocentre can provide a full run-down of smaller and more far-flung estates. All of them join together in early October to lay on the region's annual **wine festival**.

Getting away from Kelowna's crowds isn't easy, but you stand a good chance by climbing **Knox Mountain**, the high knoll that overlooks the city to the north, just five minutes' drive (or thirty minutes' walk) from downtown. It offers lovely views over the lake and town, particularly at sunset, and there's a wooden observation tower to make the most of the panorama.

Practicalities

The **bus terminal** is at the east end of town at 2366 Leckie Road on the corner of Harvey (Hwy 97), and sees off two buses daily to Calgary, Banff, Cache Creek and Kamloops respectively (☎860-3835). The **infocentre** (daily June–Aug 8am–8pm; Sept–May 9am–5pm; ☎861-1515) is five blocks back from the lake at 544 Harvey, and **bike rental** is available at *Sports Rent*, 3000 Pandosy St.

Accommodation can be a major headache in the height of summer unless you get to one of the **motels** on northbound Hwy 97 early in the morning; you'll probably find a bed here, but in a neon- and traffic-infested area well away from downtown and the lake (prices drop the further out you go). Remarkably, there's only one central downtown **hotel**, the perfectly placed and very comfortable *Willow Inn* at 235 Queensway (☎762-2122; ②) – ring ahead or book very early for summer vacancies, and don't be deterred by the adjoining bar which appears to be the headquarters of the Kelowna chapter of the Hell's Angels. The *Kelowna Backpackers Hostel*, 2343 Pandosy St (☎763-6024; ①), slightly relieves the pressure on budget rooms, but its downtown location means it fills up quickly.

If you're camping and want to stay close to the action, three **campgrounds** conveniently back onto Lakeshore Road: *Tiny Town* at Boyce Gyro Park (April–Oct; ☎762-6302; $15–20), and *Hiawatha* (year round; ☎862-8222; $19–24) and

Lakeside (year round; ☎860-4072; $20–28) at 654 Cook Rd near Rotary Beach. Arrive early at Bear Creek Provincial Park to be sure of camping space (May–Sept; $14). Most of the other campgrounds are on the other side of the lake at Westbank, a left turn off Hwy 97 on Boucherie Road just over the pontoon bridge (probably too far out if you don't have a car) – try *West Bay Beach* (March–Oct; ☎768-3004; $17.50–21).

Most **eating** places are crammed into the small downtown area. The variety is large, and a short walk should offer something to suit most tastes and budgets. Most travellers and young locals head for *Jonathan L Seagull* on Bernard St, opposite the *Paramount* cinema, which has a relaxed bar atmosphere and live music most nights – usually a singer and guitar. Despite its slick cocktail-lounge ambience, *Earl's Hollywood on Top*, 211 Bernard Ave at the corner of Abbott (☎763-2777), is good for ribs, seafood and steaks; go early to get a table on the upstairs patio. For sheer value, *Poor Boys' Restaurant* at 450 Bernard St is unbeatable: portions are huge, the decor minimal, and prices absurdly low. At the other extreme, you could splurge on seafood at *Le Papillon*, 375 Leon Ave, one of the region's top restaurants (☎763-3833; closed Sun).

Penticton

PENTICTON is a corruption of the Salish phrase *pen tak tin* – "a place to stay forever" – but this is not a sobriquet the most southerly of the Okanagan's big towns even remotely deserves. Its summer daily average of ten hours of sunshine ranks it higher than Honolulu, making tourism its biggest industry after fruit (this is "Peach City"). That, along with Penticton's proximity to Vancouver and the States, keeps prices well over the odds and ensures that the town and beaches are swarming with watersports jocks, cross-country travellers, RV skippers and lots of happy families. Off the beaches there's some festival or other playing virtually every day of the year to keep the punters entertained, the key ones being the spring-celebrating **Blossom Festival** in April and the **Peach Festival** at the end of July.

Most leisure pastimes in Penticton – water-oriented activities in particular – take place on or near Okanagan Lake, just ten blocks from the town centre. **Okanagan Beach** is the closest sand to downtown and is usually covered in oiled bodies (not to mention liberal amounts of clogging guano) for most of its one-kilometer stretch; **Skaha Beach**, 4km south of town on Skaha Lake, is a touch quieter and trendier. Both beaches close at midnight. If you don't want to laze on the beaches, you can take your sun from a cruise on the lake aboard the *Casabella Princess* which departs from 45 E Lakeshore Drive by the *Delta Hotel* (call ☎493-5551 for times; $8.50).

If you're determined to sightsee, the **museum** at 785 Main St has a panoply of predictable Canadiana (Mon–Fri 10am–5pm; donation). Just off Main Street there's the **South Okanagan Art Gallery**, which often carries high-quality shows, and – it *would* have to be the "world's something" – also qualifies as the "world's first solar-powered art gallery" (Tues–Sun 10am–5pm). More tempting perhaps, and an ideal part of a day's stopover – possibly to fit in before a sprawl on the beach – is a trip to the **Casobello Wines Vineyard**, 2km south of town off Hwy 97 on Skaha Lake Road, which has tours and free tastings every half hour (July & Aug Mon–Fri 10am–4pm). Otherwise, Penticton's main diversions are its waterslides – abundant even by Canadian standards.

Practicalities

The downtown area is small and easy to negotiate, particularly after a visit to the big **infocentre** at 185 Lakeside Drive (daily 9am–5pm, longer in summer; ☎493-4055); if it's shut there's a big map and notice-board outside, plus smaller summer offices north and south of town on Hwy 97. All three concentrate on recreational pursuits, and dozens of specialist shops around town rent out equipment for every conceivable activity. For **bikes**, look up *Riverside Bike Rental* at 75 Riverside Drive on the west side of the lakefront (May–Sept daily).

Arriving by *Greyhound*, you'll pull into the **bus depot** just off Main Street between Robinson and Ellis streets (☎493-4101); Penticton is a major intersection of routes, with buses bound for Vancouver (5 daily), Kamloops (2 daily), Nelson and points east (2 daily), and Wenatchee/Spokane (WA) in the States (1 daily; change at Osoyoos).

Although Penticton boasts a brimful of **accommodation**, digging out a room in summer isn't easy. In high season it's best to seek help from the infocentre, although you could try your luck at the many **motels** – most of the cheaper fall-backs line the messy southern approach to the town along Hwy 97. One of the best and more central choices is the *Ti-ke Shores Motel* on the lake at 914 Lakeshore Drive (May–Sept; ☎492-8769; ②–④), with luxurious doubles (cheaper off-season). Try also the *Kozy Guest House*, 1000 Lakeshore Drive (☎493-8400; ②), or the *Three Gables Hotel*, 353 Main St (☎492-3933; ③).

Most **campgrounds** have their full-up signs out continuously in summer, and you'll have trouble if you arrive without a reservation. The best and therefore busiest sites are along the lake, and the bulk of the second-rank spots near the highway on the southern approaches. Recommended are *South Beach Gardens*, 3815 Skaha Lake Rd (May–Oct; ☎492-0628; $15–20), or *Wright's Beach Camp*, south of town on Hwy 97 on Lake Skaha (May–Sept; ☎492-7120; $17–24).

Budget **eating** choices don't extend much beyond the fast-food joints and cafés bunched largely around Main Street: try *Taco Grande*, 452 Main St, for Mexican food and inexpensive breakfasts; *Elite*, 340 Main St, the best overall deal for basic burgers, soup and salads; or *Theo's*, at 687 Main St, a friendly, crowded Greek place that serves big portions. Somewhat pricier but ever popular is *Angelini's* across from the Skaha Centre on Skaha Lake Road, which also has a Greek emphasis. For something different and more upmarket, search out *Salty's Beach House*, 988 Lakeshore Drive, a restaurant that's eccentric in all departments – setting, service and menu – but delivers excellent food.

Highway 3: the border towns

British Columbia's tawdry necklace of border towns on **Highway 3** – from Hope (see p.316) to the Albertan border – provides a good reason for taking a more northerly route across the province. None amounts to much, and you'd be advised to whisk through by car or *Greyhound*; if you have to break the journey, aim to do it in **Salmo** or **Castlegar**, towns on which some of the Kootenays' charm has rubbed off. Things begin in interesting vein out of Hope, where the road climbs into the gripping mountain scenery of the Coastal Ranges, passing through **Manning Provincial Park** before dropping to **Keremeos** and **Osoyoos**, the first an appealing little fruit-growing village, the second a resort town at the heart of strange, parched desert landscapes.

After dull Princeton, the scenery picks up once more, the road following the picturesque Similkameen Valley, backed by ranks of pines and white-topped mountains.

If you're crossing over **the border** hereabouts, incidentally, don't be lulled into expecting an easy passage: if you don't hold a Canadian or US passport you can expect the sort of grilling you'd get at major entry points.

Manning Provincial Park

One of the few parks in Canada's Coast and Cascade ranges, **Manning Provincial Park** parcels up a typical assortment of mountain, lake and forest scenery about 60km south of Princeton and is conveniently bisected by Hwy 3. Even if you're just passing through it's possible to take in one of the short **trails**, the best of which is the flower-festooned Rhododendron Flats path at the park's western edge.

The most popular drive within the park is the fifteen-kilometer side road to **Cascade Lookout**, a viewpoint over the Similkameen Valley and its bowl of mountains; a gravel road carries on another 6km from here to **Blackwall Peak**, the starting point for the **Heather Trail** (10km one way), renowned for its swathes of summer wildflowers. Other manageable day hikes leave the south side of the main highway, the majority accessed from a rough road to Lightning Lake just west of the park visitor center.

Accommodation at the *Manning Park Resort* (☎840-8822; ③–④), on Hwy 3 almost exactly midway between Princeton and Hope, runs to cabins and chalets, but all these go quickly in summer. There are also several provincial **campgrounds** on and off the highway, the best on the road being *Hampton* and *Mule Deer*, 4km and 8km east of the visitor center respectively ($10). The **park visitor center**, 1km east of the resort (May–Sept 9am–8pm), has a selection of trail leaflets, and some history and natural history exhibitions.

On from Princeton

Lackluster low hills ripple around **PRINCETON**'s dispersed collection of drab, rather jerry-built houses. The **bus depot** is at the west end of things at the *Village Kitchen Restaurant*, not so far from the all-but-redundant **infocentre** (year round 9am–5pm; ☎295-3103), housed in an old Canadian Pacific rail wagon at 195 Bridge St. The **motels** – of which there are plenty – cluster around a large and grim lumber mill on the east side of town, but you're better off hanging on for Keremeos, another 67km on. If circumstances dump you in town overnight, try the *Riverside Motel* (☎295-6232; ②), 307 Thomas St, three blocks north of downtown, which has individual log cabins.

HEDLEY, an old gold-mining hamlet 42km east of Princeton, is these days just a single street with great scenery and a couple of motels. Try the *Corona Motel and Campground* (April–Oct; ☎292-8302; ①) with tent sites from $10. Just short of the village, off the highway, lies **Bromley Rock**, a lovely if oversanitized picnic stop looking down on the whitewater of the Similkameen River.

To explore some of the backcountry off the highway after Hedley, take the 21-kilometer gravel road (signed just west of Keremeos) south into the heart of **Cathedral Provincial Park**, a spectacular upland enclave with an unserviced campground and 32km of marked trails.

Keremeos

The meandering Highway 3 leads on to **KEREMEOS** and Osoyoos. In the former, the landscape lurches into a more rural mode, thanks mainly to a climate which blesses the region with the longest growing season in the country – hence the tag, "Fruit Stand Capital of Canada".

Arguably the best-situated town this side of Nelson (see p.341), Keremeos spreads over a dried-up lake bed, with hills rising up from the narrow plain on all sides. Lush, irrigated orchards surround the town, offset in spring by a lush carpet of flowers across the valley floor, and depending on the season you can pick up fruit and vegetables from stands dotted more or less everywhere. Cherries, apricots, peaches, pears, apples, plums – even grapes – all grow in abundance, and if you're not taken with the food there's the chance of **wine tastings** at the *St Laszio Vineyards*, 1km east of town on Hwy 3.

Keremeos itself is a rustic, two-street affair that's almost unspoilt by neon or urban clutter. A few shopfronts are oldish, and several make a stab at being heritage houses – the *Old Fish and Chipper* on Main St, for example. Though there's little to see or do, it's a pleasant spot to spend the night. The **infocentre** is at 415-7th Ave (June–Sept 9am–5pm; ☎499-5225).

There are about half a dozen **motels** locally: the nicest is the *Similkameen* (☎499-5984; ①), about 1km west of the center in open country surrounded by lawns and orchards. For the best of the **campgrounds**, press on 13km west on Hwy 3 to the *Lucky R* (May–Oct; ☎499-2065; $12–14.50), solitary and set amid trees and lawns on the river.

Osoyoos

Beyond Keremeos the road climbs for 46km, unfolding a dramatic view of **OSOYOOS** and a sizeable lake surrounded by bare, ocher hills. Descending, you enter one of Canada's strangest landscapes – a bona fide desert of scrub-covered hills, sand, lizards, cactus, snakes, and Canada's lowest average rainfall (around 25cm per year). Temperatures here are regularly 10°C higher than in Nelson, less than a morning's drive away, enabling exotic fruit like bananas and pomegranates to be grown, and prompting Osoyoos to declare itself the "Spanish Capital of Canada". The houses here are supposed to have been restyled to give the place an Iberian flavor to match its climate, but on the ground it's almost impossible to find any trace of the transformation.

The town is otherwise distinguished only by its position beside **Lake Osoyoos** in the Okanagan Valley – Hwy 97, which passes through the town, is the main route into the Okanagan region. In summer the place comes alive with swimmers and boaters, drawn to the warmest water of any lake in Canada, and with streams of RVs slow-tailing their way northwards.

The relative lack of crowds and strange scenery might persuade you to do your beach-bumming in Osoyoos, though even here you'll be pushed to find space in any of the town's twenty **hotels** and **motels** during high season; one of the most reasonable and most central is the *Rialto* (☎495-6022; ①) with views over the lake. Most of the motels are across the causeway on the southeastern shore of the lake, alongside the **bus stand** and the vivid pink *Pay 'n' Save*. For help, contact the **infocentre** at the junction of Hwy 3 and Hwy 97 (☎495-7142). You're more likely to get a place in one of the local **campgrounds** – try the *Cabana*

Beach (April–Oct; ☎495-7705; $15–20) at 55 East Lakeshore Drive or *Van Acres* (May–Sept; ☎495-6912; $14–20) at 7004-67th St.

Midway, Greenway and Grand Forks

At **MIDWAY**, some 65km east of Osoyoos, something of the desert landscape lingers, the hills strange, broad whalebacks cut by open valleys and covered in coarse scrub and brown-baked grass. The hamlet's handful of scattered homes looks like a windblown and wistful ghost town, making an evocative backdrop for the overgrown train tracks and tiny **railway museum** housed alongside a rusted minuscule steam engine. It's a fascinating little spot. For more background contact the **infocentre** on Hwy 3 (June–Sept 9am–6pm; ☎449-2614). To **stay**, check in to the *Midway Motor Inn*, 622 Palmerston St (☎449-2662; ①).

East out of town, the scenery along Hwy 3 begins to change from bleached grass and sagebrush to bland meandering hills. At **GREENWOOD**, however, the pines reappear, heralding a wild, battered brute of a village which has suffered from the closure of its mines and can't muster much more than a couple of old buildings and some disused mine workings. The **infocentre** is housed in the town museum on the main road at 214 South Copper St (May–Sept; ☎455-6777). You're pretty sure of a welcome in any of the local **motels**, the least expensive being the *Evening Star* (☎445-6733; ①).

GRAND FORKS is not grand at all – it's very small and very dull and little more than a perfunctory transit settlement built on a river flat. Several *Greyhound* **buses** drop in daily, probably the biggest thing to happen to the place, stopping at *Stanley's*, which is also a good choice for a snack – or you could stock up at the big *Overwaitea* supermarket alongside. The small **museum** by the traffic lights is the standard small-town model and can be seen in about the time it takes for the lights to change. Just north of town, **Christina Lake** is a modestly unspoilt summer resort with lots of swimming, boating and camping opportunities. A dozen or so motels and campgrounds sprout along its shore, with about the same number in and around the town itself, but it's hard to imagine you'd want to use them except in an emergency.

Trail and Rossland

TRAIL is home to the world's largest lead and zinc smelter, a vast industrial complex whose chimneys cast a dismal shadow over the village's few houses. **ROSSLAND**, 10km west, also has a mining foundation – gold this time, some $125 million worth of which ($2 billion at today's prices) was gouged from the surrounding hills around the turn of the century. If you're into mining heritage, a tour of the **Le Roi Gold Mine** – with 100km of tunnels – and the adjoining **Rossland Historical Museum** will stuff you with fascinating technical and geological background (mid-May to mid-Sept daily 9am–5pm; $5, or $2.50 for museum only). The **infocentre** (May–Oct 9am–8pm; ☎362-7722), at the junction of the town's two main roads, is most useful for details of the **Nancy Greene Recreation Area** northwest of town. Though best known for its world-class skiing – its **Red Mountain Ski Area** is a training ground for members of the Canadian national team – it's also excellent for hiking, an outdoor pursuit in scarce supply in these parts. There's no camping, however.

Castlegar

CASTLEGAR is a strange, diffuse place with no obvious heart, probably because roads and rivers – this is where the Kootenay meets the Columbia – make it more a transport hub than a community. In its time it was famous for its immigrant **Doukhobor** population, members of a Russian sect who fled religious persecution in 1899 and brought their pacifist-agrarian lifestyle to western Canada. Although their way of life waned after the death of their leader Peter Verigin in 1924, the Doukhobors' considerable industry and agricultural expertise transformed the Castlegar area; many locals still practise the old beliefs, and Russian is still taught in local schools.

Much of the community's heritage has been collected in the **Doukhobor Village Museum** (Wed–Sun 9am–5pm; $3), just off the main road on the right after you cross the big suspension bridge over the Kootenay River. A Doukhobor descendant is on hand to take you through the museum, which houses a winsome display of farm machinery, handmade tools and traditional Russian clothing that's intriguing as much for its alien context as for its content. As interesting as the museum, and highly recommended if you've built up a massive appetite, is the Doukhobor **restaurant** alongside. The ambience is bizarrely austere – the walls are bare but for a few crafts and rummage-sale notices – and the menu an exercise in straight-laced cuisine: Doukhobor chefs face something of a daily creative challenge, given that they can't use meat, fish or alcohol in the cooking. To meet it they produce just two set dinners daily. One brings you borsch, bread, tart and coffee; the other delivers things called *varenyky, galoopsie, pyrogy* and *nalesnici*, all tasty and shudderingly stodgy.

Castlegar's **infocentre** (year round; ☎365-6313) is at 1995-6th Ave off the main road as you leave town for Grand Forks over the Columbia bridge. The best **motel** – small, and with a nice view – is the *Cozy Pines* on Hwy 3 on the west edge of town (☎365-5613; ①–②). Closer in, the modern and attractive *Fireside* (☎365-2128; ②) is a touch more expensive. Three kilometers out of town to the west is the *Hislop's Hiway Campsite*, 1725 Mannix Rd (May–Oct; ☎365-2337; $10–12).

Salmo to Creston

A classic stretch of scenic blacktop, Hwy 3 climbs from Salmo to the fruit-growing plains around Creston via the **Kootenay Pass** – though the views are less of spectacular mountains than of a pretty tracery of creeks and rivers crashing down through forest on all sides. This is one of the highest main roads in the country – it's frequently closed by bad weather – and it has no services for 70km into Creston, so check your gas before setting out. If you're cycling, brace yourself for a fifty-kilometer uphill slog, but the reward is an unexpected and stunning lake at the pass, where there's a pull-off, picnic area and views of high peaks in the far distance.

Despite the large volume of traffic converging on it along Hwy 3 and Hwy 6, tiny **SALMO** somehow manages to retain a pioneer feel: most of its tidy wooden buildings are fronted by verandas, and in summer they're decked out with baskets of flowers. The **infocentre** (mid-June to mid-Sept; ☎357-9332) is on the corner of Hwy 6 and Fourth St, but it doesn't have a lot to promote apart from the "world's smallest telephone box", next to the *Salcrest Motel* on the south side of town, and the **museum** (May–Sept Mon–Fri 10am–4pm), a more credible attraction housed in a picturesque white-painted building at Fourth St and Railway Ave, which charts the vicissitudes of pioneer life and also hosts occasional travelling exhibitions. In winter there's **skiing** at the Salmo ski area just 2km east of town.

Buses pull in here for a long rest stop at the terminal by the *Petro-Canada* garage on the north side of the village. If you need to overnight, use either of the two central **motels**: the *Reno*, 185 Railway Ave (☎357-9937; ①), one block east of the bus terminal, or the *Salcrest* (☎357-9557; ①), at the junction of highways 3 and 6. The nearest **campground** is the *Hidden Creek Guest Ranch* (May–Oct; ☎357-2266; $7–12), 6km north of town on Hwy 6. For **food** try *Charlie's Pizza and Spaghetti House*, an old-style diner on Fourth St. Just up the road, the *Silver Dollar Pub* is the town's favorite **bar**, with pool tables, a jukebox and lots of good ol' boys in an atmospheric wooden interior. *Salmo Foods*, opposite the bar, is the best supermarket for supplies.

Don't stop in **CRESTON** unless you want a taste of the terminally bland or such sightseeing frippery as "Canada's best mural". The **infocentre** is in a log cabin (the town's only building of interest) on the east side of town at 1711 Canyon St (☎428-4342), and can help with **accommodation**, though with twenty or so motels and campgrounds to choose from, chances are you won't be fighting for a bed. The cheapest and most central spot is the *Hotel Creston* (☎428-9321; ①); motels on the town's fringes offer more salubrious, if slightly costlier alternatives. In addition to *Greyhounds* passing through on Hwy 3, *Empire Bus Lines* runs an early-morning service from here to Spokane, WA (daily except Tues & Wed).

The Kootenays

The Kootenays area is one of the most attractive and unvisited in British Columbia. It is loosely defined, essentially consisting of two major north–south valleys – the Kootenay and the Columbia, which are largely taken up by **Kootenay Lake** and **Upper** and **Lower Arrow lakes** – and three intervening mountain ranges – the Purcells, Selkirks and Monashees, whose once-rich mineral deposits formed the kernel of the province's early mining industry. **Nelson** is the key town, slightly peripheral to the Kootenays' rugged core, but a lovely place, and one of the few provincial towns that has real attractions in its own right. Scattered lakeside hamlets, notably **Kaslo** and **Nakusp**, make excellent bases for excursions into mountain scenery which in the Kootenays has a pristine quality not found elsewhere. Watery activities – canoeing and fishing in particular – are excellent, and you can also explore the ramshackle mining heritage of near-ghost towns like **Sandon** and **New Denver**, or wallow in the hot springs at Nakusp.

Getting around the region is tricky if you're without your own transport, for there are next to no public services (see the "Nelson" section for details on buses), which is a shame because the roads here are among the most scenic in a province noted for its scenery. Even with your own vehicle, there's no way to do the Kootenays justice without retracing your steps at times. You can dip in and out of the region from the Trans-Canada Highway (to the north) or Hwy 3 (to the south), but any trans-Kootenay route is more attractive than either of these main highways: the most **scenic routes** are Hwy 31A from Kaslo to New Denver, and Hwy 6 from Vernon to New Denver. Given no time constraints, your best strategy would be to enter from Creston (or Vernon) and exit at either Revelstoke (see p.431) or Creston, both of which set you up for the Canadian Rockies.

Highway 3A to Kootenay Bay

Starting from just north of Creston, **Highway 3A** picks a slow, twisting course up the eastern shore of **Kootenay Lake** to the free car ferry at Kootenay Bay. Apart from the ample scenic rewards of the lake and the mountains beyond it, the highway is almost completely empty for all of its 79km, and none of the villages marked on maps amount to anything more than scattered houses hidden in the woods. The only noteworthy sight is the **Glass House**, midway up the lake at **BOSWELL**, which ranks highly in the list of the Northwest's more bizarre offerings. Constructed entirely from embalming bottles, the house was built by a Mr Brown after 35 years in the funeral business, "to indulge", so the wonderfully po-faced pamphlet tells you, "a whim of a peculiar nature". The retired mortician travelled widely visiting friends in the funeral profession until he'd collected 500,000 bottles – that's 250 tonnes' worth – to build his lakeside retirement home. Nearby **accommodation** is provided by the *Heidelburg Inn* (☎223-8263; ②), and the *Mountain Shores Resort* (☎223-8258; ③), a combination of motel, cottages and **campground** (April–Oct; $12–15).

At **GRAY CREEK**, a few kilometers onward, check out the superb *Gray Creek Store*, which boasts the once-in-a-lifetime address of 1979 Chainsaw Ave and claims, with some justification, to be "The Most Interesting Store You've Ever Seen". The shop basically *is* Gray Creek – it's the sort of place you go to get your chainsaw fixed and where real lumberjacks come for their red-checked shirts. There are two lakeside **campgrounds** nearby, the *Old Crow* (June–Sept; ☎227-9495; $10) and the *Lakeview* (year round; ☎227-9367; $10).

CRAWFORD BAY and **KOOTENAY BAY** are names on the map that refer in the flesh to the most fleeting of settlements, the latter also being the **ferry terminal** for boats to Balfour on the west shore. As a place to stay, this side of the crossing is a touch brighter, and there's an **infocentre** (June–Sept 9am–5pm; ☎227-9267) just off the road at Crawford Bay if you need help finding some of the nicer accommodation tucked away in the woods nearby. The cheapest **motel** is the *Last Chance* (☎227-9477; ②), near the ferry dock; nearby *Wedgewood Manor* (April–Nov; ☎227-9233; ④) is upmarket and pleasantly plush, but you'll have to book ahead to secure one of its four rooms. The better of two **campgrounds** here is the nicely wooded *Kokanee Springs Resort* on Hwy 3A (☎227-9292), but Balfour has a greater choice of sites.

The thirty-minute **ferry crossing** – purportedly the longest free ferry crossing in the world – is beautiful. Free boats leave every fifty minutes from June to September, and every two hours the rest of the year, but they operate on a first-come, first-served basis, and in summer unless you're a pedestrian or bike passenger it can be a couple of sailings before your turn comes round.

Balfour and Ainsworth Hot Springs

BALFOUR is not so much the fishing village it's billed as, but rather a fairly shoddy and dispersed collection of motels, garages and cafés – albeit in verdant surroundings – designed to catch the traffic rolling on and off the Kootenay Lake ferry. RV **campgrounds** line the road to Nelson for about 2km, but the quietest are those furthest from the terminal, and much better still is Kokanee Creek Provincial Park, about 10km beyond. The handiest **motel** for the ferry is the *Balfour Beach Inn* (April–Nov; ☎229-4235; ③), convenient for the small pebbly beach just north of the terminal.

About 15km north of Balfour on Hwy 31, **AINSWORTH HOT SPRINGS** is home to some 100 residents – a town by local standards. The tasteful *Ainsworth Hot Springs Resort* (☎229-4212; ③–⑤) is ideal if you want to take in the scalding water of the **mineral springs** (daily 8.30am–9.30pm; $5), though the chalets are expensive, and local opinion rates the Nakusp hot springs (see p.340) far more highly. The nicest local **motel** is the *Mermaid Lodge* (☎229-4969; ②). Spelunkers might want to take a tour ($10) of **Cody Caves Provincial Park**, 15km up a rough side road (well signed) above town.

A touch further up the increasingly beautiful Hwy 31 comes the self-contained **Woodbury Resort** (year round; ☎353-7177; ②), a collection of motel, cottages, campground (tents $12) and watersport facilities – pitched on the lakeshore with lovely views and a small beach, it makes an attractive accommodation prospect if you're tenting. Directly opposite is the **Woodbury Mining Museum** (July–Sept daily 9am–6pm; $4), a quaint pioneer building crammed with mining regalia and the starting point for a thirty-minute underground tour of the old lead, zinc and silver workings.

Kaslo and around

KASLO must rate as one of British Columbia's most attractive and friendliest little villages. Huddled at the edge of Kootenay Lake and dwarfed by towering mountains, its half-dozen streets are lined with picture-perfect wooden homes and flower-filled gardens. It started life as a sawmill in 1889 and turned into a boomtown with the discovery of silver in 1893; diversification, and the steamers that plied the lakes, saved it from the cycle of boom and bust that ripped the heart out of so many similar towns. Kaslo remains an urbane and civilized community whose citizens work hard at keeping it that way, supporting a cultural center, art galleries, rummage sales, even a concert society. Finding your way around is no problem, nor is finding information – everyone is disarmingly helpful – but there's an **infocentre** (April–Oct daily 9am–6pm; ☎353-7323) at Fourth Ave & A St on the town's main crossroads if you need it.

The **town hall**, a distinctive green and white wooden building dating from 1898, is an architectural gem by any standards, as is the church opposite. Yet Kaslo's main attraction is the SS *Moyie*, the oldest surviving **paddle steamer** in North America, which ferried men, ore and supplies along the mining routes from 1897 until the advent of reliable roads in 1957. A museum of antiques, artefacts and photographs is due to open when the steamer's refurbishment is complete (daily 10am–4.30pm; $3). Look for the small hut alongside, the "world's smallest post office" (closed since 1970), and drop in on Kaslo's thriving **arts center**, the *Langham Cultural Society*, for theatrical performances and art exhibitions.

Kaslo makes an ideal base for tackling two of the region's major parks – Kokanee Glacier Provincial Park and the Purcell Wilderness Conservancy – and for pottering around some of the charming lakeshore communities. People at the *Langham* can advise on getting to **ARGENTA**, a refugee settlement of Quakers who came from the States to start a new life; it's also the western trailhead for the sixty-kilometer Earl Grey Pass Trail over the Purcell Mountains to Invermere.

This area, incidentally, offers a good chance of seeing **ospreys**: the Kootenays' hundred or so breeding pairs represent the largest concentration of the species in North America.

Practicalities

By far the best thing to do is visit the town's social hub, the excellent **Treehouse Restaurant** on Front Street, a warm and cozy place where you can eat superbly and easily strike up conversations. The nearby *Mariner Inn and Motel* has a beer hall, and is more of a lowlife hang-out.

The best central **accommodation** is the *Kaslo Motel* (☎353-2431; ①) – for most other options head for the marina just north of the village where, among other options, you'll find the *Beachcomber Marina* (☎353-7777; ②). For **bed and breakfast** try the *Loki Lodge* (☎353-2684; ③). More interesting accommodation possibilities are available further up the lake, most notably two rustic bed and breakfasts at Argenta – for details contact the Farleys at *Earl Grey Pass* (☎366-4472; ①), or the Pollards at *Place Cockaigne* (☎366-4394; ②).

Kaslo has a free municipal **campground** on the flat ground by the lake at the end of Front Street, past the SS *Moyie* on the right. *Mirror Lake Campground* (mid-April to mid-Oct; ☎353-7102), beautifully situated 2km south of town on the main road to Ainsworth, has more facilities and charges $10 per site. Shopping in the village is best done at the old-style *Lakeview Store* at the top of Front Street, the like of which has probably only been seen in *The Waltons*.

Kokanee Glacier Provincial Park

Kaslo is the most sensible of several possible jumping-off points for **Kokanee Glacier Provincial Park**, straddling the Selkirk Mountains to the southwest, as the access road from here – signed off Hwy 31A 5km northwest of town – offers the best views and choice of trails. (Other approaches are from Ainsworth, Hwy 6 in the Slocan Valley, and Hwy 3A between Balfour and Nelson.) The 29-kilometer Kaslo road cuts to the heart of the park, reaching the Joker Millsite parking area set amid spectacular glacier-ringed high country. Of the eleven trails in the area, the obvious **hike** from the car park runs up to Helen Deane and Kaslo lakes (8km round trip), an easy morning amble. If you're staying overnight you can pick from the usual undeveloped campgrounds (you're supposed to camp in designated sites only) and three basic summer-only **cabins** ($10; no cooking facilities) – the main one, *Slocan Chief*, is past Helen Deane Lake alongside a park ranger office.

Highway 31A and the Slocan Valley

After Kaslo you can either rattle north over gravel road to link with the Trans-Canada Highway at Revelstoke, a wild and glorious 150-kilometer drive with a ferry crossing at Galena Bay, or stay in the Kootenays and shuffle west on **Hwy 31A** through the Selkirk Mountains to the Slocan Valley. The latter road ascends from Kaslo alongside the Kaslo River, a crashing torrent choked with branches and fallen trees and hemmed in by high mountains and cliffs of dark rock that lend the drive a melancholy air. The crags' metallic sheen is indicative of the mineral wealth that fired the early growth of so many of the settlements in the region. Near its high point the road passes a series of picturesque lakes: **Fish**

Lake is deep green and has a nice picnic spot at one end; **Bear Lake** is equally pretty; and **Beaver Pond** is an amazing testament to the beaver's energy and ingenuity.

Sandon

The ghost town of **SANDON** is located 13km south of Hwy 31A, up a signed gravel side road that climbs through scenery of the utmost grandeur. Unfortunately Sandon itself is too much ghost and not enough town to suggest how it might have looked in its silver-mining heyday when it had 24 hotels, 23 saloons, an opera house and 2000 inhabitants. That it's now dilapidated rather than evocative is due mainly to a flood which swept away the earlier boardwalk settlement in 1955, leaving a partly inhabited rump that clusters around a café and **infocentre** immediately past the salmon-pink wooden building at the top of the town.

The trip is redeemed, however, if you hike the **KNS Historic Trail** (6km each way) from the site, which follows the course of the 1895 Kaslo–Slocan ore-carrying railway, past old mine works and eventually to fine views of the New Denver Glacier across the Slocan Valley to the west. Coupled with leaflets from the infocentre, the walk vividly documents the area's wild-west mining history, harking back to an era when the district – known as "Silvery Slocan" – produced the lion's share of Canada's silver. "Silver, lead, and hell are raised in the Slocan," wrote one local newspaper in 1891, "and unless you can take a hand in producing these articles, your services are not required." The immense vein of silver-rich galena that started the boom was discovered by accident in 1891 by two colorful prospectors, Eli Carpenter and Jack Seaton, when they got lost on the ridges returning to Ainsworth from Slocan Lake. Back in the bar they fell out over the find, and each raced out with his own team to stake the claim. Seaton won, and became a vastly wealthy silver baron who travelled in his own train carriage across Canada, condemning Carpenter to return to his earlier profession as a tightrope walker and to an ultimately penurious death.

New Denver and the Slocan Valley

After the Sandon turn-off Hwy 31A drops into the **Slocan Valley**, a minor but still spectacular lake-bottomed tributary between the main Kootenay and Columbia watersheds, and meets Hwy 6 at **NEW DENVER**. Born of the same silver-mining boom as Kaslo, and with a similar lakeside setting and genuine pioneer feel, New Denver is, if anything, quieter than its neighbor. The clapboard houses are in peeling, pastel-painted wood, and the tree-lined streets are mercifully free of neon, fast food and tourist trappings. As a stopover it's as good as Kaslo, for which purpose there's a single beach-hut-type **motel**, the *Valhalla Inn*, 504 Slocan Ave (☎358-2228; ①), the lake-view *Sweet Dreams Guest House* (☎358-2415; ②) and the simple *New Denver Municipal Campground* (year round; ☎358-2316; $10–12) on the south side of the village. For **food** try the *Apple Tree Sandwich Shop* on the main street. **Silvery Slocan Museum** is good for twenty minutes on the background and artefacts of the area's mining heritage. The central **infocentre** (summer only; ☎358-2631) is the place to pick up specific information on the surrounding valley.

Southbound out of New Denver, Hwy 6 follows the tight confines of the Slocan Valley for another hundred kilometers of ineffable mountain and lake landscapes.

The 125,000-acre **Valhalla Provincial Park**, on the eastern side of Slocan Lake, encapsulates the best of the scenery: a wilderness area with no developed facilities, most of it is out of reach unless you can boat across the water, though there are two trails which lead into it from the hamlet of **SLOCAN** at the south end of the lake. For a taste of the outdoors, the canter up the old railway bed from Slocan is a popular short hike, and there's more fresh air at the Mulvey Basin and Cove Creek **beaches**, each with small provincial campgrounds. Note, too, that gravel roads lead up from Hwy 6 to the more accessible heights of **Kokanee Glacier Provincial Park** to the east (p.338).

If you need to **stay** in the area, there are about half a dozen options, all in rustic settings with great mountain or lake views. Try either *Lemon Creek Lodge* (☎355-2403; ②), a motel-campground 7km south of Slocan, or the *Slocan Inn* (☎355-2223; ②) on Slocan St in Slocan itself off Hwy 6. In addition to provincial **campgrounds** at Mulvey Basin and Cove Creek (both May–Oct; $10), there's the commercial *Slocan City* on Springer St in the village (May–Oct; ☎355-2277; $10) and the unserviced *Silverton Municipal Campground* (May–Oct; free), just south of New Denver.

Highway 6: Nakusp and onward

Highway 6 may not be the most direct route through British Columbia, but it has to be one of the most dramatic. From New Denver it initially strikes north and after 30km passes **Summit Lake**, a perfect jewel of water, mountain and forest that's served by the *Three Islands Resort* **campground** (May–Sept; ☎265-3023; $11). A rough road ("Take At Your Own Risk") runs south from here into the mountains and a small winter ski area.

Another 16km beyond, **NAKUSP** is a charismatic town worth visiting for its own sake. The setting is typical of the Kootenays, with a big lake – **Upper Arrow Lake**, part of the Columbia River system – and the snowcapped Selkirk Mountains to the east for a backdrop. The nearby hot springs are the main attraction, but you could happily wander the town for a morning, or boat or swim from the public **beach**. The only actual sight in town is the **Nakusp Museum** at Sixth Ave and First St, full of the usual archive material and Victorian bric-à-brac (May–Sept; free). The helpful **infocentre**, based in the fake paddle-steamer building next door at 92 West & Sixth Ave (year round; ☎265-4234), can provide details on local fishing, boating and hiking possibilities, and – if you're driving onwards – timings for the Galena Bay and Fauquier ferries.

For a place to **stay** try the central *Leland Hotel* (☎265-4221; ①), a rather rough-and-ready retreat built in 1892, featuring an interesting downstairs bar; the owner, Klaus, offers discounts for longer stays. The *Kuskanax Lodge* (☎265-3618 or 1-800/663-0100; ③) is equally central but more upmarket, and also has a good **restaurant** – though not as good as the more expensive *Lord Minto*.

If you're only going to try the hot springs experience once in BC, **Nakusp Hot Springs**, a well-signposted complex 13km northeast of town, is the place to do it (daily June–Sept 9.30am–10pm, Oct–May 10.30am–9pm; $4.50). The manager is friendly and energetic, and it's not unusual for late-night informal parties to develop around the two outdoor pools. Unlike many similar enterprises, the natural pools are cleaned each night and are backed up by nice changing facilities. The springs are popular in the summer, partly because there's a lovely **camp-**

ground alongside (☎265-4033; $8.50). The adjoining *Cedar Chalets* (☎352-4034; ②) has seven fine rooms, but reservations are essential in high season.

On from Nakusp

Highway 23, the lesser of two onward routes from Nakusp, heads north to Revelstoke (99km), a lonely and spectacular journey which necessitates a ferry crossing halfway at Galena Bay (hourly sailings each way; free). Highway 6, however, doglegs south from Nakusp for 57 delightful kilometers to the ferry crossing at **FAUQUIER**, a handful of buildings which include a garage, a store, the *Mushroom Addition* **café** for coffee and meals, and a potentially useful **motel** – the only one for a long way – the *Alpine Lakes Motel and Restaurant* (☎269-7622; ②), bang on the lakeside near the ferry. There's a **campground** 2km back towards Nakusp, *Plum Hollow Camping* (☎269-7669; $12), marked by two big arrows sticking in the ground, and 3km beyond that the *Goose Downs* **bed and breakfast**, off the road to the west (③).

The free **ferry** across Lower Arrow Lake takes about five minutes; it departs half-hourly from 5.15am to 9.45pm and operates an intermittent shuttle throughout the night. **NEEDLES** amounts to no more than a ramp off the ferry on the other side. There's an unofficial **campground** at Whatshan Lake, 3km off the highway just after Needles, but otherwise Hwy 6 is a gloriously empty ribbon as it burrows through the staggering Monashee Mountains – though some of the time it's too hemmed in by forest for you to see anything but billions of trees. After cresting Monashee Pass, the highway begins the long descent through the **Coldstream Valley** towards the Okanagan. Snow dusts the mountains here year round, crags loom above the meadows that increasingly break the forest cover, and beautiful flower-filled valleys wind down to the highway. The first sign of life in over 100km is the *Gold Panner* **campground** (April–Nov; ☎547-2025; $11), a good spot to overnight or explore the utter wilderness of **Monashee Provincial Park** to the north. The park is reached by rough road from the hamlet of **CHERRYVILLE**, 10km further west which, despite its cartographic prominence, is just three houses, a garage and *Frank's General Store*.

LUMBY, another 20km beyond, is scarcely more substantial, although the **rooms** at the *Diamond Motor Inn* (☎547-9221; ②) are worth considering if it's late, given that Okanagan lodgings on ahead could well be packed. The town also boasts a simple riverside **campground** run by the local Lions Club (May–Oct; ☎547-9504; $7). Beyond, the road glides through lovely pastoral country: orchards, verdant meadows, low, tree-covered hills, and fine wooden barns built to resemble inverted longboats.

Nelson

NELSON is one of British Columbia's best towns, and one of the few interior settlements you could happily spend two or three days in – longer if you use it as a base for touring the Kootenays. It's home to more than its share of refugees from the Sixties, a hangover that's nurtured a friendly and close-knit community, a healthy cultural scene and a liveliness – manifest in alternative cafés, nightlife, secondhand clothes stores and the like – you'll be hard pushed to find elsewhere in the province outside Vancouver. At the same time it's a young place permeated with immense civic pride, given a further boost by the filming here of *Roxanne*,

Steve Martin's version of Cyrano de Bergerac (there's a *Roxanne* walk). Producers chose the town for its idyllic lakeside setting and 350-plus turn-of-the-century homes, factors which for once live up to the hyperbole – in this case a claim to be "Queen of the Kootenays" and "Heritage Capital of Western Canada".

Located 34km west of Balfour on Hwy 3A, the town forms a tree-shaded grid of streets laid over the hilly slopes that nudge the westernmost shores of Kootenay Lake. Most homes are immaculately kept and vividly painted, and even the commercial **buildings** along the parallel main streets – Baker and Vernon – owe more to the vintage architecture of Seattle and San Francisco than to the drab Victoriana of much of eastern Canada. If you want to add purpose to your wanderings, pick up the *Heritage Walking Tour* pamphlet from the **infocentre**, 225 Hall St (daily June–Aug 8am–8pm; Sept–May 9am–5pm; ☎352-3433), which takes you around the sort of houses many Canadians dream of retiring to, and only occasionally oversells a place – notably when it lands you in front of the jam factory and the electricity substation. Some of the town's **shops** are also worth a look, particularly those of its many artists and craftspeople, who in summer club together to present **Artwalk**, a crawl round no fewer than sixteen galleries. Most of these have regular openings and wine-glugging receptions, making for numerous free-for-all parties. *Oliver's Books* on Baker Street is excellent for maps, guides and general reading, with a bias towards the sort of New Age topics that find a ready market here.

For the most part the area owes its development to the discovery of copper and silver ore on nearby Toad Mountain at the turn of the century, and though the mines declined fairly quickly, Nelson's diversification into gold and lumber, and its roads, railway and waterways, saved it from mining's usual downside. Today mining is back on the agenda as old claims are re-explored, and even if the idea of the town's **Museum of Mines** (daily 9am–5pm; free), next to the infocentre, leaves you cold, it's worth meeting the curator, an old prospector who talks at length – and interestingly – on the quest for silver, copper and gold, past and present.

It's probably less worthwhile to trek over to the **Nelson Museum**, about twenty minutes' walk from downtown, which offers a rather haphazard display that's obviously the work of enthusiastic amateurs (summer daily 1–6pm; closed Sun in winter; $1). There are, however, odd points of interest, notably a chronicle of the original 1886 Silver King Mine that brought the town to life, as well as tantalizingly scant details on the Doukhobor (see p.334).

Practicalities

Nelson is served by *Greyhound* **buses** (☎352-3939) that run west to Penticton (for connections to Vancouver, the Okanagan and Kamloops) and east to Cranbrook (connections to Calgary via Banff or Fort Macleod). There are also infrequent minibus services to Kaslo (☎353-2492 for details) and Nakusp (☎265-3511). The depot is almost on the lakeshore, just below the town proper.

There's a reasonable spread of **accommodation**, and though all three downtown **hotels** are fairly down-at-heel, they're all reasonably priced: the *Lord Nelson*, 616 Vernon St (☎352-7211; ②) is marginally the best; the *Queen's*, 621 Baker St (☎352-5351; ①), is the least expensive and dingiest; the *Savoy*, 198 Baker St (☎352-7285; ①), comes between the two. Most of the **motels** are on Hwy 31A at the north end of town or over the miniature Forth Road bridge on the north side of the lake. Here try the *Villa Motel*, 655 Hwy 3A (☎352-5515; ③–④), with the use of an indoor pool; or the *North Shore Inn*, 687 Hwy 3A (☎352-6606; ③), where prices include a continental breakfast. The nearest **campground** is *City Tourist Park*, on the corner of High and Willow (mid-May to early Oct; ☎352-0169; from $8). If this is full, head east towards Balfour and the many sites near the ferry terminal.

The choice of **restaurants** is broad, and you can't go far wrong wandering and choosing something that looks tempting. *Stanley Baker's*, a locals' place on Baker Street next to the *Nelson Shopping Company* mall, is good for cappuccino, snacks and big, inexpensive breakfasts. The *Vienna*, an alternative café and bookstore just off Baker Street, opposite the *Bank of Montreal*, is also worth trying. For evening meals, downtown residents head for the *Main Street Diner*, 616 Baker St (closed Sun). *Bogart's*, at 198 Baker St (part of the *Savoy Hotel*), looks dubious from outside but cooks reliable pasta, ribs and seafood specials. The *Victoria Street Restaurant*, 408 Victoria St (closed Mon), has seafood, European and **vegetarian** leanings. If you're shopping for your own meals, the big **supermarkets** are in or near the mall alongside the bus depot.

North to Radium Hot Springs

Heading north from Creston and the Kootenays, Highway 95 travels through scenery as spectacular as that in the Rockies parks to the north. The route eventually follows the broad valley of the **Columbia River**, bordered on the east by the Rockies and on the west by the marginally less breathtaking **Purcell Mountains**, though for the most part access to the wilderness here is limited and you'll have to be content with enjoying it from the highway. It's a fast run if you're driving, except where the road hugs the river's dramatic bluffs and sweeping meanders. Highways 93 and 95 meet near **Cranbrook**, a focus for two US border crossings (off Hwy 1 and Hwy 93), and a town where you double back eastwards on Hwy 3 to Crowsnest Pass (see p.383) and Alberta, or continue north for Radium Hot Springs and the entrance to the Kootenay National Park (see p.434). *Greyhound* **buses** ply all these routes, connecting at Cranbrook.

East from Creston

Some forty kilometers east of Creston, buses drop off at the small *Shell* garage in unspoilt **YAHK**, no more than a few houses nestled amid the trees but a quiet stopover none the less, courtesy of the good single **motel**, *Bob's* (☎424-5581; ②). Hwy 95 branches off from Hwy 3 here and heads south for the US border (11km). Incidentally, the highway crosses a **time zone** between Moyie and Yahk – clocks go back one hour.

Following Hwy 3 northbound through fine country you reach **MOYIE**, a tiny community on the edge of lovely **Moyie Lake**, a welcome visual respite from the unending tree-covered slopes hereabouts. Though there's no motel accommodation, there are three local **campgrounds**, including the excellent one at **Moyie Lake Provincial Park** – take Munro Lake Road from the northernmost point of Moyie Lake. The private *Green River Campground* is on the lakeshore signed about 1km off Hwy 3/95 (May–Oct; ☎426-4154; $10–13.50). Another excellent option is the *Moyie River Campground,* 18km south of Cranbrook on Hwy 3/95 (April–Nov; ☎489-3047; $9–13.50).

Cranbrook

The former mining town of **CRANBROOK**, despite its pivotal location, is one of the most dismal in the province, its dreariness barely redeemed by the surrounding high mountains. A long strip of motels, neon clutter and marshalling yards dominates a downtown area otherwise distinguished only by thrift shops and closing-down sales. Local lifeblood, such as it is, flows from the motels, this being an obvious place to eat, sleep and drive away from the next morning.

The only sight to speak of is the **Cranbrook Railway Museum**, a smallish affair that revolves around the restored carriages of an old trans-Canada luxury train (daily May–Sept 9am–8pm; Oct–April noon–5pm; $5). The period buildings pushed by the infocentre at 2279 Cranbrook St (year round 9am–5pm; ☎426-5914) aren't enough to justify the trawl round the streets.

If you must stay in town – and you may have to, as there's little in the way of **accommodation** on the roads north and south – the top of the range is the *Inn of the South* at 803 Cranbrook (☎489-4301; ③), a large, modern motel on the main road. Cheaper and friendlier is the *Heritage Estate Motel* (☎426-3862; ②), near the southern edge of town and therefore removed from some of the bleaker corners. The town has a municipal **campground** at Baker Park on 14th Ave and First St (May–Sept; ☎426-2162; $10–12), though it's a good deal less appealing than Jimsmith Lake Provincial Park, located 4km southwest of town (year round; $10; no showers). Next door to the *Heritage Estate Motel* is the *Heritage Rose Dining House*, an expensive and reliable **restaurant** whose fine veranda-fronted building is an architectural oasis in these dour surroundings; the other local choice is the *Apollo*, at 1012 Cranbrook St. Opposite the latter is the *Greyhound* **bus terminal** (☎426-3331), hidden in a jungle of neon behind *McDonald's* and the *Mohawk* gas station. Bus services run east to Fernie, Sparwood and southern Alberta (2 daily); west to Nelson, Castlegar and Vancouver (3 daily); north to Kimberley, Radium, Banff and Calgary (1 daily); and south to Spokane in the US (1 daily).

East from Cranbrook

Hwy 93 leaves Hwy 95 between Fort Steele (see below) and Cranbrook, following Hwy 3 as far as Elko before branching off south for the US border (91km). An unsullied hamlet of around half a dozen houses, **ELKO** is gone in a flash, but you might stop to eat at *Wendy's Place*, a homey, backwoods spot, or to camp at the excellent *Koocanusa Lake Campground* (May–Sept; ☎529-7484; $12), signed off Hwy 93 three kilometers west of town. Hwy 3 offers colossal views of the Rockies and the fast-flowing, ice-clear Elk River, before hitting **FERNIE**, 32km north of Elko, a pleasant place of tree-lined streets and small wooden houses, surrounded by a ring of knife-edged mountains. The *Cedar Lodge* (☎423-4622; ③) is a good place to stay, or the less expensive *Inn Towner Motel* (☎423-6308; ①), at 601-2nd Ave. The **infocentre** (year round; daily 9am–5pm; ☎423-6868) stands alongside a reconstructed wooden oil derrick 2km north of town on Hwy 3. **Fernie Snow Valley**, 5km west of town and 2km off the main highway, boasts what is reputedly the longest ski season in the BC Rockies (Nov–May); out of season, adjoining **Mount Fernie Provincial Park** has plenty of hiking trails, picnic areas and campgrounds.

Hwy 3 leaves the Elk Valley at **SPARWOOD**, 29km beyond Fernie, where signs of the area's coal-mining legacy begin to appear. Close to the town – but barely visible – is Canada's largest open-cast **coal mine**, a maw capable of disgorging up to 18,000 tonnes of coal daily. Tours of the mine (July & Aug Mon–Fri at 1.30pm) leave from the local **infocentre** (daily 9am–6pm; ☎425-2423), at the junction of Hwy 3 and Aspen Drive – look for the big miner's statue. The town itself is surprisingly neat and clean, and the big *Black Nugget Motor Inn* (☎425-2236; ②) on Hwy 3 makes a convenient place to stay.

Elkford

The remainder of Hwy 3 in British Columbia is despoiled by mining; the road crests the Continental Divide 19km east of Sparwood at **Crowsnest Pass** (see p.383). Far more scenic is the drive north from Sparwood on Hwy 43, which heads upstream beside the Elk River for 35km to **ELKFORD**. Nestled against a wall of mountains to the east and more gentle hills to the west, the village claims to be the "wilderness capital of British Columbia" – ambitious, but close to the mark if you're prepared to carry on up one or other of two rough gravel roads to the north. The more easterly one follows the Elk a further 80km to **Elk Lakes Provincial Park** close to the Continental Divide, one of the wildest road-accessible spots in the province. The slightly better route to the west heads 55km into the heart of unbeatable scenery below 2792-meter **Mount Armstrong**. Both areas offer excellent chances of spotting wildlife like cougars, deer, moose, elk and members of North America's largest bighorn sheep population.

Before entering either area, however, it's essential to pick up maps and information at the Elkford **infocentre** (year round; daily 9am–5pm; ☎865-4362), located at the junction of Hwy 43 and Michel Road. They'll also be able to give directions to nearby **Josephine Falls**, a few minutes' walk from the parking area on Fording Mine Road. Whether you're staying here or pushing on north, a tent is helpful: the only accommodation options are the *Elkford Motor Inn*, next to the shopping centre at 808 Michel Rd (☎865-2211; ②), Elkford's municipal **campground** (April–Oct; ☎865-2241; $10) and wilderness campsites around Elk Lakes.

Kimberley

KIMBERLEY, a few kilometers from Cranbrook on Hwy 95A, is British Columbia's highest town (1117m), and in many ways one of its silliest, thanks to the tourist-tempting ruse of transforming itself into a Bavarian village after the imminent closure of the local mine in the 1970s threatened it with economic oblivion. The result is a masterpiece of kitsch that's almost irresistible: buildings have been given a plywood-thin veneer of authenticity, piped Bavarian music dribbles from shops with names like *The Yodelling Woodcarver*, and even the fire hydrants have been painted to look like miniature replicas of Happy Hans, Kimberley's lederhosened mascot. The ploy might seem absurd to many Europeans, but there's no doubting the energy and enthusiasm that have gone into it, nor the economic rewards that have accrued from the influx of tourists and European immigrants – Germans included. Most of the Teutonic gloss is around the **Bavarian Platzl** on Spokane Street in the small downtown area, whose fake houses compare poorly with the authentic wooden buildings and more alpine surroundings on the outskirts.

If nothing else, you can leave Kimberley safe in the knowledge that you have seen the **"World's Biggest Cuckoo Clock"**, a fraudulent affair which amounts to little more than a large wooden box that twitters inane and incessant music. The dreaded contraption performs on being fed 25¢, and people oblige often enough that Happy Hans (rather than a cuckoo) makes his noisy appearance almost continuously; when he doesn't, the council employs some unfortunate to play the accordion morning, noon and night to keep up the musical interludes.

Apart from the clock, and a small **museum** upstairs in the library just down the road, other local sights include the **Sullivan Mine**, pre-Bavarian Kimberley's main employer, which is occasionally opened up in the summer (ask at the infocentre). At **MARYSVILLE**, a couple of kilometers south of town on Hwy 95A, you can take a twenty-minute amble to see the **Marysville Waterfalls**, a series of small falls in verdant surroundings.

If you need **accommodation**, try the central *Inn of the Rockies*, 300 Wallinger Ave (☎427-2266 or 1-800/661-7559; ②), or the *North Star Motel* (☎427-5633; ②) at the northern edge of town. Drop into the twee but excellent *Chef Bernard* café and **restaurant** opposite the clock, where the owner – heartily sick of Bavaria – plays Irish fiddle music as a mark of defiance. He's also known as one of the best local chefs, and people come from miles for his special fondue evenings. A favorite budget restaurant is *La Casa Amigos*, 290 Spokane St, just down from the post office on the main crossroads. For full details of Kimberley's many summer events call in on the **infocentre** (daily 9am–6pm; ☎427-3666) at 350 Ross St, just off the main crossroads past the *Inn of the Rockies*. The key attraction is **Julyfest**, which concludes with a one-week beer festival and – almost inevitably – an international accordion championship.

Fort Steele Heritage Town

If you stick to Hwy 93/95 rather than going through Kimberley, you'll come to **Fort Steele Heritage Town** (daily 9.30am–dusk; $6), an impressively reconstructed turn-of-the-century village in a superb mountain setting. It started life in the 1860s as a provisions stop and river crossing for gold prospectors heading east to the seams on Wildhorse Creek, 6km beyond the present town site. By 1887 the Mounties had arrived to keep order, and they raised a fort under their commander, the eponymous Sam Steele. The discovery of lead and silver locally put the place on the map, but boom soon gave way to bust when the new railway ignored the town in favor of Cranbrook. Staffed by volunteers in period dress, the town consists of sixty restored buildings, including such diversions as an old-time music hall, stage coaches, blacksmiths and bakers; in summer you can watch demonstrations of weaving, quilting, ice-cream making and the like.

Fairmont Hot Springs and beyond

Back on Hwy 93/95, the Columbia Valley's scenery begins to pick up as the Rockies begin to encroach and the blanket of trees opens up into pastoral countryside. **SKOOKUMCHUCK**, marked as a town on most maps, is in fact little more than a sawmill whose chimneys belch out toxins that ride the air for miles downwind. After a few kilometers the road curves around the **Dutch Creek Hoodoos**, fantastically eroded river bluffs, and **Columbia Lake** – not one of the area's most picturesque patches of water, though the *Mountain Village*, a fine wooden **restaurant** crammed with hundreds of old bottles, makes a good meal stop just short of a colossal lumber yard at **CANAL FLATS**. Just south of the sawmill is the turn-off for **Whiteswan Lake Provincial Park**, a handkerchief-sized piece of unbeatable scenery at the end of a twenty-kilometer gravel road; the park has several campgrounds but few trails, as its main emphasis is on boating and trout fishing. The same access road continues another 30km to **Top of the World Provincial Park**, a far wilder region where you need to be completely self-sufficient – the walk-in campgrounds offer only water and firewood. Hiking in the park is good, an obvious shortish jaunt being the trail from the parking area to Fish Lake (7km one way), where there's a small cabin (summer only; small charge) and an unserviced campground. **FAIRMONT HOT SPRINGS** at the north end of Columbia Lake spills over the Columbia's flat floodplain, less a settlement than an ugly modern upmarket resort that feeds off the appeal of the hot springs themselves. The pools were commandeered from the Kootenay in 1922 for exploitation as a tourist attraction, the calcium springs (daily 8am–10pm; $4) being particularly prized for their lack of the sulphurous stench that plagues many of BC's hot dips. If you don't fancy paying around $150 to stay at the resort you could try the big **campground** one minute from the pools, though it's mainly geared to RVs (☎345-6311; $12–20), or the new *Spruce Grove Resort* 2km south of Fairmont, with inexpensive rooms and a lovely riverside campground (April–Oct; ☎345-6561; ②).

Windermere and Invermere

WINDERMERE, 15km north of Fairmont, is little more than a supermarket, filling station and campground immediately off the highway, and hardly hints at the presence of **INVERMERE**, about 1km beyond. A summer resort on Windermere Lake with the usual range of aquatic temptations, Invermere makes a pleasanter **accommodation** prospect than Radium just to the north. However, droves of anglers, boaters and beach bums mean summer vacancies can be in short supply; the central **infocentre** at Fifth St & Seventh Ave (May–Sept daily 8am–8pm; ☎342-6316) has details of bed-and-breakfast possibilities. Of the town's four **motels**, the *Lee-Jay*, 1015-13th St (☎342-9227; ②), is the most reasonable, but the *Invermere Inn* at the heart of downtown is smarter (☎342-9246; ③). The nearest provincial **campground** is 7km towards Radium at Dry Gulch Provincial Park; the private *Pantycelyn Campland* (May–Oct; ☎342-9736; $15) is on the lake and has its own private beach. Try the *Lakeside Inn* for a decent **meal** or to rent boats, bikes and watersports gear.

From Invermere a minor road climbs west into the mountains to the burgeoning **Panorama Ski Resort** (18km), whose slick facilities include only limited and expensive accommodation. In summer the chief attraction of the area is hiking, particularly if you continue up the road to the less tainted **Purcell Wilderness Conservancy**, one of the few easily accessible parts of the Purcell Mountains. If you have a tent and robust hiking inclinations, you could tackle the 61-kilometer **trail** through the area to Argenta on the northern end of Kootenay Lake (see p.337), an excellent cross-country route that largely follows undemanding valleys except when crossing the Purcell watershed at Earl Grey Pass.

All communications in southern British Columbia radiate from Vancouver; see p.311 for "Travel Details" from there.

CALGARY AND THE CANADIAN ROCKIES

Alberta is the Northwest close to its best. For many people the beauty of the **Canadian Rockies**, as they rise with awesome majesty from the rippling prairies, is the main reason to come to the region. Most visitors confine themselves to the four contiguous national parks – **Banff, Jasper, Yoho** and **Kootenay** – that straddle the southern portion of the range, a vast area whose boundaries spill over into British Columbia. Two smaller parks, **Glacier** and **Mount Revelstoke**, lie firmly in BC and not, technically, in the Rockies, but scenically and logistically they form part of the same region. Managed with remarkable efficiency and integrity, all the parks are easily accessible segments of a much wider wilderness of peaks and forests that extend from the Canada–US border northwards before merging into the ranges of the Yukon and Alaska.

If you're approaching the Rockies from the east or the States, you have little choice but to spend time in either Edmonton or Calgary, the transportation hubs for northern and southern Alberta respectively. Poles apart in feel and appearance, the two cities are locked in an intense rivalry, in which **Calgary** comes out top in almost every respect. Situated on the **Trans-Canada Highway**, less than ninety minutes from Banff National Park, it is more convenient whether you plan to take in Yoho, Kootenay, Glacier or Revelstoke, or push on to southern British Columbia and the west coast. It also has far more going for it in its own right: the weather is kinder, the Calgary Stampede is one of the country's rowdiest festivals, and the vast revenues from the oil and natural gas have been spent to good effect on its downtown skyscrapers and civic infrastructure.

Edmonton is a bleaker city, on the edge of an immense expanse of boreal forest and low hills that stretches to the border of the Northwest Territories and beyond. Bypassed by the Canadian Pacific Railway, its main importance to travellers is as a gateway to the Alaska Highway and the arctic extremities of the Yukon, and to the more popular landscapes of northern British Columbia – the **Yellowhead Highway** and Canada's last transcontinental **railway** link Edmonton to the town of Jasper and its national park in about four hours.

TOLL-FREE INFORMATION NUMBERS

Alberta Tourism ☎1-800/222-6501 within Alberta,
☎1-800/661-8888 from elsewhere in Canada and the US.
Tourism British Columbia ☎1-800/663-6000.

EDMONTON AND NORTHERN ALBERTA

Unless you're obliged to pass through downbeat **Edmonton**, there's no substantial reason to visit it. Once there, you can either head west into the Rockies and Jasper National Park, or head into the unimaginable vastness of the far northern interior. Northern Alberta contains the only all-weather road link to Yellowknife, capital of the Northwest Territories, but other than **Wood Buffalo National Park** – the largest protected area in Canada – and a surfeit of fishing possibilities, the region has nothing to waylay most visitors.

> The **telephone code** for Alberta is ☎403.

Edmonton

Alberta's provincial capital, **EDMONTON** is among the most northerly cities in North America; especially in the teeth of its bitter winters, it can seem a little too far north for comfort. Against the background of a downtown area that still has the unfinished feel of a frontier town, perhaps it's appropriate that the premier attraction for seventy percent of visitors is a shopping center, **West Edmonton Mall**.

Fort Edmonton was founded in 1795 by William Tomison for the Hudson's Bay Company and quickly expanded to compete with nearby Fort Augustus, opened earlier that year by the rival North West Company. Though it soon became a major trading post, **settlers** arrived in force only after 1870, when the company sold its governing right to the Dominion of Canada, and the city didn't become firmly established until during the Yukon gold rush of 1897, through a scam of tragic duplicity. Prompted by the city's outfitters, newspapers lured prospectors with the promise of an "All Canadian Route" to the goldfields that avoided Alaska and the dreaded Chilkoot Trail (see p.462). In the event this turned out to be a largely phantom trail across 1900 miles of intense wilderness, and hundreds of men perished as they pushed north; many of those who survived, or who never set off, ended up settling in Edmonton. World War II saw the city's role reinforced by its strategic position relative to Alaska, and its postwar growth was guaranteed by the Leduc oil strike in 1947. If Edmonton has achieved any fame since, it has been in the field of **sports**, as the home of Wayne Gretzky, the greatest player in ice-hockey history – though he has long since moved on.

Arrival and transportation

Edmonton's transportation links are second to none in western Canada. The international **airport**, 29km south of downtown off Hwy 2 (Calgary Trail), is served by many American, British and European airlines, and the majority of internal flights – especially from the Yukon and Northwest Territories – fly here in preference to Calgary; numerous shuttle flights ply between the two cities. A shuttle **bus**, the *Grey Goose Airporter*, runs downtown every half-hour from 5.15am to 12.15am, for around $13; taxis cost more like $35. Some short-hop flights use the municipal airport, north of downtown off 97th St near 118th Ave, and connected by buses with its larger rival and downtown.

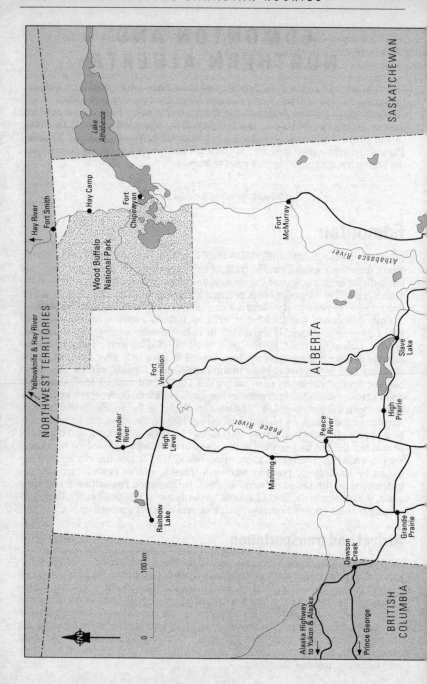

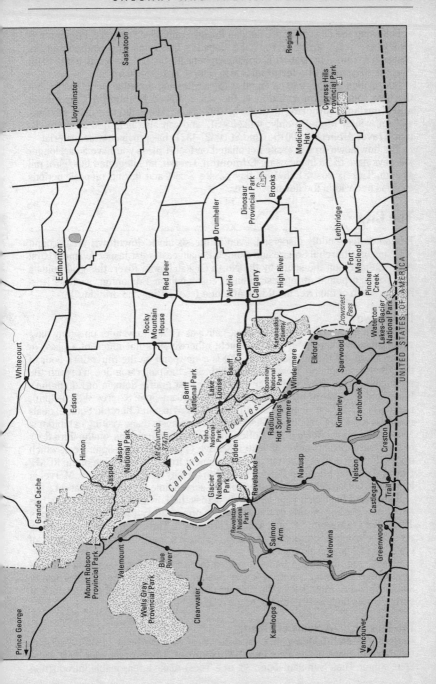

Following the closure of the famous Rockies railway via Calgary, Edmonton is also where you'll arrive if you take Canada's last remaining transcontinental passenger **train**. The station is downtown beneath the CN Tower at 10004-104th Ave; the *Greyhound* **bus terminal** is also central, at 10324-103rd St.

Information centers can be found at the airport and dotted around the city, but the best source of **information** is the well-equipped **Edmonton Convention and Tourism Authority** at no 104, 9797-Jasper Ave (summer daily 8.30am– 4.30pm; winter Mon–Fri only; ☎422-5505), who can also help find accommodation. **Travel Alberta** at 10015-102nd St (☎427-4321) has province-wide material.

The downtown area is easily negotiated on foot. Unless you have a car, longer journeys have to be made using **Edmonton Transit**, an integrated bus/light-rail system. Tickets cost $1.25–1.50, day passes $3.50, and during off-peak periods travel is free within the downtown area.

The City

Edmonton feels oddly dispersed, even in the six-block **downtown** area around Sir Winston Churchill Square and along the main east–west Jasper Avenue (101st Ave). Bounded on the south by the North Saskatchewan River, this grid holds a few assorted points of interest, though cosmopolitan Edmonton, such as it is, resides south of the river in **Old Strathcona** (see "Eating and drinking").

Downtown

Downtown Edmonton only really comes alive as a place to wander on sunny days when office workers pour out for lunch; otherwise it's not much of a place to linger. **Vista 33** (daily 10am–5pm; 50¢) is a viewpoint on the thirty-third floor of the Alberta Telephone Tower, 10020-100th St – the panorama doesn't reach the mountains, but it does open your eyes to the vast prairie domain of Edmonton's hinterland. The **Edmonton Art Gallery** (daily 10am–5pm; $2, free Wed 5–9pm), part of the Civic Centre on the north edge of Sir Winston Churchill Square, deals mainly in modern Canadian artists, though it also hosts many visiting exhibitions. More satisfyingly offbeat is the **Police Museum and Archives**, on the third floor of the central police station at 9620-103A Ave (Tues–Sat 10am–3pm; free), which traces the long arm of Albertan law enforcement from the formation of the RCMP (Royal Canadian Mounted Police) in 1873 to the city's current flatfoots. Marvel at handcuffs, old jail cells, and a stuffed rat that served time as an RCMP mascot.

If you need to stretch your legs, walk across the Low Level Bridge or take bus #51 to the glass pyramids of the **Muttart Conservatory** (Sun–Wed 11am–9pm; Thurs–Sat 11am–6pm; $4), just south of downtown. Three high-tech greenhouses reproduce tropical, temperate and arid climates; a fourth houses a potpourri of experimental botanical projects.

Finally, you might stop by for a guided tour of the domed sandstone **Alberta Legislative Building**, south of Jasper Avenue on 97th Ave and 107th St (every 30min Mon–Fri; free). Set in the manner of a medieval cathedral over an ancient shrine, it was built in 1912 on the original site of Fort Edmonton.

The Provincial Museum of Alberta

Housed in a drab building well out in the western suburbs at 12845-102nd Ave, the dated displays of the **Provincial Museum of Alberta** (summer daily 9am– 8pm; winter Tues–Sun 9am–5pm; $3, free Tues) make a reasonable introduction

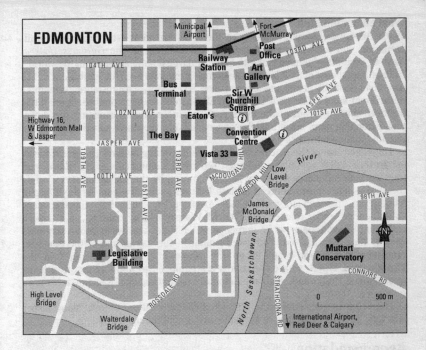

EDMONTON

Municipal Airport
Fort McMurray
Post Office
103RD AVE
Railway Station
Art Gallery
104TH AVE
Bus Terminal
Sir W Churchill Square ⓘ
JASPER AVE
101ST AVE
102ND AVE
Eaton's
Highway 16, W Edmonton Mall & Jasper ←
The Bay
Convention Centre ⓘ
JASPER AVE
Vista 33
109TH AVE
103RD AVE
MCDOUGALL HILL
River
100TH AVE
105TH AVE
GRIERSON HILL
Low Level Bridge
98TH AVE
James McDonald Bridge
North Saskatchewan
Muttart Conservatory
Legislative Building
STRATHCONA RD
CONNORS RD
N
High Level Bridge
ROSSDALE RD
0   500 m
Walterdale Bridge
International Airport, Red Deer & Calgary

to western Canada if Edmonton is your first stop in the region. Calgary, Victoria and Vancouver, however, have much better museums. To reach it by bus, take the #1, #2, #115, #116 or #120 from Jasper Ave downtown.

Natural history exhibits include painted dioramas and stuffed animals, taxidermy being the stock in trade of virtually all western Canada's museums; the best section concerns the region's bison herds and their virtual extinction. Other displays include vintage juke-boxes and a rundown of the **native peoples** of the province. In the latter collection, the "Self Torture" section contains some harrowing exhibits – nipple-stretching implements being especially eye-watering.

Fort Edmonton Park

Located southwest of the city on a deep-cut bend of the North Saskatchewan River, the 158-acre **Fort Edmonton Park** (daily 10am–6pm; $5) undertakes to re-create the history of white settlement in Edmonton during the nineteenth century. Everything has been built from scratch, and while you can't fault the attention to detail, the pristine woodwork of the supposedly old buildings hardly evokes period authenticity. Buses #32 and #123 go directly from downtown to the site, which is off the Whitemud Freeway near the Quesnell Bridge.

The heart of the complex is a facsimile of **Fort Edmonton**, a fur-trading post dominated by the Big House, home of the Chief Factor, John Rowland, head of the then ill-defined Saskatchewan District from 1828 to 1854. Edmonton's later, pre-railway era is represented by a rendition of Jasper Avenue as it appeared in 1885, while two other streets simulate 1905 and 1920, complete with rides on steam engines and tram cars to bolster the period effect.

West Edmonton Mall

"Your Adventure Awaits" announces the brochure to **West Edmonton Mall**, preparing you for a place that gets eleven mentions in the *Guinness Book of Records*, including its main claim to fame as "largest shopping mall in the world". Built at a total cost of $1.1 billion, the complex extends over the equivalent of 115 American football fields and boasts over 800 shops, 110 restaurants, and 11 department stores. The mall's effect on Edmonton has been double-edged: it has captured thirty percent of the city's retail business, thus decimating the downtown shopping area, but it has also succeeded, to everyone's surprise, in attracting nine million tourists a year.

The sheer size of the place could keep you browsing all day. The world's largest **Indoor Lake** contains a full-sized replica of Columbus's *Santa Maria*, and four working submarines – more than are owned by the Canadian navy – while the world's largest **amusement arcade** features such attractions as the "Drop of Doom", a thirteen-story "free-fall experience", and the fourteen-story "Mindbender" roller-coaster. The **World Waterpark**, by contrast, is a superb collection of swimming pools, immense water slides and wave pools (day pass $18.95; after 5pm $12.95). You could round off the day in one of the mall's 19 **cinemas**, and if you want to go the whole hog spend the night in the **Fantasyland Hotel**, where the rooms are equipped to fulfil six assorted fantasies: Roman, Hollywood, Arabian, Victorian Coach, Canadian Rail and, most intriguing of all, Truck.

The #10 **bus** goes straight to the mall, heading west out of town along Jasper Ave west of 101st St. Maps are available throughout the main building.

Accommodation

As Edmonton sees far fewer tourists than Calgary, its budget **accommodation** is considerably less burdened; unfortunately, it is also less salubrious. There are however plenty of reasonably priced beds in the big middle-ranking hotels – especially out of season. **Motels** can be found in the bleak outskirts of the city, the main concentrations being along Stony Plain Road (north of downtown) and on the Calgary Trail (south). For details of **bed and breakfast** lodgings, contact either *Edmonton Bed and Breakfast*, 13824-110th Ave (☎455-2297) or the *Gem B&B Reservation Agency*, 11216-48th Ave (☎434-6098).

Hotels and motels

Ambassador Motor Inn, 10041-106th St (☎423-1925). Mid-sized central motel with covered parking. ②.

Best Western City Centre Inn, 11310-109th St (☎479-2042 or 1-800/528-1234). Typical property of this reliable mid-priced chain. ③.

Grand Hotel, 10266-103rd St (☎422-6365). Handily located almost next to the bus terminal, but anything but grand. Clean but knocked about, it's used mainly by long-stay residents. ①.

Hotel Cecil, 10406-Jasper Ave (☎428-7001). Extremely central and convenient for the bus terminal, but you're probably taking your life in your hands here. ①.

Inn on Seventh, 10001-107th St (☎429-2861 or 1-800/661-7327). Modern, quiet and civilized, and probably the best of the middle-range hotels. ④.

Mayfair Hotel, 10815-Jasper Ave (☎423-1650). Elegant rooms with breakfast included. ④.

Quality Inn Downtown, 10209-100th Ave (☎428-6442). Reliable downtown motel with covered parking, TV, phone and breakfast included. ③–④.

Ramada Renaissance Hotel, 10155-104th St (☎423-4811 or 1-800/268-8998). Edmonton's top-of-the-pile hotel. ⑥.

Renford Inn at Fifth, 10425-100th Ave (☎423-5611 or 1-800/661-6498). Full range of facilities, including jacuzzis. ④.

Hostels and student rooms

Edmonton Youth Hostel, 10422-91st St off Jasper Ave (CHA; ☎429-0140; reservations ☎439-3139). A friendly place within walking distance of the station and bus terminal with views south over the city; however, women walking here alone at night should take care. A good source of travel information, particularly if you're heading north. Mountain bike rentals. Closed daily 10am–5pm, with a rigid midnight curfew. Members $12, non-members $16. ①.

St Joseph's College, 114th St & 89th Ave (☎492-7681). Small, cheap and popular student rooms; reservations required in summer. Well out of the center but served by several buses including the #43. ①.

University of Alberta, 97th Ave between 112th & 114th (☎492-4281). Basic institutional student rooms available in summer. ②.

YMCA, 10030-102nd Ave (☎421-9622). Men and women welcome in clean, sprightly and largely refurbished building. Three-bunk dorms $10 per person (2 nights maximum) plus private singles and doubles. ①–②.

YWCA, 10305-100th Ave (☎429-8707). Quiet and pleasant women-only accommodation with free use of swimming pool and cheap cafeteria (open to all). Dorm bunks from $10; singles from $25. ①.

Campgrounds

Androssan Campground. Located 18km east of downtown on Hwy 16; 24 free pitches, but no water or facilities other than fire pits.

Half Moon Lake Resort, Sherwood Park (☎922-3045). A private site with extensive facilities, 29km east of town on Hwy 14 and then 4km down a signposted side road.

Rainbow Valley Campground, 14340-56th Ave (mid-April–mid-Oct; ☎434-1621). Off the Whitemud Freeway at 119th St & 45th Ave in Whitemud park.

Shakers Acres Tent and Trailer Park, 21530-103rd Ave (☎447-3564). On the northwest edge of the city.

Eating and drinking

Few places stand out among Edmonton's 2000-odd **restaurants**, but if you want a bit of nocturnal zip to go with your meal you'd do best to head out to Old Strathcona, a vibrant district of café culture, nightlife and alternative arts located along 82nd (Whyte) Ave between 102nd and 105th streets – any bus marked

"University Transit Centre" from 100th St will get you there. Ethnic options – notably restaurants serving Edmonton's large Ukrainian and Eastern European populations – complement the standard steak-and-salmon offerings. Otherwise, the stalls in the *Eaton's* mall and downtown streetfront snackbars are lively at lunchtime, and all the usual fast-food, snack and breakfast options are available, the best of which are the *YWCA* and *YMCA* cafés. Beer drinkers should be sure to try the local real ale, *Big Rock*.

Cafés, snacks and bars

Café le Gare, 10308a-81st Ave. Small tea-and-coffee joint in Old Strathcona, the sort of place where you can read a book or paper for hours; poetry readings Mon nights.

Grabbajabba, 82nd Ave & 104th St. Great music and coffee at this very popular non-smoking café in the heart of Old Strathcona.

Hot Pastrami, 1044-108th St. Office-worker favorite for its deli-style food (from 6.30am) and home of the $2.50 breakfast.

Ninth Street Café, 8615-109th St. Relaxed and cozy student hang-out – generous helpings, imaginative soups and renowned desserts.

Old Strathcona Coffee Factory, 8224-104th St. Among the liveliest coffee, food and beer places in Old Strathcona. You may well have to wait, especially during the Fringe.

Old Strathcona Diner Beer and Wine Garden, 8223-104th St. Near the above, similarly friendly and casual, and with live jazz some nights. Good menu, including innovative salads.

Restaurants

Bistro Praha, 10168-100A St. A good opportunity to sample Eastern European cuisine, Edmonton style, but highbrow and expensive – better for lunch or late at night.

Café Select, 10018-106th St (☎423-0419). An excellent, intimate place, trendy without being intimidating. Serving fine simple food, it's downtown's best choice for a late-night splurge.

Mongolian Food Experience, 10160-100A St. A downtown Edmonton institution. Hugely popular lunchtime barbecues, plus a wide range of Chinese and Mongolian specialties.

Oriental Noodle House, 10718-101st St. Vietnamese and Southeast Asian food at rock-bottom prices.

Rose Bowl, 10111-117th St. Frenetic and smoky den, probably the most popular of the city's countless pizzerias.

Sceppa's Restaurant and Lounge, 10921-101st St. Coffee bar, pool table, and Edmonton's best Italian restaurant alongside.

Silk Hat, 10251 Jasper Ave (☎428-1551). First choice among Edmonton's restaurants – and also a fine place to knock back a *Molson* (the brewery's up the road) – this is a city institution whose dim, diner interior hasn't altered in 40 years. It's best known for the Fifties juke-boxes at each booth, but the inexpensive, basic food is as good as the ambience.

Strathcona Gasthaus, 10105-82nd Ave. Long-established Eastern European restaurant renowned for huge, stolid helpings and bargain-basement prices.

Veggies, 10221-82nd Ave. Good, full-blown vegetarian/non-smoking restaurant with extensive main course menu plus herbal iced teas and fruit and yogurt milkshakes.

Vi's, 112th St & 100th Ave (☎482-6402). Housed in an old residence with great views, an excellent place for a special occasion.

Nightlife and entertainment

Edmonton's enthusiastic self-promotion as the "Festival City" may have something to do with its shortage of indigenous **nightlife**. Any number of small-time spots, especially in Old Strathcona, put on live music, but clubs capable of attracting big names are thin on the ground. Stellar acts – as well as theater, ballet and opera companies – tend to appear at the University of Alberta's *Jubilee Auditorium*, 87th Ave and 114th St, and the *Coliseum*, 118th Ave and 74th St.

The best **listings** sources are the free monthlies, *Something Entertaining* and the alternative *Edmonton Bullet*, and the entertainment sections of the city's two main newspapers, the *Journal* and the *Sun*. **Tickets** for most events – including Edmonton Oilers **ice-hockey** games, played in the *Northlands Coliseum*, 118th Ave and 74th St – are available from several *BASS* outlets (☎451-8000).

Clubs, discos and live music

Blues on Whyte at the *Commercial Hotel*, 10329-82nd Ave. Widely acknowledged as one of the city's best live music clubs.

Club Malibu,10310-85th St. Top-40 disco in a converted armory.

Cook Country Saloon, 8010-103rd St. Old Strathcona country-and-western venue.

Esmeralda's at the Edmonton Inn, 11830-Kingsway Ave. Another highly rated country-and-western hoedown.

Goose Loonies, 6250-99th St. Outlying but highly popular live music club.

Sidetrack Café, 10323-112th St. Despite its disconcertingly bombed-out surroundings, this is the best of the city's live music venues and where you're most likely to see international acts of some standing.

The Sixth Street Bar, 10041-106th St. Downtown blues club with shows at 9.30pm and special 2pm Saturday jam session.

Yardbird Suite, 10203-86th Ave. Live groups nightly in the city's top jazz venue.

Yuk Yuk's, 7103-78th Ave. Assorted comedy acts every night, featuring well-known US and Canadian names.

Festivals

Hardly any area of entertainment goes uncelebrated by a festival at some time of the year in Edmonton. One of the few to merit a special pilgrimage to the city is the **Edmonton Folk Music Festival**, rated the best in North America by *Rolling Stone* – it's held at Gallagher Park (near the Muttart Conservatory) at the end of the first week in August. Also well regarded are the **International Street Performers Festival** in early July; the **International Jazz City Festival** at the end of June; and the August **Fringe Festival**, a nine-day theatrical jamboree that's the largest event of its kind in North America.

The more contrived **Klondike Days** is less compelling, a blowout that claims to be the continent's largest "outdoor entertainment" but has rather too obviously been cobbled together to steal some of Calgary's Stampede thunder. Held for ten days during July, this popular outing revolves around a re-creation of the 1890s gold-rush era, with plenty for kids, and events along the lines of the Fun Tub Race and the Hairiest Chest Competition.

Listings

Airlines *Air Canada* (☎423-1222 or 1-800/222-6596); *Canadian Airlines* (☎421-1414); *American* (☎1-800/433-7300); *Delta* (☎426-5990 or 1-800/221-1212).

Airport Information International ☎890-8382; Municipal ☎428-3991.

Bike rental *River Valley Cycle and Sports*, 9701-100A St (☎421-9125); *Campus Outdoor Centre*, University of Alberta, 116th St & 87th Ave (☎492-2767).

Books *Greenwood's*, on 82nd Ave between 103rd & 104th, is one of the city's best; *Athabasca Books*, on 105th St north of 82nd Ave, is a quality secondhand outlet.

Bus enquiries *Greyhound* (☎421-4242); bus terminal (☎421-4211).

Car rental *Rent-A-Wreck*, 10140-109th St (☎423-1755); *Thrifty*, 10036-102nd St (☎428-855); *Hertz* (☎423-3431); *Budget* (☎448-2000).

Consulates *Great Britain*, 1404-0025 Jasper Ave (☎428-0375).

Hospital Edmonton General Hospital, 1111 Jasper Ave (☎268-9111).

Police ☎423-4567.

Post office 9808-103A Ave.

Taxis *Alberta Co-op* (☎425-8310); *Checker Cabs* (☎455-2211); *Prestige* (☎462-4444); *Yellow Cabs* (☎462-3456).

Train information *VIA rail* (☎422-6032 or 1-800/561-8630).

Weather information ☎468-4940.

Northern Alberta

North of Edmonton stretches an all-but-uninhabited landscape of rippling hills, rivers, lakes, lonely farms, open prairie and the unending mantle of the northern forests. Compared to the spectacular mountain scenery to the west, northern Alberta is more akin to the monotony of the central plains of Saskatchewan and Manitoba. Unless you're fishing or boating, or just into sheer untrammelled wilderness, little here is worth detouring for, with the possible exception of **Wood Buffalo National Park** on the border with the Northwest Territories.

The two great north-flowing waterways – the **Peace River** and **Athabasca River** – that were the area's traditional arteries have been superseded by three vitally important roads. The most travelled is **Highway 16** (the Yellowhead Highway) which runs due west from Edmonton to Jasper and onwards through the Rockies to Prince George and Prince Rupert (both BC); **Highway 43–Highway 2** heads to Grande Prairie and Dawson Creek (BC) – Mile Zero of the Alaska Highway; and **Highway 43–Highway 35** (the Mackenzie Highway) bisects northern Alberta and provides its only road link to the Northwest Territories.

Direct long-haul *Greyhound* **buses** run on all these routes from Edmonton, supplemented by the *VIA* **rail** service from Edmonton to Jasper (with connections on to Vancouver or Prince Rupert). Few roads are worth travelling for their own sake, however, and for trips to Wood Buffalo National Park or Hay River (NWT) in particular **flying** can be a valuable time-saving option.

Highway 16 towards Jasper

Highway 16, or the Yellowhead Highway, is, as Edmonton's Chamber of Commerce likes to call it, "the other Trans-Canada Highway"; the second and less-travelled transcontinental route and – by comparison to the Calgary–Banff route – a longer and duller way of making for the Rocky Mountain national parks. Jasper lies 357km west of Edmonton on the highway, an easy journey by car, **bus** (4 daily; $35), or on the **train** whose tracks run parallel to the highway for its duration (Tues, Fri & Sun; $67).

Numerous **campgrounds** and **motels** service the road at regular intervals, the main concentrations being at **Edson**, halfway to Jasper, and **Hinton**. Edson's twelve motels are all much of a muchness, the cheapest being the *Cedars*, 5720-

4th Ave (☎723-4436; ①). Two nearby sites provide for campers: the *Lions Club Campground* (May–Sept; ☎723-3169; $10) on the east side of town, and the *Willmore Recreation Park* (May–Oct; ☎723-4401; $7), 6km south on 63rd St.

Highway 43–Highway 2 towards Dawson Creek (BC)

Highway 43 out of Edmonton to Grande Prairie, and **Highway 2** thereafter, ambles through terminally unexceptional towns, hills and prairie scenery on its way west to Dawson Creek (p.456). It's a mind-numbing day's journey by car or **bus** (2 daily; $55); additional bus connections run as far as Grande Prairie, 463km from Edmonton, where you may wash up if you're forced to break your journey.

Failing to live up to its evocative name, **GRANDE PRAIRIE**'s unfocused sprawl is a legacy of having the luxury of unlimited space in which to build. The **infocentre** is by Bear Creek Reservoir, off the main highway, which bypasses the main part of town to the west. Most of Grande Prairie's many **motels** are on the strip known as Richmond Avenue (100th Ave), which links the southern part of the highway bypass to downtown. All are vast affairs with bargain prices – the top-of-the-line is the *Golden Inn Hotel*, 11201-100th Ave (☎539-6000; ②), and the cheapest, the *Econo-Lodge Motor Inn*, 10909-100th Ave (☎539-4700; ①).

Canada's ultimate **cowboy bar** has to be *Kelly's Bar* in the *Sutherland Inn* at **Clairmont**, immediately north of Grande Prairie. Owned by a Calgary Stampede chuck wagon champion, it's the sort of place that has saddles for barstools and serves up shooters in bull-semen collection tubes.

Highway 35 and Peace River country

Alberta's northern reaches are accessible only from **Highway 35**, still a route for the adventurous and one which, according to Albertans, shows the real side of the province: a world of redneck homesteads, buffalo burgers, and the sort of genuine country-and-western bars where strangers on a Friday night meet silent stares but wind up being invited to the hoedown anyway. You'll find such spots more or less everywhere along the route, but very little in the way of motels, garages or campgrounds, so come prepared. The road itself is well kept and straight, allowing healthier progress than on the more serpentine Alaska Highway to the west. Two *Greyhound* **buses** run daily from Edmonton to Peace River, and one all the way to Hay River (NWT), where you can make connections for Yellowknife and Fort Smith.

If you're travelling under your own steam you'll probably have to overnight in **PEACE RIVER**, 486km from Edmonton and the starting point of Hwy 35. The largest town in the region, it has three standard **motels**: the *Peace Valley Inn*, 9609-101st St (☎624-2020; ②), with a 24-hour *Smitty's Restaurant*, the central *Crescent*, 9810-98th St (☎624-2586; ②) and the *Traveller's Motor Hotel*, 9510-100th St (☎624-3621 or 1-800/661-3227; ②–③). There's also a **campground** (May–Oct; ☎624-2120; $12) at Lion's Club Park. **MANNING**, 50km north of Peace River, is the last sizeable community for another 200km, making its pair of **motels** vital and often surprisingly busy. The *Hillcrest Motel* (☎836-3381; ②) is smaller and a shade cheaper than the *Manning Motor Inn* (☎836-2801; ②–③). For the tiny nine-pitch municipal **campground** (May–Sept; ☎836-3606; free) on the Notikewin River, turn east at the summer-only infocentre on the highway. Only a couple of basic campgrounds and the odd windblown store disturb the peace **north of Manning**, though if you're **camping** it's as well to know you can expect the unwelcome nocturnal attention of bears in these parts. Official tenting spots are *Notikewin River* (May–Sept; ☎836-2628; $7.50), a short way off the road at the junction with Hwy 692, 37km north of Manning; and *Twin Lakes Campground* (May–Sept; ☎836-2628; $7.50) another 15km up the road. The latter is close to the *Twin Lakes* eight-room **motel** (☎554-1348; ②).

As with all the larger settlements hereabouts, you're only going to stop in **HIGH LEVEL**, 199km north of Manning, as a place to bed down. Room rates begin to creep up the further north you go, and all three of the town's **motels** charge around $65. The ritziest is *Our Place Apartment Hotel* (☎926-2556; ③), followed by the *Sunset Motor Inn* (☎926-2272; ③) and the *North Grove Motel* (☎926-3771 or 1-800/582-3218; ②). Campers do best to splash out for the private facilities of *Aspen Ridge Campground* (April–Oct; ☎926-4540; $8), 3km south of the center on the main road.

Between High Level and Hay River (NWT), a string of campgrounds provide the only accommodation, and three native hamlets – Meander River, Steen River and Indian Cabins – offer only food and petrol.

Wood Buffalo National Park

Straddling the border between Alberta and the Northwest Territories, **Wood Buffalo National Park** covers an area larger than Switzerland, making it Canada's largest national park and the world's second largest protected environment. Primarily famous as home on the range for a rare free-roaming buffalo herd, it's also the last refuge of the critically endangered whooping crane – first discovered in a remote part of the park as late as 1954 – and the world's only river rookery of rare white pelicans, which usually nest on lakes.

In addition to some 46 species of mammals found in the park, including bear and lynx, the Peace-Athabasca river delta in the southeast corner boasts an enormous concentration of wildfowl and no fewer than four major migration routes overfly the area. If its wildlife is spectacular, however, the park's topography, though wild and vast in its extent, is limited to low hills, grasslands, boreal forest and marsh.

The refuge was created in 1922 to protect an estimated 1500 **wood buffalo** (*Bison bison athabascae*), a longer-legged, darker and more robust relative of the plains buffalo (*Bison bison bison*). Six years later the federal government moved some 6000 plains buffalo to the park from the now nonexistent Buffalo National Park near Wainright, Alberta, when their grazing lands were appropriated for a firing range. Most of the present herd, now down to some 3000 members, is probably a hybrid strain, and has become the subject of considerable controversy (see box). At present, however, you'll still see plenty at the roadsides, more often than not wallowing in dust to escape the ferocious mosquitoes.

Access and getting around

Getting to the park by road can be a slow business, and is possible only along a 280-kilometer stretch of Hwy 5 from Hay River (NWT) to Fort Smith. *North of 60 Bus Lines* runs **buses** from Hay River to Fort Smith (Mon–Fri only; $40 one-way; ☎874-6411), with services timed to connect with the daily *Greyhound* from Edmonton. You can also easily **fly** to Fort Smith on scheduled flights from

THE BUFFALO KILL

Clean-living Canada rarely causes international environmental outrage, but since 1990 the federal government has been at the heart of a row with conservationists. Wood Buffalo's herd of wood buffalo (a unique subspecies of the plains buffalo) is infected with highly contagious **tuberculosis** and **brucellosis**, and government scientists claim the only way to prevent the spread of the diseases to Alberta's valuable beef herds is to **kill them off**. Scientists opposed to the government plan point out that the herd has been infected for years, has kept the disease to itself, and has survived by internal regulation and natural balance. Locals point out that killing every animal would be a daunting task, given the immensity of the animals' range, and that it would presumably be fruitless if even a few were missed, as disease would erupt afresh when the herd regenerated.

The **restocking** issue has opened another can of worms, for there are just eighteen pure-bred, disease-free wood buffalo kept in captivity, and it is from these that the government intends to restart the herd. However, most experts argue that the resultant weak, inbred group would compare badly with the large and long-evolved gene pool of the present herd. Other scientists take a completely different line, maintaining that wood buffalo aren't genetically different from their plains cousins and so it wouldn't matter if they were wiped out.

The dispute has quickly become extremely messy, reflecting fundamental changes in Canadian attitudes towards the rival claims of business and the environment in a tough financial climate. Some see the hand of Canada's powerful **beef lobby** guiding the government's actions, while others see it as part of a move to relax the powerful injunctions protecting Canada's national parks and open the way for **economic growth** in what are, almost by definition, regions of depression and high unemployment. This has already started, with Alberta's government taking plains buffalo off the protected list and putting it onto restaurant menus by promoting buffalo farming to boost its northern economy.

In the saga's most ironic twist, tuberculosis and brucellosis have turned up in **farmed game animals** (mainly elk), and a huge increase in game farming has led to an explosion in the very diseases a cull of the wild herds would seek to eradicate. Animals bred in captivity are more susceptible to such diseases, and escaping farmed elk are spreading them to areas far beyond the range of Wood Buffalo's supposed culprits. At the time of writing, the federal government had appointed a committee of interested parties to review the affair; the park's buffalo, for their part, are still nibbling contentedly as the debate continues.

Edmonton (daily except Sun on *Canadian*), Hay River, Yellowknife and Vancouver, as well as on any number of wing-and-a-prayer charter planes.

Unless you're prepared to backpack or fly into the interior, the only reliable **access** to the park proper is along the 150-kilometer run of Hwy 5, its only all-weather road, through the northeastern quadrant. A 298-kilometer summer-only loop branches off Hwy 5, 8km south of Fort Smith, through the southeast corner; some stretches are impassable after heavy rain, so check conditions with the park center in Fort Smith (see below). The west leg of the loop leads to three developed **trails** – Salt River (after 15km), Rainbow Lakes (after 20km) and Pine Lake (after 65km), the latter with a nearby **campground**. Backwoods camping is allowed anywhere as long as it's at least 1500m from Pine Lake or any road or trail. **Canoeing** is wide open: the Athabasca and Peace river system was once the main route for trade from the south, and still offers limitless paddling options.

Fort Smith

Though it's actually in the Northwest Territories, **FORT SMITH** is the only conceivable base for exploring Wood Buffalo National Park. Virtually the last settlement for several hundred kilometers east and north, the town started life as a Hudson's Bay trading post, and despite being only 1km from the Alberta border, was the NWT administrative center until 1967, when the Canadian federal government moved it to Yellowknife.

Call ahead to reserve rooms in one of Fort Smith's two **hotels**: the *Pelican Rapids Inn* (☎403/872-2789; ③), with kitchenettes in every room, or the smaller *Pinecrest Hotel* (☎403/872-2320; ③). For half the price, however, you could try one of a dozen or so **B&Bs** – the best contact is *Subarctic Wilderness Adventures* (☎403/872-2467), who'll ring around for a bed or put you up themselves in their lodge with singles at around $45 with breakfast, $65 for full board. They also organize tours and **rent camping equipment**.

There's a public **campground** alongside the Slave River on the northern edge of town, though Fort Smith's stores and its two restaurants are clustered in a tiny two-block area of downtown. Drop into the **Northern Life Museum**, 110 King St, to enjoy an excellent collection of the far north's traditional artefacts, crafts and archive photographs.

Fort Smith's summer-only **infocentre** (June–Sept 9am–9pm; ☎872-2349) can supply more details on Wood Buffalo National Park.

CALGARY AND
SOUTHERN ALBERTA

Calgary is the obvious focus of southern Alberta, perfectly placed where the prairies buckle suddenly into the Rockies. In fact, with some of the continent's most awesome mountains practically on its doorstep, it takes some self-restraint to give the city the couple of days it deserves. Within day-tripping distance lie two unexpected gems: the dinosaur exhibits of the **Royal Tyrrell Museum**, near Drumheller in the strange badlands country to the east; and the **Head-Smashed-In Buffalo Jump**, a Native American site in the heart of Alberta's cowboy country to the south. This latter is most easily visited if you're following the southern route of Hwy 3 across the province, as is **Waterton Lakes National Park**, isolated well to the south of the other Canadian Rockies parks.

Calgary

Cities in North America don't come much more glittering than **CALGARY**, a likeable place whose downtown skyscrapers soared almost overnight on the back of an oil boom in the Seventies to turn it into something of a Canadian Dallas. The tight high-rise core is good for wandering, and contains the prestigious **Glenbow Museum**, while the homey wooden houses of the far-flung suburbs recall the city's pioneering frontier origins. These are further celebrated in the annual **Calgary Stampede**, a hugely popular cowboy carnival in which the whole town – and hordes of tourists – revel in a boots-and-stetson image that's still very much a way of life in the surrounding cattle country.

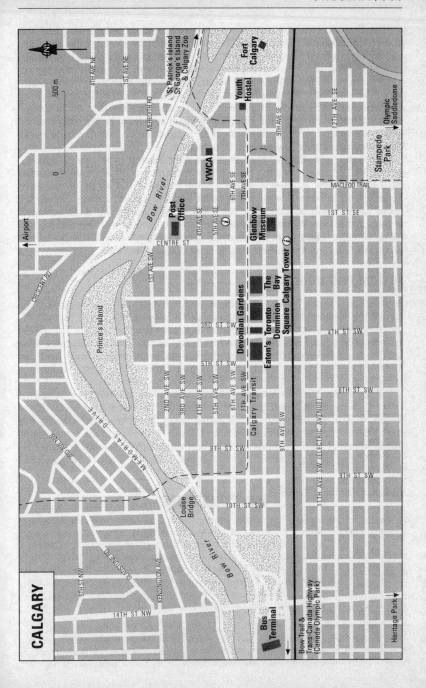

The **Blackfeet** ranged over this region for several thousand years, and it is littered with traces of old campsites, buffalo kills and pictographs; tribal lands are now locally confined to a few reserves. Whites began to gather around the confluence of the Bow and Elbow rivers from about the turn of the nineteenth century, but it wasn't until the 1870s that a North West Mounted Police fort was established here to curb the lawlessness of the whiskey traders. Christened **Fort Calgary** after the Scottish birthplace of its assistant commissioner, the new town quickly attracted ranchers and British gentlemen farmers to its low, hilly bluffs – which are indeed strongly reminiscent of Scottish moors and lowlands – and cemented an enduring Anglo-Saxon cultural bias.

Cattle and the coming of the Canadian Pacific Railway generated exceptional growth and prosperity in the early part of this century; and when the Dingman No 1 **oil** well blew, in 1914, it started a boom that enabled Calgary, by the early Seventies, to become a world energy and financial center. Falling commodity prices subsequently punctured the city's ballooning economy, but it still managed to attract the 1988 **Winter Olympics**, two weeks of much-remembered glory which, like the legacy of its oil and cattle riches, continue to lend the city the air of a brash, self-confident and apparently prospering boomtown.

Arrival and information

Approaching Calgary **by air**, you get a magnificent view of the Rockies stretching across the western horizon. The international **airport**, a modern, often half-deserted strip, is about 10km northeast of downtown – a $30 taxi ride. The widely advertised free hotel coaches tend to be elusive, but the reliable **Airporter Bus** ($7.50) departs every thirty minutes (5.30am–11.30pm) from a small booth in front of Level 1. There's a small **information center** (7am–11pm) in Level 2 (arrivals).

Calgary's brand-new **bus** terminal is comfortable but not terribly convenient; west of downtown at Eighth Ave SW and 16th St, it's a somewhat seedy thirty-minute walk to the city center. Free transit buses, however, operate during the day to the C-Train at Seventh Ave SW and Tenth St, the key to the city's central transit system. Five-dollar **taxis** for this short run are plentiful outside the terminal. **Hitching** is illegal within the city limits, following a series of gruesome

---

CHINOOKS

Winters in Calgary are occasionally moderated by **chinooks** – sudden warming winds, familiar on leeward slopes of mountains the world over, that are at their most dramatic in the plains of southwestern Alberta. Often heralded by a steely cloud band spreading from the mountains over the city, a chinook will sweep down the eastern flanks of the Rockies to raise the temperature by as much as 50°F in a couple of hours and evaporate a foot of snow in a day. The effect has to do with the way prevailing westerly winds are forced to rise over the Rockies, expanding and cooling on the way up and compressing and warming up again on the way back down, to reach Calgary both drier and warmer.

The name comes from the tribe that inhabited the area around the mouth of the Columbia River in Washington and Oregon, from where the winds seem to originate; the Chinook also lent their name to the largest species of Pacific salmon.

assaults on and by hitch-hikers. The main city **Tourist and Convention Bureau** is in the Calgary Tower, 139 Tower Centre, 101-9th Ave SW (☎262-2766 or in BC and Alberta ☎1-800/661-1678). It doles out huge amounts of information and also provide a free accommodation-finding service. Other minor offices operate on the Trans-Canada Highway and on Macleod Trail (Hwy 2) heading south, and the informative monthly *Where Calgary* is free from shops, hotels and the Tourist Bureau.

For all its rapid expansion, Calgary is a well-planned and straightforward city engineered around an inevitable grid. The metropolitan area is divided into **quadrants** (NW, NE, SE and SW) with the Bow River separating north from south, Centre Street–Macleod Trail east from west. **Downtown**, and virtually everything there is to see and do, is in a small area in or close to the SW quadrant.

City transportation

Almost everything in Calgary, barring Stampede locations and a few minor diversions, is a comfortable walk away – except in winter, when temperatures can make any excursion an ordeal. The city's much-vaunted **Plus 15 Walking System**, a labyrinthine network of enclosed walkways fifteen feet above ground, is designed to beat the freeze. It enables you to walk through downtown without setting foot outside, but is too confusing to be worth the bother when the weather's fine.

Calgary's **public transit system** is cheap, clean and efficient, comprising an integrated network of buses and the **C-Train**, the latter a cross between a bus and a train which is **free** for its downtown stretch along the length of Seventh Ave SW between Tenth St and City Hall at Third St SE.

Tickets, valid for both buses and C-Train, are available from machines on C-Train stations, from shops with a Calgary Transit sticker, and from the main **Information and Downtown Sales Centre**, 240-7th Ave SW (Mon–Fri 8.30am–5pm). The single adult fare is $1.50 (free for under-6s; 90¢ for 6–14); books of five tickets cost $6.75, ten tickets $12.50, day passes $4.50. You can pay on the bus if you have the exact change.

The sales center also provides timetables and an invaluable **information line** (☎262-1000; Mon–Fri 6am–11pm, Sat & Sun 8am–9.30pm): tell them where you are and where you want to go, and they'll give you the necessary details.

The City

Downtown Calgary lies in a self-evident cluster of mirrored glass and polished granite facades bounded by the Bow River to the north, Ninth Avenue to the south, Centre Street to the east and Eighth Street to the west. A monument to oil money, the area is about as sleek as an urban center can be; virtually everything is brand new, and the modern architecture is easy on the eye.

Any city tour should start with a trip to the **Glenbow Museum**, while a jaunt up the **Calgary Tower**, across the street, gives a literal overview of the Calgarian hinterland. Thereafter a good deal of the city lends itself to wandering on foot, whether around the mall-laden main streets or to **Prince's Island**, the nearest of many parks, and **Kensington**, the heart of Calgary's small alternative scene.

The Glenbow Museum

The excellent and eclectic collection of the **Glenbow Museum** is, aside from the Stampede, the only sight for which you'd make a special journey to Calgary. Although it's opposite the Calgary Tower at 130-9th Ave SE, the entrance is hidden alongside the Skyline Plaza complex. Built in 1966, the no-expense-spared museum (Tues–Sun 10am–6pm; $4.50, free Sat; ☎268-4100) is a testament to sound civic priorities and the cultural benefits of booming oil revenues. Its three floors of displays make a fine introduction to the heritage of the Canadian West.

The permanent collection embraces the something-for-everyone approach, starting with a section devoted to ritual and **sacred art** from around the world and an **art gallery** tracing the development of western Canadian indigenous art. Better still is the **Images of the Indian** section, an objective and fascinating look at the art that flowed back to Europe after white contact with native peoples. Two outlooks prevail – the romantic nineteenth-century image of the Indian as "noble savage" and the more forward-looking analysis of artists such as Paul Kane.

The second floor runs the gamut of western Canadian history and heritage, including an outstanding exhibit on **Native Canadian peoples**. In the **treaties** section, hidden in a corner almost as if in shame, you can read the original documents, crammed with incomprehensible jargon and legal gobbledegook; the museum text skates over the injustices with a glossary of simple facts. All facets of native **crafts** are explored, with stunning displays of carving, costumes and jewellery; the emphasis is on the original inhabitants of Alberta, but the collection also forays into the Inuit and the Metis (the offspring of native women and white fur traders, and the most marginalized group of all).

An historical chronology leads into exhibits associated with the fur trade, North West Rebellion, the Canadian Pacific, pioneer life, ranching, cowboys, oil and wheat, adding up to a glut of period paraphernalia that includes a terrifying exhibit of frontier dentistry, an absurdly comprehensive display of washing machines, and a solitary 1938 bra.

The eccentric top floor kicks off with a pointless display of Calgary Stampede merchandizing, before moving on to a huge collection of **military paraphernalia** and a dazzling display of **gems and minerals**, said to be among the world's best. These exhibits are mainly for genre enthusiasts, though the gems are worth a look if only to see some of the extraordinary and beautiful things that come out of the drab mines that fuel so much of western Canada's economy.

Other downtown sights

The **Calgary Tower** (daily 7.30am–midnight; $5), the city's favorite folly, is a good deal shorter and less imposing than the tourist material would have you believe. An obligatory tourist traipse, the 190-meter saltcellar stands in a relatively dingy area at Centre St-9th Ave SW, somewhat overshadowed by downtown's more recent sprouting. As a long-term landmark it makes a good starting point for any tour of the city, offering outstanding **views**, especially on clear days when the snow-capped Rockies fill the western horizon; whether it's worth the price of admission is another matter. Up on the observation platform you'll find a snack bar (reasonable), cocktail bar and revolving restaurant (expensive).

Any number of shopping malls lurk behind the soaring high-rises, most notably Toronto Dominion Square (Eighth Ave SW between Second and Third streets), the city's main shopping focus and the unlikely site of **Devonian Gardens** (9am–9pm; free). Like something out of an idyllic urban Utopia, the three-acre indoor garden supports a lush sanctuary of streams, waterfalls and full-sized trees, no mean feat given that it's located on the fourth floor of a glass and concrete glitter palace. Benches beside the garden's paths are perfect for picnicking on food bought in the takeaways below, while impromptu concerts are held on the small stages dotted around.

Calgary pays homage to its oil industry in the small but oddly interesting **Energeum** plonked in the main lobby of the Energy Resources Building, 640-5th Ave SW (June–Aug daily except Sat 10.30am–4.30pm; Sept–May Mon–Fri same hours; free). Its audio-visual and presentational tricks take you through the formation, discovery and drilling for coal and oil. Alberta's peculiar and problematic oil sands – granite-hard in winter, mud-soft in summer – are explained, and there's dollops of the stuff on hand for some infantile slopping around. At the **Alberta Science Centre** and **Centennial Planetarium**,11th St and Seventh Ave SW (July & Aug daily 10am–8pm; Sept–June Wed–Fri 1–5pm, Sat & Sun 10am–5pm ; $5.50), the telescopes of its small observatory are trained nightly on the moon, planets and stars (weather permitting).

Prince's Island, the Bow River and Kensington

Five minutes' walk north of downtown via a footbridge, **Prince's Island** is a popular but peaceful retreat offering plenty of trees, flowers, a snack bar, kids' playground and enough space to escape the incessant stream of joggers pounding the walkways. Between the island and downtown, the wonderful **Eau Claire Market** is a bright brash warehouse mix of food and craft market, cinemas, buskers, restaurants, walkways and panoramic terraces. All in all it brings some heart to the concrete and glass of downtown, the large communal eating area in particular a fine place to people-watch and pick up bargain take-away Chinese, Japanese, wholefood and burger snacks. The food market opens 9am to 6pm, but the complex and restaurants are open until late. Note that the tremendous new **YMCA** opposite the market has no rooms, though the superb swimming pool is open to all (daily 11.30am–1.30pm & 4.30–6.30pm; $6.50). Swimmers might be tempted by the broad, fast-flowing **Bow River** nearby, but it's for passive recreation only – the water is just two hours from its icy source in the Rockies, and its dangers are underlined by lurid signs on the banks. The river is the focus for Calgary's civilized and excellent 200-kilometer system of **recreational walkways**, asphalt paths (also available to cyclists) which generally parallel the main waterways.

A twenty-minute jaunt along the walkway system from Prince's Island, **Kensington** is a revitalized nightlife center of bars and restaurants focused on Tenth Street NW and Kensington Road. As alternative as Calgary gets, this is the city's self-proclaimed "People's Place", and the whiff of patchouli and counterculture hang in the air despite a tide of encroaching gentrification. Shops here sell healing crystals and advertise yoga and personal-growth seminars, though the older cafés, bookshops and wholefood stores are beginning to give way to trinket shops.

Fort Calgary

Fort Calgary, the city's historic nexus, stands at 750-9th Ave SE (daily 9am–5pm; site free, interpretive center $2, free Tues), a manageable eight-block walk east of downtown; you could also take bus #1 from Seventh Ave to Forest Lawn, or the C-Train free to City Hall and walk the remaining five blocks. Built by the

North West Mounted Police in 1875, the fort was the germ of the present city, and remained operative as a police post until 1914, when it was sold – inevitably – to the Canadian Pacific Railway. The whole area remained buried under railroad tracks and derelict warehouses until comparatively recently.

Period photographs in the adjoining interpretive center provide a taste of how wild Calgary still was in 1876. Even more remarkable was the ground that men in the fort were expected to cover: the log stockade was a base for operations between Fort Macleod, 160km to the south, and the similar post at Edmonton almost 400km to the north. It's not as if they had nothing to do: Crowfoot, most prominent of the great Blackfoot native chieftains of the time, commented "if the Police had not come to the country, where would we all be now? Bad men and whiskey were killing us so fast that very few of us indeed would have been left. The Police have protected us as the feathers of a bird protect it from the winter."

Only a few forlorn stumps of the original building remain, much having been torn down by the developers, and what survives is its site, now a pleasant forty-acre park contained in the angled crook of the Bow and Elbow rivers. The interpretive center traces Calgary's development with the aid of artefacts, audio-visual displays and "interpretive walks" along the river. Among the sillier things on offer – and you may never get the chance again – is the opportunity to dress up as a Mountie.

St George's Island

St George's Island is home to **Calgary Zoo, Botanical Gardens and Prehistoric Park**, all at 1300 Zoo Rd (daily 9am–dusk; $7.50), and can be reached from downtown and Fort Calgary by riverside path, by C-Train, or by car (take Memorial Drive East). This is Canada's biggest zoo, with innovative and exciting displays in which the animals are left as far as possible in their "natural" habitats. The extended North American section gives a taste of Rocky Mountain fauna.

The **Botanical Gardens** are dotted throughout the zoo, while the **Prehistoric Park** annex – a "recreated Mesozoic landscape" – is accessible by suspension bridge across the Bow River (daily mid-May to mid-Nov). Its 27 life-sized dinosaur models, none too convincing in their incongruous settings, are a poor substitute for the superb site and museum at Drumheller (see p.374), and only the fossils in two adjoining buildings are of more than fleeting interest.

Heritage Park Historical Village

A sixty-acre theme park centered on a reconstructed frontier village 16km southwest of downtown, **Heritage Park** replicates life in the Canadian West before 1914 and panders relentlessly to the myth of the "Wild West" (May–Sept daily 10am–6pm; $9.95 admission includes all rides). Full of family-oriented presentations and original costumes, this "heritage" offering – the largest of its type in Canada – is thorough enough for you never to feel obliged to see another.

The living, working museum comprises more than 100 **restored buildings**, all transported from other small-town locations. Each has been assigned to one of several communities – fur post, native village, homestead, farm and turn-of-the-century town – and most fulfil their original function. Thus you can see a working blacksmith, buy fresh bread, buy a local paper, go to church, even get married. Transportation, too, is appropriate to the period – steam trains, streetcars, horse-drawn bus, stagecoaches, and the highlight, the restored paddle-steamer **SS**

THE CALGARY STAMPEDE

An orgy of all things cowboy and cowgirl, the annual **Calgary Stampede** is a gift to Calgary's tourist industry, bringing hordes of spectators and participants into the city for the middle two weeks of July. In return the city obliges visitors by losing its collective head; all and sundry turn out in white stetsons, bolo ties, blue jeans and hand-tooled boots, and everyone appears to address one another in a bastardized cowboy slang straight out of country-and-western songs.

For all its heavily worked tourist appeal, however, the competition end of things is taken very seriously. Most of the cowboys are for real, as are the injuries – the rodeo is said to be North America's roughest – and the combined prize money is a very serious $500,000. Even the first show in 1912, masterminded by entrepreneur Guy Weadick, put up $100,000 and attracted 14,000 people to the opening parade, a line-up which included 2000 Indians in full ceremonial rig and Pancho Villa's bandits in a show erroneously billed as a swansong for the cowboy of the American West. Nowadays the ten days of **events** still kick off with a huge parade, and encompass bronco riding, bull riding, native buffalo riding, branding, calf roping, steer wrestling, cow tackling, and wild cow milking. The events run for three hours daily, with the recognized highlight, the ludicrously dangerous chuck wagon races (the "World Championship"), held over until each evening.

Nightlife is a world unto its own, with Stampede locations giving way to music, dancing and mega-cabarets which involve casts of literally thousands. There's also lots of drinking, gambling, fireworks and general partying into the small hours.

Most events take place at **Stampede Park**, southeast of downtown and best reached by C-Train to Stampede Station, which contains an amusement park, concert and show venues, bars and restaurants. Some action reverts to the Olympic Saddledome close by, and extra on-street entertainments take place throughout the city.

Accommodation during Stampede is greatly stretched, and prices for most things are hiked for the duration. **Tickets** for the key events go quickly, and cost anything between $5 and $50, but you can get most of the flavor of the thing just by being there. For ticket order forms, advance sales and **general information** write to Calgary Exhibition and Stampede, Box 1860, Station M, Calgary T2P 2L8 (☎261-0101, elsewhere in Alberta ☎1-800/661-1260) or call in person at Stampede Headquarters, 1410 Olympic Way SE, or the visitor center.

Moyie, which runs trips across the local reservoir. To get there by **car**, take either Elbow Drive or Macleod Trail south and turn right on Heritage Drive (the turn-off is marked by a huge, maroon steam engine); **bus** #53 makes the journey from downtown, or you can take the C-Train to Heritage Station and then bus #20 to Northmount.

Accommodation

Budget **accommodation** in Calgary is not plentiful, but what little exists is rarely at a premium except during Stampede (mid-July) when prepaid reservations, in central locations at least, are essential. In addition to the recommendations given below, motels abound, mostly well away from the center along Macleod Trail heading south and on the Trans-Canada heading west.

If you run into difficulties, the tourist office in the Calgary Tower is primed to hunt out rooms at short notice, or you can consult the Alberta Hotel Association's ubiquitous *Accommodation Guide.* The *Calgary Bed & Breakfast Association*, 1633-7a St (☎284-0010) have some 35 **bed and breakfast** options on their books.

Hotels and motels

Cecil, corner of Fourth Ave & Third St SE (☎266-2982). By budget standards, reasonably clean, but on a busy junction (the airport road) and with a downstairs bar with a rough reputation. No phones, TV or private baths. ②.

Hotel Regis, 124-7th Ave SE (☎262-4641). Dingy central hotel, two blocks from the Calgary Tower (and the hostel, a nicer option). Bathroom facilities are all shared and rooms only have sinks; beware the bar. ③.

Lord Nelson Inn, 1020-8th Ave SW (☎269-8262). A newish ten-story block, each room with TV and fridge, and just a block from the free C-Train. ③.

Prince Royal Inn, 618-5th Ave SW (☎263-0520 or 1-800/661-1592). A mixture of 300 studio, one- and two-room suites with full facilities and free continental breakfast. ④.

Ramada Hotel, 708-8th Ave SW (☎263-7600 or 1-800/661-8684). A large, comfortable hotel with 200 newly renovated rooms and swimming pool at the heart of downtown. ⑤.

St Louis Hotel, 430-8th Ave SE (☎262-6341). Seedy location, and extremely basic; the management is friendly, the long-term residents less so. ②.

Sandman-Quality Hotel, 888-7th Ave SW (☎237-8626 or 1-800/726-3626). Extremely handy for the free C-Train, with 300 good, dependable rooms. ⑤.

Skyline Plaza, 110-9th Ave SE (☎266-7331 or 1-800/648-7776). Not the most expensive of Calgary's smart hotels, but probably the best if you want to stay in some style. ⑦.

Travelodge, 2750 Sunridge Blvd NE (☎291-1260 or 1-800/667-3529); 2304-16th Ave (289-0211 or 1-800/255-3050); and 9206 Macleod Trail (☎253-707 or 1-800/667-3529). Three chain motels; the least expensive out-of-town choices. The first is convenient for the airport. All ③.

Westward Inn, 119-12th Ave SW (☎266-4611 or 1-800/661-9378). Amenity-loaded hotel, but a few blocks off the center of town. ⑤.

York Hotel, 636 Centre St SE (☎262-5581). Central, with good-sized rooms with TVs and baths and laundry service. ③.

Hostels and student accommodation

Calgary International Youth Hostel, 520-7th Ave SE (☎269-8239). A convenient position close to downtown, buses and two blocks east of City Hall and the free section of the C-Train. Laundry, 8-bed dorms, family rooms, cooking facilities, snack bar. Closed 10am–5pm; midnight curfew. June–Sept members $13, Oct–May $12. Non-members $16. ①.

Calgary YWCA, 320-5th Ave SE (☎263-1550). Hotel comfort for women and children only in quiet safe area; food service, pool, gym, health club and squash courts; book in summer. Singles from $27.50; dorm beds $17.50. Sleeping bag space is provided in summer. ①.

University of Calgary, 3330-24th Ave NW (☎220-3203). Way out in the suburbs, but a cheap last resort with a huge number of student rooms in the peak summer period. Take the C-Train or bus #9. The room rental office (call first) is in the Kananaskis Building on campus (24hr). Student ID card secures a 33 percent discount. ②.

Campgrounds

Bow Bend, 5227-13th Ave NW (☎288-2161). RVs only – *no* tents. Alongside parkland and the Bow River – leave the Trans-Canada at Home Rd and follow 13th Ave. Showers and laundry facilities. Mid-May to Sept only, $18.

KOA Calgary West, off Hwy 1 at the western end of the city (☎288-0411). 224 pitches, laundry, outdoor pool. Mid-April to mid-Oct, $20.

Whispering Spruce, Balzac (☎226-0097). 15min beyond the city limits on Hwy 2 north. All facilities. Mid-April to mid-Oct, $10.

Eating, drinking and nightlife

Calgary's cuisine is heavily meat-oriented; Alberta claims, with some justification, to have some of the best **steaks** in the world. With its particular immigration history, however, the city lacks the Ukrainian influences that grace cooking to the north, and prefers instead to rehash so-called "Californian cuisine".

The Toronto Dominion Square and Stephen Avenue malls, on Eighth Avenue SW between First and Third, are riddled with ethnic **takeaways** and café-style restaurants – hugely popular and perfect for lunch or snacks on the hoof. The nicest thing to do is buy food and eat it – with half of Calgary – either in the Eau Claire market or amid the greenery of Devonian Gardens. Elsewhere, the city has an impressive range of middle- to upper-bracket restaurants, where prices are low by most standards.

Calgary is no party town, except during Stampede and a brief fling in summer when the weather allows barbecues and night-time streetlife. None the less, its bars and clubs are all you'd expect of a city of this size, the vast majority of them found in four distinct areas: **Kensington**, with its varied cafés, restaurants and clubs, and the best summer evening wandering possibilities; **"Electric Avenue"**, as 11th Avenue SW between Fifth and Sixth streets is called, all identikit pubs and bars, bright, brash and very popular with the very young and trashy; **17th Avenue SW**, a quieter and more varied collection of pubs, bars, specialty shops and ethnic eating; and **downtown**, fine during the day but fairly desolate in the evening. In the specialist clubs the quality of live music is good – especially in jazz, blues and the genre closest to cowtown Calgary's heart, country. The **Country Music Association** has details of local gigs (☎233-8809). For details of the annual **Jazz Festival** (third week in June) and for daily information on who's playing where, call the **Jazz Line** (☎265-1321). Prince's Island is the venue for a **folk festival** at the end of July. **Tickets** for virtually all events are available through *BASS* (☎270-6700), and through several *Marlin Travel* offices around the city. You'll find events **listings** in Calgary's main dailies, the *Herald* (especially on Friday) and the *Sun*.

Cafés and restaurants

Bagels and Buns, 17th Ave SW near Seventh St. Informal and popular for breakfast and lunch.

Chianti Café and Restaurant, 1438-17th Ave SW (☎229-1600). Dark, noisy, and extremely popular – try to book – with pasta basics and the odd fancy dish.

Entre Nous Café, 2206-4th St SW (☎228-5525). Small, lively and congenial, big mirrors and burgundy decor giving a genuine bistro feel. Good French food; booking recommended.

Good Earth, 11th St-15th Ave. Wholefood meals and provisions.

Kaos Café, 718-17th Ave SW. Noted breakfasts, eclectic clientele; good for outside summer drinking. Live music is a draw Fri & Sat nights.

Kensington Delicafé, 1414 Kensington Rd NW. Casual and friendly, with a grown-up hippy feel. Varied menu features wholefood options, notorious desserts, huge portions and fine burgers. Also live music nightly and outdoor tables in summer.

Latin Corner, 2004-4th St SW. Small, buzzy place with good South American food.

The Roasterie, 314-10th St NW near Kensington Rd. Nice hang-out and café – no meals – newspapers, notice board and twenty kinds of coffee.

Scooza-Mi Eaterie, 1324 Centre St North. Daft name but excellent food. See also the out-of-town *Scooza-Mi II* at 6915 Macleod Trail.

Bars

Dinero's, 310 Stephen Ave Mall. Favorite office-worker hang-out for an after-work drink and Tex-Mex food, but quiet the rest of the time.

The Fox and Firkin, 11th Ave SW between Fifth & Sixth. You may have to queue for one of the biggest and most popular of the numerous "Electric Avenue" bars which, like many Calgary bars, affects the atmosphere of a British pub – noisy, crowded, tatty and fun.

O'Brien's Pub and Restaurant, 636 Centre St South Boisterous downtown bar with billiards and dancing.

Rose and Crown, 1503-4th St SW. A Calgary institution, round the corner from *The Ship and Anchor*, though the pub atmosphere is labored and the clientele grating.

St Louis Tavern, 430-8th Ave SE. Cheaper drinks and more gritty ambience than bars a few blocks away on 11th Ave (closed Sun).

The Ship and Anchor, 17th Ave SW on the corner of Fifth St. Is this the best bar in western Canada? It's certainly the best in Alberta; friendly and laid-back but jumping "neighbourhood" pub, with special Anglo-Canadian connections, darts, fine music and excellent pub food.

The Unicorn Pub, Eighth Ave SW (on the corner of Second St, downstairs in the mall). Well-known downtown pub whose cheap food brings in lunchtime punters.

Live music venues

Dusty's Saloon, 1088 Olympic Way. One of the city's better C&W spots (jam sessions on Mon nights).

Kensington Delicafé, 1414 Kensington Rd NW. Live music nightly in relaxed café/ restaurant.

The King Edward Hotel, 438-9th Ave SE. Much-loved, down-at-heel location, with consis-tently good country and R&B bands. The Saturday jam session is renowned and invariably packed – *the* blues event in the city.

Ranchman's Steak House, 9615 Macleod Trail South. A classic honkytonk, known throughout Canada, and often packed as a result. Live C&W and predictable atmosphere. Closed Sun.

Republik, 219-17th Ave SW. Currently the weirdest and most alternative nightspot in the city (jam sessions on Mon nights).

Sparkies, 1006-11th Ave SW. Sunday-night jam sessions, "alternative" music on Tuesdays, bands and "variety" nights the rest of the week.

Performing arts and cinema

The **Centre for the Performing Arts** is a dazzling new downtown complex with three performance spaces (Ninth Ave & First St SW, ☎294-7444) and the seat of the Calgary Philharmonic Orchestra. It's also base for **Theatre Calgary**, and the acclaimed *Alberta Theatre Project*, which produces five fairly avant-garde plays annually. More modest **classical concerts** are the Music at Noon offerings in the Central Library (Sept–April), and the sessions – planned and impromptu – on the small stages in Devonian Gardens. The *Lunchbox Theatre* offers a popular and wildly varied programme aimed at downtown shoppers and passers-by; perfor-mances are somewhat irregular, but tend to start at noon in the Bow Valley Square on the corner of Sixth Ave and First St SW. Calgary's **ballet** world is dominated by the young and excellent Alberta Ballet Company.

For repertory, classic and foreign **films** try the *Plaza Theatre* at 1113 Kensington Rd NW; the *National Film Board Theatre*, 222-1st St SE puts on free lunchtime shows. The **Museum of Movie Art** at the University of Calgary, 9-3600-21st St NE (Tues–Sat 9.30am–5.30pm), is home to the world's largest collec-tion of cinema posters (4000 of them, dating back to 1920).

Listings

Airlines *Air Canada*, 530-8th Ave SW (☎265-9555); *Canadian Airlines* (☎235-1161; airbus to Edmonton ☎235-8154; schedules & reservations ☎248-4888); *Time Air* (☎235-1161); *American* (☎1-800/433-7300); *America West* (☎1-800/247-5692); *Continental* (☎1-800/525-0280); *Delta* (☎265-7610); *Eastern* (☎236-2833); *KLM* (☎236-2600); *United* (☎1-800/241-6522).

Airport enquiries ☎292-8400.

Ambulance ☎261-4000.

American Express 421-7th Ave SW (☎261-5982).

Bike rental *Abominable Sports*, 640-11th Ave SW (☎266-0899). Mountain bikes $15 per day; mopeds $20 per day.

Books *Canterbury's Bookshop*, 513-8th Ave SW, is the best general bookshop. For maps and travel books, *Map Town*, 640-6th Ave SW (☎266-2241).

Bus enquiries *Greyhound* (☎265-9111); *Airporter* (☎531-3909); *Brewster*, for airport/Banff/Jasper (☎260-0719); *Red Arrow Express*, for Edmonton (☎531-0350); *Pacific Western* (☎243-2990).

Car rental *Avis* (☎269-6166); *Budget* (☎263-0505); *Hertz* (☎221-1300); *Rent-a-Wreck*, 2339 Macleod Trail (☎237-6880); *Thrifty*, 117-5th Ave SE (☎262-4400).

Consulates *British* (☎1-604/683-4421); *US*, 1000-615 Macleod Trail SE (☎266-8962).

Exchange *Calgary Foreign Exchange*, 307-4th Ave SW; *Royal Bank*, 339-8th Ave SW.

Hospital Calgary General Hospital, 841 Centre Ave East (☎268-9111).

Left luggage Facilities at the bus terminal, 850-16th St SW; $1 per 24hr.

Lost property ☎268-1600.

Pharmacy ☎253-2605 (24hr).

Police 316-7th Ave SE (☎266-1234).

Post office 220-4th Ave SE.

Rail information *Via rail* (☎1-800/561-8630); *Rocky Mtn Railtours* Calgary–Banff–Vancouver (☎1-800/665-7245).

Taxis *Associated* (☎299-1111); *Checker* (☎299-9999); *Red Top* (☎250-9222); *Yellow Cab* (☎974-1111).

Tickets Tickets for all events, shows etc from *Ticketmaster* ☎270-6700.

Weather ☎263-3333.

The Alberta Badlands

Formed by the meltwaters of the last ice age, the valley of the Red Deer River cuts a deep gash through the dulcet prairie about 140km east of Calgary, creating a surreal landscape of bare, sun-baked hills and eerie lunar flats dotted with sagebrush and scrubby, tufted grass. On their own, the **Alberta Badlands** – so anomalous in the midst of lush grasslands – would be worth a visit, but what makes them an essential detour is the presence of the **Royal Tyrrell Museum of Paleontology**. The museum is devoted to the dinosaur relics exposed by the river's erosive action, and is located 8km outside the old coal-mining town of **Drumheller**, which is also the main focus of the **Dinosaur Trail**, a road loop that explores the Red Deer Valley and surrounding badlands.

Drumheller

However you travel, you'll pass through **DRUMHELLER**, a dreary town in an extraordinary setting roughly ninety minutes' drive northeast of Calgary. As you approach it from the west, you don't realize how near you are until you come to a virulent red water tower and the road suddenly drops into a dark, hidden canyon. The otherworldliness of the gloomy, blasted landscape is heightened by its contrast to the vivid colors of the earlier wheat and grasslands. Drumheller sits at the base of the canyon, surrounded by the detritus and spoil heaps of its mining past – the Red Deer River having exposed not only dinosaur fossils but also (now exhausted) coal seams.

Drumheller is best reached by taking Hwy 2 north towards Edmonton and branching east on Hwy 72 and Hwy 9. It's an easy day trip with your own transport, and most people make straight for the Tyrrell Museum, signed from Drumheller on Hwy 838 (or "North Dinosaur Trail'). Using one of the two **Greyhound buses** daily from Calgary to Drumheller makes a day trip more of a squeeze. It's a touch too far to walk from Drumheller town center to the museum, particularly on a hot day, but *Valley Taxis* (☎823-6333) will run you there from the bus depot for about $7.

There's not much to do in the town itself, despite the best efforts of its **info-centre** at 703-2nd Ave W (May–Oct daily 9am–9pm; ☎823-6300). A limited and dog-eared selection of **accommodation** lies together a block from the bus terminal, the best of the downtown hotels being the slightly over-priced *Lodge at Drumheller* (☎823-3322; ③) opposite the hoste on Railway Ave. Other central options include the *Rockhound Motor Inn*, South Railway Drive (☎823-5302; ③), or the top-of-the-pile *Drumheller Inn* (☎823-8400; ④), a modern motel on a bluff off the Hwy 56 approach from the west; the new, tasteful log cabins of the pleasanter *Badlands Motel* (☎823-5155; ②) are 1km out of town on Hwy 838. The **youth hostel** is at the *Alexander Hotel*, 30 Railway Ave (☎823-6337), and offers a choice of 8-bed dorms (members $10, non-members $14), or private rooms (②).

Of the town's two well-situated and neighboring **campgrounds**, the larger and better is the *Dinosaur Trailer Court* (April–Oct; ☎823-3291; $14), across the river north of downtown at the junction of Hwy 56 and Hwy 838. *Shady Grove Campground* (May–Oct; ☎823-2576; $10) is a few hundred meters south, on the other side of the bridge at 25 Poplar St – closer to the town's tatty confines but with boating and swimming possibilities. The visitor center has lists of the many other private and provincial campgrounds (*Little Fish Provincial Park* the best) up and down the valley.

The tucked-away *All West* **supermarket** on First St behind the main drag stocks picnic supplies, and the *Diana* on Main St is half diner, half Chinese restaurant, but really the best eating option is the cafeteria at the museum itself.

The Royal Tyrrell Museum of Paleontology

Packed with high-tech displays, housed in a sleek building and blended skilfully into its desolate surroundings, the **Royal Tyrrell Museum** is an object lesson in museum design (May–Sept daily 9am–9pm; Oct–April Tues–Sun 10am–5pm; $5, free on Tues). It attracts half a million plus visitors a year, and its wide-ranging exhibits are likely to appeal to anyone with even a hint of scientific or natural curiosity. Although it claims the world's largest collection of complete dinosaur skeletons, the museum is far more than a load of old bones, and as well as tracing the earth's history from the year dot to the present day, it's also a leading center of study and academic research.

Laid out on different levels to suggest layers of geological time, the open-plan exhibit guides you effortlessly through a chronological progression, culminating in a huge central hall of over 200 dinosaur specimens. If there's a fault, it's that the hall is visible early on and tempts you to skip the lower-level displays, which place the dinosaurs in context by skilfully linking geology, fossils, plate tectonics, evolution and the like with Drumheller's own landscape. You also get a chance to peer into the **preparation lab** and watch scientists working on fossils in one of the world's best-equipped paleontology centers.

By far the most impressive exhibits are the **dinosaurs** themselves. Whole skeletons are immaculately displayed against three-dimensional backgrounds which persuasively depict the swamps of 60 million years ago. Some are paired with full-size plastic dinosaurs, which appear less macabre and menacing than the free-standing skeletons. Sheer size is not the only fascination: *Xiphactinus*, for example, a four-meter specimen, is striking more for its delicate and beautiful tracery of bones. Elsewhere the emphasis is on the creatures' diversity or on their staggeringly small brains, sometimes no larger than their eyes.

The museum naturally also tackles the problem of the dinosaurs' **extinction**, pointing out that around ninety percent of all plant and animal species that have ever inhabited the earth have become extinct. Leave a few minutes for the **paleo-conservatory** off the dinosaur hall, a collection of living prehistoric plants, some unchanged in 180 million years, selected from fossil records to give an idea of the vegetation that would have typified Alberta in the dinosaur age.

The Dinosaur Trail

The **Dinosaur Trail** is a catch-all circular road route of 51km embracing some of the viewpoints and lesser historic sights of the badlands and the Red Deer Valley area. The comprehensive *Visitor's Guide to the Drumheller Valley* (free from the Drumheller infocentre) lists thirty separate stop-offs, mostly on the plain above the valley, of which the key ones are: **Horsethief Canyon** (17km west of the museum) and **Horseshoe Canyon** (19km southwest of the museum on Hwy 9), two spectacular viewpoints of the wildly eroded valley, the latter with good trails to and along the canyon floor; the **Hoodoos**, slender columns of wind-sculpted sandstone, topped with mushroom-like caps (17km southeast of Drumheller on Hwy 10); the still largely undeveloped **Midland Provincial Park**, site of the area's first mines and criss-crossed by badland trails, now home to an interpretive center (daily 9am–6pm; free); and the **Atlas Coal Mine** (daily mid-May to early Sept 9am–6pm; $2), dominated by the teetering wooden "tipple", once used to sort ore and now a beautiful and rather wistful piece of industrial archeology.

Dinosaur Provincial Park

Drivers can feasibly fit in a trip to **Dinosaur Provincial Park** the same day as the Tyrrell Museum, a 174-kilometer run from Drumheller to the park, and then head back to Calgary on the Trans-Canada, which runs just south of the park. The nearest town is Brooks on the Trans-Canada, 48km west of the **Field Station of the Tyrrell Museum**, the park's obvious hub (May–Sept daily 9am–9pm; Oct–April Sat & Sun 10am–5pm). The excellent provincial **campground** in the park is open year-round, but only serviced from May to September ($6).

Nestled among some of the baddest of the badlands, this landscape is not only one of the most alien in Canada, but also one of the world's richest fossil beds and a listed UN World Heritage Site (over 300 complete skeletons have been found). The field station has a few self-guided trails and a small museum that goes over the same ground as its parent in Drumheller, leaving the real meat of the visit to the **Badlands Bus Tour**, a guided tour of the otherwise out-of-bounds dinosaur dig near the center of the park (10 tours daily May–Sept; $3.50). A few exposed skeletons have been left *in situ*, and panels give background information on the monsters. The station also organizes two-hour guided hikes.

Highway 3 and the south

The most travelled route across southern Alberta is the Trans-Canada, direct to Calgary; **Highway 3**, branching off at Medicine Hat, takes a more southerly course across the plains before finally breaching the Rockies at Crowsnest Pass. This quieter and less spectacular route into the mountains holds a trio of worthwhile diversions: the brand new **Carriage Centre** near Cardston, the marvellously monikered **Head-Smashed-In Buffalo Jump** heritage site, and **Waterton Lakes National Park**, a cross-border reserve that links with the United States' Glacier National Park.

Medicine Hat

Though **MEDICINE HAT** is barely a hundred years old, the origin of its wonderful name has already been confused. The most likely story has to do with a Cree medicine man who lost his head-dress while fleeing a battle with the Blackfoot; his followers lost heart at the omen, surrendered, and were promptly massacred. These days you rarely see the town mentioned without the adage that it "has all hell for a basement", a quotation from Rudyard Kipling coined in response to the huge reserves of natural gas that lurk below the town. Discovered by railway engineers drilling for water in 1883, the gas fields now feed a flourishing petrochemical industry which blots the otherwise park-studded downtown area on the banks of the South Saskatchewan River.

Medicine Hat may claim that its 1440 hours of summer sunshine make it Canada's sunniest city, but its main function is as a major staging post on the Trans-Canada. The least expensive of its many **motels** is the *Bel-Aire*, 633-14th St (☎527-4421; ①), conveniently situated at the junction of the Trans-Canada and Hwy 3; the *Best Western Inn*, on the Trans-Canada at 722 Redcliff Drive (☎527-3700; ③),, is more appealing.

Lethbridge

Alberta's third city, **LETHBRIDGE** is booming on the back of oil, gas and some of the province's most productive agricultural land; none of which is of much consequence to people passing through, whom the city attempts to sidetrack with the **Nikka Yuko Centennial Gardens** (May–Oct daily 9am–5pm; $5) in its southeastern corner. These five tranquil Japanese horticultural landscapes, with a placid pavilion of cypress wood perpetually laid out for a tea ceremony, were created in 1967, partly in acknowledgement of the fact that 6000 Japanese-Canadians were interned in Lethbridge during World War II.

Far removed from the gardens' decorum is **Fort Whoop-Up** (May–Sept Mon–Sat 10am–6pm, Sun noon–8pm; Oct–April Mon–Fri 8.30am–4.30pm; $2) at Indian Battle Park, a reconstruction of the wild whiskey trading post set up in 1869 by American desperadoes from Fort Benton, Montana. It was the most lucrative of the many similar forts which sprang up illegally all over the Canadian prairies, and led directly to the founding of the North West Mounted Police. It was also the scene of the last armed battle in North America between Native American tribes (fought between the Cree and Blackfoot nations in 1870).

Three *Greyhound* **buses** daily operate from Calgary to the Lethbridge bus terminal at 411-5th St S. Most of the city's **motels** are on a single strip, Mayor Macgrath Drive; the *Sandman Inn*, 421 Mayor Macgrath Drive (☎328-1111; ②), and the less expensive *Park'n'Sleep*, 1124 Mayor Macgrath Drive (☎328-5591; ①), are typical. Women alone can stay at the *YWCA*, 604-8th St S (☎329-0088; ①). The *Henderson Lake Campgrounds* (May–Oct; ☎328-5452; $11) are near Henderson Lake alongside the Nikka Yuko Gardens.

Fort Macleod and around

FORT MACLEOD catches traffic coming up from the States and down from Calgary on Hwy 2, which eases around the town center via the rebuilt wooden palisade of the **Fort Museum** (daily, May–June & Sept to mid-Oct 9am–5pm, July–Aug 9am–8pm; $3.50). One for diehard Mountie fans, this was the first fort established in Canada's Wild West by the North West Mounted Police, who got lost after being dispatched to raid Fort Whoop-Up in Lethbridge, allowing the whiskey traders to flee; finding Whoop-Up empty, they continued west under Colonel James Macleod to establish a permanent barracks on the river here.

Three daily **buses** serve the town from Lethbridge and three from Calgary, the latter continuing west to Cranbrook, Nelson and eventually to Vancouver in British Columbia. If you're stuck, the town has seven **motels**, the most central being the *Fort Motel* on Main St (☎553-3606; ②).

Head-Smashed-In Buffalo Jump

Hollywood may depict Indians trailing lone buffalo with bows and arrows; in fact, the actual methods used by Native North Americans to forage for food were often less romantic, but far more effective and spectacular. Over a period of more than 6000 years, Blackfoot hunters perfected a technique of luring buffalo herds into a shallow basin and stampeding them to their deaths over a broad cliff, where they were then butchered for meat, bone (for tools) and hide (for clothes and shelter). Such "jumps" existed all over North America, but the **Head-Smashed-In Buffalo Jump**, 18km northwest of Fort Macleod on Hwy 785, is the best preserved (May–Oct daily 9am–8pm, rest of year Tues–Sun 9am–5pm; $5; ☎553-2731). Its name, which alone should be enough to whet your appetite, is a literal description of how a nineteenth-century Blackfoot met his end after deciding the best spot to watch the jump was at the base of the cliff, apparently unaware he was about to be visited by some 500 plummeting buffalo.

The brand-new **interpretive center**, a seven-storied architectural *tour de force*, is built into the 10-meter-high and 305-meter-wide cliff near the original jump. Below it a 10-meter-deep bed of ash and bones accumulated over millennia is protected by the threat of a $50,000 fine for anyone foolish enough to rummage for souvenirs.

The facility delves deep into the history of the jump and native culture in general, its highlight being a film which attempts to recreate the thunderous death plunge using a herd of buffalo which were slaughtered, frozen and then somehow made to look like live animals hurtling to their deaths. Around the center the jump is surrounded by a couple of kilometers of **trails**, the starting point for free tours conducted by native guides. No public transportation serves the site; taxis from Fort Macleod cost about $20.

Remington-Alberta Carriage Centre

Alberta is hoping that the glittering new **Remington-Alberta Carriage Centre** (mid-May to early Sept daily 9am–8pm; otherwise daily 9am–5pm; $5), opened in 1993, will repeat the success of the Tyrrell Museum and Head-Smashed-In Buffalo Jump. Although brilliantly executed, its appeal, however, is perhaps more limited, centering on horse-drawn vehicles and evoking the atmosphere of their nineteenth-century heyday. The main hall boasts around 52 working carriages, and around 120 in passive display, the exhibits cleverly integrated with 25 "stories" that place the carriages in their social and cultural context. Additionally there's the chance to ride carriages (usually for free), see working stables and admire the magnificent Quarters and Clydesdales that make up the center's horse herd. Guides are often in period dress, and you can watch craftspeople in the process of building and renovating various carriages. The center lies immediately south of Cardston at 623 Main St (across the river from the town center), just off Hwy 2 about 50km south of Fort Macleod, and handily placed for Waterton Lakes National Park.

Waterton Lakes National Park

Waterton Lakes National Park, about 55km south of Fort Macleod, appears at first glance no more than an addendum to the much larger Glacier National Park to which it is joined across the United States border. Despite its modest acreage, however, it contains scenery – and trails – as stupendous as any of the bigger Canadian Rockies parks. Founded in 1895, it was re-launched in 1932 as an "International Peace Park" to symbolize the understated relationship between Canada and its neighbor. The two parks, however, remain separate national enclaves. Though backpackers can cross the border without formalities, to drive from one to the other you have to exit the park and pass through immigration controls, as stringent as anywhere if you're not a national of either country. A park **entry permit** for car-drivers (also valid for all other national parks in the Canadian Rockies) costs $5 for one day, $10 for four days or $30 for a full year.

The Waterton area's unique **geological history** becomes obvious on the ground once you've been able to compare its scenery with the strikingly different landscapes of Banff and Jasper national parks to the north (see p.388 and p.410). The rock of Waterton's mountains moved eastward during the formation of the Rockies (see p.386) as a single vast mass known as the Lewis Thrust. Some six kilometers thick, the monolith travelled over 70km, the result being that rocks over 1.5 billion years old from the Rockies' "sedimentary basement"– now the oldest surface rocks in the range – came to rest undisturbed on *top* of the prairies' far more recent 60-million-year-old shales. Scarcely any zone of transition exists between the two, which is why the park is often known as the place where the "peaks meet the prairies" and its landscapes as "upside-down mountains". The effect was to produce not only slightly lower peaks than to the north, but also mountains whose summits are irregular in shape and whose sedimentary formations are horizontal (very different from the steeply tilted strata and distinctive saw-tooth ridges of Banff National Park). Upper Waterton Lake by contrast (at

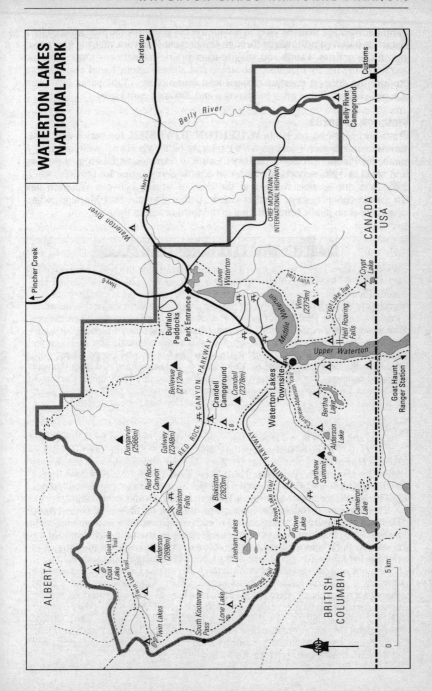

WATERTON LAKES NATIONAL PARK

Cardston

Pincher Creek

Hwy-5

Waterton River

Belly River

Belly River Campground

Customs

CANADA

USA

Chief Mountain International Highway

Lower Waterton

Middle Waterton

Vimy (2379m)

Vimy Trail

Crypt Lake Trail

Crypt Lake

Hell Roaring Falls

Upper Waterton

Park Entrance

Buffalo Paddocks

Bellevue (2112m)

Crandell Campground

Crandell (2378m)

RED ROCK CANYON PARKWAY

Dungarvin (2566m)

Galwey (2348m)

Waterton Lakes Townsite

Bertha Lake

Goat Haunt Ranger Station

Cameron-Anderson Trail

Anderson Lake

Carthew Summit

Red Rock Canyon

Blakiston Falls

Blakiston (2920m)

AKAMINA PARKWAY

Rowe Lake Trail

Lineham Lakes

Rowe Lake

Cameron Lake

Anderson (2698m)

Goat Lake Trail

Goat Lake

Twin Lake Trail

Twin Lakes

Tamarack Trail

Lone Lake

South Kootenay Pass

ALBERTA

BRITISH COLUMBIA

5 km

0

150m the Rockies' deepest lake) is a more recent phenomenon still, gouged by a glacier as it carved northwards through the present Waterton valley before expiring on the prairies. Plants and wildlife from prairie habitats co-mingle with the species of the purely montane, sub-alpine and alpine regions found elsewhere to produce the greatest diversity of **flora and fauna** of any of the parks (800 plant species – half of all that grow in Alberta – and 250 species of birds).

Waterton Townsite

From Fort Macleod, access to **WATERTON TOWNSITE**, the park's only base, accommodation source and services center, is either via Hwy 3 west and Hwy 6 south (via Pincher Creek) or on Hwy 2 south to Cardston and then west on Hwy 5. A small taxi-bus service, the *Waterton Shuttle Service* (ring for services; ☎627-2682) was due to start running at the time of writing between Waterton and *Greyhound* connections at Pincher Creek, Lethbridge and Fort Macleod; otherwise there is no public transportation to the town or within the park.

HIKING IN WATERTON LAKES PARK

Waterton Lakes Park's **trails** have a reputation as not only the best constructed in the Canadian Rockies, but also among the most easily graded, well marked and scenically routed. Bar one or two outlying hikes, three key areas contain trails and trailheads: the **townsite** itself, which has two magnificent short walks; the **Akamina Parkway**; and the **Red Rock Canyon Parkway**. Most walks are day hikes, climaxing at small alpine lakes cradled in spectacular hanging valleys. Options for backpacking are necessarily limited by the park's size, though the 36-kilometer **Tamarack Trail**, following the crenellations of the Continental Divide between the Akamina Parkway (trailhead as for Rowe Lakes – see below) and Red Rock Canyon, is rated as one of the Rockies' greatest highline treks; the 20-kilometer **Carthew–Alderson Trail** from Cameron Lake to Waterton, a popular day's outing, can be turned into a two-day trip by overnighting at the Alderson Lake campground.

Walks from the townsite
Various short loops in and around town can get you in the mood for longer excursions: try the **Prince of Wales** from the visitor center (2km) or the more demanding **Bear's Hump**, also from the center (1.2km). Another obvious, and very simple walk from the town is the **Waterton Lakeshore Trail** (13km), which follows Upper Waterton Lake's west shore across the US border to Goat Haunt; regular lake ferries sail back to the townsite, completing a lovely round trip (details on ☎859-2362).

The single most popular day's walk from the townsite, however, is the classic **Bertha Lake Trail** from Waterton, 5.8km each way (allow 3–4hr for the round trip): a short, steep hike to a busy but remarkably unsullied mountain-ringed lake. Many people break off at Lower Bertha Falls (2.9km from the townsite); if you carry on to the lake, an easy trail runs right round the lakeshore (adding about another 5km).

Another superlative walk out of Waterton is the unique **Crypt Lake Trail**, which involves a boat trip to the trailhead across Upper Waterton Lake and a crawl through a rock tunnel before the 8.7-kilometer hike to crashing waterfalls and the great glacial amphitheater containing Crypt Lake; rock walls tower 600m on three sides, casting a chill shadow that preserves small icebergs on the lake's surface throughout the summer. Allow time to catch the last boat back to Waterton (again, ferry details are on ☎859-2362). Campers should be aware that the site here is one of the most heavily used in the park's backcountry.

The town is beautifully set on Upper Waterton Lake, but offers little by way of cultural distraction (the small herd of Plains Bison in the **Bison Paddock** just north of town constitutes the only "sight"). Two scenic access roads from Waterton probe west into the park interior and provide the starting point for most trails: the **Akamina Parkway** follows the Cameron Creek valley for 20km to Cameron Lake, while the **Red Rock Canyon Parkway** weaves up Blakiston Creek for about 15km to the mouth of Red Rock Canyon (see "Practicalities" for details of car and bike rental). There are also a handful of town trails, and a trio of cracking walks – Bertha Lake, Crypt Lake and the Upper Waterton Lakeshore – start from the townsite (see box).

Information and Transportation
Everything you need to explore the park centers on Waterton Townsite. The national park **visitor center** is on Entrance Rd at the road junction to the north (mid-May to mid-Sept, daily 9am–7pm; ☎859-2445 or 859-2224). Further informa-

---

Trails from the Akamina Parkway
Most of the trails accessed by the Akamina Parkway leave from the road's end near Cameron Lake. To stretch your legs after the drive up, try either the **Akamina Lake** (0.5km) or **Cameron Lakeshore** (1.6km) trails. The best of the longer walks is to **Carthew Summit** (7.9km one way), a superb trail that switchbacks through forest before opening out into sub-alpine meadow and a final climb to a craggy summit and astounding viewpoint. The trail can be continued all the way back to Waterton Townsite (another 12km) – it's then the Carthew–Alderson Trail (see above), most of whose hard work you've done in getting up to Carthew Summit; thereafter it's largely downhill via Carthew and Alderson lakes to the townsite.

Another trail from the Akamina Parkway, however, is equally appealing – the **Rowe Lakes Trail** (5.2km one way), accessed off the Parkway 5km before Cameron Lake (it is also the first leg of the Tamarack Trail – see above). Most people walk to the Rowe Basin (where there's a backcountry campground) and then, rather than pushing on towards the Upper Rowe Lakes (1.2km beyond), either camp, turn round or – for stronger walkers – take the trail that branches right from the Upper Rowe path to walk to **Lineham Ridge** (another 3.4km). The stiffish walk is rewarded by Lineham Lake, sapphire blue in the valley far below, and a vast sea of mountains stretching to the horizon. Only come up here in good weather: it's particularly hazardous when visibility's poor and the winds are up.

Trails from the Red Rock Canyon Parkway
Most trails on the Red Rock Canyon Parkway, such as the short **Red Rock Canyon Trail** (0.7-km loop) and **Blackiston Falls** (1km), leave from Red Rock Canyon at the end of the road. The most exhilarating option from the head of the road, however, is the **Goat Lake Trail** (6.7km), which follows Bauerman Creek on an old fire road (flat and easy, but a little dull) before peeling off right at the 4.3km mark for the climb to tranquil Goat Lake and ever-improving views (there's a back-country campground at the lake). If you ignore the lake turn-off and follow the fire road another 4km you come to a junction: one trail leads north to Lost Lake (2km), the other south to the spectacular **Twin Lakes** area (3.2km). This latter option will bring you to the long-distance Tamarack Trail (see above). Walk south on this from Twin Lakes (3.1km) and you can pick up the **Blakiston Creek Trail** which will take you back to the head of the Red Rock Canyon Parkway.

tion is available from the Chamber of Commerce (☎859-2303) and, outside the visitor center's summer hours, at the park's Administration Office at 215 Mount View Rd (Mon–Fri 8am–4pm; ☎859-2477 or 859-2275). Be sure to buy the Canadian Parks Service 1:50,000 **map** *Waterton Lakes National Park* if you're going to do any serious walking. *Pat's Convenience Store*, a gas station and camping store on the corner of Mount View Rd and Waterton Ave (☎859-2266), rents out **bikes** and *Budget* **cars**. The *Royal Bank* is in Tamarack Mall on Waterton Ave, and the *Itussististukiopi Coin-Op* **laundry** is on Windflower Ave (mid-June to mid-Sept, daily 8am–10pm). *Waterton Sports and Leisure* in Tamarack Mall stocks maps, fishing licenses and general outdoors paraphernalia.

If you want to cruise the lakes contact *Waterton Shoreline Cruises* at the marina (☎859-2362 or 859-2363), an outfit that also provides the **Hikers' Water Shuttle Service**, a ferry to various trails around the lake, including a passage to the trailhead of the famed Crypt Lake walk (see box) and the hikes from Goat Haunt in the US at the southern end of Upper Waterton Lake. *Park Transport* in Tamarack Mall (☎859-2378) organizes tours, but will also lay on a **taxi** shuttle to trails on the area's two Parkways.

Accommodation

Aspen-Windflower Motel, Windflower Ave (☎859-2255). Opposite the municipal pool; motel rooms, bungalows and 8-person suites, some with kitchenettes. April to mid-Oct. ④.

Bayshore Inn, 111 Waterton Ave (☎859-2211). Just south of the marina; very comfortable hotel, 49 of whose 70 units are on the lakefront. Mid-April to mid-Oct. ④.

Crandell Mountain Lodge, 102 Mount View Rd, corner of Evergreen Ave (☎859-2288). Just 13 rooms, so more intimate than some of the town's hotels. April–Oct. ③–⑤.

El Cortez Motel, next to the Tamarack Mall at 208 Mount View Rd (☎859-2366). One of the less expensive places in town; some rooms with kitchenettes. May to mid-Oct. ②.

Kilmorey Lodge, 117 Evergreen Ave (☎859-2334). On the northern entrance to town; lakefront setting and nice old-fashioned feel. Open all year. ④.

Northland Lodge, Evergreen Ave (☎859-2353). 7 cozy rooms east of the townsite in the lee of the mountains south of Cameron Falls; some kitchenettes. Mid-May to Sept. ②.

Prince of Wales Hotel, Waterton Lake (☎859-2231). Famous and popular old hotel, whose Gothic outline you'll see in almost every picture of Waterton; worth it if you can afford it and manage to find a room. June to mid-Sept. ⑤.

Stanley Hotel, 112b Waterton Ave (☎859-2345). Old-fashioned 9-roomed hotel. Mid-May to Sept. ③.

Campgrounds

As well as the private and three park-run campgrounds detailed below, the national park provides thirteen designated **backcountry campgrounds**, with dry toilets and a surface water supply; a few also have shelters and cooking facilities. To use any, you need a free backcountry camping permit, issued on a first-come, first-served basis by the Visitor Center or Administration Office. A quota system is operated to prevent over-crowding. Unrestricted camping within the park is permitted only at Lineham Lakes, reached by a 4.2-kilometer trail off the north side of the Akamina Parkway 9.5km from Waterton.

Belly River, 1km off Chief Mountain Parkway on Hwy 6 (☎859-2224). 24-site park-operated campground. Self-registration; tap water; kitchen shelters; fireplaces. Mid-May to Sept. $6.50.

Crandell Mountain Campground, 8km west of Waterton on the Red Rock Canyon Parkway off Hwy 5 (☎859-2224). Semi-serviced park-run campground with 129 sites. Tap water; fireplaces; no showers. Mid-May to Sept. $9.50.

Homestead Campground, 3km north of Waterton Park Gateway on Hwy 6 (☎859-2247). Large 260-pitch commercial site with services, showers, pool, dancefloor and other non-rural distractions. May to mid-Sept. $12.

Riverside Campground, 5km east of Waterton Park Gateway (☎653-2888). Private; 70 sites with showers and services. Mid-May to mid-Sept. $10.

Waterton Townsite Campground, off Vimy Ave (☎859-2224). 238-site serviced park-run campground. Showers; no open fires. Mid-May to Oct. $11.75.

Eating

Fast Eddy's Gourmet Take-Out, Tamarack Mall. Sandwiches, ice cream, good cappuccino and special hikers' lunch packs.

Kootenai Brown Dining Room, Waterton Ave at the *Bayshore Inn*. Along with the *Prince of Wales'* dining rooms, one of the more elegant spots in town to treat yourself.

New Frank's Restaurant, Waterton Ave. "New" because it's been renovated: very cheap, odd combinations of breakfasts, burgers, Chinese buffet and lunch specials.

Pearl's Patio Café and Deli, Windflower Ave. Fresh baking; great for breakfast, lunch, coffee, deli-meats, picnic provisions and hikers' take-out lunches.

Pizza of Waterton, 103 Fountain Ave. Dough made daily on the premises; good pizzas to eat in or take away.

Windsor Lounge, *Prince of Wales Hotel*. One of several lounges, bars and dining rooms in this posh hotel open for non-patrons to enjoy afternoon tea, a good breakfast or a refined hour with a drink and great lake views. Dress the part, and don't come here straight off the trail.

Crowsnest Pass

The 1382-meter **Crowsnest Pass** is the most southerly of the three major routes into the Rockies and British Columbia from Alberta, and far less attractive than the Calgary and Edmonton approaches. In its early stages, however, as Hwy 3 pushes west out of Fort Macleod across glorious windblown prairie, it augurs well: the settlements are bleaker and more backwoods in appearance, and the vast unbroken views to the mountain-filled horizon appear much as they must have to the first pioneers. As the road climbs towards the pass, however, the grime and dereliction of the area's mining heritage make themselves increasingly felt. Hopes a century ago that Crowsnest's vast coal deposits might make it the "Pittsburgh of Canada" were dashed by disasters and rapid obsolescence. The Crowsnest route west is of most use as a direct route if you're hurrying to Vancouver or aim to explore the Kootenays in southern British Columbia. After breasting the pass, Hwy 3 drops into BC and follows the often spectacular Elk River Valley to join Hwy 95 at Cranbrook (see p.344).

Bellevue and the Frank Slide

Sleepy **BELLEVUE** is the first village worthy of the name after Fort Macleod; an oddball and close-knit spot with an old-world feel unusual in these parts. It's distinguished by a church the size of a dog kennel and a wooden tepee painted lemon yellow, as well as the claim to have "the best drinking water in Alberta" . None the less, it supports a small **infocentre** and the opportunity to explore – complete with hard hat and miner's lamp – the old **Bellevue Mine** (tours every half hour July & Aug daily 10am–5.30pm). The village also has one of the pass's more luxurious **campgrounds**, *Crowsnest Campground* (☎562-2932; $12), located just off the highway, with 60 sites, hot showers and a heated swimming pool.

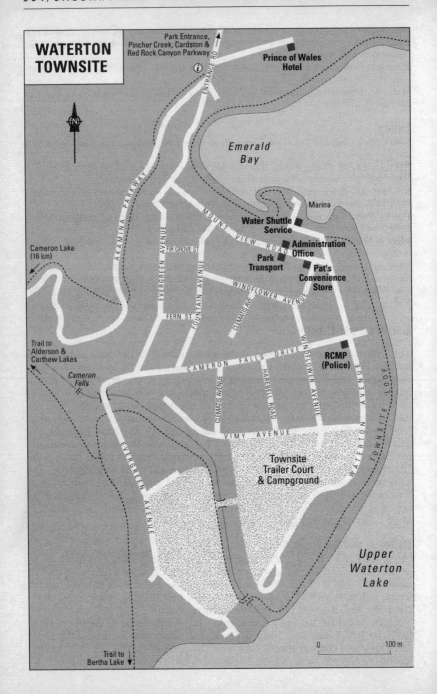

WATERTON TOWNSITE

Park Entrance,
Pincher Creek, Cardston &
Red Rock Canyon Parkway

Prince of Wales Hotel

Emerald Bay

Cameron Lake (16 km)

Marina

Water Shuttle Service

Administration Office

Park Transport

Pat's Convenience Store

Trail to Alderson & Carthew Lakes

Cameron Falls

RCMP (Police)

Townsite Trailer Court & Campground

Upper Waterton Lake

Trail to Bertha Lake

ENTRANCE RD

AKAMINA PARKWAY

EVERGREEN AVENUE

FIR GROVE ST

FOUNTAIN AVENUE

FERN ST

MOUNT VIEW ROAD

CLEMATIS AVE

WINDFLOWER AVENUE

CAMERON FALLS DRIVE

CLEMATIS AVENUE

HAREBELL ROAD

WINDFLOWER AVENUE

WATERTON AVENUE

TOWNSITE LOOP

VIMY AVENUE

EVERGREEN AVENUE

0   100 m

Dominating the skyline behind the village are the crags and vast rockfall of the **Frank Slide**, a huge landslide that has altered the contours of Turtle Mountain, once riddled with the galleries of local mines. In April 1903 some 100 million tons of rock on a front 1km long and 700m high trundled down the mountain, burying seventy people and their houses in less than two minutes. The morbidly interesting **Frank Slide Interpretive Centre**, just off the highway about 1km north of the village, highlights European settlement in the area, the coming of the Canadian Pacific Railway to Alberta, and the technology, attitudes and lives of local miners (daily mid-May to early Sept 9am–8pm; rest of year 10am–4pm; $3).

Blairmore, Coleman and the Pass

BLAIRMORE, 2km beyond the slide, is a scrappy settlement redeemed only by the walks and four winter ski runs on the hill above it. **COLEMAN** is the place to spend the night if you have to, especially if you've always wanted to be able to say you've seen "the biggest piggybank in the world". The town amounts to little – the small Crowsnest Museum, a single road, a strip of houses, three garages and a battered **motel**, the *Stop Inn* (☎562-7381; ②), a place favored by loggers. Almost as knocked about is the *Grand Union International Hostel*, 7719-17th Ave (☎562-8254; ①). More appealing is the dubiously named *Kozy Knest Kabins Triple K Motel* (☎563-5155; ②), open only from May to October and situated 8km west of Coleman on Hwy 3 beside Crowsnest Lake.

The village is handy for the **Leitch Collieries Provincial Historic Site** just off the main road, an overgrown turn-of-the-century coal mine enthusiastically described by interpretive staff (mid-May to mid-Sept daily 9am–5pm; free).

Beyond Coleman the road climbs towards **Crowsnest Pass** itself (1382m) and, after a rash of sawmills, the natural scenery finally takes center stage in a reassuring mix of lakes, mountains and trees protected by **Crowsnest Provincial Park**. A rustic provincial **campground** overlooks the lake at Crowsnest Creek, about 15km west of Coleman ($5).

THE CANADIAN ROCKIES

Few North American terrains come as loaded with expectation as the **Canadian Rockies**, and it's a relief to find that the superlatives can scarcely do credit to this sheer immensity of forests, lakes, rivers and snow-capped mountains. Although most visitors confine themselves to a handful of **national parks**, the range spans almost 1500km to the Yukon border, forming the vast watershed of the Continental Divide, which separates rivers flowing to the Pacific, Arctic and Atlantic oceans. Landscapes on such a scale make a nonsense of artificial borderlines, and the major parks are national creations that span both Alberta and British Columbia. Four of the parks – Banff, Jasper, Yoho and Kootenay – share common boundaries, and receive the attention of most of the millions of annual visitors to the Rockies.

There's little to choose between the parks in terms of scenery, and planning an itinerary that takes them all in comfortably is all but impossible. Most visitors start with **Banff National Park**, then follow the otherworldly **Icefields Parkway** north to the larger and much less busy **Jasper National Park**. From there it makes sense to continue west to **Mount Robson Provincial Park**,

THE STORY OF THE CANADIAN ROCKIES

About 600 million years ago North America was covered from Greenland to Guatemala by the vast granite mountains of the **Canadian Shield** (today restricted largely to northeast Canada). For the next 400 million years, eroded debris from the Shield – mud, sand and gravel – was washed westward by streams and rivers and deposited on the off-shore "continental slope". Heavier elements such as gravel accumulated close to the shore, lighter deposits like sand and mud were swept out to sea or left in lagoons. The enormous weight and pressure of the sediment, which built up to a depth of twenty kilometers, converted mud to shale, sand to sandstone and the natural debris of the reefs and sea bed – rich in lime-producing algae – into limestone. Two further stages were necessary, however, before these deposits – now the strata so familar in the profile of the Rockies – could be lifted from the seabed and left several thousand meters above sea level to produce the mountains we see today.

The **mountain-building** stage of the Rockies took just 100 million years, with the collision of the North American and Pacific continental plates (gigantic 50-kilometer-thick floating platforms of the earth's crust). About 200 million years ago, two separate strings of volcanic **Pacific islands**, each half the size of British Columbia, began to move eastward on the Pacific Plate towards the North American coast. When the first string arrived off the coast, the heavier Pacific Plate slid beneath the edge of the North American Plate and into the earth's molten interior. The lighter, more buoyant rock of the islands, however, stayed "afloat", detaching itself from the plate before crashing into the continent with spectacular effect. The thick orderly deposits on the continental slope were crumpled and uplifted, their layers breaking up and riding over each other to produce the coast's present-day interior and **Columbia Mountains**. Over the next 75 million years the aftershock of the collision moved inland, bulldozing the ancient sedimentary layers still further to create the Rockies' **Western Main Ranges** (roughly the mountain edge of Yoho and Kootenay national parks), and then moving further east, where some 4000 meters of uplift created the **Eastern Main Ranges** (the mountains roughly on a line with Lake Louise). Finally the detached islands "bonded" and mingled with the new mainland mountains (their "exotic" rocks can be found in geological tangles as far east as Salmon Arm in BC).

Behind the first string of islands, however, the **second archipelago** had also now crashed into the continent, striking the debris of the earlier collision. The result was geological chaos, with more folding, rupturing and uplifting of the earlier ranges. About 60 million years ago the aftershock from this encounter created the Rockies' easternmost **Front Ranges** (the distinct line of mountains that rears up so dramatically from the prairies), together with the foothills that spill around Kananaskis and Waterton lakes. The third stage of the Rockies' formation, **erosion and glaciation**, was relatively short-lived, at least three ice ages over the last 240,000 years turning the mountains into a region resembling present-day Antarctica. While only mountain summits peeked out from ice many kilometers thick, however, glaciers and the like were applying the final touches, carving sharp profiles and dumping further debris.

which protects the highest and most dramatic peak in the Canadian Rockies. Thereafter you're committed to leaving the Rockies unless you double back from Jasper to Banff to pick up the Trans-Canada Highway through the smaller **Yoho, Glacier** and **Revelstoke** national parks. Finally, **Kootenay National Park** is

---

PARK PERMITS

Motorists and motorcyclists have to buy a **vehicle permit** to stay overnight in any of the national parks covered in this chapter, or to drive the Icefields Parkway. A one-day permit, valid for all parks, costs $5 per vehicle; a four-day permit is $10 and an annual permit (valid April to March of the following year) is $30. Cyclists, pedestrians and bus or train passengers do not have to pay. There's no fee to enter provincial parks. A separate **backcountry permit**, free at any park visitor center or infocentre, is required for all overnight backcountry use.

---

more easily explored than its neighbors, though you'll have to backtrack towards Banff or loop down from Yoho to pick up the road that provides its only access. (Waterton Lakes National Park, hugging the US border, is covered on p.378.)

Though you can get around all the parks by **bus** or hitching, travelling by **car** or **bike** is the obvious way to get the most out of the region. Once there, you'd be foolish not to tackle some of the 3000km of **trails** that criss-cross the mountains, all of which are well worn and well signed. We've highlighted the best short walks and day hikes in each area, and you can get more details from the **park visitor centers**, which sell 1:50,000 topographical maps and usually offer small reference libraries of trail books; *The Canadian Rockies Trail Guide*, by Brian Patton and Bart Robinson, is invaluable for serious hiking or backpacking. Other activities – fishing, skiing, canoeing, whitewater rafting, cycling, horseriding, climbing and so on – are comprehensively dealt with in visitor centers, and you can easily **rent equipment** or sign up for organized tours in the bigger towns.

A word of **warning**: don't underestimate the Rockies. Despite the summer throngs, excellent roads and sleek park facilities, the vast proportion of parkland is wilderness and should be respected as such. See *Basics*, p.53, for more.

Kananaskis Country

Most first-time visitors race straight up to Banff, ignoring the verdant foothill region southwest of Calgary. **Kananaskis Country**, a protected area created out of existing provincial parks to take pressure off Banff, remains almost the exclusive preserve of locals, most of whom come for skiing. Kananaskis embraces a huge tract of the Rockies and has all the mountain scenery and outdoor pursuit possibilities of the parks, without the people or the commercialism. It is, however, an area without real focus, much of it remote wilderness; nothing in the way of public transportation moves out here, and the only fixed accommodation is in expensive, modern lodges – though it's idyllic camping country.

Minor roads from Calgary lead to such smaller foothill areas of the east as Bragg Creek, but the most obvious approach is to take Hwy 40, a major turn off the Trans-Canada Highway, which bisects Kananaskis's high mountain country from north to south and provides the ribbon to which most of the trails, campgrounds and scattered service centers cling. About 3km down the highway is the **Barrier Lake Information Centre** (daily 9am–5pm), where you can get a full breakdown on outdoor activities. Another 40km south of the center is a short spur off Hwy 40 to **Upper Kananaskis Lake**, probably the biggest concentration of accessible boating, fishing, camping and hiking possibilities in the region.Popular short hikes include the **Expedition Trail** (2.4km); it and many others are detailed in the definitive *Kananaskis Country Trail Guide* by Gillean Daffern, widely available in Calgary.

Banff National Park

Banff National Park is the most famous of the Canadian Rockies' parks, which makes it Canada's leading tourist attraction – so be prepared for the crowds that throng its key centers, **Banff** and **Lake Louise**, as well as the best part of its 1500km of trails, most of which suffer a continual pounding during the summer months. That said, it's worth putting up with every commercial indignity to enjoy the sublime scenery – and if you're camping or are prepared to walk, the worst of the park's excesses are fairly easily left behind.

Two popular highways offer magnificent vistas – the **Bow Valley Parkway** from Banff to Lake Louise, and the **Icefields Parkway** from Lake Louise to Jasper, transportation links that have superseded the railway that first brought the park into being. The arrival of the **Canadian Pacific** at the end of the nineteenth century brought to an end some 10,000 years of native presence in the region. Banff itself sprang to life in 1883 after three railway workers stumbled on the present town's Cave and Basin **hot springs**; within two years, the government had set aside the Hot Springs Reserve as a protected area, and in 1887 enlarged it to form Canada's first national park, the third in the world.

Banff Townsite

BANFF TOWNSITE (or just **BANFF**) is the unquestioned capital of the Canadian Rockies, and with its intense summer buzz it can be a fun and bustling base; if you've come to commune with nature, however, you'll want to get out as soon as possible. Small by European standards, it handles an immense amount of tourist traffic, much of it of the RV and mega-coach-tour variety. The Japanese presence is especially conspicuous, with a huge number of Japanese signs and menus in shops and restaurants, and backpackers are abundant in summer. Whether or not your main aim is to avoid the crowds, some contact with the town is inevitable, as it contains essential shops and services almost impossible to come by elsewhere in the park. Many of the more rewarding walks locally are some way from the town, but some surprisingly good strolls start just minutes from the main street.

Arrival and information

Banff is just ninety minutes' **drive** from Calgary on a fast, four-laned stretch of the Trans-Canada. The approach from the west is more winding, the total journey time from Vancouver being about twelve hours. From the States the quickest access is from Spokane (via Hwy 95) or Kalispell in Montana (Hwy 93).

Six daily *Greyhound* **buses** from Calgary, and five from Vancouver (via either Kamloops or Cranbrook), arrive at 100 Gopher St (☎762-6767). Services between

The **telephone code** for Banff and Jasper parks is ☎403.

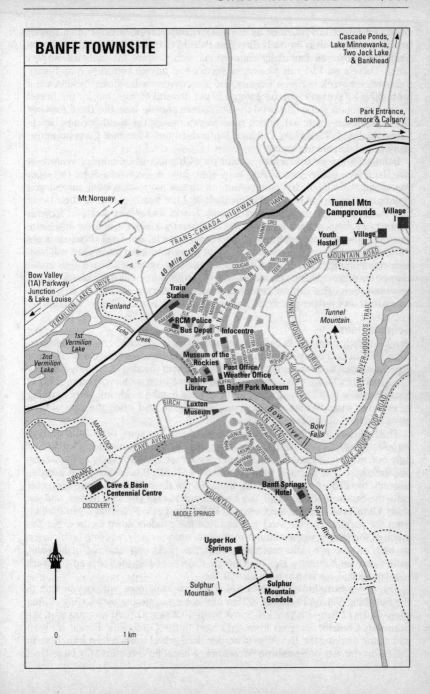

BANFF TOWNSITE

Cascade Ponds,
Lake Minnewanka,
Two Jack Lake
& Bankhead

Park Entrance,
Canmore & Calgary

Mt Norquay

Tunnel Mtn
Campgrounds

Village
I

Youth
Hostel

Village
II

TRANS-CANADA HIGHWAY

HAWK

CRES

MARMOT

BADGER

ANTELOPE

FOX

COUGAR

DEER

TUNNEL MOUNTAIN ROAD

40 Mile Creek

Bow Valley
(1A) Parkway
Junction
& Lake Louise

VERMILION LAKES DRIVE

Fenland

Echo

Creek

1st
Vermilion
Lake

2nd
Vermilion
Lake

Train
Station

RAILWAY

BIGHORN

ELK

SQUIRREL

GOPHER

RABBIT

MARTEN

MOOSE

BANFF AVENUE

RCM Police
Bus Depot

Infocentre

WOLF

LYNX

Museum of the
Rockies

Public
Library

BOW AVE

MUSKRAT

BEAVER

CARIBOU

BUFFALO

Post Office/
Weather Office

Banff Park Museum

GRIZZLY

OTTER

Tunnel
Mountain

TUNNEL MOUNTAIN DRIVE

JULIEN ROAD

BOW RIVER-HOODOOS TRAIL

BIRCH

Luxton
Museum

CAVE AVENUE

GLEN AVENUE

SPRAY AVENUE

Bow River

Bow
Falls

GOLF COURSE LOOP ROAD

MARSH LOOP

SUNDANCE

Cave & Basin
Centennial Centre

DISCOVERY

HAWK AVENUE

MOUNT NORQUAY

KOOTENAY

NAHANNI

TUZANE

RUNDLE

MIDDLE SPRINGS

MOUNTAIN AVENUE

Banff Springs
Hotel

Spray River

Upper Hot
Springs

Sulphur
Mountain

Sulphur
Mountain
Gondola

N

0   1 km

Banff and Jasper are provided by *Brewster Transportation*, which runs a single, heavily used bus daily in each direction (late May to mid-Oct, weather permitting); they also run four daily connections with Calgary International Airport (2hr). There's no *VIA* **rail** passenger service – a private company runs luxury trains once a week between Calgary and Vancouver via Banff, but tickets are a prohibitive $400. Banff is small enough to **get around** on foot, but for the hostel and campground you might need the small town **shuttle bus**, the *Banff Explorer* (June–Sept 8am– 9pm; $1), which runs on two routes: the Banff Springs Hotel–Spray Rd–Banff Rd–Buffalo Paddock Rd, and Tunnel Mountain Campgrounds–Banff hostel–Luxton Museum.

Banff's showpiece **infocentre**, a joint park-Chamber of Commerce venture at 224 Banff Ave (daily, July & Aug 8am–8pm, June & Sept 8am–6pm, Oct–May 9am–5pm; ☎762-1550), has information on almost any park-related subject you could name, including bear sightings, trails and the weather. Among their many free handouts, pick up *Banff and Vicinity Drives and Walks* and *The Icefields Parkway* for maps of park facilities, the *Backcountry Visitors' Guide* for an invaluable overview of **backpacking** trails and campgrounds, and *Trail Bicycling in the National Parks* for conditions and full list of **mountain bike** trails. Staff will help with room-hunting, and keep a constantly updated vacancies board (but aren't allowed to make specific recommendations), with a free courtesy phone to call acommodation. The central reservation service offers a fee-paying alternative (see p.394). For further practical information see also Banff "Listings" on p.397.

Gondola rides

Banff is rightly proud of its two prize **gondolas** (known elsewhere as cable-cars). High-price tickets buy you crowds, great views and commercialized summits, but also the chance to do some high-level hiking without the slog of an early-morning climb; and they'll give you a glimpse of the remote high country if you're short of time or unable to walk the trails. The best times to take a ride are early morning or evening, when wildlife sightings are more likely, and when the play of light gives an added dimension to the views.

The **Sulphur Mountain Gondola** on Mountain Ave some 5km south of town trundles skywards at a stomach-churning 51 degrees to immense views and an ugly but surprisingly good-value summit restaurant (Jan–Nov daily 8.30am–8pm, but slightly shorter hours in winter; $8.50; ☎762-2523). It takes just eight minutes to reach the 2255-meter high point, though from the restaurant a one-kilometer path, the **Summit Ridge Trail**, has been blazed to take you a bit higher, and the short **Vista Trail** leads to the viewpoint of Sanson Peak. Note that if you hike up from the parking lot (see box) you can ride the gondola down for free. Far too much of the food from the summit restaurant, unfortunately, ends up being eaten by bighorn sheep which, protected within the parks and unafraid of humans, gather here for handouts. Don't encourage them – feeding wildlife is against park regulations and can land you with a stiff fine.

The newer **Sunshine Gondola**, 18km southwest of town, whisks you 4km to the Sunshine Village Resort at 2215m and some staggering views (July & Aug Mon–Thurs 8.30am–7.30pm, Fri–Sun 8.30am–10.30pm; $12). At no extra cost, the **Standish Chairlift** leads on from the resort to the Continental Divide (2430m) and a post marking the BC–Alberta border. Two gravel **trails** return from here to the resort, by way of **Sunshine Meadows**, a beautiful and unusually large tract

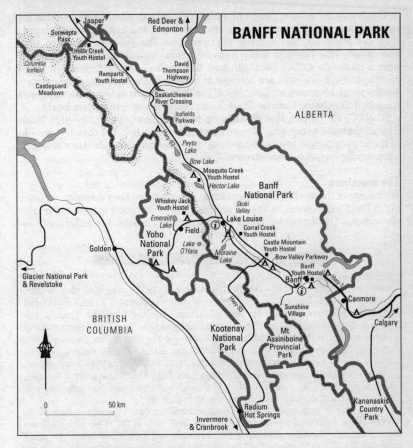

BANFF NATIONAL PARK

of alpine grassland. The shorter loop takes in Rock Isle Lake, while the longer tour (2hr) passes Grizzly and Lynx lakes before dropping to Sunshine Village.

The hot springs

Banff also boasts eight **hot springs**, and the next stop after a gondola ride on the standard itinerary is to plunge into the two currently commercialized. In early days these springs were vital to Banff's rise and popularity, their reputedly therapeutic effects being of great appeal to Canada's ailing Victorian gentry.

Dr R G Brett, chief medical officer to the Canadian Pacific Railway, used his position to secure an immensely lucrative virtual monopoly on the best springs. In 1886 he constructed the Grandview Villa, a money-spinning sanitorium promising miracle cures and wonders such as "Ice cold temperance drinks". Its handrails were reinforced by crutches abandoned by "cured" patients, though the good doctor reputedly issued crutches to all-comers whether they needed them or not.

There may be quieter places in western Canada to take the waters, but hot springs always make for a mildly bizarre experience, and even if the crowds are a pain, the prices are hardly going to cripple you. The recently renovated **Cave and Basin Hot Springs** (daily June–Sept 9am–7pm; Oct–May 9am–5pm; $3) have a moderate (32°C) pool, although the original cave and spring that gave birth to the national park are now out of bounds to the hoi-polloi. The center is southwest of downtown on Cave Ave. If you're in this part of town, you could walk the paved **Sundance Canyon Trail** (3.7km) close to the springs (see box).

At 40°C, the **Upper Hot Springs** on Mountain Ave (daily, July–Sept 10am–11pm; otherwise noon–9pm; $3) are a steamier alternative, but they receive a lot of traffic from people coming off the Sulphur Mountain Gondola. They also leave a more pungent sulphurous aftersmell.

The museums

With some of the world's most spectacular mountains on your doorstep, sightseeing in Banff might seem an absurd undertaking, yet it's good to have some rainy-day options. The downtown **Banff Park Museum** on Banff Ave bulges with two

---

HIKING NEAR BANFF TOWNSITE

Walks from downtown

Banff Townsite is one of two obvious bases for walks in the park (the other is Lake Louise), and trails around the town cater to all levels of fitness. The best short stroll from **downtown** – at least for flora and fauna – is the **Fenland Trail**, a 1.5-kilometer loop west through the montane wetlands near the First Vermilion Lake (there are three Vermilion lakes, fragments of a huge lake that once probably covered the whole Bow Valley at this point: all can be accessed off Vermilion Lakes Drive). Marsh here is slowly turning to forest, creating habitats whose rushes and grasses provide a haven for wildlife. Ospreys and bald eagles nest around the lake, together with a wide range of other birds and waterfowl, and you may also see beaver, muskrat, perhaps even coyote, elk and other deer.

For a shorter walk, and a burst of spectacular white water, pound the **Bow Falls Trail** (1km) from beneath the bridge on the south side of the river, which follows the riverbank east to a powerful set of waterfalls and rapids just below the *Banff Springs Hotel*. The Hoodoos Trail on the other side of the river offers similar views with fewer people.

The **Marsh Loop Trail** (2km) from Cave Ave leads along a boardwalk through a marshy habitat renowned for its flora: warm waters from the Cave and Basin Hot Springs immediately above have created a small, anomalous area of lush vegetation. In winter Banff's own wolf pack has been known to hunt within sight of this trail. The **Sundance Canyon Trail** (3.7km), an easy stroll to the picnic area at the canyon mouth, also starts from close to the springs; you can extend your walk along the 2.1-kilometer loop path up through the canyon, past waterfalls, and back down a peaceful wooded trail.

Day hikes near Banff

Day hikes from the town center are limited – you usually need to head a few kilometers along the Trans-Canada or to the Sunshine Village gondola area to reach trailheads that leave the flat valley floor for the heart of the mountains. Only a couple of longish ones strike out directly from town: the **Spray River Circuit**, a

floors of stuffed animals, many of which are indigenous to the park (June–Sept daily 10am–6pm; Oct–March daily except Wed & Thurs 10am–6pm; April–May Mon–Fri 1–5pm, Sat & Sun 10am–6pm; free). Hunting of game animals was banned in the park in 1890, but not before populations of moose, elk, sheep, goats and grizzlies had been severely depleted. Game wardens only arrived to enforce the injunction in 1913, and even then they didn't protect the "bad" animals – wolves, coyotes, foxes, cougars, lynx, eagles, owls and hawks – which were hunted until the 1930s as part of the park's "predator-control program". Many of the formaldehyde victims in the museum date from this period. The lovely wood-panelled **reading room** – a snug retreat, full of magazines and books on nature and wildlife – makes a perfect spot to while away a cold afternoon. In summer, by contrast, the riverside **park** behind the museum is ideal for a snooze or picnic (people also unofficially sleep here at night – you might get away with a sleeping bag, but certainly not a tent).

The nearby **Whyte Museum of the Canadian Rockies** (May–Oct daily 10am–6pm; Nov–April Tues–Sun 1–5pm; ☎762-2291; $3) contents itself with a look at the Rockies' emergence as a tourist destination through paintings and

flat, thirteen-kilometer round trip past the *Banff Springs Hotel* up the Spray River; and the **Sulphur Mountain Trail**, a 5.5-kilometer switchback that climbs to the Sulphur Mountain gondola terminal.

Park wardens at the infocentre seem unanimous in rating the **Cory Pass Trail**, combined with the **Edith Pass Trail**, as the best day hike close to Banff. The trailhead is signed 6km west of the town off the Bow Valley Parkway, 500m after the junction with the Trans-Canada. The stiff climbing involved, however, and a couple of scree passages, mean that it's not for the inexperienced or faint-hearted. The rewards are fantastic, with varied walking, a high mountain environment and spine-tingling views. From the pass itself, you can return on the Edith Pass Trail (whose start you'll have passed 1km into the Cory Pass walk), to make a total loop of a demanding 13km.

Another popular local day hike, the trail to **Cascade Amphitheatre**, starts at Mount Norquay Ski Area, 6km north of the Trans-Canada up Mount Norquay Road. This offers a medley of landscapes, ranging from alpine meadows to deep, ice-scoured valleys and a close view of the knife-edge mountains that loom so tantalizingly above town. Allow about three hours for the 7.7-kilometer walk. For the same amount of effort, you could tackle **Elk Lake** from the ski area, though at 13.5km each way it's a long day's hike; some people turn it into an overnight by using the campground 2.5km short of Elk Lake. Shorter, but harder on the lungs, is the third of Banff's popular local walks, **C Level Cirque**, reached by a four-kilometer trail from the Upper Bankhead Picnic Area on the Lake Minnewanka road east of Banff. Elsewhere, the **Sunshine Meadows** area has five high trails of between 8km and 20km, all possible as day hikes and approached either from the Sunshine Gondola or its parking area, 18km southwest of Banff.

The best **backpacking** options lie in the **Egypt Lake** area west of Banff Townsite, with longer trails radiating from the lake's campground. Once you're in the backcountry around Banff, however, the combination of trails is virtually limitless. The keenest hikers tend to march the routes that lead from Banff to Lake Louise – the **Sawback Trail** and **Bow Valley Highline**, or the tracks in the Upper Spray and Bryant Creek Valley south of the townsite.

photographs, and at the early expeditions to explore and conquer the interior peaks. Pictures of bears foraging in Banff rubbish bins and of park rangers grinning over a magnificent lynx they've just shot give some idea of how times have changed. The gleaming new complex is also home to the 2075-volume *Alpine Club of Canada* library and the 4000-volume Archives of the Canadian Rockies – the largest collection of artistic and historical material relating to the mountains.

The **Natural History Museum**, 112 Banff Ave (daily, summer 10am–10pm, winter 10am–5pm; $2) is a rather throwaway private venture that concentrates on the Rockies' geological history, with a sketchy account of its forests, flowers and minerals.

Across the river, dated displays of native history, birds and animals fill the **Luxton Museum**, a native-run enterprise attractively housed in a huge wooden stockade (entrance on Birch; daily summer 9am–9pm, winter 9am–6pm; $3.75).

The Banff Springs Hotel

At $880 a night for a suite (plus $20 for any pets), the **Banff Springs Hotel** may be way out of your league, but you can't spend much time in town without coming across at least one mention of the place, and it's hard to miss its Gothic superstructure in the flesh. Initiated in 1888, it got off to a bad start, when the architect arrived to find the place being built 180 degrees out of kilter: while the kitchens enjoyed magnificent views over the river the guest rooms looked blankly into thick forest. When it finally opened, with a rotunda to improve the views, it was the world's largest hotel.

Today the 578-room luxury pile makes ends meet from busloads of Japanese tourists, and unless you're a fan of Victorian hotel architecture and its allied knick-knacks you can easily give the organized tours a miss. A voyeuristic hour or so, however, can be spent taking a coffee or beer in the second-floor café; prices for anything else are ludicrous.

Accommodation

It's almost impossible to turn up after midday in Banff during July and August and find a bed; pre-planning is essential. Anything that can be booked has usually been snapped up, and many visitors are forced to accept top-price places ($150 plus) or backtrack as far as Canmore or even Calgary to find space. The infocentre or the **central reservation service** may be able to dig something out at short notice, the latter for a fee (☎1-800/661-1676).

The *Private Home Accommodation List* at the infocentre lists **private rooms** and **bed and breakfasts**, but don't expect too much – they're among the first places to go each day. Most of the town's **motels** are on the spur from the Trans-Canada into town, and charge uncommonly high rates for basic lodgings – typically around $140 and up for doubles: we've tried to list those that stay *under* the $100 threshold. Off-season, rates are lower.

Campgrounds are not quite as bad, but even these generally fill up by 2 or 3pm in summer – especially the 23 excellent government campgrounds, which do not take reservations. In addition to the places listed below, less-developed sites are available along both the Bow and Icefields parkways to the north. The *Banff International Youth Hostel* (see below) can book you into any of southern Alberta's smaller hostels. Note that the *Spray River Hostel* is now closed, though it still appears in some literature.

HOTELS AND MOTELS

Bow Valley View Motor Lodge, 228 Bow Ave (☎762-2261 or 1-800/661-1565). Good views from some rooms. ④.

Bumper's Inn, Banff Ave & Marmot St (☎762-3386 or 1-800/661-3518). Not central, but well priced, and with 85 rooms (some with kitchenettes) you'll have a reasonable chance of finding space. ④.

Elkhorn Lodge, 124 Spray Ave (☎762-2299). Eight rooms at the southern end of the townsite. ③.

High Country Inn, 419 Banff Ave (☎762-2236 or 1-800/661-1244). Large mid-range motel. ④.

Holiday Inn Lodge, 311 Marten St (☎762-3648). Three reasonable rooms, two cabins. ④.

Homestead Inn, 217 Lynx St (☎762-4471 or 1-800/661-1021). Mid-priced 27-room motel. ④.

Irwin's Motor Inn, 429 Banff Ave (☎762-4566 or 1-800/661-1721). Low-priced motel. ④.

Red Carpet Inn, 425 Banff Ave (☎762-4184 or 1-800/563-4609). No-frills 46-room motel. ④.

Rimrock Resort, Mountain Ave (☎762-3356 or 1-800/661-1587). Forget the *Banff Springs Hotel* if you want to do Banff in style; come instead to this superlative and magnificently situated hotel – probably the finest in the Rockies. ⑦.

Spruce Grove Motel, 545 Banff Ave (☎762-2112). The least expensive motel in town. ③.

Voyager Inn, 555 Banff Ave (☎762-3301 or 1-800/372-9288). Motel with swimming pool, and sauna. ⑤.

Woodland Village Inn, 449 Banff Ave (☎762-8534). Around 20 rooms, including lofts for up to eight people. ④.

BED AND BREAKFAST

Banff Mountain B&B, c/o Don Findlay (July & Aug; ☎762-4636). Fifteen rooms (four with private bath) in quiet rural setting within walking distance of downtown. ③.

Blue Mountain Lodge, c/o Simpson, 137 Muskrat St (☎762-5134). Ten central rooms and two cabins in central turn-of-the-century Banff landmark building. ③.

Cascade Court, 133 Spray Ave, near *Banff Springs Hotel* (☎762-2956). Two rooms with good mountain views; ten minutes' walk from town. ③.

The Holiday Lodge, 311 Marten St (☎762-3648). Seven central rooms (two with private bath); five are cabins with kitchenettes. ②

L'Auberge des Rocheurs, 402 Squirrel St (☎762-9269). Three quiet central rooms, nice views and "European" hospitality and ownership. ④.

Mrs Cowan's, 118 Otter St (☎762-3696). Nine B&B rooms with private or shared bathrooms and continental breakfast. ①–②.

Rocky Mountain B&B, c/o Kruger, 223 Otter St (☎762-4811). Eleven B&B rooms with kitchenettes and private baths just three blocks from downtown; laundry. ②–④.

Tan-Y-Bryn, c/o Cowan, 118 Otter St (☎762-3696). Eight of Banff's least expensive rooms (shared bath) in an old home on a quiet residential street three blocks short of downtown. ②.

HOSTELS

Banff International Youth Hostel, Tunnel Mountain Rd (CHA; ☎762-4122, or 237-8282 direct from Calgary). Modern 154-bed place, a 2-km slog from downtown – take the *Banff Explorer Bus* from Banff Ave in summer. Friendly staff and excellent facilities. The infoboard is a good source of advice and ride offers. Good meals available all day in the *Café Alpenglow*. Four-bed dorms cost $16 for members, $19 for non-members. ①.

Banff YWCA, 102 Spray Ave (☎762-3560). More convenient than the youth hostel – cross the river south of town and it's the first building on the left. Open to men and women, with plenty of clinically clean rooms, but they go quickly; singles $51, doubles $57, bunks $17 (bring your own sleeping bag, or rent blankets). Downstairs café has good food. ①–③.

CAMPGROUNDS

Tunnel Mountain Village I, 3km from town and 1km beyond the hostel on Tunnel Mountain Rd. Huge 622-pitch government-operated campground, the nearest to downtown, on the *Banff Explorer* bus from Banff Ave. Electricity and showers. Nearby *Tunnel Mountain Trailer Court* is reserved for RVs. *Village I* closes on Oct 1, but the nearby 223-site *Tunnel Mountain Village II*, 2.5km from town, remains open to provide walk-in winter camping. All three sites are set amid trees, with lovely views, plenty of space and short trails close at hand. Bighorn sheep, elk, and even the odd bear may drop in. From $9.50.

Two Jack Main, 13km northeast of town on Lake Minnewanka Rd. Semi-serviced 381-site park campground open May to early Sept; no showers.

Two Jack Lakeside, 12km northeast of town on the Lake Minnewanka Rd. Fully serviced 77-site park-run campground with showers; open May to early Sept.

Eating and drinking

Banff's scores of tourist **restaurants** run the gamut from Japanese and other ethnic cuisines to nouvelle-frontier grub. If your funds are limited, the *Banff Youth Hostel* and the *YWCA* cafeterias are probably the best value, while Banff Avenue is lined with good little spots for coffee and snacks, many with pleasant outdoor tables. Given Banff's huge number of summer travellers and large seasonal workforce, there are plenty of people around in summer looking for night-time action.

To stock up if you're camping, use the big *Safeway* supermarket at 318 Marten St and Elk (daily 9am–10pm), just off Banff Ave a block down from Wolf St.

Aardvarks, 304 Wolf St. Popular pizza place that gets frantic after the bars have closed (closed Sun).

Balkan Village, 120 Banff Ave. Greek outlet, renowned for big portions and belly dancing on Tues in the winter to whip things up; in summer the place turns raucous on its own, with frequent impromptu navel displays from well-oiled customers.

Barbary Coast, upstairs at 119 Banff Ave. Excellent food – pizza, steaks, burgers and salads – at good prices: the restaurant at the back is loaded with sporting memorabilia, and the highly popular bar at the front, open to 2am, also does food (occasional live music). The entrance, note, is in the mall at 119, Banff Ave.

Cake Company, 220 Bear St. Café with the usual muffins, coffee, pastries and light meals.

Edy's Back Alley, corner of Caribou and Banff Ave. The hippest (and loudest) place in town for nightlife – basement bar, food, pool and music.

Evelyn's, 201 Banff Ave (corner of Caribou). One of the best places on the strip for breakfast; excellent range of coffees.

Joe Btfspk's Diner *(sic)*, 221 Banff Ave. Tries a touch too hard to evoke period feel – all red vinyl chairs and vivid black and white floors – but it still does excellent, if slightly overpriced, food; you may have to wait at peak times.

Le Beaujolais, corner of Banff Ave and Buffalo St (☎762-2712). One of western Canada's better and more expensive restaurants. Reservations recommended.

Melissa's, 218 Lynx St. Probably Banff's most popular daytime destination, set in an old log cabin: big breakfasts, superlative *mignon* steaks, salads and burgers, plus an upstairs bar for a leisurely drink, and a summer patio for food and beer in the sun. Definitely recommended.

Rose and Crown, 202 Banff Ave. Part of a chain, combining a moderately successful pub atmosphere (darts, mock-Victorian interior) with a family-oriented restaurant. Food is of the pub-lunch variety and you can shake a leg in the adjoining nightclub and disco.

Silver City, 110 Banff Ave. Very popular bar, with dancing and live music on Friday and Saturday evenings; younger crowd than the *Rose and Crown* and *Edy's*.

Wild Bill's Legendary Saloon, 203 Banff Ave. Tex-Mex food and vegetarian dishes in the restaurant (family-oriented until 8pm); doubles as a lively bar; live entertainment six nights weekly; pool hall and games room.

Listings

Ambulance ☎762-2433.

American Express 130 Banff Ave (☎762-3207).

Bike rental *Park'n'Pedal*, 226 Bear St (☎762-3191); *Peak Experience*, 209 Bear St (☎762-0581).

Bus information 100 Gopher St (☎762-6767).

Camping equipment Rental tents etc from *Sports Rent*, 208 Bear St (☎762-8222).

Car rental *Avis*, Cascade Plaza, Wolf St (☎762-3222); *Budget*, 204 Buffalo St (☎762-2586).

Foreign exchange *Bank of America Canada*, 124 Banff Ave; *Currency Exchange* at 108 Banff Ave (Clock Tower Mall) and 317 Banff Ave (Cascade Plaza).

Hospital *Mineral Springs Hospital*, 301 Lynx St (☎762-2222).

Laundry *Cascade Plaza Coin Laundry*, 317 Banff Ave; *Laundry Company*, 203 Caribou St.

Pharmacy *Harmony Drug*, 111 Banff Ave; *Gourlay's*, 229 Bear St (Wolf & Bear Mall).

Police ☎762-2226.

Post office 204 Buffalo St (Mon–Fri 9am–5.30pm).

Taxis *Alpine* (☎762-3727); *Banff* (☎762-4444); *Mountain* (☎762-3351); *Taxi-Taxi* (☎762-3111).

Trail conditions ☎ 762-1550.

Weather ☎762-4707 or 762-2088 (24-hour recording).

Highway 1 and the Bow Valley Parkway

Two roads run parallel through the Bow Valley from Banff to Lake Louise (60km): the faster **Highway 1** (the Trans-Canada), and the quieter **Bow Valley Parkway**, on the other (north) side of the river, opened in 1989 as a special scenic route. After Banff, there's only one link between the two roads, at Castle Junction, 30km from Lake Louise. Both routes, needless to say, are staggeringly beautiful, as the mountains start to creep closer to the road. For the entire run the **Bow River**, broad and emerald green, crashes through rocks and forest, looking as close to one's image of a "mighty river" as it's possible to get. Despite the tarmac and heavy summer traffic, the surroundings are pristine and suggest the immensity of the wilderness to come. Sightings of elk and deer are common, particularly around dawn and sundown, and occasionally you'll spot moose.

Highway 1

Most people tend either to cruise Hwy 1's rapid stretch of the Trans-Canada without stopping – knowing that the road north of Lake Louise is more spectacular still – or leap out at every trail and rest stop, overcome with the grandeur of it all. On *Greyhound* or *Brewster* **buses** you're whisked through to Lake Louise in about forty minutes; if you're **driving**, try for the sake of wildlife to stick to the 90kph speed limit. The vast fences that march for kilometer after kilometer along this section of the road are designed to protect animals, not only from traffic, but from the brainless visitors who clamber out of their cars to get close to the bears occasionally glimpsed on the road. You won't have to be in the Rockies long during the summer before you're caught in a **bear jam**, when people – contrary to all park laws, never mind common sense – abandon their cars helter-skelter on the road to pursue hapless animals with cameras and camcorders.

The Bow Valley Parkway

The **Bow Valley Parkway** boasts if anything more scenic grandeur than the Trans-Canada, and offers more distractions if you're taking your time: several

---

BOW VALLEY TRAILS

Five major trails branch off the **Bow Valley Parkway**. The best short walk is the **Johnston Canyon Trail** (2.7km each way), an incredibly engineered path to a series of spray-veiled waterfalls. From the upper falls you can continue on to the seven cold-water springs of the **Ink Pots**, for a total distance of 5.8km. Another short possibility is the **Castle Crags Trail** (3.7km each way) from the signed pull-off 5km west of Castle Junction. Short but steep, and above treeline, this walk offers superlative views across the Bow Valley and the mountains beyond. Allow ninety minutes one way to take account of the stiff climb.

The best day hike is to **Rockbound Lake** (8.4km each way), a steepish climb with wild lakeland scenery at the end; allow at least two and a half hours one way. The other trails – Baker Creek (20.3km) and Pulsatilla Pass (17.1km) – serve to link backpackers with the thick network of paths in the Slate Range northeast of Lake Louise.

The two stand-out trails along **Hwy 1** are the trek to **Bourgeau Lake** (7.5km one way), which starts from a parking area 10km west of Banff – allow two and a half to three hours for the ascent – and the long day hike to **Shadow Lake** (14.3km each way), where a campground in one of the Rockies' more impressive sub-alpine basins gives access to assorted onward trails. The main trail starts from the Redearth Creek parking area 20km west of Banff (allow four hours).

---

trails, campgrounds, plus plenty of accommodation options. The largest concentration of sightseers is likely to be found at the Merrent pull-off, enjoying fantastic views of the Bow Valley and the railway winding through the mountains.

Three **lodges** are spaced equally en route, and though expensive, they may have room when Lake Louise's hotels are stretched. First is the *Johnston Canyon Resort*, 26km west of Banff (mid-May to late Sept; ☎762-2971; ③), 41 rustic cabins (some with fire and kitchenette), a shop, garage, pool and basic groceries. Next come the 21 chalets, laundry and grocery store of *Castle Mountain Village*, 32km west of Banff near Castle Junction (year-round; ☎762-3868; ④), and finally *Baker Creek Chalets*, 12km east of Lake Louise (year-round; ☎522-3761; ④–⑥), with log cabins and a good restaurant. Much the least expensive possibility is the parkway's charming **youth hostel**, *Castle Mountain Hostel*, 1.5km east of Castle Junction (year-round; closed Wed; ☎762-2367; $9). All year, you should try to call, or better still book ahead through the hostel at Banff.

Three national park **campgrounds** provide excellent retreats: *Johnston Canyon* (mid-May to mid-Sept; $7.25) is the best equipped, but still doesn't have showers; after that comes *Castle Mountain*, near Castle Junction (late June to early Sept; $7.25), and *Protection Mountain*, 5km north of Castle Junction (same details).

Lake Louise

The Banff park's other main center, **Lake Louise**, is very different to Banff – less a town than two distinct artificial resorts. The first is a small mall of shops and hotels just off the Trans-Canada known as **Lake Louise Village**. The second is the lake itself, the self-proclaimed "gem of the Rockies" and – despite its crowds and monster hotel – a sight you have to see. A third area, **Moraine Lake**, 13km south of the village, has almost equally staggering scenery and several magnificent trails. Lake Louise is 4.5km from the village on the winding Lake Louise Drive –

or, if you're walking, 2.7km on the uphill Louise Creek Trail, 4.5km via the Tramline Trail. You're better off saving the walking for around the lake, however, and taking a taxi (around $8) from the village (if anything, save the two linking trails for coming down from the lake). All three areas remain engulfed with visitors all year round; in winter people pile in for Canada's best powder **skiing**.

You may not find the prospect of staying here, at least near the lakes, all that appealing, though the lodge at Moraine Lake makes a dream treat. None the less, the mountains around offer almost unparalleled **hiking country** and the park's most popular day-use area. You'll have to weigh awesome scenery against the sheer numbers, however, for these are some of the most heavily used trails on the continent – 50,000-plus people in summer – though longer backpacking routes lead quickly away to the quieter spots.

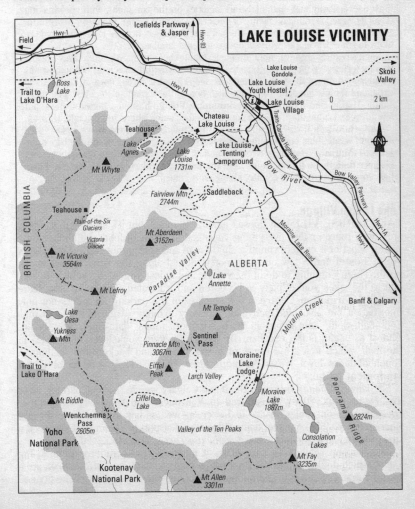

LAKE LOUISE VICINITY

WINTER IN THE ROCKIES

Six major **winter resorts** are found in the Rockies – two in Kananaskis Country, two around Banff, and one each near Lake Louise and Jasper. Along with Whistler in British Columbia, these are some of the best, the most popular and the fastest-growing areas in Canada – and not only for downhill and cross-country but also for dog-sledding, ice climbing, skating, snowmobiling, snowshoeing, canyon crawling and ice fishing. At most resorts, the **season** runs from mid-December until the end of May; conditions are usually at their best in March, when the days are getting warmer and longer, and the snow is deepest. Resort **accommodation** is hardest to come by during Christmas week, the mid-February school holidays and at Easter.

Nakiska, 25km south of the Trans-Canada Highway in Kananaskis Country, is Canada's newest resort. Developed for the 1988 Winter Olympics, it's one of the most user-friendly and state-of-the-art facilities on the continent, with snowmaking on all its varied terrain and plenty of fine cross-country skiing. **Fortress Mountain**, 15km south of Nakiska on Hwy 40, is a much smaller, homier area where you're likely to share the slopes with school groups and families.

Banff's resorts are invariably the busiest and most expensive, and heavily patronized by foreigners (especially Japanese). **Mount Norquay** has long been known as an advanced downhill area – "steep and deep" in local parlance – but has recently expanded its intermediate runs, and also boasts the Canadian Rockies' only night skiing. Higher and more exposed, **Sunshine Village** has even better scenery but few advanced runs; there's also a popular nordic center where you can take lessons.

Lake Louise's three big hills add up to Canada's most extensive resort, with downhill skiing, plus cross-country trails criss-crossing the valley and the lake area. Jasper's **Marmot Basin** is a more modest downhill area, but it's quieter and cheaper than those further south, and the park, particularly around Maligne Lake, has almost limitless cross-country skiing possibilities.

Lake Louise Village

LAKE LOUISE VILLAGE doesn't amount to much, but it's an essential supply stop, with more or less everything you need in terms of food and shelter (at a price). Most of it centers round a single mall and parking lot, with a brand-new **youth hostel** and a few outlying motels dotted along the service road to the north. There's nothing to do in the village, and unless you have a vehicle to take you to the lakes you're likely to be bored and frustrated. The smart new **Lake Louise Information Centre**, a few steps from the parking lot, offers not only information but also high-tech natural-history exhibits (daily mid-June to mid-Sept 8am–8pm, 8am–10pm in high summer; winter 9am–5pm; ☎522-3833). Almost as useful is the excellent *Woodruff and Blum* bookstore (☎522-3842) in the mall, which has a full range of **maps**, guides and background reading. A couple of doors down, *Wilson Mountain Sports* (☎522-3636) is good for **bike and equipment rental**.

Six daily *Greyhound* **buses** to Banff and Calgary stop in the mall parking lot at *The Depot* (☎522-2080); three head to Vancouver and the west. In summer *Brewster* runs one daily service to Jasper, as well as bus tours. *Pacific Western Coaches* (☎762-4558) connect daily with Calgary airport in summer. If you need a **taxi** to ferry you to the lakes, call *Lake Louise Taxi & Tours* (☎522-2020).

The Samson Mall takes care of most practical considerations. Behind *The Depot*, which doubles up as the **post office** (daily 6.30am–7pm; ☎522-3870), are a **laundromat** (☎522-2143) and public washrooms with hot showers. The general

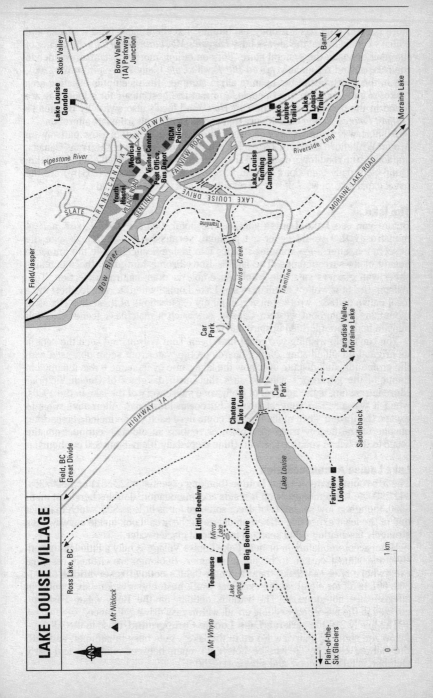

LAKE LOUISE VILLAGE

Skoki Valley

Bow Valley, (1A) Parkway Junction

Banff

Lake Louise Gondola

Pipestone River

TRANS-CANADA HIGHWAY

Medical Clinic

Youth Hostel

Visitor Center

Post Office, Bus Depot

RCM Police

FAIRVIEW ROAD

VILLAGE ROAD

SENTINEL

SLATE

Field/Jasper

Bow River

LAKE LOUISE DRIVE

Lake Louise Tenting Campground

Lake Louise Trailer

Lake Louise Trailer

Riverside Loop

Moraine Lake

Tramline

Louise Creek

MORAINE LAKE ROAD

Tramline

Car Park

Paradise Valley, Moraine Lake

HIGHWAY 1A

Field, BC Great Divide

Ross Lake, BC

Chateau Lake Louise

Car Park

Saddleback

Lake Louise

Fairview Lookout

Little Beehive

Mirror Lake

Teahouse

Big Beehive

Lake Agnes

▲ Mt Niblock

▲ Mt Whyte

Plain-of-the-Six Glaciers

0   1 km

store is good (and has a **money exchange**). Excellent basic **food** – snacks and coffee – can be had at the always busy *Laggan's Mountain Bakery*, on the corner of the mall opposite the general store. For something more substantial, wander to the relaxed and reasonably priced *Bill Peyto's Café* (daily 7am–9pm; ☎522-2200), within the youth hostel but open to all; in summer, the nice outdoor eating area makes a good place to meet people. Some of the best meals for a long way are found in the dining room of the *Post Hotel*, and locals also swear by the hotel's *Outpost Lounge*, a snug bar with fire that serves light meals from late afternoon.

A short way from the village, the **Lake Louise Gondola** runs partway up Mount Whitehorn (2669m). To reach it return to and cross over the Trans-Canada, and follow the road towards the ski area; the gondola is signed left after about 1km (June–Sept daily 9am–6pm; $7 return, $5 one way). At the top (2034m) are the usual expansive views, self-service restaurant, and several trailheads.

The lake

Before you see **Lake Louise** you see the hotel: *Chateau Lake Louise*, a 1924 monstrosity that would never get planning permission today. Yet, despite the desecration, after a few minutes it fades into insignificance beside the immense beauty of its surroundings. The lake is Kodachrome turquoise, the mountains sheer, the glaciers vast; the whole ensemble is utter natural perfection. Tom Wilson, the first white Canadian to see Lake Louise when he was led here by a local native in 1882, wrote "I never, in all my explorations of these five chains of mountains throughout western Canada, saw such a matchless scene . . . I felt puny in body, but glorified in spirit and soul."

You can't help wishing you could have been Tom Wilson, and seen the spot in its original unsullied state. Notice-boards on the waterfront seem obsessed with the profoundly dull dispute over how the lake came by its name – was it named in honor of the governor's wife, or after the fourth daughter of Queen Victoria? More interesting is the account of Hollywood's discovery of the lake in the 1920s, when it was used to suggest "exotic European locations". Alternative ways to escape the throng – two million people come here each year – include embarking on one of the nearby trails (see box), or renting an old-style **canoe** from the office to the left as you face the lake (June–Sept daily 10am–8pm; $20 per hour).

Lake Louise Accommodation

The 515-room **Chateau Lake Louise** (booking essential ☎522-3511 or 1-800/268-9411; ⑤–⑧) has a monopoly on lakeside accommodation: doubles here cost up to $550, though in low season (Oct–Dec) some go for as little as $95, which makes it one of the least expensive off-season places in the area. Look inside anyway – it's strangely fascinating – and snaffle a free cup of glacier water.

Hotel accommodation in or near Lake Louise Village is only a little less expensive, and almost certain to be full in summer. Bookings are virtually essential everywhere (you can make them through Banff's **central reservations** on ☎1-800/661-1676, for a fee); at the excellent youth hostel reservations six months in advance are not unusual. The various options on the Bow Valley Parkway, covered in the preceding section, are all within easy driving distance.

The lovely 216-site park-run **Lake Louise Campground**, close to the village – follow the signs off Fairview Rd up to the lake – gets busy in summer, and with the railway close by, it can be noisy. It's open between mid-May and early October, is fully serviced, and sites cost $9.50.

HIKES AROUND LAKE LOUISE

All the Lake Louise trails are busy in summer, but they're good for a short taste of the scenery. The two most popular end at tea houses – mountain chalets selling welcome snacks. The **Lake Agnes Trail** (3.4km), said to be the most-walked path in the Rockies, strikes off from the right (north) shore of the lake immediately past the hotel. It's a gradual climb, relieved by ever more magnificent views, and a tea house beautifully situated beside mountain-cradled Lake Agnes; allow one to two hours. Beyond the tea house you can continue on the right side of the lake and curve left around its head to climb to an easily reached pass. Here a 200-meter stroll to the left brings you to **Big Beehive**, an incredible eyrie. Almost as rewarding is the one-kilometer trail from the tea house to **Little Beehive**, a mite lower, but still privy to full-blown panoramas over the broad sweep of the Bow Valley.

Stronger walkers can return to the pass from Big Beehive and turn left to follow the steep trail down to intersect another trail; turning right leads west through rugged and increasingly barren scenery to the second tea house at the **Plain of the Six Glaciers**. Alternatively, the more monotonous **Six Glaciers Trail** leads from the hotel along the lakeshore to the same point (5.3km to the tea house).

The main appeal of the last local walk, the less used **Saddleback Trail** (3.7km one way), is that it provides access to the fine viewpoint of **Fairview Mountain**. Allow from one to two hours to Saddleback itself; the trail to the summit of Fairview strikes off right from here. Even if you don't make the last push, the Saddleback views – across to the 1200-meter wall of Mount Temple – are staggering.

The Skoki Valley

The **Skoki Valley** region east of Lake Louise offers fewer day hikes; to enjoy it you'll need a tent to overnight at any of the six campgrounds. The main access trail initially follows a gravel road forking off to the right of the Lake Louise Ski Area, off Hwy 1. Many people hike as far as **Boulder Pass**, 8.6km and 640m ascent from the parking area, as a day trip and return the same way instead of pushing on to the lodge, 8km beyond. Various well-signposted long and short trails from the lodge or the campgrounds are documented in the *Canadian Rockies Trail Guide*.

Canadian Alpine Centre and International Youth Hostel, on Village Rd just north of the mall across the river (☎522-2200). A magnificent and immensely popular new 110-bed year-round hostel run jointly with the *Canadian Alpine Club*. Reservations require the first night's fee as a **deposit** (credit card bookings accepted). 20 percent of beds are set aside for walk-ins each day (be there at the crack of dawn). 4- and 6-bed dorms cost $15 members, $20 non-members; ten double rooms. ①.

Castle Mountain Youth Hostel, 1.5km east of Castle Junction on Hwy 93 S (☎762-4122). Conveniently situated for the Bow Valley Parkway and its trails. Closed Wed off-season; dorm beds $9. ①.

Deer Lodge, on Lake Louise Drive (☎522-3747 or 1-800/661-1595). Less expensive of two downmarket alternatives to *Chateau Lake Louise* within walking distance of the lake. ⑤.

Lake Louise Inn, just north of the village mall to the right (☎522-3791 or 1-800/661-9237). The least expensive of the village hotels. ③–⑥.

Mountaineer Lodge, 101 Village Rd (☎522-3844). 80 rooms, May–Oct only. ⑤–⑦.

Paradise Lodge and Bungalows, on the Lake Louise Drive a short walk from Lake Louise (☎522-3595). Pricier of the near-lake alternatives to *Chateau Lake Louise*. Off-season rates. Mid-May to mid-Oct only. ⑥.

Post Hotel, Village Rd (☎522-3989 or 1-800/661-1586). The top hotel in the village, with a noted restaurant and bar – see p.402. ⑤–⑧.

Moraine Lake

Not quite so many people as visit Lake Louise make the thirteen-kilometer road journey to **Moraine Lake**, which is smaller than its neighbor but in many ways its scenic
superior. It also holds one of the most enticing and magnificently executed **hotels** in
the entire Rockies: if you're on honeymoon, or just want to push the boat out once,
splash out on a night or two in the *Moraine Lake Lodge* (June–Sept; ☎522-3733 or
1-800/661-8340; ⑥), a sympathetically landscaped collection of high-quality cabins. It
boasts a friendly staff and great privacy, for prices on a par with decidedly more lack-
lustre hotels in the village and near Lake Louise.

Bar the *Lodge*, its good little café and top-notch restaurant, nothing disturbs the
lake and its matchless surroundings. Until recently the scene graced the back of
Canadian $20 bills, though the illustration did little justice to the shimmering
water and the jagged, snow-covered peaks on the eastern shore that inspired the
nickname "Valley of the Ten Peaks". The peaks are now officially christened the
Wenkchemna, after the Stoney native word for "ten".

The lake, half the size of Lake Louise, is the most vivid **turquoise** imaginable.
Like Lake Louise and other big Rockies' lakes (notably Peyto on the Icefields
Parkway), the peacock blue is caused by fine particles of glacial silt, or till, known
as **rock flour**. Meltwater in June and July washes this powdered rock into the
lake, the minute but uniform particles of flour absorbing all colors of incoming
light except those in the blue-green spectrum. When the lakes have just melted in
May and June – and are still empty of silt – their color is a more normal sky blue.
You can admire the lake by walking along the east shore, from above by clambering over the great glacial moraine dam near the lodge, or from one of the **canoes
for rent** on the right just beyond the lodge and parking lot. For the best overall
perspective, however, tackle the switchback trail through the forest on the east
shore (see box).

The Icefields Parkway

The splendor of the **Icefields Parkway** (Hwy 93) can hardly be overstated: a
230-kilometer road from Lake Louise to Jasper through the heart of the Rockies,
it ranks as one of the world's ultimate drives. Its unending succession of huge
peaks, lakes and forests – capped by the stark grandeur of the Columbia Icefield
– is absolutely overwhelming. Fur traders and natives who used the route as far
back as 1800 christened it the "Wonder Trail", though the present highway only
opened in 1940 as part of a Depression-era public works program. Although about
a million people a year experience what the park blurb calls a "window on the
wilderness", for the most part you can go your own way in relative serenity.

At about its midway point the Icefields Parkway crosses from Banff into Jasper
National Park; you might turn back here, but the divide is almost completely arbitrary, and the parkway is impossible to treat as anything but a self-contained
whole, as we do here. Distances in brackets are from Lake Louise, which is virtually the only way to locate places on the road, though everything mentioned is
clearly marked off the highway by distinctive brown-green national park signs.

Access, information and planning

Tourist literature often misleadingly implies that the Icefields Parkway is highly
developed. In fact, the wilderness is extreme, with snow often closing the road
from October onwards, and there are only two points for **services**, at

HIKING: MORAINE LAKE AND PARADISE VALLEY

Moraine Lake

Each of the four basic routes in the Moraine Lake area is easily accomplished in a day, two with sting-in-the-tail additions if you want added exertion; all start from the lake, which lies at the end of Moraine Lake Road.

The easiest is the 1-kilometer amble along the lakeshore – hardly a walk at all – followed by the 2.9-kilometer stroll to **Consolation Lakes**, an hour's trip that may be busy but can provide some respite from the frenzy at Moraine Lake itself. This almost level walk ends with lovely views of a small mountain-circled lake. If you're tenting, fairly fit, or can arrange a pick-up, the highline Panorama Ridge Trail branches off the trail (signed "Taylor Lake") to run 22km to the Banff–Radium highway 7km west of Castle Junction.

The most popular walk (start as early as possible) is the **Larch Valley–Sentinel Pass Trail**, which sets off from the lake's north shore 100m beyond the lodge. A stiffish hairpin climb through forest on a broad track, with breathtaking views of the lake through the trees, brings you to a trail junction after 2.4km. Most hikers branch right, where the track levels off to emerge into Larch Valley, broad alpine upland with stands of larch (glorious in late summer and fall, as they turn) and majestic views of the encircling peaks. If you have the legs, push on to Sentinel Pass ahead, in all some two hours' walk above Moraine Lake. This is the highest point reached by a major trail in the Canadian Rockies. You can see what you're in for from the meadows – but not the airy views down into Paradise Valley from the crest of the pass. You could even continue down into Paradise Valley, a tough, scree-filled descent, and complete a superlative day's walk by picking up the valley loop (see below) back to the Moraine Lake Road.

The third option, the less walked **Eiffel Lake–Wenkchemna Pass Trail**, follows the climb from the lake as for the Larch Valley path before branching off left at the 2.4km junction. It's equally sound, virtually level, and if anything has the better scenery in the stark, glaciated grandeur to be found at the head of the Valley of the Ten Peaks. Eiffel Lake is 5.6km (allow 2–3hr) from Moraine Lake, and you don't need to go much further than the rock pile and clump of trees beyond the lake to get the best out of the walk. Ahead of you, however, a slightly rougher track continues through bleak terrain to **Wenkchemna Pass**, clearly visible 4km beyond. Having got this far, it's tempting to push on, the added climb just about worth it if lungs and weather are holding out, for the still broader views back down the Valley of the Ten Peaks. The views beyond the pass itself, however, over the Great Divide into Yoho and Kootenay parks, are disappointing.

Paradise Valley

In 1894, the mountaineer Walter Wilcox deemed **Paradise Valley** an appropriate name for "a valley of surpassing beauty, wide and beautiful, with alternating open meadows and rich forests". North of Moraine Lake, it's accessed via Moraine Lake Road about 3km from its junction with Lake Louise Drive. The walk here is a straightforward hike up one side of the valley and down the other, a loop of 18km with a modest vertical gain. Most people take in the **Lake Annette** diversion for its unmatched view of Mount Temple's 1200-meter north face (unclimbed until 1966), and many overnight at the **campground** at the head of the valley (9km from the parking area), though this is one of the busiest sites in the park. Others toughen the walk by throwing in the climb up to Sentinel Pass on the ridge south of the valley, which gives the option of continuing down the other side to connect with the Moraine Lake trails (see above).

Saskatchewan Crossing (the one place campers can stock up with groceries, 77km from Lake Louise), where the David Thompson Highway (Hwy 11) branches off for Red Deer, and at the Columbia Icefield (127km).

Though ideally you should give yourself at least three days to explore the various trails that lead off the Icefields Parkway, many are extremely short, and even allowing a day to drive the road gives you time to stop off at the half a dozen or so essential sights. Five **youth hostels** (four open year-round) and twelve excellent park **campgrounds** (two year-round) are spaced along the parkway at regular intervals. If you want more comfort, you'll have to overnight at Banff, Lake Louise or Jasper, as the only other **accommodation** – invariably booked solid – are hotels at Bow Lake, Saskatchewan Crossing, the Columbia Icefield and Sunwapta Falls. *Brewster Transportation* runs several tours and a single scheduled **bus** daily in both directions between Banff and Jasper from late May to mid-October; services at either end of the season are often weather-affected ($40 single). A word with the driver will usually get you dropped off at hostels and trailheads en route. If you're **cycling**, note that most people travel from Jasper to Banff – the grades are far more favorable – and that bikes can be rented in Jasper for one-way trips.

Between Lake Louise and the Columbia Icefield

The following are the must-sees and must-dos along the 122-kilometer stretch from Lake Louise to the Columbia Icefield: best view – Peyto Lake; best lake walk – Bow Lake; best waterfalls – Panther–Bridal Falls; best short walk – Parker Ridge. Temptations for longer walks are numerous, and the difficulty, as ever, is knowing which to choose.

The first **youth hostel** north of Lake Louise is *Mosquito Creek* (28km), a single log cabin which sleeps 38 and has basic food supplies and a wood-fired sauna (year-round; closed Tues; no phone; reservations ☎762-4122; $8). Slightly beyond is the first **campground**, *Mosquito Creek* (mid-June to mid-Sept; 32 sites; $8) and one of the parkway's two winter campgrounds (walk-in only; free after mid-Sept). Two hikes start from here: **Molar Pass** (9.8km; 3hr), a manageable day-trip with good views, and **Upper Fish Lake** (14.8km; 5hr), which follows the Molar Pass

---

HOSTEL SHUTTLE SERVICE

The *Pika Shuttle Co Ltd* (☎1-800/363-0096 in BC and Alberta) run an extremely useful daily shuttle service, connecting all thirteen youth hostels between (and including) Calgary, Banff and Jasper – including all the places on the Icefields Parkway and beyond. Typical fares are $47 for Calgary to *Whistler's* (Jasper), the longest possible journey, and $15 for the trip between Lake Louise and *Hilda Creek* hostel near the Columbia Icefield. Extra fees are payable for bikes, canoes and other cargo.

To take the shuttle, contact *Banff International Hostel* (☎762-4122) no later than 6pm the day before your desired departure with full details of your journey. Once the hostel has confirmed your booking, buy a ticket from any participating Alberta hostel, confirming the shuttle's departure time at the time of purchase. From hostels with phones, use the toll-free number to make reservations; at those without, reservations can be made through the manager. **Stand-by** tickets may be bought from the van driver at departure, subject to availability. **All passengers must have reservations at their destination hostel**.

trail for 7km before branching off and crossing the superb alpine meadows of North Molar Pass.

From the *Num-Ti-Jah Lodge* access road just beyond (37km), a great short trail sets off to **Bow Lake** and **Bow Glacier Falls** (4.3km; 1–2hr), taking in the flats around Bow Lake and climbing to some immense cliffs and several huge waterfalls beyond. The *Num-Ti-Jah Lodge*, just off the road, is one of the most famous old-fashioned lodges in the Rockies; be sure to book (May–Sept; ☎522-2167; ⑤). Another 3km up the road, just after Bow Summit (the highest point crossed by any Canadian highway), is the unmissable twenty-minute stroll to **Peyto Lake Lookout**, one of the finest vistas in the Rockies. The panorama only unfolds in the last few seconds, giving a genuinely breathtaking view of the vivid emerald lake far below; mountains and forest stretch away as far as you can see.

After 57km you reach the *Waterfowl Lake* **campground** (mid-June to mid-Sept; 116 sites; $8) and the **Chephren Lake Trail** (3.5km; 1hr), which leads to quietly spectacular scenery with a minimum of effort. **SASKATCHEWAN CROSSING** (77km) is the lowest point on the road before the icefields; the descent from Bow Summit brings you from the high subalpine ecoregion into a montane environment with its own vegetation and wildlife. Largely free of snow, the area is a favorite winter range for mountain goats, bighorn sheep and members of the deer family. The bleak settlement itself offers expensive food, petrol, spectacularly tacky gift shop and the 66-room **hotel-restaurant** *Crossing* (early March to mid-Nov; ☎761-7000; ④).

Twelve kilometers north are the *Rampart Creek* 30-bed **youth hostel**, with "the best sauna in the Rockies" (daily June–Oct; Sat & Sun rest of year with reservations, ☎439-3139; basic food store; no phone; $8), and 50-pitch **campground** (late June to early Sept; $8). The last of the Banff National Park campgrounds is the tiny 16-pitch *Cirrus Mountain* site at the 103km mark (late June to early Sept; $8). Shortly before the spectacular **Panther Falls** (113.5km) the road makes a huge hairpin climb (the so-called "Big Hill"), to open up yet more panoramic angles on the vast mountain spine stretching back towards Lake Louise.

The unmarked and often slippery 1-kilometer trail to the falls starts from the lower end of the second of two parking lots on the right. Beyond it (117km) is the trailhead to **Parker Ridge** (2.4km one way), which commands fantastic views from the summit ridge of the Saskatchewan Glacier (at 9km long the Rockies' longest). If you're only going to do one walk out of the car, make it this one – though it gets cold and windy up here, so be sure to take extra clothing. Ideally placed for this area and the Columbia Icefield 9km north – and therefore invariably busy – is the *Hilda Creek* **youth hostel** (reservations ☎439-3139; ①) 1km beyond. The setting is stunning, and accommodation (for 21) is in cozy log cabins.

The Columbia Icefield

Covering an area of 325 square kilometers, the **Columbia Icefield** is the largest collection of ice and snow in the entire Rockies. This definitive **glacier** territory holds thirteen of the thirty highest peaks in the range, including the second highest, Mount Athabasca (not visible from the road), and is one of the few Rockies icefields to be visible from a highway, with three of its six major glaciers – the Athabasca, Dome and Stutfield – within sight of the Icefields Parkway.

The busy park-run **Icefield Centre** (daily mid-June to Aug 10am–7pm, mid-May to mid-June & first two weeks of Sept 10am–5pm) provides an eerie viewpoint for the most prominent of these, the Athabasca Glacier, as well as offering information and slide shows on the glaciers and the Castleguard Caves which honeycomb the ice – Canada's most extensive, but inaccessible to the public.

You can walk onto the **Athabasca Glacier**, but full-scale expeditions are the preserve of experts unless you join an organized trip. *Brewster*'s special *Snocoaches* run 75-minute trips over the glacier (every 15min; daily, early May to mid-Oct 9am–5pm; $19.50), but they're heavily subscribed, so aim to avoid the peak midday rush. More dedicated types can sign up for the **Athabasca Glacier icewalks** (3-hr walks mid-June to early Sept daily at 12.30pm, $16; 5-hr walks Thurs & Sun 11.30am, $21). Call ☎852-4242 for details, or sign up at the front desk of the *Icefields Chalet* – be sure to bring warm clothes, boots and provisions.

The 25-room *Icefields Chalet* (☎762-6735; ③), a stop for *Brewster* services, provides a pretty low standard of **accommodation**, and has a cafeteria and restaurant. It's possible to take a Banff-bound *Brewster* bus out of Jasper in the morning, see the Icefield, and pick up the evening Jasper-bound bus later the same day.

Two unserviced but very popular **campgrounds** lie 2km and 3km south of the Icefield Centre respectively: the tent-only 33-site *Columbia Icefield* (mid-May to mid-Oct, or until the first snow; $7.25), and the 46-site *Wilcox Creek*, which takes tents and RVs (mid-June to mid-Sept; $7.25). This latter is also the trailhead for one of the best day-hikes on the entire highway, the **Wilcox Pass Trail** (4km; 335m of ascent; allow 2hr).

The path takes you steeply through thick forest before emerging suddenly on to a ridge that offers vast views over the parkway and the high peaks of the icefield (including Mount Athabasca). Beyond, the trail enters a beautiful spread of meadows, tarns and creeks, an area many people choose to halt at or wander all day without bothering to reach the pass itself.

Beyond the Columbia Icefield

If there's a change beyond the Columbia Icefield, it's a barely quantifiable lapse in the scenery's awe-inspiring intensity over the 108-kilometer stretch towards Jasper. As the road begins a gradual descent the peaks retreat slightly, taking on less dramatic profiles in the process.

Seventeen kilometers beyond the icefield is the 24-berth, 2-cabin *Beauty Creek* **youth hostel** (May–Sept, closed Tues; groups only during winter; reservations ☎439-3139;$8). Nine kilometers further is the unserviced 25-site *Jonas Creek* **campground** (mid-May to first snowfall; $7.25).

Sunwapta Falls (175km), fifteen minutes' walk through the woods from the road, may not be dramatic unless in spate, but they're interesting for the deep canyon they've cut through the surrounding valley. A short trail along the river-bank leads to more rapids and small falls downstream. If you want to put up nearby, the unserviced 35-site *Honeymoon Lake* **campground** is 4km further along the parkway (mid-June to mid-Oct; $8). Otherwise the roadside *Sunwapta Falls Resort* (mid-May to mid-Oct; ☎852-4852; ⑤) is the last of the road's **hotels**, though as you're only 52km short of Jasper it's probably worth pushing on.

One kilometer away from the last main sight, the impressive **Athabasca Falls** (where the platforms and paths show the strain of handling thousands of feet, and it's hard to feel you're in the wilderness any longer) has the excellent 40-bed *Athabasca Falls* **youth hostel** (year-round, closed Tues Oct–April; ☎852-5959; $9); the 42-site *Mount Kerkeslin* **campground**, 3km back down the road, spreads over a tranquil riverside site (mid-May to early Sept; $7.25).

BEARS

Two types of **bears** roam the Rockies – black bears and grizzlies – and you don't want to meet either. They're not terribly common in these parts (sightings are all monitored and posted at park centers), but if you're camping or walking it's essential to know how to avoid dangerous encounters, and what to do if confronted or attacked. Popular misconceptions about bears abound – that they can't climb trees, for example (they can, and very quickly) – so it's worth picking up the parks service's pamphlet *You are in Bear Country*, which cuts through the confusion and lays out some occasionally eye-opening procedures. Be prepared, and if you don't want your scalp pulled off, follow the **cardinal rules**: don't approach bears, don't feed them, and don't run.

When **hiking**, walk in a group and make noise – bears are most threatened if surprised (many people carry a whistle; the widely touted small bells, be warned, are not loud enough). Be alert when travelling into the wind, as your scent won't carry to warn bears of your approach, and stay away from dead animals and berry patches, which are important food sources. Watch for bear signs – tracks, diggings and droppings – and keep in the open as much as possible.

Camp away from rushing water, paths and animal trails, and keep the site scrupulously clean, leaving nothing hanging around in the open. Lock **food and rubbish** in a car, or hang it between two trees at least 4m above ground (many campgrounds have bear poles or steel food boxes). Take all rubbish away – don't bury it. Avoid smelly foods, fresh meat and fish, and don't cook or eat in or near the tent – lingering smells may invite unwanted nocturnal visits. Likewise, keep food off clothes and sleeping bags, and try to sleep in clean clothes at night. Bears have an acute sense of smell – avoid scented cosmetics – and may be attracted to women during menstruation, so dispose of tampons in an airtight container. They're also attracted by sex, so watch what you do in your tent if you don't want a rather drastic *coitus interruptus*.

Bears are unpredictable, and there's no guaranteed life-saving way of coping with an aggressive bear. **Calm behavior**, however, has proved to be the most successful strategy. A bear moving towards you can be considered to have it in for you, other signs being whoofing noises, snapping jaws, and the head down and ears back. A bear raised on its hind legs and sniffing is trying to identify you: absurd as it sounds, stand still and start speaking to it in low tones. Ideally, you want to make a wide detour, leave the area or wait for the bear to do so – and always leave it an escape route. Whatever you do, **don't run** (a bear can outrun a racehorse), nor scream or make sudden movements (surprising the animal is the surest way to provoke an attack). Unfortunately bears often bluff, and will charge and veer at the last moment, so though it's a fairly tall order, resist the urge to turn and run – instead back away quietly. Don't throw anything and do everything as slowly and calmly as possible. If things look ominous, put your pack on the ground as a distraction. Forget about **trees**, as black bears can climb them better than you, though grizzlies may get bored after about 4m.

If you're **attacked** things are truly grim, and quack tactics are unlikely to help you. With grizzlies, playing dead – curling up in a ball, protecting face, neck and abdomen – may be effective. Fighting back will only increase the ferocity of a grizzly attack, but a good bop to the nose will sometimes send a black bear running: it's worth a try. As a last resort only, try to intimidate the bear with anything at hand. **Chemical repellents** are available, but of unproven efficacy.

Jasper National Park

Although traditionally viewed as the second of the Rockies' big four parks, **Jasper National Park** covers an area greater than Banff, Yoho and Kootenay combined, and feels far wilder and less commercialized than its southern counterparts. Its backcountry is more extensive and less travelled, and **Jasper Townsite**, the only settlement, is far less of a resort than Banff. Most pursuits center on Jasper and the **Maligne Lake** area about 50km southeast of the townsite. Other key zones are **Maligne Canyon**, on the way to the lake, the **Icefields Parkway**, covered in the previous section, and the **Miette Hot Springs region**, an area well to the east of Jasper and visited for its springs and trails.

The park's **backcountry** is a vast hinterland scattered with countless rough campgrounds and a 1000-kilometer trail system considered among the best in the world for backpackers. Opportunities for day and half-day hikes, however, are more limited and scattered than in other parks. Most of the shorter strolls from the townsite are just low-level walks to forest-circled lakes; the best of the more exciting **day hikes** start from more remote points off the Maligne Lake road, Icefields Parkway (Hwy 93) and Yellowhead Highway (Hwy 16).

Jasper Townsite

JASPER's small-town feel comes as a relief after the razzmatazz of Banff: its streets still have the windswept, open look of a frontier town, and though the mountains don't ring it with quite the same majesty as Banff, you'll probably feel the town better suits its wild surroundings. Apart from the new **Yellowhead Museum** at 400 Pyramid Rd, with its fur trade and railroad displays (daily summer 11am–9pm; $2.50) and a **cable-car**, nothing here even pretends to be a tourist attraction; this is a place to sleep, eat and stock up.

Though Jasper doesn't get as many visitors as Banff, you have to compete with a plethora of summer travellers, and accommodation can be tight. You are also especially stuck if you don't have a vehicle; trailheads and the best scenery are a long way from downtown. Bikes can be rented at several places, however, and intermittent shuttle services can run you out of town to **Maligne Lake** and some of the more obvious attractions.

Some history

Permanent settlement first came to the Jasper area in 1811. The great explorer and trader David Thomson left **William Henry** at Old Fire Point (just outside the present townsite) while he and his companions pushed on up the valley to blaze a trail over the Athabasca Pass used by traders crossing the Rockies for over fifty years. In the meantime, Henry established **Henry House**, the first permanent European habitation in the Rockies (though its exact location has been lost). Two years later the North West Company established Jasper House, at the eastern edge of the park's present boundary. Named after Jasper Hawes, a long-time clerk there, it moved closer to Jasper Lake in 1829, when the North West and Hudson Bay companies were amalgamated.

Like other parks and their townsites, Jasper traces its real origins to the coming of the railway at the turn of the century. The Canadian Pacific had brought boom to Banff and Yoho in 1885 (when it spurned a route through the Jasper region in favor of a more southerly route; see "Field" p.422). The **Grand**

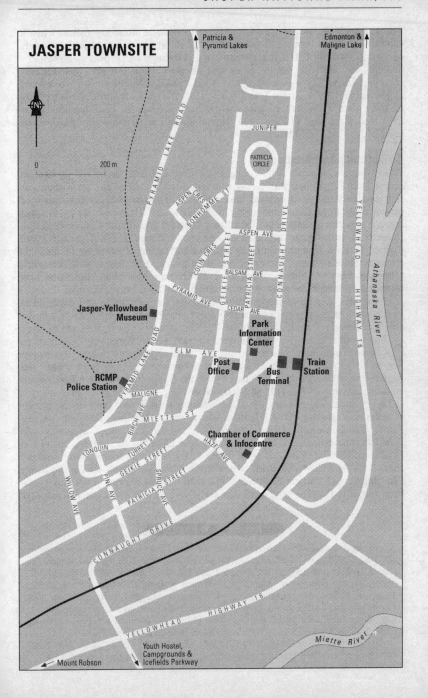

JASPER TOWNSITE

↑ Patricia &
Pyramid Lakes

Edmonton &
Maligne Lake ↑

N

0   200 m

JUNIPER

PATRICIA
CIRCLE

PYRAMID LAKE ROAD

ASPEN CRES

BONHOMME ST

ASPEN AVE

COLIN CRES

GEIKIE STREET

PATRICIA STREET

CONNAUGHT DRIVE

BALSAM AVE

PYRAMID AVE

CEDAR AVE

YELLOWHEAD HIGHWAY 16

Athabaska River

**Jasper-Yellowhead
Museum**

**Park
Information
Center**

ELM AVE

**Post
Office**

**Bus
Terminal**

**Train
Station**

**RCMP
Police Station**

PYRAMID LAKE ROAD

MALIGNE

BIRCH AVE

MIETTE ST

TONQUIN

TURRET ST

GEIKIE STREET

HAZEL AVE

**Chamber of Commerce
& Infocentre**

SPRUCE STREET

WILLOW AVE

PINE AVE

PATRICIA AVE

CONNAUGHT DRIVE

YELLOWHEAD HIGHWAY 16

Miette River

← Mount Robson

↓ Youth Hostel,
Campgrounds &
Icefields Parkway

Trunk Pacific Railway hoped for similar successes in attracting visitors when it started to push its own route west in 1902, and the Jasper Forest Park was duly created in 1908. By 1911 a tent city known as **Fitzhugh** had grown up on Jasper's present site, and the name Jasper was adopted when the site was officially surveyed. Incredibly, a second railway, the **Canadian Northern**, was completed almost parallel to the Grand Trunk line in 1913, the tracks at some points running no more than a few meters apart. Within just three years, consolidation of the lines took place west of Edmonton (ripped up rails were shipped to Europe and used in the First World War).

Arrival and transportation

Where Banff's strength is its convenience from Calgary, Jasper's is its ease of access from Edmonton, with plenty of transportation options and approaches, as well as a wide range of onward destinations. *Greyhound* (☎852-3926) runs four **buses** daily from Edmonton along the Yellowhead Highway (Hwy 16), plus onward services to Kamloops/Vancouver (4 daily) and Prince George (2 daily). *Brewster Transportation* (☎852-3332) operates services to Banff (1 daily) and Calgary (1 daily), and also runs day-trips to Banff taking in sights on the Icefields Parkway ($49.50); note, however, that weather can play havoc with *Brewster's* schedules between October and April. Both companies share the same **bus terminal**, located in the railway station building at 314 Connaught Drive.

VIA **trains** operate to Jasper from Winnipeg and Edmonton and continue to Vancouver (via Kamloops) or Prince Rupert (via Prince George). As this is the only scheduled rail route through the Rockies, summer places are hard to come by, but at other times there's little need to book a seat. **Fares** are slightly more than those of equivalent buses, and journey times considerably longer. Trains run Jasper–Edmonton (Tues, Fri & Sun); Jasper–Vancouver (Mon, Thurs & Sat); and Jasper–Prince George–Prince Rupert (Wed, Fri & Sun). The **ticket office** is open on train days only (☎852-4102 or 1-800/561-8630).

To get around locally, try the *Hiker's Wheels* service (see box) or the pricier summer-only **Jasper Area Shuttle**, which runs from the offices of *Maligne Tours*, 626 Connaught Drive (☎852-3370), out to the Jasper Tramway (via *Whistlers* campground and hostel) and Maligne Lake (via the canyon, hostel and Skyline trailheads). You can **rent bikes** at the *Whistlers Youth Hostel*, *Beyond Bikes*, 4 Cedar Ave (☎852-5922), or downtown from *Freewheel Cycles* at the *Husky Gas Station*, 611 Patricia St (☎852-3898), with the last offering a one-way rental from Jasper to Banff to let you ride the Icefields Parkway. For a **taxi** call *Heritage*

HIKER'S WHEELS

A new and inexpensive transportation service, **Hiker's Wheels**, has recently started to link Jasper with trailheads for hikers, mountain bikers and canoeists. All routes cost under $20: to the **Nigel Pass** via the Icefield infocentre and the Athabasca and Beauty Creek hostels; to **Mount Robson Provincial Park**; to the **Tonquin Valley** (for popular backpack trails); to **Maligne Lake**; and the **93a Loop**, via the Cavell youth hostel, Tonquin trailheads, Wabasso campground, Geraldine, Athabasca hostel and Wabasso Lake. The eventual aim is to serve all major trails in Jasper National Park and Mount Robson Provincial Park.

All rides *must* be pre-booked (☎852-2188), and depart from the *Hava Java Café*, 407 Patricia St. A daily bus to the Mount Edith Cavell youth hostel departs at 5pm.

Cabs (☎852-5558) or *Jasper Taxi* (☎852-3146). **Cars** can be rented through *Tilden*, 607 Connaught Drive (☎852-4972), or *Budget*, 638 Connaught Drive (☎852-3222).

Information
Both the main Travel Alberta office (Mon–Fri 9am–noon & 1–5pm; ☎852-3858), and the town's **visitor center** (daily June–Sept 8am–8pm; May 9am–6pm; ☎852-4919), are at 632 Connaught Drive on the western edge of town. Neither books accommodation, but both stock full lists. The excellent *Canadian Parks Service* **park information center**, whose amiable staff sell **maps** and have all relevant information, is at the other end of town at 500 Connaught Ave – 50m east of the station, back from the road on the left (daily, mid-June to early Sept 8am–8pm; Sept–early Dec 9am–5pm; ☎852-6176). Apply here for backcountry Park Permits and to register for backpacking trails, or out of season to the Park Administration Office at 623 Patricia St (Mon–Fri 8am–4.30pm; ☎852-6161). For weather reports call *Environment Canada* (☎852-3185). The *Reader's Choice* **bookstore**, 610 Connaught Drive (☎852-4028), has a good selection of maps and guides.

Accommodation
Beds in Jasper are not as expensive or elusive as in Banff, but accommodation is still almost unobtainable in July and August. The Chamber of Commerce has a free phone for local hotel and B&B calls, and will call around for private rooms, where you can expect to pay from $30 to $90 for a double, sometimes with breakfast thrown in. If you can afford more, or are desperate, *Banff and Jasper Central Reservations* (☎1-800/661-1676) and the office at 622 Connaught Drive (☎852-4242) may come up with something – for a fee.

Most **motels** are spaced out along Connaught Drive on the eastern edge of town, and charge well over $100 for a double room, though prices drop sharply in off-season. The four park-run **campgrounds** close to the townsite, and the three local **hostels** (joint reservations on ☎439-3139), all fill up promptly in summer, but don't forget the hostels and campgrounds strung along the Icefields Parkway.

HOTELS, MOTELS AND CHALETS
Alpine Village, 2.5km south of town on Hwy 93A (☎852-3285). An assortment of 41 serene cabins, most with great mountain views, from one-room to deluxe. May to mid-Oct. ③–⑥.

Amethyst Motor Lodge, 200 Connaught Drive (☎852-3394 or 1-800/661-9935). Almost 100 newly renovated rooms two blocks from downtown. ⑥.

Astoria Hotel, Patricia St (☎852-3351). Adequate central "alpine" hotel, one block from the railway station and bus terminal. ④.

Athabasca Hotel, 510 Patricia St (☎852-3386). Central if forbidding hotel, near the station, where the nightly entertainment and *O'Shea's Lounge* bar may keep you awake. ③–④.

Becker's Roaring River Chalets, 5km south of Jasper on Hwy 93 (☎852-3779). 72 of the best (and newest) local log cabins, most with wood-burning stoves and kitchenettes. ④–⑤.

Bonhomme Bungalows, 100 Bonhomme St (☎852-3209). Simple-looking but comfortable bungalows, chalet and lodge units, in the townsite but in a pleasant wooded setting. ③.

Chalet Patricia, 310 Patricia St (☎852-5533). Three private rooms in the town center. ②.

Lobstick Lodge, 1200 Geikie at Juniper (☎852-4431). If you're going to pay in-town, east-end motel rates, this is probably the best all-round choice. ⑥.

Marmot Lodge, 92 Connaught Drive (☎852-4471 or 1-800/661-6521). One of the biggest (106 rooms) and least expensive of the east-end motels. ⑤.

Patricia Lake Bungalows, 4.8km northwest of downtown on the Pyramid Lake Rd (☎852-3560). Motel or cabin out-of-town base. May–Sept. ③.

Pine Bungalows, 2km east of Jasper on the Athabasca River (May–Oct; ☎852-3491). Good-looking wooden cabins in forest setting, some with wood-burning stoves and kitchenettes. ③.

Sawridge Hotel Jasper, 82 Connaught Drive (☎852-5111 or 1-800/661-6427). Plush large hotel on the eastern edge of town. The in-house *Champs* disco may not be to all tastes. ⑤–⑥.

Tekarra Lodge (☎852-3058). Quiet, nicely kitsch wood cabins with wood-burning stoves, open May–Oct, located 1km south of town on the Athabasca River off Hwy 93A. ③–④.

Whistlers Inn (☎852-3361 or 1-800/282-9919). Central motel, opposite the station. ③–⑤.

BED AND BREAKFAST

A-1 Tourist Rooms, 804 Connaught Drive (☎852-3325). Three rooms with shared bathroom on main street close to bus and train. ①.

Betty Enns, 718 Connaught Drive (☎852-3640). Three rooms, private bathrooms, with use of kitchen for $10. ②.

Candice's Accommodation, 714a Patricia St (☎852-4655). A pair of rooms (shared bath) very close to downtown. ②.

Creekside Accommodation, 1232 Patricia Crescent (☎852-3530). Two bright, clean rooms (shared bath) near creek and trails. ②.

Kennedy's Holiday Rooms, 1115 Patricia Crescent (☎852-3438). Pair of rooms that share bath, patio, living room and great views. ②.

Leggett's Loft, 218 Patricia St (☎852-5807). A bright, panoramic room with private bath. ③.

Rainee's Rooms, 6 Aspen Crescent ☎(852-5181). Rooms with and without private baths. ②.

Ted Rosychuk, 1220 Cabin Creek Drive (☎852-4081). A couple of rooms, one with patio and BBQ. ②.

Three Jays Tourist Rooms, 1205 Cabin Creek Drive (☎852-3267). Two of the three rooms (shared bath) have fine views. ②.

HOSTELS

Maligne Canyon Hostel (CHA; ☎852-3584; reservations ☎439-3139). 6-bed cabins 11km east of town near Maligne Canyon (open all day, year round except Wed Oct–April). ①.

Mount Edith Cavell Hostel, Edith Cavell Rd 13km off Hwy 93A (CHA; reservations ☎439-3139). Cozier than the *Whistlers* hostel (see below), close to trails and with great views of the Angel Glacier. Sleeps 32 in two cabins; wood-burning sauna. Open mid-June to Oct all day, every day; opens up with key system for skiers in winter. ①.

Whistlers Mountain Youth Hostel (CHA; ☎852-3215; reservations ☎439-3139). Jasper's nearest youth hostel, 7km south of town (500m south of the gondola terminal) on Skytram Rd (Whistlers Mountain Rd), accessed from the Icefields Parkway (Hwy 93). The 4-km uphill walk from Hwy 93 is a killer, but shuttles run from downtown, as do taxis ($12–15). A modern place with a reputation for over-efficient management, it fills up quickly in summer, so arrive early or book. ①.

CAMPGROUNDS

Snaring River, 11km east of Jasper on Hwy 16. Simple 66-site park-run facility, dry toilets only. Mid-May to early Sept. $7.25.

Wabasso, 16km south of Jasper on Hwy 93A. 238-pitch riverside site with flush toilets, hot water, but no hot showers. Mid-May to early Sept. $9.25.

Wapiti, 4km south of the townsite and 1km south of *Whistlers* on Hwy 93. Big park-run place with flush toilets and hot showers that accepts tents but also caters for RVs. 40 sites remain open for winter camping from Oct, the park's only year-round serviced campground. $12–14.

Whistlers, 3km south of Jasper just west off Hwy 93. Jasper's main 781-site park-run campground, with all facilities (flush toilets and hot showers). If you're coming from Banff, watch for the sign; *Brewster* buses will also usually stop here. Taxis and shuttles run from Jasper. Early June to early Oct. $12–16.50.

Eating, drinking and nightlife

Options for **eating out** are restricted in Jasper, but then the town's ambience doesn't suit fine dining. Perhaps the best place for a full meal – and definitely not posh – is *Mountain Foods and Café*, opposite the station at 606 Connaught Drive (☎852-4050). The menu is cheap and varied (including vegetarian choices), the food is excellent, the staff friendly, and it's a good place to meet people; there's also a wholefood shop at the back. Also popular is the lively and far more carnivorous *Villa Caruso*, 628 Connaught Drive, where vast steaks sizzle over open grills in the windows to tempt passing trade; there's fine seafood plus pasta and pizzas if you can't face the steaks.

The best of the **cafés** is the small, non-smoking *Coco's Café;* inexpensive and trendy, with newspapers and magazines to pass the time over excellent snacks and coffees. In similar vein, but still more laid-back, the *Hava Java Café* behind the national park information center at 407 Patricia St has tables out on the lawn during summer, while the inside resembles a cozy front room (they also run the *Hiker's Wheels* service – see box on p.412). Turn left after the station for *Smitty's Restaurant*, where you can drink coffee and write postcards all day. *Nutters* at the west end of Patricia St is a **supermarket** with a wholefood bias.

Most **drinking** goes on in *O'Shea's Lounge* at the *Athabasca Hotel*, 510 Patricia St, where the "nightclub" annex has dancing and **live music**. The unpretentious *Astoria* on Connaught Drive attracts more of a thirtyish crowd, with big-screen TV, music and darts. The *Tent City* C&W evening on Friday nights is also pretty lively (at the *Jasper Park Lodge* on Lac Beauvert). The *Chaba Theatre* is a **cinema** directly opposite the station. Nightlife generally is low-key, however: most of the campgrounds and motels are too far out of town for people to get in, and the fun is generally of the make-your-own variety out at the hostel or campground.

Jasper Tramway and the lakes

With little on offer in town you need to use a bike, car or the shuttle services to get anything out of the area. The obvious trip is on the **Jasper Tramway**, 7km south of town on Whistlers Mountain Road, off the Icefields Parkway (late March to mid-Oct daily 8.30am–9.30pm; $9.65). The 2.5-kilometer cable-car ride takes seven minutes, and leaves you at an interpretive center, expensive restaurant, and a viewpoint (2285m) where you can take your bearings on much of the park. A steep trail ploughs upwards and onwards to the Whistlers summit (2470m), an hour's walk that requires warm clothes year round and reveals even more stunning views. A tough ten-kilometer trail runs the route of the tramway from *Whistlers Mountain Youth Hostel*; if you walk up, you can ride back down for $3.50. Also near the town, a winding road wends north to **Patricia** and **Pyramid lakes**, both about 5km from Jasper and racked full of rental facilities for riding, boating, canoeing, windsurfing and sailing. Food and drink is available locally, but the two lakefront lodges are usually heavily booked (the one at Pyramid Lake is open year round). Short trails, generally accessible from the approach road, include the **Patricia Lake Circle**, a 4.8-kilometer loop. Slightly closer to town on the east side of the Athabasca River, **Lake Edith** and **Lake Annette** are both busy day-use areas – the water is surprisingly warm, and in summer you can lie out on sandy beaches or grassy areas. A clutch of picnic sites are the only development, and a wheelchair-accessible trail meanders around Lake Annette (2.4km). Few other hikes from town are spectacular, but the best of the bunch,

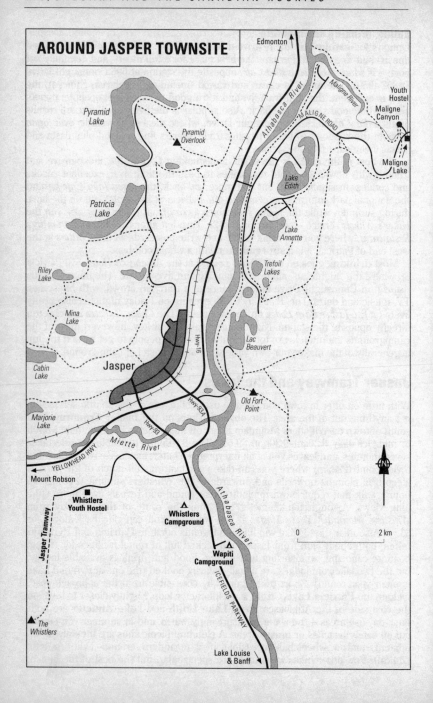

AROUND JASPER TOWNSITE

Edmonton

Athabasca River

Maligne River

MALIGNE ROAD

Youth Hostel

Maligne Canyon

Maligne Lake

Pyramid Lake

Pyramid Overlook

Lake Edith

Patricia Lake

Lake Annette

Trefoil Lakes

Riley Lake

Mina Lake

Lac Beauvert

Cabin Lake

Jasper

Hwy-16

Old Fort Point

Hwy-93A

Marjorie Lake

Hwy-93

Miette River

YELLOWHEAD HWY

Mount Robson

Whistlers Youth Hostel

Whistlers Campground

Jasper Tramway

Wapiti Campground

Athabasca River

ICEFIELDS PARKWAY

The Whistlers

N

0   2 km

Lake Louise & Banff

the **Old Fort Point Loop** (6.5km round trip), is highly recommended. Despite being just thirty minutes out of town, it's remarkably scenic, with 360° views and lots of quiet corners. To reach the trailhead (1.6km from town) use the Old Fort Exit, following Hwy 93A across the railway and Hwy 16 until you come to the Old Fort Point-Lac Beauvert turn-off: then turn left and follow the road to the parking lot beyond the bridge. The **Valley of the Five Lakes Trail** (4.6km) is also good, but the path starts 10km south of town off the Icefields Parkway. For full details of all park walks ask at the information center for the free *Day Hiker's Guide to Jasper*.

Maligne Lake road

Bumper to bumper in the summer, the **Maligne Lake road** (pronounced Ma-*leen*) runs east from Jasper for 48km, taking in a number of beautiful if overdeveloped sights. For all activities that require rental equipment, such as canoeing or fishing, reservations are essential in summer. Camping is not permitted in the main Maligne Valley itself.

A mere 11km out of Jasper, the perpetually crowded **Maligne Canyon** is the most heavily sold excursion from town, characterized by its oversized parking lot, and a tacky café/souvenir shop. Hyperbolic signs promise one of the Rockies' most spectacular gorges: in fact the canyon is deep (50m), but almost narrow enough to jump across – many people have tried and most have died in the attempt. In the end the geology is more interesting than the scenery; the violent erosive forces that created the canyon are explained on the main trail loop, an

---

OPERATION HABBAKUK

Behind every triumph of military ingenuity in World War II, there were dozens of spectacular and deliberately obfuscated failures. Few can have been as bizarre as the one witnessed by Jasper's Patricia Lake. By 1942, Allied shipping losses in the North Atlantic had become so disastrous that almost anything was considered that might staunch the flow. One Geoffrey Pike, institutionalized in a London mental hospital, put forward the idea of a vast aircraft carrier made of ice, a ship that would be naturally impervious to fire when torpedoed, and not melt from under its seamen in the icy waters of the North Atlantic.

Times were so hard the scheme was given serious consideration. Louis Mountbatten, one of the Allied Chiefs of Staff, went so far as to demonstrate the theories with ice-cubes in the bath in front of Winston Churchill at 10 Downing St. It was decided to build a 1000-tonne model somewhere very cold – Canada would be ideal – and **Operation Habbakuk** was launched. Pike was released from his hospital on special dispensation and despatched to the chilly waters of Patricia Lake. Here a substance known as pikewood was invented, a mixture of ice and wood chips (spruce chips were discovered to add more buoyancy than pine). It soon became clear, however, that the 650-meter-long and 20-story-high boat stood little chance of ever being seaworthy (never mind what the addition of 2000 crew and 26 aircraft would do for its buoyancy). Pike suggested filling the ice with air to help things along. Further complications arose when the laborers on the project, mostly pacifist Doukhobors (see p.334), became aware of the boat's proposed purpose and refused to carry on working. Spring thaws brought the project to a halt. The following season, with $75 million budgeted for the scheme, it was moved to Newfoundland, where it died a quiet death.

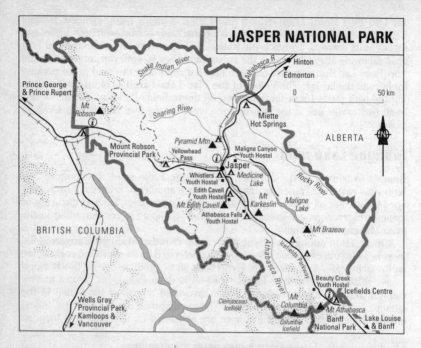

easy twenty-minute amble that can be extended to 45 minutes, or even turned into a hike back to Jasper. In winter, licensed guides lead tours (more like crawls) through the frozen canyon – contact *Maligne Tours*, 626 Connaught Drive, Jasper (☎852-3370).

Next stop is picture-perfect **Medicine Lake**, 32km from Jasper, which experiences intriguing fluctuations in level. Its waters have no surface outlet: instead the lake fills and empties through lake-bed sink-holes into the world's largest system of limestone caves. They re-emerge some 17km away towards Jasper (and may also feed some of the lakes around Jasper Townsite). When the springs freeze in winter the lake drains and sometimes disappears altogether, only to be replenished in the spring. Few people spend much time at the lake, preferring to press on to Maligne Lake, so it makes a quietish spot to escape the headlong rush down the road.

At the end of the road, 48km from Jasper, is the stunning **Maligne Lake**, 22km long and 92m deep, and surrounded by snow-covered mountains. The largest lake in the Rockies, its name comes from the French for "wicked", and was coined in 1846 by a Jesuit missionary, Father de Smet, in memory of the difficulty he had crossing the Maligne River downstream. The road peters out at a warden station, three parking lots and a restaurant flanked by a picnic area and the start of the short Lake Trail (3.2km). A small waterfront area is equipped with five berths for boats that run ninety-minute **cruises** on the lake, which give incredible views (daily May 20–June 24 hourly 10am–4pm; June 25–Sept 4 10am–5pm; Sept 5–Sept 30 10am–3pm; $27). The boats are small, however, and reservations are in order during peak times: again, contact *Maligne Tours*, who also run a bus to the

HIKING IN JASPER NATIONAL PARK

Day hikes

One of Jasper's best day hikes, the **Opal Hills Circuit** (8.2km round trip), starts from the picnic area to the left of the uppermost Maligne Lake parking lot, 48km east of Jasper. After a blood-pumping haul up the first steep slopes, the trail negotiates alpine meadows and offers sweeping views of the lake; the trip takes about four hours, but you could easily spend all day loafing around the meadows. The **Bald Hills Trail** (5.2km one way) starts with a monotonous plod along a fire road from the same parking lot, but ends with what Mary Schaffer, one of the area's first white explorers, described as "the finest view any of us had ever beheld in the Rockies"; allow four hours for the round trip. To get the best out of both walks it's essential to see them through to their conclusions.

A superlative short, sharp walk starts from Miette Hot Springs, 58km northeast of Jasper. The **Sulphur Skyline** (4km one way) offers exceptional views of knife-edged ridges, deep gorges, crags, and remote valleys. Be sure to take water with you, and allow two hours each way for the steep climb. The trailhead is signed (with others) from the **Miette Hot Springs** complex, reached from Jasper by heading 41km east on Hwy 16 and then south 17km; the *Jasper Area Shuttle* makes the trip in summer. The springs themselves are a good way to round off a day; the hottest in the Rockies, they have to be cooled for swimming (mid-June to early Sept daily 8.30am–10.30pm; $3.50).

To get to the trailhead for **Cavell Meadows** (3.8km one way), drive 7.5km south on the Icefields Parkway, then 5km along Hwy 93A and finally 14km up Mount Edith Cavell Road; a daily shuttle bus from Jasper takes bikes, so cyclists can ride back down. The scenery is mixed and magnificent; as well as Cavell's alpine meadows, you get views of Angel Glacier and the dizzying north wall of Mount Edith Cavell (named for a British nurse executed during World War I). Allow two hours round trip, and don't expect solitude.

Backpacking Trails

Jasper's system of **backpacking** trails and 111 backcountry campgrounds makes it one of the leading areas for backcountry hiking in North America. To stay overnight in the backcountry, pick up a free Park Use permit within 24 hours of your departure, from the park information center in Jasper Townsite or at the Columbia Icefield. Many popular trails operate quota systems; contact the park information office for details and book yourself a place within 21 days of departure. The office staff offer invaluable advice, and issue excellent $1 strip maps of several trails. Overnight hikes are beyond the scope of this book – talk to staff or get hold of a copy of *The Canadian Rockies Trail Guide* – but the most popular long-distance trails are the **Skyline** (44km); **Jonas Pass** (19km); and two hikes in the Tonquin Valley – **Astoria River** (19km) and **Maccarib Pass** (21km). Others to consider are Maligne Pass and the long-distance North and South Boundary trails (the latter both over 160km).

lake four times daily ($10), with drop-offs (if booked) at Maligne Canyon youth hostel ($6) and the northern ($6) and southern ends ($10) of the Skyline Trail, one of the park's three top backpacking trails (see box). Riding, fishing, rafting and guided hiking tours are also available, as are fishing tackle, rowing boat and **canoe rentals** ($30 per day, $10 per hour, $6 each additional hour). There are no accommodation or camping facilities, but two backcountry **campgrounds** can be reached by canoe.

Mount Robson Provincial Park

Mount Robson (3954m), the highest peak in the Canadian Rockies, is protected by an extensive provincial park bordering Jasper National Park to the west. Its scenery equals anything anywhere else in the Rockies, and Mount Robson itself is one of the most staggering mountains you'll ever encounter; but facilities are thin on the ground, so stock up on food and gas before entering the park.

Both road and rail links from Jasper climb through **Yellowhead Pass**, long one of the most important native and fur-trading routes across the Rockies. The pass, 20km west of Jasper Townsite, marks the boundary between Jasper and Mount Robson parks, Alberta and British Columbia, and Mountain and Pacific time zones (set your watch back one hour). This stretch of road is less dramatic than the Icefields Parkway, given over to mixed woodland – birch interspersed with firs – and mountains that sit back from the road with less scenic effect. The railway meanders alongside the road most of the way, occasionally occupied by epic freight trains hundreds of wagons long – alien intrusions in a wilderness of rocks, river and forest. Just down from the pass, **Yellowhead Lake** is the park's first landmark. Look for moose around dawn and dusk at aptly named **Moose Lake**, another 20km further west.

Mount Robson

If the first taste of the park is relatively tame, the first sight of **Mount Robson** is among the most breathtaking in the Rockies. The preceding ridges creep up in height and the massive peak itself is hidden from view until the last moment. The British explorer W B Cheadle described the mountain in 1863: "On every side the mighty heads of snowy hills crowded round, whilst, immediately behind us, a giant among giants, and immeasurably supreme, rose Robson's peak . . . We saw its upper portion dimmed by a necklace of light, feathery clouds, beyond which its pointed apex of ice, glittering in the morning sun, shot up far into the blue heaven above."

The overall impression is of immense size, thanks mainly to the colossal scale of Robson's south face – a sheer rise of 3100 meters – and to the view from the road which frames the mountain as a single mass isolated from other peaks. A spectacular glacier system, concealed on the mountain's north side, is visible if you make the backpacking hike to the Berg Lake area (see box). Local natives called the peak *Yuh-hai-has-hun* – the Mountain of the Spiral Road, an allusion to the clearly visible layers of rock that resemble a road winding to the summit. Not surprisingly, this monolith was one of the last major peaks in the Rockies to be climbed (1913), and is still considered a dangerous challenge.

Practicalities

Trains don't stop anywhere in the park, but if you're travelling by bus you can ask to be let off at Yellowhead Pass or the **Mount Robson Travel Infocentre** (May–Sept; ☎566-4325), located at the Mount Robson viewpoint near the western entrance to the park. Most of the park's few other facilities are found near the infocentre: a **café/garage** (May–Sept) and three fully serviced commercial **campgrounds**, *Emperor Ridge* (June–Sept; ☎566-4714; $11), 300m north of Hwy 16 on Kinney Lake Road; *Mount Robson Guest Ranch* (June–Sept; ☎566-4370; just

---

The **telephone code** for the Mount Robson, Yoho, Glacier, Mount Revelstoke and Kootenay parks is ☎604.

10 sites; $10), on Hargreaves Road 2km south of the highway (also with ten **cabins** for rent; ④); and *Robson Shadows Campground* (May–Oct; ☎566-4821; $10), forty nice sites on the Fraser River side of Hwy 16, 5km west of the park boundary. The only other beds in or near the park are the nine log-sided river-front cabins of *Mount Robson Lodge* (May–Oct; ☎566-4821; ③) near *Robson Shadows Campground*, and the cabins belonging to *Mount Robson Adventure Holidays* (June–Sept; ☎566-4351; ③), 16km east of the infocentre (towards Jasper), though preference for these may go to people signed up for the company's canoeing and hiking day-trips.

Backcountry camping in the park is only permitted at seven wilderness campgrounds dotted along the Berg Lake Trail (see box): to use these you have to register and pay an overnight fee at the infocentre. *Mount Robson Adventure Holidays* **rent equipment** – complete outfits start at $22 per day.

HIKING IN ROBSON PARK

Starting at the parking lot trailhead 2km north of the park infocentre, the **Berg Lake Trail** (22km each way) is the only trail to get anywhere near Mount Robson. You can do the first third or so as a comfortable day walk, passing through forest to lovely glacier-fed Kinney Lake (6.7km; campground at the lake's northeast corner). Trek the whole thing, however, and you traverse the stupendous **Valley of a Thousand Waterfalls** – the most notable being sixty-meter Emperor Falls (14.3km; campgrounds 500m north and 2km south) – and eventually enjoy the phenomenal area around **Berg Lake** itself (17.4km to its nearest, western shore). Mount Robson rises steeply from the lakeshore, its huge cliffs cradling two creaking rivers of ice, Mist Glacier and Berg Glacier – the latter, one of the Rockies' few "living" or advancing glaciers, is the source of the great icebergs that give the lake its name. Beyond the lake you can pursue the trail 2km further to Robson Pass (21.9km; campground) and another 1km to **Adolphus Lake** in Jasper National Park. Berg Lake (19.6km) and Rearguard (20.1km) campgrounds are on Berg Lake itself; with a Jasper backcountry permit you can press on to Adolphus where a less frequented site offers more in the way of solitude.

The popular day trip to **Toboggan Falls** (2km) starts from the southerly Berg Lake campground and climbs the northeast (left) side of Toboggan Creek past a series of cascades and meadows to eventual views over the lake's entire hinterland. The trail peters out after 2km, but you can easily walk on and upward through open meadows for still better views. The second trail in the immediate vicinity is **Robson Glacier** (2km), a level walk which peels off south from the main trail 1km west of Robson Pass near the park ranger's cabin. It runs across an outwash plain to culminate in a small lake at the foot of the glacier: a rougher track then follows the lateral moraine on the glacier's east side, branching east after 3km to follow a small stream to the summit of Snowbird Pass (9km total from the ranger's cabin).

Two other hikes start from Yellowhead Lake, at the other (eastern) end of the park. To get to the trailhead for **Yellowhead Mountain** (4.5km one way), follow Hwy 16 9km down from the pass and then take a gravel road 1km on an isthmus across the lake. After a steep two-hour climb through forest, the trail levels out in open country, offering sweeping views of the Yellowhead Pass area. The **Mount Fitzwilliam Trail** (13km), which leaves Hwy 16 about 1km east of the Yellowhead Mountain Trail (but on the other side of the highway), is more demanding, especially over its last half, but if you don't want to backpack to the endpoint – a truly spectacular basin of lakes and peaks – you could easily walk through the forest to the campground at **Rockingham Creek** (6km).

Yoho National Park

Wholly in British Columbia on the western side of the Continental Divide, **Yoho National Park**'s name derives from a Cree word meaning "wonder" – a testament to the awesome grandeur of the region's superlative mountains, lakes and waterfalls. At the same time it's a small park, whose intimate scale makes it perhaps the finest of the four parks. The Trans-Canada divides Yoho neatly in half, climbing from Lake Louise over the **Kicking Horse Pass** to share the broad, glaciated valley bottom of the Kicking Horse River with the old Canadian Pacific Railway. The only village, **Field** has the park center, services and limited accommodation (the nearest full-service towns are Lake Louise, 28km east, and Golden, 54km west). Other expensive accommodation is available at the central hubs, **Lake O'Hara**, the **Yoho Valley and Emerald Lake**, from which radiate most of its stunning and well-maintained trails. Thus these areas – not Field – are the focal points of the park, and get very busy in summer. Side roads lead to Emerald Lake and the Yoho Valley, so if you choose you can drive in, do a hike, and then move on at night.

Access to Lake O'Hara is far more difficult, being reserved for those on foot, or those with lodge or campground reservations (who must book on to a special bus). The five **park-run** campgrounds are the most accessible, and there's a single (road-accessible) youth hostel in the Yoho Valley. The Trans-Canada also gives direct access to short but scenic trails (see box on p.424); as these take only an hour or so, they're the best choice if you only want a quick taste of the park before moving on.

Field

No more than a few wooden houses, and backed by an amphitheater of sheer-dropped mountains, **FIELD** looks like an old-world pioneer settlement, little changed from its 1884 origins as a railway construction camp (named after Cyrus Field, sponsor of the first trans-Atlantic communication cable, who visited Yoho that year). As in other national parks, it was the railway that first spawned tourism in the area: the first hotel in Field was built by the Canadian Pacific in 1886, and within a few months 16 square kilometers at the foot of Mount Stephen (the peak to Field's east) had been set aside as a special reserve. National park status arrived in 1911, making Yoho the second of Canada's national parks.

Passenger services (other than private excursions) no longer come through Field, but the **railway** is still one of the park "sights", and among the first things you see whether you enter the park from east or west. That it came this way at all was the result of desperate political and economic horse-trading. The Canadian Pacific's chief surveyor, Sandford Fleming, wrote of his journey over the proposed Kicking Horse Pass route in 1883: "I do not think I can forget that terrible walk; it was the greatest trial I ever experienced." Like many in the company he was convinced the railway should take the much lower and more amenable Yellowhead route to the north (see "Mount Robson Provincial Park"). The railway was as much a political as a transportational tool, however, designed to unite the country and encourage settlement of the prairies. A northerly route would have ignored great tracts of valuable prairie near the US border (around Calgary), and allowed much of the area and its resources (later found to include oil and gas) to slip from the Dominion into the hands of the US. Against all engineering advice, therefore, the railway was cajoled into taking the Kicking Horse

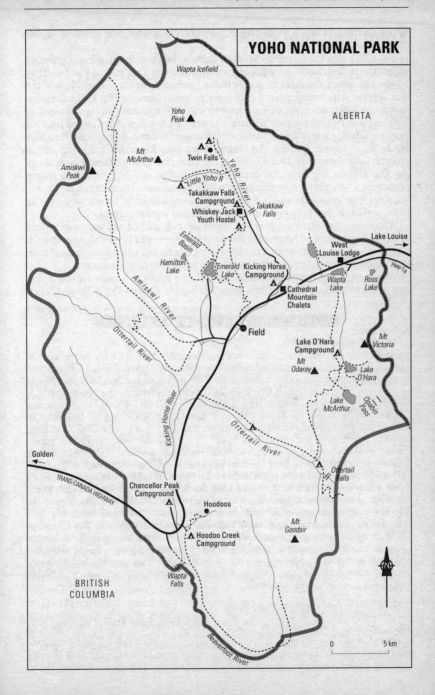

YOHO NATIONAL PARK

Wapta Icefield

ALBERTA

Yoho Peak ▲

Mt McArthur ▲ Twin Falls

Little Yoho R

Takakkaw Falls Campground

Whiskey Jack Youth Hostel

Amiskwi Peak ▲

Takakkaw Falls

West Louise Lodge

Lake Louise

Hwy-1a

Emerald Basin

Hamilton Lake

Emerald Lake

Kicking Horse Campground

Cathedral Mountain Chalets

Wapta Lake

Ross Lake

● Field

Lake O'Hara Campground

Mt Victoria ▲

Mt Odaray ▲

Lake O'Hara

Amiskwi River

Ottertail River

Kicking Horse River

Lake McArthur

Opabin Pass

Ottertail River

Ottertail Falls

Golden

TRANS-CANADA HIGHWAY

Chancellor Peak Campground

● Hoodoos

Mt Goodsir ▲

Hoodoo Creek Campground

BRITISH COLUMBIA

Wapta Falls

Beaverfoot River

N

0   5 km

route, and thus obliged to negotiate four percent grades, the greatest of any commercial railway of the time.

The result was the infamous **Spiral Tunnels**, two vast figure-of-eight galleries within the mountains (from a popular viewpoint about 7km east of Field on Hwy 1, you can watch the front of goods trains emerge from the tunnels before the rear wagons have even entered). Still more notorious was the **Big Hill**, where the line drops 330 meters in just six kilometers from Wapta Lake to the flats east of Field. The very first construction train to attempt the descent plunged into the canyon, killing three railway workers. Runaways became so common that four blasts on a whistle became the standard warning for trains careering out of control. Lady Agnes MacDonald, wife of the Canadian Prime Minister, rode down the Big Hill on the front cow-catcher of an engine in 1886, remarking that it presented a "delightful opportunity for a new sensation". Trains climbing the hill required four locomotives to pull a mere fifteen coaches: the ascent took over an hour, and exploding boilers (and resulting deaths) were recurrent.

Whatever other literature may say, there are now no *VIA rail* passenger trains to Field. The village is, however, a flag stop for *Greyhound* **buses** (5 daily in each direction) – wave them down from the *Petro-Canada* just east of the turn-off from the highway to the village, though most stop anyway to drop packages.

Yoho's **park information center**, marked by a distinctive blue roof about 1km east of Field (daily, July–Aug 8am–9pm, April–June & Sept–Oct 8.30am–4.30pm;

HIKES IN YOHO NATIONAL PARK

Hikes from Lake O'Hara

For walking purposes the Lake O'Hara region divides into five basic zones, each of which deserves a full day of exploration: Lake Oesa, the Opabin Plateau (often closed to protect its grizzlies), Lake McArthur, the Odaray Plateau and the Duchesnay Basin.

If you have time to do only one day hike, the classic (if not the most walked) trail is probably the **Opabin Plateau Trail** (3.2km one way), from the *Lake O'Hara Lodge* to Opabin Lake. Despite its brevity, you could spend hours wandering the plateau's tiny lakes and alpine meadows on the secondary trails which criss-cross the area. Most people return to O'Hara via the East Circuit Trail, but a still more exhilarating hike – and a good day's outing – is to walk the Yukness Ledge, a section of the Alpine Circuit (see below) that cuts up from the East Circuit just 400m after leaving Opabin Lake. This spectacular high-level route leads to the beautiful **Lake Oesa**, from where it's just 3.2km down to Lake O'Hara. The **Lake McArthur Trail** (3.5km one way) heads to the largest and most-photographed of the lakes in the Lake O'Hara area.

The longest and least-walked path is the **Linda Lake–Cathedral Basin** trip, past several lakes to a great viewpoint at Cathedral Platform Prospect (7.4km one way). The more challenging high-level **Alpine Circuit** (11.8km), taking in Oesa, Opabin and Schaffer lakes, is straightforward in fine weather, and when all the snow has melted; very fit and experienced walkers should have little trouble, though there's considerable exposure, and some scrambling is required. At other times it's best left to climbers, or left alone completely.

Yoho Valley and Emerald Lake hikes

The most tramped path in the Yoho Valley is the **Twin Falls Trail** (8.5km one way) from the Takakkaw Falls parking lot. This easy six-hour round trip has the reward of the Twin Falls cataract at the end, plus fine scenery and lesser waterfalls en route. If you're tenting (there are four backcountry sites up here) – or very fit – you can

☎343-6433), has displays, lectures and slide shows, and advises on trail and climbing conditions. It also gives out a useful backcountry guide and sells 1:50,000 **maps** of the park. Backcountry camping requires a permit, and if you intend to camp at Lake O'Hara (see below) it's essential to make **reservations** at the information center. The Park Administration Office in Field offers similar help and services in and out of season (Mon–Fri 8am–4.30pm; ☎343-6324).

Yoho's popularity and accessibility mean huge pressure on accommodation in late July and August; if you're really stuck, you can always make for one of the motels in Golden (see p.428). The only officially listed **rooms** in Field itself are the fourteen units of the excellent new *Kicking Horse Lodge and Café*, 100 Centre St (☎343-6303; ④), though you may strike lucky with private rooms such as *Field's Bed and Kitchen*, 310a-1st Ave (☎343-6444 or 343-6445; ③). Away from the village, but on or just off the Trans-Canada (Hwy 1) are *Cathedral Mountain Chalets* (June–Sept; ☎343-6442), 4km east of Field (leave the highway at the Takakkaw Falls turn-off), and the *West Louise Lodge* (☎343-6418; ⑥), just inside the park boundary, 11km west of Lake Louise. The most central of the five park-run **campgrounds**, *Kicking Horse* (mid-May to early Oct; $11–15), lies 5km east of Field and is fully serviced and pleasingly forested, though it echoes with goods trains rumbling through day and night. In summer a separate overflow site charges half price (no showers), but even this fills up and you should aim to arrive early.

combine Twin Falls with any of three other highly scenic walks: the Whaleback (4.5km one way; 1hr 30min), the Highline (24.4km back to Field, a two-day trek), and the Little Yoho Valley (5.3km one way; 2hr). This last is the principal goal of most backpackers; the upper reaches of the valley can also be reached directly from the Takakkaw Falls parking lot by a trail that contours above Lake Celeste. A shorter walk from the same parking lot is the Yoho Pass (10.9km; 310m vertical, 510m height loss), which links to Emerald Lake and its eponymous lodge.

From Emerald Lake the best day trip is the comparatively under-used but immensely interesting **Hamilton Lake Trail** (5.5km one way; 850m vertical; 2–3hr), leaving from the parking area at the end of Emerald Lake Road. It's demanding and steep in places, and confined to forest for the first hour or so – thereafter it's magnificent. The more modest climb to **Emerald Basin** (4.3km one way; 300m vertical; 1–2hr) also gives relative peace and quiet, following the lakeshore before climbing through forest, and ending in a small, rocky amphitheater.

Hikes from the Trans-Canada

Five short walks can be accessed off the Trans-Canada Highway. From east to west these are: **Ross Lake** (1.3km), a stunning little walk given the loveliness of the lake and the ease with which you reach it (accessed 1km south of the Great Divide picnic area); **Sherbrooke Lake** (3.1km), a peaceful sub-alpine lake accessible from the Wapta Lake picnic area (5km west of the Great Divide), where stronger walkers can peel off after 1.4km to Paget Lookout for huge views of the Kicking Horse Valley (3.5km; 520m ascent); **Mount Stephen Fossil Beds** (2.7km), a short but very steep trail, for fossil lovers only, from First St East in Field; **Hoodoo Creek** (3.1km), on the western edge of the park, accessed from the 600-meter gravel road from the Hoodoo Creek campground: the steep path leads to the weirdly eroded hoodoos themselves, pillars of glacial debris topped by protective capping stones; **Wapta Falls** (2.4km), an excellent and almost level forty-minute walk on a good trail to Yoho's largest waterfalls (by volume of water), accessed via a 1.6km dirt road 25km west of Field.

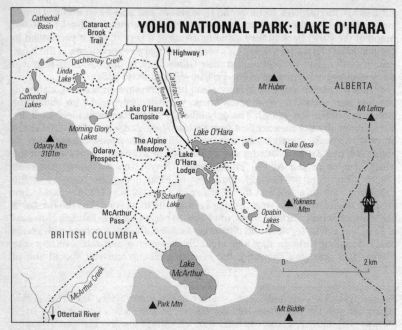

Map labels:
Cathedral Basin
Cataract Brook Trail
YOHO NATIONAL PARK: LAKE O'HARA
Highway 1
Duchesnay Creek
Linda Lake
Access Road
Cataract Brook
Mt Huber
ALBERTA
Mt Lefroy
Cathedral Lakes
Lake O'Hara Campsite
Lake O'Hara
Morning Glory Lakes
Odaray Mtn 3101m
The Alpine Meadow
Odaray Prospect
Lake O'Hara Lodge
Lake Oesa
Schaffer Lake
McArthur Pass
Yukness Mtn
Opabin Lakes
BRITISH COLUMBIA
McArthur Creek
Lake McArthur
0   2 km
Park Mtn
Mt Biddle
Ottertail River

Lake O'Hara

Backed up against the Continental Divide at the eastern edge of the park, **Lake O'Hara** is one of the Rockies' finest all-round enclaves – staggering scenery, numerous lakes, and an immense diversity of alpine and sub-alpine terrain. It's a great base for concentrated hiking: you could easily spend a fortnight exploring the well-constructed trails that strike out from the central lodge and campground. The setting is matchless, the lake framed by two of the peaks that also overlook Lake Louise across the ridge – mounts Lefroy and Victoria. The one problem is **access**, which is severely restricted to safeguard the mountain flora and fauna.

To get there, turn off the Trans-Canada onto Hwy 1A (3.2km west of the Continental Divide), cross the railway and turn right onto the gravel road leading to the parking area (1km). This road continues all the way up to the lake (13km), but it's not open to general traffic (or bikes – *no* bikes are allowed on the road or anywhere else in the Lake O'Hara region). A special **bus** runs from the parking lot up to the lake (late June to early Sept daily at 8.30am, 11.30am & 4.30pm), but priority is given to those with reservations for the lodge, campground or Alpine Club huts. Reservations are taken up to a month in advance: call in at the Field information center or phone the **reservation line** (daily ☎343-6433; cancellations ☎343-6344). If you're walking, there are no restrictions or quotas.

The picturesque **Cataract Brook Trail** (12.9km) runs roughly parallel to the road. However, it's a long way to walk before you start the proper trails from the lake (see box). Even without a reservation, it can be worth applying for stand-bys or waiting for the bus, especially when the weather's not too good and there may be no-shows for booked places. Ten of the thirty places at the campground are kept free daily and allocated on a first-come, first-served basis, but you'll have to get there early – **always** ask at the information center before you set off. To stay in one of the 23 rooms at *Lake O'Hara Lodge* (closed May and Oct–Dec; ☎343-6418; ⑦), you always need to reserve weeks in advance. Out of season you can make bookings by post to Box 1677, Banff, AB, or call ☎403/762-2118.

The Yoho Valley and Emerald Lake

Less compact an area than Lake O'Hara, the **Yoho Valley** and nearby **Emerald Lake** were formerly used by the Cree to hide their women and children while the men crossed the mountains into Alberta to trade and hunt buffalo, until the eradication of the buffalo herds, and the arrival of the railway in 1884, put paid to such ways. Now they combine to form one of the Rockies' most important backpacking zones. Though popular and easily reached – access roads head north from the

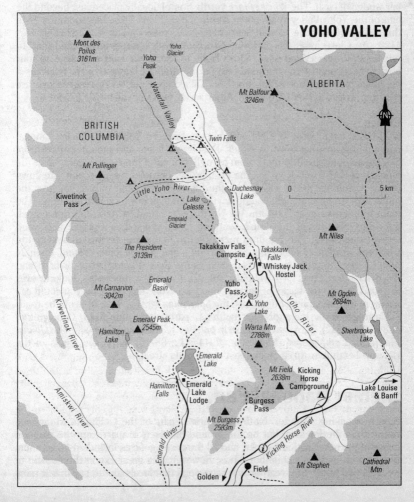

Trans-Canada up both the Emerald and Yoho valleys – the region is not, however, quite as crowded as its counterpart to the south. The scenery is equally mesmerizing, and if fewer of the trails are designed for day hikes, many of them interlock so that you can tailor walks to suit your schedule or fitness (see box on p.424).

Most trails start from the end of the Yoho Valley road at the **Takakkaw Falls** parking area (14km); the road leaves the Trans-Canada about 5km east of Field (signed from the *Kicking Horse* campground). The cascades' total 254-meter drop make them among the most spectacular road-accessible falls in the mountains: *takakkaw* is a Cree word meaning "it is wonderful".The Emerald Lake road leaves the Trans-Canada about 2km west of Field and ends, 8km on, at the *Emerald Lake Lodge* (☎343-6321 or 1-800/663-6336; ⑧), which has a **restaurant** where walking boots are certainly not in order, and a less formal **bar** for drinks and snacks. If you want to stay, advance reservations are essential, as is a willingness to part with a fair wodge of cash. The *Whiskey Jack* **youth hostel**, ideally placed just beyond the end of the Yoho Valley road, 500m south of Takakkaw Falls, has room for 27 in three dorms(mid-June to mid-Sept; ☎283-5551; reservations ☎237-8282 or 762-4122; ①). Close by is the park-run *Takakkaw Falls* **campground** (mid-June to mid-Sept; 35 unserviced sites; $10). Trails to the north (see box) lead to four further backcountry campgrounds, while the *Alpine Club of Canada* operates a members-only trail hut 8.5km north of Takakkaw Falls ($15); reservations are required – write to Box 1026, Banff, Alberta TOL OCO, or call ☎403/762-4481.

Golden

GOLDEN, 54km west of Field and midway between Yoho and Glacier national parks, is the nearest town to either. Despite its name and mountain backdrop, Golden amounts to little more than an ugly ribbon of motels and garages at the junction of Hwy 1 and Hwy 95. The town proper occupies a semi-scenic site down by the Columbia River, way below the highway strip, but only if you use the municipal campground will you do anything but look down on it from above. The main **infocentre** is at 500-10th Ave North (year round; ☎344-7125), but a small infocentre also sits at the strip's southern end disguised as a plastic and wood tepee (June–Sept). Two hundred meters north is the **bus terminal**, next to the Chinese-Canadian *Golden Palace Restaurant* – like several joints around, open 24 hours a day. All the many **motels**, such as the *Swiss Village* (☎344-2276;②) and the *Selkirk Inn*, Hwy 1 (☎ 344-6315; ②), are much of a muchness, looking over the road or onto the backs of garages opposite. None has anything you could call a view of the mountains, but at least the *Sportsman* (☎344-2915; ②) is off the road.

Campgrounds have prettier settings, particularly the *KOA Campground* (☎344-6464; $12), 3km east of the strip on Hwy 1. The town's own site, the *Golden Municipal Campground* (May–Sept; ☎344-5412; $8–10), is on the banks of the river on Tenth Ave, three blocks east of the main street.

Glacier National Park

Strictly speaking, **Glacier National Park** is part of the Columbia Mountains rather than the Rockies, but on the ground little sets it apart from the magnificence of the other national parks, and all the park agencies include it on an equal footing with its larger neighbors. It is, however, to a great extent the domain of ice, rain and snow; the weather is so atrocious that locals like to say that it rains

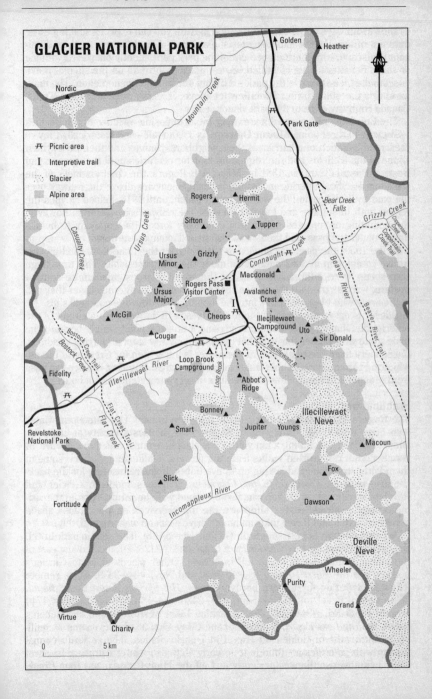

GLACIER NATIONAL PARK

Golden
Heather

Nordic

Park Gate

Picnic area
Interpretive trail
Glacier
Alpine area

Mountain Creek

Bear Creek Falls

Grizzly Creek

Rogers
Hermit

Sifton
Tupper

Copperstain Creek Trail

Connaught Creek

Ursus Creek

Ursus Minor
Grizzly

Macdonald

Casualty Creek

Rogers Pass Visitor Center

Avalanche Crest

Beaver River

Ursus Major

McGill

Cheops

Illecillewaet Campground
Uto
Sir Donald

Bostock Creek Trail
Cougar

Bostock Creek

Illecillewaet River

Loop Brook Campground

Illecillewaet R.

Beaver River Trail

Fidelity

Flat Creek Trail

Abbot's Ridge

Bonney

Illecillewaet Neve

Flat Creek

Smart
Jupiter
Youngs

Revelstoke National Park

Macoun

Slick

Fox

Fortitude

Incomappleux River

Dawson

Deville Neve

Wheeler

Purity

Virtue
Charity

Grand

0   5 km

or snows four days out of every three, and in truth you can expect a soaking three days out of five. As the name suggests, **glaciers** – 422 of them – form its dominant landscape, with fourteen percent of the park permanently blanketed with ice or snow. Scientists have identified 68 new glaciers forming on the sites of previously melted ice-sheets in the park – a highly uncommon phenomenon. The main ice-sheet, the still-growing **Illecillewaet Neve**, is easily seen from the Trans-Canada Highway or from the park visitor center.

The Columbia range's peaks are every bit as imposing as those of the Rockies – Glacier's highest point, **Mount Dawson**, is 3390m tall – and historically they've presented as much of a barrier as their neighbors. Natives and then railwaymen shunned the icefields and the rugged interior for centuries until the discovery of **Rogers Pass** (1321m) in 1881 by Major A B Rogers, the chief engineer of the Canadian Pacific. Suffering incredible hardships, navvies drove the railway over the pass by 1885, paving the way for trains which, until 1916, helped to open the region both to settlers and tourists. Despite the railway's best efforts, however, the pounding of repeated avalanches eventually forced the company to bore a tunnel under the pass, and the flow of visitors fell to almost nothing.

In the 1950s the pass was chosen as the route for the Trans-Canada Highway, whose completion in 1962 once again made the area accessible. This time huge snowsheds were built, backed up by the world's largest **avalanche-control system**. Experts monitor the slopes year round, and at dangerous times they call in the army who blast howitzers into the mountains to dislodge potential slips.

Glacier is easy enough to get to, but it doesn't tie in well with a circuit of the other parks; many people end up traversing it at some point simply because the main route west passes this way, but comparatively few stop, preferring to admire the scenery from the road. The visitor center is a flag stop for *Greyhound* **buses**, which zip through seven times a day in each direction. Entering Glacier you pass from Mountain to Pacific time – remember to set your watch back an hour.

Practicalities

The **Rogers Pass visitor center** (daily mid-June to early Oct 9am–9pm, winter 9am–5pm; ☎837-6274), 1km west of Rogers Pass, houses a variety of high-tech audio-visual aids, including a fun video on avalanche control called *Snow Wars*. In summer, staff run **guided walks** featuring flowers, wildlife and glaciers, some of them fairly strenuous and lasting up to five hours. If you're heading for the backcountry, pick up *Footloose in the Columbias*, a hiker's guide to Glacier and Revelstoke national parks; you can also buy good walking **maps**. Next to the visitor center, a **garage** and a **shop** are the only services on the Trans-Canada between Golden and Revelstoke, an hour's drive east and west respectively.

Accommodation is best sought in Golden (see p.428). The sole in-park **hotel**, the excellent *Best Western Glacier Park Lodge* (☎837-2126; ④), located just east of the visitor center, tends to be full in season. Other places close to Glacier's borders are the *Purcell Lodge* (closed May and Nov; ☎344-2639; ⑥), a remote lodge at 2180m on the eastern border; *Canyon Hot Springs Resort Campground*, 35km east of Revelstoke (May–Sept; ☎837-2420; $14–18); *Hillside Lodging*, 1740 Seward Front Rd (☎344-7281; ③), six cabins 13km west of Golden at Blaeberry River; and *Big Lake Resort*, Kinbasket Lake (May–Oct; no phone; rooms ②; tents $12), 25km west of Golden off Hwy 1 at Donald Station. The park-run **campgrounds** are *Illecillewaet* (mid-June to early Oct; also winter camping; 58 sites; $10), 3.4km west of the visitor center just off the Trans-Canada, and *Loop Brook*,

Glacier's primary renown is among serious climbers, but day-hikers and backpackers have plenty of options. Some of the park's 21 **trails** push close to glaciers for casual views of the ice – though only two spots are now safe at the toe of the Illecillewaet – and the backcountry is noticeably less busy than in the Big Four parks to the east.

The easiest short strolls off the road are the **Abandoned Rails Trail** (1.2km one way; 30min), along old rail beds to abandoned snowsheds; the **Loop Trail** (1.6km) from Loop Brook campground, full of viewpoints and features relating to the building of the railway; and the **Meeting of the Water Trail** (30min) from the Illecillewaet campground, the hub of Glacier's trail network. Six manageable day hikes from the campground give superb views onto the glaciers, particularly the **Avalanche Crest** and **Abbott's Ridge** trails.

Among the backpacking routes, the longest is the **Beaver River Trail** (30km-plus), which peels off from the highway at the Mount Shaughnessy picnic area on the eastern edge (also a favorite mountain bike route). The single best long-haul trail, however, is the **Copperstain Creek Trail** (16km), which leaves the Beaver River path after 3km, and climbs to meadows and bleak alpine tundra from where camping and onward walking options are almost endless.

2km further west (mid-June to early Sept; 19 sites; $10), which provides the luxuries of wood, water and flush toilets only on a first-come, first-served basis. If you don't manage to get into these, or want more facilities, there are three commercial campgrounds west of the park on the Trans-Canada towards Revelstoke. Free wilderness camping is allowed anywhere if you register with the visitor center and pitch more than 5km from the road.

Mount Revelstoke National Park

The smallest national park in the region, **Mount Revelstoke National Park**, is a somewhat arbitrary creation, put together at the request of local people in 1914 to protect the Clachnacudainn Range of the Columbia Mountains. The lines on the map mean little, for the superlative scenery in the 16km of no-man's-land between Glacier and Revelstoke is largely the same as that within the parks. The mountains here are especially steep, their slopes often scythed clear of trees by avalanches. You can see plenty from the Trans-Canada as it peeks out of countless tunnels – forests and snow-capped peaks aplenty, and far below, the railway and the Illecillewaet River crashing through a twisting, steep-sided gorge.

REVELSTOKE, the only community within striking range of the park, sits just outside the western boundary. Like many mountain towns, it's divided between a motel-and-garage strip along the Trans-Canada and a dispersed, frontier-type collection of houses to the rear. The river and rugged scenery roundabout redeem it, and the downtown area also has a nice feel, having been spruced up as a placatory measure following the disaster at the dam site (see below). If you're without your own vehicle, it's a good twenty-minute walk from the strip.

The main access to the park interior is the very busy **Summit Road**, or **Summit Parkway** (generally open June–Oct), which strikes north from the Trans-Canada at the town of Revelstoke and winds 26km almost to the top of

Mount Revelstoke (1938m) through forest and alpine meadows noted for glorious displays of wild flowers (best during July and August). You can also walk this stretch on the **Summit Trail** (10km one way; 4hr) from the parking lot at the base of Summit Road. Recent damage to the delicate eco-system, however, has prompted park authorities to rethink, and over the next couple of years the last 1.5km of the road will be closed to cars, leaving the choice of a walk or shuttle bus to the summit from a parking lot at Balsam Lake.

Most of the longer of the park's ten official **trails** start from the top of Summit Road; serious backpackers prefer to head to **Eagle Lake**, off Summit Road, rather than take the more popular **Miller Lake Trail** (6km one way). The award-winning **Giant Cedars Trail** is a bosky one-kilometer jaunt with ten interpretive exhibits off the road on the park's eastern edge, negotiating a tract of ancient forest crammed with 600-year-old Western Red Cedars and rough-barked Western Hemlock. **Meadows in the Sky Trail**, by contrast, is a quick loop through alpine meadows at the top of Summit Road. The *Footloose in the Columbias* booklet, available from Glacier's Rogers Pass visitor center, has further trail information.

Transportation and information

Seven daily *Greyhound* **buses** stop at the town of Revelstoke between Kamloops and Calgary; the terminal is at the west end of the strip, immediately after the big blue Columbia River bridge (☎837-5874). The **infocentre** is 200m beyond on the left (daily, July & Aug 8am–8pm, May & June 10am–6pm; ☎837-5345). Get park information there, or call in on the **Park Administration Office** at 301 Cambell Ave (Mon–Fri 8am–4.30pm; ☎837-7500) or the Rogers Pass visitor center.

Accommodation and eating

A far more amenable place to stay than Golden, the town of Revelstoke has plenty of **accommodation** – fifteen-plus motels and half a dozen campgrounds. The *Frontier* **restaurant** on the Trans-Canada, part of the eponymous motel near the infocentre, serves up superior steak-and-salad meals at reasonable prices, with friendly service and a genuine cowpoke atmosphere. In town, the *One-Twelve Restaurant* at 112 Victoria Rd is a favorite, with a pub and dance floor.

Best Western Wayside Inn, 1901 Laforme Blvd (☎837-6161 or 1-800/528-1234). The priciest and probably the best of the town's hotels. ④.

Columbia Motel, 1601-2nd St West (☎837-2191 or 1-800/663-5303). With 54 rooms one of the larger places in town; air-conditioned and heated pool in season as an extra draw. ②.

Frontier Motel and Restaurant, 122 North Nakusp Hwy (☎837-5512). On the main Trans-Canada away from the town center; good motel and first-rate food. ②.

Nelles Ranch Bed and Breakfast, Hwy 23 South (☎837-3800). Just four units on a working horse and cattle ranch 2km off the Trans-Canada Hwy. ②.

Peaks Lodge, 5km west of Revelstoke off Hwy 1 (☎837-2176). Nice small place in a reasonably rustic setting convenient for hikes, bird-watching and the like. ③.

'R' Motel, 1500 First St (☎837-2164). The cheapest motel in town. ①.

Sandman Inn, 1821 Fraser St (☎837-5271 or 1-800/726-3626). Part of a usually reliable mid-range hotel chain. ③.

Campgrounds

Revelstoke has no park-run sites. **Backcountry** camping in the park is free, with tent-pads, outhouses and food storage poles provided at Eva and Jade lakes, but isn't allowed in the Miller Lake area or anywhere within 5km of the Trans-Canada and Summit Road. Registration at the Park Administration Office is obligatory.

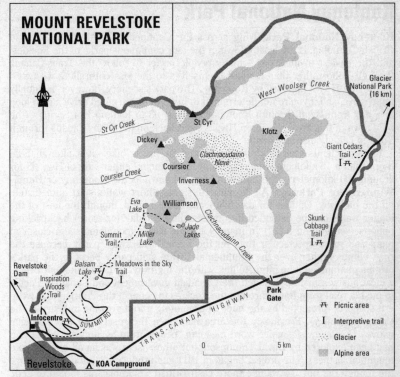

MOUNT REVELSTOKE NATIONAL PARK

The park is so small, however, that you might be better off at some of the area's more developed private **campgrounds**.

Highway Haven Motel and Campground, Three Valley Lake (☎837-2525). 20km west of Revelstoke near lake for swimming, boating etc. 30 pitches and hot showers. April–Nov. $10.

KOA Revelstoke, 5km east of Revelstoke (☎837-2085). The best of the area's campgrounds. Free showers, plus shop and swimming pool. April–Oct. $17.50.

Lamplighter Campground, off Hwy 1 before the Columbia River bridge (☎837-3385). 60 fully serviced sites. April–Oct. $12.

Williamson Lake Campground, 1818 Williamson Lake Rd (☎837-5512). Nice 36-site lakeside campground 5km from the town center. May–Sept. $16.

Revelstoke Dam

It might sound dull, but the **Revelstoke Dam** – Canada's largest, a 175-meter-tall barrier holding back the waters of the Columbia River – makes an interesting outing, 4km north of the town on Hwy 23 (daily, mid-June to early Sept 8am–8pm, mid-March to mid-June and early Sept to late Oct 9am–5pm; free). The sleek, space-age **visitor center** offers a well-put-together two-hour self-guided tour, which omits to tell you that insufficient mapping during the construction caused a landslide that threatened to swamp Revelstoke: millions had to be spent or it would have been curtains for the town. The boring bits of the tour can be skipped in favor of a lift to the top for a great view of the dam and surrounding valley.

Kootenay National Park

Kootenay National Park, lying across the Continental Divide from Banff in British Columbia, is the least known of the four contiguous parks of the Rockies, and the easiest to miss out – many people prefer to follow the Trans-Canada through Yoho rather than commit themselves to the less enthralling westward journey on Hwy 3 imposed by Kootenay. The park's scenery, however, is equally impressive, and if you're not determined to head west you could drive a neat loop in a day from Banff through Kootenay on Hwy 93 to Radium Hot Springs (the only town in this area), north on Hwy 95, and back on the Trans-Canada through Yoho to Lake Louise and Banff.

Kootenay lends itself to admiration from a car, bus or bike – it is, after all, little more than a 16-kilometer-wide ribbon of land running either side of Hwy 93 for around 100 kilometers (the highway here is known as the **Kootenay** or **Banff–Windermere Parkway**). All its numerous easy **short walks** start immediately off the highway. Options for day hikes are more limited, though the best of the longer walks can be extended into outstanding two-day (or more) backpacking options (see box on p.437) In many ways the park's mountains seem closer at hand and more spectacular than on the Icefields Parkway, partly because the road climbs higher over the Continental Divide, and partly because the park's origins guaranteed it an intimate link with the highway. In 1910 Randolph Bruce, a local businessman, persuaded the Canadian government and Canadian Pacific to push a road from Banff through the Rockies to connect the Prairies with western seaports (prompted by the hope of promoting a fruit-growing industry in the Columbia Valley). Previously the area had been the reserve of the Kootenai natives (*Kootenay* is a native word meaning "people from beyond the hills") and had been explored by David Thompson, but otherwise it was an all but inviolate mountain fastness. The project began in 1911 and produced 22km of road before the money ran out. To wangle more cash British Columbia was forced to cede 8km of land on each side of the highway to the government as a national park.

Practicalities

The only practicable access to Kootenay is on Hwy 93, a good road that leaves the Trans-Canada at Castle Junction (in Banff National Park), traverses Kootenay from north to south, and joins Hwy 95 at Radium Hot Springs at the southern entrance. Radium offers the only practical accommodation options, bar a trio of park-run campgrounds and handful of rooms at Vermilion Crossing, a summer-only huddle of shop, cabins and petrol station midway through the park. The two daily *Greyhound* **buses** east and west on the southern British Columbia route between Cranbrook, Banff and Calgary stop at Vermilion Crossing and Radium.

If you come from the east you'll hit the **Marble Canyon Information Centre** about 15km from Castle Junction (mid-June to early Sept, Fri–Mon 8.30am–8pm, Tues–Thurs 8.30am–4.30pm; no phone); coming the other way, the **West Gate Information Centre**, park warden station and ticket booth are at the southern/western end of the highway close to Radium (late June to mid-Sept daily 8am–8pm; mid-Sept to mid-Oct Sat & Sun 8am–8pm; ☎347-9505). The latter can sell you a topographical map of the park ($8.50), but both distribute the free *Backcountry Guide to Kootenay National Park*, all you need walk-wise if you're not planning anything too ambitious.

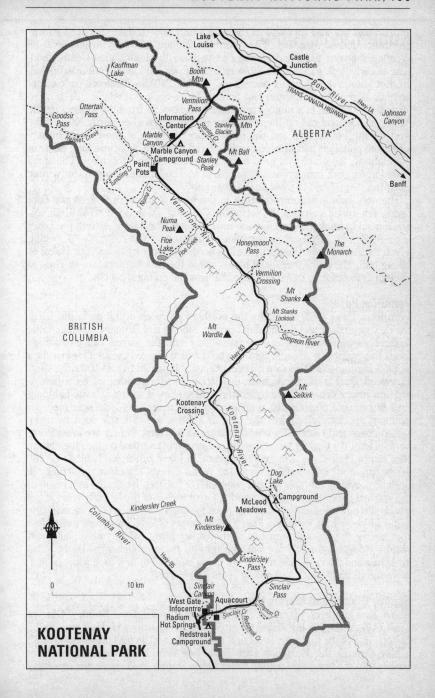

KOOTENAY NATIONAL PARK

Park staff are also on hand at the park's only two roadside serviced **camp-grounds**: *McLeod Meadows*, 25km north of Radium (mid-May to mid-Sept; 98 sites; no showers; $12), and *Marble Canyon*, near the Information Centre (mid-June to early Sept; 61 sites; no showers; $12). If you want more comforts (including hot showers) and easier access use the big 240-site *Redstreak* park campground, 3km north of Radium Hot Springs (May–Sept; ☎347-9567; $10–18); the turn-off for the site is a minor road signed off Hwy 95 from the village, by the RCMP station, and not off the main Hwy 93 which branches north 200m to the west for the hot springs and the park proper. A dozen or more **backcountry sites** with pit toilets and firewood are scattered within easy backpacking range of the highway, for which you need a free **permit** from the infocentres. The small *Dolly Varden* park campground just north of McLeod Meadows opens for **winter camping** (Sept–May; 10 sites; flush toilets only).

The only indoor **accommodation** in the heart of the park is *Kootenay Park Lodge*, ten rustic cottages at Vermilion Crossing (May–Sept; ☎762-9196; ③). You'll need to book these well in advance, similarly the *Mount Assiniboine Lodge* (Feb–April and July–Sept; reservations obligatory, ☎678-2883; ④–⑥), within which the Assiniboine Provincial Park is accessible only by helicopter, skiing or hiking trail. The four other listed hotels within the park borders, are so close to Radium as to make no difference (see "Radium Hot Springs" p.439).

Vermilion Pass

Vermilion Pass (1637m) marks the northern entrance to the park, the Great Divide's watershed and the border between Alberta and British Columbia. Little fanfare, however, accompanies the transition – only the barren legacy of a huge forest fire (started by a single lightning bolt) which ravaged the area for four days in 1968, leaving a 2400-hectare blanket of stark, blackened trunks. Take the short **Fireweed Trail** (1km) through the desolation from the parking lot at the pass to see how nature deals with such disasters, indeed how it seems to invite lightning fires to promote phoenix-like regeneration. The ubiquitous lodgepole pine, for example, specifically requires the heat of a forest fire to crack open its resin-sealed cones and release its seeds. Strange as it seems, forests are intended to burn, at least if a healthy forest is to be preserved: in montane regions the natural "fire return cycles" are a mere 42–46 years; in lower sub-alpine habitats 77–130 years; and in upper sub-alpine areas 180 years. Forests any older are actually in decline, providing few species and poor wildlife habitats. Ironically, as a result of the national parks' success in preventing forest fires over the last fifty years many woods are now over-mature, and the need for controlled burning is increasingly being addressed. At Vermilion Pass a broad carpet of lodgepole pines have taken root among the blasted remnants of the earlier forest, while young plants and shrubs ("doghair forest") are pushing up into the new clearings. Birds, small mammals and deer, elk and moose are being attracted to new food sources, and, more significantly, black and grizzly bears are returning.

Stanley Glacier and Marble Canyon

About 3km south of Vermilion Pass, the small, well-defined **Stanley Glacier Trail** (4.2km; 1hr 30min) strikes off up Stanley Creek from a parking area on the eastern side of the highway. In its first two kilometers the trail provides you with a hike through the Vermilion Pass Burn (see above), but more to the point pushes into the beautiful hanging valley below Stanley Peak. Here you can enjoy

DAY AND BACKPACKING HIKES IN KOOTENAY

If you have time and energy for only one long walk in Kootenay make it the **Kindersley Pass Trail**, a strenuous 9.8-kilometer trail that climbs to Kindersley Pass and then cuts northeast for the steep final push to Kindersley Summit. Here you can enjoy the sublime prospect of an endless succession of peaks fading to the horizon away to the northeast. Rather than double back down through the open tundra, many people push on another 2km (trail vague) and contour around the head of the Sinclair Creek valley before dropping off the ridge (the Kindersley-Sinclair Coll) to follow the well-defined **Sinclair Creek Trail** (6.4km) down to meet the highway 1km from the starting point (be sure to do the hike this way round: the Sinclair Creek trail is a long, dull climb).

Most of Kootenay's other long walks are in the park's northern half, accessed on the west side of the highway from the Marble Canyon, Paint Pots, Numa Creek and Floe Lake parking areas. The **Rockwall Trail**, a superlative thirty-kilometer (54km including approach trails) backpacking high-level trail, follows the line of the mountains here, and can be joined using four of the six trails described below. You could walk it in two days, but could easily spend longer, particularly as there are five back-country campgrounds *en route*.

From north to south on the highway, the trails start with the **Kaufmann Lake Trail** (15km one way; allow 4–6hr one way), which climbs to a classic high mountain lake. A trail from the Paint Pots runs for 2km before dividing to provide three onward options, of which the best is the **Helmet Creek Trail** (14.3km), a long day hike to the amazing Helmet Waterfalls (another intersection with the Rockwall Trail). The best of the day hikes after Kindersley Pass is the easier **Floe Lake Trail** (10.5km), up to a spellbinding lake edged by a sheer escarpment and a small glacier. There are campgrounds on the route, and another tie-in to the Rockwall Trail. The **Numa Creek Trail** (6.4km) to the north is less enthralling, as are the series of fire-road walks advertised in the park – unless you're mountain biking, therefore, ignore the Simpson River, West Kootenay, Honeymoon Pass and East Kootenay trails.

close-up views of the Stanley Glacier and its surrounding recently glaciated landscapes. The area is also known for its fossils, and for the chance to see marmots, pikas and white-tailed ptarmigan.

Marble Canyon, 8km south of Vermilion Pass, the site of a park-run **campground**, has an easy trail that's probably the most heavily trafficked of Kootenay's shorter hikes. The one-kilometer track crosses a series of log bridges over Tokumm Creek, which over 8000 years has carved through a fault in the limestone to produce a 600-meter-long and 37-meter-deep gorge. In cold weather this is a fantastic medley of ice and snow, but in summer the climax is the viewpoint from the top of the path onto a thundering waterfall as the creek pounds its way through the narrowest section of the gorge.

One of the park's better longer hikes also starts from the Marble Canyon parking lot – the **Kaufmann Lake Trail** (15km one way; 4–6hr), which follows Tokumm Creek towards the head of the valley at Kaufmann Lake (see box). The first few kilometers of the trail – easy valley and meadow walking – make an appealing hour or so's stroll.

The Paint Pots

The vivid hues of the **Paint Pots** – red, orange and mustard-colored pools renowned as one of the Rockies' more magical spots – are created by iron-laden water bubbling up from three mineral springs through clay sediments deposited on the bed of an ancient glacial lake. The pots can be reached either along the eponymous trail, which adds 2.7km onto the end of the Marble Canyon walk, or walking 1km from the Paint Pots parking area, 2km south. Either way, you pass through damp, moss-clung forest, with views across the whitewater of the Vermilion River to the snow-capped mountains beyond.

Natives from all over North America collected the colored clays from the ponds, to make into small cakes which they baked in embers. The fired clay was then ground into powder – **ochre** – and added to animal fat or fish oil to use in rock, tepee or ceremonial body painting. Ochre has always had spiritual significance for Native Americans, who saw these oxide-stained pools and their yellow-edged surroundings as inhabited by animal and thunder spirits. Standing in the quiet, rather gloomy glade, particularly on overcast days, it's easy to see why – not that the atmosphere or sanctity of the place stopped European speculators in the 1920s from mining the ochre to manufacture paint in Calgary.

The parking lot is the trailhead for three longer (day or backpack) trails, all of which kick off along the Ochre Creek Valley: Tumbling Creek Trail, Ottertail Pass Trail and the Helmet Creek-Helmet Falls Trail (see box).

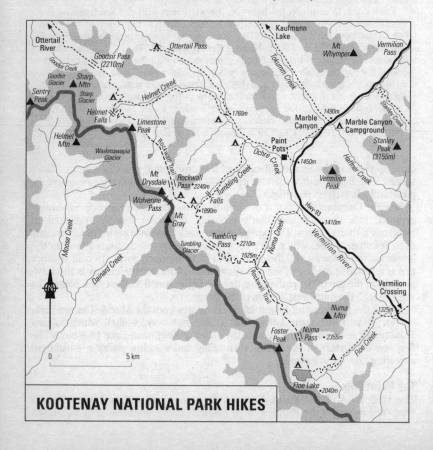

KOOTENAY NATIONAL PARK HIKES

Vermilion Crossing and Kootenay Crossing

Vermilion Crossing, 20km south of the Paint Pots Trail, is gone in a flash, but it's the only place, in summer at least, to find lodgings, petrol and food in the park. You can also stop to walk the **Verendyre Creek Trail** (2.1km), accessed west off the highway, an easy stroll, but forest-enclosed, and with only limited views of Mount Verendrye as a reward. One of the Rockies' tougher walks heads east from the Crossing, up over Honeymoon Pass and Redearth Pass to Egypt Lake and the Trans-Canada Highway in Banff National Park, while to the south equally demanding trails provide the only westside access into the wilderness of **Mount Assiniboine Provincial Park**. Sandwiched between Kootenay and Banff, the wilderness park was created in honor of Mount Assiniboine (3618m), a sabre-tooth-shaped mountain with one of the most dramatic profiles imaginable (the "Matterhorn of the Rockies", though the Stoney native name means "those who cook by placing hot rocks in water"). The **Simpson Road Trail** (8.2km) leads to the park boundary, and then divides into two paths (20km & 32km) to Lake Magog in the heart of Assiniboine.

Kootenay Crossing is no more than a ceremonial spot – it was where the ribbon was cut to open Hwy 93 in 1923 – though a clutch of short trails fan out from its park warden station, and the nearby *Dolly Varden* campground (see p.436) is the park's one specific site for winter camping. **Wardle Creek** nearby is a good place to unpack a picnic if you're determined to stick to the road; further on, the **Kootenay Valley Viewpoint** is a very popular photo-opportunity, offering one of the broadest views on the highway.

Around 11km south of the Kootenay Crossing is the **McLeod Meadows** campground (see p.436), and immediately behind it to the east the easy **Dog Lake Trail** (2.7km), much tramped as an after-dinner leg-stretcher by campers (the trail can also be accessed from the highway at the picnic area 500m south). The path offers glimpses of the Kootenay Valley through the trees, and ends in a marsh-edged lake whose temperate micro-climate makes it ideal for nature study.

Sinclair Pass

For its final rundown out of the park, the highway doglegs west through the **Sinclair Pass**, a red-cliffed gorge filled with the falling waters of Sinclair Creek and the start of the **Kindersley Pass Trail**, possibly the most scenic day hike in the park (see box). If this seems too much of a slog, Sinclair Pass offers three far easier short trails, all marked off the highway to the west. The best is the **Juniper Trail** (3.2km), accessed just 300 meters inside the park's West Gate. The trail drops to Sinclair Creek and over the next couple of kilometers touches dry canyon, arid forest slopes of juniper and Douglas Fir, and thick woods of Western Red Cedar – before emerging at the hot springs, or Aquacourt (see below), 1.4km up the road from the start.

Radium Hot Springs

RADIUM HOT SPRINGS is far less attractive than its evocative name suggests, but as the service center for Kootenay, spread across the flats of the Columbia Valley, 3km from the southern/western entrance at the junction of Hwy 93 and Hwy 95, its tacky motels and garages are likely to attract your attention.

The **hot springs** (or Aquacourt) themselves, 2km north of town off the Banff–Windermere Parkway (Hwy 93), are administered by the park authorities (May–Sept daily 8.30am–11pm; Oct–April Mon–Fri noon–9pm, Sat & Sun 9.30am–9pm;

$3.50). Natives used the springs for centuries, and commercial white development started as early as 1890 when Roland Stuart bought the area for $160. Traces of supposedly therapeutic radium found in the water turned Stuart's investment into a recreational goldmine. When the government appropriated the springs for inclusion in the national park it paid him $40,000 – a small fortune, but considerably less than what they were worth, which at the time was estimated to be $500,000. The pools today are outdoors, but serviced by a large, modern center. In summer, 4000 people per day take the plunge into the odorless 45°C waters – enough to discourage any idea of a quiet swim, though in late evening or off-season (when the hot pool steams invitingly) you can escape the bedlam and pretend more easily that the water is having some sort of soothing effect. The radium traces sound a bit worrying, but 4000 Canadians can't all be wrong.

If you have the choice, aim to stay in one of the new **motels** creeping up the Sinclair Valley around the hot springs area away from downtown – they're more expensive, but far more attractively sited than the thirty-odd motels in town. Try the big *Radium Hot Springs Resort*, 1km south of the springs (☎347-9311; ⑤) for all the trimmings; *Addison's Bungalows* (April–Oct; ☎347-9545; ③), a mix of motel and cabins nearby; or the adjacent *Mount Farnham Bungalows* (☎347-9515; ③). Almost alongside the park entrance are the *Alpen Motel* (☎347-9823; ③), and the *Kootenay* (☎347-9490; ②) and *Crescent* (☎347-9570; ②) motels. Most of the motels along the main drag in town are smaller – the cheapest are the *Tuk-In* (☎347-9464; ②) and the *Sunset* (☎347-9863; ①–②).

travel details

Trains

From Calgary to Vancouver with private *Rocky Mountain Railtours* (2 weekly July–Sept; $465 one way).

From Edmonton to Prince Rupert via Jasper and Prince George (3 weekly; 30hr); Vancouver (3 weekly; 24hr); Winnipeg via Saskatoon (3 weekly; 24hr).

From Jasper to Edmonton (3 weekly; 5hr 30min); Prince Rupert via Prince George (3 weekly; 20hr); Vancouver (daily Tues–Sun June–Oct; 17hr).

Buses

From Calgary to Edmonton (14 daily; 3hr 30min); Banff (6 daily; 1hr 40min); Lake Louise (6 daily; 2hr 35min); Vancouver via Kamloops (7 daily; 13hr); Vancouver via Vernon, Kelowna and Penticton (3 daily; 16hr); Vancouver via Fort Macleod, Cranbrook, Nelson, Osoyoos and Hope (2 daily; 24hr); Winnipeg via Lethbridge, Medicine Hat and Regina (2 daily; 24hr); Creston via Banff, Radium Hot Springs and Cranbrook (1 daily; 7hr 30min); Drumheller (2 daily; 1hr 50min); Saskatoon (2 daily; 9hr); Coutts (US; connections for Las Vegas and Los Angeles) via Fort Macleod and Lethbridge (1 daily; 4hr 30min); Dawson Creek (2 daily; 7hr 15min); Fort St John (2 daily; 9hr 15min); Prince George (2 daily; 14hr).

From Edmonton to Calgary (14 daily; 3hr 30min); Vancouver (6 daily; 14hr); Jasper (6 daily; 4hr 30min); Grande Prairie (4 daily; 6hr); Peace River (3 daily; 6hr 30min); Hay River via Peace River (1 daily; 17hr); Whitehorse (1 daily mid-May to mid-Oct; 3 weekly rest of the year; 28hr); Drumheller (1 daily; 4hr 45min); Saskatoon (4 daily; 5hr); Winnipeg (2 daily; 21hr).

Flights

From Calgary to Edmonton (every 30min; 50min); Vancouver (every 30min; 1hr 20min); Toronto (14 daily; 4hr); Montréal (12 daily; 5hr).

From Edmonton to Calgary (every 30min; 50min); Vancouver (every 30min; 1hr 25min); Toronto (10 daily; 4hr 10min); Montréal (9 daily; 5hr).

CHAPTER EIGHT

NORTH TO THE YUKON

Though much of the Northwest still has the flavor of the "last frontier", once you embark on the mainland push **north to the Yukon** you get a real feeling that you're leaving the mainstream of North American life behind you. In the popular imagination, the north figures as a perpetually frozen wasteland blasted by ferocious gloomy winters, inhabited – if at all – by hardened characters beyond the reach of civilization. In truth, it's a region where months of summer sunshine offer almost limitless opportunities for outdoor activities and an incredible profusion of flora and fauna, a country within a country the character of whose settlements has often been forged by the mingling of white settlers and **native peoples**. The indigenous hunters of the north are as varied as in the south, but two groups predominate: the **Dene**, people of the northern forests who traditionally occupied the Mackenzie River region from the Albertan border to the river's delta at the Beaufort Sea; and the arctic **Inuit** (literally "the people"), once known as the Eskimos or "fish eaters", a Dene term picked up by early European settlers and now discouraged.

The **north** is as much a state of mind as a place. People "north of 60" – the 60th Parallel – claim the right to be called **northerners**, and claim a kinship with Alaskans, but those north of the Arctic Circle look with light-hearted disdain on these "southerners". All mock the inhabitants of the northernmost corners of Alberta and such areas of the so-called Northwest, who, after all, live with the luxury of being able to get around their backcountry by road. To any outsider, however, in terms of landscape and spirit of place the north begins well south of the 60th Parallel. Thus this chapter includes not just the provinces of the "true north" – **Yukon Territory** and parts of the **Northwest Territories** – but also **northern British Columbia**.

Northern British Columbia

The two roads into the Yukon strike through northern British Columbia: the **Alaska Highway**, connecting Dawson Creek to Fairbanks in Alaska, and the **Cassiar Highway**, from near Prince Rupert to Watson Lake, on the Yukon border. Though the Cassiar's passage through the Coast Mountains offers the best landscapes, it's the Alaska Highway – serviced by daily *Greyhound* **buses** and plentiful motels and campgrounds – that is more travelled, starting in the rolling wheatlands of the Peace River country before curving into the spruce forests and sawtooth ridges of the northern Rockies. Most towns on both roads are battered and perfunctory places built around lumber mills, oil and gas plants and mining camps, though they are spawning motels and restaurants to serve the surge of summer visitors out to capture the thrill of driving the frontier highways. Equally popular are the breathtaking **sea journeys** offered by northern British Columbia. **Prince Rupert**, linked by ferry to Vancouver Island, is the springboard for boats to the magnificent **Queen Charlotte Islands** – home of the Haida people – and a vital way-station along the Inside Passage up to Alaska.

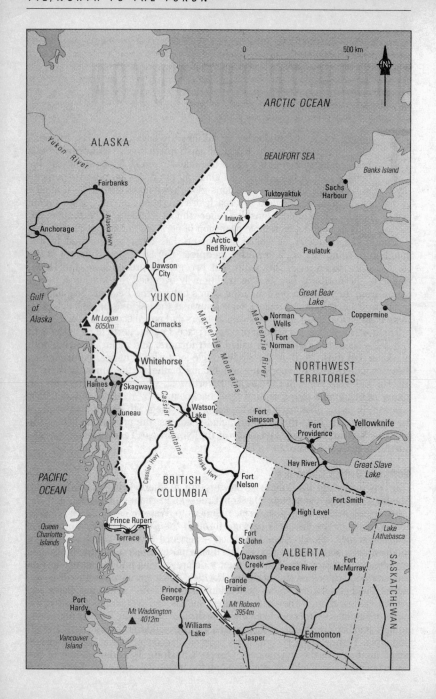

The Yukon

The Cassiar and Alaska highways converge at Watson Lake, a weather-beaten junction that straddles the 60th Parallel and marks the entrance to the **Yukon Territory** (YT), a foretaste of Alaska – though distinct and no less compelling – that is perhaps the most exhilarating and varied destination in Canada's portion of the Pacific Northwest. Taking its name from a Dene word meaning "great", it boasts the highest mountains in Canada, wild sweeps of forest and tundra, and the fascinating nineteenth-century relic, **Dawson City**. The focus of the Klondike goldrush, Dawson was also the territory's capital until that role shifted south to **Whitehorse**, a town booming on tourism and the ever-increasing exploitation of the Yukon's vast mineral resources.

Road access is easier than you might think. In addition to the Alaska Highway, which runs through the Yukon's southern reaches, the **Klondike Highway** strikes north to link Whitehorse with Dawson City. North of Dawson the recently completed **Dempster Highway** is the only road in Canada to cross the Arctic Circle, offering an unparalleled direct approach to the northern tundra and to several remote communities in the Northwest Territories. The Yukon's other major road is the short spur linking the Alaskan port of Skagway (see p.503) to Whitehorse, which shadows the **Chilkoot Trail**, a treacherous track taken by the poorest of the 1898 prospectors that is now a popular long-distance footpath.

Combining the coastal ferries with the Chilkoot Trail creates an especially fine **itinerary**. Following the old goldrush trail, the route begins at Skagway, then follows the Chilkoot to Whitehorse, before heading north to Dawson City. From there you could continue up the Dempster Highway, or travel on the equally majestic **Top of the World** into the heart of Alaska. However, many people coming up from Skagway or plying the mainland routes from British Columbia head to Alaska directly on the Alaska Highway, to enjoy views of the extraordinary and largely inaccessible mountain fastness of **Kluane National Park**.

The Northwest Territories

If the Yukon is the far north at its most accessible, the **Northwest Territories** (NWT) is the region at its most uncompromising. Just three roads nibble at the edges of this almost unimaginably vast area, which occupies a third of Canada's landmass – about the size of India – but contains only 60,000 people, almost half of whom live in or around Yellowknife, its peculiarly overblown capital. Visitors to the Pacific Northwest are likely only to be concerned with the territories' westernmost limits, and in particular the **Dempster Highway**, an adventurous and immensely rewarding trip from Dawson City across the tundra to **Inuvik**.

Most other visitors are here to fish or canoe, to hunt or watch wildlife, or to experience the **Inuit** native cultures and ethereal landscapes. More for convenience than any political or geographical reasons, the NWT is divided into **eight regions**, each with its own tourist association. We've dealt only with the region adjoining the Yukon – **Delta-Beaufort**, which embraces Inuvik and the territories' portion of the Dempster Hwy. If you intend to explore further (and there are countless flights to the more distant destinations from the Yukon and Alaska), be

TOLL-FREE INFORMATION NUMBERS

Tourism British Columbia ☎1-800/663-6000.
TravelArctic (NWT & Yukon) ☎1-800/661-0788.

certain to obtain a copy of the free *Explorers' Guide*, which summarizes accommodation options, airline connections, many of the available tours – costing anything from Can$50 to $5000 – and the plethora of outfitters who provide the equipment and back-up essential for any but the most superficial trip to the NWT.

Prince George

Rough-edged **PRINCE GEORGE**, carved from the forest to become British Columbia's third largest city, is the region's services and transport center, so you're highly likely to become acquainted with its dispersed and half-deserted downtown streets. Forestry, in the form of pulp mills, kilns, planers, plywood plants and allied chemical works, is at the core of its industrial landscape – if you ever wanted the inside story on the lumber business, this is where to find it.

Simon Fraser established a North West Trading Company post here in 1805, and named it **Fort George** in honor of the reigning George III. As a commercial nexus it quickly altered the lives of the local **Carrier Sekani** natives, who abandoned their semi-nomadic migration from winter to summer villages in favor of a permanent settlement alongside the fort. Little changed until 1914 when the arrival of the Grand Trunk Railway – later the Canadian National – spawned an influx of pioneers and loggers. The town was connected by road to Dawson Creek and the north as late as 1951, and saw the arrival of the Pacific Great Eastern Railway in 1958 – two developments that give some idea of how recent the opening up of the Canadian north has been.

The town is a disorienting open-plan network of roads and sporadic houses between Hwy 97 and a sprawling downtown area at the junction of the Fraser and Nechako rivers. As far as sight-seeing is concerned, you might as well stick to what Prince George does best and take the surprisingly popular free **tours** around some of its big mills and processing plants; to reserve a place, contact *Tourism Prince George* at either of the town's two **infocentres**: at the junction of Hwy 97 and Hwy 16 to Prince Rupert (May–Sept daily 9am–8pm; ☎563-5493), or opposite the bus terminal at 1198 Victoria St and 15th Ave (daily 9am–5pm; longer hours in summer; ☎562-3700). Company buses pick up from the centers and deliver you to one of several firms, the biggest being **Northwood Pulp and Timber**, where you are shown thousands of seedlings being grown in controlled conditions, the sawmills, and one of the continent's largest pulp mills. Outside, in a graphic illustration of the scale of Canadian forestry, logs, planks and piles of sawdust the size of small hills stretch almost as far as the eye can see.

The **telephone code** for British Columbia is ☎604.

Practicalities

Prince George is linked by **BC Rail** to Vancouver (via the Cariboo region), and by **VIA rail** to Jasper, Edmonton and beyond eastbound, and Prince Rupert (for the Prince Charlotte Islands and Inside Passage ferries) westbound. Only *VIA* drops you downtown at 1300 First Ave (☎564-5223); if you're heading for motels or the bus terminal use a taxi from either *Prince George Taxi* (☎564-4444) or *Emerald Taxi Ltd* (☎563-3333). The *BC Rail* trains arrive 5km south of downtown on Hwy 97 at the end of Terminal Blvd, but there's a free connecting bus service to various points, including the motels at the bus terminal and on Hwy 97 for a quick get-away the following day.

The town is also a staging post for *Greyhound* routes to the north (and thus Alaska), and integral to the main road routes to Dawson Creek (for the Alaska Hwy) and Prince Rupert (for the Cassiar Hwy). The *Greyhound* **bus terminal**, well south of downtown at 1566 12th Ave (☎564-5454), is close to a handful of hotels.

The best choice among the **motels** on the Hwy 97 strip is the *Spruceland Inn* (☎563-0102; ②) at the junction of Hwy 97 and 15th Ave. At the nearby *Esther's Inn* (☎562-4131; ②), one block off the highway at 1151 Commercial Drive (10th Ave), the price includes a swimming pool and jacuzzi. Closer to downtown are the *Downtown Motel*, Sixth Ave-650 Dominion St (☎563-9241; ②); the *Holiday Inn*, 444 George St (☎563-0055; ⑤); and the *Connaught Motor Inn* (☎562-4441; ②), opposite the bus terminal at 1550 Victoria St. All the **campgrounds** are some way out; at the *KOA Prince George* about 5km west on Hwy 16 (April–Oct; ☎964-7272; $14) the fee includes free hot showers and a heated outdoor pool.

With **food** don't expect much in the way of culinary sophistication and stick to good chains like *Earl's*, 15th Ave and Central St; the 1950s-style *Niners Diner* on the corner of Fifth and George; or the costlier *Cariboo Steak and Seafood Restaurant* on Fifth Ave between George and Dominion. To cheer up a night in a motel, venture out to **bars** like *Steamers*, 2595 Queensway; *JJ's*, 3601 Massey; or the *Rockpit Club*, 1380 Second Ave where some local heavy metal band is usually going through its paces.

Moving on, three *VIA rail* trains weekly run to Prince Rupert and to Edmonton via Jasper; *BC Rail* run daily trains to Vancouver in summer (3 weekly in winter) and it's well worth making a reservation on one of the more scenic of Canada's rail journeys (☎561-4033). *Greyhound* run one bus daily to Whitehorse in the Yukon, two daily to Vancouver, and two daily to Prince Rupert.

Prince George to Prince Rupert

There are two ways to make the 735-kilometer journey west from Prince George to **Prince Rupert**: neither Highway 16 nor the parallel *VIA* railway is terribly scenic until they reach the glorious river and mountain landscapes of the **Skeena Valley** 150km before Prince Rupert. Most people make this trip as a link in a much longer journey, either to reach Prince Rupert to pick up **ferries** north to Alaska or south to Port Hardy on Vancouver Island, or to join the start of the Cassiar Highway, a rough wilderness road that cuts north from the Skeena Valley to meet the Alaska Highway at Watson Lake over the Yukon border. It's also the only way to reach the Queen Charlotte Islands, accessible by ferry from Prince Rupert.

Vanderhoof to Smithers

Riding out of Prince George you're soon confronted with the relentless monotony of the Interior Plateau's rolling forests, an arboreal grind broken only by the occasional lake and the grey silhouettes of distant low-hilled horizons. At **VANDERHOOF**, 98km out, gentler patches of pasture begin to poke through the tree cover, but do little to soften the impact of the town itself. An abrupt grid of garages and motels, it's best known for its July air show and the more graceful aerial dynamics of thousands of Canadian geese at the nearby **Nechako Bird Sanctuary**. Before pushing on, grab a coffee at the *OK Café*, part of a fine collection of half-timbered heritage houses at the town's western end. If you do get stuck, or would rather stay here than Prince George, there are four inexpensive motels and a small municipal **campground** off the main highway at Stony Creek (May–Oct; ☎567-9393; $5). The **infocentre** is at 2353 Burrard Ave (year round; ☎567-2124).

Beyond here the ride becomes more verdant, so the **accommodation** possibilities of **FORT FRASER**, 50km beyond, are more attractive than those of Vanderhoof; try the quaint wooden cabins of the *Northgate Motel* (☎690-7414; ②) on the hamlet's eastern edge. If you're **camping**, hold out for the *Piper's Glen Campsite* ($8) 5km to the west, whose meadow site shelves gently to the lake.

The scenery beyond Burn's Lake picks up still more, though the run of villages continue to offer little but places to fill either the tank or the stomach. If you're going as far as to **stay** in this region aim for the excellent new *Douglas Motel* (☎846-5679; ②), just 150m out of the unspoilt hamlet of **TELKWA** on the banks of the Bulkley River. Next day, stroll up the riverfront street of heritage buildings to the handsome brown and white wood-planked **pioneer museum**.

SMITHERS, the largest place after Prince George (370km to the east), is focused on a crossroads, with an **infocentre** on one corner (year round; ☎847-9854) and a big *Super-Valu* **supermarket** on the other. If you're overnighting here, the best option is the large white-timbered *Hudson Bay Lodge* (☎847-4581; ④), outside the village as you enter from the east, though the *Florence Motel* (☎847-2678; ①) on the west side of town, or the *Sandman* on Hwy 16, part of an invariably trustworthy chain (☎847-2637; ②), charge lower rates.

The Skeena Valley

Hard on the heels of industrial Terrace, the **Skeena River** (the "River of the Mists") carves a beautiful valley through the Coast Mountains, an important trade route for natives and sternwheelers before the coming of the railway in 1912. For a couple of hours the road and railway run past a huge backdrop of snow-capped peaks half reflected in the mist-wraithed estuary. Out on the water there's a good chance of seeing the ripples of beavers and sea otters, not to mention bald eagles perched on the immense log jams. Dark valleys peel off the main river's majestic course, suggestive of a deep, untrodden wilderness and repeatedly pierced by delicate threads of waterfalls half-visible though the trees.

Shortly after Hwy 16 meets the river crashing down from the north, a couple of minor roads strike off to four nearby **Gitksan native villages** where something of the culture of the indigenous Gitksan peoples has been preserved. **'KSAN** and

Kispiox, home to the best totems and long houses, are a few kilometers off Hwy 16 on a minor road out of New Hazelton; just north of 'Ksan a road links to Kitwanga and Kitwancool. The most easterly of the Northwest Coast tribes, the Gitksan traditionally lived off fish and game rather than agriculture, and were consummate artists and carvers. Many of their traditions were eroded by the coming of whites, and by missionaries in particular, but in the 1950s the tribe's elders made a determined decision to resurrect as much of their dying culture as possible, and re-created an entire 1870 settlement at 'Ksan. Although there's a good deal of commercialism, this is the village to concentrate on – native women act as guides around several long houses, providing a commentary on the carvings, clothes, buildings and masks on show, as well as offering accounts of local history (tours daily mid-May to mid-Oct 9am–5pm; $7).

The nearest **infocentre** for the village is near New Hazelton at the junction of Hwy 16 and 62 (summer only; ☎842-6571). **Accommodation** at 'Ksan is limited to the *'Ksan Campground*, on the banks of the Skeena and Bulkley rivers (May–Oct; ☎842-5940; $9–12). At Kispiox, however, the *Sportsman's Kispiox Lodge* (☎842-6616; ①–④), *Steelhead Camp* (☎842-5435; ①) and *Kispiox Resort and Campground* (☎842-6182; ①) have a few rooms; the last two also operate as campgrounds.

Prince Rupert

There's a bracing tang of salt and fish on the air in **PRINCE RUPERT**, a distinctive port which comes as an invigorating relief after the run of characterless villages out of Prince George. A good-looking place, it has a commanding position surveying an archipelago of islands and ringed by mountains that tumble to the sea along a beautiful fjord-cut coastline. A crowd of cars, backpackers and RVs washes daily through its streets off the **Alaska, Queen Charlotte and Port Hardy ferries**, complementing the seafront's vibrant activity, and adding to the coffers of a town that's quite clearly on the up and up. There's nothing much to do, but if you're waiting for a boat it's an amiable enough spot and you'll probably bump into more fellow travellers here than almost anywhere else in northern BC.

Although you wouldn't know to look at it, the port is one of the world's largest deep-water terminals, and handles a huge volume of trade (grain, coal and fish in particular) – one reason why the old Hudson's Bay post was chosen as the terminus of Canada's second **transcontinental rail link**. The Grand Trunk Railway chairman, Charles M Hays, hoped to turn Prince Rupert into a port to rival Vancouver. In 1912 he set off for Britain to raise stock for the venture, but unfortunately chose to book a return passage on the *Titanic*. Although he went down, the railway was finished two years later – too late, in the event, to steal a march on Vancouver.

Prince Rupert's excellent little **Museum of Northern British Columbia** (May–Sept Mon–Sat 9am–9pm, Sun 9am–5pm; Oct–April Mon–Sat 10am–5pm; free), is annexed to the **infocentre** (same hours; ☎624-5637, or 1-800/667-1994 in BC) on First Ave and McBride St at the northern end of the town's tight downtown zone. It's particularly strong on the culture and history of the local **Tsimshian** natives, and has a clutch of wonderful silent archive films on topics from fishing to the building of the railway – ideal ways to whittle away a wet afternoon, of which Prince Rupert has plenty. There's also a small art gallery with a few native works, and a well-stocked bookshop, with a useful Alaskan section.

FERRIES FROM PRINCE RUPERT

Ferry terminals for both **BC Ferries** (for Port Hardy and the Queen Charlotte Islands) and the **Alaska Marine Highway** (for Skagway and Alaska Panhandle ports) are at Fairview Dock 2km southwest of town at the end of Hwy 16. Walk-on tickets for foot passengers are rarely a problem at either terminal, but advance reservations are essential if you're taking a car or want a cabin for any summer crossing. A town bus meets all incoming sailings, but for outbound sailings it's probably best to grab a **taxi** from downtown. Both operators sometimes allow backpackers to put a tent in their boats' gym or solariums.

BC Ferries operate the MV *Queen of Prince Rupert* **to Skidegate** on the Queen Charlotte Islands six times weekly in summer, less frequently in winter, a crossing which takes about 6hr 30min and costs $18 (plus $69 for cars). For booking or time-table information contact Prince Rupert's infocentre or *BC Ferries* direct on ☎624-9627. Ferries **to Port Hardy** leave four times weekly in summer and once weekly in winter for a stunning fifteen-hour cruise that costs around $90 single for walk-on passengers. To take on a car ($185) you'll need to have made a booking at least two months in advance (see also Port Hardy, p.303).

The **Alaska Marine Highway** (☎624-1744) ferries run **to Skagway** almost daily in July and August, four times weekly for the rest of the summer and in spring and fall, and twice weekly in winter (US$115; US$278–331 per car). They stop frequently en route, with the chance to go ashore for a short time, though longer stopovers must be arranged when buying a through ticket. For all Alaskan sailings turn up at least an hour before departure to go through US customs and immigration procedures, and note that though the journey takes two days there are various restrictions on the fresh food you can take on board. You can't make telephone or credit card bookings, and have to pay in person for tickets at the terminal ticket office (May–Sept daily 5am–noon; on days of sailings the rest of the year).

While you're here, check out the often-inexpensive local tours and boat trips, which can make a good way to see the offshore islands and wildlife.

A little out of town, the gondola ride to **Mount Hays** gives a bird's-eye view of the harbor and the chance to spot bald eagles – to reach it take the Wantage Rd turnoff by the *McDonald's* on Hwy 16.

Arrival

The **Greyhound station**, in the center of town at 822 Third Ave and Eighth St (☎624-5090), handles two buses to Prince George daily (about $80 one way). The **VIA rail station** is on the waterfront at First Ave and Second St (trains to Prince George Mon, Wed & Fri; information on ☎627-7589). Both *Canadian* (☎624-9181) and *BC Air* (☎624-4554) have local offices and **fly** to many BC destinations, including three scheduled flights daily to Vancouver ($325 single).

Accommodation

Finding a **place to stay** in Prince Rupert shouldn't present problems outside July and August, and if there's nothing in town, you can always backtrack along Hwy 16 to the villages beyond the Skeena Valley. The only big local **campground** is the *Park Avenue Campground*, 1750 Park Ave (year round; ☎624-5861; $9–15), west of town just 2km from the ferry terminals, but the *Parkside Resort* (see below) has fourteen sites that few people know about, and there's also the rural Prudhomme Lake provincial site (April–Nov; $8), 16km east on Hwy 16.

Aleeda, 900 Third Ave (☎627-1367). Most reasonable of the many mid-range establishments in town. ②.

Commercial, 901 First Ave (☎624-6142). Inexpensive but officially un-listed rooms of red-necked and dubious repute. ②.

Inn on the Harbour, 720 First Ave (☎624-9107). Perhaps the best all-round choice, especially if you can secure a room with a seaview. ③.

Oceanview Hotel, 950 First Ave (624-6259). Little to distinguish this place from the *Commercial*, its near neighbor. ②.

Parkside Resort, 101 11th St (☎624-9131). A smart lurid-green hotel about a kilometer out of town and more likely to have room when downtown places are full. ②.

Pioneer Rooms, 167 Third Ave (☎624-6259). The town's only decent budget option, with basic hostel-type rooms. ①.

Slumber Lodge Motor Inn, 909 Third Ave (☎627-1711). Good-value, middling motel. ③.

Eating and drinking

Fresh **fish** is the obvious thing to **eat**, preferably at the *Green Apple*, a homey shack and town institution that serves a mean halibut and chips for $6; it's at 301 McBride, just before Hwy 16 turns into town. For something a touch more upmarket, locals flock to the *Smile's Seafood Café*, at 113 George Hills Way (about 300m north of the infocentre), which has been doing a roaring trade since 1934. Next door, the *Breakers Pub* is a popular hostelry. *Bogey's*, under the *Prince Rupert* high-rise hotel on Second Ave, between Sixth and Seventh streets, is another leading **bar**; it also does decent food, and seems to be one of the few places prepared to open for breakfast.

The Queen Charlotte Islands

Ranged some 150km off the Prince Rupert coast, the archipelago of about 150 islets known as the **Queen Charlotte Islands** make an enticing diversion from the heavily travelled sea route up the Northwest coast. The islands have become something of a cult amongst travellers and environmentalists – partly for their scenery and almost legendary remoteness from the mainstream, but also because they've achieved a high profile in the battle between the forestry industry and ecology activists. At the forefront are the **Haida**, who have made the islands their home for over 10,000 years (see box). Their culture and their many deserted villages form part of the Charlottes' attraction, but many people also come to sample the immensely rich **flora and fauna** that have earned the islands the title of the "Canadian Galapagos".

The Queen Charlottes were one of only two areas in western Canada to escape the last ice age, which left many so-called **relic species** in place. Unique species not found elsewhere in the country include a fine yellow daisy, the world's largest **black bears**, and subspecies of pine-marten, deer mouse, hairy woodpecker, saw-whet owl and Stellar's jay. There are also more **eagles** here than anywhere else in the region, as well as the world's largest population of Peale's peregrine falcons and the elusive **black-footed albatross** – whose wingspan exceeds that of the largest eagles. Fish, too, are immensely plentiful, and there's a good chance of spotting whales, otters, sea-lions and other aquatic mammals.

Ferries from Prince Rupert dock near **Queen Charlotte City** on **Graham Island**, the name given to the northern of the group's two main collections of islands. Most of the Charlottes' six thousand inhabitants live either here or at **Masset** to the north, leaving the southern islands – known for convenience as **Moresby Island**

– a virtually deserted primal wilderness but for the small community at Sandspit. Accommodation is available only at Sandspit (on Moresby) and Queen Charlotte City, Tl'ell, Masset and Port Clements (on Graham) and should really be pre-booked.

The only public transportation at the time of writing is the *Evergreen Bus Line*, based at General Delivery, Masset (☎626-5678), which links Port Clements and Queen Charlotte City. Hitching is difficult, and car rental rates are among the world's highest. Unless you have a car, bike or canoe, you could have a long and expensive trip that shows you very little of what you came for.

Graham Island

Most casual visitors stick to **Graham Island**, where the bulk of the islands' roads and accommodation are concentrated along the eastern side of the island between **Queen Charlotte City** in the south and **Masset** to the north. These settlements and the villages in between – Skidegate, Tl'ell and Port Clements – shelter in the lee of the islands, away from an indented west coast that has the highest combined seismic, wind and tidal energy of any North American coastline, producing treacherous seas and a tidal range of eight meters. Much of the east coast is filled with sandy beaches and a string of provincial parks where you can appreciate the milder climes produced by the Pacific's Japanese Current, a warming stream that contributes to the islands' lush canopy of thousand-year-old spruce and cedar rainforests. On the downside, though, it drenches both sides of the islands with endless rainstorms, even in summer.

Queen Charlotte City

It would be hard to imagine anywhere less like a city than **QUEEN CHARLOTTE CITY**, a picturesque fishing village about 5km west of the Skidegate terminal for ferries to and from Prince Rupert. Most of its residents squeeze a living from the McMillan Bloedel timber giant, whose felling exploits have cleared most of the hills around the port, and who have a veto on access to many of the backcountry logging roads. For a fine overview of the place try the stroll to the top of **Sleeping Beauty Mountain**, which is reached by rough track from Crown Forest Roads near Honna Road. The village **dump** south of the houses rates as another sight for the black bears and 40-plus bald and golden eagles that gather there at dusk. Otherwise you can sign up for any number of fishing, canoeing or boating **tours** by contacting the **infocentre** at *Joy's Island Jewellers Store* (June–Sept daily 8am–6pm; Oct–May Mon–Fri 9am–5pm; ☎559-4742), about a kilometer east of town on Third Ave. The staff are incredibly knowledgeable, and there's a good selection of detailed guides and maps: Joy herself *may* let you camp on her lawn if you arrive late with nowhere to stay. There's also a **Canadian Parks Service** office for information on Moresby Island's Gwaii Haanas National Park (see p.453), west along Hwy 33 (Mon–Fri 8am–noon & 1–4.30pm; ☎559-8818). The **Ministry of Forests** in the obvious new blue building on Third Ave (☎559-8447) has information on free, primitive camp-grounds run by the Forest Service on Graham and Moresby islands.

Accommodation is scarce and demand high in summer, so try to call ahead to the splendidly restored 1910 heritage building, the *Premier Hotel*, 3101-3rd Ave (☎559-8451; ③); *Gracie's Place*, 3113-3rd Ave (☎559-4262; ②), with two homey ocean-view rooms; the *Spruce Point Lodging*, 609-6th Ave (☎559-8234; six mixed dorm beds at $17.50, otherwise B&B; ③), opposite the Chevron garage at the west end of town; or the *Hecate Inn* (☎559-4543 or 1-800/665-3350; ③), on the corner of Third Ave and Fourth St. A touch closer to the ferry terminal overlooking Bearskin Bay is the *Sea Raven Resort Motel*, 3301-3rd Ave (☎559-4423 or 1-800/665-9606; ③). For **food**, locals make for *Margaret's Café*, 3223 Wharf St, on the east side of town, or to *Claudette's Place*, 233-3rd Ave (on the west of downtown), a place with a nice patio eating area and known for its breakfasts.

THE HAIDA

The **Haida** are widely considered to have the most highly developed culture and most sophisticated art tradition of British Columbia's indigenous peoples. Extending from the Queen Charlotte Islands to south Alaska, their lands included major stands of red cedar, the raw material for their huge dugout **canoes**, intricate **carvings** and refined **architecture**. Haida trade links were built on the reputation of their skill, other BC tribes considering the ownership of an Haida canoe, for example, as a major status symbol. Renowned as traders and artists, the Haida were also feared **warriors**, paddling into rival villages and returning with canoes laden with goods, slaves and the severed heads of anyone who had tried to resist. This success at warfare was due, in part, to their use of wooden slat armor, which included a protective face visor and helmets topped with terrifying images.

Socially the Haida divided themselves into two main groups, the **Eagles** and the **Ravens**, which were further divided into hereditary kin-groups named after their original village location. Marriage within each major group – or moiety – was considered incestuous, so Eagles would always seek Raven mates and vice versa. Furthermore, descent was traced through the **female line**; a chief could not pass his property on to his sons because they would belong to a different moiety, and his inheritance passed instead to his sister's sons. Equally, young men might have to leave their childhood village to claim their inheritance from their maternal uncles.

Haida **villages** were an impressive sight, their vast cedar-plank houses dominated by fifteen-meter totem poles displaying the kin-group's unique animal crest or other mythical creatures, all carved in elegantly fluid lines. Entrance to each house was through the gaping mouth of a massive carved figure; inside, supporting posts were carved into the forms of the crest animals and most household objects were similarly decorative. Equal elaboration attended the many Haida ceremonies, such as the **mortuary potlatch**, which served as a memorial service to a dead chief and the validation of the heir's right to succession. The dead individual was laid out at the top of a carved pole near the village entrance, past which the visiting chiefs would walk wearing robes of finely woven and patterned mountain-goat wool and immense head-dresses fringed with long sea-lion whiskers and ermine skins. A hollow at the top of each head-dress was filled with eagle feathers which floated down onto the witnesses as the chiefs sedately danced.

After **European contact** the Haida population was devastated by smallpox epidemics, their numbers reduced from 6000 in 1835 to 588 by 1915. Consequently they were forced to abandon their traditional villages and gather at two sites, Masset and Skidegate. At other locations the homes and totems fell into disrepair, and only at **Ninstints**, a remote village at the southern tip of the Queen Charlottes, has an attempt been made to preserve an original Haida settlement; it has now been declared a World Heritage Site by UNESCO.

These days the Haida number around 2000, and are highly regarded in the Canadian art world; Bill Reid, Freda Diesing and Robert Davidson are among the best-known **figures**, and scores of other Haida craftspeople produce a mass of carvings and jewellery for the tourist market.

Skidegate, Tl'ell and Port Clements

Ferries dock here, but there's not much doing at **SKIDEGATE**, though you could catch up on more accessible aspects of the Haida culture at the **Queen Charlotte Islands Museum**, just north of the terminal (Tues–Sat 9am–5pm; $3). Check out, too, the **carving shed** just up the road, home to the *Loo Taas* ("Wave Eater") canoe when it's not out on hire – for a mere Can$1500 you could take a six-hour tour in the 80-meter vessel. Here or at the nearby **Skidegate Mission** is the place to inquire about permits to visit some of the 500 or more abandoned tribal villages and sites on the southern islands. In summer the Mission hosts a 6pm Thursday **seafood feast**, open to all-comers for $20.

Further along the east coast, the ranching community of **TL'ELL** 42km north, is gone in the blink of an eye, but it does hold the ten-bed *Bellis Lodge* **hostel** (☎557-4434; dorms $17; ①), and the tiny (4 rooms) *Weavers Inn Motel* (☎557-4491; ③), nearby in a lovely rural setting. Only a touch larger (by two rooms) is the *Tl'ell River Farm and Lodge* (☎559-4569 or 559-8937; ②). The *Tl'ell River House*, off Hwy 16 overlooking Tl'ell River and Hecate Strait, offers rooms, showers and a laundromat (☎557-4211 or 1-800/667-8906; ③). **Bikes and kayaks** can be **rented** from a last B&B, the *Hitunwa Kaitza*, just north of Richardson Ranch on the main road (☎557-4664; ③). **Campers** should head for the 30-site *Misty Meadows Campground*, just south of the Tl'ell River Bridge (contact the Naikoon Provincial Park office for details: ☎557-4390).

As the road cuts inland for **PORT CLEMENTS**, 20km to the northwest, it forms the southern border of the **Naikoon Provincial Park**, an enclave that extends over Graham Island's northeast corner and is designed to protect fine beach, dune and dwarf woodland habitats. There's a small **Park Centre** on the road 2km north of Tl'ell, together with a provincial **campground** (May–Oct; $8). About 8km beyond look out for the picnic site and trails at the southern tip of **Mayer Lake**, one of the nicer spots to pull over. Port Clements itself has a small museum of forestry and pioneer-related offerings, but is most famous for the world's only **Golden Spruce** tree, a 300-year-old bleached albino tree that puzzles foresters by refusing to produce anything but ordinary green-leafed saplings: a rare mutation allows the tree's needles to be bleached by sunlight. It's 6km south of the village signed off the logging road to Juskatla, a timber camp established in World War II to supply Queen Charlotte spruce for war planes. The *Golden Spruce Hotel*, 2 Grouse St (☎557-4325; ②), is Port Clements' one listed **hotel**; there's B&B at *Swan's Keep*, 197 Bayview Rd (☎557-2408; ③). For **food and drink**, the only option is the *Yakoun River Inn* on Bayview Drive.

Masset

MASSET is the biggest place on the islands, a scattered town of 1600 people, half of whom are employed by a military base built in 1971, the other half in fishing and crab canning. Most visitors come to **watch birds** at the **Delkatla Wildlife Sanctuary**, a saltwater marsh north of the village that supports 113 bird species, or to wander the neighboring village of Haida, or "Old Masset", where some six hundred natives still live and work. Many are involved in carving knick-knacks for tourists, or organizing wilderness tours, but a few are restoring and adding to the few totems still standing locally.

The **infocentre** (June–Oct daily 9am–5pm; ☎626-3982), at 1455 Old Beach Rd, has full details of wildlife and birdwatching possibilities. The Masset Village Office on Main Street also provides invaluable background (☎626-3995).

Accommodation prospects are limited to the *Naikoon Park Motel* on Tow Hill Rd, close to the beach 8km east of town (☎626-5187; ②); the *Singing Surf Inn*, 1504 Old Beach Rd (☎626-3318; ③); and a handful of B&Bs such as the *Alaska View Lodge* (☎626-3333; ③). The only **campground** around is the *Masset-Haida Lions Campground* ($8) on Tow Hill Rd, 2km north of town alongside the wildlife sanctuary. To get around call up a **taxi** (☎626-5017) or **rent a car** from *Tilden*, 1504 Old Beach Rd (☎626-3318). **Eat** at one of the two pizza and take-out places; the one **bar**, *Daddy Cool's*, Collision Ave and Main St, has live music nightly.

Moresby Island

Moresby Island is all but free from human contamination except for deserted Haida villages (one of which has the world's largest stand of totems), forestry roads and the small logging community of **SANDSPIT**, some 15km from the **Alliford Bay** terminal for the *Interisland Ferry* link with Skidegate (12 daily; 20-min crossing; $2). *Canadian Airlines* and *Trans Provincial Airlines* (☎627-1341 in Prince Rupert) fly from Prince Rupert to a small airstrip near the village.

Most locals here and on Graham Island work in Moresby's forests, and the **forestry issue** has divided the community between the Haida and ecologists – "hippies" in the local parlance – and the lumber workers (the "rednecks"). At stake are the islands' temperate rainforests and the traditional sites of the Haida, themselves politically shrewd media manipulators who have sent representatives to Brazil to advise indigenous peoples on rainforest programs. They've also occasionally provided the muscle to halt logging on the islands, and to prove a point sometimes block access to **Hotspring Island**, whose thermal pools attract many visitors. On the other hand the forests provide jobs and some of the world's most lucrative timber – a single good sitka trunk can be worth up to Can$60,000. Most of Moresby has been declared a National Park Reserve, though stiff lobbying from the logging companies leaves its position perilous.

If you're determined enough you can canoe, mountain bike or backpack the interior, but you need to be prepared to lug plenty of supplies. The **Canadian Parks Service** offices at Sandspit off Beach Rd at the north end of town (May–Sept daily 8.30am–6pm; ☎637-5362), and Queen Charlotte City (see above), have information on the new Gwaii Haanas National Park, while the **infocentre** on Beach Rd (June–Sept daily 9am–6pm; ☎637-5436) has details on tours and the limited facilities on the whole southern half of the archipelago.

As well as a couple of B&Bs, Sandspit **accommodation** options include the *Sandspit Inn* on Airport Rd near the airstrip (☎637-5334; ④), and the *Moresby Island Guest House* at 385 Alliford Bay Rd (☎637-5305; ②), overlooking the ocean at Shingle Bay 2km from the airport. Many people choose to sleep on the spit's beaches: Gray Bay has 20 official primitive **campsites** (contact the *Fletcher Challenge* forestry offices on Beach Rd; ☎637-5436). *Budget* **rental cars** can be picked up at the airport or in Sandspit at Beach and Blaine Shaw Rd (☎637-5688).

The Cassiar Highway

The 733km of the **Cassiar Highway** (Hwy 37) from the Skeena Valley east of Prince Rupert to Watson Lake just inside Yukon Territory are some of the wildest and most beautiful on any British Columbian road. Though less famous than the

Alaska Highway, the road is increasingly travelled by those who want to capture some of the adventure that accompanied the remoter reaches of its better-known neighbor in the Fifties and Sixties. Long stretches are still gravel, however, and the gas and repair facilities, let alone food and lodgings, are extremely patchy: don't contemplate the journey unless your vehicle's in top condition, with two spare tyres and spare fuel containers. The longest stretch without gas is the 240km between Meziadin Lake and Eddontenajon. The road also provides a shorter route from Prince George to the Yukon than the Alaska Highway, and as more of it is paved the number of big trucks and logging vehicles using it is on the rise – creating more potential hazards. British Columbia's *North by Northwest Tourist Association* puts out complete lists of facilities – vital accompaniments to any journey, and available from infocentres in Prince Rupert and Terrace.

If you're ready to drive the distances involved, you'll also probably be prepared to explore the highway's two main side roads to **Stewart** and to **Telegraph Creek**, and possibly the rough roads and trails that lead into two wilderness parks midway up the highway – the **Mount Edziza Provincial Park** and the **Spatsizi Plateau Wilderness Park**. If you can't face the road's entire length, the trip to Terrace offers exceptional sea and mountain **scenery**, as well as the chance to cross into Alaska at **Hyder**.

To Stewart

The Cassiar starts near Kitwanga, one of four native villages off Hwy 16, and a crossroads of the old "grease trail", named after the candlefish oil that was traded between Coast and Interior tribes. Almost immediately the road pitches into the mesmerizing high scenery of the Coast Ranges, a medley of mountains, lakes and forests that reaches a crescendo after about 100km and the side turn to **STEWART**. Here a series of immense glaciers culminates in the dramatic appearance of **Bear Glacier**, a vast sky-blue mass of ice that comes down virtually to the highway and has the strange ability to glow in the dark. Stewart itself is a shrivelled mining center sitting at the end of the Portland Canal, the world's fourth longest fjord, a natural boundary between British Columbia and Alaska that lends the town a superb peak-ringed location. Dominating its rocky amphitheater is **Mount Rainey**, whose cliffs represent one of the greatest vertical rises from sea level in the world.

The **infocentre** is housed with the local museum in the City and Fire Hall between Sixth and Seventh streets (daily May–Oct 9am–8pm; ☎636-2111). If you want to sleep over, there are two co-owned **hotels**: the *King Edward*, Fifth and Columbia (☎636-2244 or toll-free in BC ☎1-800/663-3126; ②), and the *Alpine* (☎636-2445; ②). The *King Edward*, bar one Chinese spot, is the town's only **pub** and **restaurant**. The *Stewart Lions Campground* is on Eighth Ave (May–Sept; $9–15). In summer Stewart is added to the itinerary of the Friday sailings of the *Alaska Marine Highway* ferry, so you can ride a boat to Ketchikan and thence to either Skagway or Prince Rupert, to complete a neat circular itinerary.

Hyder

Most people come to **HYDER**, population 70, simply to drink in one or both of its two bars. It's a ramshackle place 3km from Stewart on a road that crosses the **border into Alaska** with none of the usual formalities – there being nothing beyond the end of the road but 800km of wilderness. At the *Glacier Inn* the tradition is to pin a dollar to the wall in case you return broke and need a drink, and then toss back a shot of hard liquor in one and receive an "I've Been Hyderized" card. It sounds a bit of a tourist carry-on, but if you arrive out of season there's a genuine amiability about the place that warrants its claims to be the "The Friendliest Ghost Town in Alaska". The bars are open 23 hours a day, and a couple of **motels** are on hand if you want to keep on drinking: the *Sealaska Inn*, Premier Ave (☎636-9001; ③), and the *Grand View Inn* nearby (☎636-9174; ③).

Dease Lake

For several hundred kilometers beyond the Stewart junction there's nothing along the Cassiar other than the odd garage, campground, trailhead and patches of burnt or clear-cut forest etched into the Cassiar and Skeena mountains. In places, though, you can still see traces of the incredible 1900-mile Dominion Telegraph line that used to link the Dawson City goldfields with Vancouver, and of a proposed railway extension out of Prince George that was abandoned as late as 1977.

DEASE LAKE, the first place of any size, has a single **motel**, the *Northway Motor Inn* on Boulder Ave (☎771-5341; ③). Close by lies **ISKUT**, a native village offering tours into the adjacent wilderness parks, which are also accessible by float plane from Dease Lake itself. The village has the most **accommodation** options for a considerable distance; on the highway there's the *Black Sheep Motel* (April–Oct; ☎234-3141; ③). The *A-E Guest House* at Kluachon Lake 5km from the village has just three rooms and 30 tent/RV sites (May–Oct; radio phone only; ②; tents $12). Both *Red Goat Lodge* (☎234-3261; ③; tents $10) and *Iskutine Lodge* (☎234-3456; ①; tents $10) on Eddontenajon Lake, 9km south of the village, also operate as motels and campgrounds combined. In the other direction, near Stikine Grand Canyon 8km north of the village, is the 20-room *Bear Paw Ranch* (radio phone only; ③).

The road from here on is wild and beautiful, the 240km up to the Yukon border from Dease Lake among the most miraculous of what is already a superb journey. Much of this area was swamped with gold-hungry pioneers during the **Cassiar Gold Rush** of 1872–80, when the region got its name – possibly from a white prospector's corruption of *kaskamet*, the dried beaver meat eaten by local Kaska tribes. In 1877 one Alfred Freedman plucked one of the world's largest pure gold nuggets – a 72-ounce monster – from a creek east of present-day **CASSIAR**, though these days the mining has a less romantic allure, being concentrated in an open-pit **asbestos mine** 5km from the village. Most of the world's high-grade asbestos comes from here, and poisonous-looking piles of green chrysotile asbestos tailings are scattered for miles around.

Telegraph Creek

For a taste of what is possibly a more remarkable landscape than you see on the Cassiar, it's worth driving the potentially treacherous 75-kilometer side road from Dease Lake to **TELEGRAPH CREEK**, a place whose look and feel can scarcely have changed since the turn of the century, when it was a major telegraph station and trading post for the gold-rush towns to the north. The road navigates some incredible gradients and bends, twisting past canyons, old lava beds and touching on several **native villages**, notably at Tahltan River where salmon are caught and cured in traditional smokehouses and sold to passing tourists. If you're lucky you might see a Tahltan bear dog, a species now virtually extinct. Ankle high, and weighing less than a stone, these tiny animals were able to keep a bear cornered by barking and darting around until a hunter came to finish it off. Telegraph Creek itself is an object lesson in how latter-day pioneers live on the Northwest's last frontiers: it's home to a friendly mixture of city exiles, hunters, trappers and ranchers, but also a cloistered bunch of **religious fundamentalists** who have eschewed the decadent mainstream for wilderness purity. Such groups are growing in outback British Columbia, an as-yet-undocumented phenomenon that's creating friction with the easy-going types who first settled the backwoods.

Much of the village revolves around the *General Delivery* – a combined café, grocery and garage – and small adjoining **motel**, the *Stikine River Song Lodge* (☎235-3196; ②), whose eight doubles include kitchenettes.

Prince George to Dawson Creek

Dawson Creek is the launching pad for the Alaska Highway; it might not be a place where you'd choose to stop, but it's almost impossible to avoid a night here whether you're approaching from Edmonton and the east or **from Prince George** on the scenically more uplifting **John Hart Highway** (Hwy 97). Named after a former BC premier, this seemingly innocuous road is one of the north's most vital highways. Completed in 1952, it linked at a stroke the road network of the Pacific Northwest with that of the northern interior, cutting 800km off the journey from Seattle to Alaska, for example, a trip which previously had to take in a vast inland loop to Calgary. The route leads you out of British Columbia's upland interior to the so-called Peace River country, a region of slightly ridged land which belongs in look and spirit to the Albertan prairies. There's some 409km of driving, and two daily *Greyhound* **buses** make the journey.

Out of Prince George the road bends through mildly dipping hills and mixed woodland, passing small lakes and offering views to the Rockies, whose distant jagged skyline keeps up the spirits as you drive through an otherwise unbroken tunnel of conifers. About 70km on, **Bear Lake** and the **Crooked River Provincial Park** are just off the road; take the small lane just west of the park entrance to reach an idyllic patch of water fringed on its far shore by a fine sickle of sand. There's a free **campground** at the park, and the *Grizzly Inn* **motel** just beyond (☎972-4436; ③), with the road's first services after Prince George.

Both Mackenzie Junction, 152km from Prince George, and Mackenzie, 29km off the highway, are scrappy, unpleasant places, easily avoided and soon forgotten as the road climbs to **Pine Pass** (933m), one of the lower road routes over the Rockies, but spectacular all the same. The **Bijoux Falls Provincial Park**, just before it, is good for a picnic near the eponymous falls, and if you want to **camp** make sure to plump for the *Pine Valley Park Lodge* (May–Oct; $8), an immensely scenic lakeside spot that looks up to crags of massively stratified and contorted rock just below the pass. Thereafter the road drops steeply through Chetwynd to the increasingly flatter country that heralds Dawson Creek.

Dawson Creek

Arrive in **DAWSON CREEK** late and leave early: except for a small museum next to the town's eye-catching red grain hopper, and the obligatory photograph of the cairn marking **Mile Zero** of the Alaska Highway, there's nothing to do here except eat and sleep. Contact the **infocentre** at the museum, 900 Alaska Ave (daily winter 9am–6pm, longer in summer; ☎782-9595), for details of the **motels** –

and there are plenty, mostly concentrated on the Alaska Highway northeast of town. If you've climbed off a *Greyhound* at the **bus terminal**, 1201 Alaska Ave, try the new *Econo-Lodge* (☎782-9181; ③) beyond the Co-op Mall east of the Mile Zero cairn at 832-103rd Ave. You wouldn't want to linger at any of the three local **campsites**, but the most attractive is the *Mile 0 City Campground* (May–Aug; ☎782-2590; $8.50–14), about a kilometer west of the town's main spread opposite 20th St on the Alaska Highway. For something to **eat** call at the excellent *Alaska Café* on Tenth St, an attractive old wooden building completely at odds with the rest of the town. The food and ambience are good – and the bar's not bad either.

Dawson Creek to Whitehorse

Well over half of the **Alaska Highway** – a distance of about 1500km – winds through northern British Columbia from Dawson Creek to Whitehorse, the capital of the Yukon. Don't be fooled by the string of villages emblazoned across the area's maps, for there are only two towns worthy of the name en route, **Fort St John** and **Fort Nelson** – the rest are no more than a garage, a store and perhaps a motel. **Watson Lake**, on the Yukon border, is the largest of these lesser spots, and also marks the junction of the Alaska and Cassiar highways. All the way down the road, though, it's vital to book accommodation during July and August.

Driving the Alaska Highway is no longer the adventure of days past – that's now provided by the Cassiar and Dempster highways. Food, gas and lodgings are found every forty to eighty kilometers, though cars still need to be in good shape. You should drive with headlights on at all times, and take care when passing or being passed by heavy trucks. It also goes without saying that wilderness – anything up to 800km of it to each side – begins at the edge of the highway and unless you're very experienced you shouldn't contemplate any off-road exploration. Any number of guides and pamphlets are available to take you through to Fairbanks, but *The Milepost*, the road's bible, now coming up to its 50th edition, is for all its mind-numbing detail the only one you need buy.

From mid-May to mid-October daily (except Sun) a **Greyhound** bus leaves Dawson Creek in the morning and plies the road all the way to Whitehorse; it runs on Tuesday, Thursday and Saturday the rest of the year. The twenty-hour trip finishes at 5am, with only occasional half-hour meal stops, but covers the best scenery in daylight.

Dawson Creek to Fort Nelson

You need to adapt to a different notion of distance on a 2500-kilometer drive: points of interest on the Alaska Highway are a long way apart, and pleasure comes in broad changes in scenery, in the sighting of a solitary moose, or in the passing excitement of a lonely bar. Thus it's forty minutes before the benign ridged prairies around Dawson Creek prompt attention by dropping suddenly into the broad, flat-bottomed valley of the Peace River, a canyon whose walls are scalloped with creeks, gulches and deep muddy scars. Soon after comes **FORT ST JOHN**, which until the coming of the highway – when it was the field headquarters of the road's eastern construction gangs – was a trading post for local Sikanni and Beaver natives that had remained little changed since its predecessor sank into the mud of the Peace River. The ensuing shanty town received a boost when the province's largest oilfield was discovered nearby in 1955, and it's now a

THE CONSTRUCTION OF THE ALASKA HIGHWAY

The **Alaska Highway** runs northeast from Mile Zero at Dawson Creek through the Yukon Territory to Mile 1520 in Fairbanks, Alaska. Built as a military road, it's now an all-weather highway travelled by daily bus services and thousands of tourists out to recapture the thrill of the days when it was known as the "junkyard of the American automobile". It's no longer a driver's Calvary, but the scenery and the sense of pushing through wilderness on one of the continent's last frontiers remain as alluring as ever.

As recently as 1940 there was no direct land route to the Yukon or Alaska other than trails passable only to trappers. When the Japanese invaded the Aleutian Islands during World War II, however, they both threatened the traditional sea routes to the north and seemed ready for an attack on mainland Alaska – the signal for the building of the joint US–Canadian road to the north. A proposed coastal route from Hazelton in British Columbia was deemed too susceptible to enemy attack (it's since been built as the Cassiar Hwy), while an inland route bypassing Whitehorse and following the Rockies would have taken five years to build. This left the so-called **Prairie Route**, which had the advantage of following a line of airbases through Canada into Alaska – a chain known as the **Northwest Staging Route**. In the course of the war, some 8000 planes were ferried from Montana to Edmonton and then to Fairbanks on this route, where they were picked up by Soviet pilots and flown into action on the Siberian front.

Construction of the highway began on **March 9, 1942**, the start of months of misery for most of the 20,000 mainly US soldiers shanghaied to ram a road through mountains, mud, mosquito-ridden bog, icy rivers and forest during some of the harshest weather imaginable. Incredibly, crews working on the eastern and western sections met at Contact Creek, British Columbia, in September 1942, and completed the last leg to Fairbanks in October – an engineering triumph which had taken less than a year but cost around $140 million. The first full convoy of trucks to make Fairbanks managed an average 25 kph in one of the worst winters in memory.

By 1943 the highway already needed virtual rebuilding, and for seven years workers widened the road, raised bridges, reduced gradients, bypassed swampy ground and started the still-ongoing process of ironing out the vast bends (the reason why it's now only 1488 miles, for example, to the old Mile 1520 post in Fairbanks). All sorts of ideas have been put forward to explain the numerous curves – that they were to stop Japanese planes using the road as a landing strip, that they simply went where bulldozers could go at the time, or even at one point that they followed the trail of a rutting moose. Probably the chief reason is that the surveying often amounted to no more than a pointed finger aimed at the next horizon.

Although the road is widely celebrated, some sides to the story are still glossed over. Many of its toughest sections, for example, were given to black GIs, few of whom have received credit for their part in building the highway – you'll look in vain for black faces among the white officers in the archive photos of ribbon-cutting ceremonies. Another tale is the road's effect on natives on the route, scores of whom died from epidemics brought in by the workers. Yet another was the building of the controversial "Canadian Oil" or **Canol pipeline** in conjunction with the road, together with huge dumps of poisonous waste and construction junk. Wildlife en route was also devastated by trigger-happy GIs taking recreational potshots as they worked: the virtual eradication of several species was part of the reason for the creation of the Kluane Game Sanctuary, the forerunner of the Yukon's Kluane National Park.

functional settlement with all the services you need – though at just 75km into the highway it's unlikely you'll be ready to stop. If you are, there are a dozen **motels**: solid choices are the *Alexander Mackenzie Inn*, 9223-100th St (☎785-8364 or 1-800/663-8313; ③), and the *Four Seasons Motor Inn*, 9810-100th St (☎785-6647; ③). The town **infocentre** is at 9323-100th St (year round; ☎785-6037).

The next stop is **WONOWON**, 161km from Dawson, typical of the bleak settlements all the way up the road: the *Blueberry* (☎772-3322; ②) and *Pine Hill* (☎772-3340; ②) motels, wooden shacks and corrugated iron, a few wires strung between poles, rusting oil and gas storage tanks, and concrete blocks laid out as a nominal attempt at a kerb, struggle to impose some civic order on the wilderness.

PINK MOUNTAIN (226km) is much the same, with two combined motels and campgrounds – *Pink Mountain Motor Inn* (☎772-3234; rooms ②; sites $12) and the *Sportsman's Inn* (☎772-3220; rooms ②; sites $15) – and a restaurant favored by truckers (but run by hatchet-faced staff) with a reasonable **campground** across the road (☎772-3226; May–Oct; $8–20). Thirty kilometers on, however, is one of the better campgrounds hereabouts, the *Sikanni River Lodge* (☎773-6531; $10).

Thereafter the road offers immense **views** of utter wilderness in all directions, the trees as dense as ever, but noticeably more stunted than further south and nearing the limit of commercial viability. Look out for the bright "New Forest Planted" signs, presumably just a riposte from the loggers to the ecology lobby, as they are invariably backed by a graveyard of sickly-looking trees.

Fort Nelson

One of the highway's key stop-offs, **FORT NELSON** greets you with a large poster proclaiming "Jail is only the beginning – don't drink and drive", a sobering sign that hints at the sort of extremes to which people here might go to relieve the tedium of winter's long semi-twilight.

Everything in town except a small **museum** devoted to the highway's construction speaks of a frontier supplies depot, the last in a long line of trading posts attracted to a site which is fed by four major rivers and stands in the lee of the Rockies. Dour buildings stand in a battered sprawl around a windswept grid, only a single notch up civilization's ladder from the time in the late Fifties when this was still a community without power, phones, running water or doctors. Life's clearly too tough here to be geared to anything but pragmatic survival and exploitation of its huge natural gas deposits – the town has the world's second largest gas-processing plant and the huge storage tanks to prove it. Natives and white trappers live as they have for centuries, hunting beaver, wolf, wolverine, fox, lynx and mink, as well as the ubiquitous moose, which is still an important food source for many natives.

The town's many **motels** are much of a muchness and you'll be paying the same rates – about $60 for doubles worth half that – which characterize the north. The *Mini Price* a block off the highway (behind the *CIBC* bank) is central and inexpensive (☎774-2136; ①) – though location's not terribly important here – and on the town's southern approaches to the town the *Bluebell Motel* (☎774-6961; ③) is better-looking than many of the run-of-the-mill places. There's a big central **campground** beside the museum, the *Westend* (April–Nov; ☎774-2340; $11–16). The **infocentre** is at Mile 300.5 of the Alaska Hwy (summer only; ☎774-2541).

Fort Nelson to Liard Hot Springs

Landscapes divide markedly around Fort Nelson, where the highway arches west from the flatter hills of the Peace River country to meet the **northern Rockies** above the plains and plateau of the Liard River. Within a short time – once the road has picked up the river's headwaters – you're in some of the most grandiose scenery in British Columbia. Services and **motels** become scarcer, but those that exist – though they tend to be beaten-up looking places – make atmospheric and often unforgettable stops. The *Rocky Mountain Lodge* (☎232-5000; ②), 15km on, is typically dilapidated, but has an astounding position and an adjacent **campground** ($10).

TOAD RIVER, 60km beyond, has perhaps the best motel of all on this lonely stretch, the *Toad River Lodge* (☎232-5401; ②), thanks to its superlative views of thickly forested and deeply cloven mountains on all sides. Two kilometers to its north is the *Poplars Campground & Café* with tent sites and three rooms (May–Sept; ☎232-5465; rooms ②; sites $12), an equally attractive spot despite its off-putting claims to be "Home of the Foot-Long Hot Dog".

Muncho Lake, the next big natural feature, sits at the heart of a large provincial park whose ranks of bare mountains presage the barren tundra of the far north. There's a small motel and campground at the lake's southern end, but it's worth hanging on for the Strawberry Flats provincial **campground** ($8) midway up the lake or the fine *Highland Glen Lodge and Campground* (☎776-3481) for a choice of log cabin motel rooms (③) or camping sites ($10–16). A little way beyond is the less expensive *Muncho Lake Lodge*, again with rooms and campground (May–Oct; ☎776-3456; rooms ②; sites $10).

About 70km beyond the lake, the excellent *Liard River Lodge* (☎776-3341; ③), is a wonderfully cozy and friendly spot for food or a room. ("Liard" comes from the French for poplar, a ubiquitous tree in these parts.) It's also close to one of the most popular spots on the entire Alaska Highway, the **Liard Hot Springs**, whose **two thermal pools** are among the best and hottest in BC. They're reached by a short wooden walkway across steaming marsh, and are unspoilt apart from a wooden changing room and the big high-season crowds. As the marsh never freezes, it entices moose and grizzlies down to drink and graze and some 250 plant species grow in the mild microhabitat nearby, including fourteen species of orchid, lobelias, ostrich ferns and other rare boreal forest plants. The nearby provincial **campground** is one of the region's most popular, and fills up early in July and August (May–Oct; $10).

Watson Lake to Whitehorse

Beyond Liard Hot Springs the road follows the Liard River, settling into about 135km of unexceptional scenery before **WATSON LAKE**, just over the Yukon border. Created by the coming of the highway, it's neither attractive nor terribly big, but shops, motels and garages have sprung up to service the traffic congregating off the Cassiar and Campbell highways to the north and south. If you're just passing through, pull off to look at the **Alaska Highway Interpretive Centre** (daily May–Sept 8am–8pm; ☎536-7469), which as well as providing information on the Yukon also describes the highway's construction through archive photos and audio-visual displays. It's on the highway next to the *Chevron* garage

The **telephone code** for the Yukon and NWT, unless stated otherwise, is ☎403.

and close to the famous **Sign Post Forest**. This bit of gimmickry was started by a homesick GI in 1942 who erected a sign pointing the way and stating the mileage to his home in Danville, Illinois. Since then the signs have just kept on coming, and at last count numbered over 10,000.

It's still 441km from Watson Lake to Whitehorse. If you're camping there are no problems, for there are countless small government-run campgrounds along the highway. If not, you have to think more carefully to avoid being stranded. If you decide to **stay** in town the best budget choice is the *Alcan Motel* (☎536-7774; ②), with the ominous promise of "nightly entertainment". Close behind is the *Cedar Lodge Motel* (☎536-7406; ③). Both places are small, however, and you may have to plump for one of the bigger hotels, all which have rooms around $90 – the best is the *Belvedere Hotel* (☎536-7712; ⑤). The nearest **campground** is the rustic Yukon government site, 4km west of the sign forest (May–Oct; $5), but for full services use the *Gateway to Yukon RV Park and Campground* near the *Husky* garage (year round; 110 serviced, 30 unserviced sites; ☎536-7448; $10).

West of Watson Lake the road picks up more fine mountain scenery, running for hour after hour past identical combinations of snow-capped peaks and thick forest. Unlovely **TESLIN**, 263km to the west, was founded as a trading post in 1903 and now has one of the Yukon's largest Native Canadian populations, many of whom still live by hunting and fishing. The **George Johnston Museum** on the right on the way into the village (daily June–Sept 10am–8pm; $2), has a good collection of local Tlingit artefacts, plus photos of the eponymous Johnston, a Tlingit who recorded his culture on film between 1910 and 1940. If you get stuck overnight – it's 179km to Whitehorse – choose between the *Northlake Motel* (☎390-2571; ②), the *Yukon Motel* (☎390-2575; ②) with both rooms and a serviced RV park and **campground** ($10), and *Halstead's Teslin Lake Resort* (May–Sept; ☎390-2608; ②), just out of the village, which has a few rooms and a good campground.

Whitehorse

WHITEHORSE is the capital of the Yukon, home to two thirds of its population, the center of its mining and forestry industries, and a stop-off for thousands of summer visitors. Though it's the roads that bring in business today, the town owes its existence to the **Yukon River**, a 3000-kilometer artery that rises in BC's Coast Mountains and flows through the heart of the Yukon and Alaska to the Bering Sea. The floodplain and strange escarpment above the present town were long a resting point for the Dene, but the spot burgeoned into a full-blown city with the arrival of thousands of stampeders in the spring of 1898. Having braved the Chilkoot Pass (see box) to meet the Yukon's upper reaches, men and supplies then had to navigate the **Miles Canyon** and White Horse rapids southeast of the town. After the first few boats through had been reduced to matchwood, the prospectors constructed a tramway around the rapids, and in time raised a shanty town at the canyon's northern head to catch their breath before the river journey to Dawson City.

The completion of the White Pass and Yukon Railway to Whitehorse (newly named after the rapids) put the tentative settlement on a firmer footing – almost at the same time as the gold rush petered out. In the early years of this century the population dwindled quickly from about 10,000 to about 400; for forty years

THE CHILKOOT TRAIL

No single image better conjures the human drama of the 1898 gold rush than the lines of prospectors struggling over the **Chilkoot Trail**, a 53-kilometer path over the Coast Mountains between **Dyea**, north of Skagway in Alaska (see p.503), and **Bennett Lake** on the BC border south of Whitehorse. Before the rush Dyea was a small village of Chilkat Tlingit, who made annual runs over the trail to barter fish oil, clam shells and dried fish with interior Dene people for animal hides, skin clothing and copper. The Chilkat jealously guarded access to the **Chilkoot Pass**, one of only three glacier-free routes through the Coast Mountains west of Juneau. Sheer weight of numbers and a show of force from a US gunboat, however, opened the trail for stampeders to get from the ferries at the Pacific Coast ports to the Yukon River, which they then rode to the goldfields at Dawson City.

For much of 1897 the pass and border were disputed by the US and Canada until the Canadian NWMP established a storm-battered shack at the summit to enforce the fateful "ton of goods" entry requirement. Introduced because of chronic shortages in the goldfields, this obliged every man entering the Yukon to carry a ton of provisions – and was to have appalling consequences for the stampeders. Weather conditions and the fifty-degree slopes proved too severe even for horses or mules, so men had to carry supplies on their backs over as many as fifty journeys. Many died in avalanches or lost everything when temperatures dropped to -51°C and 25 meters of snow fell. Even so, the lure of gold dragged some 22,000 over the pass.

These days most people off the **ferries from Prince Rupert and the Alaska Panhandle** make the fantastic journey across the mountains by car or *Gray Line* bus on Hwy 2 from **Skagway to Whitehorse**, paralleling the old trail at a distance. More affluent tourists take the *White Pass & Yukon Railroad* (twice daily May 18–Sept 24; Skagway–White Pass by train then bus to Whitehorse; around $95).

Increasing numbers, however, walk the old trail, now preserved as a **long-distance footpath**. Its great appeal lies not only in the scenery and natural habitats – embracing coastal rainforest, tundra and subalpine boreal woodland – but also in such artefacts as old huts, rotting boots, mugs and broken bottles still scattered where they were left by the prospectors. Well marked and regularly patrolled, it is generally fit to walk between June and September. Although it takes only about four days you shouldn't launch into it lightly. There are dangers from bears, avalanches, drastic changes of weather and exhaustion – for one twelve-kilometer stretch, for example, you're advised to allow twelve hours. Excellent maps and guides are available from Skagway's Visitor Information Bureau at Second and Broadway and the *Canadian Parks Service* office at the SS *Klondike* in Whitehorse.

Before walking the path from south to north, you must pre-clear **Canadian customs** at Fraser on Hwy 2, 25km north of Skagway – which can be done by phone on ☎403/821-4111. After the time they give you to complete the trail, you must report to the Customs and Immigration Office in Whitehorse at 101 Main St (daily 8.30am–4.30pm; ☎667-6471). Immigration controls are no less lax than elsewhere.

Walk or taxi the 15km from Skagway to the trailhead at Dyea to start the walk, and then be prepared to camp, as the chance of finding space in the three cabins on the trail is almost zero. The eight **campgrounds** at intervals along the trail also become busy, but are unlikely to turn you away. No rough camping is allowed.

From Bennett Lake at the end of the trail, take a **boat** to Carcross and pick up a *Gray Line* bus to Whitehorse, or a minibus to **Log Cabin** on Hwy 2 136km south of Whitehorse to pick up a bus to either Whitehorse or Skagway. For a short taste of the *White Pass* railway you can take the train from Bennett Lake to Fraser, 8km south of Log Cabin ($17), and catch the *Gray Line* from there.

the place slumbered, barely sustained by copper mining and the paddle-wheelers that plied the river carrying freight and the occasional tourist. The second boom came with the construction of the Alaska Highway – a kickstart that prompted its repopulation (reaching a peak of 40,000), and has stood it in good stead ever since.

Arrival and information

Whitehorse's **airport** is on the bluff above the town, 5km from downtown; taxis and shuttle buses connect with downtown (the *Hillcrest* runs past the airport about hourly). The *Greyhound* **bus terminal** is at 3211 Third Ave (☎667-2223) at the extreme eastern end of downtown ten minutes' walk from Main Street – you turn left out of the terminal for the town center, something it's as well to know if you stagger off the daily *Greyhound* from Dawson Creek, which arrives at 5am.

Whitehorse's central **Visitor Information Centre** is a block east of Main St at 302 Steele St (daily May–Sept 8am–8pm; Oct–May 8.30am–5pm; ☎667-7545). Its staff are friendly and have built up an unusual **comments book**, filled with enlightening complaints and up-to-date tips from travellers coming from Alaska and the north. There is also a big **Yukon Visitor Reception Centre** for more general information on the Yukon, beside the Transportation Museum on the Alaska Hwy by the airport (daily May–Sept 8am–8pm; ☎667-2915). The *Canadian Parks Service* information office alongside the SS *Klondike* (May–Sept daily 9am–6pm; ☎667-4511) is the place to pick up information on the Chilkoot Trail. Almost as useful as these is *Books on Main*, 203 Main St, which has a full range of Yukon books, guides and pamphlets you won't find elsewhere. For an outstanding selection of **maps** visit *Jim's Toy and Gifts*, 208 Main St. **Bikes** can be rented from *The Bike Shop*, 2157-2nd Ave (☎667-6501), or *Wheels and Brakes Cyclery*, 4168-4th Ave (☎663-3760), and **canoes** from the *Kanoe People* (☎668-4899), who also organize guided day trips (from $50) and two-week expeditions on the river.

The Town

Although greater Whitehorse spills along the Alaska Highway for several kilometers, the old **downtown** core is a forty-block grid centered on Main Street and mostly sandwiched between Second and Fourth avenues. Now graced only with a handful of pioneer buildings, the place still retains the dour integrity of a frontier town, and at night the baying of timber wolves and coyotes is a reminder of the wilderness immediately beyond the city limits. Nonetheless, the tourist influx provides a fair amount of action in the bars and cafés, and the streets are more appealing than in many northern towns.

The main thing to see is the **SS Klondike** (daily May–Sept 9am–7pm; free), one of only two surviving paddle-steamers in the Yukon, now rather sadly beached at the western end of Second Ave, though it has been beautifully restored to the glory of its 1930s heyday. More than 250 stern-wheelers once plied the river, taking 36 hours to make the 700-kilometer journey to Dawson City, and five days to make the return trip against the current. The SS *Klondike* battled against the river until 1955, ferrying 300 tons of cargo a trip, until an inexperienced pilot ran her aground and condemned her to museum status. The boat has the status of a National Historic Site, and so visits are by guided tour only.

Elsewhere in town you could pop into the **MacBride Museum** at First Ave and Wood St (daily May–Oct 9am–6pm; $3.25) for the usual zoo of stuffed animals, pioneer and gold-rush memorabilia, as well as **archive photos** and a display on the Asiatic tribes who crossed the Bering Straits to settle the Americas. Resist the widely touted **stage shows**, however – a pair of expensive vaudeville acts of the banjo-plucking and frilly-knickered dancing variety.

Your money's better spent on one of the **river tours** that shoot the **Miles Canyon** 9km south of the town, otherwise reached off the Alaska Highway, or from the South Access Road which hugs the river edge beyond the SS *Klondike*. The building of a hydro-electric dam has tamed the violence of the rapids and replaced them with **Schwatka Lake**, but the two-hour trip on the MV *Schwatka* (daily 2pm & 7pm, June–Sept; $15; ☎668-2042) gives a better view of the river's potential ferocity and of the canyon's sheer walls than the viewpoints off the road.

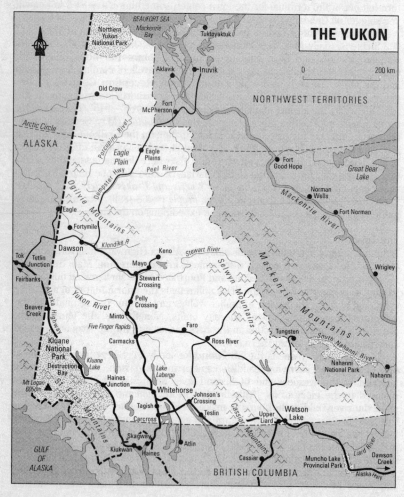

THE YUKON

Book tickets through *Atlas Tours* in town at the Westmark Hotel Mall (☎668-3161), or go straight to the dock above the dam about 3km down Canyon Road. *Youcan Voyage*, 1 Morley Rd (☎668-2927), run similar trips on the river (docking opposite the MacBride Museum), as well as six-day cruises to Dawson City. If you fancy a walk or a site for a picnic, you might stroll from the main canyon parking lot some of the 11km to Canyon City, the all-but-vanished site of the initial stage of the stampeders' tramway.

Accommodation

It's as well to call ahead in summer to reserve accommodation, especially at the excellent and newly renovated **youth hostel**, the *Fourth Avenue Residence*, 4051 Fourth Ave (☎667-4471; ①–③); it's at the far western end of Fourth Ave, a good ten-minute walk from downtown. More a hotel than a hostel, it offers a wide variety of room deals ranging from shared dorms to private doubles with TV.

Other **accommodation** runs the gamut in Whitehorse. Inexpensive, fairly grim and with live bands to serenade you through the small hours, is the *98 Hotel*, 110 Wood St (☎667-2641; ②). Only slightly better is the *Fort Yukon Hotel*, about 200m west of the bus terminal at 2163 Second Ave (☎667-2595; ②). The *Stratford Motel*, 401 Jarvis St (☎667-4243; ④), is spotlessly clean and boasts a friendly staff. Other good mid-priced places include the *Town & Mountain Hotel*, 401 Main St (☎668-7644; ④), and the *Edgewater Hotel*, 101 Main St (☎667-2572; ④). At the top of the range, two comfortable hotels belong to *Westmark*, a northern chain: the *Klondike Inn*, 2288 Second Ave (☎668-4747; ⑤), and the *Whitehorse Hotel*, Second Ave and Wood St (☎668-4700; ⑤). If you arrive late at the airport, or need an early get-away, the airstrip's nearest hotel is the *Airline Inn*, 16 Burns Rd (☎668-4330; ③).

Ask at the infocentre for their **bed and breakfast** list, or call the long-established *Baker's Bed and Breakfast*, 84 Eleventh Ave (☎633-2308; ③), *Drifters B&B*, 44 Cedar Crescent (☎633-5419; ③), or *Great North B&B*, 31 Boswell Crescent (☎668-7659; ③). The *Robert Service* **campground** has been set out specifically for tents and backpackers about fifteen minutes' walk down South Access Road (mid-May to mid-Sept; ☎668-83251; pay showers; $5). The heavily advertised *Trail of 98 RV and Campground* on the road between the Alaska Highway and downtown is as bleak as a parking lot and no good for tents.

Eating

The best of several friendly laid-back **eating** places is the *Talisman Café*, 2112 Second Ave (daily 6am–11pm; closed Sun), which serves a range of full meals, and is also a spot to while away time with a cup of coffee. Slightly more expensive and twee is *The Bistro* at 205 Main St, known for its huge breakfasts, proper *cappuccino*, and calorie-stuffed desserts. The *No Pop Sandwich Shop*, 2112 Second Ave, is altogether less cozy, but it's popular all the same and the food's good. Next door at 4123 Second Ave, the excellent hippy-ish *Alpine Bakery* (Thurs–Sat 10am–5.30pm) is usually crammed with campers; the counter greets you with the Shakespearian sentiment "one feast, one house, one mutual happiness".

Onward from Whitehorse

Whitehorse provides the main **transportation** links not only to most other points in the territory, but also to Alaska and the Northwest Territories. In summer there are thrice-daily *Canadian* **flights** to Calgary (Can$520), Edmonton (Can$450) and Vancouver (Can$450); the airline has an office at Fourth Ave and Elliot (☎668-3535). In this part of the world, it's also worth knowing the various smaller airline options that are available. *Air North* (☎668-2228) operates alarmingly old-fashioned planes between Whitehorse, Dawson City, Old Crow, Juneau and Fairbanks and issues a 21-day pass (Can$550) for travel between all five destinations. *Alkan Air* (☎668-6616) offers flights to Dawson City (Can$240), Faro, Mayo, Old Crow, Watson Lake, a handful of BC destinations, and to Norman Wells and Inuvik in the NWT (Can$470). The one and only connection to Yellowknife, a potentially vital link in any northern itinerary, is with *Delta Air* (☎668-6804; Can$360).

This is the end of the line for *Greyhound* **buses** in Canada (☎667-2223). For **Alaska and Yukon stops west of Whitehorse**, the expensive *Gray Lines'* **Alaskon Express** (☎667-2223) runs from Skagway to Whitehorse's bus terminal (daily late May to mid-Sept; US$52) and then on to Anchorage (Tues, Fri & Sat only; US$179) and Fairbanks (Tues, Fri & Sun only; US$149); note that the bus sometimes stops overnight at Beaver Creek (YT), so you may have to find the price of accommodation for certain long-haul routes into Alaska. A more ramshackle and much cheaper service in an old army bus runs to Alaska from the *Fourth Avenue Residence* (see "Accommodation").

Norline buses (☎993-5331) from the main bus terminal run to **Dawson City** (summer Mon, Wed & Fri; Sept–Oct & March–April Tues & Thurs; weekly in winter; around Can$75). *North West Stage Lines* (☎668-6975) run irregular services in old school buses **to Beaver Creek** and over gravel roads **to Faro and Ross River** about 200km northeast of Whitehorse – a journey that's particularly popular with canoeists headed for the South Macmillan River, one of Canada's best river trips.

For **car rental** try *Hertz*, 4158 Fourth Ave (☎667-2505), *Budget Car and Truck*, 4178 Fourth Ave (☎667-6200) or *Norcan*, Mile 917 Alaska Highway (☎668-2137 or 1-800/661-0445) – which unlike its competitors might rent you a car or truck suitable for gravel roads such as the Dempster and Cassiar highways.

Kluane Country

Kluane Country is the pocket of southwest Yukon on and around the 491-kilometer stretch of the Alaska Highway from Whitehorse to **Beaver Creek** at the border with Alaska. "Kluane" comes from the Southern Tutchone native word meaning a "place of many fish" after the teeming waters of the area, and of **Kluane Lake** in particular, the Yukon's highest and largest sheet of water. These days, though, the name is associated more with the wilderness of Canada's largest mountain park, the **Kluane National Park** – a region that contains the country's highest mountains, the most extensive non-polar icefields in the world, and the greatest diversity of plant and animal species in the far north. The park's main center is **Haines Junction** at the intersection of the Alaska Highway and the Haines Road. Although motels and campgrounds regularly punctuate the Alaska Highway, the only other places of any size are **Destruction Bay** and **Burwash Landing** on Kluane Lake. *Gray Line*'s **Alaskon Express** buses ply the Alaska Highway, which is also heavily hitched.

Haines Junction

A blunt and modern place with a fine mountain-circled setting, **HAINES JUNCTION** mushroomed into life in 1942 during the building of the Alaska Highway as a base for the construction of the Haines Road – a highway which connects with Skagway's sister port at Haines, 174km to the southeast. Today it's most useful as the biggest service center between Whitehorse and Tok in Alaska and as the eastern headquarters of the Kluane National Park – though the park covers a vast tract west of the Alaska Highway well to the north and south of the village. The combined *Canadian Parks Service* and Yukon government **Visitor Reception Centre** is on Logan St just off the north side of the Alaska Highway (daily May–Sept 8.30am–9pm; Oct–April 9am–5pm; ☎634-2251 or 634-2345).

If you want to stay the least expensive **motel** is the *Gateway* (☎634-2371; ②) on the junction of Haines Rd and the Alaska Highway; it also has a few serviced campsites to the rear. *Mother's Cozy Corner Motel & Restaurant* (☎634-2511; ②) lies just down the Alaska Highway on the corner of Bates Road. The simple *Pine Lake* **campground** (May–Oct; $5) is 4km west of the village signed off the Alaska Highway, or there's the bigger and more central *Kluane RV Kampground* in town (May–Sept; ☎634-2709; $8). The best place to eat is the *Village Bakery* on Logan St across from the Reception Centre.

Kluane National Park

Created in 1972 using land from the earlier Kluane Game Sanctuary, the **Kluane National Park** contains some of the Yukon's greatest but most inaccessible scenery; for the most part you have to resign yourself to seeing and walking its easterly margins from points along the Alaska Highway. Together with the neighboring Wrangell-St Elias National Park in Alaska (see p.529) the park protects the **St Elias Mountains**, though from the highway the peaks you see rearing up to the south are part of the subsidiary Kluane Range. Beyond them, and largely invisible from the road, the St Elias **Icefield Ranges** contain Mount St Elias (5488m), **Mount Logan** (5950m) – Canada's highest point – and Mount McKinley (6193m)

WALKING IN KLUANE NATIONAL PARK

Kluane's **trail system** is still in its infancy, but experienced walkers will enjoy the wilderness routes, most of which follow old mining roads or creek beds and require overnight rough camping. A few more manageable walks start from seven distinct trailheads, each mapped on separate pamphlets available at Haines's Reception Centre, where the enthusiastic staff also organize guided day walks during the summer.

Three trails start from points along a twenty-kilometer stretch of Haines Road immediately south of Haines Junction. The path nearest to the town, not surprisingly, is much the most popular walk – the nineteen-kilometer round trip **Auriol Trail**. Nearby, the **Rock Glacier Trail** is a twenty-minute jaunt to St Elias Lake; the third and longest is the **Mush Lake Road** route (21.6km one way).

North of Haines Junction, most people walk all or part of two paths that strike out from the Sheep Mountain information kiosk on Kluane Lake – either the **Sheep Mountain Ridge** (11.5km), with good chances of seeing the area's Dall sheep, or the longer **Slim's River West Trail** (28.4km) which offers a relatively easy way to see the edges of the park's icefield interior.

in Alaska, the highest point in North America. Below them, and covering half the park, is a huge base of mile-deep glaciers and icefields, home to just one permanent resident, the legendary iceworm. Unless you're prepared for full-scale expeditions, this interior is off limits, though from as little as Can$60 you can take plane **tours** over the area with *Glacier Air Tours* at Burwash Landing (☎841-5171; May 24–Sept 1); details of this and other guided tours are available from the Haines Junction Reception Centre.

On the drier, warmer ranges at the edge of the icefields a green belt of meadow, marsh, forest and fen provides sanctuary for a huge assortment of **wildlife** such as grizzlies, moose, mountain goats, and a herd of four thousand white **Dall sheep** – the animals the park originally set out to protect. These margins also support the widest spectrum of **birds** in the far north, some 150 species, including easily seen raptors like peregrine falcons, bald eagles, golden eagles and smaller birds like arctic terns, mountain bluebirds, tattlers and hawk owls.

Limited **trails** (see box) offer the chance to see some of these creatures, but the only **campground** within the park is the site at *Kathleen Lake*, on the Haines Road 16km southeast of Haines Junction ($6) – though there is plenty of hotel and camping accommodation along the Alaska Highway.

Kluane Lake

The Kluane region might keep its greatest mountains out of sight, but it makes amends by laying on the stunning **Kluane Lake** along 60km of the Alaska Highway. About 75km northwest of Haines Junction, and hot on the heels of some magnificent views of the St Elias Mountains, the huge lake (400 square kilometers) is framed on all sides by snow-covered peaks whose glaciers feed its ice-blue waters. It's not part of the national park, but there's a second park kiosk at its southern tip, the **Sheep Mountain Information Kiosk** (daily mid-May to June & first fortnight of Sept 10am–6pm; July & Aug 9am–7pm; ☎841-5161).

If you want to boat or fish, there are rental facilities at the two main settlements along the shores, Destruction Bay and Burwash Landing, each of which also has a small selection of **accommodation** to supplement the odd lodges and campgrounds along the Alaska Highway. In the smaller **DESTRUCTION BAY** (pop. 44) use the *Talbot Arm Motel* behind the *Chevron* garage (☎841-4461; ③), which also has a partly serviced **campground** ($10).

At **BURWASH LANDING**, 15km beyond, the *Burwash Landing Resort* (☎841-4441; ③) includes a big unserviced campsite (May–Oct). The best **campground** is the lovely government-run *Congdon Creek* site off the Alaska Highway, 12km south of Destruction Bay. Five kilometers further south the private *Cottonwood Park Campground* offers rather more facilities (mid-May to mid-Oct; ☎634-2739; $12).

Beaver Creek

BEAVER CREEK, Canada's westernmost settlement, is the last stop before Alaska. Following concerted lobbying from its one hundred inhabitants, however, it no longer houses the customs post – this has been moved a couple of kilometers up the road in response to complaints from the locals about the flashing lights and sirens that used to erupt whenever a tourist forgot to stop. Though the border is open twenty-four hours a day, there's a high chance you may have to stay here, particularly if you're catching the *Alaskon* **bus** service from Skagway and Whitehorse, which stops overnight at Beaver Creek on some trans-Alaskan routes. The bus company can arrange to book you into the large and expensive

Westmark Inn (May–Sept; ☎258-0560; ⑥): if that's too steep you've got the choice of booking yourself in at the eccentric *Ida's Motel* (☎862-7223; ③) or failing that, *Marvin's Inn*, General Delivery (no phone; ③).

The *Westmark* does have a large serviced **campground** ($18), though they're happier to see RVs than backpackers. Near town too there's the *Far West Holding* campground (year round; 20 partially serviced sites; ☎862-7220; $5), and a good Yukon government site 10km south at *Snag Junction* (May–Oct; $5). Also be warned that if US Customs take against you or your rucksack, they can insist on seeing at least $400 cash, and won't be swayed by any number of credit cards. For full details on border crossing and what to expect on the other side, visit the Yukon **Visitor Information Centre** (May–Sept daily 9am–9pm; ☎862-7321).

Dawson City

Few episodes in Canadian history have captured the imagination like the **Klondike gold rush**, and few places have remained as evocative of their past as **DAWSON CITY**, the stampede's tumultuous capital. For a few months in 1898 this former patch of moose pasture became one of the wealthiest and most famous places on earth, as something like 100,000 people struggled across huge tracts of wilderness to seek their fortunes in the richest goldfield of all time.

Most people now approach the town on the Klondike Highway from Whitehorse, a wonderful road through almost utter wilderness, and knowing the background to the place it's hard not to near the road's end without high expectations. Little at first, however, distinguishes its surroundings. Some 500km from Whitehorse the road wanders through low but steeply sided hills covered in spruce, aspen and dwarf firs, and then picks up a small ice-clear river – the **Klondike**. Gradually the first small spoil heaps appear on the hills to the south, and then suddenly the entire valley bottom turns into a devastated landscape of vast boulders and abandoned workings. The desolate tailings continue for several kilometers until the Klondike flows into the much broader **Yukon** and the town, previously hidden by hills, comes suddenly into view.

A good many tourists and backpackers come up here, many drawn by the boardwalks, rutted dirt streets and dozens of false-fronted wooden houses, others to canoe the Yukon, or travel the Dempster or Top of the World highways into Alaska and the Northwest Territories. After decades of decline the *Canada Parks Service* is restoring the town, now deservedly a National Historic Site, a process which is bringing about increased commercialism, new hotels – and a few misgivings about its effect on the place's character. That said, in a spot where permafrost buckles buildings, it snows in August, and temperatures drop to -60°C during winters of almost perpetual gloom, there's little real chance of Dawson losing the gritty, weather-battered feel of a true frontier town. More to the point, small-time prospecting still goes on, and there are one or two rough-and-ready bars whose hardened locals take a dim view of sharing their beers, let alone their gold, with coachloads of tourists. You could easily spend a couple of days here, one exploring the town, the other touring the old Klondike creeks to the east. If at all possible prime yourself beforehand with the background to one of the most colorful chapters in Canada's history: Pierre Berton's widely available bestseller, *Klondike – The Last Great Gold Rush 1896–1899*, is a superbly written introduction both to the period and to the place.

The Town

You should start any wander on **Front Street**, the leading edge of a street grid that runs parallel to the Yukon River and home to the impressive **visitor center** (May–Sept daily 9am–9pm; ☎993-5566). Loaded with a huge amount of material, the place also shows good introductory archive and contemporary films

THE KLONDIKE GOLD RUSH

Gold rushes in North America during the nineteenth century were nothing new, but none generated quite the delirium of the **Klondike gold rush** in 1898. Over a million people are estimated to have left home for the Yukon goldfields, the largest single one-year mass movement of people in the century. Of these about 100,000 made it to the Yukon, about 20,000 panned the creeks, 4000 found something and a couple of dozen made – and invariably lost – huge fortunes.

The **discovery of gold in 1896** on the Klondike, a tributary of the Yukon River, was the culmination of twenty years of prospecting in the Yukon and Alaska. A Hudson's Bay fur trader first noticed gold in 1842, and the first substantial report was made by an English missionary in 1863, but as the exploitation of gold was deemed bad for trade in both furs and religion neither report was followed up. The first mining on any scale took place in 1883 and gradually small camps sprang up along almost 2000 miles of river at places like Forty Mile, Sixty Mile and Circle City. All were established before the Klondike strike, but were home to only a few hundred men, hardened types reared on the earlier Californian and British Columbian gold rushes.

The discovery of the gold that started the stampede is inevitably shrouded in myth and countermyth. The first man to prospect near the Klondike River was **Robert Henderson**, a dour Nova Scotian and the very embodiment of the lone pioneer. In early 1896 he found eight cents' worth of gold in a pan scooped from a creek in the hills above present-day Dawson City. This was considered an excellent return at the time, and a sign to Henderson that the creek would make worthwhile yields. He panned out a small fortune with four companions, before returning downriver to pick up supplies.

Henderson then set about finding a route up to the creek he'd prospected, and at the mouth of the Klondike met **George Washington Carmack** and a couple of his native friends, Skookum Jim and Tagish Charley. Henderson told Carmack of his hopes for the area, and then – with a glance at the natives – uttered the phrase that probably cost him a fortune, "There's a chance for you George, but I don't want any damn Siwashes [natives] staking on that creek." Henderson wandered off into the hills, leaving Carmack, rankled by the remark, to prospect a different set of creeks – the right ones, as it turned out. On the eve of August 16 Skookum Jim found $4 of gold in a pan on Bonanza Creek, a virtually unprecedented amount at the time. Next day Carmack staked the first claim, and rushed off to register the find leaving Henderson prospecting almost barren ground on the other side of the hills.

By the end of August all of Bonanza had been staked by a hundred or so old-timers from camps up and down the Yukon. Almost all the real fortunes had been secured by the winter of 1896 when the snows and frozen river effectively sealed the region from the outside world. The **second phase** occurred after the thaw when a thousand or so miners from the West Coast arrived drawn by vague rumors emanating from the north of a big find. The headlong rush that was to make the

throughout the day, as well as organizing free tours of the town's **heritage buildings** – though these are easily seen on your own, as are the cabins which belonged to two chroniclers of the gold rush, poet **Robert Service** and the better-known **Jack London**. The local **museum** is also good for an hour, but when all is said and done it's the atmospheric streets of Dawson that are most compelling.

Klondike unique, however, followed the docking in **July 1897** of the *Excelsior* in San Francisco and the *Portland* in Seattle. Few sights could have been so stirring a proof of the riches up for grabs as the battered Yukon miners who came down the gangplanks dragging bags, boxes and sacks literally bursting with gold. The press were waiting for the *Portland*, which docked with two tons of gold on board, all taken by hand from the Klondike creeks by just a few miners. The rush was now on in earnest.

Whipped up by the media and the outfitters of Seattle and San Francisco, thousands embarked on trips that were to claim hundreds of lives. The most common route – the "poor man's route" – was to take a boat from a west coast port to Skagway, climb the dreaded **Chilkoot Pass** to pick up the Yukon River at Whitehorse, and then boat the last 500 miles to Dawson City. The easiest and most expensive route lay by boat upstream from the mouth of the Yukon in western Alaska. The most dangerous and most bogus were the "All Canadian Route" from Edmonton and overland trails through the northern wilderness.

The largest single influx came with the melting of the ice on the Yukon in May 1898 – 21 months after the first claim – when a vast makeshift armada drifted down the river. When they docked at Dawson City, the boats nestled six deep along a two-mile stretch of the waterfront. For most it was to have been a fruitless journey – every inch of the creeks having long been staked – yet in most accounts of the stampede it is clear that this was a rite of passage as much as a quest for wealth. Pierre Berton observed that "there were large numbers who spent only a few days in Dawson and did not even bother to visit the hypnotic creeks that had tugged at them all winter long. They turned their faces home again, their adventure over . . . It was as if they had, without quite knowing it, completed the job they had set out to do and had come to understand that it was not the gold they were seeking after all."

As for the gold, it's the smaller details that hint at the scale of the Klondike. The miner's wife, for example, who could wander the creek by her cabin picking nuggets from the stream bed as she waited for her husband to come home; or the destitutes during the Great Depression who could pan $40 a day from the dirt under Dawson's boardwalks; or the $1000 panned during rebuilding of the *Orpheum Theatre* in the Forties, all taken in a morning from under the floorboards where it had drifted from miners' pockets half a century before; or the $200 worth of dust panned nightly from the beermats of a Dawson saloon during 1897.

By about 1899 the rush was over, not because the gold had run out, but because the most easily accessible gold had been taken from the creeks. It had been the making of Alaska; Tacoma, Portland, Victoria and San Francisco all felt its impact; Edmonton sprang from almost nothing; and Vancouver's population doubled in a year. It was also the first of a string of mineral discoveries in the Yukon and the far north, a region whose vast and untapped natural resources are increasingly the subject of attention from multi-nationals as rapacious and determined as their grizzled predecessors.

The heritage buildings

Fuelled by limitless avarice, Dawson between 1898 and 1900 exploded into a full-blown metropolis of 30,000 people – the largest city in the Canadian west and the equal of places like Seattle and San Francisco in its opportunities for vice, decadence and good living. There were opera houses, theaters, cinemas (at a time when motion-picture houses were just three years old), steam heating, three hospitals, restaurants with French chefs, and bars, brothels and dance halls which generated phenomenal business – one Charlie Kimball took $300,000 dollars in a month from his club, and spent the lot within days. Rules of supply and demand made Dawson an expensive town, with a single two-meter frontage fetching as much in rent in a month as a four-bedroom apartment in New York cost for two years.

Only a few of the many intact **heritage buildings** around the town date from the earliest days of the rush, dozens having been lost to fire and to permafrost, whose effects are seen in some of the most appealing of the older buildings: higgledy-piggledy collapsing ruins of rotting wood, weeds and rusting corrugated iron. Elsewhere restoration projects are in full flow, and have saved wonderful wooden buildings such as the **Palace Grand Theatre** (1899) on King Street, where you can also watch the wistful award-winning black and white film, *City of Gold*, a documentary which first drew the attention of the federal government to Dawson's decline in the Fifties (daily 2.30pm; free). Nearby there's the working 1901 **Post Office** (June–Sept daily noon–6pm), *Harrington's Store* on Third Ave and Princess, with a "Dawson as They Saw It" exhibition of photos arranged by *Canadian Parks* (June–Aug daily 9am–5pm; free), and the cream and brown clapboard **Anglican Church**, built in 1902 with money collected from the miners. On Queen Street is **Diamond Tooth Gertie's Gambling House**, founded by one of the town's more notorious characters, and still operating as the only legal **casino** in Canada (July–Sept Mon–Sat 8pm–2am; $5); all proceeds go to the restoration of Dawson.

The museum

Dawson has scope for a full-blown and fully integrated museum on its past, but at present the job is done reasonably well by the **Dawson City Museum**, Fifth and Church St (June–Sept daily 10am–6pm; $4). There's an adequate historical run-through of the gold rush from the first finds; the more you know already the more you're likely to appreciate it. Fascinating old diaries and newspaper cuttings vividly document the minutiae of pioneer life and events such as the big winter freeze of 1897–98 when temperatures reputedly touched -86°C, and of the summer heat wave of 1898 when the sun shone unbroken for almost 23 hours daily, bringing temperatures in the upper thirties. The museum also shows some of the hundreds of old films that were discovered under some Dawson floorboards a few years back, and holds interesting touring exhibitions in the wood-framed rooms upstairs that once housed the council offices.

The Robert Service and Jack London cabins

The cabins of Dawson's two literary lions are only about a hundred meters apart on Eighth Avenue, about ten minutes' walk from Front Street. Most Canadians hold **Robert Service** in such high esteem that it comes as a shock actually to hear famous verses like *Songs of Sourdough* and *The Shooting of Dan McGrew*, though they do sometimes achieve a sort of inspired awfulness. Born in Preston,

England, in 1874, the poet wrote most of his gold-rush verse before he'd even set foot in the Yukon – he was posted by his bank employers to Whitehorse in 1904 and only made Dawson in 1908. He retired a rich man on the proceeds of his writing, spending his last years mainly in France, where he died in 1958. His **cabin** (June–Sept daily 10am–5pm; free) is probably cozier and better decorated than it was almost a century ago, but still gives an idea of how most people must have lived once Dawson was reasonably established. Visitors flock here in summer to hear poetry recitals in front of the cabin from a bearded eccentric dressed and mannered as the "Bard of the Yukon" (July & Aug daily at 10am & 3pm; free).

Jack London's Cabin was home to a more convincing writer, but is a less persuasive piece of reconstruction, being little more than a bleak, blank-walled and incomplete hut. London knew far more than Service of the real rigors of northern life, however, having spent time in 1897 as a ferryman on Whitehorse's Miles Canyon before moving north to spend about a year holed up on Henderson's Creek above the Klondike River. He returned home to California penniless, but loaded with a fund of material that was to find expression in books like *The Call of the Wild*, *White Fang* and *A Daughter of the Snows*. Alongside the hut, a good little museum of pictures and memorabilia is presided over by an amiable and knowledgeable curator, a writer himself (hut and museum June to mid-Sept daily 10am–noon & 1–6pm; free).

Around Dawson

While in Dawson make a point of seeing the two creeks where it all started and where most of the gold was mined – **Bonanza and Eldorado**, both over 20km away from the townsite along rough roads to the southeast. These days no big working mine survives in the region; though most of the claims are still owned and definitely out of bounds to amateurs, it's still possible to see some of the huge dredges that supplanted individual strivers. Another popular local excursion is to **Midnight Dome**, the gouged-out hill behind the town, while further afield numerous RVs, cyclists and hitch-hikers follow the **Top of the World Highway** which runs on beyond the Alaskan border to link with the Alaska Highway at Tetlin Junction.

Bonanza and Eldorado creeks

To reach **Bonanza Creek** follow the Klondike Highway – the continuation of Front St – for 4km to the junction with Bonanza Creek Road. The road threads through scenes of apocalyptic piles of boulders and river gravel for some 12km until it comes to a simple cairn marking **Discovery Claim**, the spot staked by George Carmack after he pulled out a nugget the size of his thumb, or so the story goes. Every 150 meters along the creek in front of you – the width of a claim – was to yield some 3000kg of gold, or about $25 million worth at 1900 prices. Exact amounts of gold taken out are difficult to establish because it was in miners' interests to undervalue their takings to the authorities, but most estimates suggest that around $600 million worth left the creeks between 1897 and 1904. Given a claim's huge value they were often subdivided and sold as "fractions": one miner pulled out over 100kg of gold in eight hours from a fraction – almost $1 million worth.

At Discovery Claim the road forks again, one spur running east up Eldorado Creek, if anything richer than Bonanza, the other following Upper Bonanza Road to the summit of **King Solomon's Dome**, where you can look down over smaller scarred rivulets like Hunker and Dominion creeks, before returning in a loop to the Klondike Highway via Hunker Road. As time went by and the easily reached gold was exploited, miners increasingly consolidated claims, or sold out to large companies who installed dredges capable of clawing out the bedrock and gravel. Numerous examples of these industrial dinosaurs litter the creeks, but the largest and most famous is the **No. 4 Dredge** at Claim 17 BD ("Below Discovery") off Bonanza Creek Road, which from the start of operations in 1913 was able to take as much as 25kg of gold daily. Modern mines are lucky to produce a quarter of that amount in a week.

Without a car you'll have to rent a bike or join up with one of the various **goldfield tours** run by *Gold City Tours*, Front St (☎993-5175), either to see the dredges and creeks, or to **pan for gold** yourself, at a price. Only three small fractions on Claim 6 can currently be panned free of charge – inquire at the reception center for latest locations.

Midnight Dome and Top of the World Highway

The **Midnight Dome** is the distinctive hill that rears up behind Dawson City, half-covered in stunted pines and half-eaten away by land slips. It's named because from its summit at midnight on June 21 you can watch the sun dip to the horizon before rising again straight away – Dawson being only 300km south of the Arctic Circle. The Midnight Dome Road runs 8km to its summit from the Klondike Highway just out of the town proper. It's an extremely steep haul, but more than worth the slog for the massive views over Dawson, the goldfields, the Yukon's broad meanders and the ranks of mountains stretching away in all directions. At the summer solstice there's a race to the top and lots of drink-sodden

---

THE AURORA BOREALIS

The **aurora borealis**, or Northern Lights, is a beautiful and ethereal display of light in the upper atmosphere that can be seen over large parts of northern Canada and Alaska. The night sky appears to shimmer with dancing curtains of color, ranging from luminescent monotones – most commonly appearing in green or a dark red – to fantastic veils that run the full spectrum. The display becomes more animated as it proceeds, twisting and turning in patterns called "rayed bands", and as a finale a corona sometimes appears in which rays seem to flare in all directions from a central point.

Named after the Roman goddess of dawn, the aurora was long thought to be produced by sunlight reflected from polar snow and ice, or refracted light produced in the manner of a rainbow. Research still continues into the phenomenon, but it seems the aurora is caused by **radiation** emitted as light from atoms in the upper atmosphere as they are hit by fast-moving electrons and protons. The earth's geomagnetic field certainly plays some part in the creation of the aurora, but its source would appear to lie with the **sun** – auroras become more distinct and are seen spread over a larger area two days after intense solar activity, the time it takes the "solar wind" to arrive.

You should see the northern lights as far south as Prince George in British Columbia. They are at their most dazzling from **December to March** when nights are longest and the sky darkest, though they are potentially visible year round.

and fancy-dress festivities down in Dawson. *Gold City Tours* also run regular daytime and evening tours up here.

You can snatch further broad vistas from the **Top of the World Highway** (Hwy 9), a summer-only gravel road reached by ferry from Front St across the Yukon (daily mid-May to mid-Sept, 24 hours, every 45min except Wed 5–7am; 7am–11pm the rest of the year depending on weather; free; ☎667-5644). After only 5km the road unfolds a great panorama, and after 14km another **viewpoint** looks out over the Yukon valley and the **Ogilvie Mountains** straddling the Arctic Circle. Thereafter the road runs above the tree-line as a massive belvedere and can be seen switch-backing over barren ridges way into the distance. It hits the **Alaska border** 108km from Dawson, where you can cross only when the customs post is open (May–Oct 9am–9pm). Unlike the Dempster Highway (see p.477) there's no **bus** on this route, but you should be able to hitch easily in summer because it's much travelled as a neat way of linking with the Alaska Highway at **Tok** for the roads to Fairbanks and Anchorage or the loop back to Whitehorse. Be prepared to make only about 50kph, and inquire about local difficulties and petrol availability at the Dawson visitor center.

Practicalities

Dawson City's **airport**, 19km southeast of the town on the Klondike Highway, is used by scheduled *Alkan Air* (☎668-6616) services to Inuvik (NWT), Old Crow, Mayo and Whitehorse, and by *Air North* (☎993-5110) services to Fairbanks, Whitehorse, Watson Lake and Juneau. *Norline* **buses** (☎993-5331) from Whitehorse arrive at *Arctic Drugs* on Front St (3 weekly in summer; 2 weekly in winter). Tickets for all air services, Alaska and BC ferries, and for the Dempster Highway **bus** to Inuvik, can be arranged at *Gold City Travel* on Front St (☎993-5175).

Accommodation

More and more places to stay are opening in Dawson, but the increased competition isn't bringing the prices down. The two hostels are likely to be heavily over-subscribed, as are the bed and breakfast options, though calls to the latter a couple of days in advance should secure a room. Rates are high in the half-dozen or so mid-range places, most of which look the part of old-fashioned wood- and false-fronted hotels. The main town **campground** for tents is the government *Yukon River Campground* ($5), which is on the west bank of the Yukon immediately right after the ferry crossing from the top of Front St (if you're really roughing it there is a "squatters' tent city" just past the site). The *Gold Rush Campground* in town at Fifth Ave and York is a bleak but busy place designed mainly for RVs (May–Sept; ☎993-5247; $18).

Bonanza House, near the museum on Fifth Ave (☎993-5772). Four B&B rooms with shared sitting rooms and TV. ③.

Dawson City B&B, 451 Craig St (☎993-5649). Located near the junction of the Yukon and Klondike rivers; the house has an "oriental" theme – you've been warned. ③.

Dawson City River Hostel, across the river from downtown; first left after you jump the ferry (no phone). A new CHA-affiliated collection of bunks in smart log cabins with a good view of Dawson and the river. ①.

Downtown Hotel, Second and Queen (☎993-5346 or 1-800/764-GOLD). One of the town's more plush wooden-fronted hotels, and – unlike some – open year round. ⑤.

Eldorado, Third and Princess (☎993-5451 or 1-800/661-0518). Much the same as the *Downtown*, and also open year round. ⑤.

Fifth Ave B&B, on Fifth Ave near the museum (☎993-5941). New and spacious house with shared kitchen, and rooms with and without private bathrooms. ③.

Klondike Kate's Motel, Third and King (June–Aug; ☎993-5491). Nine individual cabins: oldish and simple, but clean and warm. ③.

McLondon's Bunkhouse, Second and Princess (☎993-6164). An excellent brand-new hostel-type place with "no-nonsense rooms at no-nonsense prices". ②.

Mary's Rooms, Third and Harper (May–Sept; ☎993-6013). Very inexpensive but very ramshackle collection of spartan rooms. ②.

Northern Comfort, Sixth and Church (☎993-5271). Bed and breakfast; bike rentals available. ③.

Trail of '98 Mini-Golf, 5km out of town at the junction of the Klondike Highway and Bonanza Creek Road (☎993-6101). The best budget deal around if you can get four people together for one of the simple $40 cabins. No power or running water, but washrooms are available nearby. ②.

Triple J Hotel, Fifth and Queen (May–Oct; ☎993-5323). Rooms or cabins in old-fashioned-style hotel next to *Diamond Tooth Gertie's*. ⑤.

Westmark, Fifth and Harper (☎993-5542). Part of an up-market northern chain, and the town's swishest hotel: look out for frequent cut-price promotions to fill empty rooms. ⑥.

Westminster Hotel, Third and Queen (April–Sept; ☎993-5463). Despite the tempting old false-fronted exterior, this is a rough-house spot where the miners come in to drink long and noisily into the night. ③.

Whitehorse Cabins, Front St (mid-May to mid-Sept; ☎993-5576). Six cabins on the waterfront at the northern end of the street. ③.

White Ram B&B, Seventh and Harper (☎993-5772). Look out for the distinctive pink house. Pick-up from bus on request. ③.

Eating and nightlife

For **eating** there are a couple of good snack places on Front St – the *98 Drive In* and rather austere *Nancy's*. *Klondike Kate's* at Third and King is the friendliest and most laid-back for staples like breakfasts and straightforward dinners; the popular *Marina's*, Fifth and Harper (☎993-6800), is the best place for something a touch more special, with pizzas and excellent dinners up to about $25.

   Nightlife revolves around drinking in the main hotel bars, or an hour or so at *Diamond Tooth Gertie's* at Fourth and Queen, Canada's only legal **gambling** hall. You can also catch the almost equally touristy period-costume melodramas and vaudeville acts held at the *Palace Grand Theatre* (June–Sept nightly except Tues at 8pm; $12).

The Dempster Highway

Begun in 1959 to service northern oilfields, and completed in 1988 – by which time the accessible oil had been siphoned off – the 740-kilometer **Dempster Highway** between Dawson City and Inuvik in the Northwest Territories is the only road in Canada to cross the **Arctic Circle**, offering a tremendous journey through superb landscapes. An increasingly travelled route – which locals say means four cars an hour – it crosses the **Ogilvie Mountains** just north of Dawson before dropping down to **Eagle Plains** to provide almost unparalleled access to the sub-arctic tundra. Shortly before meeting the NWT border after

470km it rises through the **Richardson Mountains** and then drops to the drab low hills and plain of the Peel Plateau and Mackenzie River. For much of its course the road follows the path of the dog patrols operated by the Mounties in the first half of the century, taking its name from a Corporal W J D Dempster, who in March 1922 was sent to look for a patrol lost between **Fort Macpherson** (NWT) and Dawson. He found their frozen bodies just 26 miles from where they had set off.

Practicalities

The Dempster is a gravel road and the journey by **car** takes anything between twelve and fifteen hours in good conditions. It is not, however, a journey to be undertaken lightly. If you're **cycling** or motorbiking – two ever more popular ways to do the trip – you need to be prepared for rough camping, and should call at the **NWT Information Centre** on Front St in Dawson City (May–Sept 9am–7pm; ☎993-6456 or 1-800/661-0752) for practical as well as invaluable anecdotal information from the staff. If you're without your own vehicle, you might pick up a **lift** here or take the **Dempster Highway Bus Service** run by *Gold City Tours*. Departures leave from Dawson at 8am on Monday and Friday between June 14 and September 2, with an additional Wednesday service between June 26 and August 14. **Tickets** cost Can$198 one way to Inuvik (Can$350 return) and Can$99 to Eagle Plains/Arctic Circle (Can$175 same-day return). It is also worth checking that the two ferry services on the route (at Peel River and Arctic Red River) are running when bad weather threatens (☎1-800/661-0752).

In the Dempster's Yukon section there are facilities only at **Eagle Plains Hotel** (year round; ☎979-4187; rooms ⑤; camping $10), 363km to the north, and three rudimentary Yukon government **campgrounds**, at *Tombstone Mountain* (72km north of Dawson), *Engineer Creek* (194km), and *Rock River* (447km). In July and August, an information kiosk at Tombstone Mountain has details of good trails from the campground.

The only other **hotel** is the small *Tetlit Service Co-op* (☎952-2339; ⑤) in the NWT at the tiny Dene village of **Fort Macpherson** 115km south of Inuvik. There's also gasoline here, and the unserviced NWT government *Nutuiluie Campground and Information Centre* (547km from Dawson) is 3km south of the settlement (June–Sept; $5). The even tinier **Arctic Red River**, 80km south of Inuvik, also has gas and two rooms (☎953-3003; ⑤).

Dawson City to the Arctic Circle

Having come this far north it's hard to resist the temptation to cross the **Arctic Circle** 403km north of Dawson City, a journey that takes you over the most captivating stretch of the highway. At the very least you should take a short ride out of the mixed deciduous spruce woods of the boreal forests for a look at the tundra which starts beyond the **North Fork Pass**, just 79km north of Dawson. All distances given below are from Dawson City, almost the only way to locate things on the road.

After the millions of lodgepole pines in the Northwest, it's almost time for a celebration when you pass what are reputedly Canada's most northerly pines (8km). Beyond them you'll see occasional trappers' cabins: the hunting of mink, wolverine and lynx still provides the Yukon's 700 or so trappers with a $1.5 million annual income. At **Hart River** (80km) you should see part of the 1200-strong Hart River Woodland **caribou herd**; unlike the barren-ground herds further north these caribou have sufficient fodder to graze a single area instead of making seasonal migrations. **Golden eagles** and **ptarmigan** are also common on willow-lined streams such as Blackstone River (93km), as are **tundra birds** like Lapland longspurs, lesser golden plovers, mew gulls and long-tailed jaegers. At Moose Lake (105km) **moose**, needless to say, can often be seen feeding, along with numerous species of waterfowl like northern shoveller, American widgeon and the **arctic tern**, whose Arctic to Antarctic migration is the longest of any bird.

Chapman Lake (120km) marks the start of the northern Ogilvie Mountains, a region which has never been glaciated and so preserves numerous relic species of plant and insect, as well as providing an important early wintering range for the **Porcupine Caribou Herd**; as many as 40,000 caribou cross the highway in mid-October – they take four days and have right of way. Unique **butterfly** species breed at Butterfly Ridge (155km), close to some obvious caribou trails, and it should also be easy to spot Dall sheep, cliff swallows and bald eagles.

The **Arctic Circle** (403km) is marked by a battered roadside cairn and the summer home to one of the Northwest's premier eccentrics, one Harry Waldron, the self-proclaimed "Keeper of the Arctic Circle". In his late sixties, Harry sits in a rocking chair in a tuxedo with a glass of champagne and regales all comers with snippets of Robert Service, facts about the Arctic and some fairly unimpeachable views on the environment. An ex-highway worker, he started his act of his own accord, but proved so popular that he's now paid by the Yukon government to sit and do his spiel. After Harry's rocking chair, the road climbs into the Richardson Mountains to meet the border of the NWT (470km) before the less arresting flats of the Mackenzie River and the run to Inuvik.

Delta-Beaufort

The **Delta-Beaufort** region centers on **Inuvik** and embraces the mighty delta of the **Mackenzie River**, which reaches across the Beaufort Sea to Banks Island, the most westerly of Canada's arctic islands. The delta ranks as one of the Northwest's great **bird** habitats, with swans, cranes and big raptors among the many hundreds of species which either nest or overfly the region during spring and fall migration cycles. It also offers the chance of seeing pods of **beluga whales** and other big sea mammals, while native guides on Banks Island facilitate sightings of musk-ox, white fox and polar bears.

After Inuvik and the two villages on the short NWT section of the Dempster – Fort McPherson and Arctic Red River – the area's other four settlements are **fly-in communities** reached from Inuvik. Two of them, **Aklavik** and **Tuktoyaktuk**, are close by NWT standards, and are the places to fly out to for a comparatively accessible taste of aboriginal northern culture. **Sachs Harbour** (on Banks Island) and **Paulatuk** lie much further afield, and are bases for more arduous tours into the delta and arctic tundra.

Inuvik

INUVIK – "the place of man" – the furthest north you can drive on a public highway in North America, was built as a planned town in 1954 to replace Aklavik, a settlement to the west wrongly thought to be doomed to envelopment by the

Mackenzie's swirling waters and shifting mud flats. It's a strange melting pot, with native Dene, Métis and Inuvialuit living alongside the trappers, pilots, scientists and frontier entrepreneurs drawn here in the Seventies when boom followed the **oil exploration** in the delta. Falling oil prices and the rising expense of exploitation, however, soon toppled the delta's vast rigs and it seems that the oil is likely to remain largely untapped until the next century.

Wandering the town provides an eye-opening introduction to the vagaries of northern life, from the strange stilted buildings designed to prevent their heat melting the permafrost, to the all too visible signs of the **alcoholism** that affects this and many northern communities – a difficult problem, not least because the region's native groups seem to be disproportionately afflicted. Suicides here are four times the national average for Native Canadians.

On a happier note, the influence of Inuvialuit people in local political and economic life has increased, to the extent that the **Western Claims Settlement Act** of 1984 saw the government cede titles to various lands in the area, returning control that had been lost to the fur trade, the church, oil companies and southern government. A potent symbol of the local role of the church in particular resides in the town's most photographed building, the **Igloo Church**, a rather incongruous yoking of a native icon and foreign religion.

Practicalities

Canadian Airlines have scheduled **flights** daily to Inuvik from Edmonton, usually via Yellowknife, Fort Smith or Hay River (☎979-2951), and several regional companies run regular services from Whitehorse, Dawson City and numerous smaller destinations in the NWT. In summer a **bus** service operates from Dawson (see p.475) – its Inuvik office is at 175 Mackenzie Rd (☎979-4100); the **Dempster Highway** is open year round except for brief periods during the November freeze and April thaw.

For **information** on Inuvik and the region generally contact the *Delta-Beaufort Tourism Association* on Mackenzie Road (at Distributor St), a continuation of the Dempster Highway and Inuvik's main street (daily June–Sept 10am–6pm; ☎979-4321 or 979-4518).

There are only three **hotels** in town, all pricey: the *Eskimo Inn* (☎979-2801; ⑥), in central downtown; the *Finto Motor Inn* (☎979-2647; ⑥), between the airstrip and downtown; and the smarter central *Mackenzie* (☎979-2861; ⑥). *Robertson's B&B*, 48 Mackenzie Rd (☎979-311; ④), needs to be booked up to three weeks in advance during summer, as does the beautifully situated *Outlook B&B* (☎979-3789; ④), just out of town at Boot Lake. **Eating** possibilities are largely confined to the expensive hotel dining rooms – where you can gorge on char, caribou and musk-ox – unless you make for *The Back Room*, 108 Mackenzie Rd (famed for its stuffed polar bear), or *Sunriser Coffee Shop*, at no 185, whose snacks and breakfasts won't break the bank.

Inuvik may be the best place to **rent a car** for the far north, because southern firms tend not to rent vehicles for rough roads, and make hefty charges if you return a car that's obviously been over gravel: the *Budget* (☎979-2888) and *Tilden* (☎979-3383) outlets rent out suitably robust trucks and pick-ups. The two big **tour operators** in town are both worth investigating, as each runs a selection of affordable daily boat and plane tours as well as full-blown two-week expeditions: contact the *Arctic Tour Company* (☎979-2054), opposite the Igloo Church at 175 Mackenzie Rd, and *Midnight Express Tours*, 105 Mackenzie Rd (☎979-3068).

The fly-in communities

Accessible only by air except in winter, when incredible snow roads are ploughed across the frozen delta, Delta-Beaufort's four fly-in communities are close to some fascinating arctic landscapes and cultures. All are served by *Aklak Air*, Box 1190, Inuvik (☎979-3377), and all have shops, though their prices make it wise to take in your own supplies. **AKLAVIK** (pop. 800), 50km west of Inuvik on the western bank of the Mackenzie delta, means the "Place of the Barren Lands Grizzly

---

THE INUIT

They be like to Tartars, with long blacke haire, broad faces, and flatte noses, and tawnie in colour, wearing Seale skinnes . . . The women are marked in the faces with blewe streakes downe the cheekes, and round about the eies.

An officer on Frobisher's 1576 search for the Northwest Passage

Distinct from all other Canadian natives by virtue of their culture, language and Asiatic physical features, the **Inuit** are the dominant people of a **territory** that extends all the way from northern Alaska to Greenland. Nowadays increasingly confined to reserves, they once led a **nomadic** existence in one of the most hostile environments on earth, dwelling in domed **igloos** during the winter and **skin tents** in the summer, and moving around using **kayaks** (*umiaks*) or **dog sleds** (*komatik*). The latter were examples of typical Inuit adaptability – the runners were sometimes made from frozen fish wrapped in sealskin, and in the absence of wood, caribou bones were used for crossbars.

Their prey – caribou, musk-ox, seals, walruses, narwhals, beluga whales, polar bears, birds and fish – provided oil for heating and cooking, hides for clothing and tents, harpoon lines, ivory and dog harnesses. Using harpoons, bows and arrows and spears, ingenious hunting methods were devised: to catch caribou, for example, huge **inuksuits**, piles of rocks that resembled the human form, were used to steer the herd into a line of armed hunters.

The Inuit **diet** was composed totally of flesh, and every part of the animal was eaten, usually raw, from eyeballs to the heart. Delicacies included the plaited and dried intestines of seals and whole sealskins stuffed with small birds and left to putrefy until the contents had turned to the consistency of cheese. All food was **shared** and the successful hunter had to watch his catch being distributed amongst other families in the group, in accordance with specific relationships, before his own kin were allowed the smallest portion. **Starvation** was common – it was not unusual for whole villages to perish in the winter – and consequently **infanticide**, particularly of females, was employed to keep population sizes down. Elderly people who could not keep up with the travelling group were abandoned, a fate that also befell some **offenders** against the social code, though the usual way of resolving conflict was the **song-duel**, whereby the aggrieved would publicly ridicule the behavior of the other, who was expected to accept the insults with good grace.

Making **clothes**, most often of caribou hide, was a task assigned to **women** and was as essential to survival as a man's ability to hunt. Older women also **tattooed** the faces of the younger ones by threading a sinew darkened with soot through the face to make lines that radiated from the nose and mouth. Women were usually betrothed at birth and married at puberty, and both polygamy and polyandry were frequent – though female infanticide made it rare for a man to have more than two spouses. Communion with supernatural spirits was maintained by a **shaman** or

Bear". For generations it has been the home of Inuvialuit families who once traded and frequently clashed with the Gwich'in of Alaska and the Yukon. Today both live together in a town which mixes modern and traditional, and whose inhabitants are proud not to have jumped ship when they were invited to leave their sinking town for Inuvik in the Fifties. Most are happy to regale you with stories of the "Mad Trapper of Rat River", a crazed drifter who reputedly killed trappers for the gold in their teeth. After allegedly shooting a Mountie in 1931 he managed to elude capture for forty days in the dead of a brutal winter. He was

angakok, who was often a woman, and the deity who features most regularly in Inuit myth is a goddess called **Sedna**, who was mutilated by her father. Her severed fingers became seals and walruses and her hands became whales, while Sedna lived on as the mother and protector of all sea-life, capable of withholding her bounty if strict **taboos** were not adhered to. These taboos included keeping land and sea products totally separate – and so seals could never be eaten with caribou and all caribou clothing had to be made before the winter seal hunt.

Although sporadic **European contact** dates back to the Norse settlement of Greenland and some Inuit were visited by early missionaries, it wasn't until the early nineteenth century that the two cultures met in earnest. By 1860 commercial **whalers** had begun wintering around the north of Hudson Bay, employing Inuit as crew members and hunters for their food in return for European goods. Even then, the impact on the Inuit was not really deleterious until the arrival of **American whalers** in Canadian waters in 1890, when the liberal dispensing of alcohol and diseases such as smallpox and VD led to a drastic **decline in population**.

By the early decades of this century **fur traders** were encouraging the Inuit to stop hunting off the coast and turn inland using firearms and traps. The accompanying **missionaries** brought welcome medical help and schools, but put an end to multiple marriages, shamanism and other traditional practices. More changes came when Inuits were employed to build roads, airfields and other military facilities during World War II and to construct the line of radar installations known as Distant Early Warning during the Cold War era. As well as bringing **new jobs**, this also focused **government attention** on the plight of the Inuit.

The consequent largesse was not wholly beneficial: subsidized housing and welfare payments led many Inuit to abandon their hunting camps and settle in **permanent communities**, usually located in places strategic to Canada's sovereignty in the Arctic. Without knowledge of the English and French languages, these Inuit were left out of all decision-making and often lived in a totally separate part of towns that were administered by outsiders. Old values and beliefs were all but eroded by television and radio, and high levels of depression, alcoholism and violence became the norm. The 1982 European ban on imports of sealskins created mass **unemployment**, and although hunting still provides the basics of subsistence, the high cost of ammunition and fuel makes commercial-scale hunting uneconomical.

All is not gloom, however. Inuit cooperatives are increasingly successful and the production of **soapstone carvings** – admittedly a commercial adulteration of traditional Inuit ivory art – is very profitable. Having organized themselves into politically active groups and secured such **land claims** as Nunavut (a new eastern arctic territory to be created by the division of the Northwestern Territories), the Inuit are slowly rebuilding an ancient culture that was shattered in under half a century.

eventually shot on the Eagle River and is buried in town in unconsecrated ground. There's no restaurant and only one shop, but two places to **stay**: the *Daadzaii Lodge* (☎978-2252; ④) and *Bessie's Boarding and Room Rentals* (☎978-2215; ④). **Flights** from Inuvik operate daily except Sunday (Can$60 single).

TUKTOYAKTUK, or simply Tuk (pop. 1000), sits on a sandspit on the Beaufort coast about 137km north of Inuvik, and acts as a springboard both for oil workers and for tourists, outsiders who have diluted the traditional ways of the whale-hunting Karngmalit (or Mackenzie Inuit). Most casual visitors come to see whales, or to look at the world's largest concentration of **pingoes**, 1400 volcano-like hills thrown up by frost heaves across the delta's otherwise treeless flats. Tuk's only **hotels** are the *Hotel Tuk Inn* (☎977-2381; ⑤) and the *Pingo Park Lodge* (☎977-2155; ⑤). Daily **flights** from Inuvik cost Can$100 single.

PAULATUK (pop. 250), 400km east of Inuvik and among the smallest perma-nent communities of the NWT, was started by the Roman Catholic Mission in 1935 as a communal focus for the semi-nomadic Karngmalit, who despite such paternalism have fought off the adverse effects of missionaries and trader-introduced alcoholism to hang on to some of their old ways. Hunting, fishing and trapping still provide their economic staples, along with handicrafts aimed at the tourists who are out here mainly for the chance to watch or hunt big game. The *Paulatuk Hotel* has **accommodation** for twelve people (☎580-3027; ⑧) at a price. **Flights** operate twice weekly from Inuvik (Can$230 single).

The only settlement on Banks Island, **SACHS HARBOUR** (pop. 150) supports a handful of self-sufficient Inuit families who survive largely by outfitting hunters and trapping musk-ox for food and underfur (*qiviut*), which is spun and woven into clothes on sale locally. Expensive **rooms** are available at the *Icicle Inn* (☎690-4444; ⑧). There are two **flights** from Inuvik weekly (from Can$250 single).

travel details

Trains
From Prince George to Vancouver (June 15–Oct 1 daily; rest of year 3 weekly; 13hr 30min); Prince Rupert (3 weekly; 13hr); Edmonton via Jasper (3 weekly; 8hr 15min); Whitehorse (1 daily).

Buses
From Prince George to Prince Rupert (2 daily; 11hr); Edmonton via Jasper (2 daily; 9hr 45min); Dawson Creek (2 daily; 6hr 30min); Vancouver via Williams Lake and Cache Creek (2 daily; 13hr); Whitehorse (1 daily).

From Dawson Creek to Prince George (2 daily; 6hr 30min); Edmonton (2 daily; 9hr); Whitehorse (mid-May to mid-Oct 1 daily except Sun; rest of year 3 weekly; 21hr).

From Whitehorse to Anchorage (3 weekly); Dawson Creek (mid-May to mid-Oct 1 daily except Sun; rest of year 3 weekly; 21hr); Dawson City (May–Aug 3 weekly; Sept–Oct & March–April 2 weekly; rest of year 1 weekly; 7hr 30min); Skagway (mid-May to mid-Sept 1 daily except Wed & Sun; 4hr).

From Dawson City to Whitehorse (May–Aug weekly; Sept–Oct & March–April 2 weekly; rest of year 1 weekly; 7hr 30min); Inuvik (mid-June to early Sept 2–3 weekly; 12hr).

Flights
Listed below are only the main direct scheduled flights operated by the big carriers; for details on the vast range of small provincial companies operating within the north, see the town entries in the guide.

To Whitehorse from Vancouver (3 daily; 2hr 20min).

CHAPTER NINE

ALASKA

F ew regions in North America conjure up sharper images than **Alaska**; the name itself – a derivation of *Alayeska*, an Athabascan word meaning "great land of the west" – fires the imagination of many a traveller. Few who see this land of gargantuan icefields, sweeping tundra, glacially excavated valleys, lush rainforests, deep fjords and active volcanoes leave disappointed. **Wildlife** may be under threat elsewhere, but here it is abundant, with grizzly bears standing twelve feet tall, moose stopping traffic in downtown Anchorage, wolves howling in the still of the night, bald eagles soaring above the trees and fifty-plus-pound salmon leaping upstream.

The sheer size of Alaska is hard to comprehend: America's **northernmost**, **westernmost** and, because the Aleutians stretch across the 180th meridian, its **easternmost** state would, if superimposed onto the Lower 48 (the rest of the continental United States) stretch from the Atlantic to the Pacific. This vast expanse covers more than double the area of Texas, and its coastline is longer than the rest of the US combined. All but three of the nation's highest peaks are found within its boundaries and one glacier alone is larger than Switzerland.

A mere 570,000 people live in this huge state, of whom only one-fifth were actually born here. Forty percent live in Anchorage. As a rule of thumb, the more winters you have endured, the more Alaskan you are, and recent arrivals are known by the mildly abusive nickname of *cheechako* ("newcomer" in Chinook). Often referred to as the **"Last Frontier"**, Alaska in many ways mirrors the American West of the nineteenth century: an endless, undeveloped space in which to stake a claim and set up anew without interference. Or at least that's how many Alaskans would like it to be. Throughout this century tens of thousands have been lured by the promise of wealth, first by gold and then by fishing, logging and, most recently, oil. However, Alaska's 86,000 **native peoples**, who don't have the option of returning to the Lower 48 if things don't work out, have been left behind in the state's economic boom.

Environmental issues increasingly make front-page news, with the grab-it-all commercial spirit under growing pressure from federal government and "daisy

---

ACCOMMODATION PRICE CODES

All accommodation prices in this book have been coded using the symbols below, corresponding to US dollar prices in the US chapters and equivalent Canadian dollar rates in the Canadian chapters. Prices are for the least expensive double rooms in each establishment, and only include local taxes where we explicitly say so.

For a full explanation see p.46 in *Basics*.

①	up to US$30	④	US$60–80	⑦	US$130–180
②	US$30–45	⑤	US$80–100	⑧	US$180+
③	US$45–60	⑥	US$100–130		

sniffers". Recent controversies have been caused by the logging companies' practice of clear-cutting, the state's extensive road-building program, and a plan to kill off wolves – according to animal rights groups, to ensure that there are more caribou for hunters. More famously, there's also been the unholy mess created by the shipwreck of the Exxon tanker *Valdez* in 1989.

Travelling around Alaska still demands a spirit of adventure – and lots of patience if you're covering the long distances involved by road. The fastest approach is along the Alaskan Highway which cuts across British Columbia and the Yukon on its way to **Fairbanks**, a useful stepping stone to the scenic wonders of Denali National Park, home of Mount McKinley. Alternatively, the main turning off the Alaskan Highway leads to Anchorage and – more divertingly – the south coast ports of **Seward**, **Hope** and **Valdez**, as well as the magnificent national parks of Kenai Fjords and Wrangell-St Elias. You can save time by flying around Alaska's gigantic interior, but the coastal scenery is best appreciated from the ferries that slip through the elegiac fjords, glaciers and mountains bordering the Pacific, linking the area's main settlements, such as Sitka and Juneau, on the way.

If you plan to camp, you'll need the best possible gear – a strong, waterproof tent, a good sleeping bag, and cooking equipment. Binoculars are an absolute must, as, rather more mundanely, is bug spray; the **mosquito** is referred to as the "Alaska state bird", and only a repellent with 100 percent DEET keeps them off. On top of that, of course, there's the climate, though Alaska is far from the popular misconception of being one big icebox. While winter temperatures of -40°F in Fairbanks are pretty commonplace and northern towns like Barrow see no sunlight for 84 days each year, its most touristed areas, the southeast and the Kenai Peninsula, enjoy a maritime climate (45–65°F in summer) similar to that of the rest of the Pacific Northwest, meaning much more rain (in some towns 180-plus inches per year) than snow. Remarkably, the Interior in summer often gets as hot as 80°F.

Experiencing Alaska on a low budget is possible, but requires a lot of planning. The peak period of mid-June through August sees crazy room prices; May and particularly September, when tariffs are relaxed and the weather only slightly chillier, are just as good times to go. Except for around thirty **hostels**, mostly in the major towns, there is little budget **accommodation**; **transport**, thanks to the long distances, is far from cheap; and **eating and drinking** are about twenty percent more expensive than in the Lower 48. **Winter**, when hotels drop their prices by as much as half, is becoming an increasingly popular time to visit, particularly for the dazzling **aurora borealis** (see p.474).

History

Alaska has been inhabited for longer than anywhere else in the Americas; it was here, across the land bridge that spanned what is now the Bering Sea, that humans first reached the "New World", possibly as early as 40,000 BC. These first settlers can be classified into four groups, which until whites arrived lived within well-defined regions. The **Aleut**, in the inhospitable Aleutian Islands, built underground homes and hunted sea mammals such as walrus for food and clothing, while the nomadic **Athabascans** herded caribou in the Interior. The warrior **Tlingit** lived in the warmer coastal regions of the southeast, where food was plentiful, in contrast to the **Inuit** who inhabited the northwestern coast, living off fish and larger marine life. Their famous **igloo** ice-houses were seldom used as permanent dwellings, but rather as temporary lodging during hunts.

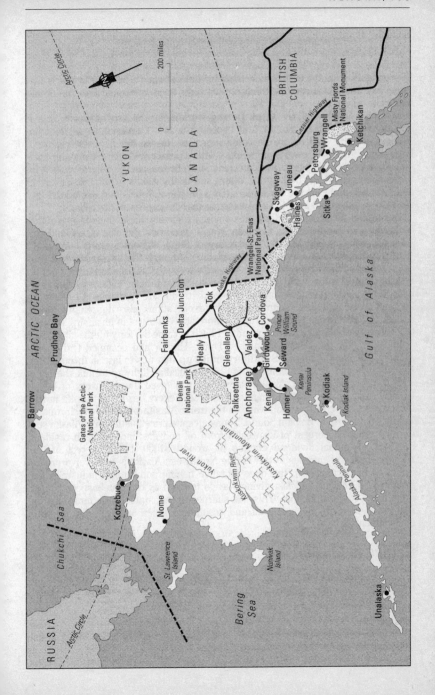

> The **area code** for the entire state of Alaska is ☎907.

Descendants of all these groups remain in Alaska today; a few live in much the same way as their ancestors, though most have been integrated into the dominant culture.

In 1741, a Dutch explorer, **Vitus Bering**, working for the Tsar of Russia, sailed into the Prince William Sound, and became the first Caucasian to set foot on Alaskan soil. He died before he could return to Russia, but his crew reported huge numbers of **sea otters** and **seals** – whose pelts were ideal for making hats – in Alaska's coastal waters. Russians, and later, Britons and Spaniards, joined in the ensuing slaughter, both of the otters and of the Aleuts, who were enslaved and forced to hunt for the fur traders. By 1799 the Russians had decimated the sea otter colonies and in doing so pressed as far east as present-day Sitka.

During the 1860s, when Russia hit economic difficulty due to the collapse of the fur trade and the disastrous Crimean War, it proposed the sale of its lands to America. On October 18, 1867, Secretary of State William Seward purchased Alaska for $7,200,000 – less than 2¢ per acre. Although the unpopular deal was referred to as **"Seward's Folly"** or "Seward's Icebox", Alaska soon turned out to be a literal **gold mine**. Gold was discovered in 1880 at Juneau, eighteen years later near Nome on the Bering Strait, and subsequently outside Fairbanks in 1902. With logging companies and commercial fishing operations also descending upon Alaska, the government began to take a more active interest in its affairs. In 1912 the Territory of Alaska was set up, and in 1959 it became the forty-ninth state.

In 1942, after the Japanese bombed Dutch Harbor and occupied two of the Aleutian Islands, the huge **US military build-up** that was to last all through the Cold War began with the construction of the Alaska Highway to link the state with the rest of America. Alaska's next boom followed the discovery of **oil** at Prudhoe Bay on the Arctic Ocean, and fortune-seekers headed to Alaska in the mid-Seventies to construct and work on the **trans-Alaska pipeline** which runs to Valdez on the Prince William Sound. Today, despite price fluctuations, Alaska still derives about 85 percent of its wealth from oil and gas; indeed, each resident receives an annual dividend cheque of around $1000. Like the rest of the resource-based economies of the Pacific Northwest, Alaska is however prone to cycles of boom and bust: the once lucrative fishing and lumber industries are presently in decline, and fast giving way to tourism as the state's second most important source of income. This has sharpened the conflict over future use of Alaskan land, with the industrial and resource lobbies in bitter dispute with environmentalists.

Getting to Alaska

The sheer remoteness of Alaska makes it expensive to reach, no matter how you travel. There is, however, no question as to which is the most **enjoyable** method – the memorable sea trip on the Alaska Marine Highway.

For further details of travel to and around Alaska, see the "Getting There" and "Getting Around" sections of *Basics*, p.5, and p.33-36.

By air

Anchorage is no longer the major air crossroads it once was, but it's still easy to **fly** to Alaska. It is however very expensive. Most but not all flights from the Lower 48 are routed through Seattle. The best service from the West Coast is operated by *Alaska Airlines*, whose money-saving package enables you to fly to such towns as Juneau, Sitka, Cordova and Fairbanks for little extra cost. Round-trip fares from Seattle are around $450.

By sea – the Alaska Marine Highway

The ferries of the state-run *Alaska Marine Highway* cover many areas otherwise only reachable by air, operating two separate and unconnected systems. The most popular route, in the southeast, runs for more than a thousand miles from Bellingham, just north of Seattle in Washington (see p.192), through a wonderland of pristine waters, towering glaciers and untouched forests to Skagway at the top of the **Inside Passage**. A similar service also starts further north at Canada's Prince Rupert (see p.447). Both routes include stops at Ketchikan, Wrangell, Petersburg, Juneau, Haines and Skagway, though many other communities, including Sitka, are served by smaller ferries in the fleet.

The whole trip takes three days and costs $245 for walk-on passengers, plus $656 for a small car. It is sometimes possible to sleep – and even to pitch a tent – on the "solarium", a covered, heated, upper deck. The **Southwest** ferry system, which charges slightly higher fares, connects the Kenai Peninsula and the Prince William Sound to the Aleutians.

For information on either route, contact the **Alaska Marine Highway**, PO Box R, Juneau, AK 99811 (see p.489). Book ahead in summer; standby space is available, but such passengers risk being off-loaded at each port of call as the ferry takes on passengers with reservations. Additional charges are levied on bicycles and kayaks.

By road

For many people, the drive up to Alaska through Canada is one of the major highlights of a visit to the state. Originally built by the military in just eight months, the **Alaska Highway**, which can be accessed from Washington, BC and Alberta – see p.458 – used to consist of 1520 fearsome miles of dirt, gravel, steep descents and thick mud. These days all but a small section is paved, with sufficient service stations, campgrounds and hotels along the way, but it remains as beautiful as ever, and still demands a spirit of adventure from drivers who attempt it. The principal alternative road route is the **Cassiar Highway** (see p.453).

The unwieldy *Milepost* (Vernon Publications; $17.95) provides mile-by-mile information on the Alaska Highway and all roads within Alaska, but almost exclusively plugs its advertisers – unless you're travelling the Alaska Highway, it's a rather bulky luxury.

No direct **buses** run to Alaska, though for around $350 total you can hop on a *Greyhound* in Seattle, and after a few transfers, reach Whitehorse in the Yukon, from where local companies such as *Alaska Direct* and the pricier *Alaskon Express* continue to Haines or Skagway in the southeast, or on the longer haul to Fairbanks and Anchorage. *Green Tortoise* (see p.12) run trips each summer from San Francisco.

Getting around Alaska

Getting around Alaska on the cheap can be tough; **public transportation** is limited, and many areas are only accessible by boat or plane, which is quick and convenient, but invariably pricey.

By bus

Anchorage is very much the hub of Alaska; from it, **buses** run to Haines and Skagway via Whitehorse, Yukon (see above), Denali, Fairbanks, Valdez (*Caribou Express*) and the Kenai Peninsula (*Seward & Homer Bus Lines*). The "big city" is also the base for tour operators such as *Gray Line of Alaska*, who run trips ranging from a half-day excursion to nearby Portage Glacier to airborne expeditions to far-flung Nome on the west coast.

By rail

The **Alaska Railroad**, constructed between 1915 and 1923 to transport supplies from ports in the Prince William Sound to the mines in the Interior, runs nearly five hundred miles north from Seward on the Kenai Peninsula to Fairbanks. Another service from Anchorage to Whittier, connects with ferries to Valdez.

By road

Visitors intending to **drive** around Alaska should bring an **emergency kit**, particularly essential in winter, as traffic can be sparse even on major routes. Conditions on the roads can change rapidly – for information, call ☎243-7675. Avalanches are a serious threat, as are collisions with wild animals, especially moose. Drivers on gravel roads are advised to keep speeds low, as rocks often fly up to shatter windscreens. Filling stations are often few and far between, and charge wildly varying prices.

By air

Travel by **plane** is not always the most expensive alternative, especially if you can map out your itinerary in advance with the state's largest operator *Alaska Airlines* who fly to most major communities and use subcontractors such as *ERA Aviation* to get to Bush towns in the Interior, or *LAB* to communities in the southeast. The other major intra-state carrier, *Mark Air*, offers particularly good connections to the west. For short-haul flights, **chartering a plane** can be an inexpensive alternative for groups. Sometimes maligned as dangerous and unreliable, the **bush**

THE ALASKA PASS

The **Alaska Pass** allows unlimited surface transportation on participating ferries, trains and buses throughout Alaska and Yukon Territory. Operators covered by the deal are the *Alaska Marine Highway*, *BC Ferries*, *Alaska Railroad*, *BC Rail*, *Alaskon Express* buses, *Greyhound* (Canada) and two other Canadian coach firms. Once you've purchased the pass, you're free to make reservations on any of the carriers mentioned.

Eight consecutive days cost $449; 21 days' travel within a 45-day period costs $899. Contact PO Box 351, Vashon, WA 98070-1351; ☎206/463-6550, US & Canada ☎1-800/248-7598, UK ☎0800/898285.

ALASKAN TRANSPORTATION AND TOUR OPERATORS

The phone numbers of the major Alaskan travel operators are listed below. Details of the specific services offered by each one can be found throughout the text of this chapter.

Air Excursions	☎907/789-5591	Gray Line of Alaska	☎907/277-5581
Alaska Airlines	☎1-800/426-0333	Kenai Coastal Tours	☎1-800/770-9119
Alaska Car Rental	☎907/225-5000	Ketchikan Air	☎907/225-6608
Alaska Direct Bus Line	☎1-800/770-6652	LAB Flying Service	☎907/766-2222
Alaska Marine Highway	☎1-800/642-0066	Mark Air	☎1-800/426-6784
		Mt McKinley Alaska Tours	☎1-800/327-7651
Alaska Maritime Tours	☎907/235-2490		
Alaska Railroad	☎1-800/544-0522	Northern Alaska Tour Company	☎907/454-8600
Alaskon Express	☎1-800/544-2206		
Backcountry Connections	☎1-800/478-5292	Princess Tours	☎907/276-7711
		Seward & Homer Bus Lines	☎907/278-0800
Caribou Express	☎907/278-5776		
Central Charters	☎1-800/478-7847	Southcentral Air	☎907/235-6172
Denali Air	☎907/683-2261	Taquan Air	☎1-800/348-1330
Denali Express	☎907/274-8539	Wrangell Mountain Air	☎1-800/478-1160
ERA Aviation	☎1-800/843-1947	White Pass and Yukon Railway	☎1-800/343-7373
Frontier Flying Service	☎907/474-0014		or ☎1-800/478-7373

planes that serve remote communities can indeed be scary at times: Alaskan weather does throw up problems and accidents can happen, but remember that the pilot wants to crash just as much as you do. A trip on a light aircraft can be the crowning glory of an Alaskan vacation.

By sea

The **Alaska Marine Highway** is a practical way to explore the southeast and the Prince William Sound/Kenai Peninsula. The only weak link in the set-up is that there's no connecting service between the southeastern and southwestern systems; but if you take a short flight from Juneau to Cordova, you can get back on the ferry.

Southeast Alaska

Southeast Alaska, cutting a 400-mile strip from the northern coast of British Columbia, and also known as the **Inside Passage**, may lack the vast openness of the Interior, but its narrow fjords, steep mountains, glaciers and thick conifer forests are awesome in their own right. All of its communities have their economic base in lumber, fishing and tourism and are set amid magnificent scenery. The state's southernmost town, **Ketchikan**, rich in Native heritage, makes a pretty introduction, tiny **Wrangell** has a pioneer air, while **Petersburg** and **Sitka** retain the respective influences of Norway and Russia. Further north are lively **Juneau**, the capital, **Haines**, with its mix of old-timers and recent arty recruits, and **Skagway**, at the northern end of the Inside Passage and thoroughly redolent of the old gold-mining days.

Although this elongated panhandle, looking out toward over a thousand rugged islands, can take months to explore, it holds surprisingly few "sights". With the exception of the **Mendenhall Glacier**, many of the most beautiful spots are expensive jaunts – none more so than **Glacier Bay National Park**.

The region's first settlers, the **Tlingit** (*Clink-it*), were confronted by Russian expansionists at the end of the eighteenth century. A steady stream of freelance profiteers, keen on tapping the region's gold, fur, fish and lumber followed, and today its small communities resound with tales of endurance, derring-do, cruelty and sheer daftness.

By far the best way to travel is on the **ferries** of the Marine Highway, though at some stage it's worth taking a **floatplane** ride. No roads connect the major towns; access by car is limited to Haines and Skagway, but only after long drives through British Columbia. For a true outdoor adventure, you can rent a **cabin** in the Tongass National Forest – which encompasses most of southeast Alaska – for around $20 per night; get details from the US Forest Service in Juneau (see p.494) or Ketchikan (see below). For the most part accessible only by floatplane, the cabins are usually booked up well in advance, but they keep a list of recently cancelled reservations.

Ketchikan and around

KETCHIKAN, the sole community on fjord-indented Revillagigedo Island, five hundred miles north of Vancouver, likes to be known as Alaska's "first city". As the first port of call for many cruise-ships, its historic downtown, wedged between the waters of the Tongass Narrows and forested Deer Mountain, becomes saturated in summer with elderly tourists. But beyond the trinket shopping it can be a delight, built into steep hills and partly propped on wooden pilings, with boardwalks and wooden staircases common thoroughfares. High points include the totem poles dotted everywhere, and a chance to view bald eagles and, if you're daft enough, bears, in the town dump. Ketchikan is also a gateway to secluded spots like the enchanted **Misty Fjords National Monument** to the north and the wild **Prince of Wales Island** to the west.

White settlers reached Ketchikan in the early 1880s. By 1886 the first of dozens of canneries had opened in what was soon to be the "salmon capital of the world". Tall forests of cedar, hemlock and spruce, which had provided timber for Tlingit homes and totems, also fed the town's sawmills. Though the timber and fishing industries have declined, the largest employer remains the massive pulp mill eight miles north.

The state's fourth largest city is a strong contender to be the nation's **wettest**; annual precipitation averages 165 inches. The tourist board shrugs it off as "liquid sunshine".

Arrival and information

Alaska Marine Highway ferries (☎225-6181) dock two miles north of downtown on Tongass Highway; city buses stop here every hour until 6.45pm. The **airport**, served by *Alaska Airlines*, is a five-minute ferry ride ($4) across the Narrows. The **visitor center** stands downtown at 131 Front St (daily 8am–5pm; ☎225-6166). Close by, in the pink building on Federal Street, is the **US Forest Service Information Center** (☎225-2148).

An incredible number of companies run excursions to the farther-flung sites: choose from expensive taxis, generic minibuses, kitsch trolleys and a luxury option in the shape of an immaculate red and white '55 Chevy (*Classic Tours*; ☎225-3091; from $35).

The prime way to see the area is by **floatplane**. *Ketchikan Air* and *Taquan Air* (both on Tongass Ave; see p.489), provide flightseeing excursions and scheduled flights to Prince of Wales Island. *Southern Exposure*, 507 Stedman St (☎225-6044), rents kayaks and organizes paddling in the Narrows – six hours costs $60 – plus longer expeditions further afield.

The Town

The bulk of Ketchikan's historic buildings lie on **Creek Street**, a rickety-looking boardwalk along Ketchikan Creek. This was a red light district until 1953; now all the former houses of ill-repute are given over to gift shops and cafés. **Dolly's House**, 24 Creek St, once the home and workplace of Dolly Arthur, the town's most famous madam, is now a small museum stuffed with saucy memorabilia (hours vary; $2; ☎225-6329). The tiny but well-curated **Tongass Historical Museum**, Dock St (Mon–Sat 8.30am–5pm, Sun 1–5pm; $1), takes a look at commercial fishing, logging and Native culture as well as hosting good temporary exhibits.

While most of the totem poles you see around town are replicas, the **Totem Heritage Center** on Deermount St exhibits 33 genuine nineteenth-century examples, recovered from abandoned Native villages (Mon–Sat 8am–5pm, Sun 9am–4pm; $2, free Sun noon–4pm). Fourteen of the best replica totem poles and a rebuilt tribal house stand in **Totem Bight State Park**, breathtakingly set on a forested strip of coast overlooking the Narrows, ten miles north of town on the Tongass Highway. The Tlingit-run **Saxman Totem Park**, three miles south of town, displays the world's largest standing collection of poles. Admission, including a chance to see sculptors at work, is free, but **guided tours** can help to decipher the images (daily 8.30am–5pm; $2).

The **Deer Mountain Salmon Hatchery**, next to the City Park at the top of Park Ave, raises and releases 300,000 king and silver salmon into the river each year. By the end of summer, the creek is teeming with returning fish who have swum upstream to spawn and die, and the banks are littered with dead fish.

Misty Fjords National Monument

Twenty-two miles east of Ketchikan on the mainland, the much-eulogized **Misty Fjords National Monument** consists of 2.3 million acres of deep fjords flanked by sheer 3000-feet glacially scoured walls topped by dense rainforest. As befits its name, the Monument is at its most atmospheric when swathed in low-lying mists. No roads lead here, but various operators run floatplane or boat trips. Fly-in/cruise-out tours with *Outdoor Alaska*, 215 Main St, Ketchikan (☎225-6044), cost $135; they also rent sea kayaks. Fourteen rustic cabins are rented by the Forest Service (☎225-2143; ①).

Metlakatla

The fishing village of **Metlakatla** stands in Alaska's only Indian reservation on Annette Island, twelve miles southwest of Ketchikan. The settlement was founded in 1887 by William Duncan, an unordained Anglican minister, after a previous community he had set up among the Tsimshian in British Columbia was shut down by church authorities (because he was prepared to accept non-believers into his community if they were willing to follow his paternalistic rules). Congress set aside the entire Annette Island as a reservation in 1891, a status the Tsimshian elected to safeguard rather than join other tribes grouped under the Alaska Native Settlement Act of 1971.

Today sleepy little Metlakatla pays homage to Duncan (who lived here until his death in 1918) in a small museum, but besides lingering round the harbor or setting out on a hike, there's not much else to see or do. The basic *Taquan Inn* (☎886-6112; ③) is the only motel on the island; if you don't fancy staying over, bear in mind that the Marine Highway ferry only makes a return journey from Ketchikan on Saturday.

Prince of Wales Island

If you're looking for a piece of Alaska that doesn't cosmeticize itself for tourists and yet is reasonably accessible, consider **Prince of Wales Island**, less than fifty miles west of Ketchikan – the third largest US island (after Kodiak and the Big Island of Hawaii). Prolific numbers of bear and deer have made this a popular hunting destination, great fishing holes punctuate its thousand-odd miles of shoreline, and 650 miles of dirt roads make for superb explorations by 4WD or mountain bike. However, the island is also a favorite with the big logging concerns, and the huge areas of clearcut can be hard to stomach.

The terminal of the *Marine Highway* **ferry** that connects the island with Ketchikan (almost daily in summer) is at **HOLLIS**, some forty miles east of the largest community, **CRAIG** (pop. 1535). There's nowhere to stay in Hollis; if you don't have any transportation, ask about the current status of the shuttle van service before you set off.

Craig sits on a small island connected to the west shore of Prince of Wales by a short causeway. It's a friendly little fishing and logging settlement; a sole totem pole, washed up on the beach and then repainted, constitutes its only "attraction". However, its bars have a reputation for bad craziness at the weekend. You can camp at the City Park or stay at *Ruthann's Hotel* (☎826-3377; ④), which also has a restaurant where an average meal costs $20. Six miles north of Craig, the Tlingit community of **KLAWOCK** features a town-center collection of 21 restored original totem poles and the island's best grocery store.

Most other communities are almost exclusively dedicated to logging. Though characterized by ramshackle clapboard houses and mobile homes, **Thorne Bay**, 43 miles northeast of Craig, stands at the end of a stunning inlet on the island's east shore that contains some nice campgrounds and beaches. Further north another jumble of temporary homes come under the name of **Coffman Cove**. This is the prime place for ocean, creek and lake fishing; Bill Pierce at *Coffman Cove Wilderness Lodge* (☎329-2249) will take you to the best holes and provide breakfast, dinner and board for around $275.

Ketchikan accommodation

Ketchikan has a wide spectrum of **hotels**, and the *Ketchikan B&B* agency (☎225-8550) arranges accommodation from around $50. The closest **campground** to town is in the attractive Ward Lake Recreation Area, five miles northwest of the ferry terminal.

Alaska Rainforest Inn, 2311 Hemlock St (☎225-9500). A mile from the ferry terminal with bunks, or rooms which sleep four. Gets a bit rowdy sometimes. ①/③.

TOTEM POLES

Contrary to the propaganda of early missionaries and legislators, southeastern tribes such as the Tlingit, Tshimsian and Haida never worshipped **totem poles** as religious objects. Totems were in fact erected to commemorate a **potlatch** (a gathering held to mark a major event such as a marriage or battle) or to pay respect to a revered elder. Composed of a series of crests depicting objects, people and animals that represented clans (ravens and eagles predominate on Tlingit poles), the totems were traditionally hewn from cedar and painted with natural mineral and vegetable pigments.

Totem pole carving all but died out between the 1880s and 1950s, during the enforcement of a law forbidding the potlatch – the core of southeast Alaskan Native culture. Since the law's repeal in 1951, and a softening in church attitude, a revival of Native culture and arts has taken place. Today active carving programs exist in several towns including Wrangell, Sitka, and particularly **Ketchikan**.

Great Alaska Cedarworks B&B, 1527 Pond Reef Rd, AK 99901 (☎247-8287). Exceptional value; one of Alaska's very best B&Bs, 11 miles north of town and only accessible by car. Two beautiful self-contained waterside cabins, great hosts and fresh-baked breads. ③.

Ketchikan Youth Hostel (AYH), in the United Methodist Church, 400 Main St (☎225-3319). Very basic hostel with beds for $7, May–Sept only. ①.

The New York Hotel, 207 Stedman St (☎225-0246). Nicely restored eight-room hotel overlooking the small-boat harbor. ⑤.

Eating and drinking in Ketchikan

Inexpensive **food** in Ketchikan is often good, with several greasy joints along Front Street serving tasty breakfasts and dinners. It's also renowned as a wild "party town", its bars teeming with commercial fishers and cannery workers eager to forget the sight and smell of raw fish.

Annabelle's Keg & Chowder House, 326 Front St (☎225-6009). Classy but relaxed atmosphere.

Chico's, 435 Dock St (☎225-2833). Great Mexican food and pizza, dinners starting at $8.50.

Diaz Chinese Restaurant, 335 Stedman St (☎225-2257). Good-value, tasty Filipino dishes.

Five Star Café, Creek St (☎247-7827). Well-prepared, healthy food, including the delightful peanut butter, tahini, honey and banana sandwich.

Potlatch Bar, 126 Thomas St (☎225-4855). Lively, no-frills pub overlooking the harbor.

Roller Bay Café, 1287 Tongass Ave (☎225-0696). Cocktails and seafood on the waterfront.

Sourdough Bar, 301 Front St (☎225-2217). Much-loved local bar, decorated with photos of shipwrecks.

Wrangell

With a population of just 2630, **WRANGELL**, the second stop on the Marine Highway System, is altogether quieter than Ketchikan, with a distinctly old-fashioned feel, in many ways untouched since the days when fur traders set up shop here in the mid-nineteenth century because of its sheltered location near the mouth of the **Stikine River**. The gorgeous Stikine – the fastest-flowing navigable stretch of water in North America – still carries some freight, but today it's best known as a popular recreation ground for anglers and kayakers.

Right in the busy harbor, accessible by a short boardwalk, **Chief Shakes Island** holds an excellent collection of totem poles and a replica tribal house filled with Tlingit blankets. The ancient rock carvings at **Petroglyph Beach**, a mile north of town on Evergreen Road, which date back as far as 7500 years, are only obscured during high tide. Also worth a visit is the **Wrangell Museum** on Second and Bevier, which does a worthy job of interpreting the carvings and local Native culture (Mon–Sat 1–4pm, and when cruise-ships are in town; $1).

Practicalities

Ferries dock right in town and usually stop over long enough to allow explorations of Chief Shakes Island.

The nearest **campground** is at **City Park**, two miles south on Zimovia Highway. Of **motels**, the comfortable *Thunderbird*, at 110 Front St (☎874-3322; ③), is the least expensive option, although the more expensive *Stikine Inn*, beside the ferry dock (☎874-3388; ⑤), has a good **bar** and **restaurant**. The First Presbyterian Church sometimes runs a summer-only **hostel** in town (☎874-3534; ①). The **visitor center** (☎874-3901) occupies the A-frame building on Outer Drive facing the harbor.

Petersburg

One highlight of an Inside Passage ferry ride is to sit up front watching the boat grope its way through the 46 tight turns of the 22-mile-long **Wrangell Narrows**. At times it feels like you can reach out and touch the steep-walled shore, and the whole deal is even more spectacular at night when the channel is floodlit.

At the north end of the channel, the pretty fishing town of **PETERSBURG** – named for Peter Buschmann, who built a cannery and dock here in 1900 and was followed by many other Norwegian immigrants – is invariably referred to as "Alaska's Little Norway". The best times to come are during the summer halibut season, when the largest fleet in the state takes to sea, and the annual **Little Norway Festival** (held the weekend nearest Norwegian Independence Day, May 17).

Practicalities

In the absence of budget **accommodation**, choices include the 24-room *Scandia House*, 110 N Nordic Drive (☎772-4281 or 1-800/722-5006; ④), and *Jewell's By The Sea B&B*, 806 Nordic Drive (☎772-3620; ④). The only central place to **camp** is along with the seasonal cannery workers at *Tent City*, a mile and a half east of town; you pay $5 for the pleasure and there are no showers. As for **food**, *Harbor Lights Pizza*, 16 Sing Lee Alley (☎772-3424), the nearby healthfood deli *Helse* (☎772-3444), and the fries-with-everything *Homestead Café*, 217 Main St (☎772-3900), all come recommended. The **visitor center** is at First and Fram (Mon–Fri 9am–5pm; ☎772-3646).

Juneau

The vibrant city of **JUNEAU** is unlike any other state capital in the Pacific Northwest. Only accessible by sea or air, it is exceptionally picturesque, hard against the **Gastineau Channel**, with steep, narrow roads clawing up into the rainforested hills behind. Gold features heavily in its history. In 1880, two prospectors – one of them Joe Juneau – made **Alaska's first gold strike** in the rainforest along the banks of the Gastineau Channel. Named Gold Creek, the camp grew rapidly. Until the last mine was shut down in 1944, this was the world's largest producer of low-grade ore – all the flat land in Juneau, stretching from downtown to the airport, is landfill from mine tailings.

Juneau took over as territorial capital from Sitka in 1906, and has retained the seat of government since statehood in 1959. However, many see the town as an inaccessible and expensive place from which to run state business. Alaskans actually voted to move the capital to the village of Willow, between Anchorage and Denali, in the Seventies, but plans were scrapped due to the high cost of literally having to build a city from scratch. Another threat emerged in January 1994 with a bid from **Wasilla**, a mid-sized town just north of Anchorage. A desperate proposal from Juneau's city fathers to construct a new purpose-built capitol funded by local taxes recently failed at the polls, leaving the whole issue wide open.

Aside from government, fishing and tourism have replaced mining. In summer, downtown is crowded with cruise-ship passengers, but there is a lot more to do in Juneau than shop for souvenirs – particularly in April, when the city hosts the annual state folk festival, one of several top-class cultural events held throughout the year.

Arrival, information and city transit

The **Marine Highway ferry terminal** (☎789-7453) is fourteen miles northwest of downtown at Auke Bay. Because the daily ferries often arrive at unearthly hours, getting into town can be a problem. A *Mendenhall Glacier Transport* bus (☎789-5460) usually leaves the terminal about fifteen minutes after the ferry arrives, dropping off at the airport and the downtown hotels ($5). Alternatively, you could walk a mile and a half along the road towards town and catch the *Capital Transit* (☎789-6901) bus #3 at Mendenhall Loop Road, which costs $1 and runs every hour from 7am. The ferry dock is not to be confused with the cruise-ship terminal, right downtown. Daily *Alaska* and *Delta* flights land at Juneau's **airport** (☎789-7281), nine miles out towards the ferry terminal; buses from the adjacent Nugget Mall go downtown. Various companies rent out cars; it's worth shopping around, but budget on at least $30 per day.

The **Davis Log Cabin**, 134 Third St, carries information about Juneau and the surrounding area (June–Sept Mon–Fri 8am–5pm Sat & Sun 10am–5pm; Oct–May Mon–Fri 8am–5pm; ☎586-2284), and there's an **information booth** at Marine Park on the waterfront, by the cruise-ship dock (May–Sept daily 9am–6pm). A 24-hour events hotline on ☎586-JUNO will keep you up to date on local events. The **Forest Service Information Center**, in Centennial Hall at the corner of Willoughby Ave and Egan Drive, has films and exhibits on the region's attractions (June–Aug daily 9am–6pm; Sept–May Mon–Sat 8am–5pm; ☎586-8751).

Juneau's Parks and Recreation Department (☎586-5226) organizes popular communal **hikes**; if you'd prefer to go it alone, invest in one of two books widely available locally: the *Juneau Trail Guide*, published by the US Forest Service ($3), or *90 Short Walks around Juneau*. The most popular treks include the steep Perseverance Trail and, over the bridge on Douglas Island, the Treadwell Mine Historic Trail. *D M Bicycles* (☎586-2277), at 217 S Franklin St, rents out **mountain bikes** and offers customized area tours. Next door, *Alaska Discovery* (☎463-5560) organizes sea-kayaking trips amid wondrous scenery. *Alaska Rainforest Tours* (☎463-3466) run all manner of local and regional tours .

Downtown Juneau

From the kiosk in Marine Park, it takes an hour and a half to follow the self-guided Juneau walking tour. Many original buildings stand in the **South Franklin Street Historic District** – Juneau never suffered the fires that destroyed many other gold towns in Alaska. The onion-domed **St Nicholas Russian Orthodox Church**, on Fifth and Gold, contains icons and religious treasures, while the excellent **Alaska State Museum**, 395 Whittier St, covers native culture, the Russian heritage and the first gold strikes. Its pride and joy is the log book in which Bering reported his first sighting of Alaska (Mon–Fri 9am–6pm, Sat & Sun 10am–6pm; $2). The smaller **City Museum** at Fourth and Main, displays relics from the mining era (summer; Mon–Fri 9am–5pm Sat & Sun 11am–5pm; $1). Also downtown, next to the cruise-ship dock, **Marine Park** is a hangout for local bohemians and the venue for Friday-night concerts throughout summer.

One of the best daytrips out of Juneau is up the narrow, twisting **Tracy Arm Fjord**. Day-long boat trips cost $125; fly-in/cruise-out experiences cost $199. Many consider this to be a better deal than the Glacier Bay trip; book on ☎463-5510 or 1-800/451-5952.

Mendenhall Glacier Area

There are certainly bigger and more spectacular glaciers in Alaska, but the twelve-mile-long, one-and-a-half-mile-wide **Mendenhall Glacier**, thirteen miles northwest of downtown, is easily the most accessible. Should your knowledge of cirques and striations be minimal, the **visitor center** (on a point this receding glacier occupied as recently as 1940) has all you need to know (daily 8.30am–6pm; ☎789-0097). Hiking trails include the **West Glacier Trail**, on which, with some caution, you can explore the ice caves.

Capital Transit buses leave for the Mendenhall hourly (Mon–Sat) from downtown; get off at Glacier Spur Road for the visitor center, or Montana Creek Road for the West Glacier trail. *Alaska Travel Adventures* (☎789-0052) run four-hour float trips on the Mendenhall River, offering wonderful views of the great lumbering flow of ice for a $75 fee that includes lunch. For a mere $60 more, however, you can participate in one of the very best excursions in all of Alaska: *Temsco Helicopters* (☎789-9501) whisk you up in the skies and land on the glacier itself, enabling you to wander around and enjoy the gaping crevasses, ultramarine pools and tumbling streams. On similarly expensive lines, *Wings of Alaska* (☎789-0790) offer one-hour flights for $100 which zoom beyond the glacier and into the **Juneau Icefield**.

If you're taking the bus back to town, get off at Glacier Hwy for a free tour of the tiny **Alaskan Brewing Co**, 5429 Shaune Drive, Lemon Creek (tours every half-hour, Tues–Sat 11am–4.30pm; ☎780-5866). Here you get a chance to consume some of their award-winning wheat-based beers, as sold throughout Alaska and in the *Brick Bar* of *Northern Exposure* fame.

Accommodation

There are plenty of motels near downtown, though it's worth trying one of Juneau's many good **B&Bs**; the *Alaska B&B Association*, 3444 Nowell St (☎586-2959), reserves rooms for $50 and up. *Mendenhall Lake Campground* (☎586-8800), accessible by buses #3 or #4 and a short hike, is spectacularly situated near the glacier, but gets cold even in summer. The smaller *Auke Village Campground* (☎789-9467), with views of the ocean, lies two miles north of the ferry terminal.

Alaskan Hotel and Bar, 167 S Franklin St (☎586-1000 or 1-800/327-9374). Pleasant old hotel in the heart of downtown, with fine bar. Twelve doubles with shared or private bath. ③.

Crondahl's B&B, 626 Fifth St (☎586-1464). Two rooms and a gourmet breakfast are on offer at this welcoming home high on the hill in downtown Juneau. ③.

Driftwood Lodge Motel, 435 Willoughby Ave (☎586-2280). One block from the waterfront; rooms include kitchenettes. Transportation to and from the airport and ferry terminal. ④.

Eagle's Nest B&B, N Douglas Hwy (☎586-6378). Cozy retreat eight miles from town on Douglas Island. TV, VCR and a DIY breakfast. ④.

Juneau International AYH Hostel, 614 Harris St (☎586-9559). Clean and comfortable, in an old home near downtown, with dorm beds for $10. ①.

Pearson's Pond Luxury B&B, 4541 Sawa Circle (☎789-3772). Spacious modern home close to Mendenhall Glacier (and a bus stop). Self-serve breakfast, outdoor spa, bicycles, rowboat, VCR, computer, and discount excursions. Smoking is seen as a heinous crime. ⑤.

Super 8 Motel, 2295 Trout St (☎789-4858). Located next to the airport, Nugget Mall and *McDonalds*. Perhaps more importantly, the Mendenhall Glacier is just a mile away. ④.

Eating and drinking

Downtown Juneau boasts a number of excellent places to eat, though they fill up very quick when cruise-ships are in town. The *McDonald's*, *BK* and *Wendy's* franchises are all represented, but the least expensive filling meals are to be had at the cafeteria in Room 241 of the Federal Building on Ninth and Glacier. For a summertime feast in beautiful surroundings, hop on one of the free buses to the *Gold Creek Salmon Bake* at the Last Chance Basin (☎586-1424). This eat-till-you-drop deal, costing $20, includes salad and delicious salmon served at sheltered outdoor tables, with live music.

Alaskan Hotel and Bar, 167 S Franklin St (☎586-1000). Great old bar, with occasional live music.

Armadillo Tex-Mex Cafe, 431 S Franklin St (☎586-1880). Huge plates of nachos start at $5.50, or try the Enchiladas Azteca, served with beans, rice and guacamole for $10.

Fiddlehead Restaurant and Bakery, 429 Willoughby Ave (☎586-3150). Known throughout the state for wholesome food. Their bread has become so popular they charge a dollar a slice, but don't let that put you off – most entrees are well under $10 and this is Juneau's finest place to eat.

Heritage Coffee and Café, 174 S Franklin St (☎586-1088). Excellent coffee, huge sandwiches.

Luna's, 210 Seward St (☎586-6990). The locals' favorite Italian restaurant. Great *calzone*.

FISH TALES

Fish, and talk of **fish**, crop up everywhere in Alaska. No self-respecting bar or café will open its doors without a mounted fifty-pound salmon, or a picture of a local with a three-hundred-pound halibut to adorn its walls. Nor does any souvenir trader set up shop without an "I Fish Therefore I Lie" T-shirt and other such fishy ephemera. No matter who you speak to, the conversation will almost inevitably get round to fish.

You'll hear the usual "one that got away" stories throughout the state, but the best tale of all involves an *Alaska Airlines* 737 that collided with a salmon while taking off from Juneau airport in 1987. This isn't just another fishy yarn. Apparently the plane startled a bald eagle, which dropped the said fish onto the cockpit, smashing glass and causing an embarrassing reschedule.

Red Dog Saloon, S Franklin St (☎463-3658). Touristy bar opposite the cruise-ship terminal with a carefully fabricated "olde worlde ambience". At night there's a much younger crowd and live music.

Taku Smokeries, 230 S Franklin St (☎463-3474). Magnificent smoked salmon and seafood. Ideal picnic food.

Near Juneau

Two islands, just a short *Marine Highway* ferry ride west of Juneau, offer visitors with time to spare a chance to experience isolated communities and remote terrain. The larger, **ADMIRALTY ISLAND**, designated a National Monument, is the only big southeastern isle not to have been scarred by logging, and also supports the region's largest bear population in the **Pack Creek Bear Refuge**. Some visitors come merely to admire the rugged scenery, though many are paddlers, attracted by the challenges and splendor of the **Cross-Admiralty Canal Route**. Ferries dock at the island's only town, **Angoon**, a Tlingit fishing community on Chatham Strait on the western side of the island, where the best of several places to stay is the *Favorite Bay Inn B&B* (☎788-3123; ③). For details on cabins, campgrounds, kayaking and hiking in bear territory, contact the Admiralty Island National Monument HQ, 8465 Old Dairy Rd, Juneau (☎586-8790).

Closer to Juneau, also on Chatham Strait, the boat stops at tiny **TENAKEE SPRINGS**, strung out along a single gravel street on the eastern shore of the more westerly **Chigahof Island**. This functions as a quiet getaway spot for Juneau residents, with its main attraction, a 106°F spring, occupying a spartan wooden bathhouse. The *Tenakee Inn* offers clean dorm beds and rooms (☎736-2241; ① & ③); rustic cabins (①) can be rented at the grocery store. There's also a free campground near town.

Just three hours away from Juneau on Chigahof's west coast, the shabby Tlingit village of **HOONAH** is surrounded by great trekking terrain, while, in town, the cultural center in the IRA Building houses a varied collection of native artefacts. Hoonah lacks a designated campground and the only place to stay charges fairly hefty prices.

Glacier Bay National Park

When Capt. George Vancouver sailed through Icy Strait in 1794, **Glacier Bay** was no more than a dent in the ice-packed coastline. Since then the Grand Pacific Glacier has receded 65 miles, to reveal a chill landscape of deep fjords lined by rock walls and fed by fifteen other receding tidewater glaciers. The flora of the bay ranges from mature spruce forests to delicate plant life, while brown and black bear, moose, mountain goats, sea otters, humpback whales, porpoise, harbor seals and thousands of birds have made the area their home.

The only way to get close to the local wildlife is on one of the spectacular **day cruises** through Glacier Bay, from the tiny little hamlet of **GUSTAVUS**, which occupies a sand spit that tapers its way into Icy Strait. Boats inch their way between the icebergs for three miles, before coming face-to-face with the massive wall of the Grand Pacific Glacier. For an additional $40 on top of the usual fee (see below), the cruise-ships can drop you off out in the park and pick you up a few days later, leaving time to explore on foot or by kayak.

Practicalities

Glacier Bay cruises alone cost $148, and before you can take one you have first to fly into Gustavus Airport. Local airlines make daily trips from Juneau for around $120 round-trip, and a little more expensively from Skagway and Haines. Larger *Alaska Airlines* planes also touch down once a day, from Juneau and Anchorage, or you can **charter** a plane from Juneau through *Air Excursions* (☎789-5591), for $220 for up to four people. Park buses from the airport to the park headquarters in Bartlett Cove (ten lonesome miles) cost $8.

A Puffin B&B in Gustavus (☎697-2258 or 1-800/478-2258 in AK; ④) features half a dozen modern cabins in a forest clearing. The friendly owners will wake those going out on a cruise for a full 5.30am breakfast and also run a tailor-made tour service (including whale-watching cruises) for independent travellers. *Salmon River Cabins* (☎697-2245; ②) are more rustic, and the *Open Gate Café* (☎697-2227) serves good food until 7pm.

Not far away, inside the park, there's a pleasant free campground, $28 dorm beds to tasteful rooms at the *Glacier Bay Lodge* (☎463-5510; ⑤). The concession company, *Glacier Bay Tours* (☎1-800/451-5952), handle bookings for park accommodation, cruises and also offer a bewildering number of packages.

Sitka

Protected from the Pacfic Ocean by dainty tree-blanketed islands, **SITKA** ranks as not just one of Alaska's prettiest towns, but also one of its most historic. Fuji-like **Mount Edgecumbe volcano** rears menacingly across Sitka Sound from the spot where Russian colonists established a fort in 1799. Three years later Tlingit warriors killed virtually all the imperial troops and their Aleut slaves, but were cannoned into submission in 1804, after which the Russians reconstructed the town, named it **Novaya Archangelsk** (New Archangel) and established it as capital of Alaska – a role it retained beyond the 1867 transfer of ownership to the US, until federal powers passed control to Juneau in 1906. Sitka today earns its keep from logging, commercial fishing and tourism; it's all too keen to pander to a taste for tacky Russianesque trivia (dancers, singers, people dressed in silly clothes etc), but has a wealth of great outdoor opportunities. Sitka also commands a fine reputation for its festivals, especially the chamber-orientated **Summer Music Festival** each June. Popular culture is celebrated in late June with the **All-Alaska Logging Championships**.

Arrival, information and getting around

Marine Highway **ferries** pass through five times per week, dropping anchor seven miles out on Halibut Point Rd (☎747-3300). Old school buses operated by *Sitka Tours* (☎747-8443) will take you downtown for $3; they also do short "stopover tours" ($8). *Alaska Airlines* offer daily service on the Seattle–Juneau–Anchorage route from the **airport** on Japonski Island, just under two miles from downtown, across O'Connell Bridge. Round-trip tickets from Juneau cost under $100 if you include a Saturday night in your stay, and the flight in and out makes for spectacular sightseeing. The **CVB** office is in the Centennial Building, 330 Harbor Drive (daily 8am–5pm; ☎747-8279).

Various companies offer **cruises** around the beautiful Pacific Islands; the least expensive way to get on the water is on a two-hour ride with *Silver Bay Cruises* (☎747-8100; $25).

The Town

Getting a grasp of Sitka's Russian past doesn't take much time. The best place to start is from the vantage point of **Castle Hill**, a rocky knob where Alaska was officially transferred to the US on October 18, 1867; a plaque marks the spot. A two-minute stroll to the heart of downtown leads to **St Michael's Cathedral** on Lincoln Street. A fine piece of rural Russian church architecture, completed in 1848 and rebuilt after a disastrous fire in 1966, it displays original icons (open when cruise-ships are in town; $1). Free tours take in the restored chapel, school room and living quarters of the large mustard-colored **Russian Bishop's House**, by the harbor – a log structure that is the oldest standing building in Alaska (daily 8.30am–4.30pm).

Four blocks further along at 104 College Drive, the **Sheldon Jackson Museum** houses the most extensive accumulation of Native artefacts in the state. All of its tools, utensils and craft objects from Aleut, Athabascan, Tlingit and, especially, Inuit peoples were collected by the Revd Sheldon Jackson on his wide-ranging travels throughout Alaska as a missionary and the territory's first General Agent of Education (summer daily 8am–5pm; otherwise Tues–Sat 10am–4pm; $2, free on Sat).

At the end of Lincoln Street, in a verdant copse between ocean and creek, **Sitka National Historic Park** embraces both the town's Tlingit heritage and its days of Russian rule. When Tsarist troops attacked a Tlingit fort on this site in 1804, the Natives withheld bombardment for six days, but after running out of gunpowder, decided to exit the fort silently at night. The next day Russians stormed the stockades only to find them empty except for a few dead children, which they alleged were murdered to accomplish the retreat in complete silence. Nothing remains of the fort, but the evocative air is enhanced by several vividly painted replica **totem poles**. A **visitor center** features good interpretive displays on what is commonly called the "Battle of Sitka", as well as hosting Native craft workshops (daily 8am–5pm; free).

Sitka's **trail system** ranges from shoreside strolls to a difficult switchback path up Mount Verstovia. Three of the nineteen Forest Service cabins (☎747-6671) in the area are reachable by trail, but are twenty to forty miles from town, making it easier to pedal there; mountain bike rental costs $20 per day from *J & D*, 203 Lincoln St (☎747-8279). The sheltered shoreline provides good **sea-kayaking** territory; *Biardaka Boats*, 201 Lincoln St (☎747-8996), offer rental, novice lessons and guided tours at reasonable prices.

Accommodation

Sitka has southeast Alaska's best range of **accommodation**, with a fine hotel, two dorm-style lodgings and twenty B&Bs. If you're looking for something a bit different, *Burgess Bauder's Lighthouse* (☎747-3056; ⑦), accessible only by boat, sleeps eight. The rustic Starrigavan campground ($5), a mile north of the ferry is the best bet for campers.

Karras B&B, 203 Kogwanton St (☎747-3978). Stunning view of the sea, great breakfasts. ③.

Sheldon Jackson College, Lincoln St campus (☎747-5220). Immaculate $25 dorms. ①.

Sitka AYH Hostel, 303 Kimshan St (☎747-8356). Spartan $6 hostel, one mile from downtown. ①.

Sitka Hotel, 118 Lincoln St (☎747-6241). Safe, clean and basic rooms downtown. ③.

Sitka House B&B, 325 Seward St (☎747-4937). Two rooms in a beautiful downtown home with breakfasts, such as baked crab, in the patio. ③.

Westmark Shee Atika, 330 Seward St (☎747-6241 or 1-800/544-0970). Fine hotel tastefully decked out with Native paintings and trimmings. ⑥.

Eating

Sitka's restaurants aren't exactly going to set gourmet tongues wagging, though there are several unusual places to dine out. For evening drinks, join the crowds in the *Westmark Shee Atika*'s bar, or the down-to-earth *Pioneer Bar* on Katlian St.

Back Door Café, behind *Old Harbor Books*, 201 Lincoln St (☎747-8856). Great coffee, plus tasty sandwiches and pastries. Daytime only.

Bayview Restaurant, upstairs at 407 Lincoln St (☎747-5440). Open 7am–7.30pm for gourmet burgers, Russian specialties, chowders and entrees such as white salmon. Reasonable prices.

Marina, 205 Harbor Drive (☎747-8840). Decent pizza and Mex food. Open until 11pm.

Nugget Restaurant, Sitka Airport Terminal (☎966-2480). One of the most popular airport cafés in North America. The pies – great creamy fruit-filled slabs of gastric ecstasy – are a must. Favorites include kiwi fruit or banana and coconut, but there are a dozen others to choose from.

Sheldon Jackson College Cafeteria, Lincoln St (☎747-2506). All-you-can-eat buffet meals: breakfast (7–8am; $4.50), lunch (11.30am–1pm; $5.50), dinner (5–6.30pm; $8).

Haines

HAINES, at the northern end of the Lynn Canal fjord on a narrow peninsula between the Chilkat and the Chilkoot inlets, seven hours by boat from Juneau, has an absolutely gorgeous setting. When the weather is clear, it is nothing short of spectacular, with snow-covered **Mount Ripinsky** rising up behind, the **Chilkoot and Chilkat mountains** hemming it in on either side, and glaciers spilling out into the deep fjord. The community itself is an interesting mix of unreconstructed rednecks and urban escapees from the Lower 48.

The Tlingit fished and traded here for years before 1881, when the first missionaries arrived and renamed the settlement for a prominent Presbyterian, Mrs F Haines. Today Haines survives on timber and fishing, and though few cruise-ships stop here it's becoming a popular tourist spot, which in mid-August hosts the cook-outs, crafts, pig-racing and log-rolling of the **Southeast Alaska Fair**. The fairgrounds also hold *Dalton City*, a small pioneer theme park notable only in that its buildings came from the movie sets of Jack London's *White Fang* which was filmed in the Haines area in 1989.

Haines is also a popular sidetrip for those motoring along the Alaska Highway – the enjoyable 151-mile drive south from Haines Junction, Yukon, hugs the **Kluane National Park** (see p.467) for much of the way.

Arrival and information

Haines' **Marine Highway terminal** (☎766-2111) is about four miles west of town. The *Haines Streetcar* shuttle service (☎766-2819; $6) meets all ferry arrivals, as do local taxis. *Alaska Direct* and *Alaskon Express* buses leave Haines three times a week in the summer for the 150-mile trip to Haines Junction in Canada, Anchorage and Fairbanks. The fifteen-mile trip to Skagway on the *Haines Water Taxi* (359 miles by road) is more like a scenic cruise than a ferry ride (☎766-3395; $29 return, $19 one-way, bikes $5).

The **visitor center**, at Second and Willard (☎766-2234; ☎1-800/478-2268 in AK, BC & YK; ☎1-800/458-3579 in the US), has all kinds of maps and information.

The Town

Apart from its art galleries and craft shops, concentrated around the visitor center, downtown Haines holds little interest. Instead, keep to the outdoor pursuits that make it a must on any Inside Passage itinerary. Two great wild **state parks** – Chilkoot Lake and Chilkat – are a mere half-hour cycle ride to the north and south of town, respectively. Chilkat in particular has some great trails and vistas, while from town, well-tramped treks lead to the summits of Mount Riley and the much more difficult Mount Ripinsky. Haines is also a popular starting point for **rafting trips**: *Chilkat Guides* (☎766-2491), on Beach Road below Fort Seward, organizes four-hour float trips ($70) down the Chilkat River (great for viewing eagles), as well as longer fly-in whitewater trips. In winter the terrain lends itself to excellent cross-country skiing and snowmobiling.

Each fall, the world's largest gathering of **bald eagles** flocks to the banks of the Chilkat River to feed on an unusually late chum salmon run (delayed by a hot spring that keeps the river from freezing). By November up to four thousand of the rare birds – as many as two dozen in one tree – are gathered along a five-mile sandbar at the **Chilkat Bald Eagle Reserve**, nine miles north of town on the Haines Highway.

In response to the general lawlessness of the gold rush era, and territorial disputes with Canada, **Fort William H Seward** was established in Haines in 1903. Half a mile west of downtown, it features fairgrounds, a reconstructed Totem Village as well as replicas of a Tlingit tribal house and a trapper's cabin. During the summer, the Chilkat Dancers perform in traditional costumes at the **Chilkat Center for the Arts**, in Fort Seward's recreational center ($7; ☎766-2160).

Accommodation

As well the usual mid-range accommodation, Haines has several **campgrounds**, such as the spotless Haines Hitchup Park, half a mile west on Main (☎766-2882), and Portage Cove, on a great scenic beach less than a mile from Fort Seward on S Front St. Chilkat State Park also has nice sites, seven miles southeast on Mud Bay Rd.

Bear Creek Camp and Hostel, two miles south on Small Tract Rd (☎766-2259). Utterly rustic lodgings; dorm beds ($12), four-person cabins ($30), including free pickup from the ferry. ①.

Hotel Haslingland and Officers Inn B&B, Fort Seward (☎766-2000, 1-800/478-2525 in US, or 1-800/542-6363 in Canada). Choice of grand old hotel or B&B in the center of the old barracks. ④.

Mountain View Motel, Fort Seward (☎766-2900). Comfortable doubles. ④.

River House B&B, Mile 1 Mud Bay Rd (PO Box 1009, AK 99827; ☎766-2060). Beautiful large cottage, one mile south of town where the Chilkat River meets the sea. ⑤.

Eating and drinking

Haines' most exciting bars and restaurants can be found in the Fort Seward area. In the evening, kayakers, cyclists and hikers frequent the friendly bar at the *Haslingland Hotel* (☎766-2000); locals stick to the more raucous joints downtown.

Bamboo Room, on Second near Main (☎766-9101). Breakfasts such as jalapeno-filled Spanish omelettes cost about $4. It's also a favorite late-night drinking hole for locals.

Chilkat Restaurant and Bakery, Fifth and Main (☎766-2920). Reasonably priced, freshly made breads, breakfasts and lunches.

Dejon Delights, Portage St, Fort Seward (☎766-2505). Take away the best smoked or pickled salmon in the state and fresh bread for the price of burger and fries.

Fort Chilkoot Potlatch, Parade Grounds, Fort Seward (☎766-2003). All-you-can-eat salmon bake on summer evenings between 5pm & 8pm.

Fort Seward Lodge, Fort Seward (☎766-2009). Specializes in good prime rib and Dungeness crab dinners.

Skagway and around

SKAGWAY, the northernmost stop on the *Marine Highway*, sprang up overnight in 1897, as a trading post serving **Klondike gold rush** pioneers about to set off on the five-hundred-mile trek to the gold fields (see p.470). It was also the last stop before the harrowing White Pass Trail, known as the "Dead Horse Trail", on which over three thousand horses perished during the winter of 1897–98 from severe weather, rugged ground and exhaustion. Having grown from one cabin to a town of twenty thousand in three months, Skagway, rife with disease and desperado violence, was reported to be "hell on earth". It boasted over seventy bars and hundreds of prostitutes, and was controlled by organized criminals, including the notorious Jefferson "Soapy" Smith, renowned for cheating hapless prospectors out of their gold. One of his scams was to operate a bogus telegraph office through which he concocted false messages from loved ones in the Lower 48 urgently demanding money, which "Soapy", of course, took responsibility for sending. He finally met a nasty end in 1899 after a shoot-out with Frank Reid, head of a vigilante group.

By 1899, the gold rush was over, but the completion in 1900 of the **White Pass and Yukon Railway** from Skagway to Whitehorse, the Yukon capital, ensured Skagway's survival. Though the railroad officially closed down in 1982, it reopened in 1988 for summer excursions, a characteristic move for one of Alaska's most tourism-conscious destinations.

The 712 residents have gone to great lengths to maintain the original appearance of their town, much of which lies in the **Klondike Gold Rush National Historic Park**, but Skagway's charm is also its curse, and in the summer it gets packed out, with as many as three cruise-ships calling in each day. However, from mid-September to early May most places in town are closed, and it becomes far more sedate, indeed almost eerie.

Many people head north from Skagway along the **Klondike Highway**, which connects with the Alaska Highway close to Whitehorse, 108 miles north (see p.461). Still more visitors come to follow the footsteps of the original prospectors (stampeders), and hike the 33-mile **Chilkoot Trail**.

Arrival, information and getting around

Marine Highway ferries (☎983-2941) arrive daily a few minutes southwest of the main thoroughfare, Broadway Street. The train station (☎983-2217), a block off Broadway St on Second Ave, offers a daily summer **rail** service to Whitehorse and the White Pass Summit. *Alaska Direct* **buses** travel daily in summer to Whitehorse, Yukon ($38), from where thrice-weekly trips run to Anchorage ($145) and Fairbanks ($125); *Alaskon Express* offer a similar service from the *Westmark Inn* on Third Ave (☎983-2241). *Haines Water Taxi* (☎983-2083; $29 round-trip, $18 one-way, bikes $5) is the easiest way to head south to Haines.

Skagway is very compact, and most of the sights can be seen easily on foot. The National Park Service **visitor center**, between Second Ave and Broadway St, holds talks, leads walking tours, and has historical displays and an impressive movie about the gold rush, as well as maps and information on the Chilkoot Trail (daily, June–Aug 8am–8pm, May & Sept 8am–6pm; ☎983-2921). Skagway's **visitor center** is in the Arctic Brotherhood Hall, detailed below (summer, Mon–Fri 9am–6pm; ☎983-2854).

The Town

The facade of the remarkable **Arctic Brotherhood Hall**, on Broadway St between Second and Third, built in 1899 by gold miners who paid their dues in nuggets, is decorated with over twenty thousand pieces of driftwood. Nearby, you can see antiques from the gold rush days at the small **Trail of 98 Museum**, on Seventh Ave, just off Broadway St (daily 8am–8pm; $2). A block away, at the corner of Sixth and Broadway, the *Days of 98 Show* is a reasonably entertaining historical musical about Soapy Smith ($14).

About one and a half miles north of town, the **Gold Rush Cemetery** is the final resting place of many of the stampeders. Among them are Soapy Smith and Frank Reid, who according to his gravestone "gave his life for the honor of Skagway"; a local prostitute, on the other hand, is remembered for "giving her honor for the life of Skagway".

From the cemetery, a short and pleasant trail leads from the cemetery to the 300-foot-high Reid Falls. The useful *Skagway Trail Map*, available from the visitor center, details other hikes in the area including those in the Dewey Lakes system, which pass pretty subalpine lakes and tumbling waterfalls, and the more difficult scramble uphill to Denver Glacier. *Sockeye Cycles*, Fifth Ave off Broadway (☎983-2851), rent out well-maintained **mountain bikes**.

The Chilkoot Trail and the Yukon Railway

One of the most popular trails in the Northwest, the 33-mile **Chilkoot Trail** is one huge "wilderness museum". Following in the footsteps of the original Klondike prospectors, it is strewn with haunting reminders of the past, including old mining dredges and gold-rush ghost towns. Starting in **Dyea**, nine miles up the highway from Skagway, and ending at **Bennett Lake** in Canada, the trail climbs through rainforest to tundra, flanked by fast-flowing streams and waterfalls.

The three- to five-day hike can be strenuous, especially the final ascent up steep scree from Sheep Camp (1000ft) to Chilkoot Pass (3550ft). You must be self-sufficient for food, fuel and shelter, and be prepared for foul weather. Campgrounds line the trail, as well as emergency shelters with stoves and firewood. There are also ranger stations at Dyea, Sheep Camp and Lindeman City; for further details, see box on p.462.

The lazy way to take in the scenery is on the **White Pass and Yukon Railway** (mid-May to late Sept; see p.489) which follows the gushing Skagway River upstream past waterfalls, ice-packed gorges and over a 1000-foot-high wooden trestle bridge, stopping at the Canadian border ($75) or on to Lake Bennett, BC ($105). There's no shortage of takers, so if you decide to go, get there early and grab a seat on the left-hand side. The company also offers a through bus-service to Whitehorse after a train ride to Fraser, BC ($99).

Accommodation

In such a touristy little town, accommodation prices run high, and places get booked up in advance. There's a pleasantly secluded campground, *Hanousek Park* (☎983-2768; $7), at Fourteenth and Broadway, near the railroad tracks.

Golden North Hotel, Broadway St (☎983-2294). Skagway's most famous hotel, built in 1898. All rooms are decorated with gold-rush antiques and have large cast-iron bathtubs. ④.

Skagway Inn B&B, Seventh and Broadway (☎983-2289). Turn-of-the-century ambience and fresh-baked breakfasts in one of Alaska's very best small inns, with very reasonable rates. ④.

Skagway International Hostel, Third and Main (☎983-2181). Homely and welcoming, one of the finest hostels in the state, despite its strict 10.30pm curfew. $10 per night. ①.

Wind Valley Lodge, 22nd and State (☎983-2236). Clean, modern motel less than a mile from downtown. Lacks the charm of the *Golden North Hotel* or *Skagway Inn*, but a good option if they are full. ④.

Eating and drinking

Most of Skagway's bars and its predominantly bland restaurants lie in the touristy area on Broadway St between Second and Seventh. The best snacks, in the form of smoked salmon, are on offer at *Dejon Delights* next to the popcorn wagon on Broadway.

Dee's Restaurant, Second Ave, off Broadway (☎983-2200). Salmon and halibut bakes, burgers and decent salads, with indoor and outdoor seating.

Northern Lights, Broadway, between Fourth and Fifth avenues (☎983-2225). Good Italian food, with pizza from $10 and pasta from $8, in a pleasant setting.

Red Onion Saloon, Second and Broadway (☎983-2222). Best bar in town. Live music, excellent pizza, and Alaskan Amber on tap.

Sweet Tooth Café, Third and Broadway (☎983-2405). Skagway's top traditional American-style café, serving breakfast, burgers and ice-cream.

Anchorage

Wedged between the two arms of the Upper Cook Inlet with the imposing Chugach Mountains to the east, **ANCHORAGE** is home to over forty percent of Alaska's population, and serves as the transportation center for the whole state. This sprawling conurbation on the edge of one of the world's great wildernesses often gets a bad press from those who live elsewhere in Alaska – many call it *Los Anchorage* – but it has its attractions, and with its beautiful setting can make a pleasant one- or two-day stopover.

By the time Captain James Cook came up what is now the Cook Inlet in 1778, in search of a Northwest Passage to the Atlantic, Russian fur-trappers had already started to settle the area, trading copper and iron for fish and furs with the Indians. Though Cook was sure that the inlet was not the Passage, he sent boats out in a southeasterly direction to investigate. When they were forced to turn back by the severe tides, Cook named this gloriously scenic stretch **Turnagain Arm**.

Anchorage itself began life in 1915 as a small tent city for construction workers on the Alaska Railroad. During the Thirties, hopefuls fleeing the Depression came pouring in from the Lower 48, and World War II – and the construction of the Alaska Highway – further boosted the city's size and importance. The opening of the airport established Anchorage – equidistant between New York and

Tokyo – as the "Crossroads of the World", and statehood in 1959 brought in yet more optimistic adventurers.

On Good Friday 1964, North America's strongest-ever **earthquake**, measuring 9.2 on the Richter scale, devastated much of downtown, but ironically Anchorage emerged richer than ever from the consequent building boom. In the early Seventies, the discovery of oil in Prudhoe Bay on Alaska's northern coast led to an influx of construction workers, earning six-figure incomes working on the trans-Alaska oil pipeline. However, Anchorage has suffered since the oil crisis in the mid-Eighties, with many big companies relocating to the Lower 48.

Many visitors try to get out of the place as quickly as possible, though even with the *Taco Bells*, *Holiday Inns*, *7-Elevens* and *Safeways* of Anytown USA, Anchorage, with its beautiful setting, still manages to let you know that you're a long way from anywhere.

Arrival, information and getting around

Anchorage International Airport lies seven miles west of town, served, in the early morning and late afternoon only, by the *People Mover* bus (see below). If you arrive at an inconvenient time you can take a taxi (around $15 to downtown) or a hotel courtesy van. The *Dynair Charter* shuttle service (☎243-3310) costs $6.50 to downtown. The train station is on the edge of town at 411 W First Ave.

Most of the major sights downtown are easily reached on foot, but the best way to get around is by bike. *Anchorage Coastal Bicycle Rentals*, 414 K St (☎279-1999), have good machines. *People Mover* buses cover the city and the surrounding area – known together as the "bowl" – between 5am and midnight, for a $1 flat fare. However, they can be very infrequent. Schedules cost $1 from the Transit Center office on Sixth and G (Mon–Fri 9am–5pm), or call *Rideline* on ☎343-6543. Numerous tours range from downtown trolley rides to flights to Nome; shop around before taking the plunge.

Information

The main information office downtown is the **Log Cabin Visitor Center**, at Fourth and F (daily, May–Sept 7.30am–7pm, Oct–April 8.30am–6pm; ☎274-3531), which has details of a pleasant and easy self-guided downtown walking tour. For a recorded message detailing events in town, call the *All About Anchorage* hotline (☎276-3200).

Diagonally across the street from the Log Cabin, the **Alaska Public Lands Information Center** has natural history information, maps, and brochures. They help plan trips into the Interior, and make reservations both for accommodation and the shuttle bus to Denali National Park – important in summer (daily 9am–7pm; ☎271-2737).

The City

In their eagerness to hightail into the "real" Alaska, visitors tend to overlook Anchorage – a blend of old and new, urban blight and rural parks – as a destination. There is, however, plenty to see in town, and it's worth spending some time here experiencing big-city Alaska, as uncompromisingly "real" as the rest of the state. The city is laid out on a grid; numbered avenues run east–west, lettered streets north–south.

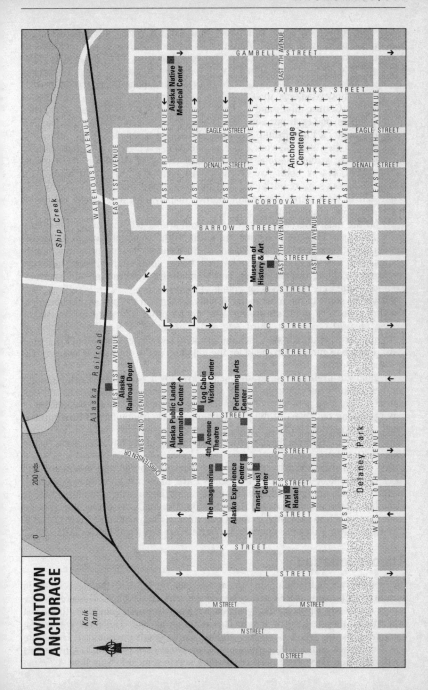

DOWNTOWN ANCHORAGE

Knik Arm

Ship Creek

200 yds

0

WAREHOUSE AVENUE

Alaska Railroad

CHRISTENSEN DR

WEST 1ST AVENUE

WEST 2ND AVENUE

WEST 3RD AVENUE

WEST 4TH AVENUE

WEST 5TH AVENUE

WEST 6TH AVENUE

WEST 7TH AVENUE

WEST 8TH AVENUE

WEST 9TH AVENUE

WEST 10TH AVENUE

EAST 1ST AVENUE

EAST 3RD AVENUE

EAST 4TH AVENUE

EAST 5TH AVENUE

EAST 6TH AVENUE

EAST 7TH AVENUE

EAST 8TH AVENUE

EAST 9TH AVENUE

EAST 10TH AVENUE

GAMBELL STREET

FAIRBANKS STREET

EAGLE STREET

DENALI STREET

CORDOVA STREET

BARROW STREET

A STREET

B STREET

C STREET

D STREET

E STREET

F STREET

G STREET

H STREET

I STREET

K STREET

L STREET

M STREET

N STREET

O STREET

Anchorage Cemetery

Delaney Park

Alaska Native Medical Center

Alaska Railroad Depot

Alaska Public Lands Information Center

Log Cabin Visitor Center

Performing Arts Center

Museum of History & Art

4th Avenue Theatre

The Imaginarium

Alaska Experience Center

Transit (bus) Center

AYH Hostel

The **Anchorage Museum of History and Art**, 121 W Seventh Ave, includes a massive oil painting of Mount McKinley by Sydney Laurence, and dioramas of Alaskan history (daily 9am–6pm; $4). **The Imaginarium**, 725 Fifth Ave, is exciting, especially for the young at heart, with hands-on displays to tell you whatever you need to know about glaciers, the Northern Lights, polar bears and the private life of the dopey-looking moose (Mon–Sat 11am–6pm; $5). At the **Alaska Experience Center**, Sixth and G, forty minutes of Alaska's best scenery, shot from choppers, planes, trains and rafts, is beamed onto a 180° wraparound screen ($6). The center's **Earthquake Theater** ($5) shows a sensible film on the 1964 disaster and then sets off your chair to simulate a 4.6 tremor (summer; daily 9am–9pm). On a more serious note, the **Wolf Song of Alaska** in the Parking Garage Mall, 414 W Sixth Ave, is the public face of a group campaigning on behalf of Alaska's most intriguing and misunderstood mammal. A donation is requested to view some worthy interpretive displays, art and videos (Mon–Sat 10am–7pm, Sun noon–5pm).

By far the most impressive range of Alaskan artefacts in town is in the private collection of the **Heritage Library Museum**, in the National Bank of Alaska on the corner of Northern Lights Blvd and C St. Exhibits include paintings, photographs, old newspapers, rare books and maps, tools and weapons and old costumes including bizarre-looking parkas made from walrus intestines (Mon–Fri noon–5pm; free; ☎265-2834 for details of tours).

As well as some of the most garish T-shirt designs on the planet, Anchorage is also home to very good **shopping**. The not-for-profit gift store in the *Alaska Native Medical Center*, on Third Ave and Gambell St, has a fine selection of authentic native crafts for sale, including jackets and moccasins (Mon–Fri 10am–2pm). For a non-garish shirt, head for the gift shop in the *4th Avenue Theatre*, 630 W Fourth Ave.

Originally a firebreak for the townsite, downtown's **Delaney Park**, running parallel to Ninth Avenue from A to P streets, also served as an airstrip and golf course. Today it's a popular spot to play baseball, tennis, soccer and basketball, or simply to hang out. West of the city the almost eerie tranquillity of **Earthquake Park**, at the end of Northern Lights Blvd, offers restorative views of the mountains, and an interpretive display provides an inkling of the havoc wrought by the 1964 earthquake.

Just fifteen minutes' drive north or east from Anchorage, the mountains and lakes of the 495,000-acre **Chugach State Park** make for great moose-spotting territory. Challenging trails traversing the park include an often treacherous scramble to the summit of 4500-foot Flattop Mountain, a spectacular vantage point from which to view the city and Cook Inlet. Half-day rafting trips in the adjacent Eagle River Valley are operated by *Eagle River Raft Trips* (☎333-3001; $40).

Accommodation

Inexpensive accommodation in Anchorage can be hard to find, especially in summer, and many places are reserved months in advance. Downtown, the hotels are nearly all prohibitively expensive from June to September, though at other times they reduce their price by as much as half. The most convenient campgrounds are *Lion's Campground*, half a mile south on Boniface Hwy from the Glenn Hwy and, a little further out, *Centennial Park* (☎333-9711), five miles north on Glenn Hwy. Free B&B reservation services include *Stay With A Friend*

(☎258-4036), *AAAB&B* (☎346-2533), and *Alaska Sourdough B&B Association* (☎563-6244).

Alaskan Samovar Inn, 720 Gambell St (☎277-1511). No-nonsense mid-priced motel. ④.

Anchorage Hotel, 330 E St (☎277-4483 or 1-800/544-0988). Small historic hotel that survived the earthquake. ⑦.

Anchorage International Hostel, 700 H St (☎276-3635). Welcoming, cozy, and very central, a block south of the Transit Center, the only gripes being the afternoon lockout and midnight curfew. Dorm beds for $10 for members, $13 for non-members – reserve well ahead in the summer. The managers also run a hostel at 2845 W 42nd St in the Spenard district (☎248-4691). ①.

Anchor Arms Motel, 433 Eagle St (☎272-9619). Budget motel offering two-room suites, some with kitchenettes, in the heart of downtown. ④.

Best Western Barratt Inn, 4616 Spenard Rd (☎243-3131 or 1-800/528-1234). Large motel with restaurant and lounge, close to the airport and Spenard district. Free 24-hour airport shuttle. ⑤.

Chelsea Inn, 3836 Spenard Rd (☎276-5002). Clean and friendly hotel on the edge of Spenard district, with free breakfast. Rooms with and without baths. ④.

Comfort Inn Heritage Suites, 111 W Warehouse Ave (☎277-6887). New hotel next to the train station and overlooking the combat fishing zone of Ship Creek. ⑥.

Inlet Inn, 539 H St (☎277-5541). Spotless small motel right downtown. ④.

Little Blue House B&B, 327 E 15th St (☎274-2583). Small rooms, few frills, but close to downtown. ③.

Sixth and B B&B, 145 W Sixth Ave (☎279-5292). Downtown Thirties home. Free use of bicycles. ④.

Snowline B&B, 11101 Snowline Drive (☎346-1631). Tucked into a quiet hillside area, twenty minutes from downtown. Continental breakfast served on outside deck. ④.

Eating

Anchorage is home to countless fast-food joints and snack bars, with plenty of small, reasonably priced cafés downtown. The best of its **restaurants**, however, are along L Street overlooking the Inlet. Cheaper ethnic food is also excellent.

Cyrano's Bookstore and Café, 413 D St (☎274-2599). Sandwiches, soups, occasional live entertainment, free papers and taped classical music in a lively bookstore (open until 2am on Saturday).

Downtown Deli, 525 W Fourth Ave (☎274-0027). Old Anchorage institution; not particularly cheap for a deli (entrees start at $7), but serving bagels and pastrami to rival New York's best.

Dynasty, 420 G St (☎279-4745). First-class Mandarin and Szechuan dishes for around ten bucks.

The Federal Building Cafeteria, Eighth and D St entrance (☎277-6736). Almost as bland as downtown's *Wendy's*, *BK* and *McDonald's*, but better value and more filling. Breakfast and lunch only.

Hogg Brothers Café, 2421 Spenard Ave (☎976-9649). Hectic diner blasting out country music while it serves big breakfasts and burgers.

Legal Pizza, 1034 W Fourth Ave (☎274-0686). Decent pizza and pasta, plus live acoustic acts.

Maharaja's, 328 G St (☎272-2233). Excellent Indian cuisine, with an all-you-can-eat lunch buffet, though quite pricey in the evening.

Simon and Seaforts, 420 L St (☎274-3502). One of the best of the mid-priced restaurants, with gorgeous views over the Inlet and wondrous seafood from around $15. Reservations recommended.

Thai Cuisine, 444 H St (☎277-8424). The best of Anchorage's many oriental restaurants.

Entertainment and nightlife

Good bars abound in downtown Anchorage, and the atmosphere varies as much as the clientele. Late at night, the main drag of **Fourth Avenue** can seem like a surreal slalom course as you swerve to avoid the terminally drunk. The other sleazy area – **Spenard**, on Spenard Rd between Northern Lights Blvd and International Airport Rd – can be fun as long as you're careful, though new hotels in the locality mean more tourists are making tracks to the better bars and clubs. Women travellers may not find the wilder side of macho Anchorage quite as endearing as many locals seem to think it is, with numerous innocent-looking bars turning out to be strip joints.

Not much can lure Alaskans indoors during the summer, so there are few summer performances, but for the rest of the year, the *Center for Performing Arts* (☎263-2787) has a huge variety of shows, plays, opera and concerts. The *Anchorage Opera* (☎279-2557) performs tragedies from late September to early October, operettas from late January to early February, and musicals at the beginning of April. In the summer, the *ACRO Theater*, 700 G Ave, has free film shows about Alaska's history and Native culture (Tues & Thurs 2pm & 3pm; ☎263-4545). *Cyrano's Cinema*, part of the restaurant and bookstore at 413 D St (see above), shows foreign and classic movies ($4; ☎274-0064). A giant screen in the glorious Art Deco *4th Avenue Theatre*, 630 W Fourth Ave (☎257-5650; free), shows Alaskana films throughout the day and a classic movie each night at 11pm.

For further details of happenings in town, call the events line on ☎263-2901.

Chilkoot Charlie's, 2435 Spenard Rd (☎272-1010). Anchorage's busiest bar; a huge, sawdust-on-the-floor, wild-time kind of place. Six bars, live music, standard bar food and lunchtime specials. "We screw the other guy and pass the savings on to you!"

Darwin's Theory, 426 G St (☎277-5322). Good, friendly downtown bar with appealing prices.

Downbeat, 3230 Seward Hwy (☎274-2328). Students' hangout underneath a restaurant, with unusually good music for this part of the world.

Jens's, 36th Ave and Arctic St (☎561-5367). Trendy, arty café-bar, south of downtown.

South of Anchorage

Besides stopping to peek at Alaska's most visited sight, the **Portage Glacier**, or driving to catch the ferry in **Whittier**, most people speed along **Turnagain Arm** south from Anchorage on the Seward Highway, believing this area lies too close to the big city to be the "true" Alaska. What they miss are some great trails, the **beluga whale lookout** at Mile 16.7 (best in midsummer) and the outdoors pursuits around **Alyeska ski resort** in **Girdwood**.

Girdwood

All that stands on the original site of **GIRDWOOD**, 37 miles south of Anchorage and destroyed by the 1964 earthquake, is an ordinary strip mall. The village now lies two miles inland in the shade of the **Alyeska ski resort**, Alaska's largest winter sports complex and the lowest-elevation ski resort in the world – Mount Alyeska's 3160-foot summit rises from just 270 feet above sea level. Until 1993 *Alyeska* resembled one of the small municipal resorts in the Rockies, but a huge investment from its Japanese owners has given it many new downhill runs, a first-class hotel and an extensive night-skiing operation. If a ski holiday in Alaska doesn't appeal, three facts about *Alyeska* may change your mind: snowfall can be as high as 750 inches, temperatures usually stay in the thirties, and it's one of the few major ski areas in the Northwest to be blessed with the visual show of the aurora borealis (see p.474).

In summer, this is prime mountain biking terrain, and *Alyeska*'s new aerial tram ($15) provides access to a stunning view of Turnagain Arm and **hiking trails**. However the best trek in the area, the three-and-a-half mile Crow Creek Trail, begins beyond the resort at the end of scenic unpaved Crow Creek Road and passes old mine works, alpine lakes, pallid mountains and Dall sheep breeding grounds.

Great-value **flightseeing** trips are run by *Alpine Air Guides* (☎783-2360); a one-hour tour costing $45 sweeps through the Girdwood valley and out over Turnagain Arm, incorporating a glacier landing. *Class V Whitewater* (☎783-2004), in a hut next to *7-Eleven*, run exhilarating wildwater rafting adventures from $75 for five hours.

Practicalities
Rooms and packages at the resort's superb *Prince Hotel* (☎783-2222; winter ⑧; summer ⑥), are complemented by half a dozen good restaurants. Not far away, *Alyeska AYH Hostel*, right on Timberline and right again on Alpina (☎783-2099; ①), has six beds for $9 in the loft of a lodge, while the nearby *Alyeska B&B* (☎783-1222; ⑥), offers luxury suites with outdoor decks in a beautiful cedar home. *Alyeska Accommodations* (☎783-2000) handle bookings for condos for $100 and up.

The best inexpensive **food** is the innocuous-looking *Lyon's Cafe and Bakery* (☎783-2000), on the Girdwood strip mall next to *7-Eleven*. Locals salivate when they talk about the Cajun food at the *Double Musky Inn* (☎783-2822) on Crow Creek Rd; budget on $30 a head. *Max's Bar* next door is lively at night.

Portage Glacier

Eleven miles south of Girdwood, a five-mile road leads to **PORTAGE GLACIER**, popular with tour buses not so much for being Alaska's most stupendous glacier, as for its proximity to Anchorage. Frustratingly, you can't see the glacier from the parking lot; if you want to get face-to-face with it you'll have to pay *Gray Line* $20 for a place on a cruise boat.

At the fascinating **visitor center** (May–Sept 9am–7pm; ☎783-2326), made memorable by its mock-up walk-through ice cave, an observation deck looks out onto iceberg-packed Portage Lake. Rangers lead hikes to search for tiny wriggly brown **ice worms** in the smaller Byron Glacier every Tuesday and Friday in summer at 7pm. The two USFS **campgrounds** ($6), a mile from the visitor center, are not surprisingly, very popular; try to get a place at *Willawaw Creek*, next to a salmon spawning observation deck and a number of beaver dams.

Whittier

Alaska Railroad trains to the port of **WHITTIER**, on the Prince William Sound, leave from a station one mile north of the glacier road turnoff on the Seward Highway (three round trips daily in summer). Take a good look at the landscape while you wait; this used to be the site of Portage town, until the 1964 earthquake dropped the level of the land by around eight feet and the area was flooded. The heavy silt deposited by the high tides makes the remaining buckled, twisted and abandoned buildings appear to be sinking, while trees stand stripped bare, killed by the onrush of saltwater.

There are no roads to Whittier; only if you plan to catch a ferry (any day but Monday) to Valdez or Cordova, is it worth taking the half-hour train ride. However, if your itinerary does bring you through, a quick trek reveals perhaps the strangest town in a state of strange towns. A mere handful of settlers eked out a living here, until the US government knocked tunnels through two massive mountains during World War II to link Whittier – and Prince William Sound – to Anchorage by rail. The army constructed a major port and fuelling station, housing its personnel in grim grey utilitarian buildings such as the landmark fourteen-story **Begich Towers**, now fitted out as apartments. As a result, most of the inhabitants of this remote outpost live in high-rise housing.

If you're unlucky to have missed your ferry connection, the town's two **motels**, the *Sportsman's Inn* (☎472-2352; ④) and the *Anchor Inn* (☎472-2354; ④) offer reasonable rooms. Both serve food, as do a number of small cafés by the harbor.

The Kenai Peninsula

Beyond Portage, Seward Highway cuts off from the south shore of Turnagain Arm to cross the **Kenai Peninsula** en route to Seward – with the Sterling Highway branching off west after about forty miles, for the trip across the peninsula to Cook Inlet. At over nine thousand square miles, the peninsula is larger than many states in the Lower 48, and offers an endless diversity of activities and scenery. Most of the major communities are accessible by public transportation, including **Homer**, at the end of the Sterling Highway. Cruises leave this artsy little town for glorious **Kachemak Bay State Park**, while on the east coast, **Seward** is the base for boat trips into the inspirational **Kenai Fjords National Park**.

Throughout the peninsula, trails branch off all along the main highways, providing excellent hiking in the **Kenai Mountains**; the four-day **Resurrection Trail** begins at the gold-mining village of **Hope**, and comes out on the Sterling Highway near the rafting center of **Cooper's Landing**.

Most Alaskans who come to the Kenai Peninsula do so to **fish**. Cast aside preconceptions of this as a tranquil activity – "combat fishing", when thousands of anglers stand elbow to elbow along the Kenai, Russian and Kasilof rivers, is intense stuff, and it takes strength and know-how to pull in a thirty-pound king salmon. Campgrounds along the rivers fill up fast, but in July and August hungry bears join in the fun and games, and most opt to stay elsewhere. Frequently changing regulations limit fishing; call the Department of Fish and Game in Juneau (☎344-0541) before you set out.

Hope

It's a good idea to swing off the busy Seward Highway, fourteen miles south of Portage, and take the paved 18-mile road that leads to the special little hamlet of **HOPE** (pop. 224), where photogenic old log buildings line a dirt main street that ends abruptly at tidal flats. Part of the original town stood on this sandy wasteland until the 1964 earthquake caused a seven-foot subsidence – the area remains unstable, so avoid walking on it.

Hope witnessed a minor boom when gold was discovered in nearby Resurrection Creek, and by 1895 as many as 3000 prospectors lived here. Most left for the Yukon during the ensuing years, but mining was still a significant employer until the Forties. Today only a few small-scale operations survive, though hundreds of tourists try their luck each year.

Other than its laid-back charm and beauty, Hope has no attractions as such, though a museum is in the offing as soon as locals get round to completing it. The town is a favorite spot for local anglers, who fish right downtown, but hikers and mountain bikers are, if anything, even better catered for. Starting just south of town, unpaved **Palmer Creek Road**, usually passable by car between late May and September, putters uphill for seven miles to the lovely six-site **Coeur d'Alene campground**. From here on you'll need a 4WD to complete the remaining five miles to the abandoned Swetmann mining camp. East of the camp, a steep **trail** leads to a hanging valley with small lakes – in midsummer the area bursts into bloom with paintbrush, columbine, monkshood and many more varieties of wildflower. Alaskan scenery doesn't get much better than this and there are usually lots of moose on view.

Near the start of Palmer Creek Road, another dirt track branches off to the right for 3.6 miles to the **Resurrection Creek Pass trailhead**. The often gruelling Resurrection hiking trail slinks up and over timberline for 38 miles to Cooper's Landing at Mile 52.3 Sterling Hwy. On foot it's a three- to four-day affair, but skilled mountain bikers can do it in a day. Several campsites line the route as well as eight cabins (bookable on ☎224-3374; ①). Two much easier trails originate at **Porcupine Campground** ($6), a mile north of town, to give great views of Turnagain Arm.

The *Seaview Bar, Café & Motel* on Main (☎782-3364; ① & ②) can look after virtually all your needs, providing clean, very basic accommodation. The owner, a keen local historian, is able to fill you in on information, and the café serves inexpensive food including an all-you-can eat barbecue for $9 on Friday and Saturday.

Seward

SEWARD, 127 miles south of Anchorage, straight down the Seward Highway, sprang to life in 1903 after engineers declared this ice-free port the ideal starting point for railroad tracks to the Interior. Since then it has been an important freight terminal, but tourism – particularly cruises into **Kenai Fjords National Park** – is now its most conspicuous business.

Seward fronts onto a classic view of the Gulf of Alaska, and is ringed by glaciers and mountains. In 1909 two pioneers bet each other to run up and down 3022-foot **Mount Marathon**; this masochistic dare has developed into an annual Fourth of July race (current record 43 minutes, 23 seconds). Most athletes accomplish the descent in ten minutes by launching themselves down the sleep slope on their butts. A good hiking trail leads to the top for a glorious view, but unlike the runners, you should allow on four hours to complete the trip. Other than that, Seward's main activities are enjoying the scenery, mingling in the busy small boat harbor, and drinking in the downtown bars.

THE GOOD SHIP MV TUSTEMENA

Although the *Alaska Marine Highway*'s southwestern ferry network is less travelled than the Inside Passage route, their ships, particularly the **MV Tustemena**, cruise arguably more fascinating scenery.

From its home port of **Seward**, the "Trusty Tusty" travels regularly to Valdez, Kodiak, Port Lions, Seldovia and Homer. Approximately eight times each summer, it makes the trip out along the Aleutian Chain as far as **Dutch Harbor/Unalaska**. This two-and-a-half-day westward voyage is not one for the faint-hearted – notoriously stormy weather causes many a stomach to churn. However, you don't have to go that far to enjoy some great marine views. The ten-hour trip west from Valdez to Seward chugs alongside whales and porpoises, past the Columbia Glacier (p.525), the tight Bainbridge Passage and, just north of Seward, craggy Resurrection Cape on the Barwell Island kittiwake rookery. The deep fjords of Kenai Fjords National Park make a fitting start for the journey to Kodiak, while the approach to Homer includes the packed rookeries in Kachemak Bay.

If you've come up from Bellingham by ferry and want more maritime travel in south central Alaska, take an *Alaska Airlines* jet from Juneau to Cordova, jump on the MV *Bartlett* to Valdez and hook up with the *Tustemena*.

Kenai Fjords National Park

Beginning just west of Seward, **KENAI FJORDS NATIONAL PARK** is a magnificent 670,000-acre region of peaks, glaciers and craggy coastline. Its towering mountains are mantled by the prodigious seven-hundred-square-mile Harding Icefield, whose retreating glaciers have cut out the dramatic fjords for which the park is named.

Eight tidewater glaciers "calve" icebergs into the sea with thunderous booms, and the fjords also hold a wealth of **marine wildlife** – sea otters, porpoises, harbor seals, stellar sea lions, plus gray, humpback, killer and minke whales – as well as the **seabird rookeries** on the cliffs of the Chiswell Islands. The best of the full-day **cruises** from Seward is conducted aboard the new boats of *Kenai Coastal Tours* (☎1-800/770-9119; $99 including lunch). If you fancy some backcountry **hiking**, *Miller's Landing* (☎224-5739) run charter boats to remote areas of the park.

Exit Glacier, down a rough dirt road which starts at Mile 3.7 Seward Hwy, is the one section of the park you can see without spending lots of money. From the ranger station at the end of the track, a half-mile stroll leads to the glacier, though if you want a more strenuous day you can walk a very steep, slippery three-mile trail to the edge of the Harding Icefield. The effort is rewarded with an adjective-defying vantage point looking out over isolated mountain peaks – **nunataks** – which interrupt the flat, pristine-white surface of the icefield.

The park's **visitor center**, in Seward's harbor, offers maps, film shows and hiking details (summer daily 8am–7pm; winter Mon–Fri 8am–5pm; ☎224-3175).

Practicalities

Alaska Railroad trains wind their way through wild rocky terrain on a daily four-hour journey from Anchorage to Seward, arriving at the depot (☎224-5550) next to the tour boats. **Marine Highway ferries** linking Valdez and Kodiak dock downtown (☎224-5485). *Seward & Homer Bus Lines* charge $32 for a one-way ride from Anchorage.

Seward's two hubs of activity, the harbor and downtown, are connected by the mile-long Fourth Avenue; if you don't feel like walking, jump on the local **trolley** (☎224-3133; $1) which also goes out as far as Exit Glacier Road. The main **visitor center** is at Mile 2, Seward Hwy (summer, daily 8am–5pm; ☎224-8051). You can also get information at the old railroad car on Third and Jefferson, though opening times can be erratic. The US Forest Service office at Fourth and Jefferson (☎224-3374) provides details on trails, campsites and cabins in the Chugach National Forest.

A couple of downtown **hotels** offer good value for money; the *New Seward Hotel*, 217 Fifth Ave (☎224-8001; ④), is the clean, unmodernized, shared-bathroom part of the plush *Best Western*, and offers a great line of kitsch toiletries, while the historic *Van Gilder Hotel* is at 308 Adams St (☎224-3079; ④ and ⑤). Out on Exit Glacier Road, the relaxing *Le Barn Appetite B&B* (☎224-8706), has rooms in a big rustic barn, and a superb café serving fresh crepes, quiches and deli sandwiches. The one **hostel** – the *Snow River AYH*, Box 425, Seward AK 99664 – is way out at Mile 16 Seward Hwy and has no phone. The most central place to **camp** is along the waterfront between the harbor and downtown.

Cafés and **restaurants** in Seward are reasonably priced. *Ray's Waterfront Bar and Grill*, by the harbor (☎224-3012), provides stunning views and big steak and seafood dinners for around $20 per person. *Breeze Inn* (☎224-5237), across the street, has tasty bar meals. Good food downtown can be found at the *Harbor Dinner Club* on Fifth Ave (☎224-3012), while *Niko's*, 133 Fourth Ave, do inexpensive burritos and pizza.

West from Seward

Although it takes barely more than ninety minutes to drive from Seward to the west coast, the route holds enough hiking trails, boating lakes and campgrounds to occupy several days. The most enjoyable stretch along the **Sterling Highway**, beginning 35 miles north of Seward, cuts through high mountains, luxuriant rainforest and parallels the Kenai River for many miles. Strung out along the curving road, **COOPER'S LANDING** encompasses numerous cafes, lodges and a small historic district, at Mile 48.7, but is best known as the launching place for **raft trips** through some glorious whitewater. Three-hour float trips cost around $40, while all-day whitewater runs will set you back $80; companies include *Alaska Rivers Co* (☎595-1226). Some thirty miles along, the small town of **Sterling** is a reasonable pit stop; *Rüdiger Thiele's* comfy and friendly **hostel**, charging $10 per night, is on Spruce Lane, Mile 76.5 Sterling Hwy (☎262-8546; ①).

The Kenai and Russian rivers are famous for their summer salmon runs, but the main base for anglers – **SOLDOTNA**, 95 miles from Seward – is a dire sort of a place with few redeeming features.

Kenai

KENAI, the peninsula's largest town and an important oil refining center, looks out over a spectacular view of the Cook Inlet, 106 miles from Seward on the Sterling Highway. The site of one of the region's oldest European settlements, Kenai celebrated its bicentennial in 1991. The town's few remaining historic buildings include the triple-domed 1846 Holy Assumption Orthodox Church (rebuilt in 1896), the 1886 Parish House, and the 1906 St Nicholas Chapel, all of which congregate along the curving dirt tracks of Old Kenai at Main and Mission streets. Within a stone's throw, the **Beluga Whale Lookout** offers the best view out over the inlet: on the far shore stands the active **Mount Redoubt volcano**, which last erupted in 1989, sending an ash cloud seven miles in the air.

Other than that, the main attraction is the **Bicentennial Visitors and Cultural Center** at the corner of Main St and N Kenai Hwy, which incorporates a reasonably sized museum that is especially strong on the town's murky Russian history (daily Mon–Fri 9am–5pm; extended weekend hours in summer; ☎283-1991). Kidnapping, assault, rape and murder of natives eventually earned the *Russian American Company* foreman in Kenai a recall to Russia to stand trial. Avenging Iliamma warriors killed several whites, including Father Juvenaly, a hapless Orthodox priest, and in the end relations were only soothed after Alexander Baranov (a company manager at Kodiak) married the daughter of a local chief.

The uncrowded **Captain Cook State Recreation Area**, 25 miles north at the end of N Kenai Rd, comprises a couple of pleasantly secluded campgrounds, a swimming area along the shores of Stormy Lake and great hiking trails along the sandy inlet beach.

Practicalities

Seward & Homer Bus Lines (see p.489) serve Kenai from Anchorage ($32 one-way) and Homer ($35 return). The **visitor center** is at 402 Overland at Main (spring & fall Mon–Fri 9am–5pm; summer Mon–Fri 9am–5pm & Sat–Sun 10am–4pm; ☎283-7989). **Accommodation** in Kenai is expensive, with options including the *Merit Inn*, 260 S Willow St (☎283-6131 or 1-800/227-6131; ⑥), the *Katmai Hotel*, 10800 Kenai Spur Hwy (☎283-6101; ⑥), and *Kenai King's Inn*, 10352 Spur Hwy (☎283-6060; ⑥). The visitor center has a list of local **B&Bs**; otherwise the only budget option is *North Star Lodge* (☎776-5259; ①–③), halfway out toward the Captain Cook SRA. Housed in an old roadhouse, thoroughly modernized in 1993, it now boasts a good café, dorm beds ($10) and basic cabins ($30); despite its

---

SALMON

"The Kings Are In". Such signs alert anglers throughout Alaska that their most prized catch – the **king** (or chinook) **salmon** – has arrived. Weighing in at an average of thirty pounds, kings grow biggest in the Kenai River, where the Alaska sport record of 97 pounds 4 ounces was taken.

In all, five different types of salmon swim up Alaska's rivers – and just to confuse matters, locals refer to each of them by two names. Besides the king/chinook, there are **red** or **sockeye** (considered the best tasting); **silver** or **coho**, the second largest variety, though the record catch is a mere 26 pounds; **pink** or **humpback**, used mostly for canning or smoking; and the ugly sibling of the family, the **dog** or **chum** salmon, which few admit to eating.

Even if you've never cast a line in your life, the temptation to go fishing, fuelled by adverts, invitations and general piscatorial banter, is quite likely to overtake you. The prime season for salmon runs from June to August, with complex sets of rules governing when and where you can fish. You'll need a licence ($30 for 14 days or $50 per year), plus an additional $20 permit if you're after king salmon. Nearly all sporting goods stores in the state sell fishing licenses.

location, right opposite a huge oil refinery, you can count on a good and inexpensive night's sleep free from noise or nasty aromas. The best **place to eat** in town, *Paradisos*, on Main next to the visitor center (☎283-2222), serves Mexican, Greek and seafood dishes.

South to Homer

The eighty or so miles of highway south to Homer hug the coast of the Cook Inlet, studded with charming fishing villages and magnificent views. Try to allow half a day for the journey, and leave Kenai on the quiet **Kalifonsky Beach Road**, which joins up with the busier Sterling Highway 25 miles south at **Kasilof**. Nine miles further on, **Clam Gulch State Recreation Area** offers camping, beaches and good clamming (licence required) between May and August. **Ninilchik State Recreation Area**, a further seventeen miles along in the shadow of the eponymous town's bluff-top Russian Orthodox Church, provides similar opportunities. The picturesque community of **ANCHOR POINT**, sixteen miles before Homer, bills itself as the most westerly point on the US highway system, and has the signpost to prove it at the end of River Road.

Homer

At the end of the Sterling Highway, **HOMER**, 226 miles from Anchorage, is the Kenai Peninsula's southernmost town to be accessible by road. It commands a truly magnificent setting, tucked beneath gently sloping verdant bluffs with a five-mile finger of land – **The Spit** – slinking out into the dark waters of Kachemak Bay, into which flow crystal-blue glacial streams, framed by dense black forest. It's so appealing that you can almost forgive the tourist board for billing it as the "Shangri-La of Alaska", while its activities and lively nightlife make this a place to scrap your itinerary and linger a few days.

Russians, drawn by the abundance of coal, were the first whites to reach the area, and by the mid-nineteenth-century, several American companies had followed suit. In 1896, **Homer Pennock**, a gold-seeker from Michigan (who dreamed of riding back home on a golden chariot), set up the community that still bears his name. For some years, every summer, young people from the Lower 48 have arrived here in droves to work on the halibut boats or in the cannery, though this tradition may disappear with the recent decline in the price and quantity of salmon in Alaska.

Homer's other main industry, **tourism**, is under no such threat. Due to its dramatic surroundings and "mild" winters (temperatures average 20–30°F), visitors flock to this pretty fishing village. The resident population, younger and more cosmopolitan than elsewhere in the state, support a thriving arts community.

Arrival, information and getting around

The *Alaska Marine Highway* office (Mon–Fri 9am–1pm; ☎235-8849) stands at the end of the Spit; **ferries** usually go to to Seldovia, Kodiak and Seward once a week and to the Aleutian Islands around eight times per summer. *Seward & Homer Bus Lines* run a daily service from Anchorage via Kenai/Soldotna for under $70 round-trip. *ERA*, *Southcentral Air* and *Mark Air* operate regular flights to

Anchorage for around $75 one way, from the **airport** two miles east of town on Kachemak Way.

Although small, Homer is quite spread out, and lacks public transit. Most hotels, restaurants and shops are in town, while almost all of the tour operators can be found five miles away along the twee boardwalks of the Spit. Getting a ride between the two seldom poses a problem, and you can rent mountain bikes from *Quiet Sports*, 141 W Pioneer Ave (☎235-8620). The main **visitor center** is on the Spit (summer, daily 9am–9pm; ☎235-5300). KBBI (890 AM) broadcast a "Bush Line", useful for offering or requesting rides.

The Town

The downtown **Pratt Museum**, 3779 Bartlett St, features high-quality works by local craftspeople, as well as Inuit and Indian artefacts, aquariums and historic Homer oddities (daily 10am–6pm; $3). Many of Homer's most popular activities, however, revolve around the **Spit**. A large proportion of the Alaskans who visit each summer come for the excellent **halibut fishing** in the "Halibut Capital of the World". These large, tasty flat fish average around fifty to one hundred pounds, but have been known to come in at over three hundred pounds; a full day's excursion with any of dozens of charter companies costs from $125. If you don't mind joining the crowds, it's cheaper and simpler to visit the **Fishing Hole**, a tiny bight on the Spit, which is stocked with salmon and offers good fishing from mid-May to mid-September. During July and August, digging for **razor clams** is a fun thing to do – regulations state you must buy a fishing licence and can keep no more than sixty of these delicious molluscs.

Skyline Drive, which runs along the top of a bluff above the town, offers glorious views of glaciers spilling into Kachemak Bay; the twenty-odd miles of the dead-end **East End Road** provide similarly good views.

Accommodation

Homer's good-value hotels and B&Bs can be fully booked in midsummer, but the visitor center on the Spit (☎235-5300) can help. There's **camping** in town, across Kachemak Bay, or on the Spit. The $3 fee for camping on the Spit doesn't seem to apply to the beach across from the *Sawlty Dog Saloon* (see below) known as "tent city", where a large summer community of "Spit-rats" resides while working in the canneries or on the boats. However most people soon get fed up with the noise, wind and fishy smells, and relocate to sites such as those run by the *Ocean Shores Motel* and *Seaside Farm*.

Driftwood Inn, 135 W Bunnel Ave (☎235-0019 or 1-800/478-8019). Homer's most pleasant motel, near downtown on the edge of the bay. Barbecue and shellfish cookouts, and a good bar opposite. ④.

Heritage Hotel, 147 E Pioneer Ave (☎235-7787 or 1-800/478-7789 in AK). Central log-built hotel; rooms without baths in the original wing, or in the extension with full facilities. ③ and ⑤.

Ocean Shores Motel, 3500 Crittenden Ave (☎235-7775). Attractive colony of lodges, cabins and huts spread over a four-acre seafront site, just off downtown. ③.

Pioneer B&B, 243 Pioneer Ave (☎235-5670). Central self-contained rooms, lots of amenities. ④.

Seaside Farm, 58335 East End Rd (☎235-7850). Lively atmosphere and a great place to meet backpackers. Clean dorms $12 a night, tent sites $6, with discount for long stays. You can also work off part of the cost by doing some work on the farm. Five miles out of town but lifts are no problem. ①.

Eating and drinking

Downtown Homer offers some of the best meal deals for budget travellers in Alaska: all-you-can-eat specials are the order of the day. For nightlife, head for the colorful bars, or to the relaxed *Pier One Theatre* (☎235-7333), next to the fishing hole on the Spit (May–Sept only), where Tom Bodett, the voice behind those catchy *Motel 6* commercials, usually records his radio show once a week.

Baghdad Café & Books, in the strip mall at 601 E Pioneer Ave (☎235-8787). Arty little coffee shop, owing more to Percy Adler (who made a movie in Alaska) than Saddam Hussein.

Café Cups, 162 W Pioneer Ave (☎235-8330). Good coffee and innovative cuisine.

Fresh Sourdough Express Bakery and Café, 1316 Ocean Drive (☎235-7571). Tasty breads and pastries, plus all-you-can-eat breakfast for $10.

Lands End Resort, at the end of the Spit (☎235-2500). Plush and pricey restaurant offering an absolutely wonderful view of the bay. Breakfast is a must.

Sawlty Dog Saloon, the Spit (☎235-9990). It's hard to miss this Homer landmark; a log-built bar with a lighthouse tower, at the end of the Spit. Rowdy, raucous and fun.

Smoky Bay Co-op Natural Food Store, Pioneer Ave and Bartlett St (☎235-7242). Wholefood shop and café with great lunches from $5.

Young's, 565 E Pioneer Ave (☎235-4002). One of the best and least expensive all-you-can-eat Chinese (with a Japanese twist) buffets that you're likely to find anywhere.

Kachemak State Park

The prime tourist attraction in the Homer area is exploring the 250,000 acres of forested mountains, glaciers, pristine fjords and inlets that comprise **Kachemak Bay State Park**, directly across the bay from Homer. Bird species here include puffin, auklets, kittiwakes and storm-petrels, and marine creatures such as seals, sea otters and whales are plentiful. *Rainbow Tours* (☎235-7272) operate two-hour sightseeing cruises to **Gull Island** – a 15,000-strong rookery. However, a longer stay reaps its rewards. The area's best trails, most of them manageable in a day, originate from the gorgeous hamlet of **Halibut Cove**. The most-travelled route, up to **Grewingk Glacier**, is an easy three-and-a-half-mile trek above the spruce and cottonwood forest to the foot of the glacier, from where you get splendid views of the bay.

The *Danny J* ferry (☎235-7847) makes two daily trips to Halibut Cove, on the south shore of the bay, via Gull Island rookery, for around $35 return, while *Central Charters* (☎1-800/478-7847) run several excursions. Pick up maps and information from the **Alaska National Marine Wildlife Refuge**, 202 Pioneer Ave in Homer (☎235-6546), which also features informative displays on birds and marine mammals. The Alaska Department of Natural Resources, which maintains the park, has stations in Homer (☎235-7024) and Herring Cove (no phone).

Halibut Cove

Reachable only by boat or floatplane, the park's sole settlement, **HALIBUT COVE** (pop. 50), nestles on high pilings in a postcard-pretty spruce-lined cove. In the Twenties, this was a thriving herring-curing village with close on one thousand residents, but today it functions as a secluded artists' colony. A good few hours can be spent browsing round the excellent **galleries**, chilling out on the rustic boardwalk, or eating **gourmet seafood** at the pricey but good *Saltry* restaurant (☎296-2223). You can't camp in the village and other **accommodation** is expensive; if money's no problem try *Halibut Cove Cabins* (☎235-7847; ⑨) or *Quiet Place Lodge B&B* (☎296-2212; ⑦).

Seldovia

Sixteen miles southwest of Homer across Kachemak Bay, the tiny fishing village of **SELDOVIA** basks in isolation. The community dwindled in importance after the Sterling Highway was extended to Homer in the Fifties, and a further setback came in 1964 when the earthquake raised sea level by four feet and obliterated much of the town. Today only a small portion of the old boardwalk remains, though one structure that emerged unharmed was the 1891 **St Nicholas Russian Orthodox Church**, high on the hill overlooking the harbor (daily 1–2pm). The village also boasts good **hiking trails**, an interesting secondhand bookstore and a small museum in the Seldovia Native Association building.

Most visitors to Seldovia spend just a few hours here on a half-day trip from Homer via Gull Island, operated by *Alaska Maritime Tours* (☎235-2490; $50). The *Marine Highway*'s *MV Tustemena* (see p.514) also stops here once a week en route between Homer and Kodiak. If you're staying over for some hiking or fishing, the best option is to **camp** for $2.50 at Ocean Park; register at the City Office by the dock.

Other **accommodation** options include the fairly basic *Seldovia Lodge* (☎234-7654; ③), the *Rowing Club Inn B&B*, on the boardwalk (☎234-7614; ⑤), and *Annie McKenzie's Boardwalk Hotel* (☎234-7818; ⑤), which also offers money-saving packages from Homer. On Main Street, the *Kachemak Kafe* (☎234-7494) serves up good inexpensive breakfast and lunch, while the *Centurion Restaurant* (☎234-7676) offers reasonable seafood dinners. For **information**, call into *Synergy Art Works* on Main Street, or phone ☎234-7816.

Kodiak Island

With thick spruce forests sprinkled along its indented coast and a rocky interior carpeted by wild grasses studded with marshes, lumpy knolls and reeded lakes, **KODIAK ISLAND** offers some of Alaska's most uncommon and pleasing landscapes. The dominant land mass in a small Gulf of Alaska archipelago some hundred miles south of the Kenai Peninsula, this is the second largest island in the US (after Hawaii's Big Island). Despite its size, no point lies more than fifteen miles from the ocean.

The island is renowned as the home of the **Kodiak bear**, a sub-species of the brown/grizzly which weighs up to 1500 pounds. Streams chock full of spawning salmon allow these monsters to thrive in the **Kodiak National Wildlife Refuge**, covering the southwestern two-thirds of the island. Roughly ten bears inhabit each square mile around Red and Fraser lakes, and bear-watching trips are big business. Apart from the bears, Kodiak provides a favorable habitat for **bald eagles**, and as many as two million seabirds nest along the fjords, bights and bays. Accommodation in nine **wilderness cabins** ($20 a night), dotted throughout the island, is drawn by lottery each year; details from Kodiak NWR, 1390 Buskin River Rd, Kodiak AK 99615 (☎487-2600).

The **Japanese Current** fosters a mild maritime climate along with plenty of rain and fog, creating poor flying conditions and the distinct possibility that your stay could be extended by a day or two. If you want to avoid delays and peak season prices, May and June are notoriously wet but September weather is usually fairly reliable.

Kodiak

All but two thousand of the island's 15,000 human population live in and around its only major town, the likeable and busy fishing port of **KODIAK** on the northeastern tip. Before Russian explorers established a community here in 1792, Aleuts and Konyag had fished the area for millennia. The capital of the tsarist Alaskan territory until 1804, Kodiak survived the transfer of Alaska to the US as a center for trappers, whale-hunters and salmon fishers. In 1939 it was just another sleepy Alaskan village, when a massive war base was created and the population rocketed to around 50,000. Today the government remains the largest single employer; the region's biggest Coastguard operation engages several thousand at its base south of town, and there's also a sizeable US Navy *SEALS* training facility.

However, most of Kodiak's wealth comes from fishing the rich waters of the Gulf, and the town maintains a fleet of over 2750 fishing vessels. Tourism definitely plays second fiddle; few cruise-ships stop, but this bustling little town, with its quality B&Bs, is a good base for exploring the island – and has an energetic nightlife too.

Two natural disasters have left their mark on Kodiak. The 1912 eruption of **Mount Novarupta** in the Katmai Range showered the town with almost two feet of thick black volcanic ash. Most residents had to be evacuated, the clean-up operation took two years, and the ash, especially conspicuous among the tightly bunched trees in Fort Abercrombie State Park, still sticks to your shoes. The force of the 1964 **earthquake** sank the town by four feet and the ensuing tidal wave destroyed canneries, the harbor and many homes.

Arrival, getting around and information

Marine Highway **ferries** on the Seward–Homer route dock once weekly at Center Ave and Marine Way downtown (☎486-3800), taking twelve hours from Homer. Both *Mark Air* and *ERA Aviation* operate daily 45-minute flights from Anchorage (costing around $300 round-trip). *Airporter* vans (☎486-7583) take you the four miles to downtown for $5. *Kodiak Tours* (☎486-5989 or 486-6635) charge $10 for a two-hour "stopover" tour.

Except for Port Lions, which is served by ferry, the most practical way to explore the island is to **fly**; *Uyak Air*'s Kodiak trips (☎486-3407), which guarantee close-up views of bears or your money back, have never had to refund the $300-plus fee. Renting a **car** enables you to get round the town of Kodiak and out along scenic Cape Chiniak Road; most rental companies slap on a 25–30¢ per mile charge, so the unlimited mileage deal offered by *National* (☎456-4751) is the best value. **Cycling** makes a great alternative; *Elkay Bicycle Shop*, 122 W Rezanof Drive (☎486-4219), rent out good bikes. Finally, **kayakers** from all over Alaska try their luck in the surrounding waters; *Wavetamer Kayak Tours* (☎486-2604; reservations preferable) arrange everything from safety-conscious two-hour outings for novices ($35) to blue-water custom expeditions.

The helpful **visitor center** is next to the ferry dock at Center Ave and Marine Way (Mon–Fri 8.30am–5pm and when the ferry is in dock; ☎486-4782).

The Town and around

Downtown Kodiak is usually lively, with plenty of comings and goings in the harbor and the adjacent bars and cafés of Marine Way. The small **Baranov Museum**, in an old Russian house opposite the dock, holds Aleut, Russian and

---

BEARS IN ALASKA

Three types of **bear** – black, brown/grizzly and polar – inhabit Alaska. Of these, the most common is the forest-dwelling **black bear**, found mostly in southeast Alaska, Prince William Sound and in the coastal mountains of south central Alaska. Weighing between 200 and 400 pounds, they can in fact be either jet black or brown. The much larger **grizzlies**, whose habitat covers all of Alaska except for the extreme southeast and far north, can be readily distinguished by their shoulder humps. They range in color from dark brown to blonde, and can weigh anything between 300 and 1500 pounds, depending on their environment; the larger ones tend to be found in coastal regions like Kodiak, where food sources are abundant, while the smaller variety eke out their food from the tundra of places such as Denali National Park. **Polar bears** frequent the pack ice of extreme northern and western Alaska; a healthy adult can scale in at over 1200 pounds.

The entire state of Alaska should be considered "bear country". If you're hiking or camping, it's crucial that you know how to avoid potentially dangerous encounters: talk to a USFS or National Park ranger before you set out, and read the Alaska Department of Fish and Games pamphlet, *Bears and You*, widely available throughout the state. The most important guidelines are given on p.409.

American pioneer artefacts such as some impressive whale bones (summer Mon–Fri 10am–4pm, Sat & Sun noon–4pm; winter Mon–Fri 11am–3pm, Sat & Sun noon–3pm; $1). Housed in St Herman's Theological Seminary, one of only three such institutions in the US, the small and rarely visited **Veniaminov Museum**, 414 Mission Rd, provides fascinating insights into the Orthodox Church and the chance to see a number of ancient icons (open by appointment; ☎486-3524; free).

Fort Abercrombie State Historical Park, etched out of lush rainforest less than four miles north, is a great place to do some seabird- and **whale-watching**, camp or take a shoreline hike: a meadow on the north end provides a dazzling blaze of color in summer. Other manageably brief **hiking trails** originate near town, notaby the steep trails to the top of Pillar and Barometer mountains. However most Kodiak trails are unmaintained and can be confusing: get precise details from the visitor center or the rangers at Fort Abercrombie. The rough and partly paved **Chiniak Highway** runs for 48 miles to Cape Greville and the Road's End Cafe, sweeping through tightly bunched spruce and passing many abandoned World War II defences plus prime vistas of Chiniak Bay.

The **Kodiak National Wildlife Refuge Visitor Center**, just past the airport at 1390 Buskin River Rd (Mon–Fri 8am–4.30pm, Sat & Sun noon–4.30pm; ☎487-2600), stocks a wealth of information on bears and the backcountry.

Accommodation

Most lodging in Kodiak is expensive, but the hotels and B&Bs are generally very good. The best place to **camp** is in Fort Abercrombie State Park, for $6.

Buskin River Inn, 1395 Airport Way (☎487-2700 or 1-800/544-2202). Good independent hotel next to the airport, four miles out. Excellent dining, a good bar and sightseeing packages. ⑥.

Kalsin Bay Inn, Mile 30 Chiniak Hwy (☎486-2659). Small rustic hotel, with a bar, restaurant and pebbly beach, thirty miles from downtown. Reservations advisable. ③.

Kodiak B&B, 308 Hope St (☎486-5367). Overlooking the harbor, and offering fresh-fish breakfasts. ④.

Shelikof Lodge, 211 Thorsheim Ave (☎486-4141). Basic but clean motel rooms downtown. Much better, and not that more expensive than the nearby *Kodiak Star*. ④.

Westmark Inn, 236 S Rezanof Drive (☎486-5712 or 1-800/544-0970). Smart rooms right downtown. ⑥.

Wintel's B&B (☎486-6935). Kodiak's premier B&B. Big yet cosy home overlooking the channel, a twenty-minute walk from downtown. Complimentary fruit basket and a great breakfast. ④.

Eating and drinking

Food in Kodiak is generally good, and not overpriced. Junk food addicts are advised that the town has the only *McDonalds* to serve **"Salmon McNuggets"**; cynics might like to know that they don't taste a lot different from the chicken variety.

Beryl's Sweet Shop, 202 Center Ave (☎486-3323). Known for its great shakes and ice-cream, but also serves good stews, sandwiches and snacks.

Buskin River Inn Restaurant, 1395 Airport Way (☎487-2700). Where the locals go for top-class seafood and steak. Inventive dishes (average $15), big desserts and a long wine list.

Henry's Sports Bar & Café, Marine Way Mall (☎486-2625). Downtown entertainment hub, open from 11am until the fun runs out. Two other bars – the *Mecca* and the *Village* – also put on music.

King's Diner, 1941 Mill Bay Rd (☎486-4100). No-nonsense café popular with locals for its huge portions. Two miles south of downtown.

Road's End, Mile 42 Chiniak Hwy (☎486-2885). Great seafood and steak dinners, snacks and desserts right at the end of the road. Also some rooms upstairs (③).

The Prince William Sound

Prince William Sound, flanked by a largely unspoiled wilderness of steep fjords and mountains, glaciers and rainforest, rests calmly at the head of the Gulf of Alaska. Sheltered by the Chugach Mountains in the north and east, and the Kenai Peninsula to the west, and with its sparkling blue waters populated by whales, porpoise, sea otters and seals, the Sound has a relatively low-key tourist industry. The only significant settlements, spectacular **Valdez**, at the end of the trans-Alaska oil pipeline, and **Cordova**, a modest and untouristy fishing community, are the respective bases from which to see the **Columbia** and **Childs glaciers**. Just behind the Chugach peaks, lies the vast and relatively untramped **Wrangell-St Elias National Park**.

SEA OTTERS

The dog-faced **sea otter** is not only one of the most amusing creatures swimming the waters of Alaska, it's also among the most amazing. Hunted to near extinction in the eighteenth century to satisfy the demands of milliners, they have now bounced back in sufficient numbers to be the curse of mollusc harvesters.

Unlike seals, sea otters possess virtually no body fat; they are protected from the cold by a magnificent coat that has an average of 650,000 hairs per square inch. Apart from humans, they're the only mammal to employ a tool for gathering food. A sea otter will dive down to the sea bed (as deep as 120 feet), with a rock tucked into its armpit, and use it to crack open the shells of its prey.

The region's first settlers, the Chugach Inuit were edged out by the more aggressive Tlingit, who in turn were displaced first by Russian trappers in search of sea otter pelts, and then by American gold prospectors and fishers. The whole marine environment was very nearly scarred for ever on Good Friday 1989, when the **Exxon Valdez** spilt its cargo of crude oil. Although the long-term effects have yet to be fully determined, the spill fortunately affected just twenty percent or so of the Prince William Sound, and so far as the tourist eye is concerned there's no visible damage.

Valdez

VALDEZ, 187 miles by road from Anchorage and the northernmost ice-free port in the Western hemisphere, lies at the head of a fjord that reaches inland twelve miles from Prince William Sound. Known as "Little Switzerland" for its stunning backdrop of steep mountains, glaciers, waterfalls and an annual snowfall of over five hundred inches, Valdez (pronounced *Valdeez*) offers great hiking, fishing and wildlife viewing.

The 1890s **gold rush** transformed Valdez from a remote whaling station into a flourishing settlement, when thousands of prospectors arrived to head up the "Valdez Trail" to the mines in the Yukon and Alaskan Interior. They arrived to find that no trail existed and that the roughly mapped-out all-American route crossed the deadly Valdez and Klutina glaciers. Only an estimated three hundred of the 3500 miners who set out completed the journey – many died from frostbite, exhaustion and falling into steep crevasses. The gold boom passed as miners found alternative routes, and Valdez came to depend on fish canneries, logging companies and occasional military use for its economic survival. Nature conspired to finish it off on Good Friday 1964. The epicenter of North America's largest **earthquake** (see p.506) was just 45 miles away. Shock waves turned the ground to quivering jelly, breaking roads, toppling buildings, and killing 33 residents. A tidal wave completed the devastation. However, the citizens of Valdez refused to be intimidated, and moved around sixty buildings to the more stable present site four miles away, where the "new" Valdez struggled on.

The town's fortunes rose again during the 1970s, when **oil** was found beneath Prudhoe Bay, and Valdez became the southern terminus of the 800-mile **trans-Alaska pipeline**, which carries one and a half million barrels of oil per day. Although winds and tides ensured that no oil from the *Exxon Valdez* made it into the port of Valdez, the spill ironically triggered an economic boom for the city as it was the most accessible site from which to direct the massive **cleanup**. The operation, which lasted into 1991, cost Exxon and the government over one hundred billion dollars. Eleven thousand workers in over one thousand boats and three hundred planes scoured the beaches; the rate for an eighteen-hour day of scrubbing rocks by hand was $24 per hour.

Arrival and information

One of the most exciting things about Valdez is getting here; both car and ferry rides are unforgettable. The turn-off at Glennallen takes you onto the scenic **Richardson Highway** and the remaining 115 miles hold epic scenery: restful alpine meadows, angry-looking waterfalls, mountain **glaciers** and the icy summit of **Thompson Pass**. *Caribou Express* **buses** from Anchorage (daily in summer, otherwise Mon, Wed & Fri) charge $80 one-way. *Alaskon Express* ply the route four times a week in high season for $95, while *Gray Line* makes the trip four or five times weekly, charging around $60 each way (☎835-2357). Many visitors arrive on the **Alaska Marine Highway** from either Whittier or Seward at the city dock at the end of Hazelet Ave (☎835-4436). If the weather is clear, the ride offers superb views of the Columbia Glacier (see below), and a chance to see lots of marine wildlife. The **airport**, with two or three daily flights to Anchorage provided by *ERA/Alaska Airlines* and *Mark Air*, lies five miles east; **taxis** (☎835-2500) are the only way to get downtown. Free tours leave several times per day from the airport's visitor center (☎835-2686); *Gray Line* buses can bring you from downtown for around $10.

The town **visitor center**, at Chenega and Fairbanks, offers a left-luggage service (daily 8am–8pm; ☎835-2330 or 1-800/770-5954).

The Town

Detailed displays on the town's checkered history in the small but excellent **Valdez Museum**, 217 Egan Drive (summer daily 9am–7pm; $2), cover the gold rush, whaling, the earthquake and a rather cheeky account of the oil spill. In addition to barbed comments about the success of the cleanup, look out for the chunk of the *Exxon Valdez* hull in which numerous serrations were cut to make souvenirs in the shape of the ill-fated tanker, and a vial of crude oil – "Do your part to help clean up the spillage!". **Valdez Library**, directly opposite the museum, runs a handy book and magazine swap box.

The **Salmon Spawning Viewpoint** on Crooked Creek, less than a mile out along the Richardson Highway, is a great spot to observe returning salmon in midsummer. Several charter companies on the harbor offer salmon- and halibut-fishing trips (about $120 per person), while *Keystone Rafting* (☎835-2606; $32) can take you down a Class III stretch of the Lowe River, beneath the Bridal Veil Falls and alongside bears fishing for salmon.

Although you only get to see what the company want you to, a nose around the **trans-Alaska pipeline terminal**, eight miles away, on the south side of the bay, is recommended. Crude oil arrives at the terminal after an 800-mile, five-day journey through the 48-inch-diameter pipeline from Prudhoe Bay, to be stored in eighteen huge tanks before being loaded onto ships. Constructed at a cost of $1.4 billion, it's the largest and most expensive facility of its kind in the world.

The Columbia Glacier

Over four miles wide at its face, and towering three hundred feet above the sea, **Columbia Glacier** is particularly spectacular when huge blocks of ice crash into the water. *Alaska Marine Highway* ferries represent the cheapest way to see this calving giant, but local cruise operators tread their way through an iceberg field to achieve a closer look. Experienced operators like *Stan Stephens* (☎835-4730 or 1-800/992-1297) point out such sights as Bligh Reef where the *Exxon Valdez* ran aground, as well as the channel the ship should have been on – there's quite a difference. Choose from an eight-hour cruise, which includes a salmon bake, for $92, and a six-hour cruise at $65.

Accommodation

Valdez has very little inexpensive accommodation, and what there is gets snapped up pretty quickly. A freephone outside the downtown visitor center connects with some of the fifty-plus **B&Bs**, while *"One Call Does It All"* (☎835-

4988 or 1-800/242-4988) or *PWS Central Reservations* (☎835-3717 or 1-800/425-2752) can book accommodation in advance.

If you want to **camp**, the Valdez Glacier Campground, seven miles from town past the airport, is somewhat impractical for those without transport, while the small *Bear Paw* campground (☎835-2372), close to the ferry terminal, is booked up early. An alternative is to join the cannery workers who spend the summer in tents on the appropriately named Hotel Hill, behind the small boat harbor. The park service requires a $5 fee, but often fails to collect. If you have an RV there should be no problem; downtown camper parks include *Eagle's Rest* (☎835-2373).

Casa de la Bellezza B&B, 333 Oumalik St (☎835-4489). Comfortable oak-floored home with a grand view of the mountains from the rear deck. Alasko-Italian breakfast and evening snacks. ④.

Cooper's Cottage B&B, 325 Mendelta St (☎835-4810). Close to the *Casa*, also a few minutes' walk to the waterfront. Courtesy mountain bikes and continental breakfast. Strongly non-smoking. ④.

Downtown B&B, 113 Galena Drive (☎835-2791 or 1-800/478-2791). Don't be fooled by the name – it's more like a small motel – but it enjoys a good location, one block from the waterfront. ④.

Totem Inn, Richardson Hwy and Meals Ave (☎835-4443). Comfortable if unexciting hotel, costing a couple of dollars less than the others. A big log fire and a reasonably priced restaurant. ⑤.

Eating

Don't schedule a gourmet night-out while in Valdez. Considering its size and wealth the town's dining options are disappointing.

Alaska Halibut House, Meals and Fairbanks (☎835-2788). Fast food, but for the most part, fresh (fried) local seafood: catch of the day and fries, $4. Also burgers and salad bar.

Mike's Pizza Palace, 210 N Harbor Drive (☎635-2368). Best place in town for steak, seafood, entrees with a Greek twist and pizza. Great view of the harbor from the bar.

Oscar's, N Harbor Drive (☎835-4700). Hybrid place next to *Mike's*, which can't seem to make up its mind whether it's a diner, fast-food joint, coffee shop or ice-cream parlor.

The Pipeline Club, at the *Valdez Motel*, 136 Egan Drive (☎835-4332). Reasonable steak and seafood dinners; Captain Hazelwood of the *Exxon Valdez* was drinking in the bar on the fateful night.

Cordova

Far quieter than Valdez, and only accessible by sea or air, **CORDOVA** is an unpretentious fishing community set in forests and mountains on the southeastern edge of the Sound. In 1906, the Irish engineer, **Michael J Heney** (who made a name for himself by building the White Pass and Yukon Railway over reputedly impassable terrain out of Skagway) chose Cordova as the port from which to ship the copper mined in Kennicott, a hundred miles northeast. The government labelled it a foolhardy idea (his proposed Copper River and Northwestern Railroad – the CR&NW – was ridiculed as "Can't Run & Never Will") and commissioned a syndicate headed by Guggenheim to lay tracks over an easier but longer route to Katalla, near Valdez. Heney, who had rejected Katalla as being prone to winter storms, and gambled on trying to cut a path through two active glaciers, was vindicated when a huge gale wrecked the Katalla pier. His crew won the race, but only after completing the elaborate **"Million Dollar Bridge"** across the glacier-walled Copper River in 1911.

Ironically after such effort, the mines became exhausted just 27 years later. Cordova shifted its dependency to fishing, but this livelihood was dealt a potentially fatal blow in 1989 with the sinking of the *Exxon Valdez*. For the next two seasons, the community reeled from the effects of the **oil spill**. Fortunately, it now seems that most of the salmon and halibut have survived, though fishers still bear a grudge against the oil companies – just read their bumper stickers.

Today the Million Dollar Bridge, heavily battered by the 1964 earthquake, cuts a lonely figure at the end of the Copper River Highway, a gravel road that traverses the wondrous **Copper River Delta**, a major homing ground for migratory birds. Right next to the bridge is **Childs Glacier**. The delta and glacier rank as two of Alaska's very best sights – relatively few tourists get to see them, but if current plans to overhaul the bridge and build a road over the old railroad tracks to Chitina are realized, you can be guaranteed that this desolate area will be mobbed.

Arrival, getting around and information

There is no road access to Cordova; **flights** land at the airport twelve miles from town on the Copper River Highway. *Alaska Airlines* offer services from Anchorage, Sitka and Juneau; *Mark Air Express* from Anchorage and Valdez. Fares are lowest if you include a Saturday in your stay. A bus between the airport and downtown costs $9 one-way.

Most people get to Cordova on the *Alaska Marine Highway*'s MV *Bartlett* **ferry** which plies the Whittier–Valdez–Cordova route three times a week. A 6am arrival and a late-night departure means you can see everything including the delta and the Childs Glacier in a day, and save money by sleeping on the boat. The ferry dock lies a mile from downtown (☎424-7333).

The tiny **Chamber of Commerce** office on First St between Adams and Browning is open fairly irregular hours (☎424-7260); when it's shut, head for the museum (see below) which keeps a rack full of information.

The Town

There are few sights in Cordova itself; the **harbor** is the core of the town's activity, particularly when the fleet is in during the in-shore fishing season. The **Cordova Historical Museum** on First and Adams has quirky exhibits on local history, including the evolution of the little ice worm which lives in the glaciers and the funky annual festival that celebrates its existence (Tues–Sat 1–5pm; free).

Less than two miles from town along the Copper River Highway, **Lake Eyak**, enveloped by woods and mountains, is a great place to go boating and jet skiing in summer.

Copper River Delta

A superb 48-mile drive along the mostly unpaved Copper River Highway leads through the wetlands of the **Copper River Delta**, a fascinating tapestry of marshes, sluggish streams, glacial sloughs and shallow ponds all backed by the heavy-shouldered Chugach Mountains. This is also one of the continent's best sites for bird-watching: it's the only known breeding ground for Canadian geese; bald eagles and sandpipers abound, and over ten percent of the world's population of trumpeter swans make their home here. Common mammals include moose, beaver and mountain goat, while bears can often be seen feasting upon berries or fishing out salmon in summer. In all, it's a wonderful – and tranquil – site for fishing, bird-watching, or **hiking** along any one of several excellent trails such as the brisk stroll up around McKinley Lake and the gambol across the wetlands at the Alaganik Slough nearby.

A visit to Cordova simply has to incorporate a trip along the entire length of the **Copper River Highway**. By far the best way to experience it is in your own vehicle: *Imperial Car Hire* (Mon–Sat ☎424-5982; Sun ☎424-7440) rent out eight-seater minivans with unlimited mileage for $60, if picked up at the airport, or $70 from town. Alternatively, *Footloose Tours* (☎424-7175) run a five-hour narrated van ride through the delta to the glacier for $38 including lunch, and rent out **mountain bikes**. Both Chitina (☎424-3524) and Cordova (☎424-3289) **air services** can take you out to far-flung cabins or fishing holes.

Specific details on the Delta and Childs Glacier (see below), including trail maps and cabin locations, can be obtained from the US Forest Service Ranger Office in the old Post Office on Second St (☎424-7661).

Childs Glacier

The engineering marvel of the **Million Dollar Bridge** – severely damaged but still crossable – marks the end of the Copper River Highway. Just one mile to the left is the best view of the dramatic **Childs Glacier**. Here the fast-flowing Copper River sweeps by the three-hundred-feet-high face of the Childs, undercutting and severing the glacier's walls and preventing its advance. As the ice walls collapse and send icebergs into the river they produce waves up to fifteen feet high at the beach on the other side. Boulders the size of your head get catapulted out of the water, so it's wise to move to the observation deck as soon as you hear the thunderous roar of cracking ice. In addition to rocks, hapless salmon also get beached producing a chase between bald eagles, bears and intrepid campers to see who gets a free dinner. It's an intriguing and special sight – especially in summer when the glacier is most active.

Accommodation

Most of Cordova's **hotels** get fully booked in summer, but **B&Bs** are a good option. There are also **forest cabins** ($20 per night) throughout the Copper River Delta, administered by the Forest Service (☎424-7661). Official **campgrounds** dot the Copper River Highway, but real back-to-nature types prefer "Hippy Cove", two miles north of town on Orca Road, where the seasonal workers hang out.

Alaskan Hotel and Bar, First St (☎424-3288). Clean simple rooms above a popular bar. Caters mostly for long stays; reserve ahead. ④.

Harborview B&B, Observation Ave (☎424-5356). Good range of big downtown rooms that come equipped with shower, TV, microwave, fridge and DIY breakfast. Well recommended. ③ & ④.

Oystercatcher B&B, Third St and Council Ave (☎424-5154). Old B&B with rooms and hearty cooked breakfasts. ③.

Reluctant Fisherman, 407 Railroad Ave (☎424-3272). Tastefully decorated rooms overlooking the harbor. ⑤.

Eating and nightlife

There are plenty of cheap places to eat and drink in town, as well as, for such an isolated community, some fairly good ones. The bar in the *Alaskan Hotel* is a favorite, as is the *Reluctant Fisherman* (see below). Cordova's annual **Iceworm Festival** in the first week of February is an excuse for much drinking and revelry.

Ambrosia Pizza, First and Council (☎424-7175). Cozy setting and huge portions of lasagne, ravioli and whopping pizzas.

Baja Taco, Nicoloff Ave (no phone). Brightly-painted school bus serving marvellously tasty burritos and tacos down by the harbor.

Killer Whale Café, First St (☎424-7733). Popular backpackers' haunt over the *Orca Bookshop*, serving soup, sandwiches and muffins at reasonable prices, and with great views over the harbor.

Powder House, Copper River Hwy (☎424-3529). Former railroad gunpowder warehouse overlooking Eyak Lake, one-and-a-half miles from town. Good value seafood bakes and live music until early in the morning.

Reluctant Fisherman, 407 Railroad Ave (☎424-7446). Great views and lunch specials (try Chef Ted's salmon chilli). The superb seafood in the evening is a bit more expensive but good.

Wrangell-St Elias National Park

Just over the (inaccessible) peaks from Valdez and Cordova, the **Wrangell-St Elias National Park** fills out the extreme southeast corner of the Alaskan Interior, on the point where four of the continent's great mountain ranges – the Wrangell, St Elias, Chugach and Alaskan – cramp up against each other. Most of the eastern border is shared with the adjoining Kluane National Park in Canada. The usually unsensationalist US National Park Service literature breaks out in a rash of (justifiable) hyperbole by saying, "Incredible. You have to see Wrangell-St Elias . . . to believe it – and even then you won't be so sure".

Everything in Wrangell-St Elias is writ large: peak after peak (including nine of the sixteen highest in the US), glacier after enormous glacier, canyon after dizzying canyon – all laced together by braided rivers, massive moraines and icy-cold lakes, with the volcanic monster of Mount Wrangell still steaming on in the background. Vegetation struggles to take hold in much of the park, though does enough to support mountain goats, Dall sheep, bears and moose throughout its environs, while the silty lowlands are traversed by three sizeable herds of caribou and numerous bison.

The park was created in 1980, and remains – in terms of access and development – in its infancy, with private landowners still holding large chunks of its putative territory. The first whites in the area came in search of gold but instead hit upon one of the continent's richest copper deposits. The mines closed after thirty frantic years of production in 1938 and today the old miners' settlement of **Kennicott**, with over thirty big disused buildings, looks like a ghost town, save for an elaborate tourist lodge. A local guide will take you on a ninety-minute tour of the buildings for $15. Kennicott lies just a few miles north of **McCarthy**, the park's main social hub and base for outfitters, situated at the end of the entrance road – though it's nothing more than a scattered little hamlet. Wrangell-St Elias is a trail-less park so in theory you can head off near enough anywhere, but *St Elias Alpine Guides* (☎277-6867) offer a number of hikes, ice climbing, mountain bike rides, raft trips and even glacier skiing. Several of the companies operating **flight-seeing trips** will also drop you off in the vast backcountry; *Wrangell Mountain Air* (☎1-800/478-1160) quote very good prices, starting at $40 for a thirty-minute flight.

Practicalities

Getting to the park is half the fun. From Glennallen, travel about 30 miles south along Richardson Highway to the Edgerton Highway (Route 10) turn-off, which tracks along the Copper River on its 32-mile journey to Chitina, the start of the rough dirt McCarthy Road through the park. This 58-mile McCarthy Road, along an old railway line (rail spikes still stick out so be wary of punctures), is hemmed in by trees which obscure the beautiful scenery, and takes at least three hours. It's a tiring journey with just one highlight, the drive across the rickety bridge high over the Kuskulana River at Mile 17. At the Kennicott River, you leave the car behind and cross the water on a hand-pulled tram – try to remember to bring gloves. From here a short walk up the hill brings you to the hamlet of McCarthy, from where a shuttle bus runs along the rough five-mile dirt road to Kennicott.

Hitching along the park road can be a hit or miss affair; if you haven't got a vehicle you take a *Backcountry Connections* van (☎1-800/478-5292; $60) from Glennallen, which is on the main Anchorage–Valdez bus route. Alternatively you can enjoy a great flight into McCarthy from Glennallen or Chitina with *Wrangell Mountain Air* (☎1-800/478-1160).

Due to their remoteness, neither McCarthy nor Kennicott are cheap places to stay. The only option for budget travellers is **camping**, which is free, but check current protocol on sites. The *Johnson Hotel/McCarthy Lodge* (☎333-5402; ⑤), evoking the atmosphere of its 1916 construction date, is very pleasant; the only other option, the *Kennecott Glacier Lodge* (☎1-800/478-2350; ⑦) is much fancier. Both offer more affordable shoulder-season specials.

The park **visitor center** is just north of **Copper Center** at Mile 105.5 Old Richardson Hwy (June–early Sept daily 8am–6pm; otherwise Mon–Fri 8am–5pm; ☎822-5235).

Interior Alaska

Falling roughly within a triangle outlined by the Glenn, Parks and Alaska highways, **Interior Alaska** lives up to every expectation as a land of great beauty. For the most part it's a rolling plateau in between the Alaska and Brooks ranges, criss-crossed by river valleys, punctuated by glaciers and with views of imposing peaks, including Mount McKinley, the nation's highest, ever present. People are hugely outnumbered by game – moose, Dall sheep, grizzly bears and herds of caribou sweep over seemingly endless swathes of taiga and tundra.

The jewel of the Interior is **Denali National Park**, some one hundred miles south of **Fairbanks**, the jumping-off point for the roadless and even wilder **Alaskan Bush**. Weather can vary enormously from day to day with even more severe seasonal variations: in winter, temperatures can drop to -50°F for days at a time, while summer days reach a sweltering 90°F. However, the major problem during the warmer months is huge mosquitoes – with attitude. Don't leave without the insect repellent.

The Mat-Su Valley

Somewhat criminally overlooked by tourists speeding north from Anchorage to Denali, the glacially contorted **Mat-Su Valley** is in fact made up of two valleys, shaped by the erosive powers of the **Matanuska and Susitna rivers** and spotted with lakes, open plateaux and towering mountains. Route 1, the main highway from Anchorage, hits the middle of the valley at Mile 35.3. Here the Parks Hwy shoots out west for seven miles to busy **Wasilla**, while antiquated **Palmer**, the other main town, lies seven miles further north on Glenn Hwy.

Palmer

The most interesting thing about **PALMER**, a sleepy little farming community, 42 miles north of Anchorage, is its history. Founded in 1916 after the construction of a railroad station, the town didn't really take off until 1935, when President F D Roosevelt drew up the unusual Matanuska Colony programme, under which 202 families from the drought-stricken Midwest were resettled here with forty-acre tracts. The failure rate was high, but many took advantage of the twenty hours of summer daylight to make this Alaska's prime agricultural region. Today Palmer is known as the home of the freak vegetable: local 125lb pumpkins and 65lb cabbages are displayed with pride at the **Alaska State Fair**, held here each year in late August. For the rest of the summer, enterprising farmers will, for a fee, show you some unusual livestock raised in the valley including reindeer, wolves and musk-ox. Better value are the many pick-your-own farms, where peaches, apples and other fruit work out at bargain prices. A popular **place to eat** is *La Fiesta Mexican Café*, 816 S Colony Way (☎746-3335), serving up authentic food in cramped surroundings. The town also features a few motels and B&Bs (*Mat-Su Valley B&B Assoc*; ☎376-7662), but the better lodging options lie around Wasilla. There's a good regional **visitor center** in the middle of town (☎746-5000 or 1-800/876-5774).

Wasilla

First impressions of rapidly growing **WASILLA**, with its fast-food joints and strip malls, tend to mark it down as an impersonal junior sibling of Anchorage. However, a couple of beautiful lakes have made the town a prime center for water sports. Over the next few years Wasilla (pop. 3666), established as a mining and railroad supply center in the Twenties, seems destined to become better known as the alternative site for Alaska's capital city. Many Alaskans feel that the town, within easy reach of both Anchorage and Fairbanks, would yield better access to politicians, who currently do their business down in Juneau. Expect to hear Wasilla to crop up in political wranglings for several years to come.

The **visitor center** occupies part of the **Dorothy G Page Museum and Historical Park**, 323 Main St, a jumble of pioneer memorabilia and old log homes (daily 10am–6pm; ☎373-9071; $3). More likely to be of interest is the **Iditarod Trail Sled Dog Race Headquarters** at Mile 2.2 Knik Rd, where "the last great race on earth" is celebrated through video screenings and walls that look like one big scrapbook (summer Mon–Fri 8am–5pm, Sat & Sun noon–5pm; otherwise Mon–Fri 9am–5pm; free). The Iditarod Trail was originally a supply route, served by dog sled, from the all-weather port of Seward to remote gold rush communities on the west coast. In 1925 part of the trail became a life-saving highway for epidemic-stricken Nome when essential serum was brought in by mushers and their huskies. These days the Iditarod is Alaska's blue riband sporting event; teams of twelve to twenty dogs race the 1049 miles from Anchorage to Nome. The winning dog-musher, quite often a woman, can expect to make the journey in ten days and pick up a prize of $50,000.

One of Wasilla's strongpoints is its good-value **accommodation**, making it a very feasible alternative to Anchorage. The lakeside *Mat-Su Resort*, 1850 Bogard Rd (☎376-3229; ② & ⑤), offers both economy and luxury rooms along with a lively well-priced bar. They'll also fix you up for the water, renting everything from pedal-boats to the latest model jet ski. Just south of town, the *Windbreak Hotel*, Mile 40.5 Parks Hwy (☎376-4484; ③), has ten clean, simple rooms and a café renowned for sating serious appetites with low-cost specials. A little further south on Fairview Loop Road, *Yukon Don's* (☎376-7472; ④), set in a converted milk barn with four themed rooms (go for the Iditarod one), a spacious lounge and a 270° view of the valleys and mountains, is one of Alaska's best-known B&Bs. The *Cottonwood Lake B&B*, three miles east of town at 4305 W Shoreline Drive (☎373-0300; ④), is a big five-bedroom lodge with a wraparound deck on the shore of a pretty lake. There's **camping** at Lake Lucille, next to the Iditarod center.

Hatcher Pass

The road up and over 3886-foot **Hatcher Pass**, the scenic highlight of the Mat-Su Valley region, runs high above the treeline through the Talkeetna Mountains, and is readily accessible from Palmer. Open only in summer, Fishhook–Willow Road, as it's officially known, twists and weaves for fifty mostly unpaved miles through high tundra, passing many old mine workings and vast memorable vistas along the way.

In this ideal hiking terrain, one of the best places to get out of the car is **Independence Mine State Park**, where a motley collection of twenty or so buildings stand in various stages of dilapidation in a starkly beautiful bowl-shaped valley. The **visitor center** (☎745-2827) and free museum, occupying the mine manager's office, can fill you in on the area's gold-mining heyday of the Thirties and nearby hiking trails. Kayaking, mountaineering, and in winter, cross-country skiing and snowmobiling, are other popular activities. One mile east of the park, the *Motherlode Lodge* (☎746-1464; ④) has a good bar and clean rooms. *Scratch's* gold-panning operation lies across the road; the real value from the $5 fee comes from Scratch's in-depth knowledge of the area rather than any gold you might accumulate. The road comes out at Mile 71 Parks Hwy near nondescript Willow, just 20 miles' drive north of Wasilla; reckon on at least six hours to make the full trip.

Talkeetna

Well beyond Wasilla, at Mile 98.7 on the Parks Highway, comes the fourteen-mile turnoff to **TALKEETNA**, a very pleasant little village that serves as the center for climbers attempting **Mount McKinley**. Its dirt roads, log cabins and small-town-Alaska feel, combined with an international flavor as mountaineers from all over the world gather to prepare for their assaults on McKinley, make for an unusual if not downright essential stop. Rumor has it that this eclectic hamlet was the model for Cicely in *Northern Exposure*, but to its credit Talkeetna doesn't use this as tour bus bait.

Above all this is a place to kick back, strolling along the beautiful sandy river banks or simply hanging out in a bar. However, at some point it's worth looking into the **Talkeetna Historical Society Museum**. Two of its three buildings are devoted to the usual pioneer, bush pilot and railroad stuff, while the other features a topographical model of Mount McKinley, detailing the different routes favored by climbers and a biography on local boy, Taras Genet, who in 1991 became the youngest person to reach the summit at age 11 (summer; daily 10am–6pm; $2). There's a great vantage point of the mountain a mile south from town, but the number one way to see McKinley is by plane (see box).

The major summer celebration – the **Moose Dropping Festival** – falls on the second weekend of July. The mere mention of the event recently caused one outraged citizen in Florida to reach for the phone and demand that the Chamber of Commerce tell him how far they actually drop the poor moose. The reply, that they tie it onto a plane, get up to 3500 feet and try to aim it onto a concrete slab, was a lie; the complainant had got his verbs and nouns mixed up, and the festival in fact focuses on the little brown balls (complete with a heavy coat of varnish) that are sold throughout the town, for use as earrings, necklaces and the like. In addition to these highly desirable lumps of Alaskana, the festival features dancing, drinking and a moose-dropping throwing competition.

Trains en route between Anchorage and Denali stop in the center of Talkeetna once a day. Hitching the fourteen miles to and from the Parks Highway rarely poses problems. The **information booth** is infrequently staffed, but the people in the museum or the filling station should be able to help you out.

Talkeetna teems with good **accommodation**. Dating back to 1917, the *Talkeetna Roadhouse* (☎733-1351; ③) bolsters its old-style atmosphere with some great home-cooking and neat, tidy rooms with shared baths. The *Swiss Alaskan Inn* (☎733-2424; ④) is the swish option, but good value, while excellent B&Bs serving huge morning meals include *River Beauty* (☎733-2741; ④), and *Belle's Cabin* (☎733-2414; ④). Perhaps the most salubrious dorm space in the state, the *K2 Bunkhouse* (☎733-2291; ①), lies off Main Street. Run by *K2 Aviation*, it costs $12 a night; priority is given to climbers so it's usually chock full from April to mid-August. Good places to **eat** include the *McKinley Deli*, which serves good pizza, and *Latitude 62* (☎733-2262), for steak and seafood dinners; **drink** in the wonderfully ancient *Fairfield Inn* on Main Street (☎733-2423; ②), which also rents out upstairs rooms. Nice as these are, be warned that the bar swings most nights until 5am.

MOUNT McKINLEY/DENALI

Long before whites reached Alaska, Athabascan Natives referred to **Mount McKinley** as **Denali**, "the Great One". Although an early adventurer renamed the mountain after the governor of Ohio who later became the 25th US president, Alaskans have never really taken to the name, and still refer to both the mountain and the park by their original title. Whatever you choose to call it, North America's tallest mountain rises from 2000-foot lowlands to a height of 20,320 feet, and on a clear day its white glow, in sharp contrast to the warm colors all around, makes for a transcendent experience.

The ice-covered giant dominates life in the village of **Talkeetna**, 153 road miles south of the park entrance, during the climbing season of mid-April to mid-August. Only 45 percent of the one thousand mountaineers who annually tackle McKinley, "the coldest mountain in the world" – and the highest, from base to peak (Everest et al. start off from a high plateau) – succeed in the ascent, thanks largely to its extreme weather conditions. Fast-swirling ice-storms can trap climbers for days, and almost every season sees at least one fatality: 1992 was one of the worst years on record with eleven fatalities.

Several companies based in Talkeetna will whisk you on a 120-mile, 90-minute "Circle McKinley" tour over moose-grazing lowlands, past moraines, alongside dazzlingly blue glaciers and (weather permitting) the 20,320-foot peak, for $150 or so. *K2 Aviation* (☎733-2291), the choice of most climbing expeditions, offers the widest range of options, including a glacier landing at base camp in planes fitted with skis.

Denali National Park

The six-million-acre wildlife reserve of **DENALI NATIONAL PARK**, 237 miles north of Anchorage, is named after the Athabascan word for its most famous denizen, **Mount McKinley**. However, the mountain is far from being the park's only attraction. In fact it's frequently surrounded by a thick blanket of cloud, and only around one quarter of visitors actually get to see the snow-covered massif. Don't let this put you off, as a ride through Denali on a shuttle bus, guarantees a chance to glimpse a vast world of tundra and taiga, glaciers and U-shaped valleys, reflective lakes and other huge mountains in the Alaskan range. Best of all is the park's vast wildlife population – most visitors return with tales of sighting grizzlies, caribou, moose and Dall sheep.

Visiting Alaska without seeing Denali is unthinkable for most travellers, and therein lies the park's only problem. In the height of summer, the visitor center and the service hotels out on Parks Highway are clogged with RVs, tour buses, screaming brats and the like. Things pick up in the park itself , and backcountry hiking remains a wonderful lonesome experience, though it's probably best if you try to get here early in the season when there are fewer people and mosquitoes.

Getting there

Driving to the Denali Park entrance (Mile 237.3 Parks Hwy) takes about five hours from Anchorage, or three from Fairbanks. **Hitching** along the Parks Highway is quite easy, especially during the summer when there are more than twenty hours of daylight. Alternatively, the easy and comfortable trains of the **Alaska Railroad** leave Anchorage daily in summer at 8.30am; the trip to the station at Denali, one and a half miles inside the park entrance, takes around eight hours and costs $90 one-way. The 8.30am departure from Fairbanks arrives at 12.30pm ($50). It's also possible to buy a through ticket from Anchorage to Fairbanks, and stop off in the park along the way, for $140. The luxurious way to arrive is in one of the (expensive) glass-domed railroad cars operated from Anchorage by *Princess Tours* (☎276-7711), and *Gray Line* (☎277-5581).

Alaska Direct Busline stops at Denali on the way between Anchorage and Fairbanks; fares from the two cities are $55 and $35 respectively. Several companies offer all-in sightseeing tours to the park: *Mt McKinley Alaska Tours* (☎1-800/327-7651) offer some of the best prices. *Denali Express* (☎274-8539) operate a van service to Denali, charging $85 from Anchorage, and an additional $25 to continue on to Fairbanks.

Sightseeing, hiking and other activities

Bar a few tour companies and RVs with special permits, the only vehicles allowed on Denali's narrow unpaved 97-mile road are yellow **shuttle buses**, a policy that ensures that the native flora and fauna remain, for the most part, undisturbed. Travel on the buses is "free" once you pay a $3 park entrance fee which is good for a week, but, and it's a big but, you may have to wait up to three days to get on one. Tickets are available up to two days in advance from the **Visitors Access Center (VAC)**, just inside the park entrance (late May to mid-Sept daily 5.45am–8pm; ☎683-1266, or 452-PARK for recorded information). The VAC also stocks a wide range of literature, and each visitor receives a copy of the *Denali Alpenglow* broadsheet; ranger-led activities include short hikes and the popular sled dog demonstration held daily at 10am, 2pm and 4pm.

Shuttle buses run to either the **Eielson Visitor Center** at mile 66 where rangers lead one-hour tundra tours each day at 1.30pm, or to aptly named **Wonder Lake** at mile 84; round trips take around eight and ten hours respectively. You can of course jump off the bus at any point along the route for a hike and return to the road and flag down the next bus to the VAC. Though the shuttle bus drivers do not perform guided tours, with up to forty pairs of watchful eyes on board, you're almost guaranteed to see the big game; a recent park questionnaire revealed that 95 percent of visitors saw **bear**, **caribou** and **Dall sheep**, 82 percent **moose** and over one-fifth, **wolves**. Other regularly sighted creatures include porcupine, snowshoe hare and arctic foxes, while over 160 bird species populate the park.

Backcountry hiking represents the best way to appreciate Denali's scenery and its inhabitants. The park is divided into 43 zones and only a designated number of hikers are allowed into each section at a time. Free permits are available, one day in advance, from the VAC's Backcountry Desk (daily 8am–8pm), who will also issue you with bear-resistant food containers. The idea is to disassociate human smells and food, thus sparing bears from becoming dependent on hikers, and hikers from becoming food for bears. It's also more than a good idea to view the five backcountry simulator programmes in the VAC before you set out across fast-flowing rivers and within sniffing distance of the grizzlies. Special camper buses – reserved for those with campground or backcountry permits – head into the park; riders are free to get off in their assigned section and start hiking. There are no trails across the tundra; just choose a good landmark and head towards it. It's not a bad idea to reconnoitre the park on a full-day bus trip in order to choose where you might like to hike on subsequent days. If there's room, buses also carry bikes; cyclists can be dropped off wherever they like, but are obliged to keep to the roads.

Just outside the park entrance, several **rafting** companies take two-hour trips down the Nenana River: all offer a gentle "scenic float", and an eleven-mile "Canyon Run" through Class III and IV rapids. *Denali Raft Adventures* (☎683-2234) usually offer the best prices; around $38 a trip. For close-up views of Mount McKinley, **flight seeing** tours cost about $120 per hour. *Denali Air* (☎683-2261) have an office at the *Denali Park Hotel*, though a better perspective is achieved by taking a flight from Talkeetna (see p.533).

In **winter**, Denali transforms itself into a ghostly snow-covered world. Motorized vehicles are banned and transport, even for park personnel is by snowshoe, skis or dog sled in temperatures often below –40°F.

Accommodation

The only hotel inside the park – the *Denali Park* – is usually booked up well in advance. Most unimaginative souls head for the busy summer-only gaggle of hotels and cabins two miles north of the park entrance at Mile 239 Parks Hwy. You can do better than this: ten miles further up the road the little coal-mining town of **HEALY** boasts a number of good B&Bs and a roadhouse-style hotel. If you get horribly stuck try *Denali Hotel and B&B Hotline* (☎1-800/345-6020, or 683-1422 locally).

For details on **camping** within the park, see box. The closest private campground outside park boundaries is *Lynx Creek* (☎683-1240), in the noisy hubbub of shops and motels, two miles north of the park entrance at Mile 239 Parks Hwy; *Denali Grizzly Bear Cabins and Campground* (☎683-2696) enjoys a more pleasing location, south of the park at Mile 231.1.

CAMPGROUNDS IN DENALI PARK

Camping is the best way to experience Denali up close, with most of the park's eight campgrounds open from May through September. The best sites are at **Wonder Lake**, where on a good day McKinley is reflected in the water; failing that, **Igloo Creek** is good for spotting Dall sheep. Try to book at one of the Alaska Public Lands Information Centers (APLIC) in Tok, Anchorage or Fairbanks; they accept reservations up to three weeks in advance and will also keep you a place on one of the special buses reserved for campers. If you fail to do so, you risk turning up in Denali and finding all buses and campgrounds booked for at least a day, meaning an expensive and irritating time in the parasitic little seasonal town outside the park. Otherwise, all sites (except Morino where you can self-register) are bookable at the main visitor center, though you may have to wait for up to three days to get a spot.

Riley Creek (year-round), Mile 0.8. 102 sites for RVs and tents; $12.

Morino, Mile 1.9. 60-person limit for people without vehicles; $3 per person.

Savage River, Mile 13. 34 sites for RVs and tents; $12.

Savage Group, Mile 13. 3 sites for groups of 9–20 people; $20.

Sanctuary River, Mile 23. 7 sites, tents only; free.

Teklanika River, Mile 29. 50 sites for RVs and tents; $12.

Igloo Creek, Mile 34. 7 sites tents only; free.

Wonder Lake (June–Sept), Mile 85. 28 sites, tents only; $12.

Denali Grizzly Bear Cabins, Mile 231 Parks Hwy (☎683-2696). Rustic and tent cabins overlooking the Nenana River. Basic models come without bedding, others have heat and sheets. ①–④.

Denali Hostel, Otto Lake Rd (☎683-1295). Nice enough hostel some ten miles north of the park, but the $24 fee sticks in the throat. ①.

Denali Mountain Lodge, 85 miles inside the park, PO Box 189, AK 99755 (☎683-2594). Located on the banks of Moose Creek, at the end of the road. The owners will get you a permit to drive right here. To minimize traffic they require at least two nights' stay and groups of four or more persons. Bring all your own supplies. ⑦.

Denali Park Hotel, opposite the train station (☎276-7234). The only hotel inside the park. Open mid-May to early Sept, reservations essential. The rooms are pretty standard, but more than anything you're paying for convenience. The operators, *ARA Services*, offer two nights for the price of one before mid-June and also run the similarly priced *McKinley Village Lodge*, Mile 224 Parks Hwy, along with the more expensive *McKinley Chalet Lodge*, Mile 239 Parks Hwy. ⑥.

Dome Home B&B, just off Mile 248.8 Parks Hwy, Healy (☎683-1239). Four-level geodesic dome with good rooms and big "Alaskan" breakfast. ④.

Happy Wanderer Hostel, Mile 239 Parks Hwy (☎683-1295). Eight beds with kitchen facilities in a mobile home. Very basic, but close to the park. $17 a night. ①.

Healy Heights B&B, Mile 248 Parks Hwy, Healy (☎683-2639). Very comfortable rustic home. Hearty breakfast and very informative owners. ④.

Historic Healy Hotel, Mile 248.8 Parks Hwy, Healy (☎683-2242). Nice, clean, simple rooms in an old railroad employees' hotel. ⑤.

McKinley–Denali Cabins, Mile 239 Parks Hwy (☎683-2733). Inexpensive heated canvas cabins in the hectic touristy jumble two miles north of the park entrance. ③.

White Moose Lodge, Mile 248 Parks Hwy, Healy (☎683-1233). Newish motel rooms in a wooded setting. ④.

Eating

All the big Denali hotels have dining rooms, but *Lynx Creek Pizza*, Mile 238.8 Parks Hwy (☎683-2547), offers the most reasonable prices in the vicinity of the park entrance. The *Box Car Café* in the *Historic Healy Hotel* (see above) serves inexpensive no-nonsense diner meals. Campers are advised to bring food from Anchorage, Wasilla or Fairbanks, as local grocery stores can be pricey.

Fairbanks

FAIRBANKS, 358 miles north of Anchorage, is at the end of the Alaska Highway from Canada and definitely at the end of the road for most tourists. Its central location makes it the focal point for the tiny villages scattered around the surrounding wilderness, and a staging post for North Slope (ie North Alaskan) villages such as **Barrow** and the oil community of **Prudhoe Bay**. These northern areas are accessible by air, and via the **Dalton Highway**, also known as the Haul Road in honor of its fast, stop-at-nothing trucks.

Fairbanks was founded accidentally when, in 1901, a steamship carrying E T Barnette, a merchant with all his wares on board, ran aground in the shallows of the Chena River. Unable to transport the supplies he was carrying, Barnette set up shop in the wilderness and catered to the few trappers and prospectors trying their luck in the area. The following year, with the beginnings of the **gold rush**, a tent city sprang up on the site, and Barnette made a mint.

In 1908, at the height of the gold stampede, the town had a population of 18,500. Due to the difficulty in retrieving gold from the frozen bedrock, most independent miners gave up, and by 1920 the population had dwindled to only 1100. The community sputtered along until World War II when several huge **military bases** were built to thwart possible Japanese attacks. Many bases remained after the war (and still do today), and the town received another major boost in the mid-Seventies when it became the transport center for the **trans-Alaska oil pipeline** project: construction and other oil-related activities brought a rush of workers seeking wages of up to $1500 per week and the population reached an all-time high. The city's economy dropped dramatically with the oil crash, and unemployment hit twenty percent before government spending put the city back on track.

Fairbanks may be flat and somewhat bland, but it's a good base for exploring a hinterland that includes gold-mining areas, hot springs and bush communities, and is surrounded by beautifully wooded rolling hills, accented by the distant Alaskan and Brooks ranges. Tourism is becoming an increasingly important earner. The spectacular **aurora borealis** is a major winter attraction, as is the **Ice Festival** in mid-March, when the North American Open Sled Dog Championships take place on the frozen downtown streets. The Festival is perhaps most famous for its ice-sculpting competition; the impressive design and detail which goes into these large works make it well worth braving the evil sub-zero temperatures.

Summer visitors should try to catch the three-day **World Inuit–Indian Olympics** in mid-July. Competitors from around the state compete in the standard dance, art and sports competitions, as well as some unusual ones like ear pulling, knuckle hop, high kick and the blanket toss, where age and wisdom often defeat youth and strength.

Fairbanks inflicts remarkable extremes of climate. Temperatures of –40°F are not uncommon, but the thermometer can rise to over 90°F in summer. Because the city sits just 188 miles south of the Arctic Circle, above which the sun neither sets during the summer nor rises during the winter equinoxes, Fairbanks also has very long days. The shortest day of the year has less than three hours of sunlight, the longest has over 21. Both can be disconcerting, and residents suffer from a high rate of depression. In summer, midnight baseball games under natural light are great fun, but stumbling out of a bar at 2am into bright sunshine can be really perturbing.

Arrival, getting around and information

Fairbanks International Airport lies about four miles southwest of downtown; there are no buses and a taxi to the center will cost around $10. Carriers offering daily flights from Anchorage include *Mark Air, Alaska Airlines, Delta*, and *United*. The city acts as a gateway for flights into the Bush; *Frontier Flying Service* (☎474-0014) operate a reliable service, weather permitting of course.

By **road**, Fairbanks is 653 miles from Haines via the Alaska Highway, and 348 miles north of Anchorage along the Parks Highway. **Alaska Railroad trains**, stopping downtown at 280 N Cushman Rd, offer the most relaxing and scenic way of travelling between Anchorage and Fairbanks, for $130 round trip (daily in summer) or $245 for a fly/rail package with *Mark Air*. *Alaska Direct* ($65) offer the least expensive **bus** fares from Anchorage, and make a stop at Denali. *Alaskon Express* make the trip four times a week from Haines ($179) and Skagway ($205) via Whitehorse, Canada. The two-day bus trip stops overnight at Beaver Creek in the Yukon, where you make your own sleeping arrangements (motel rooms ③ and up; camping $18).

Sprawling Fairbanks belies its meager population of 40,000; having a vehicle is a good idea. Two bus lines provide a reasonable service around town, but routes and schedules change frequently: call ☎459-1011 for information or collect a schedule from Transit Park between Fifth and Sixth avenues. *G O Shuttle Service* (☎474-3847) stops at all the major attractions and lets you explore them at your own pace for $20. They also run a night service to the *Howling Dog and Fox Roadhouse* (see "Drinking") for $15. Several other companies can whisk you off into the Bush and Alaska's far west. The *Northern Alaska Tour Company* (☎454-8600) are the specialists for the Arctic Circle and Prudhoe Bay, while *Gray Line* operate tours to Denali, Barrow and the Yukon.

Numbered avenues in Fairbanks run parallel to the Chena River, getting higher as you head south. The **CVB visitor center**, 550 First Ave (daily 8am–5pm; ☎456-5774), stores a vast amount of information on lodging and activities. For information on area parks, including Denali, the useful **Alaska Public Land Information Center** (APLIC) is at 250 N Cushman St (☎451-7352).

The Town

Downtown Fairbanks shouldn't take up much of your time. Besides the CVB and APLIC visitor centers, the only real stop of interest is the small **Dog Mushing Museum** in the Courthouse Building at Second and Cushman (summer, Mon–Fri 9am–6pm Sat & Sun 9am–5pm; otherwise times vary; $2). Celebrating sled dog racing through videos, memorabilia and trophies, it concentrates on the north country's other great mushing event, the **Yukon Quest** – a gruelling thousand-mile marathon from Fairbanks to Whitehorse, Yukon.

A couple of miles west on Airport Way, the forty-acre **Alaskaland** complex on the banks of the Chena River glorifies Alaskan history in a very touristy, but friendly way, and admission is free. Log cabins from Fairbanks' original down-town have been relocated here, and the "Mining Valley" and "Gold Rush Town" pay homage to the early prospectors. Two reasonable free museums cover Athabascan culture and early pioneers and the **Crooked Creek and Whiskey Island Railroad** encircles the entire park. A carousel, playgrounds and crazy golf course account for the rest of the space. Numerous free shuttle buses head out from the major hotels in town, and there is sometimes a bus from the visitor center. Round the back, Growden Field is the home of baseball's semi-pro **Fairbanks Goldpanners**, and the celebrated annual "Midnight Sun" game.

The **University of Alaska–Fairbanks (UAF) Museum**, occupying a corner of the attractive campus on the northwestern edge of town houses some of the best examples of native artefacts and pioneer relics, as well as natural and human history displays, in Alaska (summer daily 9am–7pm; otherwise times vary; $4). Also on campus, the **Large Animal Research Station** on Yankovich Road allows the opportunity to view musk oxen, caribou and reindeer up close (tours $5.50; ☎474-7207 for times). For those interested in Alaska's earthquakes and volcanoes, the **Geophysical Institute**, in the tall Elvey Building (☎474-7243), puts on an excellent tour every Thursday during summer at 2pm.

Throughout summer, the **Riverboat Discovery** (☎479-6673; $28), a restored paddle steamer based at 1975 Discovery Drive next to the airport, operates four-hour narrated tours down the Chena to the Tanana River, stopping at an Athabascan village for assorted tourist kitsch and demonstrations of native crafts. It's an expensive trip but most punters come back well satisfied.

Fox

To refer to **Fox**, eleven miles north of downtown on the Old Steese Highway, as a town is a bit of an overstatement, but around this inconsequential settlement stripped hillsides, heavy machinery, mounds of tailings and "Keep Out" signs betray the continuing seach for **gold**. Two local tours provide varying perspec-tives on the quest: **Gold Dredge #8**, Mile 9 Old Steese Hwy, centered around an impressively gigantic 1928 steel-hulled dredge, provides the more historic version along with gourmet coffee (daily 9am–6pm; $12), while the two-hour tours at the **Little El Dorado Gold Camp**, Mile 1.5 Elliot Hwy, take the fun approach, explaining the methodology behind mining and allowing ample time to pan for gold (☎479-7613 for times; $25).

With its good B&B and the excellent *Howling Dog Saloon* (both are detailed below), Fox makes a good alternative to staying in central Fairbanks. A bonus on the trip out is a good view of the **trans-Alaska pipeline** at Mile 8, Steese Hwy.

Accommodation

The dozens of motels and hotels in downtown Fairbanks, tend either to be quite pricey or pretty dodgy. **B&Bs** are plentiful, with rooms from $50; the *Fairbanks B&B Registry* (☎452-4957) has details, though the visitor center offers free phone calls and all the brochures. There are also plenty of **hostels**.

For **campers**, the *Norlite Campground*, 1660 Peger Rd (☎474-0206 or 1-800/478-0206), carries on the kitschy theme of neighboring Alaskaland, while the Alaska Division of Parks operates the Chena River State Campground (☎451-2695), a few miles south on University Ave and accessible by bus from Transit Park.

Alaska Motel, 1546 Cushman St (☎456-6393). Safest pick of the budget motels downtown. ③.

A Taste of Alaska Lodge, Eberhardt Rd, Mile 5.3 Chena Hot Springs Rd (☎488-7855). Somewhere in between a B&B and a small country lodge. Sumptuous decor and a good view of McKinley. ⑤.

Billie's Backpackers Hostel, 2895 Mack Rd (☎479-2034). Welcoming and enthusiastically run hostel. Free pickup from train station or airport, volleyball court, tent space ($7) and an all-you-can-eat evening cookout for $5. In a nice area and handy for buses to town and UAF. Bunks $14. ①.

College Bunkhouse, 1541 Westwood Way (☎479-2627). A few doors up from *Billie's* but with a slightly different atmosphere. The owner of the *Bunkhouse* is a scream and a compulsive smoker: "Yeah. We do have a no-smoking section. It's outside." ①.

Cripple Creek Resort Hotel, Ester, 5 miles south of Fairbanks (☎479-2500). The resort – a kind of adult hillbilly theme park – may not be to everyone's taste, but the rooms are good value. Bath shared between two rooms. ③.

Fairbanks AYH Hostel, 1641 Willow St (☎456-4159). Really good rooms in the manager's comfortable home. Beds $12, nice tent sites for $6. Reservations essential. ①.

Fox Creek B&B, Mile 1.1 Elliot Hwy, Fox (☎457-5494). 12 miles north of downtown. Quiet and comfortable, with big cooked breakfasts. Near the *Howling Dog Saloon* (see below). ③.

Pioneer B&B, 119 Second Ave (☎452-4628). 1906 log cabin on the edge of downtown. One of the rooms accommodates four people, making for exceptional value. ④.

Trident Apartments, 1782 Army Rd (☎479-6313 or ☎1-800/478-6313 in AK). Small but clean apartments with kitchen facilities, showers and TV. Discount for weekly stays. Close to the *Chena Pump Inn* (see below). ④.

Eating

Apart from fast-food joints, inexpensive food is hard to find in Fairbanks, although there are a number of good spots to eat, and drink, out near the university.

Café de Paris, 801 Pioneer Rd (☎456-1669). Crepes and sandwiches in an old cottage near the train station. Pricey but good. Mon–Sat 10am–3pm.

Golden Exchange Bar and Grill, 500 First Ave (☎452-1978). Great (if expensive) dinners.

Souvlaki, 112 N Turner St (☎452-5393). Good value East Mediterranean dishes including spinach pie and other vegetarian options. Next to the train station.

Two Rivers Lodge, Mile 16, Chena Hot Springs Rd (☎488-6815). A fair way out of town, but it's a pleasant drive and you'll be well rewarded with inventive steak and seafood dishes from a huge menu. They also run a shuttle service from town. Budget on around $30 a head.

Whole Earth Grocery and Deli, 3649 College Rd (☎479-2062). Healthy eating near the university.

Nightlife

Fairbanks has its decent nightspots, though none of them lies in the hard-drinking downtown district.

Hot Licks, 3549 College Rd (☎479-7813). Ice cream and espresso bar that stays open until midnight and features live jazz several nights a week.

Howling Dog Saloon, junction of Eliot and Steese Hwys, Fox (☎457-8780). An inconvenient eleven miles north of town, but perhaps the best bar in the entire North Country. Unassuming, untouristy, unpretentious and fun. Live rock and R&B bands and the ideal place to play volleyball under the midnight sun. A C&W dance hall, the *Fox Roadhouse* (☎457-8780), stands right across the street.

Pike's Landing, Mile 4.5 , Airport Rd (☎479-7113). Large and hugely popular bar/restaurant serving good light meals and cocktails on a sundeck overlooking the Chena River.

Pump House, Mile 1.3 Chena Pump Rd (☎479-8452). Even more popular than Pike's Landing. The restaurant draws in tourists for surf'n'turf dinners, while a young crowd packs the bar at night.

Outside Fairbanks: two hot springs

Legislators recently decreed that the various **hot springs** in the vicinity of Fairbanks should filter the 120–150°F waters which gush out of the frozen ground, to the extent that the spas now look, and smell, more like swimming pools than the traditional sulphur-reeking hot spots. Nevertheless they still make for a nice side trip, and are worth the effort even if it's just for the scenery on the way.

Chena Hot Springs, the most accessible and developed resort, stands in a clearing sixty miles east of Fairbanks at the end of the Chena River State Recreation Area – a bucolic swathe of **muskeg** (grassy swamp land) and forest traversed with good hiking trails and teeming with moose. Rooms at the fully equipped resort range from good-value rustic trapper cabins to luxury doubles (☎452-7867; ②–⑥), and camping costs $8. Walking in the area is especially enjoyable after a soak in the steaming natural spring waters; if you're not staying at the resort, it costs $8 per day to use the indoor pool and hot tubs. The resort also rents out canoes and mountain bikes as well as offering rafting trips.

The traditional favorite for folks from Fairbanks has been the more rustic **Circle Hot Springs**, 130 miles northeast of the city along scenic Steese Highway. It's a long drive but you pass through some pristine scenery, alongside the Chatanika River and over the 3624-feet Eagle Summit. To get to the resort, take a right at the mining village of **Central** and carry on for eight miles. In addition to taking a dip, you can go on a boat ride or pan for gold, and the area is laced with good hiking, skiing and snowmobiling trails. Accommodations range from dorm beds for $20 right up to deluxe rooms for around $100 (☎520-5113; ①–⑤).

Don't confuse the resort with the town of **CIRCLE** – a 34-mile drive over very rough roads from Central. The name was given by prospectors, who in 1893 thought they were establishing a community on the Arctic Circle; it's actually fifty miles south. Today Circle is a classic end-of-the-road community numbering seventy souls with a reputation for heavy boozing. It all adds up to a rather essential side trip.

The Dalton Highway

Built in the 1970s, to service the **trans-Alaska pipeline**, the gravel-surfaced **Dalton Highway**, or North Slope Haul Road, begins north of Fairbanks and slips and slides for 341 miles beyond the Arctic Circle to the oil facility of Prudhoe Bay on Alaska's north coast. This long, lonesome and risky road is approached from town along the Elliott Hwy, and begins 73 miles north of Fairbanks. Just beyond the city limits on the Elliott you start to get glimpses of the pipeline snaking up hills and in and out of the ground. At 188 miles north of Fairbanks a rather snappy little sign, an observation platform, a scrap of red carpet and a picnic area alert you to the fact that you've just crossed the **Arctic Circle**.

About a hundred miles inside the circle, **Disaster Creek**, in the shade of the still largely unmapped and unexplored **Brooks Range** and the **Gates of the Arctic National Park** wilderness, marks the end of the road, at least for the moment: plans to open the rest of the route to the general public have been delayed due to oil company claims that their heavy vehicles would cause too many accidents. **Prudhoe Bay**, at the end of the highway and nothing more than a collection of oil tanks and trailer homes, is also closed to visitors, and unless you can get hold of a press pass or pay $60 for a tour and some oil company propaganda. This restriction means that your journey by road comes to an end ten miles from the coast at dead-boring **Deadhorse**.

Permits to travel north beyond Disaster Creek are available from the Dept of Transport, 2301 Peger Rd, Fairbanks (☎451-2209). Many people ignore the regulations, but do bear in mind that most rental companies forbid you to take their cars on this road. In any case it's a treacherous journey. Trucks speeding along the slippery gravel track kick up frightening clouds of dust or mud which reduce visibility to absolute zero; potholes beat the hell out of the car and services, gas and repairs are non-existent. You shouldn't even think about coming here unless you've got a sturdy 4WD, a CB radio, a trunkload of supplies, and have done some careful planning.

Indeed, even driving the relatively short stretch to the Arctic Circle poses its problems – and anyway it's an awfully long drive to get to a roadsign and picnic area. If you can't resist the desire to cross the Arctic Circle, by far the best way is with the **Northern Alaska Tour Company** (☎454-8600) who'll drive you up in a minibus, supply commentary and video films (but no lunch), and fly you back down to Fairbanks for around $150 (you can save $50 by taking the minibus back, but that makes for a long, long day). The company also run a two-day tour to Prudhoe Bay for $450.

The Alaska Highway – The Final Leg

Motorists travelling north through Canada on the **Alaska Highway** reach the US border at Mile 1189.5, where there's a 24-hour customs post. Approximately 125 miles along, **TOK**, founded as a camp for crews working on the highway, today functions as a supply center for native villages, and as the gateway town for arriving travellers – including those who've arrived here from Dawson City in the Yukon, via the gravel-surfaced Top of the World Highway (see p.475). Sprawling out from the junction of the Alaska Highway, which heads west to Fairbanks, and the Glenn Hwy that snakes south to Valdez and Anchorage, Tok looks much like any other US pitstop town, except for the surrounding scenery. There's not much to do here except eat, rest and maybe attend a dog-mushing display – locals like to think of the town as the "sled-dog capital of the world". The only really essential stop, the **Alaska Public Lands Information Center** (summer daily 8am–8pm; otherwise times vary; ☎883-5667), features films, informed staff to answer questions, and can supply information on all of Alaska's parks and wilderness areas.

Most **rooms** in Tok are clean, even if some could do with a refit. The least expensive doubles can be found at the *Snowshoe Gateway Motel* (☎883-4511, or 1-800/478-4511 in AK, YK & BC; ②), though the *Golden Bear Motel* (☎883-2561; ④), makes for a more comfortable night's sleep and has a good café with an all-you-can-eat buffet. *Wildwood Kennels B&B*, Mile 1318.5 Alaska Hwy (☎883-5866; ③), featuring bed, breakfast and a cast of huskies, is a fun place to stay, while there are bunks in a big tent for $7 at the *Tok International Youth Hostel* (☎883-3745; ①), about nine miles west of Tok at Mile 1322.5. Finally, a warning to **hitchhikers**; Tok may be on an important junction, but for some reason it's hard to thumb out. People have been known to wait days.

Soon after Tok, continuing on the Alaska Hwy, the scenery unfolds to impart dramatic views of the **Alaska Range**, while the road sweeps past busy rivers and rush-infested lakes. It may come as a surprise to see a loud sign proclaiming that you have come to the end of the Alaska Highway at the otherwise unassuming little town of **DELTA JUNCTION**, 108 miles west of Tok. Technically this is accurate, as the remaining 98 miles of road to Fairbanks (the Richardson Highway) already existed when the Alaska Highway was completed in 1942. However, Fairbanks is a more fitting end to such an epic trip, and although the Delta Junction CVB do a nice line in selling "I completed the Alaska Highway" certificates, most people choose to get their endeavors endorsed at Fairbanks' visitor center.

For those who like their tourist traps coated with gooey layers of schmaltz, **NORTH POLE**, just fifteen miles before Fairbanks, is an essential stop. The town was incorporated and named in 1953 by local boosters who tried to entice toy manufacturers with the prospect that they could label their products as "Made in the North Pole". The daft idea didn't quite work out as planned. Manufacturers declined the offer, but one trader moved here, opened up *Santa Claus House* on St Nicholas Avenue – easily identified by the 22-foot Santa outside – and established the town as the self-appointed home of Santa Claus. If a child addresses a letter to "Santa Claus, North Pole", it ends up here; the store can also arrange for a letter from the red-and-white one to be sent to a child of your choice in December for $3.

travel details

Trains

The Alaska Railroad *has one daily service in each direction in summer, and one weekly service in winter between Seward on the Kenai Peninsula via Anchorage and Denali National Park; there are several trains each day between Anchorage and Whittier on the Prince William Sound.* White Pass and Yukon Railroad *has a daily service in summer from Skagway to Bennett, BC, with a through bus connection to Whitehorse. Specific departures include:*

From Anchorage to Denali National Park (1 daily summer, 1 weekly winter; 8hr); Fairbanks (1 daily summer, 1 weekly winter; 12hr); Seward (1 daily summer, 1 weekly winter; 4hr); Whittier (4 daily summer).

From Denali National Park to Anchorage (1 daily summer, 1 weekly winter; 8hr); Fairbanks (1 daily summer, 1 weekly winter; 4hr); Seward (1 daily summer, 1 weekly winter).

From Fairbanks to Anchorage (1 daily summer, 1 weekly winter; 12hr); Denali National Park (1 daily summer, 1 weekly winter; 4 hr); Seward (1 daily summer, 1 weekly winter).

From Seward to Anchorage (1 daily summer, 1 weekly winter; 4hr); Denali National Park (1 daily summer, 1 weekly winter); Fairbanks (1 daily summer, 1 weekly winter).

From Skagway to Bennett, BC, with private *White Pass and Yukon Railroad* (1 daily summer); through bus connection to Whitehorse.

From Whittier to Anchorage (4 daily summer).

Buses

Bus companies such as Alaskon Express, Seward & Homer Bus Lines, Alaska Direct, Backcountry Connections *and* Caribou Express *are detailed throughout the chapter. All routes are served less frequently in winter; the main routes in summer are:*

From Anchorage to Denali National Park and Fairbanks (1 daily); Seward and Homer (1 daily); Valdez (1 daily); Whitehorse, Haines and Skagway (3 weekly).

From Fairbanks to Denali National Park and Anchorage (1 daily); Whitehorse, Skagway and Haines (4 weekly).

Ferries

For details on the two separate services of the Alaska Marine Highway – one running along the Inside Passage in the southeast, the other covering the southwest between Cordova, Valdez, the Kenai Peninsula and the Aleutian Islands, see p.34.

PART THREE

THE
CONTEXTS

THE HISTORICAL FRAMEWORK

The **Pacific Northwest** has never had a unified history. In prehistoric times, the native peoples developed a variety of cultures geared to the region's climatic and geographical diversity, long before American settlers and the British divided the land between them. The final division was an arbitrary, typically colonial affair, but there was never a full-scale war between the two powers – the main blot on the region's history being the white man's ruinous conquest of the aboriginal population.

The Pacific Northwest is a region of intertwining histories rather than a single evolutionary thread. Not only does each of its provinces/states maintain a degree of autonomy, but each grouping of native peoples lays claim to a separate heritage that cannot be fully integrated into that of the hegemonic culture. What follows can do no more than trace the outline of a subject that can be pursued more thoroughly through some of the books recommended later.

THE BEGINNINGS

The ancestors of the native peoples of the Pacific Northwest first entered the region around twenty-five thousand years ago, when vast glaciers covered most of the North American continent, keeping the sea level far below that of today. It seems likely that these first human inhabitants crossed the land bridge linking Asia with present-day Alaska and that they were **Siberian hunter-nomads** travelling in pursuit of mammoths, hairy rhinos, bison, wild horses and sloths, the ice-age animals that made up their diet. These people left very little evidence of their passing, apart from some simple graves and the grooved, chipped stone spear-heads that earnt them the name **Fluted Point People**. In successive waves the Fluted Point People moved down through North America, across the isthmus of Panama, until they reached the southernmost tip of South America. As they settled, so they slowly developed distinctive cultures and languages.

About five thousand years ago another wave of migration passed over from Asia to Alaska. These Inuit migrants made their crossing either in skin-covered boats or on foot over the winter ice, the sea level having risen to submerge the land bridge under the waters of today's Bering Strait. Within the next thousand years the Inuit occupied the entire northern zone of the continent, moving east as far as Greenland and south to the peripheries of Yukon and Alaska, thereby displacing the earlier occupants. These first Inuits – called the **Dorset Culture** after Cape Dorset in NWT, where archeologists first identified its remains in the 1920s – were themselves assimilated or wiped out by the next wave of Inuit, who, crossing into the continent three thousand years ago, created the **Thule culture** – so-called after the Greek word for the world's northern extremity. The Thule people were the direct ancestors of today's **Inuit**.

THE NATIVE PEOPLES

Before the Europeans arrived, the **native peoples** of the Pacific Northwest – numbering perhaps 150,000 – were divided into three main language groups, Algonquian, Athapascan and Inuktitut (Inuit). Within – but not, most remarkably, co-terminus with – these linguistic groups there existed many cultures. None of these people had a written language, the wheel was unknown to them and most were reliant on the canoe, though the plains and plateau peoples to the east of the coastal mountain ranges used draught animals, the largest of which, prior to the introduction of the horse, was the dog. Over the centuries, each of the tribes developed techniques that enabled them to cope with the problems of survival posed by their environments.

THE NORTHERN PEOPLES

Immediately prior to the arrival of the Europeans, the Pacific Northwest was divided into a number of cultural zones. In the extreme north lived the nomadic **Inuit** (see also p.000), whose basic unit was the family group – the optimum arrangement for survival in the precarious conditions. The necessarily small-scale nature of Inuit life meant that they developed no formal political structures and gathered together in larger groups only if the supply of food required it – when, for example, the Arctic char were running upriver from the sea to spawn, or the caribou were migrating.

Just to the south of the Inuit, in a zone that also stretched right across the continent, lived the tribes of the **northern forests**. In the Pacific Northwest, these groups inhabited the land from central Alaska and the Yukon down to central British Columbia. This was a harsh environment too, and consequently these peoples spent most of their time in small nomadic bands following the game on which they depended. Indeed, variations between the tribes largely stemmed from the type of game they pursued: the Kutchin of the Yukon Valley combined fishing with hunting, as did the Tahltan of British Columbia, whereas the Chipewyan, their easterly neighbors, hunted deer and moose. The political structures of these tribes were also rudimentary and, although older men enjoyed a certain respect, there were no "chiefs" in any European sense of the term. In fact, decisions were generally made collectively with the opinions of successful hunters – the guarantors of survival – carrying great weight, as did those of the shaman, who was responsible for satisfying the spirits believed to inhabit every animate and inanimate object.

THE COASTAL PEOPLES

Below the nomads of the northern forests lived the **coastal peoples**, who took advantage of a kinder climate and a more abundant environment to create a sophisticated culture that stretched from southeast Alaska to Oregon. Here, a multitude of groups such as the Tlingit, Salish, Suquamish and Makah were dependent on the ocean, which provided them with a plentiful supply of food. Living a comparatively settled life, they moved only from established winter villages to summer fishing sites, and occupied giant cedar lodges, clan dwellings dominated by the hereditary chief. There was, however, little cohesion within tribes, and people from different villages – even though of the same tribe – would at times be in conflict with each other. Surplus food, especially salmon, was traded and the sizeable profits underpinned a competitive culture revolving around an intricate system of ranks and titles, which culminated in the winter **potlatch**, a giant feast where the generosity of the giver – and the eloquence of the speeches – measured the clan's success. Prestige was also conferred on clans according to the excellence of their wood-carvings, the most conspicuous manifestation being totem poles.

THE PEOPLES OF THE INTERIOR

South of the northern forests and east of the Pacific coast, specific cultures developed in response to particular climatic conditions. The nomadic hunter-gatherers of the inland valleys, like the Nez Perce, foraged for nuts and roots and mixed seasonal fishing with hunting, while the tribes round today's Klamath Lake, in southern Oregon, subsisted on plants and waterfowl and lived in semi-subterranean, earth-domed lodges. Further inland, there were the plateau tribes of the east, such as the Palouse and Spokane, whose culture echoed that of their more famous bison-dependent cousins on the prairies east of the Rockies. In the late seventeenth century, the hunting techniques of these prairie-plateau peoples were transformed by the arrival of the horse – which had made its way from Mexico, where it had been introduced by the Spanish conquistadors. On the prairies, the horse made the bison easy prey and a ready food supply spawned a militaristic culture centered on the prowess of the tribes' young braves.

THE COMING OF THE EUROPEANS

The first European sighting of the Pacific Northwest coast occurred in 1542, when a Spanish expedition sailing from Mexico dropped anchor at the mouth of the Rogue River. Stormy weather and treacherous currents prevented a landing – just as adverse conditions were later to hinder a succession of early explorers, most famously **Sir Francis Drake**, whose *Golden Hind* was buffeted up and down the Oregon coast in 1579. The Spaniards, fresh from their conquest of Mexico, were looking to extend their American empire, whereas Drake was searching for the fabled **Northwest Passage** to the Orient, by which means the English might break free of the trading restrictions imposed by the Portuguese (who controlled the Cape of Good Hope) and the Spanish (who monitored Cape Horn). Despite Drake's endeavors, the Pacific Northwest coast remained a Spanish preserve well into the eighteenth century, but the gossip of Mediterranean sea captains – one of whom, a certain Juan de Fuca, insisted he had discovered the Northwest Passage – remained to excite English nautical interest.

Meanwhile, far to the north, Russian Cossacks were moving east across Siberia bringing Mongol tribes to heel. During the reign of Peter the Great (1696–1725), they conquered the Kamchatka Peninsula and there they heard rumors from the Inuit of the proximity of today's Alaska. Doubting the veracity of this information, but curious all the same, Peter dispatched **Vitus Bering**, a Dane serving with the Russian navy, east from Kamchatka to "search for that peninsula where it [Asia] is joined to America". Bering, after whom the Strait is named, set sail in 1728, but fog prevented him from charting the coast. Twelve years later, he sailed again and, although the trip cost him his life, Bering proved – and the survivors witnessed – that Asia and America are separated by the narrowest of maritime margins.

EUROPEAN INTRUSION

In Bering's wake came traders and navy surveyors who charted the Alaskan shore. Rumours of Russian activity prompted the Spaniards in Mexico City to a reassessment of their situation, and in 1769 they launched an invasion of the Californian coast, establishing a string of Jesuit missions and fortified settlements that were eventually to blossom into cities such as San Francisco and San Diego. But in fact, the Russians posed no real threat – unlike the British who, still searching for the Northwest Passage, dispatched the illustrious **Captain Cook** to the Pacific Northwest in 1776. Cook took the easterly route, sailing round the Cape of Good Hope and across the Pacific Ocean to landfall on Vancouver Island after a year at sea. He hunted high and low for both the Northwest and Northeast (Siberian) Passage, a mission doomed to failure, and, while wintering in the Sandwich Islands (present-day Hawaii), was murdered by Polynesians. On the way home, Cook's ships dropped by Canton, where the sailors found, much to their surprise, that the Chinese were keen to buy the sea otter skins they had procured from the native Americans. News of the expedition's fortuitous discovery – and its commercial potential – spread like wild fire, and by 1790 around 30 merchants from various countries were shuttling back and forth between China and the Pacific coast.

The British Admiralty were, however, still preoccupied with the Northwest Passage and in 1791 they sent **George Vancouver** out to have another look. Although his ultimate aim was unachievable, Vancouver did chart a long stretch of coastline, including the island that bears his name. He somehow failed to notice the Columbia River – a situation remedied by the American Robert Gray shortly afterwards.

The competing claims of the three European nations as to sovereignty over the Pacific Northwest coast were settled, albeit temporarily, by the **Nuu-chah-nulth Convention** of 1790, in which the British squeezed themselves in between Russian Alaska and Spanish California. Needless to say, no-one bothered to consult the indigenous peoples, who could hardly have guessed at the catastrophe that was soon to overwhelm them. After all, they had benefited by trading furs for metal goods, and relations between them and the newcomers were often cordial. The violence, when it did occur, worked both ways.

BRITISH ASCENDANCY

In 1670 Charles II of England had established the **Hudson's Bay Company** and given it control of a million and a half square miles adjacent to Hudson Bay, itself a vast inland sea about 1500 miles east of the Pacific coast. There were two related objecties: the consolidation of the British fur trade and the encircling of New France (broadly Quebec). Montreal was well established as the center of the French fur trade and it was from here that trappers and traders, the voyageurs, launched themselves deep into the interior. Unlike their British counterparts, who waited for the furs to be brought to their stockades, many of the voyageurs adopted native dress, learnt aboriginal languages, and took wives from the tribes through which they passed. The pelts they brought back to Montreal were shipped downriver to Quebec City whence they were shipped to France.

In 1760, the British captured Montreal, marking the end of the French North American empire. With French knowledge and experience of the interior too valuable to be jettisoned, however, many of the voyageurs were employed by British merchants in the **North West Company**. Once Captain Cook's sailors had demonstrated the potential of the Chinese fur trade, the search was on for an easy way to export furs westward to the Pacific, and both companies dispatched long-haul expeditions into the Rockies, with **Alexander Mackenzie** making the first continental crossing north of Mexico in 1793. Decades of rivalry came to an end when the two companies merged to form an enlarged Hudson's Bay Company in 1821.

The Company ruled western Canada and the Pacific Northwest as a virtual fiefdom until the middle of the nineteenth century, discouraging immigration in order to protect its fur trade. It did, however, exercise its powers in the name of the British Crown and consequently, after the War of American Independence, it came to play an important role in flying the imperial flag in the face of American territorial aspirations.

THE COMING OF THE SETTLERS

By the **Louisiana Purchase** of 1803, the US bought all French lands between the Mississippi and the Rockies, from Canada to Mexico, for $15 million dollars. President Jefferson engineered the deal and it was he who bankrolled the **Lewis and Clark** expedition the following year, with the expectation that the two explorers would open up the interior to American fur traders. At that time the tribes of the Missouri basin carried their furs to Hudson's Bay Company posts in Canada, and Jefferson believed, quite rightly, that they would find it far easier to dispatch the pelts downriver to American buyers. Indeed, the President's dream was to displace the British entirely – both in the interior and along the west coast – thereby securing economic control of a continent whose potential he, unlike most of his political contemporaries, foresaw. With this in mind, his two proteges were dispatched to the

Pacific with instructions to collect every scrap of information they could find.

The expedition, consisting of 48 men, 3 boats, 4 horses, 21 bales of presents to buy goodwill and, in case that failed, rifles, a blunderbuss and a cannon, set out on May 14, 1804. Lewis and Clark ascended the Missouri, crossed the Rockies and descended the Columbia River to reach the Pacific eighteen months later. They encountered little real danger, for they evaded the warlike Sioux, but there were all sorts of problems – indiscipline among their men, treacherous whitewater rapids and just plain discomfort: they were all, for example, infested with fleas in their winter base on the west coast. They covered about 4000 miles on the outward trip, carefully mapping and describing the country and its people; their journals constitute one of the finest accounts of its sort compiled.

The Lewis and Clark expedition laid the basis for American competition with British fur traders: Clark founded the Missouri Fur Company on his return, and **John Jacob Astor** was sufficiently encouraged to site an American fur trading post, Astoria, at the mouth of the Columbia River in 1811. In the next twenty years, several factors combined to accelerate the pace of the American move westward: the opening of the Santa Fe Trail from Missouri to the far southwest (then in Mexican hands); the exploratory probings of the Rocky Mountain Fur Company, amongst whose employees was Kit Carson; and the dispatch of missionaries – most notably **Dr Marcus Whitman**, who set about Christianizing the Cayuse from his farm near today's Walla Walla in Washington. The Whitmans wrote home extolling the virtues of the **Oregon Country** (as both Washington State and Oregon were then known), firing the interest of relatives and friends. Perhaps more importantly, the Whitmans had made their long journey west by ordinary farm wagon: if they could do it, then so, it was argued, could other settler families.

THE OREGON TRAIL

The early explorers, fur traders and missionaries who travelled west from the Missouri blazed the trails that would lead thousands of American colonists to the Pacific coast. Indeed, it was Whitman himself who, in 1843, guided the first sizeable wagon train (of a thousand souls) along the **Oregon Trail** – a pioneering journey that became known to later generations as the **Great Migration**. The migrants sweated their way across the plains, chopped through forests and hauled their wagons over fast-flowing streams behind oxen that travelled at around 2mph. It was a long and hard trip, but impressions of the trail varied enormously. To some who encountered hostile natives, grizzlies, cholera or bitter weather, it was hell on earth; to others it was exhilarating – "a long picnic", wrote one. Each succeeding year a couple of thousand more emigrants followed, and soon American farmers – for the vast majority of migrants heading for the Oregon were

precisely that – were crawling all over the Willamette Valley, much to the consternation of the Hudson's Bay Company. This mass movement made Oregon an American community and was to ensure its future lay within the USA.

FIXING THE FRONTIERS

In 1783, the Treaty of Paris wrapped up the American War of Independence and recognized the United States' northern and western frontiers with British and French territory as being on the Great Lakes and along the Mississippi respectively. The Louisiana Purchase brought America's western border to the Rockies,

NATIVE AMERICANS

From the 1830s onwards, the **native Americans** of the Pacific Northwest were simply overwhelmed by the pace of events. Lacking any political or social organization beyond the immediate level of the tribe, it was not difficult for the white colonists to divide and conquer – though admittedly European-borne diseases did much of the damage, with epidemics of measles and smallpox decimating the region's indigenous population by up to seventy percent.

In the Oregon Country, the US government initially tried to move willing tribes into fairly large reservations, but as more settlers came, the tribes were forced onto smaller and smaller parcels of land. Some groups chose to resist – the Cayuse slaughtered the Whitmans, the Nez Perce killed a handful of white settlers and, most determined of all, the Modocs from the California-Oregon border fought a long-running guerrilla war against the US army – but, for the most part, the native peoples were simply swept aside. By 1880, the survivors had been consigned to **Indian Reservations** that mostly comprised the infertile land no-one else wanted. Further damage was inflicted by the **Dawes Severalty Act** of 1887, which required native Americans to select individual 160-acre reservation landholdings (lands had traditionally been held communally and land ownership was an alien concept to most of the tribes) and obliged their children to attend government or mission schools. Deprived of their traditions and independence, many lapsed into poverty, alcoholism and apathy.

In Canada, events followed a similarly depressing course. Herded onto reservations under the authoritarian paternalism of the Ministry of Indian

Affairs, Canadian native peoples were subjected to a concerted campaign of Europeanization: the potlatch was banned, and they were obliged to send their children to boarding schools for ten months of the year. In the late 1940s, the Canadian academic Frederick Tisdall estimated that no fewer than 65,000 reservation aboriginals were "chronically sick" from starvation. Further north, the Inuit were drawn into increasing dependence on the Hudson's Bay Company, which encouraged them to hunt for furs rather than food, while the twin agencies of the Christian missions and the Royal Canadian Mounted Police worked to integrate them into white culture. As in the States, the settlers brought with them diseases to which the native peoples had no natural immunity; TB, for example, was, right up until the 1960s, fifteen to twenty times more prevalent among the aboriginal population than in the rest of the population.

In recent years, both the Canadian and US governments have (somewhat intermittently) attempted to right historic wrongs, but socio-economic indicators demonstrate that native peoples remain at a significant disadvantage compared to the rest of the population. More positively, native peoples have begun to assert their identity and campaign for self-determination, especially in Canada where "Status Indians" are now represented by the **Assembly of First Nations** (AFN). Reflecting greater advocacy over the last twenty years, the Assembly has sponsored a number of legal actions over treaty rights, and has announced that its main objective is to secure an equal status with the provincial governments, a stance made clear in constitutional negotiations on the establishment of an Inuit homeland.

beyond which was Mexican-governed California, later secured for America at the end of the Mexican-American War in 1847. Meanwhile, territorial tension between Britain and the United States was partially resolved by the Anglo-American **War of 1812**: neither side was strong enough to win, but the Treaty of Ghent in 1814 formalized American recognition of the legitimacy of British North America, whose border was established along the 49th parallel west from Lake of the Woods to the Rockies.

In the Oregon Country, Astor, irritated by the failure of the Americans to trounce the English in the war of 1812, sold his trading post to the Hudson's Bay Company, who relocated their western headquarters to Vancouver, near the mouth of the Columbia River. Despite the dominant position of the Company throughout the Pacific Northwest, Britain agreed to share access to the Oregon Country with the US until the two powers could decide a final boundary. It was the influx of American farmers along the Oregon Trail that resolved the issue, and the present international frontier was fixed in 1846, following a westward extension of the original 49th parallel.

The **Oregon Territory** came into being the following year – and Washington was sliced off it in 1853. Oregon's subsequent application for US statehood was, however, delayed over the issue of slavery, with neither the existing free states nor the rival slave states eager to complicate Congressional workings with new admissions. Oregon was finally accepted as a free state in 1859, though with an appalling State Constitution that forbade free blacks from living there at all; this was rescinded after the Civil War. Thinly populated Washington only managed to assemble enough settlers to qualify for statehood in 1889. The frontier jigsaw was completed in 1867 when the US bought **Alaska** from the Russians.

AMERICAN CONSOLIDATION AND THE RUSH FOR GOLD

In 1848 **gold** was discovered in the Sierra Nevada hills. Guessing the effect the news would have in Oregon, a certain Captain Newell sailed up the Willamette River buying every spade, pick and shovel he could get his hands on. He then informed locals of the gold strike, and promptly sold their own tools back to them

– with a substantial mark-up. It was quite a scam and, in the ensuing **California gold rush**, over two thirds of able-bodied Oregonians high-tailed it south. Yet, despite the exodus, the gold rush turned out to be the making of Oregon. For the first time, there was a ready market for the farmers of the Willamette Valley – and an even closer one when gold was found at Jacksonville in 1850 – whilst Oregon lumber towns like Ashland and Roseburg boomed supplying building materials, and Portland flourished from the dramatic upturn in trade.

In the early 1860s, the story was repeated when gold was unearthed in the Oregonian interior, in the hills around John Day and Baker City. Both strikes had a dramatic impact, opening up the area east of the Cascade Mountains – and displacing the native population, who had previously been assured they'd be allowed to stay there. To feed the miners, thousands of cattle were driven over the mountains and, once they'd reached the interior, drovers found their animals thrived on the meadow grass of the valley bottoms and the plentiful supply of bunchgrass. This marked the beginning of the great cattle empires of eastern Oregon, though the ranchers' success was short-lived: the railroad reached the west in the 1880s and, at a stroke, overturned local economics. Railroad transportation meant that more money could be made from an acre sown than an acre grazed, and the cattle barons soon gave way to the farmers.

Washington followed a similar pattern, with the eastern towns of Spokane and Walla Walla prospering as supply depots for the gold and silver mines of Idaho and Montana. Here, too, the rolling grasslands of the interior were grazed by cattle until the appearance of the railroad (and the savage winter of 1881) precipitated the move over from the livestock industry to grain production. The Washington seaboard got in on the act during the **Klondike gold rush** of the 1890s, when Seattle became the jumping-off point for Alaska-bound miners, and grew to rival San Francisco.

CANADIAN CONFEDERATION

All this American activity put the wind up British North America, which was still a collection of self-governing colonies, and the discovery of gold in 1858 beside the Fraser River fuelled British anxiety. In response to the influx of American prospectors, British Columbia was hastily designated a Crown Colony – as was the Klondike when gold was struck there in 1895. Yet British North America remained incoherently structured and, as a means of keeping the US at bay, the imperial government encouraged **Confederation**. After three years of colonial debate, the British Parliament passed the **British North America Act** of 1867, which provided for a federal parliament and for each province to retain a regional government and assembly. British Columbia joined the Confederation, soon to become the **Dominion of Canada**, in 1871.

Two years later, the federal authorities created the **Mounties** (the North West Mounted Police), who came to perform a vital role in administering the Canadian west, acting both as law enforcement officers and as justices of the peace. From the 1880s, patrols diligently criss-crossed the Canadian Pacific Northwest, their influence reinforced by a knowledge of local conditions accumulated in the exercise of a great range of duties, from delivering the mail to providing crop reports. Despite a degree of autonomy, the Mounties saw themselves as an integral part of the British Empire and, more than any other organization, they ensured that these remote provinces were not poached or overrun by American traders and prospectors. They were aided in this respect by the coming of the railroad: in 1886 the first train ran from Montreal to Vancouver, opening up the west and the interior of the country to Canadian settlers.

MODERN TIMES

By 1910, the broad characteristics of today's Pacific Northwest were firmly in place. The region's economy was largely reliant on primary products, principally timber, grain and fish, but there were also pockets of manufacturing industry, especially in and around Seattle and Tacoma. Since World War II, the pace of industrialization and urbanization has quickened, alleviating dependence on logging,

THE WOBBLIES

In 1905, enthusiastic delegates to a labor congress in Chicago founded the **INDUSTRIAL WORKERS OF THE WORLD** (the IWW), the most sucessful revolutionary labor movement in US history. It was born out of frustration with the dominant union organization of the day, the *American Federation of Labor* (AFL), both for its failure to organize successful strikes and its ideological conservatism: the AFL had no political strategy and its main objective was to protect the interests of skilled workers. IWW members became known as **Wobblies**, as a result of mispronunciation of the movement's acronym by the Chinese immigrants who constituted a sizeable proportion of its members. Dedicated to the overthrow of capitalism by means of agitation and strike action, their flyers proclaimed "The working class and the employing class have nothing in common". The IWW's organizational goal was to unite the workers of individual industries – such as mining, construction and logging – within brotherhoods that would eventually be combined into the so-called **One Big Union**.

IWW membership was never large: it reached a peak of around 100,000 in 1912 – but the Wobblies managed to exercise an influence out of all proportion to their numbers. They inspired thousands of workers to actively struggle against harsh anti-strike laws, low pay and dreadful conditions. The IWW was particularly strong in Washington and Oregon, calling a series of strikes against the lumber companies. The employers frequently resorted to violence to defeat the union's causes, and in 1916, in one of several bloody incidents, seven IWW organizers were shot and many others were drowned when the Sheriff of Everett tried to prevent them disembarking from the steamboat that had brought them from Seattle.

Three years later, a (peaceful) general strike mobilized 60,000 workers and paralyzed Seattle. IWW organizers fed strikers at labor-run cafeterias, handled emergency services and delivered milk to babies so effectively that many employers feared they were witnessing the beginnings of a Bolshevik-style revolution. But in fact the Wobblies had never devised a precise political program, nor did they want to seize power, and the strike simply faded away. Indeed, the IWW was by then deeply split between radical revolutionary factions and elements that favored democratic reform. In the 1920s, the IWW began to fragment, its legacy a lasting preference in the US for large industrial unions.

fishing and farming, but not enough to insulate the Pacific Northwest from its vulnerability to a wearisome cycle of boom and bust, with prices determined by stock markets beyond local control. In this, the region mirrors much of the rest of continent and, in an attempt to speed recovery from the recessionary economics of North America and forge a separate identity, is increasingly looking toward the countries of the Pacific Rim for its future.

The dramatic landscapes for which the Pacific Northwest is famous continue to exert their influence, as in the 1980 eruption of Mount St Helens. While technology has facilitated the exploitation of harsh and inhospitable environments – through projects such as the trans-Alaska oil pipeline, completed in 1977 – in such sensitive habitats, damage wrought by incidents such as the wreck of the oil tanker *Exxon Valdez* in 1989, and the devastation caused by large-scale logging and overfishing, can be irreparable. The ongoing, and often bitter, conflict between employment imperatives (particularly in the lumber industry) and conservation issues, frequently threatens to overshadow federal political concerns emanating from seemingly remote Washington, DC or Ottawa.

NORTHWEST WILDLIFE

The Pacific Northwest boasts a wide range of natural habitats, from ice-bound polar islands in the far north to areas of sun-scorched desert along the United States border. Between these extremes the region's mountains, forests and grasslands support an incredible variety and profusion of wildlife – any brief account can only scratch the surface of what it's possible to see. National, state and provincial parks offer the best starting points, and we've listed some of the outstanding sites for spotting particular species. Don't expect to see the big attractions like bears and wolves easily, however – despite the enthusiasm of guides and tourist offices, these are encountered only rarely.

THE OCEAN

The Pacific Ocean largely determines the climate of the Northwest, keeping the coastal temperatures moderate all year round. In spring and summer, cold nutrient-rich waters rise to the surface, producing banks of cooling fog and abundant crops of phytoplankton (microscopic algae). The algae nourishes creatures such as krill (small shrimps) which provide baby food for juvenile fish. This food chain sustains millions of nesting seabirds, as well as elephant seals, sea lions and whales.

Gray whales, the most common species of whale spotted from land, were once almost hunted to the point of extinction, but have returned to the coast in large numbers. During their southward migration to breeding grounds off Mexico, from December to January (see box, p.293), they are easy to spot from prominent headlands all along the coast, and many towns – especially on Vancouver Island – have charter services offering whale-watching tours. On their way back to the Arctic Sea, in February and March, the new-born whale calves can sometimes be seen playfully leaping out of the water, or "breaching". Look for the whale's white-plumed spout – once at the surface, they usually blow several times in succession.

Humpback whales are also frequently seen, largely because they're curious and follow sightseeing boats, but also because of their surface acrobatics. They too were hunted to near-extinction, and though protected by international agreement since 1966 they still number less than ten percent of their former population.

Vancouver Island's inner coast supports one of the world's most concentrated populations of **killer whales** or **orcas**. These are often seen in family groups or "pods" travelling close to shore, usually on the trail of large fish – which on the Northwest coast means **salmon** (see box p.324). The orca, however, is the only whale whose diet also runs to warm-blooded animals – hence the "killer" tag – and it will gorge on walrus, seal and even minke, gray and beluga whales.

Another Northwest inhabitant, **sea otters** differ from most marine mammals in that they keep themselves warm with a thick soft coat of fur rather than with blubber. This brought them to the attention of early Russian and British fur traders, and by the beginning of this century they were virtually extinct. Found in numbers in Alaska (see box on p.523), they were reintroduced in 1969 to Vancouver Island's northwest coast, where they are now breeding successfully at the heart of their original range. With binoculars, it's often easy to spot these charming creatures lolling on their backs, using rocks to crack open sea urchins or mussels and eating them off their stomachs; they often lie bobbing asleep, entwined in kelp to stop them floating away.

Northern **fur seals** breed on Alaska's Pribilof Islands but are often seen off the British Columbian coast during their migrations. They are "eared seals" (like their cousins, the northern **sea lions**, who are year-round residents), and can manage rudimentary shuffling on land thanks to short rear limbs which can be rotated for forward movement. They also swim with strokes from front flippers, as opposed to the slithering, fishlike action of true seals.

TIDEPOOLS

The Pacific Northwest's shorelines are composed of three primary ecosystems: tidepools, sandy beach and estuary. You can explore **tidepools** at the twice-daily low tides (consult local newspapers for times), so long as you watch out for freak waves and take care not to get stranded by the incoming tide. You should also tread carefully – there are many small lives underfoot. Of the miles of beaches with tidepools, some of the best are at Pacific Rim National Park on Vancouver Island. Here you will find sea anemones (they look like green zinnias), hermit crabs, purple and green shore crabs, red sponges, purple sea urchins, starfish ranging from the size of a dime to the size of a hub cap, mussels, abalone and chinese-hat limpets – to name a few. Black oystercatchers, noisily heard over the surf, may be seen foraging for an unwary, lips-agape mussel. Gulls and black turnstones are also common and during summer brown pelicans dive for fish just offshore.

The life and soul of the tidepool party is the **hermit crab**. It protects its soft and vulnerable hindquarters with scavenged shells, usually those of the aptly named black turban snail. Hermit crabs scurry busily around in search of a detritus snack, or scuffle with other hermit crabs over the proprietorship of vacant snail shells.

Many of the **seaweeds** you see growing from the rocks are edible. As one would expect from a Pacific beachfront, there are also **palms** – sea palms, with 10cm-long rubbery stems and flagella-like fronds. Their thick root-like holdfasts provide shelter for small crabs. You will also find giant **kelp** washed up on shore – harvested commercially for use in thickening ice cream.

SANDY BEACHES

Long, golden sandy **beaches** may look sterile from a distance, but observe the margin of sand exposed as a gentle wave recedes, and you will see jetstreams of small bubbles emerge from numerous clams and mole crabs. Small shorebirds called sanderlings race amongst the waves in search of these morsels, and sand dollars are often easy to find along the high-tide line.

The most unusual sandy-shore bathing beauties are the **northern elephant seals**, which will tolerate rocky beaches but prefer soft sand mattresses for their rotund torsos. The males, or bulls, can reach lengths of over six meters and weigh upwards of four tons; the females, or cows, are petite by comparison – four meters long, and averaging a mere 1000 kilos in weight. They have large eyes, adapted for catching fish in deep or murky waters; indeed, elephant seals are the deepest diving mammals, capable of staying underwater for twenty minutes at a time and reaching depths of over 1000 meters, where the pressure is ninety times that at the surface. They dive deeply in order to avoid the attentions of the great white sharks who lurk offshore, for whom they are a favorite meal.

As the otter population was plundered by fur-traders, so the elephant seals were decimated by commercial whalers in the mid-nineteenth century for their blubber and hides. By the turn of the century less than a hundred remained, but careful protection has partially restored the population in many of their native Northwest habitats.

Elephant seals emerge from the ocean only to breed or moult; their name comes from the male's long trunk-like proboscis, through which they produce a resonant pinging sound that biologists call "trumpeting", which is how they attract a mate. In December and January, the bulls haul themselves out of the water and battle for dominance. The predominant, or alpha, male will do most of the mating, siring as many as fifty young pups, one per mating, in a season. Other males fight it out at the fringes, each managing one or two couplings with the hapless, defenceless females. During this time, the beach is a seething mass of ton upon ton of blubbery seals – flopping sand over their back to keep cool, squabbling with their neighbors while making rude snoring and belching sounds. The adults depart in March but the weaned pups hang around until May.

ESTUARIES

Throughout much of the Northwest, especially in the more developed south of the region, many **estuarine or rivermouth habitats** have been filled, diked, drained, "improved" with marinas or contaminated by pollutants. Those that survive intact consist of a mixture of mudflats, exposed only at low tide, and salt marsh, together forming a critical wildlife area that provides nurseries for many kinds of invertebrates and fish, and nesting and wintering grounds for many birds. Cordgrass, a dominant wetlands plant, produces five to ten times as much oxygen and nutrients per acre as does wheat.

Many interesting creatures live in the thick organic ooze, including the fat Innkeeper, a revolting-looking pink hot dog of a worm that sociably shares its burrow with a small crab and a fish, polychaete worms, clams and other goodies. Most prominent of estuary birds are the great blue herons and great egrets. Estuaries are the best place to see wintering shorebirds such as dunlin, dowitchers, least and western sandpipers and yellowlegs. Peregrine falcons and osprey are also found here.

COASTAL BLUFFS

Along the shore, coastal meadows are bright with pink and yellow sand verbena, lupines, sea rocket, sea fig and the bright orange California poppy – which, despite its name, is also found in Washington and Oregon. Slightly inland, hills are covered with coastal scrub, consisting largely of coyote brush. Coastal canyons contain broadleaf trees such as California laurel (known as myrtlewood in Oregon), alder, buckeye and oaks – and a tangle of sword ferns, horsetail and cow parsnip.

Common rainy-season canyon inhabitants include ten-centimeter-long banana slugs and rough-skinned newts. Coastal thickets also provide homes for weasels, bobcats, grey fox, racoons, black-tailed deer, quail and garter snakes, together with the reintroduced **Tule elk**, a once common member of the deer family.

RIVER VALLEYS

Like many fertile **river valleys**, the large river systems of the Northwest – near cities at least – have in places been affected by agriculture. Riparian (streamside) vegetation has been logged, wetlands drained and streams contaminated by agricultural runoff. Despite this, the riparian environment that does remain is a prime wildlife habitat, especially in the mountain parks, where conditions in many respects are still pristine. Wood ducks, kingfishers, swallows and warblers are common, as are grey fox, racoon and striped skunks. Common winter migrants include Canada geese, green-winged and cinnamon teals, pintail, shovelers and wigeon, and their refuges are well worth visiting. Don't be alarmed by the large numbers of duck-hunters – the term "refuge" is a misnomer, although many such areas do have tour routes where hunting is prohibited.

GRASSLANDS

Most of the Northwest's **grassland** is in Canada, though the popular image of the interior as a huge prairie of waving wheat is misconceived. Only ten per cent of the country is covered in true grassland, most of it in the southernmost reaches of Alberta and Saskatchewan, with spillovers in Manitoba and British Columbia – areas which lie in the rain shadow of the Rockies and are too dry to support forest.

Two grassland belts once thrived in Alberta, tallgrass prairie in the north and shortgrass in the south. Farming has now not only put large areas of each under crops, but also decimated most of the large mammals that roamed the range – pronghorns, mule deer, white-tailed deer and elk – not to mention their predators like wolves, grizzlies, coyotes, foxes, bobcats and cougars.

The most dramatic loss from the grasslands, though, has been the **bison** (or buffalo), the continent's largest land mammal. Once numbering an estimated 45 million, bison are now limited to just a few free-roaming herds (see p.361). Early prairie settlers were so struck by these extraordinary animals – the average bull stands almost two meters at the shoulder and weighs over a ton – that they believed bison, rather than the climate, had been responsible for clearing the grasslands.

Once almost as prevalent as the bison, but now almost as rare, is the **pronghorn**, a beautiful tawny-gold antelope species. Capable of speeds of over 100kph, it's the continent's swiftest land mammal, so you'll generally see nothing but distinctive white rump disappearing at speed. Uniquely adapted for speed and stamina, the pronghorn has long legs, a heart with twice the capacity of similar-sized animals, and an astonishingly wide windpipe; it also complements its respiratory machinery by running with its mouth open to gulp maximum amounts of air. Though only the size of a large dog, it has eyes larger than those of a horse, a refinement that enables it to spot predators several kilometers away. These days, however, wolves and coyotes are more likely to be after the prairie's new masters – countless small rodents such as gophers, ground squirrels and jackrabbits.

Birds have had to adapt not only to the prairie's dryness but also, of course, to the lack of extensive tree cover. Most species nest on the ground; many are also able to survive on reduced amounts of water and rely on seed-based diets, while some confine themselves to occasional ponds, lakes and "sloughs", which provide important breeding grounds for ducks, grebes, herons, pelicans, rails and many more. Other birds typical of the grassland in its natural state are the marbled godwit, the curlew, and raptors such as the **prairie falcon**, a close relation of the peregrine falcon capable of diving at speeds of up to 290kph.

BOREAL FOREST

The **boreal forest** is North America's largest single ecosystem. Stretching in a broad belt from Newfoundland to the Yukon and Alaska, it fills the area between the eastern forests, grasslands and the northern tundra, occupying a good slice of every Canadian province except British Columbia. Only certain **trees** thrive in this zone of long, cold winters, short summers and acidic soils: although the cover is not identical across the region, expect to see billions of white and black spruce, balsam fir, tamarack (larch) and jack pine, as well as such deciduous species as birch, poplar and aspen – all of which are ideal for wood pulp, making the boreal forest the staple resource of the **lumber industry**.

If you spend any time in the backcountry you'll also come across **muskeg**: neither land nor water, this porridge-like bog is the breeding ground of choice for Alaska and the Yukon's pestilential hordes of mosquitoes and blackflies. It also shelters mosses, scrub willow, pitcher plant, leatherleaf, sundew, cranberry and even the occasional orchid.

The boreal forest supports just about every animal associated with the wilderness: moose, beaver, black bear, wolf and lynx, plus a broad cross-section of small mammals and creatures like deer, caribou and coyote from transitional forest-tundra and aspen-parkland habitats to the north and south.

Wolves are still numerous in the Northwest, but hunting and harassment has pushed them to the northernmost parts of the boreal forest. Their supposed ferocity is more myth than truth. Intelligent and elusive creatures, they rarely harm humans, and it's unlikely you'll see any – though you may well hear their howling if you're out in the sticks.

Lynx are even more elusive. One of the northern forest's most elegant animals, this big cat requires a 150- to 200-square-kilometer range, making the northern wilderness one of the world's few regions capable of sustaining a viable population. Nocturnal hunters, lynx feed on deer and moose but prefer the hare, a common boreal creature that is to the forest's predators what the lemming is to the carnivores of the tundra (see p.000).

Beavers, on the other hand, are commonly seen all over the region. You may catch them at dawn or dusk, heads just above the water as they glide across lakes and rivers. Signs of their legendary activity include log jams across streams and ponds, stumps of felled saplings resembling sharpened pencils, and dens which look like domed piles of mud and sticks.

Lakes, streams and marshy muskeg margins are all favored by **moose**. A ponderous (and very short-sighted) animal with magnificent spreading antlers, it is the largest member of the deer family and is found over much of the Northwest, but especially near swampy ground, where it likes to graze on mosses and lichens. The moose is popular with hunters, and few northern bars are without their moose head – perhaps the only place you'll see this solitary and reclusive species.

Forest wetlands also offer refuge for **ducks and geese**, with loons, grebes and songbirds attracted to their undergrowth. Three species of ptarmigan – willow, rock and white-tailed – are common, and you'll see plenty of big **raptors**, including the great grey owl, the Northwest's largest owl. Many boreal birds migrate, and even those that don't, such as hawks, jays, ravens and grouse, tend to move a little way south, sometimes breaking out in mass movements known as "irruptions". Smaller birds like chickadees, waxwings and finches are particularly fond of these sporadic forays.

MOUNTAIN FORESTS

Mountain forests cover much of the Pacific Northwest and, depending on location and elevation, divide into four types: West Coast, Columbia, montane and sub-alpine.

WEST COAST FOREST

The **West Coast**'s torrential rainfall, mild maritime climate, deep soils and long growing season produce the Northwest's most impressive forests and its biggest trees. Swathes of luxuriant temperate **rainforest** cover much of Vancouver Island and the Pacific coast, dominated by Sitka spruce, western red cedar, Pacific silver fir, western hemlock, western yew and, biggest of all, **Douglas fir**, some of which tower 90m and are 1200 years old. However, these conifers make valuable timber, and much of this forest is under severe threat from logging. Some of the best stands – a fraction of the original – have been preserved on the Queen Charlotte Islands and in Vancouver Island's Pacific Rim National Park.

Below the luxuriant, dripping canopy of the big trees lies an **undergrowth** teeming with life. Shrubs and bushes like salal, huckleberry, bunchberry, salmonberry and twinberry thrive alongside mosses, ferns, lichens, liverworts, skunk cabbage and orchids. All sorts of animals can be found here, most notably the **cougar** and its main prey, the Columbian blacktail **deer**, a subspecies of the mule deer. **Birds** are legion, and include a wealth of woodland species such as the Townsend's warbler, Wilson's warbler, orange-crowned warbler, junco, Swainson's thrush and golden-crowned kinglet. Rarer birds include the rufous **hummingbird**, which migrates from its winter-

ing grounds in Mexico to feed on the forest's numerous nectar-bearing flowers.

COLUMBIA FOREST

The **Columbia forest** covers the lower slopes (400–1400m) of the Cascades, British Columbia's interior mountains and much of the Rockies. **Trees** here are similar to those of the warmer and wetter rainforest – western red cedar, western hemlock and Douglas fir – with Sitka spruce, which rarely thrives away from the coast, the notable exception. The undercover, too, is similar, with lots of devil's club (a particularly vicious thorn), azaleas, black and red twinberry, salmonberry and redberry alder. Mountain lily, columbine, bunchberry and heartleaf arnica are among the common flowers.

Few mammals live exclusively in the forests with the exception of the **red squirrel**, which makes a meal of conifer seeds, and is in turn preyed on by hawks, owls, coyotes and weasels, among others. Bigger predators roam the mountain forest, however, most notably the **brown bear**, a western variant of the ubiquitous **black bear**. Aside from the coyote, the tough, agile black bear is one of the continent's most successful carnivores and the one you're most likely to see around campgrounds and rubbish dumps. Black bears have adapted to a wide range of habitats and food sources, and their only natural enemies – save wolves, which may attack young cubs – are hunters, who bag some 30,000 annually in North America.

Scarcer but still hunted is the famous **grizzly bear**, a far larger and potentially dangerous creature distinguished by its brownish fur and the ridged hump on its back. Now extinct in many of its original habitats, the grizzly is largely confined to the remoter slopes of Alaska, the Rockies and West Coast ranges, where it feeds mainly on berries and salmon. Like other bears, grizzlies are unpredictable and readily provoked – see p.000 for tips on minimizing unpleasant encounters.

MONTANE FOREST

Montane forest covers the more southerly and sheltered reaches of Washington, Oregon and the Rockies and the dry plateaux of interior British Columbia, where spindly Douglas fir, western larch, ponderosa pine and the **lodge-**

pole pine predominate. The lodgepole requires intense heat before releasing its seeds, and huge stands of these trees grew in the aftermath of the forest fires which accompanied the building and running of the railways.

Plentiful voles and small rodents attract **coyotes**, whose yapping – an announcement of territorial claims – you'll often hear at night close to small towns. Coyotes are spreading northwards into the Yukon and Northwest Territories, a proliferation that continues despite massive extermination campaigns prompted by the coyotes' taste for livestock.

Few predators have the speed to keep up with coyotes – only the stealthy **cougar**, or wolves hunting in tandem, can successfully bring them down. Cougars are now severely depleted in North America, and the British Columbia interior and Vancouver Island are the only regions where they survive in significant numbers. Among the biggest and most beautiful of the carnivores, they seem to arouse the greatest bloodlust in hunters.

Ponderosa and lodgepole pines provide fine cover for **birds** like goshawks, Swainson's hawks and lesser species like ruby-crowned kinglets, warblers, pileated woodpeckers, nuthatches and chickadees. In the forest's lowest reaches the vegetation and birds are those of the southern prairies – semi-arid regions of sagebrush, prickly pear and bunch grasses, dotted with lakes full of common **ducks** like mallard, shoveler and widgeon. You might also see the cinnamon teal, a red version of the more common green-wing teal, a bird whose limited distribution lures birdwatchers to British Columbia.

SUBALPINE FOREST

Subalpine forests cover mountain slopes from 1300m to 2200m throughout the Rockies and the rest of the Northwest, supporting lodgepole, whitebark and limber pines, alpine fir and Engelmann spruce. It also contains a preponderance of **alpine larch**, a deciduous conifer whose vivid yellows dot the mountainsides in the fall to beautiful effect.

One of the more common animals of this zone is the **elk**, or **wapiti**, a powerful member of the deer family which can often be seen summering in large herds above the treeline. Elk court and mate during the fall, making a thin nasal sound called "bugling". You should respect their privacy, as rutting elk have notoriously unpredictable temperaments.

Small herds of **mule deer** migrate between forests and alpine meadows, using glands between their hooves to leave a scent for other members of the herd to follow. They're named after their distinctive ears, designed to provide early warning of predators. Other smaller animals which are also attracted to the subalpine forest include the golden-mantled ground squirrel, and birds such as Clark's nutcracker – both tame and curious creatures which often gather around campgrounds in search of scraps.

ALPINE ZONES

Alpine zones occur in mountains above the treeline, which in the Northwest means parts of the Cascades and Rockies, much of British Columbia and large areas of the Yukon. Plant and animal life varies hugely between summer and winter, and according to terrain and exposure to the elements – sometimes it resembles that of the tundra, at others it recalls the profile of lower forest habitats.

In spring, alpine meadows are carpeted with breathtaking displays of **wildflowers**: clumps of Parnassus grass, lilies, anemones, Indian paintbrushes, lupines and a wealth of yellow flowers such as arnica, cinquefoil, glacier lily and wood betony. These meadows make excellent pasture, attracting elk and mule deer in summer, as well as full-time residents like **Dall's sheep**, the related **bighorn** and the incredible **mountain goat**, perhaps the hardiest of Alaska and the Yukon's bigger mammals. Staying close to the roughest terrain possible, mountain goats are equipped with short, stolid legs, flexible toes and non-skid soles, all designed for clambering over near-vertical slopes, grazing well out of reach of their less agile predators.

Marmots, resembling hugely overstuffed squirrels, take things easier and hibernate through the worst of the winter and beyond. In a good year they can sleep for eight months, prey only to grizzly bears, which are strong enough and have the claws to dig down into their dens. In their waking periods they can be tame and friendly, often nibbling contentedly in the sunnier corners of campgrounds. When threatened, however, they produce a piercing and unearthly whistle. (They can also do a lot of damage: some specialize in chewing the radiator hoses of parked cars.) The strange little **pika**, a relative of the rabbit, is more elusive but keeps itself busy throughout the year, living off a miniature haystack of fodder which it accumulates during the summer.

Birds are numerous in summer, and include rosy finches, pipits and blue grouse, but few manage to live in the alpine zone year-round. One which does is the white-tailed **ptarmigan**, a plump, partridge-like bird which, thanks to its heavily feathered feet and legs, is able to snowshoe around deep drifts of snow; its white winter plumage provides camouflage. Unfortunately, ptarmigans can be as slow-moving and stupid as barnyard chickens, making them easy targets for hunters and predators.

TUNDRA

Tundra extends over much of Alaska, the northern Yukon and the Northwest Territories, stretching between the boreal forest and the polar seas. Part grassland and part wasteland, it's a region distinguished by high winds, bitter cold and **permafrost**, a layer of perpetually frozen subsoil. The tundra is not only the domain of ice and emptiness, however: long hours of summer sunshine and the thawed topsoil nurture a carpet of wildflowers, and many species of birds and mammals have adapted to the vagaries of climate and terrain.

Vegetation is uniformly stunted by poor drainage, acidic soils and permafrost, which prevents the formation of deep roots and locks nutrients in the ice. **Trees** like birch and willow can grow, but they spread their branches over a wide area, rarely reaching over a meter in height. Over ninety-nine percent of the remaining vegetation consists of perennials like **grasses** and sedges, small flowering annuals, mosses, lichens and shrubs. Most have evolved ingenious ways of protecting themselves against the elements: arctic cotton grass, for example, grows in large insulated hummocks in which the interior temperature is higher than the air outside; others have large, waxy leaves to conserve moisture or catch as much sunlight as possible. **Wildflowers** during the short, intense spring can be superlative, covering seemingly inert ground in a carpet of purple mountain saxifrage, yellow arctic poppy, indigo clusters of arctic forget-me-not and the pink buds of Jacob's ladder.

Tundra grasses provide some of the first links in the food chain, nourishing mammals such as white **arctic ground squirrels**, also known as parkas, as their fur is used by the Inuit to make parka jackets. Vegetation also provides the staple diet of **lemmings**, among the most remarkable of the arctic fauna. Instead of hibernating, these creatures live under the snow, busily munching away on shoots and consuming twice their body-weight daily – the intake they need merely to survive. They also breed prolifically, which is just as well for they are the mainstay of a long list of predators. Chief of these are **arctic white foxes**, ermines and weasels, though birds, bears and arctic wolves may also hunt them in preference to larger prey. Because they provide a food source for so many, fluctuations in the lemming populations have a marked effect on the life cycles of numerous creatures.

Caribou belong to the reindeer family and are the most populous of the big tundra mammals. They are known above all for their epic migrations, frequently involving thousands of animals, which start in March when the herds leave their wintering grounds on the fringes of the boreal forest for calving grounds to the north. The exact purpose of these migrations is still a matter for conjecture. They certainly prevent the overgrazing of the tundra's fragile mosses and lichens, and probably also enable the caribou to shake off some of the wolves that would otherwise shadow the herd (wolves have to find southerly dens at this time to bear their own cubs). The timing of treks also means that calving takes place before the arrival of biting insects, which can claim as many calves as do predators – an adult caribou can lose as much as a liter of blood a week to insects.

The tundra's other large mammal is the **musk ox**, a vast, shaggy herbivore and close cousin of the bison. The musk ox's Achilles' heel is a tendency to form lines or circles when threatened – a perfect defence against wolves, but not against rifle-toting hunters, who until the introduction of conservation measures threatened to be their undoing. The Yukon and Northwest Territories now have some of the world's largest free-roaming herds, although – like the caribou – they're still hunted for food and fur by the Inuit.

Tundra **birds** number about a hundred species and are mostly migratory. Three-quarters of these are waterfowl, which arrive first to take advantage of streams, marshes and small lakes created by surface meltwater: arctic wetlands provide nesting grounds for numerous swans, geese and ducks, as well as the loon, which is immortalized on the back of the Canadian dollar coin. The red-necked **phalarope** is a particularly specialized visitor, feeding on aquatic insects and plankton. More impressive in its abilities is the migratory **arctic tern**, whose 32,000-kilometer round trip from the Antarctic is the longest annual migration of any creature on the planet. The handful of non-migratory birds tend to be scavengers like the raven, or predators like the **gyrfalcon**, the world's largest falcon, which preys on arctic hares and ptarmigan. Jaegers, gulls, hawks and owls largely depend on the lemming: the snowy owl, for example, synchronizes its journeys south with four-year dips in the lemming population.

Fauna on the arctic **coast** has a food chain that starts with plankton and algae, ranging up through tiny crustaceans, clams and mussels, sea cucumbers and sea urchins, cod, ringed and bearded seals, to beluga whales and **polar bears** – perhaps the most evocative of all tundra creatures, but still being killed in their hundreds for "sport" despite decades of hunting restrictions. Migrating **birds** are especially common here, notably near Nunaluk Spit on the Yukon coast, which is used as a corridor and stopover by millions of loons, swans, geese, plovers, sandpipers, dowitchers, eagles, hawks, guillemots and assorted songbirds.

WILDLIFE CHECKLIST

This is by no means an exhaustive list of all the wildlife species and their habitats – it should be treated simply as an indication of the places and the times you are most likely to see certain species and types of wildlife.

Beluga, fin, humpback, blue and **minke whales**: at many points off the Northwest coast, especially off Vancouver Island's west coast and Alaska's Kenai Fjords National Park; summer.

Bison: Wood Buffalo National Park (Alberta).

Black bears: Glacier National Park (BC), Banff and Jasper national parks (BC), Kananaskis Country (Alberta), Prince William Sound (Alaska); summer.

Caribou: Dempster Highway north of Dawson City (Yukon), Denali National Park (Alaska); fall.

Dall's sheep: Sheep Mountain, Kluane National Park (Yukon) and Denali National Park (Alaska); summer.

Desert species: Cacti, sagebrush, rattlesnakes and kangaroo rats around Osoyoos (BC); summer.

Eagles and owls Boundary Bay, 20km south of Vancouver (BC); winter.

Elk: Banff and Jasper national parks (BC); Kananaskis Country (Alberta); summer.

Gray whales: Pacific Rim National Park, Vancouver Island (BC); spring and summer.

Grizzly bears: Kodiak Island and Denali National Park (Alaska), spring and summer; Glacier National Park and at Khutzeymateen Estuary, north of Prince Rupert (BC); August.

Killer whales: Robson Bight in Johnstone Strait, Vancouver Island (BC); summer.

Prairie species: Hawks, coyotes and rattlesnakes in the Milk River region (Alberta); May to June.

Salmon: Adams River sockeye salmon run near Salmon Arm (BC); October.

Seabirds: Waterfowl and seabirds in the Queen Charlotte Islands (BC), and in Kenai Fjords National Park and Kodiak Island (Alaska).

Sea otters and sea lions: off Pacific Rim National Park, Vancouver Island (BC), Kenai Fjords National Park and Prince William Sound (Alaska); spring and summer.

Wildflowers: Numerous woodland species on Vancouver Island and the Gulf Islands, and at Mount Revelstoke National Park (BC); late spring to summer.

BOOKS

Most of the following books should be readily available in the UK, US or Canada. Where two publishers are given, the first is the US publisher, the second the UK publisher.

TRAVEL

Hugh Brody *Maps and Dreams* (Pantheon; Faber, o/p). Brilliantly written account of the lives and lands of the Beaver people of north-west Canada. For further acute insights into the ways of the far north, see also Brody's *Living Arctic* (University of Washington Press; Faber).

P Browning *The Last Wilderness* (Great West Books). An engrossing description of a harsh and lonely canoe journey through the Northwest Territories.

Ranulph Fiennes *The Headless Valley* (Hodder & Stoughton, o/p). Tales of derring-do from infamous explorer, whitewater rafting down the South Nahanni and Fraser rivers of British Columbia and the NWT.

Barry Lopez *Arctic Dreams: Imagination and Desire in Northern Landscape* (Bantam; Pan). Extraordinary award-winning book, combining natural history, physics, poetry, earth sciences and philosophy to produce a dazzling portrait of the far north.

Duncan Pryde *Nununga: Ten Years of Eskimo Life* (Hippocrene; Eland). Less a travel book than a social document from a Scot who left home at 18 to live with the Inuit.

Alastair Scott *Tracks Across Alaska* (Abacus). Scott arrived in Alaska ill-equipped and inexperienced, but five months later successfully crossed the state with sled and dog team, recording his adventures on the way.

CULTURE AND SOCIETY

Don Dumond *The Eskimos and Aleuts* (Thames & Hudson). Anthropological and archeological tour-de-force on the prehistory, history and culture of northern peoples; backed up with fine maps, drawings and photographs.

Paula Fleming *The North American Indians in Early Photographs* (Phaidon). Stylized poses don't detract from a plaintive record of a way of life that has all but vanished.

Allan Gregg and Michael Posner *The Big Picture* (MacFarlane, Walter & Ross). A contemporary survey on what Canadians think of everything from sex to politics.

Paul Kane *Wanderings of An Artist among the Indians of North America* (Charles E Tuttle, o/p). Kane, one of Canada's better known landscape artists, spent three years travelling to the Pacific Coast and back in the 1840s. His witty account of his wanderings makes a delightful read – any major Canadian second-hand bookstore should have it.

Alan B Macmillan *Native Peoples and Cultures of Canada* (Douglas & McIntyre). Excellent anthology on Canada's native groups from prehistory to current issues of self-government and land claims. Well-written and illustrated throughout.

John McPhee *Coming into the Country* (Bantam). Penetrating portrait of Alaska written in the mid-1970s, but still largely relevant in a contemporary context.

Mordecai Richler *Home Sweet Home* (Triad Grafton, o/p in UK). Entertaining but occasionally whingeing anecdotes from all corners of Canada.

The True North – Canadian Landscape Painting 1896–1939 (Lund Humphries). A fascinating and well-illustrated book exploring how artists have treated northern landscapes.

HISTORY

Owen Beattie and John Geiger *The Fate of the Franklin Expedition 1845–48* (NAL Dutton; Bloomsbury). An account both of the doomed expedition to find the Northwest Passage and the discovery of artifacts and bodies still frozen in the northern ice; worth buying for the extraordinary photos.

Pierre Berton *Klondike: The Last Great Goldrush 1896–1899* (Penguin). Exceptionally readable account of the characters and epic events of the Yukon gold rush by one of Canada's finest writers.

Pierre Berton *The Arctic Grail* (Penguin). Another Berton blockbuster, this time on the quest for the North Pole and the Northwest Passage from 1818 to 1919. All the author's other books are well worth reading: see also *The Last Spike*, an account of the history and building of the transcontinental railway; *The Mysterious North: Encounters with the Canadian Frontier 1947–1954*; and *Flames across the Frontier*, retelling episodes from the often uneasy relationship between Canada and the US.

Matthew H Case *Northwest Frontier* (BCS Educational Aids). By far the most concise and readable history of pioneer Washington and Oregon in print.

Ella C Clark *Indian Legends of the Pacific Northwest* (University of California Press). Good selection of tales from several tribes, organized into thematic sections and linked by useful critical passages.

Gordon DeMarco *A Short History of Portland* (Lexikos). Thorough and charmingly written account of the city's development.

Gerald Friesen *The Canadian Prairies: A History* (University of Toronto). Stunningly well researched and surprisingly entertaining book: particularly good on the culture of the Metis and Plains Indians.

Washington Irving *Astoria* (University of Nebraska Press). An account of Oregon's first American fur-trading colony, originally published in 1839, that offers fascinating, if lengthy, insights into contemporary attitudes to the then still unsettled Northwest.

Meriwether Lewis and William Clark *The Original Journals of the Lewis and Clark Expedition, 1804–1806* (Ayer Co. Pubs, 8-volume set). Eight volumes of meticulous jottings by some of the Northwest's first inland explorers, scrupulously following President Jefferson's orders to record every detail of flora, fauna, and native inhabitant. Interesting to dip into, though booklets of extracts sold at historic sites in the Northwest are of more use to the casual reader.

Kenneth McNaught *The Penguin History of Canada* (Penguin). Recently revised and concise analysis of Canada's economic, social and political history.

James Mitchener *Alaska* (Fawcett Books). Mitchener isn't to all tastes, but there's no faulting the scope and detail of this immense popular history of the state.

National Park Service *The Overland Migrations* (NPS, US Dept of the Interior). Short but comprehensive guide to the trails that led pioneers west from the Missouri Valley in the middle of the nineteenth century.

Peter C Newman *Caesars of the Wilderness* (Penguin). Highly acclaimed and readable account of the rise and fall of the Hudson's Bay Company.

George Woodcock *A Social History of Canada* (Penguin). Erudite yet readable book about the peoples of Canada and the changes in lifestyle from wilderness to city.

NATURAL HISTORY

Tim Fitzharris and John Livingston *Canada: A Natural History* (Viking Studio). The text is prone to purple fits, but the luscious photographs make this a book to relish.

The Pocket Guide Series (Dragon's World). Clearly laid out and well-illustrated, the Pocket Book series are excellent basic handbooks for general locations of species, identification and background. Individual titles are: *The Pocket Guide to Mammals of North America* (John Burton); *The Pocket Guide to Birds of Prey of North America* (Philip Burton); *The Pocket Guide to Wild Flowers of North America* (Pamela Forey); *The Pocket Guide to Trees of North America* (Alan Mitchell); *The Pocket Guide to Birds of Western North America* (Frank Shaw).

Paul Thomas *Fur Seal Island* (Souvenir Press). The North Pacific seals' battle for survival.

Lyall Watson *Whales of the World* (Hutchinson; NAL Dutton). Encyclopedic and lavishly illustrated guide to the biggest sea mammals.

LITERATURE

Anahareo *Grey Owl and I: A New Autobiography* (Davies). Written by the Iroquois wife of Grey Owl (see below), this tells the story of their fight to save the beaver from extinction and of her shock at discovering that her husband was in fact an Englishman. Good insights into the changing life of Canada's native peoples in this century.

Margaret Atwood *Surfacing* (Fawcett Books; Virago). Canada's most eminent novelist tackles difficult subjects, but her analysis is invariably witty and penetrating. *Surfacing*, the tale of a young divorcee who returns to the Canadian wilderness to investigate the disappearance of her father, is perhaps the best of her novels with a Canadian setting – the surroundings become instrumental in an extreme voyage of self-discovery that'll leave you unable to look at the great outdoors in quite the same way again. *Cat's Eye* (Bantam; Virago) deals with a painter returning to Toronto to find herself overwhelmed by the past, a theme also explored in *Lady Oracle* (Bantam; Virago), the account of a poet confused by a life divided between London and Canada, who plans a new life in Italy after faking her death. *Wilderness Tips* (Doubleday; Bloomsbury), is her latest collection of short stories and is mainly about women looking back over the men in their lives.

Raymond Carver *What We Talk About When We Talk About Love, Cathedral, Fires* and *Elephant* (HarperCollins). Carver was born in Clatskanie, Oregon, and brought up in Yakima, Washington. Many of his terse, deceptively simple short stories are set in the Pacific Northwest; they are collected in four volumes, and some also feature in the Robert Altman film *Short Cuts*. Several volumes of his poetry, the best known *In a Marine Light* and *A New Path of the Waterfall*, were published before his untimely death in 1988.

Lovat Dickson *Wilderness Man* (Macmillan). The fascinating story of Archie Belaney, the Englishman who became famous in Canada as his adopted persona, Grey Owl. Written by his English publisher and friend, who was one of many that did not discover the charade until after Grey Owl's death.

Grey Owl *The Men of the Last Frontier, Pilgrims of the Wild; The Adventures of Sajo and Her Beaver People; Tales of an Empty Cabin* (all Macmillan). First published in the 1930s, these books romantically describe life in the wilds of Canada at a time when exploitation was changing the land forever. His love of animals and the wilderness are inspiring and his forward-thinking ecological views are particularly startling.

Hammond Innes *Campbell's Kingdom* (Carroll & Graf; Fontana). A melodrama of love and oil-drilling in the Canadian Rockies.

Ken Kesey *Sometimes a Great Notion* (Penguin). A sweaty and rain-drenched evocation of Oregon's declining timber industry provides the background for a tale of psychological quirkiness from the author of *One Flew Over the Cuckoo's Nest*

Jack London *Call of the Wild, White Fang and Other Stories* (Penguin). London spent over a year in the Yukon goldfields during the Klondike gold rush. Many of his experiences found their way into his vivid if sometimes overwrought tales of the northern wilderness.

Malcolm Lowry *Hear Us O Lord from Heaven thy Dwelling Place* (Carroll & Graf; Picador). Lowry spent almost half his writing life (1939–54) in the log cabins and beach houses he built around Vancouver. *Hear Us O Lord* is a difficult read to say the least: a fragmentary novella which among other things describes a disturbing sojourn on Canada's wild Pacific coast.

Robert Service *The Best of Robert Service* (Putnam; Running Press). Service's Victorian ballads of pioneer and gold-rush life have a certain period charm, but generally make unintentionally hilarious reading.

Audrey Thomas *The Wild Blue Yonder* (Fourth Estate). A collection of witty tales about male–female relationships.

SPECIALIST GUIDES

Don Beers *The Wonder of Yoho* (Rocky Mountain Books). Good photos and solid text extolling the delights of Yoho National Park in the Rockies.

Darryl Bray *Kluane National Park Hiking Guide* (Travel Vision). A much-needed guide to long and short walks in a park where the trail network is still in its infancy.

Ron Dalby *The Alaska Highway: An Insider's Guide* (Fulcrum). Less detailed but less dry than its main competitor, the better-known and encyclopedic *Milepost* (Northwest Books).

Neil G Carey *A Guide to the Queen Charlotte Islands* (Northwest Books). An authoritative guide to islands which are difficult to explore and ill-served by back-up literature.

John Dodd and Gail Helgason *The Canadian Rockies Access Guide* (Lone Pine). Descriptions of 115 day hikes, with degrees of difficulty, time needed, sketch maps of routes, wildlife descriptions and numerous photos.

David Dunbar *The Outdoor Traveller's Guide to Canada* (Stewart, Tabori & Chang). Too bulky to be a useful guide in the field, but a lavishly illustrated introduction to the outdoor pursuits, wildlife and geology of the best national and provincial parks.

Ben Gadd *A Handbook of the Canadian Rockies* (Corax). Widely available in western Canada's larger bookstores, this is a lovingly produced and painstakingly detailed account of walks, flora, fauna, geology and anything else remotely connected with the Rockies.

Anne Hardy *Where to Eat in Canada* (Oberon). The only coast-to-coast Canadian guide covering establishments from the smallest diner to haute-cuisine. Very subjective, but excellent details on specialties, opening hours and prices.

Ed and Lynn Henderson *Adventure Guide to the Alaska Highway* (Moorland). A reasonable though not terribly penetrating guide to the highway, how to prepare for it and what to see.

Ruth Kirk and Carmel Alexander *Exploring Washington's Past*. Every twist of the history of Washington state is examined – a fascinating read.

The Lost Moose Catalogue (Lost Moose Publishing). Highly entertaining and iconoclastic magazine-style guide and commentary on the contemporary mores of the Yukon and far north.

Teri Lydiard *The British Columbia Bicycling Guide* (Gordon Soules). Small but extremely detailed pointer to some tempting routes, backed up with good maps.

Janice E Macdonald *Canoeing Alberta* (Macdonald). A canoeist's Bible, with many detailed accounts of the province's waterways, and especially good on routes in the Rockies.

Ken Madsen and Graham Wilson *Rivers of the Yukon* (Primrose Publishing). An invaluable guide to some of the Yukon's best canoeing rivers.

Linda Moyer and Burl Willes *Unexplored Islands of the US and Canadian West Coast* (John Muir). A guide to the more intimate and homey of the Northwest's lesser known islands.

Betty Pratt-Johnson series (Adventure Publishing). The author has produced five separate books whose 157 canoeing routes provide the definitive account of how and where to canoe the lakes and rivers of British Columbia.

Tom Kirkendall and Vicky Spring *Bicycling the Pacific Coast* (Mountaineers). Detailed guide to the bike routes all the way along the coast from Mexico up to Canada. (See also Mountaineers' other backcountry cycling books – covering the Puget Sound and other parts of Washington and Oregon – and their vast list of hiking, climbing, and wildlife guides to the whole of the Northwest region). Contact The Mountaineers, 306 Second Avenue W, Seattle, WA 98119.

Bruce Obee *The Pacific Rim Explorer* (Whitecap). A good overall summary of the walks, wildlife and social history of the Pacific Rim National Park and its nearby towns. Similarly useful are *The Gulf Islands Explorer*, also by Bruce Obee, and Eliane Jones' *The Northern Gulf Islands Explorer*, both in the same series.

Gerda Pantel *The Canadian Bed and Breakfast Guide* (Fitzhenry & Whiteside). Over a thousand B&B listings (all written by the hosts) from across the country. Useful pointers as to proximity of public transport and local sights.

Brian Patton and Bart Robinson *The Canadian Rockies Trail Guide* (Summerthought). An absolutely essential guide for anyone wishing to do more than simply scratch the surface of the Rockies' walking possibilities.

Archie Shutterfield *The Chilkoot Trail: A Hiker's Historical Guide* (Alaska Northwest Books). A pithy accompaniment to the Chilkoot Trail that should be read in conjunction with Pierre Berton's *Klondike* (see above).

Sierra Club of West Canada *The West Coast Trail* (Douglas & McIntyre). Now in its sixth edition, this is probably the best of several guides to Vancouver Island's popular but demanding long-distance footpath.

William L Sullivan *Exploring Oregon's Wild Areas* (Mountaineers). Detailed guide to backpacking, climbing, rafting, and other outdoor activities across the state.

Peggy Wayburn *Adventuring in Alaska* (Sierra Club Books). A guide to the wildlife and national parks of Alaska.

INDEX

Aberdeen 187
Accommodation 46–51
Accommodation price codes 46
Addresses 69
Admiralty Island 498
Ainsworth Hot Springs 337
Aklavik 480
Alaska Highway 457–461, 542–543
Alaska Marine Highway 34–36, 192, 448
Alaska Pass 488
Albany 96
Alberta Badlands 373–376
Alert Bay 302
Amtrak 30
Anacortes 197
Anchor Point 517
Anchorage 505–510
Antelope 133
Arctic Circle 478
Argenta 337
Ashland 106
Astoria 108–110
Athabasca Glacier 408
Aurora borealis 474

Bainbridge Island 166
Baker City 129
Balfour 336
Bamfield 297
Bandon 118
Banff National Park 388–409
Banff Townsite 388–397
Banks 21
Banks Lake 227
Barkerville 311
Baseball 63
Basketball 63
Bears 409
Beaver Creek 468
Bed and breakfast 48
Bella Coola 310
Bellevue 383
Bellingham 192–193

Bend 135–138
Bhagwan Shree Rajneesh 133
Bicycles 39
Blairmore 385
Blue Mountains 126
Blue River 320
Bonanza Creek 473
Bonneville 91
Boston Bar 318
Boswell 336
Bow River 397
Bow Valley Parkway 397
Bremerton 168
Britannia Beach 307
British Columbia Forest Museum Park 282
Broken Group Islands 296–297
Brookings 120
Buffalo 361
Burns 139
Burwash Landing 468
Bus companies 32
Buses 31–33
Buses from the US 12

Cache Creek 318
Calgary 362–373
Calgary Stampede 369
Cameron Lake 289
Campbell River 299
Camping 50–51
Camping, wilderness 53–54
Canadian Rockies 385–440
Canal Flats 347
Cannon Beach 111–112
Cape Disappointment 190
Cape Flattery 183
Cape Perpetua 116
Car rental 37–38
Cariboo, The 310–311
Cars 36–38
Cascade Mountains 203–216
Cascade Locks 91
Cascades Lake Highway 137
Cashmere 214
Cassiar 455
Cassiar Highway 453–456
Castelgar 334
Cathedral Grove 289
Cave Junction 104
Centralia 174

Charleston 117
Chelan 212
Chemainus 284
Cherryville 341
Chief Joseph 130
Children, travelling with 43
Childs Glacier 528
Chilkoot Trail 462
Chinooks 364
Circle 541
Clarkston 222
Cle Elum 216
Clearwater 321
Climate 67
Clinton, BC 310
Clinton, WA 195
Coleman 385
Columbia Glacier, AK 525
Columbia Icefield 407–408
Columbia Mountains 430
Columbia River Gorge 89–90
Columbia River Scenic Highway 90
Colville National Forest 227
Concrete 210
Consulates 15
Coombs 289
Cooper's Landing 515
Coos Bay 117
Copper River Delta 527
Cordova 526–529
Cougar 209
Coulees Dam 227
Coupeville 195
Courier flights 4
Courtenay 298
Covered Bridges 96
Cowichan Lake 284
Cowichan Valley 283
Craig 492
Cranbrook 344
Crater Lake National Park 100–102
Crawford Bay 336
Credit cards 22
Creston 335
Crime 19–20
Crowsnest Pass 383–385
Cruises 5
Customs 15
Cycling 39

Dalles, The 92
Dalton Highway 541–542
Dawson City 469–473
Dawson Creek 456
Dease Lake 455
Deception Pass 196
Delta Junction 543
Delta-Beaufort 478–482
Dempster Highway 476–478
Denali National Park 534–537
Denman Island 297
Destruction Bay 468
Dinosaur Provincial Park 375
Dinosaur Trail 375
Disabled travellers 40–41
Drinking 58–62
Driving 36–38
Drumheller 373–374
Dry Falls 227
Duc Hot Springs 183
Duncan 282–283
Dungeness National Wildlife Refuge 179

Eagle Cape Wilderness 128
Eagle Plains 477
Eastsound 199
Eating 58–62
Echo 124
Edmonton 349–358
Edson 358
Electric City Coulee 227
Elgin 127
Elkford 345
Elko 344
Ellensburg 217
Embassies 15–16
Emerald Lake 427
Enterprise 127
Eugene 97–99
Everett 190

Fairbanks 537–540
Fairmont Hot Springs 347
Falkland 325
Fauquier 341
Fax 26
Fernie 344
Ferries 33–36
Ferries, Alaska Marine Highway 34, 192, 448, 487
Ferries, BC 34, 263, 303, 449

Festivals 66
Field 422
Film 64
Fishing 57–58
Flight Agents in the UK 5
Flights from Australia 7–8
Flights from Ireland 6
Flights from New Zealand 7–8
Flights from the UK 3–4
Flights from the US 9–10
Florence 116
Food foraging in Western Oregon 108
Football 63
Footpaths, long-distance 55
Forests 283
Forks 184
Fort Clatsop 110
Fort Fraser 446
Fort Macleod 377
Fort Nelson 459
Fort Rock 139
Fort St John 457
Fort Smith 362
Fort Steele Heritage Town 346
Fort Stevens State Park 110
Fox 539
Frank Slide 385
Fraser Canyon 317–318
Friday Harbor 200

Gabriola Island 287
Galiano Island 279
Ganges 278
Garibaldi Provincial Park 307
Gay travellers 45
Gibsons 305
Girdwood 510
Glacier National Park 428–431
Glide 104
Gold Bar 215
Gold Beach 119
Gold River 301
Golden 428
Graham Island 450–453
Grand Coulee Dam 226–228
Grand Forks 333
Grande Prairie 359
Grants Pass 104
Gray Creek 336
Grayland 188
Grays Harbor 187

Green Tortoise 12
Greenwood 33
Greyhound 31–33
Gustavus 498

Haida 451
Haines 501–503
Haines Junction 467
Halfway 131
Halibut Cove 519
Hatcher Pass 532
Head-Smashed-In Buffalo Jump 377–378
Healy 535
Hedley 331
Hells Canyon 131
High Desert Museum 137
High Level 360
Hiking 54–56
Hinton 358
Hitchhiking 39
Hoh Rainforest 185
Holiday operators 6
Holidays 66
Hollis 492
Homer 517–519
Hood River 92–93
Hoonah 498
Hope, AK 513
Hope, BC 316
Hornby Island 297
Horseshoe Bay 305
Hotel price codes 46
Hotels 47
Hotspring Island 453
Hurricane Ridge 182
Hyder 454

Ice hockey 63
Icefields Parkway 404–408
Ilwaco 190
Index 215
Inside Passage 303
Insurance 18–19
Inuit 480–481
Inuvik 478–479
Invermere 347
Iskut 455

Jacksonville 105
Jasper National Park 410–419
Jasper Townsite 410–415
Jasper Tramway 415

John Day 134
John Day Fossil Beds 132
John Hart Highway 456
Jordan River 281
Joseph 127–129
Juneau 494–498

Kachemak State Park 519
Kalaloch 186
Kamloops 318–320
Kananaskis Country 387
Kaslo 337–338
Kelowna 327–329
Kenai Peninsula 512–520
Kenai 515–517
Kenai Fjords National Park 514
Keremeos 332
Ketchikan 490–493
Keyport 168
Kimberley 345
Kitsap Peninsula 166–167
Klamath Falls 102
Klawock 492
Klipsan Beach 189
Klondike Gold Rush 470–
    471
Kluane Country 467–469
Kluane Lake 468
Kluane National Park 467
Kodiak 520–523
Kokanee Glacier Provincial
    Park 338
Kootenay National Park
    434–440
Kootenay Bay 336
Kootenays 335–343
'Ksan 447

La Conner 191
La Grande 126
La Push 184
Ladysmith 284
Lake Crecent 183
Lake Louise 398–403
Lake O'Hara 426
Lake Quinault 186
Langley 195
Lava Lands 137
Leadbetter Point 188
Leavenworth 214
Lesbian travellers 45
Lethbridge 376
Lewiston 222

Liard Hot Springs 460
Liberty 216
Lillooet 309
Lincoln City 113
Little Qualicum Falls 289
Long Beach, BC 295
Long Beach Peninsula, WA
    189
Longmire 205
Lopez 197
Lumby 341
Lund 306

Madeira Park 305
Madras 132
Mail 25
Makah Reservation 181
Malheur National Forest 134
Malheur National Wildlife
    Refuge 139
Maligne Canyon 417
Maligne Lake Road 417–419
Manning 359
Manning Provincial Park 321
Manzanita 112
Maps 27–28
Marble Canyon 436
Maryhill Art Museum 220
Marysville 346
Masset 452
Mat-Su Valley 530–532
Mayne Island 280
McKenzie Bridge 99
McKenzie River National
    Recreation Trail 99
Medford 105
Media 64–65
Medicine Hat 376
Medicine Lake 418
Mendenhall Glacier 496
Metlakatla 491
Midnight Dome 474
Midway 333
Miles Canyon 462
Misty Fjords National
    Monument 491
Moclips 188
Money 21–22
Mora 184
Moraine Lake 404
Moresby Island 453
Motels 47
Mount Baker 193

Mount Batchelor 136
Mount Hood 90–91
Mount Hood Loop 90
Mount McKinley 533
**Mount Rainier National
    Park** 204–206
**Mount Revelstoke National
    Park** 431–433
**Mount Robson Provincial
    Park** 420–421
Mount St Helens 207–209
Moyie 343
Multnomah Falls 90
Muncho Lake 460
MV Lady Rose 291

Nahcotta 189
Nakusp 340
Nanaimo 285–287
National Parks 52
Neah Bay 180
Needles 341
Nelson 341–343
New Denver 339
New Hazleton 447
Newcastle Island 287
Newhalem 211
Newport 115
Newspapers 64
Nez Percé 130
North Bend 216
North Pender Island 279
North Pole 543
North Umpqua River Valley
    103

Oak Harbor 196
Oakland 103
Ocean Shores 188
Ochoco National Forest 132–
    133
Okanagan 326–330
Old Man House State Park 166
Olympia 172
Olympic Peninsula 174–186
Olympic National Park 181–
    185
Ontario 130
Orcas Island 199
Oregon Trail 76
Oregon Caves 104–105
Oregon City 93
Osoyoos 332
Oysterville 189

Pacific Rim National Park
291–297
Package tours 4, 13
Paint Pots 437
Palmer 531
Palouse 223
Paradise 206
Paradise Valley 405
Parks, fees 52
Parks, National 52
Parksville 288
Passes 34–35
Passports 14
Paulatuk 482
Peace River 359
Pemberton 309
Pendleton 124–125
Penticton 329–330
Petersburg 494
Pink Mountain 459
Port Alberni 290–291
Port Angeles 179–180
Port Clements 452
Port Gamble 168
Port Hardy 303–304
Port McNeill 302
Port Orford 119
Port Renfrew 281
Port Townsend 175–178
Portage Glacier 511
Portland 77–89
Post 25
Potlatches 268
Poulsbo 168
Powell River 306
Price codes 46
Prince George 444–445
Prince of Wales Island 492
Prince Rupert 447–449
Prince William Sound 523–530
Princeton 331
Prineville 132
Pullman 223

Quadra Island 299
Qualicum Beach 288
Queen Charlotte City 450
Queen Charlotte Islands
449–453
Quesnel 311
Quinault Indian Reservation
187
Quinault Rainforest 186

Radio 65
Radium Hot Springs 439–440
Rainforests 185
Recreational vehicles (RVs) 39
Redmond 132
Remington-Alberta Carriage
Centre 378
Revelstoke 431–433
Revelstoke Dam 433
Richland 220
Roche Harbor 200
Rogers Pass 430
Rogue River 119
Roseburg 103
Roslyn 216
Rossland 333
Royal British Columbia
Museum 266–267
Royal Tyrrell Museum 374–375

Sachs Harbour 482
Salem 94–96
Salmo 334
Salmon 324, 516
Salmon Arm 323–325
Saltspring Island 278
San Juan Island 200
San Juan Islands 197–201
Sandon 339
Sandspit 453
Saskatchewan Crossing 407
Saturna Island 280
Sea Lion Caves 116
Sea to Sky Highway 306–309
Seaside 110
SEATTLE 143–165
 Accommodation 154–156
 Alki Beach 151
 Alki Point 151
 Aquarium 147
 Arrival 144
 Ballard 153
 Belltown 151
 Broadway 152
 Capitol Hill 152
 Center House 152
 Chinatown 150
 Classical music 161
 Colman Dock 147
 Columbia Center 150
 Conservatory 152
 Dance 161
 Drinking 160–161
 Eating 156–158

 Ferries 164
 Festivals 163
 Film 162
 Fishermen's Terminal 153
 Gasworks Park 153
 Gay Seattle 162
 Henry Art Gallery 153
 Hing Hay Park 150
 Hiram M Chittenden Locks 153
 History 143
 Information 144
 International District 150
 Japanese Tea Gardens 152
 Kingdome 150
 Klondike Gold Rush National Park
  148
 Lake Washington 154
 Lake Washington Ship Canal 153
 Listings 163–164
 Map 149
 Museum of Flight 151
 Museum of History and Industry
  153
 Nightlife 159–163
 Nordic Heritage Museum 153
 Occidental Park 148
 Omnidome 147
 Opera 161
 Pacific Science Center 152
 Pier 59 147
 Pike Place Market 146, 156
 Pioneer Square 148
 Rainier Tower 150
 Seattle Art Museum 147
 Seattle Center 151
 Seattle Children's Museum 153
 Smith Tower 150
 Space Needle 151
 Theater 162
 Thomas Burke Memorial Museum
  153
 Transit 144
 University District 152
 Volunteer Park 152
 Washington Park 152
 Waterfront 147
 Wing Luke Asian Museum 150
Sechelt 305
Seldovia 520
Senior Travellers 42
Sequim 178
Seward 513
Shakespeare Festival 106
Shuswap Lake 323
Sicamous 325
Sinclair Pass 439
Sisters 132
Sitka 499–500

Skagway 503–505
Skeena Valley 447
Skidegate 452
Skiing 56–57, 400
Skookumchuck 346
Slocan 340
Smithers 446
Smoking 69
Snoqualmie Falls 216
Sooke 280
South Pender Island 279
Southern Gulf Islands 277–280
Sparwood 344
Spokane 223–225
Squamish 307
Stanley Glacier 436
Steamboat 104
Stehekin 213
Stewart 454
Strathcona Provincial Park 300–301
Studying 16
Sumpter 135
Sunshine Coast 304–306
Sunwapta Falls 408
Suquamish 167
Swartz Bay (ferry) 262

Tacoma 170–172
Taholah 188
Tahsis 301
Takakkaw Falls 428
Talkeetna 532–533
Tax 21
Telegrams 26
Telegraph Cove 302
Telegraph Creek 455
Television 64
Telkwa 446
Telephones 24
Tenakee Springs 498
Teslin 461
Theater 64
Tillamook 112
Time zones 26
Tipping 62, 69
Tl'ell 452
Toad River 460
Tofino 292–293
Tok 542
Top of the World Highway 475
Tourist offices 27
Trail 333

Train from the US 11
Trains 30–31
Travellers' Cheques 22
Tri-Cities 220
Tsawwassen (ferry) 262
Tuktoyaktuk 482
Tumwater 172
Tumwater Historical Park 173
Twisp 212
Two Hot Springs 541

Ucluelet 295

Valdez 524–526
Valemount 320
VANCOUVER 231–262
 Accommodation 247–250
 Airport 233
 Aquarium 241
 Bars 254
 BC Place Stadium 237
 BC Rail 234
 Beaches 242
 Bus routes 236
 Cafés 251
 Canada Place 237
 Capilano River Park 246
 Children's Zoo 241
 Chinatown 239
 Chinese Cultural Centre 240
 Cinema 259
 Classical music 258
 Clubs 255–256
 Dance 258
 Downtown 237
 Dr Sun Yat-sen Gardens 240
 Drinking 254
 Eating 250–254
 Festivals 259
 Gastown 239
 Granville Island 242–243
 Grouse Mountain 246
 Harbour Centre 237
 History 233
 Lighthouse Park 247
 Listings 260–261
 Lonsdale Quay Market 246
 Lost Lagoon 241
 Lynn Canyon Park 246
 Maritime Museum 244
 Mount Seymour Provincial Park 247
 Museum of Anthropology 244–245
 Nightlife 254–259
 Nitobe Memorial Garden 245
 North Vancouver 245–247
 Opera 258
 Planetarium 244

 Science World 237
 SeaBus 235
 SkyTrain 235
 Stanley Park 240–241
 Theatre 258
 Tourist Information 234
 Transit 235
 Vancouver Art Gallery 237
 Vancouver Museum 243
 Vanier Park 243
 VIA rail 234
 Youth hostels 249
VANCOUVER ISLAND 262–304
Vancouver, WA 174
Vanderhoof 446
Vashon 169
Vegetarian travellers 60
Vermilion Crossing 439
Vermilion Pass 436
Vernon 326–327
VIA Rail 31
VICTORIA 264–277
Visas 14

Wahkeena Falls 90
Walking 54–56
Walla Walla 221
Wallowa Mountains 127–131
Wasilla 531
Waterton Lakes National Park 378–383
Waterton Townsite 380–383
Watson Lake 460
Weather 67
Wells 311
Wells Gray Provincial Park 321–323
Wenatchee 213
West Coast Trail 296
Westport 188
Westwold 325
Whale-watching 293, 302
Whidbey Island 194–196
Whistler 308–309
Whitehorse 461–466
Whitman Mission 221
Whittier 511
Willamette National Forest 99–100
Willamette Valley 93–102
Willapa Wildlife Refuge 188
Williams Lake 310
Windermere 347

Winslow 166
Winthrop 211
Wobblies, The 553
Wolf Haven International
  Reserve 173
Women travellers 44
Wonowon 459
Wood Buffalo National Park
  361–362

Working 16
Wrangell 493
Wrangell-St Elias National
  Park 529–530

Yahk 343
Yakima 218
Yakima Indian Reservation 219
Yakima Valley 219

Yale 317
Yellowhead Pass 420
Yoho National Park 422–
  428
Yoho Valley 427
Youth hostels 49

Zillah 219

direct orders from

		£	US$	CAN$
Amsterdam	1-85828-086-9	£7.99	US$13.95	CAN$16.99
Andalucia	1-85828-094-X	8.99	14.95	18.99
Australia	1-85828-141-5	12.99	19.95	25.99
Bali	1-85828-134-2	8.99	14.95	19.99
Barcelona	1-85828-106-7	8.99	13.95	17.99
Berlin	1-85828-129-6	8.99	14.95	19.99
Brazil	1-85828-102-4	9.99	15.95	19.99
Britain	1-85828-208-X	12.99	19.95	25.99
Brittany & Normandy	1-85828-126-1	8.99	14.95	19.99
Bulgaria	1-85828-183-0	9.99	16.95	22.99
California	1-85828-181-4	10.99	16.95	22.99
Canada	1-85828-130-X	10.99	14.95	19.99
Corsica	1-85828-089-3	8.99	14.95	18.99
Costa Rica	1-85828-136-9	9.99	15.95	21.99
Crete	1-85828-132-6	8.99	14.95	18.99
Cyprus	1-85828-182-2	9.99	16.95	22.99
Czech & Slovak Republics	1-85828-121-0	9.99	16.95	22.99
Egypt	1-85828-075-3	10.99	17.95	21.99
Europe	1-85828-159-8	14.99	19.95	25.99
England	1-85828-160-1	10.99	17.95	23.99
First Time Europe	1-85828-210-1	7.99	9.95	12.99
Florida	1-85828-184-4	10.99	16.95	22.99
France	1-85828-124-5	10.99	16.95	21.99
Germany	1-85828-128-8	11.99	17.95	23.99
Goa	1-85828-156-3	8.99	14.95	19.99
Greece	1-85828-131-8	9.99	16.95	20.99
Greek Islands	1-85828-163-6	8.99	14.95	19.99
Guatemala	1-85828-189-X	10.99	16.95	22.99
Hawaii: Big Island	1-85828-158-X	8.99	12.95	16.99
Hawaii	1-85828-206-3	10.99	16.95	22.99
Holland, Belgium & Luxembourg	1-85828-087-7	9.99	15.95	20.99
Hong Kong	1-85828-187-3	8.99	14.95	19.99
Hungary	1-85828-123-7	8.99	14.95	19.99
India	1-85828-104-0	13.99	22.95	28.99
Ireland	1-85828-179-2	10.99	17.95	23.99
Italy	1-85828-167-9	12.99	19.95	25.99
Kenya	1-85828-192-X	11.99	18.95	24.99
London	1-85828-117-2	8.99	12.95	16.99
Mallorca & Menorca	1-85828-165-2	8.99	14.95	19.99
Malaysia, Singapore & Brunei	1-85828-103-2	9.99	16.95	20.99
Mexico	1-85828-044-3	10.99	16.95	22.99
Morocco	1-85828-040-0	9.99	16.95	21.99
Moscow	1-85828-118-0	8.99	14.95	19.99
Nepal	1-85828-190-3	10.99	17.95	23.99
New York	1-85828-171-7	9.99	15.95	21.99

Pacific Northwest	1-85828-092-3	9.99	14.95	19.99
Paris	1-85828-125-3	7.99	13.95	16.99
Poland	1-85828-168-7	10.99	17.95	23.99
Portugal	1-85828-180-6	9.99	16.95	22.99
Prague	1-85828-122-9	8.99	14.95	19.99
Provence	1-85828-127-X	9.99	16.95	22.99
Pyrenees	1-85828-093-1	8.99	15.95	19.99
Rhodes & the Dodecanese	1-85828-120-2	8.99	14.95	19.99
Romania	1-85828-097-4	9.99	15.95	21.99
San Francisco	1-85828-185-7	8.99	14.95	19.99
Scandinavia	1-85828-039-7	10.99	16.99	21.99
Scotland	1-85828-166-0	9.99	16.95	22.99
Sicily	1-85828-178-4	9.99	16.95	22.99
Singapore	1-85828-135-0	8.99	14.95	19.99
Spain	1-85828-081-8	9.99	16.95	20.99
St Petersburg	1-85828-133-4	8.99	14.95	19.99
Thailand	1-85828-140-7	10.99	17.95	24.99
Tunisia	1-85828-139-3	10.99	17.95	24.99
Turkey	1-85828-088-5	9.99	16.95	20.99
Tuscany & Umbria	1-85828-091-5	8.99	15.95	19.99
USA	1-85828-161-X	14.99	19.95	25.99
Venice	1-85828-170-9	8.99	14.95	19.99
Wales	1-85828-096-6	8.99	14.95	18.99
West Africa	1-85828-101-6	15.99	24.95	34.99
More Women Travel	1-85828-098-2	9.99	14.95	19.99
Zimbabwe & Botswana	1-85828-041-9	10.99	16.95	21.99

Phrasebooks

Czech	1-85828-148-2	3.50	5.00	7.00
French	1-85828-144-X	3.50	5.00	7.00
German	1-85828-146-6	3.50	5.00	7.00
Greek	1-85828-145-8	3.50	5.00	7.00
Italian	1-85828-143-1	3.50	5.00	7.00
Mexican	1-85828-176-8	3.50	5.00	7.00
Portuguese	1-85828-175-X	3.50	5.00	7.00
Polish	1-85828-174-1	3.50	5.00	7.00
Spanish	1-85828-147-4	3.50	5.00	7.00
Thai	1-85828-177-6	3.50	5.00	7.00
Turkish	1-85828-173-3	3.50	5.00	7.00
Vietnamese	1-85828-172-5	3.50	5.00	7.00

Reference

Classical Music	1-85828-113-X	12.99	19.95	25.99
Internet	1-85828-198-9	5.00	8.00	10.00
Jazz	1-85828-137-7	16.99	24.95	34.99
Rock	1-85828-201-2	17.99	26.95	35.00
World Music	1-85828-017-6	16.99	22.95	29.99

In the USA, or for international orders, charge your order by Master Card or Visa (US$15.00 minimum order): call 1-800-253-6476; or send orders, with complete name, address and zip code, and list price, plus $2.00 shipping and handling per order to: Consumer Sales, Penguin USA, PO Box 999 – Dept #17109, Bergenfield, NJ 07621. No COD. Prepay foreign orders by international money order, a cheque drawn on a US bank, or US currency. No postage stamps are accepted. All orders are subject to stock availability at the time they are processed. Refunds will be made for books not available at that time. Please allow a minimum of four weeks for delivery.

THE LOWEST PRICE CAR RENTAL AROUND THE

AND THAT'S A PROMISE†

For convenient, low-price car rental – all around the world – choose Holiday Autos. With a network of over 4,000 locations in 42 countries, when you're off globetrotting you won't have to go out of your way to find us.

What's more, with our lowest price promise, you won't be flying round and round in circles to be sure you're getting the best price.

With Holiday Autos you can be sure of the friendly, efficient service you'd expect from the UK's leading leisure car rental company. After all, we've won the Travel Trade Gazette 'Best Leisure Car Rental Company' award and the Independent Travel Agents' 'Top Leisure Car Rental Company' award time and time again. So, we've quite a reputation to maintain.

With Holiday Autos you simply don't need to search the globe for down-to-earth low prices.

For further information see your local Travel Agent or call us direct on **0990 300 400**

Holiday Autos
WE KNOW YOU HAVE A CHOICE

†Our lowest price promise refers to our pledge to undercut by £5 any other equivalent offer made at the same price or less by an independent UK car rental company for a booking made in the UK prior to departure. Holiday Autos undercut offer is valid unless and until withdrawn by Holiday Autos.

You are
A STUDENT

You travel
THE WORLD

You want
TO SAVE MONEY

Here's how

The International Student Identity Card

Available at Student Travel Offices Worldwide.

Entitles you to discounts and special services worldwide.